READING *Our* WORLD
CONVERSATIONS *in* CONTEXT
Second Edition

Robert P. Yagelski

State University of New York at Albany

with

Amy Crouse-Powers
SUNY College of Oneonta

WADSWORTH
CENGAGE Learning

Australia ▪ Br... ...pan ▪ Korea ▪ Mexico ▪ Singapore ▪ Spain ▪ United Kingdom ▪ United States

WADSWORTH
CENGAGE Learning

Reading Our World: Conversations in Context, Second Edition
Robert P. Yagelski

Senior Publisher: Lyn Uhl

Acquisitions Editor: Kate Derrick

Development Editor: Karen Mauk

Senior Assistant Editor: Kelli Strieby

Editorial Assistant: Jake Zucker

Senior Media Editor: Cara Douglass-Graff

Marketing Manager: Jennifer Zourdos

Marketing Coordinator: Ryan Ahern

Senior Marketing Communications Manager: Stacey Purviance

Content Project Manager: Corinna Dibble

Senior Art Director: Jill Ort

Senior Print Buyer: Betsy Donaghey

Rights Acquisition Account Manager Text: Roberta Broyer

Production Service: Graphic World Inc.

Rights Acquisition Account Manager Image: Dean Dauphinais

Photo Researcher: Catherine Schnurr/ Nina Smith

Cover Designer: Anne Carter

Text Designer: Anne Carter

Cover Image: *Beach Houses,* by Kate Castelli Art and Illustration

Compositor: Graphic World Inc.

For product information and technology assistance, contact us at
**Cengage Learning Academic Resource Center,
1-800-423-0563**

For permission to use material from this text or product,
submit all requests online at **www.cengage.com/permissions.**
Further permissions questions can be e-mailed to
permissionrequest@cengage.com.

Library of Congress Control Number: 2008940877

ISBN-13: 978-1-4282-3125-2

ISBN-10: 1-4282-3125-0

Wadsworth
20 Channel Center Street
Boston, MA 02210
USA

Cengage Learning products are represented in Canada by Nelson Education, Ltd.

For your course and learning solutions, visit **www.cengage.com.**

Purchase any of our products at your local college store or at our preferred online store **www.ichapters.com.**

Printed in Canada
1 2 3 4 5 6 7 13 12 11 10 09

CONTENTS

8. COMMUNICATION   319

9. POWER   425

10. LIVING TOGETHER   523

11. RESOURCES   593

RHETORICAL CONTENTS

ANALYSIS

ARGUMENT AND PERSUASION

CAUSE-EFFECT

CLASSIFICATION

COMPARISON-CONTRAST

DEFINITION

DESCRIPTION

NARRATIVE

AUTOBIOGRAPHY

HUMOR

SATIRE

PREFACE TO INSTRUCTORS

Composition instructors know that helping student writers learn to read carefully and critically is a crucial part of helping them learn to write effectively. *Reading Our World* (formerly *The Thomson Reader*) can help composition instructors meet that challenge. Based on three fundamental principles that have emerged from research and theory in the field of composition in recent decades, *Reading Our World* can help students learn that

- *Writing and reading always occur in context.* To write well is to recognize, assess, and manage rhetorical situations effectively. To read effectively, especially the increasingly sophisticated texts, including multimedia and digital texts, that college students are asked to read today, requires readers to understand how the meaning of a text is always related to context.

- *The meaning of a text can be understood as part of ongoing conversations about important issues, questions, and ideas.* Writers and readers do not encounter texts in a vacuum. Texts are responses to other texts, and in that sense, they are part of the world of discourse—the larger conversations about life that are always happening. Because the meaning of words and texts is a function of how they are used—that is, because meaning emerges in discourse—effective writing and reading require students to be aware of the ways in which discourse shapes the meaning of texts.

- *Writing is a form of inquiry.* More than a basic skill, writing is a mode of intellectual engagement—a powerful way to explore ideas and information. Writing is a way to make sense of our lives and to deepen our understanding of the world around us.

ENHANCING THE WAY YOU TEACH

Reading Our World offers students opportunities to read and write in ways that focus on context, conversations, and inquiry. It also offers instructors opportunities to supplement their courses with trusted methods by providing

- recognizable and flexible themes for writing;
- a mix of classic authors, such as Langston Hughes, George Orwell, and Annie Dillard, and contemporary readings on topics of current interest, such as the economic considerations of vegetarianism and the cultural influence of rap music, to encourage students' engagement;
- marginalia designed to train students to be versatile, inquisitive readers by building on the discussions held every day in the classroom;
- writing activities calling for a variety of traditional and innovative papers and projects, including research papers, critical analyses, personal narratives, and multimedia documents.

With broad themes and thematic clusters that can be adapted to any instructor's preferences, *Reading Our World* can be a flexible tool that enables composition teachers to enhance their courses without having to change them wholesale.

In addition, *Reading Our World* is based on the idea that writing itself is a technology. Today's students are more familiar with technology than any previous generation, and this book incorporates into its pedagogical apparatus and its supplementary resources, English21 and InfoTrac® College Edition—important new technologies that are shaping the way we communicate. In this sense, *Reading Our World* can help students gain an understanding of how new and emerging technologies are influencing how we write and read. It can also give students valuable experience in using current and emerging technologies to create their own texts and help them appreciate the complex relationship between text and image in an increasingly multimedia world.

Informed by the belief that writing effectively and reading critically are essential, *Reading Our World* also helps students learn to navigate the complexities of contemporary life as citizens, consumers, and professionals. By helping students develop their skills and knowledge, *Reading Our World* can prepare students for writing in a changing world. The book's features have been designed to give students relevant practice in writing and reading a variety of texts in a variety of contexts so that they can develop an awareness of how writing shapes their world. It rests on the hope that students will use writing to participate in the important conversations of their time.

Attempting to incorporate all these important elements into one course can be overwhelming, but *Reading Our World* integrates the familiar with the new so that instructors can effectively help students produce smart, thoughtful, and critical writing.

WHERE DO THEMES COME FROM? AN INNOVATIVE APPROACH TO CONTENT

Most composition readers include similar themes that reflect important issues or questions in contemporary life. That's because the themes themselves are longstanding, enduring issues. But *Reading Our World* is unique among thematic readers in the way it focuses students' attention on the very idea of *themes,* inviting students to consider the following questions: Where do these themes come from? What do they reveal about how we understand the world? How do they influence the way we write and read? By encouraging students to address these questions, *Reading Our World* helps students understand how all acts of writing and reading are part of broader conversations about important issues in their lives, conversations that shape how they understand their world. In this way, *Reading Our World* helps students experience writing as engagement with the world.

Accordingly, Part 2 of *Reading Our World* (Chapters 5–12) presents reading selections that address familiar, timely, and important issues. But the organization of these chapters into *clusters,* or subthemes, highlights the contextual nature of writing and reading and helps students see how individual texts fit into ongoing conversations that shape their understanding of those texts. Each of the eight thematic chapters is divided into three clusters of three to four readings to provide a subtheme to the larger theme, reinforcing to students how broader conversations can be carried on in the form of distinct but related conversations about specific questions. For instance, the chapter on change includes a cluster of readings on scientific and technological progress, a second cluster on coming of age, and a third cluster on global climate change. All these clusters relate to the larger chapter theme of change, yet each represents a distinct discourse or conversation about an issue that reflects some kind of important change.

Forty-one of *Reading Our World*'s ninety-two readings are new to this edition, enhancing the mix of classic and contemporary readings and adding greater diversity in terms of genres, authors, and topics. Among these reading selections are conventional essays, magazine and newspaper articles (including online publications), speeches, and excerpts from blogs. These readings represent fresh variations on eight traditional themes: Identity, Understanding, Relationships, Communication, Power, Living Together, Resources, and Change. Each of these main themes is presented in the form of innovative clusters that reflect ongoing conversations about important issues related to the chapter theme. For example, instead of a separate chapter on education, a theme that regularly appears in composition readers, *Reading Our World* presents readings related to education in a cluster about Understanding; additional readings related to education appear in the chapters on Relationships, Communication, and Power. In this way, students are asked to think about how educational issues are part of other important ongoing conversations about such matters as relationships or power and how those conversations shape our understanding of education. Readings are presented in thought-provoking ways that encourage students (and teachers) to look at these themes anew and examine how the themes themselves reflect and influence the way we understand our world. Thus, *Reading Our World* encourages students' inquiry into the themes themselves to gain deeper insight into *how the very acts of writing and reading help construct those themes.* Flexible for instructors, who can select individual readings on specific topics, assign entire clusters, or create their own clusters, the themes and clusters of *Reading Our World* provide students with a groundwork for critically examining larger issues and encouraging them to enter conversations that are important to them.

The reading selections also reflect the many different discourse forms and genres that students are likely to encounter today: traditional essays, sophisticated academic analyses, editorials from various print and online sources, excerpts from books, and texts from a variety of periodicals, including newspapers, political and cultural journals, trade publications, and popular magazines. This variety helps students appreciate the many different textual forms through which writers and readers explore the important issues of the day and engage age-old questions about how we live together. In addition, these readings provide students with models of different textual forms that they themselves may be asked to write in the classroom, the workplace, and elsewhere.

ENGLISH21

The largest compilation of online resources ever organized for composition and literature courses, **English21** is a complete online support system that weaves robust, self-paced instruction with interactive assignments. Easily assignable, **English21** encourages students as they become better-prepared and successful writers. **English21** supports students through every step of the writing process, from assignment to final draft. **English21** includes carefully crafted multimedia assignments; a collection of essays; a full interactive handbook with animations, exercises, and activities; a complete research guide with animated tutorials and a link to Gale's InfoTrac® College Edition database; and a rich multimedia library with hand-selected images, audio clips, video clips, stories, poems, and plays. To learn more, visit academic.cengage.com/english21.

ENGLISH21 PLUS

Access to **English21 Plus** is available for a nominal fee when packaged with new copies of the text. **English21 Plus** includes all of the features mentioned above plus access to Wadsworth's **InSite for Writing and Research™. InSite** features an electronic peer review system, an originality checker, a rich assignment library, and electronic grade marking. To learn more, visit academic.cengage.com/english21.

THE IMPORTANCE OF CONTEXT

Instructors can sometimes find it difficult to devote class time to helping students understand the context of an essay, but because all writing occurs in context, students become more informed and effective writers when they appreciate the role of context in their writing. *Reading Our World* can help instructors solve this dilemma. It includes innovative features that provide a new and effective way to help students appreciate the crucial role of context in writing. Every reading is accompanied by *marginalia* designed to place each reading in rhetorical context and encourage students' inquiry into the importance of the various aspects of context that affect writing.

These innovative marginalia make *Reading Our World* distinctive among currently available composition readers. They advance the book's purpose of highlighting the contextual nature of writing and supporting students' inquiry into the ideas presented in each reading and into writing itself. In other words, they enable students to learn to read in more sophisticated ways by calling students' attention to the ways in which each reading can be seen as part of ongoing conversations about important issues and questions. They also foster students' awareness of their own ways of reading. Three kinds of marginalia boxes accompany the readings in *Reading Our World:*

- *Conversations* place the reading selection at hand in the context of ongoing conversations about relevant issues, problems, or themes. These marginalia call students' attention to important historical, cultural, and related background information that is essential for understanding the reading selection and encourage students to examine how contextual factors influence both the writing and reading of the text. They also make connections between the reading in question and other readings in the book.
- *Glosses,* akin to traditional footnotes, provide explanations or definitions of key concepts or terms; they also provide historical and biographical information about events, people, and texts mentioned in the reading selection and help students appreciate how writers use such information strategically as they participate in conversations about the issues they're addressing.
- *Strategies* direct students' attention to how the writer uses certain words and phrases, adopts particular styles, or employs certain forms that address the rhetorical context and reflect the relevant discourses that might influence the writer's strategic choices. These marginalia connect students' reading directly to their own development as writers.

These three kinds of marginalia function not only as sources of information and ideas about the reading selection but also as supplements to the questions and writing activities at the end of each reading selection. They help sustain the book's focus on how ideas and information are not only conveyed in writing but are also constructed *through* writing. The marginalia therefore reinforce the main ideas about writing that lie at the center of the book. Striving to point out things students should be aware of in any given reading, the marginalia do not reveal everything about the context but rather prompt the student to think more closely about the issue at hand. In this sense, they model critical reading strategies. In addition, they provide instructors with readily available materials that can easily be incorporated into their lessons.

INQUIRING ABOUT THE CONVERSATIONS

By fostering student inquiry into writing through features such as the marginalia, *Reading Our World* encourages students to ask questions about texts that will help them understand that *what* we write and read about isn't arbitrary but emerges from the ways in which we talk about ourselves, our actions, our beliefs, and the world around us. Such inquiry can help students gain insight into how language shapes what we know and do; it can deepen students' understanding of how writing and reading influence what we "see" in the world. And it provides substantive motivation and justification for learning to write effectively.

Reading Our World combines conventional pedagogical elements, such as carefully constructed questions and varied writing activities for each reading, with the innovative marginalia that explore context and encourage careful inquiry into each reading. In addition to the engaging introductory headnotes that place each reading in context, each reading selection includes three kinds of pedagogical features:

- *Understanding the Text* questions help students grasp the writer's ideas and goals, enabling them to better understand the text and consider similar strategies in their own writing.

- *Exploring the Issues* questions prompt students to delve more deeply into important issues and ideas that emerge from the reading; these questions actively engage students in pursuing these issues and ideas and encourage students to examine their own views about them as well as about the larger chapter theme or cluster topic.

- *Entering the Conversations* exercises provide varied writing activities related to the reading itself and the chapter theme. These activities include conventional assignments, such as personal narratives and formal research papers, inquiry-based projects that encourage the use of InfoTrac, and more innovative projects, such as brochures, Web sites, or PowerPoint presentations that incorporate text and images to explore a personal experience or important question related to the chapter theme. Using visuals with carefully selected questions gives students the opportunity to work with familiar media at the same time that it teaches them to critically evaluate the images in relation to the larger conversation at hand.

To encourage students to generate their own ideas about the chapter themes and to extend the conversations they have been participating in, *Reading Our World* also includes *Extending the Conversations* activities at the end of each chapter. From rearranging the given clusters to examining relevant films to selecting images to create visual essays to writing conventional academic essays, students can participate in the conversation in a variety of ways through various media.

The pedagogical features of *Reading Our World* are presented in an innovative and attractive design that makes them accessible to students and artfully combines text and image. In this sense, *Reading Our World* both reflects and models recent developments in writing and communication as multimedia technologies become increasingly common.

SUPPORTING STUDENTS' WRITING

The first four chapters of *Reading Our World* lay the foundation for the book by introducing students to key principles, including the central ideas of context and discourse. These chapters are designed to help students gain insight into the contextual nature of all writing, to train students how to "read" and choose images for their writing, to offer advice for writing in a variety of rhetorical situations, and to guide students' research on the topics they write about. Of special note is the attention devoted to visual rhetoric throughout this reader but especially in Chapter 2.

By giving students guidance in defining context, how to understand discourse, and turning a larger theme into a thesis, *Reading Our World* helps students overcome common writing difficulties at the same time that it highlights the way each theme in the book grows out of one or more discourses—discourses with which students may be unfamiliar. As composition instructors well know, students often struggle to write effectively when they are writing about unfamiliar topics or when they write in unfamiliar forms or genres. Recent theoretical work in Composition Studies has helped us understand that such difficulties result not only from students' lack of knowledge about specific topics but also from their lack of experience with—and understanding of—the discourses within which they are being asked to write. *Reading Our World* is a tool for instructors to help their students overcome this struggle.

Reading Our World also helps students learn to appreciate and negotiate the changing relationship between text and image in a world that is being reshaped by new technologies and media. Chapter 2: "Understanding Media as Contexts for Writing," guides students in "reading" images in terms of context and discourse, in using new technologies for communication, and in incorporating visual elements into their documents in a variety of media. With nearly 20 visual examples in Chapter 2 alone, students begin to see the importance of the visual in writing.

A brief research guide, Chapter 4: "Engaging in Research and Inquiry," gives students advice for conducting research, finding and using evidence effectively, and appropriately documenting sources with MLA format, including fifteen sample MLA entries. At the same time, this chapter reinforces the idea that all writing is a form of inquiry.

OTHER ANCILLARY MATERIALS

Reading Our World gives considerable support to instructors through these ancillary materials:

- **Instructor's Manual.** Containing useful synopses of every reading and suggested class activities and discussion topics, the Instructor's Manual also includes in-depth treatment of the context of the reading, providing ideas for incorporating the marginalia into discussions and for engaging students in the larger conversations about the chapter themes.
- **Companion Web site.** This site provides students with interactive exercises on the fundamentals of writing, including grammar, mechanics, and punctuation. A student paper library provides sample papers with accompanying editing and revising activities.

ACKNOWLEDGMENTS

A textbook is really an extensive collaboration involving many people, and I am grateful to everyone at Wadsworth who contributed to *Reading Our World* in some way, including the terrific people who helped design and produce this book, whose professionalism and support helped keep the project moving and who contributed so much to the quality of the final product. I am especially grateful to Karen Mauk, the development editor for this book, whose patience and insight helped guide my work for this new edition. I am also deeply indebted to Lyn Uhl, who kept this project on track through many unexpected changes and whose confidence in me never wavered throughout a sometimes difficult revision process. Corinna Dibble and Kate Mannix ushered the book through the production process, and I am thankful for their hard work to create the book you hold in your hands. I also wish to thank Amy Crouse-Powers, researcher *par excellence,* whose savvy research skills and dependability enriched this book and helped me handle the pressure of meeting deadlines. Roberta Broyer, Catherine Schnurr, and Nina Smith undertook the difficult task of securing text and visual permissions with ease.

I would also like to thank the following colleagues, as well as those who wished to remain anonymous, who gave their encouragement and constructive criticism as this book was being developed:

Trela N. Anderson, *Fayetteville State University*
Sonya C. Brown, *Fayetteville State University*
Dana Burnside, *Lehigh Carbon Community College*
Julie A. Chappell, *Tarleton State University*
Judith E. Cortelloni, *Lincoln College*
Eve Davis, *J. Sargeant Reynolds Community College*
Jo P. DeLosSantos, *Davidson County Community College*

Jason De Polo, *North Carolina A&T State University*
Sharon George, *College of Charleston*
Owen W. Gilman, Jr., *Saint Joseph's University*
D. Alexis Hart, *Virginia Military Institute*
Miles McCrimmon, *J. Sargeant Reynolds Community College*
Terry Pollard, *Mississippi Gulf Coast Community College*
Paula Sebastian, *Bellevue College*
Helen Sitler, *Indiana University of Pennsylvania*
Alissa Skovira, *The University of Akron*
Judith L. Steele, *Mid-America Christian University*
Matt Theado, *Gardner-Webb University*
Jenara Turman, *University of Nebraska at Kearney*

Carol Forman-Pemberton, my codirector at the Capital District Writing Project, deserves special thanks for her genuine support and patience as I completed the project, even when she had many pressures of her own to deal with. Thanks, too, to the other teachers in the Capital District Writing project, who have become valued colleagues and continue to teach me so much about writing and teaching. My students over the years, especially the students in the English teacher education program at the State University of New York at Albany, also continue to teach me about writing and give me the motivation to learn more. I also wish to thank my sons, Adam and Aaron, who are always willing to listen to my rants and whose own rants convey insights that deepen my thinking and writing. And most important, I wish to thank my wife, Cheryl, whose selfless love, support, and confidence always sustain me, whose smile lights even the most difficult day of writing, and whose impact on this book—and on all my writing—is profound.

INTRODUCTION TO STUDENTS

The first thing you need to know about writing is that it matters.

If you're reading this book for a college composition course, then you are living proof that writing matters. In most colleges and universities, composition courses are the only courses required of *all* students, regardless of their majors. Obviously, the people who set college graduation requirements believe that writing matters.

So do state lawmakers. In most states, high school students are required to take four years of English to receive a high school diploma. Other than social studies, English is the only subject that most states require students to study for four years. Perhaps that's because lawmakers believe that writing and reading are the most important skills for students to develop. Doing well in school is largely a matter of writing and reading well. That's especially true in college, where you are asked to read and write increasingly sophisticated texts.

The second thing you need to know about writing is that it matters. It matters more than you probably think. Here are a few ways in which writing matters:

- *Writing is a powerful means of communicating ideas and information.* The book you are holding in your hands is proof of that. Any book is. Just think for a moment about how effectively writing can convey complicated ideas or information—through books, newspapers, Web pages, text messages, blogs, and all sorts of other documents and media. Writing makes those ideas available to readers in other places and at other times. It's really a remarkable thing. You are reading this book, which contains so many ideas, many months after I have written these words.

- *Writing is a powerful tool for learning.* It is no coincidence that schools and colleges require students to learn how to write well because writing and reading are central to academic learning. When you write, you use your mind in ways that differ from listening or talking or watching. You engage in an important kind of thinking that can result in greater learning about any subject. Researchers have spent countless hours studying how writing facilitates learning, but if you've spent any time writing, and if you've paid attention, you already know that writing is a unique learning tool. The more effectively you write, the more you will learn, and the more likely you are to be successful in school and beyond.

- *Writing is a powerful means of self-expression.* There are few ways to express your ideas that are as effective as writing. An essay, a poem, a personal letter, a letter to a newspaper editor, a story, a memo, a report, a blog post, an e-mail message—all these can be ways for a writer to make a statement, share a feeling, express an opinion, explain a point of view, stake a claim, provide information, explore an idea, or issue a challenge. Writing can be a way to present yourself to others, to convey a sense of who you are. Writing allows writers to do these things more effectively and more widely than other common means of communication. You can shout your opinion about a political issue to a group of people on a street corner, but a carefully written letter to a newspaper editor has the potential to reach a much wider audience, and with greater impact.

- *Writing is a social activity.* When you write, you are connecting with others. In that sense, writing is always social, even if you're doing it in a small isolated cabin by some pond in the forest, far away from the nearest town. Even if you're only writing for your teacher, you are engaging in a social act that inherently connects you and your teacher. And when you follow rules for writing certain kinds of texts—like job letters or science reports or editorial essays—you are using forms of writing that have been developed over many years by many different people. When you write about a philosophical question for your philosophy class, you are using ideas that have been around for thousands of years, and you are engaging in a conversation about philosophy that has been going on for just as long. In all these ways, writing is a deeply social activity.

- *Writing is a political act.* Obviously, writing about a controversial political issue can be seen as a political act. But any time you write anything that is important to you and is likely to be read by someone else, you are engaging in a potentially political act that can have consequences for you and for others. Writing can be a means to challenge power or resist oppression. That's why slave owners in the American South before the Civil War made it a crime to teach Blacks to read and write. Writing was a way for slaves to exchange ideas that might provoke them to resist White domination; it was a way for slaves to oppose slavery without necessarily taking up arms. Why do governments regulate and control publications and media? For the same reasons that slave owners made it illegal for slaves to read and write. Why do high school principals sometimes censor student newspapers? Ditto. Because of the potential political power of writing.

- *Writing is a way to participate in the world around you.* Whether you are writing a job application, a letter to the editor of your local newspaper, a message on a blog, or an essay for one of your classes, you are engaging with the world around you. Writing is not just a solitary intellectual activity; because of the power of writing to affect others, writing is also an *act*—a way to participate in important activities. As many of the readings in this book will illustrate, writing can make things happen. It can change the world—in big, dramatic ways as well as in small but no less important ways.

So writing matters. And it matters more today than ever because the globalized and increasingly technological world you are living in is so profoundly shaped by writing—in forms both new and old.

This book is intended to help you write and read more effectively in a complicated and changing world. It is designed to help you gain insight into the most important aspects of writing and to help you learn to manage many different kinds of writing tasks. I hope it will also help you gain a deeper appreciation for the power of writing and the ways it matters in your life.

PART

1

Writing *in* Context

What Is "Good" Writing?

WHEN I WAS IN COLLEGE, I BEGAN WRITING ARTICLES FOR NEWSPAPERS AND MAGAZINES. ONE DAY, I STOPPED AT MY LOCAL GAS STATION AND THE OWNER, WHOM MY FAMILY HAD KNOWN FOR YEARS, MENTIONED THAT HE HAD READ AN ARTICLE OF MINE IN A MAGAZINE TO WHICH HE SUBSCRIBED. HE ASKED ME SOME QUESTIONS ABOUT THE PIECE, AND WE CHATTED FOR A WHILE. IT WAS FUN FOR ME TO TALK ABOUT A PIECE OF WRITING I HAD DONE MONTHS EARLIER WITH A GUY WHO USUALLY

discussed car problems with me. As I was leaving, he said, "You're a good writer." I was proud to hear that, but I was also surprised. It was the first time anyone had said that about writing I had done outside school. The only feedback I had previously received on my writing was from teachers, who usually pointed out problems and gave grades. But the gas station owner read my article because he was interested in the topic, not because he wanted to evaluate the writing. It was the first time I had the experience of connecting with a reader for reasons other than grading.

At the time, I assumed that if I was a good writer in school, then I must also be a good writer outside school. I assumed that good writing is good writing, no matter what the circumstances. Was I right? I don't think so. Here's why.

Writing Depends on Context

You probably do much more writing and reading in a day than you realize: reading the morning paper, sending a text message, checking your e-mail, writing a letter to your school's financial aid department, paging through a recent issue of a newsmagazine in the dentist's office, filling out a job application. All these are common but important literate activities that require a certain level of skill and knowledge. Yet in many

ways, they are not the same kind of writing and reading expected in school. What counts as good writing in a text message or a letter to your financial aid officer obviously may differ from what counts as good writing in school. That's because good writing is always related to the context of the writing. There's really no such thing as good writing in general. Writing can only be judged good in a particular situation. What makes a letter to your financial aid officer effective will not necessarily be the same as what will earn you an A on a research report in your biology class. By the same token, writing that works in your biology class may earn you a low grade in a history class. Of course, some aspects of good writing will apply no matter what the context (I'll address some of those aspects in Chapter 3). But those aspects—which include things like correct grammar, proper form, and coherent paragraphs—do not by themselves make writing good. It's much more complicated than that.

Good Writing Fits the Rhetorical Situation

What is good writing, then? How can we know when we've produced a good piece of writing? The short answer is that good writing is an appropriate response to a given situation. Writing is good when it fits the context. This means that good writers examine the writing situation, or what theorists call the *rhetorical situation,* and try to address it effectively. Writing is good because it somehow connects with readers in a given rhetorical situation. It is good if it communicates something meaningful to those readers in that situation. The gas station owner liked my magazine article in part because that article spoke to his interests and met his expectations for an article in that magazine at that point in time. This book includes many reading selections that might be considered good writing in terms of the writing style or the ideas conveyed by the writer. But mostly, the selections in this book are examples of writing that is effective within specific rhetorical situations. And to understand what makes that writing good requires that you understand something about those rhetorical situations.

Effective Writers Take Audience into Account

Of course, different readers can respond very differently to the same piece of writing. The gas station owner liked my article, but his mechanic might have considered it boring. You probably have disagreed with a classmate about whether a piece of writing is good or not. Maybe your best friend doesn't like your favorite book. Scholars debate the quality of Shakespeare's writing. And you certainly have had teachers who prefer a certain kind of writing that other teachers disliked. Does that mean that good writing is completely subjective? No. But it does mean that the question of what is good writing is complicated and that readers are always part of the equation. Writers must take that complexity into account.

In my experience as both a professional writer and a teacher of writing, I have learned that the easiest part of learning to write well is learning the basic rules of writing. It may be boring to learn some of the rules of grammar or to run a spelling check on the draft of an essay, but those aspects of writing are really not very difficult. What's challenging is learning how to assess the rhetorical situation for your writing and to respond effectively to the context within which you're writing. The most effective writers are those who understand the importance of context in writing. And the first step is to examine what context in writing is.

Defining Context in Writing

The Jungle by Upton Sinclair is one of those books that people say changed the world. It's one of my favorite examples of the power— and the complexity—of writing. And it can help us better understand the role of context in writing. There are two useful ways to think about context: (1) as a conversation among readers and writers and (2) as the right moment for writing. The story of *The Jungle* can help us understand both.

THE RHETORICAL SITUATION
The idea of the rhetorical situation, which dates back to the ancient Greek philosophers, helps explain the relationships among the key elements of communication in writing (or speaking): the writer (or speaker), the writer's (or speaker's) subject, and the audience. The image of a triangle has traditionally been used to represent these relationships between a writer and his or her subject, between a writer and an audience, and between the audience and the subject. These relationships shape how meaning is conveyed in a text.

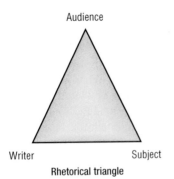

Audience

Writer   Subject

Rhetorical triangle

The Jungle was published in 1906, but this wrenching story about the travails of a Lithuanian immigrant named Jurgis Rudkus in Chicago's meat-packing plants at the turn of the twentieth century still moves readers today. When it was first published, it helped create a national uproar that led to the passage of food safety laws that continue to protect Americans a century later. Its **descriptions** of the horrible conditions and the poor treatment of workers inside meat-packing plants outraged many readers. Initially, many publishers refused to publish the novel, which first appeared in serial installments in a socialist newspaper called *Appeal to Reason*. But the demand for the novel was so great that one publisher decided to print it—although only after verifying the novel's descriptions of the Chicago meat-packing plants. The meat-packing industry tried to discredit Sinclair and his novel. But eventually, congressional hearings revealed that Sinclair's harrowing depiction of working in the meat-packing plants was accurate, and Congress subsequently passed the law establishing the Food and Drug Administration (FDA) to oversee the food industry. In effect, Sinclair's novel moved an entire nation to address serious health and safety issues related to the food industry.

POWERFUL DESCRIPTION

Here's a sample of the kind of description in Sinclair's novel that provoked such a public outcry in 1906. In this passage, Jonas (the uncle of Jurgis's wife) is describing to his family what he experienced in the meat-packing plants:

> Jonas had told them how the meat that was taken out of the pickle would often be found sour, and how they would rub it up with soda to take away the smell, and sell it to be eaten on free-lunch counters; also of all the miracles of chemistry which they performed, giving to any sort of meat, fresh or salted, whole or chopped, any color and any flavor and any odor they chose. In the pickling of hams they had an ingenious apparatus, by which they saved time and increased the capacity of the plant—a machine consisting of a hollow needle attached to a pump; by plunging this needle into the meat and working with his foot a man could fill a ham with pickle in a few seconds. And yet, in spite of this, there would be hams found spoiled, some of them with an odor so bad that a man could hardly bear to be in a room with them. To pump into these the packers had a second and much stronger pickle which destroyed the odor—a process known to the workers as "giving them thirty per cent." Also, after the hams had been smoked, there would be found some that had gone to the bad. Formerly these had been sold as "Number Three Grade," but later on some ingenious person hit upon a new device, and now they would extract the bone, about which the bad part generally lay, and insert in the hole a white-hot iron. After this invention there was no longer Number One, Two, and Three Grade—there was only Number One Grade.

Because of the growth of food processing in the United States at the time, such descriptions caused great concern among American consumers. But the novel contains even more disturbing descriptions about how food was processed and how workers were mistreated. The impact of such writing is partly a function of the context: These descriptions were so disturbing to many readers at the time because increasing numbers of Americans were eating processed food.

Context as Conversation

How did one novel have such a big impact? You might answer that question by saying that *The Jungle* was just good writing. But that wouldn't really explain the novel's impact. To do that, we have to look a little more closely at the circumstances surrounding the novel and the era in which it was written. The novel fueled a national debate about how food was processed in the United States at the beginning of the twentieth century. But Sinclair did not create the problems he described in his book, nor was he the first person to write about them. In a sense, when Upton Sinclair wrote *The Jungle*, he was joining a conversation about these issues that was already going on. And the power of his book was partly a matter of how it fit into that conversation.

Here's what I mean. When Upton Sinclair's novel appeared, the U.S. Congress was already debating a bill that would regulate the

MORE THAN ONE CONVERSATION

When writers write about a topic of interest and importance, they are often joining several "conversations" at once. Sinclair was actually joining several related conversations, as I'll discuss a little later. It's important to understand that the contexts of writing can be complicated, and often, writers may be focusing attention on one conversation while they are actually part of several. How readers respond, then, will be partly a result of which conversations they believe they are taking part in.

food industry. Many Americans were concerned about the safety of food produced by the rapidly growing food processing industry. But the big food producers didn't want regulations, and they helped stall the bill in Congress. The descriptions of the terrible conditions in the meat-packing plants in *The Jungle* helped energize a national debate that was already occurring and put pressure on Congress to pass the bill. People began talking and writing about Sinclair's novel as part of that debate. If that debate had not been happening, *The Jungle* might not have received the attention it did, and it might not have affected so many readers as deeply as it did, no matter how engaging its story. In other words, Sinclair was writing about something people cared about, something they were already talking and thinking and reading about. He was joining a conversation that mattered to him and to his readers. If we think about context in this way, we can see that *context includes more than just a topic that interests readers at a given point in time; it also includes what people are saying and thinking in general about that topic at that time.*

Although it is rare for a book or article to have the wide impact that Sinclair's novel had, the basic elements of this example apply to all writing. When you write an essay for an English class, you are responding to a specific rhetorical situation (usually a response to a question or writing prompt), much as Sinclair did. Your audience will be much smaller than his was, and your purpose may be very different, but you are still writing for an audience (even if that audience is only your teacher or your classmates) and you still have a purpose (even if your immediate purpose is only to earn a good grade). How effective your essay is depends in large part on how well you respond to the elements of that rhetorical situation. How good your essay is depends on how well it fits the context. And the same is true of any writing you do.

It is helpful to think of writing as part of a conversation. When you write an essay for a course, you are taking part in ongoing conversations about your topic that influence what you write and how your readers will respond. What you learn about your topic and how you understand the issues you are writing about will be influenced by those conversations. Like Sinclair, you have to address your topic in a way that fits those ongoing conversations.

The Right Timing: Understanding Historical Context

So the impact of *The Jungle* can be explained in part by understanding the context as an ongoing conversation about food safety in the United States at that time. But there's more to the story. The descriptions in Sinclair's novel of the living and working conditions in the food industry appalled many readers at a time when Americans were already worried about the larger problems of immigration and the effects of industrialization. **The early years of the twentieth century** were marked by the rapid growth of industry as well as a wave of immigration that was profoundly changing American society. Some Americans wanted to limit immigration. Others, like Sinclair himself, were deeply concerned about the treatment of immigrants and the exploitation of workers by American industry. So *The Jungle* was not only part of the national debate about food safety; it was also part of other important conversations about immigration, industrialization, and the protection of workers.

These conversations mattered to Sinclair as a writer. He hoped his novel would help Americans see how workers were exploited by American industry. He believed that the problems in the meat-packing plants depicted in his novel were really the fault of the American capitalist system. As a socialist, he believed sweeping economic and political reforms were needed to protect Americans from what he saw as the evils of capitalism. Sinclair hoped that his story would convert many readers to his view that capitalism was bad for American workers. In writing *The Jungle*, he was participating in the national debates about the American political and economic system and about individual worker's rights. In fact, **these debates had really been going on among philosophers and political thinkers for centuries.** Famous philosophers like Plato and Karl Marx wrote about these same basic issues, and their ideas influenced writers like Sinclair. Ultimately, Sinclair hoped that his writing would help sway American opinion about industrialization and capitalism. So he was actually disappointed that the public reaction to his book focused on the food industry. He was hoping for a workers' revolution, not for the formation of the FDA. Amazingly, despite the great impact of his novel, Sinclair felt he had failed in his primary goal: to convince Americans to resist the rise of industrial capitalism.

Why did readers react so strongly to *The Jungle*'s descriptions of the food processing plants but largely ignore the novel's message about capitalism? We can explain this "failure" if we think about context as including the historical moment. While American readers at that time were ready for a story about the food processing industry, they were not as ready for a critique of capitalism. The national debate about food safety made it an issue that readers knew about and were concerned about. Those debates shaped readers' reaction to *The Jungle* more directly than the ongoing debates about workers' rights and capitalism. At that moment in time, more readers were more in tune with food safety as a problem than with industrialization or capitalism as important issues. As a result, Sinclair's novel was read by more peo-

USING HISTORICAL CONTEXT
Notice how I'm giving important background information here to help you understand the historical context within which Sinclair was writing. Readers need to appreciate the historical context just as much as writers do. Usually, we don't think about historical context when we're writing because we're writing in the present. But when we examine a text like *The Jungle*, we can more easily see how important historical context can be. Without your realizing it, historical context influences your writing. For example, you will sometimes write about topics that are controversial right now—topics that interest readers today but perhaps not in a week or a year. In other words, historical context influences your choice of subject matter for your writing. In addition, beliefs and attitudes may be related to historical context. For instance, if you write about gender today, you will be writing to readers whose attitudes about gender are probably different from the attitudes of readers twenty or thirty years ago, and your own attitudes about gender will likely reflect the times. In these and other ways, historical context is an integral part of all the writing and reading we do.

ONGOING CONVERSATIONS
This is another important point about context: The conversations that writers are joining are usually conversations with long histories. When Sinclair wrote about workers' rights, he was drawing on ideas that had been debated for many years—ideas about the nature of government, about civil society, about individual rights, and related matters. The specific issues may have changed over time, but the fundamental questions did not. Many of the essays in this book are part of important conversations that have been going on for many centuries.

CULTURE AS CONTEXT

Another important component of context is culture, and food is a good example of how issues and ideas can be shaped by culture. Think of the significance of food in important religious and cultural rituals: the Jewish rules for kosher food, the meatless meals during the Catholic celebration of Lent, the fasting among Muslims during Ramadan. Think also of the cultural meaning of certain foods: a hot dog at a Fourth of July picnic or the lamb slaughtered for an important event, such as a wedding, in many Arab nations. These examples help us see that our attitudes about things like food are deeply shaped by the culture we live in. Inevitably, then, culture shapes our writing and reading, too. For Sinclair, part of the challenge was that capitalism was widely accepted in American culture, so it may be that American readers were less likely to respond to his criticisms of capitalism than to his descriptions of the food processing plants.

ple as part of **the conversation about food safety** and not as a critique of capitalism as he had hoped. Thus, Sinclair was able to connect with his audience in one sense but not in another. Like all writers, Sinclair could write in a way that was appropriate for the context, but he could not control readers' reactions.

Does that mean Sinclair's novel was not good writing? You'll have to answer that for yourself. But I hope you'll see that there is no easy "yes" or "no" answer to that question. To be effective in any writing task, a writer must examine context and try to respond to it appropriately. Your challenge in doing so may not be as great as Sinclair's, but it is fundamentally the same kind of challenge. And it is the kind of challenge that makes writing so meaningful and worthwhile.

Context and Reading

Everything in this chapter about the importance of context for writers also applies to readers. When you read a text, you read it in a specific context. That context includes:

- when and why you are reading the text (for a class assignment, for your own pleasure or knowledge, for your job)
- your background (your age, gender, ethnic or racial identity, and so on)
- your beliefs and values (religious, ethical, and so on)
- your experiences (with the topic as well as with texts like the one you're reading)
- your knowledge (about the topic and related matters)

All these factors influence how you read that text. For example, imagine reading a newspaper editorial about a controversial issue that you have strong feelings about. Your response to that editorial is likely to be shaped not only by your own opinion, but also by many of the factors I just mentioned. Now think about a textbook in an introductory sociology course. When you read that textbook, you are probably reading it as someone who is not an expert in sociology, and that will influence how you read it. So part of your challenge as a reader is to place that text in the larger context of the field of sociology.

Now back to *The Jungle*. Think about the different ways you can read that one text:

- as a story about immigrants
- as a critique of American capitalism
- as a literary work that explores certain themes
- as a historical artifact that had an important role in the formation of the FDA
- as a reflection of ideas and conditions at a certain point in American history
- as an example of the power of writing
- as an example of the importance of context in writing

What you know about *The Jungle* and the context in which it was written affects how you read it. When and why you read the book will also affect how you read it. Similarly, your own background and your identity shape how you read it. Context matters—for writers *and* readers.

Discourse and Why It Is Important

If you think about writing as a matter of participating in ongoing conversations about important or interesting issues, you are more likely to pay attention to some of the complex elements of context that I have been describing; as a result, you are more likely to write effectively in the various rhetorical situations you encounter. But this idea of writing as conversation can also help us see that writing is not just a matter of discussing relevant topics or questions that are part of ongoing conversations; it is also a matter of understanding how language is used in those conversations. It is a matter of what theorists call *discourse*. In other words, the ongoing conversations that writers participate in often involve different ways of using language that affect what they write and how readers understand what they write. Let me explain with an example.

Early in 2005, a controversy erupted in the small town of Glens Falls in upstate New York. A year earlier, a local artist had been commissioned by the school district to paint a mural that covered the entire wall of an elementary school's main hallway. The artist decided his mu-

Details from a school mural by Esmond Lyons in Glens Falls, NY.

© Esmond Lyons, 2004.

ral should depict the region around Glens Falls, and he asked the students for their ideas about what he should include in the mural.

One of the suggestions he received was to include an image of a man who stood every day in the town square holding a sign that said, "Support Our Troops." The man, who claimed to be encouraging people to support the U.S. soldiers fighting in Iraq at the time, became a kind of local celebrity. For more than two years he stood with his sign on the town square every day. Anyone living in Glens Falls would know about him, so the students felt he should be depicted in the mural. The artist agreed, and he painted a tiny image of the man in one section of the mural. However, on the mural, the artist painted the man's sign to read "Blessed Are the Peace Makers Who Make Peace" instead of "Support Our Troops" (see photo on p. 9). After the mural was finished, some town residents and members of the school board complained about the artist's representation of the man's sign. They argued that the artist's change to the man's sign amounted to a political statement against the war in Iraq, which they believed was inappropriate for a school mural. To understand why they interpreted the change in that way, we have to examine what the two phrases—"Support Our Troops" and "Blessed Are the Peace Makers Who Make Peace"— might mean in this context.

Words Acquire Meaning within Discourses

At first glance, these phrases seem straightforward. To "Support Our Troops" obviously means offering some kind of support for them; that support might include verbal expressions of support, encouragement, or perhaps sending them letters or packages. Similarly, "Blessed Are the Peace Makers Who Make Peace" seems to be an obvious statement of praise for people who work for peace. But, of course, these two phrases have additional meanings depending on how and when they are used and who uses them. In other words, what these phrases mean depends on their *use in context.* In 2005, "Support Our Troops" was generally understood to be a statement of support not only for the troops themselves but also for the war in Iraq and the policies of the American government; by contrast, "Blessed Are the Peace Makers Who Make Peace" in reference to the war was understood to be a statement against the war and U.S. government policies. These meanings resulted from the way these phrases were used at that historical moment. Moreover, if the artist had painted "Blessed Are the Peace Makers Who Make Peace" somewhere else on his mural, it would not likely have been interpreted as

CONTEXT AND IMAGES
Context affects not only words but images, too. Consider the yellow ribbon with the phrase "Support Our Troops" that became a common sight in the United States after the invasion of Iraq in 2003. That image symbolized support for U.S. policies in Iraq and came to represent a certain political viewpoint. Its meaning was shaped by the contexts in which it was used and by the historical circumstances. It's also worth noting that the yellow ribbon came from a popular song from the 1970s, "Tie a Yellow Ribbon 'round the Old Oak Tree," in which a woman is waiting for her lover to return home after a long absence. In this case, several different discourses are "blended" to give the yellow ribbon its symbolic meaning.

Support Our Troops

© Scott Heiner/istockphoto.com

an antiwar statement. But putting it on the sign of the man who was well known as a supporter of the war effort gave it meaning as an antiwar statement.

The point is that context influences the meaning of words. Both writers and readers rely on context for those meanings. Those two phrases—"Support Our Troops" and "Blessed Are the Peace Makers Who Make Peace"—were part of ongoing national conversations about U.S. foreign policy and about the war in Iraq. How those phrases are used in such conversations gives them certain meanings or significance. Scholars use the term *discourse* to describe this process of meaning arising from the way language is used in various situations. The idea of discourse helps us identify special uses of language to see how the meanings of words and phrases are related to the way they are used by certain groups of people in certain situations.

Writers Are Always "within" Discourse

What does all this have to do with you as you sit down to write an essay for your history or psychology class? Well, in writing such an essay, not only are you participating in ongoing conversations about history or psychology, but your understanding of the ideas and issues you're writing about is influenced by the discourses of those academic fields. What you say in your essay about a topic in psychology, for example, will be determined in part by the discourse of psychology. That discourse includes the important issues that define the field of psychology, the views and values of those in the field, and the significance of certain ideas or words within the field. When you write that psychology paper, you are—whether you realize it or not—part of that discourse. And to write that paper effectively means that you can "enter the discourse" of psychology effectively. To write well in a specific field about a specific topic requires that you have some sense of the important ideas in that field; it also requires that you understand the language of that field to some extent. In psychology, for example, you would probably need to know what terms like the *unconscious* or *ego* mean because they are important ideas in that field. And what those terms mean in psychology is not necessarily what they mean in other contexts. If you use the term *ego* in a discussion with psychology majors, they will likely assume that you are referring to a part of the human subconscious that famed psychologist Sigmund Freud identified. If you use the term in casual conversation with some friends, they are likely to assume that you're referring to a personality trait (for example, someone's "big ego").

Throughout this book, I refer to the idea of participating in conversations about various issues. Participating in these conversations is also a matter of entering the discourses that shape those conversations. As you gain experience as a writer and reader, you will also be learning about various discourses. Your ability to write well and to read effectively depends in large part on your knowledge of these discourses. Even the matter of *what* you write about is shaped by discourse. The

JARGON

We tend to think of jargon as a negative thing, but actually, jargon can serve useful purposes. Sometimes special words or phrases are needed to refer to ideas or developments that are difficult to capture with more common words. One example is *discourse*. Some people might protest the use of this term, which sounds academic and may confuse many readers. Why not use a more common term like *language*? In some ways, the term *language* can convey some of what is meant by *discourse,* but it doesn't quite capture the complexity of the idea of discourse as it has come to be understood by scholars. So this kind of jargon is actually an efficient and easy way for scholars to convey their ideas to one another. As a college student, you will be introduced to specialized terms like *discourse* within the different academic disciplines you will study. Each discipline has specialized terms that might seem like so much jargon but which actually help people in those fields communicate effectively with each other.

important questions, ideas, and problems in a given academic field or in the society at large are determined in part by the discourses we are subject to. So having a sense of how discourses work is part of becoming a more sophisticated and effective writer and reader.

Where Do Themes Come From?

Like many other composition textbooks, this one is organized around topics or *themes*. If you look at the Contents, you'll see that each chapter from 5 through 12 has a main theme: understanding, communication, relationships, and so on. And within each chapter are clusters of readings that reflect other themes related to the main theme of the chapter. These themes should be familiar to you. They are not only common themes in writing classes, but they also reflect important issues in society in general. And it's worth asking where these themes come from.

That question may seem silly. You might wonder what difference it makes to ask why education, for example, or identity is considered an important issue to read and write about. Most composition textbooks include readings devoted to these themes, and it would be difficult to find a teacher or a student who would argue that these themes are not important. But examining how these specific themes have come to be considered important can help us better understand the key point of this chapter: that writing is best understood in context. If we look at how and why certain issues seem important to most readers and writers while other issues do not, we can gain a better sense of how the writing and reading we do is part of an ongoing process that affects how we understand the world around us. Let me explain what I mean.

Pick up almost any U.S. newspaper and you'll find the same main sections: news, editorials and opinion, sports, and business/money. There are usually sections devoted to arts or lifestyle as well, and many newspapers include a section on travel. Most also include classified ads and comics. These sections—which are really themes—have become so commonplace in modern news media that you probably think of them as natural. Even local television news includes versions of these themes: national news, local news, sports, and weather. But in a sense, these sections divide the world into categories, and they convey implicit messages about what's important. So it's worth wondering why most newspapers have the same main sections. Is it because we all see the world in more or less the same way, and newspapers simply describe the world around us (as many journalists claim)? Or do the sections of a newspaper reflect a certain view of the world? I think it's a little bit of both—and more.

Think about the fact that most newspapers have a business section and a sports section, implying that these activities—business and sports—are important and that readers should pay attention to them. The very existence of these sections, no matter what stories they contain, places value on these activities. It tells us that business matters, for example. The business section directs our attention toward certain events, activities, ideas, and issues that are somehow classified as "business." The same is true of the other sections of the newspaper. But it's also worth thinking about what might be left out of these common sections of a newspaper. For example, why isn't there a section devoted to, say, environmental issues? Or one devoted to communication? Why is there a business section but not a labor section?

You might answer that these issues—the environment, communication, or labor—are included in the other main sections of the newspaper. For instance, a story about an environmental problem in a local river might be included in the local news section, or a story about toxic waste at a local factory might be included in the business section. That may be true. But what if such stories were included in a separate section called The Environment? How would that change the way we read those stories? Would a story on toxic waste at a local factory have a different meaning if it were included in a section on the environment as opposed to the section on business? What difference would that make? For one thing, any story appearing in the business section is implicitly defined as a business issue. The focus of the story would therefore not necessarily be on environmental protection or conservation but on the implications of the toxic waste for business and perhaps for the economy in general. In a sense, a value judgment is being made simply by placing the story in the business section: The environment is being defined in economic terms, and business is perhaps given greater value than environmental protection. On the other hand, placing that story in a section on the environment might suggest that the focus of attention is the environment itself rather than the activities of business or the economy; it would convey a message that the environment matters. Would that affect how readers understood the issue? Such questions help us see that how we categorize the world reflects our values and beliefs; it reflects what we think is important. So *themes are not just groups of topics or subjects; themes reflect our understanding of the world.*

The same principle applies to this book. When I began to compile the Contents, I started with main themes that seemed important for a first-year writing course: education, politics, identity, and so on. But as I reviewed individual reading selections and tried to decide which themes they fit best, I began to realize that I might be influencing what those selections mean to a reader. For example, if I took an essay

THE WORLD OF THE NEWSPAPER
USA Today, the largest circulation newspaper in the United States, includes the main sections seen at the upper left in this image: News, Travel, Money, Sports, Life, Tech, and Weather. Consider what these categories suggest about the world around us. Where do these sections—or themes—come from?

USA Today home page

like E. B. White's famous "Once More to the Lake" and put it in a chapter about relationships, it would imply that the focus of White's essay is on relationships of some kind. Maybe that *is* the focus of his essay. But it's also an essay about an important place, so it could fit nicely into Chapter 10: Living Together. If I had included a chapter on memory, it could have fit there, too, since the essay is based on White's childhood memories. Or I might have included it in a chapter on growing up. If so, then you might be inclined to read it as a story about growing up and getting older.

There are three important points to keep in mind here. First, any piece of writing can have many themes. E. B. White's essay is so often reprinted in textbooks precisely because it explores several complex themes that engage different readers. The second point is that what a piece of writing means will depend on context. Readers may see a certain meaning in White's essay just because it is placed in a chapter on spaces or relationships. Students may read it a certain way because of how their teacher presents it to them. Understanding an essay is therefore partly a matter of paying attention to the context in which you are reading it as well as trying to understand the context within which it was written. Third, a reader's experience and viewpoint can also affect what an essay means. Different readers may see different meanings in the same text depending on who they are and how they view the subject of the essay at that time.

This book is designed to help you explore the contexts of writing and reading in just these ways. I have organized the book into themes and subthemes in a way that I hope will call your attention to how context affects the meaning we make as writers and readers. Throughout this book, you will be asked questions that will focus your attention on how an essay or an article fits into a context and how its messages may be related to that context. These questions will focus your attention on how ideas and viewpoints develop over time as a result of the way writers and readers use language to examine and understand the world around them. Being aware of these messages is part of being a critical and sophisticated reader. It is also essential for being an effective writer.

So what does it mean to be a good writer? Part of the answer to that question, as I discovered when I began writing for different audiences, like the gas station owner in my hometown, is that good writers understand the importance of context. Your success as a writer, in school as well as outside the classroom, is partly a matter of your ability to recognize that context and make the choices in your writing that best fit that context. This book can help you learn to do that.

Chapter 2
Understanding Media as Contexts for Writing

FIRST BEGAN TO APPRECIATE THE IMPORTANCE OF IMAGES IN THE EARLY 1980S WHEN I WAS A NEW TEACHER OF WRITING. ONE OF THE BOOKS ASSIGNED TO THE FIRST-YEAR COMPOSITION CLASS I WAS TEACHING INCLUDED A PROVOCATIVE ESSAY CALLED "THE BOSTON PHOTOGRAPHS" BY WRITER AND FILMMAKER NORA EPHRON. THE ESSAY WAS ABOUT A SERIES OF DRAMATIC PHOTOGRAPHS TAKEN AT THE SCENE OF A FIRE AT A HIGH-RISE APARTMENT BUILDING IN BOSTON IN 1975. AS THE PHOTOGRAPHER WATCHED the firefighters trying to rescue residents stranded on the upper floors of the building, he noticed a young woman and her small child standing on the fire escape with a fireman who was reaching desperately for a rescue ladder. Suddenly, as the photographer was snapping pictures of the scene, the fire escape gave way, and the woman and her child plunged many stories to the street below. The woman was killed, but her child, who landed on top of her, survived.

The next day, three photographs showing the horrifying scene were published in newspapers

Stanley Forman, *The Boston Photographs,* 1975

© Stanley J. Forman, Pulitzer Prize, Spot News, 1976

© Stanley J. Forman, Pulitzer Prize, Spot News, 1976

© Stanley J. Forman, Pulitzer Prize, Spot News, 1976

around the world, sparking a controversy that raged for weeks. Many people were upset that the photos were published, arguing that they were not only unnecessary, because a fire at the apartment building in Boston would normally not have been news anywhere else, but also that the photos sensationalized the event and violated the woman's privacy at the moment of her death. Editorials criticizing or supporting the decision to publish the photos appeared in many newspapers around the United States.

I asked the students in my class to take up the controversy. Their assignment was to decide whether to publish the photographs and then to write a brief statement explaining their decision. The discussion in class that day was lively and intense, and there was no consensus about whether the newspaper editors were right to publish the photographs. Some students argued that the photos were published just to sell newspapers. Others argued that the photos merely documented a tragic event. Some students asked whether the story about the fire would have been different without the photos. Others pointed out that newspapers in other states and countries would not even have published a story about a fire in Boston without those dramatic photos. A few students argued that the photos were an intrusion on an intimate, private moment for the woman who died, and some asked whether the controversy would have been any different if the woman had survived. Whatever their opinion about the decision, *all* the students agreed that the riveting photos had a profound impact on anyone who saw them.

That discussion highlighted for me the impact that images can have on us. Those photographs affected readers in ways that the written text of the news articles did not. Even though the articles about the fire described the scene and informed readers that the woman died, somehow the images of the woman and her child falling seemed to have greater power than writing alone. Why?

There is no easy way to answer that question. But as a writer and a reader, you should appreciate not only the power of images to convey feelings, ideas, and information but also *how* images do so. We live in a multimedia world in which we are bombarded with images of all kinds—in television commercials, in magazine and newspaper advertisements, on billboards, on flyers and posters, on clothing, and on the Internet. Increasingly, as new technologies evolve, images are not only more common in communication but also more important. In addition, with these new technologies, writers can more easily combine images with text to help make their messages more effective. These capabilities mean that writers can create documents in which images, text, and even sound work together to convey complex messages and ideas.

IMAGES AS INFORMATION

A few years ago, a scholar named Gunther Kress pointed out that "the visual is becoming more prominent in the landscape of public communication."[1] Kress argued that images and text can convey information differently, and new technologies enable writers to take advantage of the power of both image and text more effectively than ever before. He used the example of a textbook to make his point. Textbooks today, like the one you're reading now, make use of images in different ways from textbooks thirty or forty years ago, which usually included a few illustrations to supplement the text. Today, according to Kress, images are used to convey important information rather than simply to illustrate.

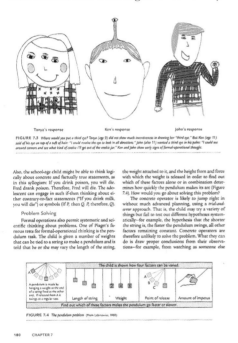

A typical textbook. From *Psycholinguistics*, 2nd Edition by Dan I. Slobin. Copyright © 1979, 1974 by Scott, Foresman and Company. Reprinted by permission of Addison Wesley Longman, Inc.

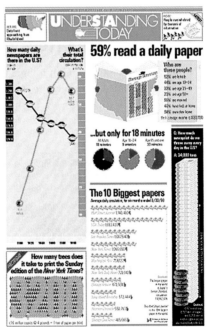

Imitation of *USA Today* front page by Nigel Holmes, from *Understanding USA* by Richard Saul Wurman.

[1]Gunther Kress, "'English' at the Crossroads: Rethinking Curricula of Communication in the Context of the Turn to the Visual." In Gail E. Hawisher and Cynthia L. Selfe (Eds.), *Passions, Pedagogies, and 21st Century Technologies* (Logan: Utah State University Press, 1999), pp. 66–88.

Keep in mind that when we examine images in communication, we're really examining another component of *context*. The technological media we use for communication are not just tools but are also an integral part of the context of writing. If you are using the Internet to communicate a message, that technological context can influence your decisions as a writer. Learning to incorporate images into your writing and becoming familiar with new technologies for communication are part of the process of learning to write in context and to assess different rhetorical situations.

What all this means for writers is that they have more sophisticated tools to accomplish their purposes in writing and more opportunities to reach audiences through different media. It also means that both writers and readers face new challenges as they communicate with one another in various media. They have to develop a better understanding of how a medium can influence a message or place limitations on a writer. They also have to understand how images convey messages and how the visual can be an important part of a writing task. That's what this chapter is about. It will help you understand the importance of the visual in communication today, and it will give you some ideas for using visual elements in your own writing tasks.

"Reading" Images

When we view an image, we are not only making sense of the visual elements of that image, but we are also looking for messages that the image might convey. In other words, we can "read" images for what they

Subhankar Banerjee, Arctic National Wildlife Refuge

say to us. And learning to read images is part of being an informed reader and writer. Reading images involves three main considerations:

- context
- background knowledge
- perspective

Images in Context

The impact and meaning of an image are always related to context. For example, consider the photograph by Subhankar Banerjee on page 18. Most people wouldn't need to know much about the photograph to appreciate the beauty of this wilderness scene. Obviously, how you react to this photograph is influenced by your feelings about wilderness and perhaps by your prior life experiences.

But how might the meaning of this photograph change if you knew that it was taken in the Arctic National Wildlife Refuge (ANWR) in Alaska in 2002 and that ANWR has been the subject of controversy because of various bills before the U.S. Congress that would allow oil drilling there? How would that influence the way you read this photo? Would its message about wilderness be different if you did not know about those controversies? Consider that in 2004 Senator Barbara Boxer from California used this and similar photographs during a debate in the U.S. Senate about oil drilling in ANWR. For Boxer, these images refuted a statement made by Gale A. Norton, who was secretary of the interior, that the refuge is "a flat white nothingness." In the context of those debates, these photographs were not just depictions of natural beauty; they also acquired a certain political significance.

The point is that we read an image within a specific context that can significantly influence what that image might mean. Obviously, we can discuss the technical merits of Subhankar Banerjee's photograph, such as how he positions the elements in the scene—the water, the vegetation in the foreground, the distant mountains, and the clouds—to convey certain messages about wilderness. We might discuss the color or lighting of the scene in the same way. A photographer or an artist uses such elements to convey what he or she sees in the scene. This use of various visual elements is sometimes called *composition*. But the political significance of that photograph does not come from the composition of the photograph itself; rather, it comes from the context within which it is seen.

Context, of course, includes *time,* or *historical context* (see page 6 in Chapter 1). For example, here's an airline advertisement that appeared in the 1970s,

Extra hands assure extra luxuries on DELTA *Royal Service Flights*

Not two, but three alert stewardesses assure you of every attention in the brief span of a Delta Royal Service Flight. So linger over your luncheon or dinner with its complimentary champagne and choice of entrée (*tenderloin steak to order, Rock Cornish hen, or seafood on appropriate days*). There's also music by Muzak, fast baggage handling and beverage service for the discerning passengers who specify these luxurious flights.

These flights serve:
NEW YORK · WASHINGTON · ATLANTA · HOUSTON · CHICAGO
MIAMI · NEW ORLEANS · DALLAS · PHILADELPHIA
BALTIMORE · MEMPHIS · DETROIT

Delta's DC-8 Jetliners are on their way!

Delta advertisement from the 1970s

when attitudes about women in American culture were very different. At that time, this image of a smiling, well-dressed woman serving passengers would have been considered a positive one by most readers. But what messages about women might be read in this image today? Your answer to that question is influenced by current attitudes or beliefs regarding gender roles—attitudes or beliefs that may be different from those of the 1970s. It is in this sense that the historical moment influences what an image might mean to viewers.

This photograph also illustrates an important point made earlier: that images and text can work together to convey powerful messages differently than the image or text alone could convey. In this case, the text below the paragraph is intended to shape the message of the photograph. The second paragraph of the text emphasizes qualities that many Americans at that time might have associated with women (*attractive, considerate, orderly, courteous, poised);* in conjunction with that text, the photo, which shows a woman helping a young child, suggests motherhood. Without that paragraph, the photograph would still convey certain messages about women and specifically about flight attendants, but the text in the ad "frames" those messages so that viewers are more likely to read the image as the airline intended. Of course, context comes into play here again. Today, the words used to describe the stewardess—*attractive, orderly, poised*—might carry negative connotations when applied to women that those words might not have carried for most readers in the 1970s. So readers today might read this advertisement very differently, and no doubt many would find this ad offensive. This example helps us see not only the importance of historical context in how we read images but also the ways in which attitudes and values can change over time, which also affects the meaning of an image.

The Role of Background Knowledge

Very often, the messages you see in an image are shaped by background knowledge. Here's a simple example. The impact of the photograph below depends in large part on your knowing that the man is

President George W. Bush at Mount Rushmore

President George W. Bush and that the background shows Mount Rushmore, the famous national monument in South Dakota where the faces of four U.S. presidents—George Washington, Thomas Jefferson, Theodore Roosevelt, and Abraham Lincoln—are carved into a mountainside. Because Mount Rushmore is widely associated with patriotism, viewers of this photo who are familiar with Mount Rushmore are likely to read a patriotic message. Without that background knowledge, however, the patriotic message may be lost on a viewer who might see this photo as simply showing a man speaking in front of a large sculpture.

Here's a slightly more complicated example. Do you get the joke in the comic strip below, from 2005? If not, it may be because you need background knowledge that you don't have. To appreciate the humor, you have to be familiar with events of the time—specifically, the public debates about the Iraq war, especially the criticisms of the Bush administration's lack of a "mission goal" in that war. But to fully appreciate the humor, you also have to be familiar with Herman Melville's classic novel *Moby Dick*. The main character, a nineteenth century sea captain named Ahab, is killed in his fanatical pursuit of a white whale named Moby Dick by becoming entangled in the harpoon lines. The cartoonist is relying on readers' familiarity with the story of Ahab and Moby Dick. Only if you know that story and are also familiar with the debate about mission goals in Iraq will the humor and message of this comic strip be clear to you. Without that knowledge, what this comic strip means to you may be different from what the artist intended.

So background knowledge can incorporate a variety of elements:

- general knowledge about a subject
- familiarity with current events
- familiarity with public discussions about current events
- cultural knowledge (in the form of literature or art)
- historical knowledge

Perspective

How you read an image is also influenced by your own viewpoint or perspective. Your values, beliefs, and opinions about the subject matter will shape the way you react to an image. Let's return to the photograph of President Bush, for example (page 21). Obviously, your opinion of the President would affect your reaction to this photograph. In addition, your political viewpoint will influence your reaction. Someone with a conservative viewpoint is likely to read this photo differently from a liberal. A Bush supporter is more likely to read a straightforward and positive patriotic message in this photo than someone who voted against Bush. Even if these two people see more or less the same message in the photograph (that is, a patriotic message about George W. Bush), their political viewpoints will affect how they interpret and react to that message. The Bush opponent is more likely to reject the photo's patriotic message, for instance, or he or she might read the message as an ironic one. (We could do the same sort of analysis of the comic strip on page 21.) If you use images in your writing, keep in mind that readers may respond very differently to those images. Anticipating those responses is part of analyzing your audience (see page 37 in Chapter 3).

Putting It All Together: Reading Complex Images

Photographers, artists, and designers use these principles of context, background knowledge, and perspective to try to reach their intended audiences and convey their messages effectively. Understanding these principles can help you read images more critically and carefully. And it can make you aware of how your own response to an image is perhaps more complicated than it might seem. Let's look at one more example, a poster (top left) from a consumer and environmental advocacy group called Adbusters. What messages do you read in this poster?

The text on the poster sends an obvious message about curbing consumption. But there may be other, less obvious messages as well. The poster recalls the famous military recruiting advertisements during World War II such as the one shown here (bottom left). Those advertisements were thought to convey a sense of patriotic duty, suggesting that citizenship included self-sacrifice for one's country. The poster about curbing consumption relies on your familiarity with those World War II recruiting advertisements and their patriotic messages. But in this case, there is a twist: You are not being recruited for military service but for opposition to consumer culture. In making this twist, the poster suggests that reducing the consumption of consumer goods is patriotic, an idea that might strike many Americans as counterintuitive because it is widely believed that economic consumption is good for America.

In this case, then, a seemingly simple message—curb your consumption—is more complex and relies on a complicated set of associations and background knowledge for its impact. Moreover, a viewer's response to this poster may not be a straightforward matter of that viewer's political viewpoint. In other words, patriotism is often associated with a conservative political viewpoint, but in this case, it is associated with a more progressive argument against consumerism. So even conservative viewers who consider themselves very patriotic may have a more complicated reaction to the image. To appreciate this complexity, consider your own reaction to this poster. Do you find its message appealing or valid? Why or why not? How you answer those questions might enable you to understand better why the image has the impact on you that it does. Throughout this book, you will be asked similar questions about different images and texts. Understanding your own reactions to images and texts is an important part of understanding how messages are communicated through them.

Using Images in Your Writing

As a writer today, you have the advantage of powerful, accessible, and easy-to-use technologies that were unavailable to writers even five or ten years ago. Word processing programs enable writers to incorporate images into documents very easily and to control document layout and design. Used in conjunction with color printers, these programs enable writers to create professional-looking documents of all kinds: flyers, posters, brochures, and reports with tables, graphs, and other images. Other programs like PowerPoint® that enable users to create slide shows are now routinely used in schools and businesses. Desktop publishing programs allow users to create documents with very sophisticated visual elements. In addition, the Internet has become a rich venue for publishing that allows you to take advantage of visual elements as well as sound to convey your messages effectively to a variety of audiences.

Although these tools are accessible and relatively easy to use, they require you to consider various issues—such as color, layout, and composition—that writers have traditionally not had to worry about. With these new possibilities, then, come new challenges for both writers and readers.

Deciding to Use Images

In deciding whether to incorporate images into an assignment, the first step is to ask whether images would enable you to convey your message to your audience more effectively than text alone. Sometimes

© Robert Yagelski

© Robert Yagelski

adding an image just to illustrate your text may not make your writing more effective. However, in some cases, an image can enhance the impact of your writing. *The Boston Photographs* on pages 15 and 16 surely enhanced Nora Ephron's essay by allowing her readers to experience the power of those photos directly. If you're writing about, say, a controversy over a proposal to build a new big-box retail store in your town, including well-composed photographs of the stream or meadow on the proposed building site can help you make a more effective argument against the proposal, especially if your audience includes people who share your environmental concerns. So your decision to incorporate photographs should always take your audience and your purpose into account.

If you decide that images will make your writing more effective, select them carefully. In the previous example of an argument against a proposed big-box retail store, a poorly done photograph of the proposed site won't do much to enhance your argument, but a carefully composed photo that might evoke a reader's sense of the site's beauty will likely have a more appropriate effect on your readers. Or let's say you live in a coastal town that is considering allowing more development on a natural public beach. Which of the photographs on this page might work better if you wished to write an essay opposing such development? Which would work better if you were in favor of the development? Your answer to those questions depends on your audience, the message you want to convey to that audience, the specific points you want to make about the proposed development, and **your own sense of responsibility as a writer.** If you wished to emphasize the natural beauty of the location, the first photograph would make sense. If you believe that the development would be consistent with what is already there, then the second photograph would help you convey your point by showing that some homes already exist at that site.

Selecting Images

The considerations discussed in the previous section apply to *any* kind of image you decide to use—not only photographs but sketches, paintings, cartoons, graphs, or logos as well. Sometimes deciding which kind of image to use is important. In some cases, a graph or chart is an obvious choice. For example, the graph below is from a report by the testing company ACT about the readiness of high school graduates for college-level academic work. The graph shows the percentage of high school graduates who meet the criteria for readiness for college-level math based on the math courses they took in high school. Presenting this information in the form of a graph effectively conveys the differences between students who took few math courses in high school and students who took more math, including more advanced courses. This same information could easily be presented in the text itself, but it might have more impact on a reader in the form of a graph. Obviously, a photograph or other kind of image would not work as well in this case. Given the audience and purpose of the ACT report, using a graph makes sense.

Sometimes deciding which kind of image to use isn't so clear cut. For example, let's say you were writing a research paper examining the social, economic, and environmental effects of the automobile on U.S. society. Both of the images on page 26 convey messages about such effects, but which would be most appropriate for your paper?

In answering that question, you would, as always, consider your purpose and audience. But in deciding

THE ETHICS OF USING IMAGES

The decision to use an image in a document is not just a technical or strategic decision; it is also an ethical one. Although both photographs on page 24 may have been taken at the same beach, neither shows the whole scene. Which photo you select and how you use it in your document can affect the messages you convey about the scene. Selecting the first photograph, for instance, may convey the beauty of the beach but it may also be misleading because it seems to show no development at all along the beach. The second photo might suggest a housing development where one does not really exist. As a writer in this instance, you would have to decide how best to use one or both of these photographs to accomplish your purpose without misleading your audience or misrepresenting the circumstances surrounding the issue. It is important to think about your rhetorical decisions as ethical decisions. As a writer you should always consider the ethical implications of your decisions. In such cases, it's a good idea to ask yourself not only whether the image will make your document more effective but also whether it is the right thing to do.

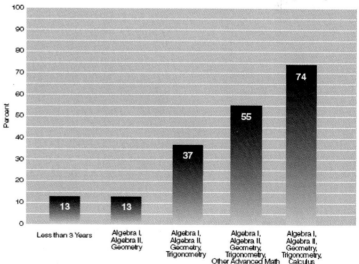

*2004 ACT-tested High School Graduates Meeting
College Algebra Benchmark by Mathematics Course Sequence*

What was that bump?

www.adbusters.org

© Clarita/Morguefile.com

between these two images, you would also want to consider the different impact a photograph and a poster might have on readers. The photograph depicts a real scene, whereas the poster makes a comment through a color sketch. Readers might see the photograph as more "objective" and real; the photograph might thus be a more effective choice if you wanted to take a balanced view of the subject. In this case, the type of image—not just what the image depicts—is an important consideration.

Considering Layout and Design

If you are using photographs, charts, graphs, or other visual elements in your assignment, you'll need to think about how to incorporate those elements effectively into your document. In many cases, you may simply be able to insert a photograph or chart into the text of your paper (which is easy to do with most word processing programs). Documents with more sophisticated formats, such as brochures, flyers, web pages, or PowerPoint presentations, require you to think more carefully about layout and design. Here are a few simple principles to keep in mind:

- *Design should be appropriate to your purpose.* Flashy images, unconventional fonts, or an unusual page layout would probably not be appropriate for a research paper for your sociology class. By contrast, if you are building a web site devoted to, say, progressive music, you might consider a more unconventional design to convey a sense of the unconventional nature of the music. The point is to design your document so that it meets your purposes for your intended audience. An inappropriate design will undermine your document's ability to convey your message effectively.

- *Less is more.* Too many visual elements in a report or essay may overwhelm your reader and weaken the impact of the images. Select only those images that you think will enhance your text. Also, remember that a crowded page or screen can be hard to read. Graphic designers understand the value of "white space"—that is, leaving blank areas around graphics and text to make it easier for readers to make sense of what's on the page. Try not to put too many elements on a single page. The idea is to make it easier for your readers to understand the ideas and information on the page.

- *Symmetry and balance can enhance your design.* Good designers strive for a page or screen that is visually balanced. Often, the elements on a page are arranged in a pattern that directs a reader's eyes first to the most important material and then to the less important material. These patterns tend to make it easier for readers to get the message. For example, the front page of a newspaper is usually divided into three or four main columns; text and graphics are positioned within or across these columns in a basic rectangular pattern. (When we read a print text in English, our eyes move from left to right and top to bottom. Accordingly, designers will often lay out a page to take advantage of this "natural" movement of a reader's eyes.) Other common patterns include *radial* design, in which several elements are arranged around a main image or graphic, and *collage,* in which a number of different images and graphics along with blocks of text overlap on the page. Whatever pattern you use, the main principle to remember is that it should help readers or viewers understand your message and find the information you are trying to convey.

- *Use contrast.* On a well-designed page of a print document or a web site, contrasting elements are arranged in a visually appealing and efficient way. For example, the blue box shown here at the top of the page can be used for a main heading or title, while the lighter box on the left side might be used to highlight key points or references (or links on a web site). Both boxes contrast nicely with the main text, which is placed in a white box. This contrast makes the various kinds of information on the page easier for a reader to access.

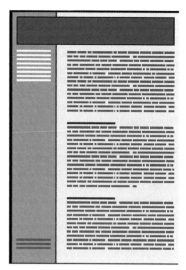

Contrast design example

A WORD ABOUT POWERPOINT

Today, it is common for teachers to allow or assign students to use programs like PowerPoint for in-class presentations and projects. If you have the opportunity to use PowerPoint, you can apply the principles discussed in this chapter to your presentation. One advantage of programs like PowerPoint is that they provide ready-made templates for you to use that follow the advice about symmetry, layout, and color given in this chapter. If you are making a presentation with PowerPoint, keep in mind it is ineffective to simply read what is on a slide. It is much more effective to use the images and words on your slides to supplement what you are saying (or reading). For example, if you are making a presentation about suburban sprawl in a geography class, you might show a slide with a chart that indicates the increase in sprawl in the past few decades and the loss of open space as a result. While your audience views that chart, you can be talking about some of the consequences of that growth (rather than simply reading the chart to the audience). In this way, PowerPoint can enhance your presentation rather than *become* the presentation.

CONSIDERING OTHER MEDIA FOR WRITING

Many different media are available to writers today. In addition to traditional print media, such as newspapers, magazines, and books, and the established media of television and radio, the Internet and other electronic technologies such as text messaging provide a wide array of outlets for communication that did not exist even a decade ago. Through television, film, the Internet, and print media, you are exposed to countless messages every day, and making sense of those messages is an important part of making your way in the world, both inside and outside the classroom. Consider, for example, how important the web site *YouTube.com* has become for conveying messages through videos. The principles discussed in this chapter for reading images and for designing documents apply in general to many of these different media. For example, interpreting the way a television commercial tries to convey its message is similar to reading a photograph, as discussed earlier (see page 18). Learning to interpret messages critically in a variety of media is part of being an informed reader and can also help you become a more effective writer.

For detailed advice about designing documents, consult a handbook or a more specialized guide for the medium you're working with. But keep in mind that the design of your document will have a lot to do with how effectively it conveys your messages or information to your intended audience.

Using Color

For most assignments, you may not have to deal with color, but many documents can be enhanced through the careful use of color. This is especially true of web pages. Here are a few general guidelines for using color:

- *Use color only if it will enhance your document.* Using colored fonts or graphics in a biology lab report or a history paper may look nice but will likely contribute little to the effectiveness of the paper. On the other hand, a web page without any color is likely to be unappealing and ineffective in addressing your intended audience.

- *Choose colors carefully.* Colors can be very effective in creating a certain mood or "feel" to a document, but poorly selected or inappropriate colors will probably make your document less effective. Consider audience and purpose when selecting colors. Bright yellow lettering on a red background is probably a poor choice for a brochure about a church retreat or a food service for senior citizens, for example. In general, professional graphic artists suggest using subtle colors for the majority of a document, reserving brighter colors for emphasizing specific elements or ideas.

- *Use colors according to a pattern or scheme.* In well-designed documents, you'll notice that a few colors are used throughout the document, perhaps in various shades. Too many different colors create visual confusion.

It's important to keep in mind that black-and-white images can be just as effective as color images, and in some cases, they can be more appropriate. Consider this photograph of the World War II Nazi concentration camp

© AP Photo

World War II concentration camp

at Auschwitz. The use of a black-and-white format for this photograph helps convey the terrible sense of loss and emptiness that we associate with that place; in this case, black and white may be more appropriate to the subject than color.

Combining Text and Image

To communicate effectively means combining visual elements with your text in ways that take advantage of the power of both writing and images. You can often convey messages visually without using words, and your words can have greater impact when combined with carefully selected images or when presented visually in certain ways. The "essay" on page 30 is an example of a writer's effective use of the visual in combination with his words to make a point. It appeared on the editorial page of the *New York Times*. Like other essays in the editorial section of a newspaper, this one makes an argument—in this case, about some of the implications and risks of our common uses of computers. The writer, Evan Eisenberg, could have made his argument in a conventional essay, but he chose to use a visual format to make his point. He relies on his audience's familiarity with computers and particularly with the kinds of error messages that often appear in "dialogue boxes" on the computer screen. And he combines his text with visual elements to convey his point. In evaluating the effectiveness of this essay, consider the following questions:

- What specific point or criticism do you think Eisenberg is making in this editorial essay?
- In what ways do the visual elements—the computer screen "look" of the essay and the dialogue box graphics—contribute to his argument?
- What specific messages or information are conveyed by the visual elements in this essay?
- In what ways does the text rely on the visual elements for its meaning? (In other words, would the text in the dialogue boxes be understandable without the visual elements?)
- How might Eisenberg's argument be different if he had not included the visual elements?

This example illustrates a writer's careful use of the visual in combination with his text. Each component of this essay—the visual and the textual—conveys important information and contributes to Eisenberg's main point.

As a reader, you can learn to become more aware of how the visual and the textual can be used in combination to convey messages. That awareness makes you a more informed, sophisticated, and careful reader. As a writer, that awareness can help you take advantage of the power of both images and text.

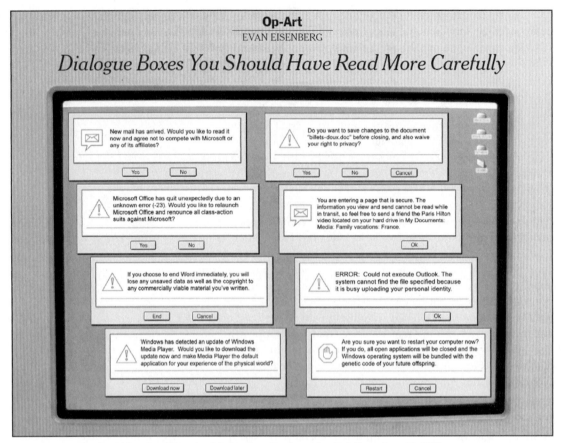

"Dialogue Boxes You Should Have Read More Carefully," by Evan Eisenberg. *New York Times,* Sept. 30, 2004.

DURING THE 1980S, I WAS A FACULTY ADVISER TO A STUDENT CHAPTER OF AMNESTY INTERNATIONAL, A WELL-KNOWN HUMAN RIGHTS ORGANIZATION. AMONG THE MOST IMPORTANT ACTIVITIES WE ENGAGED IN WERE LETTER-WRITING CAMPAIGNS ON BEHALF OF POLITICAL PRISONERS AROUND THE WORLD. HERE'S HOW IT WORKED. WHENEVER AMNESTY INTERNATIONAL LEARNED ABOUT A PERSON BEING IMPRISONED ILLEGALLY OR TORTURED FOR POLITICAL REASONS anywhere in the world, it would alert its members by sending brief newsletters called "Action Alerts" by mail. These Action Alerts described the imprisoned person, explained the circumstances, and provided information about the government offices or officials to whom we were being asked to write; they also included suggestions for writing effective letters to those officials. When our chapter received an Action Alert, we'd meet to discuss the situation, talk about strategies we could use in our letters, write and share drafts, and help each other with revisions. At the end of the meeting, we would have a dozen or so letters to send off on behalf of the imprisoned person.

Amnesty International had learned that publicizing cases of illegal imprisonment or torture was one of the most effective ways to help prisoners. It also knew that if a government received hundreds or thousands of letters about such a case, it was usually more likely to reconsider its actions against the prisoner in question. Often, such letter-writing campaigns resulted in a trial for the prisoner or even in the prisoner's release; sometimes they saved a prisoner's life.

My students learned important lessons about writing by participating **IN THOSE LETTER-WRITING CAMPAIGNS,** which is why I'm sharing this story with you. They learned that writing is a powerful medium for communicating ideas and information. Letters were an effective way to express our concerns about troubling government actions and to convey to people in power that others around the world were aware of what was happening. This was real writing that had real consequences. It was a way for the students to enter important conversations that mattered to people all over the world—and especially to the political prisoners on whose behalf we were writing. But in joining those conversations about specific cases of political prisoners, my students were also taking part in larger conversations about human rights, about government policies, and about individual responsibility. As I noted in Chapter 1, writing is really a matter of joining conversations about issues that matter in our lives, whether you are writing a letter to a government official about a political prisoner, an entry on a blog about an environmental policy, a letter to the editor of a newspaper about a local land-use controversy, or an essay for your economics course. We write because we need to be part of these conversations that affect our lives. And writing well means entering these conversations in effective and knowledgeable ways.

CHANGING TECHNOLOGIES FOR WRITING AND COMMUNICATION
Keep in mind that these letter-writing campaigns were happening before the Internet became such an important medium for communication. Today, such campaigns are managed through web sites maintained by organizations like Amnesty International, and the process is not only much faster but also more effective because of the power of the Internet to communicate instantly to millions of people all over the world. In the 1980s, we did not have access to the Internet, so we wrote letters.

During our letter-writing campaigns, my students were also learning some important lessons about *how* to write effectively—lessons
that you will learn as you engage in the writing assignments in your
composition course:

- *Writers write for specific rhetorical situations.* As I explained in
  Chapter 1, all writing is done in context, and to be effective,
  writers must write in ways that fit the context. By writing letters
  as part of the Amnesty International campaigns, my students
  were learning how to take context into account—assessing the
  rhetorical situation, learning about their audience, and writing letters that addressed their audience under those special
  circumstances. Good writing means being able to assess the
  rhetorical situation and respond to it appropriately.

- *Purpose guides a writer's decisions.* Whether you are writing a letter
  that you hope will help free an illegally held prisoner, a report
  for your economics course, or an essay in your composition
  class, you are writing for a specific purpose. That purpose should
  shape the choices you make as you draft and revise your text.

- *Form fits purpose.* You have probably learned in school how to
  write book reports, business letters, science reports, research
  papers, and various kinds of essays, such as narratives or arguments. The reason for learning to write in these different forms
  is to be able to use them for specific purposes in appropriate
  situations. When you write a business letter to apply for a job,
  the reader expects your letter to follow a certain format. A science report also follows a certain format that has become a
  standard way for scientists to communicate the results of their
  research to each other. My students were writing a certain kind
  of persuasive letter to convince a government official to act in a
  certain way. All these forms serve specific purposes. Good writers learn to write in different forms and use those forms appropriately for a variety of purposes.

- *Writing is a process.* All writers move through a process from the
  time they conceive an idea to the finished text. In the letter-
  writing campaigns, my students were given topics to write about,
  but they still had to go through the various steps of the writing
  process, including generating ideas for their letters, organizing
  and developing their ideas in their drafts, getting help from
  other readers to improve their drafts, and revising and editing
  the letters before sending them to their intended audience.
  You move through these same steps for any writing you do. To
  write well is partly a matter of learning to manage that process
  effectively.

- *Writers adopt a style that is appropriate for the context.* The specific
  choices writers make about their writing style are guided by
  their sense of what is appropriate for the specific situation. My

students had to adopt a relatively formal writing style for their letters, and sometimes they had to use special words depending on the government or country they were writing to. An informal writing style would not have been effective in those situations. Writing style is a tool writers use to achieve their purposes in specific situations. To write effectively means adapting your writing style to the context, no matter what kind of writing you're engaged in.

- *Effective writers use technology appropriately.* Today, writers have at their disposal all kinds of powerful technologies, including computers with sophisticated word processing programs, the Internet, and various kinds of multimedia tools. My students were using technologies available to them at the time: typewriters, word processors, and basic pen and paper. You will have to make choices about which technologies make sense for you, not only for writing your drafts but also for doing research and sharing your writing with readers. Part of the challenge of writing well today is learning to use these new and powerful technologies effectively.

The rest of this chapter provides a brief overview of these important aspects of writing. It offers some basic advice to help you complete whatever writing tasks you are engaged in.

Theme into Thesis

It may sound obvious, but the writer's first job is to decide what to write about. As you probably know from your own experience, finding a topic is not always easy. In many cases, you may be provided with a topic, such as in a course assignment that specifies a topic or in the letter-writing campaigns I described earlier. But even when you are given a topic, what you say about that topic is up to you. A big part of your task is to determine what main idea or point you will make about your topic. That main idea or point is your *thesis*. For any writing activity, whether or not your topic is provided, you must develop a thesis.

Developing your thesis may be a little easier if you keep in mind that when you're writing, you're participating in a conversation about an important issue or *theme*. Many of the exercises in Chapters 5 through 12 offer specific suggestions for writing activities that will help you identify a thesis for your essay. But the principle guiding these activities applies to *any* writing situation: Your thesis grows out of your effort to enter a conversation about an important issue in a specific rhetorical situation. In other words, *your thesis is your contribution to the conversation about the issue you're writing about.*

What does that mean in practical terms? Well, let's say your composition instructor asks you to write an essay about an important experience you had as a teenager. That's a pretty open-ended assignment (which is not uncommon in composition courses), so part of the challenge is to consider *why* you might want to write about such an experience (aside from having to complete the assignment to earn a good grade for the course). If you think about the assignment as part of an ongoing conversation about adolescence and the challenges of being a teenager, then your purpose becomes easier to identify; you want to add something to those conversations. For example, many parents, educators, and others have concerns about how teens often feel overly sensitive about their physical appearance, which can lead to common problems like low self-esteem or more serious problems like eating disorders or the use of substances like steroids. The popular media are full of stories about these issues. Maybe you played a sport in high school and felt pressure to use steroids or other substances to enhance your physique and performance. In deciding to write about your experience, you would be identifying a specific topic that is part of these ongoing conversations about a theme (problems in adolescence) that matters to many people in our society. So as you decide just how to approach writing about your experience, you would want to consider how your specific experience might add to these conversations. Your *thesis* would be your contribution to those conversations about the *theme* of the challenges of being a teen; it is the statement you are making about that theme. Accordingly, you would want to tell your story in a way that focuses attention on how the pressure to look a certain way or to perform athletically at a high level affects teenagers.

Developing your thesis is really a matter of exploring your topic in a way that meets the needs of the rhetorical situation. In writing about the pressures on teen athletes, for example, you would want to consider what your experience might reveal about those pressures. Let's say you were on a track-and-field team on which some of the other players used steroids and encouraged their teammates to do so. You might ask yourself a series of questions to identify important events or issues related to your experience:

- What exactly was the nature of your experience on that team? What pressures did you feel? How did steroids come into play?
- What happened to athletes who took steroids? What happened to those who didn't? What reasons did athletes have for taking steroids or refusing to do so?
- What role did the coaches or parents play in the situation?
- Were there any key moments in your experience, such as someone getting hurt or getting caught with steroids? What led up to those moments? What resulted from them?
- What did you learn about athletics from this experience? What did you learn about teenagers? What did you learn about yourself?

In trying to answer such questions, you would not only generate material for your essay, but you would also begin to formulate the main point you wish to make about that experience. As you explore the experience and its consequences, you are working toward the statement you want to make about it. That is, you're working toward your thesis.

Keep in mind that your thesis need not be a one-sentence statement of your main point, but sometimes it can be helpful to make such a statement. In our example, it might look like this:

> Teenagers are often unprepared to deal with the pressures that are created by the high value our society places on success in athletics.

Or maybe like this:

> Teens cheat in sports by taking steroids because of their need to succeed in a highly competitive environment.

It can be a good idea to write out your thesis in this way to keep it in mind as you develop your essay. But this issue of steroid use among teen athletes is very complicated, and one sentence might not quite do justice to that complexity. Boiling your experience down to one sentence may not enable you to capture the complexity of the experience and the issues it raises. If that's the case, it can be helpful to write a brief paragraph that summarizes your thesis. A few sentences are all you need. The point is to identify what you want to say about your experience.

It's important to note that **your thesis can change** as you develop your essay. In fact, if you carefully explore your topic, it is likely that you will learn more about the issues and perhaps gain insight into your experience that you didn't have previously. Your opinion or perspective may change as a result of writing about the experience. For example, in writing about experiences with steroid use on your high school track-and-field team, you may have started out blaming your teammates who took steroids, especially if they caused problems for you or other team members. But as you explore your experience and develop your thesis, you may come to the realization that those students were responding to the same pressure all teens can feel and therefore had understandable reasons for deciding to take steroids. You may still believe they were wrong, but you may now appreciate the difficulties they faced and the complexities of the situation in a way that perhaps you had not done previously. As a result, you may find your thesis changing slightly as you develop your essay. That's good. It means that you are learning and developing a more complicated and sophisticated viewpoint about the issue.

Because your essay is your contribution to the ongoing conversations about an important issue—in this case, the issue of steroid use among teens—it makes sense to consider what others are saying and

WRITING AS INQUIRY
If your thesis changes as you develop your essay, it's an example of what writing teachers mean when they talk about "writing as inquiry": By writing about a topic, you are engaging in inquiry into the topic that can result in your gaining new insights into that topic. You are *learning* about your topic by writing. (See Chapter 1 for more on this topic.)

QUESTIONS TO ASK YOURSELF AS YOU DEVELOP YOUR THESIS
- What general question, issue, or problem am I exploring in this essay?
- What is the current status of this question, issue, or problem? What is being said (or written) about it?
- What are my general beliefs or opinions about this question, issue, or problem?
- What do I know about it? What do I want to know about it?
- What experiences have I had that might be related to this question, issue, or problem?
- What specific concerns do I have about it?
- Who might share my concerns?
- What do I have to say about the question, issue, or problem?

writing about the issue as you develop your thesis. In this way, reading what has been written about your topic is part of the process of developing your thesis. (Chapter 4 describes how research can be an integral part of *any* writing task, not just research papers.) And considering what your audience knows and believes is also part of the process. In other words, as you develop your thesis, you are considering how to present that thesis effectively to your audience. Doing so may change your own viewpoint. So part of developing your thesis involves assessing the rhetorical situation.

Assessing the Rhetorical Situation

Assessing a rhetorical situation is both straightforward and complex. (See Chapter 1 for an explanation of *rhetorical situation.*) The basic elements of any rhetorical situation—*writer, subject,* and *audience*—are usually pretty obvious, but the closer you look at those elements, the more complicated they can become. Effective writing depends on the extent to which you can assess those elements appropriately and fit your writing to the situation.

For example, your composition teacher may ask you to write a persuasive essay about a current issue on your campus—let's say, a proposal to restrict alcohol sales at all athletic events. Here's a look at the rhetorical situation for this assignment:

- *Audience.* Your audience might include members of your campus community as well as local residents and officials who might have concerns about the sale of alcohol at sporting events and fans who attend those events. The first step is to try to identify that audience and consider their connection to the controversy. What's at stake for them in this situation? What do they know and think about it?

- *Subject.* Your subject may seem obvious—in this case, you're writing about the proposed policy regarding alcohol sales at sporting events. But as you develop your thesis, it's important to look more carefully at that subject. How did the controversy about alcohol sales at sporting events arise in the first place? Were there incidents that led to concerns about alcohol sales at sporting events on your campus? If so, what happened? Did members of the community question campus policies? Is this a recent issue or one that has been of concern for some time? Just what would the new policy do? Who would be affected by it and how? Such questions help you explore the subject you're writing about and may lead you to a different perspective on that subject than the one you started with.

- *Writer.* Looking at the issue and the circumstances surrounding it leads to questions about your own interest in or connection to the issue. Why does this issue concern you? Are you a sports fan who regularly attends games on your campus? Have you had any experiences that are relevant to the current controversy? How would the new policy affect you? Do you have something to say about it? In short, consider your purposes or motivation for writing about the issue as well as your experiences with or connection to it. Consider, too, your credibility as someone who has something to say about the issue.

As you explore these elements of the rhetorical situation, you may find that the immediate situation (writing about a proposed campus policy to a local audience) may actually be broader than it seems. Alcohol consumption by young people, especially on college campuses, is a national issue that has been addressed by officials on college campuses around the country and by state and federal officials, as well as by organizations like SADD (Students Against Drunk Driving). The behavior of fans at sporting events also concerns Americans in general. So in writing about your campus's proposed policy regarding alcohol consumption at sporting events, you're actually writing about larger issues that concern a much broader audience. And in joining the debate in your community about alcohol consumption at sporting events, you are also joining the ongoing conversations in American society about youth, sports, alcohol, and related social issues. So it makes sense to take into account what has been said in those conversations—the local ones in your community as well as the larger ones in the society in general. That's part of the process of assessing the rhetorical situation.

The more carefully you explore these elements of the rhetorical situation, the more likely you are to identify important questions, concerns, and viewpoints relevant to your topic. You can therefore make more informed decisions about what to include in your essay, what to leave out, how to present your position and the positions of others involved in the issue, and what style or voice to use to best convey your point, or thesis, to your intended audience.

Knowing Your Audience

Identifying your audience is only the first step in deciding how to address that audience effectively. Knowing something about your audience and anticipating what your audience knows and believes are also crucial components of assessing the rhetorical situation. Let's return to the example of writing an essay about a proposed change in the policy regarding alcohol consumption at athletic events on your campus.

Let's say you intend your essay for your campus newspaper. In that case, you would have a pretty good idea about your audience because it would be a relatively local audience composed of students and fac-

---

QUESTIONS TO ASK YOURSELF WHEN ASSESSING RHETORICAL CONTEXT

- *Audience:* Who is my audience? What connection to the topic does my audience have? What do they know about my subject? What do they need to know?
- *Subject:* What is the issue? What are the circumstances surrounding the issue? Why is this issue important or interesting to me and to my audience?
- *Writer:* What is my interest in this issue? What connection do I have to the issue? What contribution to the conversations or debates about this issue can I make? What special insight or authority do I have for writing about this issue?

SHADES OF MEANING

Words are not neutral; they often have shades of meaning that go beyond the literal dictionary definition (see the section *Discourse and Why It Is Important* on page 9 in Chapter 1). Some words and phrases will send powerful messages to certain audiences, and as a writer, you need to take those messages into account. For example, in the heated debates about abortion, *pro-choice* and *pro-abortion* technically mean the same thing: They generally refer to people who support legal abortion. But these two phrases carry very different messages depending on the context and the audience. For some people who oppose abortion, *pro-choice* can be considered a misleading term. For people who consider themselves pro-choice, the term *pro-abortion* can seem misleading. These differences are a result of how these terms are used in ongoing conversations about controversial issues. Writers should be aware of these complexities when they are choosing words and refining their writing style.

ulty in your campus community and perhaps some members of the surrounding community. Even such a specific audience could be very diverse, and you could never really know exactly who your readers might be, what they know, and how they might feel about the issue. But you could safely assume a great deal about what they might know about the local situation. For example, they would probably be familiar with the proposed policy change and with any incidents that might have led to it. They would also be familiar with some of the viewpoints people have expressed about the situation in the local media. In writing for such an audience, then, you would probably not need to include a great deal of background information about the situation. A reference to the policy change would be enough.

Writers always make assumptions about what their intended audience might know about their topic. But sometimes it can be tricky to anticipate what your audience knows. For instance, if you wanted to write a letter to the editor of a much larger publication—say, *USA Today* or a sports-related web site like ESPN.com—about the issue of alcohol consumption at college athletic events, you could not assume that readers of such a publication would be familiar with the situation on your campus. You would have to decide how much background information to include for these readers. Even with such a large audience, though, you could make some assumptions about what they know. Readers of *USA Today* would likely be familiar with the general problem of alcohol abuse on college campuses because it is a much-discussed problem in national media. They might also know about well-publicized incidents involving alcohol abuse at college sporting events, particularly if those incidents took place at colleges with high-profile sports teams. So as a writer, you might refer to such incidents as a way to set the stage for your own thesis, and you wouldn't necessarily need to fill in much background information.

QUESTIONS TO ASK YOURSELF WHEN ANALYZING AUDIENCE

- Do I have a specific audience in mind for this particular writing task? If so, who is that audience?
- What do I know about my audience that is relevant to my topic? Is there anything about my audience that I should find out before finishing this writing task?
- What can I assume my audience knows about that topic? What background information about my topic should I provide for them?
- What beliefs or opinions will my audience likely have regarding my topic? Do I need to take these beliefs or opinions into account in my writing?
- What is my connection to my audience, if any? Does that connection matter for my writing task? If so, how? What might my audience know about me? Does it matter whether or not they know me?
- What interest in my topic does my audience have?
- What ideas or language might be especially controversial for my audience? Should I avoid these ideas or language in my writing?
- How do I want my audience to react to my writing?

The point is that you always have to try to anticipate what your audience might know about your topic, even when that audience is large and diverse. And you also should have a sense of what their expectations might be. For example, readers of *USA Today* would not expect a very formal writing style in a brief editorial essay or letter to the editor. On the other hand, your sociology instructor might expect a more formal academic style for an assignment on the same topic. In short, as you examine your audience, you must consider that audience in the context of the rhetorical situation as a whole.

Keep in mind, too, that your sense of audience can be shaped by a variety of complicated factors having to do with the identities of your readers—things like race, gender, religion, sexual orientation, ethnicity, age, income, and so on. For example, if your primary audience is composed of students in your composition class, which includes several international students, you would want to be aware of how they might respond to a reference to Americans as "we." Referring to Americans in that way might alienate your international classmates.

How you address your audience in a piece of writing will help determine how effective your writing will be for the specific rhetorical situation you're in. Making your best guess about your audience will probably mean that you will have a better chance of achieving your purpose in that rhetorical situation.

Managing the Writing Process

The great American writer Ernest Hemingway was once asked in an interview about the famous last chapter of his novel *A Farewell to Arms,* which has been the subject of a great deal of discussion among literary critics over the years. Hemingway told the interviewer that he rewrote the chapter thirty-eight times. When asked why, Hemingway replied that he had to get the words right.

I like to tell that story to students to emphasize the role of revision in effective writing. It's unlikely that you will find yourself having to revise something three dozen times, as Hemingway did, but that story can teach us that even the greatest writers must work through the process of writing carefully and assiduously. Part of being an effective writer is learning how to manage that process efficiently. The most important thing to remember is that there is no formula for engaging in the writing process. Writing is not a step-by-step, paint-by-number activity. It's much messier than that. And part of the challenge is accepting some messiness and uncertainty in writing.

Most writing involves some version of three main activities: generating, gathering, and organizing ideas and/or information; writing the draft; and revising and editing. Often, these three activities are called *prewriting, drafting,* and *rewriting.* Whatever they're called, keep in mind that at some point in any writing task, you'll have to come up with ideas and collect information, organize those ideas and information in a draft, and rewrite that draft so it is effective and correct.

The biggest mistake student writers make is trying to do all these activities at once. Many students wait until the last minute and then try to complete their assignment in a single draft, essentially collapsing all these activities—prewriting, drafting, and revising—into one writing session. The result is usually a less effective text and a tedious and unenjoyable writing experience. You have probably done this; most students have (I did when I was a student!). But it's rarely a good idea because writing well requires more kinds of thinking than most

WRITING UNDER PRESSURE
Sometimes you have a tight deadline, so you have to complete a writing assignment at the last minute. But some students rationalize their procrastination by claiming that they do their best work under pressure. I don't buy it. Students who say this usually wait until the last minute to begin their writing, which leaves little time to engage in all the activities described in this chapter. Inevitably, they have to cut corners—perhaps gathering insufficient information on their topic, rushing their draft, revising quickly or not at all, or even plagiarizing, which is more tempting when the pressure is on. Don't kid yourself like this. Starting your writing assignments a little earlier can make your task easier because it enables you to break the task up into sections rather than trying to do it all at once. And it usually means that you will produce better writing.

people can do at once. (Multitasking may be a trend these days, but it doesn't necessarily help writers write well.) Writers can do a better job if they complete the writing task in parts. Spending some time generating ideas or collecting information can mean that writing the first draft will be a little easier than if you try to think of ideas at the same time that you're actually writing the essay. Similarly, writing a rough draft without worrying about things like spelling and grammar will usually enable you to concentrate on making your point rather than stopping to correct errors or look up a word in the dictionary. You can go back later to fix spelling or punctuation errors—*after* you've done the hard work of organizing your ideas into a coherent, readable draft. Managing your writing process in this way usually means allowing yourself sufficient time to complete these various activities and to revise your draft before your deadline.

Learning through Writing

Learning to manage your own writing process is not a matter of just identifying the steps you should take as you complete an assignment; writing is also a form of inquiry—a means of exploring your ideas and learning new concepts or information. When you write carefully about a topic, you come to know that topic better; you might also come to learn more about yourself and the world around you in the process. That's one reason students are asked to write reports and papers not just in English or composition courses but in all disciplines.

Often, students will tell me, "I know what I want to say, but I just can't find the words." Well, that's not quite true. Rarely is an idea for an essay or a report completely worked out in your mind before you begin writing. In fact, our own ideas are often not entirely clear to us; they get worked out in our heads as we write about those ideas. In addition, ideas can change as a result of the act of writing because through writing we are learning more about a topic than we knew when we started working on it. So once you identify your thesis, remember that it may change as you explore your topic further. In the end, your finished paper is not just an expression of your thesis; it is also a reflection of what you have learned through writing.

Thinking of writing as a process of inquiry also means that you may have to do research at any point in the process. (Research techniques are discussed in detail in Chapter 4.) Often, especially when writing research papers, students proceed with the idea that they must first collect as much information about their topic as they can before they start writing. Then they write their papers based on that information. But the act of writing your draft may reveal gaps in your information, or it may raise questions about your topic that you cannot answer without further research. If that happens, it's a sign that you're learning as you write, and you have to explore your topic further. You may have to stop writing your draft and go back to gather more information or change your plan for organizing your paper.

Using Form and Structure

In many ways, writing an effective essay is a little bit like constructing a building. For both tasks you need a solid foundation, a clear sense of purpose, and a sound structure. When constructing a building, a builder must have a good foundation and sturdy frame so that all the pieces fit together properly and the building will be strong. The same is true of writing. No matter what your writing task, you need a solid structure for your ideas and information. In other words, you have to organize your ideas and information appropriately for your audience and for the writing task at hand.

How you organize your text is influenced by several factors. One is the form or genre within which you're writing. For example, if you're writing a lab report for a chemistry class, you will probably follow a very specific format for organizing the information in that report, including an explanation of the purpose of the lab experiment, a description of the methods you used in your experiment, an overview of your results, and a discussion of those results. For such an assignment, organizing your writing can be fairly easy because you are following a clear (and perhaps required) format. But when you are writing in a less rigid format—say, a personal narrative or a critical analysis—you will have to find an effective way to organize your writing. Here are some tips for doing so:

- *Consider form or genre.* Many writing assignments specify common forms or genres, as I've already noted. For example, in your composition class you might be asked to write a persuasive essay on a topic of current interest. Your instructor might specify that you include both pro and con arguments on your topic, and you may even be required to include a specific number of arguments for and against your position on your topic. In such cases, use your assignment guidelines to help you decide how to organize your essay. If you must include one counterargument for every argument in favor of your position, for instance, then you can easily organize your essay around each main argument followed by one counterargument. You simply have to decide which of the main arguments comes first, which comes next, and so on.
- *Start big.* Every piece of writing you are likely to complete will have a few main ideas and several supporting ideas or information for each main idea. So if you can figure out how to organize your main ideas, you can usually decide rather easily where the supporting material should go. For example, let's say you were writing a report for a sociology course about the growth of youth sports in the United States. And let's imagine

that after doing some research, you decide that you want to make three main points in your report: (1) that several key factors have led to the growing participation in sports, (2) that many problems have emerged as more kids play team sports, and (3) that there are several important benefits for kids who participate in sports. Let's imagine further that you have some interesting information about the rapid growth of lacrosse as a scholastic sport as well as very good statistical information about the rise in illegal steroid use by teens. Now, how will you organize all this information and these main points? First, decide the order in which you should discuss your three main points. Then decide which of those three main points is best supported by the other information you have. If you decide to discuss the factors that influence the growth in sports participation first, then you would probably discuss the growing popularity of lacrosse early in your report because that information clearly supports your point about the increase in sports participation in general. The information about steroids will come later, probably in the section about problems with participation in sports. The point is that if you begin with your main ideas, the task of organizing even a very long paper is easier.

- *Consider purpose and audience when you organize your writing.* Considering your audience and your purpose in addressing that audience can help you make good decisions about organizing your writing. For example, imagine that you are writing a persuasive essay for an audience of your classmates about, say, the benefits of nuclear power, and you suspect that most of your classmates are opposed to nuclear power. In that case, you might begin your essay with information about nuclear power that would address their concerns. If you know that they are worried about global warming, for instance, you might begin by emphasizing the need for energy sources that do not produce the greenhouse gases that contribute to global warming. For an audience that supports nuclear power, on the other hand, you might make the point about global warming later in your essay. In short, deciding how to organize a piece of writing is really a matter of considering how best to present your information or ideas to your intended audience to achieve your purpose as a writer.

- *Use an outline to help you "see" the structure of your essay.* An outline can often help you get a better sense of how to organize your writing more effectively. Even a very simple outline can help you decide which ideas or information to put first, which to put next, and so on. More detailed outlines with subheadings can help when you have a great deal of information to include in your essay or report. But outlines don't need to be rigid. I like to begin with a simple outline of the main ideas, or "pieces," of my essay, just to get a better sense of how these pieces might fit together. As I gather more information and develop my ideas, I fill in my outline with more detail, putting the new information where it seems to fit best. Sometimes I have to rearrange my outline as I work on my draft because I find that an idea doesn't fit well where I thought it would. So an outline can be flexible. It's a tool that helps you see how your essay is organized so that you can more easily make adjustments if necessary.

Revising Is Not Editing

When you revise a piece of writing, you are doing more than correcting spelling or punctuation errors or tinkering with sentences. Genuine revising is a crucial part of exploring your topic, developing your thesis, and working out your ideas fully; it is an integral part of addressing your audience effectively. I first learned this lesson about revising when I wrote one of my first magazine articles while I was in college.

Like many students, I wrote a lot of my course assignments in one draft, but I still earned good grades for most assignments (see *Writing under Pressure* on page 39). So when I started writing for magazines, I thought I knew what I was doing. For one assignment, the magazine editor asked me to write about the challenges of providing good health care in rural areas, which was then a topic of national concern. So I did my research, wrote the article, and sent it to the editor by my deadline. I had essentially written the article in one draft from start to finish, and then I did some editing for minor errors and awkward sentences. I assumed the article was finished and the next step was to see it in print (and receive my check!).

A few weeks later, however, an envelope arrived from the editor. It contained five single-spaced pages of questions, comments, and suggestions for revising my article. There were no errors in my article—no misspellings or punctuation errors—nor were there problems with my writing style. I had made sure of that. Instead, the editor's letter posed many questions that he assumed readers of his magazine would ask—questions that I had not answered sufficiently in my article. He made many comments about sections that worked well and sections that didn't. And he offered numerous detailed sugges-

THE FIVE-PARAGRAPH ESSAY AND OTHER MYTHICAL BEASTS
In high school you were probably asked to write a five-paragraph essay with a first paragraph that introduced your thesis followed by three "body" paragraphs, each discussing one main idea, and a concluding paragraph that restated your thesis. Such an assignment makes organizing a piece of writing easy because all you really have to do is identify your thesis and three main points about that thesis; the required five-paragraph structure does the rest: you just plop the right information into one of the five paragraphs. But few writing tasks are so simple when it comes to organizing our writing. In fact, outside of school, you will probably never see anything that looks like a five-paragraph essay. Most common forms of writing—including business letters, research papers, narratives, reviews, and even lab reports—can vary dramatically in how they are organized. There is no one "right" way to organize a personal narrative or a research paper, for example. So as a writer you will have to make decisions about the best way to organize your writing. However, there are some common approaches to organization that fit one form or another. For example, narratives are often organized chronologically, so that a story is told from beginning to end. Such a method for organization would not necessarily work for a lab report or a persuasive essay, but you can become familiar with common strategies for organization if you pay attention to how writers organize the essays included in Chapters 5 through 12 in this textbook. As a writer, part of your task when organizing your writing is to try to identify the methods that might be appropriate for the specific writing task you are completing.

tions for revisions—large and small—to improve the article. In effect, the editor was telling me to revise extensively if I wanted to have my article published in his magazine (and if I wanted to get paid for my work). Never had a teacher read my writing so carefully, and never had a teacher asked me to revise so extensively.

At first, I was stunned. Did this mean I was a poor writer? Well, no. As I reread the editor's letter and considered his various questions, comments, and suggestions, I began to see that I had indeed neglected to address many important issues in my article. I could see that I did not consider what readers of the magazine might need to know. I had obviously left out important information, which meant I had to do additional research. I had also included some unnecessary information that I could eliminate. In short, I was rethinking my article in ways that took my audience and purpose more fully into account. And as I began revising the manuscript, I was doing so with my readers in mind. I used the editor's questions and comments and suggestions as a guide for revising, but I also made revisions that he didn't suggest. I was really *rewriting* my article. And the result was not only a better article for that situation but also a better experience for me as a writer because I learned a great deal more about my subject as well as about the act of writing.

The most important lesson I learned was that revising is not just the editing you do after you finish writing a draft; **REVISING IS AN INTEGRAL PART OF THE PROCESS OF WRITING** because it is through revising that you can really begin to see where your writing is going. If you want to learn to write well in various rhetorical situations—outside school as well as in school—then you will eventually have to learn how to revise effectively. And the best way to do that is by taking your writing seriously and engaging in your own writing process genuinely and honestly. If you do that, you will find yourself returning to your drafts, as Hemingway did, to make them better. And eventually, they *will* become better.

Using Technology

Today, most student writers have access to computers with sophisticated word processing programs that can make many aspects of the writing process easier. A program like Microsoft Word makes it easy to save drafts. You can also track your changes using special features of such programs so that you can see what revisions you've made; other features enable you to have a classmate or friend make suggestions or comments without changing your main text. You can also use spelling check or grammar check features to help with editing. It is a good idea to become familiar with these many capabilities of word processing programs to make your writing process more efficient. Try them out and use what works best for you. In addition, e-mail is an easy and effective way to share writing and exchange comments about drafts in progress. Many composition instructors now use e-mail or web-based programs such as Blackboard so that students can easily share drafts of their writing. These technologies can help you make your writing process more efficient.

We live in a technology-rich world that offers an amazing variety of tools for writers that go well beyond word processing. For writers, the Internet offers a wealth of information for research (which I'll discuss

---

QUESTIONS TO ASK YOURSELF WHEN REVISING

There are no hard-and-fast rules for revising, but you can make the process a little easier if you break it up into several steps. The basic idea is to start with the big issues and work toward the smaller ones. I like to think of the process as having three main parts: revising for meaning, revising for strategy, and revising for style.

Revising for Meaning. After you've completed your rough draft, read through to see whether you've addressed your topic sufficiently.
- Have I included everything I intended to include in this essay or paper?
- Is anything missing? If so, what?
- Have I included anything that is unnecessary or irrelevant? Can I leave anything out without weakening my draft?
- Is my thesis clear? Is anything confusing about my main ideas?
- Do I need to rethink my ideas or gather more information?
- Do I maintain my focus throughout the text? Do I drift off my main idea anywhere in the draft?

Revising for Strategy. Once you are satisfied that you have addressed the big questions, you can begin to narrow your focus to address matters of structure and strategy. At this stage, concern yourself with whether your paper is written in a way that makes your point clear and conveys your ideas effectively to your readers.
- Is the paper organized in a way that will make sense to my intended audience? Do I move effectively from one main point to the next? Are any parts of the paper out of place? If so, where might they work better?
- Do I make clear transitions from one main section to the next?
- Does the introduction set up my paper effectively? Does it provide a good sense of what the paper will be about?
- Does the conclusion wrap up my main ideas effectively? Does it emphasize the ideas or the point I want to leave my readers with?
- Have I addressed my audience in ways that make sense for my topic and thesis? Have I taken my audience's perspective sufficiently into account (what they might know, what they might need to know, and so on)? (See *Knowing Your Audience* on page 37.)

Revising for Style. Now you can focus on your prose. At this point, you want to work with sentences, rhythm, word choice, and the rules of standard written English. You want to bring your voice out effectively and appropriately for the rhetorical situation. Move through your draft sentence by sentence and try to craft each sentence so that it is as effective as possible.
- Are there any confusing passages? If so, how can I rewrite specific sentences to make these passages clearer?
- Is my voice strong and consistent throughout the paper? Are there sections where my voice seems less effective?
- Can any sentences be improved by restructuring them or eliminating words or phrases that aren't essential?
- Can I improve any passages with more appropriate word choice?

In your composition class, you may be asked to share drafts of your writing with classmates so that you can get feedback on how to improve your draft. Sharing your drafts before they are finished is one of the most effective ways to improve your writing, and it is also a good way to develop your revision skills. If you are not asked to share your drafts in your composition class, consider finding a friend or family member who might offer useful feedback on your drafts. Or visit the writing center on your campus, where you can get feedback from trained writing tutors.

A WORD ABOUT SPELLING CHECKERS AND GRAMMAR CHECKERS

Many students like to run the spelling and grammar checking features that are included with most word processing programs. These features can find misspelled words and suggest corrections; they can also find many kinds of punctuation and grammar errors. But be careful when you use these features. They do not always find all the errors or problems in your drafts, and sometimes they suggest corrections that may actually create new errors. If you do use these features, make sure you review the suggestions for correcting errors before you make any changes to your draft. And be especially careful with the thesaurus feature on your word processing program. Very often, the thesaurus will suggest a word that is inappropriate for the context.

in Chapter 4) and also provides access to audiences that were unavailable to most writers in the past. You may already have experience with blogs and other web-based forums where you can share your writing and communicate with different audiences. Or perhaps you maintain your own web site where you publish your writing. It is likely that your composition instructor will encourage (or even require) you to explore these opportunities for online writing. Many of the exercises in this book will also encourage you to venture online to engage in various kinds of writing. If you do, keep in mind that writing in these new media enables you to enter conversations that are reshaping our world today.

These new technologies are also changing the way we combine text with images and sound. I discussed technology in Chapter 2, but it is important to remember that for some kinds of writing tasks, you do not need to limit yourself to text alone. The nature of the task and the rhetorical situation will help you determine whether you can or should use images, graphics, or other kinds of media to achieve your purpose and address your audience effectively.

Writing as Inquiry

A FEW YEARS AGO, A STUDENT OF MINE NAMED KRISTEN DECIDED TO WRITE AN ARGUMENT IN FAVOR OF BECOMING A VEGETARIAN. SHE INTENDED HER ARGUMENT FOR A GENERAL AUDIENCE, SUCH AS THE READERS OF A WIDELY CIRCULATED PUBLICATION LIKE *USA TODAY*. SHE WANTED TO PERSUADE HER READERS THAT BECOMING A VEGETARIAN IS A GOOD IDEA BECAUSE A VEGETARIAN DIET IS HEALTHIER THAN A DIET THAT INCLUDES MEAT.

As she looked into the issue, however, she began to see that it was more complicated than she first thought. Her research into the health benefits of a vegetarian diet revealed that it is possible to have a healthy diet that includes meat and that there are actually some health risks to a vegetarian diet. That led her to examine arguments *against* becoming a vegetarian, and she began to explore other points of view, which deepened her understanding of the issue. She also began to encounter environmental arguments for becoming a vegetarian that she hadn't previously considered. She learned, for example, that raising beef cattle, chickens, and hogs on a large scale causes serious environmental damage. As a result, Kristen began to develop an ethical argument for becoming a vegetarian that she considered more powerful than her original argument based on health benefits. Her basic opinion about becoming a vegetarian did not change— she was still in favor of it—but her argument shifted from a focus on individual health benefits to larger social, environmental, and ethical concerns. As a result of her writing about becoming a vegetarian, she gained a better understanding of the issue—and I think she wrote a more effective paper, too.

Many of the assignments in this book ask you to engage in inquiry about a topic to understand it better, just as Kristen did. When Kristen examined opposing viewpoints that her readers might have, she was exploring her topic with her audience and her purpose in mind, and they shaped her exploration. By writing a more informed argument, she was able to participate more effectively in our society's larger conversations about diet and health and social responsibility. Ultimately, that's an important part of your goal whenever you write—to communicate effectively and knowledgeably about a given topic.

Writing is not just a matter of putting your thoughts or ideas down on paper; it is also a means of exploring those thoughts or ideas, a way to inquire into a topic. I'd like you to think of research in this same way: Research is part of the process of learning about something through writing, as Kristen did.

Conducting Research

Researching a topic is a process of inquiry through which you not only gather information and develop ideas about your topic but also gain a greater understanding of it. This is why I think it's a mistake to approach your research as a separate activity from your writing. Conducting research is an integral part of the writing process.

Here are a few main principles to help you understand this process of researching a topic:

- *Conducting research is not a linear process.* It may be possible in some cases to gather all the information you need before you actually begin writing a draft of your paper, but if you are genuinely engaged with your topic, it is more likely that as you start writing you will find you need to do more research. As you revise a draft for the second or third time, you might discover that you need some information that you don't have, so you need to go back to the library or the Internet to find that information. When Kristen began to see an ethical and environmental argument in favor of vegetarianism rather than simply a health-related argument, she had to do more research to gain a better understanding of the ethical and environmental issues. In short, research can lead to more research. It's all part of the process of exploring your topic for your intended audience.

- *Research depends on the nature of the writing assignment.* Although it's probably true that you don't need to do formal research for every writing assignment, it's also true that you may need to do research for assignments that are not, strictly speaking, research papers. For example, if you're writing a letter to the editor of your school newspaper about a local controversy, you may have to do some research to gather information about that controversy. Similarly, you may be asked to write a paper for a psychology class on an experience you had with, say, a school guidance counselor; that assignment may require you to find information about school guidance counselors. Putting together a web page for a student organization you belong to may require you to examine the web sites of similar organizations. So almost any writing activity may require you to look for information or consult sources.

  Obviously, some kinds of writing require specialized kinds of research. A report for your chemistry class may require you to consult certain scientific journals. Your sociology instructor may ask you to use only certain kinds of academic books or articles for a paper on government drug policies, whereas your communications instructor may ask you to examine sources from the popular press for an assignment on the news coverage of political campaigns. In each case, the nature of the assignment makes certain kinds of sources useful or necessary and other sources inappropriate. It's your job as a writer to determine what kinds of sources you need to explore for your assignment. So doing research doesn't mean just going to the Internet and doing a Google search or checking your library's listings for your topic; it means identifying the *kinds* of sources that are most appropriate and relevant to your assignment.

- *An open mind can mean greater learning.* If you begin your research with the idea that you already know exactly what kinds of information you need, you may miss an opportunity to explore your topic fully and understand it better. For example, let's say you are writing a paper for a criminology class about reasons for the rising prison population in the United States. After making some notes about your topic and reading your course textbook, you have compiled a list of the kinds of information you need for your paper, including statistical data about the prison population, information about changes in state laws that have led to higher incarceration rates, and information about different incarceration rates for different racial groups. So you set off looking for sources with that kind of information. After finding the information, you write your paper, focusing on just those reasons that are discussed in the sources you have found. But let's say that one of your sources mentions the fact that most new prisons are being built in rural areas. When you were developing your list of information that you had to find, you hadn't thought about the matter of *where* prisons are being built. So that wasn't on your list, and you didn't include it in your paper. But if you then went back to look for additional sources that relate specifically to this matter of where prisons are being built, you might find that there is another important reason for the increasing prison population in the United States that has to do with the economics of the criminal justice system. Exploring that issue might enhance your understanding of your topic—and lead to a better paper.

   The point is that even if you begin your research with a good idea of the kinds of information or sources you need to find, keeping an open mind about your research will likely mean that you'll learn more about your topic and therefore be more likely to write an effective paper.

Tools for Your Inquiry

You are fortunate to live at a time when the tools available to writers for their research are much more powerful and extensive than what was available even a few years ago. In addition to traditional sources like books, newspapers, and journals available through your library, the Internet is a vast resource that provides ready access to an astonishing variety of information. Moreover, traditional print sources, such as newspaper and magazine articles and even books, are increasingly available in digital form, either on CD-ROMs or online. I can remember spending hours in the library as an undergraduate student laboriously paging through indexes like *The Reader's Guide to Periodical Literature* to find sources that looked useful, checking the card catalog, and then plodding through the library stacks to find those articles or books

CURIOSITY IN RESEARCH
Curiosity is an important component of the research process. Research—and writing in general—is a way to satisfy your curiosity about questions or issues or ideas that are important or interesting to you. Research should be a process of allowing your curiosity to guide you. Follow your questions and hunches. Look to see what's around the next corner, even if that direction doesn't seem to be the one you're going in. A course assignment is likely to be much more enjoyable if you allow yourself to be curious about your topic. Not knowing exactly what you will learn is part of what makes research—and writing—interesting and worthwhile.

WHAT COUNTS AS A SOURCE?

The short answer is "almost anything." The right sources for a writing assignment depend on the nature of that assignment. If you're writing about the effects of government policies on farming in your state, then it would make sense to talk to an expert in your state agriculture department or your local agriculture extension service in addition to consulting more conventional sources, such as journal articles or books about farm policy. For a PowerPoint presentation on hip-hop culture for your sociology class, you might visit hip-hop web sites or talk to local musicians. For an assignment in his history course, my son visited the Saratoga Battlefield National Monument in upstate New York to speak to the museum curator there about that famous Revolutionary War battle. The point is that you should seek relevant information and ideas wherever they might be. The library or the Internet may not always be the best places to find sources for your assignment. Be curious and creative as you research your topic.

on the shelves. Usually, the library didn't have all the sources I needed for my paper, and often, a list of twenty potential sources would result in only four or five articles or books that I could actually find. If those articles or books weren't exactly what I needed, then I'd have to go back to *The Reader's Guide* to try to find more sources.

Today, you can log onto the Internet, go to the web site for your school's library, and find hundreds and even thousands of sources in online indexes like *The Reader's Guide* or more specialized databases for various subjects. Once you find relevant sources in an index or database, you can often read the full article online—without ever getting up from your desk. You can also check to see if your library has any of the books you need before you actually go to the library to check them out. These many online resources can be a gold mine for a writer.

The variety and extensive nature of these resources also mean greater challenges for writers in determining which sources are credible and useful. The rest of this chapter offers some general advice to help you identify, assess, and cite sources for your writing. In the following section, we'll examine some of the tools you can use for your research. Later, we'll discuss how to cite your sources.

The Library and the Internet

Many of the resources that were once available only through your library are now available on the Internet. Today, most college and university libraries offer access to the library's holdings and many indexes, databases, and other kinds of resources and research services through their web sites. So "going to the library" to do research might mean logging onto the Internet and using your library's web site to search for sources. But there remain important differences between using your library and using the Internet for research:

- A university or college library will usually provide access to specialized indexes and databases that are not always available on the web.
- Libraries carefully evaluate the resources they provide, which is not always true of resources available on the Internet.
- Libraries provide access to books; various reference guides; and newspaper, magazine, or journal articles that are not always available on the Internet.

So it's still a good idea to begin your research at your library or on your library's web site.

Using Indexes and Databases

An *index* is basically a listing of published books and articles; a *database* is the same thing, although it may contain more information than an index. For many assignments that require research, you may need to consult one of the many different indexes or databases to find sources. When you use an index or database, you are looking for information about books and articles that might be relevant to your topic. A listing in an index or database will usually provide the title of the book or article; the author (if available); the journal, magazine, or other publication in which the article appeared; the publisher; the date of publication; and the length of the article. Using this information, you can decide whether the article or book is likely to be useful in your research. If the title sounds relevant to your topic, if the article is from a reputable source or written by a well-known author in the field, or if the article was written during a relevant time period for your topic, then you might consider reading the selection. At that point, you would go to your library (or the Internet) to find that article or book.

A visit to your library's web site will reveal that there are dozens of indexes and databases available to you. Obviously, the first step is to decide which ones to search. Because searching a database for information can be time-consuming, this step is important. You don't want to spend time searching through a database only to discover that it does not list the kinds of sources you need for your project. If you're not sure what a database contains, ask your librarian.

KINDS OF INDEXES AND DATABASES
There are two basic kinds of indexes and databases: general and specialized. General indexes are just that: very general listings of sources on a broad range of topics. *The Reader's Guide to Periodical Literature* is one of the oldest and best-known general indexes; it includes listings of articles published in many popular and commercial magazines, journals, and newspapers. InfoTrac College Edition is a newer general index that offers listings similar to *The Reader's Guide* but includes many contemporary digital as well as academic sources. For many academic writing assignments, you might need to consult a specialized index or database that contains listings of publications related to a specific academic discipline, such as psychology, sociology, or medicine. *Psychological Abstracts,* for example, contains listings of articles from professional and academic journals in psychology; similarly, the *MLA International Bibliography* includes sources for the study of literature and literary theory. Such specialized indexes and databases are useful in finding materials that would not usually appear in popular newspaper or magazine articles.

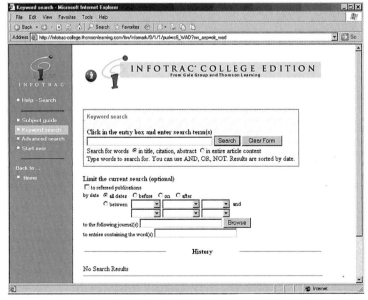

InfoTrac screen shot. From INFOTRAC ONEFILE PLUS by Thomson Gale, © 2005, Gale Group. Reprinted by permission of the Gale Group.

A WORD ABOUT WIKIPEDIA

In recent years, Wikipedia, which describes itself as "the free encyclopedia that anyone can edit," has become one of the world's most extensive and popular online resources. Chances are that you have used Wikipedia for some of your school assignments. If so, then you know how much information is available at that web site. But you may not know that Wikipedia has been controversial. Because Wikipedia is written and edited by thousands of volunteers who may not be experts in the subjects they are writing about, many educators are skeptical of the accuracy of the information in Wikipedia. In addition, critics have identified bias in some Wikipedia entries. However, some studies have shown Wikipedia to be generally as reliable as more traditional sources, such as *Encyclopedia Britannica*. The managers of Wikipedia acknowledge that some of the encyclopedia's entries are questionable, incomplete, undocumented, or controversial, and they will usually indicate such problems at the beginning of such entries. If you use Wikipedia as a source for your writing, be aware of these issues and make your decisions about the reliability of its information accordingly. Moreover, check with your instructor about whether he or she will accept Wikipedia as a source for your course assignments.

The basic task of searching an index or database is straightforward: You look for titles of articles or books that seem relevant to your topic. Most databases have similar basic search functions. For example, the keyword search screen for InfoTrac is on page 51.

This screen allows you to search the Info-Trac database using a keyword. Suppose you're writing a report on alternative energy. You can begin by using *alternative energy* as your keyword. You might also try searching for related terms, such as *solar power, wind power, sustainable energy,* or *renewable energy.* Notice the blue bar on the left side of the screen, which has several options for other kinds of searches that will allow you to search by subject, journal type, and similar factors. You may have to try these different search functions to see which ones will yield the most useful results for your topic.

Your database search will yield a list of articles, and you will have to select which articles might be useful for your paper. Review the list to see whether it is worth finding the article itself. If your library has access to that article, you can go to the article directly.

Databases such as InfoTrac College Edition can be extremely useful in finding information and materials you need for your project. But using these databases can also be time-consuming. Often, there is no substitute for just spending time searching a database for what you need, so be sure to leave yourself sufficient time for your research.

Searching the Internet

The Internet is becoming an increasingly important resource for research. That's not surprising because the Internet contains an unimaginable amount of information and is growing rapidly. But searching the Internet is different in two important ways from searching materials in your library or on your library's web site:

1. The Internet is not organized into neat databases and indexes such as those in your library. To find relevant materials on the Internet requires different strategies than you would use when searching for materials in your library. The most common method of searching the Internet is to use a *search engine* such as Google. Search engines work more or less like an index or database you might find at your library, but they generally do not limit their searches to specific kinds of materials, such as academic journals or newspapers, as indexes or databases do. Instead, a typical search with a search engine will turn up many

different kinds of materials—and usually far more material than you could possibly sort through for your research.

2. Because the Internet is largely unregulated and anyone with access to it can put up a web site, materials on the Internet cannot be considered as trustworthy as the materials you might find at your library. Whereas your librarians evaluate materials before including them in the library's collections, no one is required to evaluate materials before they are posted to the web. So it is important to evaluate the credibility of materials you find on the web.

A search engine is a program that searches the Internet according to specific criteria and then indexes what it finds. Google (http://www.google.com) is one of the better known search engines. (Google also has an excellent scholarly search engine at http://scholar.google.com that provides access to scholarly sources on the web.) Other popular search engines include http://www.ask.com and http://www.yahoo.com. Search engines use different criteria for finding materials on the Internet, so it is good practice to use more than one when doing Internet research.

Like more formal indexes or databases, Internet search engines allow you to search by keyword, and many of them allow you to refine your searches. Let's say you are writing an essay about an emergency you had with your dog, and you wanted to find more information about emergency medical care for animals. You might begin your search with terms like *veterinary medicine* or *animal care*. Such terms by themselves are likely to turn up many thousands of web sites. When I was writing this chapter in 2008, for example, a search for *veterinary medicine* turned up more than 6 million sites! So you want to be as specific as possible. You might include *all* of these search terms as keywords: *veterinary medicine, emergency,* and *animal care*. But using such general terms will likely turn up too many sites for you to visit and evaluate, so it's a good idea to narrow your search even further by being more specific. You might focus on pets or dogs, for instance. Or you might focus only on animal care in the United States or on a specific kind of situation, such as *dog sprayed by a skunk*. The more specific your search terms, the better your results are likely to be.

In addition to search engines, you can also use online encyclopedias, such as Wikipedia.com, Answers.com, or Britannica.com. The web sites of many organizations also contain resource pages with links to specific kinds of information.

Evaluating Internet Resources

Once you find relevant materials on the Internet, you need to determine whether they are credible or trustworthy, which can sometimes be tricky. Because anyone can put up a web site, and because there is no official review process for web sites, it's important to be cautious

AN IMPORTANT SEARCH TRICK
Here is a strategy for using search engines more efficiently. If you place your search terms in quotation marks, the search engine will look for exactly those words in that order. For example, if you search for *veterinary medicine,* your search will turn up sites with both those words as well as sites that have either one word or the other; however, placing that term in quotation marks (*"veterinary medicine"*) will yield only sites with the term *veterinary medicine.* Using quotation marks in this way can help you narrow your search and find more relevant web sites.

when deciding whether to use material from a web site, even if that material looks reliable. Here are some guidelines for evaluating Internet sources.

- *Who sponsors the web site?* Obviously, a university web site, the site of a respected news organization like the *New York Times* or CNN, a government web site, or the site of a well-known organization like the Red Cross or the American Heart Association is likely to contain reliable and trustworthy information. Such sites make it easy to determine who the sponsor is. But often, it isn't clear who sponsors a site, and in these cases, you should try to determine the sponsor before deciding whether to use the information. You can do this in several ways:
  - Check the Internet address, or URL, which can provide information about the site's sponsor.
  - Read the "About" page, which many web sites include and which often contains information about the site's sponsor.
  - Check the bottom of the home page, which often has copyright information about the site.

  If you cannot determine who sponsors the site, it is probably best not to use the information you find there.

- *What is the purpose of the site?* In the case of a recognizable web site, such as *USA Today* or a university web site, the purpose is usually very clear. But for less familiar sites, the site's purpose is not always obvious. Is it an informational site—for example, the site of a consumer advocacy group intended to provide consumers with information about certain kinds of products? Is its purpose to sell a product? Often, by exploring the site for a few moments, you can determine the site's general purpose, which can help you decide whether the information on the site is trustworthy.

- *Who is the author?* If you find an article or some other kind of document on a web site, look for the name of the author. Sometimes information about the author is included with the article, but if not, you can search the Internet to find out more about that author. Many articles and pages on web sites list no author; however, that isn't necessarily a problem because many organizations include material on their web sites that is produced by staff members, who are not always listed as authors. But if there is no author and you already have questions about the web site, you probably should be skeptical about using material from that site.

- *Is the web site current?* The web sites of news organizations, universities, and other reliable organizations are usually updated regularly, often several times daily. But many web sites are rarely, if ever, updated. That can be a problem if the information you find on that site relates to a topic of current interest. Check the bottom of the home page of a web site for a date. Most reliable web sites list the date when they were last updated. If there is no such date, don't assume the information on the site is current.

- *Is there evidence of bias?* Sometimes it's easy to determine that a web site reflects a certain point of view. But often, bias is subtle. For example, White supremacist organizations have sponsored web sites about Martin Luther King, Jr., that seem credible at first glance. But a closer look reveals that these sites are intended to look like an objective resource about King's life while concealing their real purpose: to raise questions about King and his work and to convey misinformation about him. Even if a site seems credible, always check for signs of bias, especially if you are unfamiliar with the organization or person sponsoring the site.

- *Is the information on the web site accurate?* Even if a web site passes these other tests and seems trustworthy, you should still be cautious about trusting the information you find there if you know little about the site or its sponsors. It's a good idea to check the accuracy of the site by corroborating its information elsewhere. For example, if you're writing a paper about the Civil Rights Movement and you find a web site that contains historical information, check a few of the facts on that site by referring to a history book or similar reference book or by visiting a web site that you know is trustworthy. You might, for instance, check the dates listed for Martin Luther King, Jr.'s, life or information about the passage of the Voting Rights Act. Checking a few facts in this way can help you determine whether you can trust other information on the site.

Other Source Material

Many of the exercises and assignments in this book ask you to write about topics that require you to look beyond the library and the Internet in your research. For example, an essay about a controversy surrounding a new big-box retail store proposed for your town may require you to talk to local officials and residents to get information and hear various points of view. The library or Internet might provide relevant information about similar controversies in other towns, but they may not have information about the specific situation in your town. For an assignment like this, you might need to interview people from the town or look at town records, such as the minutes of town council meetings. It might also be a good idea to get information from organizations involved in the controversy. It's worth considering these three kinds of sources for writing assignments that you might not be able to complete using traditional sources.

READING INTERNET ADDRESSES
The address of a web site is referred to as a URL (Uniform Resource Locator). You can often learn a lot from the address itself. The suffix of a URL conveys important information: *.com* means the web site is a commercial or business site; *.edu* means the site is an educational institution (university web sites end in *.edu,* for example); *.org* means the site is sponsored by a nongovernmental organization; *.gov* means it's a government web site. A site with a *.edu* suffix is likely to be relatively trustworthy because it is probably sponsored by a university or college. A *.org* site may also be trustworthy, but organizations sometimes have interests and agendas that might make you skeptical about the information included on the site. For example, a site for a political action committee might reflect a very conservative or liberal political viewpoint, which may affect the kind of information the site contains. A site for an environmental group is likely to favor information that supports its perspective. A *.com* site may mean that the site is a moneymaking venture, so information on the site may reflect the business's efforts to sell its products. Keep these things in mind when you're visiting web sites for your research.

INTERNET HOAXES

Hoaxes have become common on the Internet, but they're not always easy to identify.

This photograph (top right) began circulating on the Internet shortly after the power outage in the northeastern United States in August 2003 and was said to have been taken from a satellite during the power outage, but it was actually a hoax. The actual satellite photos are below. The lesson is clear: Be cautious about using information and materials you find on the Internet.

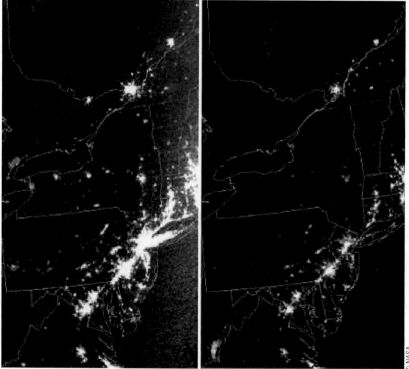

Interviews

Interviewing is an art that can take many years to master, but here are a few guidelines to keep in mind if you do any interviewing:

- Carefully prepare your questions in advance. Create a list of the most important questions you want to ask. Try to keep your questions brief.

- Do your homework. Try to learn something about the person you're interviewing and about your topic so that you don't waste time asking about information you should already know.
- Allow the person to do most of the talking. The biggest mistake inexperienced interviewers make is talking too much.
- Take notes or use a tape recorder. If you use a tape recorder, be sure to ask the person for permission to do so.
- Check your information. Before leaving the interview, be sure to check important facts with the person and also check the spelling of important names you might use in your writing.

Public Records and Documents

For many writing assignments, the best information may be located in town, state, or federal documents. Often, these documents can only be found in a public building and may not be available on the Internet. If you need to examine such materials for your research, check with the appropriate office about how you can access the materials. Find out whether you can make photocopies of the documents, which can save time. For state or federal documents, this process can be time-consuming, so plan ahead.

Materials from Organizations

Let's say you are creating a web site about the loss of wetlands in your region and its effects on local wildlife populations. For such an assignment, it would be a good idea to search your library or the Internet for information about wetland loss in general. But for your local situation, there may be better sources, such as the local or state chapter of the Audubon Society or a similar environmental organization. Often, these organizations have publications, such as flyers or pamphlets, that they distribute to the public. They may also have reports about issues that concern them. Such documents may not be available in libraries or on the Internet, and the only way to get them may be through the organization itself. Usually, a phone call or e-mail is the best first step to find out what resources the organization has and how you can access them.

Working with Source Material

No matter how you obtain information through your research, you will have to use that information appropriately and effectively in your writing. That means three things: (1) deciding which information to include in your paper; (2) integrating that information properly into your own writing; and (3) avoiding plagiarism. Here are some guidelines for each of these:

- *Deciding which information to include.* If you do your research diligently and allow your curiosity to guide you, you will probably gather more information than you need. So you must decide which information is most important or useful for your assignment. Like other important decisions in your writing, deciding what to use should be influenced by your purpose and your audience. Sometimes the information you gather might be interesting and relevant but unnecessary. For example, let's say that in doing research for a report on the popularity of orchids, you meet a gardener who invented a new method for growing rare species of orchids. The story of that gardener is interesting, but it may not be relevant to your paper, which focuses on the popularity of orchids. However, that same story might be important to include if you were writing an article for the newsletter of your local gardening association. The key is to be careful and discerning in selecting material to include. Don't include irrelevant information just because it seems interesting.

- *Integrating information into your writing.* Incorporating source material effectively into a piece of writing can be a difficult challenge for many students because students often allow the source material, rather than the purpose of the assignment and their own ideas about the material, to guide them. The most important thing to keep in mind is that you are using sources to help accomplish *your* purpose in your assignment. So you should use information you collect to help explain an idea, support a point, describe a problem or situation, document an event, or make an argument. Let's return to the example of a report on the popularity of orchids. Let's say you found several articles about the environmental damage that large-scale orchid growing causes, and you want to include in your report some information about the environmental implications of orchid growing. You may need to summarize what you learned about this problem from the articles you found, and you may even use quotations from those articles to help describe the problem. In this case, you are using source material (the articles you found) to document a problem (the environmental damage caused by orchid growing) that you believe should be included in your report about the popularity of orchids. What you say about those articles is determined by your purpose in your report and by your decisions as a writer about what is important to include and what can be left out; it is determined as well by your sense of what your audience will want or need to know about the environmental damage caused by orchid growing. If you allow your purpose and audience to guide you, you are likely to make more effective choices about which source material to use.
- *Avoiding plagiarism.* Plagiarism is essentially the act of presenting someone else's ideas or words as your own. The most egregious

example of plagiarism is having someone else write a paper for you and then submitting it to your instructor as if you had written it yourself. That is dishonest and unethical, and in most colleges it will result in serious consequences if you are caught. But there are many other forms of plagiarism, and often students plagiarize without intending to or even knowing that they are doing so. Usually, that is because they are not careful in using their source material. The basic rule of thumb when using source material is this: *When in doubt, cite your source.* Any time you use information from a source, cite that source (according to the guidelines in this chapter). If you use specific words from a source, place those words in quotation marks to indicate to your readers that those words came from your source. If you use sources as described under "Integrating Information into Your Writing," guided by your purpose and your audience, you are less likely to plagiarize inadvertently. (Check your college library web site for information about citing sources and avoiding plagiarism. Also, be familiar with your college or university's policy on intellectual or academic honesty.)

Citing Sources

If you use any kind of source for a writing assignment, you must cite that source. Citing a source means two things: (1) letting readers know that a quotation, an idea, or information in your text came from that source and (2) including information about that source in a bibliography or works cited page. There are different ways of citing sources, but one of the most common for most college writing assignments is MLA (Modern Language Association). Generally, MLA is used in the humanities (e.g., history, philosophy, English).

The following section includes some guidelines for citing common kinds of sources. (For complete guidelines, consult the *MLA Handbook for Writers of Research Papers.*) Whichever style you use, keep in mind that the primary purposes of citing your sources properly are (1) to credit and document the source of your information and (2) to enable readers to find the source.

Parenthetical (In-Text) Citations Using MLA Style

A parenthetical citation tells a reader that you have cited a source. For example, let's say you're writing an essay about the popularity of mountain climbing, and you want to discuss some of the history of American mountaineering. You want to include in your essay the fact that there were five unsuccessful American attempts to climb K2, the world's second highest mountain, before the successful 1978 expedition—something you learned about on page 6 of a book called *The Last Step: The*

American Ascent of K2 by Rick Ridgeway. How would you use a parenthetical citation to cite your source?

Here's what a sentence citing information (but no quotation) from Ridgeway's book might look like in your essay:

> Before the Americans finally climbed K2 in 1978,
> five previous expeditions had failed to reach
> that mountain's elusive summit (Ridgeway 6).

Notice that the parenthetical citation contains only the author's last name and the page reference with no punctuation between them. (Also notice that the parentheses are placed *inside* the final period of the sentence.) If you mention Ridgeway's name in your sentence, then you only have to include the page reference in parentheses:

> As famed mountaineer Rick Ridgeway explains
> in <u>The Last Step: The American Ascent of K2</u>,
> American climbers failed to reach K2's elusive
> summit in five previous attempts before the
> successful American expedition in 1978 (6).

This information tells a reader that you found this information on page 6 of Ridgeway's book. If the reader wants more information about that book, he or she will find it in your bibliography or works cited page. (The format for bibliographic or works cited entries is discussed in the next section.)

Here are some additional guidelines for parenthetical citations using MLA style:

- *In general, include the least amount of necessary information in parentheses.* If you can, include the author's name or the title of the work in your sentence, and place only the page reference in parentheses.
- *If the work you're citing has no listed author, include the title in parentheses.* Let's say you have a document called "Helping the Homeless" from the organization Habitat for Humanity. If you were using information from page 2 of that document, your parenthetical citation would look like this: ("Helping the Homeless" 2).

Compiling a Bibliography or Works Cited Page

If you cite a source in your paper, you should include a bibliography or works cited page. For example, let's return to our example of citing information from Rick Ridgeway's book in a paper about the popularity of mountaineering. Here's what the entry in your bibliography would look like in MLA style:

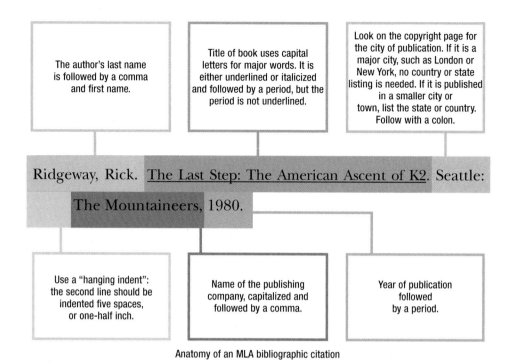

Anatomy of an MLA bibliographic citation

> Ridgeway, Rick. The Last Step: The American Ascent of
>
> K2. Seattle: The Mountaineers, 1980.

The basic information you need for a citation in a bibliography or works cited page is similar. When doing your research, therefore, be sure to record this information so that it is available when you begin compiling your bibliography. Also remember that your bibliography should be in alphabetical order regardless of which style you're using.

In the following sections, examples are provided for common kinds of sources in MLA format.

Sample MLA Citations
Printed Resources

1. Book with One Author

> Gibaldi, Joseph. MLA Handbook for Writers of Research
>
> Projects. 5th ed. New York: The Modern Language
>
> Association, 1999.

2. Book with a Corporate Author

> American Allergy Association. <u>Allergies in Children</u>. New
>
> York: Random House, 1998.

Use this type of entry when the book wasn't written by an individual but was produced by an organization. In this case, the name of the organization is placed where the author's name would go.

3. Book with Multiple Authors

> Lowi, Theodore J., Benjamin Ginsberg, and Steve
>
> Jackson. <u>Analyzing American Government: American</u>
>
> <u>Government, Freedom and Power</u>. 3rd ed. New York:
>
> Norton, 1994.

If there are more than three authors, include only the first author's name and add *et al.*: Jones, Robert, et al.

4. Article, Essay, or Story from an Anthology or Collection

> Jackson, Shirley. "The Lottery." <u>The Norton Anthology</u>
>
> <u>of Literature by Women</u>. Ed. Sandra M. Gubar. New
>
> York: Norton, 1985. 1872–1880.

5. Article from an Encyclopedia

> Franklin, Mark N. "Voting Behavior." <u>The Encyclopedia of</u>
>
> <u>Democracy</u>. 1995 ed. 782–783.

6. Magazine Article

> Wallace, David Foster. "Host." <u>The Atlantic Monthly</u>. April
>
> 2005: 51–77.

7. Journal Article

> Warner, Megan B., et al. "The Longitudinal Relationship
>
> of Personality Traits and Disorders." <u>Journal of</u>
>
> <u>Abnormal Psychology</u> 113 (2004): 217–227.

The number that follows the title of the journal is the volume number; the number in parentheses is the date of publication. The last numbers are the page numbers.

8. Newspaper Article

> Gladstone, Valerie. "Shiva Meets Martha Graham, at a Very
>
> High Speed." <u>New York Times</u> 10 Aug. 2003, New
>
> England ed., sec. 2: 3.

9. Personal Interview

> Powers, Jonathan. Personal interview. 23 Feb. 1989.

Web or Other Computer Resources

1. Article, Essay, or Story from an Online Database

> Edmondson, Elie A. "Martin Amis Writes Postmodern
>
> Man." <u>Critique</u> 42 (2001): 145. <u>Expanded Academic</u>
>
> <u>ASAP</u>. Gale Group Databases. SUNY Oneonta Lib.,
>
> Oneonta, NY. 13 Nov. 2008 <http://infotrac.
>
> galegroup.com>.

When you use a reference from an online database, you not only include the date of the publication but also the date you retrieved the source. Note that in MLA style, you also provide the name of the library from which you retrieved the information.

2. Entry in an Online Encyclopedia

> "Angelfish." <u>Microsoft Encarta Encyclopedia Online</u>. 2005.
>
> Microsoft Corp. 24 Jan. 2008 <http://encarta.msn.
>
> com/encyclopedia_761555978/Angelfish.html>.

Notice that there is no author, so the title of the article is placed first.

3. Newspaper Article from an Online Service or Database

> Louv, Richard. "Reseeding Environmentalism." <u>The</u>
>
> <u>Oregonian</u> 27 Mar. 2005, sunrise edition, commen-
>
> tary forum: E01. <u>LexisNexis</u>. SUNY Oneonta Lib.,
>
> Oneonta, NY. 9 Apr. 2008 <http://www.lexis-nexis.
>
> com/universe>.

4. Unsigned Article on a Web Site

> "Aboard the Underground Railroad: A National Register
>
> Travel Itinerary." National Park Service: Our Shared
>
> History African American Heritage. US Park Service.
>
> 12 Apr. 2008 <http://www.cr.nps.gov/nr/travel/
>
> underground/>.

Notice that in this example MLA style requires including the sponsor of the web site (in this case, the U.S. Park Service).

5. Signed Personal Web Site

> Nathanson, Betty. <u>Dejavu Standard Poodles</u>. 2 Feb. 2008
>
> <http://community-2.webtv.net/bnathanson/
>
> dejavustandard/>.

6. Personal E-mail

> Stonebraker, Gabriel. Personal e-mail. 16 June 2005.

PART

2

Themes *for* Writing *and* Inquiring

Chapter 5 Identity

HESE TWO HEADLINES APPEARED ON THE *NEW YORK TIMES*
WEB SITE ON THE SAME DAY IN 2004:

"HISPANICS RESIST RACIAL GROUPING BY CENSUS"
"IDENTITY THEFT IS EPIDEMIC: CAN IT BE STOPPED?"

"Hispanics Resist Racial Grouping by Census" reported on a woman named Kathia Mendez, who was raised in the Dominican Republic, where she was known as an Indian, a term often used in that country to refer to people of mixed race who do not have indigenous roots. In the United States, however, Mendez is more likely considered Black or Hispanic. But when she filled out the U.S. Census Bureau's questionnaire, she checked the box for Some Other Race. "I'm not black and I'm not white; we don't define ourselves that way," she told the reporter.

> But when she filled out the U.S. Census Bureau's questionnaire, she checked the box for Some Other Race. "I'm not black and I'm not white; we don't define ourselves that way," she told the reporter.

Kathia Mendez is a good example of someone who doesn't seem to fall into the categories we use to describe racial or ethnic identity, and her situation helps reveal the complexities of such categories. Is she Hispanic because she is from a country where Spanish is spoken? Is she Black because of her skin color? Is she Indian because of her ethnic heritage? Is she Dominican because of where she was born? Is she American because she has been a resident of the United States for nine years? And would she be an "American" if she had remained in the Dominican Republic, which is also in the Americas? Such questions indicate how difficult it can be to pin down one's identity.

Reading about Mendez, I couldn't help thinking about a former student of mine named Donna who was born and raised in New York City but whose parents had immigrated to the United States from Haiti before she was born. In school, Donna was often described as African American, the term that many people prefer to Black. But Donna told me that her parents rejected the term African American. They considered themselves Black Americans, not African Americans, because they were from a Caribbean country, not from Africa. So they are Black, American, and Haitian, but not African American. Like Mendez, Donna helps us see that identity is a much more complicated matter than we might think, especially when we so casually use terms like African American or Hispanic. As these situations suggest, racial identity also has something to do with where we are born and where we live as well as with how we look and how we speak. Sorting out all these characteristics isn't always easy.

Stories like Mendez's also raise the question of why we even need such categories. Why is it important to describe someone as Black or White, Asian or Latina, European or Native American? And what are the consequences of being categorized in these ways? As the readings in this chapter reveal, how we categorize one another does matter—often in very obvious ways, such as when certain groups of people are denied the rights available to other groups, as has been the case with Black Americans, Native Americans, Asian Americans, women, and other groups in the United States for much of its history. And consider that many people like Kathia Mendez, who have been categorized as Hispanic, have been opposed to a U.S. government proposal to eliminate the category of Some Other Race from the U.S. Census. These people argue that none of the other categories used by the Census Bureau accurately describes who they are. This is not just a matter of words because the decision by the Census Bureau about this category will directly affect the lives of millions of Americans by influencing government decisions about issues like education funding and various kinds of government benefits. Identity matters.

But identity is about more than race and ethnicity. It's also about gender, sexual orientation, age, social class, and national origin. It's about religious background and belief: We can be Muslim, Christian, Hindu, Jewish, Buddhist, atheist. It can be about political ideology: conservative, liberal, socialist, libertarian, anarchist. It's about the roles we play in our families and communities: mother, daughter, father, son, uncle, neighbor. It's also about the activities we take part in that help define who we are: student, teacher, writer, doctor, climber, athlete, activist, social worker, carpenter. And it can also be about the choices we make as consumers, including financial and business transactions that are increasingly shaped by new technologies that make it possible to steal someone's identity.

The very idea of identity theft seems odd. After all, your identity is yours. It's unique, isn't it? How can someone steal your identity? According to the *New York Times* article mentioned earlier, "Identity Theft Is Epidemic: Can It Be Stopped?", in our consumer-oriented society identity is often a matter of numbers: your Social Security number, bank account numbers, driver's license number, credit card account numbers. These numbers are, in a sense, who you are when it comes to things like buying a car, getting a loan, renting an apartment, or saving money from your paycheck in a bank account. They are your identity. And they can be stolen and used by someone else. This kind of theft has become a multibillion dollar problem in recent years as more and more important financial transactions are conducted through electronic means, including the Internet. It's another reminder not only that our identities are important but also that they are shaped by a variety of complex factors, including technology.

This chapter explores the complexity of identity. Each of the three clusters looks at identity from a different angle. The first cluster asks you to think about the many different ways we define ourselves, offering three different perspectives on what it means to claim an identity for yourself. The second cluster shifts the focus to how others define us and what the consequences of those definitions might be. And the third cluster explores the idea that each of us can have more than one identity.

I hope all of the clusters prompt you to think about how we use common categories, such as race, class, gender, ethnicity, sexual preference, and nationality, to define ourselves and each other. In a sense, in creating this chapter, I simply rearranged categories of identity that we already use. But of course, I couldn't really avoid

> **After all, your identity is yours. It's unique, isn't it? How can someone steal your identity?**

those categories because they have become so deeply ingrained in our thinking about ourselves and each other. They have become powerful lenses through which we see and understand each other. And that's part of the point of this chapter: to help you look more closely at the categories we so often use without often thinking about what they really mean. I also wanted to organize this chapter in a way that might call your attention to how artificial yet powerful our ways of defining each other can be. Most important, what I hope you'll see in this chapter are the interesting ways in which writers work within and against these categories to help us understand ourselves. As you read through the selections in this chapter, pay attention to how writing itself enables these authors to define themselves—and consider how your own writing and reading define you.

CREATING OUR SELVES

HAVE YOU EVER HEARD SOMEONE TALKING ABOUT HOW SHE "FOUND HERSELF"? OR PERHAPS YOU'VE HEARD SOMEONE DESCRIBING A TIME IN HIS LIFE WHEN HE DIDN'T KNOW WHO HE WAS. IT'S A RELATIVELY COMMON WAY OF TALKING ABOUT HOW PEOPLE CAN COME TO A

new understanding of themselves. For a long time, though, I was puzzled by such talk. How could you not know who you are? How do you find yourself? Where were you before you found yourself? The question of who you are seemed simple, even silly, to me. You are who you are. Aren't you?

Well, yes and no. Think about it like this: Are you the same person at school as you are at home or at work or with a group of your closest friends? Do you just act differently in each of these settings? Or are you somehow a different person in each of these settings? My guess is that your answer to these questions is something like, well, yes and no. You probably have a sense of yourself that stays pretty much the same no matter where you are or what you're doing. But I'd bet that if you spoke to the different people you interact with in different settings—your coworkers, your family members, your classmates, your neighbors—you might be surprised to find out that these different people think somewhat differently about "who you are." In some ways, you are always you. But your identity is not necessarily constant. It can relate to the different roles you have in your life (such as daughter or son, student, professional, friend) and the different contexts in which you live your life (work, home, school, community). And in each of these situations, you have some control over who you are. In other words, to some extent, you can "create" your self.

If this all sounds too abstract or fuzzy, the reading selections in this cluster may help to make it more concrete. For example, Sojourner Truth, a Black American activist for women's rights in the nineteenth century, poses a seemingly straightforward question in her famous speech: "Ain't I a Woman?" As you'll see, the answer to this question is not as simple as it seems. Of course she's a woman. But what exactly did that mean when women were not allowed to

vote, when they were not allowed to own property in many regions, when they were seen as inferior to men? In asking that question, Sojourner Truth begins to create a new way of defining what it means to be a woman. She creates a new kind of female self, one who challenges the conventional way of understanding who a woman is. In the same way, the other authors in this cluster challenge us to reexamine our familiar ways of thinking about identity—about what it means to be a Native American or a rural dweller or a woman or whomever. They help us see that we can indeed create ourselves, but we don't do so in isolation and we don't have complete control over our identities.

There is both power and risk in this ability to create ourselves. Some aspects of our identities may seem out of our control, such as our sex. But how we define sex or gender and what those definitions mean to others can make all the difference, as Sojourner Truth encourages us to see in her speech. Yes, she is a woman, but she wants to define that identity in a certain kind of way, despite the fact that others may define it differently. Thus, the effort to create a self is always a kind of struggle between how we as individuals understand our identities and how others do. As you read the selections in this cluster, consider how these authors deal with that struggle.

Consider, too, how the very act of writing is an act of creating a self. N. Scott Momaday may be Kiowa, for example, because he was born with that racial and ethnic identity, but he also creates a certain kind of self as a Kiowa in writing his essay about Rainy Mountain. Through the act of writing, he claims a certain way of understanding who he is as a Kiowa. And the same is true of the other authors. Each uses writing as a way to imagine their identities and to present themselves to us. I hope they help you see that you engage in the same act of self-creation whenever you write.

In 1851, the following address was delivered *by a former slave named Sojourner Truth (1797–1883) to the Women's Rights Convention in Akron, Ohio. By that time, Truth was a famous abolitionist and activist for women's rights. The previous year, a book by Oliver Gilbert titled* The Narrative of Sojourner Truth, *based on Gilbert's interviews with Truth, was*

Ain't I A Woman?

SOJOURNER TRUTH

published, and it brought national attention to Truth. It told the story of a domestic servant named Isabella who in 1843 changed her name, left her work and her home, and journeyed through the country preaching about God's salvation. Over time, she began to speak out forcefully about women's voting rights, the abolition of slavery, and social justice. Along with her fame came controversy, and accounts of her 1851 speech in Ohio suggest that some of the convention's organizers did not want her to speak, fearing that her presence would negatively influence public opinion about their efforts to gain the right to vote for women. But Truth did speak, and Frances Gage, one of the convention leaders, recorded Truth's words. The speech has become a classic American expression of women's rights. And it has helped make Sojourner Truth a symbol of the struggle for equality and justice.

Well, children, where there is so much racket there must be something out of kilter. I think that 'twixt the negroes of the South and the women at the North, all talking about rights, the white men will be in a fix pretty soon. But what's all this here talking about?

That man over there says that women need to be helped into carriages, and lifted over ditches, and to have the best place everywhere. Nobody ever helps me into carriages, or over mud-puddles, or gives me any best place! And ain't I a woman? Look at me! Look at my arm! I have ploughed and planted, and gathered into barns, and no man could head me! And ain't I a woman? I could work as much and eat as much as a man—when I could get it—and bear the lash as well! And ain't I a woman? I have borne thirteen children, and seen most all sold off to slavery, and when I cried out with my mother's grief, none but Jesus heard me! And ain't I a woman?

Then they talk about **THIS THING IN THE HEAD;** what's this they call it? [member of audience whispers, "intellect"] That's it, honey. What's that got to do with women's rights or negroes' rights? If my cup won't

SOJOURNER TRUTH, "AIN'T I A WOMAN?" (1851).

But controversy remains. There is some question about the accuracy of Gage's text. Truth did not read or write, so there was no "official" version of her speech. And some newspaper accounts at the time contradict Gage's text. But it is Gage's text that has become the accepted version of Truth's speech, and it is worth thinking about why. In other words, what is it about this version of Sojourner Truth's speech that seems to touch people even today? What does this speech say about what it means to be a woman? What does it say about the importance of claiming the right to define "woman" in a certain way—or claiming the right to define any kind of identity? And does it matter that this version of the speech may not be exactly what Sojourner Truth said in 1851? ◹

STRATEGIES: THIS "THING" AN INTELLECT
In this part of her speech (par. 3), Sojourner Truth seems to forget the word for *intellect*. It's possible that she may have genuinely forgotten the word for "this thing in the head." It may also be that this is just the way Frances Gage, the person who wrote down the speech, remembered it. But it's also possible that Truth may have feigned not knowing the word *intellect*. If that were true, what might her purpose have been? What point might she have been making by pretending to forget the word for intellect?

CONVERSATIONS: WOMEN'S RIGHTS
When she gave this now-famous speech in 1851, Sojourner Truth was actively engaged in a national movement to help women gain the right to vote in the United States. It might surprise you that the struggle for women's voting rights continued until 1920, when the U.S. Congress passed the Nineteenth Amendment, extending the right to vote to all women. But the movement for women's rights continued through the twentieth century and gained momentum in the 1970s and 1980s, when activists were proposing the Equal Rights Amendment to the U.S. Constitution, which would extend women's rights beyond voting into other areas of law, including employment and taxation. Perhaps it isn't surprising that Sojourner Truth has once again become a revered figure for women's rights. Her famous 1851 speech has become part of the ongoing conversations about women's rights and social justice today. Consider what this speech, delivered when it was illegal for women to vote, might contribute to that conversation.

hold but a pint, and yours holds a quart, wouldn't you be mean not to let me have my little half measure full?

Then that little man in black there, he says women can't have as much rights as men, 'cause Christ wasn't a woman! Where did your Christ come from? Where did your Christ come from? From God and a woman! Man had nothing to do with Him.

If the first woman God ever made was strong enough to turn the world upside down all alone, these women together ought to be able to turn it back, and get it right side up again! And now they is asking to do it, the men better let them.

Obliged to you for hearing me, and now old Sojourner ain't got nothing more to say.

Understanding the Text

1. What is Sojourner Truth's definition of *woman,* based on her words in this speech?

2. What main arguments does Truth make in favor of women's rights? Do you find these arguments convincing? Why or why not?

3. What evidence does Truth offer to support her view of women? What do you think her evidence suggests about her beliefs and values?

Exploring the Issues

1. This speech was originally delivered at a women's rights convention in 1851. How effectively do you think Sojourner Truth addressed that audience? Why do you think her words still have an impact on readers today?

2. In her speech, Truth used common language to make a point about a very complex issue—namely, how women were understood in a White, male-dominated society. In what ways do you think her use of common language influences her message? Do you find this kind of language effective in this case? Why or why not?

3. Sojourner Truth makes an argument in favor of women's rights. Evaluate her argument. How effectively do you think she makes her case in this very brief speech? How persuasively does she support her case?

Do you think her main points are still valid today? Explain.

Entering the Conversations

1. Drawing on Sojourner Truth's speech and any other relevant text, write an essay in which you define *woman.*

2. Rewrite Truth's speech for a contemporary audience.

INFOTRAC

3. Using InfoTrac College Edition and any other relevant sources, explore the history of the women's rights movement in the United States. Find out more about the movement to gain voting rights for women in the late nineteenth and early twentieth centuries, and look into the more recent women's movements in the late twentieth century. What were the key events of these movements? What obstacles did they face? What were the main arguments made on behalf of women's rights? Then write a report in which you discuss what you learned in your research. Alternatively, create a web site based on your research.

Suffragettes picketing outside jail, 1917

Suffragettes during march for the vote, 1912

4. These photographs were taken in 1912 and 1917, a few years before the Nineteenth Amendment was passed, which gave women in the United States the legal right to vote. Examine what these photographs might reveal about the women's rights movement in the early twentieth century. What ideas do you think these photographs communicate? What do the photos emphasize? What's missing? What do the photos suggest about the *suffragettes,* the term used to describe the women who fought for women's rights? Write an essay in which you analyze the messages in these photographs.

Where you are born can be a big part of your identity. I remember the first time I began to realize this. I grew up near the Pocono Mountains of northeastern Pennsylvania and then lived for several years in northern New England before moving to Ohio. During my first winter in Ohio, I felt a subtle homesickness that I assumed was

THE Way TO *Rainy* Mountain

just a result of missing my family and friends. But the feeling became intense one day when I was looking at photographs from Vermont. I kept coming back to one photograph of a very ordinary scene of an empty, snow-covered farm field on a low hillside. The photo had been taken in Vermont, but the scene could have been almost anywhere in the northeastern United States. It suddenly occurred to me that what was so powerful about the photograph was that it showed the typical landscape I had lived in for so many years. I had become so accustomed to that landscape that I almost didn't notice it—until I left. And I missed it almost in the same way I missed family and friends. That landscape is in some ways a part of who I am.

In the following essay, N. Scott Momaday (b. 1934) writes about that same kind of connection to a place. But perhaps in some ways, Momaday, a Native American,

N. SCOTT MOMADAY

A single knoll rises out of the plain in Oklahoma, north and west of the Wichita range. For my people, the Kiowas, it is an old landmark, and they gave it the name Rainy Mountain. The hardest weather in the world is there. Winter brings blizzards, hot tornadic winds arise in the spring, and in summer the prairie is an anvil's edge. The grass turns brittle and brown, and it cracks beneath your feet. There are green belts along the rivers and creeks, linear groves of hickory and pecan, willow and witch hazel. At a distance in July or August the steaming foliage seems almost to writhe in fire. Great green and yellow grasshoppers are everywhere in the tall grass, popping up like corn to sting the flesh, and tortoises crawl about on the red earth, going nowhere in the plenty of time. Loneliness is an aspect of the land. All things in the plain are isolate; there is no confusion of objects in the eye, but *one* hill or *one* tree or *one* man. To look upon that landscape in the early morning, with the sun at your back, is to lose the sense of proportion. Your imagination comes to life, and this, you think, is where Creation was begun.

I returned to Rainy Mountain in July. My grandmother had died in the spring, and I wanted to be at her grave. She had lived to be very

N. Scott Momaday, "The Way to Rainy Mountain" from *The Reporter* (1967). Reprinted by permission of University of New Mexico Press.

describes a deeper connection to the land than I could understand. He describes the central importance of place not only to his own identity as an individual but to the identity of his people as a whole. Whereas my ancestors left their native Poland to immigrate to the United States, Momaday's ancestors, like so many other Native Americans, were forced from their homeland and had to abandon the land they identified with as well as their lifestyle. In that regard, their very identity was threatened. As you read, consider the role that place *plays in Momaday's sense of himself as a person and especially as a Native American. It might help to think about your own sense of connection to a specific place—your birthplace, for example—as you read Momaday's description of Rainy Mountain.*

Born to a Kiowa father and a mother who was part Cherokee, N. Scott Momaday is the author of several books of poetry, a Pulitzer Prize–winning novel, and a collection of Kiowa legends called The Way to Rainy Mountain *(1969), in which the following essay first appeared.* ▼

old and at last infirm. Her only living daughter was with her when she died, and I was told that in death her face was that of a child.

I like to think of her as a child. When she was born, the Kiowas were living the last great moment of their history. For more than a hundred years they had controlled the open range from the Smoky Hill River to the Red, from the headwaters of the Canadian to the fork of the Arkansas and Cimarron. In alliance with the Comanches, they had ruled the whole of the Southern Plains. War was their sacred business, and they were the finest horsemen the world has ever known. But warfare for the Kiowas was pre-eminently a matter of disposition rather than of survival, and they never understood the grim, unrelenting advance of the U.S. Cavalry. When at last, divided and ill provisioned, they were driven onto the Staked Plains in the cold of autumn, they fell into panic. In Palo Duro Canyon they abandoned their crucial stores to pillage and had nothing then but their lives. In order to save themselves, they surrendered to the soldiers at Fort Sill and were imprisoned in the old stone corral that now stands as a military museum. My grandmother was spared the humiliation of those high gray walls by eight or ten years, but she must have known from birth the affliction of defeat, the dark brooding of old warriors.

Her name was Aho, and she belonged to the last culture to evolve in North America. Her forebears came down from the high country in western Montana nearly three centuries ago. They were a mountain people, a mysterious tribe of hunters whose language has never been classified in any major group. In the late seventeenth century they began a long migration to the south and east. It was a journey toward the dawn, and it led to a golden age. Along the way the Kiowas were befriended by the Crows, who gave them the culture and religion of the Plains. They acquired horses, and their ancient nomadic spirit was suddenly free of the ground. They acquired Tai-me, the sacred sun-dance doll, from that moment the object and symbol of their worship, and so shared in the divinity of the sun. Not least, they acquired the sense of destiny, therefore courage and pride. When they entered upon the Southern Plains they had been transformed. No longer were they slaves to the simple necessity of survival; they were a lordly and dangerous society of fighters and thieves, hunters and priests of the sun. According to their origin myth, they entered the world through a hollow log. From one point of view, their migration was the fruit of an old prophecy, for indeed they emerged from a sunless world.

Though my grandmother lived out her long life in the shadow of Rainy Mountain, the immense landscape of the continental interior lay like memory in her blood. She could tell of the Crows, whom she had never seen, and of the Black Hills, where she had never been. I wanted to see in reality what she had seen more perfectly in the mind's eye, and drove fifteen hundred miles to begin my pilgrimage.

Devil's Tower

Yellowstone, it seemed to me, was the top of the world, a region of deep lakes and dark timber, canyons and waterfalls. But, beautiful as it is, one might have the sense of confinement there. The skyline in all directions is close at hand, the high wall of the woods and the deep cleavages of shade. There is a perfect freedom in the mountains, but it belongs to the eagle and the elk, the badger and the bear. The Kiowas reckoned their stature by the distance they could see, and they were bent and blind in the wilderness.

Descending eastward, the highland meadows are a stairway to the plain. In July the inland slope of the Rockies is luxuriant with flax and buckwheat, stonecrop and larkspur. The earth unfolds and the limit of the land recedes. Clusters of trees, the animals grazing far in the distance, cause the vision to reach away and wonder to build upon the mind. The sun follows a longer course in the day, and the sky is immense beyond all comparison. The great billowing clouds that sail upon it are shadows that move upon the grain like water, dividing light. Farther down, in the land of the Crows and the Blackfeet, the plain is yellow. Sweet clover takes hold of the hills and bends upon itself to cover and seal the soil. There the Kiowas paused on their way; they had to come to the place where they must change their lives. The sun is at home on the plains. Precisely there does it have the certain character of a god. When the Kiowas came to the land of the Crows, they could see the dark lees of the hills at dawn across the Bighorn River, the profusion of light on the grain shelves, the oldest deity ranging after the solstices. Not yet would they veer southward to the cauldron of the land that lay below; they must wean their blood from the northern winter and hold the mountains a while longer in their view. They bore Tai-me in procession to the seat.

A dark mist lay over the Black Hills, and the land was like iron. At the top of a ridge I caught sight of **DEVIL'S TOWER** upthrust against the gray sky as if in the birth of time the core of the earth had broken through its crust and the motion of the world was begun. There are things in nature that engender an awful quiet in the heart of man; Devil's Tower is one of them. Two centuries ago, because of their need to explain it, the Kiowas made a legend at the base of the rock. My grandmother said:

> "Eight children were there at play, seven sisters and their brother. Suddenly the boy was struck dumb; he trembled and began to run upon his hands and feet. His fingers became claws, and his body was covered with fur. There was a bear where the boy had been. The sisters were terrified; they ran, and the bear after them. They came to the stump of a great tree, and the tree spoke to them. It bade them climb upon it, and as they did so, it began to rise into the air. The bear came to kill them, but they were just beyond its reach. It reared against the tree and scored the bark all around with its claws. The seven sisters were borne into the sky, and they became the stars of the Big Dipper."

From that moment, and so long as the legend lives, the Kiowas have kinsmen in the night sky. Whatever they were in the mountains, they could be no more. However tenuous their well-being, however much they had suffered and would suffer again, they had found a way out of the wilderness.

My grandmother had a reverence for the sun, a holy regard that now is all but gone out of mankind. There was a wariness in her, and an ancient awe. She was a Christian in her later years, but she had come a long way about, and she never forgot her birthright. As a child she had been to **THE SUN DANCES;** she had taken part in that annual rite, and by it she had learned the restoration of her people in the presence of Tai-me. She was about seven when the last Kiowa sun dance was held in 1887 on the Washita River above Rainy Mountain Creek. The buffalo were gone. In order to consummate the ancient sacrifice—to impale the head of a buffalo bull upon the Tai-me tree— a delegation of old men journeyed into Texas, there to beg and barter for an animal from the Goodnight herd. She was ten when the Kiowas came together for the last time as a living sun-dance culture. They could find no buffalo; they had to hang an old hide from the sacred tree. Before the dance could begin, a company of soldiers rode out from Fort Sill under orders to disperse the tribe. Forbidden without cause the essential act of their faith, having seen the wild herds slaughtered and left to rot upon the ground, the Kiowas backed away forever from the tree. That was July 20, 1890, at the great bend of the Washita. My grandmother was there. Without bitterness, and for as long as she lived, she bore a vision of deicide.

Now that I can have her only in memory, I see my grandmother in the several postures that were peculiar to her: standing at the wood stove on a winter morning and turning meat in a great iron skillet; sitting at the south window, bent above her beadwork, and afterwards,

10

GLOSS: THE SUN DANCE
Usually performed during the summer solstice, the sun dance was an important religious ritual of self-sacrifice and renewal among many of the Native American tribes of the Plains, including the Kiowas. During the ceremony, men seeking to cleanse themselves spiritually for the good of the tribe would fast, dance, pray, and have their chests or backs pierced in a way that resulted in their being suspended by their flesh to attain a trancelike state of purity. When the U.S. Army took control of Native American lands during the nineteenth century, it often banned the ritual.

when her vision failed, looking down for a long time into the fold of her hands; going out upon a cane, very slowly as she did when the weight of age came upon her; praying. I remember her most often at prayer. She made long, rambling prayers out of suffering and hope, having seen many things. I was never sure that I had the right to hear, so exclusive were they of all mere custom and company. The last time I saw her she prayed standing by the side of her bed at night, naked to the waist, the light of a kerosene lamp moving upon her dark skin. Her long black hair, always drawn and braided in the day, lay upon her shoulders and against her breasts like a shawl. I do not speak Kiowa, and I never understood her prayers, but there was something inherently sad in the sound, some merest hesitation upon the syllables of sorrow. She began in a high and descending pitch, exhausting her breath to silence; then again and again—and always the same intensity of effort, of something that is, and is not, like urgency in the human voice. Transported so in the dancing light among the shadows of her room, she seemed beyond the reach of time. But that was illusion; I think I knew then that I should not see her again.

HOUSES ARE LIKE SENTINELS IN THE PLAIN, old keepers of the weather watch. There, in a very little while, wood takes on the appearance of great age. All colors wear soon away in the wind and rain, and then the wood is burned gray and the grain appears and the nails turn red with rust. The window panes are black and opaque; you imagine there is nothing within, and indeed there are many ghosts, bones given up to the land. They stand here and there against the sky, and you approach them for a longer time than you expect. They belong in the distance; it is their domain.

Once there was a lot of sound in my grandmother's house, a lot of coming and going, feasting and talk. The summers there were full of excitement and reunion. The Kiowas are a summer people; they abide the cold and keep to themselves, but when the season turns and the land becomes warm and vital they cannot hold still; an old love of going returns upon them. The aged visitors who came to my grandmother's house when I was a child were made of lean and leather, and they bore themselves upright. They wore great black hats and bright ample shirts that shook in the wind. They rubbed fat upon their hair and wound their braids with strips of colored cloth. Some of them painted their faces and carried the scars of old and cherished enmities. They were an old council of warlords, come to remind and be reminded of who they were. Their wives and daughters served them well. The women might indulge themselves; gossip was at once the mark and compensation of their servitude. They made loud and elaborate talk among themselves, full of jest and gesture, fright and false alarm. They went abroad in fringed and flowered shawls, bright beadwork and German silver. They were at home in the kitchen, and they prepared meals that were banquets.

STRATEGIES: DESCRIPTION AND THEME
Paragraph 12 is a good example of how a writer can use description to do more than just provide readers with an image of a place or a thing. In this paragraph, Momaday shifts abruptly from his memories of his grandmother in the previous paragraphs to a description of houses on the plains. But this description seems different from descriptions earlier in the essay of the various places Momaday has visited, such as Yellowstone or the Black Hills. Is it different? If so, in what way? What idea or point do you think Momaday is trying to convey through this description?

There were frequent prayer meetings, and nocturnal feasts. When I was a child I played with my cousins outside, where the lamplight fell upon the ground and the singing of the old people rose up around us and carried away into the darkness. There were a lot of good things to eat, a lot of laughter and surprise. And afterwards, when the quiet returned, I lay down with my grandmother and could hear the frogs away by the river and feel the motion of the air.

Now there is a funereal silence in the rooms, the endless wake of some final word. The walls have closed in upon my grandmother's house. When I returned to it in mourning, I saw for the first time in my life how small it was. It was late at night, and there was a white moon, nearly full. I sat for a long time on the stone steps by the kitchen door. From there I could see out across the land; I could see the long row of trees by the creek, the low light upon the rolling plains, and the stars of the Big Dipper. Once I looked at the moon and caught sight of a strange thing. A cricket had perched upon the handrail, only a few inches away. My line of vision was such that the creature filled the moon like a fossil. It had gone there, I thought, to live and die, for there, of all places, was its small definition made whole and eternal. A warm wind rose up and purled like the longing within me.

The next morning, I awoke at dawn and went out on the dirt road to Rainy Mountain. It was already hot, and the grasshoppers began to fill the air. Still, it was early in the morning, and birds sang out of the shadows. The long yellow grass on the mountain shone in the bright light, and a scissortail hied above the land. There, where it ought to be, at the end of a long and legendary way, was my grandmother's grave. She had at last succeeded to that holy ground. Here and there on the dark stones were ancestral names. Looking back once, I saw the mountain and came away.

HAVE YOU EVER SEEN A REAL INDIAN?

AMERICAN INDIAN COLLEGE FUND
EDUCATION IS STRENGTH

© American Indian College Fund

American Indian College Fund Advertisement

Understanding the Text

1. Momaday writes that he returned to Rainy Mountain when his grandmother died. What significance does he see in his grandmother's life? What does he mean when he writes that "the immense landscape of the continental interior lay like memory in her blood"? What "pilgrimage" does his grandmother's death prompt Momaday to make? Why is this pilgrimage important to him?

2. What do we learn about the history of the Kiowa people in this essay? Why is this history important to Momaday? What purpose do you think it serves in this essay and in helping Momaday convey a sense of his identity?

3. At the conclusion of this essay, Momaday has returned to his grandmother's house near Rainy Mountain. Why do you think he focuses on that specific place? What importance does that house have for him? What connection does he see between that house and the larger landscape of the Plains where his people once lived? What do you think that connection might suggest about his sense of himself as a Native American?

Exploring the Issues

1. Periodically in this essay, Momaday includes information about the history of the Kiowas as well as other Native American tribes. What sense of the Kiowas as a people does he convey through this information? What are the Kiowas like based on Momaday's descriptions of them? In what ways are their characteristics related to the land where they live? What point do you think Momaday is making about the importance of the land in our sense of identity?

2. What event or events does Momaday use to organize his essay? Why do you think he orga-

nizes the essay in this way? How effectively do you think this way of organizing the essay helps him convey his ideas?

3. In many ways, Momaday's essay is not only about a sense of place but also about a sense of time. How does Momaday use time in this essay? What role does the past play in his understanding of himself? What is the relationship between the past and the present for him? Do you think the sense of time that he conveys is universal, or does it apply only to Native Americans? Explain.

4. Compare the descriptions in the first and last paragraphs of this essay. In what ways do you think they are similar? In what ways are they different? What do you think Momaday means when he writes in the very last sentence of this essay that he "saw the mountain and came away"? What main point do you think he wishes to convey with that final sentence?

Entering the Conversations

1. Write an essay in which you describe a place that is important to you. Like Momaday, try to convey a sense of that importance through your descriptions of that place, and include any historical or background information that you think your readers will need to help them understand the importance of that place.

2. Write an essay for an audience of your classmates about an important memory you have of a family member or of your family in general.

3. In a group of classmates, share the essays you wrote for Question 2. Discuss the significance of the memories that each of you has written about. What might these essays suggest about the importance of memory to our sense of self?

4. Using the Internet and relevant sources at your library, find photographs or other illustrations that you think would be appropriate for Momaday's essay. Select these images so that they not only illustrate the landscape that Momaday describes but also communicate what you believe are his main points about the importance of the land and the connections between the land and one's identity. Then use the images you have selected to make a photo essay or a web site. In other words, try to create a visual version of Momaday's words. Alternatively, create a visual document representing a place that is important to your identity.

INFOTRAC

5. Using InfoTrac College Edition, the Internet, and any other relevant sources, examine a controversy over the use of a specific place, such as Devil's Tower (see *Context: Devil's Tower* on page 76). In recent years, as development has occurred in many places that were once considered wilderness, such controversies have become increasingly common. If possible, focus on such a controversy in the region where you live. Try to find out what the focus of the controversy is and how it has developed over time. Try to understand the arguments of all sides in the controversy. Then write a report based on your research. In your report, provide sufficient background and present the main arguments in the controversy. Draw conclusions about the importance of place on the basis of what you have learned about this controversy.

6. On the basis of your research for Question 5, write a letter to the editor of a newspaper in your region expressing your views about the controversy.

This essay offers a twist on the old saying *that you are what you eat. Award-winning fiction writer Bobbie Ann Mason (b. 1940) recalls growing up in rural Kentucky in the 1950s, and she focuses our attention on the food that her family ate. For Mason, her family's diet was a reflection of their rural identity. And that diet was not just about nutrition and*

Being Country

health. It was also about social status, and it was central to Mason's sense of herself. But as she tells us in this passage, she wasn't entirely happy about it. In sharing these memories, Mason addresses old questions about the relationship between our identities and the places where we live, but she also reminds us that our attitudes toward place are complicated by prevailing ideas about social class and geographical regions. For example, as a young girl, Mason felt that being "country" meant being backward and somehow having less status than people from the nearby town with its "centers of pleasure," including places to shop and eat and be entertained. Those places seemed more glamorous to Mason than her country life. It's worth thinking about whether that difference between city and country might have changed since Mason's childhood in the 1950s. Do the city and the country still represent what they once did? Do they still matter in our identities as they seem to have mattered to Mason when she was young?

BOBBIE ANN MASON

One day Mama and Granny were shelling beans and talking about the proper method of drying apples. I was nearly eleven and still entirely absorbed with the March girls in *Little Women*. Drying apples was not in my dreams. Beth's death was weighing darkly on me at that moment, and I threw a little tantrum—what Mama called a hissy fit.

"Can't y'all talk about anything but food?" I screamed.

There was a shocked silence. "Well, what else is there?" Granny asked.

Granny didn't question a woman's duties, but I did. I didn't want to be hulling beans in a hot kitchen when I was fifty years old. I wanted to *be* somebody, maybe an airline stewardess. Also, I had been listening to the radio. I had notions.

Our lives were haunted by the fear of crop failure. We ate as if we didn't know where our next meal might come from. All my life I have had a recurrent food dream: I face a buffet or cafeteria line, laden with beautiful foods. I spend the entire dream choosing the foods I want. My anticipation is deliciously agonizing. I always wake up just as I've made my selections but before I get to eat.

The Simple Life, with Paris Hilton and Nicole Ritchie

CONVERSATIONS: THE CITY AND THE COUNTRY

In the old fable about the city mouse and the country mouse, a mouse from the city and a mouse from the country visit each other's homes and each learns to appreciate his home. The fable may tell us something about the longstanding tensions between city life and country life in Western culture. For most of its history, the United States was largely a rural nation. According to the U.S. Census Bureau, before 1920, most of the population lived in rural areas. In 1990, however, more than 75 percent of Americans were city dwellers. Not everyone agrees that these changes represent progress, and many scholars, artists, and critics have examined the relative benefits and drawbacks to a nation defined by cities rather than by a more rural existence. Examine how Mason presents this contrast between the city and the country. In what ways does Mason's depiction of each depend on stereotypes about the city and the country? How does Mason challenge those stereotypes? Consider, too, how the stereotypes might be part of the larger conversations in our society about city and country. For example, in 2003, a television series called *The Simple Life* focused on two wealthy women from the city who take up a rural lifestyle. How might this image from that show draw on, challenge, or reinforce stereotypes about city and country? Or consider the two photographs on page 83 by Peter Menzel, who traveled the world photographing people with all their possessions. What do these two photographs suggest about city and rural life?

Bobbie Ann Mason has enjoyed much acclaim for her fiction, especially for her collection of short stories Shiloh and Other Stories *(1983) and her novel* In Country *(1984). The following essay originally appeared in* Clear Springs: A Memoir *(1999).* ☑

Working with food was fraught with anxiety and desperation. In truth, no one in memory had missed a meal—except Peyton Washam on the banks of Panther Creek wistfully regarding his seed corn. But the rumble of poor Peyton's belly must have survived to trouble our dreams. We were at the mercy of nature, and it wasn't to be trusted. My mother watched the skies at evening for a portent of the morrow. A cloud that went over and then turned around and came back was an especially bad sign. Our livelihood—even our lives—depended on forces outside our control.

I think this dependence on nature was at the core of my rebellion. I hated the constant sense of helplessness before vast forces, the continuous threat of failure. Farmers didn't take initiative, I began to see; they reacted to whatever presented itself. I especially hated women's part in the dependence.

My mother allowed me to get spoiled. She never even tried to teach me to cook. "You didn't want to learn," she says now. "You were a lady of leisure, and you didn't want to help. You had your nose in a book."

I believed progress meant freedom from the field and the range. That meant moving to town, I thought.

10   Because we lived on the edge of Mayfield, I was acutely conscious of being country. I felt inferior to people in town because we grew our food and made our clothes, while they brought whatever they needed. Although we were self-sufficient and resourceful and held clear title to our land, we lived in a state of psychological poverty. As I grew older, this acute sense of separation from town affected me more deeply. I began to sense that the fine life in town—celebrated in mag-

CONVERSATIONS: THE CITY AND THE COUNTRY continued

Caven family, American Canyon, California

Regzen family, Ulaanbaatar, Mongolia

azines, on radio, in movies—was denied us. Of course we weren't poor at all. Poor people had too many kids, and they weren't landowners; they rented decrepit little houses with plank floors and trash in the yard. "Poor people are wormy and eat wild onions," Mama said. We weren't poor, but we were country.

We had three wardrobes—everyday clothes, school clothes, and Sunday clothes. We didn't wear our school clothes at home, but we could wear them to town. When we got home from church, we had to change back into everyday clothes before we ate Mama's big Sunday dinner.

"Don't eat in your good clothes!" Mama always cried. "You'll spill something on them."

Mama always preferred outdoor life, but she was a natural cook. At harvest time, after she'd come in from the garden and put out a wash, she would whip out a noontime dinner for the men in the field—my father and grandfather and maybe some neighbors and a couple of hired hands: fried chicken with milk gravy, ham, mashed potatoes, lima beans, field peas, corn, slaw, sliced tomatoes, fried apples, biscuits, and peach pie. This was not considered a banquet, only plain hearty food, fuel for work. All the ingredients except the flour, sugar, and salt came from our farm—the chickens, the hogs, the milk and butter, the Irish potatoes, the beans, peas, corn, cabbage, apples, peaches. Nothing was processed, except by Mama. She was always butchering and plucking and planting and hoeing and shredding and slicing and creaming (scraping cobs for the creamed corn) and pressure-cooking and canning and freezing and thawing and mixing and shaping and baking and frying.

We would eat our pie right on the same plate as our turnip greens so as not to mess up another dish. The peach cobbler oozed all over the turnip-green juice and the pork grease. "It all goes to the same

CONVERSATIONS: FOOD
Notice Mason's descriptions of hamburgers in paragraph 15: She writes that hamburgers bought in town were "better." In this passage, Mason is describing a scene from her childhood in the 1950s, but she wrote this memoir in the 1990s. Attitudes about food—about what is healthy and desirable in a diet— have changed considerably in that time and so has the nature of the American diet. Today, food is also part of a larger conversation about environmental sustainability. How might the changing context regarding attitudes toward food affect the way you read this passage?

place," Mama said. It was boarding-house reach, no "Pass the peas, please." Conversation detracted from the sensuous pleasure of filling yourself. A meal required meat and vegetables and dessert. The beverages were milk and iced tea ("ice-tea"). We never used napkins or ate tossed salad. Our salads were Jell-O and slaw. We ate "poke salet" and wilted lettuce. Mama picked tender, young pokeweed in the woods in the spring, before it turned poison, and cooked it a good long time to get the bitterness out. We liked it with vinegar and minced boiled eggs. Wilted lettuce was tender new lettuce, shredded, with sliced radishes and green onions, and blasted with hot bacon grease to blanch the rawness. "Too many fresh vegetables in summer gives people the scours," Daddy said.

Food was better in town, we thought. It wasn't plain and everyday. The centers of pleasure were there—**THE HAMBURGER** and barbecue places, the movie shows, all the places to buy things. Woolworth's, with the pneumatic tubes overhead rushing money along a metallic mole tunnel up to a balcony; Lochridge & Ridgway, with an engraved sign on the third-story cornice: STOVES, APPLIANCES, PLOWS. On the mezzanine at that store, I bought my first phonograph records, brittle 78s of big-band music—Woody Herman and Glenn Miller, and Glen Gray and his Casa Loma Orchestra playing "No Name Jive." A circuit of the courthouse square took you past the grand furniture stores, the two dime stores, the shoe stores, the men's stores, the ladies' stores, the banks, the drugstores. You'd walk past the poolroom and an exhaust fan would blow the intoxicating smell of hamburgers in your face. Before she bought a freezer, Mama stored meat in a rented food locker in town, near the ice company. She stored the butchered calf there, and she fetched hunks of him each week to fry. But hamburgers in town were better. They were greasier, and they came in waxed-paper packages.

At the corner drugstore, on the square, Mama and Janice and I sat at filigreed wrought-iron tables on a black-and-white mosaic tile floor, eating peppermint ice cream. It was very cold in there, under the ceiling fans. The ice cream was served elegantly, in paper cones sunk into black plastic holders. We were uptown.

The A&P grocery, a block away, reeked of the rich aroma of ground coffee. Daddy couldn't stand the smell of coffee, but Mama loved it. Daddy retched and scoffed in his exaggerated fashion. "I can't stand that smell!" Granny perked coffee, and Granddaddy told me it would turn a child black. I hated coffee. I wouldn't touch it till I was thirty. We savored store-bought food—coconuts, pineapples, and Vienna sausages and potted meat in little cans that opened with keys. We rarely went to the uptown A&P. We usually traded at a small mom-and-pop grocery, where the proprietors slapped the hands of black children who touched the candy case. I wondered if they were black from coffee. . . .

15

Understanding the Text

1. In paragraph 7, Mason writes, "I think this dependence on nature was at the core of my rebellion." What specifically does she mean by "dependence on nature" in this passage? Why does she rebel against this? What might this rebellion suggest about Mason's sense of herself as a rural person?

2. Mason devotes much of this brief essay to descriptions of and references to food. Why do you think she does so? What importance does food have in her sense of identity? Why was the source of her food so important?

3. What was special about the town, according to Mason? What do you think Mason intended the town to represent as she describes it in this essay? Do you think cities and towns still represent the same things to most people today? Explain.

Exploring the Issues

1. At one point in her essay, Mason writes that she and her family lived in a state of "psychological poverty," though she also tells us that her family was not poor. Where did her feeling of being poor come from? What might this psychological poverty suggest about how people develop a sense of identity in American society?

2. Mason writes that her mother insisted that her family was not poor; they were "country." What do you think is the difference between being poor and being country, based on Mason's descriptions? What might this essay suggest about American attitudes toward social class? How does this distinction between poor and country fit in with your own sense of social class?

3. Mason's prose has been described by some critics as straightforward and down-to-earth. Do you agree with that description? Why or why not? Cite specific passages from her essay to support your answer.

4. Mason wrote this essay in the late 1990s, about forty years after the experiences she describes in it. She describes her feelings about "being country" as a young girl. What do you think is Mason's attitude about being country today, based on this essay? Do you think she wishes to present her experiences as a rural dweller in a positive way? Explain, citing specific passages from the essay to support your answer.

Entering the Conversations

1. Write an essay based on memories of your own childhood. In your essay, try to focus on a particular aspect of your upbringing and how the place where you were raised might have influenced your sense of your own identity.

2. Visit several web sites or blogs devoted to country life and analyze them in terms of the image they present of rural life and the assumptions they seem to make about living in the country. Try to get a sense of the audience they are trying to reach. Then write a report on the basis of your analysis.

3. Write a contemporary version of the old fable of the city mouse and the country mouse (see Conversations: The City and the Country on page 82.)

INFOTRAC

4. Using InfoTrac College Edition and any other relevant resources, examine the changes that have occurred in the United States regarding the relationship between rural and urban life. As a starting point for thinking about this topic, look at Conversations: The City and the Country on page 82. Try to find out how life has changed in American cities and in rural areas in the past decades, and identify the major challenges facing urban and rural dwellers today. Then write a report on the basis of your research.

5. On the basis of your research for Question 4, write a letter to your senator or state representative (or some other appropriate political representative) in which you express your concerns about important issues facing urban or rural dwellers in your region of the country.

6. Write a letter to the editor of your local newspaper or another publication you think is appropriate in which you discuss what it means to be from the city or from the country today.

DEFINING EACH OTHER

N THE PAST FEW DECADES, THE TERM *THE OTHER* HAS BECOME AN INCREASINGLY COMMON ONE IN DISCUSSIONS ABOUT DIFFERENCE, DIVERSITY, PREJUDICE, AND RACISM. IT IS EVEN SOMETIMES USED AS AN ODD-SOUNDING VERB: YOU CAN BE "OTHERED"—THAT IS, YOU CAN BE categorized as "other" than something, which usually means less than or inferior to that something. Most often, people belonging to minority groups or nonmainstream cultures are "othered" in this way, but the idea can apply to any person or group treated in a way that reflects prejudice or bias. All of us have probably been in circumstances in which we have been The Other, but it's clear that some groups have long been categorized as Other in systematic ways that are damaging and disturbing.

> Most often, people belonging to minority groups or nonmainstream cultures are "othered" in this way, but the idea can apply to any person or group treated in a way that reflects prejudice or bias.

It's worth thinking about what this idea of The Other says about how we respond to each other's identities. In discussions of injustices based on such things as race, gender, ethnicity, religion, and culture, this term has acquired a particular kind of meaning. It suggests something more than prejudice. To have prejudice is to dislike or have negative feelings about someone or something; conversely, we can have a prejudice in favor of something—for example, a sports fan can be prejudiced toward a favorite team. But to consider someone as an Other is to place that person in a category that is separate from ourselves and, importantly, somehow inferior to ourselves. It is to consider that person's identity undesirable in some way. It is to define another in ways that the person would never define himself or herself. And it is to do all these things in subtle ways that might not be apparent. The ways in which we define The Other can be less visible than, say, racism, which is often much more obvious and recognizable. We can, for instance, assume someone is less than we are without seeming to treat that person in an openly disparaging or racist way. So this idea of The Other serves the useful purpose of describing a specific way of categorizing people on the basis of prejudices or biases about certain identities.

If the idea of The Other seems vague to you, the three essays in this cluster may help you get a better handle on it. Each writer addresses a slightly different way in which the category of The Other can emerge in our interactions with each other. Some of these categories are more obvious than others. For example, Gregory Jay writes about race, though his focus is not on so-called minority races but on how Whiteness becomes the category by which other races are measured. In a sense, he examines how various races are implicitly "othered" by the assumed dominance of Whiteness as a racial category. Similarly, Maxine Hong Kingston and Dagoberto Gilb describe racial categories—Asian and Hispanic—that are often defined as The Other. But they also help us see less obvious ways in which people are defined as Other—for example, as immigrants or women. All these essays thus give us concrete ways of seeing The Other. They call our attention to how we constantly categorize people in ways that emphasize difference, and they may also help us gain insight into the consequences of this "othering."

"My aunt haunts me," Maxine Hong Kingston (b. 1940) writes at the end of the following essay. Yet Kingston does not even know her aunt's name, nor has she ever met her aunt. She only knows bits and pieces of the story her mother has told her about her aunt, whose very existence her family has tried to forget. Kingston's essay offers a vivid and compelling

No Name Woman

picture of how our identities can be shaped by those around us, especially members of our families and our communities, and by the traditions and history of our culture. Kingston's aunt was a Chinese woman and as such was expected to be a certain kind of person who acted in certain accepted ways. But her actions prompted her family and neighbors to give her other identities: adulterer, betrayer, suicide. Her story is a stark reminder that we don't necessarily control our identities. And if you think that the story Kingston tells about her aunt is extreme, a closer look at what it means to be a woman or a man in our society today will reveal that, like Kingston's aunt, we are all subject to expectations and beliefs that shape who we are and who we can be.

Kingston's essay is also about the stories we tell each other and ourselves about who we are. As Kingston writes about her aunt, she is also telling a story about herself as a Chinese American woman. And as you'll see, it isn't an easy story to tell. It makes me wonder about our need to try to define ourselves even as we are being

MAXINE HONG KINGSTON

"Y**ou must not tell anyone," my mother said, "what I am** about to tell you. In China your father had a sister who killed herself. She jumped into the family well. We say that your father has all brothers because it is as if she had never been born.

"In 1924 just a few days after our village celebrated seventeen hurry-up weddings—to make sure that every young man who went 'out on the road' would responsibly come home—your father and his brothers and your grandfather and his brothers and your aunt's new husband sailed for America, the Gold Mountain. It was your grandfather's last trip. Those lucky enough to get contracts waved good-bye from the decks. They fed and guarded the stowaways and helped them off in Cuba, New York, Bali, Hawaii. 'We'll meet in California next year,' they said. All of them sent money home.

"I remember looking at your aunt one day when she and I were dressing; I had not noticed before that she had such a protruding melon of a stomach. But I did not think, 'She's pregnant,' until she began to look like other pregnant women, her shirt pulling and the

defined by others. If you've ever felt that you have been unfairly labeled by other people as something that you believe you are not—a nerd or a jock or worse—then you might begin to get a sense of Kingston's need to understand her aunt's story and how it might affect her own sense of self. Maxine Hong Kingston is a widely acclaimed author of many articles, essays, and books, including Tripmaster Monkey: His Fake Book *(1989),* The Fifth Book of Peace *(2003), and the award-winning* The Woman Warrior: Memoirs of a Girlhood among Ghosts *(1976), in which the following excerpt first appeared.* ◪

STRATEGIES: TELLING STORIES
Kingston has been both praised and criticized for the way she uses fictional techniques in telling stories about her life and her family. Some critics have charged that her writing is not really autobiographical because she incorporates fictional elements into her narratives. Others have hailed her innovative blending of fiction and nonfiction. As you read this essay about her aunt, consider how Kingston's narrative style and the techniques she uses for telling her story might influence your reaction to that story.

white tops of her black pants showing. She could not have been pregnant, you see, because her husband had been gone for years. No one said anything. We did not discuss it. In early summer she was ready to have the child, long after the time when it could have been possible.

"The village had also been counting. On the night the baby was to be born the villagers raided our house. Some were crying. Like a great saw, teeth strung with lights, files of people walked zigzag across our land, tearing the rice. Their lanterns doubled in the disturbed black water, which drained away through the broken bunds. As the villagers closed in, we could see that some of them, probably men and women we knew well, wore white masks. The people with long hair hung it over their faces. Women with short hair made it stand up on end. Some had tied white bands around their foreheads, arms, and legs.

"At first they threw mud and rocks at the house. Then they threw eggs and began slaughtering our stock. We could hear the animals scream their deaths—the roosters, the pigs, a last great roar from the ox. Familiar wild heads flared in our night windows; the villagers encircled us. Some of the faces stopped to peer at us, their eyes rushing like searchlights. The hands flattened against the panes, framed heads, and left red prints. 5

"The villagers broke in the front and the back doors at the same time, even though we had not locked the doors against them. Their knives dripped with the blood of our animals. They smeared blood on the doors and walls. One woman swung a chicken, whose throat she had slit, splattering blood in red arcs about her. We stood together in the middle of our house, in the family hall with the pictures and tables of the ancestors around us, and looked straight ahead.

"At that time the house had only two wings. When the men came back, we would build two more to enclose our courtyard and a third one to begin a second courtyard. The villagers pushed through both wings, even your grandparents' rooms, to find your aunt's, which was also mine until the men returned. From this room a new wing for one of the younger families would grow. They ripped up her clothes and shoes and broke her combs, grinding them underfoot. They tore her work from the loom. They scattered the cooking fire and rolled the new weaving in it. We could hear them in the kitchen breaking our bowls and banging the pots. They overturned the great waist-high earthenware jugs; duck eggs, pickled fruits, vegetables burst out and mixed in acrid torrents. The old woman from the next field swept a broom through the air and loosed the spirits-of-the-broom over our heads. 'Pig.' 'Ghost.' 'Pig,' they sobbed and scolded while they ruined our house.

"When they left, they took sugar and oranges to bless themselves. They cut pieces from the dead animals. Some of them took bowls that were not broken and clothes that were not torn. Afterward we swept up the rice and sewed it back up into sacks. But the smells from the spilled preserves lasted. Your aunt gave birth in the pigsty that night.

The next morning when I went up for the water, I found her and the baby plugging up the family well.

"Don't let your father know that I told you. He denies her. Now that you have started to menstruate, what happened to her could happen to you. Don't humiliate us. You wouldn't like to be forgotten as if you had never been born. The villagers are watchful."

Whenever she had to warn us about life, my mother told stories that ran like this one, a story to grow up on. She tested our strength to establish realities. Those in the emigrant generations who could not reassert brute survival died young and far from home. Those of us in the first American generations have had to figure out how the invisible world the emigrants built around our childhoods fit in solid America.

The emigrants confused the gods by diverting their curses, misleading them with crooked streets and false names. They must try to confuse their offspring as well, who, I suppose, threaten them in similar ways—always trying to get things straight, always trying to name the unspeakable. The Chinese I know hide their names; sojourners take new names when their lives change and guard their real names with silence.

Chinese-Americans, when you try to understand what things in you are Chinese, how do you separate what is peculiar to childhood, to poverty, insanities, one family, your mother who marked your growing with stories, from what is Chinese? What is Chinese tradition and what is the movies?

If I want to learn what clothes my aunt wore, whether flashy or ordinary, I would have to begin, "Remember Father's drowned-in-the-well sister?" I cannot ask that. My mother has told me once and for all the useful parts. She will add nothing unless powered by Necessity, a riverbank that guides her life. She plants vegetable gardens rather than lawns; she carries the odd-shaped tomatoes home from the fields and eats food left for the gods.

Whenever we did frivolous things, we used up energy; we flew high kites. We children came up off the ground over the melting cones our parents brought home from work and the American movie on New Year's Day—*Oh, You Beautiful Doll* with Betty Grable one year, and *She Wore a Yellow Ribbon* with John Wayne another year. After the one carnival ride each, we paid in guilt; our tired father counted his change on the dark walk home.

Adultery is extravagance. Could people who hatch their own chicks and eat the embryos and the heads for delicacies and boil the feet in vinegar for party food, leaving only the gravel, eating even the gizzard lining—could such people engender a prodigal aunt? To be a woman, to have a daughter in starvation time was a waste enough. My aunt could not have been the lone romantic who gave up everything for sex. Women in the old China did not choose. Some man had commanded her to lie with him and be his secret evil. I wonder whether he masked himself when he joined the raid on her family.

Perhaps she encountered him in the fields or on the mountain where the daughters-in-law collected fuel. Or perhaps he first noticed her in the marketplace. He was not a stranger because the village housed no strangers. She had to have dealings with him other than sex. Perhaps he worked an adjoining field, or he sold her the cloth for the dress she sewed and wore. His demand must have surprised, then terrified her. She obeyed him; she always did as she was told.

When the family found a young man in the next village to be her husband, she stood tractably beside the best rooster, his proxy, and promised before they met that she would be his forever. She was lucky that he was her age and she would be the first wife, an advantage secure now. The night she first saw him, he had sex with her. Then he left for America. She had almost forgotten what he looked like. When she tried to envision him, she only saw the black and white face in the group photograph the men had taken before leaving.

The other man was not, after all, much different from her husband. They both gave orders: she followed. "If you tell your family, I'll beat you. I'll kill you. Be here again next week." No one talked sex, ever. And she might have separated the rapes from the rest of living if only she did not have to buy her oil from him or gather wood in the same forest. I want her fear to have lasted just as long as rape lasted so that the fear could have been contained. No drawn-out fear. But women at sex hazarded birth and hence lifetimes. The fear did not stop but permeated everywhere. She told the man, "I think I'm pregnant." He organized the raid against her.

On nights when my mother and father talked about their life back home, sometimes they mentioned an "outcast table" whose business they still seemed to be settling, their voices tight. In a commensal tradition, where food is precious, the powerful older people made wrongdoers eat alone. Instead of letting them start separate new lives like the Japanese, who could become samurais and geishas, the Chinese family, faces averted but eyes glowering sideways, hung on to the offenders and fed them leftovers. My aunt must have lived in the same house as my parents and eaten at an outcast table. My mother spoke about the raid as if she had seen it, when she and my aunt, a daughter-in-law to a different household, should not have been living together at all. Daughters-in-law lived with their husbands' parents, not their own; a synonym for marriage in Chinese is "taking a daughter-in-law." Her husband's parents could have sold her, mortgaged her, stoned her. But they sent her back to her own mother and father, a mysterious act hinting at disgraces not told me. Perhaps they had thrown her out to deflect the avengers.

20　　She was the only daughter; her four brothers went with her father, husband, and uncles "out on the road" and for some years became western men. When the goods were divided among the family, three of the brothers took land, and the youngest, my father, chose an education. After my grandparents gave their daughter away to her husband's family, they had dispensed all the adventure and all the property. They expected her alone to keep the traditional ways, which her brothers, now among the barbarians, could fumble without detection. The heavy, deep-rooted women were to maintain the past against the flood, safe for returning. But the rare urge west had fixed upon our family, and so my aunt crossed boundaries not delineated in space.

The work of preservation demands that the feelings playing about in one's guts not be turned into action. Just watch their passing like cherry blossoms. But perhaps my aunt, my forerunner, caught in a slow life, let dreams grow and fade and after some months or years went toward what persisted. Fear at the enormities of the forbidden kept her desires delicate, wire and bone. She looked at a man because she liked the way the hair was tucked behind his ears, or she liked the question-mark line of a long torso curving at the shoulder and straight at the hip. For warm eyes or a soft voice or a slow walk—that's all—a few hairs, a line, a bright-ness, a sound, a pace, she gave up family. She offered us up for a charm that vanished with tiredness, a pigtail that didn't toss when the wind died. Why, the wrong lighting could erase the dearest thing about him.

It could very well have been, however, that my aunt did not take subtle enjoyment of her friend, but, a wild woman, kept rollicking com-pany. Imagining her free with sex doesn't fit, though. I don't know any women like that, or men either. Unless I see her life branching into mine, she gives me no ancestral help.

To sustain her being in love, she often worked at herself in the mir-ror, guessing at the colors and shapes that would interest him, chang-ing them frequently in order to hit on the right combination. She wanted him to look back.

On a farm near the sea, a woman who tended her appearance reaped a reputation for eccentricity. All the married women blunt-cut their hair in flaps about their ears or pulled it back in tight buns. No non-sense. Neither style blew easily into heart-catching tangles. And at their weddings they displayed themselves in their long hair for the last time. "It brushed the backs of my knees," my mother tells me. "It was braid-ed, and even so, it brushed the backs of my knees."

At the mirror my aunt combed individuality into her bob. A bun 25
could have been contrived to escape into black streamers blowing in the wind or in quiet wisps about her face, but only the older women in our picture album wear buns. She brushed her hair back from her forehead, tucking the flaps behind her ears. She looped a piece of thread, knotted into a circle between her index fingers and thumbs, and ran the double strand across her forehead. When she closed her fingers as if she were making a pair of shadow geese bite, the string twisted together catching the little hairs. Then she pulled the thread away from her skin, ripping the hairs out neatly, her eyes watering from the needles of pain. Opening her fingers, she cleaned the thread, then rolled it along her hairline and the tops of her eyebrows. My

CONVERSATIONS: FEMALE BEAUTY

In paragraph 25, Kingston provides a vivid description of two traditional practices among Chinese women to create a certain physical appearance considered beautiful. The first is the removal of some hair along the forehead and temples; the other is the binding of feet, which was done because small feet were considered desirable. Although these practices may seem odd or even extreme to people outside Chinese culture, every culture—including contemporary American culture—has its own peculiar practices related to certain beliefs about physical beauty. Consider, for example, the practice of waxing, by which hair is removed from certain parts of the body. This practice has become increasingly common in the United States in recent years, and both men and women will pay hefty sums to have their bodies waxed, which is not always a pleasant experience.

mother did the same to me and my sisters and herself. I used to believe that the expression **"CAUGHT BY THE SHORT HAIRS"** meant a captive held with a depilatory string. It especially hurt at the temples, but my mother said we were lucky we didn't have to have our **FEET BOUND** when we were seven. Sisters used to sit on their beds and cry together, she said, as their mothers or their slave removed the bandages for a few minutes each night and let the blood gush back into their veins. I hope that the man my aunt loved appreciated a smooth brow, that he wasn't just a tits-and-ass man.

Once my aunt found a freckle on her chin, at a spot that the almanac said predestined her for unhappiness. She dug it out with a hot needle and washed the wound with peroxide.

More attention to her looks than these pullings of hairs and pickings at spots would have caused gossip among the villagers. They owned work clothes and good clothes, and they wore good clothes for feasting the new seasons. But since a woman combing her hair hexes beginnings, my aunt rarely found an occasion to look her best. Women looked like great sea snails—the corded wood, babies, and laundry they carried were the whorls on their backs. The Chinese did not admire a bent back; goddesses and warriors stood straight. Still there must have been a marvelous freeing of beauty when a worker laid down her burden and stretched and arched.

Such commonplace loveliness, however, was not enough for my aunt. She dreamed of a lover for the fifteen days of New Year's, the time for families to exchange visits, money, and food. She plied her secret comb. And sure enough she cursed the year, the family, the village, and herself.

Even as her hair lured her imminent lover, many other men looked at her. Uncles, cousins, nephews, brothers would have looked, too, had they been home between journeys. Perhaps they had already been restraining their curiosity, and they left, fearful that their glances, like a field of nesting birds, might be startled and caught. Poverty hurt, and that was their first reason for leaving. But another, final reason for leaving the crowded house was the never-said.

30 She may have been unusually beloved, the precious only daughter, spoiled and mirror-gazing because of the affection the family lavished on her. When her husband left, they welcomed the chance to take her back from the in-laws; she could live like the little daughter for just a while longer. There are stories that my grandfather was different from other people, "crazy ever since the little Jap bayoneted him in the head." He used to put his naked penis on the dinner table, laughing. And one day he brought home a baby girl, wrapped up inside his brown western-style greatcoat. He had traded one of his sons, probably my father, the youngest, for her. My grandmother made him trade back.

When he finally got a daughter of his own, he doted on her. They must have all loved her, except perhaps my father, the only brother who never went back to China, having once been traded for a girl.

Brothers and sisters, newly men and women, had to efface their sexual color and present plain miens. Disturbing hair and eyes, a smile like no other, threatened the ideal of five generations living under one roof. To focus blurs, people shouted face to face and yelled from room to room. The immigrants I know have loud voices, unmodulated to American tones even after years away from the village where they called their friendships out across the fields. I have not been able to stop my mother's screams in public libraries or over telephones. Walking erect (knees straight, toes pointed forward, not pigeon-toed, which is Chinese-feminine) and speaking in an inaudible voice, I have tried to turn myself American-feminine. Chinese communication was loud, public. Only sick people had to whisper. But at the dinner table, where the family members came nearest one another, no one could talk, not the outcasts nor any eaters. Every word that falls from the mouth is a coin lost. Silently they gave and accepted food with both hands. A preoccupied child who took his bowl with one hand got a sideways glare. A complete moment of total attention is due everyone alike. Children and lovers have no singularity here, but my aunt used a secret voice, a separate attentiveness.

She kept the man's name to herself throughout her labor and dying; she did not accuse him that he be punished with her. To save her inseminator's name she gave silent birth.

He may have been somebody in her own household, but intercourse with a man outside the family would have been no less abhorrent. All the village were kinsmen, and the titles shouted in loud country voices never let kinship be forgotten. Any man within visiting distance would have been neutralized as a lover—"brother," "younger brother," "older brother"—115 relationship titles. Parents researched birth charts probably not so much to assure good fortune as to circumvent incest in a population that has but one hundred surnames. Everybody has eight million relatives. How useless then sexual mannerisms, how dangerous.

As if it came from an atavism deeper than fear, I used to add "brother" silently to boys' names. It hexed the boys, who would or would not ask me to dance, and made them less scary and as familiar and deserving of benevolence as girls.

But, of course, I hexed myself also—no dates. I should have stood up, both arms waving, and shouted out across libraries, "Hey, you! Love me back." I had no idea, though, how to make attraction selective, how to control its direction and magnitude. If I made myself American-pretty so that the five or six Chinese boys in the class fell in love with me, everyone else—the Caucasian, Negro, and Japanese boys—would too. Sisterliness, dignified and honorable, made much more sense.

Attraction eludes control so stubbornly that whole societies designed to organize relationships among people cannot keep order, not even when they bind people to one another from childhood and raise them together. Among the very poor and the wealthy, brothers married their adopted sisters, like doves. Our family allowed some romance, paying adult brides' prices and providing dowries so that their sons and daughters could marry strangers. Marriage promises to turn strangers into friendly relatives—a nation of siblings.

In the village structure, spirits shimmered among the live creatures, balanced and held in equilibrium by time and land. But one human being flaring up into violence could open up a black hole, a maelstrom that pulled in the sky. The frightened villagers, who depended on one another to maintain the real, went to my aunt to show her a personal, physical representation of the break she made in the "roundness." Misallying couples snapped off the future, which was to be embodied in true offspring. The villagers punished her for acting as if she could have a private life, secret and apart from them.

If my aunt had betrayed the family at a time of large grain yields and peace, when many boys were born, and wings were being built on many houses, perhaps she might have escaped such severe punishment. But the men—hungry, greedy, tired of planting in dry soil, cuckolded—had been forced to leave the village in order to send food-money home. There were ghost plagues, bandit plagues, wars with the Japanese, floods. My Chinese brother and sister had died of an unknown sickness. Adultery, perhaps only a mistake during good times, became a crime when the village needed food.

The round moon cakes and round doorways, the round tables of graduated size that fit one roundness inside another, round windows and rice bowls—these talismans had lost their power to warn this family of the law: a family must be whole, faithfully keeping the descent line by having sons to feed the old and the dead who in turn look after the family. The villagers came to show my aunt and lover-in-hiding a broken house. The villagers were speeding up the circling of events because she was too shortsighted to see that her infidelity had already harmed the village, that waves of consequences would return unpredictably, sometimes in disguise, as now, to hurt her. This roundness had to be made coin-sized so that she would see its circumference: punish her at the birth of her baby. Awaken her to the inexorable. People who refused fatalism because they could invent small resources insisted on culpability. Deny accidents and wrest fault from the stars.

⁴⁰ After the villagers left, their lanterns now scattering in various directions toward home, the family broke their silence and cursed her. "Aiaa, we're going to die. Death is coming. Death is coming. Look what you've done. You've killed us. Ghost! Dead Ghost! Ghost! You've never been born." She ran out into the fields, far enough from the house so that she could no longer hear their voices, and pressed herself against the earth,

her own land no more. When she felt the birth coming, she thought that she had been hurt. Her body seized together. "They've hurt me too much," she thought. "This is gall, and it will kill me." With forehead and knees against the earth, her body convulsed and then relaxed. She turned on her back, lay on the ground. The black well of sky and stars went out and out forever; her body and her complexity seemed to disappear. She was one of the stars, a bright dot in blackness, without home, without a companion, in eternal cold and silence. An agoraphobia rose in her, speeding higher and higher, bigger and bigger; she would not be able to contain it; there would be no end to fear.

Flayed, unprotected against space, she felt pain return, focusing her body. This pain chilled her—a cold, steady kind of surface pain. Inside, spasmodically, the other pain, the pain of the child, heated her. For hours she lay on the ground, alternately body and space. Sometimes a vision of normal comfort obliterated reality: she saw the family in the evening gambling at the dinner table, the young people massaging their elders' backs. She saw them congratulating one another, high joy on the mornings the rice shoots came up. When these pictures burst, the stars drew yet further apart. Black space opened.

She got to her feet to fight better and remembered that old-fashioned women gave birth in their pigsties to fool the jealous, pain-dealing gods, who do not snatch piglets. Before the next spasms could stop her, she ran to the pigsty, each step a rushing out into emptiness. She climbed over the fence and knelt in the dirt. It was good to have a fence enclosing her, a tribal person alone.

Laboring, this woman who had carried her child as a foreign growth that sickened her every day, expelled it at last. She reached down to touch the hot, wet, moving mass, surely smaller than anything human, and could feel that it was human after all—fingers, toes, nails, nose. She pulled it up on to her belly, and it lay curled there, butt in the air, feet precisely tucked one under the other. She opened her loose shirt and buttoned the child inside. After resting, it squirmed and thrashed and she pushed it up to her breast. It turned its head this way and that until it found her nipple. There, it made little snuffling noises. She clenched her teeth at its preciousness, lovely as a young calf, a piglet, a little dog.

She may have gone to the pigsty as a last act of responsibility: she would protect this child as she had protected its father. It would look after her soul, leaving supplies on her grave. But how would this tiny child without family find her grave when there would be no marker for her anywhere, neither in the earth nor the family hall? No one would give her a family hall name. She had taken the child with her into the wastes. At its birth the two of them had felt the same raw pain of separation, a wound that only the family pressing tight could close. A child with no descent line would not soften her life but only trail after her, ghostlike, begging her to give it purpose. At dawn the villagers on their way to the fields would stand around the fence and look.

45 Full of milk, the little ghost slept. When it awoke, she hardened her breasts against the milk that crying loosens. Toward morning she picked up the baby and walked to the well.

Carrying the baby to the well shows loving. Otherwise abandon it. Turn its face into the mud. Mothers who love their children take them along. It was probably a girl; there is some hope of forgiveness for boys.

*   *   *

"Don't tell anyone you had an aunt. Your father does not want to hear her name. She has never been born." I have believed that sex was unspeakable and words so strong and fathers so frail that "aunt" would do my father mysterious harm. I have thought that my family, having settled among immigrants who had also been their neighbors in the ancestral land, needed to clean their name, and a wrong word would incite the kinspeople even here. But there is more to this silence: they want me to participate in her punishment. And I have.

In the twenty years since I heard this story I have not asked for details nor said my aunt's name; I do not know it. People who comfort the dead can also chase after them to hurt them further—a reverse ancestor worship. The real punishment was not the raid swiftly inflicted by the villagers, but the family's deliberately forgetting her. Her betrayal so maddened them, they saw to it that she would suffer forever, even after death. Always hungry, always needing, she would have to beg food from other ghosts, snatch and steal it from those whose living descendants give them gifts. She would have to fight the ghosts massed at crossroads for the buns a few thoughtful citizens leave to decoy her away from village and home so that the ancestral spirits could feast unharassed. At peace, they could act like gods, not ghosts, their descent lines providing them with paper suits and dresses, spirit money, paper houses, paper automobiles, chicken, meat, and rice into eternity—essences delivered up in smoke and flames, steam and incense rising from each rice bowl. In an attempt to make the Chinese care for people outside the family, **CHAIRMAN MAO** encourages us now to give our paper replicas to the spirits of outstanding soldiers and workers, no matter whose ancestors they may be. My aunt remains forever hungry. Goods are not distributed evenly among the dead.

My aunt haunts me—her ghost drawn to me because now, after fifty years of neglect, I alone devote pages of paper to her, though not origamied into houses and clothes. I do not think she always means me well. I am telling on her, and she was a spite suicide, drowning herself in the drinking water. The Chinese are always very frightened of the drowned one, whose weeping ghost, wet hair hanging and skin bloated, waits silently by the water to pull down a substitute.

GLOSS: CHAIRMAN MAO
Mao Zedong was the Communist leader of China from 1949 to 1976. In his efforts to consolidate Communist control over China, Mao instituted a variety of policies intended to change longstanding Chinese cultural traditions. In this paragraph, Kingston is referring to one such policy by which the Chinese Communist government promoted the honoring of outstanding citizens who devoted themselves to the state rather than honoring one's ancestors, which is an ancient tradition in China.

Understanding the Text

1. In the beginning of this essay, Kingston describes in detail the villagers' raid on her family's home in China in the 1920s. Why does Kingston's mother tell her this story? What importance does the story have for Kingston's mother? Does it have the same importance for Kingston? Explain.

2. In many ways, this essay focuses on the desire to preserve family and cultural traditions and some of the consequences of preserving those traditions. In paragraph 21, Kingston writes, "The work of preservation demands that the feelings playing about in one's guts not be turned into action." What does Kingston mean by that statement? What does the statement indicate about an individual's responsibility in Chinese culture? What might it suggest about the connections between an individual's identity and his or her family and cultural traditions?

3. In paragraph 29, Kingston writes that one reason the uncles, cousins, nephews, and brothers in her family left their home in China was "the never-said." Elsewhere in the essay, she tells us that her mother warned her not to mention her aunt, the "no name woman," who died without speaking the name of the man who had fathered her baby. Kingston refers to other secrets and silences in her family's history. What is the importance of these secrets and silences? What do they reveal about the cultural traditions with which Kingston's family grew up?

4. What effect did her family's cultural traditions regarding relationships between men and women and regarding sexuality have on Kingston as a young girl? What might these effects suggest about how individuals develop an identity?

Exploring the Issues

1. In a sense, this essay is about how the ability to bear children affects women's sense of identity. This aspect of being a woman is what ultimately led to Kingston's aunt's death. Yet bearing children is also considered miraculous and wonderful. What do you think Kingston is saying about how cultures treat this special part of a woman's identity? What might this essay suggest about the way women are defined within communities or cultures?

2. How would you describe Kingston's narrative voice in this essay? In what ways do you think her voice helps convey her own views about her family's history and traditions? Cite specific passages to support your answer.

3. What aspects of a woman's identity as described in this essay do you think are unique to Chinese culture? How do the attitudes toward women that Kingston describes compare with attitudes toward women in your own culture?

4. In telling the story of her aunt, Kingston offers several different scenarios to explain what happened and why. This is one example of the blending of fiction and nonfiction techniques for which Kingston is well known as a writer. Examine the effectiveness of this technique in this essay. To what extent do you think it enhances or weakens Kingston's effort to convey her ideas? Do you think the essay would have been as effective if she had not used this kind of technique and simply explained that no one is really sure just what happened to her aunt?

Entering the Conversations

1. Write an essay in which you tell some of your own family history as a way to explore your identity.

Focus your essay on a specific event, experience, or person that you consider important in your family life and describe it in a way that will help readers understand its significance to you and your family.

2. Create a web site, blog, or photo essay based on the essay you wrote for Question 1.

 INFOTRAC

3. Using InfoTrac College Edition, your library, and any other relevant resources, try to find out about family traditions in a culture other than your own. If possible, visit the office for international students on your campus to gather information about that culture or to talk to someone you might know from another culture. Write a report in which you describe some of the most important traditions related to family life in the culture you have studied. Compare those traditions to the traditions in your own culture. Try to draw conclusions about important similarities and differences in these traditions and what they might suggest about the role of family in various cultures.

4. Popular television shows often focus on families. *The Bill Cosby Show, Malcolm in the Middle, Roseanne,* and even the animated series *The Simpsons* are some of the many successful television sitcoms that focus on families or family life. Select several such shows and examine the ways in which they present these families. What do these shows reveal about families and family identity? What attitudes or beliefs about families do these shows convey? Most important, what do these shows suggest about how our families influence our own sense of identity? Write an essay in which you address these questions. In your essay, analyze what these shows reveal about the connection between our identities and our families.

Dagoberto Gilb (b. 1950) has focused much of his writing on his Chicano identity. One critic noted that what he found most impressive about Gilb's essays is "his measured indignation at the inability of white America to grasp Chicano beliefs or culture." I was struck by that comment not only because it so nicely describes the distinctive quality of Gilb's writing,

You Know Him BY His Labors, BUT Not His Face

DAGOBERTO GILB

but also because it says something interesting about how people understand others from backgrounds that differ from their own. In a sense, Gilb's writing is an effort to define his Chicano identity and to resist the ways in which mainstream America defines that identity. That is not a straightforward task because for many people, Chicano is associated with other kinds of identities, such as immigrant or migrant worker, that can be thought of as negative—as "Other" (a term discussed in the introduction to this cluster on page 86). In the following essay, as in much of his writing, Gilb challenges such attitudes. Here, he asks his readers to go beyond the surface, to consider the humanity that can be hidden behind labels like "immigrant." As you read this thoughtful and unusual essay, you might consider whether Gilb is

The one who left wasn't the only one sleeping on a stained twin mattress under a carpet remnant in the room near the stench of sewage, wasn't the only one making shadows from a single light bulb dangling by a wire, who laughed at that old snoring dog, who liked to praise that dinner of beans and rice and chiles, not the only one who shared a torn love seat to watch a fuzzy TV with so many brothers drinking beer and soda and sisters getting married and having babies, that crowd of aunts, uncles, cousins, nephews and nieces, not the only one with unfaded scars and bad teeth, not the only one who complained about that so-loud radio always somewhere, not the only one who could pick out the best used retread tires.

He wasn't the only one loving a mother who wore that same house-dress and apron, warming tortillas in the morning and early evening, who was still a beautiful woman.

He was the one who left and he will never stop loving her either. He had to leave behind a wife. The one who left had to leave behind his children. It was as though where he was going was a distant uncle's place, a man not blood, on his father's side, or it was the ex-husband of his godmother.

Somebody close to somebody else, somebody known but who is not in the family. That rich man has a successful construction business, or is a landowner, or he is just from "the States." He is the one many have seen drinking, laughing, talking loud in his language. He wouldn't live in even the nicest house in Mexico.

5 In "the States," there is work that pays and that is what the one who left needs and wants and he knows how to work, he is not afraid of any work, of earning. He is the one who left and he met good people, and bad people, and it was always dirty and mean, the same clothes no matter where or when or what. And that rich man does have lots of work. The one who left sweeps the sawdust and scrubs the cement and masonry tools and coils the hoses.

He stoops low for the cinder blocks and he lifts a beam that has to be set high. He pushes the wheelbarrow and pounds spikes with a flattened waffle-face metal hammer and he pulls out pins with its claws. He hauls the trash scraps and he digs the plumbing trench.

He always says yes and he means yes. He is a **CHEAP WAGE**, and he is quiet because he is far from home, **AS PAPERLESS AS BIRTH**, and he not only acts grateful, he is grateful, because there is always worse at home.

The one who left is nobody special, and he knows it himself.

There are so many others just like him, hungry, even hungrier once they've been paid. His only home is work and job. His only trust, his only confidence, is the work, the job.

10 The one who left lives near streets in the States that were the first and are now the last. He shops at markets where others who left go.

He does not go to banks, but of course he wants to. He does not have a driver's license, but of course he wants one. He does not have a phone, but of course he wants one. He wants his family to be with him.

He learned early to live like a shadow watching a single light bulb and now he moves with almost a natural invisibility, carefully crossing into the light of night, not really seen when he's working in the sun.

He is someone who left his mother to get work.

He left his wife to find work.

15 He left his children to get work.

His citizenship is not in Mexico or in "the States" but is at a job.

He is not a part-time citizen, a temporary citizen.

He is loyal to work, and he is a patriot of its country.

He does not want to leave it in three years, or in six years. Like everyone else, he wants to become wealthy in his country.

challenging your own attitudes about people who may be different from you.

Dagoberto Gilb is the author of Gritos: Essays *(2003), which was a finalist for the National Book Critics Circle Award, as well as three other books of fiction. The following essay was first published in the* Los Angeles Times *in 2004.* ◹

STRATEGIES: DESCRIPTION WITH A PURPOSE
The scene Gilb describes in the opening paragraphs of this essay is detailed and vivid, but it is not identified as a specific place at a particular time. Why? What do you think Gilb tries to accomplish with this description? What do the details he includes suggest about the people being described? In what ways might this description be different if it were given a specific place and time? Keep these questions in mind as you read the rest of this essay, and consider how this description helps convey Gilb's message.

CONVERSATIONS: ILLEGAL IMMIGRATION
In paragraph 7, Gilb describes the "one who left" as a "cheap wage" and "as paperless as birth." The descriptions might seem vague, but they have significance in the context of the ongoing debates about illegal immigration in the United States. Such debates have a long history in the United States, but they intensified in the years since 2000, as the U.S. economy struggled through a recession. Some Americans believe that illegal immigrants take jobs away from U.S. citizens. Others argue that immigrants do work that most Americans refuse to do. In recent decades, several plans to grant an amnesty to some illegal immigrants have been proposed. In early 2004, for example, President George W. Bush announced plans to reform immigration laws so that some illegal immigrant workers could acquire legal status. But many people opposed the plan. As these debates continue, many immigrants remain "paperless," like the man Gilb describes here—that is, they have no papers to document their status as legal immigrants and are therefore often referred to as "undocumented immigrants." Consider how the meaning of Gilb's essay is shaped by this context and by the ongoing conversations about immigration. Consider as well how he relies on that context as he chooses his words and develops his ideas in this essay.

Understanding the Text

1. Who is "the one who left" that Gilb describes in the opening paragraph? What is noteworthy about him, if anything? Why does Gilb describe him as "nobody special" later in the essay (par. 8)?

2. Who is the "somebody close to somebody else" that Gilb describes in the fourth paragraph? In what ways is he different from the people described elsewhere in this essay? Why are these differences important?

3. What is the significance of work to the people described in this essay? Why does Gilb write that the "person who left" is "loyal to work, and he is a patriot of its country"? What does this suggest about immigrant workers?

Exploring the Issues

1. Examine Gilb's decision not to identify the people in this essay in more specific terms. What effect do you think this decision has on Gilb's essay? What effect did it have on you as a reader? Do you think the essay would have been more or less effective if Gilb had identified specific people in specific locations? Explain.

2. Notice how Gilb ends this essay: "Like everyone else, he wants to become wealthy in his country." Why do you think he ends with this line? What point do you think he is making? What might this line suggest about the similarities and differences between the immigrant worker described in this essay and the people in the United States that he works for? Do you agree with Gilb that "everyone else" wants to become wealthy? Why or why not?

3. What do you think this essay suggests about the United States and about Americans? What do you think it suggests about Mexico? Do you think Gilb is criticizing one or both of these countries? Explain, citing specific passages from the essay to support your answer.

Entering the Conversations

1. Write an essay in which you express your views about immigration. Be sure to support your position appropriately. (You may wish to do some research about immigration for this assignment, as described in Question 4.)

2. In a group of classmates, share the essays you wrote for Question 1. What main arguments do you and your classmates present regarding immigration? What do these arguments suggest about how you define *American* and *immigrant*? In what ways might Gilb's essay influence your position on immigration or the positions of your classmates?

3. Try to find a friend or family member who is an immigrant or whose ancestors immigrated to the United States. Or visit the office for international students on your campus to meet someone from another country who might be willing to talk to you about his or her experiences. Interview this person and try to get a sense of what it has been like to come to the United States from somewhere else. Or get a sense of how the fact that their parents or grandparents were immigrants has affected their sense of who they are. Then write an essay on the basis of this interview in which you explore the identity of *immigrant*. If you are yourself an immigrant, write an essay about your experiences in coming to the United States.

 INFOTRAC

4. Search InfoTrac College Edition, the Internet, and other relevant resources for information and viewpoints regarding immigration in the United States. (Currently, many advocacy groups both for and against greater restrictions on immigration to the United States maintain web sites, so be aware that much information about immigration on the web is presented from these viewpoints.) Try to identify the main arguments for and against greater or fewer restrictions on immigration, and focus specifically on illegal immigrant workers and their role in these arguments. Then write a report on the basis of your research. In your report, provide an overview of these debates about immigration, and try to draw conclusions about how attitudes toward people of certain races, ethnicity, cultural backgrounds, religious beliefs, and national origin seem to influence the ongoing debates about immigration.

5. On the basis of your research for Question 4, write a letter to the editor of your local newspaper or another appropriate publication in which you express your views about immigration.

Alternatively, create a blog or web site devoted to this issue.

For many people, race is the most powerful aspect of identity. Certainly, it is among the most complex and controversial ways that we define ourselves and each other. The history of relations among races, not just in the United States but around the world, is an often sobering story of conflict, discrimination, and violence. In the United

Who Invented *White* People?

States, the legacy of slavery seems to influence any discussion of race, and very often, discussions of race relations and racial identity focus on what it means to be Black in America. But in the past decade or so, a number of scholars and social critics have argued that when it comes to addressing the complexities and problems associated with race, we should be focusing attention not exclusively on Blacks or Latinos or Native Americans or people of color; rather, we should be looking at Whiteness. One of those scholars is Gregory Jay (b. 1952), a professor of English at the University of Wisconsin at Milwaukee. Like many other scholars interested in understanding race, Jay believes that the way we tend to discuss issues related to race makes Whiteness invisible. Whenever we discuss race, we discuss people of color but not Whiteness itself. And that's a problem, he believes, because it assumes that Whiteness is the

GREGORY JAY

"What is it for? What parts do the invention and development of whiteness play in the construction of what is loosely described as 'American'?"
    —Toni Morrison, *Playing in the Dark: Whiteness and the Literary Imagination*

This week we celebrate Martin Luther King, Jr. day. What should our celebration focus on, and how can we best continue the work that he began? For most of us, Dr. King represents the modern Civil Rights Movement. That Movement was a struggle against the legal and social practices of racial discrimination—against everything from separate drinking fountains, white and colored public bathrooms, and segregated schools and lunch counters to the more subtle, everyday prejudices of ignorance and injustice that are common in America. The Civil Rights Act of 1965 is among Dr. King's greatest legacies, transforming the face of America more decisively than almost any other legislation since the Civil War. Dr. King gave his life for

standard by which other races are understood. In other words, according to Jay, when we examine how various racial categories are understood, we also have to look at Whiteness as a racial category; to avoid examining Whiteness as a racial category is to give it special status. In this way, how *we discuss race both conveys and reinforces certain messages about the status of various racial categories.*

In his provocative essay, which was originally delivered as a speech on Martin Luther King, Jr., Day in 1998, Jay explores how the racial category of White emerged from historical and cultural developments. He argues that only by understanding "where White people came from" can we hope to address longstanding conflicts and injustices associated with race. It is a challenging task, one that reminds us that there are profound consequences to how we define others. ◪

the fight against injustice, and as we survey the changes in the thirty years since then we must say that his was a great and glorious victory.

Yet the promised land still eludes us. Once the crude legal structures of discrimination were torn down, Americans faced the fact that changing the laws did not change the feelings and beliefs of individuals, black or white. Beyond the abstract words of law and legislation, real people continued to carry with them the history of racism, whether as victims of its horrors or as beneficiaries of its privileges. To this day, racial discrimination remains pervasive in America. The old-boy networks at major corporations ensure the continuation of white male dominance. Banks regularly discriminate against minorities in business and housing loans. Homeowners and apartment owners refuse to sell or rent across color lines, partly because of the threats and violence that still occur when they do. Parents express discomfort or outright rage when children love or marry across the lines of race. Government subsidizes white suburban life with everything from freeway construction and business tax exemptions to mortgage write-offs while starving urban neighborhoods and cutting welfare programs. Ivy league schools give preference to the children of alumni and wealthy donors for admission, which, given the fact that the alumni and donors are overwhelmingly white, means that white applicants have an artificially easy time getting into the best colleges, and thus into the best jobs. It is hard to have many alumni of color, after all, when in the past colleges refused to enroll people of African or Asian or Hispanic descent, and placed strict quotas on Jews as well. Most of us could pluck similar examples out of the newspaper every day. This is not the legacy that Dr. King envisioned when he stood on the mountain top and saw his dream.

What keeps racism alive in America? I don't pretend to be the one to know the answer to this question. It's a question, however, that every one of us needs to ask. We need to ask it not only of ourselves, looking into our hearts, but to ask it of each other—to ask our friends, our family, our coworkers, and our church members. But in talking about race, what, exactly, should we talk about? I want to propose today that we talk about whiteness. Too often in America, we talk about race as if it were only something that people of color have, or only something we need to talk about when we talk about African Americans or Asian Americans or American Indians or Latino Americans. One thing that has changed radically since the death of Dr. King is that most white people do not want to call themselves white people, or see themselves in racial terms. From the days of the founding fathers until the Civil Rights movement, "white" was a common term in the law as well as society. Federal, state, and local officials regularly passed laws containing the word "white," defining everything from slavery and citizenship to where people could sit on a bus. Today, the movement against racism has had the unexpected effect of letting whiteness off the hook. Over and over we hear people say that "race shouldn't matter," that we should, or even do, have a "color blind society." What has happened, I think, is that we have instead created a blindness to whiteness, or been blinded by whiteness itself. As the title of Cornel West's best selling book insists, *Race Matters*, and to that I would add that whiteness still matters the most.

The trouble, then, with the **DR. MARTIN LUTHER KING, JR. HOLIDAY,** with Black History Month, and such token expressions of concern is that they once more ghettoize the question of race. Worse, they tend to make race a black matter, something that we only discuss when we talk about African Americans, as if they were the only ones with a race. By distracting our glance, such tokenism once more blinds us to the race that is all around us, to what Herman Melville, in *Moby Dick*, called "the whiteness of the whale." The great white whale of racism is a white invention. It was white people who invented the idea of race in the first place, and it is white people who have become obsessed and consumed by it until, like Captain Ahab, they have become entangled so deeply in pursuing its nature that they self-destruct in the process. As the Nobel prize winning black author Toni Morrison has argued, in her wonderful book titled *Playing in the Dark: Whiteness and the Literary Imagination,* Melville and the other great writers of the American tradition tell the story of whiteness over and over. White identity defines itself against the backdrop of an African or colored presence: Ishmael and Queequeg in *Moby Dick,* Huck and Jim in *Huckleberry Finn,* right on up through Bill Cosby and what's-his-name on *I Spy* or any number of black-white buddy films in Hollywood. Ironically, white Americans can only define themselves by comparison to that which they are not, and so whiteness depends on blackness for its very definition.

Where did white people come from, anyway? Who invented whiteness? Scholars of race generally agree that the modern meaning of whiteness emerges in the centuries of European colonialism and imperialism that followed the Renaissance. Now granted, human begins have always clustered themselves in groups—families, clans, tribes, ethnic populations, nation states, etc.—and these groups have regularly been the source of discrimination and violence. At times it seems that an "us versus them" mentality starts on every playground and extends into every neighborhood, society, and government. Since human beings appear to require a sense of identity, and since identity is constructed by defining whom and what you are different from, it may be that the politics of difference will never be erased from human affairs.

That said, why did something called "racial" difference become so important in people's sense of their identity? Before the age of exploration, group differences were largely based on language, religion, and geography. The word "race" referred rather loosely to a population group that shared a language, customs, social behaviors, and

5

CONVERSATIONS: MARTIN LUTHER KING, JR., DAY
Jay uses Martin Luther King, Jr., Day as the occasion for his examination of whiteness. Although there seems to be an obvious connection between a holiday that celebrates the famous civil rights leader and a discussion of race, the matter is more complex than it might seem. Martin Luther King, Jr., Day has been a U.S. national holiday since 1986, but it remained controversial for a number of years. Some states resisted declaring the holiday, notably Arizona, which did not approve the holiday until 1992; New Hampshire, which changed its "Civil Rights Day" to "Martin Luther King Day" in 1999; and Utah, which changed "Human Rights Day" to "Martin Luther King, Jr., Day" in 2000. Consider how Jay relies on the complex historical background to this holiday in making his argument. Consider as well how the historical context might influence the way readers might respond to Jay's argument. What does Jay add to the ongoing conversations about race in the United States?

The Human Race Machine, Nancy Burson,
2000

other cultural characteristics—as in the French race or the Russian
race or the Spanish race (differences we might now call "ethnic" rather than "racial"). As European adventurers, traders, and colonists accelerated their activities in Africa and Asia and the Americas, there
emerged the need to create a single large distinction for differentiat-
ing between the colonizers and the colonized, or the slave traders
and the enslaved. At first, religious distinctions maintained their pre-
eminence, as the Africans and American Indians were dubbed pa-
gans, heathens, barbarians, or savages—that is, as creatures without
the benefits of Christian civilization or, perhaps, even as creatures
without souls. Efforts to Christianize the Indians and the Africans,
however, were never separate from efforts to steal their lands or exploit their labor. To justify such practices, Europeans needed a difference greater than religion, for religious justification melted away
once the Indian or African converted.

NOW THE EUROPEAN HAD ALWAYS REACTED A BIT HYSTERICALLY TO THE DIF-
FERENCES OF SKIN COLOR AND FACIAL STRUCTURE BETWEEN THEMSELVES
AND THE POPULATIONS ENCOUNTERED IN AFRICA, ASIA, AND THE AMERICAS
(see, for example, Shakespeare's dramatization of racial conflict in
Othello and *The Tempest*). Beginning in the 1500s, Europeans began
to develop what became known as "scientific racism," the attempt to
construct a biological rather than cultural definition of race. Biological races were said to predict and determine the cultural traits of
peoples, so that cultural differences could be "explained" on a "scientific" basis. Scientific racism divided the world's populations into
a few large species or groups. By the nineteenth century, race scientists settled on the term "Caucasians," first used as a synonym for
Europeans in 1807, probably because the term's association with the
Near East and Greece suited white people's desire to see themselves
as having originated in the Golden Age of Classical Civilization. Caucasian usually appeared in a list of "major" race groups including
also Mongolian (people of Asian descent), Ethiopian (people of African descent), and American Indian.

The fantasy of a "white race" with historical origins in Classical
Civilization white-washed the complexion of Greece and Rome
(whose people were a mixture of Mediterranean, Semitic, and African populations each bringing unique cultural traditions to the table). Postulating a direct biological descent from this Classical fantasy to the present helped justify contemporary racist practices.
White plantation owners in the American South, for example, built
their plantations according to Neo-Classical architecture (as did the
architects of our nation's capitol), so that the slave master's mansion
would recall the Parthenon of Ancient Greece, suggesting a racial
continuity between the Classical forefathers and the slave owners. In
the construction of whiteness, it was regularly said that slavery and
democracy were not a contradiction, since the ancient Greeks had

themselves been slave owners and regularly persecuted races considered "barbarians." What was good enough for the original whites, it was thought, was good enough for the people of Virginia and South Carolina and Mississippi (an argument that was not widely contested by white Americans in the North).

Whiteness, then, emerged as what we now call a "pan-ethnic" category, as a way of merging a variety of European ethnic populations into a single "race," especially so as to distinguish them from people with whom they had very particular legal and political relations— Africans, Asians, American Indians—that were not equal to their relations with one another as whites. But what of America as the great "melting pot"? When we read our history, we come to see that the "melting pot" never included certain darker ingredients, and never produced a substance that was anything but white. Take, for example, that first and most famous essay on the question "What is an American?" In 1781, an immigrant Frenchman turned New York farmer named Hector St. Jean de Crèvecoeur published his book *Letters from an American Farmer.* Here are some lines from its most quoted pages:

> . . . whence came all these people? They are a mixture of English, Scotch, Irish, French, Dutch, Germans, and Swedes. From this promiscuous breed, that race now called Americans have arisen. What, then, is the American, this new man? He is neither an European nor the descendant of an European; hence that strange mixture of blood, which you will find in no other country. I could point out to you a family whose grandfather was an Englishman, whose wife was Dutch, whose son married a French woman, and whose present four sons have now four wives of different nations. *He* is an American, who, leaving behind him all his ancient prejudices and manners, receives new ones from the new mode of life he has embraced, the new government he obeys, and the new rank he holds. . . . The Americans were once scattered all over Europe; here they are incorporated into one of the finest systems of populations which has ever appeared.

No longer a European, the American represents a new race made from the stock of various European nations. No mention is made of Africans or Indians, perhaps because this new American race does indeed receive new prejudices from the new mode of life it has embraced. Crèvecoeur candidly describes the process by which the American race originated as a white race; or rather, the way in which the descendants of Europeans constructed a myth of themselves as a white race with special claim on the answer to the question "What is an American?" An American was a white man. Just as importantly, America was that place where the downtrodden classes of Europe

CONVERSATIONS: THE IRISH IN AMERICA
In paragraph 11, Jay discusses the history of the Irish people and how they have been viewed both in Europe and in the United States. The status of the Irish has long been a matter of cultural and political controversy and conflict, complicated by longstanding religious tensions between Catholics and Protestants. These controversies continue to be the focus of attention today. The film *Gangs of New York* (2002) portrays some of the history of the Irish in New York. It's worth considering what a film like this one might suggest about the struggles of a people to define itself and to resist being defined in certain ways. In this essay, Jay is arguing in part that how we discuss race makes a difference. Since popular films are a medium by which these discussions take place, we might consider how they influence such discussions.

STRATEGIES: USING EXAMPLES TO ILLUSTRATE A POINT
In paragraphs 12 and 13, Jay is discussing complex theoretical ideas related to what he calls the "social construction" of reality. (If you're interested in exploring these ideas further, you can consult the work of Pierre Bourdieu and Peter Berger, two important theorists who have written about social construction theory.) Here, Jay provides several general but concrete examples of how his own racial "whiteness" might affect his daily life. Consider how effectively these brief examples help you understand his larger abstract point about the privileges of the racial category of whiteness.

could throw off the oppression of aristocrats and attain not only fraternal equality among themselves, but superiority over those who were not of the new white race. When the Constitution of the United States was written, it thus specifically enshrined slavery into law and denied citizenship to enslaved Africans. When the Naturalization Act of 1789 was made law, it stipulated that only "whites" were eligible for naturalization as citizens (a clause persistently contested by people of Chinese and Japanese ancestry for the next 150 years).

In a fascinating, provocative book called *How the Irish Became White*, Noel Ignatiev describes this process of Europeans becoming white in the case of the Irish immigrants of the nineteenth century. Ireland was a colony devastated by English imperialism, and by a racial stereotyping of the Irish as backward, primitive, savage, and barbarian (in no small measure because of their Catholicism). When the Irish set foot in America, they were still subject to much of the racial prejudice and discrimination they had suffered at home at the hands of the British. Irish immigrants to America occupied a position only just above that of the blacks, alongside whom they often labored on the docks or railroads. For the Irish, becoming white would offer many advantages, not least of which would be the elimination of their major competitors for jobs. The Irish began to organize the exclusion of Northern free blacks from shipyard or factory employment, and continued this discrimination in later generations when the Irish dominated the police and firemen's unions in most cities. The Irish formed a key ingredient in the pro-slavery coalition that sat at the core of the Democratic Party in America before the Civil War, and which was brought to full power by the Indian killer and Southern patriot Andrew Jackson. White working class men, many of them Irish, opposed the abolition of slavery because of the threat they believed free blacks would pose to their economic prosperity, just as they opposed the extension of slavery into the new territories because of the threat slavery would pose to the creation of high wage jobs in the West. The hostility between the Irish and the blacks that lives on until today has its roots in this early history of how the Irish became white, and of how various Irish-dominated institutions in urban America—especially police and fire departments and labor unions—prospered through racial discrimination.

Whiteness, of course, is a delusion—as the insane Captain Ahab of *Moby Dick* demonstrates. Scientists today agree that there is no such thing as "race," at least when analyzed in terms of genetics or behavioral variation. Every human population is a mongrel population, full of people descended from various places and with widely differing physical qualities. Racial purity is the most absurd delusion, since intermarriage and miscegenation have been far more the norm than the exception throughout human ethnic history. "Race," then, is what academics like to call a "socially constructed" reality. Race is a reality in the sense that people experience it as real and base much of their behavior on it. Race, however, is only real because certain social institutions and practices make it real. Race is real in the same way that a building or a religion or a political ideology is real, as each is the result of human effort, not a prescription from nature or God. Thus the concept of race can have little or no foundation, yet it can still be the force that makes or breaks someone's life, or the life of a people or a nation.

For white people, race functions as a large ensemble of practices and rules that give white people all sorts of small and large advantages in life. Whiteness is the source of many privileges, which is one reason people have trouble giving it up. It is important to stress that to criticize whiteness is not necessarily to engage in a massive orchestration of guilt. Guilt is often a distracting and mistaken emotion, especially when it comes to race. White people are fond of pointing out that as individuals they have never practiced discrimination, or that their ancestors never owned slaves. White people tend to cast the question of race in terms of guilt in part because of the American ideology of individualism, by which I mean our tendency to want to believe that individuals determine their own destinies and responsibilities. In this sense it is un-American to insist that white Americans benefit every day from their whiteness, whether or not they intend to do so. But that is the reality. Guilt, then, has nothing to do with whiteness in this sense of benefiting from structural racism and built-in privileges. I may not intend anything racial when I apply for a loan, or walk into a store, or hail a cab, or ask for a job—but in every circumstance my whiteness will play a role in the outcome, however "liberal" or "anti-racist" I imagine myself to be. White men have enormous economic advantages because of the disadvantages faced by women and minorities, no matter what any individual white men may intend. If discrimination means that fewer qualified applicants compete with you for the job, you benefit. You do not have to be a racist to benefit from being white. You just have to look the part.

The privileges of whiteness are the not-so-secret dirty truth about race relations in America. Three decades after Dr. King, we should be able to see that our blindness to whiteness has crippled us in our walk toward equality and justice and freedom. As the national conversation on race continues, let us resolve to make whiteness an issue, and not just on this holiday or during Black History Month. When we talk about race in America, we should be talking about the invention of whiteness, and about what David Roediger calls the **"ABOLITION OF WHITENESS."** From this perspective, the end of racism will not come when America grants equal rights to minorities. Racism will end only with the abolition of whiteness, when the white whale that has been the source of so many delusions is finally left to disappear beneath the sea of time forever.

CONVERSATIONS: THE ABOLITION OF WHITENESS
Jay's reference in paragraph 14 to the work of David Roediger is one example of how scholars and critics use each other's work to continue discussions of issues like race. Roediger is a well-known historian and author of *Towards the Abolition of Whiteness* (1994). Jay's reference to Roediger's work helps him make his point in this paragraph. What else might this reference accomplish?

Understanding the Text

1. In what ways have people become blind to whiteness, according to Jay? What are the consequences of this blindness? Do you agree with him? Why or why not?

2. Explain Jay's statement that "ironically, white Americans can only define themselves by comparison to that which they are not, and so whiteness depends on blackness for its very definition." What is ironic about this situation? What are the implications of this idea in Jay's view?

3. According to Jay, where did the racial category of whiteness come from? What evidence does he offer to support his analysis of the emergence of white as a racial category? How persuasive do you find this evidence?

4. What are the privileges of whiteness, according to Jay? How does our blindness to whiteness affect these privileges? Do you think Jay is right about the privileges of whiteness? Explain. You might draw on your own experience or the experiences of people you know to support your answer.

Exploring the Issues

1. Throughout this essay, Jay refers to and quotes from various scholars and other authors who have written about race. Examine these references. Who are the authors Jay refers to? What kind of credibility or expertise do they have? How effectively do you think Jay uses these references to support his arguments? What might the specific references Jay uses suggest about the audience Jay imagined for this essay?

2. In paragraph 5, Jay writes, "Since human beings appear to require a sense of identity, and since identity is constructed by defining whom and what you are different from, it may be that the politics of difference will never be erased from human affairs." Do you think Jay is right? Explain, drawing on other readings in this chapter to support your answer. If Jay is right that we will always define ourselves as different from others, what might this mean for our efforts to eliminate some of the terrible effects of racism and racial conflict?

3. Writing about race can be a difficult task, especially because it is such a sensitive issue for many people and because it remains among the most charged and controversial issues in American culture. Certainly, Jay must have known that by making his argument about whiteness he risked angering many readers. What evidence do you see that Jay tried to be sensitive to readers of certain backgrounds or beliefs? Do you think he wrote this essay in a way that is intended to provoke certain readers? Explain, citing specific passages from his essay to support your answer.

4. How do you describe Jay's voice in this essay? In what ways do you think his voice contributes to or detracts from his argument? Provide examples from his essay to support your answer.

Entering the Conversations

1. Write an essay in which you discuss how your racial identity has affected your life. In your essay, define your race as you understand it and draw on your experiences to describe how it has impacted your life and your relationships with others.

2. In a group of classmates, share the essays you wrote for Question 1. Identify similarities and differences in the way race seems to have been a factor in your lives. Try to draw conclusions about the way we use race to define one another.

3. Write an essay for your local newspaper expressing your thoughts on the occasion of Martin Luther King, Jr., Day.

4. At one point in his essay, Jay writes, "Since human beings appear to require a sense of identity, and since identity is constructed by defining whom and what you are different from, it may be that the politics of difference will never be erased from human affairs." Write an essay in which you respond to this point. What are the consequences of this point of view? What does it mean in terms of our collective efforts to combat racism and solve racial conflict? To what extent do you think Jay is right? Try to address such questions in your essay.

DIVERSE SELVES, MULTIPLE IDENTITIES

EVERY FOUR YEARS DURING THE U.S. PRESIDENTIAL ELECTION, WE HEAR A LOT ABOUT "THE AMERICAN PEOPLE." I OFTEN WONDER WHAT THAT PHRASE MEANS. WHO EXACTLY ARE *THE AMERICAN PEOPLE* ANYWAY? POLITICIANS LIKE TO USE THE PHRASE AS IF WE ARE all essentially the same, as if the differences among us are irrelevant. But hearing someone say "the American people" always reminds me of how diverse the people of the United States really are.

Try this little experiment: Make a list of people you know, such as your close friends, family members, coworkers, people in clubs or organizations you belong to, or neighbors—anyone you see regularly. Then, next to each name, write down a description of who that person is. Include any important details about that person. Chances are that even on a short list, you'll have many different kinds of people. For example, on my list would be people who are White, Black, Asian, and Hispanic; people from several different parts of the United States and a few from other countries; people who are Catholic, Jewish, Buddhist, and Protestant; people of many different ages and people who do many different things for a living; and people with different political views. Many of the people I am thinking of fall into several of these categories at the same time. For example, one of my coworkers is a bilingual Catholic, Hispanic woman from the northeastern United States. One of my students is also a bilingual Catholic woman, but her mother is from Spain whereas her father is an Irish American. The more I think about the people I know, the more diverse they seem to become.

The readings in this cluster call attention to that kind of diversity. They explore different racial, ethnic, and cultural identities. And they reveal that none of us has a single identity; rather, each of us has many identities related to important aspects of our lives, such as race, national origin, gender, ethnicity, age, and so much else. In many ways, I find this to be the most fascinating aspect of the whole idea of *identity*: the multiplicity of identities that a single person can have and the many different ways that those identities can affect a person's life. My race might be the most important aspect of my identity in some contexts, but in other situations, my age or gender or perhaps the fact that I am a father or a teacher may be more important. That's part of the richness and the challenge of living in a diverse society. We can be many things to many people.

But although this kind of diversity is often celebrated, the multiple identities we each have can often complicate our lives in less desirable ways. The writers whose essays appear in this cluster explore that complexity and the challenges it can bring to individuals who sometimes struggle with different identities. My hope is that these readings not

> That's part of the richness and the challenge of living in a diverse society. We can be many things to many people.

only help you appreciate this complexity in others but also enable you to see it in yourself.

I also hope these readings call your attention to the many issues that relate to *identity*. For example, the essays in this cluster address such issues as immigration and assimilation, culture, national identity, multiculturalism, and racism. To some extent, *identity* is a term that helps us make sense of age-old questions about who we are. But it is also a term that can divert our attention from other ways of seeing the world and other people around us. Imagine, for example, if we strictly adhered to the Zen Buddhist ideal of "erasing the self." What if we stopped focusing on identity as an issue? How would that change the way we understand and interact with each other?

What if you woke up one morning and discovered that you were a different race? If that sounds far-fetched, you'll want to read the following essay by Erin Aubry Kaplan (b. 1961), which first appeared in LA Weekly *in 2003. Kaplan, a journalist, tells the story of Wayne Joseph, who lived his life believing that he was a Black man until he*

Black Like I Thought I Was

took a DNA test when he was fifty-one years old. (A DNA test identifies a person's genetic makeup, which can be matched with people of similar racial backgrounds.) That test indicated that Joseph actually had no Black blood in him. He is Indo-European and Native American, but not Black. Understandably, the results of the DNA test shocked Joseph and left him deeply uncertain about his own identity. After living his entire life as a Black person, he was now faced with the knowledge that he was not Black. How could he suddenly give up a part of his identity that was so central to his life and his way of understanding himself?

If Wayne Joseph's experience raised hard questions for him, it raises similarly hard questions for all of us. As Joseph asks at the end of this essay, "The question ultimately is, are you who you say you are, or are you who you are genetically?" What makes someone

ERIN AUBRY KAPLAN

Wayne Joseph is a 51-year-old high school principal in Chino whose family emigrated from the segregated parishes of Louisiana to central Los Angeles in the 1950s, as did mine. Like me, he is of Creole stock and is therefore on the lighter end of the black color spectrum, a common enough circumstance in the South that predates the multicultural movement by centuries. And like most other black folk, Joseph grew up with an unequivocal sense of his heritage and of himself; he tends toward black advocacy and has published thoughtful opinion pieces on racial issues in magazines like *Newsweek*. When Joseph decided on a whim to take a new ethnic DNA test he saw described on a *60 Minutes* segment last year, it was only to indulge a casual curiosity about the exact percentage of black blood; virtually all black Americans are mixed with something, he knew, but he figured it would be interesting to make himself a guinea pig for this new testing process, which is offered by a Florida-based company called DNA Print Genomics Inc. The experience would at least be fodder for another essay for *Newsweek*. He got his kit in the mail, swabbed his mouth per the instructions and sent off the DNA samples for analysis.

Now, I have always believed that what is now widely considered one of slavery's worst legacies—the Southern "one-drop" rule that indicted anyone with black blood as a nigger and cleaved American society into black and white with a single stroke—was also slavery's only upside. Of course I deplore the motive behind the law, which was rooted not only in white paranoia about **MISCEGENATION,** but in a more practical need to maintain social order by keeping privilege and property in the hands of whites. But by forcing blacks of all complexions and blood percentages into the same boat, the law ironically laid a foundation of black unity that remains in place today. It's a foundation that allows us to talk abstractly about a "black community" as concretely as we talk about a black community in Harlem or Chicago or South-Central (a liberty that's often abused or lazily applied in modern discussions of race). And it gives the lightest-skinned among us the assurance of identity that everybody needs in order to feel grounded and psychologically whole—even whites, whose **PUBLIC NON-ETHNICITY IS REALLY ETHNICITY WRIT SO LARGE** and influential it needs no name. Being black may still not be the most advantageous thing in the world, but being nothing or being neutral— the rallying cry of modern-day multiculturalists—has never made any emotional or real-world sense. Color marks you, but your membership in black society also gives you an indestructible house to live in and a bed to rest on. I can't imagine growing up any other way.

Wayne Joseph can't, either. But when the results of his DNA test came back, he found himself staggered by the idea that though he still qualified as a person of color, it was not the color he was raised to think he was, one with a distinct culture and definitive place in the American struggle for social equality that he'd taken for granted. Here was the unexpected and rather unwelcome truth: Joseph was 57 percent Indo-European, 39 percent Native American, 4 percent East Asian—and zero percent African. After a lifetime of assuming blackness, he was now being told that he lacked even a single drop of black blood to qualify.

"My son was flabbergasted by the results," says Joseph. "He said, 'Dad, you mean for 50 years you've been passing for black?'" Joseph admits that, strictly speaking, he has. But he's not sure if he can or wants to do anything about that at this point. For all the lingering effects of institutional racism, he's been perfectly content being a black man; it has shaped his worldview and the course of his life in ways that cannot, and probably should not, be altered. Yet Joseph struggles to balance the intellectual dishonesty of saying he's black with the unimpeachable honesty of a lifelong experience of *being* black. "What do I do with this information?" he says, sounding more than a little exasperated. "It was like finding out you're adopted. I don't want to be disingenuous with myself. But I can't conceive of living any other way. It's a question of what's logical and what's visceral."

Race, of course, has always been a far more visceral matter than a logical one. We now know that there is no such thing as race, that

Black or White or Asian or any other race? Is Joseph Black because he was raised as a Black person? Is he Black because for his entire life other people accepted him as a Black person? And does race overshadow other important aspects of his—or anyone's—identity? Such questions highlight the complexity of race as an identity. But we might also ask why race matters so much in the first place. Isn't Joseph the same person now that he was before his DNA test? Keep that question in mind as you read about his remarkable experience. ◩

GLOSS: MISCEGENATION
Miscegenation is the mixing of races through marriage and/or sexual relations. The term has long been used to refer to the mixing of Blacks and Whites in the United States.

CONVERSATIONS: WHITENESS
Kaplan states that the "public non-ethnicity" of White people is "really ethnicity writ so large and influential it needs no name." Compare this statement with Gregory Jay's idea that whiteness is "invisible" (see page 103).

5

GLOSS: FAUSTIAN PROTAGONIST
Dr. Faustus is a famed character in a German legend who makes a deal with the Devil in return for power. The term *Faustian bargain* is used to refer to morally or ethically questionable deals in which someone gains something by selling out in some way. A Faustian protagonist is someone who makes such a deal.

humans are biologically one species; we know that an African is likely to have more in common genetically with a European thousands of miles away than with a neighboring African. Yet this knowledge has not deterred the racism many Europeans continue to harbor toward Africans, nor the wariness Africans harbor toward Europeans. Such feelings may never be deterred. And despite all the loud assertions to the contrary, race is still America's bane, and its fascination; Philip Roth's widely acclaimed last novel set in the 1990s, *The Human Stain,* features a **FAUSTIAN PROTAGONIST** whose great moral failing is that he's a black man who's been passing most of his life for white (the book was made into a movie in 2003).

Joseph recognizes this, and while he argues for a more rational and less emotional view of race for the sake of equity, he also recognizes that rationality is not the same thing as fact. As much as he might want to, he can't simply refute his black past and declare himself white or Native American. He can acknowledge the truth but can't quite apply it, which makes it pretty much useless to other, older members of his family. An aunt whom he told about the test results only said that she wasn't surprised. "When I told my mother about the test, she said to me, 'I'm too old and too tired to be anything else,'" recalls Joseph. "It makes no difference to her. It's an easy issue."

After recovering from the initial shock, Joseph began questioning his mother about their lineage. He discovered that, unbeknownst to him, his grandparents had made a conscious decision back in Louisiana to *not* be white, claiming they didn't want to side with a people who were known oppressors. Joseph says there was another, more practical consideration: Some men in the family routinely courted black women, and they didn't want the very public hassle such a pairing entailed in the South, which included everything from dirty looks to the ignominy of a couple having to separate on buses and streetcars and in restaurants per the Jim Crow laws. I know that the laws also pointedly separated mothers from sons, uncles from nephews, simply because one happened to be lighter than the other or have straighter hair. Determinations of race were entirely subjective and imposed from without, and the one-drop rule was enforced to such divisive and schizophrenic effects that Joseph's family—and mine—fled Louisiana for the presumably less boundary-obsessed West. But we didn't flee ourselves, and didn't expect to; we simply set up a new home in Los Angeles. The South was wrong about its policies but it was right about our color. It had to be.

Joseph remains tortured by the possibility that maybe nobody is right. The essay he thought the DNA test experience would prompt became a book that he's already 150 pages into. He doesn't seem to know how it'll end. He's in a kind of limbo that he doesn't want and that I frankly wouldn't wish on anyone; when I wonder aloud about taking the $600 DNA test myself, Joseph flatly advises against it. "You don't want to know," he says. "It's like a genie coming out of a bottle. You can't put it back in." He has more empathy for the colorblind crowd than he had before, but isn't inclined to believe that the Ward Connerlys and other professed racial conservatives of the world have the best interests of colored people at heart. "I see their point, but race *does* matter, especially with things like medical research and other social trends," he says of **CONNERLY'S PROPOSITION 54,** the much-derided state measure that seeks to outlaw the collection of ethnic data that will be voted on in the recall election next Tuesday. "Problems like that can't just go away." For the moment, Joseph is compelled to try to judge individually what he knows has always been judged broadly, to reconcile two famously opposed viewpoints of race not for the sake of political argument—he has made those—but for his own peace of mind. He's wrestling with a riddle that will likely outlive him, though he doesn't worry that it will be passed on to the next generation—his ex-wife is black, enough to give his children the firm ethnic identity he had and that he embraced for most of his life. "The question ultimately is, are you who you say you are, or are you who you are genetically?" he muses. The logical—and visceral—answer is that it's not black and white.

CONVERSATIONS: CONNERLY'S PROPOSITION 54
In 2003, Californians defeated Proposition 54, the Racial Privacy Initiative, a state ballot initiative that would have made it illegal for the government to collect any information regarding the race of individual citizens. Ward Connerly, a regent of the University of California, was a leader in the effort to pass Proposition 54. He argued that ignoring race altogether would benefit Blacks and other minorities. Consider how Wayne Joseph's experience might influence someone's view of an initiative like Proposition 54 and the idea of "color blindness." What is the significance of his experience in view of Proposition 54?

Understanding the Text

1. Why does Wayne Joseph struggle with the question of whether to tell people that he is Black or not? What do you think his struggle with this question suggests about him? What does it suggest about race as an aspect of our identity?

2. How did Joseph's family come to be identified as Black? Why is this part of their history important? What might it suggest about how race is defined and treated in American society?

3. What does Kaplan mean when she writes at the end of paragraph 7 that "the South was wrong about its policies but it was right about our color. It had to be." Do you think she's right? Explain.

Exploring the Issues

1. In paragraph 7, Kaplan tells some of the history of Wayne Joseph's family and of her own family. Why do you think she includes this reference to her own background in an article that is about Joseph? What advantages and disadvantages do you see to Kaplan including this information about herself? How does this knowledge about Kaplan affect the way you read this article?

2. Kaplan writes in paragraph 2 that being Black gives someone "an indestructible house to live in and a bed to rest on." Examine her use of metaphor to make this point.

What does this metaphor of a house suggest about racial identity? Do you find the metaphor effective in this case? Explain.

3. Near the end of her article, Kaplan refers to Proposition 54 (see *Conversations: Connerly's Proposition 54* on page 113). Examine how this context might affect the way readers react to Kaplan's article. Given that Proposition 54 would have effectively outlawed official records of a person's race, does Proposition 54 affect the significance of Wayne Joseph's experiences in any way?

Entering the Conversations

1. Write an essay in which you discuss whether Wayne Joseph should continue to identify himself as a Black man even after DNA testing shows that he is not. In your essay, support your position on Joseph's decision and discuss your view of the role of race in our identities and the importance of racial identity in contemporary society.

2. In a group of classmates, share the essays you wrote for Question 1. Try to identify the main arguments in support of Joseph's decision to continue identifying himself as a Black man and the arguments against that decision. Debate these positions with your group members, and try to draw conclusions about the way race is used as a category in contemporary society.

INFOTRAC

3. In this essay, Kaplan criticizes a movement that has come to be called *multiculturalism,* which is a general view that celebrates diversity and promotes racial, ethnic, and cultural tolerance. She writes that "being nothing or being neutral—the rallying cry of modern-day multiculturalists—has never made any emotional or real-world sense." Using InfoTrac College Edition and any other appropriate resources, find out about multiculturalism. What is this movement? How did it get started? What are the main views and goals of people that Kaplan calls "multiculturalists"? What impact has it had on American society? Try to address such questions in your research. You might consider speaking to someone on your campus who has expertise in these issues (for example, a professor who specializes in cultural studies or African American studies). Write a report providing a description of multiculturalism and its impact on American society. Draw your own conclusions about whether or not Kaplan is right in her criticisms of multiculturalism.

4. Write an essay for an audience of your classmates in which you tell the story of an incident or experience in which your racial identity was somehow important.

5. Create a web site, PowerPoint presentation, or other kind of document that conveys your sense of racial identity.

I grew up in a family whose Polish traditions *were kept alive by my grandmother and a few other relatives of her generation. My great grandparents were immigrants who came to the United States from Poland at the turn of the twentieth century, and as far as my grandmother was concerned, Polish was the way we should describe ourselves. In fact, in the*

Crossing THE Border WITHOUT Losing Your Past

small Pennsylvania town where I grew up, people often described themselves as Polish, Lithuanian, Ukrainian, Czech, or some other eastern European nationality, even though they were all born and raised in the United States. For my father's generation, however, being Polish wasn't necessarily something to be celebrated, partly because of the prejudice against eastern European immigrants that was held by people of other nationalities in that part of Pennsylvania during the first half of the twentieth century. My father liked to say that we weren't Polish; we were Americans. And over the years, our Polish identity seems to have faded.

Writer Oscar Casares (b. 1964) also has a family history that includes immigration to the United States. But his Mexican identity remains a central part of who he is.

OSCAR CASARES

Along with it being DIEZ Y SEIS DE SEPTIEMBRE, **Mexican** Independence Day, today is my father's 89th birthday. Everardo Issasi Casares was born in 1914, a little more than a hundred years after Miguel Hidalgo y Costilla rang the church bells of Dolores, summoning his parishioners to rise up against the Spaniards.

This connection has always been important in my family. Though my father was born in the United States, he considers himself a Mexicano. To him, ancestry is what determines your identity. If you have Mexican blood, you are Mexican, whether you were born in Mexico City or New York City. This is not to say he denies his American citizenship—he votes, pays taxes and served in the Army. But his identity is tied to the past. His family came from Mexico, so like them he is Mexicano, punto, end of discussion.

In my hometown, Brownsville, Tex., almost everyone I know is Mexicano: neighbors, teachers, principals, dropouts, doctors, lawyers, drug

Indeed, although he and his parents were born and continue to live in the United States, Casares refuses to use the label Mexican American. He prefers Mexican to describe himself. As I read this essay, I wondered why Casares' family has held onto its immigrant roots, while my family— and the other families where I grew up—have not. Does it have to do with time? It has been 100 years since my ancestors immigrated to the United States, whereas Casares' ancestors were more recent arrivals. Is it skin color? All my ancestors were White, whereas Casares and his family are not. Is it language? My family gave up the Polish language long before I was born, but Spanish continues to be spoken in the region of the United States where Casares and his family live. I'm not sure what the answer is, but my family history and Casares' reflect some of the complexities of the identities that we claim for ourselves and that others assign to us. Chances are that your own identity is just as complex.

Oscar Casares is a fiction writer whose collection of stories, Brownsville: Stories, *was published in 2003. This essay first appeared in the* New York Times *in 2003.* ☑

STRATEGIES: LANGUAGES
In the opening paragraph, Casares includes a brief Spanish phrase, "diez y seis de septiembre," without translating it into English. Writers sometimes include quotations in other languages in this way if they wish to preserve the quotation's original language. But here, Casares is not quoting from a text in another language; rather, he is using Spanish for this phrase (which means "September 16," the date in 1810 when Father Hidalgo, a Catholic priest, began a rebellion in the town of Dolores against the Spanish rulers in Mexico). Consider why Casares would include a Spanish phrase without translation in an essay written in English and published in an English-language newspaper, the *New York Times,* many of whose readers do not understand Spanish. What might he be trying to suggest by doing so? What do you think he is revealing about his attitudes toward his readers?

dealers, priests. Rich and poor, short and tall, fat and skinny, dark- and light-skinned. Every year our Mexican heritage is celebrated in a four-day festival called Charro Days. Men grow beards; mothers draw moustaches on their little boys and dress their little girls like Mexican peasants; the brave compete in a jalapeño-eating contest. But the celebration also commemorates the connection between two neighboring countries, opening with an exchange of gritos (traditional cowboy calls you might hear in a Mexican movie) between a representative from Matamoros, Mexico, standing on one side of the International Bridge and a Brownsville representative standing on the other.

Like many Americans whose families came to this country from somewhere else, many children of Mexican immigrants struggle with their identity, as our push to fully assimilate is met with an even greater pull to remain anchored to our family's country of origin. This is especially true when that country is less than a quarter of a mile away—the width of the Rio Grande—from the new one. We learn both cultures as effortlessly as we do two languages. We learn quickly that we can exist simultaneously in both worlds, and that our home exists neither here nor there but in the migration between these two forces.

But for Mexican-Americans and other immigrants from Spanish-speaking countries who have been lumped into categories like Latino or Hispanic, this struggle has become even more pronounced over the last few years as we have grown into the largest minority group in the United States. Our culture has been both embraced and exploited by advertisers, politicians and the media. And as we move, individually, from our small communities, where our identity is clear, we enter a world that wants to assign us a label of its choosing.

When I left Brownsville in 1985 to start school at the University of Texas at Austin one of the first things I was asked was, "What are you?" "I'm Mexican," I told the guy, who was thrown off by my height and light skin. "Really, what part of Mexico are you from?" he asked, which led me to explain I was really from Brownsville, but my parents were Mexican. "Really, what part of Mexico?" Here again I had to admit they weren't really born in Mexico and neither were my grandparents or great-grandparents. "Oh," he said, "you're Mexican-American, is what you are."

Mexican-American. I imagined a 300-mile-long hyphen that connected Brownsville to Austin, a bridge between my old and new world. Not that I hadn't seen this word combination, Mexican-American, on school applications, but I couldn't remember the words being spoken to me directly. In Brownsville, I always thought of myself as being equally Mexican and American.

When I graduated that label was again redefined. One of my first job interviews was at an advertising agency, where I was taken on a tour: the media department, the creative department, the account-service department, the Hispanic department. This last department specialized in marketing products to Spanish-speaking consumers. In the group were men and women from Mexico, Puerto Rico and California, but together they were Hispanic. I was hired to work in another department, but suddenly, everyone was referring to me as Hispanic.

HISPANIC? WHERE WAS THE MEXICAN IN ME? Where was the hyphen? I didn't want to be Hispanic. The word reminded me of those Mexican-Americans who preferred to say their families came from Spain, which they felt somehow increased their social status. Just hearing the word Hispanic reminded me, too, of people who used the word Spanish to refer to Mexicans. "The Spanish like to get wild at their fiestas," they would say, or "You Spanish people sure do have a lot of babies."

In this same way, the word Hispanic seemed to want to be more user friendly, especially when someone didn't want to say the M word: Mexican. Except it did slip out occasionally. I remember standing in my supervisor's office as he described calling the police after he saw a car full of "Mexicans" drive through his suburban neighborhood.

Away from the border, **THE WORD MEXICAN** had come to mean dirty, shiftless, drunken, lustful, criminal. I still cringe whenever I think someone might say the word. But usually it happens unexpectedly, as though the person has pulled a knife on me. I feel the sharp words up against my gut. Because of my appearance, people often say things in front of me they wouldn't say if they knew my real ethnicity—not Hispanic, Latino or even Mexican-American. I am, like my father, Mexican, and on this day of independence, I say this with particular pride.

10

CONVERSATIONS: ETHNIC LABELS

Throughout his essay, Casares devotes much attention to the different terms that can be used to identify himself: Mexican, Mexican-American, Latino, and Hispanic. In this paragraph, he discusses some of the reasons he does not prefer the term Hispanic to refer to himself, and he explains some of the connotations of that term. In explaining why he rejects this term, Casares is taking part in a much larger set of conversations about racial and ethnic identity that have been going on in American society for many years. He reminds us that certain terms may mean different things to different people and that the meanings of terms can evolve. Just as the term *Negro,* which was once an accepted term for Blacks, came to be seen as a negative label, Hispanic has taken on negative meanings when it is used to refer to people who come from Spanish-speaking countries. As a person of Mexican descent, Casares is obviously aware of the complexity of these terms. As a writer, he must be aware of the different meanings, both positive and negative, that these terms might have for different readers. (The readings in Chapter 8, *The Politics of Language,* may help you further explore the ways in which words can acquire various political meanings.)

STRATEGIES: FIGURATIVE LANGUAGE

This paragraph includes a wonderful example of a writer skillfully using figurative language to help convey several ideas. Casares opens the paragraph with an explanation of the negative meanings of the word Mexican, including "criminal." A few sentences later, he uses the metaphor of a knife to help convey how he feels when he thinks about someone calling him a "Mexican." But notice how Casares subtly creates an image of a criminal, perhaps a mugger, pulling a knife suddenly on a victim. And he twists the expected meaning of this image so that he, the Mexican, becomes the victim, and the hypothetical person calling him "Mexican" becomes the criminal wielding the knife. Consider how Casares manipulates this metaphor and relies on prejudices against Mexicans to convey several messages in this passage.

Understanding the Text

1. Why is it important for Casares to identify himself as Mexican rather than as Mexican-American or Hispanic? What differences does he see among these ways of defining his ethnic or racial identity? Do you think these differences are important? Explain.

2. Given that neither Casares nor his parents were born in Mexico, what is the role of their family history in how Casares identifies himself as Mexican? Do you agree with him that this history is as important to his identity as his American citizenship? Why or why not?

3. In paragraph 5, Casares writes that immigrants from Spanish-speaking countries "have been lumped into categories like Latino or Hispanic." Who has done this lumping? Why? What might this lumping suggest about how racial or ethnic labels are used?

Exploring the Issues

1. In the opening paragraph, Casares refers to Mexican Independence Day, which celebrates Mexico's independence from Spain. Later, Casares discusses why he dislikes the term *Hispanic* as a way to refer to himself. What connection does Casares make between this history of Mexico and the term *Hispanic*? Why is this connection important to him? What does it suggest about race, ethnicity, and national origin as aspects of our identities?

2. Casares discusses several different labels for his identity (such as Mexican-American,

Latino, Hispanic) and how the meanings of those labels can change or be redefined. What do you think the changing meanings of these labels suggests about how we describe our own identities and the identities of others?

3. Casares draws heavily on his own experiences as a person of Mexican descent in the United States to support his points and to explain his views. Evaluate his use of these experiences. How effectively do you think he uses them to make his points and convey his ideas?

Entering the Conversations

1. Write an essay in which you describe your own ethnic or racial identity.

2. Select a term that is used to identify people of a particular race, ethnicity, or nationality and write an essay in which you research the meanings and uses of that term. In your essay, provide some history of that term and how it has been used. Try to identify the meanings it has for different people. Draw conclusions

about the use of such labels when referring to one's identity. (You may have to do some research for this assignment depending on the term you choose.)

3. Create a web site or photo essay depicting your identity or identities.

4. In a group of classmates, share the projects you created for Question 3. What do these projects indicate about how each of you understands his or her identity? What conclusions can you draw about the many different identities we can have?

5. In recent decades, discussions of immigration in the United States have focused on people of Hispanic descent, in part because of the large numbers of people from Mexico who cross illegally into the United States. Photos like this one have become common in newspapers and magazines and on web sites. Using this photo and others depicting immigrants that you find in print or online, write an essay in which you analyze the way immigrants are portrayed in the media today.

USA–Mexico border wall: Undocumented immigrants prepare to cross illegally over, under, or through the 10-foot-high steel wall, 1993.

As I was writing this book, I happened to have a conversation with a former student of mine who had been living in Sweden for the past several years. He was born and raised in the United States, but he and his wife, who is Swedish, had decided to raise their family in Sweden because they consider it a safer, more tolerant society than the United States today. My former student believes this is the right choice for his family, but it was not an easy decision for him because

American Dreamer

he considers himself an American, not a European or a Swede.

I was thinking about him as I read the following essay by Bharati Mukherjee (b. 1940), an immigrant from India who is a naturalized U.S. citizen and who unequivocally describes herself as an American. Mukherjee has strong views on what it means to be American—and on the issue of identity in general. For her, to be an American has less to do with one's culture or race than it does with the ideals that are reflected in the U.S. Constitution. In her view, America is as much an idea as it is a place. I think my former student would agree with her, yet his understanding of the idea of America has led him to a different conclusion about what it means to be an American. I don't know whether Mukherjee's essay would change his mind. It may change yours.

Bharati Mukherjee is an acclaimed writer whose books include The Middleman and Other Stories

BHARATI MUKHERJEE

The United States exists as a sovereign nation. "America," in contrast, exists as a myth of democracy and equal opportunity to live by, or as an ideal goal to reach.

I am a naturalized U.S. citizen, which means that, unlike native-born citizens, I had to prove to the U.S. government that I merited citizenship. What I didn't have to disclose was that I desired "America," which to me is the stage for the drama of self-transformation.

I was born in Calcutta and first came to the United States—to Iowa City, to be precise—on a summer evening in 1961. I flew into a small airport surrounded by cornfields and pastures, ready to carry out the two commands my father had written out for me the night before I left Calcutta: Spend two years studying creative writing at the Iowa Writers' Workshop, then come back home and marry the bridegroom he selected for me from our caste and class.

In traditional Hindu families like ours, men provided and women were provided for. My father was a patriarch and I a pliant daughter. The neighborhood I'd grown up in was homogeneously Hindu,

(1988) and Jasmine *(1999). This essay appeared in* Mother Jones *magazine in 1997.* ▾

Bengali-speaking, and middle-class. I didn't expect myself to ever disobey or disappoint my father by setting my own goals and taking charge of my future.

5   When I landed in Iowa 35 years ago, I found myself in a society in which almost everyone was Christian, white, and moderately well-off. In the women's dormitory I lived in my first year, apart from six international graduate students (all of us were from Asia and considered "exotic"), the only non-Christian was Jewish, and the only nonwhite an African-American from Georgia. I didn't anticipate then, that over the next 35 years, the Iowa population would become so diverse that it would have 6,931 children from non-English-speaking homes registered as students in its schools, nor that Iowans would be in the grip of a cultural crisis in which resentment against immigrants, particularly refugees from Vietnam, Sudan, and Bosnia, as well as unskilled Spanish-speaking workers, would become politicized enough to cause the Immigration and Naturalization Service to open an "enforcement" office in Cedar Rapids in October for the tracking and deporting of undocumented aliens.

In Calcutta in the '50s, I heard no talk of "identity crisis"—communal or individual. The concept itself—of a person not knowing who he or she is—was unimaginable in our hierarchical, classification-obsessed society. One's identity was fixed, derived from religion, caste, patrimony, and mother tongue. A Hindu Indian's last name announced his or her forefathers' caste and place of origin. A Mukherjee could *only* be a Brahmin from Bengal. Hindu tradition forbade intercaste, interlanguage, interethnic marriages. Bengali tradition even discouraged emigration: To remove oneself from Bengal was to dilute true culture.

Until the age of 8, I lived in a house crowded with 40 or 50 relatives. My identity was viscerally connected with ancestral soil and genealogy. I was who I was because I was Dr. Sudhir Lal Mukherjee's daughter, because I was a Hindu Brahmin, because I was Bengali-speaking, and because my *desh*—the Bengali word for homeland—was an East Bengal village called Faridpur.

The University of Iowa classroom was my first experience of coeducation. And after not too long, I fell in love with a fellow student named Clark Blaise, an American of Canadian origin, and impulsively married him during a lunch break in a lawyer's office above a coffee shop.

That act cut me off forever from the rules and ways of upper-middle-class life in Bengal, and hurled me into a New World life of scary improvisations and heady explorations. Until my lunch-break wedding, I had seen myself as an Indian foreign student who intended to return to India to live. The five-minute ceremony in the lawyer's office suddenly changed me into a transient with conflicting loyalties to two very different cultures.

10   The first 10 years into marriage, years spent mostly in my husband's native Canada, I thought of myself as an expatriate Bengali perma-

nently stranded in North America because of destiny or desire. My first novel, *The Tiger's Daughter*, embodies the loneliness I felt but could not acknowledge, even to myself, as I negotiated the no man's land between the country of my past and the continent of my present. Shaped by memory, textured with nostalgia for a class and culture I had abandoned, this novel quite naturally became an expression of the expatriate consciousness.

It took me a decade of painful introspection to put nostalgia in perspective and to make the transition from expatriate to immigrant. After a 14-year stay in Canada, I forced my husband and our two sons to relocate to the United States. But the transition from foreign student to U.S. citizen, from detached onlooker to committed immigrant, has not been easy.

The years in Canada were particularly harsh. Canada is a country that officially, and proudly, resists cultural fusion. For all its rhetoric about a cultural "mosaic," Canada refuses to renovate its national self-image to include its changing complexion. It is a New World country with Old World concepts of a fixed, exclusivist national identity. Canadian official rhetoric designated me as one of the "visible minority" who, even though I spoke the Canadian languages of English and French, was straining "the absorptive capacity" of Canada. Canadians of color were routinely treated as "not real" Canadians. One example: In 1985 a terrorist bomb, planted in an Air-India jet on Canadian soil, blew up after leaving Montreal, killing 329 passengers, most of whom were Canadians of Indian origin. The prime minister of Canada at the time, Brian Mulroney, phoned the prime minister of India to offer Canada's condolences for India's loss.

Those years of race-related harassments in Canada politicized me and deepened my love of the ideals embedded in the American Bill of Rights. I don't forget that the architects of the Constitution and the Bill of Rights were white males and slaveholders. But through their declaration, they provided us with the enthusiasm for human rights, and the initial framework from which other empowerments could be conceived and enfranchised communities expanded.

I am a naturalized U.S. citizen and I take my American citizenship very seriously. I am not an economic refugee, nor am I a seeker of political asylum. I am a voluntary immigrant. I became a citizen by choice, not by simple accident of birth.

15 **YET THESE DAYS, QUESTIONS SUCH AS WHO IS AN AMERICAN AND WHAT IS AMERICAN CULTURE ARE BEING POSED** with belligerence, and being answered with violence. Scapegoating of immigrants has once again become the politicians' easy remedy for all that ails the nation. Hate speeches fill auditoriums

CONVERSATIONS: ANTI-IMMIGRATION SENTIMENTS
In this paragraph, Mukherjee describes the increasing opposition in the United States to immigration and the violence associated with the prejudice and bigotry that sometimes accompanies anti-immigration movements. Mukherjee wrote this essay in 1997, when concerns about immigration—both legal and illegal—were high among many Americans. Some states, notably California, considered legislation to limit immigration or to make it more difficult for illegal immigrants to receive social services in the United States. Consider whether the situation regarding immigration in the United States has changed much since Mukherjee wrote this essay. Are her concerns about anti-immigration sentiments still valid? How might developments since 1997 affect the way we read her essay today? She writes in the following paragraph that "it is imperative that we come to some agreement about who 'we' are, and what our goals are for the nation, now that our community includes people of many races, ethnicities, languages, and religions." Is that statement still valid today?

CONVERSATIONS: THE AMERICAN MELTING POT

In paragraph 21, Mukherjee refers to the common metaphors of the melting pot and the mosaic to describe the diversity of American society. Consider how these images draw on those same metaphors. What do they communicate about American culture? About diversity?

© Christine Thresh, 2001

We the People quilt, 2002

© Chien-Chi Chang/Magnum Photos

Kindergarten graduation in Chinatown, New York City, 1996

GLOSS: MICHAEL FAY'S CANING

Michael Fay was the son of an American living and working in Singapore in 1994 when he was arrested for vandalism. The legal punishment for such a crime in Singapore was caning— that is, being flogged on the buttocks with a wooden cane. His sentence provoked an outcry among many Americans who viewed it as barbaric. But as Mukherjee notes, people in Singapore supported it.

for demagogues willing to profit from stirring up racial animosity. An April Gallup poll indicated that half of Americans would like to bar almost all legal immigration for the next five years.

The United States, like every sovereign nation, has a right to formulate its immigration policies. But in this decade of continual, large-scale diasporas, it is imperative that we come to some agreement about who "we" are, and what our goals are for the nation, now that our community includes people of many races, ethnicities, languages, and religions.

The debate about American culture and American identity has to date been monopolized largely by Eurocentrists and ethnocentrists whose rhetoric has been flamboyantly divisive, pitting a phantom "us" against a demonized "them."

All countries view themselves by their ideals. Indians idealize the cultural continuum, the inherent value system of India, and are properly incensed when foreigners see nothing but poverty, intolerance, strife, and injustice. Americans see themselves as the embodiments of liberty, openness, and individualism, even as the world judges them for drugs, crime, violence, bigotry, militarism, and homelessness. I was in Singapore in 1994 when the American teenager **MICHAEL FAY** was sentenced to caning for having spraypainted some cars. While I saw Fay's actions as those of an individual, and his sentence as too harsh, the overwhelming local sentiment was that vandalism was an "American" crime, and that flogging Fay would deter Singapore youths from becoming "Americanized."

Conversely, in 1994, in Tavares, Florida, the Lake County School Board announced its policy (since overturned) requiring middle school teachers to instruct their students that American culture, by which the board meant European-American culture, is inherently "superior to other foreign or historic cultures." The policy's misguided implication was that culture in the United States has not been affected by the American Indian, African-American, Latin-American, and Asian-American segments of the population. The sinister implication was that our national identity is so fragile that it can absorb diverse and immigrant cultures only by recontextualizing them as deficient.

Our nation is unique in human history in that the founding idea of "America" was in opposition to the

20

tenet that a nation is a collection of like-looking, like-speaking, like-worshiping people. The primary criterion for nationhood in Europe is homogeneity of culture, race, and religion—which has contributed to blood-soaked balkanization in the former Yugoslavia and the former Soviet Union.

America's pioneering European ancestors gave up the easy homogeneity of their native countries for a new version of utopia. Now, in the 1990s, we have the exciting chance to follow that tradition and assist in the making of a new American culture that differs from both the enforced assimilation of a **"MELTING POT"** and the Canadian model of a multicultural "mosaic."

The multicultural mosaic implies a contiguity of fixed, self-sufficient, utterly distinct cultures. **MULTICULTURALISM,** as it has been practiced in the United States in the past 10 years, implies the existence of a central culture, ringed by peripheral cultures. The fallout of official multiculturalism is the establishment of one culture as the norm and the rest as aberrations. At the same time, the multiculturalist emphasis on race- and ethnicity-based group identity leads to a lack of respect for individual differences within each group, and to vilification of those individuals who place the good of the nation above the interests of their particular racial or ethnic communities.

We must be alert to the dangers of an "us" vs. "them" mentality. In California, this mentality is manifesting itself as increased violence between minority, ethnic communities. The attack on Korean-American merchants in South Central Los Angeles in the wake of the Rodney King beating trial is only one recent example of the tragic side effects of this mentality. On the national level, the politicization of ethnic identities has encouraged the scapegoating of legal immigrants, who are blamed for economic and social problems brought about by flawed domestic and foreign policies.

We need to discourage the retention of cultural memory if the aim of that retention is cultural **BALKANIZATION.** We must think of American culture and nationhood as a constantly re-forming, transmogrifying "we."

25   In this age of **DIASPORAS,** one's biological identity may not be one's only identity. Erosions and accretions come with the act of emigration. The experience of cutting myself off from a biological homeland and settling in an adopted homeland that is not always welcoming to its dark-complexioned citizens has tested me as a person, and made me the writer I am today.

I choose to describe myself on my own terms, as an American, rather than as an Asian-American. Why is it that hyphenation is imposed only on nonwhite Americans? Rejecting hyphenation is my refusal to categorize the cultural landscape into a center and its peripheries; it is to demand that the American nation deliver the promises of its dream and its Constitution to all its citizens equally.

CONVERSATIONS: MULTICULTURALISM
Since the 1980s, the idea of multiculturalism has become an influential way of thinking about diversity and differences related to race, ethnicity, culture, gender, and other important aspects of identity. But in recent years, many observers have criticized the idea of multiculturalism, which seems to promote tolerance and celebrate diversity, on the grounds that it actually reinforces problematic attitudes about race, ethnicity, culture, and so on. Here, especially in paragraph 22, Mukherjee weighs in on this important conversation, offering her own criticism of multiculturalism. You might compare Mukherjee's position on multiculturalism to Erin Aubry Kaplan's discussion of it in her essay (par. 2 on page 111).

GLOSSES: CULTURAL BALKANIZATION
The term *balkanization* has been used since World War I to describe the breaking up of a nation into several smaller, hostile states or regions, as occurred after World War I on the Balkan Peninsula, a region that includes Greece, Bulgaria, Albania, and the former Yugoslavia (which now includes Croatia, Serbia, and Bosnia). Here, Mukherjee expands the use of the term to refer to cultural identity rather than nation-states.

DIASPORAS
Diaspora originally referred to the dispersing of the Jewish people after the Babylonian exile. It is now often used, as Mukherjee uses it here, to refer to the scattering of any people with a common origin or cultural background.

My rejection of hyphenation has been misrepresented as race treachery by some India-born academics on U.S. campuses who have appointed themselves guardians of the "purity" of ethnic cultures. Many of them, though they reside permanently in the United States and participate in its economy, consistently denounce American ideals and institutions. They direct their rage at me because, by becoming a U.S. citizen and exercising my voting rights, I have invested in the present and not the past; because I have committed myself to help shape the future of my adopted homeland; and because I celebrate racial and cultural mongrelization.

What excites me is that as a nation we have not only the chance to retain those values we treasure from our original cultures but also the chance to acknowledge that the outer forms of those values are likely to change. Among Indian immigrants, I see a great deal of guilt about the inability to hang on to what they commonly term "pure culture." Parents express rage or despair at their U.S.-born children's forgetting of, or indifference to, some aspects of Indian culture. Of those parents I would ask: What is it we have lost if our children are acculturating into the culture in which we are living? Is it so terrible that our children are discovering or are inventing homelands for themselves?

Some first-generation Indo-Americans, embittered by racism and by unofficial "glass ceilings," construct a phantom identity, more-Indian-than-Indians-in-India, as a defense against marginalization. I ask: Why don't you get actively involved in fighting discrimination? Make your voice heard. Choose the forum most appropriate for you. If you are a citizen, let your vote count. Reinvest your energy and resources into revitalizing your city's disadvantaged residents and neighborhoods. Know your constitutional rights, and when they are violated, use the agencies of redress the Constitution makes available to you. Expect change, and when it comes, deal with it!

30   As a writer, my literary agenda begins by acknowledging that America has transformed me. It does not end until I show that I (along with the hundreds of thousands of immigrants like me) am minute by minute transforming America. The transformation is a two-way process: It affects both the individual and the national-cultural identity.

Others who write stories of migration often talk of arrival at a new place as a loss, the loss of communal memory and the erosion of an original culture. I want to talk of arrival as gain.

Understanding the Text

1. What does Mukherjee mean when she writes that America is "the stage for the drama of self-transformation"? Why is this self-transformation important to her?

2. What differences does Mukherjee see between how identity is understood in her native India and how it is understood in the United States? Why are these differences important to her?

3. Why does Mukherjee believe it is necessary for Americans to come to some agreement about who they are, about what "America" is? Do you agree with her? Why or why not? What might your answer to that question suggest about your own views regarding what it means to be an American?

4. What is distinctive about America, according to Mukherjee? Do you think most Americans would agree with her? Do you? Explain.

Exploring the Issues

1. Mukherjee presents her experiences in this essay. What kinds of experiences does she describe? What do these experiences suggest about her as a person? What might they suggest about the nature of identity? How effectively do you think she uses her experiences in this essay?

2. In paragraph 7, Mukherjee states that her "identity was viscerally connected with ancestral soil and genealogy." In the essay by Erin Aubry Kaplan on page 110 in this cluster, Wayne Joseph uses the same term—visceral—in discussing his identity (par. 4 and par. 8 in Kaplan's essay). Look up the meaning of this term and evaluate how Mukherjee (and Joseph) use it in this context. What does this term suggest about identity?

3. At several points, Mukherjee challenges and criticizes other immigrants, including those from her native India, for their complaints about losing their cultural identity. What effect do you think these criticisms have on the essay as a whole? How did they affect your sense of Mukherjee as the author of this essay?

4. This essay was published in *Mother Jones,* a magazine that covers political and cultural issues from a progressive perspective. Based on this essay, what assumptions do you think Mukherjee made about her audience? In what ways does she seem to address readers of *Mother Jones*? Does knowing something about *Mother Jones* change the way you read this essay? Explain, citing specific passages to support your answers.

Entering the Conversations

1. Write an essay in which you define cultural identity. You may wish to consult sources to help you understand the idea of culture and the ways in which it is understood by various scholars and critics.

2. Write an essay for an audience of your classmates in which you define what it means to be an American.

3. Rewrite the essay you wrote for Question 3 as an op-ed (opinion) piece for your local newspaper or some other publication that reaches an audience outside your school.

4. The images below were published during the 2004 U.S. presidential election. Consider what they communicate about American cultural identity. Drawing on these photos and others you can find that reflect your ideas about American identity, create a photo essay or web site that defines American identity as you understand it.

© AP Photo/Ted S. Warren

© AP Photo/Eric Gay

The 2008 presidential campaign was in *many ways a lesson in the complexities of identity in the United States. As is usual during presidential campaigns,* the candidates tried to emphasize various identities depending on which voters they were trying to woo. *A candidate campaigning in Indiana might play up his Midwestern roots. A candidate addressing a meeting of leaders of the Baptist church might present herself as a devout Christian. And of course all the candidates talked at some point*

Mixed Messenger

about being Americans. But if being an American is always a complicated matter, it was even more so in 2008. In that election, the candidates running for their party's nomination reflected America's diversity perhaps more than in any campaign in history. There were traditional white men like Senator John McCain of Arizona and Senator John Edwards of North Carolina, but there was also a woman—(Senator Hillary Clinton), a Latino (New Mexico Governor Bill Richardson), and a Mormon

PEGGY ORENSTEIN

A few weeks ago, while stuck at the Chicago airport with my 4-year-old daughter, I struck up a conversation with a woman sitting in the gate area. After a time, she looked at my girl—who resembles my Japanese-American husband—commented on her height and asked, "Do you know if her birth parents were tall?"

Most Americans watching **BARACK OBAMA'S CAMPAIGN,** even those who don't support him, appreciate the historic significance of an African-American president. But for parents like me, Obama, as the first biracial candidate, symbolizes something else too: the future of race in this country, the paradigm and paradox of its simultaneous intransigence and disappearance. It's true that, over the past months, Obama has increasingly positioned himself as a black man. That's understandable: insisting on being seen as biracial might alienate African-American leaders and voters who have questioned his authenticity. White America, too, has a vested interest in seeing him as black; it's certainly a more exciting, more romantic and more

CONVERSATIONS: THE 2008 U.S. PRESIDENTIAL CAMPAIGN
At the time Orenstein's essay was published, Senator Barack Obama from Illinois was among several candidates seeking the nomination of the Democratic Party for president, and his biracial background was the focus of much attention in the popular press and among many groups of Americans, including African Americans, some of whom debated whether Obama could really be considered African American (as Orenstein notes in the next paragraph). These many different conversations about Obama's racial identity were part of the larger conversation about race that Americans have been having since before the Civil War, and they underscore the complexity of that conversation. Orenstein's perspective on that conversation is shaped by her experience as the mother of a biracial child. Consider how your own identity might shape your participation in that conversation.

ORENSTEIN, PEGGY. "MIXED MESSENGER," NEW YORK TIMES, APRIL 6, 2008 SUNDAY. REPRINTED BY PERMISSION OF THE *NEW YORK TIMES*.

concrete prospect than the "first biracial president." Yet, even as he proves his **BLACK CRED,** it may be the senator's dual identity, and his struggles to come to terms with it, that explain his crossover appeal and that have helped him to both embrace and transcend race, winning over voters in Birmingham, Iowa, as well as Birmingham, Ala.

Mixed-race marriages were illegal in at least 16 states when Obama was born, though the taboo was historically inconsistent—white men could marry Asian women in some places, for instance, while marriages like mine, which go the other way, were forbidden. Since 1967, when those laws were declared unconstitutional, the rate of interracial marriage among all groups has skyrocketed. And those couples have children. Of the seven million Americans who identified themselves as mixed-race in the 2000 census (the first in which it was possible to do so), nearly half were under the age of 18. Almost 5 percent of Californians now identify themselves as mixed-race; by comparison, fewer than 7 percent are African-American. Hawaii, Obama's childhood home, is the most diverse state in the Union: 21 percent of residents identified as "Hapa," a Hawaiian word meaning "half" that has gone from being a slur against mixed-race Asians to a point of pride—and has increasingly been adopted by multiracials of all kinds on the Mainland.

But the rise of multiracialism is not all Kumbaya choruses and "postracial" identity. The **N.A.A.C.P.** criticized **THE CENSUS CHANGE,** fearing that since so few in the black community are of fully African descent, mass attrition to a mixed-race option could threaten political clout and Federal financing. Mexican-Americans, a largely mixed-race group, fought to be classified as white during the first half of the 20th century; during the second half, they fought against it.

5   Among Asians, Japanese-Americans in Northern California have argued over "how Japanese" the contestants for the Cherry Blossom Queen must be (the answer so far: 50 percent, which is less rigid than San Francisco's Miss Chinatown U.S.A., whose father must be Chinese, but more strict than the 25 percent Chinese required to be Miss Los Angeles Chinatown).

Hapas muddy discussions of affirmative action and the gathering of health-care statistics. When a Centers for Disease Control researcher who called to survey me about my daughter's vaccinations asked about her race, I answered, Caucasian and Asian. There was a pause, then she asked, "Which would you mainly identify her as?"

More than anything, though, Hapas remind us that, while racism is real, "race" is a shifting construct. Consider: Would Obama still be seen as "black enough" if the wife by his side were white? And don't get my husband started on why Tiger Woods—whose mother is three-quarters Asian and whose father was one-quarter Chinese and half African-American—is rarely hailed as the first Asian-American golf superstar.

Race is thrust on Hapas based on the shades of their skin, the shapes of their eyes, their last names. (Quick: **WHAT RACE IS APOLO OHNO?** How

(former Massachusetts Governor Mitt Romney). But the candidate who seemed to complicate the question of identity more than any other was Illinois senator Barack Obama, whose father is Kenyan, whose mother is a White American, and who was born into a Muslim family but is a practicing Christian. Indeed, Senator Obama may have reflected America's diversity, but the many different reactions to him seemed to underscore the complexities of that diversity.

Writer Peggy Orenstein was especially sensitive to these different reactions to Obama's identity, because, like Obama's parents, she herself is part of a mixed-race marriage. In the following essay, which was first published in the New York Times *in 2008 when the presidential campaign was in full swing, she discusses the different reactions to Senator Obama's identity as a way to examine the complicated question of identity in American culture. Orenstein raises questions about multiculturalism in the United States, but Orenstein is also interested in how our ideas about race are changing. I hope her essay will also cause you to wonder about how we define and claim our identities in an increasingly diverse world.*

STRATEGIES: USING SLANG

When Orenstein writes in paragraph 2 that Obama is trying to prove "his black cred," she is using a slang term for the more formal term "credibility." In an essay that is written in standard English for a traditional publication such as the *New York Times,* such a use of slang stands out. Consider what effect this use of slang has on you as a reader. How might it influence your sense of Orenstein's own credibility as a writer? In what ways might it strengthen—or weaken—her essay?

GLOSS: N.A.A.C.P.
The National Association for the Advancement of Colored People, which was founded in 1909 by several prominent African-American activists, including Ida Wells-Barnett and W.E.B. DuBois, has promoted equal rights for people of color. According to its mission statement, the purpose of the organization "is to ensure the political, educational, social, and economic equality of rights of all persons and to eliminate racial hatred and racial discrimination."

CONVERSATIONS: THE 2000 U.S. CENSUS
Every ten years, the U.S. Government undertakes a census of the nation's population. Traditionally, this census includes information about the racial and ethnic background of Americans, and the categories used in the census have changed over time. As Orenstein notes, the 2000 U.S. Census was the first one that included a "mixed-race" category, which was controversial. Note that such a policy change is shaped not only by a changing American population but also by changing attitudes about race.

GLOSS: FAMOUS MIXED-RACE PEOPLE
Orenstein mentions several well-known people who are, like her daughter, biracial, including the professional golfer Tiger Woods; Apolo Ohno, who won five Olympic medals for speed skating in 2002 and 2006; and actress Meg Tilly.

about Meg Tilly? Both are half-Asian.) But ethnicity, an internal sense of culture, place and heritage—that's more of a choice. Cultivating it in our children could be the difference between a Hapa Nation that's a rich, variegated brown and one that fades to beige. I know that challenge firsthand. Because we are trying to raise our daughter as bicultural, much in our family is up for grabs, from the food we eat—and what we say before and after eating it—to the holidays we celebrate to whether we call her rear end a tushie or an *oshiri*.

For the moment, she attends a Jewish preschool (where, as it happens, a quarter of her class, not to mention an assistant rabbi, is Hapa) and identifies so strongly with my heritage that my husband has begun to feel uneasy. He recently suggested that, for balance, we enroll her in Dharma school at the Japanese Buddhist church. Let me be clear: he is an atheist who grew up Methodist; I hew to a kind of social-relativist concept of "oneness." And our daughter is going to spend her days shuttling between two temples?

I sometimes wonder what will happen in another 50 years. Will my grandchildren "feel" Jewish? Japanese? Latino? African-American? Will they be pluralists? "Pass" as Anglo? Refuse categorization? Will Hapa Nation eventually make tracking "race" impossible? Will it unite us? Or will it, as some suggest, further segregate African-Americans from everyone else? The answer to all these questions may be yes. Regardless, watching Senator Obama campaigning with his black wife, his Indonesian-Caucasian half-sister, his Chinese-Canadian brother-in-law and all of their multiculti kids, it seems clear that the binary, black-and-white—not to mention black-or-white—days are already behind us.

10

Understanding the Text

1. What does Senator Barack Obama symbolize to Orenstein? In what sense does his importance as a presidential candidate go beyond his identity as a Black American in Orenstein's view?

2. What is the history of mixed-race marriage in the United States? Why is this history important to Orenstein? What does it suggest to her about Americans' attitudes about race?

3. In paragraph 4 Orenstein refers to a change in the U.S. Census that allowed Americans to indicate their race as "mixed." Why was that change significant in Orenstein's view? To what extent does that policy change underscore Orenstein's main point about race in this essay?

4. What is *Hapa?* How has the use of this term changed over time? Why do you think Orenstein uses it instead of more traditional terms?

5. What does Orenstein mean when she writes in paragraph 7 that "while racism is real, 'race' is a shifting construct"? In what way is this idea important to her point in this essay?

Exploring the Issues

1. In paragraph 6 Orenstein writes that "Hapas muddy discussions of affirmative action and the gathering of health-care statistics." She suggests here that the complexities of racial identity can affect public policies such as affirmative action. What might this situation reveal about the role of race in contemporary American society? Why does

one's racial identity really matter?

2. Orenstein reveals much about her own family in this essay. She describes the racial backgrounds of herself and her husband as well as their religious beliefs and their efforts to raise their daughter as biracial. What does Orenstein's own family situation suggest about the challenges we face in the United States today when it comes to race? What might her experience tell us about racism? To what extent do you think Orenstein's experience reflects American culture today? Do you think her essay would be less effective if she had not included information about her family? Explain.

3. Do you think the racial identity of the president of the United States matters? Why or why not? What might your answer to this question reveal about your own beliefs regarding the role of race in contemporary American society?

4. In what ways do you think one's racial identity is related to other aspects of identity, such as religion, culture, geographical location, and gender? In describing her own family's experience, Orenstein refers to several such factors, including religious upbringing, language, and food. How do you think these factors complicate our sense of racial identity? Can race be separated from these other factors? Explain.

Entering the Conversations

1. Write an essay in which you tell the story of your own racial identity. In your essay,

try to explore the role your racial identity plays in your life.

2. Visit the web sites of several organizations that are somehow linked to racial identity, such as the N.A.A.C.P. Try to get a sense of how these organizations define their racial identities. How do they seem to understand the role of race in American society? What exactly do these organizations do and how do their activities relate to their sense of the role of race? Then write a report for an audience of your classmates about what you learned through your research on these organizations. In your report, describe how the organizations you investigated seem to understand race and its role in contemporary American life. Draw conclusions on the basis of your research about how we understand race today.

3. Select several popular television shows and watch several episodes of each to get a sense of how race is portrayed and talked about in these shows. Try to select well-known shows that reach a wide viewing audience and focus your attention on the roles played by characters of different racial identities. Also pay close attention to how race is explicitly discussed by characters or how it figures into the plots of various episodes. On the basis of your experience with these television shows, write an essay in which you present an analysis of the treatment of race on television. In your analysis, describe any important commonalities or differences among the TV shows you reviewed in their portrayal of race and try to draw conclusions about attitudes toward race that are suggested by these shows.

Alternatively, do a similar analysis using print, online, or television advertisements.

4. Write an argument for or against affirmative action or other race-based policies. For this assignment you will probably have to research affirmative action or other race-based policies you might be examining. For your research, look into recent controversies involving affirmative action policies, such as the controversies over race-based ad-

missions policies at the University of Michigan and other American universities and professional schools (such as law schools and medical schools). Also consider talking to faculty members at your school who might have expertise in affirmative action policy (for example, faculty members in political science, sociology, or public planning). On the basis of your research, write an essay in which you make an argument in favor of or opposition to affirmative action policies. Focus on a specific policy (such as college admissions), and base your argu-

ment not only on your research but also on your own sense of the importance of race in such decisions.

5. On the basis of the research you did for Question 4, write a letter to the Dean of Admissions at your school expressing your views about college admissions policies regarding race. In your letter, explain your position on race-based admissions policies and urge your school to adopt policies that reflect your position. (For this assignment, you may have to research your school's admissions policies.)

Extending the Conversations

1. Drawing on several of the essays in this chapter, define *identity* and discuss its importance in our lives. Try to identify the various aspects of identity that you consider important, referring where appropriate to the essays in this chapter.

2. Several of the writers in this chapter, including Erin Aubry Kaplan and Bharati Mukherjee, directly address the issue of multiculturalism in their essays. Several other writers, such as Peggy Orenstein and Oscar Casares, implicitly discuss the diversity of American society. Drawing on several of the essays in this chapter, write an essay in which you present your own view of multiculturalism in contemporary American society. (For this essay, you may wish to do some research on multiculturalism as a movement or an idea. See the box labeled "Conversations: Multiculturalism" on page 121.)

3. Many writers in this chapter describe changes or transformations in the way they understand themselves and describe their identities. Let's assume this chapter was not called "Identity" but was called something like "Transformations." Select several of the essays in the chapter (or from other chapters) in which the authors describe some kind of important change or transformation in their sense of identity, and write an essay about these transformations. Try to examine these transformations so that you can draw conclusions about our identities and about how we can change over time.

4. Identify an issue—a problem or controversy or question—that emerges for you from one or more of the readings in this chapter. For example, several of the essays in this chapter discuss immigration. Identify such an issue that is important to you and, drawing on the relevant essays, discuss the issue and why it is significant. Present your own view of the issue and draw conclusions about the way the essays you have selected address that issue.

5. Write a dialogue involving Erin Aubry Kaplan, Oscar Casares, Bharati Mukherjee, or a combination of writers whose essays appear in this chapter about what it means to be an American. Alternatively, select several authors from this chapter and write a dialogue in which they address an issue or problem that emerges from their essays.

6. Several of the essays in this chapter describe places that are important to the author (for example, Bobbie Ann Mason, N. Scott Momaday). Write an essay in which you discuss the importance of place in identity. Draw on any authors in this chapter that seem appropriate to help support your points about place and identity.

7. Watch television commercials for a week or so, trying to vary your viewing habits so that you are seeing commercials that air during many different kinds of shows (such as sporting events, prime-time sitcoms, weekend news shows). Try to identify commercials that seem to have something to do with being an American. Select several such commercials and write an analysis of the way they seem to present the identity of an American.

8. Do the same kind of assignment described in Question 7 for another aspect of identity, such as race, gender, ethnicity, or culture.

9. In recent years, a number of new drugs have appeared on the market to treat male sexual dysfunction—for example, Viagra and Cialis. These drugs have been the focus of extensive advertising campaigns on television, radio, the Internet, and in print media. Examine some advertisements for these drugs in terms of what they might suggest about male and female identities. Write an essay in which you analyze such advertisements, drawing conclusions about the messages they seem to convey about being a man or a woman.

10. Working with a group of classmates, create an advertisement for a car or truck that depicts a certain kind of identity. Consider creating a web site or use the desktop publishing capabilities of your word processing program to create a print advertisement.

(You might review Chapter 2 of this book for advice on using images and visual elements in your ads.)

11. Select several popular songs and analyze them for what they suggest about identity.

12. Many popular films tell the story of someone whose identity changes in some way, either by personal choice or because of forces beyond an individual's control. In *American Beauty* (1999), for instance, the main character is a successful family man living in an American suburb who decides that his life is meaningless and sets about changing himself in several ways, which creates conflict with his wife, his coworkers, and others in his life. Select several such films that portray someone whose identity seems to change in important ways and write an essay in which you discuss how the films depict these changes. Draw conclusions about what these films might say about identity.

13. Visit several blogs and read them to get a sense of the writer's identity in each one. Consider how each writer presents himself or herself: what they reveal about their lives, how they describe themselves and their experiences, and their writing style or voice. Then write an essay in which you analyze how writers of blogs create their identities online and draw conclusions about the role of online technologies in creating identities.

Chapter **6** Understanding

Bettmann/CORBIS

MY DOG, SUMMIT, A TWELVE-YEAR-OLD GOLDEN RETRIEVER, IS LYING ON THE FLOOR NEAR MY DESK. SHE'S SNOOZING AT THE MOMENT, AS SHE OFTEN DOES WHEN I'M WRITING IN THE MORNING, BUT SOMETIMES I THINK SHE UNDERSTANDS WHAT I'M DOING. SHE SEEMS TO KNOW THAT EVERY MORNING AFTER I'VE FINISHED BREAKFAST

and poured a second cup of coffee, I'll sit down at my desk. So she follows me from the kitchen into my study and settles into a comfortable position near my desk. After an hour or two, she'll get up and look at me, as if to say, "Are you finished yet?" If I go into the kitchen for another cup of coffee, she won't move, though. She seems to know that I'm not yet finished writing. But if it's around noon, she'll follow me, expecting me to let her outside. And after I let her back in, she'll lie down in her customary spot near the kitchen table as I eat lunch. Sometimes, she'll pick up her head and stare at me with what seems to be a knowing expression on her face. And I can't help but wonder, "What is she thinking?"

> In other words, our daily lives are shaped so profoundly by our own thoughts, which seem to rush through our minds in a constant stream.

It may seem silly to wonder about what a dog might be thinking or even whether a dog *can* think. But we do. If you've spent any time with a dog or a cat or maybe a larger animal like a horse, you've probably asked yourself the same question. But why would we even bother to ask such a question? Maybe it's because of our own experience as thinkers. In other words, our daily lives are shaped so profoundly by our own thoughts, which seem to rush through our minds in a constant stream. And that constant stream of thought is an important part of how we experience the world around us and, more important still, how we experience ourselves in the world. It's only natural to wonder if animals like Sum-

mit, with whom we develop close bonds, might also *think* in some way.

Of course, philosophers, psychologists, and other theorists have been thinking about thinking for a long time. "I think; therefore I am," René Descartes, the influential eighteenth century philosopher, famously declared. What Descartes was saying is that the capacity to understand ourselves as beings in the world is what makes us human; in a sense, it's our intellect that gives us our very existence, for without this capacity to think in this way, we would not be aware of ourselves as we are. We'd be more like my dog, Summit, who certainly can learn and maybe can even *know,* but who is not aware of herself as a being in the way we humans are.

If you think about thinking like this for a while, soon you'll start wondering about related matters, like learning and knowing and education. Are these all the same thing? Philosophers and psychologists say no. They see important differences among these most basic cognitive activities. *Learning* something isn't the same thing as *knowing* something. And learning is not necessarily the same thing as *education;* in other words, you don't need formal education to learn something, and you know a great many things that you learned outside school. And of course, there's also the matter of *understanding.* What exactly does it mean to understand something? Is that the same thing as knowing? If not, what does learning or education have to do with understanding?

Now, I wasn't really thinking about all this when I first began to put together this chapter. Instead, I was trying to come up with a theme that would be a good category for some of the essays in this chapter about education. For instance, the essay by Paulo Freire called "The Banking Concept of Education" is one that I really wanted to include because it raises some important issues about education that I believe students should think about. But when you read Freire's essay (which is a very challenging piece of writing), you'll quickly see that it's not just about formal education. It's also about knowing and learning more broadly. His critique of formal education is based on certain ideas about knowing and learning—and yes, understanding—that he believes make us truly human. So to place his essay in a chapter about education makes sense, but it doesn't quite do justice to the complexity and the depth of his ideas.

The same is true of an essay like Maya Angelou's. This famous excerpt from her autobiography, *I Know Why the Caged Bird Sings,* describes her eighth-grade graduation ceremony at a racially segregated school in the American South in the 1930s. If you read it carefully, you realize that Angelou isn't just writing about the ritual of graduating from school or even about formal education in general. She's also describing an epiphany: a new and profound insight into who she was as a young Black girl. She's describing how she came to a different understanding about herself in society. So the category of education seemed too limited to classify this essay, too.

What Angelou and Freire and the other authors in this chapter are really writing about is how we understand ourselves and the world around us and how we come to that understand-ing. But they do so in the context of many different yet related conversations. The first cluster, for example, includes essays in which the writers describe personal journeys that lead to new ways of understanding themselves. You might say that these essays are part of a neverending process of learning that we all experience. The focus of the second cluster, "Schooling," is obvious, but I hope the essays in this cluster complicate and challenge your ideas about formal education. These essays are about formal education in some way, but they push us to think differently about what happens in schools and what we should expect from education. The third cluster, "Belief," shifts attention to the connection between what we think we know and what we believe. I might

> Learning something isn't the same thing as knowing something. And learning is not necessarily the same thing as education.

have called this cluster "Faith" or "Spirituality," and you might consider whether such a title for the cluster would have changed the way you read these essays, which examine how we as human beings make sense of our place in the world around us.

All three clusters are intended to get you to think in new ways about thinking. And I hope the readings in this chapter also help you appreciate the power of writing in our neverending efforts to understand ourselves and our world.

LEARNING

N 1995, POP SINGER ALANIS MORISSETTE RELEASED A SONG TITLED "YOU LEARN." HERE'S A PORTION OF THE LYRICS TO THAT SONG:

I recommend biting off more than you
    can chew to anyone
I certainly do
I recommend sticking your foot in your
    mouth at any time
Feel free
Throw it down (the caution blocks you
    from the wind)
Hold it up (to the rays)
You wait and see when the smoke clears
You live you learn
You love you learn
You cry you learn
You lose you learn
You bleed you learn
You scream you learn

In a sense, Morissette's song is one kind of answer to the question: What does it mean to learn? In her song, she suggests that we are learning all the time just by living. She suggests, too, that learning isn't always easy or obvious. In fact, we may learn most from our most difficult experiences.

Morissette's song repeats an insight that philosophers and psychologists have long known: We learn through experience. In fact, some philosophies and theories, such as the "pragmatist" philosophy of John Dewey and William James, are based on the idea that experience is central to all learning. This may seem commonsensical, but scholars have long tried to understand just how we do learn by experience.

The essays in this cluster might be considered part of that longstanding effort to examine how we learn from experience. They provide four angles on Morissette's song, for each essay describes a challenging or unusual circumstance that led to some important learning on the part of the writer. Take the essay by D. Winston Brown, for example. In some ways, his story about a frightening and potentially deadly experience is typical. It's an example of how we can learn important lessons by living through very difficult circumstances. In that sense, Brown's essay is one we can all relate to. But Brown's story is also one that examines part of what it means to be a Black man in American society, and that complicates his essay. I can understand how he learned something important about himself through his experience because I have gone through difficulties too, and I believe I learned from them. But I am a White man, and I have never been in a situation in which my life was directly at risk because of the prospect of violence. So I can't really say I know what that's like. But I can learn vicariously from Brown. In other words, the insights he has gained through his experience can be shared with me—and with you—through his writing, even if we can never really know what it's like to stare down the barrel of a gun.

Brown's essay is also a gripping story, and it reminds us that we often make sense of our experiences by telling stories. And if we learn by telling stories to each other, then we also learn through writing. By writing about their experiences, writers can gain insight into those experiences. Writing itself is learning.

The essays by Richard Wright and Annie Dillard are as compelling as Brown's, though in different ways. Each of these writers explores a different kind of experience that led to a new way of thinking, a new understanding of something. Sometimes the learning described in these essays is subtle, such as when Dillard gains insight into how to live by paying attention to a weasel that she observed near her home. Sometimes the learning arises from a lifetime of work and reflection. And sometimes the learning is dramatic, as was the case for Richard Wright, who had to fight racism to pursue a kind of learning that many of us take for granted.

But you don't need to have that kind of dramatic experience to learn. As Morissette's song suggests, learning happens. You just have to pay attention. I hope these essays help you do so.

ALANIS MORISSETTE, "YOU LEARN" FROM *JAGGED LITTLE PILL*.

When I was in the seventh grade, I bought a paperback copy of Battle Cry, *a novel by Leon Uris about the experiences of a group of young American marines fighting in the Pacific theater during World War II. I enjoyed reading military history and fiction, and I often read novels like* Battle Cry. *In school one day, during a study*

THE Library Card

period, my teacher noticed me reading and asked about the book. She borrowed it from me, returning it at the end of the day. As she gave it back to me, she asked, "Do you think you can handle this?" At the time, I assumed she was referring to the graphic descriptions of violence and sex in the book. But as I look back on that incident, I see that she was monitoring my reading. If she considered the book inappropriate for me, she may have contacted my parents. It's possible that the school might have tried to prevent me from reading the book.

I thought of that incident as I read the following excerpt from Richard Wright's autobiography, Black Boy *(1945). In this compelling passage, Wright describes his efforts to obtain books from a library at a time when it was risky for Blacks to do so. His story is about the impact of racism on the lives of Black Americans, which affected even what and how they*

RICHARD WRIGHT

ne morning I arrived early at work and went into the bank lobby where the Negro porter was mopping. I stood at a counter and picked up the Memphis *Commercial Appeal* and began my free reading of the press. I came finally to the editorial page and saw an article dealing with one **H. L. MENCKEN.** I knew by hearsay that he was the editor of the *American Mercury*, but aside from that I knew nothing about him. The article was a furious denunciation of Mencken, concluding with one, hot, short sentence: Mencken is a fool.

I wondered what on earth this Mencken had done to call down upon him the scorn of the South. The only people I had ever heard denounced in the South were Negroes, and this man was not a Negro. Then what ideas did Mencken hold that made a newspaper like the *Commercial Appeal* castigate him publicly? Undoubtedly he must be advocating ideas that the South did not like. Were there, then, people other than Negroes who criticized the South? I knew that during the Civil War the South had hated northern whites, but I had not encountered such hate during my life. Knowing no more of Mencken than I did at that moment, I felt a vague sympathy for him. Had not the

read. But it is also about the impact that reading can have on a person. Wright explores the effects of his reading on his sense of who he was as a Black man, and he describes how his reading helped him learn some difficult lessons. In many ways, his reading—as well as the writing he eventually did—changed him dramatically; it helped him gain a new understanding of himself. And it represented a challenge to the Whites who controlled the southern communities like the one where Wright grew up. In this regard, Wright's passage helps us understand why there have always been attempts to control what people read and write. It also helps us see why people will resist efforts to control their reading and writing.

Richard Wright (1908–1960) is considered one of the foremost American writers of the twentieth century. In addition to his autobiography, Black Boy, *he was author of a number of collections of stories, works of nonfiction, and novels, including* Native Son *(1940) and* Uncle Tom's Children *(1938). He was a passionate voice for the victims of oppression and a controversial figure in part because of his sympathies for the Communist Party.* ⬇

GLOSS: H. L. MENCKEN
Henry Louis Mencken (1880–1956), who is mentioned in the first paragraph, was one of the best-known writers and political observers of his time. A prolific author of newspaper columns as well as poetry and books of social commentary, he was known for his sharp wit and often biting criticisms of public figures and human nature. In paragraph 61, Wright offers his own description of Mencken's writing.

South, which had assigned me the role of a non-man, cast at him its hardest words?

Now, how could I find out about this Mencken? There was a huge library near the riverfront, but I knew that Negroes were not allowed to patronize its shelves any more than they were the parks and playgrounds of the city. I had gone into the library several times to get books for the white men on the job. Which of them would now help me to get books? And how could I read them without causing concern to the white men with whom I worked? I had so far been successful in hiding my thoughts and feelings from them, but I knew that I would create hostility if I went about the business of reading in a clumsy way.

I weighed the personalities of the men on the job. There was Don, a Jew; but I distrusted him. His position was not much better than mine and I knew that he was uneasy and insecure; he had always treated me in an offhand, bantering way that barely concealed his contempt. I was afraid to ask him to help me get books; his frantic desire to demonstrate a racial solidarity with the whites against Negroes might make him betray me.

Then how about the boss? No, he was a Baptist and I had the suspicion that he would not be quite able to comprehend why a black boy would want to read Mencken. There were other white men on the job whose attitudes showed clearly that they were Kluxers or sympathizers, and they were out of the question.

There remained only one man whose attitude did not fit into an anti-Negro category, for I had heard the white men refer to him as a "Pope lover." He was an Irish Catholic and was hated by the white southerners. I knew that he read books, because I had got him volumes from the library several times. Since he, too, was an object of hatred, I felt that he might refuse me but would hardly betray me. I hesitated, weighing and balancing the imponderable realities.

One morning I paused before the Catholic fellow's desk.

"I want to ask you a favor," I whispered to him.

"What is it?"

"I want to read. I can't get books from the library. I wonder if you'd let me use your card?"

He looked at me suspiciously.

"My card is full most of the time," he said.

"I see," I said and waited, posing my question silently.

"You're not trying to get me into trouble, are you, boy?" He asked, staring at me.

"Oh, no sir."

"What book do you want?"

"A book by H. L. Mencken."

"Which one?"

"I don't know. Has he written more than one?"

5

10

15

"He has written several."

"I didn't know that."   20

"What makes you want to read Mencken?"

"Oh, I just saw his name in the newspaper," I said.

"It's good of you to want to read," he said. "But you ought to read the right things."

I said nothing. Would he want to supervise my reading?   25

"Let me think," he said. "I'll figure out something."

I turned from him and he called me back. He stared at me quizzically.

"Richard, don't mention this to the other white men," he said.

"I understand," I said. "I won't say a word."

A few days later he called me to him.   30

"I've got a card in my wife's name," he said. "Here's mine."

"Thank you, sir."

"Do you think you can manage it?"

"I'll manage fine," I said.

"If they suspect you, you'll get in trouble," he said.   35

"I'll write the same kind of notes to the library that you wrote when you sent me for books," I told him. "I'll sign your name."

He laughed.

"Go ahead. Let me see what you get," he said.

That afternoon I addressed myself to forging a note. Now, what were the names of books written by H. L. Mencken? I did not know any of them. I finally wrote what I thought would be a foolproof note: *Dear Madam: Will you please let this nigger boy*—I used the word "nigger" to make the librarian feel that I could not possibly be the author of the note—*have some books by H. L. Mencken?* I forged the white man's name.

40   I entered the library as I had always done when on errands for whites, but I felt that I would somehow slip up and betray myself. I doffed my hat, stood a respectful distance from the desk, looked as unbookish as possible, and waited for the white patrons to be taken care of. When the desk was clear of people, I still waited. The white librarian looked at me.

"What do you want, boy?"

As though I did not possess the power of speech, I stepped forward and simply handed her the forged note, not parting my lips.

"What books by Mencken does he want?" she asked.

"I don't know, ma'am," I said, avoiding her eyes.

"Who gave you this card?"

"Mr. Falk," I said.   45

"Where is he?"

"He's at work, at the M—— Optical Company," I said. "I've been in here for him before."

"I remember," the woman said. "But he never wrote notes like this."

CONVERSATIONS: RACIAL SLURS

Wright tells us in paragraph 39 that when he forged the note to the librarian, he used the word "nigger." Notice how that racially charged word, which we consider a slur, carries several meanings in this scene. What are those meanings? Consider what that word might have meant in 1945, when Wright's book was published, compared to today. Consider, too, how Wright uses the word as a tool in this context. What might this scene reveal about the way political and historical context influences the meaning of words?

50   Oh, God, she's suspicious. Perhaps she would not let me have the books? If she had turned her back at that moment, I would have ducked out the door and never gone back. Then I thought of a bold idea.

"You can call him up, ma'am," I said, my heart pounding.

"You're not using these books, are you?" she asked pointedly.

"Oh, no, ma'am. I can't read."

"I don't know what he wants by Mencken," she said under her breath.

55   I knew now that I had won; she was thinking of other things and the race question had gone out of her mind. She went to the shelves. Once or twice she looked over her shoulder at me, as though she was still doubtful. Finally she came forward with two books in her hand.

"I'm sending him two books," she said. "But tell Mr. Falk to come in next time, or send me the names of the books he wants. I don't know what he wants to read."

I said nothing. She stamped the card and handed me the books. Not daring to glance at them, I went out of the library, fearing that the woman would call me back for further questioning. A block away from the library I opened one of the books and read a title: *A Book of Prefaces*. I was nearing my nineteenth birthday and I did not know how to pronounce the word "preface." I thumbed the pages and saw strange words and strange names. I shook my head, disappointed. I looked at the other book; it was called *Prejudices*. I knew what that word meant; I had heard it all my life. And right off I was on guard against Mencken's books. Why would a man want to call a book *Prejudices*? The word was so stained with all my memories of racial hate that I could not conceive of anybody using it for a title. Perhaps I had made a mistake about Mencken? A man who had prejudices must be wrong.

When I showed the books to Mr. Falk, he looked at me and frowned.

"That librarian might telephone you," I warned him.

60   "That's all right," he said. "But when you're through reading those books, I want you to tell me what you get out of them."

That night in my rented room, while letting the hot water run over my can of pork and beans in the sink, I opened *A Book of Prefaces* and began to read. I was jarred and shocked by the style, the clear, clean, sweeping sentences. Why did he write like that? And how did one write like that? I pictured the man as a raging demon, slashing with his pen, consumed with hate, denouncing everything American, extolling everything European or German, laughing at the weaknesses of people, mocking God, authority. What was this? I stood up, trying to realize what reality lay behind the meaning of the words . . . Yes, this man was fighting, fighting with words. He was using words as a weapon, using them as one would use a club. Could words be weapons? Well, yes, for here they were. Then, maybe, perhaps, I could use them as a weapon? No. It frightened me. I read on and what amazed

STRATEGIES: DETAILS
Notice the details in the first sentence of paragraph 61. Writers often use details not only to describe a scene or event but also to convey messages about that scene or event. What messages do these details convey?

me was not what he said, but how on earth anybody had the courage to say it.

Occasionally I glanced up to reassure myself that I was alone in the room. Who were these men about whom Mencken was talking so passionately? Who was Anatole France? Joseph Conrad? Sinclair Lewis, Sherwood Anderson, Dostoevski, George Moore, Gustave Flaubert, Maupassant, Tolstoy, Frank Harris, Mark Twain, Thomas Hardy, Arnold Bennett, Stephen Crane, Zola, Norris, Gorky, Bergson, Ibsen, Balzac, Bernard Shaw, Dumas, Poe, Thomas Mann, O. Henry, Dreiser, H. G. Wells, Gogol, T. S. Eliot, Gide, Baudelaire, Edgar Lee Masters, Stendhal, Turgenev, Huneker, Nietzsche, and scores of others? Were these men real? Did they exist or had they existed? And how did one pronounce their names?

I ran across many words whose meanings I did not know, and I either looked them up in a dictionary or, before I had a chance to do that, encountered the word in a context that made its meaning clear. But what strange world was this? I concluded the book with the conviction that I had somehow overlooked something terribly important in life. I had once tried to write, had once reveled in feeling, had let my crude imagination roam, but the impulse to dream had been slowly beaten out of me by experience. Now it surged up again and I hungered for books, new ways of looking and seeing. It was not a matter of believing or disbelieving what I read, but of feeling something new, of being affected by something that made the look of the world different.

As dawn broke I ate my pork and beans, feeling dopey, sleepy. I went to work, but the mood of the book would not die; it lingered, coloring everything I saw, heard, did. I now felt that I knew what the white men were feeling. Merely because I had read a book that had spoken of how they lived and thought, I identified myself with that book. I felt vaguely guilty. Would I, filled with bookish notions, act in a manner that would make the whites dislike me?

I forged more notes and my trips to the library became frequent. 65 Reading grew into a passion. My first serious novel was Sinclair Lewis's *Main Street.* It made me see my boss, Mr. Gerald, and identify him as an American type. I would smile when I saw him lugging his golf bags into the office. I had always felt a vast distance separating me from the boss, and now I felt closer to him, though still distant. I felt now that I knew him, that I could feel the very limits of his narrow life. And this had happened because I had read a novel about a mythical man called George F. Babbitt.

The plots and stories in the novels did not interest me so much as the point of view revealed. I gave myself over to each novel without reserve, without trying to criticize it; it was enough for me to see and feel something different. And for me, everything was something different. Reading was like a drug, a dope. The novels created moods in which I lived for days. But I could not conquer my sense of guilt, my

CONVERSATIONS: FAMOUS NOVELS

Wright refers to two novels by Theodore Dreiser, one of the best-known American novelists in the first half of the twentieth century. Dreiser's novels, especially *Sister Carrie* and *An American Tragedy,* are considered sharp criticisms of American capitalism. Wright himself came to sympathize with the anticapitalist views of the Communist Party. In a sense, Wright's reading helped shape his political and social views—as well as his own novels. His descriptions of the novels he read can be seen as an example of how fiction can be part of the broader discussions of social and political issues that are carried on in our society through the political process and the press.

CONVERSATIONS: JIM CROW

In the brief scene in paragraph 76, Wright describes some of the risks he faced as his anger about the way he was treated by Whites increased because of his reading. This scene gives us a glimpse into what life was like in the American South in the 1930s and 1940s, when Jim Crow laws (which Wright mentions earlier in par. 74) were in effect. These laws prohibited Blacks from certain activities and rights (such as voting) and created a climate of tension and fear, as Wright suggests in this passage. It's worth considering how Wright's reading was a challenge to the Jim Crow culture of the American South and how it might therefore be seen as subversive. This is what writers sometimes mean when they discuss the power of literacy.

feeling that the white men around me knew that I was changing, that I had begun to regard them differently.

Whenever I brought a book to the job, I wrapped it in newspaper—a habit that was to persist for years in other cities and under other circumstances. But some of the white men pried into my packages when I was absent and they questioned me.

"Boy, what are you reading those books for?"

"Oh, I don't know, sir."

"That's deep stuff you're reading, boy." 70

"I'm just killing time, sir."

"You'll addle your brains if you don't watch out."

I read **DREISER'S JENNIE GERHARDT AND SISTER CARRIE** and they revived in me a vivid sense of my mother's suffering; I was overwhelmed. I grew silent, wondering about the life around me. It would have been impossible for me to have told anyone what I derived from these novels, for it was nothing less than a sense of life itself. All my life had shaped me for the realism, the naturalism of the modern novel, and I could not read enough of them.

Steeped in new moods and ideas, I bought a ream of paper and tried to write; but nothing would come, or what did come was flat beyond telling. I discovered that more than desire and feeling were necessary to write and I dropped the idea. Yet I still wondered how it was possible to know people sufficiently to write about them? Could I ever learn about life and people? To me, with my vast ignorance, my Jim Crow station in life, it seemed a task impossible of achievement. I now knew what being a Negro meant. I could endure the hunger and I had learned to live with hate. But to feel that there were feelings denied me, that the very breath of life itself was beyond my reach, that more than anything else hurt, wounded me. I had a new hunger.

In buoying me up, reading also cast me down, made me see what 75 was possible, what I had missed. My tension returned, new, terrible, bitter, surging, almost too great to be contained. I no longer *felt* that the world about me was hostile, killing; I *knew* it. A million times I asked myself what I could do to save myself, and there were no answers. I seemed forever condemned, ringed by walls.

I did not discuss my reading with Mr. Falk, who had lent me his library card; it would have meant talking about myself and that would have been too painful. I smiled each day, fighting desperately to maintain my old behavior, to keep my disposition seemingly sunny. But some of the white men discerned that I had begun to brood.

"Wake up there, boy!" Mr. Olin said one day.

"Sir!" I answered for the lack of a better word.

"You act like you've stolen something," he said.

80 I laughed in the way I knew he expected me to laugh, but I resolved to be more conscious of myself, to watch my every act, to guard and hide the new knowledge that was dawning within me.

If I went north, would it be possible for me to build a new life then? But how could a man build a life upon vague, unformed yearnings? I wanted to write and I did not even know the English language. I bought English grammars and found them dull. I felt that I was getting a better sense of the language from novels than from grammars. I read hard, discarding a writer as soon as I felt that I had grasped his point of view. At night the printed page stood before my eyes in sleep.

Mrs. Moss, my landlady, asked me one Sunday morning:

"Son, what is this you keep on reading?"

"Oh, nothing. Just novels."

85 "What you get out of 'em?"

"I'm just killing time," I said.

"I hope you know your own mind," she said in a tone which implied that she doubted if I had a mind.

I knew of no Negroes who read the books I liked and I wondered if any Negroes ever thought of them. I knew that there were Negro doctors, lawyers, newspapermen, but I never saw any of them. When I read a Negro newspaper I never caught the faintest echo of my preoccupation in its pages. I felt trapped and occasionally, for a few days, I would stop reading. But a vague hunger would come over me for books, books that opened up new avenues of feeling and seeing, and again I would forge another note to the white librarian. Again I would read and wonder as only the naïve and unlettered can read and wonder, feeling that I carried a secret, criminal burden about with me each day.

That winter my mother and brother came and we set up housekeeping, buying furniture on the installment plan, being cheated and yet knowing no way to avoid it. I began to eat warm food and to my surprise found that regular meals enabled me to read faster. I may have lived through many illnesses and survived them, never suspecting that I was ill. My brother obtained a job and we began to save toward the trip north, plotting our time, setting tentative dates for departure. I told none of the white men on the job that I was planning to go north; I knew that the moment they felt I was thinking of the North they would change toward me. It would have made them feel that I did not like the life I was living, and because my life was completely conditioned by what they said or did, it would have been tantamount to challenging them.

I could calculate my chances for life in the South as a Negro fairly 90 clearly now.

I could fight the southern whites by organizing with other Negroes, as my grandfather had done. But I knew that I could never win that way; there were many whites and there were but few blacks. They were strong and we were weak. Outright black rebellion could never win. If I fought openly I would die and I did not want to die. News of lynchings were frequent.

CONVERSATIONS: THE DECLINE OF READING In 2004, A National Endowment for the Arts (NEA) released a report indicating that fewer Americans were reading novels, stories, plays, and poems. According to the NEA report, 10 percent fewer Americans were reading such literature in 2002 than in 1982. When the report was released, many observers and educators expressed alarm at these figures, suggesting that a decline in reading literature was detrimental to American society, which requires an educated citizenry to keep democracy healthy. It is interesting to consider the reaction to the NEA report in the context of this passage (par. 88) from Richard Wright's autobiography, which shows how reading literature could be risky in some ways and has also been controlled in our own country.

I could submit and live the life of a genial slave, but that was impossible. All of my life had shaped me to live by my own feelings, and thoughts. I could make up to **BESS** and marry her and inherit the house. But that, too, would be the life of a slave; if I did that, I would crush to death something within me, and I would hate myself as much as I knew the whites already hated those who had submitted. Neither could I ever willingly present myself to be kicked, as Shorty had done. I would rather have died than do that.

I could drain off my restlessness by fighting with **SHORTY AND HARRISON.** I had seen many Negroes solve the problem of being black by transferring their hatred of themselves to others with a black skin and fighting them. I would have to be cold to do that, and I was not cold and I could never be.

I could, of course, forget what I had read, thrust the whites out of my mind, forget them; and find release from anxiety and longing in sex and alcohol. But the memory of how my father had conducted himself made that course repugnant. If I did not want others to violate my life, how could I voluntarily violate it myself?

95   I had no hope whatever of being a professional man. Not only had I been so conditioned that I did not desire it, but the fulfillment of such an ambition was beyond my capabilities. Well-to-do Negroes lived in a world that was almost as alien to me as the world inhabited by whites.

What, then, was there? I held my life in my mind, in my consciousness each day, feeling at times that I would stumble and drop it, spill it forever. My reading had created a vast sense of distance between me and the world in which I lived and tried to make a living, and that sense of distance was increasing each day. My days and nights were one long, quiet, continuously contained dream of terror, tension, and anxiety. I wondered how long I could bear it.

GLOSS: BESS, SHORTY, AND HARRISON
Bess was a woman with whom Wright was in love and whom he describes elsewhere in his autobiography, *Black Boy,* from which this passage is excerpted. Shorty and Harrison are friends of his who are also described elsewhere in *Black Boy.*

Understanding the Text

1. What prompted Wright to try to obtain books from the library? What might this episode reveal about Wright as a person?

2. What is Wright's reaction to the books he reads by H. L. Mencken (par. 61–63)? Why do you think he focuses attention on Mencken's writing? What does Wright mean when he writes that reading Mencken's book convinced him that he "had somehow overlooked something terribly important" in his life? What was it that he had overlooked?

3. Why does Wright say that "reading was like a drug, a dope" for him? What does this simile suggest about reading? Do you think this is an appropriate simile to describe the effects of reading on him? Why or why not?

4. What dilemma does reading lead to for Wright? What does he realize as a result of confronting this dilemma? How does he resolve it? What does his dilemma suggest about the circumstances within which Blacks lived in the American South?

Exploring the Issues

1. In a sense, this excerpt from Wright's autobiography is a description of the effect of reading on one person. Examine the sections in this passage (par. 63–65 or par. 73, for example) in which Wright describes how he was affected by the specific books he read. What were the effects of these books on him? How did they change his thinking? Were there similarities in the way the different books he read affected him? Explain.

2. Imagine if you were prevented from having access to books, newspapers, the Internet, or other sources of information you use regularly. What impact might that have on your life? What might Wright's difficulties obtaining books tell us about reading and writing and their roles in our society?

Entering the Conversations

1. In paragraph 63, Wright tells us that after reading H. L. Mencken's book, he "hungered for books, new ways of looking and seeing." Write an essay about a time you experienced new ways of looking and seeing as a result of reading a book or having a profound experience.

2. Given Wright's descriptions about the power that Whites had over Blacks during the time he was growing up, I might have put this essay in Chapter 9 on power. Using Wright's essay and any of the essays in Chapter 9 that seem appropriate, write an essay in which you discuss the relationship between power and learning. In what ways did the power dynamics between Whites and Blacks affect Wright's learning? What do his experiences tell us about how such dynamics can hinder learning or result in certain kinds of learning?

 INFOTRAC

3. Throughout history, there have been many attempts to control what people read and even whether they can read. Today, we continue to see efforts to control reading and writing—from attempts by totalitarian governments to ban certain kinds of books to efforts by individuals and groups in the United States to prohibit schools from assigning certain books to students. Using InfoTrac College Edition and other appropriate resources, examine previous and current efforts to control writing and reading. Try to find examples of attempts to ban certain kinds of reading materials, and examine those examples to understand the reasons for them. Write a report in which you describe such efforts to control reading and writing. Describe these situations and explain the views of the people involved.

Draw conclusions about reading and writing on the basis of the examples you discuss.

4. This painting by Jacob Lawrence (1917–2000), an African American artist interested in the struggles of freedom during the Civil Rights Movement, depicts a scene entitled *The Library* (1960). Write an essay in which you analyze the messages this painting communicates about libraries and reading.

Jacob Lawrence, *The Library*, 1960

I have seen a weasel in the wild only once in my life, while I was sitting on the shore of a remote lake in the Adirondack Mountains in New York. The weasel appeared suddenly on a brush pile near the shore. Like Dillard, I found that brief encounter exhilarating. It was an unexpected moment of wonder when I was close to a wild creature that I had previously seen only in photographs—an opportunity to experience the wild more intimately than most of us usually do. But for

Living LIKE Weasels

Dillard, the chance encounter with a weasel takes on much greater meaning. It prompts her to reflect on her life in a profound way and to raise questions about the choices she has made about how to live. These seem to be weighty issues to ponder as a result of a brief glimpse of a wild creature. But perhaps that's part of what makes Dillard such a respected and popular writer. If you read carefully, you'll see that her vivid descriptions are more than descriptions; they are part of her efforts to explore complex ideas with seemingly simple prose. With careful choices of words, Dillard directs our attention to seemingly obvious things in which she sees great significance. Just as Dillard's observations of her surroundings can reveal surprises and insights, paying careful attention to her words can reward you with surprises and insights as

ANNIE DILLARD

A weasel is wild. Who knows what he thinks? He sleeps in his underground den, his tail draped over his nose. Sometimes he lives in his den for two days without leaving. Outside, he stalks rabbits, mice, muskrats, and birds, killing more bodies than he can eat warm, and often dragging the carcasses home. Obedient to instinct, he bites his prey at the neck, either splitting the jugular vein at the throat or crunching the brain at the base of the skull, and he does not let go. One naturalist refused to kill a weasel who was socketed into his hand deeply as a rattlesnake. The man could in no way pry the tiny weasel off, and he had to walk half a mile to water, the weasel dangling from his palm, and soak him off like a stubborn label.

And once, says Ernest Thompson Seton—once, a man shot an eagle out of the sky. He examined the eagle and found the dry skull of a weasel fixed by the jaws to his throat. The supposition is that the

well. Her essay reminds us that learning can happen unexpectedly and in the most mundane circumstances.

Annie Dillard (b. 1945) is the author of a number of books, including the award-winning Pilgrim at Tinker Creek *(1974) and* Teaching a Stone to Talk *(1982), in which the following essay was first published.* ◪

STRATEGIES: DESCRIPTION
In paragraphs 4 and 5, Dillard describes the area around her home, which she tells us is in "suburbia." Notice the kinds of details she includes in this description. Consider how these details focus your attention on specific aspects of her surroundings and how they convey a sense of Dillard's suburbia.

STRATEGIES: RHYTHM
Dillard begins paragraph 6 with a single word: *So.* That one-syllable word, which is not a complete sentence by itself, slows down the pace of this passage and changes the rhythm of her prose. It also serves as a transition from the description of the area around her home (par. 4 and 5) to the narrative about her encounter with the weasel. Notice that Dillard uses the word by itself again at the end of paragraph 10. Compare these two uses of the word. Do they accomplish the same things in each case? Dillard's use of the word *so* is a good example of a writer manipulating rhythm to achieve an effect or signal an important shift in a passage.

eagle had pounced on the weasel and the weasel swiveled and bit as instinct taught him, tooth to neck, and nearly won. I would like to have seen that eagle from the air a few weeks or months before he was shot: was the whole weasel still attached to his feathered throat, a fur pendant? Or did the eagle eat what he could reach, gutting the living weasel with his talons before his breast, bending his beak, cleaning the beautiful airborne bones?

*   *   *

I have been reading about weasels because I saw one last week. I startled a weasel who startled me, and we exchanged a long glance.

Twenty minutes from my house, through the woods by the quarry and across the highway, is Hollins Pond, a remarkable piece of shallowness, where I like to go at sunset and sit on a tree trunk. Hollins Pond is also called Murray's Pond; it covers two acres of bottomland near Tinker Creek with six inches of water and six thousand lily pads. In winter, brown-and-white steers stand in the middle of it, merely dampening their hooves; from the distant shore they look like miracle itself, complete with miracle's nonchalance. Now, in summer, the steers are gone. The water lilies have blossomed and spread to a green horizontal plane that is terra firma to plodding blackbirds, and tremulous ceiling to black leeches, crayfish, and carp.

5   This is, mind you, suburbia. It is a five-minute walk in three directions to rows of houses, though none is visible here. There's a 55 mph highway at one end of the pond, and a nesting pair of wood ducks at the other. Under every bush is a muskrat hole or a beer can. The far end is an alternating series of fields and woods, fields and woods, threaded everywhere with motorcycle tracks—in whose bare clay wild turtles lay eggs.

So. I had crossed the highway, stepped over two low barbed-wire fences, and traced the motorcycle path in all gratitude through the wild rose and poison ivy of the pond's shoreline up into high grassy fields. Then I cut down through the woods to the mossy fallen tree where I sit. This tree is excellent. It makes a dry, upholstered bench at the upper, marshy end of the pond, a plush jetty raised from the thorny shore between a shallow blue body of water and a deep blue body of sky.

The sun had just set. I was relaxed on the tree trunk, ensconced in the lap of lichen, watching the lily pads at my feet tremble and part dreamily over the thrusting path of a carp. A yellow bird appeared to my right and flew behind me. It caught my eye; I swiveled around—and the next instant, inexplicably, I was looking down at a weasel, who was looking up at me.

*   *   *

Weasel! I'd never seen one wild before. He was ten inches long, thin as a curve, a muscled ribbon, brown as fruitwood, soft-furred, alert. His face was fierce, small and pointed as a lizard's; he would have made a good arrowhead. There was just a dot of chin, maybe two brown hairs' worth, and then the pure white fur began that spread down his underside. He had two black eyes I didn't see, any more than you see a window.

The weasel was stunned into stillness as he was emerging from beneath an enormous shaggy wild rose bush four feet away. I was stunned into stillness twisted backward on the tree trunk. Our eyes locked, and someone threw away the key.

Our look was as if two lovers, or deadly enemies, met unexpectedly on an overgrown path when each had been thinking of something else: a clearing blow to the gut. It was also a bright blow to the brain, or a sudden beating of brains, with all the charge and intimate grate of rubbed balloons. It emptied our lungs. It felled the forest, moved the fields, and drained the pond; the world dismantled and tumbled into that black hole of eyes. If you and I looked at each other that way, our skulls would split and drop to our shoulders. But we don't. We keep our skulls. So.

He disappeared. This was only last week, and already I don't remember what shattered the enchantment. I think I blinked, I think I retrieved my brain from the weasel's brain, and tried to memorize what I was seeing, and the weasel felt the yank of separation, the careening splashdown into real life and the urgent current of instinct. He vanished under the wild rose. I waited motionless, my mind suddenly full of data and my spirit with pleadings, but he didn't return.

Please do not tell me about "approach-avoidance conflicts." I tell you I've been in that weasel's brain for sixty seconds, and he was in mine. Brains are private places, muttering through unique and secret tapes—but the weasel and I both plugged into another tape simultaneously, for a sweet and shocking time. Can I help it if it was a blank?

What goes on in his brain the rest of the time? What does a weasel think about? He won't say. His journal is tracks in clay, a spray of feathers, mouse blood and bone: uncollected, unconnected, loose-leaf, and blown.

*   *   *

I would like to learn, or remember, how to live. I come to Hollins Pond not so much **TO LEARN HOW TO LIVE** as, frankly, to forget about it. That is, I don't think I can learn from a wild animal how to live in particular—shall I suck warm blood, hold my tail high, walk with my footprints precisely over the prints of my hands?—but I might learn

10

CONVERSATIONS: LEARNING TO LIVE
In his classic book, *Walden,* Henry David Thoreau (1817–1862) explains his reasons for living alone in a small cabin in the forest this way: "I went into the woods because I wished to live deliberately, to front only the essential facts of life, and see if I could not learn what it had to teach, and not, when I came to die, discover that I had not lived." I wondered if Dillard had this passage in mind when she wrote, "I would like to learn, or remember, how to live" (par. 14). If so, she would be joining a longstanding conversation in Western culture about our relationship to the land.

something of mindlessness, something of the purity of living in the physical senses and the dignity of living without bias or motive. The weasel lives in necessity and we live in choice, hating necessity and dying at the last ignobly in its talons. I would like to live as I should, as the weasel lives as he should. And I suspect that for me the way is like the weasel's: open to time and death painlessly, noticing everything, remembering nothing, choosing the given with a fierce and pointed will.

15   I missed my chance. I should have gone for the throat. I should have lunged for that streak of white under the weasel's chin and held on, held on through mud and into the wild rose, held on for a dearer life. We could live under the wild rose wild as weasels, mute and uncomprehending. I could very calmly go wild. I could live two days in the den, curled, leaning on mouse fur, sniffing bird bones, blinking, licking, breathing musk, my hair tangled in the roots of grasses. Down is a good place to go, where the mind is single. Down is out, out of your ever-loving mind and back to your careless senses. I remember muteness as a prolonged and giddy fast, where every moment is a feast of utterance received. Time and events are merely poured, unremarked, and ingested directly, like blood pulsed into my gut through a jugular vein. Could two live that way? Could two live under the wild rose, and explore by the pond, so that the smooth mind of each is as everywhere present to the other, and as received and as unchallenged, as falling snow?

We could, you know. We can live any way we want. People take vows of poverty, chastity, and obedience—even of silence—by choice. The thing is to stalk your calling in a certain skilled and supple way, to locate the most tender and live spot and plug into that pulse. This is yielding, not fighting. A weasel doesn't "attack" anything; a weasel lives as he's meant to, yielding at every moment to the perfect freedom of single necessity.

I think it would be well, and proper, and obedient, and pure, to grasp your one necessity and not let it go, to dangle from it limp wherever it takes you. Then even death, where you're going no matter how you live, cannot you part. Seize it and let it seize you up aloft even, till your eyes burn out and drop; let your musky flesh fall off in shreds, and let your very bones unhinge and scatter, loosened over fields, over fields and woods, lightly, thoughtless, from any height at all, from as high as eagles.

Understanding the Text

1. How does Dillard encounter the weasel? Why is this encounter unusual or remarkable to her? What was it about this encounter that made such an impression on Dillard?

2. What do you think Dillard learns about herself in thinking about her encounter with the weasel?

3. What does Dillard believe she can learn from an animal like a weasel? Why does she believe that she missed her chance to live like a weasel? What does this reveal about her and her views about modern living?

Exploring the Issues

1. Dillard begins this essay with a description of weasels. What does this description suggest about weasels? Why do you think Dillard begins in this way? What ideas are introduced in this beginning that will become important in her essay?

2. In paragraph 10, Dillard describes in detail the look she exchanged with the weasel. Examine this description for what it seems to suggest about the weasel and about Dillard. Look especially at the figures of speech she uses in her description (for example, she describes the encounter as if "two lovers, or deadly enemies, met unexpectedly"). What do you think she is trying to convey through such figures of speech and through her choice of details?

3. Assess Dillard's use of metaphor in this essay—not only the specific metaphors she uses to describe scenes she has witnessed

but also the metaphor of living like a weasel. What ideas does that metaphor allow Dillard to convey? How effectively do you think that metaphor conveys her ideas?

4. How would you describe the tone of this essay? In additional to her detailed descriptions of her surroundings and her encounter with the weasel, Dillard also includes thoughts about how she lives her life and raises questions about how she should do so. What impact do these thoughts and questions have on the essay? How did you react to them? What might your reaction suggest about you as a reader?

Entering the Conversations

1. In an essay intended for your classmates, describe an encounter you had with wildlife or something else that struck you as special in some way. Write your essay in a way that might convey an idea or insight you gained from that encounter. Try also to convey a sense of what you learned about yourself.

2. Writers have long examined the idea that we humans can learn a great deal from nature. Dillard's essay can be seen as an example of such learning. Drawing on her essay and on any other essays that seem appropriate, write an essay in which you discuss how these writers understand nature and how and what they learn from their encounters with the natural world. (For this assignment, you might consider using the following essays: Scott Russell Sanders, "Stillness"; M. Scott Momaday, "The Way to Rainy Mountain"; E. B. White,

"Once More to the Lake"; or Melissa Pierson, "Losing Home."

INFOTRAC

3. Many educators argue that environmental education should be a required part of the school curriculum. One justification they offer for this requirement is that through environmental education students not only can learn more about preserving the environment but they can also learn about themselves, as Dillard did in this essay. Using InfoTrac College Edition and any other relevant resources, find out what environmental education is and how its proponents justify it. Try to find examples of schools and colleges where environmental education is a part of the curriculum. If possible, interview people in your own school who are involved in environmental education. Then, on the basis of your research, write a proposal in which you make a case for or against an environmental education curriculum at your school. (If your school already has such a curriculum, you can make a proposal for changing it in ways that you believe would improve it.) In your proposal, draw on your research to support your specific recommendations. Draw also on Dillard's essay and others like it.

4. Visit one or more blogs that focus on the environment in some way. Analyze the discussion on the blogs for how they seem to address our interactions with the natural world. Then, write an essay reporting on these blogs and what they seem to suggest about the lessons we learn as a result of our interactions with nature.

I once met a building contractor, a man about my age, who was not only a skilled builder but also seemed to have led a rich and interesting life. We talked as he worked one day, and somehow we stumbled onto the topic of gun ownership. I was surprised to learn that my contractor friend kept a handgun in his bedroom. When I asked why, he told

Both Sides of a Gun Barrel

me that a few years earlier, while walking alone on a city street, he had been beaten and robbed by three young men, one of whom had a gun. Ever since that night, my friend owned a gun—for protection, he said. Sometimes when I hear one of those all-too-frequent news reports about a shooting in a city neighborhood or a rural town, I think of that contractor and wonder whether he would ever actually use his gun if someone broke into his home. Thankfully, few of us ever have the opportunity to find out what it is like to point a loaded gun at another human being—or to have a loaded gun pointed at us. Writer D. Winston Brown is one of those few.

In the following essay, Brown tells the disturbing story of his experiences with guns as a young man living in a violent world. What Brown learns through these experiences is life-changing, but the lessons did not come easily. Like many young

D. WINSTON BROWN

I had risen early and removed every particle of dust and dirt from my 1979 Datsun 200SX. By the time I left the house shortly before noon, the car gleamed under the Alabama sunlight. I picked up Garrett, a friend with a penchant for Pink Floyd and bottled beer, and we drove to meet other friends, the whole time watching the daylight grow heavy and settle on the candy-apple-red sparkle.

As each hour passed and we changed locations—a clean car on a Saturday required frequent changes of venue—I never parked in the shade and, as dusk approached, sought out spots under streetlights. The car gleamed as we drank beer at each stop, in each new neighborhood. I drove the car slow; I played the music loud. Cameo was out then: the album with "Word Up" and "Candy." The crowd changed as the hours passed: two people riding, three people riding. We rode and drank and smoked and long after the sun had tired of us, a guy named Spoon, a classmate, climbed into the backseat. Spoon sat in the middle so he could stretch his long skinny arm between the front seats. Garrett and I, in the front seats, watched as Spoon pointed out the way to Annetta Simon's house. Spoon's idea. He knew her, said we needed to meet her.

D. WINSTON BROWN, "BOTH SIDES OF A GUN BARREL," CREATIVE NONFICTION, 2005. REPRINTED WITH THE PERMISSION OF CREATIVE NONFICTION.

I remember that his elbow was huge compared to the rest of his arm, like a tennis ball skewered on a mop handle. I remember we rode slowly through the night as if we were on the prowl. I remember the heat remained just shy of 99 degrees that night, and I fell in love with how the chill of beer on the back of my throat felt like time stopping before a slow drag of warm air delivered a thaw. I remember we were at a stoplight when Spoon slid his thin arm forward again, low, until I found myself transfixed by the gleam of a silver handgun, .38 caliber, which sat softly in the cushion of his palm.

I had seen guns before but never in my car.

5   This was not a year; this was a time. People were wearing **GUESS JEANS WITH LEATHER POCKET FLAPS** or Levi's 501 Blues. Polo was destroying Izod, and hip-hop was just beginning to strip the veneer from the unconscious ease of life. And guns—guns were not yet a fashion statement. So when Spoon reached his arm forward with his hand cradling the silver weapon, I possessed no preconstructed, cool response.

"Shit, Spoon. What the hell is that?"

"It's a gun," Spoon said.

"I know it's a gun," I said. "But what the fu-"

"Chill out," Spoon said. "I thought we could use it to scare-"

10   "Spoon," I said, "I ain't down for using no gun on a girl. If she don't want to-"

"Chill," Spoon said again. "I don't have to force any girls to do anything." He leaned his long head forward between the seats. "I thought we could get, I mean, scare them niggers who came by the school last week."

There had been a fight: Garrett and me versus three boys who'd come to our school as it was letting out. Garrett had walked out the door with his arm around the girlfriend of one of the boys. He had told her a joke, and they were laughing as they emerged from the school. I was behind them when I saw the boys approach. They were man-boys compared to us. Their blue jeans were creased and starched. Gold hung from their necks: herringbones wide as Band-Aids and rope chains weighed down by crosses. With each step, their faces curled into hardened scowls.

They shoved Garrett from behind. I dropped my books and ran toward them. From there, it progressed like most any fight, a slow-motion blur of fists and cuss words and falling and kicking. We, surprisingly, held our own. It slammed to a halt, all of the jumbled confusion, when one of the boys pulled out a gun. It looked old and dull and more like a prop than a weapon, but there was no denying it was a gun. He held his arm straight and placed the barrel inches away from my head. What he said I don't remember. I fixated on the gold-nugget rings he wore on three of his fingers. I remember thinking that as long as I could see the shine of those rings I was still alive. I heard someone cry, "No." I heard someone's sneakers squeak in the doorway behind me. Down the block, a car's engine revved. The moment flooded with isolated

people, Brown was caught up in the violence that sometimes mars our neighborhoods, but it was his father's own terrifying encounters with violence that helped Brown make sense of his experience with guns. His essay is an example of the painful lessons that can sometimes be learned as a result of decisions we make. Brown hopes his essay will help other young Black men learn from his experiences. It may also complicate the way you think about the causes of violence and its effects on young people.

D. Winston Brown's short fiction has appeared in many publications and earned him numerous awards. The following essay, which first appeared in the journal Creative Nonfiction, *was reprinted in* Utne *and in the* Best American Nonrequired Reading 2007.

STRATEGIES: SETTING THE SCENE
Notice the details Brown uses in paragraph 5 to set the scene for the events he is about to describe. He does not indicate the year when these events occurred, but he selects details carefully to evoke a sense of the 1980s as he experienced them. Consider how these details not only evoke that time but also help establish the mood of this essay. Consider, too, how Brown's descriptions help convey a sense of tension. If you have heard your writing teacher talk about using details carefully to convey a message, this passage is a good example of what he or she meant.

CONVERSATIONS: FACT OR FICTION

In this passage, Brown seems to suggest that we can never completely trust our memories of an event, especially when that event is as traumatic as having your life threatened. But the idea that our memories are untrustworthy raises questions about the accuracy and truth of a story. We accept Brown's story as factual because he tells us it happened to him. But the question of what is fact or fiction is not always straightforward. James Boswell's famous biography of the great British writer Samuel Johnson, published in 1791 and considered by many critics to be the greatest biography ever written, has been questioned by scholars who have found serious inaccuracies in it and who suggest that Boswell invented many of the events he describes in the book. More recently, controversies have emerged over books that have been presented as memoirs but were found to contain fabricated information or events. One of the best known of these controversies occurred in 2005 and involved the writer James Frey, whose memoir about his life as a drug dealer, *A Million Little Pieces* (2003), was promoted by the popular television talk show host Oprah Winfrey. After journalists raised questions about the accuracy of Frey's book, he admitted on Oprah's show that much of what he wrote in his book did not happen as he described it, but he insisted that the basic truth of his story was still valid. As you read Brown's story about his own life, it's worth considering Brown's statement in this paragraph that his memory of his own experiences seems unclear. How might that change the way you read his essay? Should it? To what extent must a story be factual to be true?

sounds: squeaks, gasps, jangled keys, running feet. I struggled to hear what I didn't want to hear—the crack of the gun when it fired.

It never came.

A gun to the head. A crowd of witnesses. A world slowed down to a single moment. What did I feel? I asked myself that for days, weeks, years. I tried sometimes to re-create the moment in my head, but memory and desire are too strong to be kept separated; they blend and produce mutated offspring. **THE FACTS ALWAYS CHANGED WHEN I TRIED TO REMEMBER.** Even when other students told me what they'd seen—that I'd stood motionless, didn't blink, didn't flinch or cower—it felt unfamiliar, nothing like the perfectly still free-fall I felt whenever I tried to remember on my own.

There was one person, Jeremy McGetty, who witnessed that after-school brawl and described how I'd reacted in one word: *reconciled*. I asked him to elaborate. "Reconciled with the possibility," he told me, "of both living and dying." Then, revising slightly, he said, "Reconciled with dying."

Reconciled became a refrain in my head. It didn't fit. A decent student with a middle-class background, a product of an insulated private school, I was not supposed to be someone who reconciled his life with dying. I knew people who had, maybe, reconciled, at least with their situations. They didn't come to school often. But my older brother and I were on our way to being third-generation college graduates. I knew my destiny because my family taught it to me, day after day, in deed and word. I thought about being reconciled with parental guidance. With the expectation of table manners. With Christmases where gifts crowded around the tree. But not with death. Yet, when I thought of it—of that description of my reaction—my blood surged: I felt pleased, thrilled even, that in that moment I had not retreated, not shrunk. I reconciled.

I can recall few details of the six days that passed between my conversation with Jeremy McGetty and seeing that gun in my car. I can still clearly see the gleaming gun.

But this is not about guns. This is not a celebration of violence, nor is it a refutation of guns or violence. It is not that simple. Black boys, guns, anger. No matter the economic class of the boys, no matter the education, no matter the professional position, we seldom lose that head-nod to another brother or that anger, caged and carried in spines, which skirts just below the skin, racing or prodding alongside blood. But this is not about anger either—at least not in the simple sense. There is no simple answer to how a gun in my car became a primal summons.

To understand something, anything, about that moment requires   20
another story, one in which I am only a witness.

I was 12. It was late, and I was asleep.

When my father woke me, he didn't tickle me or nudge me or call me one of his many nicknames. He used my name—Daryl—and repeated his request for me to wake up and dress only once. His tone was unrecognizable, and the request was a commandment.

For years after, when I talked about this night, I described my father's voice—depending on the audience—as alternately stark or angry or full of rage, sometimes loud, sometimes louder. It took nearly a decade for me to know that his voice was reconciled.

My father drove a long, brown Buick LeSabre. Alone on the backseat, I felt like the sole person on a church pew. We passed through empty streets with no regard for streetlights or stop signs. My mother sat in the front passenger seat without a single comment about our speed.

Something had happened to my brother at a party. He was older, a   25
junior in high school, and he was indestructible, so my parents' level of quiet concern didn't alarm me. Instead, I sat on the backseat with my mind excited by what I'd seen my father place next to him on the seat: his gun. My history with this gun: I'd seen my father fire it into the sky on the Fourth of July, and once I'd snuck into my parents' bedroom, with my brother, and peered into my father's file cabinet at the gun. My brother had clapped his hands, a loud smack I just knew was gunfire. I had dropped to the floor and held my breath until I heard his taunting laughter.

When we arrived at our destination, my father swept up the gun and rushed out of the car. People crowded the driveway. I saw my brother. He looked fine. He and a friend, I learned, had been attacked by a gang: BAQ. This gang was the terror of Birmingham then, and because my brother had taken them on and emerged with only bruises and scrapes—minus one Armitron calculator watch—he would become even more one-dimensional to me: indestructible, tough, cool.

My father had walked away as my mother and I walked toward the house. He and his gun had climbed back into the car and disappeared. While he was gone, and after I'd nosed my way into complete knowledge of what had happened to my brother, I began to create scenarios in my head: my father riding with his lights out; my father finding the BAQ members, draped by slinky women in short skirts and hanging out on car hoods, drinking beer; my father pulling out his gun, demanding the return of my brother's calculator watch. I drifted toward the street and listened for gunfire, but the night offered only unbroken silence.

When my father returned, he did it as if he'd only been to the store for a pack of cigarettes. He didn't tell where he'd been, and no one asked. I waited for him to say something. The mood evolved into jokes and laughter, and the men drank beer. I felt cheated; my curiosity was not satisfied. When we drove home, we did it slowly. I leaned forward to glimpse the gun, but the seat between my parents held nothing. Finally, I stretched out and fell asleep.

There is nothing original in that anecdote. A man, his son, and the need to protect. At 12, I didn't understand that level of protection. But I understood embarrassment. I understood pride. Protection was pushing someone when they pushed me. It was also associated with things: gold chains, a new pair of Nikes, clean cars with bumping stereos. These things, I learned, deserved protection, deserved my blood if need be. We all knew this, and we all knew an infraction—like stepping on someone's new Air Jordans—meant a fight was inevitable. Years later, fists would turn to knives, and knives would turn to guns, but when I was 12, a father, a gun, and a gang-attacked brother were only exciting.

30   You never know exactly how one story will fit on top of another, how the brain will create its own truth to satisfy your deepest needs. Things may happen discretely, days apart, months apart, cities and decades and neighborhoods apart, but history collapses, then memory, and nothing ever remains discrete. Isolation is the lie we tell ourselves to comfort ourselves, but connections stretch the prisms we see through to allow more in, and more always changes things. Long before my father carried his gun as a weapon, history had constructed my prism, as it had for so many other young black boys. It was an unspoken history, so I didn't truly comprehend why I instinctively bristled at the word *nigger* or why the white guard at the jewelry store followed my father, my brother, and me while we shopped for a Christmas gift for my mother, or what it meant when some white child, some innocent classmate at my 98 percent white private school, said he couldn't come spend the night because his grandfather told him that he "didn't need to be going to no nigger's house in a nigger neighborhood." He said *black,* but I heard *nigger* even then, and I hit him. It's that anger—history's long and subtle voice—that, when it is misunderstood, becomes a simmering hostility.

Years later, I would deromanticize that night, unravel the cowboy dreams I'd dressed it in and begin the work of understanding what my father did, what my father had been willing to do. But first, I would have to encounter my car, Garrett, Spoon, me, and the gun.

I didn't consciously think about my father and his gun when Spoon stretched his weapon forward like an offering. I merely accepted it. In my hand, the gun felt heavy, solid. It contained no fun, no play, and we rode the next few blocks in silence. Not a reflective silence. Reflection would have demanded too much of me. I spent those few blocks divorcing myself from what I was about to do. There was justice to be exacted—and revenge. I thought of him only as The Boy.

What I know now and couldn't have known then is that we—so many young, black boys—had moved beyond simply being frightened by the brutal world. Progress in this country since the first slaves, though slow and incremental and often delivered reluctantly, had nonetheless been steady. Each decade, each era, you could mark notables: **BUFFALO SOLDIERS, MARCUS GARVEY, A.C. POWELL, *BROWN V. BOARD*, WRIGHT, ELLISON, MARTIN, MALCOLM, CIVIL RIGHTS LEGISLATION.** Then something died. Hard to pin exactly what and where, but the effect was crushing. Maybe, as James Baldwin writes in *The Fire Next Time*, psychological death happened first when black soldiers returned from World War II in search of home but, instead, lost hope as **AMERICA SPURNED THEM.** If so, that same death knell finally tolled as the '60s expired, when we, the ghost children of Dynamite Hill and American capitalism, sensed a similar loss of hope. Faith and charity were scarce, too. We no longer asked, Why hast Thou forsaken me? We accepted our forsakenness, assumed it as a status quo that would never bend but might, one day, break. Not that we gave up on God; we just no longer waited on divine intervention. If God had not rescued this country from its black heart, how could he help a black man put food on the table, buy a house, feel good about bringing a son into a country that had spent the better part of its youth denying those sons the right to be men? No one needed to tell us of this legacy; its impatient and simmering anger fell into our bones. Without a reason for patient faith, we fell into the acquisition of now—of seizing everything and every dream, now. For many boys, life and death fell, with the weight of a Bible, into the hand that wielded the gun. We were not adrift, not without direction, but we knew, without knowing, the invisible barrier that often stood between possibility and us. This was an old war, and we didn't know how to fight it. So we fought and killed each other. We battled over gold chains and gym shoes, over ghetto blasters and Gazelles and four-finger gold rings. These things symbolized style, and style was manhood.

What we have learned to fight for, to protect, is not an easy path to trace. What makes it real? The list is far too long: the atrocity of slavery; the 1921 race riots in Tulsa; the inherited memory of lynching; the murders of Medgar Evers and Emmett Till; burned-in mental images of water cannons blasting people down sidewalks, police dogs ripping the clothes of marchers, children locked into paddy wagons. Just pick one from this short list. I came to understand why I took that gun from Spoon only after hearing for the first time a story that I'd heard at least 20 times before.

GLOSS: THE CIVIL RIGHTS MOVEMENT
The people and events Brown mentions in this paragraph figure prominently in the American Civil Rights Movement. The Buffalo Soldiers were Blacks, including many former slaves, who served in the U.S. Army in the 19th and 20th centuries and fought in campaigns against American Indians in the western United States as well as in the Spanish–American War, in the Philippines, and in World Wars I and II. Marcus Garvey was a controversial Black leader in the early 20th century who promoted Black separatism. Adam Clayton Powell, a controversial U.S. Representative from Harlem, served in Congress from 1944 to 1970 and promoted civil rights. Richard Wright, Ralph Ellison, and James Baldwin are critically acclaimed African American writers. Martin Luther King, Jr., and Malcolm X were prominent leaders in the Civil Rights Movement. *Brown v. Board* refers to the landmark Supreme Court decision in 1954 striking down the segregation of American schools. In paragraph 34, Brown refers to other important events in the Civil Rights Movement, including the murders of the Black civil rights activist Medgar Evers in Mississippi in 1963 by a White man and Emmett Till, a fourteen-year-old who was beaten to death in Mississippi in 1955 by White men for allegedly whistling at a White woman.

CONVERSATIONS: VIOLENCE AND RACISM
In this paragraph, Brown reviews some of the history of racism in the United States to help explain why young Black men have sometimes been caught up in the kind of violence he himself experienced. In doing so, Brown is joining a longstanding, complicated, and contentious conversation in the United States about racism, race relations, justice, and equality. Notice that Brown refers to key figures and events in the Civil Rights movement in the United States. Consider what those references might suggest about how Brown understands his place in this ongoing conversation. What might his story contribute to the conversation?

35   It takes place on Dynamite Hill. It involves a boy, a garage where several men sit in a car without closing the garage door or turning on any lights, and a bedroom closet full of guns. Dynamite Hill was a thriving neighborhood filled with blacks of all classes and professions. In the middle of it all was a lawyer who became a target for racists during the late '50s. Arthur Davis Shores was a small man physically, but he fought with a savage intellect to make significant changes: He stood up to racism one court case at a time. In return, his house was dynamited—several times. It probably would have happened more often had it not been for the men who decided to maintain a protective vigil, across the street in the dark garage. My grandfather, a high school football coach, was one of them.

Every day, close to dusk, a car would back into my grandparents' garage. The door would remain open. Three, sometimes four, men would pile into the car as darkness came. My grandmother, also a schoolteacher, would cook a meal or snacks to get them through the night. The men never took the key out of the ignition. They had lookouts who walked the sidewalks. They communicated with walkie-talkies. My father, a boy of 10 or 11, also had a role. Every evening he was responsible for going into my grandparents' bedroom closet and retrieving the weapons. Not handguns, but rifles. The men didn't mean simply to deter—they meant to kill, if necessary.

I don't know everything they did during those nights. But I do know three things. One: My father, already proficient with guns, was a child nonetheless and still prone to concentration lapses. The story he tells involves him hurriedly swooping the rifles into his arms without first checking the safeties. One of the rifles fires and a hole opens in the ceiling, scarring the house my grandmother keeps immaculate. Two: The hole, for a long time, is not repaired. My grandmother hates guns and wants the hole to be a reminder. Three: Later that night, a call comes in over the walkie-talkie. A lookout sees someone walking near Mr. Shores' house, and he believes he saw the person toss something that was lit. The men rush from the garage. My father follows. They surround the suspect. He's white, a teenager. Guns are drawn. The interrogation reveals that the suspect lives blocks away, and he is out walking so that his mother won't catch him smoking a cigarette. He tells them he tossed the cigarette butt in the grass. The white boy goes home; the black men resume their vigil. My father is now a witness.

My grandfather and his partners wielded violence to protect. I don't assume that senseless killing didn't happen prior to my teenage years, but I do know that I lived through an evolution, one where guns became common, where boys wanting to be men no longer fought one another but shot to kill. And over what? Not for social change or to protect a neighbor. But over jewelry. Over cars. Over trendy gym shoes. Over blocks of faded, cracked pavement.

But I'd not yet arrived at these thoughts the night Spoon and Garrett watched me play with the silver gun while we sat at a red light. I felt I'd been given something I needed. We drove until we saw a group of teenagers. They were laughing and joking. Then Spoon pointed to someone who'd drifted away from the crowd. I recognized him. My hand tightened around the gun. I wanted him to feel what I'd felt, and I wanted to feel the power he'd felt. I pulled the car to a stop. He was running before I fully extended my arm. I fired. He kept running toward the crowd. I fired again, followed him with the gun's barrel, sliding my arm along the door, and fired again. People ran, open-mouthed, and they looked like puppets, toys, not real. I kept The Boy in sight. I fired until the gun emptied, and then **I HEARD THE SCREAMS,** noticed the fear of the people running.

40   I've never gotten over how good it felt, the physicality of that un-challenged power; it threw me into some sort of high. I remember driving away, all three of us whooping in the electric delight of conquest. I remember drinking a beer and feeling as if my blood still vibrated from firing the gun. I loved feeling like that, but then—as quick as a book slammed shut—I feared it. That fear crept through me when I watched the late, late news that night and when I read the newspaper the next morning. When I went to school Monday, I spent several classes glancing at the door, expecting to see policemen crash through.

Nothing happened. Life went on.

My friends, the ones who knew, just laughed. They treated me like a victorious general. They nosed around intently for facts, and they laughed when they learned I'd hit nothing. I became something different to them, and to myself. I fired no more guns during high school or after. I don't really know what happened to Spoon. He dropped out of high school, and I saw him a few times, hanging outside of parties or at George Ward Park on Sundays. Garrett became a drug addict whose ravaged body quit a few years shy of his 25th birthday. As for me, I heard the clap of that gun for years in my sleep, until it eventually faded.

Then, when I heard my father's story again, I thought of my twisted attempt at manhood, at pride. Somewhere along the way, my father succeeded in handing down to me a better ideal of manhood. I went on to college and a career, but I know so many others who didn't. I still see them occasionally, and I remember how we were all boys, at some point, who dreamed of manhood. Unfortunately, America has a long history of discouraging its darker-hued sons from becoming men, and from that discouragement has risen a legacy of anger. Anger at poll taxes. At separate but equal. At the murder of **AMADOU DIALLO.** At the murder of **JAMES BYRD JR.** At the language and practice of racism in all its old guises and modern disguises.

STRATEGIES: ESTABLISHING PACE AND RHYTHM
This essay contains many passages in which Brown describes a scene or narrates the events of his past. Notice how Brown uses sentence structure and word choice in this paragraph to create a rhythm that quickens the pace of the scene. His sentences in this passage are mostly short and simple, and he avoids multisyllabic words, which would slow readers down. These strategies enable him to narrate these events in a way that is intended to make the scene more vivid.

GLOSS: AMADOU DIALLO AND JAMES BYRD, JR.
Amadou Diallo was a 23-year-old immigrant from Guinea who was shot by New York City police in 1999 as they searched for a crime suspect near Diallo's home; he was unarmed at the time and not connected to the crime being investigated. James Byrd, Jr., was a 49-year-old Black man who was tortured and murdered by three White men in Jasper, Texas, in 1998; the men were later charged and convicted under a hate crime law.

I don't know who said it first, but I remember my father telling me something he said his father told him: A man ain't nothin' but a man. As children do, I shrugged it off when I was young, but, as children do, I recalled it later and began the difficult work of understanding his stories and what they meant to me, for me. Sometimes, I suppose, what a society fractures in its sons is something only a father can heal. This is not to discount mothers, but it often takes a man to guide a boy into becoming a man.

45   These days, when I look at boys dressed in identical brand-name clothes; boys who speak perfect English in public spaces; or boys with their baseball caps tilted to the side, their jeans slung low, their teeth encased in platinum and diamonds, their heads covered in perfect cornrows or their biceps adorned with R.I.P. tattoos, I know all they want in life is to be men—and I know they are doubtful or scared they may not be given the chance. The truth about those dragons that lie in wait for them fuels a naked and aggressive and urgent ambition to compete in America's marketplace. This need manifests as an electric vitality that permeates American culture, giving it life and allowing its consumers to come close to the void—to play in the darkness—without risk. Meanwhile, the black boys who huddle like alchemists, creating and recreating opportunity where it doesn't exist, allow our real (and historical) anger to propel us at a furious pace toward dreams we refuse to defer. And though it is not possible, we do want to put down that anger gifted to us by a generation and a country that have yet to fulfill their obligation to show us how to prosper and evolve while dealing with and standing in the darker legacy of our manhood. Until this happens, as many ingredients shall fuel us—a deep and buried anger being one of them—as have contributed to the complex and tragic creation of these United States.

Understanding the Text

1. Early in his essay, Brown tells us that a friend who saw another young man hold a gun held to Brown's head described Brown's reaction as "reconciled." What did he mean? Why is Brown pleased by his friend's use of that word at the time? How does Brown's reaction to that word relate to his larger point in this essay?

2. In paragraph 19, Brown states that "there is no simple answer to how a gun in my car became a primal summons." What does he mean by that statement? In what sense was the gun a "primal summons"? What does that term suggest about Brown's role in that incident and about the roles of the other young men? And why is there no simple reason for that gun being in Brown's car?

3. What does the story of Brown's brother have to do with Brown's own story about his encounters with guns? What does he mean when he writes, in paragraph 31, that he would eventually "deromanticize" the night he witnessed his father bring out a gun to protect his brother? Why is it important that Brown "deromanticize" that event?

4. What is the difference between Brown's experience with guns and his father's and grandfather's experiences with guns? When does Brown come to realize this differ-ence? Why is this difference significant to Brown?

5. What does Brown learn from his experience with guns? How does he relate his experience to the young Black men he describes in the essay's final paragraph?

Exploring the Issues

1. Brown tells us that more than one story is required to understand the pivotal moment of the main story in the essay. Examine the stories Brown tells in this essay and how they relate to one another. How does each story help Brown make his point in the essay? What themes or ideas do these stories enable Brown to explore? How effectively do you think Brown weaves these stories together?

2. In paragraph 15, Brown writes, "I tried sometimes to re-create the moment in my head, but memory and desire are too strong to be kept separated; they blend and produce mutated offspring. The facts always changed when I tried to remember." Later, in paragraph 30, he writes, "You never know exactly how one story will fit on top of another, how the brain will create its own truth to satisfy your deepest needs." What do you think Brown is saying about memory in these passages? If our memory of an experience is not dependable, how do we really know what happened? Does it matter? What do you think Brown's essay suggests about the "truth" of the stories we tell about our lives? What might his essay suggest about the purposes of telling stories?

3. In telling the stories of his father's and grandfather's experiences with guns and violence, Brown refers to an "evolution" that took place by the time he was a teen (see par. 38). What does Brown mean by this term? How does he explain the changes he describes in the gun violence that his father's and grandfather's generations experienced and the gun violence of his own generation? Do you think his explanation is valid? Why or why not?

4. Throughout this essay, Brown refers to manhood and the process of becoming a man. In the final paragraph of the essay he also refers to "the darker legacy of our manhood." What does "manhood" mean to Brown? What is its "darker legacy" for him and other Black men? What does this idea of manhood have to do with the violence Brown experienced in his youth and the violence he sees among young Black men today? What might Brown's essay suggest about the role of gender in how we understand ourselves and our experiences?

Entering the Conversations

1. Write an essay about an experience you had, perhaps a very difficult experience, that helped you learn something important or helped you gain a better understanding of yourself.

2. In a sense, Brown's essay is an attempt to explain the violence that he sees among young Black men and to understand the historical factors that might have contributed to that violence. Violence among young people—and especially among young Black men—is a controversial topic that has been addressed not only by writers like Brown but also by social scientists, politicians, and educators. Using InfoTrac and other appropriate sources, look into this question of youth violence and especially the question of race and violence. How prevalent is youth violence? Are there different rates of violence among young people of different racial backgrounds? Try to find information to answer such questions. Also, try to find out what social scientists have learned about the causes and effects of this

violence. Then, write a report in which you present what you have learned about this topic.

3. On the basis of your research for Question 2, write an editorial essay for a newspaper in your region in which you offer your own perspective on youth violence and what can be done to stop it.

4. Many films and television shows address the same topics of violence and racism that Brown explores in his essay. Select several such films and/or television shows, such as the Academy Award–winning film *Crash* (2006) or the television show *The Wire,* and examine the way they portray violence and its connection to race. How do they seem to explain this connection? How is violence depicted in them? Then write an essay on the basis of your analysis. In your essay, describe the way violence and its connection to racism are presented in the films or shows you viewed, and look for similarities and differences among the films and shows. Draw conclusions

about how the relationship between violence and race seems to be depicted in mainstream media.

Alternatively, select a single recent film or television show and write a review in which you focus on the film's or show's portrayal of violence and its connection to race.

5. Write an analysis of Brown's narrative technique in this essay. In your analysis, examine how Brown organizes his narrative and incorporates the stories of his brother, father, and grandfather. Look also at how Brown uses language, especially descriptive detail and rhythm, to help him tell his story. Draw conclusions about the effectiveness of Brown's technique. In your analysis, you might compare Brown's writing with other writers in this textbook who also use narrative techniques in their essays.

6. Rewrite the essay you wrote for Question 1 using some of what you learned about Brown's narrative technique for Question 5.

SCHOOLING

MOST AMERICANS SHARE THE EXPERIENCE OF GOING TO SCHOOL. APPROXIMATELY 96 PERCENT OF SCHOOL-AGED CHILDREN (UP TO ABOUT THE AGE OF SIXTEEN) ATTEND SCHOOL, AND STATES HAVE VARIOUS LAWS THAT MANDATE SCHOOL ATTENDANCE.

That means just about everyone you know has been to school. And the experience of school is remarkably similar, whether you're in a small rural town like Pinedale, Wyoming, or a huge city like Los Angeles. There are obvious differences between these situations, but the basic elements of schooling are the same for everyone: the courses, the curriculum, the way classrooms look, the way the school day is structured, and, of course, the tests, the homework, the rules, the extracurricular activities, and the ceremonies like school assemblies and graduation. I'm guessing that nothing in this list sounds unfamiliar to you. And I find that pretty remarkable: Despite the great focus on diversity in our culture in recent decades and despite the great value that Americans place on individuality, if you look at schools, what you see is sameness.

At least, that's what I see. But there's more to schooling than meets the eye, and that's what this cluster of readings is all about. These essays go beyond "readin', writin', and 'rithmetic." They examine some of the complicated learning that occurs in school that is not always obvious and not always intended. These writers prompt us to look more closely at what we are learning in school, and they help us see that we learn much more in school than the material we study for tests. And what we learn in schools may not always be positive or beneficial.

Maya Angelou's description of her eighth-grade graduation, for example, is not a typical essay of celebration and hope, as you might expect in an essay about a graduation. For Angelou, graduating from a segregated school in the American South was a hard lesson in some of the realities of being Black in the United States. In some ways, that lesson contradicted the lessons she had learned in her classes. And because of that contradiction, Angelou's essay asks us to rethink some of our most basic beliefs about what education is for and who benefits from it. Like Angelou, famed education theorist Paulo Freire prompts us to rethink our beliefs about education. But his purpose is somewhat more pointed: He offers a harsh critique of formal education and of the way he believes it indoctrinates students into becoming passive learners. In Freire's view, formal education serves the primary purpose of maintaining an unfair and unjust status quo. Essayist Richard Rodriguez writes about how education can shape the way we think about ourselves, and in some ways, his autobiographical essay offers a concrete example of Freire's theories about education. He asks us to consider the consequences of schooling and wonders whether its opportunities require some students to pay too dearly. Likewise, celebrated poet and activist Adrienne Rich challenges our usual ways of thinking about how schooling provides opportunities for students. She addresses the way women have been treated unequally in schools and calls on women to resist that treatment.

The longer I have been involved in education, the more complicated schooling seems to get and the less convinced I am that everything we ask students to do in school is worth their time or effort. (Indeed, you may feel that much of what I ask you to do in this book is useless!) I have been teaching for more than two decades, and, like the authors in this cluster, I have learned that the most important learning that happens in schools often has little to do with the formal curriculum or those standardized tests that we all sweat through. These authors invite us to examine what some theorists have called "the hidden curriculum" of schools and to question what happens in schools. I'm guessing that you have done some of that questioning already. I hope these essays prompt you to continue such questioning.

When we think of graduation, we tend to think of celebration, recognition, and a sense of possibility. We think about the future. And the hopefulness we associate with graduation is a reflection of our belief in the benefits of an education and the idea that it creates opportunities for those who are willing to work hard. Certainly, that's how Maya Angelou (b. 1928)

Graduation

was thinking about her eighth-grade graduation in the excitement leading up to the ceremony. But that ceremony didn't live up to her expectations. Instead, it forced her to face some of the disturbing realities of growing up as a Black person in the segregated American South in the 1930s. The future for Black graduates wasn't the same future of possibility and opportunity that was open to Whites in her small town of Stamps, Arkansas—or for that matter, in any other American town. Her graduation story is thus a reminder that some of our beliefs about schooling may not necessarily conform to the realities we face. And it suggests that the never-ending conversations in our society about education may encourage beliefs about schooling that are problematic and misleading. Angelou's essay asks, Does success in school really lead to opportunity? The answer to that question, if we pay attention to

MAYA ANGELOU

The children in Stamps trembled visibly with anticipation. Some adults were exited too, but to be certain the whole young population had come down with graduation epidemic. Large classes were graduating from both the grammar school and the high school. Even those who were years removed from their own day of glorious release were anxious to help with preparations as a kind of dry run. The junior students who were moving into the vacating classes' chairs were tradition-bound to show their talents for leadership and management. They strutted through the school and around the campus exerting pressure on the lower grades. Their authority was so new that occasionally if they pressed a little too hard it had to be overlooked. After all, next term was coming, and it never hurt a sixth grader to have a play sister in the eighth grade, or a tenth-year student to be able to call a twelfth grader Bubba. So all was endured in a spirit of shared understanding. But the graduating classes themselves were the nobility. Like travelers with exotic destinations on their minds, the graduates were remarkably forgetful. They came to school without their books, or tablets or even pencils. Volunteers fell over themselves to secure replacements for the missing equipment. When accepted, the willing workers might or might not be thanked, and it was of no importance to the pregraduation rites. Even teachers were respectful of the now quiet and aging seniors, and tended to speak to them, if not as equals, as beings only slightly lower than themselves. After tests were returned and grades given, the student body, which acted like an extended family, knew who did well, who excelled, and what piteous ones had failed.

Unlike the white high school, Lafayette County Training School distinguished itself by having neither lawn, nor hedges, nor tennis court, nor climbing ivy. Its two buildings (main classrooms, the grade school and home economics) were set on a dirt hill with no fence to limit either its boundaries or those of bordering farms. There was a large expanse to the left of the school which was used alternately as a baseball diamond or basketball court. Rusty hoops on swaying poles represented the permanent recreational equipment, although bats and balls could be borrowed from the P.E. teacher if the borrower was qualified and if the diamond wasn't occupied.

Over this rocky area relieved by a few shady tall persimmon trees the graduating class walked. The girls often held hands and no longer bothered to speak to the lower students. There was a sadness about them, as if this old world was not their home and they were bound for higher ground. The boys, on the other hand, had become more friendly, more outgoing. A decided change from the closed attitude they projected while studying for finals. Now they seemed not ready to give up the old school, the familiar paths and classrooms. Only a small percentage would be continuing on to college—one of the South's A & M (agricultural and mechanical) schools, which trained Negro youths to be carpenters, farmers, handymen, masons, maids, cooks and baby nurses. Their future rode heavily on their shoulders, and blinded them to the collective joy that had pervaded the lives of the boys and girls in the grammar school graduating class.

Parents who could afford it had ordered new shoes and readymade clothes for themselves from Sears and Roebuck or Montgomery Ward. They also engaged the best seamstresses to make the floating graduating dresses and to cut down secondhand pants which would be pressed to a military slickness for the important event.

Oh, it was important, all right. Whitefolks would attend the ceremony, and two or three would speak of God and home, and the Southern way of life, and Mrs. Parsons, the principal's wife, would play the graduation march while the lower-grade graduates paraded down the aisles and took their seats below the platform. The high school seniors would wait in empty classrooms to make their dramatic entrance.

5

Angelou, is, "It depends." The question for you is, "On what?"

As you'll see, Angelou manages to retrieve hope from what seems to be an almost hopeless situation, and her ability to find that hope may be one reason that this excerpt from her autobiography, I Know Why the Caged Bird Sings *(1970), is so widely read and so often reprinted. In a sense, Angelou's story is a classic American tale of success, and ironically it makes it easy to overlook the fact that her race is perhaps the biggest reason that she had to struggle to attain that success. But how can you read this story without feeling uneasy about how American schools encouraged racism? And if you're paying attention, you'll notice that we're having the same conversations about schools and race today—more than sixty years after Angelou's eighth-grade graduation and more than thirty years after she published this account of it. What might that say about schooling and learning?* ▼

*   *   *

In the Store I was the person of the moment. The birthday girl. The center. Bailey had graduated the year before, although to do so he had had to forfeit all pleasures to make up for his time lost in Baton Rouge.

My class was wearing butter-yellow piqué dresses, and Momma launched out on mine. She smocked the yoke into tiny crisscrossing puckers, then shirred the rest of the bodice. Her dark fingers ducked in and out of the lemony cloth as she embroidered raised daisies around the hem. Before she considered herself finished she had added a crocheted cuff on the puff sleeves, and a pointy crocheted collar.

I was going to be lovely. A walking model of all the various styles of fine hand sewing and it didn't worry me that I was only twelve years old and merely graduating from the eighth grade. Besides, many teachers in Arkansas Negro schools had only that diploma and were licensed to impart wisdom.

The days had become longer and more noticeable. The faded beige of former times had been replaced with strong and sure colors. I began to see my classmates' clothes, their skin tones, and the dust that waved off pussy willows. Clouds that lazed across the sky were objects of great concern to me. Their shiftier shapes might have held a message that in my new happiness and with a little bit of time I'd soon decipher. During that period I looked at the arch of heaven so religiously my neck kept a steady ache. I had taken to smiling more often, and my jaws hurt from the unaccustomed activity. Between the two physical sore spots, I suppose I could have been uncomfortable, but that was not the case. As a member of the winning team (the graduating class of 1940) I had outdistanced unpleasant sensations by miles. I was headed for the freedom of open fields.

10   Youth and social approval allied themselves with me and we trammeled memories of slights and insults. The wind of our swift passage remodeled my features. Lost tears were pounded to mud and then to dust. Years of withdrawal were brushed aside and left behind, as hanging ropes of parasitic moss.

My work alone had awarded me a top place and I was going to be one of the first called in the graduating ceremonies. On the classroom blackboard, as well as on the bulletin board in the auditorium, there were blue stars and white stars and red stars. No absences, no tardinesses, and my academic work was among the best of the year. I could say the preamble to the Constitution even faster than Bailey. We timed ourselves often: "We the people of the United States in order to form a more perfect union . . ." I had memorized the Presidents of the United States from Washington to Roosevelt in chronological as well as alphabetical order.

My hair pleased me too. Gradually the black mass had lengthened and thickened, so that it kept at last to its braided pattern, and I didn't have to yank my scalp off when I tried to comb it.

Louise and I had rehearsed the exercises until we tired out ourselves. Henry Reed was class valedictorian. He was a small, very black boy with hooded eyes, a long, broad nose and an oddly shaped head. I had admired him for years because each term he and I vied for the best grades in our class. Most often he bested me, but instead of being disappointed I was pleased that we shared top places between us. Like many Southern Black children, he lived with is grandmother, who was as strict as Momma and as kind as she knew how to be. He was courteous, respectful and soft-spoken to elders, but on the playground he chose to play the roughest games. I admired him. Anyone, I reckoned, sufficiently afraid or sufficiently dull could be polite. But to be able to operate at a top level with both adults and children was admirable.

His valedictory speech was entitled **"TO BE OR NOT TO BE."** The rigid tenth-grade teacher had helped him write it. He'd been working on the dramatic stresses for months.

15   The weeks until graduation were filled with heady activities. A group of small children were to be presented in a play about buttercups and daisies and bunny rabbits. They could be heard throughout the building practicing their hops and their little songs that sounded like silver bells. The older girls (nongraduates, of course) were assigned the task of making refreshments for the night's festivities. A tangy scent of ginger, cinnamon, nutmeg and chocolate wafted around the home economics building as the budding cooks made samples for themselves and their teachers.

In every corner of the workshop, axes and saws split fresh timber as the woodshop boys made sets and stage scenery. Only the graduates were left out of the general bustle. We were free to sit in the library at the back of the building or look in quite detachedly, naturally, on the measures being taken for our event.

Even the minister preached on graduation the Sunday before. His subject was, "Let your light so shine that men will see your good works and praise your Father, Who is in Heaven." Although the sermon was purported to be addressed to us, he used the occasion to speak to backsliders, gamblers and general ne'er-do-wells. But since he had called our names at the beginning of the service we were mollified.

Among Negroes the tradition was to give presents to children going only from one grade to another. How much more important this was when the person was graduating at the top of the class. Uncle Willie and Momma had sent away for a Mickey Mouse watch like Bailey's. Louise gave me four embroidered handkerchiefs. (I gave her crocheted doilies.) Mrs. Sneed, the minister's wife, made me an undershirt to wear for graduation, and nearly every customer gave me a

CONVERSATIONS: "TO BE OR NOT TO BE"
I'm sure you recognized this line, perhaps the most famous line from Shakespeare's play, *Hamlet*. It has become part of Western culture. In selecting that line for the title of his valedictory speech, Henry is calling attention to certain ideas that we associate with that famous play. Consider what those ideas are and how Angelou uses them later in her essay. You might also think about what this reference means to you as a reader—and whether or not that meaning matches what Angelou seems to intend.

nickel or maybe even a dime with the instruction "Keep on moving to higher ground," or some such encouragement.

Amazingly the great day finally dawned and I was out of bed before I knew it. I threw open the back door to see it more clearly, but Momma said, "Sister, come away from that door and put your robe on."

20   I hoped the memory of that morning would never leave me. Sunlight was itself young, and the day had none of the insistence maturity would bring it in a few hours. In my robe and barefoot in the backyard, under cover of going to see about my new beans, I gave myself up to the gentle warmth and thanked God that no matter what evil I had done in my life He had allowed me to live to see this day. Somewhere in my fatalism I had expected to die, accidentally, and never have the chance to walk up the stairs in the auditorium and gracefully receive my hard-earned diploma. Out of God's merciful bosom I had won reprieve.

Bailey came out in his robe and gave me a box wrapped in Christmas paper. He said he had saved his money for months to pay for it. It felt like a box of chocolates, but I knew Bailey wouldn't save money to buy candy when we had all we could want under our noses.

He was as proud of the gift as I. It was a soft-leather-bound copy of a collection of poems by Edgar Allan Poe, or, as Bailey and I called him, "Eap." I turned to "Annabel Lee" and we walked up and down the garden rows, the cool dirt between our toes, reciting the beautifully sad lines.

Momma made a Sunday breakfast although it was only Friday. After we finished the blessing, I opened my eyes to find the watch on my plate. It was a dream of a day. Everything went smoothly and to my credit, I didn't have to be reminded or scolded for anything. Near evening I was too jittery to attend to chores, so Bailey volunteered to do all before his bath.

Days before, we had made a sign for the Store, and as we turned out the lights Momma hung the cardboard over the doorknob. It read clearly: CLOSED. GRADUATION.

25   My dress fitted perfectly and everyone said that I looked like a sunbeam in it. On the hill, going toward the school, Bailey walked behind with Uncle Willie, who muttered, "Go on, Ju." He wanted him to walk ahead with us because it embarrassed him to have to walk so slowly. Bailey said he'd let the ladies walk together, and the men would bring up the rear. We all laughed, nicely.

Little children dashed by out of the dark like fireflies. Their crepe-paper dresses and butterfly wings were not made for running and we heard more than one rip, dryly, and the regretful "uh uh" that followed.

The school blazed without gaiety. The windows seemed cold and unfriendly from the lower hill. A sense of ill-fated timing crept over me, and if Momma hadn't reached for my hand I would have drifted back to Bailey and Uncle Willie, and possibly beyond. She made a few slow jokes about my feet getting cold, and tugged me along to the now-strange building.

Around the front steps, assurance came back. There were my fellow "greats," the graduating class. Hair brushed back, legs oiled, new dresses and pressed pleats, fresh pocket handkerchiefs and little handbags, all homesewn. Oh, we were up to snuff, all right. I joined my comrades and didn't even see my family go in to find seats in the crowded auditorium.

The school band struck up a march and all classes filed in as had been rehearsed. We stood in front of our seats, as assigned, and on a signal from the choir director, we sat. No sooner had this been accomplished than the band started to play the national anthem. We rose again and sang the song, after which we recited the pledge of allegiance. We remained standing for a brief minute before the choir director and the principal signaled to us, rather desperately I thought, to take our seats. The command was so unusual that our carefully rehearsed and smooth-running machine was thrown off. For a full minute we fumbled for our chairs and bumped into each other awkwardly. Habits change or solidify under pressure, so in our state of nervous tension we had been ready to follow our usual assembly pattern: the American national anthem, then the pledge of allegiance, then the song every Black person I knew called the Negro national Anthem. All done in the same key, with the same passion and most often standing on the same foot.

Finding my seat at last, I was overcome with a presentiment of worse   30
things to come. Something unrehearsed, unplanned, was going to happen, and we were going to be made to look bad. I distinctly remember being explicit in the choice of pronoun. It was "we," the graduating class, the unit, that concerned me then.

The principal welcomed "parents and friends" and asked the Baptist minister to lead us in prayer. His invocation was brief and punchy, and for a second I thought we were getting on the high road to right action. When the principal came back to the dais, however, his voice had changed. Sounds always affected me profoundly and the principal's voice was one of my favorites. During assembly it melted and lowed weakly into the audience. It had not been in my plan to listen to him, but my curiosity was piqued and I straightened up to give him my attention.

He was talking about **BOOKER T. WASHINGTON,** our "late great leader," who said we can be as close as the fingers on the hand, etc. . . . Then he said a few vague things about friendship and the friendship of kindly people to those less fortunate than

CONVERSATIONS: THE MEANING OF BOOKER T. WASHINGTON
A famous Black educator who helped establish the Tuskegee Institute in 1881, Washington is often invoked as an inspiration for the way he overcame hardship to find great success. He came to be known as "The Great Accommodator" for his view that Blacks should strive to improve their economic and personal prospects rather than struggle for equal rights with Whites. Such views made Washington controversial among many Blacks because he was seen as giving in to White prejudice and dominance. Many believed that true equality could never be achieved through the kind of approach Washington advocated. How might that knowledge of Washington affect the way readers react to this passage? And consider how the principal was participating in a certain kind of conversation about race relations by referring to Washington in his speech. In other words, what does the principal's reference to Booker T. Washington really mean in the context of his graduation speech?

themselves. With that his voice nearly faded, thin, away. Like a river diminishing to a stream and then to a trickle. But he cleared his throat and said, "Our speaker tonight, who is also our friend, came from Texarkana to deliver the commencement address, but due to the irregularity of the train schedule, he's going to, as they say, 'speak and run.'" He said that we understood and wanted the man to know that we were most grateful for the time he was able to give us and then something about how we were willing always to adjust to another's program, and without more ado—"I give you Mr. Edward Donleavy."

Not one but two white men came through the door off-stage. The shorter one walked to the speaker's platform, and the tall one moved to the center seat and sat down. But that was our principal's seat, and already occupied. The dislodged gentleman bounced around for a long breath or two before the Baptist minister gave him his chair, then with more dignity than the situation deserved, the minister walked off the stage.

Donleavy looked at the audience once (on reflection, I'm sure that he wanted only to reassure himself that we were really there), adjusted his glasses and began to read from a sheaf of papers.

35   He was glad "to be here and to see the work going on just as it was in the other schools."

At the first "Amen" from the audience I willed the offender to immediate death by choking on the word. But Amens and Yes, sir's began to fall around the room like rain through a ragged umbrella.

He told us of the wonderful changes we children in Stamps had in store. The Central School (naturally, the white school was Central) had already been granted improvements that would be in use in the fall. A well-known artist was coming from Little Rock to teach art to them. They were going to have the newest microscopes and chemistry equipment for their laboratory. Mr. Donleavy didn't leave us long in the dark over who made these improvements available to Central High. Nor were we to be ignored in the general betterment scheme he had in mind.

He said that he had pointed out to people at a very high level that one of the first-line football tacklers at Arkansas Agricultural and Mechanical College had graduated from good old Lafayette County Training School. Here fewer Amen's were heard. Those few that did break through lay dully in the air with the heaviness of habit.

CONVERSATIONS: RACE, SPORTS, AND INTELLIGENCE

In paragraph 37, Angelou describes the graduation speech given by the White superintendent, Donleavy, to his Black audience. In his speech, Donleavy makes a clear distinction between the opportunities waiting for Black graduates, which are mostly in athletics, and the opportunities available to Whites, which include just about every other kind of career. Does this speech sound familiar? It reminds me of more recent controversies that have been sparked by comments about race and intelligence. In 1987, for example, Al Campanis, a former baseball star and a successful executive with the Los Angeles Dodgers, suggested in a television interview that the reason there weren't more Black managers, coaches, and team owners in professional baseball is that Blacks may not have the necessary intelligence to do such jobs. More recently, in 2004, former star football player Paul Horning argued in an interview that the college he attended, Notre Dame, which has a reputation for high academic standards, should "loosen up" those standards to attract better Black athletes, suggesting that good Black athletes are incapable of meeting high academic standards. Although the comment provoked immediate criticism and condemnation, it's not too different from the attitude reflected in the comments of Superintendent Donleavy at Angelou's graduation more than sixty years earlier. Think about how these attitudes shape our conversations about race and equal rights and how they might shape the meaning of Angelou's story.

He went on to praise us. He went on to say how he had bragged that "one of the best basketball players at Fisk sank his first ball right here at Lafayette County Training School."

40   The white kids were going to have a chance to become Galileos and Madame Curies and Edisons and Gauguins, and our boys (the girls weren't even in on it) would try to be Jesse Owenses and Joe Louises.

Owens and the Brown Bomber were great heroes in our world, but what school official in the white-goddom of Little Rock had the right to decide that those two men must be our only heroes? Who decided that for Henry Reed to become a scientist he had to work like George Washington Carver, as a bootblack, to buy a lousy microscope? Bailey was obviously always going to be too small to be an athlete, so which concrete angel glued to what country seat had decided that if my brother wanted to become a lawyer he had to first pay penance for his skin by picking cotton and hoeing corn and studying correspondence books at night for twenty years?

The man's dead words fell like bricks around the auditorium and too many settled in my belly. Constrained by hard-learned manners I couldn't look behind me, but to my left and right the proud graduating class of 1940 had dropped their heads. Every girl in my row had found something new to do with her handkerchief. Some folded the tiny squares into love knots, some into triangles, but most were wadding them, then pressing them flat on their yellow laps.

On the dais, the ancient tragedy was being replayed. Professor Parsons sat, a sculptor's reject, rigid. His large, heavy body seemed devoid of will or willingness, and his eyes said he was no longer with us. The other teachers examined the flag (which was draped stage right) or their notes, or the windows which opened on our now-famous playing diamond.

Graduation, the hush-hush magic time of frills and gifts and congratulations and diplomas, was finished for me before my name was called. The accomplishment was nothing. The meticulous maps, drawn in three colors of ink, learning and spelling decasyllabic words, memorizing the whole of *The Rape of Lucrece*—it was for nothing. Donleavy had exposed us.

45   We were maids and farmers, handymen and washerwomen, and anything higher that we aspired to was farcical and presumptuous.

Then I wished that Gabriel Prosser and Nat Turner had killed all whitefolks in their beds and that Abraham Lincoln had been assassinated before the signing of the Emancipation Proclamation, and that Harriet Tubman had been killed by that blow on her head and Christopher Columbus had drowned in the *Santa Maria*.

It was awful to be a Negro and have no control over my life. It was brutal to be young and already trained to sit quietly and listen to charges brought against my color with no chance of defense. We should all be dead. I thought I should like to see us all dead, one on top of the other. A pyramid of flesh with the whitefolks on the bottom, as the broad base, then the Indians with their silly tomahawks and teepees and wigwams and treaties, the Negroes with their mops and recipes and cotton sacks and spirituals sticking out of their mouths. The Dutch children should all stumble in their wooden shoes and break their necks. The French should choke to death on the Louisiana Purchase (1803) while silkworms ate all the Chinese with their stupid pigtails. As a species, we were an abomination. All of us.

Donleavy was running for election, and assured our parents that if he won we could count on having the only colored paved playing field in that part of Arkansas. Also—he never looked up to acknowledge the grunts of acceptance—also, we were bound to get some new equipment for the home economics building and the workshop.

He finished, and since there was no need to give any more than the most perfunctory thank-you's, he nodded to the men on the stage, and the tall white man who was never introduced joined him at the door. They left with the attitude that now they were off to something really important. (The graduation ceremonies at Lafayette County Training School had been a mere preliminary.)

50   The ugliness they left was palpable. An uninvited guest who wouldn't leave. The choir was summoned and sang a modern arrangement of "Onward, Christian Soldiers," with new words pertaining to graduates seeking their place in the world. But it didn't work. Elouise, the daughter of the Baptist minister, recited "Invictus," and I could have cried at the impertinence of "I am the master of my fate, I am the captain of my soul."

My name had lost its ring of familiarity and I had to be nudged to go and receive my diploma. All my preparations had fled. I neither marched up to the stage like a conquering Amazon, nor did I look in the audience for Bailey's nod of approval. Marguerite Johnson, I heard the name again, my honors were read, there were noises in the audience of appreciation, and I took my place on the stage as rehearsed.

I thought about colors I hated: ecru, puce, lavender, beige and black.

There was shuffling and rustling around me, then Henry Reed was giving his valedictory address, "To Be or Not to Be." Hadn't he heard the whitefolks? We couldn't *be,* so the question was a waste of time. Henry's voice came out clear and strong. I feared to look at him. Hadn't he got the message? There was no "nobler in the mind" for Negroes because the world didn't think we had minds, and they let us know it. "Outrageous fortune"? Now, that was a joke. When the ceremony was over I had to tell Henry Reed some things. That is, if I still cared. Not "rub," Henry, "erase." "Ah, there's the erase." Us.

Henry had been a good student in elocution. His voice rose on tides of promise and fell on waves of warnings. The English teacher had helped him to create a sermon winging through Hamlet's soliloquy. To be a man, a doer, a builder, a leader, or to be a tool, an unfunny joke, a crusher of funky toadstools. I marveled that Henry could go through with the speech as if we had a choice.

I had been listening and silently rebutting each sentence with my eyes closed; then there was a hush, which in an audience warns that something unplanned is happening. I looked up and saw Henry Reed, the conservative, the proper, the A student, turn his back to the audience and turn to us (the proud graduating class of 1940) and sing, nearly speaking, 55

> "Lift ev'ry voice and sing
> Till earth and heaven ring
> Ring with the harmonies of Liberty . . ."

It was the poem written by James Weldon Johnson. It was the music composed by J. Rosamond Johnson. It was the Negro national anthem. Out of habit we were singing it.

Our mothers and fathers stood in the dark hall and joined the hymn of encouragement. A kindergarten teacher led the small children onto the stage and the buttercups and daisies and bunny rabbits marked time and tried to follow:

> "Stony the road we trod
> Bitter the chastening rod
> Felt in the days when hope, unborn, had died.
> Yet with a steady beat
> Have not our weary feet
> Come to the place for which our fathers sighed?"

Each child I knew had learned that song with his ABC's and along with "Jesus Loves Me This I Know." But I personally had never heard it before. Never heard the words, despite the thousands of times I had sung them. Never thought they had anything to do with me.

On the other hand, the words of Patrick Henry had made such an impression on me that I had been able to stretch myself tall and trembling and say, "I know not what course others may take, but as for me, give me liberty or give me death."

And now I heard, really for the first time:

> "We have come over a way that with tears has been watered,
> We have come, treading our path through the blood of the slaughtered."

CONVERSATIONS: SONGS, POETRY, AND HOPE

In paragraph 55 and the following paragraphs, Angelou describes a stirring scene in which her classmate began singing a song that Angelou refers to as "the Negro national anthem." She includes excerpts from the song itself, which was based on a poem by James Weldon Johnson. It is common for speakers at graduations to quote from well-known songs or poems. In that sense, Angelou describes a rather typical graduation scene. But this particular song adds a twist to that typical scene because of the song's association with the Black struggle for equal rights. Thus, Henry's singing the song is part of the American ritual of graduation at the same time that it challenges that ritual. Consider how different that song would sound to a Black person compared with a White person, especially in Arkansas in the 1930s or 1940s. How does it sound today? Consider, too, how Angelou's description of that compelling moment at her graduation seems both timeless and specific.

60   While echoes of the song shivered in the air, Henry Reed bowed his head, said "Thank you," and returned to his place in the line. The tears that slipped down many faces were not wiped away in shame.

We were on top again. As always, again. We survived. The depths had been icy and dark, but now a bright sun spoke to our souls. I was no longer simply a member of the proud graduating class of 1940; I was a proud member of the wonderful, beautiful Negro race.

Oh, Black known and unknown poets, how often have your auctioned pains sustained us? Who will compute the lonely nights made less lonely by your songs, or the empty pots made less tragic by your tales?

If we were a people much given to revealing secrets, we might raise monuments and sacrifice to the memories of our poets, but slavery cured us of that weakness. It may be enough, however, to have it said that we survive in exact relationship to the dedication of our poets (include preachers, musicians and blues singers).

Understanding the Text

1. Why, specifically, was Angelou so excited about her upcoming graduation from eighth grade? In what way is this excitement central to the story that Angelou tells?

2. Why does Angelou state that graduation "was finished for me before my name was called. The accomplishment was nothing"? What led her to that conclusion?

3. Why is the Negro National Anthem important to this story? What do you think is the significance of Henry's decision to begin singing the song at that point in the ceremony? How does the song influence the way you read the final paragraphs of Angelou's story?

Exploring the Issues

1. Angelou devotes the first half of this essay to a description of the events leading up to the graduation ceremony. How effective do you think this description is? What role does it play in the narrative of the graduation itself? What expectations does it set up for the rest of the essay?

2. In paragraphs 44–47, Angelou refers to several famous literary works, important historical figures, and events. Why does she do so? What effect do these spe-

cific references have? What do you think Angelou meant them to convey? How might they relate to her overall theme in this essay?

3. In some ways, this essay is about the beliefs that Americans have about schooling. What are those beliefs? Do you think Angelou shares those beliefs? In what ways do you think she challenges them?

Entering the Conversations

1. Write an essay for an audience of your classmates in which you tell the story of your high school graduation (or your graduation from another school or program). Try to tell the story in a way that develops or emphasizes important ideas that you want to convey about the experience to your readers.

2. Imagine that you have been invited to give the address at the graduation ceremony at your old high school. Write that address.

3. In a group of classmates, compare your addresses written for Question 2. What similarities or differences can you identify in these graduation speeches? What do the speeches convey about education? Consider differences in the learning situations that each classmate came from—an urban or rural school, a school with a very diverse student population, a

wealthy suburban school, and so on. Now, based on your discussion, write a brief analysis of graduation speeches in which you discuss the main features of that very specialized genre and discuss the purposes that these speeches serve in American culture.

4. Consider the images below and how they depict education. The photograph on the left shows Black students being prevented by National Guard troops from entering high school in Little Rock, Arkansas, a famous standoff that led to a nationwide controversy about segregation in American schools. The other two images are from the web site of Arkansas State University, available on the Internet in 2004. What values do the images communicate regarding schooling? Find images online or in print media that you think reflect the state of education in the United States today when it comes to race. Write an essay discussing the messages those images communicate and draw your own conclusions about the current state of education in the United States, discussing what you believe are the basic values regarding education in the United States.

Alternatively, create a web site or multimedia presentation reflecting your views about the current state of education.

A White student passes through an Arkansas National Guard line as Elizabeth Eckford is turned away, 1957.

FPG/Hulton Archive/Getty Images

ARKANSAS STATE UNIVERSITY
Jonesboro, Arkansas

CREATING LEADERS.

personal
CREATING LEADERS.

FUTURE STUDENTS

© Arkansas State University.

Unless you're an educator (and even if you are an educator), you may never have heard of Paulo Freire (1921–1997). Yet he is one of the most influential education theorists of the twentieth century. At the center of his theories of education is the notion that schooling should be about becoming "fully human," which means understanding that

THE *Banking* Concept OF Education

reality is not fixed but is a process in which individual human beings participate. In other words, we don't simply live in the world as it is; we create it. Being fully human is knowing that we have the capacity to change the world through our active participation. But conventional schooling, according to Freire, teaches students to be passive components of the status quo and in doing so it "dehumanizes" them. This conventional approach to schooling, which Freire calls the "banking concept of education," thus helps maintain the status quo, with all its inequalities and injustices.

Now, if this seems abstract to you, consider that Freire was jailed in his native Brazil in the 1960s for the "subversive" act of developing literacy programs for rural peasants. He was subsequently exiled by the military dictatorship that ruled Brazil at the time, but his ideas about "liberatory" education began

PAULO FREIRE

A careful analysis of the teacher-student relationship at any level, inside or outside the school, reveals its fundamentally *narrative* character. This relationship involves a narrating Subject (the teacher) and patient, listening objects (the students). The contents, whether values or empirical dimensions of reality, tend in the process of being narrated to become lifeless and petrified. Education is suffering from narration sickness.

The teacher talks about reality as if it were motionless, static, compartmentalized, and predictable. Or else he expounds on a topic completely alien to the existential experience of the students. His task is to "fill" the students with the contents of his narration—contents which are detached from reality, disconnected from the totality that engendered them and could give them significance. Words are emptied of their concreteness and become a hollow, alienated, and alienating verbosity.

The outstanding characteristic of this narrative education, then, is the sonority of words, not their transforming power. "Four times four is sixteen; the capital of Pará is Belém." The student records, memorizes, and repeats these phrases without perceiving what four times four really means, or realizing the true significance of "capital" in the affirmation "the capital of Pará is Belém," that is, what Belém means for Pará and what Pará means for Brazil.

Narration (with the teacher as narrator) leads the students to memorize mechanically the narrated content. Worse yet, it turns them into "containers," into "receptacles" to be "filled" by the teacher. The more completely she fills the receptacles, the better a teacher she is. The more meekly the receptacles permit themselves to be filled, the better students they are.

5   Education thus becomes an act of depositing, in which the students are the depositories and the teacher is the depositor. Instead of communicating, the teacher issues communiqués and makes deposits which the students patiently receive, memorize, and repeat. This is the "banking" concept of education, in which the scope of action allowed to the students extends only as far as receiving, filing, and storing the deposits. They do, it is true, have the opportunity to become collectors or cataloguers of the things they store. But in the last analysis, it is the people themselves who are filed away through the lack of creativity, transformation, and knowledge in this (at best) misguided system. For apart from inquiry, apart from the praxis, individuals cannot be truly human. Knowledge emerges only through invention and re-invention, through the restless, impatient, continuing, hopeful inquiry human beings pursue in the world, with the world, and with each other.

In the banking concept of education, knowledge is a gift bestowed by those who consider themselves knowledgeable upon those whom they consider to know nothing. Projecting an absolute ignorance onto others, a characteristic of the ideology of oppression, negates education and knowledge as processes of inquiry. The teacher presents himself to his students as their necessary opposite; by considering their ignorance absolute, he justifies his own existence. The students, alienated like the slave in the Hegelian dialectic, accept their ignorance as justifying the teacher's existence—but, unlike the slave, they never discover that they educate the teacher.

The *raison d'être* of libertarian education, on the other hand, lies in its drive towards reconciliation. Education must begin with the solution of the teacher-student contradiction, by reconciling the poles of the contradiction so that both are simultaneously teachers *and* students.

This solution is not (nor can it be) found in the banking concept. On the contrary, banking education maintains and even stimulates the contradiction through the following attitudes and practices, which mirror oppressive society as a whole:

a. the teacher teaches and the students are taught;

b. the teacher knows everything and the students know nothing;

c. the teacher thinks and the students are thought about;

to influence other educators. The publication of his now-famous book Pedagogy of the Oppressed, *which appeared in English in 1970 and in which the following essay first appeared, brought his ideas to a worldwide audience. By the time he returned to Brazil in the 1980s as an internationally prominent voice for education reform, Brazil was once again under civilian rule, and he became minister of education for the city of São Paulo. He remained in Brazil and continued to push for education reform until his death.*

The first time I read the following essay, I don't think I fully understood his complicated ideas. Maybe that's because Freire's essay is less about schooling and more fundamentally about how we understand ourselves as beings in the world. In that sense, it is really a philosophical text that addresses age-old questions: Who are we? How do we know the world? What is our relationship to the world? What is reality? Don't be put off by some of the difficulties of Freire's essay. His ideas are sometimes hard to understand, and his writing can be challenging as well. So you may need to work through his essay carefully. But I think you'll find that it's worth the effort. As you read, ask yourself whether Freire's ideas, which grew out of his experiences in South America, are valid for American schools. That's a question that many educators— those who agree with Freire and those who don't—have asked. In trying to answer it, you will be joining one of the most vigorous conversations about education that continues today, so many years after Freire first presented his ideas in this essay. ◪

d. the teacher talks and the students listen—meekly;

e. the teacher disciplines and the students are disciplined;

f. the teacher chooses and enforces his choice, and the students comply;

g. the teacher acts and the students have the illusion of acting through the action of the teacher;

h. the teacher chooses the program content, and the students (who were not consulted) adapt to it;

i. the teacher confuses the authority of knowledge with his or her own professional authority, which she and he sets in opposition to the freedom of the students;

j. the teacher is the Subject of the learning process, while the pupils are mere objects.

It is not surprising that the banking concept of education regards men as adaptable, manageable beings. The more students work at storing the deposits entrusted to them, the less they develop the critical consciousness which would result from their intervention in the world as transformers of that world. The more completely they accept the passive role imposed on them, the more they tend simply to adapt to the world as it is and to the fragmented view of reality deposited in them.

10   The capability of banking education to minimize or annul the students' creative power and to stimulate their credulity serves the interests of the oppressors, who care neither to have the world revealed nor to see it transformed. The oppressors use their "humanitarianism" to preserve a profitable situation. Thus they react almost instinctively against any experiment in education which stimulates the critical faculties and is not content with a partial view of reality but always seeks out the ties which link one point to another and one problem to another.

Indeed, the interests of the oppressors lie in "changing the consciousness of the oppressed, not the situation which oppresses them";[1] for the more the oppressed can be led to adapt to that situation, the more easily they can be dominated. To achieve this end, the oppressors use the banking concept of education in conjunction with a paternalistic social action apparatus, within which the oppressed receive the euphemistic title of "welfare recipients." They are treated as individual cases, as marginal persons who deviate from the general configuration of a "good, organized, and just" society. The oppressed are regarded as the pathology of the healthy society, which must therefore adjust

---

CONVERSATIONS: THE PROBLEMS WITH SCHOOLS

Freire's criticisms of formal schooling have influenced many well-known educational theorists, including Henri Giroux, Peter McLaren, and bell hooks. (Essays by bell hooks appear on page 256 and page 515 in this book.) If those names don't ring any bells for you, it's probably because you haven't read the kind of educational theory that they write. Their articles and books—and the articles and books of their critics—amount to a lively but specialized conversation about education among academics and theorists. It's worth asking whether that conversation is different from the larger public conversations about education reform that are always occurring in the popular media and in political campaigns. We always seem to be hearing about crises in our schools and about various government programs to improve education. For example, in 2001, President George W. Bush signed into law a sweeping education reform bill that has come to be known as No Child Left Behind. But what supporters of that law say is wrong with schools seems very different from Freire's list. Why? If Freire is such an internationally known and influential education theorist and reformer, why do his ideas seem to have been left out of the public discussions about education reform efforts such as No Child Left Behind? What might that tell us about how different ideas reach different audiences at different times?

these "incompetent and lazy" folk to its own patterns by changing their mentality. These marginals need to be "integrated," "incorporated" into the healthy society that they have "forsaken."

The truth is, however, that the oppressed are not "marginals," are not people living "outside" society. They have always been "inside"— inside the structure which made them "beings for others." The solution is not to "integrate" them into the structure of oppression, but to transform that structure so that they can become "beings for themselves." Such transformation, of course, would undermine the oppressors' purposes; hence their utilization of the banking concept of education to avoid the threat of student *conscientização.*[°]

The banking approach to adult education, for example, will never propose to students that they critically consider reality. It will deal instead with such vital questions as whether Roger gave green grass to the goat, and insist upon the importance of learning that, on the contrary, *Roger gave green grass to the rabbit.* The "humanism" of the banking approach masks the effort to turn women and men into automatons—the very negation of their ontological vocation to be more fully human.

Those who use the banking approach, knowingly or unknowingly (for there are innumerable well-intentioned bank-clerk teachers who do not realize that they are serving only to dehumanize), fail

CONVERSATIONS: CLASSROOMS AND LEARNING

This photograph depicts a typical college classroom. Consider how this scene might illustrate some of Freire's criticisms of what he calls the "banking concept of education." What does it reveal about schooling?

Cartoons are often used to critique public education. Consider whether the criticism of schooling made by Mike Keefe's cartoon coincides with Freire's critique of formal schooling. Consider, too, whether the medium of a cartoon can convey such criticisms as effectively as a conventional academic essay.

[°]**conscientização** According to Freire's translator, "The term *conscientização* refers to learning to perceive social, political, and economic contradictions, and to take action against the oppressive elements of reality."

to perceive that the deposits themselves contain contradictions about reality. But, sooner or later, these contradictions may lead formerly passive students to turn against their domestication and the attempt to domesticate reality. They may discover through existential experience that their present way of life is irreconcilable with their vocation to become fully human. They may perceive through their relations with reality that reality is really a *process*, undergoing constant transformation. If men and women are searchers and their ontological vocation is humanization, sooner or later they may perceive the contradiction in which banking education seeks to maintain them, and then engage themselves in the struggle for their liberation.

15   But the humanist, revolutionary educator cannot wait for this possibility to materialize. From the outset, her efforts must coincide with those of the students to engage in critical thinking and the quest for mutual humanization. His efforts must be imbued with a profound trust in people and their creative power. To achieve this, they must be partners of the students in their relations with them.

The banking concept does not admit to such partnership—and necessarily so. To resolve the teacher-student contradiction, to exchange the role of depositor, prescriber, domesticator, for the role of student among students would be to undermine the power of oppression and serve the cause of liberation.

Implicit in the banking concept is the assumption of a DICHOTOMY BETWEEN HUMAN BEINGS AND THE WORLD: a person is merely *in* the world, not *with* the world or with others; the individual is spectator, not re-creator. In this view, the person is not a conscious being (*corpo consciente*); he or she is rather the possessor of *a* consciousness: an empty "mind" passively open to the reception of deposits of reality from the world outside. For example, my desk, my books, my coffee cup, all the objects before me—as bits of the world which surrounds me—would be "inside" me, exactly as I am inside my study right now. This view makes no distinction between being accessible to consciousness and entering consciousness. The distinction, however, is essential: the objects which surround me are simply accessible to my consciousness, not located within it. I am aware of them, but they are not inside me.

It follows logically from the banking notion of consciousness that the educator's role is to regulate the way the world "enters into" the students. The teacher's task is to organize a process which already occurs spontaneously, to "fill" the students by mak-

CONVERSATIONS: THE NATURE OF REALITY

In paragraph 17, when Freire refers to a "dichotomy between human beings and the world," he is participating in an age-old philosophical conversation about the nature of reality and how (or if) we can come to know that reality. This conversation has been occurring at least since the time of the ancient Greek philosophers and has preoccupied some of the world's greatest minds ever since. To anyone who has studied philosophy, Freire's discussion of "consciousness" may sound familiar. If his discussion seems abstract to you, it may help to keep in mind that what Freire calls the "banking concept of education" is based on the assumption that knowledge exists separately from the knower. In other words, reality is "out there," separate from us, and we can know it only through careful observation—for example, through science. We can only describe what is real; we can't create or change it. Although this may sound abstract, it's actually the idea on which modern science—and modern education—is based. And part of what Freire is trying to do in this essay is to challenge this way of thinking about knowledge. For Freire, believing that reality is "objective," as modern science asks us to do, makes it possible for all kinds of injustices to seem "natural" or "inevitable." But understanding reality as something we can change means that we can eliminate those injustices. You might think about it in this way: This is where philosophy meets real life.

ing deposits of information which he or she considers to constitute true knowledge.[2] And since people "receive" the world as passive entities, education should make them more passive still, and adapt them to the world. The educated individual is the adapted person, because she or he is better "fit" for the world. Translated into practice, this concept is well suited to the purposes of the oppressors, whose tranquility rests on how well people fit the world the oppressors have created, and how little they question it.

The more completely the majority adapt to the purposes which the dominant minority prescribe for them (thereby depriving them of the right to their own purposes), the more easily the minority can continue to prescribe. The theory and practice of banking education serve this end quite efficiently. Verbalistic lessons, reading requirements,[3] the methods for evaluating "knowledge," the distance between the teacher and the taught, the criteria for promotion: everything in this ready-to-wear approach serves to obviate thinking.

The bank-clerk educator does not realize that there is no true security in his hypertrophied role, that one must seek to live *with* others in solidarity. One cannot impose oneself, nor even merely co-exist with one's students. Solidarity requires true communication, and the concept by which such an educator is guided fears and proscribes communication. 20

Yet only through communication can human life hold meaning. The teacher's thinking is authenticated only by the authenticity of the students' thinking. The teacher cannot think for her students, nor can she impose her thought on them. Authentic thinking, thinking that is concerned about *reality*, does not take place in ivory tower isolation, but only in communication. If it is true that thought has meaning only when generated by action upon the world, the subordination of students to teachers becomes impossible.

Because banking education begins with a false understanding of men and women as objects, it cannot promote the development of what Fromm calls "biophily," but instead produces its opposite: "necrophily."

> While life is characterized by growth in a structured, functional manner, the necrophilous person loves all that does not grow, all that is mechanical. The necrophilous person is driven by the desire to transform the organic into the inorganic, to approach life mechanically, as if all living persons were things. . . . Memory, rather than experience; having, rather than being, is what counts. The necrophilous person can relate to an object—a flower or a person—only if he possesses it; hence a threat to his possession is a threat to himself; if he loses possession he loses contact with the world. . . . He loves control, and in the act of controlling he kills life.[4]

Oppression—overwhelming control—is necrophilic; it is nourished by love of death, not life. The banking concept of education, which serves the interests of oppression, is also necrophilic. Based on a mechanistic, static, naturalistic, spatialized view of consciousness, it transforms students into receiving objects. It attempts to control thinking and action, leads women and men to adjust to the world, and inhibits their creative power.

When their efforts to act responsibly are frustrated, when they find themselves unable to use their faculties, people suffer. "This suffering due to impotence is rooted in the very fact that the human equilibrium has been disturbed."[5] But the inability to act which causes people's anguish also causes them to reject their impotence, by attempting

> . . . to restore [their] capacity to act. But can [they], and how? One way is to submit to and identify with a person or group having power. By this symbolic participation in another person's life, [men have] the illusion of acting, when in reality [they] only submit to and become part of those who act.[6]

25   Populist manifestations perhaps best exemplify this type of behavior by the oppressed, who, by identifying with charismatic leaders, come to feel that they themselves are active and effective. The rebellion they express as they emerge in the historical process is motivated by that desire to act effectively. The dominant elites consider the remedy to be more domination and repression, carried out in the name of freedom, order, and social peace (that is, the peace of the elites). Thus they can condemn—logically, from their point of view—"the violence of a strike by workers and [can] call upon the state in the same breath to use violence in putting down the strike."[7]

Education as the exercise of domination stimulates the credulity of students, with the ideological intent (often not perceived by educators) of indoctrinating them to adapt to the world of oppression. This accusation is not made in the naïve hope that the dominant elites will thereby simply abandon the practice. Its objective is to call the attention of true humanists to the fact that they cannot use banking educational methods in the pursuit of liberation, for they would only negate that very pursuit. Nor may a revolutionary society inherit these methods from an oppressor society. The revolutionary society which practices banking education is either misguided or mistrusting of people. In either event, it is threatened by the specter of reaction.

Unfortunately, those who espouse the cause of liberation are themselves surrounded and influenced by the climate which generates the banking concept, and often do not perceive its true significance or its dehumanizing power. Paradoxically, then, they utilize this same instrument of alienation in what they consider an effort to liberate. Indeed, some "revolutionaries" brand as "innocents," "dreamers," or even "reactionaries" those who would challenge this educational practice. But one does not liberate people by alienating them. Authentic liberation—the process of humanization—is not another deposit to be made in men. Liberation is a praxis: the action and reflection of men and women upon their world in order to transform it. Those truly committed to the cause of liberation can accept neither the mechanistic concept of consciousness as an empty vessel to be filled, nor the use of banking methods of domination (propaganda, slogans—deposits) in the name of liberation.

Those truly committed to liberation must reject the banking concept in its entirety, adopting instead a concept of women and men as conscious beings, and consciousness as consciousness intent upon the world. They must abandon the educational goal of deposit-making and replace it with the posing of the problems of human beings in their relations with the world. "Problem-posing" education, responding to the essence of consciousness—*intentionality*—rejects communiqués and embodies communications. It epitomizes the special characteristic of consciousness: being *conscious of,* not only as intent on objects but as turned in upon itself in a Jasperian "split"—consciousness as consciousness *of* consciousness.

Liberating education consists in acts of cognition, not transferrals of information. It is a learning situation in which the cognizable object (far from being the end of the cognitive act) intermediates the cognitive actors—teacher on the one hand and students on the other. Accordingly, the practice of problem-posing education entails at the outset that the teacher-student contradiction be resolved. Dialogical relations—indispensable to the capacity of cognitive actors to cooperate in perceiving the same cognizable object—are otherwise impossible.

Indeed, problem-posing education, which breaks with the vertical patterns characteristic of banking education, can fulfill its function as the practice of freedom only if it can overcome the above contradiction. Through dialogue, the teacher-of-the-students and the students-of-the-teacher cease to exist and a new term emerges: teacher-student with students-teachers. The teacher is no longer merely the-one-who-teaches, but one who is himself taught in dialogue with the students, who in turn while being taught also teach. They become jointly responsible for a process in which all grow. In this process, arguments based on "authority" are no longer valid; in order to function, authority must be *on the side of* freedom, not *against* it. Here, no one teaches another, nor is anyone self-taught. People teach each other, mediated by the world, by the cognizable objects which in banking education are "owned" by the teacher.

The banking concept (with its tendency to dichotomize everything) distinguishes two stages in the action of the educator. During the first, he cognizes a cognizable object while he prepares his lessons in his study or his laboratory; during the second, he expounds to his students about that object. The students are not called upon to know, but to memorize the contents narrated by the teacher. Nor do the students practice any act of cognition, since the object towards which that act should be directed is the property of the teacher rather than a medium evoking the critical reflection of both teacher and students. Hence in the name of the "preservation of culture and knowledge" we have a system which achieves neither true knowledge nor true culture.

The problem-posing method does not dichotomize the activity of the teacher-student: she is not "cognitive" at one point and "narrative" at another. She is always "cognitive," whether preparing a project or engaging in dialogue with the students. He does not regard cognizable objects as his private property, but as the object of reflection by himself and the students. In this way, the problem-posing educator constantly re-forms his reflections in the reflection of the students. The students—no longer docile listeners—are now critical co-investigators in dialogue with the teacher. The teacher presents the material to the students for their consideration, and reconsiders her earlier considerations as the students express their own. The role of the problem-posing educator is to create, together with the students, the conditions under which knowledge at the level of the *doxa* is superseded by true knowledge, at the level of the *logos*.

Whereas banking education anesthetizes and inhibits creative power, problem-posing education involves a constant unveiling of reality. The former attempts to maintain the *submersion* of consciousness; the latter strives for the *emergence* of consciousness and *critical intervention* in reality.

Students, as they are increasingly posed with problems relating to themselves in the world and with the world, will feel increasingly challenged and obliged to respond to that challenge. Because they apprehend the challenge as interrelated to other problems within a total context, not as a theoretical question, the resulting comprehension tends to be increasingly critical and thus constantly less alienated. Their response to the challenge evokes new challenges, followed by new understandings; and gradually the students come to regard themselves as committed.

35   Education as the practice of freedom—as opposed to education as the practice of domination—denies that man is abstract, isolated, independent, and unattached to the world; it also denies that the world exists as a reality apart from people. Authentic reflection considers neither abstract man nor the world without people, but people in their relations with the world. In these relations consciousness and world are simultaneous: consciousness neither precedes the world nor follows it.

La conscience et le monde sont dormés
d'un même coup: extérieur par essence à la

conscience, le monde est, par essence relatif à elle.[8]

In one of our culture circles in **CHILE,** the group was discussing (based on a codification) the anthropological concept of culture. In the midst of the discussion, a peasant who by banking standards was completely ignorant said: "Now I see that without man there is no world." When the educator responded: "Let's say, for the sake of argument, that all the men on earth were to die, but that the earth itself remained, together with trees, birds, animals, rivers, seas, the stars . . . wouldn't all this be a world?" "Oh no," the peasant replied emphatically. "There would be no one to say: 'This is a world.'"

The peasant wished to express the idea that there would be lacking the consciousness of the world which necessarily implies the world of consciousness. *I* cannot exist without a *non-I*. In turn, the *not-I* depends on that existence. The world which brings consciousness into existence becomes the world *of* that consciousness. Hence, the previously cited affirmation of Sartre: *"La conscience et le monde sont dormés d'un même coup."*

As women and men, simultaneously reflecting on themselves and on the world, increase the scope of their perception, they begin to direct their observations towards previously inconspicuous phenomena:

> In perception properly so-called, as an explicit awareness [*Gewahren*], I am turned towards the object, to the paper, for instance. I apprehend it as being this here and now. The apprehension is a singling out, every object having a background in experience. Around and about the paper lie books, pencils, ink-well, and so forth, and these in a certain sense are also "perceived," perceptually there, in the "field of intuition"; but whilst I was turned towards the paper there was no turning in their direction, nor any apprehending of them, not even in a secondary sense. They appeared and yet were not singled out, were not posited on their own account. Every perception of a thing has such a zone of background intuitions or background awareness, if "intuiting" already includes the state of being turned towards, and this also is a "conscious experience," or more briefly a "consciousness of" all indeed that in point of fact lies in the co-perceived objective background.[9]

That which had existed objectively but had not been perceived in its deeper implications (if indeed it was perceived at all) begins to "stand out," assuming the character of a problem and therefore of challenge. Thus, men and women begin to single out elements from their "background awarenesses" and to reflect upon them. These elements are now objects of their consideration, and, as such, objects of their action and cognition.

CONVERSATIONS: CHILE IN THE 1960S
In paragraph 36, Freire refers to his literacy work with peasants in Chile in the 1960s. At the time, Chile was experiencing political tensions, which worsened after socialist leader Salvadore Allende was elected president in 1970. In 1973, Allende was killed in a coup led by Chile's military. Subsequently, the military leader who took control of the nation, Augusto Pinochet, declared martial law. Many people believed that Allende's overthrow was orchestrated in a plot that involved the U.S. CIA. In the years that followed, many Allende supporters and others who criticized or opposed the government were persecuted; thousands disappeared or were executed in what the Chilean government claimed was an effort to protect the nation from communist subversion. How might this context have shaped Freire's ideas about education and freedom? And how might this context lead some of Freire's critics to complain that his education theories are too political?

STRATEGIES: TALKING PHILOSOPHY
In paragraph 38, Freire includes a long quotation from well-known twentieth century German philosopher Edmund Husserl. Elsewhere, Freire includes quotations from other famous philosophers, including Jean-Paul Sartre, Reinhold Niebuhr, and Erich Fromm. What does Freire accomplish with these quotations and references? What do these quotations suggest about Freire's sense of his audience? Who might be familiar with such philosophers? What do these references reveal about Freire's sense of his purpose in writing this essay?

In problem-posing education, people develop their power to perceive critically *the way they exist* in the world *with which* and *in which* they find themselves; they come to see the world not as a static reality, but as a reality in process, in transformation. Although the dialectical relations of women and men with the world exist independently of how these relations are perceived (or whether or not they are perceived at all), it is also true that the form of action they adopt is to a large extent a function of how they perceive themselves in the world. Hence, the teacher-student and the students-teachers reflect simultaneously on themselves and the world without dichotomizing this reflection from action, and thus establish an authentic form of thought and action.

40   Once again, the two educational concepts and practices under analysis come into conflict. Banking education (for obvious reasons) attempts, by mythicizing reality, to conceal certain facts which explain the way human beings exist in the world; problem-posing education sets itself the task of demythologizing. Banking education resists dialogue; problem-posing education regards dialogue as indispensable to the act of cognition which unveils reality. Banking education treats students as objects of assistance; problem-posing education makes them critical thinkers. Banking education inhibits creativity and domesticates (although it cannot completely destroy) the *intentionality* of consciousness by isolating consciousness from the world, thereby denying people their ontological and historical vocation of becoming more fully human. Problem-posing education bases itself on creativity and stimulates true reflection and action upon reality; thereby responding to the vocation of persons as beings who are authentic only when engaged in inquiry and creative transformation. In sum: banking theory and practice, as immobilizing and fixating forces, fail to acknowledge men and women as historical beings; problem-posing theory and practice take the people's historicity as their starting point.

Problem-posing education affirms men and women as beings in the process of *becoming*—as unfinished, uncompleted beings in and with a likewise unfinished reality. Indeed, in contrast to other animals who are unfinished, but not historical, people know themselves to be unfinished; they are aware of their incompletion. In this incompletion and this awareness lie the very roots of education as an exclusively human manifestation. The unfinished character of human beings and the transformational character of reality necessitate that education be an ongoing activity.

Education is thus constantly remade in the praxis. In order to *be*, it must *become*. Its "duration" (in the Bergsonian meaning of the word) is found in the interplay of the opposites *permanence* and *change*. The banking method emphasizes permanence and becomes reactionary; problem-posing education—which accepts neither a "well-behaved" present nor a predetermined future—roots itself in the dynamic present and becomes revolutionary.

Problem-posing education is revolutionary futurity. Hence, it is prophetic (and, as such, hopeful). Hence, it corresponds to the historical nature of humankind. Hence, it affirms women and men as beings who transcend themselves, who move forward and look ahead, for whom immobility represents a fatal threat, for whom looking at the past must only be a means of understanding more clearly what and who they are so that they can more wisely build the future. Hence, it identifies with the movement which engages people as beings aware of their incompletion—an historical movement which has its point of departure, its Subjects and its objective.

The point of departure of the movement lies in the people themselves. But since people do not exist apart from the world, apart from reality, the movement must begin with the human-world relationship. Accordingly, the point of departure must always be with men and women in the "here and now," which constitutes the situation within which they are submerged, from which they emerge, and in which they intervene. Only by starting from this situation—which determines their perception of it—can they begin to move. To do this authentically they must perceive their state not as fated and unalterable, but merely as limiting—and therefore challenging.

Whereas the banking method directly or indirectly reinforces   45
men's fatalistic perception of their situation, the problem-posing method presents this very situation to them as a problem. As the situation becomes the object of their cognition, the naïve or magical perception which produced their fatalism gives way to perception which is able to perceive itself even as it perceives reality, and can thus be critically objective about that reality.

A deepened consciousness of their situation leads people to apprehend that situation as an historical reality susceptible of transformation. Resignation gives way to the drive for transformation and inquiry, over which men feel themselves to be in control. If people, as historical beings necessarily engaged with other people in a movement of inquiry, did not control that movement, it would be (and is) a violation of their humanity. Any situation in which some individuals prevent others from engaging in the process of inquiry is one of violence. The means used are not important; to alienate human beings from their own decision-making is to change them into objects.

This movement of inquiry must be directed towards humanization—the people's historical vocation. The pursuit of full humanity, however, cannot be carried out in isolation or individualism, but only in fellowship and solidarity; therefore it cannot unfold in the antagonistic relations between oppressors and oppressed. No one can be authentically human while he prevents others from being so. Attempting *to be more* human, individualistically, leads to *having more,* egotistically, a form of dehumanization. Not that it is not fundamental *to have* in order *to be* human. Precisely because it *is* necessary, some men's *having* must not be allowed to constitute an obstacle to others' *having*, must not consolidate the power of the former to crush the latter.

Problem-posing education, as a humanist and liberating praxis, posits as fundamental that the people subjected to domination must fight for their emancipation. To that end, it enables teachers and students to become Subjects of the educational process by overcoming authoritarianism and an alienating intellectualism; it also enables people to overcome their false perception of reality. The world—no longer something to be described with deceptive words—becomes the object of that transforming action by men and women which results in their humanization.

Problem-posing education does not and cannot serve the interests of the oppressor. No oppressive order could permit the oppressed to begin to question: Why? While only a revolutionary society can carry out this education in systematic terms, the revolutionary leaders need not take full power before they can employ the method. In the revolutionary process, the leaders cannot utilize the banking method as an interim measure, justified on grounds of expediency, with the intention of *later* behaving in a genuinely revolutionary fashion. They must be revolutionary—that is to say, dialogical—from the outset.

NOTES

[1]Simone de Beauvoir, *La pensée de droite, aujourd'hui* (Paris); ST, *El pensamiento político de la derecha* (Buenos Aires, 1963), p. 34.

[2]This concept corresponds to what Sartre calls the "digestive" or "nutritive" concept of education, in which knowledge is "fed" by the teacher to the students to "fill them out." See Jean-Paul Sartre, "Une idée fondamentale de la phénomenologie de Husserl: L'intentionalité," *Situations* I (Paris, 1947).

[3]For example, some professors specify in their reading lists that a book should be read from pages 10 to 15—and do this to "help" their students!

[4]Erich Fromm, *The Heart of Man* (New York, 1966), p. 41.

[5]Ibid., p. 31.

[6]Ibid.

[7]Reinhold Niebuhr, *Moral Man and Immoral Society* (New York, 1960), p. 130.

[8]Sartre, op. cit., p. 32. [The passage is obscure but could be read as "Consciousness and the world are given at one and the same time: the exterior world as it enters consciousness is relative to our ways of seeing and understanding that world."—Editors' note]

[9]Edmund Husserl, *Ideas—General Introduction to Pure Phenomenology* (London, 1969), pp. 105–06.

Understanding the Text

1. Summarize the "banking concept of education," as Freire understands it. What are the main features of this kind of education?

2. What is the "teacher-student contradiction," according to Freire? Why is it important for his criticism of conventional schooling? Do you agree with him? Why or why not?

3. In what ways is education "the exercise of domination," as Freire sees it?

4. What is "liberating education" or "problem-posing education" according to Freire? How is this kind of education different from the banking concept of education that Freire criticizes? Do you think problem-posing education, as Freire describes it, would solve the problems he sees with conventional education? Explain.

5. What does Freire mean when he says that problem-posing education should foster a "critical intervention in reality"? In what sense can students "intervene" in reality, as Freire sees it? Why is this intervention so important to him?

6. Why does Freire's problem-posing approach to education describe people as "beings in the process of becoming"? What exactly does that mean? Why is that important in his approach to education?

Exploring the Issues

1. What does Freire mean when he describes students as "oppressed" and teachers as "oppressors"? Using Freire's ideas, explain how you as a student might be described as oppressed within formal schooling. Cite specific passages from his essay to support your answer.

2. Review Freire's list of the ten "attitudes and practices" of conventional education listed in paragraph 8. Does this list sound at all familiar to you? Do you think it accurately describes schools you have attended? Explain.

3. In paragraph 41, Freire discusses *permanence* and *change.* He claims that conventional education, which he describes as the "banking model of education," emphasizes permanence, whereas his problem-posing approach to education is based on the possibility of change. Based on your own experiences as a student and your own knowledge of education, do you think Freire is right on this point? Why or why not? Refer to your own experiences as well as to specific passages from Freire's essay to support your answer.

4. What would Freire's problem-posing method of education mean for American schools? What exactly do you think it would look like if it were applied to American schools? What specific changes would it lead to? Do

you think it would work? Why or why not?

5. Freire's educational theories and proposed reforms have been criticized as too political. Based on this essay, do you think those criticisms are justified? Explain.

6. Why do you think Freire's ideas about education have been so influential? What appeal do you see in his theories? What might the appeal of his ideas in Western nations like the United States suggest to you about the problems facing the educational systems in those nations?

Entering the Conversations

1. Write a conventional essay in which you explain Freire's ideas about education. In your essay, summarize his criticisms of what he calls the "banking concept of education" and describe his "problem-posing" method. Explain his basic ideas regarding knowledge and reality and how those ideas figure into his criticisms of conventional education. Draw your own conclusions about the effectiveness of his proposed method of education.

2. Rewrite the essay you wrote for Question 1 for a general audience, such as readers of a publication such as *USA Today* or the readers of your local newspaper.

3. Using Freire's ideas about education, write an analysis of your own school (you can choose to analyze your high school or your college). In your essay, summarize what you believe are the most important of Freire's ideas. Then apply those ideas to your own experiences in your school. In what ways might Freire's ideas help explain your experiences? What do his ideas reveal about the school you attended? On the basis of your critique, draw conclusions about any changes that you believe should be made to your school.

4. In a group of classmates, compare the essays you wrote for Question 3. In what ways do your essays describe similar or different problems in the schools you attended? On the basis of your discussion, try to draw conclusions about the usefulness of Freire's ideas about education or about problems you see with his ideas.

INFOTRAC

5. Using InfoTrac College Edition, the Internet, your library, and any other relevant sources, try to determine whether Freire's ideas have been applied to schools in the United States or elsewhere. Examine how those schools have used Freire's ideas. Try to find reviews or criticisms of Freire's work that might help you gain a better understanding of some of the benefits or drawbacks of using his ideas about education in an American school setting. Then write a report for your classmates in which you describe these efforts and evaluate their effectiveness.

6. Using appropriate technology and working with several classmates, create a video or photo collage that illustrates Freire's criticisms of the banking concept of education. Alternatively, create a web site with the same purpose.

In the following essay, Richard Rodriguez (b. 1944) writes that "education requires radical self-reformation." In a sense, Hunger of Memory *(1982), the autobiography in which this essay first appeared, is Rodriguez's explanation of that statement. And his explanation is a sobering one. He shares his experiences as the son of Mexican immigrants*

THE Achievement OF Desire

who becomes a successful student in American schools, pursuing his education all the way to doctoral studies in English literature. Such academic success is usually celebrated, but Rodriguez writes movingly of the profound personal costs of his success. In doing so, Rodriguez joins a longstanding and often intense set of conversations about schooling in America. Those conversations have in recent decades often focused on the rigid and even oppressive nature of formal education in the United States. Many scholars have argued that schools reflect a narrow set of values that exclude students like Rodriguez, who come from diverse backgrounds. But Rodriguez complicates the issue by describing how a "non-mainstream" student like himself could achieve success in schools.

When it was first published, Hunger of Memory *received much attention—and criticism—and it eventually became an important part of national discussions about*

RICHARD RODRIGUEZ

I stand in the ghetto classroom—"the guest speaker"—attempting to lecture on the mystery of the sounds of our words to rows of diffident students. "Don't you hear it? Listen! The music of our words. *'Sumer is icumen in. . . .'* And songs on the car radio. We need Aretha Franklin's voice to fill plain words with music—her life." In the face of their empty stares, I try to create an enthusiasm. But the girls in the back row turn to watch some boy passing outside. There are flutters of smiles, waves. And someone's mouth elongates heavy, silent words through the barrier of glass. Silent words—the lips straining to shape each voiceless syllable: *"Meet meee late err."* By the door, the instructor smiles at me, apparently hoping that I will be able to spark some enthusiasm in the class. But only one student seems to be listening. A girl, maybe fourteen. In this gray room her eyes shine with ambition. She keeps nodding and nodding at all that I say; she even takes notes. And each time I ask a question, she jerks up and down in her desk like a marionette, while her hand waves over the bowed heads of her classmates. It is myself (as a boy) I see as she faces me now (a man in my thirties).

bilingual education in the United States. Since then, Rodriguez's voice has continued to be heard in discussions about education. He has worked for the Pacific News Service in San Francisco and has appeared as an essayist on PBS's The News Hour *with Jim Lehrer. He has also written essays for newspapers and magazines and has authored several other books, including* Days of Obligation: An Argument with My Mexican Father *(1993), which was nominated for the Pulitzer Prize in nonfiction.* ◪

The boy who first entered a classroom barely able to speak English, twenty years later concluded his studies in the stately quiet of the reading room in the British Museum. Thus with one sentence I can summarize my academic career. It will be harder to summarize what sort of life connects the boy to the man.

With every award, each graduation from one level of education to the next, people I'd meet would congratulate me. Their refrain always the same: "Your parents must be very proud." Sometimes then they'd ask me how I managed it—my "success." (How?) After a while, I had several quick answers to give in reply. I'd admit, for one thing, that I went to an excellent grammar school. (My earliest teachers, the nuns, made my success their ambition.) And my brother and both my sisters were very good students. (They often brought home the shiny school trophies I came to want.) And my mother and father always encouraged me. (At every graduation they were behind the stunning flash of the camera when I turned to look at the crowd.)

As important as these factors were, however, they account inadequately for my academic advance. Nor do they suggest what an odd success I managed. For although I was a very good student, I was also a very bad student. I was a "scholarship boy," a certain kind of scholarship boy. Always successful, I was always unconfident. Exhilarated by my progress. Sad. I became the prized student—anxious and eager to learn. Too eager, too anxious—an imitative and unoriginal pupil. My brother and two sisters enjoyed the advantages I did, and they grew to be as successful as I, but none of them ever seemed so anxious about their schooling. A second-grade student, I was the one who came home and corrected the "simple" grammatical mistakes of our parents. ("Two negatives make a positive.") Proudly I announced—to my family's startled silence—that a teacher had said I was losing all trace of a Spanish accent. I was oddly annoyed when I was unable to get parental help with a homework assignment. The night my father tried to help me with an arithmetic exercise, he kept reading the instructions, each time more deliberately, until I pried the textbook out of his hands, saying, "I'll try to figure it out some more by myself."

When I reached the third grade, I outgrew such behavior. I became more tactful, careful to keep separate the two very different worlds of my day. But then, with ever-increasing intensity, I devoted myself to my studies. I became bookish, puzzling to all my family. Ambition set me apart. When my brother saw me struggling home with stacks of library books, he would laugh, shouting: "Hey, Four Eyes!" My father opened a closet one day and was

5

CONVERSATIONS: BILINGUAL EDUCATION

Rodriguez's first language was Spanish, but he writes here that he was proud to be losing his Spanish accent. He tells us that he tried to emulate his teachers, who spoke English. The elementary school classrooms he attended were really "English-only" classrooms, in which Spanish-speaking students were required to do their work in English. In part because of the difficulties faced by such students, many schools throughout the country implemented bilingual education programs, in which students could be taught in both English and their first language. Proponents of these programs argued that students would learn the content of the curriculum better if they studied in their first language, and eventually they would be able to learn in English, too. Critics of these programs argued that bilingual education placed students like Rodriguez at a disadvantage because it treated them differently from "mainstream" students and delayed their learning of English. After his book *Hunger of Memory* was published, Rodriguez became an outspoken opponent of bilingual education. Consider how his criticisms of bilingual education relate to his experiences as a student.

startled to find me inside, reading a novel. My mother would find me reading when I was supposed to be asleep or helping around the house or playing outside. In a voice angry or worried or just curious, she'd ask: "What do you see in your books?" It became the family's joke. When I was called and wouldn't reply, someone would say I must be hiding under my bed with a book.

(How did I manage my success?)

What I am about to say to you has taken me more than twenty years to admit: *A primary reason for my success in the classroom was that I couldn't forget that schooling was changing me and separating me from the life I enjoyed before becoming a student.* That simple realization! For years I never spoke to anyone about it. Never mentioned a thing to my family or my teachers or classmates. From a very early age, I understood enough, just enough about my classroom experiences to keep what I knew repressed, hidden beneath layers of embarrassment. Not until my last months as a graduate student, nearly thirty years old, was it possible for me to think much about the reasons for my academic success. Only then. At the end of my schooling, I needed to determine how far I had moved from my past. The adult finally confronted, and now must publicly say, what the child shuddered from knowing and could never admit to himself or to those many faces that smiled at his every success. ("Your parents must be very proud. . . .")

I

At the end, in the British Museum (too distracted to finish my dissertation) for weeks I read, speed-read, books by modern educational theorists, only to find infrequent and slight mention of students like me. (Much more is written about the more typical case, the lower-class student who barely is helped by his schooling.) Then one day, leafing through **RICHARD HOGGART'S *THE USES OF LITERACY*,** I found, in his description of the scholarship boy, myself. For the first time I realized that there were other students like me, and so I was able to frame the meaning of my academic success, its consequent price—the loss.

Hoggart's description is distinguished, at least initially, by deep understanding. What he grasps very well is that the scholarship boy must move between environments, his home and the classroom, which are at cultural extremes, opposed. With his family, the boy has the intense pleasure of intimacy, the family's consolation in feeling public alienation. Lavish emotions texture home life. *Then,* at school, the instruction bids him to trust lonely reason primarily. Immediate needs set the pace of his parents' lives. From his mother and father the boy learns to trust spontaneity and nonrational ways of knowing. *Then,* at school, there is mental calm. Teachers emphasize the value of a reflectiveness that opens a space between thinking and immediate action.

CONVERSATIONS: HOGGART'S SCHOLARSHIP BOY
Notice how Rodriguez uses Richard Hoggart's book *The Uses of Literacy* in this passage and elsewhere in this essay. In a way, Rodriguez is engaging in a conversation about literacy and education that Hoggart was also engaging in. Rodriguez relies heavily on Hoggart's ideas in his discussion of his own experiences as a "scholarship boy," a term he borrows from Hoggart. Consider how this use of Hoggart's ideas and even his phrases helps Rodriguez make his points.

STRATEGIES: SUMMARY
Rodriguez devotes much attention to
summarizing and highlighting the ideas
of Richard Hoggart, as expressed in
Hoggart's book *The Uses of Literacy*.
Examine Rodriguez's summaries of
Hoggart's ideas and consider how the
summaries help him make sense of his
own experiences as a young student. This
is a good example of how a writer can
use a summary strategically to
accomplish his or her purpose in an
essay.

Years of schooling must pass before the boy will be able to sketch   10
the cultural differences in his day as abstractly as this. But he senses
those differences early. Perhaps as early as the night he brings
home an assignment from school and finds the house too noisy for
study.

> He has to be more and more alone, if he is going to "get on."
> He will have, probably unconsciously, to oppose the ethos of
> the hearth, the intense gregariousness of the working-class
> family group. Since everything centers upon the living-room,
> there is unlikely to be a room of his own; the bedrooms are
> cold and inhospitable, and to warm them or the front room,
> if there is one, would not only be expensive, but would re-
> quire an imaginative leap—out of the tradition—which most
> families are not capable of making. There is a corner of the
> living-room table. On the other side Mother is ironing, the
> wireless is on, someone is singing a snatch of song or Father
> says intermittently whatever comes into his head. The boy has
> to cut himself off mentally, so as to do his homework, as well
> as he can.[1]

The next day, the lesson is as apparent at school. There are even rows
of desks. Discussion is ordered. The boy must rehearse his thoughts
and raise his hand before speaking out in a loud voice to an audience
of classmates. And there is time enough, and silence, to think about
ideas (big ideas) never considered at home by his parents.

Not for the working-class child alone is adjustment to the classroom
difficult. Good schooling requires that any student alter early childhood habits. But the working-class child is usually least prepared for
the change. And, unlike many middle-class children, he goes home
and sees in his parents a way of life not only different but starkly opposed to that of the classroom. (He enters the house and hears his
parents talking in ways his teachers discourage.)

Without extraordinary determination and the great assistance of
others—at home and at school—there is little chance for success.
Typically most working-class children are barely changed by the classroom. The exception succeeds. The relative few become scholarship
students. Of these, Richard Hoggart estimates, most manage a fairly
graceful transition. Somehow learn to live in the two very different worlds of their day. There are some others, however, those Hoggart pejoratively terms "scholarship boys," for whom success comes
with special anxiety. Scholarship boy: good student, troubled son.
The child is "moderately endowed," intellectually mediocre, Hoggart
supposes—though it may be more pertinent to note the special qualities of temperament in the child. High-strung child. Brooding. Sensitive. Haunted by the knowledge that one *chooses* to become a student.
(Education is not an inevitable or natural step in growing up.) Here

is a child who cannot forget that his academic success distances him from a life he loved, even from his own memory of himself.

Initially, he wavers, balances allegiance. ("The boy is himself [until he reaches, say, the upper **FORMS**] very much of *both* the worlds of home and school. He is enormously obedient to the dictates of the world of school, but emotionally still strongly wants to continue as part of the family circle.") Gradually, necessarily, the balance is lost. The boy needs to spend more and more time studying, each night enclosing himself in the silence permitted and required by intense concentration. He takes his first step toward academic success, away from his family.

From the very first days, through the years following, it will be with his parents—the figures of lost authority, the persons toward whom he feels deepest love—that the change will be most powerfully measured. A separation will unravel between them. Advancing in his studies, the boy notices that his mother and father have not changed as much as he. Rather, when he sees them, they often remind him of the person he once was and the life he earlier shared with them. He realizes what some Romantics also know when they praise the working class for the capacity for human closeness, qualities of passion and spontaneity, that the rest of us experience in like measure only in the earliest part of our youth. For the Romantic, this doesn't make working-class life childish. Working-class life challenges precisely because it is an *adult* way of life.

The scholarship boy reaches a different conclusion. He cannot afford to admire his parents. (How could he and still pursue such a contrary life?) He permits himself embarrassment at their lack of education. And to evade nostalgia for the life he has lost, he concentrates on the benefits education will bestow upon him. He becomes especially ambitious. Without the support of old certainties and consolations, almost mechanically, he assumes the procedures and doctrines of the classroom. The kind of allegiance the young student might have given his mother and father only days earlier, he transfers to the teacher, the new figure of authority. "[The scholarship boy] tends to make a father-figure of his form-master," Hoggart observes.

But Hoggart's calm prose only makes me recall the urgency with which I came to idolize my grammar school teachers. I began by imitating their accents, using their diction, trusting their every direction. The very first facts they dispensed, I grasped with awe. Any book they told me to read, I read—then waited for them to tell me which books I enjoyed. Their every casual opinion I came to adopt and to trumpet when I returned home. I stayed after school "to help"—to get my teacher's undivided attention. It was the nun's encouragement that mattered most to me. (She understood exactly what—my parents never seemed to appraise so well—all my achievements entailed.) Memory gently caressed each word of praise bestowed in the class-

GLOSS: FORMS
"Forms" is a British term that refers to school grades. "Upper forms" would be equivalent to American high school grades 9–12.

15

room so that compliments teachers paid me years ago come quickly to mind even today.

The enthusiasm I felt in second-grade classes I flaunted before both my parents. The docile, obedient student came home a shrill and precocious son who insisted on correcting and teaching his parents with the remark: "My teacher told us. . . ."

I intended to hurt my mother and father. I was still angry at them for having encouraged me toward classroom English. But gradually this anger was exhausted, replaced by guilt as school grew more and more attractive to me. I grew increasingly successful, a talkative student. My hand was raised in the classroom; I yearned to answer any question. At home, life was less noisy than it had been. (I spoke to classmates and teachers more often each day than to family members.) Quiet at home, I sat with my papers for hours each night. I never forgot that schooling had irretrievably changed my family's life. That knowledge, however, did not weaken ambition. Instead, it strengthened resolve. Those times I remembered the loss of my past with regret, I quickly reminded myself of all the things my teachers could give me. (They could make me an educated man.) I tightened my grip on pencil and books. I evaded nostalgia. Tried hard to forget. But one does not forget by trying to forget. One only remembers. I remembered too well that education had changed my family's life. I would not have become a scholarship boy had I not so often remembered.

20   Once she was sure that her children knew English, my mother would tell us, "You should keep up your Spanish." Voices playfully groaned in response. "¡Pochos!" my mother would tease. I listened silently.

After a while, I grew more calm at home. I developed tact. A fourth-grade student, I was no longer the show-off in front of my parents. I became a conventionally dutiful son, politely affectionate, cheerful enough, even—for reasons beyond choosing—my father's favorite. And much about my family life was easy then, comfortable, happy in the rhythm of our living together: hearing my father getting ready for work; eating the breakfast my mother had made me; looking up from a novel to hear my brother or one of my sisters playing with friends in the backyard; in winter, coming upon the house all lighted up after dark.

But withheld from my mother and father was any mention of what most mattered to me: the extraordinary experience of first-learning. Late afternoon: in the midst of preparing dinner, my mother would come up behind me while I was trying to read. Her head just over mine, her breath warmly scented with food. "What are you reading?" Or, "Tell me all about your new courses." I would barely respond, "Just the usual things, nothing special." (A half smile, then silence. Her head moving back in the silence. Silence! Instead of the flood of intimate sounds that had once flowed smoothly between us, there was this silence.) After dinner, I would rush to a bedroom with papers and books. As often as possible, I resisted parental pleas to "save lights" by coming to the kitchen to work. I kept so much, so often, to myself. Sad. Enthusiastic. Troubled by the excitement of coming upon new ideas. Eager. Fascinated by the promising texture of a brand-new book. I hoarded the pleasures of learning. Alone for hours. Enthralled. Nervous. I rarely looked away from my books—or back on my memories. Nights when relatives visited and the front rooms were warmed by Spanish sounds, I slipped quietly out of the house.

It mattered that education was changing me. It never ceased to matter. My brother and sisters would giggle at our mother's mispronounced words. They'd correct her gently. My mother laughed girlishly one night, trying not to pronounce *sheep* as *ship*. From a distance I listened sullenly. From that distance, pretending not to notice on another occasion, I saw my father looking at the title pages of my library books. That was the scene on my mind when I walked home with a fourth-grade companion and heard him say that his parents read to him every night. (A strange-sounding book—*Winnie the Pooh*.) Immediately, I wanted to know, "What is it like?" My companion, however, thought I wanted to know about the plot of the book. Another day, my mother surprised me by asking for a "nice" book to read. "Something not too hard you think I might like." Carefully I chose one, Willa Cather's *My Antonia*. But when, several weeks later, I happened to see it next to her bed unread except for the first few pages, I was furious and suddenly wanted to cry. I grabbed up the book and took it back to my room and placed it in its place, alphabetically on my shelf.

*   *   *

"Your parents must be very proud of you." People began to say that to me about the time I was in sixth grade. To answer affirmatively, I'd smile. Shyly I'd smile, never betraying my sense of the irony: I was not proud of my mother and father. I was embarrassed by their lack of education. It was not that I ever thought they were stupid, though stupidly I took for granted their enormous native intelligence. Simply, what mattered to me was that they were not like my teachers.

But, "Why didn't you tell us about the award?" my mother demanded, her frown weakened by pride. At the grammar school ceremony several weeks after, her eyes were brighter than the trophy I'd won. Pushing back the hair from my forehead, she whispered that I had "shown" the *gringos*. A few minutes later, I heard my father speak to my teacher and felt ashamed of his labored, accented words. Then guilty for the shame. I felt such contrary feelings. (There is no simple roadmap through the heart of the scholarship boy.) My teacher was so soft-

25

spoken and her words were edged sharp and clean. I admired her until it seemed to me that she spoke too carefully. Sensing that she was condescending to them, I became nervous. Resentful. Protective. I tried to move my parents away. "You both must be very proud of Richard," the nun said. They responded quickly. (They were proud.) "We are proud of all our children." Then this afterthought: "They sure didn't get their brains from us." They all laughed. I smiled.

*   *   *

Tightening the irony into a knot was the knowledge that my parents were always behind me. They made success possible. They evened the path. They sent their children to parochial schools because the nuns "teach better." They paid a tuition they couldn't afford. They spoke English to us.

For their children my parents wanted chances they never had—an easier way. It saddened my mother to learn that some relatives forced their children to start working right after high school. To *her* children she would say, "Get all the education you can." In schooling she recognized the key to job advancement. And with the remark she remembered her past.

As a girl new to America my mother had been awarded a high school diploma by teachers too careless or busy to notice that she hardly spoke English. On her own, she determined to learn how to type. That skill got her jobs typing envelopes in letter shops, and it encouraged in her an optimism about the possibility of advancement. (Each morning when her sisters put on uniforms, she chose a bright-colored dress.) The years of young womanhood passed, and her typing speed increased. She also became an excellent speller of words she mispronounced. "And I've never been to college," she'd say, smiling, when her children asked her to spell words they were too lazy to look up in a dictionary.

Typing, however, was dead-end work. Finally frustrating. When her youngest child started high school, my mother got a full-time office job once again. (Her paycheck combined with my father's to make us—in fact—what we had already become in our imagination of ourselves—middle class.) She worked then for the (California) state government in numbered civil service positions secured by examinations. The old ambition of her youth was rekindled. During the lunch hour, she consulted bulletin boards for announcements of openings. One day she saw mention of something called an "anti-poverty agency." A typing job. A glamorous job, part of the governor's staff. "A knowledge of Spanish required." Without hesitation she applied and became nervous only when the job was suddenly hers.

30   "Everyone comes to work all dressed up," she reported at night. And didn't need to say more than that her co-workers wouldn't let

her answer the phones. She was only a typist, after all, albeit a very fast typist. And an excellent speller. One morning there was a letter to be sent to a Washington cabinet officer. On the dictating tape, a voice referred to urban guerrillas. My mother typed (the wrong word, correctly): "gorillas." The mistake horrified the anti-poverty bureaucrats who shortly after arranged to have her returned to her previous position. She would go no further. So she willed her ambition to her children. "Get all the education you can; with an education you can do anything." (With a good education *she* could have done anything.)

When I was in high school, I admitted to my mother that I planned to become a teacher someday. That seemed to please her. But I never tried to explain that it was not the occupation of teaching I yearned for as much as it was something more elusive: I wanted to *be* like my teachers, to possess their knowledge, to assume their authority, their confidence, even to assume a teacher's persona.

In contrast to my mother, my father never verbally encouraged his children's academic success. Nor did he often praise us. My mother had to remind him to "say something" to one of his children who scored some academic success. But whereas my mother saw in education the opportunity for job advancement, my father recognized that education provided an even more startling possibility: it could enable a person to escape from a life of mere labor.

In Mexico, orphaned when he was eight, my father left school to work as an "apprentice" for an uncle. Twelve years later, he left Mexico in frustration and arrived in America. He had great expectations then of becoming an engineer. ("Work for my hands and my head.") He knew a Catholic priest who promised to get him money enough to study full time for a high school diploma. But the promises came to nothing. Instead there was a dark succession of warehouse, cannery, and factory jobs. After work he went to night school along with my mother. A year, two passed. Nothing much changed, except that fatigue worked its way into the bone; then everything changed. He didn't talk anymore of becoming an engineer. He stayed outside on the steps of the school while my mother went inside to learn typing and shorthand.

By the time I was born, my father worked at "clean" jobs. For a time he was a janitor at a fancy department store. ("Easy work; the machines do it all.") Later he became a dental technician. ("Simple.") But by then he was pessimistic about the ultimate meaning of work and the possibility of ever escaping its claims. In some of my earliest memories of him, my father already seems aged by fatigue. (He has never really grown old like my mother.) From boyhood to manhood, I have remembered him in a single image: seated, asleep on the sofa, his head thrown back in a hideous corpselike grin, the evening newspaper spread out before him. "But look at all you've accomplished," his best friend said to him once. My father said nothing. Only smiled.

35   It was my father who laughed when I claimed to be tired by reading and writing. It was he who teased me for having soft hands. (He seemed to sense that some great achievement of leisure was implied by my papers and books.) It was my father who became angry while watching on television some woman at the Miss America contest tell the announcer that she was going to college. ("Majoring in fine arts.") "College!" he snarled. He despised the trivialization of higher education, the inflated grades and cheapened diplomas, the half education that so often passed as mass education in my generation.

It was my father again who wondered why I didn't display my awards on the wall of my bedroom. He said he liked to go to doctors' offices and see their certificates and degrees on the wall. ("Nice.") My citations from school got left in closets at home. The gleaming figure astride one of my trophies was broken, wingless, after hitting the ground. My medals were placed in a jar of loose change. And when I lost my high school diploma, my father found it as it was about to be thrown out with the trash. Without telling me, he put it away with his own things for safekeeping.

*   *   *

CONVERSATIONS: SCHOOLING AND CULTURAL DIVERSITY
In paragraph 38, Rodriguez describes leaving home for college, but in many ways he had already left home. His American education created a distance between him and his family. Rodriguez's experience suggests some of the reasons that people from minority backgrounds sometimes distrust American schooling, which some critics believe does not sufficiently value students' cultural and ethnic backgrounds. In view of Rodriguez's experience, consider this advertisement from the American Indian College Fund, which supports colleges run by American Indian tribes. The caption reads: "If I stay on the rez I can use my education to help my people." How might this ad support—or complicate—Rodriguez's analysis of his own educational experience?

These memories slammed together at the instant of hearing that refrain familiar to all scholarship students: "Your parents must be proud. . . ." Yes, my parents were proud. I knew it. But my parents regarded my progress with more than mere pride. They endured my early precocious behavior—but with what private anger and humiliation? As their children got older and would come home to challenge ideas both of them held, they argued before submitting to the force of logic or superior factual evidence with the disclaimer, "It's what we were taught in our time to believe." These discussions ended abruptly, though my mother remembered them on other occasions when she complained that our "big ideas" were going to our heads. More acute was her complaint that the family wasn't close anymore, like some others she knew. Why weren't we close, "more in the Mexican style"? Everyone is so private, she added. And she mimicked the yes and no answers she got in reply to her questions. Why didn't we talk more? (My father never asked.) I never said.

I was the first in my family who asked to leave home when it came time to go to college. I had been admitted to Stanford, one hundred miles away. My departure would only make physically apparent the separation that had occurred long before. But it was going too far. In the months preceding my leaving, I heard the question my mother never asked except indirectly. In the hot kitchen, tired at the end of her workday, she demanded to know, "Why aren't the colleges here in Sacramento good enough for you? They are for your brother and sister." In the middle of a car ride, not turning to face me, she wondered, "Why do you need to go so far away?" Late at night, ironing, she said with disgust, "Why do you have to put us through this big expense? You know your scholarship will never cover it all." But when September came there was a rush to get everything ready. In a bedroom that last night I packed the big brown valise, and my mother sat nearby sewing initials onto the clothes I would take. And she said no more about my leaving.

Months later, two weeks of Christmas vacation: the first hours home were the hardest. ("What's new?") My parents and I sat in the kitchen for a conversation. (But, lacking the same words to develop our sentences and to shape our interests, what was there to say? What could I tell them of the term paper I had just finished on the "universality of Shakespeare's appeal"?) I mentioned only small, obvious things: my dormitory life; weekend trips I had taken; random events. They responded with news of their own. (One was almost grateful for a family crisis about which there was much to discuss.) We tried to make our conversation seem like more than an interview.

II

From an early age I knew that my mother and father could read and write both Spanish and English. I had observed my father making his way through what, I now suppose, must have been income tax forms. On other occasions I waited apprehensively while my mother read onion-paper letters airmailed from Mexico with news of a relative's illness or death. For both my parents, however, reading was something done out of necessity and as quickly as possible. Never did I see either of them read an entire book. Nor did I see them read for pleasure. Their reading consisted of work manuals, prayer books, newspaper, recipes.

Richard Hoggart imagines how, at home,

> . . . [the scholarship boy] sees strewn around, and reads regularly himself, magazines which are never mentioned at school, which seem not to belong to the world to which the school introduces him; at school he hears about and reads books never mentioned at home. When he brings those books into the house they do not take their place with other books which the family are reading, for often there are none or almost none; his books look, rather, like strange tools.

In our house each school year would begin with my mother's careful instruction: "Don't write in your books so we can sell them at the end of the year." The remark was echoed in public by my teachers, but only in part: "Boys and girls, don't write in your books. You must learn to treat them with great care and respect."

OPEN THE DOORS OF YOUR MIND WITH BOOKS, read the red and white poster over the nun's desk in early September. It soon was apparent to me that reading was the classroom's central activity. Each course had its own book. And the information gathered from a book was unquestioned. READ TO LEARN, the sign on the wall advised in December. I privately wondered: What was the connection between reading and learning? Did one learn something only by reading it? Was an idea only an idea if it could be written down? In June, CONSIDER BOOKS YOUR BEST FRIENDS. Friends? Reading was, at best, only a chore. I needed to look up whole paragraphs of words in a dictionary: Lines of type were dizzying, the eye having to move slowly across the page, then down, and across. . . . The sentences of the first books I read were coolly impersonal. Toned hard. What most bothered me, however, was the isolation reading required. To console myself for the loneliness I'd feel when I read, I tried reading in a very soft voice. Until: "Who is doing all that talking to his neighbor?" Shortly after, remedial reading classes were arranged for me with a very old nun.

At the end of each school day, for nearly six months, I would meet with her in the tiny room that served as the school's library but was actually only a storeroom for used textbooks and a vast collection of *National Geographics.* Everything about our sessions pleased me: the smallness of the room; the noise of the janitor's broom hitting the edge of the long hallway outside the door; the green of the sun, lighting the wall; and the old woman's face blurred white with a beard. Most of the time we took turns. I began with my elementary text. Sentences of astonishing simplicity seemed to me lifeless and drab: "The boys ran from the rain . . . She wanted to sing . . . The kite rose in the blue." Then the old nun would read from her favorite books, usually biographies of early American presidents. Playfully she ran through complex sentences, calling the words alive with her voice, making it seem that the author somehow was speaking directly to me. I smiled just to listen to her. I sat there and sensed for the very first time some possibility of fellowship between a reader and a writer, a communication, never *intimate* like that I heard spoken words at home convey, but one nonetheless *personal.*

One day the nun concluded a session by asking me why I was so reluctant to read by myself. I tried to explain; said something about the way written words made me feel all alone—almost, I wanted to add but didn't, as when I spoke to myself in a room just emptied of furniture. She studied my face as I spoke; she seemed to be watching more than listening. In an uneventful voice she replied that I had nothing to fear. Didn't I realize that reading would open up whole new worlds? A book could open doors for me. It could introduce me to people and show me places I never imagined existed. She gestured toward the bookshelves. (Bare-breasted African women danced, and the shiny hubcaps of automobiles on the back covers of the *Geographic* gleamed in my mind.) I listened with respect. But her words were not very influential. I was thinking then of another consequence of literacy, one I was too shy to admit but nonetheless trusted. Books were going to make me "educated." *That* confidence enabled me, several months later, to overcome my fear of the silence.

45   In fourth grade I embarked upon a grandiose reading program. "Give me the names of important books," I would say to startled teachers. They soon found out that I had in mind "adult books." I ignored their suggestion of anything I suspected was written for children. (Not until I was in college, as a result, did I read *Huckleberry Finn* or *Alice's Adventures in Wonderland.*) Instead, I read *The Scarlet Letter* and Franklin's *Autobiography.* And whatever I read I read for extra credit. Each time I finished a book, I reported the achievement to a teacher and basked in the praise my effort earned. Despite my best efforts, however, there seemed to be more and more books I needed to read. At the library I would literally tremble as I came upon whole shelves of books I hadn't read. So I read and I read and I read: *Great Expectations;* all the short stories of Kipling; *The Babe Ruth Story;* the entire first volume of the *Encyclopedia Britannica* (A–ANSTEY); the *Iliad; Moby Dick; Gone with the Wind; The Good Earth; Ramona; Forever Amber; The Lives of the Saints; Crime and Punishment; The Pearl. . . .* Librarians who initially frowned when I checked out the maximum ten books at a time started saving books they thought I might like. Teachers would say to the rest of the class, "I only wish the rest of you took reading as seriously as Richard obviously does."

But at home I would hear my mother wondering, "What do you see in your books?" (Was reading a hobby like her knitting? Was so much reading even healthy for a boy? Was it the sign of "brains"? Or was it just a convenient excuse for not helping about the house on Saturday mornings?) Always, "What do you see . . . ?"

What *did* I see in my books? I had the idea that they were crucial for my academic success, though I couldn't have said exactly how or why. In the sixth grade I simply concluded that what gave a book its value was some major idea or theme it contained. If that core essence could be mined and memorized, I would become learned like my teachers. I decided to record in a notebook the themes of the books that I read. After reading *Robinson Crusoe,* I wrote that its theme was "the value of learning to live by oneself." When I completed *Wuthering Heights,* I noted the danger of "letting emotions get out of control." Rereading these brief moralistic appraisals usually left me disheartened. I couldn't believe that they were really the source of reading's value. But for many more years, they constituted the only means I had of describing to myself the educational value of books.

In spite of my earnestness, I found reading a pleasurable activity. I came to enjoy the lonely good company of books. Early on weekday

---

CONVERSATIONS: READING

In 2007, the National Endowment for the Arts (NEA) released a report called *To Read or Not To Read,* indicating a general decline in reading among American teenagers and adults. The report set off a national debate about the state of literacy among Americans, but that debate was really part of a seemingly endless conversation about whether American students read enough, write well enough, and learn enough. In this passage, Rodriguez describes himself as an unusually avid reader. His reading habits may strike you as remarkable because few young people read as much as Rodriguez did when he was a student. But later, in paragraph 47, Rodriguez raises questions about the value of the reading he did. How might his questions fit into the more recent conversations in the United States about whether Americans read enough?

mornings, I'd read in my bed. I'd feel a mysterious comfort then, reading in the dawn quiet—the blue-gray silence interrupted by the occasional churning of the refrigerator motor a few rooms away or the more distant sounds of a city bus beginning its run. On weekends I'd go to the public library to read, surrounded by old men and women. Or, if the weather was fine, I would take my books to the park and read in the shade of a tree. A warm summer evening was my favorite reading time. Neighbors would leave for vacation and I would water their lawns. I would sit through the twilight on the front porches or in backyards, reading to the cool, whirling sounds of the sprinklers.

I also had favorite writers. But often those writers I enjoyed most I was least able to value. When I read William Saroyan's *The Human Comedy*, I was immediately pleased by the narrator's warmth and the charm of his story. But as quickly I became suspicious. A book so enjoyable to read couldn't be very "important." Another summer I determined to read all the novels of Dickens. Reading his fat novels, I loved the feeling I got—after the first hundred pages—of being at home in a fictional world where I knew the names of the characters and cared about what was going to happen to them. And it bothered me that I was forced away at the conclusion, when the fiction closed tight, like a fortune-teller's fist—the futures of all the major characters neatly resolved. I never knew how to take such feelings seriously, however. Nor did I suspect that these experiences could be part of a novel's meaning. Still, there were pleasures to sustain me after I'd finish my books. Carrying a volume back to the library, I would be pleased by its weight. I'd run my fingers along the edge of the pages and marvel at the breadth of my achievement. Around my room, growing stacks of paperback books reenforced my assurance.

50   I entered high school having read hundreds of books. My habit of reading made me a confident speaker and writer of English. Reading also enabled me to sense something of the shape, the major concerns, of Western thought. (I was able to say something about Dante and Descartes and Engels and James Baldwin in my high school term papers.) In these various ways, books brought me academic success as I hoped that they would. But I was not a good reader. Merely bookish, I lacked a point of view when I read. Rather, I read in order to acquire a point of view. I vacuumed books for epigrams, scraps of information, ideas, themes—anything to fill the hollow within me and make me feel educated. When one of my teachers suggested to his drowsy tenth-grade English class that a person could not have a "complicated idea" until he had read at least two thousand books, I heard the remark without detecting either its irony or its very complicated truth. I merely determined to compile a list of all the books I had ever read. Harsh with myself, I included only once a title I might have read several times. (How, after all, could one read a book more than once?)

And I included only those books over a hundred pages in length. (Could anything shorter be a book?)

There was yet another high school list I compiled. One day I came across a newspaper article about the retirement of an English professor at a nearby state college. The article was accompanied by a list of the "hundred most important books of Western Civilization." "More than anything else in my life," the professor told the reporter with finality, "these books have made me all that I am." That was the kind of remark I couldn't ignore. I clipped out the list and kept it for the several months it took me to read all of the titles. Most books, of course, I barely understood. While reading Plato's *Republic,* for instance, I needed to keep looking at the book jacket comments to remind myself what the text was about. Nevertheless, with the special patience and superstition of a scholarship boy, I looked at every word of the text. And by the time I reached the last word, relieved, I convinced myself that I had read *The Republic.* In a ceremony of great pride, I solemnly crossed Plato off my list.

III

The scholarship boy pleases most when he is young—the working-class child struggling for academic success. To his teachers, he offers great satisfaction; his success is their proudest achievement. Many other persons offer to help him. A businessman learns the boy's story and promises to underwrite part of the cost of his college education. A woman leaves him her entire library of several hundred books when she moves. His progress is featured in a newspaper article. Many people seem happy for him. They marvel. "How did you manage so fast?" From all sides, there is lavish praise and encouragement.

In his grammar school classroom, however, the boy already makes students around him uneasy. They scorn his desire to succeed. They scorn him for constantly wanting the teacher's attention and praise. "Kiss Ass," they call him when his hand swings up in response to every question he hears. Later, when he makes it to college, no one will mock him aloud. But he detects annoyance on the faces of some students and even some teachers who watch him. It puzzles him often. In college, then in graduate school, he behaves much as he always has. If anything is different about him it is that he dares to anticipate the successful conclusion of his studies. At last he feels that he belongs in the classroom, and this is exactly the source of the dissatisfaction he causes. To many persons around him, he appears too much the academic. There may be some things about him that recall his beginnings—his shabby clothes; his persistent poverty; or his dark skin (in those cases when it symbolizes his parents' disadvantaged condition)—but they only make clear how far he has moved from his past. He has used education to remake himself.

It bothers his fellow academics to face this. They will not say why exactly. (They sneer.) But their expectations become obvious when they are disappointed. They expect—they want—a student less changed by his schooling. If the scholarship boy, from a past so distant from the classroom, could remain in some basic way unchanged, he would be able to prove that it is possible for anyone to become educated without basically changing from the person one was.

55   Here is no fabulous hero, no idealized scholar-worker. The scholarship boy does not straddle, cannot reconcile, the two great opposing cultures of his life. His success is unromantic and plain. He sits in the classroom and offers those sitting beside him no calming reassurance about their own lives. He sits in the seminar room—a man with brown skin, the son of working-class Mexican immigrant parents. (Addressing the professor at the head of the table, his voice catches with nervousness.) There is no trace of his parents' in his speech. Instead he approximates the accents of teachers and classmates. Coming from *him* those sounds seem suddenly odd. Odd too is the effect produced when *he* uses academic jargon—bubbles at the tip of his tongue: "*Topos* . . . negative capability . . . vegetation imagery in Shakespearean comedy." He lifts an opinion from Coleridge, takes something else from Frye or Empson or Leavis. He even repeats exactly his professor's earlier comment. All his ideas are clearly borrowed. He seems to have no thought of his own. He chatters while his listeners smile—their look one of disdain.

When he is older and thus when so little of the person he was survives, the scholarship boy makes only too apparent his profound lack of *self*-confidence. This is the conventional assessment that even Richard Hoggart repeats:

> [The scholarship boy] tends to over-stress the importance of examinations, of the piling-up of knowledge and of received opinions. He discovers a technique of apparent learning, of the acquiring of facts rather than of the handling and use of facts. He learns how to receive a purely literate education, one using only a small part of the personality and challenging only a limited area of his being. He begins to see life as a ladder, as permanent examination with some praise and some further exhortation at each stage. He becomes an expert imbiber and doler-out; his competence will vary, but will rarely be accompanied by genuine enthusiasms. He rarely feels the reality of knowledge, of other men's thoughts and imaginings, on his own pulses. . . . He has something of the blinkered pony about him.

But this is criticism more accurate than fair. The scholarship boy is a very bad student. He is the great mimic; a collector of thoughts, not a thinker; the very last person in class who ever feels obliged to have an opinion of his own. In large part, however, the reason he is such a bad student is because he realizes more often and more acutely than most other students—than Hoggart himself—that education requires radical self-reformation. As a very young boy, regarding his parents, as he struggles with an early homework assignment, he knows this too well. That is why he lacks self-assurance. He does not forget that the classroom is responsible for remaking him. He relies on his teacher, depends on all that he hears in the classroom and reads in his books. He becomes in every obvious way the worst student, a dummy mouthing the opinions of others. But he would not be so bad—nor would he become so successful, a *scholarship* boy—if he did not accurately perceive that the best synonym for primary "education" is "imitation."

Those who would take seriously the boy's success—and his failure—would be forced to realize how great is the change any academic undergoes, how far one must move from one's past. It is easiest to ignore such considerations. So little is said about the scholarship boy in pages and pages of educational literature. Nothing is said of the silence that comes to separate the boy from his parents. Instead, one hears proposals for increasing the self-esteem of students and encouraging early intellectual independence. Paragraphs glitter with a constellation of terms like *creativity* and *originality*. (Ignored altogether is the function of imitation in a student's life.) **RADICAL EDUCATIONALISTS** meanwhile complain that ghetto schools "oppress" students by trying to mold them, stifling native characteristics. The truer critique would be just the reverse: not that schools change ghetto students too much, but that while they might promote the occasional scholarship student, they change most students barely at all.

From the story of the scholarship boy there is no specific pedagogy to glean. There is, however, a much larger lesson. His story makes clear that education is a long, unglamorous, even demeaning process—*a nurturing never natural to the person one was before one entered a classroom.* At once different from most other students, the scholarship boy is also the archetypal "good student." He exaggerates the difficulty of being a student, but his exaggeration reveals a general predicament. Others are changed by their schooling as much as he. They too must re-form themselves. They must develop the skill of memory long before they become truly critical thinkers. And when they read Plato for the first several times, it will be with awe more than deep comprehension.

The impact of schooling on the scholarship boy is only more apparent to the boy himself and to others. Finally, although he may be laughable—a blinkered pony—the boy will not let his critics forget their own change. He ends up too much like them. When he speaks, they hear themselves echoed. In his pedantry, they trace their own. His ambitions are theirs. If his failure were singular, they might readily pity him. But he is more troubling than that. They would not scorn him if this were not so.

CONVERSATIONS: RADICAL EDUCATIONALISTS
In discussing the effects of his experiences in school, Rodriguez mentions "radical educationalists" who argue that "ghetto schools 'oppress' students by trying to mold them." Here, Rodriguez directly joins a lively debate about education reform that has been going on in the United States since public schooling came to be widespread during the nineteenth century. In particular, Rodriguez is referring to more recent discussions among scholars and theorists who believe that schooling in the United States reflects White middle-class values and compromises students, like Rodriguez, who come from different backgrounds. The writings of Paulo Freire, whose essay appears earlier in this cluster, have been influential in these professional discussions about education. Consider how Rodriguez's story carries certain kinds of meaning when it is read in the context of those discussions.

IV

60   Like me, Hoggart's imagined scholarship boy spends most of his years
in the classroom afraid to long for his past. Only at the very end of his
schooling does the boy-man become nostalgic. In this sudden change
of heart, Richard Hoggart notes:

> He longs for the membership he lost, "he pines for some
> Nameless Eden where he never was." The nostalgia is the
> stronger and the more ambiguous because he is really "in
> quest of his own absconded self yet scared to find it." He
> both wants to go back and yet thinks he has gone beyond
> his class, feels himself weighted with knowledge of his own
> and their situation, which hereafter forbids him the simpler
> pleasures of his father and mother.

According to Hoggart, the scholarship boy grows nostalgic because
he remains the uncertain scholar, bright enough to have moved from
his past, yet unable to feel easy, a part of a community of academics.

This analysis, however, only partially suggests what happened to me
in my last year as a graduate student. When I traveled to London to
write a dissertation on English Renaissance literature, I was finally
confident of membership in a "community of scholars." But the pleasure that confidence gave me faded rapidly. After only two or three
months in the reading room of the British Museum, it became clear
that I had joined a lonely community. Around me each day were dour
faces eclipsed by large piles of books. There were the regulars, like
the old couple who arrived every morning, each holding a loop of the
shopping bag which contained all their notes. And there was the historian who chattered madly to herself. ("Oh dear! Oh! Now, what's
this? What? Oh, my!") There were also the faces of young men and
women worn by long study. And everywhere eyes turned away the moment our glance accidentally met. Some persons I sat beside day after
day, yet we passed silently at the end of the day, strangers. Still, we
were united by a common respect for the written word and for scholarship. We did form a union, though one in which we remained distant from one another.

More profound and unsettling was the bond I recognized with
those writers whose books I consulted. Whenever I opened a text that
hadn't been used for years, I realized that my special interests and
skills united me to a mere handful of academics. We formed an exclusive—eccentric!—society, separated from others who would never
care or be able to share our concerns. (The pages I turned were stiff
like layers of dead skin.) I began to wonder: Who, beside my dissertation director and a few faculty members, would ever read what I
wrote? And: Was my dissertation much more than an act of social
withdrawal? These questions went unanswered in the silence of the
Museum reading room. They remained to trouble me after I'd leave

the library each afternoon and feel myself shy—unsteady, speaking simple sentences at the grocer's or the butcher's on my way back to my bed-sitter.

Meanwhile my file cards accumulated. A professional, I knew exactly how to search a book for pertinent information. I could quickly assess and summarize the usability of the many books I consulted. But whenever I started to write, I knew too much (and not enough) to be able to write anything but sentences that were overly cautious, timid, strained brittle under the heavy weight of footnotes and qualifications. I seemed unable to dare a passionate statement. I felt drawn by professionalism to the edge of sterility, capable of no more than pedantic, lifeless, unassailable prose.

Then nostalgia began.

After years spent unwilling to admit its attractions, I gestured nostalgically toward the past. I yearned for that time when I had not been so alone. I became impatient with books. I wanted experience more immediate. I feared the library's silence. I silently scorned the gray, timid faces around me. I grew to hate the growing pages of my dissertation on genre and Renaissance literature. (In my mind I heard relatives laughing as they tried to make sense of its title.) I wanted something—I couldn't say exactly what. I told myself that I wanted a more passionate life. And a life less thoughtful. And above all, I wanted to be less alone. One day I heard some Spanish academics whispering back and forth to each other, and their sounds seemed ghostly voices recalling my life. Yearning became preoccupation then. Boyhood memories beckoned, flooded my mind. (Laughing intimate voices. Bounding up the front steps of the porch. A sudden embrace inside the door.)

For weeks after, I turned to books by educational experts. I needed to learn how far I had moved from my past—to determine how fast I would be able to recover something of it once again. But I found little. Only a chapter in a book by Richard Hoggart. . . . I left the reading room and the circle of faces.

*   *   *

I came home. After the year in England, I spent three summer months living with my mother and father, relieved by how easy it was to be home. It no longer seemed very important to me that we had little to say. I felt easy sitting and eating and walking with them. I watched them, nevertheless, looking for evidence of those elastic, sturdy strands that bind generations in a web of inheritance. I thought as I watched my mother one night: Of course a friend had been right when she told me that I gestured and laughed just like my mother. Another time I saw for myself: my father's eyes were much like my own, constantly watchful.

But after the early relief, this return, came suspicion, nagging until I realized that I had not neatly sidestepped the impact of schooling. My desire to do so was precisely the measure of how much I remained an academic. *Negatively* (for that is how this idea first occurred to me): my need to think so much and so abstractly about my parents and our relationship was in itself an indication of my long education. My father and mother did not pass their thinking about the cultural meanings of their experience. It was I who described their daily lives with airy ideas. And yet, *positively:* the ability to consider experience so abstractly allowed me to shape into desire what would otherwise have remained indefinite, meaningless longing in the British Museum. If, because of my schooling, I had grown culturally separated from my parents, my education finally had given me ways of speaking and caring about that fact.

My best teachers in college and graduate school, years before, had tried to prepare me for this conclusion, I think, when they discussed texts of aristocratic pastoral literature. Faithfully, I wrote down all that they said. I memorized it: "The praise of the unlettered by the highly educated is one of the primary themes of 'elitist' literature." But, "the importance of the praise given the unsolitary, richly passionate and spontaneous life is that it simultaneously reflects the value of a reflective life." I heard it all. But there was no way for any of it to mean very much to me. I was a scholarship boy at the time, busily laddering my way up the rungs of education. To pass an examination, I copied down exactly what my teachers told me. It would require many more years of schooling (an inevitable miseducation) in which I came to trust the silence of reading and the habit of abstracting from immediate experience—moving away from a life of closeness and immediacy I remembered with my parents, growing older—before I turned unafraid to desire the past, and thereby achieved what had eluded me for so long—the end of education.

NOTES

[1]All quotations in this essay are from Richard Hoggart, *The Uses of Literacy* (London: Chatto and Windus, 1957), chapter 10. [Author's note]

Understanding the Text

1. Why does Rodriguez say that his family's support for him and the encouragement of his grammar school teachers do not adequately explain his academic success? How does he explain his success?

2. In paragraph 7, Rodriguez states that success in school separated him from his life at home. He offers several anecdotes that reveal how his relationship with his family changed as he became more successful in school. In what ways did that relationship change? Why did it change, in his view? How does he feel about these changes? Do you agree with him? Why or why not?

3. What is the primary effect of schooling on the student, especially the working-class student, according to Rodriguez? Do you think he is right? Explain.

4. Who is the "scholarship boy"? What distinguishes this kind of student? Why is this idea of the scholarship boy so important to Rodriguez?

5. What was the role of reading in Rodriguez's life as a young student? How is his reading different from his parents' reading? Why does he describe himself as "not a good reader" but "bookish"?

6. Why does Rodriguez eventually quit school before completing his doctoral program? What does this decision suggest about Rodriguez as a person? About his values?

Exploring the Issues

1. In the opening two paragraphs of this essay, Rodriguez describes a scene in which he is speaking to a classroom full of teenage students, one of whom reminds him of himself twenty years earlier. He "summarizes" his academic career in a single sentence (par. 2) and then writes, "It will be harder to summarize what sort of life connects the boy to the man." Examine how these two paragraphs introduce this essay. What tone does Rodriguez set in his introduction? What expectations does he create for you as a reader? What does he reveal about himself as a person? How might the sense you get of him in these two paragraphs influence the way you read the rest of the essay?

2. Rodriguez describes his life at home and his life at school as two separate worlds. How does he characterize these separate worlds? What are the main features of each, in his view? Why does he believe that success and comfort in one requires losing the other? Do you agree with him? Why or why not? What do Rodriguez's experiences suggest about schooling?

3. Rodriguez devotes much attention to describing his parents and telling his readers about their experiences and lives. What do we learn about his mother and father? What details does Rodriguez provide about them? What do his descriptions of his parents contribute to this essay? How do they help Rodriguez make his main points?

4. In some ways, this essay is a conventional autobiography in which Rodriguez tells the story of his experiences as a student more or less in chronological order. But he doesn't strictly follow a timeline of his life, and he often includes commentary about his experiences from his perspective many years after the events he is describing happened. Examine how Rodriguez tells his story and look in particular at how he organizes his essay. What does he emphasize? What do you think he leaves out? How effectively does he narrate his experiences to make his point?

Entering the Conversations

1. Write an essay in which you tell the story of your own experience as a student—your own educational autobiography. Try to tell your story in a way that emphasizes what you believe was most important about your experience, and use your experience to make a point—in the way Rodriguez uses his experiences to make a point about education.

2. In a group of classmates, share the essays you wrote for Question 1. What kinds of experiences in schools did you and your classmates focus on in your essays? What similarities and differences can you identify among these experiences? What conclusions can you draw about schooling from these experiences?

3. On the basis of your discussions in Question 2, write an essay for an audience of your classmates in which you offer your own view of schooling. In your essay, identify what you see as the problems and the benefits of schooling as you experienced it, and propose changes in schools that you

believe should be made. Draw on Rodriguez's essay, your classmates' essays, and any other relevant texts to help you make your points. Alternatively, write your essay as an editorial page essay for your local newspaper.

4. Interview a student whose first language is not English but who has attended American schools. (If you don't know someone like this, you might contact the office in your school that supports international students.) Try to get a sense of that person's

experience as a student in English-speaking schools. Write an essay on the basis of your interview, presenting this person's experience and drawing your own conclusions on the basis of that experience. (If you are a student whose first language is not English, write your essay based on your own experience.)

5. Rodriguez writes in his essay that "education requires radical self-reformation." Explain what he means and respond to his statement.

A few years ago, I had the good fortune to be at a writing awards dinner at which Adrienne Rich (b. 1929) was the keynote speaker. The event was a typical banquet in which student writers were celebrated for award-winning essays. Faculty members and parents were there, and the atmosphere was polite and celebratory. When Rich spoke, she

Taking Women Students Seriously

ADRIENNE RICH

also celebrated the winning writers, congratulating them on their accomplishments and encouraging them to continue writing. But she went on to say that writing wasn't about winning awards. It was about making change. "Write as if your life depended upon it," she told her audience, with great conviction in her voice.

Adrienne Rich has always written as if her life depends upon it. For Rich, writing is a way to fight for justice and to raise her voice in support of those she believes have been victimized. She is not only an internationally acclaimed poet, with sixteen books of poetry to her credit; she is also one of the most vocal and respected proponents of feminism. The following essay, which was first delivered as a talk to a gathering of women academics in 1978, has become a well-known critique of the treatment of women in education. It reflects some of the power of Rich's voice that has made

I see my function here today as one of trying to create a context, delineate a background, against which we might talk about women as students and students as women. I would like to speak for a while about this background, and then I hope that we can have, not so much a question period, as a raising of concerns, a sharing of questions for which we as yet may have no answers, an opening of conversations which will go on and on.

When I went to teach at Douglass, a women's college, it was with a particular background which I would like briefly to describe to you. I had graduated from an all-girls' school in the 1940s, where the head and the majority of the faculty were independent, unmarried women. One or two held doctorates, but had been forced by the Depression (and by the fact that they were women) to take secondary school teaching jobs. These women cared a great deal about the life of the mind, and they gave a great deal of time and energy—beyond any limit of teaching hours—to those of us who showed special intellectual interest or ability. We were taken to libraries, art

her the influential thinker and writer that she is. As you read, consider whether her arguments about gender in education have the same force today as they did in 1978.

In addition to poetry, for which she has won numerous awards, Adrienne Rich has written several books of essays, has won a MacArthur Foundation "genius" grant, and has taught writing at many colleges and universities, including Rutgers University and Stanford University. ▼

CONVERSATIONS: OPEN ADMISSIONS
Open admissions policies, which began at the City University of New York (CUNY) system in 1969, changed the criteria for students seeking admission to college, guaranteeing that students who graduated from accredited high schools would be admitted to CUNY. Many other colleges and universities followed CUNY's lead in implementing open admissions policies. These controversial policies enabled many students to attend college who previously would have been denied admission. Many educators believe that open admissions policies have made college more accessible to Americans; critics have argued that the policies have watered down the college curriculum and diminished the value of a college degree. In recent years, many colleges and universities, including CUNY, have eliminated open admissions policies. Consider what Rich's references to the SEEK program and to open admissions suggest about her own views about such programs and about higher education in general.

museums, lectures at neighboring colleges, set to work on extra research projects, given extra French or Latin reading. Although we sometimes felt "pushed" by them, we held those women in a kind of respect which even then we dimly perceived was not generally accorded to women in the world at large. They were vital individuals, defined not by their relationships but by their personalities; and although under the pressure of the culture we were all certain we wanted to get married, their lives did not appear empty or dreary to us. In a kind of cognitive dissonance, we knew they were "old maids" and therefore supposed to be bitter and lonely; yet we saw them vigorously involved with life. But despite their existence as alternate models of women, the *content* of the education they gave us in no way prepared us to survive as women in a world organized by and for men.

From that school, I went on to Radcliffe, congratulating myself that now I would have great men as my teachers. From 1947 to 1951, when I graduated, I never saw a single woman on a lecture platform, or in front of a class, except when a woman graduate student gave a paper on a special topic. The "great men" talked of other "great men," of the nature of Man, the history of Mankind, the future of Man; and never again was I to experience, from a teacher, the kind of prodding, the insistence that my best could be even better, that I had known in high school. Women students were simply not taken very seriously. Harvard's message to women was an elite mystification: we were, of course, part of Mankind; we were special, achieving women, or we would not have been there; but of course our real goal was to marry—if possible, a Harvard graduate.

In the late sixties, I began teaching at the City College of New York—a crowded, public, urban, multiracial institution as far removed from Harvard as possible. I went there to teach writing in the SEEK Program,° which predated **OPEN ADMISSIONS** and which was then a kind of model for programs designed to open up higher education to poor, black, and Third World students. Although during the next few years we were to see the original concept of SEEK diluted, then violently attacked and betrayed, it was for a short time an extraordinary and intense teaching and learning environment. The characteristics of this environment were a deep commitment on the part of teachers to the minds of their students; a constant, active effort to create or discover the conditions for learning, and to educate ourselves to meet the needs of the new college population; a philosophical attitude based on open discussion of racism, oppression, and the politics of literature and language; and a belief that learning in the classroom could not be isolated from the student's experience as a member of an urban minority group in white

°An acronym for "Search for Education, Elevation, and Knowledge."

America. Here are some of the kinds of questions we, as teachers of writing, found ourselves asking:

(1) What has been the student's experience of education in the inadequate, often abusively racist public school system, which rewards passivity and treats a questioning attitude or independent mind as a behavior problem? What has been her or his experience in a society that consistently undermines the selfhood of the poor and the nonwhite? How can such a student gain that sense of self which is necessary for active participation in education? What does all this mean for us as teachers?

(2) How do we go about teaching a canon of literature which has consistently excluded or depreciated nonwhite experience?

(3) How can we connect the process of learning to write well with the student's own reality, and not simply teach her/him how to write acceptable lies in standard English?

When I went to teach at Douglass College in 1976, and in teaching   5
women's writing workshops elsewhere, I came to perceive stunning
parallels to the questions I had first encountered in teaching the so-
called disadvantaged students at City. But in this instance, and against
the specific background of the women's movement, the questions
framed themselves like this:

(1) What has been the student's experience of education in schools which reward female passivity, indoctrinate girls and boys in stereotypic sex roles, and do not take the female mind seriously? How does a woman gain a sense of her *self* in a system—in this case, patriarchal capitalism—which devalues work done by women, denies the importance and uniqueness of female experience, and is physically violent toward women? What does this mean for a woman teacher?

(2) How do we, as women, teach women students a canon of literature which has consistently excluded or depreciated female experience, and which often expresses hostility to women and validates violence against us?

(3) How can we teach women to move beyond the desire for male approval and getting "good grades" and seek and write their own truths that the culture has distorted or made taboo? (For women, of course, language itself is exclusive: I want to say more about this further on.)

In teaching women, we have two choices: to lend our weight to the forces that indoctrinate women to passivity, self-depreciation, and a sense of powerlessness, in which case the issue of "taking women students seriously" is a moot one; or to consider what we have to work

CONVERSATIONS: THE OTHER
In this paragraph, Rich argues that women must be taken seriously or they risk remaining "always the Other, the defined, the object, the victim." This term, the Other, has become a common one in academic discussions of cultural diversity. It refers to the ways in which nonmainstream groups, as defined by race, ethnicity, class, or, as in this case, gender, can be understood and treated as something other than normal. An entire body of academic research and cultural criticism has developed around this idea. To use the term "the Other" is to refer implicitly to that research and criticism. Adrienne Rich is one of the scholars who have helped make this term part of our ongoing discussions about diversity and difference. (To read more about this idea of "the Other," see the introduction to Cluster 2, Defining Each Other, of Chapter 5 on page 86.)

against, as well as with, in ourselves, in our students, in the content of the curriculum, in the structure of the institution, in the society at large. And this means, first of all, taking ourselves seriously: Recognizing that central responsibility of a woman to herself, without which we remain always **THE OTHER**, the defined, the object, the victim; believing that there is a unique quality of validation, affirmation, challenge, support, that one woman can offer another. Believing in the value and significance of women's experience, traditions, perceptions. Thinking of ourselves seriously, not as one of the boys, not as neuters, or androgynes, but as *women*.

Suppose we were to ask ourselves, simply: What does a woman need to know? Does she not, as a self-conscious, self-defining human being, need a knowledge of her own history, her much-politicized biology, an awareness of the creative work of women of the past, the skills and crafts and techniques and powers exercised by women in different times and cultures, a knowledge of women's rebellions and organized movements against our oppression and how they have been routed or diminished? Without such knowledge women live and have lived without context, vulnerable to the projections of male fantasy, male prescriptions for us, estranged from our own experience because our education has not reflected or echoed it. I would suggest that not biology, but ignorance of our selves, has been the key to our powerlessness.

But the university curriculum, the high-school curriculum, do not provide this kind of knowledge for women, the knowledge of Womankind, whose experience has been so profoundly different from that of Mankind. Only in the precariously budgeted, much-condescended-to area of women's studies is such knowledge available to women students. Only there can they learn about the lives and work of women other than the few select women who are included in the "mainstream" texts, usually misrepresented even when they do appear. Some students, at some institutions, manage to take a majority of courses in women's studies, but the message from on high is that this is self-indulgence, soft-core education: the "real" learning is the study of Mankind.

If there is any misleading concept, it is that of "coeducation": that because women and men are sitting in the same classrooms, hearing the same lectures, reading the same books, performing the same laboratory experiments, they are receiving an equal education. They are not, first because the content of education itself validates men even as it invalidates women. Its very message is that men have been the shapers and thinkers of the world, and that this is only natural. The bias of higher education, including the so-called sciences, is white and male, racist and sexist; and this bias is expressed in both subtle and blatant ways. I have mentioned already the exclusiveness of grammar itself: "The student should test himself on the above questions"; "The poet is representative. He stands among partial men for the complete man." Despite a few half-hearted departures from custom, what the linguist

Wendy Martyna has named "He-Man" grammar prevails throughout the culture. The efforts of feminists to reveal the profound ontological implications of **SEXIST GRAMMAR** are routinely ridiculed by academicians and journalists, including the professedly liberal *Times* columnist, Tom Wicker, and the professed humanist, Jacques Barzun. Sexist grammar burns into the brains of little girls and young women a message that the male is the norm, the standard, the central figure beside which we are the deviants, the marginal, the dependent variables. It lays the foundation for androcentric thinking, and leaves men safe in their solipsistic tunnel-vision.

10 Women and men do not receive an equal education because outside the classroom women are perceived not as sovereign beings but as prey. The growing incidence of rape on and off the campus may or may not be fed by the proliferations of pornographic magazines and X-rated films available to young males in fraternities and student unions; but it is certainly occurring in a context of wide-spread images of sexual violence against women, on billboards and in so-called high art. More subtle, more daily than rape is the verbal abuse experienced by the woman student on many campuses—Rutgers for example—where, traversing a street lined with fraternity houses, she must run a gauntlet of male commentary and verbal assault. The undermining of self, of a woman's sense of her right to occupy space and walk freely in the world, is deeply relevant to education. The capacity to think independently, to take intellectual risks, to assert ourselves mentally, is inseparable from our physical way of being in the world, our feelings of personal integrity. If it is dangerous for me to walk home late of an evening from the library, *because I am a woman and can be raped,* how self-possessed, how exuberant can I feel as I sit working in that library? How much of my working energy is drained by the subliminal knowledge that, as a woman, I test my physical right to exist each time I go out alone? Of this knowledge, Susan Griffin has written:

> . . . more than rape itself, the fear of rape permeates our lives. And what does one do from day to day, with *this* experience, which says, without words and directly to the heart, *your existence, your experience, may end at any moment.* Your experience may end, and the best defense against this is not to be, to deny being in the body, as a self, to . . . avert your gaze, make yourself, as a presence in the world, less felt.°

°From Griffin's *Rape: The Power of Consciousness* (New York, 1979).

CONVERSATIONS: SEXIST GRAMMAR
When Rich accuses journalists and academics of using sexist grammar, as she does in this paragraph, she is joining a debate about grammar rules and conventions that was raging among educators and activists in the 1970s and 1980s. The debate sometimes focused on the use of *he* as a generic pronoun to refer to "anyone" or "one." Here's an example: "Anyone can climb a mountain if he has the desire and the will." Traditionally, this use of *he* was considered proper. But activists like Rich protested such "correct" uses of pronouns, arguing that they reinforce the idea that women are less important than men and that "the male is the norm," as Rich writes. Today, it is often considered inappropriate to use the male pronoun *he* in this way. Instead, writers employ what is called nonsexist language, as in this example: "Anyone can climb a mountain if he or she has the desire and the will." Often, writers will simply rewrite sentences to avoid the indefinite pronoun altogether: "Anyone with the desire and will can climb a mountain." This debate about the pronoun *he* is a good example of how language rules and conventions often reflect certain values that are controversial or problematic.

Finally, rape of the mind. Women students are more and more often now reporting sexual overtures by male professors—one part of our overall growing consciousness of sexual harassment in the workplace. At Yale a legal suit has been brought against the university by a group of women demanding an explicit policy against sexual advances toward female students by male professors. Most young women experience a profound mixture of humiliation and intellectual self-doubt over seductive gestures by men who have the power to award grades, open doors to grants and graduate school, or extend special knowledge and training. Even if turned aside, such gestures constitute mental rape, destructive to a woman's ego. They are acts of domination, as despicable as the molestation of the daughter by the father.

But long before entering college the woman student has experienced her alien identity in a world which misnames her, turns her to its own uses, denying her the resources she needs to become self-affirming, self-defined. The nuclear family teaches her that relationships are more important than selfhood or work; that "whether the phone rings for you, and how often," having the right clothes, doing the dishes, take precedence over study or solitude; that too much intelligence or intensity may make her unmarriageable; that marriage and children—service to others—are, finally, the points on which her life will be judged a success or a failure. In high school, the polarization between feminine attractiveness and independent intelligence comes to an absolute. Meanwhile, the culture resounds with messages. During Solar Energy Week in New York I saw young women wearing "ecology" T-shirts with the legend: CLEAN, CHEAP AND AVAILABLE; a reminder of the 1960s antiwar button which read: CHICKS SAY YES TO MEN WHO SAY NO. Department store windows feature female mannequins in chains, pinned to the wall with legs spread, smiling in positions of torture. Feminists are depicted in the media as "shrill," "strident," "puritanical," or "humorless," and the lesbian choice—the choice of the woman-identified woman—as pathological or sinister. The young woman sitting in the philosophy classroom, the political science lecture, is already gripped by tensions between her nascent sense of self-worth, and the battering force of messages like these.

Look at a classroom: look at the many kinds of women's faces, postures, expressions. Listen to the women's voices. Listen to the silences, the unasked questions, the blanks. Listen to the small, soft voices, often courageously trying to speak up, voices of women taught early that tones of confidence, challenge, anger, or assertiveness, are strident and unfeminine. Listen to the voices of the women and the voices of the men; observe the space men allow themselves, physically and verbally, the male assumption that people will listen, even when the majority of the group is female. Look at the faces of the silent, and of those who speak. Listen to a woman groping for language in which to express what is on her mind, sensing that the terms of academic discourse are not her language, trying to cut down her thought to the dimensions of a discourse not intended for her *(for it is not fitting that a woman speak in public)*; or reading her paper aloud at breakneck speed, throwing her words away, deprecating her own work by a reflex prejudgment: *I do not deserve to take up time and space.*

As women teachers, we can either deny the importance of this context in which women students think, write, read, study, project their own futures; or try to work with it. We can either teach passively, accepting these conditions, or actively, helping our students identify and resist them.

One important thing we can do is *discuss* the context. And this   15
need not happen only in a women's studies course; it can happen anywhere. We can refuse to accept passive, obedient learning and insist upon critical thinking. We can become harder on our women students, giving them the kinds of "cultural prodding" that men receive, but on different terms and in a different style. Most young women need to have their intellectual lives, their work, legitimized against the claims of family, relationships, the old message that a woman is always available for service to others. We need to keep our standards very high, not to accept a woman's preconceived sense of her limitations; we need to be hard to please, while supportive of risk-taking, because self-respect often comes only when exacting standards have been met. At a time when adult literacy is generally low, we need to demand more, not less, of women, both for the sake of their futures as thinking beings, and because historically women have always had to be better than men to do half as well. A romantic sloppiness, an inspired lack of rigor, a self-indulgent incoherence, are symptoms of female self-depreciation. We should help our women students to look very critically at such symptoms, and to understand where they are rooted.

Nor does this mean we should be training women students to "think like men." Men in general think badly: in disjuncture from their personal lives, claiming objectivity where the most irrational passions seethe, losing, as Virginia Woolf observed, their senses in the pursuit of professionalism. It is not easy to think like a woman in a man's world, in the world of the professions; yet the capacity to do that is a strength which we can try to help our students develop. To think like a woman in a man's world means thinking critically, refusing to accept the givens, making connections between facts and ideas which men have left unconnected. It means remembering that every mind resides in a body; remaining accountable to the female bodies in which we live; constantly retesting given hypotheses against lived experience. It means a constant critique of language, for as Wittgenstein (no feminist) observed, "The limits of my language are the lim-

GUERRILLA GIRLS' POP QUIZ.

Q. If February is Black History Month and March is Women's History Month, what happens the rest of the year?

A. Discrimination.

Courtesy of www.guerrillagirls.com

A PUBLIC SERVICE MESSAGE FROM **GUERRILLA GIRLS** 532 LAGUARDIA PL #237, NY 10012

CONVERSATIONS: BREAKING SILENCES

These two images might be considered current examples of women breaking their silences, as Rich urges them to do in this paragraph. Consider how these images might convey Rich's message about women. Consider, too, that these images appeared in 2004, whereas Rich made her call for women to fight discrimination in 1978.

Courtesy of www.guerrillagirls.com

its of my world." And it means that most difficult thing of all: listening and watching in art and literature, in the social sciences, in all the descriptions we are given of the world, for the silences, the absences, the nameless, the unspoken, the encoded—for there we will find the true knowledge of women. And in breaking those silences, naming our selves, uncovering the hidden, making ourselves present, we begin to define a reality which resonates to *us*, which affirms *our* being, which allows the woman teacher and the woman student alike to take ourselves, and each other, seriously: meaning, to begin taking charge of our lives.

Understanding the Text

1. What kinds of experiences did Rich have in school as both a student and a teacher? What did these experiences teach her about education?

2. What does Rich mean when she insists that women must think of themselves *as women*? Why is this important to her? What are the consequences of failing to do so in her view?

3. What are Rich's main criticisms of education as it relates to women? Do you agree with her? Why or why not?

4. What connection does Rich see between the physical abuse of women and the way women are treated in classrooms? Do you think this connection is valid? Why or why not? Is Rich's criticism valid today? Explain.

5. What solutions does Rich offer to the problems she describes in this article? Do you think these solutions have been tried in the twenty-five years since Rich first wrote this essay? Can they achieve Rich's goals? Explain.

Exploring the Issues

1. Rich devotes the first several paragraphs of her essay to an overview of her own education as a young woman. What purpose does this overview serve in this essay? How does it help set up Rich's main argument? How did it influ-

ence your sense of Rich as the writer of this essay? Does it give her greater (or less) credibility, in your view? Explain.

2. Examine the questions Rich lists in paragraphs 4–5, which she tells us were posed to students at City College of New York and later at Douglass College. What do these questions indicate about the purposes of education as Rich and her colleagues understood them? Do you think these are appropriate questions to pose to students? Why or why not? What might your answer to that question suggest about your own views regarding schooling? In answering these questions, you might compare Rich's views with those of other writers in this book whose essays are about education in some way, including Paulo Freire (page 176) and Min Zhan Lu (page 371).

3. What kinds of evidence does Rich offer to support her claims about the treatment of women in education? Evaluate her evidence. How valid do you find it? How persuasively do you think she supports her positions?

4. This essay is adapted from a talk that Rich gave to women academics in 1978. Assess how Rich addresses this audience. What does she assume about her audience? In what ways does she define her audience as special or different? How effectively do you think she speaks to this audience in this essay? Do you

think her essay would be as effective for a different audience? Explain, citing specific passages from the essay to support your answer.

Entering the Conversations

1. Write an essay in which you discuss your own experiences in schools in terms of gender. How has your gender affected your schooling, in your view? What kinds of opportunities, obstacles, or challenges have you had as a result of being a man or a woman in school? In your essay, try to draw conclusions about the role of gender in schooling. If appropriate, refer to Rich's essay or to any other relevant essay in this book.

2. In a group of classmates, share the essays you wrote for Question 1. What similarities and differences can you identify among the views of your classmates regarding gender in education? What conclusions can be drawn from the experiences of your classmates about the role of gender in education?

3. Organize a classroom forum in which you debate the validity of Rich's argument about women in education. Agree to a format (for example, each participant can speak for three minutes followed by questions from other participants). Try to identify the main issues regarding gender in education that emerge from the forum. Alternatively, write an essay responding to Rich's viewpoint about women in education.

INFOTRAC

4. Using InfoTrac College Edition and any other appropriate resources, examine the role of gender in education today. Narrow the focus of your research to a specific issue involving gender, such as the experiences of women in certain academic fields (such as physics or philosophy), the position of women in school administration, or women's athletics. Explore that specific issue, trying to determine the current state of the issue regarding gender and identifying changes in the status of women in recent decades. Then write a report on the basis of your research.

5. Many popular films have depicted women in education—for example, *Mona Lisa Smile* (2003), *Legally Blonde* (2001), and *Educating Rita* (1983). Focusing on one or more such films, write an essay in which you discuss how women in education are portrayed in film (and other popular media). What attitudes regarding women in education are conveyed in these films? What conclusions can you draw about what these films might say about the status of women in American society?

BELIEF

N 1999, WELL-KNOWN SCHOLARS GEORGE LAKOFF AND MARK JOHNSON PUBLISHED A BOOK CALLED *PHILOSOPHY IN THE FLESH*, IN WHICH THEY WROTE,

Living a human life is a philosophical endeavor. Every thought we have, every decision we make, and every act we perform is based upon philosophical assumptions so numerous we couldn't possibly list them all. We go around armed with a host of presuppositions about what is real, what counts as knowledge, how the mind works, who we are, and how we should act. Such questions, which arise out of our daily concerns, form the basic subject matter of philosophy.

That quotation is as good a definition of philosophy as I've ever encountered, and it conveys very well why philosophy has been an important area of human inquiry for thousands of years. What Lakoff and Johnson state so well in this passage is that we seem to have a basic need to understand who we are and what we do. And philosophy, that age-old subject that is so often poked fun at for being impractical, is the result of that need.

But a closer look at this passage reveals that it might also serve as a description of religion, which is also based on some of those same questions about what is real, who we are, and how we should act. So is science. Although we tend to think of philosophy, religion, and science as different kinds of endeavors, in a very basic way they are all based on fundamental *beliefs*. It is those beliefs that enable us to make sense of the world around us and our place in that world. And those beliefs help determine what we know about the world.

The essays in this cluster all examine this connection between knowing and believing. At least that's how I see them. They reveal that knowing and believing are intimately related to each other.

This may all seem very abstract and, well, philosophical. But as these authors try to help us see, what we *think* we know and what we believe shape our day-to-day decisions about how we live. As Lakoff and Johnson suggest in the passage I quoted, we base everything we do on our assumptions about the world—that is, on what we believe to be true. And if these issues were not important, we wouldn't still be talking and writing and arguing and wondering about them after so many centuries of religious, philosophical, and scientific inquiry.

> **You don't have to look far for evidence of the fact that what we believe and what we think we know are deadly serious matters.**

As you read the essays in this cluster, you might keep in mind that they address issues that lead to some of the most intense and even deadly disagreements and conflicts among human beings. You don't have to look far for evidence of the fact that what we believe and what we think we know are deadly serious matters. As I am writing these words, the world is witnessing countless armed conflicts that have their origins in disagreements about basic beliefs—sometimes religious beliefs, sometimes cultural or political beliefs. I hope these essays can help you gain some insight into these hard questions. And I hope they help you think in useful ways about your own beliefs and how they shape your world.

I can remember as a young child asking my grandmother, who was a very religious person, questions about religious matters that puzzled me. Often, her response was, "You just have to have faith." I'm sure many people have heard such a comment. It seems natural to question some of the things we are taught to believe as children, and it is not unusual

Salvation

for people to experience great doubt about what they have been taught as they get older and learn more about themselves and the world. In the following essay, Langston Hughes (1902–1967) writes about that kind of doubt. But for Hughes, the religious doubt he experienced was dramatic and frightening. He writes of a time in his church when he was asked to declare his faith publicly as a Christian. It was an agonizing moment for Hughes, who was just twelve years old at the time, for he was not sure what he was supposed to be feeling. He was unable to wholeheartedly embrace the faith that everyone else in the church seemed to embrace. And the consequences of that inability were profound.

In a sense, this brief excerpt from Hughes's autobiography, The Big Sea *(1940), is about the public and private aspects of religious faith. It seems likely that Hughes would not have experienced this*

LANGSTON HUGHES

I was saved from sin when I was going on thirteen. But not really saved. It happened like this. There was a big revival at my Auntie Reed's church. Every night for weeks there had been much preaching, singing, praying, and shouting, and some very hardened sinners had been brought to Christ, and the membership of the church had grown by leaps and bounds. Then just before the revival ended, they held a special meeting for children, "to bring the young lambs to the fold." My aunt spoke of it for days ahead. That night I was escorted to the front row and placed on the mourners' bench with all the other young sinners, who had not yet been brought to Jesus.

My aunt told me that when you were saved you saw a light, and something happened to you inside! And Jesus came into your life! And God was with you from then on! She said you could see and hear and feel Jesus in your soul. I believed her. I had heard a great many old people say the same thing and it seemed to me they ought to know. So I sat there calmly in the hot, crowded church, waiting for Jesus to come to me.

The preacher preached a wonderful rhythmical sermon, all moans and shouts and lonely cries and dire pictures of hell, and then he sang a song about the ninety and nine safe in the fold, but one little lamb was left out in the cold. Then he said: "Won't you come? Won't you come to Jesus? Young lambs, won't you come?" And he held out his arms to all us young sinners there on the mourners' bench. And the little girls cried. And some of them jumped up and went to Jesus right away. But most of us just sat there.

A great many old people came and knelt around us and prayed, old women with jet-black faces and braided hair, old men with work-gnarled hands. And the church sang a song about the lower lights are burning, some poor sinners to be saved. And the whole building rocked with prayer and song.

5   Still I kept waiting to *see* Jesus.

Finally all the young people had gone to the altar and were saved, but one boy and me. He was a rounder's son named Westley. Westley and I were surrounded by sisters and deacons praying. It was very hot in the church, and getting late now. Finally Westley said to me in a whisper: "God damn! I'm tired o' sitting here. Let's get up and be saved." So he got up and was saved.

Then I was left all alone on the mourners' bench. My aunt came and knelt at my knees and cried, while prayers and song swirled all around me in the little church. The whole congregation prayed for me alone, in a mighty wail of moans and voices. And I kept waiting serenely for Jesus, waiting, waiting—but he didn't come. I wanted to see him, but nothing happened to me. Nothing! I wanted something to happen to me, but nothing happened.

I heard the songs and the minister saying: "Why don't you come? My dear child, why don't you come to Jesus? Jesus is waiting for you. He wants you. Why don't you come? Sister Reed, what is this child's name?"

"Langston," my aunt sobbed.

10   "Langston, why don't you come? Why don't you come and be saved? Oh, Lamb of God! Why don't you come?"

Now it was really getting late. I began to be ashamed of myself, holding everything up so long. I began to wonder what God thought about Westley, who certainly hadn't seen Jesus either, but who was now sitting proudly on the platform, swinging his knickerbockered legs and grinning down at me, surrounded by deacons and old women on their knees praying. God had not struck Westley dead for taking his name in vain or for lying in the temple. So I decided that maybe to save further trouble, I'd better lie, too, and say that Jesus had come, and get up and be saved.

So I got up.

Suddenly the whole room broke into a sea of shouting, as they saw me rise. Waves of rejoicing swept the place. Women leaped in the air.

wrenching moment if he had not been among believers in church, who set certain expectations regarding faith and salvation. His story asks us to think about the relationship between religion as a social institution, with its doctrines that shape what we believe, and our individual faith. To what extent is our faith our own? To what extent is it a function of social convention and upbringing? These are not easy questions, and Hughes's essay may prompt you to wrestle with them.

Hughes was a prolific poet, essayist, fiction writer, and playwright who is considered one of the key figures in the great American literary movement of the 1920s called the Harlem Renaissance. The experience described in the following essay took place in Missouri, where Hughes was born. ⬇

CONVERSATIONS: REVIVAL MEETINGS
The meeting that Hughes attended at his Auntie Reed's church was part of a much larger movement in the late nineteenth and early twentieth centuries in the United States that some historians call the Second Great Awakening. This movement was characterized by an increase in religious activity in response to concerns about the immoral state of society. An important component of this movement was "revival meetings," such as the one Hughes describes in this essay, which were often organized by traveling preachers and sometimes attracted thousands of people for several days of preaching and worship. Today, religion remains as important—and controversial—as it was in Hughes's lifetime, and you might consider what Hughes's essay contributes to our longstanding debates about religion and faith.

CONVERSATIONS: RELIGION AND FILM
Many films have been made about religion and religious themes, and a few have focused on the character of the traveling preacher and the kind of revival meeting described in this essay. One such film was *Leap of Faith* (1992), which starred Steve Martin as Jonas Nightingale, a con artist who used high-tech gimmicks to convince people at his revival meetings that they were "saved" and to encourage them to contribute cash to his traveling church. Martin's character is part of a longstanding tradition in stories and film that pokes fun at religious revivals and calls into question the faith of people caught up in such movements. But Hughes's essay presents this revival meeting in a very serious way and complicates popular views about religious revivals.

My aunt threw her arms around me. The minister took me by the hand and led me to the platform.

When things quieted down, in a hushed silence, punctuated by a few ecstatic "Amens," all the new young lambs were blessed in the name of God. Then joyous singing filled the room.

That night, for the first time in my life but one for I was a big boy twelve years old—I cried. I cried, in bed alone, and couldn't stop. I buried my head under the quilts, but my aunt heard me. She woke up and told my uncle I was crying because the Holy Ghost had come into my life, and because I had seen Jesus. But I was really crying because I couldn't bear to tell her that I had lied, that I had deceived everybody in the church, that I hadn't seen Jesus, and that now I didn't believe there was a Jesus anymore, since he didn't come to help me.

15

Understanding the Text

1. What expectations does Hughes have about the revival meeting that he was attending with his aunt? Where did these expectations come from? What might they suggest about religious faith and religious events like the meeting at his aunt's church?

2. What prevents Hughes from going up to the preacher during the revival meeting? What do you think Hughes's hesitation reveals about him as a person?

3. What role does Westley play in this experience? In what ways do you think Westley helps Hughes convey his perspective on faith and religion?

Exploring the Issues

1. What main ideas about religion and faith do you think Hughes is trying to convey in this essay? Do you agree with him? Why or why not?

2. In this essay, Hughes describes an experience that happens during a relatively short time—a few hours at most. Examine how he conveys a sense of time. What moments during the experience does he emphasize? How does he describe those moments? How does his manipulation of time in this essay help him convey his ideas about faith?

3. How would you describe Hughes's voice in this essay? He is describing an experience he had when he was twelve years old, but he wrote this passage when he was nearly forty. Do you think he tries to capture the voice of a twelve-year-old boy? Explain, citing specific passages to support your answer.

Entering the Conversations

1. Write an essay in which you describe your own understanding of faith. In your essay, define faith as you understand it, drawing on your own experiences and on Hughes's essay (or any other relevant essay or book) to support your explanation.

2. In a group of classmates, share your essays from Question 1. How does each of you define faith? What similarities and differences can you identify among your respective ideas about faith? What questions about faith might be raised by the essays that each of you wrote?

3. Write an essay in which you describe an important experience you have had involving your faith or religion.

4. Interview several people you know about their views regarding religion and faith. Try to determine whether they see any distinction between religion and faith. Then write a report for your classmates about what you learned through your interviews.

5. Create a visual document (such as a web site or photo essay) that reflects your view of faith.

6. In recent years, several popular television shows have focused on issues of faith. Shows like *Touched by an Angel,* for example, assume a certain kind of understanding of faith and spirituality. Select one or more such shows and examine how they present faith, spirituality, or religion. Then write an essay in which you discuss these shows and what they seem to suggest about faith in contemporary culture.

The United States was founded as a haven *not only for those who sought political freedom but also for those fleeing religious persecution, and most Americans hold dear the principle that they are free to engage in any religious practice they choose. But although the idea of religious freedom is fundamental to American life, religious tolerance is less so, as Joel*

Learning True Tolerance

Engardio explains in the following essay. As a member of a religious minority, Jehovah's Witnesses, whose beliefs often led to their being treated as outcasts in their own communities, Engardio understands what it is like to experience religious intolerance first-hand. He also knows what it means to stand up for your own principles. His deep belief in the basic value of tolerance grows out of that experience.

JOEL ENGARDIO

I was raised as a JEHOVAH'S WITNESS. **If I ever knocked on your** door when you were mowing the lawn or taking a nap, please excuse me. I understand: A kid with a *Watchtower* magazine on your front porch isn't a Girl Scout with cookies, but, hey, you didn't have to sic your dog on me.

I believe how we treat the people we dislike the most and understand the least—Jehovah's Witnesses, for example—says a lot about the freedoms we value in America: religion, speech and personal liberty. And all of these freedoms rely on one thing: tolerance.

I learned this as a kid when I went door-knocking with my mom. We were preaching that Jehovah's kingdom was coming soon to solve the world's problems. I prayed no one from school was behind those doors. Dogs I could run from. It was hard enough being singled out as the kid who didn't celebrate Christmas or didn't say the Pledge of Allegiance. There was little tolerance for my explanation that we only worshipped God, and that God wasn't Ameri-

GLOSS: JEHOVAH'S WITNESSES
The Jehovah's Witnesses are a Christian religious sect that began as a small Bible study group in Pennsylvania in the 1870s and grew to a worldwide religion of 90,000 congregations. Jehovah's Witnesses adhere to a strict interpretation of the Bible and believe that a new earthly paradise will be created by God after the Armageddon. Members of Jehovah's Witnesses are expected to spread their beliefs by distributing information about their faith, as Engardio mentions in this paragraph when he apologizes for knocking on people's doors. In paragraph 3, Engardio also refers to the religion's strict prohibition against its members participating in other religious or secular rituals, such as Christmas or the reciting of the Pledge of Allegiance to the American flag in school, that are not officially part of Jehovah's Witness doctrine.

JOEL ENGARDIO, "LEARNING TRUE TOLERANCE," FROM NPR, WEEKEND EDITION, NOVEMBER 25, 2007.

can. There was no tolerance when I told my third-grade class that Santa Claus was pagan and a lie.

Still, I didn't have a bad childhood. Our Saturday morning ministry meant sacrificing my Saturday morning cartoons, but our 10 o'clock coffee break was a blessing. That's when we would gather at Dunkin' Donuts, trying not to get powdered sugar on our suits and dresses, while we told stories and laughed. We always knew when you were "home but hiding."

5   As a teenager, I decided fitting in at school and in life was worth sacrificing some principles. So I never became a Jehovah's Witness. That was the first time I broke my mom's heart. The second time was when I told her I am gay.

Obviously, I don't agree with my mom's belief that same-sex relationships are wrong. But I tolerate her religion because she has a right to her beliefs. And I like it that **MY MOM DOESN'T POLITICIZE HER BELIEFS.** She has never voted for a law that discriminates against gay people, or against anyone who isn't a Jehovah's Witness. Her Bible tells her to love, above all.

My belief in tolerance led to a documentary film I made about Jehovah's Witnesses, and my mom actually likes it. The message is about being open to letting people have views we don't like, so in that sense, it could also be about Muslims, gay people or NASCAR race fans. The point is the people we don't understand become less scary when we get to know them as real people. We don't have to be each other's **CUP OF TEA,** but tolerance lets a variety of kettles peacefully share the stove.

I believe our capacity to tolerate both religious and personal difference is what will ultimately give us true liberty—even if it means putting up with an occasional knock on the door.

CONVERSATIONS: RELIGION AND POLITICS
When Engardio writes that his mother doesn't "politicize her beliefs," he is entering an old and very contentious debate in American culture about the relationship between religion and politics. Although the U.S. Constitution provides for the separation of church and state, it does not expressly forbid a citizen from voting on the basis of his or her religious beliefs. In recent presidential elections, many issues have become controversial because voters approach them on the basis of their religious beliefs, including abortion, prayer in public schools, and same-sex marriage. Engardio's statements in this paragraph raise questions about whether it is really possible to keep religion out of politics.

STRATEGIES: METAPHOR
Engardio's last sentence in paragraph 7 includes the cliché about something being a person's "cup of tea." Clichés are often metaphors, and in this case Engardio extends the metaphor to include both cups and kettles. What do you think Engardio is saying through the use of this metaphor?

Engardio's essay raises some unsettling questions about religious practice and religious freedom in our increasingly diverse culture. The treatment he endured as a Jehovah's Witness reveals that freedom and tolerance are not the same thing. And his experience, unfortunately, is not unique. After the terrorist attacks on the United States on September 11, 2001, reports of discrimination, abuse, and even violence directed at Muslims proliferated in many parts of the United States. In recent years, there have been several well-publicized cases in which government agents accused members of religious sects of illegal activities, such as the case of the Fundamentalist Church of Jesus Christ and the Latter Day Saints in Texas in 2008, whose children were taken away from their parents because of charges of sexual abuse that were never substantiated. Many critics saw these cases not as the enforcement of the law but as the persecution of people whose religious beliefs differed from the American mainstream—in other words, as religious intolerance.

Engardio understands another kind of intolerance: intolerance of gays and others whose sexual preferences make them a minority in mainstream American society. But as Engardio sees it, intolerance of gays and intolerance of members of a religious group are the same thing, and he argues that we will never know true freedom until we replace intolerance with tolerance.

A program strategist for the American Civil Liberties Union, Engardio is also a documentary filmmaker and essayist whose writing has appeared in publications such as the New York Times *and* USA Today. *This essay was recorded for the National Public Radio "This I Believe" series in 2007.* ◪

Understanding the Text

1. What significance does Engardio see in the treatment he received as a Jehovah's Witness?

2. In what sense does freedom require tolerance according to Engardio? Do you think he's right? Why or why not?

3. In Engardio's view, what is a primary reason for intolerance? What is the best way to eliminate intolerance?

Exploring the Issues

1. In paragraphs 6 and 7, Engardio refers to his mother's views about same-sex marriage as well as her reaction to his documentary film about Jehovah's Witnesses. What points is Engardio making about tolerance in these paragraphs? How does his use of the example of his mother help him make these points? How effective do you think this strategy is in helping Engardio convey his ideas to his readers?

2. In paragraph 6, Engardio writes that his mother does not "politicize her beliefs," but many Americans would contend that it is impossible to keep religion and politics separate. Do you think it is possible? Explain. How would you respond to Engardio's views about this issue?

3. Although tolerance is usually considered an admirable and desirable quality, some religious groups expressly forbid tolerating people who hold certain beliefs or engage in

certain kinds of lifestyle choices. For example, some religious groups actively oppose same-sex marriage, and there have been many cases in history of people being persecuted or even put to death for their beliefs. Given these views, do you think it is possible to achieve the kind of tolerance that Engardio describes in this essay? Explain.

Entering the Conversations

1. Write an essay in which you discuss your most basic belief. (You might write this essay in the form of a "This I Believe" essay like Engardio's. Visit the National Public Radio web site, www.npr.org, for more information about this essay series.)

2. In paragraph 7, Engardio mentions the documentary film he has made about Jehovah's Witnesses, called *Knocking,* which was broadcast on the Public Broadcasting System (PBS) in 2007. If possible, watch Engardio's film and write a review of it. In your review, draw conclusions about whether Engardio's film reflects the views on tolerance that he expresses in this essay. (You can find information about the film at www. knocking.org.)

3. Engardio suggests in this essay that it is important to keep one's religious beliefs from influencing one's political participation. His essay recalls the old cliché that religion and politics don't mix. But religion

and politics often do seem to mix in American society (see "Conversations: Religion and Politics" on page 229). Write an essay in which you explore this issue of the relationship between religion and politics. In your essay, consider what the American tradition of the separation of Church and state means for the role of religion in politics. Also, consider recent controversies about the religious views of political candidates. (For example, during the 2008 U.S. presidential election, the religious views of Democratic candidate Senator Barack Obama became an issue for many voters.) Try to draw your own conclusions about the role of one's religious beliefs in American political life. (You may wish to do some research for this assignment.)

Alternatively, write an essay about a time when your own religious views or the religious views of someone you know influenced how you or they voted in an election or participated in some political activity (such as attending a town board meeting).

4. Write an essay about an experience you had that had something to do with tolerance. In your essay, tell the story of that experience so that your readers will understand how tolerance (or intolerance) was an important part of the experience.

Alternatively, create a web site, photo essay, or some other kind of multimedia presentation in which you explore the idea of tolerance.

You've probably heard the old saying that *you should never mix religion and politics. Maybe the saying should be changed slightly: don't mix religion and science. In recent years, intense controversies about such issues as the teaching of evolution in schools and the use of stem cells for scientific research suggest that science and religion can clash when it comes to*

Taking Science on Faith

important matters of education, health, and similar concerns. But these controversies are nothing new. Science and religion have been in conflict for hundreds of years. In 1633, the great Italian astronomer Galileo, who is sometimes called the father of modern science, was tried for heresy by religious authorities for defending the idea that the earth revolved around the sun. Nearly 300 years later, in 1925, a high school teacher named John Scopes was put on trial in Tennessee for teaching evolution. Because important ideas like evolution can seem to threaten religious beliefs, it is unlikely that conflicts between science and religion will ever cease.

For physicist Paul Davies, however, these conflicts may serve a larger purpose: they may help us figure out the most basic questions about the nature of the universe—questions that are at the heart of the field of physics. Davies believes that science and religion are similar in one

PAUL DAVIES

Science, we are repeatedly told, is the most reliable form of knowledge about the world because it is based on testable hypotheses. Religion, by contrast, is based on faith. The term **"DOUBTING THOMAS"** well illustrates the difference. In science, a healthy skepticism is a professional necessity, whereas in religion, having belief without evidence is regarded as a virtue.

The problem with this neat separation into "non-overlapping magisteria," as **STEPHEN JAY GOULD** described science and religion, is that science has its own faith-based belief system. All science proceeds on the assumption that nature is ordered in a rational and intelligible way. You couldn't be a scientist if you thought the universe was a meaningless jumble of odds and ends haphazardly juxtaposed. When physicists probe to a deeper level of subatomic structure, or astronomers extend the reach of their instruments, they expect to encounter additional elegant mathematical order. And so far this faith has been justified.

The most refined expression of the rational intelligibility of the cosmos is found in the laws of physics, the fundamental rules on which nature runs. The laws of gravitation and electromagnetism, the laws that regulate the world within the atom, the laws of motion—all are

PAUL DAVIES, "TAKING SCIENCE ON FAITH," *NEW YORK TIMES*, NOVEMBER 24, 2007, SECTION A: COLUMN 0, OP-ED. REPRINTED BY PERMISSION OF THE *NEW YORK TIMES*.

important way: They are both based on faith. Although many people would strenuously disagree with that idea, Davies believes we must recognize this similarity between religion and science if we want to answer fundamental questions about the existence of the universe. Whether you agree or not, his essay may raise complicated questions for you about the relationships—and differences—among religion, faith, science, and knowledge.

Paul Davies is a professor of physics and director of Beyond: the Center for Fundamental Concepts in Science at Arizona State University. He has written more than two dozen books, including The Mind of God, *as well as numerous articles on science for many publications, including* The Economist, *the* New York Times, *and the* Guardian. *In 1995, he won the Templeton Prize, a prestigious award that recognizes important work in science and religion.* ◪

GLOSS: DOUBTING THOMAS
The term "doubting Thomas" (par. 1) refers to one of Jesus Christ's twelve apostles who did not believe his fellow apostles when they told him that Jesus had risen from the dead. An account in the Bible indicates that Thomas required physical proof before he would believe that Jesus had arisen.

GLOSS: STEPHEN JAY GOULD
Biologist and best-selling author Stephen Jay Gould (1941–2002) (par. 2) was well-known for exploring complex and often controversial scientific topics for a general audience in books such as *The Mismeasure of Man* (1981), which examines the history of standardized testing and psychometrics. His many essays for *Natural History* magazine were reprinted in best-selling books like *Ever Since Darwin* (1977) and *The Panda's Thumb* (1980).

---

expressed as tidy mathematical relationships. But where do these laws come from? And why do they have the form that they do?

WHEN I WAS A STUDENT, the laws of physics were regarded as completely off limits. The job of the scientist, we were told, is to discover the laws and apply them, not inquire into their provenance. The laws were treated as "given"—imprinted on the universe like a maker's mark at the moment of cosmic birth—and fixed forevermore. Therefore, to be a scientist, you had to have faith that the universe is governed by dependable, immutable, absolute, universal, mathematical laws of an unspecified origin. You've got to believe that these laws won't fail, that we won't wake up tomorrow to find heat flowing from cold to hot, or the speed of light changing by the hour.

Over the years I have often asked my physicist colleagues why the laws of physics are what they are. The answers vary from "that's not a scientific question" to "nobody knows." The favorite reply is, "There is no reason they are what they are—they just are." The idea that the laws exist reasonlessly is deeply anti-rational. After all, the very essence of a scientific explanation of some phenomenon is that the world is ordered logically and that there are reasons things are as they are. If one traces these reasons all the way down to the bedrock of reality—the laws of physics—only to find that reason then deserts us, it makes a mockery of science.

Can the mighty edifice of physical order we perceive in the world about us ultimately be rooted in reasonless absurdity? If so, then nature is a fiendishly clever bit of trickery: meaninglessness and absurdity somehow masquerading as ingenious order and rationality.

Although scientists have long had an inclination to shrug aside such questions concerning the source of the laws of physics, the mood has now shifted considerably. Part of the reason is the growing acceptance that the emergence of life in the universe, and hence the existence of observers like ourselves, depends rather sensitively on the form of the laws. If the laws of physics were just any old ragbag of rules, life would almost certainly not exist.

A second reason that the laws of physics have now been brought within the scope of scientific inquiry is the realization that what we long regarded as absolute and universal laws might not be truly fundamental at all, but more like local bylaws. They could vary from place to place on a mega-cosmic scale. A God's-eye view might reveal a vast patchwork quilt of universes, each with its own distinctive set of bylaws. In this "multiverse," life will arise only in those patches with bio-friendly bylaws, so it is no surprise that we find ourselves in a Goldilocks universe—one that is just right for life. We have selected it by our very existence.

The multiverse theory is increasingly popular, but it doesn't so much explain the laws of physics as dodge the whole issue. There has to be a physical mechanism to make all those universes and be-

5

stow bylaws on them. This process will require its own laws, or meta-laws. Where do they come from? The problem has simply been shifted up a level from the laws of the universe to the meta-laws of the multiverse.

10   Clearly, then, **BOTH RELIGION AND SCIENCE ARE FOUNDED ON FAITH**—namely, on belief in the existence of something outside the universe, like an unexplained God or an unexplained set of physical laws, maybe even a huge ensemble of unseen universes, too. For that reason, both monotheistic religion and orthodox science fail to provide a complete account of physical existence.

This shared failing is no surprise, because the very notion of physical law is a theological one in the first place, a fact that makes many scientists squirm. Isaac Newton first got the idea of absolute, universal, perfect, immutable laws from the Christian doctrine that God created the world and ordered it in a rational way. Christians envisage God as upholding the natural order from beyond the universe, while physicists think of their laws as inhabiting an abstract transcendent realm of perfect mathematical relationships.

And just as Christians claim that the world depends utterly on God for its existence, while the converse is not the case, so physicists declare a similar asymmetry: the universe is governed by eternal laws (or meta-laws), but the laws are completely impervious to what happens in the universe.

It seems to me there is no hope of ever explaining why the physical universe is as it is so long as we are fixated on immutable laws or meta-laws that exist reasonlessly or are imposed by divine providence. The alternative is to regard the laws of physics and the universe they govern as part and parcel of a unitary system, and to be incorporated together within a common explanatory scheme.

In other words, the laws should have an explanation from within the universe and not involve appealing to an external agency. The specifics of that explanation are a matter for future research. But until science comes up with a testable theory of the laws of the universe, its claim to be free of faith is manifestly bogus.

STRATEGIES: USING PERSONAL EXPERIENCE TO MAKE A POINT
In paragraph 4 Davies refers to his own experience as a student of science and as a practicing scientist. This strategy of drawing on personal experience is one that writers commonly use to help make a point, and it's worth considering how effectively Davies uses it here to help make his point.

CONVERSATIONS: RELIGION AND SCIENCE
When Davies writes in paragraph 10 that "both religion and science are founded on faith," he is joining the continuing debate about the relationship between science and religion. As a prominent scientist and award-winning author, Davies is particularly well-suited to take part in this debate (see the introduction to this essay on page 231 for biographical information about Davies); he has written many books and articles about some of the complicated issues in the debate. Davies's background as an internationally known scientist may give him much credibility among many readers, but that same background may make other readers skeptical of his views. In this regard, Davies is a good example of the complexities writers face in trying to convey their messages to an audience, and this essay, which was published in a respected international newspaper, is a good example of how tricky a rhetorical situation can be (see "Assessing Rhetorical Context" in Chapter 3).

Understanding the Text

1. In what sense is science a "faith-based belief system," according to Davies? What fundamental belief provides the basis for science? Why is this idea of science as a belief system important in Davies's view? What are the most important implications of this view?

2. Why were questions about the reasons for the existence of the laws of physics discouraged or ignored among scientists according to Davies? Why are such questions now being asked? What might this change suggest about the nature of science?

3. Why does Davies believe that neither science nor religion can completely explain the existence of the physical universe? What is his solution to finding an answer to the question of where the universe comes from? Do you find his solution acceptable? Why or why not? What might your answer to this question suggest about your own beliefs?

Exploring the Issues

1. Davies claims that science is a "faith-based belief system" similar to religion in its requirement that scientists believe in the inherent order of the universe. Does Davies find this situation acceptable? Does he wish science to be free of faith? Explain, citing specific passages from his essay to support your answer.

2. Science and religion have often been in conflict. Perhaps the best example of this conflict is the ongoing debate about the teaching of evolution in public schools. Some people believe that "creationism," or the belief that God created the world, should be taught in biology classes along with (or in place of) the theory of evolution, which is a scientific explanation of the origins of life. Many scientists argue that creationism should not be taught in biology classes because it is not science. How does Davies account for these conflicts between science and religion? Do you think he offers a possible solution? Explain.

3. In paragraph 9, Davies writes, "There has to be a physical mechanism to make all those universes and bestow by-laws on them." On what basis does Davies make this statement? Do you think he is right? Isn't this statement just a reflection of his own beliefs? If so, do you think it weakens Davies' argument for "an explanation from within the universe" (par. 14)? Why or why not?

Entering the Conversations

1. Write an essay expressing your own views about science and religion.

2. In a group of classmates, share the essays you wrote for Question 1. Look for similarities and differences in the way you and your classmates seem to understand religion and science and their roles in our lives. Based on your discussion, try to draw conclusions about conflicts between science and religion.

3. As the introduction to this reading indicates (see page 231), in recent years there have been several controversies involving science and religion, including the debate about teaching evolution or creationism in schools, the controversy over the use of fetal stem cells for medical research, and the continuing debate about when life begins, which is part of the conflicts over abortion. Select one such controversy and examine the roles that religion and science seem to have in that controversy. Look into the basic issues in the controversy and examine the arguments from various sides. Try to get a sense of whether those involved in the controversy base their positions on scientific or religious views. If possible, interview several people who may be involved in the controversy or have knowledge of it (such as a faculty member at your school). Then write a report on the basis of your research. In your report, explain the controversy, its history, and the main issues involved. Describe the roles of religion and science in the controversy as you understand it. Draw conclusions about the relationship between religion and science on the basis of your examination of that controversy.

4. On the basis of your research for Question 2, write a letter to a person or an organization involved in the controversy you examined and offer your own suggestions for resolving the controversy.

5. Write an essay about a time when religion enabled you to understand something that science could not, or a time when science enabled you to understand something that religion could not.

The United States is one of the most religious nations in the world. Polls show that less than 3% of Americans identify themselves as atheists and that atheists are distrusted by Americans more than any other group of people. Such polls may not be surprising because a belief in God is woven into the very fabric of American social and

God and Girls in Thailand

political life. God is mentioned in the Declaration of Independence, and prayers are often said at public events. "In God We Trust" is printed on American currency. For most Americans, there is no question about the existence of God. In recent years, the publication of several books by prominent scholars who are deeply critical of religion (such as The God Delusion *by biologist Richard Dawkins and* There Is a God *by philosopher Anthony Flew) have sparked an intense debate about the existence of God. But although the question of the existence of God is settled for the vast majority of Americans, it is in fact a very old question that has preoccupied some of the world's greatest thinkers. John Allen Paulos is one of them. He is an atheist, but as the following essay suggests, that doesn't mean he has stopped wrestling with the most fundamental questions about who we are and how we should live. In the following essay,*

JOHN ALLEN PAULOS

I **found myself at loose ends** IN A BEACH TOWN IN THAILAND ON CHRISTMAS MORNING, 2006. Away from my family in Philadelphia, I was visiting a friend who was planning an early retirement in Southeast Asia. While wandering near the edge of town, I spotted a spirit house, a sort of miniature temple mounted on a pedestal like a bird house. Although irreligious, I noted the fruit offerings strewn around it and was attracted to its makeshift beauty.

Pausing at the shrine, I saw a small Internet café just beyond it, empty except for three nubile young women who were giggling and periodically running up to one or another of the many computers in the room. The desire for my morning Diet Coke, the need to check my email, and the palpable mirth bubbling out of the women drew me into the place.

Despite the goings-on, I first took care of my caffeine and correspondence demands. Soon, however, I noticed there were Webcams on all the computers. It was obvious that the young women were multi-tasking, sending instant messages and occasional pictures in

JOHN ALLEN PAULOS, "GOD AND GIRLS IN THAILAND," EXCERPT FROM IRRELIGION: A MATHEMATICIAN EXPLAINS WHY THE ARGUMENTS FOR GOD JUST DON'T ADD UP. HILL AND WANG 2007.

Paulos shares an unusual experience he had to ponder these questions. In doing so, he joins the age-old effort to make sense of human life. His essay raises additional questions about where our ethics and morality come from. If not from God, then where? He may not have a simple answer to that question, but his essay may cause you to join him in pondering it.

Paulos, a renowned mathematician who teaches at Temple University, has written several best-selling books about math in our lives, including Irreligion: A Mathematician Explains Why the Arguments for God Just Don't Add Up *(2007). This essay was published on the web site* 3 Quarks Daily *in 2008.* ▼

STRATEGIES: ESTABLISHING A SCENE
In the opening paragraphs of his essay, Paulos describes the setting where the experience that is the focus of this essay takes place. But Paulos may be doing more here than simply setting the scene. Notice that although the events he describes in the rest of the essay occur in a small Internet café, the first thing he describes in the essay is a temple. Consider why Paulos would focus our attention on that temple first, rather than on the café. Writers often choose details carefully to convey messages or help explore their ideas, and Paulos may be telling us more here than what he saw on that Christmas morning.

quick succession to nine farangs (Thai for Western foreigners) scattered around the world.

Feeling unmoored and a bit voyeuristic, I eavesdropped and soon gleaned that the girls had met the men on their earlier trips to Thailand. (Perhaps sexist-sounding, "girls" nevertheless seems the more apt term for them.) I noted with amusement that when new pictures of their admirers appeared on the various monitors, the girls would chortle, and the English "expert" among them would write something endearing. The three girls would then quickly move on to the samey (Thai for boyfriend or husband) of another of the girls. Each girl seemed to have three.

Seeing my obvious interest, the girls started to ask me what certain words in the e-mails meant. "Sawatee (hello), Mr. Diet Coke, what 'pine for you' mean?" I explained that "pine for you" meant "miss you very much," that "obsessed with you" meant "think about you all the time," and so on. The men seemed strangely oblivious to the girls' limited English vocabulary. They also seemed lovesick, lonely, and mooning over their "true loves" at Christmas.

After I proved myself as a translator, the girls asked me what else they could say. I suggested that they write how lonely the beach was without their boyfriends and helped them a bit with their spelling. My lines elicited good responses from their sameys, causing them to laugh uproariously. They pumped me for more good lines, which I happily provided. The girl who had distractedly taken my money for the Diet Coke now offered me another one gratis as well as various coconut candies, which I accepted, and some fried insects, which I declined.

Christopher Moore, a Bangkok-based novelist whose compelling mysteries are set in Thailand, once jokingly remarked to me that Thai has no common word or phrase to describe integrity of a rigid, abstract type, but many frequently used terms for "fun." And great fun it was helping the girls dupe farangs on three continents out of their money via the Western Union office in town. (Perhaps "dupe" is the wrong word since I think the bargain was a fair one and inexpensive at that: a Yuletide fantasy for a few dollars.)

After a while, however, the pain underlying the men's instant messages began to weigh on me. The girls had taken to reading me all the messages, and it was clear that most of the men were somewhat forlorn. They seemed to be unmarried, isolated, and searching for a connection, for some sort of emotional salvation. My supercilious attitude toward them and the idealized fantasies they had constructed was morphing into empathy. In very different circumstances fortunately, I nevertheless could acknowledge some kinship with them. After all, I had myself entered the café to make some email re-connections of my own. The girls too, I began to see, felt a bit more than their charmingly mercenary behavior might suggest.

Since it took place on Christmas day, this vignette comes to mind when I meet people who seem to have a fierce yearning to believe, whether in a person or a divinity. Even if aware of the illogic and gaping holes in the arguments for God, they may continue to believe as willfully and needfully as these farangs believed in their Thai girlfriends, their goddesses.

10 So what of my role which, despite my rationale above, was problematic? I was doing the opposite of what I often do in my professional life, which is to espouse critical thinking, numeracy, skepticism. Here on the Gulf of Siam I was facilitating a **CHIMERA,** albeit an emotional one with which I have considerably more sympathy than its religious analogue.

Why? I'm not sure. It may simply be that, though **I DON'T BELIEVE IN GOD,** I do believe in love, even deluded love. Or maybe it was a lark. Or perhaps I saw the incident as a telling sidelight on the effects of globalization, on mixing spirit houses with Diet Cokes. All I'm sure of is that I don't want to scoff too much at yearning and need, whether it be for love or for a divinity. I just don't possess the latter.

GLOSS: CHIMERA
In Greek mythology, the chimera was a creature made up of the parts of different animals. The term is used to refer to something that is illusory or doesn't exist.

CONVERSATIONS: BELIEF IN GOD
In this paragraph, Paulos refers to the human "yearning and need" for love or a divinity. As the introduction to this reading selection indicates (see page 235), Paulos is an internationally known scholar who has written a book about the existence of God. He is therefore one of several well-known thinkers who have joined the age-old debate about God. Over the years, many of the world's leading philosophers have been part of this debate, including Blaise Pascal (1623–1662), Emmanuel Kant (1724–1804), Soren Kierkegaard (1813–1855), and Freidrich Neitzsche (1844–1900). Like Paulos, these philosophers recognized the human need to understand the reasons for our existence. His essay suggests that some of the most basic questions about human existence are never entirely resolved. In this sense, his essay might be seen as part of a never-ending conversation about who we are.

Understanding the Text

1. Why does Paulos become interested in what the girls he sees in the Internet café are doing? What is it that attracts his interest in their activities? What do you think this scene reveals about Paulos himself? Do you think he intends to reveal anything about himself here? Explain.

2. Why does Paulos begin to have second thoughts about helping the girls in the café? How do Paulos's misgivings relate to his main point in the essay?

3. What is the chimera that Paulos believes he was facilitating by his actions in the café? Why is he troubled by this idea? What conclusions does he draw from the experience? Do these conclusions seem appropriate given the events he has described? Why or why not?

Exploring the Issues

1. In paragraph 7, Paulos writes that the girls duped the men with whom they were communicating. But then he includes the following statement in parentheses: "Perhaps 'dupe' is the wrong word since I think the bargain was a fair one and inexpensive at that: a Yuletide fantasy for a few dollars." What is the "bargain" that Paulos is referring to here and why does he describe it as "fair"? Why do you think he places this statement in parentheses? Would it have been different if he did not use the parentheses? Explain.

2. In describing his encounter with the girls in the Internet café and his efforts to help them communicate with men through e-mail, Paulos calls his behavior "problematic" (see par. 10) and suggests that what he did may have been unethical. Why does he feel that way? What might his feelings suggest about human relationships and our responsibilities in dealing with other people—especially people we do not know? Do you agree with him? Why or why not?

3. In the final paragraph of this essay, Paulos wonders about the cause of his feelings about his experience in the café, and he writes, "It may simply be that, though I don't believe in God, I do believe in love, even deluded love." Why do you think he mentions here that he is an atheist? How might this paragraph—and this essay—be different if he had simply written, "I believe in love" and not mentioned that he doesn't believe in God?

Entering the Conversations

1. In this essay, Paulos suggests that one can believe in basic human moral or ethical principles without believing in God. Write an essay about something you believe in. Consider organizing your essay around a personal experience as Paulos does.

2. The introduction to this reading selection mentions the recent debates about the existence of God (see page 235). Look into these debates and especially the discussions about books about religion by well-known scholars, including John Allen Paulos. If possible, read several of the books in this debate (or portions of them) and examine some of the reviews and essays written about those books. Try to get a sense of the main issues in the debate. Then write a report on the basis of your research. In your report, describe the recent debate and summarize the positions of the major figures in the debate. Identify the main issues. Draw conclusions about belief, faith, and religion.

Alternatively, select one of the books in this debate and write a review of it.

3. On the basis of your research for Question 2, write an essay in which you offer your position about the existence of God. In your essay, discuss the main reasons for your position and try to incorporate into your discussion the views of the authors you read as part of your research.

4. Create a web site that is intended to be a resource for people interested in learning more about the current debates about the existence of God and the role of religion in human life. (For this assignment you may need to do research as described in Question 2).

5. Write a response to Paulos in which you offer your own interpretation of the experience in the Internet café that he describes in his essay.

Extending the Conversations

1. Drawing on the readings in this chapter, write an essay in which you discuss the differences between knowing and believing.

2. The title of the third cluster in this chapter is *"Belief,"* which names the theme that I see in these readings. But these essays are about other themes—some directly related to the idea of belief, some not. Identify an important idea or theme that you see in the readings in this cluster. Then write an essay in which you explore that idea or theme, drawing on the readings in this cluster where appropriate. Alternatively, select an important theme that you see in this chapter and write an essay for an audience of your classmates in which you draw on several readings in the chapter to discuss that theme.

3. This chapter makes a distinction between *learning* and *schooling*. Write an essay in which you draw on your own experience as a student to explore this distinction between learning and schooling. To what extent did your experiences in school result in your learning something of value? How much true learning do you believe you did in school? What specific experiences do you think contributed most to your learning? Did you learn anything of importance in school that was not part of the formal curriculum? Try to address such questions in your essay and draw conclusions about the relationship between learning and schooling.

Alternatively, write a letter to the school board in the district in which you attended school (or the principal if you attended a private school) expressing your views about how schools can truly contribute to students' learning. In your letter, refer to your own experiences as a student to support your viewpoint, and propose specific changes you believe your school should make to enhance student learning.

4. Identify what you see as a compelling theme that runs through the readings in this chapter. Select four (or more) essays that explore that theme in some way, and write an essay in which you discuss that theme, drawing on those four (or more) essays. Write your essay in a way that participates in a conversation about that theme. In other words, write it for an audience who would have an interest in that theme.

5. Select several authors in this chapter and write a dialogue in which they explore the relationship between knowing and believing.

6. Drawing on several essays in this chapter for your ideas, write an essay for your local newspaper or another appropriate publication with a general audience in which you discuss the changes that should be made to schools so they foster what you believe to be true learning and understanding of the world.

7. Select an important theme that you see in the readings in this chapter and create a PowerPoint presentation in which you explore that theme, drawing on any relevant essays in the chapter.

8. Every university and most schools now have web sites, many of which are very sophisticated and extensive. Select several school or university web sites and examine the way they present their school or university. What kinds of images do they present? What information do they include? How do they address visitors to the web site? How do they seem to assume that visitors will use these sites? What general impressions are conveyed about the specific school or university and about education in general? Then write a report of your investigation, describing the web sites you reviewed and presenting your conclusions about what these sites reveal about their schools and about education. Alternatively, create a web site on the basis of your investigation. Construct your web site as a resource for students, parents, and others who may wish to learn about schools or universities through the Internet. On your web site, provide tips for such an audience about how to view school or university web sites. Or create a new web site for your school or university based on the results of your investigation.

9. In the introduction to Cluster 1 of this chapter, I included some of the lyrics from Alanis Morissette's song "You Learn." Select several songs that you think convey important insights about learning, understanding, or spirituality, and write an essay in which you discuss these themes as they are explored in these songs. Alternatively, write your own song about what it means to learn or understand something.

10. Select several popular television shows in which science seems to play an important role. For example, the popular program *CSI* depicts the work of criminal investigators who use scientific methods to solve crimes. *The X Files* included a character (Scully) who was a physician and who believed in science as a means of answering questions and solving problems. Examine such shows for what they seem to suggest about science. Then write a review essay in which you discuss what you have learned from your analysis. Draw conclusions about how science is portrayed in the media as a way of knowing the world.

11. Many films and television shows have spiritual themes that explore our beliefs about God, the afterlife, and spirituality in general. Among such films are *Michael,* about an angel living on Earth, and *Bruce Almighty,* a comedy in which a man is temporarily given God's powers. Some recent television shows have explored similar themes—for example, *Touched by an Angel.* These films are not based directly on Bible stories or explicit religious doctrines, yet, they do explore themes associated with established religions, most commonly Christianity. Select one or more such films and examine the way they explore themes of spirituality. What ideas about spirituality do they seem to convey? What religious beliefs do they reflect? Write an analysis of the films you have selected in which you try to answer such questions. Draw conclusions about what these films might suggest about our cultural attitudes regarding knowing and believing.

12. Many popular films tell stories of people who have experienced some kind of change or important kind of learning in their lives. The classic film by Orson Welles, *Citizen Kane,* for example, tells the story of a wealthy publisher who learns some difficult lessons as he pursues his quest for power and influence. Similarly, the main characters in the more recent film version of the popular fantasy trilogy *The Lord of the Rings* experience great trials that ultimately change them. Select one or several films that you believe tell the story of an important learning experience, and write an essay in which you discuss what the main character (or characters) learned and how that learning happened. In your essay, draw conclusions about what it means to learn. Consider writing your essay as a review essay that might appear in a popular magazine or on a web site devoted to film.

13. Many films depict schools, including many classic films, such as *To Sir with Love* or *The Paper Chase.* Other well-known films that deal directly with schooling in some way include *Animal House, The Dead Poets' Society, The Breakfast Club, Stand and Deliver,* and *Dangerous Minds.* Although these films are very different, they all include familiar images of schools and they all portray teachers, students, and conventional school activities in ways that are familiar to most Americans. Choose one or more such films and examine what they seem to suggest about school and about learning. Then write an essay in which you present your analysis, drawing conclusions about what these films reveal about American attitudes and values regarding schooling and education.

14. Write a script of a film or play that tells the story of an important kind of learning or spiritual transformation.

Chapter 7 Relationships

© Paul Kaye; Cordaiy Photo Library Ltd./CORBIS

AT THE END OF HIS CLASSIC FILM *ANNIE HALL* (1973), WOODY ALLEN, SPEAKING AS THE CHARACTER ALVIE SINGER, TELLS AN OLD JOKE ABOUT A MAN WHO GOES TO THE DOCTOR, COMPLAINING THAT HIS BROTHER THINKS HE'S A CHICKEN. WHEN THE DOCTOR ASKS WHETHER THE MAN HAS HAD HIS BROTHER HOSPITALIZED, THE MAN REPLIES, "I WOULD, BUT we need the eggs." Allen then explains that relationships are just like that: They're crazy and illogical, but we all need them.

When I began putting together the chapters of this book, it seemed obvious that I should include a chapter on relationships, for what could be more important or fundamental to human life than relationships? As Woody Allen says, we all need the eggs. And as his film *Annie Hall* makes clear, relationships are extremely complicated, often difficult, and sometimes painful. No wonder writers have been writing about them forever. This is indeed rich ground for writers to till.

There is nothing more central to our lives than our relationships with other people. Entire sections of bookstores are devoted to relation-

> **Entire sections of bookstores are devoted to relationships of all kinds: romantic, parental, family, professional.**

ships of all kinds: romantic, parental, family, professional. And entire professions are devoted to them as well; for example, much of psychology focuses on relationships between individuals and groups. Most of us will devote a great deal of time and energy in our lives to developing and maintaining our relationships with others, and most of us will spend some time dealing with the damage that can be done in a relationship.

But the term *relationships* doesn't necessarily refer exclusively to people. We can have a relationship with a pet, a place (our hometown or college campus), an activity (a sport like football or swimming), an organization (the military or a political party), or a thing (a car or motorcycle). We might even have a relationship to a time or

era, like the 1960s. As humans, we *relate to* so many things. And the complexity of our many relationships is perhaps a big reason we so often write about them. We want—and need—to understand relationships because they are so much a part of being human. We want to examine the complexities and wonders and challenges of relationships.

The reading selections in this chapter reflect some of the complexities as well as the challenges of relationships. The truth is that almost any of the readings in this book could be placed in this chapter because all of them are about some kind of relationship. And it's a pretty good bet that the writers whose essays are included in this chapter didn't start out with the goal of writing about relationships. Instead, they had some experience, person, event, or problem that they wanted to explain or explore. So what's the point of having a chapter with such a broad theme? That's a question I'd like you to think about as you read through the selections in this chapter.

I'd argue that placing readings in this chapter affects how you understand them and therefore helps shape what they mean to you. For example, the first essay in the chapter, "Attila the Honey I'm Home," by Kristin van Ogtrop, is about a modern woman's efforts to have both a career and a family. In that sense, it might fit nicely under the theme of "Work" or "Lifestyle" or "Women." It might even fit into Chapter 12 on Change. But placing it in a chapter about relationships gives it a certain significance and perhaps suggests how you should read it. And it's worth asking whether van Ogtrop intended it to be read as an essay about relationships—rather than as an essay about work or family or lifestyle or women. The point is that essays like van Ogtrop's address rich and complicated issues that are really part of many different conversations that we, as members of a society, are always having. And what her essay, or any essay, "means" is determined in part by what conversation it fits into.

Each of the three clusters in this chapter offers a slightly different way to think about relationships. The first focuses on love, which is perhaps the most profound expression of a relationship. I wanted to find essays that might get you thinking about the many different kinds of love we can experience in our lives. The second cluster, "Complicating Relationships," includes readings that examine ways we can encounter various kinds of obstacles in relationships, and it raises questions about how relationships are affected by beliefs, values, traditions, and even laws. The third cluster asks you to rethink your understanding of relationships in general. These four essays pose questions about some of our most basic values regarding relationships among people and even our relationship to the natural world.

> **As humans, we relate to so many things.**

In reading these essays, you are joining a complex conversation that humans have long been having. When you watch a film like Woody Allen's *Annie Hall* or listen to a love song or read a newspaper editorial about same-sex marriage, you are participating in that conversation about how we relate to one another. The significance of the readings in this chapter will be determined in part by how you have been participating in that conversation. Pay attention to how you read—and pay attention to how these writers have joined that conversation.

EXPLORING LOVE

IT IS POSSIBLE THAT MORE HAS BEEN WRITTEN ABOUT LOVE THAN ABOUT ANY OTHER TOPIC. IT HAS BEEN THE SUBJECT OF COUNTLESS STORIES, PLAYS, POEMS, SONGS, AND FILMS, AND IT SEEMS AT TIMES TO CONSUME US. BUT FOR ALL THE ATTENTION WE GIVE IT, LOVE REMAINS AS MYSTERI- OUS AND HARD TO DEFINE AS EVER. MAYBE THAT'S WHY

so many writers have turned their attention to it. Or maybe it's because love is as important as anything else we can experience in our lives.

The essays in this cluster offer three very different perspectives on love. I selected them because I wanted to highlight how complex and multifaceted love can be. We can experience many different kinds of love, so it seems important to pay attention to what we might call the diversity of love. But I also wanted to find essays that help us

> We are drawing from a huge well of cultural traditions and stories that help us make sense of this crazy thing called love.

see that when we write or talk about love, we are drawing from a huge well of cultural traditions and stories that help us make sense of this crazy thing called love. Writers rely on that cultural well to convey their ideas about love.

For example, Kristin van Ogtrop's essay, "Attila the Honey I'm Home," assumes that readers are familiar with the traditional American family, with a wife and children and a working husband who supports them. The title itself draws on the image of the husband returning home from a day's work, which has become part of American culture and is reflected in countless films and television shows. But van Ogtrop turns that familiar image on its head: in her essay it is the wife returning from work and saying that familiar line, "Honey, I'm home." That twist wouldn't mean much

if van Ogtrop wasn't able to count on her readers being familiar with the image of the traditional American family. In other words, she dips into the well of cultural tradition to help make her point. And notice that she also assumes that readers will know who Attila is. The name of Attila the Hun, a fifth century warlord who terrorized Europe and Asia, has become shorthand for someone who is mean and nasty—usually a man, but in this case another twist. Again, van Ogtrop relies on shared cultural knowledge between her and her readers.

The other essays in this cluster also rely on a shared cultural background, though that background differs slightly for each essay. The essay by bell hooks, for instance, draws on both Western and Eastern cultural traditions in examining what we mean by love in a larger sense—not romantic love, but the kind of love described by religious thinkers and philosophers. In this case, she assumes her readers will have a sense of what that kind of love is, even if they are unfamiliar with the Buddhist tradition that she refers to in her dialogue with Buddhist teacher Thich Nhat Hanh.

As a reader, you may often be unaware of how much background knowledge you bring to a piece of writing. And you may not realize that your reaction to an essay may reflect your culture as much as your individual experiences or preferences. But I hope these essays help you become more sensitive to how much knowledge and experience you draw on as a reader and how deeply that knowledge and experience can shape the way you read. I hope, too, that these essays give you some insight into this wonderful and complicated thing called love.

At first glance, this essay by a successful *magazine editor is about what it takes to be a career woman and mother in the United States today. Kristin van Ogtrop (b. 1964) writes vividly about balancing the roles of wife, mother, and successful professional. But in describing her hectic struggles to balance her many responsibilities, van Ogtrop is also*

Attila THE Honey I'm Home

KRISTIN VAN OGTROP

implicitly describing the challenges of certain kinds of love: for family, for spouse, for career, and for self. Van Ogtrop's love for her family is reflected in her constant efforts to meet her family's needs and in her feelings of guilt that perhaps she doesn't always do so. In complaining about her husband, for example, she admits to feeling that she is perhaps not the wife she could be. In this sense, she is describing some of the challenges spouses face in trying to maintain a marriage. Van Ogtrop also raises questions about the nature of these kinds of love and perhaps about the costs of love, too.

The images van Ogtrop shares from her life are familiar ones in our society's ongoing discussions about what is often called the "balancing act"—that is, the effort of men and especially women to balance career and family and marriage. As you read, you might consider why these images are

I t's a typical night:

I arrive home from work, after first stopping to pick up my two boys from my friend Gabrielle's house, where my nanny has left them on a play date. It's seven thirty. No one has had a bath. Foolishly, I have promised that we will make milk shakes. The boys have eaten dinner. I haven't. My husband is at a basketball game and won't be home until ten.

Owen, who is six, tosses a bouquet of flowers—a gift from Gabrielle's garden—onto the grass as we get out of the car. Three-year-old Hugo sees the moon. I mention that the sun is out, too; he runs from one end of the front walk to the other, trying to find it, getting closer to the street with each lap.

Owen says he wants the milk shake *now*.

I unlock the front door and step in. George the cat meows and rubs against my legs, begging to be fed.

I walk back outside to pick up the flowers, the wet towel (swimming lessons), and my own two bags from work (contents: three unread newspapers, two magazines, a birthday party invitation for Owen, a

familiar and what they tell us about our society's attitudes and expectations regarding love.

Kristin van Ogtrop has been an editor at a number of magazines, including Glamour, Vogue, *and* Travel & Leisure, *and has written for many others, including* Seventeen *and* Outside. *She is currently managing editor of* Real Simple *magazine. This essay appeared in* The Bitch in the House: 26 Women Tell the Truth about Sex, Solitude, Work, Motherhood, and Marriage, *edited by Cathi Hanauer (2002).* ◪

STRATEGIES: FIRST-PERSON DESCRIPTION
In these opening paragraphs and throughout her essay, van Ogtrop describes scenes from her daily life. Consider what these various scenes tell us about who van Ogtrop is and the kind of life she leads. What specific details does she choose to share with her readers? Why do you think she shares these details?

present for the party, and a folder of work that, ever the optimist, I'm hoping to do tonight).

Back into the house with flowers, towel, bags. As I put my keys in the bowl next to the front door (small attempt at order), I knock over a framed picture beside it. The glass in the frame shatters.

Hugo calls, insistent, for me to come back outside.

Owen hovers behind me, barefoot. He wants to know why, when you combine chocolate and vanilla, does the ice cream turn brown instead of white?

I maneuver Owen around the broken glass and ask him to get the Dustbuster as I begin to pick up the shards. He disappears into the kitchen for what seems like ten minutes. I glance out for Hugo, whose voice is fainter but *definitely* still audible. George stands on his hind legs, clawing holes in the screen.

Owen reappears with the Dustbuster, revving the motor. He wants to know exactly how long until we make the milk shake, and are we sure we even have chocolate ice cream?

I am talking in my Mr. Rogers voice as my desperation rises. Any minute now my head is going to blast off my body, burst through the screen door, and buzz around my little town, eventually losing steam before landing with a thud somewhere near the train station, where it will be run over by one of my smiling neighbors being picked up by what I imagine are calm spouses who will drive them calmly home to houses calm and collected where the children are already bathed and ready for bed.

As for me, it's time to start yelling.

*   *   *

The next day:

I get up at 5:30 to leave the house at 6:00, to be driven to the TV studio for hair and makeup at 6:45, to go on the air, live, at 7:40. I'm the executive editor of an enormously popular women's magazine and am appearing as an "expert" on a local morning show to discuss "what your wallet says about you." I have a hairstylist I've never met and he makes the back of my head look ridiculous, like a ski jump. At 7:25 the segment producer hands me the anchor's script; it contains five questions that weren't part of yesterday's pre-interview. I make up answers that sound informed-clever-peppy enough for morning TV with two minutes to spare. Total airtime: ninety seconds.

By the time I get to the office at 8:30 I have six voice mail messages (boss, nanny, human resources manager, unhappy writer, underling editor wanting guidance, my mother), twenty-seven e-mails, and, on my chair, a 4,000-word article I need to edit by the end of the day. I run to the cafeteria to get something to eat, then call boss and nanny and answer most of the e-mails before my 9:30 meeting.

At 10:45 two fact-checkers come into my office to describe the 15
problems of a recent story, which kept them at work until 4:00 A.M.
the night before. Are fact-checkers or editor to blame? Editor, I decide, and call her in. She is flustered and defensive, and starts to cry.
My tissue box is empty, so I hand her a napkin. We talk (well, I talk;
she nods) about the fact that she's made similar mistakes in the past,
and perhaps this isn't the job for her. After she leaves I call the human
resources manager to discuss the problematic editor, a looming legal
problem, and staff salaries.

I have lunch at my desk and a second cup of coffee while I edit the
piece, until two editors visit to complain about coworkers. A third
tells me she is overloaded. A fourth confesses her marital problems
and starts to cry; now I'm out of napkins, too. I give her the number
of a counseling service and suggest she use it. Someone calls to ask
about the presentation I'm giving tomorrow; I haven't even begun to
think about it, which probably should worry me but somehow
doesn't.

I finish the edit and drop it in my out box. Before leaving the office
at 5:30 I pick up all the paper that blankets my desk and divide it into
four discrete piles for the morning. I very well might forget to look
through the piles and something will get overlooked, but when I return to work, the neat stacks will make me feel organized and calm.
And at work, I usually am.

Here are a few things people have said about me at the office:

- "You're unflappable."
- "Are you ever in a bad mood?"
- "You command respect as soon as you walk into a room."
- "Your straightforward, no-nonsense style gets things done."
- "You're good at finessing situations so people don't boil over."

Here are things people—OK, the members of my family—have
said about me at home:

- "Mommy is always grumpy."
- "Why are you so tense?"
- "You just need to relax."
- "You don't need to yell!"
- "You're too mean to live in this house and I want you to go
  back to work for the rest of your life!"

That last one is my favorite. It's also the saddest, because it captures 20
such a painful truth: too often I'm a better mother at work than I am
at home. Of course, at work, no one shouts at me for five minutes
straight in what parents universally refer to as an "outside voice." No
one charges into my office, hands outstretched, to smear peanut butter all over my skirt or Vaseline all over my favorite needlepoint rug.
At work, when someone is demanding something of me, I can say,

"I'll call you back" or "Let's talk about that in the next meeting." When people don't listen to me, they do so after they've left my office, not right in front of me. Yet even if shouting and random acts of destruction were to become the norm at work, I probably would not respond with the angry tantrums that punctuate so many nights at home. We have our own form of chaos in the office, after all. I work with creative people—temperamental, flaky, "difficult"—but my job is to be the eye of the storm.

So why this angel-in-the-office, horror-at-home division? Shouldn't the skills that serve me so well at work help me at the end of the day? My friend Chrissie, heroic stay-at-home mother of four, has one explanation: My behavior simply reproduces, in the adult world, the perfect-at-school/demon-at-home phenomenon that is acted out daily among children throughout America. I am on my best behavior at work, just as Owen is on his best behavior at school, but at home we have to ask him seven times to put on his shoes and by the seventh time it's no longer a request but a shouted, boot-camp command. And I am on my worst behavior at home because that's where I can "unwind" after spending eight (or ten, or fourteen) hours at the office keeping my cool.

Arlie Russell Hochschild has other ideas about this apparently widespread condition. In her 1997 book *TIME BIND: WHEN WORK BECOMES HOME AND HOME BECOMES WORK,* she writes, "In this new model of family and work life, a tired parent flees a world of unresolved quarrels and unwashed laundry for the reliable orderliness, harmony, and managed cheer of work." At the office, I do manage, in all senses of the word. I am paid to be bossy—a trait that, for better and worse, has always been a predominant part of my personality. But at home, that bossiness yields unpleasant dividends, both from two boys who are now officially Grade A backtalkers and from a husband who frequently lets me know he's not someone I need to supervise. Still, the impulse isn't likely to go away, as long as I remain the only one in our household who knows where the library books/soccer cleats/car keys have gone—and what to do with them. At home I am wife, mother, baby-sitting and housekeeping manager, cook, social secretary, gardener, tutor, chauffeur, interior decorator, general contractor, and laundress. That many roles is exhausting, especially at those times when my mind is still in work mode. The other night I said to Hugo, "Do you want to put on your pj's in Owen's office?" It's a messy juggling act, and when a ball drops, I'm never laughing.

Last Friday I picked up the cheery note that Owen's kindergarten teacher, Ms. Stenstrom, sends at the end of every week. "We had an exciting morning!" it began. "We finished our touch unit by guessing

---

CONVERSATIONS: THE "BALANCING ACT"

Throughout this essay, van Ogtrop includes vivid descriptions of her hectic days as a mother and a career woman. If these scenes are familiar to you, it may be because popular media often depict such scenes as typical in modern American life, especially for women. For example, the kinds of women's magazines that van Ogtrop herself edits publish articles about how women can balance their roles as mothers, wives, and professionals. In this paragraph, van Ogtrop refers to Arlie Hochschild's book *Time Bind: When Work Becomes Home and Home Becomes Work* (1997), one of many such books published in the 1980s and 1990s as increasing numbers of women pursued careers. Books like Hochschild's are part of an ongoing discussion about the implications of these changes in American society and the challenges they present not only to women but also to the society as a whole. Consider how van Ogtrop's essay fits into that larger discussion and how van Ogtrop herself seems to be participating in it.

what was in all the bags—thanks for sending in SUCH mysterious objects!" I had forgotten that Owen was supposed to have taken something interesting to touch in a brown paper bag to school that day. Standing alone in the kitchen, I started to cry. I read the note again, feeling miserable for Owen, miserable for me, miserable for lovely, infinitely patient Ms. Stenstrom. Then I climbed the stairs, cornered Dean, and cried some more. Is that appropriate? To cry for an hour and then have a long, tedious, completely unproductive discussion with an equally sleep-deprived husband about All The Things We're Doing Wrong? How did I turn into this?

*   *   *

Start with my mother, end with my father. In 1976, when I was twelve, fully two-thirds of all American households that consisted of married couples with children had one parent staying home full-time, according to the U.S. Census Bureau. My mother was one of those parents. With her tuna cashew casserole recipe, I won the 4-H Ready Foods Contest at the Delaware State Fair when I was in fourth grade. From my mother I learned that when you assemble a place setting, the knife should be one thumb-knuckle distance from the edge of the table; when you arrange flowers in a vase, the largest blooms should be at the bottom; when you hem a skirt, you should turn the ends of the fabric under twice. From my mother I also learned that grades are important, that feelings are neither right nor wrong, and that I am capable of just about anything I make up my mind to do.

College, graduate school, first jobs (art gallery, film production company); they all happened without much planning. Along the way I met Dean, and for a few years nothing else mattered. Then, when I was twenty-seven, I landed at *Vogue*—and suddenly found myself living on a planet where I spoke the native tongue. Dean left graduate school and got a magazine job, too. Of course, while he and I were fetching coffee and confirming the spelling of proper names (standard duties for editor wanna-bes, for a salary dangerously close to minimum wage), our closest friends were finishing law school and business school and accepting $100,000 jobs and getting pregnant and buying houses. I despaired: we would never have children! never buy a house! never pay off my student loan!

But I got promoted. I got pregnant. By the time Owen was a year old, the charms of our romantic brownstone floor-through in Brooklyn were obliterated by overflowing closets and a litter box in the living room. For the sake of matrimonial harmony Dean allowed himself to be talked into the suburbs (hello! nearly the happiest day in my life!). Our once-minuscule salaries got bigger, our once-mansionlike house eventually felt smaller, but we're still here; our choice has stuck.

I left *Vogue* and had job after job, and as I moved from one magazine to another, this thought formed on the border of my consciousness. It got less peripheral, gradually bigger, until it was large and
clear as day: in spite of years of training, I had not become my mother. I was my father, with ovaries. I have his square shoulders and his
ease with strangers; I also have his extraordinarily short fuse. Like my
father, I am polite to people in the workplace because I am trying to
charm them, to win them over—and to be fair, to do the right thing.
At work I give people the benefit of the doubt. At home there is no
such thing. At home I—like my father—blame first, ask questions
later. My mother is the soul of patience. My mother is nothing like
this.

I can still arrange flowers and set a table, but I can't remember how
my mother disciplined without raising her voice. Where my kids are
concerned, I am volatile but deeply sentimental, like my father. I
keep locks of their hair, a drawer full of their drawings. And when
they're asleep, I kneel beside their beds in atonement for my sins,
press my nose to their sweaty blond heads, and ask forgiveness for my
take-no-prisoners parenting style.

I work because I have to financially, and because I love to. Like my
dad, I get enormous personal satisfaction from career success. But
the smoothness with which my career flows makes life at home even
harder to manage. Like me, my father is missing the microchip that
processes chaos. When his three daughters were small, he would
come home from work (by six, in time for family dinner) and pour
himself a drink before he'd even taken off his tie. The drink was not
a reward for a hard day's work, but a buttress for what he'd face over
the next four hours. On a recent visit to our house, while attempting
to work an ice maker that had been broken for four months, he announced, "If I lived in this house, I'd have to drink all day long." Ice
makers, you see, don't stay broken for four months in his house. My
father has a wife.

*   *   *

Ah, a wife. Sometimes when describing the work my nanny does to   30
women of another generation who find my life perplexing, I say, "Basically, she's a wife," and wonder if it's horribly sexist or insulting to
use that description. Lauren does wash the kids' clothes, make their
dinner, help with homework, cuddle after naps. She does not, however, write notes to the teacher or plan vacations or figure out where
we're going to put the hamster Owen desperately wants. And Dean,
God bless him, is terrible at those things. I used to think it was lack of
training; now I think it's that Y chromosome. Dean is spectacular at
spelling Kyrgyzstan and remembering who won the 1976 World Series. Ask him the first name of Hugo's nursery school teacher and

he's stumped. Ask him to remember to pick up cat food and it goes in one ear and out the other; on really frustrating days he'll deny ever being told at all (note to self: don't say anything important if the sports section is within ten feet). So there are duties—and they seem to number in the thousands—that fall in the vast gray area that is not-husband-not-nanny, and therefore they are mine.

I come home on an average Tuesday to find the Scholastic book order form submerged in a pile of drawings and Pokémon cards and disemboweled pens on the kitchen counter. I look at the pictures of Clifford paperbacks, boxed sets, games. How many Clifford books do we already have, anyway? Did I order a Clifford cassette the last time, or was I just considering it? Did Dean's sister give Owen a Clifford CD-ROM for Christmas? The questions (unanswerable without a substantial investment of house searching or phone calling) start to jam my circuits, and I think I might burst into tears. I just can't make one

---

CONVERSATIONS: THE CHANGING ROLES OF AMERICAN WOMEN

In paragraph 33 and the following paragraphs, van Ogtrop describes some of her duties as a mother and wife, comparing herself with her father and mother and their roles as husband and wife. Obviously, the roles of women have changed since van Ogtrop's childhood. Examine what these two images might say about those changes. The first image is from an advertisement from 1963. The second is an ad from early 2000. What messages do they convey about who women are? What do they say about the expectations for women in American society?

Pledge advertisement

Secret antiperspirant advertisement, 2004

more decision. I have a sudden, overwhelming desire to be George Banks, the clueless and routinized father in *Mary Poppins,* when he bursts into the house at six on the dot singing, "I feel a surge of deep satisfaction!" Slippers, sherry, pipe at 6:01. Then: "It's 6:03, and the heirs to my dominion/are scrubbed and tubbed, and adequately fed/And so I'll pat them on the head, and send them off to bed/How lordly is the life I lead!" George at least has a song's length of ignorant bliss before he learns that the children have gone missing. . . .

Unfortunately, the fantasy doesn't quite sustain me as the bathwater sloshes all over the floor and the choice of *Bread and Jam for Frances* over *If You Give a Moose a Muffin* results in fraternal civil war. That's when the exhaustion wins. I call to Dean, who has just arrived home from work, "I can't deal with this anymore!" and he steps in before I really start to yell. I wash my face and brush my teeth and fall into bed the minute I can make a break for it, the millisecond Hugo is finished with his nightly forty-five minutes of getting in and out, in and out of bed. I crawl under the covers like a woman who has walked forty miles through a snowstorm, and remember all over again that—pathetic or not—this really is my favorite moment of the day.

*   *   *

And so there's the guilt. This is one area in which my father and I differ. He has never Wrestled with His Identity as a Parent. He has never, as far as I know, overcompensated for anything. He didn't ever play duck-duck-goose after work, as I did two nights ago, even though it was dark and the grass was wet and I would rather—who are we kidding?—have been inside with a glass of wine. The guilt seems centered on the things I'm missing in my children's lives. I know I miss much, because I feel it: there is a purity to their everyday world that makes my heart ache. When I walk into one of their schools, I feel as if I'm walking into a church; the halls are filled with noble souls who are trying to save the world. I am not of that world in the way that non-working mothers are—I'm more a frequent visitor—and I suspect that my guilt and sadness about that are part of what makes me so cranky at home.

But my guilt is diminishing as I evolve, and I consider the process of shedding it a significant act of liberation. The older my kids get, the more I'm beginning to realize that they're happy and smart and loving, despite the fact that Mom works. I am trying to eliminate the stubborn fear that children of working mothers grow up to be unhappy adults. I'm making progress, although I'm occasionally derailed by news items like the one I recently saw in the *Wall Street Journal* that described the math scores of children who don't have two parents at home from 6:00 to 9:00 P.M. (Let's just say the chances of Owen and Hugo ever reaching AP calculus are slim.)

There's guilt where my marriage is concerned, too, but it's a Mo-   35
bius strip: guilt and resentment, and more guilt because of the resentment. We are just like many two career, multiple-child couples I know.
I could write a script for one of our arguments and pass it out to half
of my suburban neighbors (the 51 percent in my town with working
moms); simply change the names and everyone could act out the
same neat little domestic drama. Whereas Dean and I used to argue
about money and where to live, we now bicker constantly about one
thing: who is doing more. Before we had children we were broke but
had fun doing effortless activities that didn't cost a dime, like sleeping in. Now we have money but no time together (and, obviously, no
sleeping in). We are still partners, but often partners in martyrdom,
burning ourselves at the stake on a bonfire of diapers that need to be
changed, mittens that need to be found, plumbers who need to be
called. We often have a semifight at three in the afternoon to see who
is least required at the office and can take the 5:58 train to relieve the
nanny. During the week we are rarely, if ever, both home awake with
the kids at the same time. Although Dean points out that this is true
of most working parents we know, it troubles me that, schedule-wise,
we might as well be divorced with joint custody. Because we spend
many weekend nights with friends and their children, we eat dinner
together as a foursome only about once a week, not five or six times
as was the norm in our own childhoods. Is this the worst thing in the
world? Is this damaging to my children in the long run? As with everything, it depends on who you ask.

It's these questions without answers that make me insane. Most
work questions somehow have ready answers, and when I doubt my
abilities as an editor, the moments are fleeting. I doubt my skills as a
mother every day. I measure myself against a Platonic motherhood
ideal and I'm always coming up short. You could argue that the doubt
itself makes me try harder, means I continue to strive. But the doubt
is also what makes me irrational, moody, even angry when faced with
the chaos that accompanies such fundamental childhood joys as
jumping on Mommy and Daddy's newly made bed.

*   *   *

Was my mother ever this angry? It's hard to believe, and scares
me when I contemplate it. When I was little, reading a book on the
hammock or playing foursquare in the driveway, was my mom actually looking forward to the day when I would go away to college so
she could have the house to herself? Didn't she love me more than
that?

This, I fear, is how it will be: I will love my children, but my love for
them will always be imperfect, damaged by my rigid personality and
the demands of my work. I will never be able to share the surprise

they feel when they find a cicada in the grass, because stopping to marvel at the cicada means I will miss my morning train. I will never fully love, without qualifiers, the loud, messy place that is the home of two energetic boys. The years will pass, Owen and Hugo will grow, and I will continue to dream about the time I can walk in the front door and feel relaxed.

I will long for a time when I will never yell at my kids just because I am late. Long to be a mother who simply doesn't care that there's Vaseline on my needlepoint rug. To be on my best behavior at home, just as I am at work; to treat my family with the same kindness and respect that I at least pretend to give everyone in my office.

40   Because before I know it, my boys will be grown. The house will be spotless, and so will I: nice, calm, both at work and at home. Four little feet jumping on the bed will be a distant memory. And things like cicadas will have lost their magic, and my children will be gone for good.

Understanding the Text

1. What does van Ogtrop tell us about the kind of person she is? Why is this information important to her main point in this essay? What was your reaction to van Ogtrop as a person as she presents herself in this essay? How might your sense of her as a person affect your response to her main point in this essay?

2. About half way through her essay (par. 23), van Ogtrop describes a scene in which she breaks down in tears after realizing that she forgot to send something to school with her son. Why is this incident so important to van Ogtrop? What does she mean when she writes at the end of the paragraph, "How did I turn into this?"

3. In what ways does van Ogtrop compare herself with

her father? What does this comparison reveal about her as a person? Is the comparison flattering to van Ogtrop? Is it important that it be flattering? Explain.

4. In the third-to-last paragraph of this essay, van Ogtrop writes that she fears her love for her children "will always be imperfect." What does she mean? What solution to this problem does she find, if any? Do you think she is right? Why or why not?

Exploring the Text

1. What do the scenes van Ogtrop describes from her family life suggest about her social class and economic status? What might they reflect about her cultural background? Is she a typical American? Would these scenes be familiar to *all* Americans? Explain. What audience do you think van

Ogtrop is writing to? What does she assume about her readers' social and cultural background?

2. Do you think van Ogtrop expects readers to sympathize with her when she describes her daily struggles and her sometimes failed efforts to keep her cool at home? Why or why not? Cite specific passages to support your answer.

3. What might this essay reveal about the kind of love family members have for each other? What might it reveal about love that parents have for their children? About love between two partners in a marriage?

4. In some ways, van Ogtrop's essay might be seen as the price one pays for pursuing a career and trying to raise a family at the same time. What do you think her essay suggests about our society's attitudes regarding the importance of career and family?

Entering the Conversations

1. Write an essay in which you describe an experience that you believe reveals some of the challenges of love.

2. In a group of your classmates, share the essays you wrote for Question 1. What kinds of experiences did you and your classmates write about? What similarities and differences can you identify among these essays? How might you explain the differences in these essays? What do you think the essays reveal about our society's attitudes about love and relationships in families?

3. Using van Ogtrop's essay as a primary source and drawing on any other appropriate sources, write an essay for an audience of your classmates in which you define *love*. Alternatively, write an editorial essay for your local newspaper in which you define love

in the context of the changing American family.

INFOTRAC

4. Using InfoTrac College Edition and any other appropriate resources, examine the changing role of women in American society and especially the role of women in the workplace. Try to find information about women who pursue careers and raise families at the same time. What challenges do these women and their families face? How typical is van Ogtrop's situation? How typical are the struggles she describes in this essay? What have women done to address these challenges? Try to answer such questions in your research. Then write a report in which you describe the changing role of American women. In your report, present what you learned through your research and discuss implications of the changing role of American women for families, marriage, and the workplace.

5. Review several issues of popular women's magazines, such as the ones that van Ogtrop has worked for (e.g., *Glamour*). What do they suggest about the balancing act that van Ogtrop describes in her essay? How do they discuss love and marriage and careers for women? What values regarding family and career do they seem to support? Write a report of your review of these magazines in which you discuss what you found and draw conclusions about how love, marriage, family, and career are discussed in contemporary American society. Alternatively, create a web site in which you present your conclusions.

6. Select a popular television show that you think depicts the balancing act that van Ogtrop describes. Write an essay in which you discuss how this television show presents the balancing act of modern women, and draw your own conclusions about what this show might suggest about the place of women in contemporary society.

One of the most influential Black women *scholars in the United States today, bell hooks (b. 1952) is well known for her provocative and unconventional writing about race, gender, education, and culture in well-received books like* Talking Back *(1989) and* Teaching to Transgress *(1994). She is perhaps less well known as a prominent*

ON Building A Community OF Love

student of Buddhism who has written widely on Buddhist ideas about love, relationships, and community. In the following essay, hooks presents a dialogue with Thich Nhat Hanh, one of the world's foremost teachers of Zen Buddhism, who first gained international attention in the 1960s for his peace activism against the Vietnam War. As hooks tells us in this essay, Thich Nhat Hanh's writings profoundly influenced her own writing, especially her book All about Love *(2001). In this dialogue, she invites Nhat Hanh to explore with her the concepts of love and community from a Buddhist perspective. In doing so, she and Nhat Hanh raise questions about the nature of love among people in a community—questions that go beyond any single religious or cultural perspective. Their examination of Buddhist ideas about love and community can help us think more broadly about what*

BELL HOOKS

As teacher and guide Thich Nhat Hanh has been a presence in my life for more than twenty years. In the last few years I began to doubt the heart connection I felt with him because we had never met or spoken to one another, yet his work was ever-present in my work. I began to feel the need to meet him face to face, even as my intuitive self kept saying that it would happen when the time was right. My work in love has been to trust that intuitive self that kept saying that it would happen when the time was right. My work in love has been to trust that intuition knowledge.

Those who know me intimately know that I have been contemplating the place and meaning of love in our lives and culture for years. They know that when a subject attracts my intellectual and emotional imagination, I am long to observe it from all angles, to know it inside and out.

In keeping with the way my mind works, when I began to think deeply about the metaphysics of love I talked with everyone around me about it. I talked to large audiences and even had wee one-on-one

BELL HOOKS, "ON BUILDING A COMMUNITY OF LOVE: BELL HOOKS MEETS WITH THICH NHAT HANH TO ASK: HOW DO WE BUILD A COMMUNITY OF LOVE?" FROM *SHAMBHALA SUN ONLINE*, JANUARY 2000. FROM THE *SHAMBHALA SUN* MAGAZINE: WWW.SHAMBHALA-SUN.COM. REPRINTED BY PERMISSION.

conversations with children about the way they think about love. I talked about love in every state. Indeed, I encouraged the publishers of my new book *All About Love: New Visions* to launch it with postcards, t-shirts, and maybe even a calendar with the logo "Love in every state." I talked about love everywhere I traveled.

To me, all the work I do is built on a foundation of loving-kindness. Love illuminates matters. And when I write provocative social and cultural criticism that causes readers to stretch their minds, to think beyond set paradigms, I think of that work as love in action. While it may challenge, disturb and at times even frighten or enrage readers, love is always the place where I begin and end.

5   A central theme of all about love is that from childhood into adulthood we are often taught misguided and false assumptions about the nature of love. Perhaps the most common false assumption about love is that love means we will not be challenged or changed. No doubt this is why people who read writing about racism, sexism, homophobia, religion, etc. that challenges their set assumptions tend to see that work as harsh rather than loving.

Of all the definitions of love that abound in our universe, a special favorite of mine is the one offered in *THE ROAD LESS TRAVELED* BY PSYCHOANALYST M. SCOTT PECK. Defining love as "the will to extend one's self for the purpose of nurturing one's own or another's spiritual growth," he draws on the work of Erich Fromm to emphasize again and again that love is first and foremost exemplified by action—by practice—not solely by feeling.

FROMM'S *THE ART OF LOVING* was published when I was four years old. It was the book I turned to in my late teens when I felt confused about the nature of love. His insistence that "love is the active concern for the life and growth of that which we love" made sense to me then and it still does. Peck expands this definition. Knowing that the world would be a paradise of peace and justice if global citizens shared a common definition of love which would guide our thoughts and action, I call for the embrace of such a common understanding in all about love: new visions. That common understanding might be articulated in different words carrying a shared meaning for diverse experiences and cultures.

Throughout the more than twenty years that I have written on the subject of ending domination in whatever form it appears (racism, sexism, homophobia, classism), I have continually sought those paths that would lead to the end of violence and injustice. Since so much of my thinking about love in my late teens revolved around familial and romantic love, it was not until I was in my early twenties writing feminist theory that I began to think deeply about love in relation to domination.

we mean when we talk about love among members of a community.

This essay can also help us think about how we talk and write about love. The form of the dialogue, which hooks has used in many of her academic books, is as old as Plato's famous dialogues, written more than 2,500 years ago, in which the great philosopher Socrates offers his wisdom by engaging in dialogue with his peers or his students. hooks's dialogues do not follow a strict question-and-answer format but involve a give-and-take by two people interested in understanding a complicated idea. As you read, consider how this form might help hooks accomplish her goals as a writer. Consider, too, how the non-Western cultural perspective that she and Nhat Hanh take might complicate your own ideas about love and community.

Born Gloria Watkins, bell hooks is currently distinguished professor of English at City College of the City University of New York. The following dialogue first appeared in 2000 in Shambhala Sun Online, *a publication devoted to Buddhism.* ◙

CONVERSATIONS: LOVE
In Chapter 1 of *All about Love* (2001), bell hooks writes, "Imagine how much easier it would be for us to learn how to love if we began with a shared definition. The word 'love' is most often defined as a noun, yet all the more astute theorists of love acknowledge that we would all love better if we used it as a verb." In this dialogue with Thich Nhat Hanh, hooks refers to definitions of love from M. Scott Peck and Erich Fromm, two very popular writers whose work focuses on love and emotional well-being. In doing so, she not only helps her readers better understand her way of defining love, but she also places her essay in the context of a much larger conversation about love and relationships.

STRATEGIES: PERSONAL VOICE
hooks is well known for the way she
draws on personal experience and adopts
a personal voice in her writing, even
when she is writing about complicated
theoretical topics for an academic
audience. In her book *Talking Back,* she
argues that "if we are to reach our people
and all people . . . we must understand
that the telling of one's personal story
provides a meaningful example, a way for
folks to identify and connect." Here in
paragraph 9, as she often does in her
writing, hooks shares some of her own
experiences to introduce her dialogue
with Thich Nhat Hanh. Some scholars
have criticized hooks for this personal
writing style. Consider the potential
impact of this personal approach on
readers. What do you think this approach
might help hooks achieve in her writing?
What problems do you see with her
personal style?

During my first years in college Martin Luther King's message of love as the path to ending racism and healing the wounds of racial domination had been replaced by a black power movement stressing militant resistance. While King had called for nonviolence and compassion, this new movement called on us to harden our hearts, to wage war against our enemies. Loving our enemies, militant leaders told us, made us weak and easy to subjugate, and many turned their backs on King's message.

Just as the energy of a racially-based civil rights liberation struggle   10
was moving away from a call for love, the women's movement also launched a critique of love, calling on females to forget about love so that we might seize power. When I was nineteen participating in feminist consciousness-raising groups, love was dismissed as irrelevant. It was our "addiction to love" that kept us sleeping with the enemy (men). To be free, our militant feminist leaders told us, we needed to stop making love the center of our imaginations and yearnings. Love could be a good woman's downfall.

These two movements for social justice that had captured the hearts and imagination of our nation—movements that began with a love ethic—were changed by leaders who were much more interested in questions of power. By the late seventies it was no longer necessary to silence discussions of love; the topic was no longer on any progressive agenda.

Those of us who still longed to hold on to love looked to religions as the site of redemption. We searched everywhere, all around the world, for the spiritual teachers who could help us return to love. My seeking led me to Buddhism, guided there by the Beat poets, by personal interaction with Gary Snyder. At his mountain home I would meet my first Buddhist nun and walk mindfully with her, all the while wondering if my heart could ever know the sweet peace emanating from her like a perfume mist.

My seeking led me to the work of a Buddhist monk Martin Luther King had met and been touched by—Thich Nhat Hanh. The first work I read by this new teacher in my life was a conversation book between him and Daniel Berrigan, *The Raft Is Not the Shore.*

At last I had found a world where spirituality and politics could meet, where there was no separation. Indeed, in this world all efforts to end domination, to bring peace and justice, were spiritual practice. I was no longer torn between political struggle and spiritual practice. And here was the radical teacher—a Vietnamese monk living in exile—courageously declaring that "if you have to choose between Buddhism and peace, then you must choose peace."

CONVERSATIONS: THE CIVIL RIGHTS MOVEMENT AND THE WOMEN'S MOVEMENT
In this section of her essay, hooks explains how two important
social and political movements in the United States in the 1960s
and 1970s shaped her ways of thinking about love and
relationships. She traces a pendulous swing of people involved in
the Civil Rights and the women's movements from love to hate and
back to love. It might be difficult for us today to understand the
intense debates within these movements about how to relate to
one's opponents. For example, some Black leaders openly called
for violence against Whites to combat the violence of White racism.
Some, including Martin Luther King, Jr., disagreed, promoting
instead a nonviolent approach based on a belief in equality, justice,
and love. Obviously, this experience deeply affected hooks and
helped shape her ideas about love and hate. Do you think hooks
speaks effectively about these issues to readers who were not
alive during the social movements she describes in this passage?

Unlike white friends and comrades who were often contemptuous [15] of me because I had not traveled to the East or studied with important teachers, Thich Nhat Hanh was calmly stating: "Buddhism is in your heart. Even if you don't have any temple or any monks, you can still be a Buddhist in your heart and life." Reading his words I felt an inner rapture and could only repeat, "Be still my heart." Like one wandering in the desert overcome by thirst, I had found water. My thirst was quenched and my spiritual hunger intensified.

For a period of more than ten years since leaving home for college I had felt pulled in all directions by anti-racist struggle, by the feminist movement, sexual liberation, by the fundamentalist Christianity of my upbringing. I wanted to embrace radical politics and still know god. I wanted to resist and be redeemed. *The Raft Is Not the Shore* helped strengthen my spiritual journey. Even though I had not met with Thich Nhat Hanh he was the teacher, along with Chögyam Trungpa Rinpoche, who were my chosen guides. Mixing the two was a fiery combination.

As all became well with my soul, I began to talk about the work of **THICH NHAT HANH** in my books, quoting from his work. He helped me bring together theories of political recovery and spiritual recovery. For years I did not want to meet him face to face for fear I would be disappointed. Time and time again I planned to be where he was and the plan would be disrupted. Our paths were crossing but we were never meeting face to face.

Then suddenly, in a marvelous serendipitous way, we were meeting. In his presence at last, I felt overwhelmed with gratitude that not only was I given the blessing of meeting him, but that a pure spirit of love connected us. I felt ecstatic. My heart jumped for joy—such union and reunion to be in the presence of one who has tutored your heart, who has been with you in spirit on your journey.

The journey is also to the teacher and beyond. It is always a path to the heart. And the heart of the matter is always our oneness with divine spirit—our union with all life. As early as 1975, Thich Nhat Hanh was sharing: "The way must be in you; the destination also must be in you and not somewhere else in space or time. If that kind of self-transformation is being realized in you, you will arrive."

Walking on love's path on a sunny day on my way to meet my teacher, I meet Sister Chan Khong. She too has taught me. She felt my [20] heart's readiness. Together we remembered the teacher who is everywhere awakening the heart. As she writes at the end of *Learning True Love*, "I am with you just as you have been with me, and we encourage each other to realize our deepest love, caring and generosity . . . together on the path of love."

* * *

GLOSS: THICH NHAT HANH
In 1966, Thich Nhat Hanh, a Buddhist monk, was forced to leave his native Vietnam because of his activism against the war then raging in his homeland. He has since become one of the world's foremost Buddhist teachers and peace activists. He established Plum Village in France, a center for the study and practice of what he calls "engaged Buddhism," which has several satellite centers around the world. He is author of dozens of books about Buddhism and about working toward peace.

bell hooks: I began writing a book on love because I felt that the United States is moving away from love. The civil rights movement was such a wonderful movement for social justice because the heart of it was love—loving everyone. It was believing, as you taught us yesterday, that we can always start anew; we can always practice forgiveness. I don't have to hate any person because I can always start anew, I can always reconcile. What I'm trying to understand is why are we moving away from this idea of a community of love. What is your thinking about why people are moving away from love, and how we can be part of moving our society towards love?

Thich Nhat Hanh: In our own Buddhist **SANGHA,** community is the core of everything. The sangha is a community where there should be harmony and peace and understanding. That is something created by our daily life together. If love is there in the community, if we've been nourished by the harmony in the community, then we will never move away from love.

The reason we might lose this is because we are always looking outside of us, thinking that the object or action of love is out there. That is why we allow the love, the harmony, the mature understanding, to slip away from ourselves. This is, I think, the basic thing. That is why we have to go back to our community and renew it. Then love will grow back. Understanding and harmony will grow back. That's the first thing.

The second thing is that we ourselves need love; it's not only society, the world outside, that needs love. But we can't expect that love to come from outside of us. We should ask the question whether we are capable of loving ourselves as well as others. Are we treating our body kindly—by the way we eat, by the way we drink, by the way we work? Are we treating ourselves with enough joy and tenderness and peace? Or are we feeding ourselves with toxins that we get from the market—the spiritual, intellectual, entertainment market?

So the question is whether we are practicing loving ourselves? Because loving ourselves means loving our community. When we are capable of loving ourselves, nourishing ourselves properly, not intoxicating ourselves, we are already protecting and nourishing society. Because in the moment when we are able to smile, to look at ourselves with compassion, our world begins to change. We may not have done anything but when we are relaxed, when we are peaceful, when we are able to smile and not to be violent in the way we look at the system, at that moment there is a change already in the world.

So the second help, the second insight, is that between self or no-self there is no real separation. Anything you do for yourself you do for the society at the same time. And anything you do for society you do for yourself also. That insight is very powerfully made in the practice of **NO-SELF.**

25

GLOSSES:
SANGHA

Sangha is a Buddhist term referring to a community or group, such as members of a temple or church. It is also used to refer to larger communities and even to humanity as a whole. Sangha is one of the "three treasures" that Buddhists believe are available to all people; the other two are the Buddha himself and the *dharma,* which refers to the Buddha's teachings.

NO-SELF

When Thich Nhat Hanh writes about "the practice of no-self," he is referring to the Buddhist belief in the fundamental unity of all beings. Buddhist practice is a process of trying to understand the self, through meditation and study, to realize that, ultimately, there is no self but only a unity of all life of which each self is inherently a part. Later, in paragraph 33, Nhat Hanh refers to "interbeing," which is another term for the unity of all beings; in other words, according to Buddhist teachings, each being is inherently a part of every other being.

bell hooks: I think one of the most wonderful books that Martin Luther King wrote was *Strength to Love*. I always liked it because of the word "strength," which counters the Western notion of love as easy. Instead, Martin Luther King said that you must have courage to love, that you have to have a profound will to do what is right to love, that it does not come easy.

Thich Nhat Hanh: Martin Luther King was among us as a brother, as a friend, as a leader. He was able to maintain that love alive. When you touch him, you touch a **BODHISATTVA,** for his understanding and love was enough to hold everything to him. He tried to transmit his insight and his love to the community, but maybe we have not received it enough. He was trying to transmit the best things to us—his goodness, his love, his nonduality. But because we had clung so much to him as a person, we did not bring the essence of what he was teaching into our community. So now that he's no longer here, we are at a loss. We have to be aware that crucial transmission he was making was not the transmission of power, of authority, of position, but the transmission of the dharma. It means love.

bell hooks: Exactly. It was not a transmission of personality. Part of why I have started writing about love is feeling, as you say, that our culture is forgetting what he taught. We name more and more streets and schools after him but that's almost irrelevant, because what is to be remembered is that strength to love.

That's what we have to draw courage from—the spirit of love, not the image of Martin Luther King. This is so hard in the West because we are such an image and personality driven culture. For instance, because I have learned so much from you for so many years of my life, people kept asking me whether I had met you in person.

Thich Nhat Hanh: (laughs) Yes, I understand.

bell hooks: And I said yes, I have met him, because he has given his love to me through his teachings, through mindfulness practice. I kept trying to share with people that, yes, I would like to meet you some day, but the point is that I am living and learning from his teaching.

Thich Nhat Hanh: Yes, that's right. And that is the essence of interbeing. We had met already in the very non-beginning (laughs). Beginning with longing, beginning with blessings.

bell hooks: Except that you have also taught that to be in the presence of your teacher can also be a moment of transformation. So people say, is it enough that you've learned from books by him, or must you meet him, must there be an encounter?

Thich Nhat Hanh: In fact, the true teacher is within us. A good teacher is someone who can help you to go back and touch the true teacher within, because you already have the insight within you. In Buddhism we call it buddhanature. You don't need someone to transfer buddhanature to you, but maybe you need a friend who

30

35

GLOSS: BODHISATTVA

In Buddhism, a *bodhisattva* is a being that, while not yet fully enlightened, is actively striving toward that goal. Conventionally, the term is applied to hypothetical beings with a high degree of enlightenment and power, but as hooks and Nhat Hanh use it in this dialogue, it also refers to people who have made a formal commitment to Buddhist practice and study. Bodhisattva literally means "enlightenment being" in Sanskrit.

can help you touch that nature of awakening and understanding working in you.

So a good teacher is someone who can help you to get back to a teacher within. The teacher can do that in many different ways; she or he does not have to meet you physically. I feel that I have many real students whom I have not met. Many are in cloisters and they never get out. Others are in prison. But in many cases they practice the teachings much better than those who meet me every day. That is true. When they read a book by me or hear a tape and they touch the insight within them, then they have met me in a real way. That is the real meeting.

bell hooks: I want to know your thoughts on how we learn to love a world full of injustice, more than coming together with someone just because they share the same skin or the same language as we do. I ask this question of you because I first learned about you through Martin Luther King's homage to your compassion towards those who had hurt your country.

Thich Nhat Hanh: This is a very interesting topic. It was a very important issue for the Buddha. How we view justice depends on our practice of looking deeply. We may think that justice is everyone being equal, having the same rights, sharing the same kind of advantages, but maybe we have not had the chance to look at the nature of justice in terms of no-self. That kind of justice is based on the idea of self, but it may be very interesting to explore justice in terms of no-self.

bell hooks: I think that's exactly the kind of justice Martin Luther King spoke about—a justice that was for everyone whether they're equal or not. Sometimes in life all things are not equal, so what does it mean to have justice when there is no equality? A parent can be just towards a child, even though they're not equal. I think this is often misunderstood in the West, where people feel that there can be no justice unless everything is the same. This is part of why I feel we have to relearn how we think about love, because we think about love so much in terms of the self.

40 **Thich Nhat Hanh:** Is justice possible without equality?

bell hooks: Justice is possible without equality, I believe, because of compassion and understanding. If I have compassion, then if I have more than you, which is unequal, I will still do the just thing by you.

Thich Nhat Hanh: Right. And who has created inequality?

bell hooks: Well, I think inequality is in our minds. I think this is what we learn through practice. One of the concepts that you and Daniel Berrigan spoke about in *The Raft Is Not the Shore* is that the bridge of illusion must be shattered in order for a real bridge to be constructed. One of the things we learn is that inequality is an illusion.

Thich Nhat Hanh: Makes sense (laughs).

bell hooks: Before I came here I had been struggling with the question of anger toward my ex-boyfriend. I have taken my vows as a bodhisattva, and so I always feel very depressed when I have anger. I had come to a point of despair because I had so much difficulty with my anger in relation to this man. So yesterday's dharma talk about embracing our anger, and using it, and letting it go, was very essential for me at this moment. 45

Thich Nhat Hanh: You want to be human. Be angry, it's okay. But not to practice is not okay. To be angry, that is very human. And to learn how to smile at your anger and make peace with your anger is very nice. That is the whole thing—the meaning of the practice, of the learning. By taking a look at your anger it can be transformed into the kind of energy that you need—understanding and compassion. It is with negative energy that you can make the positive energy. A flower, although beautiful, will become compost someday, but if you know how to transform the compost back into the flower, then you don't have to worry. You don't have to worry about your anger because you know how to handle it—to embrace, to recognize, and to transform it. So this is what is possible.

bell hooks: I think this is what people misunderstand about Martin Luther King saying to love your enemies. They think he was just using this silly little phrase, but what he meant was that as Black Americans we need to let our anger go, because holding on to it we hold ourselves down. We oppress ourselves by holding on to anger. My students tell me, we don't want to love! We're tired of being loving! And I say to them, if you're tired of being loving, then you haven't really been loving, because when you are loving you have more strength. As you were telling us yesterday, we grow stronger in the act of loving. This has been, I think, a very hurting thing for Black Americans—to feel that we can't love our enemies. People forget what a great tradition we have as African-Americans in the practice of forgiveness and compassion. And if we neglect that tradition, we suffer.

Thich Nhat Hanh: When we have anger in us, we suffer. When we have discrimination in us, we suffer. When we have the complex of superiority, we suffer. When we have the complex of inferiority, we

CONVERSATIONS: ANGER AND ACTIVISM
Throughout this dialogue, Thich Nhat Hanh refers to the importance of love and compassion in dealing with anger and conflict. During the Vietnam War, he preached this same message of love in his activism against the war, even in the face of violence. But other Buddhists took a different path in opposing the war. In 1963, hundreds of newspapers around the world published images like this one depicting a Buddhist monk after he set himself on fire to protest the war. Consider how such a form of protest, which received a great deal of attention at the time, might complicate Thich Nhat Hanh's ideas about the path to peace. How might this historical context have influenced Nhat Hanh's ideas? How might it affect the way you read this essay? Consider, too, the impact of such an image as compared to the written or spoken words of an activist like Thich Nhat Hanh.

© Bettmann/Corbis

Buddhist monk committing ritual suicide, 1963

suffer also. So when we are capable of transforming these negative things in us, we are free and happiness is possible.

If the people who hurt us have that kind of energy within them, like anger or desperation, then they suffer. When you see that someone suffers, you might be motivated by a desire to help him not to suffer anymore. That is love also, and love doesn't have any color. Other people may discriminate against us, but what is more important is whether we discriminate against them. If we don't do that, we are a happier person, and as a happier person, we are in a position to help. And anger, this is not a help.

50 **bell hooks:** And lastly, what about fear? Because I think that many white people approach black people or Asian people not with hatred or anger but with fear. What can love do for that fear?

Thich Nhat Hanh: Fear is born from ignorance. We think that the other person is trying to take away something from us. But if we look deeply, we see that the desire of the other person is exactly our own desire—to have peace, to be able to have a chance to live. So if you realize that the other person is a human being too, and you have exactly the same kind of spiritual path, and then the two can become good practitioners. This appears to be practical for both.

The only answer to fear is more understanding. And there is no understanding if there is no effort to look more deeply to see what is there in our heart and in the heart of the other person. The Buddha always reminds us that our afflictions, including our fear and our desiring, are born from our ignorance. That is why in order to dissipate fear, we have to remove wrong perception.

bell hooks: And what if people perceive rightly and still act unjustly?

Thich Nhat Hanh: They are not able yet to apply their insight in their daily life. They need community to remind them. Sometimes you have a flash of insight, but it's not strong enough to survive. Therefore in the practice of Buddhism, **SAMADHI** is the power to maintain insight alive in every moment, so that every speech, every word, every act will bear the nature of that insight. It is a question of cleaning. And you clean better if you are surrounded by sangha—those who are practicing exactly the same.

55 **bell hooks:** I think that we best realize love in community. This is something I have had to work with myself, because the intellectual tradition of the West is very individualistic. It's not community-based. The intellectual is often thought of as a person who is alone and cut off from the world. So I have had to practice being willing to leave the space of my study to be in community, to work in community, and to be changed by community.

Thich Nhat Hanh: Right, and then we learn to operate as a community and not as individuals. In Plum Village, that is exactly what we try to do. We are brothers and sisters living together. We try to operate like cells in one body.

GLOSS: SAMADHI
A Sanskrit term for "meditative absorption," *samadhi* refers to a state of mind that Buddhists try to achieve through meditation.

bell hooks: I think this is the love that we seek in the new millennium, which is the love experienced in community, beyond self.

Thich Nhat Hanh: So please, live that truth and disseminate that truth with your writing, with your speaking. It will be helpful to maintain that kind of view and action.

bell hooks: Thank you for your open-hearted example.

Thich Nhat Hanh: You're welcome. Thank you.

60

Understanding the Text

1. How does hooks define love? How does her understanding of love play a role in her own writing and in her work as a teacher and a cultural critic? How might your own understanding of love differ from hooks's? In what ways might your understanding of love influence your reaction to this essay?

2. What experiences did hooks have as a young woman that shaped her thinking about love? In what ways did those experiences influence her?

3. Why, according to hooks, was her encounter with the writings of Thich Nhat Hanh, Chögyam Trungpa Rinpoche, and other Buddhist teachers so important in the development of her thinking about social justice and her involvement in the Civil Rights and women's movements?

4. How does Thich Nhat Hanh define *community*? How does he understand the relationship between individuals and communities? What role does love play in that relationship, according to him?

Exploring the Issues

1. How would you describe the voices of bell hooks and Thich Nhat Hanh in this dialogue? What role does each voice play? What similarities and differences can you "hear" in their voices? How do you think these similarities or differences might strengthen or weaken this essay?

2. How effective do you think the form of a dialogue is to convey a point or examine an idea? Cite specific passages to support your answer.

3. In paragraph 26, Thich Nhat Hanh refers to "the practice of no-self," which is explained in *Gloss: No-Self* on page 260. Some scholars have pointed out that it is similar to the Christian idea of the Holy Trinity of God the Father, Jesus, and the Holy Spirit. Consider how a reader's religious beliefs and upbringing might shape his or her response to this dialogue between bell hooks and Thich Nhat Hanh. In what ways do you think Nhat Hanh's references to Buddhist beliefs might help him achieve his goals with readers? What obstacles might his references to Buddhist beliefs present for non-Buddhist readers? How did you react to these references? What might your answer to that question reveal about you as a reader?

4. This essay was originally published in *Shambhala Sun*, a Buddhist magazine. Throughout their dialogue, both hooks and Nhat Hanh use many specialized terms from Buddhist teachings, such as *sangha* and *samadhi*, which would be familiar to readers of *Shambhala Sun*. Examine the effect of these terms on you as a reader. Do you need to understand these terms if you are to understand the basic points that hooks and Nhat Hanh make about love and community? If you are unfamiliar with these terms, did you find the essay difficult to follow? If hooks and Nhat Hanh had their discussion without using these terms, would the essay have been different in any way? Explain. What might this essay help us understand about the role of specialized language in a piece of writing? What might it suggest about what readers need to know to make sense of any piece of writing?

Entering the Conversations

1. In the opening section of this essay, hooks writes about the great influence of the writings of Thich Nhat Hanh and other Buddhist teachers on her. In an essay intended for an audience of your classmates, describe the effect of a book or writer that was especially important to you in some way.

INFOTRAC

2. Search InfoTrac College Edition as well as the Internet for resources on Buddhism and especially on Buddhist ideas about love. Then, drawing on these sources as well as on this essay by bell hooks, write a report in which you examine how love is understood by

Buddhism and by Christianity (or another religious tradition of interest to you). What similarities and differences can you identify in how these religious traditions understand love? How does the understanding of love in each tradition seem to affect its religious practices? What conclusions can you draw about religious or cultural differences when it comes to the idea of love?

3. Drawing on this essay and any other relevant sources, write an essay in which you discuss the power of love. Alternatively, create a visual representation (such as a web site or a photo essay) of the power of love.

4. Several films in recent years have focused on the encounter of Westerners with Buddhism. In the film *Beyond Rangoon* (1995), two American women are traveling in Myanmar (formerly Burma), where protests, led by internationally famous activist Aung San Suu Kyi (whose es-

say appears in Chapter 9), against the military government were violently suppressed. The film examines Buddhist ideas about life and death and is based in part on the notion that a Westerner can learn about life and love by seeing the world as a Buddhist. *Seven Years in Tibet* (1997), based on the famous book of that same title by Heinrich Harrer, tells the story of a German climber trapped in Tibet at the start of World War II. He develops a close relationship with the Dalai Lama and through that relationship comes to understand the world differently. Focusing on these or similar films, write an analysis of how Buddhist ideas are portrayed in contrast to a Western perspective. What do the films suggest about Buddhism? About Western culture? What questions do they raise about culture and community? In your analysis, draw conclusions about how culture affects the way we talk about love.

Losing a family member or any loved one is *perhaps the most difficult experience a person can have. But although it is an experience that we all share, it is different for each of us. For writer Eric Liu, the death of his father was painful not only because he lost the father he dearly loved but also because it forced him to confront himself in a way he had never done*

Song FOR My Father

before. In the following essay, which is excerpted from his memoir, The Accidental Asian *(1998), Liu tells the story of his family life as his father suffered from a fatal kidney disease, but the story is really about him as he struggles with his own sense of identity and self-esteem. His father's illness helped him appreciate the special person his father was, and his respect for his father deepened as he watched his father deal with his illness. But ironically, the experience also shook Liu's faith in himself. In this sense, Liu's essay is as much about the complexities and pains of love as it is about the power of love and our need for it.*

When I first read the book in which Liu's essay appears, I was struck by the emotional power of Liu's story and his spare, clean prose. I immediately decided it should be included in this textbook. At first it seemed to fit best in Chapter 5, which focuses on identity, for Liu's story is about his struggle

ERIC LIU

In the summer of 1977, "the Liu's family," as Dad called us, took a weeklong trip to Ocean City, New Jersey. Mom had researched and planned the trip months in advance. We rented a modest "cottage," a converted garage with a kitchen, that was a few blocks from the boardwalk. After spending the day on the beach, we'd come back to the cottage for dinner. My mother, to save money, had prepared a cooler full of fruit and Chinese food. We'd eat, talk, putter around, and then Andrea and I would fall asleep with our stuffed animals on the foldout bed. Early one morning, we awakened to the strange, plaintive cry of a man walking down the boardwalk, a faraway cry that sounded to my parents like "Sweeeet-heart," and to us kids like "Sweeeet Tarts."

I will always think of that trip as a time of pure, boundless joy. I was nine. This was our first family vacation, our first six-hour drive, the first time I had ever touched and smelled the sea. My mother's recollections are more bittersweet. Just a few weeks before we were to leave, my father was informed that he was ill, life-threateningly ill, and that he would have to begin treatments immediately. He and Mom decid-

ERIC LIU, "SONG FOR MY FATHER," *THE ACCIDENTAL ASIAN: NOTES OF A NATIVE SPEAKER* BY ERIC LIU, PAGES 24–32. NEW YORK: VINTAGE BOOKS, 1999. REPRINTED BY PERMISSION OF RANDOM HOUSE, INC.

to understand his Chinese heritage and his identity as an Asian-American. But like any good piece of writing that delves into important human issues, Liu's essay is about many things, including love. What it means to you will depend on your own racial and ethnic background, your experiences with your own identity, and even what your writing instructor might say about this essay. I hope this essay will help you think in new ways about love—as well as about identity and loss and family and the many other things that make human life so complex and wonderful.

A former speechwriter and policy advisor for President Bill Clinton, Eric Liu is founder of the journal The Next Progressive *and author of numerous books, including* The True Patriot *(2008). He teaches at the University of Washington.* ◨

ed to go ahead with the vacation. But while my sister and I ate cotton candy and collected shells those endless August afternoons, they knew that life would be changed forever come September.

At least a year before that trip, Baba had begun to suffer wrenching headaches and fatigue, which he attributed to the stress of work. It got so bad that he would come home at lunchtime just to lie down for an hour. When finally he went to the doctor, the news could not have been more stunning: the cause of his symptoms was kidney failure, or, technically, end-stage renal disease. The doctors speculated that medication he'd taken in China as a child had damaged his kidneys, but they couldn't be sure. Now the deterioration was beyond repair. His body was no longer capable of cleansing itself. His blood was choking on its own pollutants.

I can't point now to a single moment when I realized that my father was sick. I remember that at a certain juncture that fall Dad started taking trips to the hospital in Westchester County, about an hour away, to begin dialysis treatments. He and Mom must have explained to me what was going on, because I also remember going to the hospital with them one cloudy day to behold the bulky, squat artificial-kidney machine with its dials and switches arrayed in something like a face. Having just seen *Star Wars,* I called it R2D2. The doctor laughed, my parents smiled.

Yet I don't remember now how Dad reacted to his diagnosis. Was it despair, resolve, denial? I don't remember when Dad asked that his sickness remain a family secret, though I do remember feeling we had taken a sacred vow of silence. We kept that vow, all of us, until his death. I don't remember when Dad decided he wanted to switch to home dialysis. (We kept the machine hidden in a closet.) I don't remember whether Mom had reservations about taking on the risks, the responsibility. I can only see how nervous she was the first time she helped hook him up to the machine at home. Was I scared that day? I don't remember.

I think my father would be glad to know that I don't remember these things. He tried to shield my sister and me from the pain of his sickness—not the physical pain, which he would sometimes express, but the psychic pain, which he shared only with Mom. He did so, it now seems, for his own sake as much as ours. He was too proud to be incapacitated, too private to reveal his infirmity. He could not imagine letting a disease break his stride; amazingly, it hardly did. He went about the business of his daily life, going to the office, mowing the lawn, fixing up the house, playing catch, helping us with homework, shopping for groceries, as if nothing were wrong.

Baba did not want to be treated differently for being sick. He thought his coworkers and bosses and friends and neighbors would smother him with patronizing concern, and from this belief spilled an ink-dark secrecy. We couldn't tell anyone. This was why Dad went to the hospital in Westchester: so nobody local would know. It's why

5

we had a code word for the kidney machine: so we wouldn't give Dad away.

The rest of us swallowed the illogic whole. This was what Baba wanted, after all, what he had asked of us. It didn't feel like he was controlling us or even really imposing on us. Never did I think to ask him: What's the worst thing that would happen if people found out? Wouldn't people understand? Why do you think your place in the world is so tenuous? Instead, secrecy became the warp and woof of our family life. We became adept at making excuses for the fact that Mom and Dad were occupied and our house off-limits so much of the time. We learned to have plausible explanations always at the ready. On a few occasions we had to contort ourselves to keep the truth from observant friends. Yet after a while it all became unremarkable: the sickness, the silence that surrounded it, and the silence that surrounded the silence.

Every family has its own culture, and ours, in many ways, was characteristically Chinese American: stir-fried flavors, invented traditions, inside jokes in a hybrid tongue. But **OUR FAMILY CULTURE ALSO INCLUDED THIS:** The pulse and hum of the kidney machine, as it pumped my father's blood through a filter three nights a week, five hours a night. Quarterly trips to the shipping depot across the river to pick up boxes of artificial-kidney devices, saline solution, Betadine, tubes, pads, tape, and other supplies, then bring them back, unload them into the basement, and crush the dozens of empty boxes that had molded and sagged there. Long-sleeved shirts for Dad, even in summer, to hide the scabrous fistula and needle wounds in his left forearm. The habit of keeping half an ear open at all times for the sudden, grating alarm that the machine would sound if something in Dad's blood chemistry was off. Being asked by Mom to pray, though I'd never known how to pray, when Dad was hospitalized for one of several episodes of pneumonia. Incorporating those superficially Christian prayers into the intricate, many-tiered complex of superstitions I had erected to ward off further calamity.

10   The stereotype holds that the Chinese mind is clannish, suspicious, haunted, obsessed with face. And in the way we responded to my father's situation perhaps my family fit the stereotype. We were insular and secretive, sometimes profoundly irrational. Anxieties that could not be named circled us like ghosts. We fashioned an elaborate front, and behind that front there was often sorrow and foreboding. But the truth is, there was also happiness—a true and tender happiness. In our self-enclosed domain, we came to forget the fundamental troubles. We forgot about things like mortality, things that might make the latticework of our existence seem unbearably fragile. We did not record the past or prepare for the worst. Instead, we lived the unknowing bliss of the moment. Was this typically Chinese? Or was it, rather, typically American?

For a while I had a theory that my father's actions, on some level, had been motivated by the dread of racial stigma. I conjectured that

---

STRATEGIES: USING DETAILS AND SENTENCE STRUCTURE
Writing teachers often emphasize the use of carefully chosen details to describe a scene, an event, or a feeling. In a sense, you might read paragraph 9 as a list of details vividly describing what Liu calls "our family culture" that developed around his father's illness. But if you look carefully at the specific details Liu has chosen, you'll see that he is doing more here than describing the impact of his father's illness on his family's life. He is also conveying something important about family love. Notice too that all but a few of the sentences in this paragraph are sentence fragments. Why do you think Liu uses sentence fragments here instead of complete sentences? What effect do you think these fragments have on a reader?

his secrecy, far from being "typically Chinese" behavior, was actually a preemptive strike against *anti-Chinese* behavior: a way to fit in, to hide his difference, to insure against mistreatment. But my mother dismissed the notion. Dad wasn't a fearful victim, she said. And this wasn't about the fear of racial discrimination. After all, he had concealed the facts from *Chinese* friends as well. His only sin was that he was too proud to let others know he was sick.

I realized, as Mom insisted on this, that it was I, not my father, who had conflated the desire to hide the disease with the desire to downplay difference of another kind. It was I, not my father, who had boxed against the shame and shadow of racial stigma. I had my own set of reasons for going along with the family charade: as a Chinese boy in an American world, I wanted generally to project a *normal* image, to cloak any handicap, real or imagined. As a Chinese boy in an American world, I was accustomed to facades.

I wish I knew what Dad thought. I have, in so many ways, learned from my father: learned to be assertive, to be kind, to disarm with charm. Also: to be mindful of appearances, to keep things in the family, to never depend on the kindness of others. I learned how to live only in the present. This I learned perhaps too well. For so much of my inheritance today seems depthless and desultory. Where my father disdained cheap emotions, I deal in nostalgia and sugary sentimentality. Where my father knew how to salvage dignity from great dreams that had been eaten away, I have mainly a talent for mythmaking. Where my father seemed to have an endless reserve of inner strength and self-knowledge, I have but an echoing well.

To fill the hollow, I look sometimes to Chineseness. Where does my Chineseness lie? In my looks, surely. In my culture, vestigially. In my behavior, too? I have been told, in the years since my father died, that I have been the prototypical Confucian son, a textbook example of filial loyalty to my mother. But if that is true, is it because Chinese values seeped down into me? Or is it because I am the first child and only son of a widow, whom I love, who has become perhaps my closest friend? I find it difficult to separate out the part of my behavior shaped by ethnicity and the part shaped by my situation. I also find it, after a while, pointless. The longer I stare in the mirror, looking for telltale evidence of Chineseness behind the epicanthic fold of the eye, the more I suspect that the truth is to be found in my peripheral field of vision.

What is **CHINESENESS**? It is anything, everything, and ultimately nothing. In the end, Chineseness does nothing to explain the courage my father summoned to endure fourteen years of dialysis, 15

CONVERSATIONS: WHAT IS CHINESENESS?

As American society becomes increasingly diverse, questions about racial, ethnic, and cultural identity often seem to take on added significance. As Liu indicates in this essay (and in the book *The Accidental Asian* from which this essay is taken), he struggled with questions about how "Chinese" or how "American" he was—or should be. Such questions are part of a much larger and more complicated set of discussions that are always taking place in the United States about what it means to be an American. Sometimes these discussions focus on immigration, sometimes on language, sometimes on schooling (see the essay by Richard Rodriguez on page 191, for example). Often, these discussions reveal an uneasiness among Americans about their identities, an uneasiness like Liu's. Perhaps it is because the United States was founded as a nation of immigrants when Europeans first settled in North America and pushed Native Americans off the land on which they were living. Whatever the reason, it's worth thinking about what Liu's essay might contribute to this never-ending effort to make sense of who we are.

more years than the doctors had ever thought possible. It does nothing to explain the horror, the all-consuming vacuum of his sudden, unexpected death in the middle of what seemed like a manageable bout of infection. Nor does it explain my mother's determination, in the aftermath, to face herself and "to experience life," as she says, without illusion. It does nothing, for the Liu's family, to ease the phantom pain of our missing limb—or to explain why, despite the pain, I can still giggle out loud at the mere thought of Baba. When your father, who was Chinese, has died, Chineseness seems an irrelevance: an inert container, just one among many, for holding the memories of shared experience. When your father has died, you realize this: it is the liquid of memory, not the cup we drink it from, that gives our lives content and reveals our humanity.

The last time I saw my father before the weekend he died, we were on our way home together. It was the Friday before Memorial Day. He was on assignment in New York City, I was coming up from Washington, and we decided to meet in Manhattan and then take the commuter train back to Poughkeepsie. It was a windy day, and we met at a new Chinese noodle shop near his office. Baba took obvious ethnic pride in this small shop: it was clean, modern, bustling, efficient, and served huge steaming bowls of spicy noodle soup for what seemed a pittance. Our conversation was animated. I remember, in this restaurant, slipping into Chinese more freely. As I sat across a small table from my father, I thought to myself, this is our future: Dad had just begun an exciting new job, I was a year into my postgraduate life in politics. We ate heartily, even sloppily. When we stepped out of the shop, the wind had picked up and the skies were churning. We caught a cab just before the rain arrived.

Sometimes I'll think of that afternoon, or think of all that my father and I imagined doing together, or think of something he once said to me, or look into a photograph of him, or wonder what he would think of the person I have become, and I'll lose myself in reminiscence, straining to recall the timbre of his voice, the arpeggio of his laughter, the sound of his sleep, and before I even realize that I have opened my mouth and drawn a breath, I will hear the word float off my lips; "Baba?"

Understanding the Text

1. Why did Liu's family keep his father's illness a secret? What was the impact of the silence that Liu writes about in paragraph 8? What do you think this silence suggests about Liu and his family?

2. In paragraph 10, Liu describes the "sorrow and foreboding" his family felt as they dealt with his father's illness. But he also writes that they felt a "true and tender happiness." What was the source of that happiness? What do you think it reveals about families? About love?

3. What does Liu's family's "Chineseness" have to do with his father's illness? Why is the issue of their racial identity important to Liu? What does he learn about his racial identity as a result of this experience?

4. In his description of the last time he saw his father, Liu writes that his father took "obvious ethnic pride" in the Chinese noodle shop where they met for lunch. Why? Why do you think Liu shares this detail about his last meeting with his father? What do you think this pride has to do with Liu's main points in this essay?

Exploring the Issues

1. What do you think Liu learns about his father—and about himself—as a result of his father's illness? What does his experience reveal about love? Cite specific passages from the essay to support your answer.

2. In paragraph 14, Liu describes himself looking at his own image in a mirror as he searches for answers about himself. Then he writes, "The longer I stare in the mirror, looking for telltale evidence of Chineseness behind the epicanthic fold of the eye, the more I suspect that the truth is to be found in my peripheral field of vision." What do you think he means by that statement? What truth is he referring to? And how can that truth be found in his "peripheral vision"?

3. In some ways, this essay is about memory and our efforts to make sense of past experience, sometimes through writing. As Liu describes his childhood experiences in this essay, he also tells us that there is much he cannot remember. And near the end of his essay, he writes that "it is the liquid of memory, not the cup we drink it from, that gives our lives content and reveals our humanity." What does this statement say about Liu's beliefs about memory and its importance in our lives? How do you think it relates to the final paragraph of the essay, in which Liu describes what happens when he remembers his deceased father? Do you agree with Liu about memory? Why or why not? What do you think Liu believes is the role of writing in dealing with our memories?

4. Liu describes his family life in some detail in this essay. What image of his family do you think he most wants to convey to his readers? What do you think his essay reveals about families in general? How are Liu's family experiences similar to or different from what other American families experience? Do these similarities or differences matter? Explain.

Entering the Conversations

1. Write an essay about your family. In your essay, try to convey a sense of what your family means to you.

2. In a group of classmates, share the essays you wrote for Question 1. Compare your various experiences with your families and try to identify commonalities among those experiences. What do these experiences suggest about families? Try to draw conclusions about the roles families play in our lives and the nature of family love.

3. Several of the essays in this chapter describe families or address family issues in some way: Anna Quindlen's "Say Farewell to Pin Curls," Kristin van Ogtrop's "Attila the Honey I'm Home," and David Brooks's "The Power of Marriage," among others. Select several of these or other appropriate essays and compare their views on family life and the roles of families in our lives. On the basis of your analysis of these essays, write an essay in which you draw conclusions about views of the family in American culture. In your essay, draw on your own experiences and other appropriate resources.

4. Create a multimedia document, such as a PowerPoint presentation or a web site, in which you present your view of family love.

5. Write a letter to a member of your family explaining what you have learned about love from that person.

6. Liu's essay presents a loving portrait of his family, but we often hear news reports about problems with American families. Those reports often focus on the changing nature of the American family. For example, such reports sometimes include statistics about the number of single-parent households in the United States or about divorce rates and the increase in so-called "blended" families that are created when two previously married people with children remarry and bring their families together. Using InfoTrac, the Internet, your library, and other appropriate sources, investigate the state of the American family. Try to identify the ways in which the family seems to be changing. Also try to determine whether attitudes about families are changing. Then write a report on the basis of your research. In your report, describe the state of the family in American culture and draw conclusions about its role in our lives.

7. Create a pamphlet, video, web site, or similar document intended to provide advice about family life and its complexities.

COMPLICATING RELATIONSHIPS

RECENTLY, I WAS SHARING SOME STORIES WITH A COLLEAGUE ABOUT GROWING UP. SHE AND HER HUSBAND HAD JUST MOVED BACK TO HER HOME-TOWN AFTER LIVING IN ANOTHER STATE FOR SEVERAL YEARS, AND THEY WERE LIVING IN A HOUSE OWNED BY HER MOTHER

until they could find a house of their own. She also mentioned that the month before she and her husband moved into the house, her sister and her sister's "partner" had moved out. As we talked further, I learned that my colleague's father lived in a nearby town with *his* partner. Her father, it turns out, is gay—something he revealed when my colleague was only about ten years old. Eventually, I learned, her parents divorced, and her mother raised her and her sister. This all struck me as an unusual family history, very different from my own family's story. But increasingly, what were once unusual and unconventional

> But increasingly, what were once unusual and unconventional relationships are becoming more common.

relationships are becoming more common. Today, about half of all marriages in the United States end in divorce, which means that there are a great many people who grow up without both parents living in the same home or who grow up in "blended" families—that is, families created when two divorced people with children remarry. You probably know adults who live with their parents—maybe returning home after finishing college. Or maybe you know a single woman raising an adopted child. Or a gay couple raising a family. Indeed, as I am writing this, some states are engaged in intense debates about whether to make same-sex marriages legal.

These developments can challenge our usual ways of thinking about relationships. The debates about same-sex

marriage, for example, sometimes call into question our ideas about *family* and *marriage*. Opponents of same-sex marriage will sometimes argue that these marriages are not natural. Others point out that marriage is a social convention that is as much about economic and legal arrangements as it is about raising families or being in love. Such discussions reveal the complexities of human relationships.

The reading selections in this cluster highlight some of these complexities. David Brooks's essay, for example, is an argument in favor of same-sex marriage, which is likely to remain a controversial issue in the United States for some time. The other readings in this cluster reveal that even the most common and conventional kinds of relationships can be more complicated than we may think. William Jelani Cobb's essay, for instance, explores how marriage among Black slaves in the pre–Civil War American South was tightly controlled and often forbidden, suggesting that the institution of marriage has been used for many different political, social, and economic purposes. Anna Quindlen examines how the complex relationships between a parent and her adolescent children can change over time. And Laura Kipnis asks us to reexamine our society's uneasiness with romantic relationships between college professors and their students. Yet these four essays barely scratch the surface when it comes to complicating relationships.

As you read these selections, think about the way that we engage in discussions about relationships: What can our language reveal about our values and beliefs? These writers can help us appreciate the fact that when we talk about matters like marriage, we are part of our society's attempts to make sense of the complexities of relationships.

College can be an intense experience, with students and professors often working very closely together. So it isn't really very surprising that students and professors will sometimes find themselves in romantic relationships. But such relationships are usually frowned upon and often expressly prohibited by school policies. Professor Laura

Off Limits: Should Students Be Allowed to Hook Up with Professors?

Kipnis (b. 1956) asks why. In this provocative essay, she questions policies forbidding faculty members from having romantic relationships with students, challenging us to reexamine our attitudes about such relationships. As she points out in her essay, colleges are concerned about protecting students from the coercion that can occur if a student feels vulnerable to a faculty member. Professors, after all, have some authority and power over students. But Kipnis thinks the issue is less about protecting students than about regulating behavior. She examines the changing circumstances on university campuses

LAURA KIPNIS

The burning academic question of the day: Should we professors be permitted to "hook up with" our students, as the kids put it? Or they with us? In the olden days when I was a student (back in the last century) hooking up with professors was more or less part of the curriculum. (OK, I went to art school.) But that was a different era, back when sex—even when not so great or someone got their feelings hurt—fell under the category of experience, rather than injury and trauma. It didn't automatically impede your education; sometimes it even facilitated it.

But such things can't be guaranteed to turn out well—what percentage of romances do?—so colleges around the country are formulating policies to regulate such interactions, to protect against the possibility of romantic adversity. In 2003, the University of California's nine campuses ruled to ban consensual relationships between professors and any students they may "reasonably expect" to have future academic responsibility for; this includes any student known to have an interest in any area within the faculty member's expertise. But while engineering students may still pair-bond with professors of Restoration drama in California, many campuses are moving to prohibit all romance between any professor and any student.

FEMINISM has taught us to recognize the power dynamics in these kinds of relationships, and this has evolved into a dominant paradigm, the new propriety. But where once the issue was coercion or quid pro quo sex, in institutional neo-feminism the issue is any whiff of sexuality itself—or any situation that causes a student to "experience his or her vulnerability." (Pretty much the definition of sentience, I always thought.) "The unequal institutional power inherent in this relationship heightens the vulnerability of the student and the potential for coercion," the California code warns, as if any relationship is ever absent vulnerability and coercion. But the problem in redressing romantic inequalities with institutional blunt instruments is that it just confers more power on the institutions themselves, vastly increasing their reach into people's lives.

Ironically, the vulnerability of students has hardly decreased under the new paradigm; it's increased. As opportunities for venting injury have expanded, the variety of opportunities to feel injured have correspondingly multiplied. Under the "offensive environment" guidelines, students are encouraged to regard themselves as such exquisitely sensitive creatures that an errant classroom remark impedes their education, such hothouse flowers that an unfunny joke creates a lasting trauma—and will land you, the unfunny prof, on the carpet or in the national news.

5   My own university is thankfully less prohibitive about student-professor couplings: You may still hook up with students, you just can't harass them into it. (How long before hiring committees at these few remaining enclaves of romantic license begin using this as a recruiting tool? "Yes the winters are bad, but the students are friendly.") But don't think of telling them jokes! Our harassment guidelines warn in two separate places that inappropriate humor violates university policy. (Inappropriateness—pretty much the definition of humor, I always thought.)

and in our society in general, arguing that our concerns about faculty members romancing their students reflect our general uneasiness about sexuality.

Perhaps just as interesting as her argument is the way Kipnis presents it. As you read, pay attention to Kipnis's writing style and the voice she creates in her essay. In a sense, she is taking part in a conversation about love and sex that people have been having for centuries, but she is doing so in a way that seems very contemporary. Consider whether she is speaking to you.

Laura Kipnis is a professor in the School of Communication at Northwestern University and a well-known cultural critic. She is the author of Against Love: A Polemic *(2003) and* Bound and Gagged: Pornography and the Politics of Fantasy in America *(1996). This essay was first published in* Slate, *an online magazine, in 2004.* ◪

CONVERSATIONS: FEMINISM AND SEXUALITY
When Kipnis writes that "feminism has taught us to recognize the power dynamics in these kinds of relationships," she is not referring to one specific theory called *feminism;* rather, she is referring to an ongoing set of conversations over the past three decades or so about gender and specifically about the role of women in society. Feminism can thus refer to academic theories about gender, to the women's movement for equal rights, and to a general social perspective on gender roles. Often, feminism refers to a belief that women have been limited in a society defined and controlled by men; sometimes, the term is used more broadly to refer to a critical perspective on power relations among men and women and on the dynamics of gender roles in society. It can be used as both a positive and a negative term. Here, Kipnis calls feminism a "paradigm," which means a broad way of thinking about the world. Consider how her use of the term reflects these many conversations about gender and what it reveals about her own perspective about gender. Consider, too, how those conversations shape the meaning of a term like *feminism* and create a specialized language that a writer like Kipnis can use to make her point.

STRATEGIES: USING PERSONAL EXPERIENCE
In this section of her essay, Kipnis describes her experience at a workshop on sexual harassment that she attended on her campus. Writers often use their own experiences to help illustrate a point or explore an issue. Compare Kipnis's use of this strategy with the way other writers in this chapter use it (for example, Anna Quindlen on page 284).

Seeking guidance, realizing I was clinging to gainful employment by my fingernails, I signed up for a university sexual-harassment workshop. (Also two e-mail communiqués from the dean advised that non-attendance would be noted.) And what an education I received—though probably not the intended one.

Things kicked off with a "Sexual Harassment Pretest," administered by David, an earnest mid-50ish psychologist, and Beth, an earnest young woman with a masters in social work. It consisted of unanswerable true-false questions like: "If I make sexual comments to someone and that person doesn't ask me to stop, then I guess that my behavior is probably welcome." Everyone seemed grimly determined to play along—probably hoping to get out by cocktail hour—until we were handed a printed list of "guidelines." No. 1: "Do not make unwanted sexual advances."

Someone demanded querulously from the back, "But how do you know they're unwanted until you try?" (OK, it was me.) David seemed oddly flummoxed by the question, and began anxiously jangling the change in his pants pocket. "Do you really want me to answer that?" he asked.

Another person said helpfully, "What about smoldering glances?" Everyone laughed. A theater professor guiltily admitted to complimenting a student on her hairstyle that very afternoon (one of the "Do Nots" on the pretest) but wondered whether as a gay male, not to have complimented her would be grounds for offense. He started mimicking the female student, tossing her mane around in a "notice my hair" manner. People shouted suggestions for other pretest scenarios for him to perform. Rebellion was in the air. Someone who studies street gangs whispered to me, "They've lost control of the room." David was jangling his change so frantically you had to strain to hear what anyone was saying.

10

My attention glued to David's pocket, I recalled a long-forgotten pop psychology guide to body language that identified change-jangling as an unconscious masturbation substitute. (And isn't **CAPTAIN QUEEG'S** habit of toying with a set of steel marbles in his pants pocket diagnosed by the principal mutineer in Herman Wouk's *Caine Mutiny* as closet masturbation?) If the very leader of our sexual harassment workshop was engaging in potentially offensive public masturbatory-like behavior, what hope for the rest of us!

Let's face it: Other people's sexuality is often just weird and creepy. Sex is leaky and anxiety-ridden; intelligent people can be oblivious about it. Of course the gulf between desire and knowledge has long been a tragicomic staple; these campus codes do seem awfully optimistic about rectifying the condition. For a more pessimistic account, peruse some recent treatments of the student-professor hook-up theme—Coetzee's *Disgrace;* Francine Prose's *Blue Angel;* Mamet's *Oleanna*—in which learning has an inverse relation to self-knowledge, in which pro-

GLOSS: CAPTAIN QUEEG
Captain Queeg is the main character in *The Caine Mutiny,* a 1952 novel by Herman Wouk about a mutiny aboard an American military ship during World War II. Another character calls attention to Queeg's habit of handling steel marbles that he keeps in his pants pocket.

fessors are emblems of sexual stupidity, and such disasters ensue that it's hard not to read these as cautionary tales, even as they send up the new sexual correctness.

Of course, societies are always reformulating the stories they tell about intergenerational desire and the catastrophes that result, from Oedipus to faculty handbooks. The details vary, also the kinds of catastrophes prophesized—once it was plagues and crop failure, these days it's trauma and injury. Even over the last half-century the narrative has drastically changed. Consider the Freudian account, yesterday's contender as big explanatory story: Children desire their parents, this desire meets up with prohibitions—namely the incest taboo—and is subject to repression. But the desire persists nevertheless, occasionally burbling to the surface in the form of symptoms: that mysterious rash, that obsessional ritual.

Today, intergenerational desire remains the dilemma; what's shifted is the direction of arrows. In the updated version, parents (and parent surrogates) do all the desiring, children are innocent victims. What's excised from the new story is the most controversial part of the previous one: childhood sexuality. Children are returned to innocence, a far less disturbing (if less complex) account of childhood.

Excising student sexuality from campus romance codes just extends the same presumption. But students aren't children. Whether or not it's smart, plenty of professors I know, male and female, have hooked up with students, for shorter and longer durations. (Female professors do it less, and rarely with undergrads.) Some act well, some are assholes, and it would definitely behoove our students to learn the identifying marks of the latter breed early on, because post-collegiate life is full of them too. (Along with all the well-established marriages that started as student-teacher things, of course—another social reality excised from the story.)

Let's imagine that knowledge rather than protectionism (or institutional power enhancement) was the goal of higher education. Then how about workshops for the students too? Here's an idea: "10 Signs That Your Professor Is Sleeping With You To Assuage Mid-Life Depression and Will Dump You Shortly Afterward." Or, "Will Hooking Up With a Prof Really Make You Feel Smarter: Pros and Cons." No doubt we'd all benefit from more self-knowledge about sex, but until the miracle drug arrives that cures the abyss between desire and intelligence, universities might try being educational instead of regulatory on the subject.

15

CONVERSATIONS: NOVELS ABOUT STUDENT–TEACHER RELATIONSHIPS
In paragraph 11, Kipnis mentions three well-known novels that describe relationships between students and their teachers. Notice how Kipnis uses these references to make her point, describing these novels as "cautionary tales." What might these references suggest about how art and literature help shape our ways of understanding issues like relationships between professors and students?

Understanding the Text

1. What is the main reason that universities adopt policies prohibiting romantic relationships between a student and a faculty member? What is Kipnis's complaint about such policies?

2. What changes does Kipnis see in attitudes toward romantic relationships and toward sexuality as a result of feminism? What problems have these changes brought about in her view? Do you agree with her? Why or why not?

3. Kipnis writes that she received an education by attending the sexual-harassment workshop at her university, "though probably not the intended one." What did she learn at that workshop? In what sense was what she learned unintended?

4. What is "the new sexual correctness" that Kipnis refers to? In what way does this point support her main argument about university policies prohibiting relationships between professors and students?

5. What does Kipnis mean when she states that university policies governing student–teacher relationships "excise student sexuality from campus romance codes"? In what sense do these policies eliminate sexuality as Kipnis sees it? Why, in her view, is this a problem?

Exploring the Issues

1. How would you characterize Kipnis's writing style? What kind of language does she use? What effect do you think her style is intended to have on readers? What effect did it have on you? Did it make you more or less inclined to take her seriously? Cite specific passages to support your answer.

2. Kipnis briefly discusses humor in this essay, pointing out that jokes with sexual content are considered inappropriate for professors to tell in class. Examine Kipnis's own use of humor. What kinds of humor does she use in making her point? How does this humor contribute to her voice in the essay? How did you respond to her humor? Did you find it effective? Why or why not?

3. Kipnis argues that there is a "new sexual correctness" on college campuses today. Do you agree with her? Why or why not? How might your own experiences and observations of campus life support or complicate her position?

4. In paragraph 3, Kipnis suggests that feminism has influenced our attitudes about gender and sexuality to the degree that an "institutional neo-feminism" has given universities more power to regulate students' sexual behavior. This is a complicated point that requires some understanding of feminism (see *Conversations: Feminism and Sexuality* on page 275).

Examine Kipnis's reasoning here. Identify what she sees as positive in feminism as well as what seems problematic to her. Then evaluate her point. Do you find her point a valid one? Do you agree with her? Why or why not?

Entering the Conversations

1. Write an editorial for your school newspaper in which you take a position on the issue of romantic relationships between students and their professors.

2. With a group of classmates, examine your college's or university's policies regarding romantic relationships between faculty members and students. Compare its policy with policies at other schools. If possible, interview administrators at your college and perhaps at other colleges for their views about these policies. Try to find out why the policies are in place and the justifications for the specific provisions of the policies. Write a report for an audience of your classmates about these policies, explaining what is allowed and what is prohibited under the policies. Draw conclusions about the appropriateness or effectiveness of such policies.

3. On the basis of your research for Question 2 and working with a group of classmates, rewrite your school's policy regarding romantic relationships between faculty members and students to reflect your views about such relationships.

INFOTRAC

4. In her essay, Kipnis mentions several novels that describe romantic relationships between students and teachers, including *Blue Angel* by Francine Prose and *Disgrace* by J. M. Coetzee. Using InfoTrac College Edition, find reviews of these novels and any other books about relationships between students and teachers. Write an analysis of these reviews. In your analysis, provide an overview of what these reviews say about relationships between faculty members and students, and try to draw conclusions about our culture's attitudes regarding such relationships.

5. In her book *Against Love,* Kipnis writes, "We live in sexually interesting times, meaning a culture which manages to be simultaneously hypersexualized and to retain its Puritan underpinnings, in precisely equal proportions." In paragraph 4 of this essay, Kipnis echoes this statement, offering a critique of what she sees as our society's current attitude toward the treatment of children and young adults. Her critique is consistent with the arguments of some cultural critics who have expressed concern over what they see as a trend toward excessive "political correctness." Consider both sides of this debate and then write an essay in which you offer your perspective. What are the ways in which we, as a society, overprotect our young people? In what ways should we be a little less uptight?

The state of Vermont allowed gay couples to *enter into legal "civil unions," which angered opponents of same-sex marriage who believed that* civil union *is just another term for marriage. In San Francisco, hundreds of gay couples were married by city officials, igniting a firestorm of protest from opponents of same-sex marriage around the country and*

THE Power OF Marriage

resulting in a legal fight that ended with a U.S. court disallowing the marriages. In Massachusetts, the governor enforced a centuries-old law that seemed to make same-sex marriages illegal in that state, which angered supporters of same-sex marriage. In 2004, some public opinion polls indicated that a majority of Americans were opposed to making same-sex marriages legal, but the same polls often suggested that Americans did not necessarily oppose certain legal rights for same-sex couples. These controversies about same-sex marriage were often portrayed in the media as black-and-white: liberals in favor of same-sex marriage, conservatives opposed to it. But well-known conservative writer David Brooks (b. 1961) argues that supporting same-sex marriage is actually a proper conservative position. His essay seems to complicate the easy, either-or way that the controversy is often presented in popular media.

DAVID BROOKS

Anybody who has several sexual partners in a year is committing spiritual suicide. He or she is ripping the veil from all that is private and delicate in oneself, and pulverizing it in an assembly line of selfish sensations.

But marriage is the opposite. Marriage joins two people in a sacred bond. It demands that they make an exclusive commitment to each other and thereby takes two discrete individuals and turns them into kin.

Few of us work as hard at the vocation of marriage as we should. But marriage makes us better than we deserve to be. Even in the chores of daily life, married couples find themselves, over the years, coming closer together, fusing into one flesh. Married people who remain committed to each other find that they reorganize and deepen each other's lives. They may eventually come to the point when they can say to each other: "Love you? I am you."

Today marriage is in crisis. Nearly half of all marriages end in divorce. Worse, in some circles, marriage is not even expected. Men and women shack up for a while, produce children and then float off to shack up with someone else.

5 Marriage is in crisis because marriage, which relies on a culture of fidelity, is now asked to survive in a culture of contingency. Today, individual choice is held up as the highest value: choice of lifestyles, choice of identities, choice of cellphone rate plans. Freedom is a wonderful thing, but the culture of contingency means that the marriage bond, which is supposed to be a sacred vow till death do us part, is now more likely to be seen as an easily canceled contract.

Men are more likely to want to trade up, when a younger trophy wife comes along. Men and women are quicker to opt out of marriages, even marriages that are not fatally flawed, when their "needs" don't seem to be met at that moment.

Still, even in this time of crisis, every human being in the United States has the chance to move from the path of contingency to the path of marital fidelity—except homosexuals. Gays and lesbians are banned from marriage and forbidden to enter into this powerful and ennobling institution. A gay or lesbian couple may love each other as deeply as any two people, but when you meet a member of such a couple at a party, he or she then introduces you to a "partner," a word that reeks of contingency.

You would think that faced with this marriage crisis, **WE CONSERVATIVES** would do everything in our power to move as many people as possible from the path of contingency to the path of fidelity. But instead, many argue that gays must be banished from matrimony because gay marriage would weaken all marriage. A marriage is between a man and a woman, they say. It is women who domesticate men and make marriage work.

Well, if women really domesticated men, heterosexual marriage wouldn't be in crisis. In truth, it's moral commitment, renewed every day through faithfulness, that "domesticates" all people.

10 Some conservatives may have latched onto biological determinism (men are savages who need women to tame them) as a convenient way to oppose gay marriage. But in fact we are not animals whose lives are bounded by our flesh and by our gender. We're moral creatures with souls, endowed with the ability to make covenants, such as the one Ruth made with Naomi: "Where you go I will go, and where you stay I will stay. Your people will be my people and your God my God. Where you die I will die, and there I will be buried."

The conservative course is not to banish gay people from making such commitments. It is to expect

In considering Brooks's argument, pay attention to how he takes part in the intense conversations in American society about this controversy—and about sexuality in general. Think about how he uses common terms like liberal *or* conservative *and how such terms might convey subtle meanings. Think, too, about how he connects religion and politics. A close look at his essay might reveal why he is such a widely read columnist for the* New York Times, *in which this essay first appeared in 2003.* ▼

CONVERSATIONS: CONTROVERSIES ABOUT SEXUAL PREFERENCE
When I read Brooks's opening paragraph, especially his statement about "spiritual suicide," I could not help think that he was making a subtle reference to the controversial view of some conservative and religious leaders that homosexuality is immoral. Public statements in the 1980s and 1990s by some religious leaders that AIDS, a disease that disproportionately affects gay people, is a punishment for homosexual activity ignited intense reactions in the midst of ongoing debates about sexual orientation. How might these debates influence the way readers will react to Brooks's point here? How do these debates help shape the meaning of a phrase like "spiritual suicide"?

STRATEGIES: ETHOS AND AUDIENCE
In paragraph 8, Brooks clearly identifies himself as a conservative and addresses his readers as "we conservatives." Readers who are familiar with Brooks's writing would not be surprised by such a statement because he is well-known for his conservative views. But this essay appeared on the editorial page of the *New York Times,* a widely circulated newspaper that is generally considered liberal in its viewpoint. As a result, Brooks's address to his readers as "we conservatives" seems somewhat surprising—even intentionally provocative. Maybe Brooks intended it that way, trying to take advantage of his reputation as a conservative. Establishing a reputation among readers is known as *ethos.* It's worth considering how ethos can be influenced by the context of a piece of writing. In this case, how is Brooks's phrase "we conservatives" affected by the fact that he is writing for a newspaper that is generally considered liberal? Would it have the same effect if his essay appeared in a conservative publication?

CONVERSATIONS: RELIGION AND MARRIAGE
In making his argument about same-sex marriage, Brooks makes many religious references. For example, in paragraph 10 he refers to the biblical account of Ruth and Naomi, women who are thought by many to have been lesbians. He makes it clear that his political stance is conservative, and he closely allies his politics with his religion. The public debates in the United States about same-sex marriage often include religious and moral arguments, and many religious leaders have made public statements condemning laws that allow same-sex marriage. When the state of Vermont made civil unions legal, some religious leaders called the law immoral. Given the way religion has played a role in debates about same-sex marriage, how does Brooks's use of religious references affect his argument?

that they make such commitments. We shouldn't just allow gay marriage. We should insist on gay marriage. We should regard it as scandalous that two people could claim to love each other and not want to sanctify their love with marriage and fidelity.

When liberals argue for gay marriage, they make it sound like a really good employee benefits plan. Or they frame it as a civil rights issue, like extending the right to vote.

Marriage is not voting. It's going to be up to conservatives to make the important, moral case for marriage, including gay marriage. Not making it means drifting further into the culture of contingency, which, when it comes to intimate and sacred relations, is an abomination.

Understanding the Text

1. How does Brooks define marriage in this essay? Do you think his understanding of marriage is widely shared by Americans? Explain.

2. What support does Brooks offer for his assertion that marriage is in crisis? How persuasive do you find this support?

3. What are Brooks's main points in favor of same-sex marriage? What differences does he see in the conservative and liberal positions on this issue?

Exploring the Issues

1. Brooks begins this essay with a provocative statement about sexual promiscuity, stating clearly his belief that anyone who has more than one

sexual partner in a year is "committing spiritual suicide." Why do you think he begins his essay in this way? What do you think he hopes to accomplish with such a provocative opening? What reaction do you think he expects from readers? How might this opening influence the way readers read the rest of his essay? How did it affect the way you read his essay? What might your reaction reveal about you as a reader?

2. In paragraph 5, Brooks makes a distinction between fidelity in a marriage and what he calls "the culture of contingency," which values individual freedom above all else. In what ways does this culture of contingency weaken marriage, according to Brooks? Do you agree with him? Why or why not? Do you think he fairly and

accurately represents the current situation with marriage as a choice between fidelity and freedom? Explain.

3. Notice how Brooks defines the main positions on same-sex marriage as liberal and conservative. Consider whether Brooks's representation of this debate is accurate. Are there really only two positions on this issue—conservative and liberal? What exactly do those two terms—*conservative* and *liberal*—mean here? In what ways might these two terms affect how readers react to Brooks's argument?

Entering the Conversations

1. Write an essay for an audience of your classmates in which you state and defend your position on same-sex marriage.

2. Rewrite the essay you wrote for Question 1 for the editorial page of your local newspaper.

INFOTRAC

3. In paragraph 12, Brooks criticizes liberal arguments in favor of same-sex marriage, saying that liberals look at gay marriage primarily as a civil rights issue. Using InfoTrac College Edition and other appropriate resources, find essays by others who promote or oppose gay marriage and consider their reasons for their positions. Try to identify the main arguments for and against same-sex marriage. Then write a report on the state of the controversy, describing the most common positions on the issue and analyzing the arguments on each side. Try to draw conclusions about how the ongoing public conversations about same-sex marriage are carried on. Alternatively, create a web site on which you present the results of your search and analysis. Be sure to include appropriate links to relevant web sites.

4. Consider what the photograph below conveys about marriage and about gay couples. What do you think is being suggested about same-sex marriage in this image? How might this image draw on the ongoing controversies about same-sex marriage to convey its meaning?

5. Write an essay in which you discuss what you believe is the relationship between religious belief and marriage as a legal arrangement. What role does religion play in marriage? To what extent is marriage a legal rather than a religious matter? Try to address such questions in your essay.

6. In a group of classmates, share the essays you wrote for Question 5. Identify the main points of agreement and disagreement among your group members about the relationship between religion and marriage. Try to draw conclusions about the role of religion in marriage in contemporary American society.

© Constantine Manos/Magnum Photos

First legally married gay couple in Provincetown, MA, 2004

When I was growing up in the late 1960s and early 1970s, my mother often gave my three sisters "permanents," just as Anna Quindlen (b. 1953) describes her mother giving her one in the following essay. As Quindlen suggests, getting a "perm" could be quite a production. I remember my sisters spending hours in the bathroom with towels draped over

Say Farewell TO Pin Curls

their shoulders, making faces because of the nasty smell of the special chemicals dripping from their wet hair. They bickered with my mother as she applied the chemicals and always complained when they had to get a perm. Perms are not as popular as they once were, but Quindlen reminds us that teens and their parents still bicker about hair and dress styles. What makes her essay more than just a memory of growing up is that she explores what these conflicts about appearance— whether they are over hair styles or body piercings or clothes—can tell us about the relationships between parents and their kids. As you read Quindlen's essay, think about how your own experiences with family and your own sense of identity might shape the way you respond to her insights.

GLOSS: MAY PROCESSION
May Procession is a Catholic Church tradition in honor of Mary, mother of Jesus Christ.

ANNA QUINDLEN

This balmy stretch from Easter until the end of school in June always reminds me of my mother messing around with my hair. Too often the kitchen smelled like the wallpaper was being chemically removed because of the fumes from Tonette, the home permanent for little girls.

Afterward my head looked perpetually surprised. The thick straight bangs belied the ebullient frizz on either side, so that my face was a window with a flat shade and ruffled cafe curtains. We all had bangs then, so that our hair would not be in our faces, a habitual complaint by the mothers and the nuns. When my hair was in my face my mother referred to me as Veronica Lake.

Easter, **MAY PROCESSION,** class pictures, graduation. Pin curls, braids, ribbons, rollers. There exists not a single photo of significance from my childhood that shows my head as it was in nature. Occasionally the day was warm or wet enough to cause the phony curl to release before the end of the afternoon. This is why I look more or less normal in first-communion photographs, except for the veil and the hands prayerfully folded. Sitting here today I can re-create in my mind the sensation of bobby pins poking my scalp, the way sleeping on rollers feels like having a shoe box for a pillow. We were groomed then like baby beauty queens.

This is no longer my life, not as a person, not as a parent. I messed with my children's hair only when they were babies, to cut the boys' curls—they cried, I cried—and to secure the weirdly overweening topknot my daughter had for her first year. Still reeling from the counterculture internecine warfare of the late 1960s, I made a deal with myself: no fighting over clothes and hair. (I reserve the right to go ballistic about tats and piercings.) "My hair like Jesus wore it/Hallelujah I adore it/Hallelujah Mary loved her son/Why don't my mother love me?" That was the title song from the first Broadway rock musical, and the question of the time. Fathers threatened to throw sons with ponytails out of the house. What was the point of that?

5   It is one measure of the **LOOSEY-GOOSEY CHILD REARING** with which our parents sometimes reproach us—"I always let my babies cry themselves to sleep!"—that we have eliminated the barbershop as a battleground. In this way I have acquired a son with a mohawk. I do not like this, although apparently everyone else finds it flattering. Some middle-school boys even wrote a song about it. He has agreed to buzz it back into a more conventional hairstyle in time for the prom.

The prom was the last time I remember letting my mother mess around with my hair. She created a braided bun woven with costume-jewelry pearls and was moved to tears by her skill and my altered appearance. I was luckier than those of my classmates who'd gone to the beauty parlor and came out with immense helmet-hair updos, looking like a cross between the bride and her own grandmother. For graduation my hair hung naturally, long and straight, in my face as I stepped to the podium. I cut it all off three weeks after my mother died, an act not of fashion but of self-abnegation. For a time all my brothers had hair longer than mine. It drove our father nuts.

It occurred to me, looking at mohawk man and his equally unfettered siblings—two atheists, two vegetarians, three writers, three actors, one jock, and all in just three humans!—that there was a sad point to all that sectioning and spraying my mother did. She was trying to ease me, from the head down, into a life of masquerade. A quiet soul who had somehow found herself with a daughter so extroverted that it could be counted as a clinical diagnosis, she must have understood that conformity was my inevitable uncomfortable fate. The conventions of so-called femininity were every bit as rigid, as painful and as false as those manic ringlets that made a brave show until they fell of their own weight. My mother could not have envisioned a future free of girdles and garter belts, deference and duty, permanent waves and teasing combs, a future of freedom. But that future was foretold in those boys who let their hair fall to their shoulders, the world according to the Kinks: "Girls will be boys and boys will be girls, it's a mixed up, muddled up, shook up world."

Anna Quindlen is an award-winning writer whose books include the novels Blessings *(2002) and* One True Thing *(1996). She is a regular columnist for* Newsweek *magazine, in which this essay first appeared in 2003.* ▼

STRATEGIES: WORD CHOICE

I love the first line of paragraph 2: "Afterward my head looked perpetually surprised." Here, Quindlen is describing the appearance of her hair after her mother gives her a permanent. We might expect a description of someone's face as "surprised," not one's hair or head. But Quindlen chooses an adjective—surprised—that we would not usually associate with the appearance of hair. Writing teachers sometimes describe such word choices as "fresh" or "lively."

CONVERSATIONS: VERONICA LAKE

Veronica Lake was a well-known actress in the 1950s. How is she presented in this photograph? What does this photograph suggest about women? About a woman's appearance, especially her hair? Do you think this is the kind of image Quindlen had in mind when writing this paragraph?

Veronica Lake

I don't know that it's necessarily easier to take freedom as your birthright, to think if someone looks twice at the cockscomb of hair sprouting above the shaved sides that it's their problem, dude. There are still standards. They are simply looser ones. And there's a tyranny of freedom, too, so that nonconformism becomes the new conformity. But I think this is the better way; a tie, it has always seemed to me, is nothing but a noose with a pleasing pattern. My daughter and her girlfriends all have this trick of making an impromptu bun with their long hair, quick as a wink, and it looks beautiful and unstudied (unsprayed!) and not at all as though they are trying to be miniature adults, which is how I look in so many of those pictures. My boys do their own buzz cuts with clippers they keep in the bathroom. The irony is that I wish they'd let their hair grow longer. But I try to keep my mouth shut. The hair wars, thank God, are over.

CONVERSATIONS: LOOSEY-GOOSEY PARENTING

During the past three or four decades, experts such as Benjamin Spock, Penelope Leach, T. Berry Brazelton, Richard Ferber, and William Sears have sold millions of books with advice to parents about how to raise children "the right way." Sometimes, the advice offered by such experts has been controversial and has contradicted traditional attitudes about raising children. In paragraph 5 Quindlen offers her own thoughts in the context of this age-old conversation between one generation of parents and the next. In doing so, she reminds us that what we think about child rearing is influenced by historical context, by culture, and by age.

CONVERSATIONS: THE GENERATION GAP

At the end of paragraph 7, when Quindlen writes about a future that was "foretold in those boys who let their hair fall to their shoulders, the world according to the Kinks: 'Girls will be boys and boys will be girls, it's a mixed up, muddled up, shook up world,'" she is referring to the 1960s and early 1970s, when young men began to wear long hair, often in protest against their parents' values and in violation of accepted dress codes. Some observers called this conflict between young people and their parents "the Generation Gap." Today, we sometimes hear about Generation X and how it differs from its parents' generation, which is often called the "Baby Boom" generation, or "the Boomers." These photos reflect those generational conflicts.

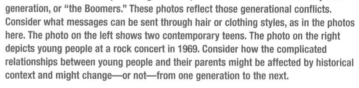

Consider what messages can be sent through hair or clothing styles, as in the photos here. The photo on the left shows two contemporary teens. The photo on the right depicts young people at a rock concert in 1969. Consider how the complicated relationships between young people and their parents might be affected by historical context and might change—or not—from one generation to the next.

© Margo Silver/Getty Images

© David Hurn/Magnum Photos

Understanding the Text

1. Quindlen tells us that she does not like her son's mohawk haircut. Why, then, does she do nothing to get him to change it? What might this suggest about Quindlen as a parent?

2. In paragraph 7, Quindlen describes her mother as "a quiet soul" with an extroverted daughter to whom she tried to teach the conventions of femininity. Why does Quindlen focus attention on her mother in this way? Why does she contrast herself to her mother? How is this contrast important to her main point about growing up and about parenting?

3. Quindlen discusses conformity among teens and what she calls "the tyranny of freedom." What does she mean by that phrase? What point does she make about the social pressures that kids experience as they grow up? Do you think she's right about the "tyranny of conformity"? Why or why not?

Exploring the Issues

1. Quindlen draws on memories of her childhood as a girl raised in a Catholic family. How does Quindlen's upbringing as a Catholic shape her sense of her identity? In what ways might this essay differ if she had been raised as a Jew or Muslim or atheist? Do Quindlen's insights about

parent–teen relationships depend on her upbringing as a Catholic? Or do you think they apply regardless of one's religious or cultural background? Explain.

2. In paragraph 4, Quindlen writes that she will not fight with her children about clothes and hair. But then she makes the following statement, which she places in parentheses: "I reserve the right to go ballistic about tats and piercings." Why do you think she includes this statement about tattoos and body piercings? How are those different from hairstyles and clothes? Do you think this statement strengthens or weakens Quindlen's argument? Explain.

3. Quindlen writes about her experiences as a daughter growing up in the 1960s, and she describes some of her experiences with her own son and daughter. How might her experiences have differed from a boy's experiences? Do you think Quindlen adequately accounts for gender in her discussion of the relationships between generations? Explain.

4. As the reading's introduction indicates, this essay was first published in *Newsweek,* a weekly magazine with a large and diverse audience. Who do you think Quindlen believes is in that audience? What kind of readers do you think she is addressing in this essay? Cite specific passages to support your answer.

Entering the Conversations

1. Write an essay for an audience of your classmates about an experience in which you have had some kind of conflict with your parents or other important adults in your life who are of an older generation. Tell the story of that conflict in a way that might help your readers gain insight into relationships.

2. In a group of classmates, share the essays you wrote for Question 1. Compare the experiences you each wrote about and try to identify the similarities and differences among those experiences. What might the experiences of your group suggest about relationships between parents and children? Between people of different generations? How might factors such as religious upbringing, racial or ethnic identity, or gender influence these relationships?

 INFOTRAC

3. Using InfoTrac College Edition or other appropriate resources, look for contemporary articles or books about raising children today. In particular, try to find articles in newspapers or magazines intended specifically for parents and try to find reviews of books about parenting. Review these materials to get a sense of the main perspectives in American culture today about raising children.

What are the important questions and challenges that parents face today? What kinds of advice and support do they receive? Then write a report on the basis of your research, drawing conclusions regarding attitudes about raising children in our culture today. Alternatively, explore differences in attitudes toward child rearing in different cultures. How do views about raising children in American culture differ from views in other cultures? Write a report describing those differences.

4. On the basis of your research for Question 3, create a pamphlet addressed to parents with advice on raising their children today. Alternatively, create a web site with advice for parents. Be sure to pay attention to the design of your site (see Chapter 2 in this book).

5. Write an essay for a general audience (such as readers of your local newspaper) based on your own experience in which you offer your perspective on parent–child relationships, particularly regarding a child's independence from his or her parents.

6. Rewrite Quindlen's essay from the point of view of her child.

Western culture has many stories of forbidden *love. In high school, you may have read Shakespeare's* Romeo *and* Juliet, *perhaps the most famous story of forbidden love. Many popular films are based on this same theme. Often, in considering such stories, we focus on the depth of love between the two main characters and on their great efforts to overcome obstacles to*

THE *Other* L-Word

their love. In Shakespeare's famous play, for example, Romeo and Juliet risk losing their families and even their lives to be together. Yet a closer look at these stories reveals that things may be more complicated than they seem. Romeo and Juliet fall in love against the backdrop of a complex social and political scene. In this sense, Shakespeare's play isn't just about the intensity of romantic love; it is also about how relationships can be deeply influenced by circumstances that can even determine whether two people can be together. In the same way, the following essay by historian William Jelani Cobb explores how historical context can affect love and family. Cobb focuses on Black slaves in the American South before the Civil War. In describing the great legal, cultural, and practical obstacles that slaves had to overcome to be with their loved ones, Cobb reminds us that even something that seems as straightforward as love between two people

WILLIAM JELANI COBB

They have been together for a millennium—or at least look as if they have. They are seated beside each other, arms touching, him shoeless and her head wrapped in cloth and God only knows what they've seen. They are barely past the bitter years of slavery and to tell the truth, it's still hard to tell the difference. The photograph is grainy and slightly out of focus, but you can still make out the weathered lines of years and experience on their faces. And you can still sense the connection forged of those years.

The picture speaks of a quiet fortitude, togetherness in the crucible of slavery, an intimacy that is rarely seen in our discussions of black history.

Sometimes it seems like there's a civil war going on between black men and black women. It's ironic that Valentine's Day takes place during Black History Month, but those two events manage to overlap without ever coinciding—as if there is no love or romance within our collective history in this country. We know of husbands sold away from wives and wives taken from husbands to face the sexual exploitation of white overseers. We know of black men and women who were bred like livestock.

WILLIAM JELANI COBB, "THE OTHER L-WORD." REPRINTED BY KIND PERMISSION OF THE AUTHOR.

must be understood in terms of the broader circumstances surrounding a relationship. In this case, forbidden love takes on great political, cultural, and racial significance.

William Jelani Cobb is an associate professor of history at Spelman College. This essay was first published in 2004 at Africana.com. ◪

STRATEGIES: VISUAL DESCRIPTION
In the opening paragraph, Cobb describes an old photograph. Initially, he doesn't explicitly tell us that the photo depicts two elderly former slaves who are apparently married or in love, but we can figure that out as we read further. It is not unusual for writers to include vivid descriptions in an essay to help make a point or highlight an event or activity. Here, though, Cobb is describing a photograph as if it were a scene he might be witnessing. Consider what his description might accomplish in his essay. Consider, too, why he might have included this verbal description instead of the photograph itself.

CONVERSATIONS: BLACK MEN VS. BLACK WOMEN
Cobb states at the beginning of paragraph 6, "Filtered through lens of popular media, it seems like there's a civil war going on between black men and black women." Here, he is referring to films, television shows, books, and articles that suggest a strain in relationships between Black men and women in American society. Popular films like *Waiting to Exhale* (1995) depict Black women as dissatisfied with the state of the romantic relationships they have with Black men. Other films, such as *Jungle Fever* (1991) and *Mississippi Masala* (1991), portray the criticism Black men are sometimes subject to when they become romantically involved with women who are not Black. Notice how Cobb uses this larger conversation about Black male–female relationships to introduce his discussion about the importance of romantic love among Black slaves in the United States before the Civil War. Consider, too, how these conversations shape the meaning of Cobb's essay.

But what we rarely speak of is love in the context of adversity.

The question goes loudly unasked: who needed love more than the enslaved? Beyond the uprisings and the daily resistance, outside of the escapes, arsons and thefts, the most subversive act committed by enslaved black people may have been daring to love each other. The ten-plus generations of black men and women who lived through the ordeal of slavery went to extraordinary lengths to give meaning to their own lives, to construct relationships that might, if only momentarily, dull the pain of forced servitude, to care for others in a society which sought to make black love a contradiction in terms. And that reality is all but lost in our present love deficit.

Filtered through lens of popular media, it seems like there's a **CIVIL WAR GOING ON BETWEEN BLACK MEN AND BLACK WOMEN.** African Americans are the least likely segment of the population to marry and have a divorce rate that exceeds fifty percent. We are also far less likely to remarry after a divorce than members of other groups. Black radio's airwaves are congested with loveless ballads; rappers boldly declare themselves love-proof—and thereby pain-proof—and disgruntled sirens sing songs of fiscal obligation. In an era where baby-daddies and baby-mamas replace husbands and wives, it's easy to see the destructive legacy of slavery, segregation, incarceration playing itself out. But that's only half of the history—and we've never needed to hear the other side of the story more urgently.

The truth is that marriage and family were extremely important to enslaved black people—despite the obvious difficulties that confronted their relationships. Slave marriages were given no legal recognition, but slaves constructed binding traditions of their own. In addition to **"JUMPING THE BROOM,"** they also presented each other with blankets whose acceptance indicated that they were now considered married within the community. Others, who could not find a willing clergyman or who had been denied permission to marry, simply married themselves. Still, recognition of their union was important enough that ex-slaves besieged the Freedman's Bureau with requests for marriage ceremonies after emancipation. Three Mississippi counties accounted for 4627 marriages in a single year. The end of slavery also brought with it literally thousands of black people wandering throughout the South in search of husbands and wives who had been sold away from them.

Prior to emancipation, individuals went to great lengths to maintain their relationships. One of the most common causes of slave escapes was to see loved ones on distant plantations. One man set out before sunrise each Sunday morning and walked the entire day to spend a few hours with his wife

CONVERSATIONS: "JUMPING THE BROOM"
"Jumping the broom" (par. 7) is a ritual that some scholars believe developed because marriages among slaves were not a
slave couple who were marrying stood together, with broom laid on the ground in front of them, and jumped over the broom,
symbolized their new life together and the "sweeping away" of their old ones. This ritual has regained popularity in recent year,
Black couples. Consider how this ritual is depicted in these images. What aspects of marriage are portrayed or emphasized in ea

Levon Lewis, *Jumping the Broom*

Modern-day couple practicing the jumping the broom
ritual

before having to walk back in time to begin the next day's work.
George Sally, enslaved on a sugar plantation in Louisiana, ignored
the slaveholder's demands and left to visit his wife—an offense for
which he was arrested. (He later stated that he did not mind being
arrested for seeing his wife.) Others risked their lives to protect their
spouses. While sexual exploitation of married black women by overseers was a constant concern, it was not unheard of for husbands to
kill whites who had attacked their wives. One unnamed slave attacked
an overseer who had attempted to whip his wife and was himself
forced to flee into the woods for eleven months.

William Grose, a slave in Loudon County, Virginia, married a free
black woman— against the wishes of the plantation owner, who feared
that she might help him escape. William was sold to a widower in New
Orleans, who demanded that he take another woman as his wife. He
wrote in his autobiography, "I was scared half to death, for I had one
wife whom I liked and didn't want another." The couple managed to

remain in contact and his wife traveled to New Orleans and found work as a domestic in the family that had bought William. When their relationship was discovered, she was forced to leave New Orleans. Incredibly, William devised a plan to escape and fled to Canada where he and his wife were reunited.

Some black couples managed, despite all odds, to construct long, close-knit unions. In the 1930s, Barbara, a woman who was born into slavery in North Carolina, told an interviewer the story of how she had met her husband Frank:

> I seen Frank a few times at the Holland's Methodist Church . . . After a while Frank becomes a butcher and he was doing pretty good . . . so he comes to see me and we courts for a year. We was sitting in the kitchen at the house when he asks me to have him. He told me that he knows that he wasn't worthy, but that he loved me and that he'd do anything he could to please me and that he'd always be good to me. When I was fourteen when I got married and when I was fifteen my oldest daughter was born. I had three after her and Frank was as proud of them as could be. We was happy. We lived together fifty-four years and we was always happy, having only a little bit of argument.

Lucy Dunn, who had also been a slave in North Carolina, told a similar tale:

> It was in the little Baptist church where I first seen Jim Dunn and I fell in love with him then, I reckons. He said that he loved me then too, but it was three Sundays 'fore he asked to see me home. We walked that mile home in front of my mother and I was so happy that I ain't thought it was even a half mile. We ate cornbread and turnips for dinner and it was night before he went home. Mother wouldn't let me walk with him to the gate, so I just sat there on the porch and said goodnight.
>
> He come over every Sunday for a year and finally he proposed. That Sunday night I did walk with Jim to the gate and stood under the honeysuckles that was smelling so sweet. I heard the big old bullfrogs a-croakin' by the river and the whipper-wills a hollerin' in the woods. There was a big yellow moon and I reckon Jim did love me. Anyhow, he said so and asked me to marry him and he squeezed my hand.

She told her suitor that she would have to think about his proposal. She and her mother spent the week discussing the seriousness of marriage. Lucy told her mother that she understood but, "I intends to make a go of it anyhow."

"On Sunday my mother told Jim and you ought to have seen that black boy grin." They were married a week later. "We lived together fifty-five years and we always loved each other . . . we had our fusses and our troubles, but we trusted in the lord and we got through." The old woman wiped away tears as she spoke of her husband. "I loved him during life and I love him now, though he's been dead for twelve years. I thinks of him all the time, but it seems like we're young again when I smell honeysuckles or see a yellow moon."

One hundred and thirty-nine years past slavery, we may have something left to learn from those enslaved generations. Near the end of her interview, Barbara spoke a truth that may be more valid now than when she first said it: "My mother died near twenty years ago and father died four years later. He had not cared to live since mother left him. I've heard some of the young people laugh about slave love, but they should envy the love which kept mother and father so close together in life and even held them in death."

Understanding the Text

1. Why does Cobb state that "the most subversive act committed by enslaved black people may have been daring to love each other"? In what ways would love between two slaves have been "subversive"? What do you think this subversiveness suggests about love and marriage?

2. In what specific ways were marriage and family important to slaves, according to Cobb?

3. What do we learn in this essay about the difficulties slaves encountered in trying to maintain loving family relationships? In what ways are these difficulties important to Cobb's main point?

4. What lessons does Cobb draw from the stories he shares about romantic love between slaves? Do you think these lessons are reasonable ones based on the stories he shares? Explain.

Exploring the Issues

1. Cobb includes excerpts from narratives by slaves and anecdotes about relationships between slaves. What purposes do these excerpts and anecdotes serve? What does Cobb accomplish by including them? In what ways do you think they strengthen or weaken his essay?

2. In paragraph 6, Cobb refers to popular media portrayals of relationships between Black men and women. (See *Conversations: Black Men vs.*

Black Women on page 290.) In the same paragraph, he writes, "We are also far less likely to remarry after a divorce than members of other groups." Who is the "we" in this sentence? What might it suggest about Cobb's audience? About him? Do you think you are part of Cobb's intended audience? Explain.

3. What do you think Cobb's essay suggests about the nature of love? What might it suggest about the role of race and culture in romantic and family relationships? About the way laws affect such relationships?

Entering the Conversations

1. Interview several married couples you know about the circumstances of their relationships. Try to identify any obstacles they may have faced, no matter how small, to their relationship. Then write a report for your classmates in which you tell the stories of the couples you have interviewed and explain the circumstances surrounding their relationships. In your report, try to identify any common problems the couples faced and draw conclusions about some of the factors that can influence a relationship.

INFOTRAC

2. Using InfoTrac College Edition, the Internet, and any other relevant resources, research the laws concerning

marriage in the United States or in other nations. Look into the history of such laws. What are the legal restrictions on marriage? What specific aspects of a relationship do laws seem to affect? For example, do they affect a couple's financial status, professional life, or family situations? How might these laws affect different people differently? In other words, do the laws apply differently to people of different races, ages, or ethnic backgrounds? Do they differ for men and women? Do they allow for same-sex relationships? What are the implications of these laws for people in love? Try to answer such questions in your research. Then write a report on the basis of your research.

3. Write an essay analyzing the portrayal of romantic love in one or more popular films that focus on troubled or forbidden relationships (for example, *Mississippi Masala, Jungle Fever, Lolita*). How do these films depict romantic love? What do they reveal about our society's attitudes regarding love and marriage? Try to address such questions, drawing your own conclusions about the nature of the relationships.

4. Select several contemporary songs that address obstacles to romantic relationships. Write a review of these songs in which you discuss what they seem to suggest about the nature of love. Alternatively, write your own song about forbidden love.

RETHINKING RELATIONSHIPS

ONCE HEARD SOMEONE SAY THAT YOU'LL UNDERSTAND YOUR PARENTS BETTER ONCE YOU HAVE CHILDREN OF YOUR OWN. IF THAT'S TRUE, IT'S PROBABLY BECAUSE HAVING CHILDREN PROMPTS PARENTS TO RETHINK THE RELATIONSHIPS BETWEEN PARENTS AND CHILDREN.

The four essays in this cluster ask you to rethink the perspectives on relationships presented in the essays in the two previous clusters in this chapter—just as new parents may rethink their relationships with their own parents. I decided to create this cluster after rereading the essays in the first two clusters and realizing that there was much more to say about relationships. The conversations we are always having in our society about relationships often include perspectives that challenge conventional wisdom. In an important way, that's how attitudes and beliefs can be changed.

> The conversations we are always having in our society about relationships often include perspectives that challenge conventional wisdom.

Judy Syfers Brady's essay, "Why I Want a Wife," is a good example. In that essay, Brady pushes her readers to take a hard look at the roles of husband and wife in a conventional marriage. And it's pretty clear that she doesn't like what she sees. She wants us to reconsider the way we typically think about husbands and wives. You may disagree, but there's no doubt that many Americans see those roles much differently now than they did in the early 1970s when Brady's essay was first published. And it's perspectives like Brady's that helped change our collective minds.

The other writers in this cluster also look at familiar aspects of relationships from unusual angles. David Sedaris shares an experience from his childhood that highlights the role of peer groups in our young lives, but his experience may reveal far more about his relationship with his family and how that relationship shapes his interactions with others. In sharing his experience, he explores how deeply our sense of identity can be shaped by our relationships with family and peers, but he also explores how our perspective on our relationships can change over time. His essay is funny, but it raises serious questions about how even short-lived relationships can have a lasting impact on us. Jaimie Epstein offers a new twist on a very old theme. She discusses her experience with online dating and discovers that some very old-fashioned concerns influence her use of the newest technology for social connections. And for Anthony Doerr, a telescope leads him to perhaps the biggest question of all when it comes to relationships: What is our relationship to the universe?

What I like about this cluster is that the four essays continue the larger conversations about relationships that we are always having, but they do so in ways that won't let us off the hook. Their unusual perspectives don't let us get too comfortable with our own thinking about what relationships are and what they should be. And they help us see why there always seems to be another way to look at our relationships. In this sense, this final cluster is a good example of how writing can be much more than a means of communication; it is also a means of rethinking who we are and reexamining the world around us.

This essay, which was published in the inaugural issue of Ms. *magazine in 1971, is one of the most widely reprinted essays ever written. It shows up in countless college writing textbooks, in books about women's issues, on feminist web sites, and in speeches about gender and women's rights. I first came across the essay in the early 1980s,*

Why I Want A Wife

when I was a new writing teacher. When I first assigned it to my students, it sparked the most intense discussion we had all semester. More than twenty years later, I am still using the essay in some of my classes, and the discussions it provokes are just as intense as that first one. The obvious question is: Why? What is it about this essay that has made it so interesting, engaging, and provocative to readers for so many years? I won't answer that question because I'm sure you'll come up with your own answers. But I will ask you to think about whether this is the same essay today that it was in 1971, when the women's rights movement was just gaining momentum and feminism was a relatively new (and challenging) way of thinking about gender for most Americans. It's rare for an essay to stay relevant for so many years, but this one seems to have remained so. Is that because the

JUDY SYFERS BRADY

I belong to that classification of people known as wives. I am A Wife. And, not altogether incidentally, I am a mother.

Not too long ago a male friend of mine appeared on the scene fresh from a recent divorce. He had one child, who is, of course, with his ex-wife. He is looking for another wife. As I thought about him while I was ironing one evening, it suddenly occurred to me that I, too, would like to have a wife. Why do I want a wife?

I would like to go back to school so that I can become economically independent, support myself, and if need be, support those dependent upon me. I want a wife who will work and send me to school. And while I am going to school I want a wife to take care of my children. I want a wife to keep track of the children's doctor and dentist appointments. And to keep track of mine, too. I want a wife to make sure my children eat properly and are kept clean. I want a wife who will wash the children's clothes and keep them mended. I want a wife who is a good nurturing attendant to my children, who arranges for their schooling, makes sure that they have an adequate social life with their peers, takes them to the park, the zoo, etc. I want a wife who takes care of the chil-

JUDY SYFERS BRADY, "WHY I WANT A WIFE." FROM "WHY I WANT A WIFE" BY JUDY BRADY (SYFERS). MS. MAGAZINE (1973). REPRINTED BY PERMISSION OF THE AUTHOR.

dren when they are sick, a wife who arranges to be around when the children need special care, because, of course, I cannot miss classes at school. My wife must arrange to lose time at work and not lose the job. It may mean a small cut in my wife's income from time to time, but I guess I can tolerate that. Needless to say, my wife will arrange and pay for the care of the children while my wife is working.

I want a wife who will take care of my physical needs. I want a wife who will keep my house clean. A wife who will pick up after my children, a wife who will pick up after me. I want a wife who will keep my clothes clean, ironed, mended, replaced when need be, and who will see to it that my personal things are kept in their proper place so that I can find what I need the minute I need it. I want a wife who cooks the meals, a wife who is a good cook. I want a wife who will plan the menus, do the necessary grocery shopping, prepare the meals, serve them pleasantly, and then do the cleaning up while I do my studying. I want a wife who will care for me when I am sick and sympathize with my pain and loss of time from school. I want a wife to go along when our family takes a vacation so that someone can continue to care for me and my children when I need a rest and change of scene.

5   I want a wife who will not bother me with rambling complaints about a wife's duties. But I want a wife who will listen to me when I feel the need to explain a rather difficult point I have come across in my course of studies. And I want a wife who will type my papers for me when I have written them.

I want a wife who will take care of the details of my social life. When my wife and I are invited out by my friends, I want a wife who takes care of the baby-sitting arrangements. When I meet people at school that I like and want to entertain, I want a wife who will have the house clean, will prepare a special meal, serve it to me and my friends, and not interrupt when I talk about things that interest me and my friends. I want a wife who will have arranged that the children are fed and ready for bed before my guests arrive so that the children do not bother us. I want a wife who takes care of the needs of my guests so that they feel comfortable, who makes sure that they have an ashtray, that they are passed the hors d'oeuvres, that they are offered a second helping of the food, that their wine glasses are replenished when necessary, that their coffee is served to them as they like it. And I want a wife who knows that sometimes I need a night out by myself.

I want a wife who is sensitive to my sexual needs, a wife who makes love passionately and eagerly when I feel like it, a wife who makes sure that I am satisfied. And, of course, I want a wife who will not demand sexual attention when I am not in the mood for it. I want a wife who assumes the complete responsibility for birth control, because I do

essay is just a good piece of writing? Or is it because the issues it addresses and the questions it raises are just as important today as they were in the 1970s? Obviously, readers still find the essay engaging, but are they reading it the same way today as readers read it in 1971? Keep those questions in mind as you read.

Judy Syfers Brady (b. 1937) continues to write today, focusing much of her attention on cancer and advocating for cancer patients. ◢

STRATEGIES: DETAILS
Brady tells us in paragraph 2 that she was ironing clothes one evening when she decided that like her recently divorced friend, she, too, would like a wife. Carefully chosen details can not only help describe a scene but also carry messages that an author wishes to convey to a reader. What do these two details—that she was ironing and that it was in the evening—convey in this context?

CONVERSATIONS: MARRIAGE AND DIVORCE
When Brady wrote this essay in 1971, most Americans lived in traditional households—that is, families made up of a husband, wife, and children. In 1970, more than twice as many Americans lived in traditional families as those living in single or nontraditional households. Today, about the same number of Americans live in traditional families as in single households. Divorce is more common as well, with about half of all marriages today ending in divorce. Consider how these changes in American family lifestyles might affect the way we read this essay.

STRATEGIES: HYPERBOLE
Some critics point out that Brady seems to be creating an unrealistic picture of a typical wife, that she intentionally exaggerates to make her point. Such a strategy, which is often called *hyperbole,* can call readers' attention to common things that they may usually overlook. Would you say that Brady employs hyperbole in this essay? If so, does it work?

CONVERSATIONS: A WOMAN'S PLACE
These two photos of women in the 1950s seem to depict some of what Brady describes in her essay about a woman's role in the home. What do you think these images convey about women? Consider the extent to which these images reflect not only a particular era but also a particular culture and socioeconomic status.

© Bettmann/CORBIS

© H. Armstrong Roberts/CORBIS

not want more children. I want a wife who will remain sexually faithful to me so that I do not have to clutter up my intellectual life with jealousies. And I want a wife who understands that my sexual needs may entail more than strict adherence to monogamy. I must, after all, be able to relate to people as fully as possible.

If, by chance, I find another person more suitable as a wife than the wife I already have, I want the liberty to replace my present wife with another one. Naturally, I will expect a fresh, new life; my wife will take the children and be solely responsible for them so that I am left free.

When I am through with school and have a job, I want my wife to quit working and remain at home so that my wife can more fully and completely take care of a wife's duties.

10   My God, who *wouldn't* want a wife?

Understanding the Text

1. Brady tells us that she began wanting a wife while thinking about a recently divorced friend of hers who is looking for a new wife. Why is her friend's situation important in terms of Brady's point in this essay?

2. According to Brady's descriptions of a wife, what are a wife's primary responsibilities? What are a husband's responsibilities? What do these different responsibilities suggest about marriage? About gender?

3. On what grounds would a husband seek to end his marriage to his wife, according to this essay? Are these grounds reasonable, in your view? Does Brady intend them to be? Explain.

Exploring the Issues

1. How would you summarize Brady's main point in this essay? Point to specific passages that you think reveal her point. Do you agree with her? Why or why not?

2. What kind of picture of a wife does Brady create? Do you think this picture is accurate, even today? Why or why not? Do you think Brady intended this picture to be accurate? Explain.

3. How would you describe the tone of this essay? Do you find the tone effective, given Brady's point? Explain, citing specific passages to support your answer.

4. This essay was first published in *Ms.* magazine, which was intended to be a voice for the women's movement in the early 1970s. Who do you think Brady assumed her audience would be? Was she writing to men as well as to women? Explain.

Entering the Conversations

1. Write a response to Brady's essay.

2. In a group of classmates, share your responses to Brady's essay. What are the main points of agreement and disagreement about her essay? In what ways do the men and women in your group react differently to her essay, if at all? Try to draw conclusions about how gender or other factors might influence the way readers react to Brady's essay.

3. Write an essay in which you analyze Brady's essay. Focus on her rhetorical strategy and examine how she makes her point. Try to describe the key elements of her strategy. Assess the effectiveness of her approach. In your analysis, you might compare Brady's essay with other essays in this chapter that also deal with relationships in an unusual or provocative way.

4. Talk to several married couples you know as well as to people who have been divorced. Get their perspectives on marriage and specifically on the roles of husbands

"Ah! Here it is!"

"If something is bothering you about our relationship, Lorraine, why don't you just spell it out."

and wives in a marriage. Try to learn how they feel about those roles and the challenges facing married couples today. Then write an essay for an audience of your classmates in which you discuss what you learned about marriage from your conversations. Draw your own conclusions about the roles of husbands and wives in marriage.

5. What do the cartoons on the preceding page say about marital relationships? About the problems married couples face? About how married couples relate to each other? Where do you think the ideas about marriage portrayed in these cartoons come from? Write an analysis in which you address such questions.

6. Many popular films and TV shows depict marital relationships. Select several films or TV shows that you think reveal important ideas about gender roles and write an analysis of these films or shows. In your analysis, discuss what you think these films or shows reveal about contemporary attitudes regarding men and women.

Not long ago my nephew, who was thirteen years old at the time, got into a fight at school. He punched another boy who had bullied him for some time. Both kids were suspended from school, as required by school policy, but the school principal confided to my nephew that he was justified in confronting the bully. It turns out that my nephew had been the object

Consider THE Stars

of ridicule by the bully and his friends, and though he endured the ridicule for a long time without doing anything, it clearly bothered him. He told his parents, "I just don't understand why they don't like me."

I thought about my nephew when I read the following essay by writer David Sedaris. In the essay, Sedaris describes an encounter he had with a popular kid at his school when he was twelve years old. Although the circumstances of Sedaris's experience were somewhat different from the bullying that my nephew experienced, both my nephew and Sedaris were dealing with the seemingly timeless desire to be accepted by a peer group. If you attended school (and almost everyone does), then you will recognize the situation Sedaris describes in his essay. Sedaris's

GLOSS: HUGH
Hugh is Sedaris's friend, who regularly appears in his writing.

DAVID SEDARIS

Every night before going to bed, HUGH steps outside to consider the stars. His interest is not scientific—he doesn't pinpoint the constellations or make casual references to Canopus; rather, he just regards the mass of them, occasionally pausing to sigh. When asked if there's life on other planets, he says, "Yes, of course. Look at the odds."

It hardly seems fair we'd get the universe all to ourselves, but on a personal level I'm highly disturbed by the thought of extraterrestrial life. If there are, in fact, billions of other civilizations, where does that leave our celebrities? If worth is measured on a sliding scale of recognition, what would it mean if we were all suddenly obscure? How would we know our place?

*   *   *

In trying to make sense of this, I think back to a 1968 Labor Day celebration at the Raleigh Country Club. I was at the snack bar, listening to a group of sixth-graders who lived in another part of town and sat discussing significant changes in their upcoming school year. According to the girl named Janet, neither Pam Dobbins nor J. J. Jackson had been invited to the Fourth of July party hosted by the Duffy

essay is a little bit like remembering our own school days. And he takes us back to those days with his trademark humor. But Sedaris's story also poses some intriguing questions about the role of peer relationships in how we think about ourselves. Perhaps surprisingly, Sedaris does not hold a grudge against the popular student who shunned him. Instead, his memories of that student continue to shape how Sedaris thinks about himself. His essay can help us understand the power of peer relationships in our lives and perhaps prompt us to rethink what it means to be "popular."

David Sedaris is an award-winning humorist and author of a number of essays and books, including the best-selling Me Talk Pretty One Day *(2000) and* Dress Your Family in Corduroy and Denim *(2004), in which the following essay appeared.* ◪

twins, who later told Kath Matthews that both Pam *and* J. J. were out of the picture as far as the seventh grade was concerned. "Totally, completely out," Janet said. "Poof."

I didn't know any Pam Dobbins or J. J. Jackson, but the reverential tone of Janet's voice sent me into a state of mild shock. Call me naive, but it had simply never occurred to me that other schools might have their own celebrity circles. At the age of twelve, I thought the group at E. C. Brooks was if not nationally known, then at least its own private phenomenon. Why else would our lives revolve around it so completely? I myself was not a member of my school's popular crowd, but I recall thinking that, whoever they were, Janet's popular crowd couldn't begin to compete with ours. But what if I was wrong? What if I'd wasted my entire life comparing myself with people who didn't really matter? Try as I might, I still can't wrap my mind around it.

*   *   *

They banded together in the third grade. Ann Carlsworth, Christie Kaymore, Deb Bevins, Mike Holliwell, Doug Middleton, Thad Pope: they were the core of the popular crowd, and for the next six years my classmates and I studied their lives the way we were supposed to study math and English. What confused us most was the absence of any specific formula. Were they funny? No. Interesting? Yawn. None owned pools or horses. They had no special talents, and their grades were unremarkable. It was their dearth of excellence that gave the rest of us hope and kept us on our toes. Every now and then they'd select a new member, and the general attitude among the student body was "Oh, pick me!" It didn't matter what you were like on your own. The group would *make* you special. That was its magic.

So complete was their power that I actually felt honored when one of them hit me in the mouth with a rock. He'd gotten me after school, and upon returning home, I ran into my sister's bedroom, hugging my bloody Kleenex and crying, "It was Thad!!!"

Lisa was one grade higher than me, but still she understood the significance. "Did he *say* anything?" she asked. "Did you save the rock?"

My father demanded I retaliate, saying I ought to knock the guy on his ass.

"Oh, Dad."

"Aww, baloney. Clock him on the snot locker and he'll go down like a ton of bricks."

"Are you talking to *me?*" I asked. The archaic slang aside, who did my father think I was? Boys who spent their weekends **MAKING BANANA NUT MUFFINS** did not, as a rule, excel in the art of hand-to-hand combat.

"I mean, come on, Dad," Lisa said. "Wake up."

The following afternoon I was taken to Dr. Povlitch for X-rays. The rock had damaged one of my

5

10

STRATEGIES: USING DETAILS
In this passage, Sedaris describes himself as a seventh-grader who spent his weekends "making banana nut muffins" and therefore did not "excel in the art of hand-to-hand combat." He could have described himself simply as a boy who was not aggressive or strong. Instead, he uses these details, which add both humor and a concrete sense of what he was like when he was twelve years old. This use of detail is an example of what writing teachers sometimes describe as *showing* and not *telling*. But Sedaris is doing more with these details than just describing himself. Consider how these details also help set the scene for the events to follow.

bottom teeth, and there was some question over who would pay for the subsequent root canal. I figured that since my parents had conceived me, delivered me into the world, and raised me as a permanent guest in their home, they should foot the bill, but my father thought differently. He decided the Popes should pay, and I screamed as he picked up the phone book.

"But you can't just . . . *call* Thad's house."

"Oh yeah?" he said. "Watch me."   15

There were two Thad Popes in the Raleigh phone book, a Junior and a Senior. The one in my class was what came after a Junior. He was a Third. My father called both the Junior and the Senior, beginning each conversation with the line "Lou Sedaris here. Listen, pal, we've got a problem with your son."

He said our last name as if it meant something, as if we were known and respected. This made it all the more painful when he was asked to repeat it. Then to spell it.

A meeting was arranged for the following evening, and before we left the house, I begged my father to change his clothes. He'd been building an addition to the carport and was wearing a pair of khaki shorts smeared with paint and spotted here and there with bits of dried concrete. Through a hole in his tattered T-shirt, without squinting, it was possible to see his nipple.

"What the hell is wrong with this?" he asked. "We're not staying for dinner, so who cares what I'm wearing?"

I yelled for my mother, and in the end he compromised by changing his shirt.   20

*   *   *

From the outside, Thad's house didn't look much different from anyone else's—just a standard split-level with what my father described as a totally inadequate carport. Mr. Pope answered the door in a pair of sherbet-colored golf pants and led us downstairs into what he called "the rumpus room."

"Oh," I said, "this is nice!"

The room was damp and windowless and lit with hanging Tiffany lampshades, the shards of colorful glass arranged to spell the words *Busch* and *Budweiser.* The walls were paneled in imitation walnut, and the furniture looked as though it had been hand-hewn by settlers who'd reconfigured parts of their beloved Conestoga wagon to fashion such things as easy chairs and coffee tables. Noticing the fraternity paddle hanging on the wall above the television, my father launched into his broken Greek, saying *"Kalispera sas adhelfosl."*

When Mr. Pope looked at him blankly, my father laughed and offered a translation. "I said, 'Good evening, brother.' "Oh . . . right," Mr. Pope said. "Fraternities are Greek."

25   He directed us toward a sofa and asked if we wanted something to drink. Coke? A beer? I didn't want to deplete Thad's precious cola supply, but before I could refuse, my father said sure, we'd have one of each. The orders were called up the staircase, and a few minutes later Mrs. Pope came down, carrying cans and plastic tumblers.

"Well, *hello* there," my father said. This was his standard greeting to a beautiful woman, but I could tell he was just saying it as a joke. Mrs. Pope wasn't unattractive, just ordinary, and as she set the drinks before us, I noticed that her son had inherited her blunt, slightly upturned nose, which looked good on him but caused her to appear overly suspicious and judgmental.

"So," she said. "I hear you've been to the dentist." She was just trying to make small talk, but because of her nose, it came off sounding like an insult, as if I'd just had a cavity filled and was now looking for someone to foot the bill.

"*I'll* say he's been to the dentist," my father said. "Someone hits you in the mouth with a rock and I'd say the dentist's office is pretty much the first place a reasonable person would go."

Mr. Pope held up his hands. "Whoa now," he said. "Let's just calm things down a little." He yelled upstairs for his son, and when there was no answer he picked up the phone, telling Thad to stop running his mouth and get his butt down to the rumpus room ASAP.

30   A rush of footsteps on the carpeted staircase and then Thad sprinted in, all smiles and apologies. The minister had called. The game had been rescheduled. "Hello, sir, and you are . . . ?"

He looked my father in the eye and firmly shook his hand, holding it in his own for just the right amount of time. While most handshakes mumbled, his spoke clearly; saying both *We'll get through this as quickly as possible* and *I'm looking forward to your vote this coming November.*

I'd thought that seeing him without his group might be unsettling, like finding a single arm on the sidewalk, but Thad was fully capable of operating independently. Watching him in action, I understood that his popularity was not an accident. Unlike a normal human being, he possessed an uncanny ability to please people. There was no sucking up or awkward maneuvering to fit the will of others. Rather, much like a Whitman's sampler, he seemed to offer a little bit of everything. Pass on his athletic ability and you might partake of his excellent manners, his confidence, his coltish enthusiasm. Even his parents seemed invigorated by his presence, uncrossing their legs and sitting up just a little bit straighter as he took a seat beside them. Had the circumstances been different, my father would have been all over him, probably going so far as to call him son—but money was involved, so he steeled himself.

"All right, then," Mr. Pope said. "Now that everyone's accounted for, I'm hoping we can clear this up. Sticks and stones aside, I suspect this all comes down to a little misunderstanding between friends."

I lowered my eyes, waiting for Thad to set his father straight. *"Friends?* With *him?"* I expected laughter or the famous Thad snort, but instead he said nothing. And with his silence, he won me completely. A little misunderstanding—that's *exactly* what it was. How had I not seen it earlier?

The immediate goal was to save my friend, and so I claimed to have   35
essentially thrown myself in the path of Thad's fast-moving rock.

"What the hell was he throwing rocks for?" my father asked. "What the hell was he throwing them *at?"*

Mrs. Pope frowned, implying that such language was not welcome in the rumpus room.

"I mean, Jesus Christ, the guy's got to be a complete idiot."

Thad swore he hadn't been aiming at anything, and I backed him up, saying it was just one of those things we all did. "Like in Vietnam or whatever. It was just friendly fire."

My father asked what the hell I knew about Vietnam, and again   40
Thad's mother winced, saying that boys picked up a lot of this talk by watching the news.

"You don't know what you're talking about," my father said.

"What my wife meant . . . ," Mr. Pope said.

"Aww, baloney."

The trio of Popes exchanged meaningful glances, holding what amounted to a brief, telepathic powwow. "This man crazy," the smoke signals read. "Make heap big trouble for others."

I looked at my father, a man in dirty shorts who drank his beer   45
from the can rather than pouring it into his tumbler, and I thought, *You don't belong here.* More precisely, I decided that he was the reason I didn't belong. The hokey Greek phrases, the how-to lectures on mixing your own concrete, the squabble over who would pay the stupid dentist bill—little by little, it had all seeped into my bloodstream, robbing me of my natural ability to please others. For as long as I could remember, he'd been telling us that it didn't matter what other people thought: their judgment was crap, a waste of time, baloney. But it did matter, especially when those people were *these* people.

"Well," Mr. Pope said, "I can see that this is going nowhere."

My father laughed. "Yeah, you got that right." It sounded like a parting sentence, but rather than standing to leave, he leaned back in the sofa and rested his beer can upon his stomach. "We're all going nowhere."

At this point I'm fairly sure that Thad and I were envisioning the same grim scenario. While the rest of the world moved on, my increasingly filthy and bearded father would continue to occupy the rumpus-room sofa. Christmas would come, friends would visit, and the Popes would bitterly direct them toward the easy chairs. "Just ignore him," they'd say. "He'll go home sooner or later."

In the end, they agreed to pay for half of the root canal, not because they thought it was fair but because they wanted us out of their house.

*   *   *

50   Some friendships are formed by a commonality of interests and ideas: you both love judo or camping or making your own sausage. Other friendships are forged in alliance against a common enemy. On leaving Thad's house, I decided that ours would probably be the latter. We'd start off grousing about my father, and then, little by little, we'd move on to the hundreds of other things and people that got on our nerves. "You hate olives," I imagined him saying. "I hate them, too!"

As it turned out, the one thing we both hated was me. Rather, I hated me. Thad couldn't even summon up the enthusiasm. The day after the meeting, I approached him in the lunchroom, where he sat at his regular table, surrounded by his regular friends. "Listen," I said, "I'm really sorry about that stuff with my dad." I'd worked up a whole long speech, complete with imitations, but by the time I finished my mission statement, he'd turned to resume his conversation with Doug Middleton. Our perjured testimony, my father's behavior, even the rock throwing: I was so far beneath him that it hadn't even registered.

Poof.

*   *   *

The socialites of E. C. Brooks shone even brighter in junior high, but come tenth grade, things began to change. Desegregation drove a lot of the popular people into private schools, and those who remained seemed silly and archaic, deposed royalty from a country the average citizen had ceased to care about.

Early in our junior year, Thad was jumped by a group of the new black kids, who yanked off his shoes and threw them in the toilet. I knew I was supposed to be happy, but part of me felt personally assaulted. True, he'd been a negligent prince, yet still I believed in the monarchy. When his name was called at graduation, it was I who clapped the longest, outlasting even his parents, who politely stopped once he'd left the stage.

55   I thought about Thad a lot over the coming years, wondering where he went to college and if he joined a fraternity. The era of the **BIG MAN ON CAMPUS** had ended, but the rowdy houses with their pool tables and fake moms continued to

---

CONVERSATIONS: CHANGING VIEWS OF COLLEGE FRATERNITIES
When Sedaris wonders in this passage whether Thad joined a fraternity in college, he notes that the "era of Big Man on Campus had ended" and fraternity members were "now viewed as date rapists and budding alcoholics." He is referring to some of the changes that have occurred in the social life on college campuses since the mid-twentieth century, when fraternities and sororities were widely viewed as desirable social organizations in which many students sought to be members. At one time, the phrase "Big Man on Campus" was used to refer to a popular person on a college campus, usually a member of a popular fraternity. Over time, it came to mean anyone who is important in some way. By the 1980s and 1990s, changes in the student populations at many colleges and universities as well as changing attitudes about alcohol use began to reshape the role of fraternities and sororities and influenced how many people thought of them. Instances of injuries and even death as a result of drinking alcohol that occurred at some fraternities and increasing reports of date rape led some colleges to restrict fraternity activities or even close down some fraternities. Notice how Sedaris refers to these complex developments in a single sentence by using a few phrases such as "Big Man on Campus" and "date rape." This is a good example of how discourse can shape the meanings of certain words and phrases, as discussed in Chapter 1 (see pages 10–11). Sedaris can rely on the meanings that these phrases have acquired to help make his point in this passage—and to participate in a larger conversation about college life.

serve as reunion points for the once popular, who were now viewed as date rapists and budding alcoholics. I tell myself that while his brothers drifted toward a confused and bitter adulthood, Thad stumbled into the class that changed his life. He's the poet laureate of Liechtenstein, the surgeon who cures cancer with love, the ninth-grade teacher who insists that the world is big enough for everyone. When moving to another city, I'm always hoping to find him living in the apartment next door. We'll meet in the hallway and he'll stick out his hand, saying, "Excuse me, but don't I—*shouldn't* I know you?" It doesn't have to happen today, but it *does* have to happen. I've kept a space waiting for him, and if he doesn't show up, I'm going to have to forgive my father.

THE ROOT CANAL THAT WAS SUPPOSED TO LAST FOR TEN YEARS has now lasted for over thirty, though it's nothing to be proud of. Having progressively dulled and weakened, the tooth is now a brownish gray color the **CONRAN'S CATALOG** refers to as "Kabuki." It's hanging in there, but just barely. While Dr. Povlitch worked out of a converted brick house beside the Colony Shopping Center, my current dentist, Docteur Guig, has an office near the Madeleine, in Paris. On a recent visit, he gripped my dead tooth between his fingertips and gently jiggled it back and forth. I hate to unnecessarily exhaust his patience, so when he asked me what had happened, it took me a moment to think of the clearest possible answer. The past was far too complicated to put into French, so instead I envisioned a perfect future, and attributed the root canal to a little misunderstanding between friends.

STRATEGIES: ORGANIZING A NARRATIVE

In the final paragraph of his story, Sedaris refers to the tooth that was damaged by a rock, as he described near the beginning of the story (see paragraph 6). In doing so, he brings us to the present day while at the same time reminding us of the incident that led to his story in the first place. This common strategy of referring back to a key moment in the story is an effective way to conclude a narrative. It enables the writer not only to remind readers of something important in the story but also to highlight a main theme or idea. Here, Sedaris uses his visit to the dentist to connect past and present and convey a message about the event that occurred in his childhood. Notice too that his narrative is organized chronologically; that is, he tells the story from beginning to end without moving back and forth in time as some writers do in their narratives (for example, see "Both Sides of a Gun Barrel" by D. Winston Brown on page 152).

GLOSS: CONRAN'S CATALOGUE

Conran is an international retailer of high-end home products, which it sells through an extensive catalogue as well as in its stores.

Understanding the Text

1. What accounted for the popularity of the popular crowd at Sedaris's school? What was the source of their power? What do you think Sedaris is trying to say about the nature of popularity through his descriptions of the popular kids?

2. Why does Sedaris believe that he and Thad had become friends as a result of the meeting with their parents? What does this belief say about Sedaris and his hopes and desires as a twelve-year-old? What do you think he learns when he discovers that Thad did not consider him a friend?

3. Near the end of his narrative, Sedaris tells us that he's still waiting to encounter Thad, whom he expects to be a successful or important person. Sedaris also writes that if he doesn't encounter Thad, he will have to forgive his father. Why does he expect Thad to be a successful person? What significance does Thad continue to have for Sedaris? And why would he have to forgive his father if Thad is not a successful person? Why has he not forgiven his father yet?

Exploring the Issues

1. Sedaris is well known for his humorous narratives about his own life, and he uses humor even when he is writing about serious issues. What is the source of Sedaris's humor in this essay? How effective do you think Sedaris's humor is? Do you think the essay would be more or less effective if Sedaris had told this story without using humor as he does? Explain.

2. At times in this passage, Sedaris paints a less-than-flattering picture of his family, especially his father. For example, in paragraph 18, he presents an image of his father as somewhat gruff and

unsophisticated as well as unconcerned about his dress and physical appearance, and later he describes his father's embarrassing behavior when he meets with Thad's parents. What is the effect of this depiction of his father in the essay? How might the essay have been different if Sedaris had described his father in a more neutral way? What do you think these descriptions suggest about how Sedaris feels about his family and especially his father? Do you think he intends to criticize or ridicule his father in these descriptions or is he simply poking fun? Explain, citing specific passages from the essay to support your answer.

3. The first two paragraphs briefly describe Hugh looking at the stars in the night sky and Sedaris's reaction to Hugh's comment that there must be life on other planets. But the rest of the essay focuses exclusively on Sedaris's experience with his schoolmate Thad and includes nothing about Hugh. Why do you think Sedaris begins his essay in this way? How do the first few paragraphs influence the way you read his story? How might they shape Sedaris's themes or main ideas in the story? And why do you think Sedaris titled the essay "Consider the Stars"? How might that title help shape the meaning of the essay?

Entering the Conversations

1. Write an essay in which you tell the story of a relationship that influenced you and how you think of yourself.

INFOTRAC

2. In many ways, Sedaris's story is about the role of peer groups among children and adolescents, and a great deal of research and attention has been devoted to the importance of social relationships

with peers, especially in schools. Using InfoTrac and other appropriate sources, investigate some of what has been learned about peer groups among school students. Try to identify important research on the role of social relationships in schools, and get a sense of prevailing views among educators about the impact of students' social relationships on academic work and other aspects of school life. Then, write a report on the basis of your research. In your report, describe what you learned about peer groups in schools and draw conclusions about the role of peer groups.

3. On the basis of the research you did for Question 2, create a pamphlet or web site (or similar document) containing advice for middle or high school students about social relationships and peer groups.

4. Today, many middle and high school students increasingly maintain social relationships and peer groups online through text messaging, social networking sites like MySpace, and blogs, and in recent years a great deal of attention has been devoted to this trend. In some cases, controversies have emerged because of online bullying, and some schools have established policies regarding the use of social networking sites. Examine the use of these technologies among students today and write an essay in which you offer your view of the role such technologies play in students' social lives. Draw on your own experience with these technologies, if appropriate.

5. Write a letter to the parents of middle or high school students at the school you attended, giving them advice about how to deal with their children's peer groups and social relationships. In your letter, address the use of online technologies like text messaging and MySpace and draw on your own experience to support the advice you are giving.

Recently, a friend of mine decided to try an *online dating service after going through a divorce. She had been married for more than ten years, so dating wasn't something she had done in a long time, and as a middle-aged woman she worried that she would have trouble meeting new men. An online dating service seemed like an easy way for her to*

Sentence Sensibility

solve this problem. So she registered for one of the increasing number of such services, created a profile, and reviewed the list of possible matches she received. She was surprised (and not entirely pleased) to find her ex-husband listed among those matches! He had apparently signed up for the same online dating service.

I'm not sure exactly what to make of my friend's experience with online dating (maybe it suggests that she and her ex-husband really were a good match!), but my guess is that her experience isn't entirely unique. According to one study published in 2008, online dating is the third most popular use of the Internet (after music and gaming). But online dating does raise interesting questions about how we use technologies to conduct our relationships with one another. Freelance writer Jaimie Epstein offers one look at how online technologies can play a role in our relationships. Like my

JAIMIE EPSTEIN

I promise this is on topic, so PLEASE BEAR WITH ME. . . . One day, as a cure for a broken heart, a heart that had only barely survived a head-on collision with another heart, a heart just out of intensive care, bruised and limping and still shying at the sound of any traffic, I decided to go online to find distraction in the arms of other, virtual men and maybe, as a bonus, a suitable replacement for the one no longer in my life, to meet someone the normal way, as opposed to the archaic, anachronistic, so 1970s way I had met HIM—I'd had my skis (nearly) charmed off me at 10,000 feet by my instructor, who was trying, with a dribble of luck but gallons of patience, to teach me how to jump turn on telemark skis. A broken heart, like the crack of dawn, can't be fixed, said a wise friend, but I was hoping that the splint of male attention might at least encourage healing—and it would mean I'd have less time to waste obsessing over you-know-whom.

I didn't realize, however, WHAT A HUGE BOULDER I WOULD BE ROLLING UPHILL—what with my being a "literary person," a sometime editor of this column, someone whose ear is as tuned to the pitch of language as a cellist's is to music—until the misplaced modifiers, dyslexic spellings and grievous abuses of syntax started pouring in. One seeker of

JAIMIE EPSTEIN, "SENTENCE SENSIBILITY," *NEW YORK TIMES*. ON LANGUAGE; JULY 22, 2007. REPRINTED BY PERMISSION OF THE *NEW YORK TIMES*.

friend, Epstein was prompted to go online to look for a companion, but she finds that her rather traditional attitudes about language got in the way of her online search for a mate. Her essay, which appeared in the New York Times *in 2008, is lighthearted and humorous, but it addresses complex issues about how we judge others—in this case, on the basis of the way they write. It also may cause us to wonder about the role of language in our relationships as well as about our attitudes regarding "proper" language.* ◲

a woman to call his own allowed that the last book he had read was "Atonement," which was about to earn him a gold star, **IAN MCEWAN** having his own section on my bookshelves, except that he didn't quit while he was ahead—he had to add that it was written by . . . **IAN MC-GREGOR!** O.K., no big deal, you say, they're both Brits, it's hard to keep all the Ians (or, um, Ewans!) straight, you know what/whom he meant and at least he reads something besides **GAWKER.** Well, yeah, but couldn't he have malappropriated a lesser writer's name, one whose first and last aren't tattooed on my forehead, one not sitting on a pedestal in front of my computer? Couldn't he have checked his sources?

Speaking of mis-namers, I am sure the Spielbergs and the Kings of the world are used to the "Steven or Stephen?" flip of the spelling coin, and some of my closest friends have been known to lose one of my "i"s, but you'd think that a man trying to impress a woman would get her name right. Well, you would be wrong. After an intense flurry of e-mailing that involved the seductive vocabulary of maple farming—"splitting maul"! "peavey"!—and even more seductive pictures of said maple farmer, I decided that we had reached the point in our relationship where I really needed him to spell my name correctly, and I told him so in a gentle mama-bear-like way. Next thing I know I get a quick response: "oops, bad timing—I just started a new relationship"! O.K., maybe he did, or maybe he took offense at my comment about the grin of satisfaction slathered over his end-of-the-work-day face in his latest photo attachment: "for all i know you've just put a family of four through a wood chipper!" (Dude, where's your sense of humor? **DID YOU NOT LOVE "FARGO"**?) But maybe he was one of those men who would sooner ask for directions than have their punctuation or grammar corrected. Can you spell "thin-barked"?

I know what you're thinking: No wonder she's single, no wonder she got dumped, who would want to feel those eyes/ears of judgment upon his every utterance? (Please include a RECENT photo and a list of the five things you can't live without when you e-mail your diatribe to me at pninup-grrrl@findlove.com.) But just imagine what it's like to be afflicted with an excess language-sensitivity gene. I mean, how would you feel if someone extolled your "skillful verbage"? Maybe he liked the way I threw my verbs around, but my nose picked up a whiff of "garbage." And what about

---

STRATEGIES: ADDRESSING AN AUDIENCE

This essay was originally published in a column called "On Language" that appears regularly in the *New York Times*. When Epstein writes at the beginning of her essay that it is "on topic," she is alerting her readers that her topic may not seem appropriate for a column about language. She knows that her readers expect a certain kind of topic for that column and she anticipates their possible objections to a topic that may seem more appropriate for a column about relationships. This is a good example of how rhetorical context can directly shape a writer's decisions about what to include and how to address an audience (see "Assessing Rhetorical Context" on page 37 in Chapter 3).

STRATEGIES: USING ALLUSIONS

You might not have recognized the reference in paragraph 2 to the ancient Greek myth of Sisyphus, a king who was punished by the gods for his misdeeds by having to roll a huge boulder up a hill; each time he nears the top, the boulder rolls back down again. His punishment has come to symbolize futility of effort because he never completes his task. Here, Epstein refers to Sisyphus's boulder in a humorous way. Such a reference, or literary *allusion,* is usually intended to convey some point or meaning. Epstein uses such allusions—to movies, clichés, and famous people as well as to literary texts—throughout this essay. Consider the effect of these allusions on readers. And consider how Epstein uses an allusion in this paragraph. What, exactly, is her "boulder"? Is she just poking fun at herself or making a more serious point about relationships?

the onomatopoeticist who enjoyed the "slurshing sound of the waves"? "Slurshing" made me think "drink sloppily and quickly," and combined with the motion of the water, the effect of his words was to produce welling seasickness, not the soothing rock and roll of the ocean crashing and uncrashing with romantic abandon along the shore of a secluded beach that he must have been aiming for.

5   Uh-oh, I just ended a sentence with a preposition! Hey, I know I fall far short of the lofty standards upheld by **STRUNK AND WHITE, FOWLER, BERNSTEIN AND GARNER.** It's not like, whoops, I mean as if (see!), I'm perfect, as if I have, after all these years, mastered the subtlety of who/whom, as if I never use "media" in the singular or accidentally type "their" when I mean "there," as if I ever get the comma or not before "too" 100 percent right. I know people don't proofread their myriad daily e-mail messages, and I have certainly been chagrined to discover, say, that I fired off "bike" when I meant "back," but isn't dating online like sending out your résumé, aren't you trying to sell yourself to a potential employer (i.e., friend, lover, hand-to-hold-until-the-end-of-time)? When you write to a new someone, that someone who just might be the answer to your dreams (yeah, right), don't you want to show him/her that you care, that you are paying attention?

Alas, there does not appear to be a 12-step program for usage addicts, but while pondering what to do about my little weakness, I recalled that my baby brother, while working on his Ph.D. in math, once mentioned an "encumber" in a letter to me (yes, a real letter—it was eons ago), referring to the green vegetable, sometimes peeled, sometimes not, that you slice into salads or turn into raita to accompany your Indian feast. His spelling, if that's possible, has only devolved since (maybe that's why he finds numbers so elegant), but I still love him as much as I always have. So, channeling sibling tolerance, I began to leap over stray commas and words-run-into-periods and managed to go out with a cool downtown daddy-o "tommorow" who has "distain" for organized religion. And guess what? I even enjoined myself! Unfortunately, I won't be able to discuss the financial wizard who basically wanted to know whether I could squat his weight (160; I can) because his affliction would indeed be off topic.

CONVERSATIONS: HUMOR AND CULTURE

In sharing this anecdote about her online interaction with a potential date, Epstein includes her response to the man's photograph ("for all i know you've just put a family of four through a wood chipper!"), which she claims she meant as a joke. In explaining that joke, Epstein writes, "Did you not love '*Fargo*'?" Here, she is referring to a popular movie, *Fargo*, released in 1996, which includes a well-known scene showing a criminal disposing of his partner's body in a wood chipper. Obviously, you need to be familiar with the movie to understand the humor here, which might reveal something about the nature of humor. In a sense, such jokes require that we be part of larger conversations in our society that include movies, music, and other elements of popular culture. Allusions to movies like the one Epstein makes in this paragraph also reveal how movies and other elements of popular culture acquire certain kinds of meanings as they become part of our social interactions (including our humor).

GLOSSES: EWAN, MCGREGOR, AND GAWKER

Novelist Ian McEwan has written many award-winning novels, including *Atonement* (2001). Actor Ewan McGregor played the role of Obi-Wan Kenobi in the film *Star Wars Episode III: Revenge of the Sith* (2005). Gawker is a web site focused on media gossip and popular culture.

STRUNK AND WHITE, FOWLER, BERNSTEIN AND GARNER

Here, Epstein is referring to three well-known and respected books on writing style and grammar usage.

Understanding the Text

1. What is it about the incorrect use of language by some of the men in the online dating service to which Epstein subscribed that bothered her so much? Was it just that these men made errors in their writing, or it was something more? What do you think Epstein's emphasis on correct language in this case might suggest about relationships?

2. What does Epstein mean when she writes that she is "afflicted with an excess language-sensitivity gene" (see paragraph 4)? Do you think she's making a serious point here? Explain.

3. Why does Epstein believe that using correct language is important when communicating with someone in online dating services? Do you agree with her? Why or why not?

Exploring the Issues

1. Epstein writes in an almost conversational style, seeming to address her readers directly as if she were telling her story excitedly over lunch or a cup of coffee or sharing it online. She uses words, phrases, and constructions that seem more appropriate for informal writing or text messaging than for a column in a prestigious newspaper like the *New York Times*. Assess her writing style. How would you describe it? What kind of voice emerges from her writing? What elements of her writing contribute to her style? Do you think her style is appropriate for her subject? Explain. Do you find her writing style effective? Why or why not? What might your reaction to

her style reveal about you as a reader? Cite specific passages from the essay in your answer.

2. Epstein seems to poke fun at her own personality quirks, especially her obsession with language. In paragraph 4, for example, she writes, "I know what you're thinking: No wonder she's single, no wonder she got dumped, who would want to feel those eyes/ears of judgment upon his every utterance?" And she describes her failings in relationships as well. What picture of Epstein emerges from this essay? How does she present herself as a person? Do you think she intends for her readers to like her? Explain, citing specific passages from the essay to support your answer.

3. What point do you think Epstein is making about relationships in this essay? What does language have to do with romantic relationships, in her view? Do you think she's right? Why or why not?

Entering the Conversations

1. Write an essay about your own experiences with technology in your own relationships. For example, if you have used online dating services, you might write an essay about that experience. If you use social networking sites such as Facebook or MySpace, you might base your essay on those experiences. In your essay, try to draw conclusions about the role of technology in our relationships with one another.

2. Identify several references that Epstein makes to rules of usage and style. For example, in para-

graph 5 she writes that she has not "mastered the subtlety of who/whom, as if I never use 'media' in the singular or accidentally type 'their' when I mean 'there'." Refer to a handbook (such as *Fowlers*) or other appropriate source to look up these rules. Then write a brief guide for writers focused on what you consider to be the most important such rules that Epstein refers to in her essay.

3. Using the guide you created for Question 2, review a draft of your own writing for errors or problems related to those rules.

INFOTRAC

4. As the introduction to this essay indicates (see page 309), online dating has grown considerably in the past decade or so and is now an established part of American culture. Using InfoTrac, the Internet, and other appropriate sources, investigate online dating services. Look into the different kinds of online dating services, how people tend to use them, and how they have grown or changed in recent years. Try to find studies or analyses of these services to get a sense of what experts say about them. Then, write a report on the basis of your research. In your report, present what you learned about online dating services and draw conclusions about how they might influence social relationships.

5. On the basis of your research for Question 4, create a web site or other appropriate document that serves as a guide to online dating.

This essay might seem a surprising choice in a chapter of readings about relationships. Writer Anthony Doerr describes a photograph taken by the Hubble telescope, which orbits the earth like a satellite and is used by astronomers to explore the universe in a way that is not possible from the surface of the earth. Doerr believes that the

Window OF Possibility

photograph, which is called the Hubble Ultra Deep Field, is "the most incredible photograph ever taken." He explains why in this essay, and in doing so he addresses some age-old questions about our place in the universe. As he notes in his essay, the more we learn about the universe, the bigger it seems to become. And questions about our place in it seem to take on a different tone. But Doerr believes that contemplating the universe is an essential part of being human.

STRATEGIES: USING ANALOGY
Writers often use analogy to explain a complex concept or principle. Here, Doerr compares the Milky Way with a bucket of marbles to help us appreciate the enormous number of stars in the Milky Way. He uses the same strategy several times in this essay. Do these analogies help you understand the ideas he is conveying? You might consider whether his essay would be less effective without these analogies.

ANTHONY DOERR

We live on Earth. Earth is a clump of iron and magnesium and nickel, smeared with a thin layer of organic matter, and sleeved in vapor. It whirls along in a nearly circular orbit around a minor star we call the sun.

I know, the sun doesn't *seem* minor. The sun puts the energy in our salads, milkshakes, hamburgers, gas tanks, and oceans. It literally makes the world go round. And it's huge: The Earth is a chickpea and the sun is a beach ball. The sun comprises 99.9 percent of all the mass in the solar system. Which means Earth, Mars, Jupiter, Saturn, etc., all fit into that little 0.1 percent. But, truly, our sun is exceedingly minor. Almost incomprehensibly minor.

We call our galaxy the **MILKY WAY.** There are at least 100 billion stars in it and our sun is one of those. A hundred billion is a big number, and humans are not evolved to appreciate numbers like that, but here's a try: If you had a bucket with a thousand marbles in it, you would need to procure 999,999 more of those buckets to get a billion marbles. Then you'd have to repeat the process

By focusing our attention on a special photograph of the night sky, he is really encouraging us to focus on ourselves, to think about our relationship to those trillions of stars that astronomers look at through the Hubble telescope, and to think about our relationships to one another on this very small planet we inhabit. These are big questions that we may not often spend time contemplating, but Doerr believes there is value in doing so. His essay might persuade you of this value.

Anthony Doerr is the author of three collections of short fiction, for which he has won numerous prizes, including the prestigious O. Henry Prize, which he won three times. This essay appeared in Orion *magazine in 2007.* ◪

STRATEGIES: ORGANIZING AN ESSAY
In this paragraph, Doerr introduces what can be considered the main focus of his essay: the Hubble Ultra Deep Field photograph. But notice that he does so about halfway through the essay. Often, writing teachers advise students to establish their focus and introduce their main ideas in the beginning of an essay and then provide background or supporting information in the following paragraphs. That is a common way to organize an essay, but it isn't the only way, as Doerr's essay suggests. Consider why he might have decided to introduce the photograph so far into his essay rather than at the beginning. For example, he could have begun his essay with paragraph 12 and then followed that with the information in paragraphs 1–11. How might that have affected his essay? Would it have changed his main point in any way?

a hundred times to get as many marbles as there are stars in our galaxy.

That's a lot of marbles.

So. The Earth is massive enough to hold all of our cities and oceans and creatures in the sway of its gravity. And the sun is massive enough to hold the Earth in the sway of its gravity. But the sun itself is merely a mote in the sway of the gravity of the Milky Way, at the center of which is a vast, concentrated bar of stars, around which the sun swings (carrying along Earth, Mars, Jupiter, Saturn, etc.) every 230 million years or so. Our sun isn't anywhere near the center; it's way out on one of the galaxy's minor arms. We live beyond the suburbs of the Milky Way. We live in Nowheresville.

But still, we are in the Milky Way. And that's a big deal, right? The Milky Way is at least a major *galaxy*, right?

Not really. Spiral-shaped, toothpick-shaped, sombrero-shaped—in the visible universe, at any given moment, there are hundreds of thousands of millions of galaxies. Maybe as many as 125 billion. There very well may be more galaxies in the universe than there are stars in the Milky Way.

So. Let's say there are 100 billion stars in our galaxy. And let's say there are 100 billion galaxies in our universe. At any given moment, then, assuming ultra-massive and dwarf galaxies average each other out, there might be 10,000,000,000,000,000,000,000 stars in the universe. That's 1.0×10 to the twenty-second power. That's 10 sextillion.

Here's a way of looking at it: there are enough stars in the universe that if everybody on Earth were charged with naming his or her share, we'd each get to name a trillion and a half of them.

Even that number is still impossibly hard to comprehend—if you named a star every time your heart beat for your whole life, you'd have to live about 375 lifetimes to name your share.

Last year, a handful of astronomers met in London to vote on the top ten images taken by the Hubble Telescope in its sixteen years in operation. They chose some beauties: the Cat's Eye Nebula, the Sombrero Galaxy, the Hourglass Nebula. But conspicuously missing from their list was the **HUBBLE ULTRA DEEP FIELD IMAGE.** It is, I believe, the most incredible photograph ever taken.

In 2003, Hubble astronomers chose a random wedge of sky just below the constellation Orion and, during four hundred orbits of the Earth, over the course of several months, took a photograph with a million-second-long exposure. It was something like peering through an eight-foot soda straw with one big, superhuman eye at the same wedge of space for eleven straight nights.

What they found there was breathtaking: a shard of the early universe that contains a bewildering array of galaxies and pre-galactic lumps. Scrolling through it is eerily similar to peering at a drop of pond water through a microscope: one expects the galaxies to start squirming like paramecia. It bewilders and disorients; the dark patches swarm with questions. If you peered into just one of its black corners, took an Ultra Deep Field of the **ULTRA DEEP FIELD,** would you see as much all over again?

What the Ultra Deep Field image ultimately offers is a singular glimpse at ourselves. Like **COPERNICUS'S** *On the Revolutions of the Celestial Spheres,* it resets our understanding of who and what we are.

15 As of early April 2007, astronomers had found 204 planets outside our solar system. They seem to be everywhere we look. Chances are, many, many stars have planets or systems of planets swinging around them. What if *most* suns have solar systems? If our sun is one in 10 sextillion, could our Earth be one in 10 sextillion as well? Or the Earth might be one—just *one,* the only one, *the* one. Either way, the circumstances are mind-boggling.

The Hubble Ultra Deep Field is an infinitesimally slender core-sample drilled out of the universe. And yet inside it is enough vastness to do violence to a person's common sense. How can the window of possibility be so unfathomably large?

Take yourself out to a field some evening after everyone else is asleep. Listen to the migrant birds whisking past in the dark; listen to the creaking and settling of the world. Think about the teeming, microscopic worlds beneath your shoes—the continents of soil, the galaxies of bacteria. Then lift your face up.

The night sky is the coolest Advent calendar imaginable: it is composed of an infinite number of doors. Open one and find ten thousand galaxies hiding behind it, streaming away at hundreds of miles per second. Open another, and another. You gaze up into history; you stare into the limits of your own understanding. The past flies toward you at the speed of light. Why are you here? Why are the stars there? Is it even remotely possible that our one, tiny, eggshell world is the only one encrusted with life?

The Hubble Ultra Deep Field image should be in every classroom in the world. It should be on the president's desk. It should probably be in every church, too.

20 "To sense that behind anything that can be experienced," Einstein once said, "there is a something that our mind cannot grasp and whose beauty and sublimity reaches us only indirectly and as a feeble reflection, this is religiousness."

Whatever we believe in—God, children, nationhood—nothing can be more important than to take a moment every now and then and accept the invitation of the sky: to leave the confines of ourselves and fly off into the hugeness of the universe, to disappear into the inexplicable, the implacable, the reflection of that something our minds cannot grasp.

CONVERSATIONS: THE HUBBLE ULTRA DEEP FIELD IMAGE
This is the image that Doerr is referring to in his essay. When the essay was first published, this photograph accompanied it. You might consider whether the presence of the photograph changes Doerr's essay in any way. Would you read the essay differently if you could not see this photograph? Conversely, how does Doerr's essay influence the way you "read" this photograph? Think also about how a photograph like this one is part of our efforts to understand the nature of the universe and our relationship to it.

ESA/S. Beckwith (STScI)/HUDF Team/NASA

GLOSS: COPERNICUS
In 1539, Polish astronomer Nicholaus Copernicus (1473–1543) wrote *On the Revolutions of the Celestial Spheres,* which challenged the prevailing belief that the sun revolved around the earth. In place of that view, Copernicus proposed a "heliocentric" theory in which the sun was the center of our solar system. His ideas, which were extremely controversial at the time, eventually revolutionized astronomy and changed our understanding of the solar system and our place in it.

Understanding the Text

1. In what sense does Doerr describe the sun as "minor"? Why is that point important in this essay?

2. Why does Doerr describe the earth and our solar system as "Nowheresville"? What point is he making?

3. What exactly is the Hubble Ultra Deep Field image? Why is it so important to Doerr? Do you think his sense of its importance is justified? Explain.

4. Why does Doerr believe that the Hubble Ultra Deep Field photograph should be in every classroom and church in the world? What purpose would the photograph serve if it were in those many classrooms and churches, in Doerr's view? Do you agree with him? Why or why not?

Exploring the Issues

1. In the first half of his essay, Doerr includes many facts and statistics about stars, planets, galaxies, and the sun. What purpose do these facts and figures serve in this essay? How do they help Doerr make his main point? How effective do you think these facts and figures are in helping Doerr make that point? Explain.

2. In paragraph 14, Doerr writes, "What the Ultra Deep Field image ultimately offers is a singular glimpse at our-

selves." What do you think he means by that statement? In what sense can a photograph of space provide a "glimpse of ourselves"? What might such a statement suggest about how we know and learn? What might it suggest about the role of photography and other visual media in how we understand ourselves?

3. Doerr is a fiction writer, not a scientist, yet this essay is about an important scientific event (the creation of the Hubble Ultra Deep Field photograph) and includes extensive discussion of specialized information from astronomy. How credible do you find Doerr as the writer of an essay on a topic that is apparently a scientific one, even though he is not a scientist? Does it matter that he is not a scientist? Explain. If you find him credible, what do you think accounts for his credibility in this essay?

Entering the Conversations

1. Write an essay about an experience that revealed something important to you about your relationship to the universe.

2. Visit the web site of the Hubble telescope (http://hubblesite.org/) and other Internet sites related to the work done with the Hubble. Try to get a sense of how the

Hubble is used and what people think about it. Then write an essay in which you offer your own views about the role of the Hubble (and perhaps similar technologies) in our understanding of ourselves as human beings.

3. Write a letter to an official of your school encouraging the school to display the Hubble Ultra Deep Field photograph. In your letter, draw on Doerr's essay to support your position. Alternatively, if you disagree with Doerr's viewpoint, write a response to him explaining why.

4. In a group of classmates, discuss Doerr's suggestion that all classrooms and churches should include a copy of the Hubble Ultra Deep Field photograph. Is there general agreement that Doerr is right? If not, what are the points of disagreement? Try to determine what factors seem to influence your classmates' views about Doerr's suggestion and about our relationship to the universe. Then write an essay in which you offer your own views about how we think about our relationship to the universe.

5. Create a visual representation (for example, a photo essay, web site, or PowerPoint presentation) conveying your sense of the place of humans in the universe.

Extending the Conversations

1. Select two or more of the essays in this chapter and examine the way each writer addresses his or her intended audience. Look specifically at the writer's use of language, the organization of the essay, and the kinds of references and information the writer uses. Then write an analysis of the essays you have selected. In your analysis, use specific references to passages in the essays to illustrate your points and draw conclusions about effective strategies for addressing audience in writing.

2. Select several of the essays in this chapter that you think offer insight into the idea of relationships and write an essay in which you examine what those essays suggest about relationships.

3. Drawing on the essays in this chapter and any other relevant resources, create a pamphlet for a specific audience (such as students at your school or people at your workplace) in which you offer advice about relationships.

4. Norman Rockwell is well known for his paintings depicting American life. But he is sometimes criticized for depicting an idealized (and unrealistic) vision that excludes much of American society. Write an analysis of this image in which you discuss what it says about American family life. In your analysis, evaluate this image from a specific perspective. For example, you might take a feminist perspective. Or you might write in the context of the recent controversies about

same-sex marriages. What can be said about this painting from that perspective? Draw conclusions about the values reflected in this image based on the perspective you have adopted. Alternatively, create a visual representation (for example, a photo essay or a web site) of family life as a response to Rockwell's painting.

5. Find several magazine advertisements that have something to do with love—for example, advertisements for diamond engagement rings or for Mother's Day flowers. Examine these advertisements for the way they portray love and try to identify what they suggest about the nature of love. Focus especially on the way they use images to convey their messages. Then write an analysis of these advertisements, drawing conclusions about the way love is portrayed. Discuss what you think these advertisements reveal about popular attitudes regarding love. Alternatively, identify several television commercials that portray love in some

Norman Rockwell, *Family at Dinner Table*

way and write a similar analysis of these commercials.

6. Select an issue related to relationships that is addressed by the readings in this chapter (for example, same-sex marriage, parent–teen relationships) and search the Internet for sites that focus on that issue. Identify several such sites and then write an analysis of the sites, examining how they address the issue and how they portray themselves. For example, does a web site for an advocacy group try to convey an image of objectivity or authority about the issue it addresses? Draw conclusions about how the issue is portrayed on Internet sites and how ideas are conveyed through these sites. Alternatively, create your own web site for the issue you have identified. (Consult Chapter 2 about visual media.)

7. View several popular television talk shows that often focus their programs on relationships (for example, *The Oprah Winfrey Show* or *Dr. Phil*). What might these shows suggest about relationships in contemporary society? Write an essay in which you try to address such questions. In your essay, describe the shows you viewed and discuss what you think they suggest about attitudes regarding relationships. Alternatively, create a self-help guide (in the form of a pamphlet, a web site, or some other appropriate document) based on the advice about relationships that was presented in these shows.

8. Select one or more recent popular films that you think convey a powerful message about love and write an essay in which you discuss that message and how the film or films convey it.

EVEN BEFORE I GET OUT OF BED IN THE MORNING, I AM COMMUNICATING. I USUALLY ASK MY WIFE, CHERYL, IF SHE WANTS TO SHOWER FIRST. WHILE SHE'S IN THE SHOWER, I TURN ON THE RADIO. DURING THE NEXT HOUR, I WILL LISTEN TO NEWS REPORTS AS I MAKE BREAKFAST AND GET READY FOR THE DAY. DURING THAT HOUR, CHERYL AND I WILL TALK about our plans for the day, the menu for dinner, errands we have to run, items in the news. When my son gets up, he usually turns on the television to get the latest sports news, and sometimes I'll ask him to turn down the volume so I can hear the radio better. Later, after everyone has left for work or school, I'll read the local newspaper as I finish my coffee. Once I sit down at my desk to work, I'll check my e-mail and read and respond to various messages. I might also check a web site or two for more news updates or log onto the web-based discussion board that I have set up for one of my classes to read the mes-

> As my description of my typical morning suggests, we communicate almost constantly in many different ways.

sages that my students have posted. On some mornings, the phone will ring, and I'll talk to a family member or a colleague. Later, as I'm leaving home for campus, I may write a brief note and stick it on the refrigerator door to remind us of things we need to buy at the grocery store. On the way to campus, I read road signs or traffic lights, signal to other drivers when I want to turn, place a parking pass on my car windshield, and slow down to signal to pedestrians on campus that they can cross the road. And of course, there's much, much more. You probably do many of the same things that I just described.

As my description of my typical morning suggests, we communicate almost constantly in many different ways. Obviously, we talk to one another. But we also read and write in various media, including notes, newspapers and magazines, e-mail, signs, and text messaging. We listen to the radio and watch television. We talk on telephones. We "read" various kinds of images, from basic symbols like a red traffic light or a rest room sign to more sophisticated visual texts such as music videos or political advertisements. We use body language to let others know that we like or dislike them, that we're interested in what they're saying or doing, that we're uncertain or hesitant, or even that we are angry or threatening. My dog can tell by my facial expression whether or not she should approach me to be petted or stay where she is, and of course, we humans do the same kind of thing with facial expressions all the time. We send messages with our clothes: that we're conventional, hip, practical, conservative, alluring, even knowledgeable. If I am hiking in cold weather in the mountains, the clothes I choose will send a message to my hiking companions that I am prepared (or not) and that I know something about being in the mountains (or not). We might be communicating to others by the kind of car we drive. A gas–electric hybrid car like the Toyota Prius, for example, might be a statement about protecting the environment. In church or temple, we bow our heads, and at sporting events we raise our arms in the air. We fly our nation's flag from our porches, and we wear black to funerals. We drape an American flag over the casket of a military veteran, and we shoot rifles into the air at a veteran's burial. We yawn at meetings, and we kiss our loved ones good night. We never stop using an astonishing array of tools to communicate.

So it's no surprise that scholars, philosophers, scientists, linguists, and psychologists have long been trying to understand communication. More than 2,500 years ago, Aristotle wrote a famous treatise known as the *Rhetoric*, in which he explains the process of persuading an audience through speech (or writing). In a way, Aristotle's book, which is still read today, was one of the first textbooks on using language—similar in many respects to the textbook you're reading right now. Aristotle offered advice to speakers so that they could communicate ideas more effectively to their audiences—advice that is still followed today. In the centuries since then, countless others have tried to understand the complexities of communication. Philosophers have devoted their careers to studying human language, and many scientists have done the same. Neurophysiologists use state-of-the-art technologies such as CAT scans to map the human brain in their efforts to understand speech and visual communication. Scholars devise new theories such as semiotics (the study of signs), to explain communication. Linguists describe the thousands of different human languages in their quest to understand speech. Biologists document the many ways in which animals send messages to one another. Yet, even as we continue to communicate with one another about this amazing activity we call communication, we remain daunted by its complexity.

The readings in this chapter expose some of that complexity. Each of the three clusters focuses on some aspect of communication: the po-

litical nature of language, the power of literacy, and the potential for communication in nonverbal forms. But it wasn't easy to narrow the subject of communication to these three clusters. So, despite the variety of these readings, there's much more about communication that I wasn't able to include here. Keep that in mind as you read about the wonder, the power, the challenge,

> Yet, even as we continue to communicate with one another about this amazing activity we call communication, we remain daunted by its complexity.
>
> Keep that in mind as you read about the wonder, the power, the challenge, and the limits of the many ways we communicate with one another.

and the limits of the many ways we communicate with one another. I hope these essays help you appreciate the subtleties of various forms of communication, such as advertising or music, that affect you every day. I hope, too, that this chapter reinforces a message that I have been trying to send throughout this book: Writing is a wondrous form of communication whose power you can harness in your own life.

THE POLITICS OF LANGUAGE

WHEN I WAS A NEW GRADUATE STUDENT IN THE EARLY 1980S, I UNEXPECTEDLY GOT MY FIRST REAL LESSON IN THE POLITICS OF LANGUAGE. I WAS WALKING DOWN THE HALL TOWARD MY OFFICE ONE AFTERNOON, AND I PASSED THREE WOMEN WHO WERE ALSO NEW GRADUATE STUDENTS. I KNEW THEM WELL FROM CLASSES WE WERE TAKING TOGETHER. AS I PASSED THEM, I SAID, "HI, GIRLS." ALL THREE WOMEN LOOKED

surprised, and one said indignantly, "Girls?!" At the time, I didn't quite understand either their surprise or their indignation. I had grown up in a small, working-class town where women were regularly referred to as "girls." The women who worked in my grandmother's small catering business, all of whom were older than fifty, were known to everyone as "the girls." None of them ever took offense at the term. So what was wrong with calling my three friends, who were in their twenties, "girls"?

To answer that question is to begin to examine the many ways in which even the most ordinary language is political. Words can carry powerful messages that go well beyond dictionary definitions. And those political messages relate to cultural and historical circumstances. In other words, the political meaning of a word depends on context.

My friends helped teach me that lesson by making me aware that the word *girl* is not a neutral term for women, as I had used it. Rather, it is a word that for many people, including my three friends, reflects a sexist view of women. By that time in the early 1980s, the women's movement had helped make people sensitive to the sexism in common expressions, which often emphasize male over female or reflect a negative or even degrading view of women. For example, when I was growing up, it was not only common to refer to all women as girls, but it was also common to hear women referred to as "babes," "foxes," and similar terms that we now consider insulting. The women's movement helped us see that those terms send powerful messages about the status of women—messages that reduce women to physical objects and suggest that the value of a woman is a function of her physical attractiveness to men. Although *girl* didn't necessarily carry such an obviously degrading

message in the early 1980s, it could easily be understood as derogatory when it was used to refer to women because it implied the immaturity of a young girl rather than the maturity of an adult.

But the politics of language does not refer only to the meaning of words. The decision to speak in a certain language or to use a certain dialect can also send powerful messages. During the last few U.S. presidential elections, for example, the candidates sometimes spoke in Spanish to audiences in California, Texas, and Florida, where Spanish-speaking people make up a significant percentage of the population. A candidate's use of Spanish in public speeches is intended to send a message to Spanish-speaking citizens that they matter. It can also send less positive messages, such as the suggestion that citizens are being pandered to during an election campaign.

The writers whose essays are included in this cluster will help you explore these obvious and not-so-obvious ways in which language can be political. They provide examples of some of the ways in which we use language to make statements, political and otherwise. Two of them, Amy Tan and Gloria Anzaldúa, share their experiences as bilingual women whose ways of using their different languages reveal how language can be a tool for control as well as a means of empowerment. Deborah Tannen looks at important gender differences in our uses of language. And Gary Sloan focuses our attention on how politicians try to use language for their own purposes. All these writers are concerned with how words can convey different meanings and reflect various political viewpoints. The lessons they can teach may serve you well in a world that is so profoundly shaped by the politics of language.

All of Amy Tan's novels have something to do with China, where her mother was born, and in each one, the Chinese language and cultural heritage are central to the story. The following essay may help explain why. In this essay, Tan (b. 1952) describes her struggles as a student whose mother's "broken" English wasn't spoken in schools and often caused problems

Mother Tongue

for both Tan and her mother. It quickly becomes clear that despite the difficulties she experienced with her mother, Tan sees something special in her mother's language. It also becomes clear that Tan appreciates the complexities of the different "Englishes" that she learned. She understands, for example, that people can suffer discrimination because they speak in a dialect that is not Standard English. And she knows that a person's language can send different messages to different people, some of which arise from bias and prejudice. Tan's experiences can help us understand why the charged debates about Standard English and bilingual education can have such important consequences for individuals. In a sense, her essay is a vivid personal portrayal of the politics of language. But this essay is also a statement of her own love affair with her language heritage— and with language in general.

AMY TAN

I am not a scholar of English or literature. I cannot give you much more than personal opinions on the English language and its variations in this country or others.

I am a writer. And by that definition, I am someone who has always loved language. I am fascinated by language in daily life. I spend a great deal of my time thinking about the power of language—the way it can evoke an emotion, a visual image, a complex idea, or a simple truth. Language is the tool of my trade. And I use them all—all the Englishes I grew up with.

Recently, I was made keenly aware of the different Englishes I do use. I was giving a talk to a large group of people, the same talk I had already given to half a dozen other groups. The nature of the talk was about my writing, my life, and my book, *The Joy Luck Club*. The talk was going along well enough, until I remembered one major difference that made the whole talk sound wrong. My mother was in the room. And it was perhaps the first time she had heard me give a lengthy speech, using the kind of English I have never used with her. I was saying things like, "The intersection of memory upon imagination"

Award-winning writer Amy Tan is the author of four novels, including The Joy Luck Club *(1989), which was a* New York Times *bestseller that was translated into twenty-five languages and made into a movie. The following essay first appeared in the* Threepenny Review *in 1990.* ◻

and "There is an aspect of my fiction that relates to thus-and-thus"—a speech filled with carefully wrought grammatical phrases, burdened, it suddenly seemed to me, with nominalized forms, past perfect tenses, conditional phrases, all the forms of standard English that I had learned in school and through books, the forms of English I did not use at home with my mother.

Just last week, I was walking down the street with my mother, and I again found myself conscious of the English I was using, the English I do use with her. We were talking about the price of new and used furniture and I heard myself saying this: "Not waste money that way." My husband was with us as well, and he didn't notice any switch in my English. And then I realized why. It's because over the twenty years we've been together I've often used that same kind of English with him, and sometimes he even uses it with me. It has become our language of intimacy, a different sort of English that relates to family talk, the language I grew up with.

5　　So you'll have some idea of what this family talk I heard sounds like, I'll quote what my mother said during a recent conversation which I videotaped and then transcribed. During this conversation, my mother was talking about a political gangster in Shanghai who had the same last name as her family's, Du, and how the gangster in his early years wanted to be adopted by her family, which was rich by comparison. Later, the gangster became more powerful, far richer than my mother's family, and one day showed up at my mother's wedding to pay his respects. Here's what she said in part:

"Du Yusong having business like fruit stand. Like off the street kind. He is Du like Du Zong—but not Tsung-ming Island people. The local people call putong, the river east side, he belong to that side local people. That man want to ask Du Zong father take him in like become own family. Du Zong father wasn't look down on him, but didn't take seriously, until that man big like become a mafia. Now important person, very hard to inviting him. Chinese way, came only to show respect, don't stay for dinner. Respect for making big celebration, he shows up. Mean give lots of respect. Chinese custom. Chinese social life that way. If too important won't have to stay too long. He come to my wedding. I didn't see, I heard it. I gone to boy's side, they have YMCA dinner. Chinese age I was nineteen."

You should know that my mother's expressive command of English belies how much she actually understands. She reads the *Forbes* report, listens to *Wall Street Week*, converses daily with her stockbroker, reads all of Shirley MacLaine's books with ease—all kinds of things I can't begin to understand. Yet some of my friends tell me they understand 50 percent of what my mother says. Some say they understand 80 to 90 percent. Some say they understand none of it, as if she were speaking pure Chinese. But to me, my mother's English is perfectly clear, perfectly natural. It's my mother tongue. Her language, as I

STRATEGIES: USING DIALECT
In paragraph 6, Tan quotes her mother, whose first language is Chinese, to give us an example of what Tan calls her "family talk." Fiction writers often use dialects like this to help convey a sense of their characters. Such uses of dialect are less common in nonfiction writing, in part because writers often try to avoid embarrassing the people they are quoting, who may feel they sound unintelligent by speaking in dialect. (Tan expresses this view in par. 8 and 9.) In fact, many newspapers and magazines edit quotations so that they do not contain dialects. Consider what messages Tan is sending about dialects by quoting her mother as she does here.

hear it, is vivid, direct, full of observation and imagery. That was the language that helped shape the way I saw things, expressed things, made sense of the world.

* * *

Lately, I've been giving more thought to the kind of English my mother speaks. Like others, I have described it to people as "broken" or "fractured" English. But I wince when I say that. It has always bothered me that I can think of no way to describe it other than "broken," as if it were damaged and needed to be fixed, as if it lacked a certain wholeness and soundness. I've heard other terms used, "limited English," for example. But they seem just as bad, as if everything is limited, including people's perceptions of the limited English speaker.

I know this for a fact, because when I was growing up, my mother's "limited" English limited *my* perception of her. I was ashamed of her English. I believed that her English reflected the quality of what she had to say. That is, because she expressed them imperfectly her thoughts were imperfect. And I had plenty of empirical evidence to support me: the fact that people in department stores, at banks, and at restaurants did not take her seriously, did not give her good service, pretended not to understand her, or even acted as if they did not hear her.

My mother has long realized the limitations of her English as well. When I was fifteen, she used to have me call people on the phone to pretend I was she. In this guise, I was forced to ask for information or even to complain and yell at people who had been rude to her. One time it was a call to her stockbroker in New York. She had cashed out her small portfolio and it just happened we were going to go to New York the next week, our very first trip outside California. I had to get on the phone and say in an adolescent voice that was not very convincing, "This is Mrs. Tan." 10

And my mother was standing in the back whispering loudly, "Why he don't send me check, already two weeks late. So mad he lie to me, losing me money."

And then I said in perfect English, "Yes, I'm getting rather concerned. You had agreed to send the check two weeks ago, but it hasn't arrived."

Then she began to talk more loudly. "What he want, I come to New York tell him front of his boss, you cheating me?" And I was trying to calm her down, make her be quiet, while telling the stockbroker, "I can't tolerate any more excuses. If I don't receive the check immediately, I am going to have to speak to your manager when I'm in New York next week." And sure enough, the following week there we were in front of this astonished stockbroker, and I was sitting there redfaced and quiet, and my mother, the real Mrs. Tan, was shouting at his boss in her impeccable broken English.

CONVERSATIONS: SECOND-LANGUAGE LEARNERS

Like many second-language learners, Tan sometimes struggled with language in school, as she describes in paragraph 15. In the past few decades, educators have paid much more attention to the challenges facing students whose first language is other than English or who live in households where other languages are spoken. Bilingual education programs, in which students are taught in their first language rather than in English, are intended to address the needs of such students, but they have long been controversial and have recently been abandoned by many states. Tan's description in this paragraph provides a vivid example of some of the difficulties facing second-language learners.

We used a similar routine just five days ago, for a situation that was far less humorous. My mother had gone to the hospital for an appointment, to find out about a benign brain tumor a CAT scan had revealed a month ago. She said she had spoken very good English, her best English, no mistakes. Still, she said, the hospital did not apologize when they said they had lost the CAT scan and she had come for nothing. She said they did not seem to have any sympathy when she told them she was anxious to know the exact diagnosis, since her husband and son had both died of brain tumors. She said they would not give her any more information until the next time and she would have to make another appointment for that. So she said she would not leave until the doctor called her daughter. She wouldn't budge. And when the doctor finally called her daughter, me, who spoke in perfect English—lo and behold—we had assurances the CAT scan would be found, promises that a conference call on Monday would be held, and apologies for any suffering my mother had gone through for a most regrettable mistake.

15   I think my mother's English almost had an effect on limiting my possibilities in life as well. Sociologists and linguists probably will tell you that a person's developing language skills are more influenced by peers. But I do think that the language spoken in the family, especially in immigrant families which are more insular, plays a large role in shaping the language of the child. And I believe that it affected my results on achievement tests, IQ tests, and the SAT. While my English skills were never judged as poor, compared to math, English could not be considered my strong suit. In grade school I did moderately well, getting perhaps B's, sometimes B-pluses, in English and scoring perhaps in the sixtieth or seventieth percentile on achievement tests. But those scores were not good enough to override the opinion that my true abilities lay in math and science, because in those areas I achieved A's and scored in the ninetieth percentile or higher.

CONVERSATIONS: TESTING ENGLISH

Few educational issues have been more controversial than standardized testing, and in this section of her essay, Tan provides a glimpse into that controversy. The examples of test items that Tan includes in these two paragraphs (16 and 17) suggest some of the complexities of standardized testing that critics have often cited. When this essay was first published in 1990, standardized testing was becoming more widespread as many states tried to address concerns about low standards in public education. In the late 1990s and the first few years of the twenty-first century, the trend accelerated as federal education policy encouraged states to require standardized testing in core subjects, including English. Consider what Tan's experiences with tests might suggest about the challenges of testing students' language knowledge and skill.

This was understandable. Math is precise; there is only one correct answer. Whereas, for me at least, the answers on English tests were always a judgment call, a matter of opinion and personal experience. Those tests were constructed around items like fill-in-the-blank sentence completion, such as, "Even though Tom was _____, Mary thought he was _____." And the correct answer always seemed to be the most bland combinations of thoughts, for example "Even though Tom was shy, Mary thought he was charming," with the grammatical structure "even though" limiting the correct answer to some sort of semantic opposites, so you wouldn't get answers like, "Even though Tom was foolish, Mary thought he was ridiculous." Well, according to my mother, there were very few limitations as to what Tom could have been and what Mary might have thought of him. So I never did well on tests like that.

The same was true with word analogies, pairs of words in which you were supposed to find some sort of logical, semantic relationship—for example, "*Sunset* is to *nightfall* as _____ is to _____." And here you would be presented with a list of four possible pairs, one of which showed the same kind of relationship: *red* is to *spotlight, bus* is to *arrival, chills* is to *fever, yawn* is to *boring*. Well, I could never think that way. I knew what the tests were asking, but I could not block out of my mind the images already created by the first pair, "*sunset* is to *nightfall*"—and I would see a burst of colors against a darkening sky, the moon rising, the lowering of a curtain of stars. And all the other pairs of words—red, bus, spotlight, boring—just threw up a mass of confusing images, making it impossible for me to sort out something as logical as saying: "A sunset precedes nightfall" is the same as "a chill precedes a fever." The only way I would have gotten that answer right would have been to imagine an associative situation, for example, my being disobedient and staying out past sunset, catching a chill at night, which turns into feverish pneumonia as punishment, which indeed did happen to me.

*   *   *

I have been thinking about all this lately, about my mother's English, about achievement tests. Because lately I've been asked, as a writer, why there are not more Asian Americans represented in American literature. Why are there few Asian Americans enrolled in creative writing programs? Why do so many Chinese students go into engineering? Well, these are broad sociological questions I can't begin to answer. But I have noticed in surveys—in fact, just last week—that Asian students, as a whole, always do significantly better on math achievement tests than in English. And this makes me think that there are other Asian American students whose English spoken in the home might also be described as "broken" or "limited." And perhaps they also have teachers who are steering them away from writing and into math and science, which is what happened to me.

Fortunately, I happen to be rebellious in nature and enjoy the challenge of disproving assumptions made about me. I became an English major my first year in college, after being enrolled as pre-med. I started writing nonfiction as a free-lancer the week after I was told by my former boss that writing was my worst skill and I should hone my talents toward account management.

20   But it wasn't until 1985 that I finally began to write fiction. And at first I wrote using what I thought to be wittily crafted sentences, sentences that would finally prove I had mastery over the English language. Here's an example from the first draft of a story that later made its way into *The Joy Luck Club,* but without this line: "That was my mental quandary in its nascent state." A terrible line, which I can barely pronounce.

Fortunately, for reasons I won't get into today, I later decided I should envision a reader for the stories I would write. And the reader I decided upon was my mother, because these were stories about mothers. So with this reader in mind—and in fact she did read my early drafts—I began to write stories using all the Englishes I grew up with: the English I spoke to my mother, which for lack of a better term might be described as "simple"; the English she used with me, which for lack of a better term might be described as "broken"; my translation of her Chinese, which could certainly be described as "watered down"; and what I imagined to be her translation of her Chinese if she could speak in perfect English, her internal language, and for that I sought to preserve the essence, but neither an English nor a Chinese structure. I wanted to capture what language ability tests can never reveal: her intent, her passion, her imagery, the rhythms of her speech, and the nature of her thoughts.

Apart from what any critic had to say about my writing, I knew I had succeeded where it counted when my mother finished reading my book and gave me her verdict: "So easy to read."

Understanding the Text

1. What are "all the Englishes" that Tan grew up with? What exactly does Tan mean by Englishes? What differences are there among the different Englishes she uses? Why are these differences important to her?

2. Tan shares several anecdotes about her mother's use of "broken" or "limited" English in dealing with bankers, doctors, and other professional people. What do these anecdotes reveal about what Tan calls the "limitations" of her mother's English? Why are

these limitations important to Tan? What do they suggest about our uses of language? What do they suggest about our attitudes toward language differences?

3. Why is the fact that Asian American students seem to do better in math and science than in other school subjects important to Tan? What does it suggest to her about the role of language in the learning of such students? Do you think she is right? Why or why not?

4. Why does Tan believe that her mother is the best reader for her stories and novels?

What might this suggest about a writer's audience?

Exploring the Issues

1. In the first two paragraphs, Tan identifies herself as "someone who has always loved language," and not as "a scholar of English or literature." Why do you think Tan begins her essay in this way? How did this beginning affect your view of Tan as the author of this essay? Did it give her more or less credibility, in your view? Explain.

2. In paragraph 3, Tan describes a talk she was giving about her novel *The Joy Luck*

Club, and she describes the language she was using in that talk as the "standard English that I had learned in school and through books." Do you think Tan is criticizing "school English" in her essay? If so, do you think her criticism is valid? Explain, citing specific passages from the text and drawing on your own experience with English to support your answer.

3. Examine Tan's descriptions of her mother. What kind of person is Tan's mother? What characteristics does Tan focus on in her descriptions of her mother? Why do you think Tan emphasizes these characteristics? How might her descriptions of her mother contribute to her main point in this essay?

4. In paragraph 20, Tan shares the following sentence from a draft of one of her stories: "That was my mental quandary in its nascent state." Tan calls this sentence a "terrible line." What do you think she finds terrible about this sentence? Do you agree with her? Why or why not? What might Tan's opinion of this sentence suggest about her views about writing style?

Entering the Conversations

1. Write an essay for an audience of your classmates describing an experience in which your use of language was important. The experience can be a time when your use of language was problematic or troubling, a time when your language put you at some kind of advantage or disadvantage, or a time when language played a central role in some event. Describe the experience in a way that helps your readers understand what you might have learned about language through that experience.

2. In a group of classmates, share the essay you wrote for Question 1. Discuss what the experiences you and your classmates described might suggest about language. What was political about the way language was used in your experiences? What conclusions can you draw from your discussion?

INFOTRAC

3. Using InfoTrac College Edition and any other relevant resources, investigate the challenges facing second-language learners in schools today and the programs that educators are developing to address those challenges. Find out what educators have learned about how best to help second-language learners. Write a report on the basis of your research.

4. Try to find someone who is a second-language learner.

(See *Conversations: Second Language-Learners* on page 326.) Interview this person about his or her experiences with language in school as well as outside school. How has that language affected schoolwork or social activities that are done in English? What problems or difficulties has this person experienced? Then write an essay in which you describe the person you interviewed and his or her experiences as a second language-learner. Draw conclusions about the politics of language from your interview.

5. Write an essay in which you present your position on the question of requiring only English in schools, workplaces, government meetings, and elsewhere. (The movement to adopt such requirements is known as the English Only movement. You may want to learn more about it by visiting the web sites of groups that support such requirements.) Explain why you think English should be (or should not be) the exclusive language used in certain circumstances. What are the advantages of requiring (or not requiring) English only? What problems do you see with having different languages in school or the workplace? Try to address such questions in your essay.

Writer and linguist Deborah Tannen (b. 1945) *is perhaps best known for her 1990 book* You Just Don't Understand: Women and Men in Conversation, *which was on the New York Times bestseller list for a remarkable four years. In that book, which some critics described as revolutionizing the way we understand communication between*

Sex, Lies AND Conversation

men and women, Tannen examines the central role that gender plays in communication. Her work helped popularize the idea of sexual politics in the 1990s and emphasized the differences in the way men and women communicate. The following article, which first appeared in the Washington Post *in 1990, is a shorter version of the analysis that Tannen developed in* You Just Don't Understand. *In this article, Tannen describes the differences in the way men and women communicate and she explains how those differences contribute to problems in male–female relationships. Such problems are often the focus of jokes and popular sitcoms, but Tannen helps us see that the consequences of communication problems in relationships are anything but funny. She also helps us see that the politics of language can play out in the most ordinary interactions between friends and couples, and she reminds us that language, one*

DEBORAH TANNEN

I was addressing a small gathering in a suburban Virginia living room—a women's group that had invited men to join them. Throughout the evening, one man had been particularly talkative, frequently offering ideas and anecdotes, while his wife sat silently beside him on the couch. Toward the end of the evening, I commented that women frequently complain that their husbands don't talk to them. This man quickly concurred. He gestured toward his wife and said, "She's the talker in our family." The room burst into laughter; the man looked puzzled and hurt. "It's true," he explained. "When I come home from work I have nothing to say. If she didn't keep the conversation going, we'd spend the whole evening in silence."

This episode crystallizes the irony that although American men tend to talk more than women in public situations, they often talk less at home. And this pattern is wreaking havoc with marriage.

The pattern was observed by political scientist Andrew Hacker in the late '70s. Sociologist Catherine Kohler Riessman reports in her book *Divorce Talk* that most of the women she interviewed—but only a few of the men—gave lack of communication as the reason for their divorces. Given the current divorce rate of nearly 50 percent, that amounts to millions of cases in the United States every year—a virtual epidemic of failed conversation.

In my own research, complaints from women about their husbands most often focused not on tangible inequities such as having given up the chance for a career to accompany a husband to his, or doing far more than their share of daily life-support work like cleaning, cooking, social arrangements and errands. Instead, they focused on communication: "He doesn't listen to me," "He doesn't talk to me." I found, as Hacker observed years before, that most wives want their husbands to be, first and foremost, conversational partners, but few husbands share this expectation of their wives.

5   In short, the image that best represents the current crisis is the **STEREOTYPICAL CARTOON SCENE** of a man sitting at the breakfast table with a newspaper held up in front of his face, while a woman glares at the back of it, wanting to talk.

LINGUISTIC BATTLE OF THE SEXES

How can women and men have such different impressions of communication in marriage? Why the widespread imbalance in their interests and expectations?

In the April, 1990 issue of *American Psychologist,* Stanford University's **ELEANOR MACCOBY REPORTS THE RESULTS OF HER OWN AND OTHERS' RESEARCH** showing that children's development is most influenced by the social structure of peer interactions. Boys and girls tend to play with children of their own gender, and their sex-separate groups have different organizational structures and interactive norms.

I believe these systematic differences in childhood socialization make talk between women and men like **CROSS-CULTURAL COMMUNICATION,** heir to all the attraction and pitfalls of that enticing but difficult enterprise. My research on men's and women's conversations uncovered patterns similar to those described for children's groups.

For women, as for girls, intimacy is the fabric of relationships, and talk is the thread from which it is woven. Little girls create and maintain friendships by exchanging secrets; similarly, women regard conversation as the cornerstone of friendship. So a woman expects her husband to be a new and improved version of a best friend. What is important is not the individual subjects that are discussed but the sense of closeness, of a life shared, that emerges when people tell their thoughts, feelings, and impressions.

10   Bonds between boys can be as intense as girls', but they are based less on talking, more on doing

of the most complex aspects of human life, is further complicated by gender.

A professor of linguistics at Georgetown University, Deborah Tannen is the author of nineteen books, including books about communication for popular audiences, such as The Argument Culture: Stopping America's War of Words *(1999) and* I Only Say This Because I Love You: Talking to Your Parents, Partner, Sibs, and Kids When You're All Adults *(2002), as well as scholarly works focusing on communication, such as* Gender and Discourse *(1994).* ▼

STRATEGIES: USING RESEARCH TO SUPPORT A POINT
Notice Tannen's reference in paragraph 7 to Eleanor Maccoby's research on gender differences in children's social interactions. Tannen uses this reference to help build her case for recognizing the importance of gender differences in adult communication. She makes note of the fact that Maccoby is a researcher at Stanford University, one of the most prestigious American universities. Consider how this reference helps Tannen not only support her point about gender differences but also establish her own credibility as an authority on gender and communication.

GLOSS: CROSS-CULTURAL COMMUNICATION
The term *cross-cultural communication* refers to communication between people of different cultures. In paragraph 8, Tannen applies the term to communication between people of different genders within the same culture. She will then use the term in this new sense throughout her article, especially in her conclusion. This is an example of how terms can acquire different meanings as people use them in new ways.

CONVERSATIONS: CARTOONS AND SOCIAL PROBLEMS
Tannen ends the opening section of this article (par. 5) with a reference to a "stereotypical cartoon scene" such as the one in this cartoon. Tannen's reference to cartoons in this instance suggests the role that cartoons can play in communicating important social and cultural attitudes and trends. The fact that Tannen, an accomplished scholar of linguistics, would make such a reference also suggests the importance of cartoons as a means of communication.

"If I were a car, you could find the words."

things together. Since they don't assume talk is the cement that binds a relationship, men don't know what kind of talk women want, and they don't miss it when it isn't there.

Boys' groups are larger, more inclusive, and more hierarchical, so boys must struggle to avoid the subordinate position in the group. This may play a role in women's complaints that men don't listen to them. Some men really don't like to listen, because being the listener makes them feel one-down, like a child listening to adults or an employee to a boss.

But often when women tell men, "You aren't listening," and the men protest, "I am," the men are right. The impression of not listening results from misalignments in the mechanics of conversation. The misalignment begins as soon as a man and a woman take physical positions. This became clear when I studied videotapes made by psychologist Bruce Dorval of children and adults talking to their same-sex best friends. I found that at every age, the girls and women faced each other directly, their eyes anchored on each other's faces. At every age, the boys and men sat at angles to each other and looked elsewhere in the room, periodically glancing at each other. They were obviously attuned to each other, often mirroring each other's movements. But the tendency of men to face away can give women the impression they aren't listening even when they are. A young woman in college was frustrated: Whenever she told her boyfriend she wanted to talk to him, he would lie down on the floor, close his eyes, and put his arm over his face. This signaled to her, "He's taking a nap." But he insisted he was listening extra hard. Normally, he looks around the room, so he is easily distracted. Lying down and covering his eyes helped him concentrate on what she was saying.

Analogous to the physical alignment that women and men take in conversation is their topical alignment. The girls in my study tended to talk at length about one topic, but the boys tended to jump from topic to topic. The second-grade girls exchanged stories about people they knew. The second-grade boys teased, told jokes, noticed things in the room and talked about finding games to play. The sixth-grade girls talked about problems with a mutual friend. The sixth grade boys talked about 55 different topics, none of which extended over more than a few turns.

LISTENING TO BODY LANGUAGE

Switching topics is another habit that gives women the impression men aren't listening, especially if they switch to a topic about themselves. But the evidence of the 10th-grade boys in my study indicates otherwise. The 10th-grade boys sprawled across their chairs with bodies parallel and eyes straight ahead, rarely looking at each other. They looked as if they were riding in a car, staring out the windshield. But they were talking about their feelings. One boy was upset because a girl had told him he had a drinking problem, and the other was feeling alienated from all his friends.

15   Now, when a girl told a friend about a problem, the friend responded by asking probing questions and expressing agreement and understanding. But the boys dismissed each other's problems. Todd assured Richard that his drinking was "no big problem" because "sometimes you're funny when you're off your butt." And when Todd said he felt left out, Richard responded, "Why should you? You know more people than me."

Women perceive such responses as belittling and unsupportive. But the boys seemed satisfied with them. Whereas women reassure each other by implying, "You shouldn't feel bad because I've had similar experiences," men do so by implying, "You shouldn't feel bad because your problems aren't so bad."

There are even simpler reasons for women's impression that men don't listen. Linguist Lynette Hirschman found that women make more listener-noise, such as "mhm," "uhuh," and "yeah," to show "I'm with you." Men, she found, more often give silent attention. Women who expect a stream of listener noise interpret silent attention as no attention at all.

Women's conversational habits are as frustrating to men as men's are to women. Men who expect silent attention interpret a stream of listener noise as overreaction or impatience. Also, when women talk to each other in a close, comfortable setting, they often overlap, finish each other's sentences and anticipate what the other is about to say. This practice, which I call "participatory listenership," is often perceived by men as interruption, intrusion and lack of attention.

A parallel difference caused a man to complain about his wife, "She just wants to talk about her own point of view. If I show her another view, she gets mad at me." When most women talk to each other, they assume a conversationalist's job is to express agreement and support. But many men see their conversational duty as pointing out the other side of an argument. This is heard as disloyalty by women, and refusal to offer the requisite support. It is not that women don't want to see

CONVERSATIONS: BODY LANGUAGE
This image from a popular advertising campaign for the Apple iPod music player might be seen as an example of how body language can communicate feelings or thoughts. The exuberance and joy suggested by the dancing silhouette body in this advertisement would be familiar to most consumers. In paragraphs 12 and 13, Tannen is talking about more subtle forms of body language that send often complex messages in various social situations. Consider how we learn to "read" body language, like dancing, and how that learning is part of communication between men and women.

© The Advertising Archives

other points of view, but that they prefer them phrased as suggestions and inquiries rather than as direct challenges.

20   In his book *Fighting for Life*, Walter Ong points out that men use "agonistic" or warlike, oppositional formats to do almost anything; thus discussion becomes debate, and conversation a competitive sport. In contrast, women see conversation as a ritual means of establishing rapport. If Jane tells a problem and June says she has a similar one, they walk away feeling closer to each other. But this attempt at establishing rapport can backfire when used with men. Men take too literally women's ritual "troubles talk," just as women mistake men's ritual challenges for real attack.

THE SOUNDS OF SILENCE

These differences begin to clarify why women and men have such different expectations about communication in marriage. For women, talk creates intimacy. Marriage is an orgy of closeness: you can tell your feelings and thoughts, and still be loved. Their greatest fear is being pushed away. But men live in a hierarchical world, where talk maintains independence and status. They are on guard to protect themselves from being put down and pushed around. This explains the paradox of the talkative man who said of his silent wife, "She's the talker." In the public setting of a guest lecture, he felt challenged to show his intelligence and display his understanding of the lecture. But at home, where he has nothing to prove and no one to defend against, he is free to remain silent. For his wife, being home means she is free from the worry that something she says might offend someone, or spark disagreement, or appear to be showing off; at home she is free to talk.

The communication problems that endanger marriage can't be fixed by mechanical engineering. They require a new conceptual framework about the role of talk in human relationships. Many of the psychological explanations that have become second nature may not be helpful, because they tend to blame either women (for not being assertive enough) or men (for not being in touch with their feelings). A SOCIOLINGUISTIC APPROACH by which male-female conversation is seen as cross-cultural communication allows us to understand the problem and forge solutions without blaming either party.

Once the problem is understood, improvement comes naturally, as it did to the young woman and her boyfriend who seemed to go to sleep when she wanted to talk. Previously, she had accused him of not listening, and he had refused to change his behavior, since that would be admitting fault. But then she learned about and explained to him the differences in women's and men's habitual ways of aligning themselves in conversation. The next time she told him she wanted to talk, he began, as usual, by lying down and covering his eyes. When the familiar negative reaction bubbled up, she reassured herself that he really was listening. But then he sat up and looked at her. Thrilled,

---

CONVERSATIONS: THE DIVORCE RATE
According to the U.S. Census Bureau, about 50 percent of all marriages in the United States will end in divorce. There is some disagreement about that figure. Some experts prefer to use the figure from the National Center for Health Statistics for divorces per capita, which was 0.40 percent in 2002. In other words, for every 1,000 people in the United States, there are four divorces. This divorce rate has been at least 0.40 percent since 1972; it has been declining slightly since 1981. Consider how Tannen's essay might influence our understanding of divorce.

CONVERSATIONS: SOCIOLINGUISTIC APPROACH
In discussing communication problems in marriages, Tannen advocates a "sociolinguistic approach," which refers to a theoretical perspective on language that emphasizes social and cultural context in communication, rather than understanding language exclusively as a psychological or physiological matter. In fact, Tannen's mention earlier in this paragraph (par. 22) of "psychological explanations" might be seen as a subtle argument in favor of a sociolinguistic instead of a psychological approach to explain communication difficulties between men and women. This is an example of the way that scholars carry on professional conversations about important issues in their academic fields.

she asked why. He said, "You like me to look at you when we talk, so I'll try to do it." Once he saw their differences as cross-cultural rather than right and wrong, he independently altered his behavior.

Women who feel abandoned and deprived when their husbands won't listen to or report daily news may be happy to discover their husbands trying to adapt once they understand the place of small talk in women's relationships. But if their husbands don't adapt, the women may still be comforted that for men, this is not a failure of intimacy. Accepting the difference, the wives may look to their friends or family for that kind of talk. And husbands who can't provide it shouldn't feel their wives have made unreasonable demands. Some couples will still decide to divorce, but at least their decisions will be based on realistic expectations.

In these times of resurgent ethnic conflicts, the world desperately   25
needs cross-cultural understanding. Like charity, successful cross-cultural communication should begin at home.

Understanding the Text

1. Why are differences in the ways men and women communicate important, according to Tannen? What are the larger implications of these differences?

2. Examine the major differences in the ways men and women communicate with each other as Tannen describes them in this essay. What do you think they suggest about gender roles in contemporary Western society? Do you think Tannen is suggesting that we reexamine or question these gender roles? Explain, citing specific passages to support your answer.

3. How do "misalignments in the mechanics of conversation" affect the way men and women talk to each other, according to Tannen? How does she account for these misalignments? Do you think she is right, based on your own experiences? Explain.

4. In Tannen's view, how do the main differences in the way men and women communicate contribute to marriage difficulties? How can these problems be remedied, according to Tannen? What do you think her discussion of these problems suggests about language? About gender?

Exploring the Issues

1. In a sense, Tannen's solution to the communication problems between men and women comes down to understanding the differences in how men and women communicate. How convincing do you find this solution? Based on your own experiences, do you think this is a feasible solution? Why or why not?

2. Tannen's writing has been described as accessible and readable, even though she writes about complex issues from a scholarly perspective. Evaluate Tannen's writing style. How would you describe it? What are its most noticeable features? Do you find her style accessible and readable? Explain, citing specific examples to support your answer.

3. Throughout this essay, Tannen refers to her own research on social interactions between boys and girls. Keeping in mind that Tannen is a well-known linguistics scholar, what effect did these references to her research have on you as a reader? Do they strengthen or weaken her essay in any way? Did they influence your sense of Tannen as an author? Explain. What might your answers to these questions reveal about you as a reader?

4. This essay was first published in 1990. Yet the book that is based on the ideas in this article, *You Just Don't Understand: Women and Men in Conversation,* continues to be read today. Do you think Tannen's ideas about gender and communication still apply today? Why or why not? Has anything changed since 1990 that might affect the validity of Tannen's ideas? Explain. What might the continuing popularity of her book say about gender and communication in contemporary society?

Entering the Conversations

1. Identify the main characteristics of the way women talk and the way men talk, as Tannen describes them in this essay. Now listen to several conversations among your friends or family members. If possible, tape-record the conversations. (Be sure to ask for the participants' permission first.) Then analyze the conversations using Tannen's ideas. Try to determine whether the conversations fall into the patterns that Tannen describes for men and women. Write a report about your informal study of the conversations you observed. In your report, describe those conversations (where they occurred, who participated) and present your analysis of them, using Tannen's ideas. Draw conclusions about the usefulness of Tannen's ideas for understanding communication between men and women.

2. Based on your work for Question 1 and drawing on Tannen's essay, create a pamphlet for an audience of students at your school (or another audience you wish to address) with advice about how to communicate with members of the opposite sex. Alternatively, create a web site for the same purpose.

3. Write your own analysis of gender differences in communication based on your experiences and your own perspective on how men and women communicate with one another.

4. Select several popular television sitcoms, such as *The King of Queens* or *Everybody Loves Raymond,* and watch several episodes, focusing on how the couples are portrayed in the shows and especially on how they communicate. What characterizes the ways that the male and female characters talk to one another in these shows? Are there similarities and differences in the way the shows portray male–female communication, especially among married couples? What might these shows suggest about cultural attitudes regarding communication between men and women? What might they suggest about the politics of language? Try to address these questions. Then write an essay in which you present your analysis to an audience of your classmates. Alternatively, write a letter to the editor of your local newspaper in which you express your opinion about the portrayal of male–female relationships on popular television shows.

I grew up in a home where my parents and grandparents sometimes used Polish, though only my grandparents really spoke that language. Often, they spoke Polish to refer to specific cultural or religious traditions, such as special holiday rituals. Sometimes, Polish was part of those rituals, such as the Polish Christmas carols that were sung at special

How to Tame a *Wild* Tongue

holiday church services. And once in a while, Polish words were used when English ones didn't seem quite right, such as when my grandmother referred to a close friend as pani, *a term that seemed to have a special meaning that the English word* friend *didn't quite capture. I never paid much attention to these uses of Polish, maybe because my siblings and I were expected to learn "proper" English. But I think Polish was a way for my grandmother to hold onto a sense of herself as a Pole.*

I thought about my grandmother when I first read Gloria Anzaldúa's (1942–2004) provocative essay. Like my grandmother, Anzaldúa uses language—in this case, Chicano Spanish—to maintain her sense of identity. But Anzaldúa goes well beyond my grandmother's efforts to preserve her ethnic heritage. She uses a number of languages, dialects, styles, voices, and textual forms to create an

GLORIA ANZALDÚA

"**W**e're going to have to control your tongue," the dentist says, pulling out all the metal from my mouth. Silver bits plop and tinkle into the basin. My mouth is a motherlode.

The dentist is cleaning out my roots. I get a whiff of the stench when I gasp. "I can't cap that tooth yet, you're still draining," he says.

"We're going to have to do something about your tongue," I hear the anger rising in his voice. My tongue keeps pushing out the wads of cotton, pushing back the drills, the long thin needles. "I've never seen anything as strong or as stubborn," he says. And I think, how do you tame a wild tongue, train it to be quiet, how do you bridle and saddle it? How do you make it lie down?

Who is to say that robbing a people of
its language is less violent than war?
—*Ray Gwyn Smith*[1]

GLORIA ANZALDÚA, "HOW TO TAME A WILD TONGUE." FROM *BORDERLANDS/LA FRONTERA: THE NEW MESTIZA.* COPYRIGHT © 1987, 1999 BY GLORIA ANZALDÚA. REPRINTED BY PERMISSION OF AUNT LUTE BOOKS.

exuberant and defiant statement about herself, her people, and their language. Anzaldúa's essay, which was first published in her book Borderlands/La Frontera *(1987), presents a view of language as a way to declare one's autonomy and to resist being silenced. Raised in the borderlands of southwest Texas, she embraced a variety of languages and dialects, including various regional versions of Spanish and Native American languages as well as Standard English. You may find her unusual approach to writing disconcerting at times. But Anzaldúa would not have wanted it any other way, for she used her writing to challenge our ideas about who we are and how we speak to one another. That provocative approach characterizes all her writing, including* This Bridge Called My Back: Radical Writings by Women of Color *(1981), in which she wrote that she felt compelled to write "because I must keep the spirit of my revolt and myself alive."* ◘

I remember being caught speaking Spanish at recess—that was good for three licks on the knuckles with a sharp ruler. I remember being sent to the corner of the classroom for "talking back" to the Anglo teacher when all I was trying to do was tell her how to pronounce my name. "If you want to be American, speak 'American.' If you don't like it, go back to Mexico where you belong."

"I want you to speak English. *Pa' hallar buen trabajo tienes que saber hablar el inglés bien. Qué; vale toda tu educación si todavía hablas inglés con un 'accent,'*" my mother would say, mortified that I spoke English like a Mexican. At Pan American University, I and all Chicano students were required to take two speech classes. Their purpose: to get rid of our accents.

Attacks on one's form of expression with the intent to censor are a violation of the First Amendment. *El Anglo con cara de inocente nos arrancó la lengua.* Wild tongues can't be tamed, they can only be cut out.

Overcoming the Tradition of Silence

Ahogadas, escupimos el oscuro.
Peleando con nuestra propia sombra
el silencio nos sepulta.

En boca cerrada no entran moscas. "Flies don't enter a closed mouth" is a saying I kept hearing when I was a child. *Ser habladora* was to be a gossip and a liar, to talk too much. *Muchachitas bien criadas,* well-bred girls don't answer back. *Es una falta de respeto* to talk back to one's mother or father. I remember one of the sins I'd recite to the priest in the confession box the few times I went to confession: talking back to my mother, *hablar pa' 'tras, repelar. Hociocona, repelona, chismosa,* having a big mouth, questioning, carrying tales are all signs of being *mal criada.* In my culture they are all words that are derogatory if applied to women—I've never heard them applied to men.

*   *   *

The first time I heard two women, a Puerto Rican and a Cuban, say the word *"nosotras,"* I was shocked. I had not known the word existed. Chicanas use *nosotros* whether we're male or female. We are robbed of our female being by the masculine plural. Language is a male discourse.

> And our tongues have become
> dry   the wilderness has
> dried out our tongues   and
> we have forgotten speech.
>   —*Irena Klepfisz*[2]

Even our own people, other Spanish speakers *nos quieren poner candados en la boca.* They would hold us back with their bag of *reglas de academia.*

Oyé como ladra:
el lenguaje de la frontera
Quien tiene boca se equivoca.
—*Mexican saying*

"*Pocho,* cultural traitor, you're speaking the oppressor's language by   10
speaking   English, you're ruining the Spanish language," I have been
accused by various Latinos and Latinas. Chicano Spanish is considered
by the purist and by most Latinos deficient, a mutilation of Spanish.

But Chicano Spanish is a border tongue which developed naturally.
Change, *evolución, enriquecimiento de palabras nuevas por invención o*
adopción have created variants of Chicano Spanish, *un nuevo lenguaje.*
Un lenguaje que corresponde a un modo de vivir. Chicano Spanish is not
incorrect, it is a living language.

For a people who are neither Spanish nor live in a country in which
Spanish is the first language; for a people who live in a country in
which English is the reigning tongue but who are not Anglo; for a
people who cannot entirely identify with either standard (formal,
Castilian) Spanish nor standard English, what recourse is left to them
but to create their own language? A language which they can connect
their identity to, one capable of communicating the realities and values true to themselves—a language with terms that are neither *espa-*
ñol ni inglés, but both. We speak a patois, a forked tongue, a variation
of two languages.

Chicano Spanish sprang out of the Chicanos' need to identify ourselves as a distinct people. We needed a language with which we could
communicate with ourselves, a secret language. For some of us, language is a homeland closer than the Southwest—for many Chicanos
today live in the Midwest and the East. And because we are a complex, heterogeneous people, we speak many languages. Some of the
languages we speak are

1. Standard English
2. Working class and slang English
3. Standard Spanish
4. Standard Mexican Spanish
5. North Mexican Spanish dialect
6. Chicano Spanish (Texas, New Mexico, Arizona, and California
   have regional variations)
7. Tex-Mex
8. *Pachuco* (called *caló*)

My "home" tongues are the languages I speak with my sister and
brothers, with my friends. They are the last five listed, with 6 and
7 being closest to my heart. From school, the media, and job situations, I've picked up standard and working class English. From
Mamagrande Locha and from reading Spanish and Mexican litera-

ture, I've picked up Standard Spanish and Standard Mexican Spanish. From *los recién llegados,* Mexican immigrants, and *braceros,* I learned the North Mexican dialect. With Mexicans I'll try to speak either Standard Mexican Spanish or the North Mexican dialect. From my parents and Chicanos living in the Valley, I picked up Chicano Texas Spanish, and I speak it with my mom, younger brother (who married a Mexican and who rarely mixes Spanish with English), aunts, and older relatives.

15   With Chicanas from *Nuevo México* or *Arizona* I will speak Chicano Spanish a little, but often they don't understand what I'm saying. With most California Chicanas I speak entirely in English (unless I forget). When I first moved to San Francisco, I'd rattle off something in Spanish, unintentionally embarrassing them. Often it is only with another Chicana *tejano* that I can talk freely.

*   *   *

Words distorted by English are known as anglicisms or *pochismos.* The *pocho* is an anglicized Mexican or American of Mexican origin who speaks Spanish with an accent characteristic of North Americans and who distorts and reconstructs the language according to the influence of English.[3] Tex-Mex, or Spanglish, comes most naturally to me. I may switch back and forth from English to Spanish in the same sentence or in the same word. With my sister and my brother Nune and with Chicano *tejano* contemporaries I speak in Tex-Mex.

From kids and people my own age I picked up *Pachuco. Pachuco* (the language of the zoot suiters) is a language of rebellion, both against Standard Spanish and Standard English. It is a secret language. Adults of the culture and outsiders cannot understand it. It is made up of slang words from both English and Spanish. *Ruca* means girl or woman, *vato* means guy or dude, *chale* means no, *simón* means yes, *churro* is sure, talk is *periquiar, pigionear* means petting, *que gacho* means how nerdy, *ponte águila* means watch out, death is called *la pelona.* Through lack of practice and not having others who can speak it, I've lost most of the *Pachuco* tongue.

CHICANO SPANISH

Chicanos, after 250 years of Spanish/Anglo colonization, have developed significant differences in the Spanish we speak. We collapse two adjacent vowels into a single syllable and sometimes shift the stress in certain words such as *maíz/maiz, cohete/cuete.* We leave out certain consonants when they appear between vowels: *lado/lao, mojado/mojao.* Chicanos from South Texas pronounce *f* as *j* as in *jue (fue).* Chicanos use "archaisms," words that are no longer in the Spanish language, words that have been evolved out. We say *semos, truje, haiga, ansina,* and *naiden*. We retain the "archaic" *j*, as in *jalar*, that derives from an earlier *h* (the French *halar* or the Germanic *halon* which was lost to standard Spanish in the sixteenth century), but which is still found in several regional dialects such as the one spoken in South Texas. (Due to geography, Chicanos from the Valley of South Texas were cut off linguistically from other Spanish speakers. We tend to use words that the Spaniards brought over from Medieval Spain. The majority of the Spanish colonizers in Mexico and the Southwest came from Extremadura—Hernán Cortés was one of them—and Andalucía. Andalucians pronounce *ll* like a *y*, and their *d*'s tend to be absorbed by adjacent vowels: *tirado* becomes *tirao*. They brought *el lenguaje popular, dialectos y regionalismos*.)[4]

Chicanos and other Spanish speakers also shift *ll* to *y* and *z* to *s*.[5] We leave out initial syllables, saying *tar* for *estar, toy* for *estoy, hora* for *ahora* (*cubanos* and *puertorriqueños* also leave out initial letters of some words). We also leave out the final syllable such as *pa* for *para*. The intervocalic *y*, the *ll* as in *tortilla, ella, botella*, gets replaced by *tortia* or *toriya, ea, botea*. We add an additional syllable at the beginning of certain words: *atocar* for *tocar, agastar* for *gastar*. Sometimes we'll say *lavaste las vacijas*, other times *lavates* (substituting the *ates* verb endings for the *aste*).

We use anglicisms, words borrowed from English: *bola* from ball, *carpeta* from carpet, *máchina de lavar* (instead of *lavadora*) from washing machine. Tex-Mex argot, created by adding a Spanish sound at the beginning or end of an English word such as *cookiar* for cook, *watchar* for watch, *parkiar* for park, and *rapiar* for rape, is the result of the pressures on Spanish speakers to adapt to English. 20

We don't use the word *vosotros/as* or its accompanying verb form. We don't say *claro* (to mean yes), *imagínate*, or *me emociona*, unless we picked up Spanish from Latinas, out of a book, or in a classroom. Other Spanish-speaking groups are going through the same, or similar, development in their Spanish.

LINGUISTIC TERRORISM

> *Deslenguadas. Somos los del español deficiente.* We are your linguistic nightmare, your linguistic aberration, your linguistic *mestisaje*, the subject of your *burla*. Because we speak with tongues of fire we are culturally crucified. Racially, culturally, and linguistically *somos huérfanos*—we speak an orphan tongue.

Chicanas who grew up speaking Chicano Spanish have internalized the belief that we speak poor Spanish. It is illegitimate, a bastard language. And because we internalize how our language has been used against us by the dominant culture, we use our language differences against each other.

Chicana feminists often skirt around each other with suspicion and hesitation. For the longest time I couldn't figure it out. Then it dawned on me. To be close to another Chicana is like looking into the mirror. We are afraid of what we'll see there. *Pena.* Shame. Low estimation of self. In childhood we are told that our language is wrong. Repeated attacks on our native tongue diminish our sense of self. The attacks continue throughout our lives.

Chicanas feel uncomfortable talking in Spanish to Latinas, afraid of their censure. Their language was not outlawed in their countries. They had a whole lifetime of being immersed in their native tongue; generations, centuries in which Spanish was a first language, taught in school, heard on radio and TV, and read in the newspaper.

25   If a person, Chicana or Latina, has a low estimation of my native tongue, she also has a low estimation of me. Often with *mexicanas y latinas* we'll speak English as a neutral language. Even among Chicanas we tend to speak English at parties or conferences. Yet, at the same time, we're afraid the other will think we're *agringadas* because we don't speak Chicano Spanish. We oppress each other trying to out-Chicano each other, vying to be the "real" Chicanas, to speak like

CONVERSATIONS: THE GROWING SPANISH-SPEAKING MINORITY
Anzaldúa writes in paragraph 26 that Spanish-speaking people will constitute the largest minority in the United States by 2000. According to the U.S. Census Bureau, the proportion of the U.S. population described as Hispanic grew from about 9 percent in 1990 to more than 13 percent in 2002, making it the largest minority in the United States by a slight margin. (Blacks represented about 12 percent of the total population, according to the 2000 Census.) This graphic illustrates how many Spanish speakers are widely distributed in the United States. Consider the significance of Anzaldúa's statement about the Spanish-speaking minority in the United States in terms of her argument about language in this essay. Why is this fact important to her? How does it contribute to her argument?

Language: [Spanish or Spanish Creole ▾]   Show data: ⦿ by county ○ by zip code
State: [Mainland US ▾]

Number of Speakers
(by county)
☐ 0
☐ 1-99
☐ 100 - 499
☐ 500 - 999
☐ 1,000 - 4,999
☐ 5,000 - 19,999
☐ 20,000 - 49,999
☐ 50,000 - 99,999
☐ 100,000 - 499,999
☐ 500,000 - 999,999
☐ 1,000,000 - 3,500,000

Modern Language Association. www.mla.org <http://www.mla.org>

Spanish-speaking people in the United States

Chicanos. There is no one Chicano language just as there is no one Chicano experience. A monolingual Chicana whose first language is English or Spanish is just as much a Chicana as one who speaks several variants of Spanish. A Chicana from Michigan or Chicago or Detroit is just as much a Chicana as one from the Southwest. Chicano Spanish is as diverse linguistically as it is regionally.

By the end of this century, Spanish speakers will comprise the biggest minority group in the United States, a country where students in high schools and colleges are encouraged to take French classes because French is considered more "cultured." But for a language to remain alive it must be used.[6] By the end of this century English, and not Spanish, will be the mother tongue of most Chicanos and Latinos.

* * *

So, if you want to really hurt me, talk badly about my language. Ethnic identity is twin skin to linguistic identity—I am my language. Until I can take pride in my language, I cannot take pride in myself. Until I can accept as legitimate Chicano Texas Spanish, Tex-Mex, and all the other languages I speak, I cannot accept the legitimacy of myself. Until I am free to write bilingually and to switch codes without having always to translate, while I still have to speak English or Spanish when I would rather speak Spanglish, and as long as I have to accommodate the English speaker rather than having them accommodate me, my tongue will be illegitimate.

I will no longer be made to feel ashamed of existing. I will have my voice: Indian, Spanish, white. I will have my serpent's tongue—my woman's voice, my sexual voice, my poet's voice. I will overcome the tradition of silence.

> My fingers
> move sly against your palm
> Like women everywhere, we speak in code. . . .
> —*Melanie Kaye/Kantrowitz*[7]

"VISTAS," CORRIDOS, Y COMIDA: MY NATIVE TONGUE

In the 1960s, I read my first Chicano novel. It was *City of Night* by John Rechy, a gay Texan, son of a Scottish father and a Mexican mother. For days I walked around in stunned amazement that a Chicano could write and could get published. When I read *I Am Joaquín*[8] I was surprised to see a bilingual book by a Chicano in print. When I saw poetry written in Tex-Mex for the first time, a feeling of pure joy flashed through me. I felt like we really existed as a people. In 1971, when I started teaching High School English to Chicano students, I tried to supplement the required texts with works by Chicanos, only to be reprimanded and forbidden to do so by the principal. He

CONVERSATIONS: CHICANO LITERATURE

Anzaldúa describes her struggles to teach and study Chicano literature in the early 1970s. Today, many universities have programs devoted to Chicano literature and related literatures, and works by Chicano writers are assigned in many secondary schools. But Anzaldúa wrote this essay in the late 1980s, when many literary scholars were challenging traditional ideas about which "great" literary works should be assigned in schools and universities. The idea of the "canon" of great literature, which for many years was limited to works by White European writers (mostly male writers), influenced the school curriculum for most of the twentieth century until scholars began to argue for including works by women and by writers of color who had not previously been represented in English courses and literature programs. Anzaldúa's brief description of her experiences here is a reference to this much larger discussion about what literature should be taught in schools, a discussion that has been occurring for many decades.

claimed that I was supposed to teach "American" and English literature. At the risk of being fired, I swore my students to secrecy and slipped in Chicano short stories, poems, a play. In graduate school, while working toward a Ph.D., I had to "argue" with one adviser after the other, semester after semester, before I was allowed to make Chicano literature an area of focus.

Even before I read books by Chicanos or Mexicans, it was the Mexican movies I saw at the drive-in—the Thursday night special of $1.00 a carload—that gave me a sense of belonging. *"Vámonos a las vistas,"* my mother would call out and we'd all—grandmother, brothers, sister, and cousins—squeeze into the car. We'd wolf down cheese and bologna white bread sandwiches while watching Pedro Infante in melodramatic tearjerkers like *Nosotros los pobres,* the first "real" Mexican movie (that was not an imitation of European movies). I remember seeing *Cuando los hijos se van* and surmising that all Mexican movies played up the love a mother has for her children and what ungrateful sons and daughter suffer when they are not devoted to their mothers. I remember the singing-type "westerns" of Jorge Negrete and Miquel Aceves Mejía. When watching Mexican movies, I felt a sense of homecoming as well as alienation. People who were to amount to something didn't go to Mexican movies, or *bailes,* or tune their radios to *bolero, rancherita,* and *corrido* music.

*   *   *

The whole time I was growing up, there was *norteño* music sometimes called North Mexican border music, or Tex-Mex music, or Chicano music, or *cantina* (bar) music. I grew up listening to *conjuntos,* three- or four-piece bands made up of folk musicians playing guitar, *bajo sexto,* drums, and button accordion, which Chicanos had borrowed from the German immigrants who had come to Central Texas and Mexico to farm and build breweries. In the Rio Grande Valley, Steven Jordan and Little Joe Hernández were popular, and Flaco Jiménez was the accordion king. The rhythms of Tex-Mex music are those of the polka, also adapted from the Germans, who in turn had borrowed the polka from the Czechs and Bohemians.

I remember the hot, sultry evenings when *corridos*—song of love and death on the Texas-Mexican borderlands—reverberated out of cheap amplifiers from the local *cantinas* and wafted in through my bedroom window.

Corridos first became widely used along the south Texas/Mexican border during the early conflict between Chicanos and Anglos. The *corridos* are usually about Mexican heroes who do valiant deeds against the Anglo oppressors. Pancho Villa's song, *"La cucaracha,"* is the most famous one. *Corridos* of John F. Kennedy and his death are still very popular in the Valley. Older Chicanos remember Lydia Mendoza, one of the great border *corrido* singers who was called *la Gloria de Tejas*. Her *"El tango negro,"* sung during the great Depression, made her a singer of the people. The ever-present *corridos* narrated one hundred years of border history, bringing news of events as well as entertaining. These folk musicians and folk songs are our chief cultural mythmakers, and they made our hard lives seem bearable.

I grew up feeling ambivalent about our music. Country-western and rock-and-roll had more status. In the fifties and sixties, for the slightly educated and *agringado* Chicanos, there existed a sense of shame at being caught listening to our music. Yet I couldn't stop my feet from thumping to the music, could not stop humming the words, nor hide from myself the exhilaration I felt when I heard it.

*   *   *

35   There are more subtle ways that we internalize identification, especially in the forms of images and emotions. For me food and certain smells are tied to my identity, to my homeland. Woodsmoke curling up to an immense blue sky; woodsmoke perfuming my grandmother's clothes, her skin. The stench of cow manure and the yellow patches on the ground; the crack of a .22 rifle and the reek of cordite. Homemade white cheese sizzling in a pan, melting inside a folded *tortilla*. My sister Hilda's hot, spicy *menudo, chile colorado* making it deep red, pieces of *panza* and hominy floating on top. My brother Carito barbequing *fajitas* in the backyard. Even now and 3,000 miles away, I can see my mother spicing the ground beef, pork, and venison with *chile*. My mouth salivates at the thought of the hot steaming *tamales* I would be eating if I were home.

> *Si le preguntas a mi mamá, "¿Qué eres?"*

> Identity is the essential core of who
> we are as individuals, the conscious
> experience of the self inside.
> —*Gershen Kaufman*[9]

Nosotros los Chicanos straddle the **BORDERLANDS.** On one side of us, we are constantly exposed to the Spanish of the Mexicans, on the other side we hear the Anglos' incessant clamoring so that we forget our language. Among ourselves we don't say *nosotros los americanos, o nosotros los españoles, o nosotros los hispanos.* We say *nosotros los mexicanos* (by *mexicanos* we do not mean citizens of Mexico; we do not mean a national identity, but a racial one). We distinguish between *mexicanos del otro lado* and *mexicanos de este lado.* Deep in our hearts we believe that being Mexican has nothing to do with which country one lives in. Being Mexican is a state of soul—not one of mind, not one of citizenship. Neither eagle nor serpent, but both. And like the ocean, neither animal respects borders.

CONVERSATIONS: LANGUAGE PRACTICES
Notice that many of the words Anzaldúa uses in this essay, such as *tejano, cantina,* and *fajita,* which have become commonly used in English, are italicized throughout the essay. It is a common editorial practice to italicize words from another language when writing in formal English. Perhaps Anzaldúa's editors used italics because it is standard in publishing to do so. But Anzaldúa also insists on writing in a way that does not have "to accommodate the English speaker" (par. 27). You might consider how common editorial practices for Standard English, like italicizing foreign words, might be examples of the "linguistic terrorism" that Anzaldúa criticizes in her essay. Consider, too, how effective her use of untranslated Spanish is as a strategy to combat linguistic terrorism.

STRATEGIES: METAPHOR
Here, as elsewhere in her essay, Anzaldúa refers to the "borderlands," the region where she grew up in southwest Texas along the U.S.–Mexico border. But she uses the term *borderland* to refer to more than that region. Here, it is a metaphor for the way she and her people used language. It is also a metaphor for her very identity as a Chicana. What other meanings does this term have for Anzaldúa?

Dime con quien andas y te diré; quien eres.
(Tell me who your friends are and I'll tell you who you are.)
—*Mexican saying*

Si le preguntas a mi mama, "¿Qué eres?" te dirá, "Soy mexicana." My brothers and sister say the same. I sometimes will answer *"soy mexicana"* and at others will say *"soy Chicana" o "soy tejana."* But I identified as *"Raza"* before I ever identified as *"mexicana"* or "Chicana."

As a culture, we call ourselves Spanish when referring to ourselves as a linguistic group and when copping out. It is then that we forget our predominant Indian genes. We are 70–80 percent Indian.[10] We call ourselves Hispanic[11] or Spanish-American or Latin American or Latin when linking ourselves to other Spanish-speaking peoples of the Western hemisphere and when copping out. We call ourselves Mexican-American[12] to signify we are neither Mexican nor American, but more the noun "American" than the adjective "Mexican" (and when copping out).

Chicanos and other people of color suffer economically for not acculturating. This voluntary (yet forced) alienation makes for psychological conflict, a kind of dual identity—we don't identify with the Anglo-American cultural values and we don't totally identify with the Mexican cultural values. We are a synergy of two cultures with various degrees of Mexicanness or Angloness. I have so internalized the borderland conflict that sometimes I feel like one cancels out the other and we are zero, nothing, no one. *A veces no soy nada ni nadie. Pero hasta cuando no lo soy, lo soy.*

40   When not copping out, when we know we are more than nothing, we call ourselves Mexican, referring to race and ancestry; *mestizo* when affirming both our Indian and Spanish (but we hardly ever own our Black) ancestry; Chicano when referring to a politically aware people born and/or raised in the United States; *Raza* when referring to Chicanos; *tejanos* when we are Chicanos from Texas.

Chicanos did not know we were a people until 1965 when **CESAR CHAVEZ** and the farmworkers united and *I Am Joaquín* was published and *la Raza Unida* party was formed in Texas. With that recognition, we became a distinct people. Something momentous happened to the Chicano soul—we became aware of our reality and acquired a name and a language (Chicano Spanish) that reflected that reality. Now that we had a name, some of the fragmented pieces began to fall together—who we were, what we were, how we had evolved. We began to get glimpses of what we might eventually become.

Yet the struggle of identities continues, the struggle of borders is our reality still. One day the inner struggle will cease and a true integration take place. In the meantime, *tenémos que hacer la lucha. ¿Quién está protegiendo los ranchos de mi gente? ¿Quién está tratando de cerrar la*

GLOSS: CESAR CHAVEZ
In 1962, well-known and sometimes controversial labor activist Cesar Chavez (1927–1993) founded the union that eventually became the United Farm Workers. He worked on behalf of migrant farm workers in the American Southwest and especially in California, most of whom were Spanish-speaking.

fisura entre la India y el blanco en nuestra sangre? El Chicano, si, el Chicano que anida como un ladrón en su propia casa.

* * *

Los Chicanos, how patient we seem, how very patient. There is the quiet of the Indian about us.[13] We know how to survive. When other races have given up their tongue we've kept ours. We know what it is to live under the hammer blow of the dominant *norteamericano* culture. But more than we count the blows, we count the days the weeks the years the centuries the aeons until the white laws and commerce and customs will rot in the deserts they've created, lie bleached. *Humildes* yet proud, *quietos* yet wild, *nosotros los mexicanos-Chicanos* will walk by the crumbling ashes as we go about our business. Stubborn, persevering, impenetrable as stone, yet possessing a malleability that renders us unbreakable, we, the *mestizas* and *mestizos,* will remain.

NOTES

[1]Ray Gwyn Smith, *Moorland Is Cold Country,* unpublished book.

[2]Irena Klepfisz, *"Di rayze aheym*/The Journey Home," in *The Tribe of Dina: A Jewish Women's Anthology,* Melanie Kaye/Kantrowitz and Irena Klepfisz, eds. (Montpelier, VT: Sinister Wisdom Books, 1986), 49.

[3]R. C. Ortega, *Dialectología Del Barrio,* trans. Hortencia S. Alwan (Los Angeles, CA: R. C. Ortega Publisher & Bookseller, 1977), 132.

[4]Eduardo Hernandéz-Chávez, Andrew D. Cohen, and Anthony F. Beltramo, *El Lenguaje de los Chicanos: Regional and Social Characteristics of Language Used by Mexican Americans* (Arlington, VA: Center for Applied Linguistics, 1975), 39.

[5]Hernandéz-Chávez, xvii.

[6]Irena Klepfisz, "Secular Jewish Identity: Yidishkayt in America," in *The Tribe of Dina,* Kaye/Kantrowitz and Klepfisz, eds., 43.

[7]Melanie Kaye/Kantrowitz, "Sign," in *We Speak in Code: Poems and Other Writings* (Pittsburgh, PA: Motheroot Publications, Inc., 1980), 85.

[8]Rodolfo Gonzales, *I Am Joaquín/Yo Soy Joaquín* (New York, NY: Bantam Books, 1972). It was first published in 1967.

[9]Gershen Kaufman, *Shame: The Power of Caring* (Cambridge, MA: Schenkman Books, Inc., 1980), 68.

[10]John R. Chávez, *The Lost Land: The Chicano Images of the Southwest* (Albuquerque, NM: University of New Mexico Press, 1984), 88–90.

[11]"Hispanic" is derived from *Hispanis (España,* a name given to the Iberian peninsula in ancient times when it was a part of the Roman Empire) and is a term designated by the U.S. government to make it easier to handle us on paper.

[12]The Treaty of Guadalupe Hidalgo created the Mexican-American in 1848.

[13]Anglos, in order to alleviate their guilt for dispossessing the Chicano, stressed the Spanish part of us and perpetrated the myth of the Spanish Southwest. We have accepted the fiction that we are Hispanic, that is Spanish, in order to accommodate ourselves to the dominant culture and its abhorrence of Indians. Chávez, 88–91.

Understanding the Text

1. In what ways is language a male discourse, as Anzaldúa describes it in paragraph 7? Why is this idea important to her? Do you agree with her? Why or why not?

2. What is the importance of Chicano Spanish, according to Anzaldúa? What does her view of this language suggest about language in general?

3. How does Anzaldúa explain the way that Chicano Spanish has developed? What is its relationship to English? Why is this relationship important, in her view? What might it reveal about how languages are viewed and how they are used?

4. Why does Anzaldúa wish "to write bilingually and to switch codes without having always to translate," as she states in paragraph 27? What does this desire suggest about language? Do you think she is right? Why or why not?

5. What is the significance of Mexican film and the various forms of music that Anzaldúa describes from her youth? How do these relate to the Chicano Spanish language that she spoke? How do they contribute to her larger argument about that language?

6. At the end of her essay, Anzaldúa declares that one day "the struggle of identities" for Chicanos will end and "a true integration" will take place. What exactly does she mean by that statement? How would language be part of a true integration?

Exploring the Issues

1. What is the effect of including Spanish words and phrases throughout an essay that is mostly written in English as Anzaldúa does? How might this use of Spanish contribute to her main purpose in this essay? What effect did her using several languages have on you as a reader?

2. Examine how Anzaldúa describes the different languages she speaks. What does she emphasize in these descriptions? What is important to her about each language? What might her descriptions suggest about her view of language? What do you think they might suggest about language as a political tool?

3. In a sense, Anzaldúa's essay is as much about English as it is about Chicano Spanish. What view of English does Anzaldúa present in this essay? How do you think Anzaldúa's view of English—and of language in general—might contribute to larger debates about requiring Standard English in schools?

4. What is the relationship of language to identity as Anzaldúa understands it? She describes herself variously as Chicana, Spanish, Mexican, *mestiza,* and *tejano,* and she describes a variety of languages and dialects that she uses with various people. How do these different identities and languages relate to one another? What might the complexities of language and dialect that Anzaldúa describes suggest about the role of language in our sense of self?

Entering the Conversations

1. In paragraph 27, Anzaldúa writes, "I am my language." Write an essay in which you develop that idea from your own experience and based on your own views about language and identity. Alternatively, write the same essay in an unconventional form, using whatever slang, dialects, or languages you think might help you convey your point—as Anzaldúa does in her essay.

2. Write an essay describing an experience in which you were the victim of what Anzaldúa calls "linguistic terrorism."

3. In a group of classmates, discuss Anzaldúa's approach to writing. How effective do you and your classmates find her writing style, especially her use of different languages and textual forms? What appeals to you and your classmates about her style? What is difficult or ineffective about it? Discuss how your reactions to her writing might reveal your own views—and prejudices—about language.

4. In paragraph 17, Anzaldúa describes some of the slang terms of *Pachuco,* which she describes as a secret slang language of rebellion used by young people. Consider the slang that you or people you know speak or once spoke. What purpose do these dialects serve? Do they matter? How does it make a person feel to speak such a dialect? Then write an essay in which you describe this slang and explain its uses in your life or in the lives of others you know.

5. Using Anzaldúa's essay and any other appropriate essay from this book (or elsewhere), write a letter to the superintendent of your local schools in which you present your views about how language should be taught in schools. Should only Standard English be taught? If so, why? Should other languages and "nonstandard" dialects be part of the school curriculum? Why or why not? How might Anzaldúa's essay serve as a model for the way language should be taught in schools? How might it support an argument for teaching only Standard English? Try to address such questions in your letter. Alternatively, write a letter to the editor of your local newspaper or another publication of your choice in which you express your views about teaching Standard English in schools.

Shortly after the war in Iraq began in March *2003, a number of slogans began appearing on bumper stickers, in newspapers and magazines, on the Internet, and on billboards throughout the United States. Perhaps the most common of these slogans was "Support Our Troops," but other slogans were also popular: "Home of the Brave," "United We Stand,"*

Sleuthing *Patriotic* Slogans

"God Bless America." At the time, these slogans were obviously referring to the war in Iraq and what President George W. Bush called "the war on terror." They were usually interpreted as expressions of patriotism. But writer Gary Sloan wondered just what these slogans really mean. Writing a few months after the United States and its allies invaded Iraq, Sloan offered a careful, if lighthearted, analysis of some of the most common patriotic slogans at the time. His essay is a good example of the use of irony in political writing. But it has a special twist: Sloan is a retired English professor, and he draws on his expertise as a grammarian to analyze political slogans. His analysis calls attention to the ways in which the larger political meanings of slogans often have little to do with grammar or the technical definitions of words. And he helps us see how language acquires meaning in specific historical and cultural contexts.

GARY SLOAN

In this best of times and worst of times, the American landscape is dotted with signs, billboards, posters and stickers emblazoned with patriotic slogans. In my hometown, merchants have scrawled on their display windows a smorgasbord of venerable shibboleths: "United We Stand," "Support the Troops," "Pray for the Troops," "Let Freedom Ring," "Home of the Brave," "God Bless America." Taped on many windows is a flyer that reads: "Pro-America Rally in Railroad Park. Bring lawn chairs, flags, and snacks. Dress patriotic."

When I read the flyer, I thought: Shouldn't that be "Dress *patriotically?*"

Because I have spent much of my life studying and teaching language, I respond inappropriately to patriotic slogans: I parse them grammatically and try to explicate them the way I would an obscure fragment in an essay. Like Hamlet, I sometimes become sicklied over with the pale cast of thought when I shouldn't be thinking at all. The slogans are designed to evoke warm feelings of camaraderie and unity, not grimaces and cocked brows.

Yet I persist in my folly. To wit: Many patriotic slogans are in the imperative mood. They issue a command ("Support the Troops,"

GARY SLOAN, "SLEUTHING PATRIOTIC SLOGANS." FROM *ALTERNET*, APRIL 10, 2003. REPRINTED BY PERMISSION.

As you read this essay, it's worth remembering that it was originally published in Alternet.org, an Internet site that describes itself as a progressive news source. The intended audience for this essay, then, very likely had specific political views about the war in Iraq that Sloan certainly was aware of (and perhaps shared). You might consider how the political views of an audience might shape the meaning of a slogan. Consider, too, how well the irony in Sloan's essay would work with a more conservative audience as compared to a liberal one. ▼

CONVERSATIONS
CLICHÉS AND QUOTATIONS
In the opening sentence, Sloan recalls a famous line from Charles Dickens's novel *A Tale of Two Cities* (1859): "It was the best of times, it was the worst of times." Many readers will recognize this reference to that famous novel about politics and self-sacrifice that takes place during the French Revolution in the late eighteenth century. In the novel, the main character, Sydney Carton, gives up his life so that the woman he loves can be with her husband, whose life is spared by Carton's sacrifice. But many readers may not recognize this reference to Dickens's novel. Consider how Sloan's use of this reference (which is technically called an *allusion*) might enhance the meaning of this paragraph. What might Sloan wish to suggest with such an allusion? What would his paragraph lose if he had not included this allusion? Will his point be clear to readers who don't recognize the allusion? Sloan makes allusions to other well-known literary works in this essay. Consider the effects of those allusions as well.

GRAMMAR
In paragraph 4, Sloan uses a technical grammar term, the *imperative mood*, which refers to statements that are commands. In paragraph 7, he uses another grammar term, the *subjunctive mood*, which is a verb form that describes a possible or desired action or state, not a factual or actual one. (A typical example of subjunctive mood is a statement like this one: "I wish I were home right now.") Sloan is a retired English professor, so he can be expected to be familiar with such technical terms. But he wrote this essay for a much broader audience, not for linguists or grammarians. Consider what purposes his use of these technical terms might serve in this essay. What might they accomplish that less technical terms would not?

GLOSS: THE DELPHI ORACLE
The Oracle at Delphi was Pythia, priestess of the god Apollo in ancient Greek mythology, who resided at the city of Delphi around 1400 B.C. and gave predictions about the future that her listeners often could not make sense of and interpreted in various ways.

"Pray for the Troops"). Commands are risky. They create resistance in natural-born rebels and in patriophobes (those with an excessive fear of patriotism).

Are "Let Freedom Ring" and "United We Stand" logically compatible? If everyone exercises freedom of speech and conscience, will we all stand united? Instead of assenting to the war against Iraq, some may opt to ring their dissent. How does one "Support the Troops"? Letters? Pep rallies? Boxes of homemade cookies? Can one support the troops by urging them to obey their consciences even if their consciences conflict with their orders?

"Home of the Brave." Hmm. Brave in what sense? Obviously, many Americans aren't physically brave. Millions are afraid to walk the streets at night or open their doors to strangers. If "brave" refers to moral courage, might the bravest Americans be those who resist the will of the majority? Might it require more bravery to protest Operation Iraqi Freedom than to support it?

"God Bless America" is almost as inscrutable as the utterances of a **DELPHI ORACLE**. Grammatically, the words are in the subjunctive mood. They express a wish or a prayer: "Please, God, bless America," or "May God bless America."

The real conundrum: What do the words mean? In what sense is God to bless America? With good health, bouncing babies, supportive spouses? Good schools? High IQs? Philosophical wisdom? Fat paychecks, sirloin steaks, sport utility vehicles, faster computers, more cable channels, bigger boom boxes? Competitive Superbowls? Better face lifts and liposuction? Speedier cruise missiles, smarter smart bombs, stealthier stealth bombers? Continued monopoly of the planet's natural resources?

And does "America" mean Americans? If so, does it comprise all Americans, including murderers, rapists, thieves, swindlers, embezzlers, muggers, liars, cheats, bullies, pederasts, pornographers, conceited airheads, slobs, slum lords, domestic tyrants, bigots and racists?

Or does "America" refer to land, spacious skies and amber waves of grain? Or to some platonic ideal of government embodied in the Declaration of Independence and the Constitution, worthy of being blessed even if some Americans aren't?

Now, if I can just figure out how to dress patriotic.

CONVERSATIONS: SLOGANS

In all these photographs, the slogan "Support Our Troops" is used, but consider how the meaning of the slogan might differ in each case. How might Sloan's analysis of such slogans help us understand how their meaning can change depending on the context of their use?

© Chitose Suzuki/AP Photo

© 2003 David McNew/Getty Images

© Sandy Huffaker/Getty Images

Understanding the Text

1. What does Sloan mean when he writes that he "responds inappropriately to patriotic slogans"? Why does he describe his responses as "folly"? Do you believe him? Why or why not?

2. In paragraph 8, Sloan asks "What do the words mean?" What do you think his answer is? Do you think he really does not know? Do you agree with him?

3. How would you summarize Sloan's main point about slogans?

Exploring the Issues

1. How does Sloan present himself in this essay? What kind of person does he seem to be? What authority does he seem to have for making these kinds of statements about slogans? Do you think he wishes to be taken seriously? Explain, citing specific passages to support your answer.

2. Sloan's essay is a careful analysis of the way language is used in political slogans. His analysis rests on a knowledge of formal grammar and linguistic concepts. How effective do you find his analysis of these common slogans? Does his careful reading of such slogans offer us insights into language use that we could not otherwise gain? Does Sloan's grammatical analysis lead to a useful understanding of the political uses of language? Does it make us aware of aspects of our language use that we would otherwise miss?

3. How would you describe Sloan's strategy in making his point about political slogans and about political language in general? Does he state his position explicitly? If so, where do you see that statement in his essay? If not, how do you know what his point is? How effective do you think this essay is in conveying Sloan's point? To what extent do you think your answer to that question depends on your own political beliefs? Explain.

Entering the Conversations

1. Write a response to Sloan's essay about political slogans.

2. With a group of classmates, write several slogans related to what you believe are the most important current political issues.

3. Listen to a political speech. (You can find transcripts or audiotapes of major speeches from the most recent presidential election on the Internet or in your school library.) Identify any statements that you

would describe as political slogans and analyze the way the candidate uses those slogans in his or her speech. What do you think the candidate means by those slogans? Are the slogans being directed to a particular audience?

4. Each of these images shows a vehicle sporting bumper stickers. Consider what overall message each driver might be sending by the selection of specific bumper stickers. What conclusions can you draw about the driver? What purposes do you think each driver might have had in placing these particular bumper stickers on the vehicle? How effective are these bumper stickers in conveying specific messages to others?

© Dave G. Houser/Corbix

© Richard Hamilton Smith/Corbis

WRITING MATTERS

ONCE HAD A STUDENT WHO GOT INTO TROUBLE IN HIGH SCHOOL FOR WRITING AN ESSAY THAT CRITI-CIZED SCHOOL POLICIES PROHIBITING STUDENTS FROM EXPRESSING OPINIONS CRITICAL OF THE SCHOOL. THE ESSAY DID NOT CONTAIN ANY PROFANE LANGUAGE OR VIO-LENT IMAGES, NOR DID IT BELITTLE ANY TEACHERS OR SCHOOL OFFICIALS. BUT THE STUDENT'S TEACHER TOOK

it to the principal, and the student and her parents were summoned to the principal's office to address "the problem."

What exactly was the problem in this case? Well, I can't speak for the principal, but it seems clear that part of the problem was *writing* itself. Or to put it another way, this student got into trouble because of the power of writing. The school authorities must have feared those written words for some reason. Otherwise, why would they take the essay so seriously? In some important way, that essay mattered. And it mattered because writing matters. You may have heard your English teachers extolling the power of writing as a positive, beneficial thing. And it is. But the power of writing is more complicated than that. So it's no surprise that efforts to control writing through censorship and other means have a long history. Consider the case of acclaimed novelist Salman Rushdie, a British citizen of Indian descent, whose best-selling novel, *The Satanic Verses* (1988), deeply offended many Muslims. In 1989, the Ayatollah Khomeini of Iran, one of the world's great Muslim spiritual leaders at the time, declared the book blasphemous and called for Rushdie's death. Rushdie was forced to live in hiding until the Ayatollah's decree was rescinded in 1998. Rushdie's experience is a frightening reminder of the power of the written word and the consequences writing can sometimes have.

The power of writing can matter in many different, often dramatic ways. For example, it has been said that when President Abraham Lincoln met Harriet Beecher Stowe, he commented, "So this is the little lady who started the war." Stowe, of course, is the author of *Uncle Tom's Cabin* (1852), a best-selling novel about the lives of Black slaves that was believed to have influenced the view of many Americans about slavery at that time. Lincoln's comment

suggests the power of a story like Stowe's to shape opinions and affect public debate about important issues. Or consider Thomas Paine's pamphlet *Common Sense,* which was published in 1776 and is estimated to have sold 500,000 copies—at a time when there were only 2.5 million people living in the American colonies. Some historians believe that *Common Sense,* which was Paine's vigorous case for independence from England, was a key factor in generating support for the rebellion against England.

So it's no wonder that there have long been efforts to control what is written and what is read. And don't think that efforts to control writing are limited to governments or religious leaders. If you went to an American elementary or secondary school, chances are your experience there was shaped by censorship. Each year, political organizations, religious groups, parents, and others challenge books used in schools. Sometimes these challenges focus on well-known controversies, such as the debate about teaching creationism along with evolution. But consider this list of the most commonly challenged books in American schools during the 1990s: *The Adventures of Huckleberry Finn* by Mark Twain, *The Catcher in the Rye* by J. D. Salinger, *I Know Why the Caged Bird Sings* by Maya Angelou, *Of Mice and Men* by John Steinbeck, and *Forever* by Judy Blume. *The Diary of Anne Frank* and *Harry Potter and the Goblet of Fire,* a huge international bestseller, have also been favorite targets of censors. These books are considered examples of great writing by many critics, but they must also be examples of the power of writing—a power that is sometimes threatening to many people.

The following essays can help us understand that power. And they remind us that the power of writing can be deeply personal at the same time that it is political and cultural.

I like to read the letters to the editor of my local newspaper. Most of them have to do with issues that matter only to the people in the region where I live, such as town council decisions on building projects, school budgets, tax increases, problems with local roads, or local political controversies. These may seem like minor issues, but they

Nobody Mean *More* to Me Than You and the *Future* Life of Willie Jordan

matter enough to people living in the region to prompt them to express their views in the public forum of the newspaper's editorial page. The letters to the editor not only provide a forum for opinions, but they also can provoke readers to think about an issue, take up a local cause, or join the conversation about an important local matter. For the students that June Jordan (1936–2002) describes in the following essay, though, writing a letter to the editor of a local newspaper was a much bigger matter. You might even say it was a matter of life and death.

Jordan describes her experience with a college English class she

JUNE JORDAN

Black English is not exactly a linguistic buffalo; as children, most of the thirty-five million Afro-Americans living here depend on this language for our discovery of the world. But then we approach our maturity inside a larger social body that will not support our efforts to become anything other than the clones of those who are neither our mothers nor our fathers. We begin to grow up in a house where every true mirror shows us the face of somebody who does not belong there, whose walk and whose talk will never look or sound "right," because that house was meant to shelter a family that is alien and hostile to us.

As we learn our way around this environment, either we hide our original word habits, or we completely surrender our own voice, hoping to please those who will never respect anyone different from themselves: Black English is not exactly a linguistic buffalo, but we should understand its status as an endangered species, as a perishing, irreplaceable system of community intelligence, or we should expect its extinction, and, along with that, the extinguishing of much that constitutes our own proud, and singular identity.

What we casually call "English," less and less defers to England and its "gentlemen." "English" is no longer a specific matter of geography or an element of class privilege; more than thirty-three countries use this tool as a means of "international communication."[1] Countries as disparate as Zimbabwe and Malaysia, or Israel and Uganda, use it as their non-native currency of convenience. Obviously, this tool, this "English," cannot function inside thirty-three discrete societies on the basis of rules and values absolutely determined somewhere else, in a thirty-fourth other country, for example.

In addition to that staggering congeries of non-native users of English, there are five countries, or 333,746,000 people, for whom this thing called "English" serves as a native tongue.[2] Approximately ten percent of these native speakers of "English" are Afro-American citizens of the U.S.A. I cite these numbers and varieties of human beings dependent on "English" in order, quickly, to suggest how strange and how tenuous is any concept of "Standard English." Obviously, numerous forms of English now operate inside a natural, an uncontrollable, continuum of development. I would suppose "the standard" for English in Malaysia is not the same as "the standard" in Zimbabwe. I know that standard forms of English for Black people in this country do not copy that of whites. And, in fact, the structural differences between these two kinds of English have intensified, becoming more Black, or less white, despite the expected homogenizing effects of television[3] and other mass media.

Nonetheless, white standards of English persist, supreme and unquestioned, in these United States. Despite our multilingual population, and despite the deepening Black and white cleavage within that conglomerate, white standards control our official and popular judgments of verbal proficiency and correct, or incorrect, language skills, including speech. In contrast to India, where at least fourteen languages co-exist as legitimate Indian languages, in contrast to Nicaragua, where all citizens are legally entitled to formal school instruction

taught at the State University of New York at Stony Brook in 1984. The lessons the students in her class learned went well beyond the classroom. The brother of one of Jordan's students was killed in a confrontation with police, which the students in the class interpreted as an example of police violence against Blacks in their city. Ultimately, they decided to combat that violence by writing letters to the editor of a local newspaper to express their outrage about the incident. The difficult debates among Jordan's students about whether to write that letter in Black English or Standard English can tell us a great deal about the politics of language in American society, about the power of writing, and about the limits to that power.

Whenever I assign this essay in my classes, I ask my students to decide whether they would choose to write the letters to the newspaper as Jordan's students did. I also ask them to justify their decision. It is always a hard decision for them. As you read this essay, think about what decision you might have made in this case—and why.

June Jordan was a poet, essayist, and professor of English at the University of California at Berkeley. Her works include On Call: New Political Essays *(1985) and* June Jordan's Poetry for the People: A Revolutionary Blueprint *(1995). This essay was first published in the* Harvard Educational Review *in 1988.* ▾

---

[1] *English Is Spreading, but What Is English?* A presentation by Professor S. N. Sridahr, Dept. of Linguistics, S.U.N.Y. at Stony Brook, April 9, 1985; Dean's Conversation among the Disciplines.

[2] Ibid.

[3] *New York Times*, March 15, 1985, Section One, p. 14: Report on study by Linguistics at the University of Pennsylvania.

STRATEGIES: IDENTIFYING AN AUDIENCE
Notice Jordan's use of the first person in the first paragraph. She writes that "Afro-Americans living here depend upon this language for our discovery of the world." Later in the paragraph, she writes that "we should understand its [Black English's] status as an endangered species." Who is the *we* in this sentence? Is it the same *we* as in the previous sentence or is Jordan addressing two different audiences here? It is not unusual for an author to address several different audiences in a piece of writing, but in this case, consider the possibility that Jordan may be sending different messages to different readers.

CONVERSATIONS: BLACK ENGLISH AND STANDARD ENGLISH
For many years, educators, scholars, politicians, and others have debated about how the English language should be taught in schools. In the 1990s, a controversy erupted in Oakland, California, when school officials there declared *Ebonics,* another term for Black English, to be a separate dialect of English and not just slang. They adopted a policy to treat Black English as a foreign language, and they directed schools to teach students who spoke Black English as if Standard English were their second language. The public outcry eventually prompted school officials to drop the policy, but it also provoked a great deal of discussion about Black English, Standard English, and language in general as well as about the responsibilities of schools in teaching English to students of diverse racial, cultural, and linguistic backgrounds. Although Jordan's essay was published several years before the controversy in Oakland, it is part of a debate about English that has been going on for decades in the United States. In particular, in the early part of her essay, Jordan challenges the idea that there is one correct "standard" version of English that should be taught in schools. This debate continues today, and it's worth thinking about how persuasive Jordan's argument is so many years after she wrote it. It's also worth thinking about why this issue of standard English continues to be so controversial. (The essays by Amy Tan and Gloria Anzaldúa earlier in this chapter also address this issue.)

in their regional or tribal languages, compulsory education in America compels accommodation to exclusively white forms of "English." White English, in America, is "Standard English."

This story begins two years ago, I was teaching a new course, "In Search of the Invisible Black Woman," and my rather large class seemed evenly divided between young Black women and men. Five or six white students also sat in attendance. With unexpected speed and enthusiasm we had moved through historical narratives of the nineteenth century to literature by and about Black women, in the twentieth. I had assigned the first forty pages of Alice Walker's *The Color Purple,* and I came, eagerly, to class that morning:

"So!" I exclaimed, aloud. "What did you think? How did you like it?"

The students studied their hands, or the floor. There was no response. The tense, resistant feeling in the room fairly astounded me.

At last, one student, a young woman still not meeting my eyes, muttered something in my direction:

"What did you say?" I prompted her.

"Why she have them talk so funny. It don't sound right."

"You mean the language?"

Another student lifted his head: "It don't look right, neither. I couldn't hardly read it."

At this, several students dumped on the book. Just about unanimously, their criticisms targeted the language. I listened to what they wanted to say and silently marveled at the similarities between their casual speech patterns and Alice Walker's written version of Black English.

But I decided against pointing to these identical traits of syntax; I wanted not to make them self-conscious about their own spoken language—not while they clearly felt it was "wrong." Instead I decided to swallow my astonishment. Here was a negative Black reaction to a prize winning accomplishment of Black literature that white readers across the country had selected as a best seller. Black rejection was aimed at the one irreducibly Black element of Walker's work: the language—Celie's Black English. I wrote the opening lines of *The Color Purple* on the blackboard and asked the students to help me translate these sentences into Standard English:

You better not never tell nobody but God. It'd kill your mammy.
Dear God,

I am fourteen years old. I have always been a good girl. Maybe you can give me a sign letting me know what is happening to me.

Last spring after Little Lucious come I heard them fussing. He was pulling on her arm. She say it too soon, Fonso. I
aint well. Finally he leave her alone. A week go by, he pulling
on her arm again. She say, Naw, I ain't gonna. Can't you see
I'm already half dead, an all of the children.[4]

Our process of translation exploded with hilarity and even hysterical,   15
shocked laughter: The Black writer, Alice Walker, knew what she was
doing! If rudimentary criteria for good fiction includes the manipulation of language so that the syntax and diction of sentences will tell
you the identity of speakers, the probable age and sex and class of
speakers, and even the locale—urban/rural/southern/western—
then Walker had written, perfectly. This is the translation into Standard English that our class produced:

> *Absolutely, one should never confide in anybody besides God.*
> *Your secrets could prove devastating to your mother.*
> Dear God,
> I am fourteen years old, I have always been good. But
> now, could you help me to understand what is happening
> to me?
> Last spring, after my little brother, Lucious, was born, I
> heard my parents fighting. My father kept pulling at my
> mother's arm. But she told him, "It's too soon for sex,
> Alfonso. I am still not feeling well." Finally, my father left her
> alone. A week went by, and he began bothering my mother,
> again: Pulling her arm. She told him, "No, I won't! Can't you
> see I'm already exhausted from all of these children?"

(Our favorite line was "It's too soon for sex, Alfonso.")

Once we could stop laughing, once we could stop our exponen-
tially wild improvisations on the theme of Translated Black English,
the students pushed me to explain their own negative first reactions
to their spoken language on the printed page. I thought it was probably akin to the shock of seeing yourself in a photograph for the
first time. Most of the students had never before seen a written fac-
simile of the way they talk. None of the students had ever learned
how to read and write their own verbal system of communication:
Black English. Alternatively, this fact began to baffle or else bemuse
and then infuriate my students. Why not? Was it too late? Could
they learn how to do it, now? And, ultimately, the final test question,
the one testing my sincerity: Could I teach them? Because I had
never taught anyone Black English and, as far as I knew, no one,
anywhere in the United States, had ever offered such a course, the
best I could say was "I'll try."

---

[4]Alice Walker, *The Color Purple*, p. 11, Harcourt Brace, N.Y.

He looked like a wrestler.

He sat dead center in the packed room and, every time our eyes met, he quickly nodded his head as though anxious to reassure, and encourage, me.

20   Short, with strikingly broad shoulders and long arms, he spoke with a surprisingly high, soft voice that matched the soft bright movement of his eyes. His name was Willie Jordan. He would have seemed even more unlikely in the context of Contemporary Women's Poetry, except that ten or twelve other Black men were taking the course, as well. Still, Willie was conspicuous. His extreme fitness, the muscular density of his presence underscored the riveted, gentle attention that he gave to anything anyone said. Generally, he did not join the loud and rowdy dialogue flying back and forth, but there could be no doubt about his interest in our discussions. And, when he stood to present an argument he'd prepared, overnight, that nervous smile of his vanished and an irregular stammering replaced it, as he spoke with visceral sincerity, word by word.

That was how I met Willie Jordan. It was in between "In Search of the Invisible Black Woman" and "The Art of Black English." I was waiting for Departmental approval and I supposed that Willie might be, so to speak, killing time until he, too, could study Black English. But Willie really did want to explore Contemporary Women's poetry and, to that end, volunteered for extra research and never missed a class.

Towards the end of that semester, Willie approached me for an independent study project on South Africa. It would commence the next semester. I thought Willie's writing needed the kind of improvement only intense practice will yield. I knew his intelligence was outstanding. But he'd wholeheartedly opted for "Standard English" at a rather late age, and the results were stilted and frequently polysyllabic, simply for the sake of having more syllables. Willie's unnatural formality of language seemed to me consistent with the formality of his research into South African apartheid. As he projected his studies, he would have little time, indeed, for newspapers. Instead, more than 90 percent of his research would mean saturation in strictly historical, if not archival, material. I was certainly interested. It would be tricky to guide him into a more confident and spontaneous relationship both with language and apartheid. It was going to be wonderful to see what happened when he could catch up with himself, entirely, and talk back to the world.

September, 1984: Breezy fall weather and much excitement! My class, "The Art of Black English," was full to the limit of the fire laws. And, in Independent Study, Willie Jordan showed up, weekly, fifteen minutes early for each of our sessions. I was pretty happy to be teaching, altogether!

I remember an early class when a young brother, replete with his ever present pork-pie hat, raised his hand and then told us that most of what he'd heard was "all right" except it was "too clean." "The brothers on the street," he continued, "they mix it up more. Like 'fuck' and 'mother-fuck.' Or like 'shit.'" He waited, I waited. Then all of us laughed a good while, and we got into a brawl about "correct" and "realistic" Black English that led to Rule 1.

Rule 1: *Black English is about a whole lot more than mothafuckin.*

As a criterion, we decided, "realistic" could take you anywhere you want to go. Artful places. Angry places. Eloquent and sweettalkin places. Polemical places. Church. And the local Bar & Grill. We were checking out a language, not a mood or a scene or one guy's forgettable mouthing off.

It was hard. For most of the students, learning Black English required a fallback to patterns and rhythms of speech that many of their parents had beaten out of them. I mean *beaten*. And, in a majority of cases, correct Black English could be achieved only by striving for *incorrect* Standard English, something they were still pushing at, quite uncertainly. This state of affairs led to Rule 2.

Rule 2: *If it's wrong in Standard English it's probably right in Black English, or, at least, you're hot.*

It was hard. Roommates and family members ridiculed their studies, or remained incredulous, "You *studying* that shit? At school?" But we were beginning to feel the companionship of pioneers. And we decided that we needed another rule that would establish each one of us as equally important to our success. This was Rule 3.

Rule 3: *If it don't sound like something that come out somebody mouth then it don't sound right. If it don't sound right then it ain't hardly right. Period.*

This rule produced two weeks of compositions in which the students agonizingly tried to spell the sound of the Black English sentence they wanted to convey. But Black English is, preeminently, an oral/spoken means of communication. *And spelling don't talk.* So we needed Rule 4.

Rule 4: *Forget about the spelling. Let the syntax carry you.*

Once we arrived at Rule 4 we started to fly because syntax, the structure of an idea, leads you to the world view of the speaker and reveals her values. The syntax of a sentence equals the structure of your consciousness. If we insisted that the language of Black English adheres to a distinctive Black syntax, then we were postulating a profound difference between white and Black people, *per se*. Was it a difference to prize or to obliterate?

There are three qualities of Black English—the presence of life, voice, and clarity— that testify to a distinctive Black value system that we became excited about and self-consciously tried to maintain.

1. Black English has been produced by a pre-technocratic, if not antitechnological, culture. More, our culture has been constantly threatened by annihilation or, at least, the swallowed blurring of assimilation. Therefore, our language is a system constructed by peo-

ple constantly needing to insist that we exist, that we are present. Our language devolves from a culture that abhors all abstraction, or anything tending to obscure or delete the fact of the human being who is here and now/the truth of the person who is speaking or listening. Consequently, *there is no passive voice construction possible in Black English.* For example, you cannot say, "Black English is being eliminated." You must say, instead, "White people eliminating Black English." The assumption of the presence of life governs all of Black English. Therefore, overwhelmingly, *all action takes place in the language of the present indicative.* And every sentence assumes the living and active participation of at least two human beings, the speaker and the listener.

2. A primary consequence of the person-centered values of Black English is the delivery of voice. If you speak or write Black English, your ideas will necessarily possess that otherwise elusive attribute, *voice.*

3. One main benefit following from the person-centered values of Black English is that of *clarity.* If your idea, your sentence, assumes the presence of at least two living and active people, you will make it understandable because the motivation behind every sentence is the wish to say something real to somebody real.

*   *   *

As the weeks piled up, translation from standard English into Black English or vice versa occupied a hefty part of our course work.

Standard English (hereafter S.E.): "In considering the idea of studying Black English those questioned suggested—"
(What's the subject? Where's the person? Is anybody alive in there, in that idea?)

Black English (hereafter B.E.): "I been asking people what you think about somebody studying Black English and they answer me like this."

But there were interesting limits. You cannot "translate" instances of Standard English preoccupied with abstraction or with nothing/nobody evidently alive, into Black English. That would warp the language into uses antithetical to the guiding perspective of its community of users. Rather you must first change those Standard English sentences, themselves, into ideas consistent with the person-centered assumptions of Black English.

GUIDELINES FOR BLACK ENGLISH

1. Minimal number of words for every idea: This is the source for the aphoristic and/or poetic force of the language; eliminate every possible word.

2. Clarity: If the sentence is not clear it's not Black English.

3. Eliminate use of the verb *to be* whenever possible. This leads to the deployment of more descriptive and, therefore, more precise verbs.

4. Use *be* or *been* only when you want to describe a chronic, ongoing state of things.

   He *be* at the office, by 9. (He is always at the office by 9.)
   He *been* with her since forever.

5. Zero copula: Always eliminate the verb *to be* whenever it would combine with another verb in Standard English.

   S.E.: She is going out with him.
   B.E.: She going out with him.

6. Eliminate *do* as in:

   S.E.: What do you think? What do you want?
   B.E.: What you think? What you want?

   Rules number 3, 4, 5, and 6 provide for the use of the minimal number of verbs per idea and, therefore, greater accuracy in the choice of verb.

7. In general, if you wish to say something really positive, try to formulate the idea using emphatic negative structure.

   S.E.: He's fabulous.
   B.E.: He bad.

8. Use double or triple negatives for dramatic emphasis.

   S.E.: Tina Turner sings out of this world.
   B.E.: Ain nobody sing like Tina.

9. Never use the *-ed* suffix to indicate the past tense of a verb.

   S.E.: She closed the door.
   B.E.: She close the door. Or, she have close the door.

10. Regardless of international verb time, only use the third person singular, present indicative, for use of the verb *to have*, as an auxiliary.

    S.E.: He had his wallet then he lost it.
    B.E.: He have him wallet then he lose it.
    S.E.: He had seen that movie.
    B.E.: We seen that movie. Or, we have see that movie.

11. Observe a minimal inflection of verbs. Particularly, never change from the first person singular forms to the third person singular.

    S.E.: Present Tense Forms: He goes to the store.
    B.E.: He go to the store.
    S.E.: Past Tense Forms: He went to the store.
    B.E.: He go to the store. Or, he gone to the store. Or, he been to the store.

12. The possessive case scarcely ever appears in Black English. Never use an apostrophe ('s) construction. If you wander into a possessive case component of an idea, then keep logically consistent: *ours, his, theirs, mines.* But, most likely, if you bump into such a component, you have wandered outside the underlying world-view of Black English.

    S.E.: He will take their car tomorrow.
    B.E.: He taking they car tomorrow.

13. Plurality: Logical consistency, continued: If the modifier indicates plurality then the noun remains in the singular case.

    S.E.: He ate twelve doughnuts.
    B.E.: He eat twelve doughnut.
    S.E.: She has many books.
    B.E.: She have many book.

14. Listen for, or invent, special Black English forms of the past tense, such as: "He losted it. That what she felted." If they are clear and readily understood, then use them.

15. Do not hesitate to play with words, sometimes inventing them: e.g. "astropotomous" means huge like a hippo plus astronomical and, therefore, signifies real big.

16. In Black English, unless you keenly want to underscore the past tense nature of an action, stay in the present tense and rely on the overall context of your ideas for the conveyance of time and sequence.

17. Never use the suffix *-ly* form of an adverb in Black English.

    S.E.: The rain came down rather quickly.
    B.E.: The rain come down pretty quick.

18. Never use the indefinite article *an* in Black English.

    S.E.: He wanted to ride an elephant.
    B.E.: He want to ride him a elephant.

19. Invariant syntax: in correct Black English it is possible to formulate an imperative, an interrogative, and a simple declarative idea with the same syntax:

B.E.: You going to the store?
　　　You going to the store.
　　　You going to the store!

Where was Willie Jordan? We'd reached the mid-term of the semester. Students had formulated Black English guidelines, by consensus, and they were now writing with remarkable beauty, purpose, and enjoyment:

I ain hardly speakin for everybody but myself so understan that.— Kim Parks

Samples from student writings:

Janie have a great big ole hole inside her. Tea Cake the only thing that fit that hole . . .

That pear tree beautiful to Janie, especial when bees fiddlin with the blossomin pear there growing large and lovely. But personal speakin, the love she get from staring at that tree ain the love what starin back at her in them relationship. (Monica Morris)

Love is a big theme in, *They Eye Was Watching God.* Love show people new corners inside theyself. It pull out good stuff and stuff back bad stuff . . . Joe worship the doing uh his own hand and need other people to worship him too. But he ain't think about Janie that she a person and ought to live like anybody common do. Queen life not for Janie. (Monica Morris)

In both life and writin, Black womens have varietous experience of love that be cold like a iceberg or fiery like a inferno. Passion got for the other partner involve, man or woman, seem as shallow, ankle-deep water or the most profoundest abyss. (Constance Evans)

Family love another bond that ain't never break under no pressure. (Constance Evans)

You know it really cold / When the friend you / Always get out the fire / Act like they don't know you / When you in the heat. (Constance Evans)

Big classroom discussion bout love at this time. I never take no class where us have any long arguin for and against for two or three day. New to me and great. I find the class time talkin a million time more interestin than detail bout the book. (Kathy Esseks)

40   As these examples suggest, Black English no longer limited the students, in any way. In fact, one of them, Philip Garfield, would shortly "translate" a pivotal scene from Ibsen's *Doll's House,* as his final term paper.

Nora: I didn't gived no shit. I thinked you a asshole back then, too, you make it so hard for me save mines husband life.

Krogstad: Girl, it clear you ain't any idea what you done. You done exact what I once done, and I losed my reputation over it.

Nora: You asks me believe you once act brave save you wife life?

Krogstad: Law care less why you done it.

Nora: Law must suck.

Krogstad: Suck or no, if I wants, judge screw you wid dis paper.

Nora: No way, man. (Philip Garfield)

But where was Willie? Compulsively punctual, and always thoroughly prepared with neatly typed compositions, he had disappeared. He failed to show up for our regularly scheduled conference, and I received neither a note nor a phone call of explanation. A whole week went by. I wondered if Willie had finally been captured by the extremely current happenings in South Africa: passage of a new constitution that did not enfranchise the Black majority, and militant Black South African reaction to that affront. I wondered if he'd been hurt, somewhere. I wondered if the serious workload of weekly readings and writings had overwhelmed him and changed his mind about independent study. Where was Willie Jordan?

One week after the first conference that Willie missed, he called: "Hello, Professor Jordan? This is Willie. I'm sorry I wasn't there last week. But something has come up and I'm pretty upset. I'm sorry but I really can't deal right now."

I asked Willie to drop by my office and just let me see that he was okay. He agreed to do that. When I saw him I knew something hideous had happened. Something had hurt him and scared him to the marrow. He was all agitated and stammering and terse and incoherent. At last, his sadly jumbled account let me surmise, as follows: Brooklyn police had murdered his unarmed, twenty-five-year-old brother, Reggie Jordan. Neither Willie nor his elderly parents knew what to do about it. Nobody from the press was interested. His folks had no money. Police ran his family around and around, to no point. And Reggie was really dead. And Willie wanted to fight, but he felt helpless.

*   *   *

With Willie's permission I began to try to secure legal counsel for the Jordan family. Unfortunately Black victims of police violence are truly numerous while the resources available to prosecute their killers are truly scarce. A friend of mine at the Center for Constitutional

Rights estimated that just the preparatory costs for bringing the cops into court normally approaches $180,000. Unless the execution of Reggie Jordan became a major community cause for organizing, and protest, his murder would simply become a statistical item.

Again, with Willie's permission, I contacted every newspaper and media person I could think of. But the William Bastone feature article in *The Village Voice* was the only result from that canvassing.   45

Again, with Willie's permission, I presented the case to my class in Black English. We had talked about the politics of language. We had talked about love and sex and child abuse and men and women. But the murder of Reggie Jordan broke like a hurricane across the room.

There are few "issues" as endemic to Black life as police violence. Most of the students knew and respected and liked Jordan. Many of them came from the very neighborhood where the murder had occurred. All of the students had known somebody close to them who had been killed by police, or had known frightening moments of gratuitous confrontation with the cops. They wanted to do everything at once to avenge death. Number One: They decided to compose personal statements of condolence to Willie Jordan and his family written in Black English. Number Two: They decided to compose individual messages to the police, in Black English. These should be prefaced by an explanatory paragraph composed by the entire group. Number Three: These individual messages, with their lead paragraph, should be sent to *Newsday*.

The morning after we agreed on these objectives, one of the young women students appeared with an unidentified visitor, who sat through the class, smiling in a peculiar, comfortable way.

Now we had to make more tactical decisions. Because we wanted the messages published, and because we thought it imperative that our outrage be known by the police, the tactical question was this: Should the opening, group paragraph be written in Black English or Standard English?

I have seldom been privy to a discussion with so much heart at the   50
dead heat of it. I will never forget the eloquence, the sudden haltings of speech, the fierce struggle against tears, the furious throwaway, and useless explosions that this question elicited.

That one question contained several others, each of them extraordinarily painful to even contemplate. How best to serve the memory of Reggie Jordan? Should we use the language of the killers—Standard English—in order to make our ideas acceptable to those controlling the killers? But wouldn't what we had to say be rejected, summarily, if we said it in our own language, the language of the victim,

---

CONVERSATIONS: POLICE VIOLENCE

Jordan writes in this passage (par. 47) that few issues are "as endemic to Black life as police violence." She wrote that line in 1988, but the issue of police violence against Blacks and other minority populations is a very old one. In the years since her essay was published, there have been several highly publicized instances of such violence, including the beating of Rodney King by Los Angeles police in 1991 and the beating of Abner Louima by New York City police in 1997. In both cases, Black men were severely beaten by White officers, provoking outrage and protest, especially among minority groups. In addition, a number of controversies arose in the late 1990s regarding the police practice of "racial profiling," in which police pay greater attention to people of certain racial or ethnic backgrounds on the assumption that those people are more likely to commit certain crimes. You might consider whether things have changed since Jordan's essay was published and whether readers today might understand the issue of police violence differently than readers in the 1980s.

Reggie Jordan? But if we sought to express ourselves by abandoning our language wouldn't that mean our suicide on top of Reggie's murder? But if we expressed ourselves in our own language wouldn't that be suicidal to the wish to communicate with those who, evidently, did not give a damn about us/Reggie/police violence in the Black community?

At the end of one of the longest, most difficult hours of my own life, the students voted, unanimously, to preface their individual messages with a paragraph composed in the language of Reggie Jordan. *"At least we don't give up nothing else. At least we stick to the truth: Be who we been. And stay all the way with Reggie."*

It was heartbreaking to proceed, from that point. Everyone in the room realized that our decision in favor of Black English had doomed our writings, even as the distinctive reality of our Black lives always has doomed our efforts to "be who we been" in this country.

I went to the blackboard and took down this paragraph, dictated by the class:

> . . . YOU COPS!
>
> WE THE BROTHER AND SISTER OF WILLIE JORDAN, A FELLOW STONY BROOK STUDENT WHO THE BROTHER OF THE DEAD REGGIE JORDAN. REGGIE, LIKE MANY BROTHER AND SISTER, HE A VICTIM OF BRUTAL RACIST POLICE, OCTOBER 25, 1984. US APPALL, FED UP, BECAUSE THAT ANOTHER SENSELESS DEATH WHAT OCCUR IN OUR COMMUNITY. THIS WHAT WE FEEL, THIS, FROM OUR HEART, FOR WE AIN'T STAYIN' SILENT NO MORE.

55   With the completion of this introduction, nobody said anything. I asked for comments. At this invitation, the unidentified visitor, a young Black man, ceaselessly smiling, raised his hand. He was, it so happens, a rookie cop. He had just joined the force in September and, he said he thought he should clarify a few things. So he came forward and sprawled easily into a posture of barroom, or fireside, nostalgia:

"See," Officer Charles enlightened us, "most times when you out on the street and something come down you do one of two things. Over-react or under-react. Now, if you under-react then you can get yourself kilt. And if you over-react then maybe you kill somebody. Fortunately it's about nine times out of ten and you will over-react. So the brother got kilt. And I'm sorry about that, believe me. But what you have to understand is what kilt him: Over-reaction. That's all. Now you talk about Black people and white police but see, now, I'm a cop myself. And (big smile) I'm Black. And just a couple months ago I was on the other side. But see it's the same for me. You a cop, you the ultimate authority: the Ultimate Authority. And you on the street, most of the time you can only do one of two things: over-react or under-react. That's all it is with the brother. Over-reaction. Didn't have nothing to do with race."

That morning Officer Charles had the good fortune to escape without being boiled alive. But barely. And I remember the pride of his smile when I read about the fate of Black policemen and other collaborators, in South Africa. I remember him, and I remember the shock and palpable feeling of shame that filled the room. It was as though that foolish, and deadly, young man had just relieved himself of his foolish, and deadly, explanation, face to face with the grief of Reggie Jordan's father and Reggie Jordan's mother. Class ended quietly. I copied the paragraph from the blackboard, collected the individual messages and left to type them up.

NEWSDAY rejected the piece.

The Village Voice could not find room in their "Letters" section to print the individual messages from the students to the police.

60   None of the TV news reporters picked up the story.

Nobody raised $180,000 to prosecute the murder of Reggie Jordan. Reggie Jordan is really dead.

I asked Willie Jordan to write an essay pulling together everything important to him from that semester. He was still deeply beside himself with frustration and amazement and loss. This is what he wrote, unedited, and in its entirety:

> Throughout the course of this semester I have been researching the effects of oppression and exploitation along racial lines in South Africa and its neighboring countries. I have become aware of South African police brutalization of native Africans beyond the extent of the law, even though the laws themselves are catalyst affliction upon Black men, women, and children. Many Africans die each year as a result of the deliberate use of police force to protect the white power structure.
>
> Social control agents in South Africa, such as policemen, are also used to force compliance among citizens through both overt and covert tactics. It is not uncommon to find bold-faced coercion and cold-blooded killings of Blacks by South African police for undetermined and/or inadequate reasons. Perhaps the truth is that the only reasons for this heinous treatment of Blacks rests in racial differences. We should also understand that what is conveyed through the media is not always accurate and may sometimes be construed as the tip of the iceberg at best.
>
> I recently received a painful reminder that racism, poverty, and the abuse of power are global problems which are by no means unique to South Africa. On October 25, 1984, at approximately 3:00 P.M. my brother, Mr. Reginald Jordan, was shot and killed by two New York City policemen from the 75th precinct in the East New York section of Brooklyn. His life ended at the age of twenty-five. Even up to this cur-

GLOSS: *NEWSDAY*
One of New York City's most widely read publications, *Newsday* is also one of the largest newspapers in the United States in terms of circulation.

rent point in time the Police Department has failed to provide my family, which consists of five brothers, eight sisters, and two parents, with a plausible reason for Reggie's death. Out of the many stories that were given to my family by the Police Department, not one of them seems to hold water. In fact, I honestly believe that the Police Department's assessment of my brother's murder is nothing short of ABSOLUTE BULLSHIT, and thus far no evidence had been produced to alter perception of the situation.

Furthermore, I believe that one of three cases may have occurred in this incident. First, Reggie's death may have been the desired outcome of the police officer's action, in which case the killing was premeditated. Or, it was a case of mistaken identity, which clarifies the fact that the two officers who killed my brother and their commanding parties are all grossly incompetent. Or, both of the above cases are correct, i.e., Reggie's murderers intended to kill him and the Police Department behaved insubordinately.

Part of the argument of the officers who shot Reggie was that he had attacked one of them and took his gun. This was their major claim. They also said that only one of them had actually shot Reggie. The facts, however, speak for themselves. According to the Death Certificate and autopsy report, Reggie was shot eight times from point-blank range. The Doctor who performed the autopsy told me himself that two bullets entered the side of my brother's head, four bullets were sprayed into his back, and two bullets struck him in the back of his legs. It is obvious that unnecessary force was used by the police and that it is extremely difficult to shoot someone in his back when he is attacking or approaching you.

After experiencing a situation like this and researching South Africa I believe that to a large degree, justice may only exist as rhetoric. I find it difficult to talk of true justice when the oppression of my people both at home and abroad attests to the fact that inequality and injustice are serious problems whereby Blacks and Third World people are perpetually short-changed by society. Something has to be done about the way in which this world is set up. Although it is a difficult task, we do have the power to make a change.

—Willie J. Jordan, Jr.

EGL 487, Section 58, November 14, 1984

It is my privilege to dedicate this book to the future life of Willie J. Jordan, Jr.

August 8, 1985

Understanding the Text

1. Why does Jordan believe Black English is an endangered species? What importance do her concerns about Black English have to her overall argument in this essay? Keeping in mind that this essay was first published in 1988, do you think Jordan's concerns about Black English as an endangered species are still valid? Explain.

2. What is the role of Standard English in the story that Jordan tells? What does Jordan's experience with her students suggest about Standard English? Do you think she makes a persuasive case for her own views of Standard English? Why or why not?

3. What is Jordan's purpose in having her students "learn" Black English? What do you think they ultimately learn about Black English and about language in general?

4. In what ways do you think the differences between Black English and Standard English that Jordan's students identified are important? What might these differences suggest about English?

5. Why do Jordan's students ultimately decide to submit their letters to *Newsday* with a note written in Black English? Why does Jordan believe that their decision

"doomed" their letters? Do you agree with the students? With Jordan? Why or why not? What might your answers to these questions suggest about your own views regarding Standard English?

Exploring the Issues

1. Jordan is telling two stories in this essay: the story of her class and the story of Willie Jordan and his brother. Examine how Jordan tells these two stories and how she weaves them together. How exactly do they relate to one another? How does Jordan connect them? How effectively do you think Jordan uses these two stories to convey her main ideas about race and language?

2. How does Jordan portray Black English in this essay? What does she emphasize about Black English? How does she compare it with Standard English? What do you think Jordan is trying to suggest about language and race by the way she presents Black English and Standard English in this essay? Do you think she's right? Explain.

3. Jordan tells us that there were five or six White students in her "rather large class." Although she refers repeatedly to her students throughout the essay, she never mentions the White students again. Why do you

think she refers to them briefly near the beginning of the essay but nowhere else in the essay? What effect might their presence in her class have had on the discussions about whether to write the letter to *Newsday* in Black English? In what ways might her essay have been different if she had included more description of their role in her class discussions?

4. What do you think Jordan wishes to suggest by ending her essay as she does? Do you think her ending is hopeful in any way? Do you think she intended it to be? Explain, citing specific passages to support your answer.

Entering the Conversations

1. With a group of classmates, decide whether Jordan's students were right to submit the letters to *Newsday* with an introductory letter written in Black English. Or should they have written it in Standard English? Try to reach consensus in your group, identifying the main reasons for your group's position. Then write a statement as a group in which you state and explain your group's position.

2. Write an essay in which you state and defend your own position about the decision made by June Jordan's students.

INFOTRAC

3. Using InfoTrac College Edition, your library, and any other appropriate resources, explore the controversy surrounding Black English, or Ebonics. Try to find sources that present various sides of the controversy about whether or not Black English is a legitimate dialect or simply a slang version of Standard English. If possible, speak to an expert on your campus, such as a professor of English or linguistics. You might also speak to people who use Black English or who grew up or live in areas where many people speak Black English. Then write a report in which you present the findings of your research. In your report, define Black English and provide an overview of what is known or believed about the uses of Black English. Try to present the main arguments for and against defining Black English as a distinct dialect of English (rather than as slang), and draw conclusions about its use in schools or other settings.

4. Examine some examples of contemporary music, such as hip-hop, in which Black English is used. Then write an analysis of the songs you selected using the rules for Black English developed by Jordan and her students. Determine whether the lyrics of songs using Black English conform to the rules described in this essay. Try to draw conclusions about the way musicians use Black English. For example, what can they do with Black English that they could not do with Standard English in their music?

Min Zhan Lu's (b. 1946) remarkable story *about learning to read and write in Chinese Communist schools never fails to provoke vigorous discussion in my classes. Many of my American students are amazed that schooling can be as overtly political as Lu's was. They often comfort themselves by pointing out that such obvious indoctrination does not happen in*

FROM Silence TO Struggle

MIN ZHAN LU

American schools. Yet Lu's essay often prompts these same students to look more closely at their experiences in American schools. Often, they are surprised to find some similarities between the way they were taught to write and read and the way Lu was taught. In some ways, the discussion my students and I have about Lu's essay are similar to debates about formal schooling that have been occurring in the United States since modern public schools developed in the nineteenth century. Some scholars trace the rise of public schooling in the United States to the rise of industrialized capitalism, and they make a connection between how writing has been taught in American schools and the needs of the capitalist workplace. Is that connection the same as the obvious political purposes that schooling served in Lu's case? You'll have to answer that question for yourself.

If Lu's essay is about the political nature of writing instruction, it is also about the tensions that can

Imagine that you enter a parlor. You come late. When you arrive, others have long preceded you, and they are engaged in a heated discussion. . . . You listen for a while, until you decide that you have caught the tenor of the argument; then you put in your oar. Someone answers; you answer him; another comes to your defense; another aligns himself against you, to either the embarrassment or gratification of your opponent, depending upon the quality of your ally's assistance. However, the discussion is interminable. The hour grows late, you must depart. And you do depart, with the discussion still vigorously in progress.

  —*Kenneth Burke,* The Philosophy of Literary Form

Men are not built in silence, but in word, in work, in action-reflection.

  —*Paulo Freire,* Pedagogy of the Oppressed

My mother withdrew into silence two months before she died. A few nights before she fell silent, she told me she regretted the way she had raised me and my sisters. I knew she was referring to the way we had been brought up in the midst of two conflicting worlds—the world of home, dominated by the ideology of the Western human-

arise when the literacy we learn at home conflicts with the literacy taught in school. Like Lu, many American students learn to read and write at home in different ways and in different languages from what is expected in schools. As you read Lu's compelling story of the challenges she faced, you might consider whether the way you have been taught to write in schools reflects values or beliefs that conflict with your upbringing at home.

Min Zhan Lu is a professor of English at the University of Wisconsin at Milwaukee. Her many articles and books about writing instruction include Representing the "Other": Basic Writers and the Teaching of Basic Writing *(1999). She has also written a memoir titled* Shanghai Quartet: The Crossings of Four Women of China *(2001). The following essay first appeared in 1987 in* College English, *a professional journal devoted to issues in the teaching of English. Because Lu is addressing an audience of academics with expertise in language and literacy, she sometimes uses words in a specialized way. As you read, pay attention to terms that may be unfamiliar to you—terms that Lu's intended audience would understand but that a more general audience may not.* ▼

CONVERSATIONS: THE CULTURAL REVOLUTION

In 1966, Chinese Communist leader Mao Zedong (whose name is written as Mao Tse-tung by Lu) initiated a series of attacks on Communist Party leaders and their supporters that he claimed were intended to rid Chinese society of the influences of capitalism and Western culture. The resulting purge of party leaders, intellectuals, businesspeople, and others led to the persecution of many Chinese people by Mao's followers and especially by the Red Guard, an organization of mostly young people who were loyal to Mao. These purges seriously disrupted China and weakened its economy, and in some cases, armed conflict between factions erupted. People like Lu's family, who were successful businesspeople, spoke English, or had other connections to Western culture, suffered greatly during this "revolution," which lasted in various forms until after Mao's death in 1976.

istic tradition, and the world of a society dominated by Mao Tse-tung's Marxism. My mother had devoted her life to our education, an education she knew had made us suffer political persecution during the Cultural Revolution. I wanted to find a way to convince her that, in spite of the persecution, I had benefited from the education she had worked so hard to give me. But I was silent. My understanding of my education was so dominated by memories of confusion and frustration that I was unable to reflect on what I could have gained from it.

This paper is my attempt to fill up that silence with words, words I didn't have then, words that I have since come to by reflecting on my earlier experience as a student in China and on my recent experience as a composition teacher in the United States. For in spite of the frustration and confusion I experienced growing up caught between two conflicting worlds, the conflict ultimately helped me to grow as a reader and writer. Constantly having to switch back and forth between the discourse of home and that of school made me sensitive and self-conscious about the struggle I experienced every time I tried to read, write, or think in either discourse. Eventually, it led me to search for constructive uses for such struggle.

From early childhood, I had identified the differences between home and the outside world by the different languages I used in each. My parents had wanted my sisters and me to get the best education they could conceive of—Cambridge. They had hired a live-in tutor, a Scot, to make us bilingual. I learned to speak English with my parents, my tutor, and my sisters. I was allowed to speak Shanghai dialect only with the servants. When I was four (the year after the Communist Revolution of 1949), my parents sent me to a local private school where I learned to speak, read, and write in a new language—Standard Chinese, the official written language of New China.

In those days I moved from home to school, from English to Standard Chinese to Shanghai dialect, with no apparent friction. I spoke each language with those who spoke the language. All seemed quite "natural"—servants spoke only Shanghai dialect because they were servants; teachers spoke Standard Chinese because they were teachers; languages had different words because they were different languages. I thought of English as my family language, comparable to the many strange dialects I didn't speak but had often heard some of my classmates speak with their families. While I was happy to have a special family language, until second grade I didn't feel that my family language was any different than some of my classmates' family dialects.

My second grade homeroom teacher was a young graduate from a missionary school. When she found out I spoke English, she began to practice her English on me. One day she used English when

5

asking me to run an errand for her. As I turned to close the door behind me, I noticed the puzzled faces of my classmates. I had the same sensation I had often experienced when some stranger in a crowd would turn on hearing me speak English. I was more intensely pleased on this occasion, however, because suddenly I felt that my family language had been singled out from the family languages of my classmates. Since we were not allowed to speak any dialect other than Standard Chinese in the classroom, having my teacher speak English to me in class made English an official language of the classroom. I began to take pride in my ability to speak it.

This incident confirmed in my mind what my parents had always told me about the importance of English to one's life. Time and again they had told me of how my paternal grandfather, who was well versed in classic Chinese, kept losing good-paying jobs because he couldn't speak English. My grandmother reminisced constantly about how she had slaved and saved to send my father to a first-rate missionary school. And we were made to understand that it was my father's fluent English that had opened the door to his success. Even though my family had always stressed the importance of English for my future, I used to complain bitterly about the extra English lessons we had to take after school. It was only after my homeroom teacher had "sanctified" English that I began to connect English with my education. I became a much more eager student in my tutorials.

What I learned from my tutorials seemed to enhance and reinforce what I was learning in my classroom. In those days each word had one meaning. One day I would be making a sentence at school: "The national flag of China is red." The next day I would recite at home, "My love is like a red, red rose." There seemed to be an agreement between the Chinese "red" and the English "red," and both corresponded to the patch of color printed next to the word. "Love" was my love for my mother at home and my love for my "motherland" at school; both "loves" meant how I felt about my mother. Having two loads of

CONVERSATIONS: THE COLOR RED
Lu discusses the various meanings that the color *red* had for her as a Chinese student. During most of the twentieth century, red was the color associated with communism; to be called a "red" in the United States was to be labeled a Communist or Communist sympathizer. For Chinese Communists, red symbolized the revolution, and it is the dominant color of the Chinese flag (shown here). It is interesting to think about how the meanings associated with the color red have changed since Lu was a young student in the 1950s, especially after the break-up of the former Soviet Union, which, along with China, was the other great Communist power. Many Communist movements continue to use the color to signify revolution, but in the United States, the color no longer is so clearly associated with communism. Today, for example, political observers often speak of the "red" states, which are considered more conservative, and the "blue" states, considered more liberal. This map shows the states that voted for George W. Bush in red and those that voted for John Kerry in blue in the 2004 U.S. presidential election.

© Jeremy Homer/CORBIS

Chinese flag

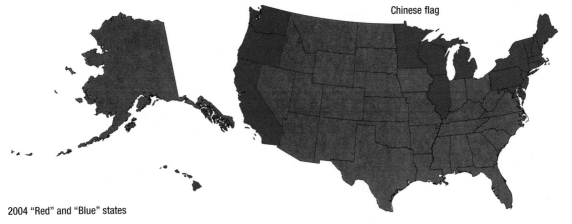

2004 "Red" and "Blue" states

homework forced me to develop a quick memory for words and a sensitivity to form and style. What I learned in one language carried over to the other. I made sentences such as, "I saw a red, red rose among the green leaves," with both the English lyric and the classic Chinese lyric—red flower among green leaves—running through my mind, and I was praised by both teacher and tutor for being a good student.

Although my elementary schooling took place during the fifties, I was almost oblivious to the great political and social changes happening around me. Years later, I read in my history and political philosophy textbooks that the fifties were a time when "China was making a transition from a semi-feudal, semi-capitalist, and semi-colonial country into a socialist country," a period in which "the Proletarians were breaking into the educational territory dominated by Bourgeois Intellectuals." While people all over the country were being officially classified into Proletarians, Petty-bourgeois, National-bourgeois, Poor-peasants, and Intellectuals, and were trying to adjust to their new social identities, my parents were allowed to continue the upper middle-class life they had established before the 1949 Revolution because of my father's affiliation with British firms. I had always felt that my family was different from the families of my classmates, but I didn't perceive society's view of my family until the summer vacation before I entered high school.

First, my aunt was caught by her colleagues talking to her husband over the phone in English. Because of it, she was criticized and almost labeled a Rightist. (This was the year of the Anti-Rightist movement in which the Intellectuals became the target of the "socialist class-struggle.") I had heard others telling my mother that she was foolish to teach us English when Russian had replaced English as the "official" foreign language. I had also learned at school that the American and British Imperialists were the arch-enemies of New China. Yet I had made no connection between the arch-enemies and the English our family spoke. What happened to my aunt forced the connection on me. I began to see my parents' choice of a family language as an anti-Revolutionary act and was alarmed that I had participated in such an act. From then on, I took care not to use English outside home and to conceal my knowledge of English from my new classmates.

10   Certain words began to play important roles in my new life at the junior high. On the first day of school, we were handed forms to fill out with our parents' class, job, and income. Being one of the few people not employed by the government, my father had never been officially classified. Since he was a medical doctor, he told me to put him down as an Intellectual. My homeroom teacher called me into the office a couple of days afterwards and told me that my father couldn't be an Intellectual if his income far exceeded that of a Capitalist. He also told me that since my father worked for Foreign Impe-

rialists, my father should be classified as an Imperialist Lackey. The teacher looked nonplussed when I told him that my father couldn't be an Imperialist Lackey because he was a medical doctor. But I could tell from the way he took notes on my form that my father's job had put me in an unfavorable position in his eyes.

The Standard Chinese term **"CLASS"** was not a new word for me. Since first grade, I had been taught sentences such as, "The Working class are the masters of New China." I had always known that it was good to be a worker, but until then, I had never felt threatened for not being one. That fall, "class" began to take on a new meaning for me. I noticed a group of Working-class students and teachers at school. I was made to understand that because of my class background, I was excluded from that group.

Another word that became important was "consciousness." One of the slogans posted in the school building read, "Turn our students into future Proletarians with socialist consciousness and education!" For several weeks we studied this slogan in our political philosophy course, a subject I had never had in elementary school. I still remember the definition of "socialist consciousness" that we were repeatedly tested on through the years: "Socialist consciousness is a person's political soul. It is the consciousness of the Proletarians represented by Marxist Mao Tse-tung thought. It takes expression in one's action, language, and lifestyle. It is the task of every Chinese student to grow up into a Proletarian with a socialist consciousness so that he can serve the people and the motherland." To make the abstract concept accessible to us, our teacher pointed out that the immediate task for students from Working-class families was to strengthen their socialist consciousnesses. For those of us who were from other class backgrounds, the task was to turn ourselves into Workers with socialist consciousnesses. The teacher never explained exactly how we were supposed to "turn" into Workers. Instead, we were given samples of the ritualistic annual plans we had to write at the beginning of each term. In these plans, we performed "self-criticism" on our consciousnesses and made vows to turn ourselves into Workers with socialist consciousnesses. The teacher's division between those who did and those who didn't have a socialist consciousness led me to reify the notion of "consciousness" into a thing one possesses. I equated this intangible "thing" with a concrete way of dressing, speaking, and writing. For instance, I never doubted that my political philosophy teacher had a socialist consciousness because she was from a steelworker's family (she announced this the first day of class) and was a Party member who wore grey cadre suits and talked like a philosophy textbook. I noticed other things about her. She had beautiful eyes and spoke Standard Chinese with such a pure accent that I thought she should be a film star. But I was embarrassed that I had noticed things that

GLOSS: CLASS

The idea of *class* is central to the Marxist political ideology under which Lu grew up in Communist China. Within that ideology, *class* refers to categories that identify people in terms of their relative positions in an economic and political system. In Lu's experience, there were clear delineations among various classes within a Marxist system. But the idea of class in U.S. society isn't so clear-cut. Some people use it to refer to income level; for others, it reflects types of work or working conditions, regardless of income. For example, a worker in an automobile factory might be classified as "working class" even though he or she might earn more money than a teacher or a sales manager, who would be considered "middle class." You might think about the importance of the idea of social class in Lu's experience and how your own experiences might shape the way you react to the stories she tells.

ought not to have been associated with her. I blamed my observation on my Bourgeois consciousness.

At the same time, the way reading and writing were taught through memorization and imitation also encouraged me to reduce concepts and ideas to simple definitions in literature and political philosophy classes, we were taught a large number of quotations from Marx, Lenin, and Mao Tse-tung. Each concept that appeared in these quotations came with a definition. We were required to memorize the definitions of the words along with the quotations. Every time I memorized a definition, I felt I had learned a word: "The national red flag symbolizes the blood shed by Revolutionary ancestors for our socialist cause"; "New China rises like a red sun over the eastern horizon." As I memorized these sentences, I reduced their metaphors to dictionary meanings: "red" meant "Revolution" and "red sun" meant "New China" in the "language" of the Working Class. I learned mechanically but eagerly. I soon became quite fluent in this new language.

As school began to define me as a political subject, my parents tried to build up my resistance to the "communist poisoning" by exposing me to the "great books"—novels by Charles Dickens, Nathaniel Hawthorne, Emily Brontë, Jane Austen, and writers from around the turn of the century. My parents implied that these writers represented how I, their child, should read and write. My parents replaced the word "Bourgeois" with the word "cultured." They reminded me that I was in school only to learn math and science. I needed to pass the other courses to stay in school, but I was not to let the "Red doctrines" corrupt my mind. Gone were the days when I could innocently write. "I saw the red, red rose among the green leaves," collapsing, as I did, English and Chinese cultural traditions. "Red" came to mean Revolution at school, "the Commies" at home, and adultery in *The Scarlet Letter*. Since I took these symbols and metaphors as meanings natural to people of the same class, I abandoned my earlier definitions of English and Standard Chinese as the language of home and the language of school. I now defined English as the language of the Bourgeois and Standard Chinese as the language of the Working class. I thought of the language of the Working class as someone else's language and the language of the Bourgeois as my language. But I also believed that, although the language of the Bourgeois was my real language, I could and would adopt the language of the Working class when I was at school. I began to put on and take off my Working class language in the same way I put on and took off my school clothes to avoid being criticized for wearing Bourgeois clothes.

15   In my literature classes, I learned the Working-class formula for reading. Each work in the textbook had a short "Author's Biography": "X X X, born in 19— in the province of X X, is from a Worker's family. He joined the Revolution in 19—. He is a Revolutionary realist with a passionate love for the Party and Chinese Revolution. His work

expresses the thoughts and emotions of the masses and sings praise to the prosperous socialist construction on all fronts of China." The teacher used the "Author's Biography" as a yardstick to measure the texts. We were taught to locate details in the texts that illustrated these summaries, such as words that expressed Workers' thoughts and emotions or events that illustrated the Workers' lives.

I learned a formula for Working-class writing in the composition classes. We were given sample essays and told to imitate them. The theme was always about how the collective taught the individual a lesson. I would write papers about labor-learning experiences or school-cleaning days, depending on the occasion of the collective activity closest to the assignment. To make each paper look different, I dressed it up with details about the date, the weather, the environment, or the appearance of the Master-worker who had taught me "the lesson." But as I became more and more fluent in the generic voice of the Working-class Student, I also became more and more self-conscious about the language we used at home.

For instance, in senior high we began to have English classes ("to study English for the Revolution," as the slogan on the cover of the textbook said), and I was given my first Chinese-English dictionary. There I discovered the English version of the term "class-struggle." (The Chinese characters for a school "class" and for a social "class" are different.) I had often used the English word "class" at home in sentences such as, "So and so has class," but I had not connected this sense of "class" with "class-struggle." Once the connection was made, I heard a second layer of meaning every time someone at home said a person had "class." The expression began to mean the person had the style and sophistication characteristic of the Bourgeoisie. The word lost its innocence. I was uneasy about hearing that second layer of meaning because I was sure my parents did not hear the word that way. I felt that therefore I should not be hearing it that way either. Hearing the second layer of meaning made me wonder if I was losing my English.

My suspicion deepened when I noticed myself unconsciously merging and switching between the "reading" of home and the "reading" of school. Once I had to write a report on *The Revolutionary Family,* a book about an illiterate woman's awakening and growth as a Revolutionary through the deaths of her husband and all her children for the cause of the Revolution. In one scene the woman deliberated over whether or not she should encourage her youngest son to join the Revolution. Her memory of her husband's death made her afraid to encourage her son. Yet she also remembered her earlier married life and the first time her husband tried to explain the meaning of the Revolution to her. These memories made her feel she should encourage her son to continue the cause his father had begun.

I was moved by this scene. "Moved" was a word my mother and sisters used a lot when we discussed books. Our favorite moments in novels were moments of what I would now call internal conflict, moments which we said "moved" us. I remember that we were "moved" by Jane Eyre when she was torn between her sense of ethics, which compelled her to leave the man she loved, and her impulse to stay with the only man who had ever loved her. We were also moved by Agnes in *David Copperfield* because of the way she restrained her love for David so that he could live happily with the woman he loved. My standard method of doing a book report was to model it on the review by the Publishing Bureau and to dress it up with detailed quotations from the book. The review of *The Revolutionary Family* emphasized the woman's Revolutionary spirit. I decided to use the scene that had moved me to illustrate this point. I wrote the report the night before it was due. When I had finished, I realized I couldn't possibly hand it in. Instead of illustrating her Revolutionary spirit, I had dwelled on her internal conflict, which could be seen as a moment of weak sentimentality that I should never have emphasized in a Revolutionary heroine. I wrote another report, taking care to illustrate the grandeur of her Revolutionary spirit by expanding on a quotation in which she decided that if the life of her son could change the lives of millions of sons, she should not begrudge his life for the cause of Revolution. I handed in my second version but kept the first in my desk.

20   I never showed it to anyone. I could never show it to people outside my family, because it had deviated so much from the reading enacted by the jacket review. Neither could I show it to my mother or sisters, because I was ashamed to have been so moved by such a "Revolutionary" book. My parents would have been shocked to learn that I could like such a book in the same way they liked Dickens. Writing this book report increased my fear that I was losing the command over both the "language of home" and the "language of school" that I had worked so hard to gain. I tried to remind myself that, if I could still tell when my reading or writing sounded incorrect, then I had retained my command over both languages. Yet I could no longer be confident of my command over either language because I had discovered that when I was not careful—or even when I was—my reading and writing often surprised me with its impurity. To prevent such impurity, I became very suspicious of my thoughts when I read or wrote. I was always asking myself why I was using this word, how I was using it, always afraid that I wasn't reading or writing correctly. What confused and frustrated me most was that I could not figure out why I was no longer able to read or write correctly without such painful deliberation.

I continued to read only because reading allowed me to keep my thoughts and confusion private. I hoped that somehow, if I watched myself carefully, I would figure out from the way I read whether I had really mastered the "languages." But writing became a dreadful chore. When I tried to keep a diary, I was so afraid that the voice of school might slip in that I could only list my daily activities. When I wrote for school, I worried that my Bourgeois sensibilities would betray me.

The more suspicious I became about the way I read and wrote, the more guilty I felt for losing the spontaneity with which I had learned to "use" these "languages." Writing the book report made me feel that my reading and writing in the "language" of either home or school could not be free of the interference of the other. But I was unable to acknowledge, grasp, or grapple with what I was experiencing, for both my parents and my teachers had suggested that, if I were a good student, such interference would and should not take place. I assumed that once I had "acquired" a discourse, I could simply switch it on and off every time I read and wrote as I would some electronic tool. Furthermore, I expected my readings and writings to come out in their correct forms whenever I switched the proper discourse on. I still regarded the discourse of home as natural and the discourse of school alien, but I never had doubted before that I could acquire both and switch them on and off according to the occasion.

When my experience in writing conflicted with what I thought should happen when I used each discourse, I rejected my experience because it contradicted what my parents and teachers had taught me. I shied away from writing to avoid what I assumed I should not experience. But trying to avoid what should not happen did not keep it from recurring whenever I had to write. Eventually my confusion and frustration over these recurring experiences compelled me to search for an explanation: how and why had I failed to learn what my parents and teachers had worked so hard to teach me?

I now think of the internal scene for my reading and writing about *The Revolutionary Family* as a heated discussion between myself, the voices of home, and those of school. The review on the back of the book, the sample student papers I came across in my composition classes, my philosophy teacher—these I heard as voices of one group. My parents and my home readings were the voices of an opposing group. But the conversation between these opposing voices in the internal scene of my writing was not as polite and respectful as the parlor scene Kenneth Burke has portrayed (see epigraph). Rather, these voices struggled to dominate the discussion, constantly incorporating, dismissing, or suppressing the arguments of each other, like the battles between the hegemonic and counterhegemonic forces described in Raymond Williams' *Marxism and Literature* (108–14).

CONVERSATIONS: WRITING AND READING AS SOCIAL ACTS
In this paragraph, Lu is describing the impact of her struggle to write her book report on *The Revolutionary Family*. In doing so, she expresses her fears that she could no longer control her "home language" and her "school language." She writes that "my reading and writing in the 'language' of either home or school could not be free of the interference of the other." This is a compelling example of what scholars sometimes mean when they refer to the social nature of language. It is also an example of what theorists mean when they discuss the "instability" of meaning in writing—in other words, the ways in which the meaning of a text is not completely within the control of the writer but is determined by context. In this case, Lu is influenced by the languages of school and home, and she cannot control those influences completely, even though she is aware of them. In this regard, although she may be writing her own essay, her writing is not completely individual but is always a social act because it is done in the context of the practices and expectations of others. As a scholar of rhetoric and composition, Lu is aware of these issues. In paragraphs 24 and 27, she discusses them directly and uses her own experience to illustrate the social nature of language. Furthermore, in making references to the writing of Kenneth Burke and Raymond Williams, two famous scholars who explored issues in language, she is extending the ongoing scholarly conversations about the nature of writing and the problem of meaning.

25   When I read *The Revolutionary Family* and wrote the first version of my report, I began with a quotation from the review. The voices of both home and school answered, clamoring to be heard. I tried to listen to one group and turn a deaf ear to the other. Both persisted. I negotiated my way through these conflicting voices, now agreeing with one, now agreeing with the other. I formed a reading out of my interaction with both. Yet I was afraid to have done so because both home and school had implied that I should speak in unison with only one of these groups and stand away from the discussion rather than participate in it.

My teachers and parents had persistently called my attention to the intensity of the discussion taking place on the external social scene. The story of my grandfather's failure and my father's success had from my early childhood made me aware of the conflict between Western and traditional Chinese cultures. My political education at school added another dimension to the conflict: the war of Marxist-Maoism against them both. Yet when my parents and teachers called my attention to the conflict, they stressed the anxiety of having to live through China's transformation from a semifeudal, semi-capitalist, and semi-colonial society to a socialist one. Acquiring the discourse of the dominant group was, to them, a means of seeking alliance with that group and thus of surviving the whirlpool of cultural currents around them. As a result, they modeled their pedagogical practices on this utilitarian view of language. Being the eager student, I adopted this view of language as a tool for survival. It came to dominate my understanding of the discussion on the social and historical scene and to restrict my ability to participate in that discussion.

To begin with, the metaphor of language as a tool for survival led me to be passive in my use of discourse, to be a bystander in the discussion. In Burke's "parlor," everyone is involved in the discussion. As it goes on through history, what we call "communal discourses"—arguments specific to particular political, social, economic, ethnic, sexual, and family groups—form, re-form and transform. To use a discourse in such a scene is to participate in the argument and to contribute to the formation of the discourse. But when I was growing up, I could not take on the burden of such an active role in the discussion. For both home and school presented the existent conventions of the discourse each taught me as absolute laws for my action. They turned verbal action into a tool, a set of conventions produced and shaped prior to and outside of my own verbal acts. Because I saw language as a tool, I separated the process of producing the tool from the process of using it. The tool was made by someone else and was then acquired and used by me. How the others made it before I acquired it determined and guaranteed what it produced when I used it. I imagined that the more experienced and powerful members of the community were the ones responsible for making the tool. They were the ones who participated in the discussion and fought with opponents. When I used what they made, their labor and accomplishments would ensure the quality of my reading and writing. By using it, I could survive the heated discussion. When my immediate experience in writing the book report suggested that knowing the conventions of school did not guarantee the form and content of my report, when it suggested that I had to write the report with the work and responsibility I had assigned to those who wrote book reviews in the Publishing Bureau, I thought I had lost the tool I had earlier acquired.

Another reason I could not take up an active role in the argument was that my parents and teachers contrived to provide a scene free of conflict for practicing my various languages. It was as if their experience had made them aware of the conflict between their discourse and other discourses and of the struggle involved in reproducing the conventions of any discourse on a scene where more than one discourse exists. They seemed convinced that such conflict and struggle would overwhelm someone still learning the discourse. Home and school each contrived a purified space where only one discourse was spoken and heard. In their choice of textbooks, in the way they spoke, and in the way they required me to speak, each jealously silenced any voice that threatened to break the unison of the scene. The homogeneity of home and of school implied that only one discourse could and should be relevant in each place. It led me to believe I should leave behind, turn a deaf ear to, or forget the discourse of the other when I crossed the boundary dividing them. I expected myself to set down one discourse whenever I took up another just as I would take off or put on a particular set of clothes for school or home.

Despite my parents' and teachers' attempts to keep home and school discrete, the internal conflict between the two discourses continued whenever I read or wrote. Although I tried to suppress the voice of one discourse in the name of the other, having to speak aloud in the voice I had just silenced each time I crossed the boundary kept both voices active in my mind. Every "I think . . ." from the voice of home or school brought forth a "However . . ." or a "But . . ." from the voice of the opponents. To identify with the voice of home or school, I had to negotiate through the conflicting voices of both by restating, taking back, qualifying my thoughts. I was unconsciously doing so when I did my book report. But I could not use the interaction comfortably and constructively. Both my parents and my teachers had implied that my job was to prevent that interaction from happening. My sense of having failed to accomplish what they had taught silenced me.

To use the interaction between the discourses of home and school 30 constructively, I would have to have seen reading or writing as a process in which I worked my way towards a stance through a dialectical process of identification and division. To identify with an ally, I would have to have grasped the distance between where he or she stood and where I was positioning myself. In taking a stance against an opponent, I would have to have grasped where my stance identified with the stance of my allies. Teetering along the "wavering line of pressure and counter-pressure" from both allies and opponents, I might have worked my way towards a stance of my own (Burke, *A Rhetoric of Motives* 23). Moreover, I would have to have understood that the voices in my mind, like the participants in the parlor scene, were in constant flux. As I came into contact with new and different groups of people or read different books, voices entered and left. Each time I read or wrote, the stance I negotiated out of these voices would always be at some distance from the stances I worked out in my previous and my later readings or writings.

I could not conceive such a form of action for myself because I saw reading and writing as an expression of an established stance. In delineating the conventions of a discourse, my parents and teachers had synthesized the stance they saw as typical for a representative member of the community. Burke calls this the stance of a "god" or the "prototype"; Williams calls it the "official" or "possible" stance of the community. Through the metaphor of the survival tool, my parents and teachers had led me to assume I could automatically reproduce the official stance of the discourse I used. Therefore, when I did my book report on *The Revolutionary Family*, I expected my knowledge of the official stance set by the book review to ensure the actual stance of my report. As it happened, I began by trying to take the official stance of the review. Other voices interrupted. I answered back. In the process, I worked out a stance approximate but not identical to the official stance I began with. Yet the experience of having to labor to realize my knowledge of the official stance or to prevent myself from wandering away from it frustrated and confused me. For even though I had been actually reading and writing in a Burkean scene, I was afraid to participate actively in the discussion. I assumed it was my role to survive by staying out of it.

*   *   *

Not long ago, my daughter told me that it bothered her to hear her friend "talk wrong." Having come to the United States from China with little English, my daughter has become sensitive to the way English, as spoken by her teachers, operates. As a result, she has amazed her teachers with her success in picking up the language and in adapting to life at school. Her concern to speak the English taught in the classroom "correctly" makes her uncomfortable when she hears people using "ain't" or double negatives, which her teacher considers "improper." I see in her the me that had eagerly learned and used the discourse of the Working class at school. Yet while I was torn between the two conflicting worlds of school and home, she moves with seeming ease from the conversations she hears over the dinner table to her teacher's words in the classroom. My husband and I are proud of the good work she does at school. We are glad she is spared the kinds of conflict between home and school I experienced at her age. Yet as we watch her becoming more and more fluent in the language of the classroom, we wonder if, by enabling her to "survive" school, her very fluency will silence her when the scene of her reading and writing expands beyond that of the composition classroom.

For when I listen to my daughter, to students, and to some composition teachers talking about the teaching and learning of writing, I am often alarmed by the degree to which the metaphor of a survival tool dominates their understanding of language as it once dominated my own. I am especially concerned with the way some composition classes focus on turning the classroom into a monological scene for the students' reading and writing. Most of our students live in a world similar to my daughter's, somewhere between the purified world of the classroom and the complex world of my adolescence. When composition classes encourage these students to ignore those voices that seem irrelevant to the purified world of the classroom, most students are often able to do so without much struggle. Some of them are so adept at doing it that the whole process has for them become automatic.

However, beyond the classroom and beyond the limited range of these students' immediate lives lies a much more complex and dynamic social and historical scene. To help these students become actors in such a scene, perhaps we need to call their attention to voices that may seem irrelevant to the discourse we teach rather than encourage them to shut them out. For example, we might intentionally complicate the classroom scene by bringing into it discourses that stand at varying distances from the one we teach. We might encourage students to explore ways of practicing the conventions of the discourse they are learning by negotiating through these conflicting voices. We could also encourage them to see themselves as responsible for forming or transforming as well as preserving the discourse they are learning.

As I think about what we might do to complicate the external and internal scenes of our students' writing, I hear my parents and teachers saying: "Not now. Keep them from the wrangle of the marketplace until they have acquired the discourse and are skilled at using it." And I answer: "Don't teach them to 'survive' the whirlpool of crosscurrents by avoiding it. Use the classroom to moderate the currents. Moderate the currents, but teach them from the beginning to struggle." When I think of the ways in which the teaching of reading and writing as classroom activities can frustrate the development of students, I am almost grateful for the overwhelming complexity of the circumstances in which I grew up. For it was this complexity that kept me from losing sight of the effort and choice involved in reading or writing with and through a discourse.

Works Cited

Burke, Kenneth. *The Philosophy of Literary Form: Studies in Symbolic Action.* 2nd ed. Baton Rouge: Louisiana State UP, 1967.

——. *A Rhetoric of Motives.* Berkeley: U of California P, 1969.

Freire, Paulo. *Pedagogy of the Oppressed.* Trans. M. B. Ramos. New York: Continuum, 1970.

Williams, Raymond. *Marxism and Literature.* New York: Oxford UP, 1977.

Understanding the Text

1. What does Lu mean when she states that this essay is "my attempt to fill up that silence with words" (par. 2)? What silence is she referring to? What led to that silence? In what ways do you think Lu's essay achieves this goal of filling the silence?

2. What were the chief differences between what Lu calls the "discourse of home" and the "discourse of school"? Why were these differences so important to Lu? What might these different discourses suggest about writing?

3. In what ways does school help define Lu as a "political subject"? How do reading and writing contribute to her becoming such a subject? Do you think schooling in the United States defines students as political subjects? Why or why not?

4. Why is writing a book report on *The Revolutionary Family* so difficult and important for Lu? What does she learn through this experience? What does this experience reveal about writing and about language in general?

5. What does Lu mean when she writes about taking an "active role in the argument" (par. 26–28)? What argument is occurring here? How can Lu take an active role in it? What main point do you think she is making about writing in this passage?

6. What is the "metaphor of the survival tool" that Lu uses to refer to language in this article? In what ways was language a survival tool for her? Why does she worry that her daughter and other students see language as a survival tool? Do you think her concern is valid? Why or why not?

Exploring the Issues

1. Lu goes into great detail to describe some of her struggles with reading and writing in school and at home. In paragraphs 15 through 20, she describes specific assignments she completed that were difficult for her because of the different expectations for reading and writing in school and at home. Examine these passages carefully. In what ways were reading and writing really different for Lu at home compared to school? What do you think these scenes reveal about reading and writing?

2. In paragraph 28, Lu writes that in her experiences in China, "Home and school each contrived a purified space where only one discourse was spoken and heard." Explain what Lu means by this statement. Do you think the statement applies to your own experience? Explain.

3. At the end of her essay, Lu writes that she believes that composition teachers should teach students "from the beginning to struggle." Why does she advocate such an approach to teaching writing? What would that kind of teaching mean for student writers, in your view? Do you agree with her? Why or why not?

Entering the Conversations

1. Write an essay describing an experience in which writing or reading was especially difficult or risky for you.

2. In a group of classmates, share the essays you wrote for Question 1. What similarities and differences can you identify in the various experiences you and your classmates wrote about? What do your essays suggest about writing? On the basis of your essays, try to draw conclusions about the political nature of writing and its role in our lives.

3. Some critics charge that many American college professors teach in ways that are too political or that compromise students who disagree with their professors on certain political issues. There have been controversies on some campuses in which specific professors have been accused of overtly political teaching. Using the Internet, your library, and any other appropriate resources, try to find instances of such controversies and determine why complaints were filed against the professor. If such a controversy occurred on your own campus, include that in your research. Also, find editorials or essays in which the writers offer their views about such political teaching. (Many web sites are devoted to these issues.) Then, drawing on your research, write an essay in which you express your views about the political nature of teaching—and especially about teaching writing.

4. On the basis of your research for Question 3, write a letter to the president of your college expressing your views about the political nature of teaching on your campus.

5. Arrange to talk to someone on your campus who was educated in a country other than the United States. (You might visit your campus office for international students or your writing center to find such a person.) If possible, arrange to talk to more than one such person. Find out what their experiences with school were like, especially regarding the way they were taught to write. Get their impressions and opinions about those experiences and how they feel about schooling in the United States. Write a report for your classmates about your interviews. Provide some information about each person you spoke to (where they are from, when they came to the United States and why, and so forth), and describe their experiences with writing instruction in their home country and in the United States. Draw conclusions about how writing is taught and how it might affect individual students. Alternatively, if you are a person who was educated in a country other than the United States, write an essay in which you describe your experiences, comparing how you were taught to read and write there to how writing is taught in the United States.

A few years ago, I had the opportunity to *teach a writing class in a prison. My students ranged in age from their teens to their fifties; they were incarcerated for all kinds of crimes, from auto theft and drug trafficking to murder. Many of them could hardly write a correct sentence. But all of them worked hard on their writing, and some of*

Becoming A Poet

them took advantage of the *assignments I gave to tell the stories of their often sad and difficult lives. I often felt that the power of their writing did not lie so much in what they wrote about but in the fact that for a few hours each week they could escape the dull yet dangerous lives they led in prison and become something other than inmates. Writing gave them a way to feel human again.*

Maybe because of that experience I have found this essay by Jimmy Santiago Baca (b. 1952) to be especially powerful. In this essay, which is taken from his autobiography, Working in the Dark: Reflections of a Poet of the Barrio (1992), *Baca describes his own difficult life growing up in the American Southwest, a life characterized by crime and trouble with the law. His descriptions of his horrific experiences while in prison are especially powerful, and they sometimes make me wonder*

JIMMY SANTIAGO BACA

On weekend graveyard shifts at St. Joseph's Hospital I worked the emergency room, mopping up pools of blood and carting plastic bags stuffed with arms, legs, and hands to the outdoor incinerator. I enjoyed the quiet, away from the screams of shotgunned, knifed, and mangled kids writhing on gurneys outside the operating rooms. Ambulance sirens shrieked and squad car lights reddened the cool nights, flashing against the hospital walls: gray—red, gray—red. On slow nights I would lock the door of the administration office, search the reference library for a book on female anatomy and, with my feet propped on the desk, leaf through the illustrations, smoking my cigarette. I was seventeen.

One night my eye was caught by a familiar-looking word on the spine of a book. The title was *450 Years of Chicano History in Pictures*. On the cover were black-and-white photos: Padre Hidalgo exhorting Mexican peasants to revolt against the Spanish dictators; Anglo vigilantes hanging two Mexicans from a tree; a young Mexican woman with rifle and ammunition belts crisscrossing her breast; César Chávez and field workers marching for fair wages; Chicano railroad workers

JIMMY SANTIAGO BACA, "BECOMING A POET." FROM *WORKING IN THE DARK: REFLECTIONS OF A POET OF THE BARRIO* (1992). PUBLISHER: RED CRANE BOOKS. REPRINTED BY PERMISSION.

laying creosote ties; Chicanas laboring at machines in textile factories; Chicanas picketing and hoisting boycott signs.

From the time I was seven, teachers had been punishing me for not knowing my lessons by making me stick my nose in a circle chalked on the blackboard. Ashamed of not understanding and fearful of asking questions, I dropped out of school in the ninth grade. At seventeen I still didn't know how to read, but those pictures confirmed my identity. I stole the book that night, stashing it for safety under the slop sink until I got off work. Back at my boardinghouse, I showed the book to friends. All of us were amazed; this book told us we were alive. We, too, had defended ourselves with our fists against hostile Anglos, gasping for breath in fights with the policemen who outnumbered us. The book reflected back to us our struggle in a way that made us proud.

Most of my life I felt like a target in the cross hairs of a hunter's rifle. When strangers and outsiders questioned me I felt the hang-rope tighten around my neck and the trapdoor creak beneath my feet. There was nothing so humiliating as being unable to express myself, and my inarticulateness increased my sense of jeopardy, of being endangered. I felt intimidated and vulnerable, ridiculed and scorned. Behind a mask of humility, I seethed with mute rebellion.

5   Before I was eighteen, I was arrested on suspicion of murder after refusing to explain a deep cut on my forearm. With shocking speed I found myself handcuffed to a chain gang of inmates and bused to a holding facility to await trial. There I met men, prisoners, who read aloud to each other the works of Neruda, Paz, Sabines, Nemerov, and Hemingway. Never had I felt such freedom as in that dormitory. Listening to the words of these writers, I felt that invisible threat from without lessen—my sense of teetering on a rotting plank over swamp water where famished alligators clapped their horny snouts for my blood. While I listened to the words of the poets, the alligators slumbered powerless in their lairs. Their language was the magic that could liberate me from myself, transform me into another person, transport me to other places far away.

And when they closed the books, these Chicanos, and went into their own Chicano language, they made barrio life come alive for me in the fullness of its vitality. I began to learn my own language, the bilingual words and phrases explaining to me my place in the universe. Every day I felt like the paper boy taking delivery of the latest news of the day.

Months later I was released, as I had suspected I would be. I had been guilty of nothing but shattering the windshield of my girlfriend's car in a fit of rage.

Two years passed. I was twenty now, and behind bars again. The federal marshals had failed to provide convincing evidence to extradite me to Arizona on a drug charge, but still I was being held. They had ninety

about the men in my prison writing class and what they went through. But Baca's essay is really more about writing than it is about his hard life as a young criminal and an inmate. His essay includes some of the most provocative descriptions of writing that I have ever encountered. Thankfully, few of us have known the degradation and humiliation that Baca suffered in prison, so perhaps we have not experienced the power of writing in the way he has. Yet, I think most of us have known moments when we can feel some of that power. And certainly Baca's essay might help us think about what writing can mean in a person's life. I selected this essay for this cluster partly because I hope it will help you gain a sense of what writing might mean in your life.

In addition to his autobiography, Working in the Dark: Reflections of a Poet of the Barrio *(1992),* Jimmy Santiago Baca *has written several volumes of poetry, including* Black Mesa Poems *(1987), and has received numerous awards for his writing.* ▼

days to prove I was guilty. The only evidence against me was that my girlfriend had been at the scene of the crime with my driver's license in her purse. They had to come up with something else. But there was nothing else. Eventually they negotiated a deal with the actual drug dealer, who took the stand against me. When the judge hit me with a million-dollar bail, I emptied my pockets on his booking desk: twenty-six cents.

One night in my third month in the county jail, I was mopping the floor in front of the booking desk. Some detectives had kneed an old drunk and handcuffed him to the booking bars. His shrill screams raked my nerves like a hacksaw on bone, the desperate protest of his dignity against their inhumanity. But the detectives just laughed as he tried to rise and kicked him to his knees. When they went to the bathroom to pee and the desk attendant walked to the file cabinet to pull the arrest record, I shot my arm through the bars, grabbed one of the attendant's university textbooks, and tucked it in my overalls. It as the only way I had of protesting.

10   It was late when I returned to my cell. Under my blanket I switched on a pen flashlight and opened the thick book at random, scanning the pages. I could hear the jailer making his rounds on the other tiers. The jangle of his keys and the sharp click of his boot heels intensified my solitude. Slowly I enunciated the words . . . p-o-n-d, ri-pple. It scared me that I had been reduced to this to find comfort. I always had thought reading a waste of time, that nothing could be gained by it. Only by action, by moving out into the world and confronting and challenging the obstacles, could one learn anything worth knowing.

Even as I tried to convince myself that I was merely curious, I became so absorbed in how the sounds created music in me and happiness, I forgot where I was. Memories began to quiver in me, glowing with a strange but familiar intimacy in which I found refuge. For a while, a deep sadness overcame me, as if I had chanced on a long-lost friend and mourned the years of separation. But soon the heartache of having missed so much of life, that had numbed me since I was a child, gave way, as if a grave illness lifted itself from me and I was cured, innocently believing in the beauty of life again. I stumblingly repeated the author's name as I fell asleep, saying it over and over in the dark: Words-worth, Words-worth.

Before long my sister came to visit me, and I joked about taking her to a place called Kubla Khan and getting her a blind date with this *vato* named Coleridge who lived on the seacoast and was *malías* on morphine. When I asked her to make a trip into enemy territory to buy me a grammar book, she said she couldn't. Bookstores intimidated her, because she, too, could neither read nor write.

Days later, with a stub pencil I whittled sharp with my teeth, I propped a **RED CHIEF NOTEBOOK** on my knees and wrote my first words. From that moment, a hunger for poetry possessed me.

STRATEGIES: USING DETAILS
Throughout this essay, Baca uses physical details to convey a sense of his experiences. But sometimes the details he selects do more than describe the scene. Here, for example, he tells us that the notebook he was writing in was a Red Chief notebook, which was a common brand of notebook often used in schools. Consider what message that detail might convey in this scene and how it might relate to Baca's larger point about literacy and identity. What would he lose in this passage if he had simply mentioned that he had a notebook without specifying that it was a Red Chief notebook?

Until then, I had felt as if I had been born into a raging ocean where I swam relentlessly, flailing my arms in hope of rescue, of reaching a shoreline I never sighted. Never solid ground beneath me, never a resting place. I had lived with only the desperate hope to stay afloat; that and nothing more.

But when at last I wrote my first words on the page, I felt an island   15
rising beneath my feet like the back of a whale. As more and more words emerged, I could finally rest: I had a place to stand for the first time in my life. The island grew, with each page, into a continent inhabited by people I knew and mapped with the life I lived.

I wrote about it all—about people I had loved or hated, about the brutalities and ecstasies of my life. And, for the first time, the child in me who had witnessed and endured unspeakable terrors cried out not just in impotent despair, but with the power of language. Suddenly, through language, through writing, my grief and my joy could be shared with anyone who would listen. And I could do this all alone; I could do it anywhere. I was no longer a captive of demons eating away at me, no longer a victim of other people's mockery and loathing, that had made me clench my fist white with rage and grit my teeth to silence. Words now pleaded back with the bleak lucidity of hurt. They were wrong, those others, and now I could say it.

Through language I was free. I could respond, escape, indulge; embrace or reject earth or the cosmos. I was launched on an endless journey without boundaries or rules, in which I could salvage the floating fragments of my past, or be born anew in the spontaneous ignition of understanding some heretofore concealed aspect of myself. Each word steamed with the hot lava juices of my primordial making, and I crawled out of stanzas dripping with birth-blood, reborn and freed from the chaos of my life. The child in the dark room of my heart, that had never been able to find or reach the light switch, flicked it on now; and I found in the room a stranger, myself, who had waited so many years to speak again. My words struck in me lightning crackles of elation and thunderhead storms of grief.

*   *   *

When I had been in the county jail longer than anyone else, I was made a trustee. One morning, after a fistfight, I went to the unlocked and unoccupied office used for lawyer-client meetings, to think. The bare white room with its fluorescent tube lighting seemed to expose and illuminate my dark and worthless life. And yet, for the first time, I had something to lose—my chance to read, to write; a way to live with dignity and meaning, that had opened for me when I stole that scuffed, secondhand book about the Romantic poets. In prison, the abscess had been lanced.

"I will never do any work in this prison system as long as I am not allowed to get my G.E.D." That's what I told the reclassification panel.

The captain flicked off the tape recorder. He looked at me hard and said, "You'll never walk outta here alive. Oh, you'll work, put a copper penny on that, you'll work."

20   After that interview I was confined to deadlock maximum security in a subterranean dungeon, with ground-level chicken-wired windows painted gray. Twenty-three hours a day I was in that cell. I kept sane by borrowing books from the other cons on the tier. Then, just before Christmas, I received a letter from Harry, a charity house samaritan who doled out hot soup to the homeless in Phoenix. He had picked my name from a list of cons who had no one to write to them. I wrote back asking for a grammar book, and a week later received one of Mary Baker Eddy's treatises on salvation and redemption, with Spanish and English on opposing pages. Pacing my cell all day and most of each night, I grappled with grammar until I was able to write a long true-romance confession for a con to send to his pen pal. He paid me with a pack of smokes. Soon I had a thriving barter business, exchanging my poems and letters for novels, commissary pencils, and writing tablets.

One day I tore two flaps from the cardboard box that held all my belongings and punctured holes along the edge of each flap and along the border of a ream of state-issue paper. After I had aligned them to form a spine, I threaded the holes with a shoestring, and sketched on the cover a hummingbird fluttering above a rose. This was my first journal.

CONVERSATIONS: WRITING AND IMAGINATION
In this and the following paragraphs, Baca offers vivid descriptions of how he felt when he was writing. Consider what these images might suggest about writing and about the connections between writing and thinking. Compare Baca's descriptions with Min Zhan Lu's account of writing in her essay on page 371. How does each writer complicate our views of the power of writing?

Whole afternoons I wrote, unconscious of passing time or whether it was day or night. Sunbursts exploded from the lead tip of my pencil, words that grafted me into awareness of who I was; peeled back to a burning core of bleak terror, an embryo floating in the image of water, I cracked out of the shell wide-eyed and insane. Trees grew out of the palms of my hands, the threatening otherness of life dissolved, and I became one with the air and sky, the dirt and the iron and concrete. There was no longer any distinction between the other and I. Language made bridges of fire between me and everything I saw. I entered into the blade of grass, the basketball, the con's eye, and child's soul.

At night I flew. I conversed with floating heads in my cell, and visited strange houses where lonely women brewed tea and rocked in wicker rocking chairs listening to sad Joni Mitchell songs.

Before long I was frayed like a rope carrying too much weight, that suddenly snaps. I quit talking. Bars, walls, steel bunk, and floor bristled with millions of poem-making sparks. My face was no longer familiar to me. The only reality was the swirling cornucopia of images in my mind, the voices in the air. Mid-air a cactus blossom would appear, a snake-flame in blinding dance around it, stunning me like a guard's fist striking my neck from behind.

25   The prison administrators tried several tactics to get me to work. For six months, after the next monthly prison board review, they

sent cons to my cell to hassle me. When the guard would open my cell door to let one of them in, I'd leap out and fight him—and get sent to thirty-day isolation. I did a lot of isolation time. But I honed my image-making talents in that sensory-deprived solitude. Finally they moved me to death row, and after that to "nut-run," the tier that housed the mentally disturbed.

As the months passed, I became more and more sluggish. My eyelids were heavy, I could no longer write or read. I slept all the time.

One day a guard took me out to the exercise field. For the first time in years I felt grass and earth under my feet. It was spring. The sun warmed my face as I sat on the bleachers watching the cons box and run, hit the handball, lift weights. Some of them stopped to ask how I was, but I found it impossible to utter a syllable. My tongue would not move, saliva drooled from the corners of my mouth. I had been so heavily medicated I could not summon the slightest gesture. Yet inside me a small voice cried out, I am fine! I am hurt now but I will come back! I am fine!

Back in my cell, for weeks I refused to eat. Styrofoam cups of urine and hot water were hurled at me. Other things happened. There were beatings, shock therapy, intimidation.

Later, I regained some clarity of mind. But there was a place in my heart where I had died. My life had compressed itself into an unbearable dread of being. The strain had been too much. I had stepped over that line where a human being has lost more than he can bear, where the pain is too intense, and he knows he is changed forever. I was now capable of killing, coldly and without feeling. I was empty, as I have never, before or since, known emptiness. I had no connection to this life.

But then, the encroaching darkness that began to envelop me forced me to reform and give birth to myself again in the chaos. I withdrew even deeper into the world of language, cleaving the diamonds of verbs and nouns, plunging into the brilliant light of poetry's regenerative mystery. Words gave off rings of white energy, radar signals from powers beyond me that infused me with truth. I believed what I wrote, because I wrote what was true. My words did not come from books or textual formulas, but from a deep faith in the voice of my heart.

I had been steeped in self-loathing and rejected by everyone and everything—society, family, cons, God, and demons. But now I had become as the burning ember floating in darkness that descends on a dry leaf and sets flame to forests. The word was the ember and the forest was my life.

* * *

I was born a poet one noon, gazing at weeds and creosoted grass at the base of a telephone pole outside my grilled cell window. The words I wrote then sailed me out of myself, and I was transported and metamorphosed into the images they made. From the dirty brown blades of grass came bolts of electrical light that jolted loose my old self; through the top of my head that self was released and reshaped in the clump of scrawny grass. Through language I became the grass, speaking its language and feeling its green feelings and black root sensations. Earth was my mother and I bathed in sunshine. Minuscule speckles of sunlight passed through my green skin and metabolized in my blood.

Writing bridged my divided life of prisoner and free man. I wrote of the emotional butchery of prisons, and of my acute gratitude for poetry. Where my blind doubt and spontaneous trust in life met, I discovered empathy and compassion. The power to express myself was a welcome storm rasping at tendril roots, flooding my soul's cracked dirt. Writing was water that cleansed the wound and fed the parched root of my heart.

I wrote to sublimate my rage, from a place where all hope is gone, from a madness of having been damaged too much, from a silence of killing rage. I wrote to avenge the betrayals of a lifetime, to purge the bitterness of injustice. I wrote with a deep groan of doom in my blood, bewildered and dumbstruck; from an indestructible love of life, to affirm breath and laughter and the abiding innocence of things. I wrote the way I wept, and danced, and made love.

Understanding the Text

1. What role do books play in Baca's life? To what extent do you think the impact of books on Baca was related to his circumstances? In other words, would books have meant as much to him if he had not been in prison and suffered abuse there? Explain.

2. What does Baca mean when he writes, "Through language I was free"? In what sense was he free, even when he was in prison? What kind of freedom did his writing give him? What do you think Baca's experiences might suggest about writing in general?

3. Why was Baca subject to such terrible abuse while in prison? Why did his demand about getting a GED result in such harsh treatment? What do you think this experience might suggest about learning? About writing?

4. How does Baca use writing to pull himself out of the terrible state he was in while in prison? What changed in him as a result of his writing? Do you find his descriptions of how he used writing believable? Explain, citing specific passages to support your answer.

Exploring the Issues

1. Assess Baca's writing style in this essay. What features of his writing stand out for you? How effective do you find his writing? How might Baca's writing style reflect his own beliefs about writing and its importance in his life?

2. In paragraph 24, Baca describes his mental state in solitary confinement as one in which his "only reality was the swirling cornucopia of images in my mind, the voices in the air." Given his description, his condition could easily be taken as mental illness. However, his earlier descriptions of his writing (for example, in par. 22), which he presents as happy moments, sound very similar to the description in paragraph 24. Examine the way Baca describes his mental state when he was writing and at other times as well. What metaphors and images does he use? What ideas do you think he is trying to convey about writing? What might his experience suggest about language and our sense of self in general? Do you find his descriptions effective? Do you think they accurately convey a sense of the experience of writing?

3. Baca has been acclaimed as a writer who speaks powerfully for Chicanos and for people of color in general. In what ways do you think this essay reflects Baca's desire to speak for his people? Based on this

essay, do you think Baca's reputation as a poet of Chicanos and people of color is justified? Why or why not?

4. Baca describes his experiences and his writing as deeply connected to his identity as a Chicano who grew up in a barrio in the south-western United States. Do you think he imagined his primary audience for this essay to be Chicanos? In what ways might he have been trying to address a wider audience? Do you think you are part of the audience that Baca imagined for this essay? Explain, citing specific passages to support your answers.

Entering the Conversations

1. Write an essay describing an experience in which writing somehow made a difference in your life. Alternatively, write an essay in which you discuss the role that writing has played in your life.

2. In a group of classmates, share the essays you wrote for Question 1. What similarities and differences can you identify among your classmates regarding the role of writing in your lives? What might your essays suggest about writing?

3. In his essay, Baca describes learning about Chicano history through reading and through conversations with other inmates. This passage suggests the importance of telling the story of a people. Write an essay in which you tell your version of the story of your family or some other group or community that you identify with.

4. Write an essay in which you compare Baca's ideas about the connections between writing and identity with the ideas of Gloria Anzaldúa, whose essay begins on page 337.

5. Write an essay that explains how writing can be a means to freedom. Alternatively, create a web site or some other visual document that reflects your sense of how writing can make a person free.

6. Locate a blog or online discussion group devoted to writing and follow the conversations there for a time. Then, write an essay presenting an analysis of those conversations. Draw conclusions about how the people in those conversations understand the power of writing.

If you pay any attention to the political conversations in the mainstream American media, you are undoubtedly familiar with political talk show hosts like Rush Limbaugh, Bill O'Reilly, and Ann Coulter. To many critics, these and other well-known media figures have become symbols of what is wrong with political discourse in contemporary

Just Us Folks

American society. Their talk shows, critics charge, undermine American democracy by poisoning the minds of voters and diverting voters' attention from legitimate political debate. In 2004, comedian Jon Stewart appeared on the CNN political talk show Crossfire *and scolded the show's co-hosts, Tucker Carlson and Paul Begala, for "hurting America" with their political discussions, which Stewart criticized as "theater" rather than genuine debate.*

Historian Susan Jacoby would likely agree with Stewart, but in her view political talk shows like Crossfire *are a symptom of a much more fundamental problem in American culture. In the following essay, which is excerpted from her book* The Age of American Unreason *(2008), Jacoby describes what she believes is the dumbing down of American culture. In Jacoby's view, anti-intellectualism and anti-rationalism are undermining American democracy itself.*

SUSAN JACOBY

The word is everywhere, a plague spread by the President of the United States, television anchors, radio talk show hosts, preachers in megachurches, self-help gurus, and anyone else attempting to demonstrate his or her identification with ordinary, presumably wholesome American values. Only a few decades ago, Americans were addressed as people or, in the more distant past, ladies and gentlemen. Now we are all folks. Television commentators, apparently confusing themselves with the clergy, routinely declare that "our prayers go out to those folks"—whether the folks are victims of drought, hurricane, flood, child molestation, corporate layoffs, identity theft, or the war in Iraq (as long as the victims are American and not Iraqi). Irony is reserved for fiction. **PHILIP ROTH,** in *The Plot Against America*—a dark historical reimagining of a nation in which **CHARLES LINDBERGH** defeats Franklin D. Roosevelt in the 1940 presidential election—confers the title "Just Folks" on a Lindbergh program designed to de-Judaize young urban Jews by sending them off to spend their summers in wholesome rural and Christian settings.

SUSAN JACOBY, "JUST US FOLKS," FROM JACOBY, SUSAN. *THE AGE OF AMERICAN UNREASON,* PAGES 3–30. NEW YORK: RANDOM HOUSE, 2008. REPRINTED WITH PERMISSION OF RANDOM HOUSE, INC.

While the word "folks" was once a colloquialism with no political meaning, there is no escaping the political meaning of the term when it is reverently invoked by public officials in twenty-first century America. After the terrorist bombings in London on July 7, 2005, President Bush assured Americans, "I've been in contact with our homeland security folks and I instructed them to be in touch with local and state officials about the facts of what took place here and in London and to be extra vigilant as our folks start heading to work." Bush went on to observe that "the contrast couldn't be clearer, between the intentions of those of us who care deeply about human rights and human liberty, and those who've got such evil in their heart that they will take the lives of innocent folks." **THOSE EVIL TERRORISTS. OUR INNOCENT FOLKS.**

The specific political use of folks as an exclusionary and inclusionary signal, designed to make the speaker sound like one of the boys or girls, is symptomatic of a debasement of public speech inseparable from a more general erosion of American cultural standards. Casual, colloquial language also conveys an implicit denial of the seriousness of whatever issue is being debated: talking about folks going off to war is the equivalent of describing rape victims as girls (unless the victims are, in fact, little girls and not grown women). Look up any important presidential speech in the history of the United States before 1980, and you will not find one patronizing appeal to folks. Imagine: We here highly resolve that these folks shall not have died in vain . . . and that government **OF THE FOLKS, BY THE FOLKS, FOR THE FOLKS,** shall not perish from the earth. In the 1950s, even though there were no orators of Lincoln's eloquence on the political scene, voters still expected their leaders to employ dignified, if not necessarily erudite, speech. Adlai Stevenson may have sounded too much like an intellectual to suit the taste of average Americans, but proper grammar and respectful forms of address were mandatory for anyone seeking high office. The gold standard of presidential oratory for adult Americans in the fifties was the memory of Roosevelt, whose patrician accent in no way detracted from his extraordinary ability to make a direct connection with ordinary people. It is impossible to read the transcripts of FDR's famous fireside chats and not mourn the passing of a civic culture that appealed to Americans to expand their knowledge and understanding instead of pandering to the lowest common denominator. Calling for sacrifice and altruism in perilous times, Roosevelt would no more have addressed his fel-

Jacoby's wit is sharp but her argument is based on a deep belief in the traditional values of American democracy. You may well disagree with her. But her essay offers insight into the role of written communication in our political and cultural lives.

An independent scholar and a writer for the Washington Post, *Susan Jacoby is author of eight books on American politics and culture. She is also a political blogger and director of the Center for Inquiry, a nonpartisan think tank that promotes rationalism in political and cultural life.* ▼

GLOSS: PHILIP ROTH AND CHARLES LINDBERGH
Acclaimed American writer Philip Roth (b. 1933), mentioned in paragraph 1, is best known for his collection of stories, *Goodbye, Columbus* (1959), and the novel *Portnoy's Complaint* (1969). His fiction often explores the nature of Jewish identity in a secular world. In *The Plot Against America* (2004), Roth writes a fictional history of the United States in which Charles Lindbergh, who many people believed was anti-Semitic, becomes president in 1940 of a nation in which anti-Jewish sentiment becomes increasingly accepted. Charles Lindbergh became an American hero in 1927 when he was the first person to fly an airplane alone across the Atlantic Ocean. Although he opposed the U.S. entry into WWII, Lindbergh served as a pilot in the U.S. armed forces. Think about how Jacoby uses the references to Roth and Lindbergh here. What point is she making about the word "folks" in this passage? In what ways does the reference to Roth's novel help her make that point?

CONVERSATIONS: OF THE FOLKS, BY THE FOLKS, FOR THE FOLKS
The well-known phrase "of the people, by the people, for the people"—which is sometimes mistakenly attributed to the U.S. Constitution—was spoken by President Abraham Lincoln on November 19, 1863, in Gettysburg, Pennsylvania, the site of the great Civil War battle that took place in July of that year. Lincoln's speech, which has come to be known as "The Gettysburg Address," is generally considered one of the greatest political speeches in American history. Jacoby assumes that her readers not only recognize these famous words but also understand their significance. Lincoln's words have special meaning within that conversation, and Jacoby relies on that meaning to make her point here.

low citizens as folks than he would have uttered an obscenity over the radio. To keep telling Americans that they are just folks is to expect nothing special—a ratification and exaltation of the quotidian that is one of the distinguishing marks of anti-intellectualism in any era.

The debasement of the nation's speech is evident in virtually everything, on every subject, broadcast and podcast on radio, television, and the Internet. In this true, all-encompassing public square, homogenized language and homogenized thought reinforce each other in circular fashion. As **GEORGE ORWELL** noted in 1946, "A man may take to drink because he feels himself a failure, and then fail all the more completely because he drinks. It is rather the same thing that is happening to the English language. It becomes ugly and inaccurate because our thoughts are foolish, but the slovenliness of our language makes it easier for us to have foolish thoughts." In this continuous blurring of clarity and intellectual discrimination, political speech is always ahead of the curve—especially because today's media possess the power to amplify and spread error with an efficiency that might have astonished even Orwell. Consider the near-universal substitution, by the media and politicians, of "troop" and "troops" for "soldier" and "soldiers." As every dictionary makes plain, the word "troop" is always a collective noun; the "s" is added when referring to a particularly large military force. Yet each night on the television news, correspondents report that "X troops were killed in Iraq today." This is more than a grammatical error; turning a soldier—an individual with whom one may identify—into an anonymous-sounding troop encourages the public to think about war and its casualties in a more abstract way. Who lays a wreath at the Tomb of the Unknown Troop? It is difficult to determine exactly how, why, or when this locution began to enter the common language. Soldiers were almost never described as troops during the Second World War, except when a large military operation (like the Allied landing on D-Day) was being discussed, and the term remained extremely uncommon throughout the Vietnam era. My guess is that some dimwits in the military and the media (perhaps the military media) decided, at some point in the 1980s, that the word "soldier" implied the masculine gender and that all soldiers, out of respect for the growing presence of women in the military, must henceforth be called troops. Like unremitting appeals to folks, the victory of troops over soldiers offers an impressive illustration of the relationship between fuzzy thinking and the debasement of everyday speech.

By debased speech, I do not mean bad grammar, although there is 5 plenty of that on every street corner and talk show, or the prevalence of obscene language, so widespread as to be deprived of force and meaning at those rare times when only an epithet will do. Nor am I talking about Spanglish and so-called Black English, those favorite targets of cultural conservatives—although I share the conservatives' belief that

---

CONVERSATIONS: GEORGE ORWELL
Here, Jacoby quotes from George Orwell's famous essay, "Politics and the English Language," which appears on page 454 of this textbook. Orwell's analysis has become a standard way of understanding political language and propaganda. Jacoby's reference to Orwell's essay is a way not only for her to participate in a longstanding conversation about language and politics but also to signal to readers her own position in that conversation.

public schools ought to concentrate on teaching standard English. But the standard of standard American English, and the ways in which private speech now mirrors the public speech emanating from electronic and digital media, is precisely the problem. Debased speech in the public square functions as a kind of low-level toxin, imperceptibly coarsening our concept of what is and is not acceptable until someone says something so revolting—**DON IMUS'S** notorious description of female, African-American college basketball players as "nappy-headed hos" is the perfect example—that it produces a rare, and always brief, moment of public consciousness about the meaning and power of words. Predictably, the Imus affair proved to be a missed opportunity for a larger cultural conversation about the level of all American public discourse and language. People only wanted to talk about bigotry—a worthy and vital conversation, to be sure, but one that quickly degenerated into a comparative lexicon of racial and ethnic victimology. Would Imus have been fired for calling someone a faggot or a dyke? What if he had only called the women hos, without the additional racial insult of nappy-headed? And how about Muslims? Didn't **ANN COULTER** denigrate them as "ragheads" (a slur of which I was blissfully unaware until an indignant multiculturalist reported it on the op-ed page of *The New York Times*). The awful reality is that all of these epithets, often accompanied by the F-word, are the common currency of public and private speech in today's America. They are used not only because many Americans are infected by various degrees of bigotry but because all Americans are afflicted by a poverty of language that cheapens humor and serious discourse alike. The hapless Imus unintentionally made this point when he defended his remarks on grounds that they had been made within a humorous context. "This is a comedy show," he said, "not a racial rant."

Wrong on both counts. Nothing reveals a lack of comic inventiveness more reliably than the presence of reflexive epithets, eliciting snickers not because they exist within any intentional "context" but simply because they are crass words that someone is saying out loud. Part of Imus's audience was undoubtedly composed of hard-core racists and misogynists, but many more who found his rants amusing were responding in the spirit of eight-year-olds laughing at farts. Imus's "serious" political commentary was equally pedestrian. He frequently enjoined officials who had incurred his displeasure to "just shut up," displaying approximately the same level of sophistication as **VICE PRESIDENT DICK CHENEY** when he told Sen. Patrick J. Leahy on the Senate floor, "Go fuck yourself." As the genuinely humorous **RUSSELL BAKER** observes, previous generations of politicians (even if they had felt free to issue the physically impossible Anglo-Saxon injunction in a public forum) would have been shamed by their lack of verbal inventiveness. In the 1890s, Speaker of the House Thomas Reed took care of one opponent by observing that "with a few more brains he

GLOSSES: IMUS AND COULTER
Popular radio talk show host Don Imus caused a storm of controversy in 2007 when he described the members of the Rutgers University women's basketball team as "nappy-headed hos." As a result of that comment, he was fired by CBS, which owned his radio show. Conservative political critic Ann Coulter caused a similar controversy by describing Iranians as "ragheads" in 2006. Consider how these examples help Jacoby expose what she calls "the awful reality of these epithets."

CHENEY AND BAKER
United States Vice President Dick Cheney was overheard making this remark during an argument in the U.S. Senate in 2004. Russell Baker is a political humorist who uses music to parody current political events.

could be a halfwit." Of another politician, Reed remarked, "He never opens his mouth without subtracting from the sum of human intelligence." Americans once heard (or rather, read) such genuinely witty remarks and tried to emulate that wit. Today we parrot the witless and halfwitted language used by politicians and radio shock jocks alike.

The mirroring process extends far beyond political language, which has always existed at a certain remove from colloquial speech. The toxin of commercially standardized speech now stocks the private vault of words and images we draw on to think about and to describe everything from the ridiculous to the sublime. One of the most frequently butchered sentences on television programs, for instance, is the incomparable Liberace's cynically funny, "I cried all the way to the bank"—a line he trotted out whenever serious critics lambasted his candelabra-lit performances as kitsch. The witty observation has been transformed into the senseless catchphrase, "I laughed all the way to the bank"—often used as a non sequitur after news stories about lottery winners. In their dual role as creators of public language and as microphones amplifying and disseminating the language many Americans already use in their daily lives, the media constitute a perpetuum mobile, the perfect example of a machine in which cause and effect can never be separated. A sports broadcaster, speaking of an athlete who just signed a multiyear, multimillion dollar contract says, "He laughed all the way to the bank." A child idly listening—perhaps playing a video game on a computer at the same time—absorbs the meaningless statement without thinking and repeats it, spreading it to others who might one day be interviewed on television and say, "I laughed all the way to the bank," thereby transmitting the virus to new listeners. It is all reminiscent of the exchange among Alice, the March Hare, and the Mad Hatter in *Alice's Adventures in Wonderland.* "Then you should say what you mean," the March Hare tells Alice. "I do," Alice hastily replied; "at least—at least I mean what I say—that's the same thing, you know." The Hatter chimes in, "Not the same thing a bit! Why, you might just as well say that 'I see what I eat' is the same thing as 'I eat what I see.'" In an ignorant and anti-intellectual culture, people eat mainly what they see.

Understanding the Text

1. What is the political meaning of the word *folks* today, according to Jacoby? Why does this meaning of the word concern her? What does the common use of that word in American political discourse reveal about American

society, in her view? What might her analysis of this word suggest about political language?

2. What is the effect of using the word *troops* instead of *soldiers,* in Jacoby's view? Why is such a substitution a problem, as she sees it? Do you agree? Why or why not?

3. Jacoby writes that "the standard of standard American English, and the ways in which private speech now mirrors the public speech emanating from electronic and digital media, is precisely the problem." What does she mean by that statement? How does the word *folks* illustrate this problem, in her view?

4. Why does Jacoby reject Don Imus's explanation for his use of a racial epithet as comedy? What does such a use of language reveal about American culture, in her view? Do you agree? Explain.

Exploring the Issues

1. In this essay, Jacoby offers a harsh critique of the way language is used in political discussions, especially the widespread use of words like *folks* that she believes are more suitable for casual conversation. Assess Jacoby's own use of language. How would you describe her word choice and the level of sophistication of her vocabulary and sentence structure? Do you think her own use of language is consistent with her views about the proper use of language in political discussions? Explain, citing specific passages from her essay to support your answer.

2. Jacoby criticizes the kind of humor used by radio "shock jocks" like Don Imus (see par. 5 and 6). What exactly is the basis of her criticism about this kind of humor? What do you think her criticism of the humor of shock jocks suggests about humor in American life in general? Do you think Jacoby is right about this issue? Explain.

3. Throughout this essay, Jacoby makes many references to historical events, important political and cultural figures, books, essays, and recent political events. Examine these references. What do they suggest about the assumptions Jacoby makes about her readers? What effect do you think they have on readers? What effect did they have on you? What do you think they suggest about

Jacoby as a writer and as a person? Do you think they reflect her own viewpoint as expressed in this essay? Explain.

Entering the Conversations

1. Write an essay in which you respond to Jacoby's critique of language use in contemporary American culture. In your essay, summarize the main points of Jacoby's critique and take a position on it, explaining why you agree or disagree with her. Draw from your own experience as well as your own analysis of the way language is used in the mainstream media today.

2. In a group of classmates, share the essays you wrote for Question 1. Try to identify points of agreement or disagreement with Jacoby. Also, try to determine how the political views of your classmates might influence their reactions to Jacoby's essay.

3. Jacoby maintains a blog on the web site of the *Washington Post* called "The Secularist's Corner," which describes itself as "not always polite conversation on religion, politics, and society with Susan Jacoby." Visit Jacoby's blog and review the discussions there. (You can find her blog by visiting the *Washington Post* web site or using an Internet search engine such as Google.) Explore the site and review its mission statement and descriptions of Jacoby and the purpose of the site. Get a sense of the topics that Jacoby and her readers address in their discussions, and pay attention to the nature of those discussions. Then write an essay in which you offer an analysis of Jacoby's blog.

Describe the nature of the discussions that take place on her blog. In particular, determine whether those discussions are characterized by the rationalism that she claims to believe in.

Alternatively, participate in Jacoby's blog for a time and write an essay about your experience. Draw conclusions from your experience about the nature of "rationalist" debate.

4. Watch several popular political talk shows, such as *Crossfire* or *The O'Reilly Factor,* to get a sense of the nature of discussion on those shows. Pay particular attention to the way language is used on those shows. Then, write an analysis of language use on the shows you watched. In your essay, describe the word choice and general nature of conversation on those shows, and evaluate the level of that conversation as you see it. Draw conclusions about whether Jacoby's criticisms are valid for the shows you watched.

5. Select a recent political speech by a prominent politician (such as the president or a well-known senator) and analyze that speech using Jacoby's critique as a guide. Try to draw conclusions on the basis of your analysis about whether Jacoby's criticisms of American political speech are valid.

6. Write an essay in which you compare the speech you selected for Question 5 with President Abraham Lincoln's Gettysburg Address. In your essay, analyze the way each speaker uses language, and draw conclusions about the nature of political speech today as compared to Lincoln's era.

BEYOND WORDS

THE OLD SAYING THAT A PICTURE IS WORTH A THOU-SAND WORDS IS ONE WAY TO DESCRIBE THE POWER OF AN IMAGE TO COMMUNICATE. CONSIDER THE PHOTOGRAPHS ON PAGE 56, FOR EXAMPLE. THEY WERE TAKEN FROM A SATELLITE JUST BEFORE AND DURING THE MASSIVE

power outage in the eastern United States and Canada in August 2003. Imagine what you might say about these photographs. There is a lot to say, perhaps about the extent of our electricity usage, about the impact of a blackout on society, about our interconnectedness, about patterns of development in North America. And much more. Or think about it this way: How might you use these photographs to make a statement about, say, energy conservation or the need for changes in the way the power system is managed? A picture can indeed be worth a thousand words.

But it isn't just pictures that are worth a thousand words. All kinds of images can be used to send all kinds of messages. Think about a road sign like this one:

This sign communicates important information to drivers about road conditions—in this case, that there is a down-grade—and indicates specifically to truckers that they will have to shift gears to negotiate the down-grade safely. All this information is communicated without words.

Or think about the American flag. It can be used to com-municate patriotism, national pride, ownership (as in the case of a flag painted on the side of a U.S. Army vehicle), remembrance (as when athletes wear flags on their uni-forms to honor fallen soldiers), even danger (an upside-down flag is a sign of emergency). When protesters burn American flags, they are making a powerful and often controversial statement. And it's no surprise that many Americans believe that burning the flag should be illegal. Or how about the flag shown on this page. This image changes the familiar symbol of the American flag to make a statement about the role of corporations in American society. How difficult would it be to write an essay that

© Chris Simpson/Getty Images

makes such a statement as dramatically and concisely as this image does?

We can communicate just as effectively with sound as well. Think of a siren, for example. Or think of "Taps" played at a funeral. Did you ever notice the music playing in a store at the mall? If you're shopping at a store like The Gap, you're likely to hear hip-hop or other popular music that appeals to young people. But you wouldn't hear that kind of music in a fine jewelry store or a hardware store, where the customers are likely to be much older. Obviously, the music in stores like these is carefully selected to create a certain atmosphere for customers; it tells customers that this is their kind of store. Of course, music can communicate more provocative messages as well, such as the antiwar protest songs of the 1960s and 1970s or the music of a rapper making a statement about racial injustice.

The following essays explore some of the ways in which we communicate beyond words. They ask you to think carefully about how we send and receive mes-sages through various me-dia other than writing. Grow-ing up in today's multimedia world, you are constantly bombarded with messages of all kinds: visual, aural, textual. And your ability to make sense of these mes-sages—and sometimes even to resist them—can profoundly shape your life. These essays can help you appreciate how.

As Bakari Kitwana writes in the following *essay, the well-known rapper Chuck D of the rap group Public Enemy declared in 1988 that rap music is "the Black CNN." Chuck D may have been making a point about rap music's role in describing the realities of life facing Black people in contemporary society. But by the turn of the new century, it became*

THE Challenge OF *Rap* Music

clear that rap music had become something even bigger than the Black CNN. Its influence seems to be far-reaching. The sounds of rap music blare from everywhere on the radio dial, from hip-hop stations to mainstream top 40 stations. Rappers themselves are no longer exclusively Black but reflect a diversity of racial and ethnic categories. Eminem, who is White, is among the world's most popular rappers, and rappers from Africa, Asia, and South America have found success. Young people of every color and income level now wear hip-hop clothing styles that were once seen only in a few Black neighborhoods in a few big cities. Big mainstream corporations like McDonald's and Coca-Cola use rap music in their television commercials. All of these developments seem to give strength to Kitwana's description of rap music as a cultural movement. Kitwana helps us see that music can communicate and influence in ways that go well beyond the lyrics of

BAKARI KITWANA

Mr. Mayor, imagine this was your backyard
Mr. Governor, imagine it's your kids that starve
imagine your kids gotta sling crack to survive,
swing a Mac to be live . . .

—Nas, *"I Want to Talk to You"*

In June 2001, Rush Communications CEO Russell Simmons convened a hip-hop summit in New York City. With the theme "Taking Back Responsibility," the summit focused its agenda on ways to strengthen rap music's growing influence. The 300 participants included major rap artists and industry executives as well as politicians, religious and community leaders, activists, and scholars. Few forces other than rap music, now one of the most powerful forces in American popular culture, could bring together such a diverse gathering of today's African American leaders. In many ways, the summit signaled hip-hop as the definitive cultural movement of our generation.

As the major cultural movement of our time, hip-hop (its music, fashion, attitude, style, and language) is undoubtedly one of the core

songs. He shows us that hip-hop as a musical style sends larger messages about race, gender, and social issues as well as about money and success. It has also emerged in film, television, and clothing styles, revealing that music can work in connection with other media to communicate effectively to many different audiences. Kitwana's arguments about hip-hop thus help us gain insight into the many different ways we can communicate with and beyond words.

Writer and editor Bakari Kitwana has written about hip-hop culture for a variety of publications, including the Village Voice, The Source, *and the* Progressive. *He is the author of* The Rap on Gangsta Rap *(1994),* Why White Kids Love Hip Hop *(2005), and* The Hip Hop Generation *(2002), in which this essay first appeared.* ◩

influences for young African Americans born between 1965 and 1984. To fully appreciate the extent to which this is true, think back for a moment about the period between the mid-1970s and the early 1980s, before rap became a mainstream phenomenon. Before MTV. Before BET's Rap City. Before the Fresh Prince of Bel Air. Before *House Party* I or II. It is difficult now to imagine Black youth as a nearly invisible entity in American popular culture. But in those days, that was the case. When young Blacks were visible, it was mostly during the six o'clock evening news reports of crime in urban America.

In contrast, today it is impossible not to see young Blacks in the twenty-first century's public square—the public space of television, film, and the Internet. Our images now extend far beyond crime reports. For most of our contemporaries, it's difficult to recall when this was not the case. Because of rap, the voices, images, style, attitude, and language of young Blacks have become central in American culture, transcending geographic, social, and economic boundaries.

To be sure, professional athletes, especially basketball players, have for decades been young, Black, highly visible, and extremely popular. Yet, their success just didn't translate into visibility for young Blacks overall. For one thing, the conservative culture of professional sports, central to their identity, was often at odds with the rebellious vein inherent in the new Black youth culture. While household-name ball players towed the generic "don't do drugs and stay in school" party line, rappers, the emissaries of the new Black youth culture, advocated more anti-establishment slogans like "fuck the police." Such slogans were vastly more in synch with the hard realities facing young Blacks—so much so that as time marched on and hip-hop culture further solidified its place in American popular culture, basketball culture would also come to feel its influence.

Largely because of rap music, one can tune in to the voices and find the faces of America's Black youth at any point in the day. Having proven themselves as marketable entertainers with successful music careers, rappers star in television sit-coms and film and regularly endorse corporate products (such as Lil'Kim—Candies, Missy Elliot—the Gap, and Common, Fat Joe, and the Goodie Mob—Sprite). In the mid-1980s, a handful of corporations began incorporating hip-hop into their advertisement spots. Most were limited to run-of-the-mill product endorsements. By the late 1990s, however, ads incorporating hip-hop—even those promoting traditionally conservative companies—became increasingly steeped in the subtleties of hip-hop culture. Setting the standard with their extremely hip-hop savvy 1994 Voltron campaign, Sprite broke away from the straight-up ce-

5

CONVERSATIONS: RAP AS A CULTURAL MOVEMENT
The idea that a form of music can be thought of as a "cultural movement" is not new. In the 1950s and 1960s, rock-n'-roll music was seen as a youth movement in reaction to some of the values of their parents' generation. Rock-n'-roll music seemed to express the rebellious views of young people at the same time that it also seemed to influence their views. Certain styles of dress, slang, and social practices (such as popular dances called "sock hops") came to be associated with rock-n'-roll. This is the sense in which Kitwana describes hip-hop as a cultural movement. In this essay, Kitwana is joining an expanding conversation among scholars, critics, and others about the importance of hip-hop as such a movement. But this ongoing conversation has often been contentious, too, with some critics offering harsh condemnations of what they believe is the glorification of violence, sexism, and even racism by hip-hop artists.

lebrity endorsement format. Says Coca-Cola global marketing manager Darryl Cobbin, who was on the cutting edge of this advertising strategy: "I wanted to usher in a real authenticity in terms of hip-hop in advertising. We wanted to pay respect to the music *and* the culture. What's important is the value of hip-hop culture, not only as an image, but as a method of communication."

By the late 1990s, advertisers like the Gap, Nike, AT&T, and Sony soon followed suit and incorporated hip-hop's nuances into their advertising campaigns. As a result, the new Black youth culture resonates throughout today's media, regardless of what companies are selling (from soft drinks and footwear to electronics and telecommunications).

Of course, none of this happened overnight. In fact, more important than the commercialization of rap was the less visible cultural movement on the ground in anyhood USA. In rap's early days, before it became a thriving commercial entity, dj party culture provided the backdrop for this off-the-radar cultural movement. What in the New York City metropolitan area took the form of dj battles and MC chants emerged in Chicago as the house party scene, and in D.C. it was go-go. In other regions of the country, the local movement owed its genesis to rap acts like Run DMC, who broke through to a national audience in the early 1980s. In any case, by the mid-1980s, this local or underground movement began to emerge in the form of cliques, crews, collectives, or simply kids getting together primarily to party, but in the process rhyming, dj-ing, dancing, and tagging. Some, by the early 1990s, even moved into activism. In large cities like Chicago, San Francisco, Houston, Memphis, New Orleans, Indianapolis, and Cleveland and even in smaller cities and suburban areas like Battle Creek, Michigan, and Champaign, Illinois, as the '80s turned to the '90s, more and more young Blacks were coming together in the name of hip-hop.

In the early 1980s, the "in" hip-hop fashion for New York City Black youth included Gazelles (glasses), sheepskins and leather bombers (coats), Clarks (shoes), nameplates, and name belts. In terms of language, Five Percenter expressions like "word is bond" were commonplace. These hip-hop cultural expressions in those days were considered bizarre by Black kids from other regions of the country. A student at the University of Pennsylvania at the time, Conrad Muhammad, the hip-hop minister, speaks to this in reminiscing on the National Black Students Unity Conference he organized in 1987:

> Jokers were getting off buses with shower caps on, perms and curls. MTV and BET had not yet played a role in standardizing Black youth culture the way they do today. Young people from different cities weren't all dressing the same way. Brothers

CONVERSATIONS: HIP-HOP FASHION
Images like this one showing young people in hip-hop fashions have become commonplace in recent years, especially in advertisements for clothing. Consider what images like this suggest about hip-hop as a cultural movement. Does this image convey the same kinds of messages about hip-hop that Kitwana argues for in this essay?

© Brand X Pictures/Alamy

and sisters were stepping off buses saying "we're from the University of Nebraska, Omaha." "We're from University of Minnesota." "We're from Cal Long Beach."

But by the early to mid-1990s, hip-hop's commercialized element had Black kids on the same page, regardless of geographic region. In this hip-hop friendly national environment, hip-hop designers like Enyce, Mecca, and FUBU were thriving, multi-platinum sales for rap artists were routine (and dwarfed the 1980s mark of success: gold sales), and hip-hop expressions like "blowin' up," "representin'," and "keepin' it real" worked their way into the conversational language of Black youth around the country. Contrast this to the mid-1980s when even those deep into hip-hop didn't see the extent to which a national cultural movement was unfolding.

10   "Before the Fresh Fest Tour of 1984, few folks were defining hip-hop culture as hip-hop culture," says Hashim Shomari, author of *From the Underground: Hip-Hop as an Agent of Social Change.* "That was a relatively 1990s phenomenon." Practitioners like Africa Bambaataa, Grandmaster Flash, Fab-Five Freddy, Chuck D, and KRS-One were on the frontlines of those who saw the need to flesh out the definitions. Also, it wasn't until the early 1990s that breakthrough books like Joseph Eure and James Spady's *Nation-Conscious Rap* (1991), Michael Gonzales and Havelock Nelson's *Bring the Noise: A Guide to Rap Music and Hip-Hop Culture* (1991), and Tricia Rose's *Black Noise: Rap Music and Black Culture in Contemporary America* (1994) began to discuss hip-hop as an influential culture that went beyond the commercial.

Without question, rap's national exposure played a key role in the uniform way in which the local cultural manifestations evolved. More recently, given rap's commercial success, alongside limited employment options beyond minimum wage-jobs for young Blacks, hip-hop's cultural movement at the local level is increasingly marked by an entrepreneurial element. On the West Coast, East Coast, in southern and northern cities, and in rural and suburban areas in between, young Blacks are pressing their own CDs and selling them "out the trunk" regionally.° many of them are hoping to eventually put their city on the hip-hop map. What all this around the way activity has in common is that kids are tuned in to the same wavelength via hip-hop, some aspiring to be the next Air Jordan of hip-hop, others engaging in what is to them a way of life without commercial popular culture

---

°My emphasis here is on Black youth—no disrespect to the countless folks of other racial and ethnic groups down with hip-hop. This is not to say that Latino and to a lesser extent Asian and Native American youth have not been influential in and touched by hip-hop culture. Neither is it meant to ignore the distinctiveness of Caribbean Americans. More recently white kids, a large segment of hip-hop's listening audience, are jumping into the fray. Nevertheless, rap music indisputably remains dominated by Black youth in both its commercial and local manifestations. [Author's note]

aspirations, and still others tuning in as a basic engagement with the youth culture of our time.

The commercialized element of this cultural movement and the off-the-radar one fuel each other. The underground element provides a steady stream of emerging talent that in turn gets absorbed into commercialization. That new voice and talent again inspires more discussion (about the art form, new styles, trends, language, and larger issues and themes) and more talent at the local level, which later infuses the commercial manifestation of the cultural movement. Case in point: the more recent wave of talent (say, Master P out of New Orleans, Eve from Philly, and Nelly from St. Louis) is similar to the much earlier waves like the Geto Boys out of Houston and Compton's NWA. Those earlier waves of talent (the Geto Boys, NWA, Too Short, E-40, and others) most certainly provided inspiration for the No Limit Soldiers and Ruff Ryders, who came later. Like the earliest waves of artists, each group represents its distinct region, while tapping into the national movement. In turn, Master P, Eve, and Nelly will influence the next wave of talent breaking from the margins into the mainstream.

It's not exactly a chicken-or-egg question, however. Hip-hop as a culture indisputably emerged in the South Bronx in the late 1970s, and in other parts of the northeast shortly thereafter, before branching out around the country in the early 1980s. What's arguable is the extent to which hip-hop would have become the national cultural movement that it is today without commercialization.

In 1988, rapper Chuck D of the rap group Public Enemy described rap music as "the Black CNN." This was certainly true at the grassroots level at the time. However, the decade of the 1990s proved even more profound as rap music became thoroughly accepted and promoted in mainstream American popular culture. As such, rap provided the foundation for a resounding young Black mainstream presence that went far beyond rap music itself.

Understanding the degree to which the local and commercial are   15
deeply entrenched and interdependent, one can begin to grasp the far-reaching effects of hip-hop on young Blacks. As the primary vehicle through which young Blacks have achieved a national voice and presence, rap music transmits the new Black youth culture to a national audience. And in the same way as the mainstream media establishes the parameters for national discussion for the nation at large, rap music sets the tone for Black youth. As the national forum for Black youth concerns and often as the impetus for discussion around those issues, rap music has done more than any one entity to help our generation forge a distinct identity.

Another important aspect of what makes rap so substantive in the lives of young Blacks is its multilingual nature. In addition to beaming out hip-hop culture, rap also conveys elements of street culture, prison culture, and the new Black youth culture. Often all of these elements overlap within rap's lyrics and visual images. In the process, images and ideas that define youth culture for this generation—such as designer clothes, like Sean Jean, Phat Farm, and Tommy Hilfiger, ever-changing styles of dress, and local colloquialisms—are beamed out to a captive national audience. Also transmitted are cues of personal style, from cornrows and baby dreads to body piercing and tattoos.

And finally, even more important than fashion, style, and language, the new Black culture is encoded within the images and lyrics of rap and thus help define what it means to be young and Black at the dawn of the millennium. In the process, rap music has become the primary vehicle for transmitting culture and values to this generation, relegating Black families, community centers, churches, and schools to the back burner.

To be sure, rap marked a turning point, a shift from practically no public voice for young Blacks—or at best an extremely marginalized one—to Black youth culture as the rage in mainstream popular culture. And more than just increasing Black youth visibility, rap articulated publicly and on a mass scale many of this generation's beliefs, relatively unfiltered by the corporate structures that carried it. Even when censored with bleeps or radio-friendly "clean" versions, the messages were consistent with the new Black youth culture and more often than not struck a chord with young Blacks, given our generation's unique collective experiences. At the same time, the burgeoning grassroots arts movement was underway. All was essential to rap's movement into the mainstream and its emergence as the paramount cultural movement of our time.

*   *   *

Although hip-hop has secured its place as a cultural movement, its biggest challenge lies ahead. In the late 1980s when gangsta rap first emerged, community activists and mainstream politicians of the civil rights generation began to challenge rap's content. This criticism forced a dialogue that revealed one of the Black community's best kept secrets, the bitter generational divide between hip-hop generationers and our civil rights/Black power parents.

20   The key concern was Black cultural integrity: how have the very public images of young Blacks in hip-hop music and culture affected the larger Black community? Central to this discussion was the pervasive use of offensive epithets in rap lyrics, such as "nigga," "bitch," and "ho," all of which reinforce negative stereotypes about Blacks. What was the price of this remarkable breakthrough in the visibility of young Blacks in the mainstream culture? Had young rappers simply transferred images of young Black men as criminals from news reports to entertainment? And finally, had the growing visibility of

young Black entertainers further marginalized young Black intellectuals and writers, who have remained nearly invisible?

A handful of responses emerged. The response from the rap industry was unanimous: free speech is a constitutional right. The predominant response from rap artists themselves was a proverbial head in the sand. Most reasoned that the older generation was out of touch with the concerns of hip-hop generationers. Just as our parents' generation was unfamiliar with the music, the thinking went, when it came to other matters of our generation, particularly issues involving hip-hop, they, likewise, didn't know what they were talking about. By and large, the question of rap's attack on Black cultural integrity went unaddressed. In fact, the use of incendiary words like "nigga" and "bitch" has become so commonplace in rap's lyrics that today even those in rap's growing white audience routinely use them when referring to each other and often their Black peers (a matter Spike Lee vaguely touched on in the film *Bamboozled*).

Lately, as the theme of the Simmons summit "Taking Back Responsibility" suggests, hip-hop is again undertaking the critical task of questioning its relationship to the community. David Mays, publisher of the hip-hop magazine *The Source*, and Reverend Al Sharpton held a series of summits eight months prior to the Simmons summit, which called for a code of conduct in light of arrests of numerous rappers and the growing association of rappers with criminality. Minister Conrad Muhammad, dubbed the hip-hop minister for the moral voice he's long brought to the hip-hop community, felt the Mays-Sharpton gathering didn't go far enough. Muhammad called for a summit of Black rap artists, rap industry executives, and activists to discuss ways of holding the hip-hop industry accountable to the Black community. Appalled by Muhammad's moral challenge to the rap industry, Simmons countered Muhammad with a call for his own summit to be held within a few weeks of the Muhammad one.

Simmons, a major player in the rap industry who earlier began flexing his political muscle by reaching out to Democratic party insiders like Hillary Clinton in her bid for the U.S. Senate, brought together the largest and most media-celebrated summit to date. Joining rap industry insiders were African American notables like minister Louis Farrakhan, NAACP-head Kweisi Mfume, U.S. Representative Cynthia McKinney, and scholars Cornel West and Michael Eric Dyson.

The Simmons event was impressive in terms of sheer numbers and diverse backgrounds. But where it most seriously came up short was in its failure to incorporate the grassroots segment of hip-hop's cultural movement, especially hip-hop generation activists. When hip-hop's true influence as a cultural movement is finally understood, events like these will recognize that the very same synergy at the heart of hip-hop's commercial success has also informed our generation's activists and political theorists. Just as some record executives can

---

CONVERSATIONS: OFFENSIVE LYRICS
In this passage, Kitwana refers to some of the criticisms of hip-hop music by parents' groups, religious organizations, and women's groups. As Kitwana suggests, these criticisms have focused on what many people consider offensive lyrics, including obscenities, racial epithets, and language that denigrates women. Some advocates for hip-hop have argued that these lyrics reflect the realities of contemporary Black life and call attention to the injustices many Blacks face. In acknowledging these criticisms here, Kitwana might be seen to be offering his response to such criticisms and to encourage advocates for hip-hop to address those criticisms. Consider how your own sense of this debate might influence the way you read this passage and react to Kitwana's view.

give us a blueprint for blowin' up rap acts, the ideas that our generation's activists hold about maximizing rap's potential for social change have been seasoned in their day-to-day work and experience. If our generation's cultural movement is to evolve to have a meaningful political impact, the local segments of hip-hop's cultural movement—from hip-hop generation activists to local entrepreneurs to the everyday hip-hop kids on the block—must not only be brought to the table, but must have a major voice.

*   *   *

25   Furthermore, rather than centering the discussion within our own generation—*and,* yes, including the expertise and insight of our parents' generation—the invitation-only Simmons summit turned to the mostly liberal-integrationist civil rights leadership and music industry executives. The result was predictable: a combination of the traditional music industry call for free speech, which allows for continued blockbuster sales without disrupting the minstrel-esque proven formula for success, and the traditional civil rights activist call for young voters to support Democratic candidates for public office. Neither of these same-game-with-another-name reforms challenge civil righters or industry insiders to do anything different than what they are already doing. Moreover, pushing activists of the civil rights generation to the forefront of this effort is tantamount to casting older-generation R&B singers like Dionne Warwick and Lionel Richie as leads in a 'hood film or featuring them at a concert alongside ODB or Lil' Kim.

Until hip-hop is recognized as a broad cultural movement, rather than simply an influential moneymaker, those who seek to tap into hip-hop's potential to impact social change should not expect substantive progress. A unified front between hip-hop's commercial and grassroots sectors on the issue of sociopolitical action would change the nature of the dialogue. For example, in the same way that the hip-hop community as a cultural movement inherently answered the question, "what is hip-hop culture?" a new inclusive framework inevitably would answer the question, "what do we mean by politicizing the hip-hop generation?" Is our goal to run hip-hop generationers for office, to turn out votes for Democrats and Republicans, to form a third party, or to provide our generation with a more concrete political education?

Understanding the Text

1. Why does Kitwana believe that hip-hop is "the definitive cultural movement of our generation," as he puts it? What evidence does he provide to support that statement? Do you agree with him? Why or why not?

2. What factors does Kitwana identify as important in the rise of hip-hop? What do you think these factors and the rise of hip-hop suggest about the role of music in contemporary society?

3. What specific effects has the rise of hip-hop as a national movement had on contemporary society, according to Kitwana? Why are these effects important, in his view? Do you think he's right? Explain.

4. What does Kitwana see as the challenges facing hip-hop music today? What goals does he believe hip-hop should seek to achieve? What does Kitwana's discussion of these challenges and goals suggest about his view of hip-hop and of Black America in general?

Exploring the Issues

1. Throughout this essay, Kitwana uses the first person. For example, in paragraph 3 he writes that "it is impossible not to see young Blacks in the twenty-first century's public square," and he then goes on to state that "our images now extend far beyond crime reports." Who is Kitwana referring to here when he mentions "*our* images"? What might his use of the first person suggest about his sense of his intended audience? How did you react to his use of the first person in this essay? What might your answer to that question suggest about you as a reader?

2. Throughout this essay, Kitwana includes quotations from books and articles as well as from statements by various artists and critics. Examine these quotations. Who are the people that Kitwana quotes? Do they have anything in common? What might his choices of quotations suggest about his sense of his audience? How effective do you think these specific quotations are in helping Kitwana make his argument about hip-hop as a cultural movement?

3. In paragraphs 22–25, Kitwana criticizes the meeting organized by Russell Simmons (first described in par. 1). Examine these criticisms. What exactly concerns Kitwana about this event? What significance does he see in the event? To whom does Kitwana seem to be addressing his criticisms in this passage? What might this passage suggest about Kitwana's sense of purpose for this essay? How effectively do you think he accomplishes that purpose? Explain.

Entering the Conversations

1. Write an essay in which you describe the influence of hip-hop music on contemporary society from your perspective. In your essay, describe the role of hip-hop in your own life and the lives of your friends, family, or others you know. Draw on Kitwana's essay and any other relevant sources to discuss this role and what you see as the impact that hip-hop music has had.

2. Select several popular hip-hop artists that you believe have been influential in the current music scene. Write an essay in which you analyze their songs for their themes and messages. In your essay, identify what you see as the main themes that these artists address in their music and discuss what those themes might suggest about hip-hop as a musical form and as a cultural movement.

3. Create a photo essay or a web site that defines hip-hop as a cultural movement. Use any images, sounds, and text that you think best reflect your view of hip-hop as a cultural movement and its influence on contemporary society.

4. Write an essay intended for your local newspaper (or another appropriate publication) in which you express your view about the debates over the lyrics of some hip-hop songs. In your essay, discuss your position about lyrics that some people consider offensive and explain why you believe they should or should not be subject to any form of censorship (such as banning songs from some radio stations or preventing the sale of CDs to children or teens).

5. Many colleges now offer courses in hip-hop culture. With a group of classmates, write a proposal for such a course at your school. (If your school already has such a course, you might write a proposal to change it in some way or to add an additional course.) In your proposal, identify the topics or issues your course on hip-hop would address and describe the assignments, readings, activities, and other features of the course. In addition, write a rationale or justification for the course that explains why you believe your school should offer such a course and what benefits it would offer students.

Like so many people, I use my television remote control to change channels when a commercial comes on. But not always. I find some commercials funny and interesting. I suspect you do too. There's no question that although many commercials are silly and some are even insulting, others are creative and entertaining. My guess is that you probably don't

Jesus IS A Brand of Jeans

think twice about talking about your favorite commercials with your friends just as you might talk about a favorite TV show.

Writer Jean Kilbourne asks us to think twice about advertising. In the following essay, she offers a provocative critique of all forms of advertising and raises serious questions about the impact of advertising on how we live our lives. In her view, advertising profoundly shapes the way we understand ourselves and even affects our ability to find happiness. But the real power of advertising lies in our belief that advertising really doesn't affect us. Kilbourne's analysis can help us appreciate some of the many different and complex forms of communication by which we convey messages to each other.

Jean Kilbourne (b. 1943) is author of Can't Buy My Love: How Advertising Changes the Way We Think and Feel *(2000) and creator of the award-winning film* Killing Us Softly: Advertising's Image of Women *(1979).* ▼

JEAN KILBOURNE

A recent ad for Thule car-rack systems features a child in the backseat of a car, seatbelt on. Next to the child, assorted sporting gear is carefully strapped into a child's carseat. The headline says: "We Know What Matters to You." In case one misses the point, further copy adds: "Your gear is a priority."

Another ad features an attractive young couple in bed. The man is on top of the woman, presumably making love to her. However, her face is completely covered by a magazine, open to a double-page photo of a car. The man is gazing passionately at the car. The copy reads, "The ultimate attraction."

These ads are meant to be funny. Taken individually, I suppose they might seem amusing or, at worst, tasteless. As someone who has studied ads for a long time, however, I see them as part of a pattern: just two of many ads that state or imply that products are more important than people. Ads have long promised us a better relationship via a product: *buy this and you will be loved.* But more recently they have gone beyond that proposition to promise us a relationship with the product itself: *buy this and it will love you.* The product is not so much the means to an end, as the end itself.

JEAN KILBOURNE, "JESUS IS A BRAND OF JEANS," FROM JEAN KILBOURNE, "JESUS IS A BRAND OF JEANS," *NEW INTERNATIONALIST,* SEPTEMBER 2006, ISSUE 393, PAGES 10–12. REPRINTED BY PERMISSION OF THE *NEW INTERNATIONALIST.*

After all, it is easier to love a product than a person. Relationships with human beings are messy, unpredictable, sometimes dangerous. "When was the last time you felt this comfortable in a relationship?" asks an ad for shoes. Our shoes never ask us to wash the dishes or tell us we're getting fat. Even more important, products don't betray us. "You can love it without getting your heart broken," proclaims a car ad. One certainly can't say that about loving a human being, as love without vulnerability is impossible.

The all-new Mazda6.
Go your own way.

5   We are surrounded by hundreds, thousands of messages every day that link our deepest emotions to products, that objectify people and trivialize our most heartfelt moments and relationships. Every emotion is used to sell us something. Our wish to protect our children is leveraged to make us buy an expensive car. A long marriage simply provides the occasion for a diamond necklace. A painful reunion between a father and his estranged daughter is dramatized to sell us a phone system. Everything in the world—nature, animals, people—is just so much stuff to be consumed or to be used to sell us something.

The problem with advertising isn't that it creates artificial needs, but that it exploits our very real and human desires. Advertising promotes a bankrupt concept of *relationship*. Most of us yearn for committed relationships that will last. We are not stupid: we know that buying a certain brand of cereal won't bring us one inch closer to that goal. But we are surrounded by advertising that yokes our needs with products and promises us that *things* will deliver what in fact they never can. In the world of advertising, lovers are things and things are lovers.

It may be that there is no other way to depict relationships when the ultimate goal is to sell products. But **THIS APPARENTLY BOTTOMLESS CONSUMERISM NOT ONLY DEPLETES THE WORLD'S RESOURCES, IT ALSO DEPLETES OUR INNER RESOURCES.** It leads inevitably to narcissism and solipsism. It becomes difficult to imagine a way of relating that isn't objectifying and exploitative.

TUNED IN

Most people feel that advertising is not something to take seriously. Other aspects of the media are serious—the violent films, the trashy talk shows, the bowdlerization of the news. But not advertising! Although much more attention has been paid to the cultural impact of advertising in recent years than ever before, just about everyone still feels personally exempt from its influence. What I hear more than anything else at my lectures is: "I don't pay attention to ads . . . I just tune them out . . . they have no effect on me." I hear this most from people wearing clothes emblazoned with logos. In truth, we are all influenced. There is no way to tune out this much information, especially when it is designed to break through the "tuning out" process. As advertising

© The Advertising Archives

© The Advertising Archives

critic Sut Jhally put it: "To not be influenced by advertising would be to live outside of culture. No human being lives outside of culture."

Much of advertising's power comes from this belief that it does not affect us. As **JOSEPH GOEBBELS** said: "This is the secret of propaganda: those who are to be persuaded by it should be completely immersed in the ideas of the propaganda, without ever noticing that they are being immersed in it." Because we think advertising is trivial, we are less on guard, less critical, than we might otherwise be. While we're laughing, sometimes sneering, the commercial does its work.

Taken individually, ads are silly, sometimes funny, certainly nothing to worry about. But cumulatively they create a climate of cynicism that is poisonous to relationships. Ad after ad portrays our real lives as dull and ordinary, commitment to human beings as something to be avoided. Because of the pervasiveness of this kind of message, we learn from childhood that it is far safer to make a commitment to a product than to a person, far easier to be loyal to a brand. Many end up feeling romantic about material objects yet deeply cynical about other human beings.

10

STRATEGIES: STATING A THESIS

In paragraphs 6 and 7, Kilbourne states the main point of her essay—her thesis. The rest of her essay can be seen as her attempt to explain and support her claim that advertising has a negative impact on how we view our relationships with one another. In a way, Kilbourne has organized her essay as writing teachers often instruct students to organize a conventional academic essay: with the thesis clearly stated in the introduction and the supporting points presented coherently in the following paragraphs. She then reinforces her thesis in her conclusion, where she also identifies some of the implications of her claims. Consider the effectiveness of Kilbourne's strategy of clearly stating her thesis in the introductory section of her essay. How well might this strategy help persuade her readers that her thesis is right? How effectively might it convince readers to continue reading her essay?

GLOSS: JOSEPH GOEBBELS

Joseph Goebbels (1897–1945) was Adolf Hitler's Minister for Public Enlightenment and Propaganda for the Nazi Party that controlled Germany in the 1930s and 1940s. Goebbels's ability to develop effective propaganda is considered to be one of the reasons for Hitler's rise to power.

UNNATURAL PASSIONS

We know by now that advertising often turns people into objects. Women's bodies—and men's bodies too these days—are dismembered, packaged and used to sell everything from chainsaws to chewing gum, champagne to shampoo. Self-image is deeply affected. The self-esteem of girls plummets as they reach adolescence partly because they cannot possibly escape the message that their bodies are objects, and imperfect objects at that. Boys learn that masculinity requires a kind of ruthlessness, even brutality.

Advertising encourages us not only to objectify each other but to feel passion for products rather than our partners. This is especially dangerous when the products are potentially addictive, because addicts do feel they are in a relationship with their substances. I once heard an alcoholic joke that Jack Daniels was her most constant lover. **WHEN I WAS A SMOKER,** I felt that my cigarettes were my friends. Advertising reinforces these beliefs, so we are twice seduced—by the ads and by the substances themselves.

The addict is the ideal consumer. Ten percent of drinkers consume over sixty per cent of all the alcohol sold. Most of them are alcoholics or people in desperate trouble—but they are also the alcohol industry's very best customers. Advertisers spend enormous amounts of money on psychological research and understand addiction well. They use this knowledge to target children (because if you hook them early they are yours for life), to encourage all people to consume more, in spite of often dangerous consequences for all of us, and to create a climate

STRATEGIES: USING PERSONAL
EXPERIENCE
This essay is an analysis of advertising's
impact as well as an argument for
resisting that impact. It is not a personal
essay in which Kilbourne focuses on her
own experience. But in paragraph 12,
Kilbourne refers directly to her own
experience as a smoker. Even in more
formal analyses or arguments, writers
sometimes use their own experience to
help support a claim or illustrate a point.
Consider whether Kilbourne's reference to
her own smoking enhances her argument.
Does it give her more or less credibility to
make an argument against advertising?

of denial in which all kinds of addictions flourish. This they do with full
intent, as we see so clearly in the "secret documents" of the tobacco
industry that have been made public in recent years.

The consumer culture encourages us not only to buy more but to
seek our identity and fulfillment through what we buy, to express our
individuality through our "choices" of products. Advertising corrupts
relationships and then offers us products, both as solace and as substitutes for the intimate human connection we all long for and need.

In the world of advertising, lovers grow cold, spouses grow old, children grow up and away—but possessions stay with us and never
change. Seeking the outcomes of a healthy relationship through
products cannot work. Sometimes it leads us into addiction. But at
best the possessions can never deliver the promised goods. They can't
make us happy or loved or less alone or safe. If we believe they can,
we are doomed to disappointment. No matter how much we love
them, they will never love us back.

Some argue that advertising simply reflects societal values rather than
affecting them. Far from being a passive mirror of society, however, advertising is a pervasive medium of influence and persuasion. Its influence is cumulative, often subtle and primarily unconscious. A former

15

editor-in-chief of *Advertising Age,* the leading advertising publication in North America, once claimed: "Only eight per cent of an ad's message is received by the conscious mind. The rest is worked and re-worked deep within, in the recesses of the brain."

Advertising performs much the same function in industrial society as myth did in ancient societies. It is both a creator and perpetuator of the dominant values of the culture, the social norms by which most people govern their behaviour. At the very least, advertising helps to create a climate in which certain values flourish and others are not reflected at all.

Advertising is not only our physical environment, it is increasingly our spiritual environment as well. By definition, however, it is only interested in materialistic values. When spiritual values show up in ads, it is only in order to sell us something. Eternity is a perfume by Calvin Klein. Infiniti is an automobile, and Hydra Zen a moisturizer. Jesus is a brand of jeans.

Sometimes the allusion is more subtle, as in the countless alcohol ads featuring the bottle surrounded by a halo of light. Indeed products such as jewellery shining in a store window are often displayed as if they were sacred objects. Advertising co-opts our sacred symbols in order to evoke an immediate emotional response. Media critic **NEIL POSTMAN** referred to this as "cultural rape."

20   It is commonplace to observe that consumerism has become the religion of our time (with advertising its holy text), but the criticism usually stops short of what is at the heart of the comparison. Both advertising and religion share a belief in transformation, but most religions believe that this requires sacrifice. In the world of advertising, enlightenment is achieved instantly by purchasing material goods. An ad for a watch says, "It's not your handbag. It's not your neighbourhood. It's not your boyfriend. It's your watch that tells most about who you are." Of course, this cheapens authentic spirituality and transcendence. This junk food for the soul leaves us hungry, empty, malnourished.

© The Advertising Archives

CONVERSATIONS: NEIL POSTMAN
One of the most influential critics of popular culture, Neil Postman (1931–2003) was the author of many books examining important components of popular culture as well as significant developments that shape contemporary society, including *Amusing Ourselves to Death: Public Discourse in the Age of Show Business* (1985), *Technopoly: The Surrender of Culture to Technology* (1992), and *The End of Education: Redefining the Value of School* (1995). His ideas influenced public discussions about issues like the uses of technology, the training of teachers, and advertising. When Kilbourne refers to Postman here, she not only contributes to those discussions, but also signals her own position as a critic of popular culture.

SUBSTITUTE STORIES

Human beings used to be influenced primarily by the stories of our particular tribe or community, not by stories that are mass-produced and market-driven. As George Gerbner, one of the world's most respected researchers on the influence of the media, said: "For the first time in human history, most of the stories about people, life and val-

ues are told not by parents, schools, churches, or others in the community who have something to tell, but by a group of distant conglomerates that have something to sell."

Although it is virtually impossible to measure the influence of advertising on a culture, we can learn something by looking at cultures only recently exposed to it. In 1980 the Gwich'in tribe of Alaska got television, and therefore massive advertising, for the first time. Satellite dishes, video games and VCRs were not far behind. Before this, the Gwich'in lived much the way their ancestors had for generations. Within 10 years, the young members of the tribe were so drawn by television they no longer had time to learn ancient hunting methods, their parents' language or their oral history. Legends told around campfires could not compete with Beverly Hills 90210. Beaded moccasins gave way to Nike sneakers, and "tundra tea" to Folger's instant coffee.

As multinational chains replace local character, we end up in a world in which everyone is Gapped and Starbucked. Shopping malls kill vibrant downtown centres locally and create a universe of uniformity internationally. We end up in a world ruled by, in John Maynard Keynes's phrase, the values of the casino. On this deeper level, rampant commercialism undermines our physical and psychological health, our environment and our civic life, and creates a toxic society.

Advertising creates a world view that is based upon cynicism, dissatisfaction and craving. Advertisers aren't evil. They are just doing their job, which is to sell a product; but the consequences, usually unintended, are often destructive. In the history of the world there has never been a propaganda effort to match that of advertising in the past 50 years. More thought, more effort, more money goes into advertising than has gone into any other campaign to change social consciousness. The story that advertising tells is that the way to be happy, to find satisfaction—and the path to political freedom, as well—is through the consumption of material objects. And the major motivating force for social change throughout he world today is this belief that happiness comes from the market.

Understanding the Text

1. What pattern does Kilbourne see in advertising in recent years? What is the significance of this pattern, in her view? Why does it worry her? Do you think she's right? Explain.

2. Why doesn't Kilbourne believe people who tell her that they are not affected by advertising? What is her response to such claims? Why is it important to her to make the case that we are all affected by advertising?

3. What does advertising teach us about relationships, according to Kilbourne? How does advertising convey messages about relationships? What is the cumulative effect of advertising on us, in her view? How does she believe can we combat this effect? What do you think Kilbourne's argument suggests about human be-

ings and the role of communication in our beliefs about ourselves and the world around us?

4. In what sense is an addict the "ideal consumer," according to Kilbourne? What does this point suggest about advertising? What does it suggest about Kilbourne's views regarding a consumer culture? Do you agree with her? Why or why not?

5. What function does Kilbourne believe advertising serves in contemporary society? Why is it important to recognize this function, in her view? What do you think such a claim suggests about contemporary society?

6. What does Kilbourne mean when she writes that "Jesus is a brand of jeans"? Do you think she intended that statement (which is also the title of her essay) to be provocative? Explain.

Exploring the Issues

1. Kilbourne argues that advertising "exploits our very real and human desires" and "promotes a bankrupt concept of *relationship*." In what ways does advertising have these effects, according to Kilbourne? Evaluate this claim. How does she support it? How convincingly do you think she makes this claim? Do you agree with her? Why or why not? What might your response to her argument reveal about you as a reader— and as a consumer?

2. When it was first published in the *New Internationalist* in 2006, Kilbourne's article included many examples of print and television advertisements. She refers to some of these ads in her essay, but many of them were included as examples that she does not discuss directly. How important do you think these examples of ads are in helping

Kilbourne support her claims about the impact of advertising? Would her essay be more or less effective without these examples of ads? Explain, citing specific ads and/or passages from her essay in your answer.

3. In paragraph 15, Kilbourne writes that possessions "can't make us happy or loved or less alone or safe. If we believe they can, we are doomed to disappointment." Earlier, in paragraph 6, she, writes, "Most of us yearn for committed relationships that will last." What do you think these and similar statements reveal about Kilbourne's views about human beings? What do they seem to suggest about her own values? How do such statements contribute to your sense of Kilbourne as a person? Do they make you more or less inclined to accept her analysis of advertising? Explain.

Entering the Conversations

1. Write a response to Kilbourne in which you either support her position or offer an alternative view of advertising in contemporary society.

2. In a group of classmates, share the essays you wrote for Question 1. Determine the extent to which your classmates agree or disagree with Kilbourne. Identify the main points of agreement or disagreement among you and your classmates about advertising and its role in our lives. Then, on the basis of this discussion, make appropriate revisions to the essay you wrote for Question 1.

3. Select several current television, print, or Internet ads and analyze them for the messages you believe they convey about what is important. On the basis of your own analysis, evaluate Kilbourne's argument and draw your own conclusions about what these ads might reveal about the current state of American culture.

4. Create an advertisement (in print or video format) that conveys a sense of your own beliefs about relationships and your own basic values about living. For your ad, select a product that somehow symbolizes your beliefs and values.

5. Keep a record of all the advertising you encounter in a day or a week. Try to keep track of every ad you might see, such as billboards or magazine ads, or hear on the radio or watch on television. Also, keep track of the general content of the ads you encounter. For example, note whether the ad is about music or cars or clothing. Then, write a report for an audience of your classmates about your daily experience with advertising. In your report, describe the records you kept and give specific examples of ads you encountered. Offer your own analysis of the content and messages of these ads. Try to draw conclusions about the presence and impact of advertising in your life.

6. On the basis of the report you wrote for Question 5, create a pamphlet, web page, or other appropriate document or presentation intended to be a consumer's guide to advertising. In your document, offer tips for dealing with the messages conveyed by advertising.

If a picture is worth a thousand words, as *the old saying goes, what is the worth of the images of jets crashing into the World Trade Center in New York City on September 11th, 2001? I remember standing with some colleagues that morning in front of a television watching silently as those images were replayed again and again. Millions of people around the world were doing the same thing at that very moment. Many of us were left speechless by those images. Words seemed inadequate to express what we felt. The pictures said it all.*

But what exactly did those pictures say? In the millions of words that were spoken and written about what happened on September 11, 2001, many different interpretations of those events have emerged. Everyone agrees that those famous images depict terrible attacks that took place on that day, but as Farhad Manjoo reveals in this essay, some people are still

---

STRATEGIES: WORD CHOICE
Manjoo uses the term *outré*, which means unconventional or bizarre, in the first sentence of this essay. Consider why he would use this unusual word here instead of a more common term like "bizarre." How might this term fit into his main point in this essay?

How Photos Support Your Own "Reality"

FARHAD MANJOO

In the summer of 2006, I met Philip Jayhan, a member of the self-described 9/11 "Truth Movement," at Conspiracy Con, an annual Northern California gathering of adherents to **OUTRÉ** ideas. Jayhan is a clean-cut, chain-smoking fellow in his middle 40s with dusty blond hair and a quick, meandering, argumentative style. When I told him I believed the official theory of 9/11, he raised an eyebrow in a way that suggested more sorrow than anger. Then, on his laptop, he pulled up his Web site, LetsRoll911.org, and played the video clip that long ago prompted him to question everything.

The scene—**IT WAS FILMED BY ONE OF THE MANY TV CAMERAS AIMED AT THE WORLD TRADE CENTER TOWERS THAT MORNING**—begins with the hulking silver mass of the South Tower filling the frame. In slow motion, Flight 175, the second plane to hit the World Trade Center, jerks into the picture. Then, near the front of the fuselage, an indistinctly shaped bright gleam appears on the undercarriage of the plane. This illuminated slice, Jayhan believes, is the exhaust plume of a missile.

The entire sequence takes place over the course of just a few frames of video—in less than a split second at the film's full speed. But Jayhan

arguing about what the pictures actually show. Manjoo's essay reveals not only the power of images to convey messages but also the complexity of that power. When we look at an image, we all look at the same thing, but we don't necessarily all see the same thing. Or maybe we don't all agree on what we see. Whatever the case, Manjoo helps us understand that we can't always believe what we see—or maybe it's that we see only what we believe. Read his essay and decide for yourself.

Farhad Manjoo (b. 1978) is the author of True Enough: Learning to Live in a Post-Fact Society *(2008) and a staff writer for* Salon *magazine, where the following essay appeared in 2008.* ◢

CONVERSATIONS: TECHNOLOGY AND TRUTH

In paragraph 2, Manjoo refers to one of many different videos taken of the planes crashing into the World Trade Center towers on September 11, 2001. As Manjoo goes on to explain, many people disagree about what those images actually show, but it is obvious that videos made with portable video cameras, photographs taken with cell phones, and independent films like *Loose Change* made by conspiracy theorists (which Manjoo mentions in par. 6) have become a central part of the many discussions and debates about the events of that day. Consider how those debates might be different if no video footage or photographic images of the disaster at the World Trade Center existed.

© Associated Press Television News Limited/Getty

says that in this quick moment, we're witnessing something dastardly: Just before Flight 175 hits the building, a missile jettisons from the plane, falls a few feet away, and then flies straight at the tower.

I couldn't see it. For me, the video was too blurry, drained of color; like so much about 9/11 and its aftermath, the sequence seemed lost in shades of gray. And when I looked into Jayhan's theory later, I saw that several thorough investigations have ruled out the possibility of a missile on Flight 175.

Yet Jayhan remains a believer, and he is not alone. Polls show that a large percentage of Americans question the official story of 9/11; an unbelievable number suspect, like Jayhan does, that the government had a hand in the attack.   5

Here's what's most interesting about this movement: 9/11 conspiracy theorists—from Jayhan to the provocateurs who produced the popular film "Loose Change"—all rely on photos to make their case, the same images that the rest of us use to support our version of the story.

More photos used to mean better proof—a better representation of the "truth." You might reason, for instance, that if only we had better photographic evidence from the Kennedy assassination than **ABRAHAM ZAPRUDER'S ICONIC 26-SECOND FILM,** we'd know exactly what happened there. We wouldn't argue—as many Kennedy researchers do—about what Zapruder's film means: Does it prove that there are two shooters there, or just one? Does it show that Oswald had enough time to get off three shots, or just the opposite?

In the decades since Kennedy's death, we've achieved photographic ubiquity. Today, billions of tiny cameras record everything, and broadcast it all immediately online. The world, now, is constantly watched, each of us Zapruder himself.

Strangely, though, all these images have not pushed us toward greater collective agreement about what has happened, or what is happening, in the major controversies of the day. Sept. 11 is a primary exhibit, but in other issues, too, photos seem to prompt more disagreement than agreement: Images did not settle, for instance, **WHAT REALLY HAPPENED BETWEEN AMERICAN AND IRANIAN BOATS ON THE STRAIT OF HORMUZ** in January. Indeed, the brilliant pictures that now come at us daily often only blur the truth, casting reality itself wide open for debate.

10   One cause of this is a phenomenon psychologists call "selective perception," which was described, most famously, in a study by social scientists Albert Hastorf and Hadley Cantril in the early 1950s. The pair set out to determine how an Ivy League football championship game—in which Princeton trounced Dartmouth—had been perceived so differently by fans of the opposing teams. Each campus was in an uproar over what each described as the other side's blatantly unsportsmanlike play.

Hastorf and Cantril showed a film clip of the game to groups at each school—two fraternities at Dartmouth and two eating clubs at Princeton. They asked the students to act as unbiased referees, marking down all infractions they could spot. The results were remarkable: The Dartmouth fans mainly noticed Princeton's errors, while the Princeton fans concentrated on Dartmouth's.

The fans weren't deliberately overlooking things, Hastorf and Cantril stress. This was a matter of visual perception: Each side, that is, really did "see" a completely different game. When one Dartmouth alumnus was shown a film of the game, he decided it must have been badly edited. He'd heard that his side had played dirty, but where were those parts on the movie? He simply could not see them.

To understand how opposing fans saw the game so differently, consider what a football game really is: organized chaos. "There's an instant before it collapses into some generally agreed-upon fact when a football play, like a traffic accident, is all conjecture and fragments and partial views," Michael Lewis points out in *The Blind Side,* his fantastic exploration of the modern game. But it's not just car accidents and football plays that are like this; nearly everything is.

Think about a schoolyard at recess, a baseball game, a political debate. Think about a confrontation at sea, a presidential assassination, a terrorist attack. Or just think about all that happened to you yesterday: Every "thing" that occurs is really a million smaller things involving a million people. But which of the million things, and which of the million people, do we notice? And which do we overlook?

15   Hastorf and Cantril argued that it is the stratified structure of football, and of life, that explains the difference between what the Dartmouth fans "saw" and what the Princeton fans "saw" when they watched an identical movie of the season-ending game. There are countless "occurrences" during a football game, but we only notice one of these occurrences "when that happening has significance," they wrote.

The rub is that not everyone finds the same things significant, so even if we're watching the same event, you and I might see different things. What you notice in a photograph or a video is a function of a personalized calculus—an idiosyncratic, unconscious filter, built up over a lifetime, that you apply to all that you take in. When the Dartmouth alumnus watched the film of the game, he interpreted the images through a mind reared at Dartmouth. To him, the idea of a

GLOSS: THE ZAPRUDER FILM
A short film of the assassination of President John F. Kennedy in November 1963 was made by a spectator named Abraham Zapruder, who was in the crowd as Kennedy's motorcade drove along the streets of Dallas, Texas. This film has become one of the most important parts of the ongoing debate about Kennedy's death. Like 9/11, Kennedy's assassination inspired many conspiracy theories, and the Zapruder film has been examined countless times for evidence of such a conspiracy.

GLOSS: INCIDENT IN THE STRAIT OF HORMUZ
In January 2008, an apparent confrontation between several Iranian gunboats and American warships in the Strait of Hormuz near the coast of Iran sparked an international controversy. The Iranian government denied U.S. allegations that the Iranian gunboats threatened U.S. warships. Both sides presented videos of the incident to support their claims.

Dartmouth footballer playing dirty did not—could not—register. So he didn't see it.

Which brings us back to 9/11-doubter Philip Jayhan. Jayhan has long harbored a deep distrust of the government and of the institutions that exert power on the world. Given his worldview, it's clear Jayhan really believes that he sees a missile shooting out from Flight 175.

Or, to put it more accurately, he *really does see it*. A billion things happened to a million people on 9/11, and if you watch all the videos and listen to all of the audio, there's a lot that you'll find significant, and there's a lot you'll overlook. Some of it you've really got to puzzle out. Jayhan puzzles it out according to his own thoughts about how things work in society. And as a consequence of his ideas about the world generally, he is naturally prone to seeing something in those pictures that I—as a consequence of my own vastly different beliefs about the world—do not.

There are, of course, many other ways in which pictures deceive us today—through digital manipulation, for example, or as a result of selective viewing (when blogs you favor only show you pictures of an event that support your view).

Together, these forces have diminished the power of photographic proof. We think that what we see in pictures—or what we hear on tape—gives us a firm hold on fact. But increasingly, the pictures and the sounds we find ourselves believing may only be telling us one version of true.   20

Understanding the Text

1. Why has the presence of so many cameras not made it easier to determine what happened during important events, according to Manjoo? What does this suggest about video evidence, in his view?

2. What is selective perception? Why is this idea important to Manjoo? What does he believe it reveals about the debates surrounding important events like 9/11? Do you agree with him? Why or why not?

3. What does the study of fan perceptions of the football game between Dartmouth College and Princeton University suggest about how human beings experience various events? How does that study help us understand controversies like 9/11?

4. In what ways has the power of photographic proof been diminished, according to Manjoo? What might that development suggest about the role of images in our understanding of events? Do you agree with Manjoo that photographic proof has been diminished? Why or why not?

Exploring the Issues

1. In the first few paragraphs of this essay, Manjoo describes a conversation he had with Philip Jayhan, who believes that there is evidence that 9/11 was the result of a U.S. government conspiracy. Examine how Manjoo presents Jayhan and other conspiracy theorists. Do you think he presents them fairly? Does he intend to criticize them? What purpose does his description of these conspiracy theorists have in this essay?

2. Manjoo uses a variety of information to support his claims and illustrate his points. For example, he cites opinion polls, studies of perception, and various experts throughout his essay. How effectively do you think the evidence he presents supports his claims? Do you find his evidence credible? Explain. What might Manjoo's use of evidence indicate about his intended audience?

3. Examine how Manjoo addresses his audience in this essay. At times he seems to be addressing his readers directly (see par. 14, for example). What effect does this approach have on you as a reader? Do you find it effective? Explain. What might Manjoo's style in this essay suggest about his assumptions about his audience? In answering that question, you might consider visiting the web site for *Salon* magazine to get a sense of the magazine's style, content, and intended audience.

4. Manjoo suggests in this essay that much of what people "see" in an image or an event is a result of what they believe, even when there is evidence that they might be mistaken. What does this suggest about what is true and what is not? What does it suggest about how we determine what is or is not true?

Entering the Conversations

1. Write an essay for an audience of your classmates in which you offer your own perspective on the events that occurred on September 11, 2001. In your essay, use any photographs, videos, or other such evidence to support your position. Draw on Manjoo's essay as well.

2. In a group of classmates, share the essays you wrote for Question 1. Identify points of agreement and disagreement about the events of September 11, 2001, and try to get a sense of how your classmates interpret those events. Try to determine why each person in your group believes what he or she believes about 9/11. What conclusions might you draw from your group's discussion about how we come to our beliefs about important events?

3. Visit several web sites devoted to the events of September 11, 2001 (including some of the sites Manjoo mentions in his essay) and review those sites to get a sense of the perspective that each promotes. Try to determine what kind of evidence each site seems to rely on to support its point of view. Then write an essay in which you present an analysis of these web sites. In your essay, describe the sites you visited and the way they use evidence to support their views. Draw conclusions about how evidence, especially video or photographic evidence, shapes our understanding of specific events or our opinions of those events.

4. Write an essay about an experience you had in which there was disagreement about what actually happened. In your essay, explore the disagreement and try to understand why it occurred. Also, try to draw conclusions about what your experience suggests about how we know what is true and what isn't.

5. Rewrite the essay you wrote for Question 4 from the point of view of another person who was part of that experience.

Extending the Conversations

1. Several writers in this chapter address issues that have to do with language differences. For example, Gloria Anzaldúa describes her uses of Chicano Spanish and several related languages to make a statement about the connection between those languages and her identity. Other writers explore similar issues related to Standard English, including June Jordan and Amy Tan. Drawing on several of these essays, write an essay exploring language differences and their impact on contemporary life. In what ways do you think language differences come into play in our lives today? What problems might be associated with language differences? Try to address such questions in your essay and draw conclusions about the role of language in our lives.

2. Identify what you think is an important theme that runs through this chapter. Then select several of the readings in which this theme is explored and, drawing from those essays, write an essay discussing that theme. Alternatively, create a PowerPoint presentation or other appropriate multimedia text in which you explore your theme.

3. Drawing on the readings in this chapter, write a letter to graduating seniors at your high school in which you offer them advice about communicating in the world after high school. In your letter, share what you have learned about how to communicate effectively in various settings (school, work, and so on), and offer what you think is the advice that they most need to be effective communicators. Draw on any of the readings in this chapter or any other appropriate resources. Alternatively, create a pamphlet, web site, or some other kind of document for the same purpose.

INFOTRAC

4. Write a conventional academic essay in which you discuss what you believe are the implications of recent technological developments (such as the Internet, cell phones, various wireless devices) on the way we communicate in contemporary society. Draw on any of the readings in this chapter and, using InfoTrac College Edition and other appropriate sources, do any additional research that you think would be useful. In your essay, trace the history of the device or technology you have selected and describe its implications for communication today. Discuss what you think its impact will be in the future and draw your own conclusions about its benefits and disadvantages.

5. Write an essay about the power of music as a medium for communication. Draw on any relevant essays in this chapter and use any other appropriate sources. If possible, create a web site or multimedia presentation (using a program like PowerPoint) based on your essay. Incorporate into your web site or presentation clips from songs or music videos, as appropriate.

6. Select several popular television commercials and write an analysis of the messages they send about some idea or issue that is important to you (such as patriotism, race, gender, and so on). In your analysis, focus on how the commercials use images, sounds, colors, and words to convey their messages; draw conclusions about television commercials as a medium for communication. If possible, create a multimedia presentation that focuses on the same analysis (using PowerPoint or some other program or medium).

7. Identify several common visual symbols or images and write an essay analyzing what those symbols mean and how they are used to communicate ideas, beliefs, information, and so forth. Draw on any appropriate essays in this chapter to support your analysis.

8. If you have access to a camera, take several photographs that illustrate an important idea or belief of yours. Use those photographs to create a photo essay or web site that conveys that idea or belief.

9. Select one or more films and write an essay in which you examine the role music plays in these films. How might music be used to communicate important social messages, and how do these films portray or use music as a medium?

© Hulton-Deutsch Collection/CORBIS

T HE PRESIDENT OF THE UNITED STATES IS SOMETIMES CALLED THE MOST POWERFUL MAN IN THE WORLD. WHAT EXACTLY DOES THAT MEAN? I SUSPECT THAT FOR MANY PEOPLE IT MEANS THAT THE PRESIDENT IS THE COMMANDER IN CHIEF OF THE WORLD'S MOST POWERFUL MILITARY FORCE.

He is the one who decides whether to use that awesome military power, which has an almost unimaginable capacity for destruction. Or maybe it means that the president has the ability to influence government policies that affect the lives of millions of people. For example, in 2003, President George W. Bush proposed an education reform program called No Child Left Behind. Using his substantial influence as president, Bush was able to turn that proposal into new laws and policies affecting what children are taught in schools, how they are evaluated, and how schools are funded. It is no exaggeration to

> It seems pretty clear that the men who wrote the U.S. Constitution in 1787 understood the risks of giving one person too much power.

say that No Child Left Behind has changed schools in important ways and therefore has touched the lives of millions of American schoolchildren. The ability to have such an impact on the lives of others is surely one way to define power.

But the more you think about power, the more you begin to see power in many different aspects of your life. A police officer has the power to arrest you and take away your physical freedom, if only temporarily. A judge has the power to send you to jail, assuming you have done something to justify incarceration. Your boss may have the power to hire or fire employees. A building inspector has the power to approve or deny your request to build a garage or a deck on your property. A teacher has the power to evaluate your performance in a class by assigning you a grade. A doctor has the power to prescribe medication. A

minister has the power to marry two people—or to influence the spiritual lives of a congregation.

Of course, with such power usually comes responsibility. The president's authority to send troops into war is tempered by the fact that his decision can lead to the deaths of many people. An arrest record can have serious consequences, which is why the law prevents a police officer from arresting someone without just cause. Grades matter to students for a variety of reasons, including remaining eligible for loans, gaining admission to a school, graduating, or finding a job. As a result, a teacher must justify students' grades or face the possibility of having unfair grades changed by a principal or dean. And there are limits to power. It seems pretty clear that the men who wrote the U.S. Constitution in 1787 understood the risks of giving one person too much power, so they placed various limits on a president's power. The three branches of government that you learned about in your social studies classes—legislative, judicial, and executive—are intended to "check" one another so that one branch does not acquire too much power. Because of such careful provisions in the Constitution, even with all his power, the president cannot declare war, for example, without the consent of Congress, and his policy proposals, such as education reform initiatives, must be approved by Congress as well.

When I began thinking about this chapter, I was thinking mostly about this kind of political power, partly because we tend to think of power in either political or physical terms. In fact, I might have called this chapter "Politics" or "Government" because many of the essays have to do with the power of governments, or political power, in some way. These essays prompt us to think carefully about the power that government has in our lives. But I also wanted you to think about these essays more broadly. If you read them as investigations into power in general, and not just as essays about political power, how would that change their meaning? For example, Wendell Berry's essay, published shortly after the terrible events of September 11, 2001, indirectly criticizes the U.S. government for many of its economic and social policies. In that sense, we can read this essay as a statement of his political beliefs or as a political criticism of the way the U.S. government wields its power over citizens. But what is Berry saying more broadly about governmental power in our lives? What does his essay suggest about the connection between power and our basic beliefs about how we should live together on the earth? If you approach Berry's essay with those questions in mind, you may read it as something more than a political statement, and it may teach you something more fundamental about the complexities of power in human life.

That's how I'd like you to approach all the essays in this chapter: as essays about specific kinds of power or particular examples of power, but also as essays about power in general—what it is and why we should pay attention to it. As you'll see, not all the essays focus on government. Some deal with more nebulous kinds of power: the power of ideas, of racism and prejudice, of individual acts of resistance, of morality. Writers like Henry David Thoreau, bell hooks, and Martin Luther King, Jr., may address governmental power in their essays, but they also ask you to think about the less obvious ways that various kinds of power can affect

> If you read them as investigations into power in general, and not just as essays about political power, how would that change their meaning?

how we live. And of course, all these writers share one other quality: They have all taken advantage of another kind of power, the power of writing.

WHAT IS POWER?

N 1971, PSYCHOLOGY PROFESSOR PHILIP ZIMBARDO CONDUCTED THE FAMOUS STANFORD PRISON EXPERIMENT. ZIMBARDO WAS INTERESTED IN UNDERSTANDING THE PSYCHOLOGY OF PRISON LIFE, so he designed an experiment to see how ordinary people would react to the conditions of prison. He recruited twenty-four young male college students as volunteers, half of whom were assigned to be "guards" and half "inmates." The volunteers were to live for two weeks in campus offices that were altered to resemble a prison. But Zimbardo and his research team had to stop the experiment after only six days because the mock prison began to function like a real one. Volunteers who served as guards quickly became abusive and a few even displayed sadistic behaviors; many of the "inmates" suffered severe stress and emotional trauma. The most frightening aspect of this famous experiment was how quickly average young men adapted to roles in which they exercised power over other people. Although none of the volunteers had any experience in law enforcement or corrections, and although they were not given any specific instructions about how to run the "prison," the "guards" almost immediately began to develop strategies and techniques to gain complete psychological and physical control over the "inmates." They devised methods that are widely used in real prisons: stripping prisoners naked; making them use numbers instead of names; requiring prisoners to wear degrading identical uniforms; taking away the prisoners' ability to make even the most basic decisions, such as going to the bathroom; and confining prisoners to small, isolated rooms. Zimbardo's experiment has been used to explain the behavior of Nazi soldiers and prison guards in World War II and other situations in which ordinary people participated in unspeakable abuses against other human beings. His experiment is a compelling exploration of the nature of power and an example of the frightening capacity of human beings to wield power over one another.

Zimbardo's experiment offers some disturbing answers to the question, What is power? When we think about power, certainly we think about the use of physical means to exercise control over others, as prison guards sometimes do. Power can also be psychological or emotional control, which the "guards" in Zimbardo's experiment exercised over the "inmates" by denying them certain basic elements of human dignity or trying to strip away their sense of identity. The resistance of some of those "inmates" to the guards' demands might also be seen as a kind of power: the power of one's own integrity or sense of dignity, the ability to stand up for yourself, to fight back against oppression. As the lead researcher who carried out the experiment, Zimbardo also held a kind of power: the power to conduct such an experiment and to end it as well. What was the source of his power? His status as a scholar at an internationally renowned university? His successful record as a researcher? His knowledge? Maybe his own sense of human dignity and empathy for others, which must have been part of the reason he ended his experiment? Or maybe it was fear: fear of the harm that he might be causing to the volunteers. Certainly fear is a formidable kind of power.

If the Zimbardo experiment raises questions about the nature of power, the four readings in this cluster raise additional ones. Mary Crow Dog's autobiographical essay might seem to be another example of the kind of power that Zimbardo witnessed among the volunteers in his famous experiment: the use of physical force to control or subdue others. Crow Dog experienced that kind of power firsthand. But her essay also explores other kinds of power that emerge from a sense of one's dignity and identity. Zachary Scott-Singley describes his unsettling experiences as an American soldier in Iraq and in those descriptions we can see some of the many different ways that military power can be wielded by individual soldiers under trying circumstances; we also see the power of caring and love. President John F. Kennedy's essay describes poetic language as power, and the writers of the satiric newspaper *The Onion* reveal that satiric humor can be a kind of power to make sense of and deal with political events that affect our lives.

Such a brief selection of readings couldn't possibly explore the many different kinds of power we might encounter in our lives, but these readings nevertheless provide a rich and intriguing set of answers to the question, What is power? I hope they'll help you appreciate the complexities of power in your own life—as well as the power of writing to help you make sense of it all.

If we read this excerpt from Mary Crow Dog's autobiography as an essay about power, we will probably focus on the cruel ways that the sisters who ran the Indian boarding school she attended exercised their power over the students there in the 1960s. But if we look past Crow Dog's descriptions of the physical abuse that took place at her boarding

Civilize Them WITH A Stick

school, we'll see that there's more to her story than the use of power by White Americans to rob Indian children of their language or identity, for her story is also about the power of the human desire to survive. And it is a story about the power of language to help establish and maintain one's identity (which is one reason why teachers at Indian boarding schools tried so hard to prevent Indian children from speaking their native languages) as well as the capacity of language to bear witness to the abuses of power. Crow Dog's story itself is a way to fight the power of those who abused her and the other Indian children who attended her boarding school; through her writing, she not only asserts her dignity as a Lakota woman, but she also exposes the abuse of power so that others might find the strength to resist such abuse as she herself did. I suspect her story will stir strong emotions in you. I also hope it will help you appreciate how you might use writing both to

MARY CROW DOG

. . . Gathered from the cabin, the wickiup, and the tepee,
partly by cajolery and partly by threats;
partly by bribery and partly by force,
they are induced to leave their kindred
to enter these schools and take upon themselves
the outward appearance of civilized life.
                    —Annual report of the Department of Interior, 1901

It is almost impossible to explain to a sympathetic white person what a typical old Indian boarding school was like; how it affected the Indian child suddenly dumped into it like a small creature from another world, helpless, defenseless, bewildered, trying desperately and instinctively to survive and sometimes not surviving at all. I think such children were like the victims of Nazi concentration camps trying to tell average, middle-class Americans what their experience had been like. Even now, when these schools are much improved, when the buildings are new, all gleaming steel and glass, the food tolerable, the teachers well trained and well intentioned, even trained in child psychology— unfortunately the psychology of white children, which is different from

MARY CROW DOG, "CIVILIZE THEM WITH A STICK," FROM *LAKOTA WOMAN*. BY MARY CROW DOG AND RICHARD ERDOES, PAGES 28–41. NEW YORK: GROVE PRESS, 1960.

resist and to wield power in your own life.

This essay first appeared in Lakota Woman *(1990), Mary Crow Dog's best-selling auto-biography, which was co-written with Richard Erdoes. Crow Dog, who was born Mary Brave Bird in 1953 on the Rosebud Indian Reservation in South Dakota, writes on her web site, "I have spent most of my life fighting for Native American rights. . . . The struggle is never over." ◪*

GLOSS: ST. FRANCIS SCHOOL AND INDIAN BOARDING SCHOOLS
In paragraph 2, Crow Dog mentions the St. Francis school, which was one of many schools established specifically for Indian children by the U.S. government and by Catholic or Christian organizations. Often established by missionaries on Indian reservations in the late nineteenth century, Indian boarding schools increased in number through the twentieth century. By the 1960s, as many as 60,000 Indian children were attending such schools each year. However, many Indian boarding schools began to close in the 1980s and 1990s. Today, approximately 10,000 Indian children attend boarding schools. These schools have always been controversial, in part because they originally tried to "re-educate" Indian children in order to assimilate them into White American culture and thereby eliminate Indian culture. The most famous such school was in Carlisle, Pennsylvania, where thousands of Indian children from various parts of the American West were sent to be "civilized" from 1879 to 1918. The St. Francis Mission, established in South Dakota in 1885 by the Jesuit Society, an order of Catholic priests, eventually became the St. Francis School in 1972, which Mary Crow Dog attended.

ours—the shock to the child upon arrival is still tremendous. Some just seem to shrivel up, don't speak for days on end, and have an empty look in their eyes. I know of an eleven-year-old on another reservation who hanged herself, and in our school, while I was there, a girl jumped out of the window, trying to kill herself to escape an unbearable situation. That first shock is always there. . .

The mission school at **ST. FRANCIS** was curse for our family for genera-tions. My grandmother went there, then my mother, then my sisters and I. At one time or other every one of us tried to run away. Grandma told me once about the bad times she had experienced at St. Francis. In those days they let students go home only for one week every year. Two days were used up for transportation, which meant spending just five days out of three hundred and sixty-five with her family. And that was an improvement. Before grandma's time, on many reservations they did not let the students go home at all until they had finished school. Anybody who disobeyed the nuns was severely punished. The building in which my grandmother stayed had three floors, for girls only. Way up in the attic were little cells, about five by five by ten feet. One time she was in church and instead of praying she was playing jacks. As punishment they took her to one of those little cubicles where she stayed in darkness because the windows had been boarded up. They left her there for a whole week with only bread and water for nourishment. After she came out she promptly ran away, together with three other girls. They were found and brought back. The nuns stripped them naked and whipped them. They used a horse buggy whip on my grandmother. Then she was put back into the attic—for two weeks.

My mother had much the same experiences but never wanted to talk about them, and then there I was, in the same place. The school is now run by the BIA—the Bureau of Indian Affairs—but only since about fifteen years ago. When I was there, during the 1960s, it was still run by the Church. The **JESUIT FATHERS** ran the boys' wing and the **SISTERS OF THE SACRED HEART** ran us—with the help of the strap. Nothing had changed since my grand-mother's days. I have been told recently that even in the '70s they were still beating children at that school. All I got out of school was being taught how to pray. I learned quickly that I would be beaten if I failed in my devotions or, God forbid, prayed the wrong way, espe-cially prayed in Indian to Wakan Tanka, the Indian Creator.

The girls' wing was built like an F and was run like a penal institution. Every morning at five o'clock the sisters would come into our large dor-mitory to wake us up, and immediately we had to kneel down at the sides of our beds and recite the prayers. At six o'clock we were herded into the church for more of the same. I did not take kindly to the discipline and to marching by the clock, left-right, left-right. I was never one to like being forced to do something. I do something because I feel like doing it. I felt this way always, as far as I can remember, and my sister Barbara felt the same way. An old medicine man once told me: "Us Lakotas are not like dogs who can be trained, who can be beaten and keep on wagging their tails, licking the hand that whipped them. We are like cats, little cats, big cats, wildcats, bobcats, mountain lions. It doesn't matter what kind, but cats who can't be tamed, who scratch if you step on their tails." But I was only a kitten and my claws were still small.

5   Barbara was still in the school when I arrived and during my first year or two she could still protect me a little bit. When Barb was a seventh-grader she ran away together with five other girls, early in the morning before sunrise. They brought them back in the evening. The girls had to wait for two hours in front of the mother superior's office. They were hungry and cold, frozen through. It was wintertime and they had been running the whole day without food, trying to make good their escape. The mother superior asked each girl, "Would you do this again?" She told them that as punishment they would not be allowed to visit home for a month and that she'd keep them busy on work details until the skin on their knees and elbows had worn off. At the end of her speech she told each girl, "Get up from this chair and lean over it." She then lifted the girls' skirts and pulled down their underpants. Not little girls either, but teenagers. She had a leather strap about a foot long and four inches wide fastened to a stick, and beat the girls, one after another, until they cried. Barb did not give her that satisfaction but just clenched her teeth. There was one girl, Barb told me, the nun kept on beating and beating until her arm got tired.

I did not escape my share of the strap. Once, when I was thirteen years old, I refused to go to Mass. I did not want to go to church because I did not feel well. A nun grabbed me by the hair, dragged me upstairs, made me stoop over, pulled my dress up (we were not allowed at the time to wear jeans), pulled my panties down, and gave me what they called "swats"—twenty-five swats with a board around which Scotch tape had been wound. She hurt me badly.

My classroom was right next to the principal's office and almost every day I could hear him swatting the boys. Beating was the common punishment for not doing one's homework, or for being late to school. It had such a bad effect upon me that I hated and mistrusted every white person on sight, because I met only one kind. It was not until much later that I met sincere white people I could relate to and be friends with. Racism breeds racism in reverse.

The routine at St. Francis was dreary. Six A.M., kneeling in church for an hour or so; seven o'clock, breakfast; eight o'clock, scrub the floor, peel spuds, make classes. We had to mop the dining room twice every

GLOSS: THE JESUITS AND THE SISTERS OF THE SACRED HEART
Jesuits (par. 3) are members of the Society of Jesus, an order of Roman Catholic priests founded in the sixteenth century. Sisters of the Sacred Heart (par. 3) are an order of Roman Catholic nuns.

day and scrub the tables. If you were caught taking a rest, doodling on the bench with a fingernail or knife, or just rapping, the nun would come up with a dish towel and just slap it across your face, saying, "You're not supposed to be talking, you're supposed to be working!" Monday mornings we had cornmeal mush, Tuesday oatmeal, Wednesday rice and raisins, Thursday cornflakes, and Friday all the leftovers mixed together or sometimes fish. Frequently the food had bugs or rocks in it. We were eating hot dogs that were weeks old, while the nuns were dining on ham, whipped potatoes, sweet peas, and cranberry sauce. In winter our dorm was icy cold while the nuns' rooms were always warm.

I have seen little girls arrive at the school, first-graders, just fresh from home and totally unprepared for what awaited them, little girls with pretty braids, and the first thing the nuns did was chop their hair off and tie up what was left behind their ears. Next they would dump the children into tubs of alcohol, a sort of rubbing alcohol, "to get the germs off." Many of the nuns were German immigrants, some from Bavaria, so that we sometimes speculated whether Bavaria was some sort of Dracula country inhabited by monsters. For the sake of objectivity I ought to mention that two of the German fathers were great linguists and that the only Lakota–English dictionaries and grammars which are worth anything were put together by them.

10   At night some of the girls would huddle in bed together for comfort and reassurance. Then the nun in charge of the dorm would come in and say, "What are the two of you doing in bed together? I smell evil in this room. You girls are evil incarnate. You are sinning. You are going to hell and burn forever. You can act that way in the devil's frying pan." She would get them out of bed in the middle of the night, making them kneel and pray until morning. We had not the slightest idea what it was all about. At home we slept two and three in a bed for animal warmth and a feeling of security.

The nuns and the girls in the two top grades were constantly battling it out physically with fists, nails, and hair-pulling. I myself was growing from a kitten into an undersized cat. My claws were getting bigger and were itching for action. About 1969 or 1970 a strange young white girl appeared on the reservation. She looked about eighteen or twenty years old. She was pretty and had long, blond hair down to her waist, patched jeans, boots, and a backpack. She was different from any other white person we had met before. I think her name was Wise. I do not know how she managed to overcome our reluctance and distrust, getting us into a corner, making us listen to her, asking us how we were treated. She told us that she was from New York. She was the first real **HIPPIE OR YIPPIE** we had come

---

CONVERSATIONS: HIPPIES, YIPPIES, BLACK PANTHERS, YOUNG LORDS, AND WEATHERMEN

In this passage, Crow Dog mentions some of the important groups expressing resistance to mainstream American culture in the 1960s and 1970s. Some of these groups, such as the Weathermen and the Black Panthers, explicitly advocated violent resistance to racism and government oppression, while other groups, like the hippies, supported alternative lifestyles as a form of resistance to mainstream society. Later in her essay, Crow Dog tells us that she was part of the Indian resistance movement at Wounded Knee in 1973. In a sense, in telling us about her encounter with the White woman she identifies as a hippie, she is referring to the larger conversations about racism, social justice, and peace that were occurring in the United States during that time. And writing her story about her experiences at the Indian boarding school might be seen as part of the continuing conversations about those important events.

across. She told us of people called the **BLACK PANTHERS, YOUNG LORDS, AND WEATHERMEN.** She said, "Black people are getting it on. Indians are getting it on in St. Paul and California. How about you?" She also said, "Why don't you put out an underground paper, mimeograph it. It's easy. Tell it like it is. Let it all hang out." She spoke a strange lingo but we caught on fast.

Charlene Left hand Bull and Gina One Star were two full-blood girls I used to hang out with. We did everything together. They were willing to join me in a Sioux uprising. We put together a newspaper which we called the *Red Panther.* In it we wrote how bad the school was, what kind of slop we had to eat—slimy, rotten, blackened potatoes for two weeks—the way we were beaten. I think I was the one who wrote the worst article about our principal of the moment, Father Keeler. I put all my anger and venom into it. I called him a goddam wasicun son of a bitch. I wrote that he knew nothing about Indians and should go back to where he came from, teaching white children whom he could relate to. I wrote that we knew which priests slept with which nuns and that all they ever could think about was filling their bellies and buying a new car. It was the kind of writing which foamed at the mouth, but which also lifted a great deal of weight from one's soul.

On Saint Patrick's Day, when everybody was at the big powwow, we distributed our newspapers. We put them on windshields and bulletin boards, in desks and pews, in dorms and toilets. But someone saw us and snitched on us. The shit hit the fan. The three of us were taken before a board meeting. Our parents, in my case my mother, had to come. They were told that ours was a most serious matter, the worst thing that had ever happened in the school's long history. One of the nuns told my mother, "Your daughter really needs to be talked to." "What's wrong with my daughter?" my mother asked. She was given one of our *Red Panther* newspapers. The nun pointed out its name to her and then my piece, waiting for mom's reaction, after a while she asked, "Well, what have to got to say to this? What do you think?"

My mother said, "Well, when I went to school here, some years back, I was treated a lot worse than these kids are. I really can't see how they can have any complaints, because we was treated a lot stricter. We could not even wear skirts halfway up our knees. These girls have it made. But you should forgive them because they are young. And it's supposed to be a free country, free speech and all that. I don't believe what they done is wrong." So all I got out of it was scrubbing six flights of stairs on my hands and knees, every day. And no boy-side privileges.

The boys and girls were still pretty much separated. The only time one could meet a member of the opposite sex was during free time, between four and five-thirty, in the study hall or on benches or the volleyball court outside, and that was strictly supervised. One day Charlene and I went over to the boys' side. We were on the ball team

and they had to let us practice. We played three
extra minutes, only three minutes more than we
were supposed to. Here was the nuns' opportunity
for revenge. We got twenty-five swats. I told Charlene, "We are getting too old to have our bare asses
whipped that way. We are old enough to have babies. Enough of this shit. Next time we fight back."
Charlene only said, "Hoka-hay!"

We had to take showers every evening. One little
girl did not want to take her panties off and one of
the nuns told her, "You take those underpants
off—or else!" But the child was ashamed to do it.
The nun was getting her swat to threaten the girl.
I went up to the sister, pushed her veil off, and knocked her down. I
told her that if she wanted to hit a little girl she should pick on me,
pick one her own size. She got herself transferred out of the dorm a
week later.

In a school like this there is always a lot of favoritism. **AT ST. FRAN-
CIS IT WAS STRONGLY TINGED WITH RACISM.** Girls who were near-white,
who came from what the nuns called "nice families," got preferen-
tial treatment. They waited on the faculty and got to eat ham or eggs
and bacon in the morning. They got the easy jobs while the skins,
who did not have the right kind of background—myself among
them—always wound up in the laundry room sorting out ten bushel
baskets of dirty boys' socks every day. Or we wound up scrubbing the
floors and doing all the dishes. The school therefore fostered fights
and antagonism between whites and breeds, and between breeds
and skins. At one time Charlene and I had to iron all the robes and
vestments the priests wore when saying Mass. We had to fold them
up and put them into a chest in the back of the church. In a corner,
looking over our shoulders, was a statue of the crucified Savior, all
bloody and beaten up. Charlene looked up and said, "Look at that
poor Indian. The pigs sure worked him over." That was the closest I
even came to seeing Jesus.

I was held up as a bad example and didn't mind. I was old enough
to have a boyfriend and promptly got one. At the school we had an
hour and a half for ourselves. Between the boys' and the girls' wings
were some benches where one could sit. My boyfriend and I used to
go there just to hold hands and talk. The nuns were very uptight
about any boy-girl stuff. They had an exaggerated fear of anything
having even the faintest connection with sex. One day in religion
class, an all-girl class, Sister Bernard singled me out for some remarks,
pointing me out as a bad example, an example that should be shown.
She said that I was too free with my body. That I was holding hands
which meant that I was not a good example to follow. She also said

that I wore unchaste dresses, skirts which were too short, too sugges-
tive, shorter than regulations permitted, and for that I would be punished. She dressed me down before the whole class, carrying on and
on about my uchastity.

I stood up and told her, "You shouldn't say any of those things,
miss. You people are a lot worse than us Indians. I know all about you,
because my grandmother and my aunt told me about you. Maybe
twelve, thirteen years ago you had a water stoppage here in St. Francis. No water could get through the pipes. There are water lines right
under the mission, underground tunnels and passages where in my
grandmother's time only the nuns and priests could go, which were
off-limits to everybody else. When the water backed up they had to go
through all the water lines and clean them out. And in those huge
pipes they found the bodies of newborn babies. And they were white
babies. They weren't Indian babies. At least when our girls have babies, they don't do away with them that way, like flushing them down
the toilet, almost."

"And that priest they sent here from Holy Rosary in Pine Ridge   20
because he molested a little girl. You couldn't think of anything better than dump him on us. All he does is watch young women and girls
with that funny smile on his face. Why don't you point him out for an
example?"

Charlene and I worked on the school newspaper. After all we had
some practice. Every day we went down to Publications. One of the
priests acted as the photographer, doing the enlarging and developing. He smelled of chemicals which had stained his hands yellow.
One day he invited Charlene into the darkroom. He was going to
teach her developing. She was developed already. She was a big girl
compared to him, taller too. Charlene was nicely built, not fat, just
rounded. No sharp edges anywhere. All of sudden she rushed out of
the darkroom, yelling to me, "Let's get out of here! He's trying to feel
me up. That priest is nasty." So there was this too to contend with—
sexual harassment. We complained to the student body. The nuns
said we just had a dirty mind.

We got a new priest in English. During one of his first classes he
asked one of the boys a certain question. The boy was shy. He spoke
poor English, but he had the right answer. The priest told him, "You
did not say it right. Correct yourself. Say it over again." The boy got
flustered and stammered. He could hardly get out a word. But the
priest kept after him: "Didn't you hear? I told you to do the whole
thing over. Get it right this time." He kept on and on.

I stood up and said, "Father, don't be doing that. If you go into an
Indian's home and try to talk Indian, they might laugh at you and say,
'Do it over correctly. Get it right this time!'"

He shouted at me, "Mary, you stay after class. Sit down right now!"

I stayed after class, until after the bell. He told me, "Get over here!"   25

He grabbed me by the arm, pushing me against the blackboard, shouting, "Why are you always mocking us? You have no reason to do this."

I said, "Sure I do. You were making fun of him. You embarrassed him. He needs strengthening, not weakening. You hurt him. I did not hurt you."

He twisted my arm and pushed real hard. I turned around and hit him in the face, giving him a bloody nose. After that I ran out of the room, slamming the door behind me. He and I went to Sister Bernard's office. I told her, "Today I quit school. I'm not taking any more of this, none of this shit anymore. None of this treatment. Better give me my diploma. I can't waste any more time on you people."

Sister Bernard looked at me for a long, long time. She said, "All right, Mary Ellen, go home today. Come back in a few days and get your diploma." And that was that. Oddly enough, that priest turned out okay. He taught a class in grammar, orthography, composition, things like that. I think he wanted more respect in class. He was still young and unsure of himself. But I was in there too long. I didn't feel like hearing it. Later he became a good friend of the Indians, a personal friend of myself and my husband. He stood up for us during **WOUNDED KNEE** and after. He stood up to his superiors, stuck his neck way out, became a real people's priest. He even learned our language. He died prematurely of cancer. It is not only the good Indians who die young, but the good whites, too. It is the timid ones who know how to take care of themselves who grow old. I am still grateful to that priest for what he did for us later and for the quarrel he picked with me—or did I pick it with him?—because it ended a situation which had become unendurable for me. The day of my fight with him was my last day in school.

GLOSS: WOUNDED KNEE

In 1973, the Indian activist organization called the American Indian Movement (AIM) seized the town of Wounded Knee on the Pine Ridge Reservation in South Dakota to protest what they alleged was police brutality against Native Americans as well as abuses by the Bureau of Indian Affairs, which managed the reservation. U.S. Marshalls and U.S. military personnel sealed off the town for 71 days until a settlement to end the siege was reached. The incident received international press coverage. Mary Crow Dog, who was among the Indians who participated in the takeover of Wounded Knee, gave birth to her first child during the siege.

Understanding the Text

1. In paragraph 3, Crow Dog describes herself as a kitten when she was a student at the board school. What does she mean? What is the significance of this metaphor in Crow Dog's story about her experiences?

2. What does Crow Dog tell us is the effect of her experiences with physical violence on her? Why is this effect important, in her view? Do you agree? Why or why not?

3. Why does Crow Dog get into trouble for writing a school newspaper? What do you think her anecdote about this experience reveals about

her? What does it reveal about the nuns who ran her boarding school? About her mother? About writing?

4. Why does Crow Dog leave the boarding school after her altercation with the young priest? What do you think her departure under those circumstances reveals about her? How do you think she has changed as a result of her experiences at the school?

Exploring the Issues

1. Crow Dog devotes most of this essay to her experiences at the Indian boarding school she attended as a child, but the first few paragraphs focus on the experiences her mother and grandmother had in the same school. Why do you think Crow Dog includes her mother's and grandmother's experiences in an essay focused on her own experience? What effect do you think her descriptions of her mother's and grandmother's experience might have on readers? How do they help Crow Dog convey her main ideas about her own experiences?

2. In paragraph 9, Crow Dog writes, "For the sake of objectivity I ought to mention that two of the German fathers were great linguists and that the only Lakota-English dictionaries and grammars which are worth anything were put together by them." Do you think Crow Dog is objective in her depiction of the sisters and priests at the boarding school she attended? Do you think she really intends to be? Explain. Why do you think she would include this statement in any essay that really has nothing to do with linguistics?

3. What do you think is the main point that Crow Dog hopes to convey to readers about her experiences in the boarding school? What pur-

poses might she be trying to achieve in telling her story? How effectively do you think she conveys her ideas about her experiences?

Entering the Conversations

1. Write an essay about a time when you felt subjected to control or power against your will. Tell the story of that experience in a way that not only describes the incident but also conveys how you felt at the time. Try also to convey a sense of how power was used (or abused) in that experience.

2. Write an essay in which you discuss the various kinds of power that are evident in Mary Crow Dog's story. In your essay, try to answer the question, What is power?

INFOTRAC

3. Part of Mary Crow Dog's story is about the importance of language to Native Americans and their sense of identity. As she suggests in paragraph 9, the Lakota language is not widely used and is disappearing as a result. Many other Native American languages and the languages of other ethnic minorities have suffered the same fate. Using InfoTrac, your library, and other relevant resources, investigate the role of language in Native American life—or select another language that is disappearing and investigate that language. Try to learn some-

thing about the language itself and the nation or ethnic group who speaks it, and find out the extent to which the language continues to be used today. Try to find out whether there have been any efforts to preserve the language (such as the writing of the Lakota-English dictionary that Mary Crow Dog mentions in par. 9). If possible, talk to someone who speaks that language or is familiar with it, or interview a professor at your school who may have expertise in linguistics or anthropology. Then, write a report on the basis of your research about the language you examined. In your report, describe the state of that language today. Draw conclusions about the power of language and its connection to identity.

4. Write an essay in which you define and analyze power in school settings. Draw on your own experience, Mary Crow Dog's essay, and any other relevant sources (including other essays in this textbook, such as Paulo Freire's essay, "The Banking Concept of Education," on page 176) to examine the nature of power and how it is used (and possibly abused) in schools. Draw conclusions about the role of power in schooling.

5. On the basis of your analysis of power in schooling for Question 4, create a web site, pamphlet, or other appropriate document intended to be a guide to help students understand power in schools.

First-hand accounts of war are as old as *civilization. Some accounts are famous, such as Julius Caesar's* Commentaries about the Gallic Wars. *More recent wars, especially the Vietnam War, have spawned many books by common soldiers about their often-harrowing experiences in battle. Like other autobiographical accounts of war by*

A Soldier's Thoughts

soldiers, Zachary Scott-Singley's writings about his experiences in Iraq in 2005 include disturbing descriptions of the horrors of war and the often regrettable decisions of soldiers who must act quickly in confusing and deadly circumstances. Scott-Singley writes about such events with deep emotion, and his narratives reveal some of the complexities of power: military power, physical power, and the power of fear as well as the power of hope.

Scott-Singley's accounts also reveal another kind of power: the power of new communications technologies like the Internet. The following passages were originally posted to Scott-Singley's blog, and in that regard, his first-hand accounts of war differ from the many others that have been written over the centuries. Today, thousands of "milblogs" maintained by soldiers provide a real-time window into the experience of war that never before existed. Their stories, instantly available to millions of readers

ZACHARY SCOTT-SINGLEY

APRIL 29, 2005—MEMORIES OF DEATH

There is good out there even though at times it all seems bleak. There is also death. How many have dealt in death? Some would call it murder. Well, I have a confession to make, my platoon and I have had over 192 confirmed kills during our first deployment here (during the war on our way to capture Baghdad). We targeted people and then they just disappeared. Why? They were going to kill me. I had my orders and they had theirs. We were mortal enemies because we were told that we were. There are some who would tell me to not think about what I had to do, or it will drive you insane.

For me, however, I can't help but think about it. They were men like me. Some of them were even conscripted into military service. **WHAT MADE THEM FIGHT?** Were they more scared of their leader than of us? What has become of their families? How could I forget or not think about all that I have done? Should I wash my hands of it all like Pontius Pilate? I think not. My choices have been made, my actions irreversible. So live I will, for we were the victors. Right? The ones who survived. It is our victory, and our burden to carry. And I bear it

ZACHARY SCOTT-SINGLEY, "A SOLDIER'S THOUGHTS," IN *THE BEST AMERICAN NONREQUIRED READING 2006*, PAGES 21–27. EDITED BY DAVE EGGERS. BOSTON: HOUGHTON MIFFLIN, 2006.

with pride and with the greatest of remorse. Do you think that there is a special place in hell for people like me? Or will God judge me to have been a man of honor and duty?

When they told us how many we had killed my first thought was pride. Pride for such a high number. How does one feel pride for killing? Two years later and my thoughts are changed, transformed if you will. Those were just numbers so long ago when I first heard them. Now, however, I know that they were men with families like mine. It is crazy that we humans can be so destructive. There are people out there lining up to become martyrs, to kill themselves in order to kill others, and yet you still have people who fight tooth and nail to live for just one more minute longer. We are an oxymoron, humanity that is. What makes someone look down the sights of a rifle to take aim on a fellow human being? What does it take to pull the trigger? I have done those things. I have done them and would do it again if it meant returning to my wife and children again. Some of you may think that I am a beast and you are probably right. I am. I will kill, I will take aim and fire, I will call fire upon you from afar with rockets and bombs or anything I can get my hands on if it means that I will see my family one more time.

But, I will also choose to dwell on and live with my choices. I chose to enlist as a soldier. My time has been served and now it is becoming overtime, but I won't just run away. As much as I would love to just be done (and rightly so now that I have been **INVOLUNTARILY EXTENDED**). One thing is all I ask of you. I ask that you not judge me. Let me be my own judge, for my judgment is harsher than any you could give me anyway. For I will always have those memories to remind me of what I have done and what I am. Please know that I pray for peace every day, that and to see my family again.

MAY 4, 2005—IT WAS STILL DARK . . .

5   It was still dark. I got dressed in that darkness. When I was ready I grabbed an MRE (meal ready to eat) and got in the truck. I was going to go line the truck up in preparation for the raid we were about to go on. The targets were three houses where **RPG** attacks had come from a few days prior. Sitting there in that darkness listening to the briefing on how we were to execute the mission, I let my mind wander from the briefing and said a prayer. "Just one more day, God, let me live one more day and we will go from there . . . " It was the same prayer I said every day because every day I did the same thing. I left the base. With a small team I would go out each day on different missions. I was their translator.

throughout the world, display the power of this new medium of the Internet to communicate. In this regard, the Internet is a brand-new way for soldiers to tell very old stories about human conflict and resilience—and about the complexities of power.

Scott-Singley served as a sergeant in the U.S. Army's 3rd Infantry Division in Iraq. As of 2008, he continued to maintain his blog, where the following accounts first appeared. They were reprinted in Best American Nonrequired Reading of 2006. ◪

STRATEGIES: ESTABLISH VOICE
Blogs tend to be written in much less formal style than, say, articles published in a newspaper or reports written for your college classes. But that doesn't mean that bloggers do not employ sophisticated strategies to make their writing effective for their intended audience. In paragraphs 2 and 3, for instance, Scott-Singley poses hard questions about his own moral responsibilities as a soldier, and he raises doubts about himself as a soldier and a person. Notice how those questions focus our attention on the complex moral issues he is struggling with and also involve his readers directly in that struggle, making the moral issues seem very real and pressing. This strategy is a way for him to establish his voice as a soldier who thinks carefully about his experiences, to focus attention on important moral issues, and to convey a sense of urgency about those issues.

GLOSS: INVOLUNTARY EXTENSIONS OF DUTY
When Scott-Singley writes, in paragraph 4, that he has "been involuntarily extended," he is referring to a U.S. military policy during the Iraq War by which soldiers were ordered to remain in Iraq after their designated tours of duty were complete. Through this policy, a soldier might be ordered to remain in the military even after his or her contract had expired, as happened to Scott-Singley (see par. 15). This policy became controversial as the Iraq War continued and many soldiers were ordered to return to Iraq for second, third, and even fourth tours of duty.

GLOSS: RPG
RPG refers to rocket-propelled grenade, a common and deadly shoulder-fired weapon used in the Iraq War that launches an explosive at a target.

CONVERSATIONS: SADDAM
Scott-Singley refers in this passage to Saddam Hussein, who ruled Iraq as President from 1979 to 2003, when he was removed from power as a result of the U.S. military invasion of Iraq. Hussein was subsequently tried for crimes against the Iraqi people, convicted, and executed. In 2002 and 2003, the U.S. government charged that Hussein's efforts to develop weapons of mass destruction justified the military invasion to remove him from power. An international controversy surrounded those charges, which were disputed by some governments, including some U.S. allies. Many people opposed the military invasion of Iraq because they did not believe the U.S. government's claims about Saddam Hussein. Notice that Scott-Singley refers here only to "Saddam." Because of the ongoing controversy about the Iraq War, Scott-Singley can assume his readers know who "Saddam" is. Indeed, that single name carries many meanings as a result of the extensive and often contentious debates about Saddam Hussein and the impact of the U.S. invasion.

GLOSS: AK-47
The AK-47 military assault rifle, which was developed and manufactured by the former Soviet Union and continues to be produced in Russia, is one of the most widely used military weapons in the world. It is popular among the insurgents who battled the U.S. military forces and its allies in Iraq.

There were different people to meet each day. There were some who would kill you if they could. They would look at you and you could see the hate in their eyes. I also met with people who would have given me everything they owned. People that were so thankful to us because we had rid them of **SADDAM**. Well, this day was not really much different from all those other days so far. After the briefing we all got into our assigned seats and convoyed out to the raid site. I was to go in directly after the military police that would clear the building.

The raid began without a hitch. Inside one of the courtyards of one of the houses, talking to an Iraqi woman, checking to see if her story correlated with what the detained men had said, I heard gunfire. It was automatic gunfire. Ducking next to the stone wall I yelled at the woman to get inside her house, and when the gunfire stopped I peeked my head around the front gate. I saw a soldier amongst the others who was pulling rear security by our vehicles. This soldier I saw was still aiming his M249 (a fully automatic belt-fed machine gun) at a black truck off in the distance. His was the weapon I had heard.

I ran up near his position and overheard the captain in charge of the raid asking what had happened and why had this soldier opened fire. The soldier kept his weapon aimed and answered that he was sure he had seen a man holding an **AK-47** in the back of the black truck. I was amongst the four (along with the soldier who had fired on the black truck) who had been selected to go and see what was up with that truck.

We were out of breath when we got to the gun truck nearest to the black civilian truck (a gun truck is a HUMMWV, sometimes called a Hummer by civilians, with a .50-caliber machine gun on its roof). There was a group of four Iraqis walking towards us from the black truck. They were carrying a body. When I saw this I ran forward and began to speak (in Arabic) to the man holding the body but I couldn't say a word.

There right in front of me in the arms of one of the men I saw a small boy (no more than three years old). His head was cocked back at the wrong angle and there was blood. So much blood. How could all that blood be from that small boy? I heard crying too. All of the Iraqi men standing there were crying and sobbing and asking me WHY? Someone behind me started screaming for a medic. It was the young soldier (around my age) who had fired his weapon. He screamed and screamed for a medic until his voice was hoarse and a medic came just to tell us what I already knew. The boy was dead. I was so numb.

10

I stood there looking at that little child, someone's child (just like mine), and seeing how red the clean white shirt of the man holding the boy was turning. It was then that I realized that I had been speaking to them, speaking in a voice that sounded so very far away. I heard my voice telling them (in Arabic) how sorry we were. My mouth was saying this but all my mind could focus on was the hole in the child's head. The white shirt covered in bright red blood. Every color was so bright. There were other colors too. The glistening white pieces of the child's skull still splattered on that so very white shirt. I couldn't stop looking at them even as I continued telling them how sorry we were.

I can still see it all to this very day. The raid was over, there were no weapons to be found, and we had accomplished nothing except killing a child of some unknowing mother. Not wanting to leave yet, I stayed as long as I could, talking to the man holding the child. I couldn't leave because I needed to know who they were. I wanted to remember. The man was the brother of the child's father. He was the boy's uncle, and he was watching him for his father who had gone to the market. They were carpenters and the soldier who had fired upon the truck had seen someone holding a piece of wood and standing in the truck bed.

Before I left to go back to our base I saw the young soldier who had killed the boy. His eyes were unfocused and he was just standing there, staring off into the distance. My hand went to my canteen and I took a drink of water. That soldier looked so lost, so I offered him a drink from my canteen. In a hoarse voice he quietly thanked me and then gave me such a thankful look, like I had given him gold.

Later that day those of us who had been selected to go inspect the black truck were filling reports out about what we had witnessed for the investigation. The captain who had led the raid entered the room we were in and you could see that he was angry. He said, "Well this is just great! Now we have to go and give that family bags of money to shut them up." I wanted to kill him. I sat there trembling with my rage. Some family had just lost their beautiful baby boy and this man, this COMMISSIONED OFFICER in the United States Army is worried about trying to pay off the family's grief and sorrow. He must not have been a father, otherwise he would know that money doesn't even come close . . . I wanted to use my bare hands to kill him, but instead I just sat there and waited until the investigating officer called me into his office.

To this day I still think about that raid, that family, that boy. I won- [15] der if they are making attacks on us now. I would be. If someone took the life of my son or my daughter nothing other than my own death would stop me from killing that person. I still cry too. I cry when the memory hits me. I cry when I think of how very far away I am from my family who needs me. I am not there just like the boy's father wasn't there. I pray every day for my family's safety and just that I was with them. I have served my time, I have my nightmares, I have enough blood on my hands. My contract with the Army has been involuntarily extended. I am not asking for medicine to help with the nightmares or for anything else, only that the Army would have held true to the contract I signed and let me be a father, a husband, a daddy again.

MAY 29, 2005—MY THOUGHTS ON MONSTERS

There is a place where the skies are blue, the water is clean, and life is good. This place cannot be found where I am at. Over here almost every single morning begins with violence, explosions, and people being killed. Over here the locals can't make enough money because it is so unsafe to be out and working. Over here things are different. Down is often up and up isn't down but sideways. In Iraq there are some who want only to see their children grow up, to grow old with their loved ones.

There are also monsters here. "Monsters?" you say. "Those can't be real." I tell you that they are. I have seen with my own eyes that they are. The worst part is that they look just like people. They aren't, though. They think that the way to do things is to violently end their lives. Most of the time they end up destroying and devastating those regular people who love their families. People who work honestly, those who have hearts. The monsters, however, are hard to spot because like I said, they look like regular people.

I have spoken with these monsters, seen their eyes. I wonder how you can fit so much hate in there. Maybe that is why they blow themselves up. They just can't contain all that hate . . .

Want to know what it is like to be one? I have come close before. Close, because I wanted to kill so badly, to destroy those same monsters, but I realized something. You are only a monster if you let yourself become one.

20   So now I dream not about monsters but about that place. It is so very far away that it doesn't seem like it is real anymore. That place is called home. I just hope that I make it back there.

JUNE 17, 2005—STICKS AND STONES BUT WORDS CAN NEVER HURT

I can't stop thinking about what a major said to me the other day: "The whole country of Iraq, every man, woman, and child . . . Kill every one of them and it still won't be worth one American's life."

Perhaps this is why we won't win here, because so many feel that the life of an Iraqi doesn't even register when compared to that of an American. This kind of mindset permeates the thoughts of many of the soldiers here in Iraq.

So often I hear, "I gotta go f— guard Hajji!" from the soldiers assigned the duty of watching over the Iraqi workers who are working on our base. Another thing I hear so very often is, "I'm gonna go shoot me some Hajji." The soldiers who say these things speak as if the Iraqi people were some kind of animal to be hunted. You might tell me that terrorists are nothing more than animals to be hunted but if you look at the statistics **MOST OF THOSE KILLED ARE CIVILIANS** not foreign fighters.

It is time to wake up and realize that there are more important things than the **MICHAEL JACKSON TRIAL.** There are things like the value of a human life or the value of an *entire* nation that has been kicked so many times by tyrants that it may look downtrodden and useless but under it all there is the beauty of LIFE.

OCTOBER 27, 2005—OUR WALK THROUGH LIFE

25 What is the human condition? Here in Iraq we fight terrorists and insurgents. We give them names (hajji, towelhead, raghead) to peel away their humanity. We focus only on the horrible things that have happened so that we can bring ourselves to kill, but in doing so we too become changed. No longer do we fit in when we get home. We become outsiders and misfits amongst our own families and distance ourselves as others distance themselves from us.

Alone, it becomes easier with time to be that way. You can't let others know the things you have done because they would never understand and it would only serve to make us even more alone.

We must build as well; we become so proficient at building that we could be engineers. Walls are our specialty, so we build them thick and high around ourselves. These walls shut out all the pain and hurt we feel when others can't seem to understand why we are the way we are, or when they judge and condemn us as if they were God himself. The walls don't just keep those things out, but they serve to keep so much in as well. All of it, the guilt, the pain, and the fears we have can be kept deep inside where nobody will have to see them except ourselves.

That is OK, though, because from there we can learn one last and important skill, that of the beast tamer. Like a monster everything we keep inside locked away can take on a mind of its own, creating even more pain. Some of us fall apart at this point, hitting the ground so hard that we decide we cannot get up. And so it ends.

The rest of us learn tricks to keep that beast inside so that nobody will ever have to see how much of a monster we have become. In doing so we can continue our walk through life. That is the soldier's cost of war, and it is ours to bear alone until the end.

CONVERSATIONS: CIVILIAN CASUALTIES
The questions of how many Iraqis were killed in the Iraq War and how many were civilians were intensely debated as the war continued and as military actions and terrorist bombings took more and more lives there. According to Iraq Body Count, an organization that tracked the numbers of civilians killed in Iraq during the war, 84,000–92,000 civilians were killed there between 2003, when the U.S.-led coalition forces invaded Iraq, and June 2008. Some estimates by other organizations were much higher. In 2006, for example, the World Health Organization estimated that between 104,000 and 223,000 civilians had been killed in Iraq to that point. By comparison, slightly more than 4,000 U.S. military personnel had been killed in Iraq as of the summer of 2008. The debates about the numbers of deaths in Iraq were part of the larger debates about the war itself. These casualty figures were used in various ways to support arguments for or against the war. Consider how Scott-Singley's reference to these figures helps him establish his own position about the war in this passage.

GLOSS: MICHAEL JACKSON TRIAL
In this paragraph, Scott-Singley refers to the 2005 trial of pop singer Michael Jackson for the sexual molestation of a child. Jackson was acquitted of the charges, but his arrest and trial caused an international sensation and around-the-clock coverage by some news organizations. What point does Scott-Singley make by using this reference here?

Understanding the Text

1. What causes Scott-Singley to continue to think about the people killed by his unit in Iraq? How does he feel about the deaths caused by his unit? What do you think his questions about these people reveal about him and his attitudes about war?

2. In paragraph 4, Scott-Singley writes that he "won't just run away." What does he mean by that statement? What do you think that statement reveals about him? What might it suggest about the purpose of his blog?

3. Why do you think Scott-Singley wants to know more about the child who was killed during the military raid he was on (see par. 12)? Why is this information important to him?

4. Who are the monsters that Scott-Singley claims to have encountered in Iraq? What do you think Scott-Singley's discussion of these monsters reveals about his view of human beings? Do you agree with him? Why or why not?

5. What is the cost of war to the soldier, according to Scott-Singley? What does this cost suggest about human beings?

Exploring the Issues

1. At several points in these passages, Scott-Singley includes vivid descriptions of incidents that occurred while he was serving in Iraq (see par. 7–12, for instance). Evaluate these descriptions. What details does Scott-Singley provide? What images or events does he seem to emphasize in these descriptions? What mes-sages do you think these descriptions are meant to convey to readers? Do you find these descriptions effective? Why or why not?

2. These entries first appeared on Scott-Singley's blog. Do you think that makes any difference in terms of Scott-Singley's writing style? Explain. How would you describe his style? What characteristics of his writing contribute most to that style? Do you find his writing style effective? Why or why not?

3. In paragraph 15, Scott-Singley wonders whether the family of the child who was killed on the raid he participated in are now attacking the U.S. soldiers there. He then writes that he himself would be making attacks on the people who had taken the life of his own child if he were in that unfortunate situation. Why do you think he includes this statement here? What does it reveal about him? What does it suggest about his view of the insurgents he was fighting in Iraq? What might it suggest about war in general?

Entering the Conversations

1. Write an essay about one of the most trying experiences of your life.

2. In a group of classmates, share the essays you wrote for Question 1 and discuss what they seem to suggest about the nature of power in our lives.

3. Write an essay in which you discuss what Scott-Singley's blog entries suggest about power. In your essay, you might compare Scott-Singley's essay with other essays in this textbook and analyze the similarities and differences in the messages they convey about power.

4. Visit Scott-Singley's blog and several other "milblogs" maintained by soldiers. Review the entries on these blogs to get a sense of the bloggers' voices, interests, and the purposes of their blogs. Then write an essay in which you evaluate these blogs and draw conclusions about their uses. In your essay, discuss what you think these blogs reveal about power.

INFOTRAC

5. "Milblogs" like Scott-Singley's became controversial during the Iraq War. Using InfoTrac, the Internet, and other appropriate resources, investigate the controversy surrounding blogs by soldiers and the efforts to control or suppress such blogs. Look into how these blogs have been used and examine the criticisms of them that some people have made. If possible, interview a milblogger about why he or she maintains a blog. Then write a report on the basis of your research. In your report, discuss the nature of milblogs and the efforts to control them, and provide an overview of the controversy surrounding them. Draw conclusions from your research about what milblogs reveal about the power of the Internet.

6. On the basis of your research for Question 5, post a message to a blog in which you express your opinion about milblogs.

On a cold, windy January day in 1961, *famed American poet Robert Frost recited a poem titled "The Gift Outright" at the inauguration of President John F. Kennedy. That moment has become part of American myth.*

Frost died in January 1963, almost exactly two years after Kennedy's inauguration. In October of that year, President Kennedy gave

Power AND Poetry

the following address at a special tribute to Frost that was held at Amherst College in Massachusetts. In his address, Kennedy makes the connection between poetry and political power that was implied by Frost's presence at Kennedy's inauguration. As Kennedy sees it, poets are essential for democracy because they use language not so much to exercise power but to question it and challenge those who wield it. Kennedy makes a case for appreciating this power of poetry. I hope he convinces you, for it may be that we too often forget about this important power, even though it is all around us: not only in poems like Frost's but also in the music we listen to, the advertising jingles we hear, and the language of accomplished orators like Kennedy himself.

John F. Kennedy was the 35th president of the United States, serving from January 1961, to November 1963, when he was assassinated while visiting Dallas, Texas, just a month after delivering the following address. ▼

JOHN F. KENNEDY

This day, devoted to the memory of Robert Frost, offers an opportunity for reflection which is prized by politicians as well as by others and even by poets. For Robert Frost was one of the granite figures of our time in America. He was supremely two things: an artist and an American. **A NATION REVEALS ITSELF NOT ONLY BY THE MEN IT PRODUCES** but also by the men it honors, the men it remembers.

In America our heroes have customarily run to men of large accomplishments. But today this college and country honor a man whose contribution was not to our size but to our spirit; not to our political beliefs but to our insight; not to our self-esteem but to our self-comprehension.

In honoring Robert Frost we therefore can pay honor to the deepest sources of our national strength. That strength takes many forms, and the most obvious forms are not always the most significant.

The men who create power make an indispensable contribution to the nation's greatness, but the men who question power make a contribution just as indispensable, especially when that questioning is disinterested, for they determine whether we use power or power uses us. Our national strength matters; but the spirit which informs and

JOHN F. KENNEDY, "POWER AND POETRY," EXCERPTED FROM SPEECH GIVEN OCTOBER 1963 AT AMHERST COLLEGE.

STRATEGIES: RHETORICAL CONTEXT
When Kennedy refers to "this day," he is referring to October 27, 1963, when a special ceremony was held at Amherst College in Amherst, Massachusetts, to honor Robert Frost, who died earlier that year. Keep in mind that this essay was originally delivered as a speech at that ceremony. Kennedy connects that ceremony honoring a single poet to a much larger conversation about the role of art in a nation's political life. This conversation has been going on for many centuries—at least since the days of Plato, who famously warned that poets should be restricted from politics because their use of poetic language couldn't be trusted to help us seek truth. As you'll see in the following paragraphs, Kennedy does not completely agree with Plato's argument. By implicitly connecting his comments about Robert Frost to this larger question of the role of poetry in political life, Kennedy makes his speech something more than just a tribute to Frost. By this strategy, writers can use a specific event, such as a ceremony honoring a special person, to make a larger point.

CONVERSATIONS: HONORING MEN (AND WOMEN)
At the end of paragraph 1, Kennedy states that "a nation reveals itself not only by the men it produces but also by the men it honors, the men it remembers." In 1963, when Kennedy gave this speech, such a statement would probably not cause much of a stir. Today, however, we consider such language sexist. If you were writing a sentence like Kennedy's today, you would be expected to use nonsexist language: for example, "A nation reveals itself not only by the men and women it produces but also by the men and women it honors, the men and women it remembers." Or, to make the sentence more concise, you might write, "A nation reveals itself not only by the people it produces but also by those it honors, those it remembers." Changes in the conventions of writing style, including how to refer to gender, reflect changes in our attitudes and values about important matters like gender, race, age, and ethnicity. In a sense, these changes are a result of the conversations we are always having as a society about what we value.

GLOSS: ACQUAINTED WITH THE NIGHT
Kennedy quotes here the first line of a poem by Robert Frost titled "Acquainted With the Night." Consider how this quotation helps Kennedy make his point here about Frost's poetry.

GLOSS: A LOVER'S QUARREL WITH THE WORLD
Robert Frost is reputed to have said that he would like his tombstone to read, "He had a lover's quarrel with the world." *A Lover's Quarrel With the World* is also the title of a documentary film about Frost that was released in 1963.

controls our strength matters just as much. This was the special significance of Robert Frost.

He brought an unsparing instinct for reality to 5 bear on the platitudes and pieties of society. His sense of the human tragedy fortified him against self-deception and easy consolation.

"I have been," he wrote, "one **ACQUAINTED WITH THE NIGHT**." And because he knew the midnight as well as the high noon, because he understood the ordeal as well as the triumph of the human spirit, he gave his age strength with which to overcome despair.

At bottom he held a deep faith in the spirit of man. And it is hardly an accident that Robert Frost coupled poetry and power, for he saw poetry as the means of saving power from itself.

When power leads man towards arrogance, poetry reminds him of his limitations. When power narrows the areas of man's concern, poetry reminds him of the richness and diversity of his existence. When power corrupts, poetry cleanses, for art establishes the basic human truths which must serve as the touchstones of our judgment. The artist, however faithful to his personal vision of reality, becomes the last champion of the individual mind and sensibility against an intrusive society and an officious state. The great artist is thus a solitary figure. He has, as Frost said, **"A LOVER'S QUARREL WITH THE WORLD."** In pursuing his perceptions of reality he must often sail against the currents of his time. This is not a popular role. If Robert Frost was much honored during his lifetime, it was because a good many preferred to ignore his darker truths. Yet, in retrospect, we see how the artist's fidelity has strengthened the fiber of our national life.

If sometimes our great artists have been the most critical of our society, it is because their sensitivity and their concern for justice, which must motivate any true artist, make them aware that our nation falls short of its highest potential.

I see little of more importance to the future of our country and our 10 civilization than full recognition of the place of the artist. If art is to nourish the roots of our culture, society must set the artist free to follow his vision wherever it takes him.

We must never forget that art is not a form of propaganda; it is a form of truth. And as **MR. MACLEISH** once remarked of poets, "There is nothing worse for our trade than to be in style."

In free society art is not a weapon, and it does not belong to the sphere of polemics and ideology. Artists are not engineers of the soul. It may be different elsewhere. But in a democratic society the highest duty of the writer, the composer, the artist, is to remain true to himself and to let the chips fall where they may. In serving his vision of the truth, the artist best serves his nation. And the nation which disdains the mission of art invites the fate of Robert Frost's hired man—the fate of having **"NOTHING TO LOOK BACKWARD TO WITH PRIDE, AND NOTHING TO LOOK FORWARD TO WITH HOPE."**

I look forward to a great future for America—a future in which our country will match its military strength with our moral strength, its wealth with our wisdom, its power with our purpose.

I look forward to an America which will not be afraid of grace and beauty, which will protect the beauty of our national environment, which will preserve the great old American houses and squares and parks of our national past, and which will build handsome and balanced cities for our future.

15   I look forward to an America which will reward achievement in the arts as we reward achievement in business or statecraft.

I look forward to an America which will steadily raise the standards of artistic accomplishment and which will steadily enlarge cultural opportunities for all our citizens.

And I look forward to an America which commands respect throughout the world, not only for its strength but for its civilization as well.

And I look forward to a world which will be safe, not only for democracy and diversity but also for personal distinction.

GLOSS: MR. MACLEISH
Archibald MacLeish (1892–1982) was a Pulitzer Prize-winning American poet who also served in the U.S. government during World War II and believed that poets had a duty to become involved in public life.

STRATEGIES: USING QUOTATIONS
Throughout his speech, Kennedy quotes several people, including Robert Frost himself. In this paragraph, Kennedy includes a line from one of Frost's poems titled "The Death of the Hired Man," in which Frost describes a dying farmhand who seems to have led a sad and hard life. This common strategy enables a writer to use another's words to help make or reinforce an important point. But writers can use quotations in different ways. Here, Kennedy assumes his audience will be familiar with the poem from which he is quoting in order to understand his point about the nation's fate; without a sense of that poem's subject matter, the audience will probably not understand Kennedy's point. By contrast, when Kennedy quotes Frost in paragraph 8, he does so in a way that enables his audience to understand his point even if they are unfamiliar with the source of that quotation. Consider the differences between these two uses of quotations.

Understanding the Text

1. Why does Kennedy believe it is important to honor people like Robert Frost? What does honoring such people indicate about a nation? What specifically is worth honoring about Robert Frost? What significance does Frost have, in Kennedy's view? Kennedy gave this speech in 1963. Do you think his views about a person like Frost still apply today? Explain.

2. What does Kennedy mean when he writes that Frost "saw poetry as the means of saving power from itself" (see par. 7)? In what sense can poetry save power from itself? What does this statement suggest about the nature of power? What does it suggest about the power of poetry?

3. Why are great artists critical of society, according to Kennedy? What does this kind of criticism reveal about poetry and other forms of artistic expression? What does it reveal about artists?

4. What is the connection that Kennedy sees between art and democracy? Why are writers and other artists important in a democracy, in his view? Do you think Kennedy is right? Why or why not?

Exploring the Issues

1. How would you define the power of poetry as Kennedy understands it? Do you think poetry has a kind of power that other forms of writing do not? Explain, citing passages from the essay to support your answer.

2. Many critics have praised John F. Kennedy's abilities as a speaker. Based on the text of this speech, evaluate Kennedy's speaking abilities. What are the most important characteristics that you think make this speech effective (or ineffective, depending upon your opinion)? What features of this text suggest that it was originally written as a speech rather than an essay? Does it work well as an essay, in your view? Explain. (If possible, find a link to a recording of Kennedy's speech on the Internet and include a listening to that recording in your analysis.)

3. What is the vision of American democracy that Kennedy presents in this speech? What role does poetry—and art in general—play in that vision? Do you think this vision is shared by many Americans today? Explain.

Entering the Conversations

1. Write an essay in which you offer your own thoughts about the power of poetry—or any kind of writing. Alternatively, write a poem (or song) about the power of poetry.

2. Read some of Robert Frost's poetry and write an essay in which you offer your own analysis of the power and significance of Robert Frost's poetry. Select several well-known poems by Frost or perhaps choose some of your own favorites (if you are familiar with his poetry). In your analysis, draw conclusions about whether you think Kennedy's evaluation of Frost's poetry is valid. Draw conclusions as well about the power of poetry—or language in general.

3. Many of the writers whose essays are included in this textbook are known for the political significance of their writing—for example, George Orwell (whose essay appears on page 454 of this textbook), bell hooks (pages 256, 515), and Paulo Freire (page 176). Select one or more of these writers (or a writer whose writing does not appear in this textbook) and write an essay in which you discuss the political significance of his or her writing. In your essay, draw conclusions about the power of writing.

4. In his speech, which he delivered in 1963, Kennedy argues that poets and other artists play a special role in a democratic society. Write an essay in which you consider the relevance of Kennedy's argument today. Do poets play the special role today that Kennedy believed they did in the 1960s? Do other kinds of artists play that role today? How might the role of artistic expression—whether through poetry, music, or other forms of art—have changed in the four decades since Kennedy gave his speech? Address such questions in your essay and draw conclusions about the role of poetry or other forms of art in the political life of contemporary American society. Draw on Kennedy's speech and other relevant essays from this textbook (such as Jimmy Santiago Baca's "Becoming a Poet" on page 386) to support your position.

Alternatively, create a web page, PowerPoint presentation, or some other kind of multimedia document that conveys your view about the significance of poetry or some other art form today.

5. On the basis of your work for Question 4, write a letter to the dean or president of your school to express your view about the importance of poetry or other forms of artistic expression. In your letter, state and support your position about whether your school's curriculum should include (or not include) courses or other requirements that would enable students to learn to appreciate these forms of artistic expression.

Political humor has a long tradition in American culture. Americans have always used humor to criticize the foibles of those in power, perhaps to defuse some of the anxiety we feel about how political power is used by those who hold it. In fact, some of the most revered writers in American literary history were famous in their day for their political satire, most

Bill OF Rights Pared Down TO A *Manageable* Six

notably Mark Twain. You can get a sense of his brand of political humor in some sections of his best-known novel, The Adventures of Huckleberry Finn, *in which minor characters serve as vehicles for Twain's biting criticisms of political officials. Today, the stand-up monologue, in which a comedian pokes fun at current political events, is a standard part of the acts of popular television comedians like David Letterman and Jay Leno. And the growing popularity of comedians like Jon Stewart and Stephen Colbert, whose humor focuses on politics, indicates that Twain's spirit is alive and well today.*

The following article, taken from the satiric newspaper The Onion, *is a good example of the kind of political humor that seems to have*

THE ONION

Washington, DC

Flanked by key members of Congress and his administration, President Bush approved Monday a streamlined version of the Bill of Rights that pares its 10 original amendments down to a "tight, no-nonsense" six.

A Republican initiative that went unopposed by congressional Democrats, the revised Bill of Rights provides citizens with a "more manageable" set of privacy and due-process rights by eliminating four amendments and condensing and/or restructuring five others. The Second Amendment, which protects the right to keep and bear arms, was the only article left unchanged.

Calling the historic reduction "a victory for America," Bush promised that the new document would do away with "bureaucratic impediments to the flourishing of democracy at home and abroad."

resurged in popularity in recent years. Like Jon Stewart and Stephen Colbert, The Onion *relies on satire and irony for its humor. But what lies beneath the barbs and tongue-in-cheek lines are serious ideas about what is wrong with the way power is used in the United States today. Perhaps it takes this kind of offbeat but unflinching humor to make us more aware of the consequences of power. In that regard, humor, and especially satire, is an important kind of power itself. It is no coincidence that satirists, from Twain to Jon Stewart, can profoundly influence the political views of Americans. In fact, polls show that among many younger Americans, Stewart's TV show,* The Daily Show, *is the primary source of political information. That is surely a reflection of the power of political satire.*

The following article appeared in The Onion *in December 2002.* ⊡

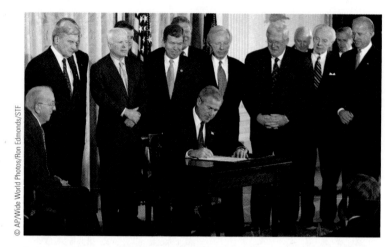

© AP/Wide World Photos/Ron Edmonds/STF

As supporters look on, Bush signs the Bill of Rights Reduction and Consolidation Act

"It is high time we reaffirmed our commitment to this enduring symbol of American ideals," Bush said. "By making the Bill of Rights a tool for progress instead of a hindrance to freedom, we honor the true spirit of our nation's forefathers."

The Fourth Amendment, which long protected citizens' homes against unreasonable search and seizure, was among the eliminated amendments. Also stricken was the Ninth Amendment, which stated that the enumeration of certain Constitutional rights does not result in the abrogation of rights not mentioned.

"Quite honestly, I could never get my head around what the Ninth Amendment meant anyway," said outgoing House Majority Leader Dick Armey (R-TX), one of the leading advocates of the revised Bill of Rights. "So goodbye to that one."

Amendments V through VII, which guaranteed the right to legal counsel in criminal cases, and guarded against double jeopardy, testifying against oneself, biased juries, and drawn-out trials, have been condensed into Super-Amendment V: The One About Trials.

Attorney General John Ashcroft hailed the slimmed-down Bill of Rights as "a positive step."

"Go up to the average citizen and ask them what's in the Bill of Rights," Ashcroft said. "Chances are, they'll have only a vague notion. They just know it's a set of rules put in place to protect their individual freedoms from government intrusion, and they assume that's a good thing."

Ashcroft responded sharply to critics who charge that the Bill of Rights no longer safeguards certain basic, inalienable rights.

"We're not taking away personal rights; we're increasing personal *security*," Ashcroft said. "By allowing for greater government control over the particulars of individual liberties, the Bill of Rights will now offer expanded personal freedoms whenever they are deemed appro-

STRATEGIES: USING STYLE TO CREATE HUMOR

This article is written in a way that mimics standard journalistic writing style. This paragraph, for example, seems to report the elimination of two amendments from the Bill of Rights in the straightforward, objective style of a newspaper article. Consider how this writing style contributes to the satiric humor of this article. Do you need to know that the statements in this paragraph aren't true for this writing style to be effective as humor? Consider, too, how the authors of this article rely on their readers' background knowledge—for example, about the Bill of Rights and about the presidency of George W. Bush—to make their "fake" journalism humorous.

5

10

Bush works on revisions to the Bill of Rights

CONVERSATIONS: VISUAL HUMOR
Consider how the photograph on this page, which seems to show President Bush "editing" the Bill of Rights, conveys its humor. What specific elements of this image might make it humorous? What knowledge must readers have to understand the humor in the image? You might compare this use of a photograph to other uses of visual elements in political satire, such as television's popular *The Daily Show,* in which comedians satirize current political events by posing as "real" journalists. To what extent might *The Onion* and *The Daily Show* use visual elements in similar ways in their satire? What are the differences in their uses of visual humor?

priate and unobtrusive to the activities necessary to effective operation of the federal government."

Ashcroft added that, thanks to several key additions, the Bill of Rights now offers protections that were previously lacking, including the right to be protected by soldiers quartered in one's home (Amendment III), the guarantee that activities not specifically delegated to the states and people will be carried out by the federal government (Amendment VI), and freedom of Judeo-Christianity and non-combative speech (Amendment I).

According to U.S. Sen. Larry Craig (R-ID), the original Bill of Rights, though well-intentioned, was "seriously outdated."

"The United States is a different place than it was back in 1791," Craig said. "As visionary as they were, the framers of the Constitution never could have foreseen, for example, that our government would one day need to jail someone indefinitely without judicial review. There was no such thing as suspicious Middle Eastern immigrants back then."

15 Ashcroft noted that recent FBI efforts to conduct investigations into "unusual activities" were severely hampered by the old Fourth Amendment.

"The Bill of Rights was written more than 200 years ago, long before anyone could even fathom the existence of wiretapping technology or surveillance cameras," Ashcroft said. "Yet through a bizarre fluke, it was still somehow worded in such a way as to restrict use of these devices. Clearly, it had to go before it could do more serious damage in the future."

The president agreed.

CONVERSATIONS: THE FOURTH AMENDMENT
The statement attributed to Attorney General John Ashcroft in paragraph 16 relates to a serious point that has been made by supporters of tougher measures to fight terrorism. The original text of the Fourth Amendment reads, "The right of the people to be secure in their persons, houses, papers, and effects, against unreasonable searches and seizures, shall not be violated, and no Warrants shall issue, but upon probable cause, supported by Oath or affirmation, and particularly describing the place to be searched, and the persons or things to be seized." Some law enforcement and antiterrorism experts argue that these restrictions hamper their efforts to protect the nation against terrorism and that the protections guaranteed by the Fourth Amendment must sometimes be limited so that efforts to fight terrorism can be effective. Civil liberties advocates disagree, arguing that limiting these protections opens the door to abuses of power by the police and other law enforcement agencies. You might consider how this context gives force to the humor of this article. Consider, too, the extent to which this kind of satire can actually contribute to serious discussions about government power and individual rights.

"Any machine, no matter how well-built, periodically needs a tune-up to keep it in good working order," Bush said. "Now that we have the bugs worked out of the ol' Constitution, she'll be purring like a kitten when Congress reconvenes in January—just in time to work on a new round of counterterrorism legislation."

"Ten was just too much of a handful," Bush added. "Six civil liberties are more than enough."

Understanding the Text

1. According to this article, what justification is offered for revising the Bill of Rights? What legitimate criticisms, if any, do you think the authors of this article are making of President Bush and members of the U.S. Congress?

2. In what sense might the Bill of Rights be a "hindrance to freedom"? Do you think there is a serious argument to be made in support of this position? Explain.

3. What do you think this article suggests about the average American and his or her understanding of the U.S. Constitution? Do you think the authors are right about Americans? Why or why not?

4. How does this article portray U.S. political leaders? Do you think this portrait is justified? Explain.

Exploring the Issues

1. What must readers know about the Bill of Rights in order to understand the satire in this article? Will the satire "work" for readers who are unfamiliar with the Bill of Rights? Explain.

2. What do you think this article suggests about the con-sequences of power in U.S. politics?

3. How would you describe the humor of this article? What exactly makes it humor-ous? Did you find it humor-ous? Explain, citing specific passages to support your an-swer. What might your reac-tion to this article reveal about you as a reader? What might it reveal about your political views?

4. How important do you think the photographs in-cluded with this article are? How much do they contribute to the effectiveness of the arti-cle's satire?

Entering the Conversations

1. Write your own satiric arti-cle about a current political is-sue or event that you believe is important.

2. In a group of classmates, share the articles you wrote for Question 1. Identify any common satiric strategies that you and your classmates used to convey your criticisms in your articles. Discuss those criticisms and how effectively they are conveyed through satire. Try to draw conclusions about the use of satire to con-vey a serious message about power and politics.

3. Watch several episodes of *The Daily Show* or another tele-vision show that includes politi-cal satire. (Many television shows that are not necessarily political satires sometimes in-clude political satire, like *The Simpsons*.) Or, listen to a radio show that includes political sat-ire. What issues do these shows tend to focus on? How do they convey their points about politics and government? Then write an essay for an au-dience of your classmates in which you report on what you found. In your essay, describe the shows you watched or lis-tened to and discuss the politi-cal messages they send. Draw conclusions about satire as a medium for discussion of seri-ous issues. Alternatively, write a script for your own political satire for television or radio.

4. Find several political car-toons from newspapers or mag-azines and analyze them for the messages they convey. Then write an essay in which you present your analysis. Include in your essay the cartoons you selected and discuss the mes-sages each cartoon conveys. Try to explain how the cartoon-ists use satire to convey a seri-ous point. Alternatively, create your own political cartoon that conveys a point about the con-sequences of power in contem-porary American political life.

THE PROCESS OF POWER

I F YOU'VE EVER ATTENDED A SCHOOL BOARD MEETING, OBSERVED A TRIAL, OR WATCHED CONGRESSIONAL HEARINGS ON C-SPAN, YOU HAVE WITNESSED THE PROCESS OF GOVERNMENTAL OR POLITICAL POWER. THE MEMBERS OF YOUR LOCAL SCHOOL BOARD, FOR EXAMPLE, ARE GIVEN AUTHORITY TO MAKE IMPORTANT DECISIONS ABOUT FUNDING PROGRAMS,

hiring and firing teachers and administrators, establishing curriculum guidelines, and adopting school policies. While these decisions may seem minor compared to, say, the decision of the U.S. Congress to approve the appointment of a secretary of state or a Supreme Court justice, they nevertheless affect the lives of many people in your school district. Such "minor" decisions reflect the power that is entrusted to government officials or school officials by the residents of a town or state or nation. What is striking is that even when such decisions are not popular, they are almost always accepted. In other words, Americans are generally confident that the process of power in their towns, school districts, cities, and states is fair and is working, even when they disagree with a decision or a policy. In fact, it's probably fair to say that most Americans pay little attention to the thousands of "minor" decisions made each day by officials in their school districts, towns or cities, and states. The process of power goes on, and most of us don't even notice it because we assume it's working the way it should.

That's probably a good thing. It says something important about the way political or governmental power functions in American society. But the process of power is often more subtle and more complicated and sometimes more pernicious than we might realize. And that's what the readings in this cluster focus on. While we tend to notice the "big" ways in which power is wielded in the United States, such as the decision to go to war or the transfer of power after a presidential election, we may not be as aware of the many ways in which governmental power can directly affect our lives. I was reminded of this in a rather striking way a few months after the horrific terrorist attacks of September 11,

2001, when the U.S. Border Patrol set up a checkpoint on Interstate 87 about seventy-five miles south of the Canadian border in upstate New York. I have been traveling that stretch of highway for many years, so on my way home from a hiking trip in early 2002, I was surprised to find myself stopped at the checkpoint. The Border Patrol agents and several New York State police officers were questioning drivers and inspecting some cars. Despite my surprise, I realized that this new checkpoint was the result of new government policies implemented after September 11, 2001, as part of President George W. Bush's "war on terror." These policies reflect the power of the government to affect or even control various aspects of our lives. Drivers like me have little choice but to stop our cars at a checkpoint like that one in upstate New York.

Because power can so directly affect our lives, many writers warn us to be vigilant. Wendell Berry's essay, for example, calls our attention to the ways in which government can abuse its power even when it seems to be acting on behalf of citizens. In the same way, George Orwell, in what has become one of the most famous essays ever written in English, focuses our attention on how governments and groups can use language to obscure their abuses of power. And Lani Guinier shows us that even with the many protections included in the U.S. Constitution, the abuse of power is still possible. These essays remind us that we should not take for granted the processes of power.

They also remind us that writing itself is one of the most effective ways to hold governments accountable for the power that we give them. As you read these essays, think about how the power of writing can be part of the processes of power.

Few modern writers have been as influential as George Orwell (1903–1950). Chances are that you have already read some of his writing—perhaps his famous novels 1984 *(1949) or* Animal Farm *(1945). Orwell, born as Eric Blair, reached the height of his career as a writer during and shortly after World War II, which profoundly reshaped*

Politics AND THE
English Language

GEORGE ORWELL

the world's political landscape and gave rise to great fears about government power. Orwell was especially concerned about the rise of totalitarian governments after the war, particularly in nations like East Germany (which was officially known as the German Democratic Republic) and Poland that were under the influence of the communist government of the Soviet Union. Orwell considered these governments and their leaders a grave threat to liberty throughout the world, and much of his writing is devoted to exposing the implications of such power.

At first glance, the following essay seems to be about writing and about using language carefully, and many English teachers present it that way. But Orwell wished to examine how language can be used to acquire and maintain power. He helps us see that language can be used to control us without our realizing it. He also helps us see that understanding the

Most people who bother with the matter at all would admit that the English language is in a bad way, but it is generally assumed that we cannot by conscious action do anything about it. Our civilization is decadent and our language—so the argument runs—must inevitably share in the general collapse. It follows that any struggle against the abuse of language is a sentimental archaism, like preferring candles to electric light or hansom cabs to aeroplanes. Underneath this lies the half-conscious belief that language is a natural growth and not an instrument which we shape for our own purposes.

Now, it is clear that the decline of a language must ultimately have political and economic causes: it is not due simply to the bad influence of this or that individual writer. But an effect can become a cause, reinforcing the original cause and producing the same effect in an intensified form, and so on indefinitely. A man may take to drink because he feels himself to be a failure, and then fail all the more completely because he drinks. It is rather the same thing that is happening to the English language. It becomes ugly and inaccurate because our thoughts are foolish, but the slovenliness of our language makes it easier for us to have foolish thoughts. The point is that the process is reversible. Modern English, especially written English, is full of bad habits which spread by imitation and which can be avoided if one is willing to take the necessary trouble. If one gets rid of these habits one can think more clearly, and to think clearly is a necessary first step toward political regeneration: so that the fight against bad English is not frivolous and is not the exclusive concern of professional writers. I will come back to this presently, and I hope that by that time the meaning of what I have said here will have become clearer. Meanwhile, here are five specimens of the English language as it is now habitually written.

These five passages have not been picked out because they are especially bad—I could have quoted far worse if I had chosen—but because they illustrate various of the mental vices from which we now suffer. They are a little below the average, but are fairly representative examples. I number them so that I can refer back to them when necessary:

1. I am not, indeed, sure whether it is not true to say that the Milton who once seemed not unlike a seventeenth-century Shelley had not become, out of an experience ever more bitter in each year, more alien *[sic]* to the founder of that Jesuit sect which nothing could induce him to tolerate.

    Professor Harold Laski (Essay in *Freedom of Expression*)

2. Above all, we cannot play ducks and drakes with a native battery of idioms which prescribes egregious collocations of vocables as the Basic *put up with* for *tolerate* or *put at a loss* for *bewilder.*

    Professor Lancelot Hogben (*Interglossia*)

3. On the one side we have the free personality: by definition it is not neurotic, for it has neither conflict nor dream. Its desires, such as they are, are transparent, for they are just what institutional approval keeps in the forefront of consciousness; another institutional pattern would alter their number and intensity; there is little in them that is natural, irreducible, or culturally dangerous. But *on the other side,* the social bond itself is nothing but the mutual reflection of these self-secure integrities. Recall the definition of love. Is not this the very picture of a small academic? Where is there a place in this hall of mirrors for either personality or fraternity?

    Essay on psychology in *Politics* (New York)

complexities of language is one way to resist power. So this essay is not only about political power; it is also about the power of language to shape our understanding of the world.

Orwell wrote this essay just after World War II ended. If you think Orwell's concerns about the political uses of language are no longer valid, consider that after the terrorist attacks of September 11, 2001, the U.S. Congress passed the Patriot Act, which expanded the power of some government agencies and which many critics believed undermined the constitutional rights of Americans; the name of the act is an example of the kind of language that Orwell expressed concerns about in this essay.

This essay was originally published in a journal called Horizon *in 1946.* ◪

CONVERSATIONS: LANGUAGE AND STYLE
Throughout this essay, Orwell uses sophisticated language and includes many words and phrases that were more common in 1946, when this essay was published, than they are today. In paragraph 1, for example, he refers to "archaism," a relatively uncommon word meaning something old or outdated. He also mentions "hansom cabs," which is a kind of horse-drawn carriage. In some cases, Orwell's word choices reflect the style of his time, which may strike you as difficult to read; Orwell also writes in British style, which is somewhat different from American English. You may need to consult your dictionary to help you understand specific passages. This essay reminds us that writing styles and conventions change over time, though we usually don't notice it until we read an essay like this one, which is from a very different historical moment.

4. All the "best people" from the gentlemen's clubs, and all the frantic fascist captains, united in common hatred of Socialism and bestial horror at the rising tide of the mass revolutionary movement, have turned to acts of provocation, to foul incendiarism, to medieval legends of poisoned wells, to legalize their own destruction of proletarian organizations, and rouse the agitated petty-bourgeoisie to chauvinistic fervor on behalf of the fight against the revolutionary way out of the crisis.

Communist pamphlet

5. If a new spirit is to be infused into this old country, there is one thorny and contentious reform which must be tackled, and that is the humanization and galvanization of the B.B.C. Timidity here will bespeak canker and atrophy of the soul. The heart of Britain may be sound and of strong beat, for instance, but the British lion's roar at present is like that of Bottom in Shakespeare's *A Midsummer Night's Dream*—as gentle as any sucking dove. A virile new Britain cannot continue indefinitely to be traduced in the eyes or rather ears, of the world by the effete languors of Langham Place, brazenly masquerading as 'standard English.' When the Voice of Britain is heard at nine o'clock, better far and infinitely less ludicrous to hear aitches honestly dropped than the present priggish, inflated, inhibited, schoolma'amish arch braying of blameless bashful mewing maidens!

Letter in *Tribune*

Each of these passages has faults of its own, but, quite apart from avoidable ugliness, two qualities are common to all of them. The first is staleness of imagery; the other is lack of precision. The writer either has a meaning and cannot express it, or he inadvertently says something else, or he is almost indifferent as to whether his words mean anything or not. This mixture of vagueness and sheer incompetence is the most marked characteristic of modern English prose, and especially of any kind of political writing. As soon as certain topics are raised, the concrete melts into the abstract and no one seems able to think of turns of speech that are not hackneyed: prose consists less and less of *words* chosen for the sake of their meaning, and more and more of *phrases* tacked together like the sections of a prefabricated henhouse. I list below, with notes and examples, various of the tricks by means of which the work of prose construction is habitually dodged:

DYING METAPHORS

5 A newly invented metaphor assists thought by evoking a visual image, while on the other hand a metaphor which is technically "dead" (e.g. *iron resolution*) has in effect reverted to being an ordinary word and can generally be used without loss of vividness. But in between these two classes there is a huge dump of worn-out metaphors which have

lost all evocative power and are merely used because they save people the trouble of inventing phrases for themselves. Examples are: *Ring the changes on, take up the cudgel for, toe the line, ride roughshod over, stand shoulder to shoulder with, play into the hands of, no axe to grind, grist to the mill, fishing in troubled waters, on the order of the day, Achilles' heel, swan song, hotbed.* Many of these are used without knowledge of their meaning (what is a "rift," for instance?), and incompatible metaphors are frequently mixed, a sure sign that the writer is not interested in what he is saying. Some metaphors now current have been twisted out of their original meaning without those who use them even being aware of the fact. For example, *toe the line* is sometimes written as *tow the line.* Another example is *the hammer and the anvil,* now always used with the implication that the anvil gets the worst of it. In real life it is always the anvil that breaks the hammer, never the other way about: a writer who stopped to think what he was saying would avoid perverting the original phrase.

OPERATORS OR VERBAL FALSE LIMBS

These save the trouble of picking out appropriate verbs and nouns, and at the same time pad each sentence with extra syllables which give it an appearance of symmetry. Characteristic phrases are *render inoperative, militate against, make contact with, be subjected to, give rise to, give grounds for, have the effect of, play a leading part (role) in, make itself felt, take effect, exhibit a tendency to, serve the purpose of, etc., etc.* The keynote is the elimination of simple verbs. Instead of being a single word, such as *break, stop, spoil, mend, kill,* a verb becomes a *phrase,* made up of a noun or adjective tacked on to some general-purpose verb such as *prove, serve, form, play, render.* In addition, the passive voice is wherever possible used in preference to the active, and noun constructions are used instead of gerunds (*by examination of* instead of *by examining*). The range of verbs is further cut down by means of the *-ize* and *de-* formations, and the banal statements are given an appearance of profundity by means of the *not un-* formation. Simple conjunctions and prepositions are replaced by such phrases as *with respect to, having regard to, the fact that, by dint of, in view of, in the interests of, on the hypothesis that;* and the ends of sentences are saved by anticlimax by such resounding commonplaces as *greatly to be desired, cannot be left out of account, a development to be expected in the near future, deserving of serious consideration, brought to a satisfactory conclusion,* and so on and so forth.

PRETENTIOUS DICTION

Words like *phenomenon, element, individual* (as noun), *objective, categorical, effective, virtual, basic, primary, promote, constitute, exhibit, exploit, utilize, eliminate, liquidate,* are used to dress up a simple statement and give an air of scientific impartiality to biased judgments. Adjectives like *epoch-making, epic, historic, unforgettable, triumphant, age-old, inevi-*

table, inexorable, veritable, are used to dignify the sordid process of international politics, while writing that aims at glorifying war usually takes on an archaic color, its characteristic words being: *realm, throne, chariot, mailed fist, trident, sword, shield, buckler, banner, jackboot, clarion.* Foreign words and expressions such as *cul de sac, ancien régime, deus ex machina, mutatis mutandis, status quo, gleichschaltung, weltanschauung,* are used to give an air of culture and elegance. Except for the useful abbreviations *i.e., e.g.,* and *etc.,* there is no real need for any of the hundreds of foreign phrases now current in the English language. Bad writers, and especially scientific, political, and sociological writers, are nearly always haunted by the notion that Latin or Greek words are grander than Saxon ones, and unnecessary words like *expedite, ameliorate, predict, extraneous, deracinated, clandestine, subaqueous* and hundreds of others constantly gain ground from their Anglo-Saxon numbers.[1] The jargon peculiar to Marxist writing (*hyena, hangman, cannibal, petty bourgeois, these gentry, lackey, flunkey, mad dog, White Guard,* etc.) consists largely of words translated from Russian, German, or French; but the normal way of coining a new word is to use Latin or Greek root with the appropriate affix and, where necessary, the size formation. It is often easier to make up words of this kind (*deregionalize, impermissible, extramarital, non-fragmentary* and so forth) than to think up the English words that will cover one's meaning. The result, in general, is an increase in slovenliness and vagueness.

MEANINGLESS WORDS

In certain kinds of writing, particularly in art criticism and literary criticism, it is normal to come across long passages that are almost completely lacking in meaning.[2] Words like *romantic, plastic, values, human, dead, sentimental, natural, vitality,* as used in art criticism, are strictly meaningless, in the sense that they not only do not point to any discoverable object, but are hardly ever expected to do so by the reader. When one critic writes, "The outstanding feature of Mr. X's work is its living quality," while another writes, "The immediately striking thing about Mr. X's work is its peculiar deadness," the reader

---

[1] An interesting illustration of this is the way in which the English flower names which were in use till very recently are being ousted by Greek ones, *snapdragon* becoming *antirrhinum, forget-me-not* becoming *myosotis,* etc. It is hard to see any practical reason for this change of fashion: it is probably due to an instinctive turning-away from the more homely word and a vague feeling that the Greek word is scientific [Orwell's note].

[2] Example: "Comfort's catholicity of perception and image, strangely Whitmanesque in range, almost the exact opposite in aesthetic compulsion, continues to evoke that trembling atmospheric accumulative hinting at a cruel, an inexorably serene timelessness. . . . Wrey Gardiner scores by aiming at simple bull's-eyes with precision. Only they are not so simple, and through this contended sadness runs more than the surface bittersweet of resignation" (*Poetry Quarterly*) [Orwell's note].

accepts this as a simple difference of opinion. If words like *black* and *white* were involved, instead of the jargon words *dead* and *living*, he would see at once that language was being used in an improper way. Many political words are similarly abused. The word *Fascism* has now no meaning except in so far as it signifies "something not desirable." The words *democracy, socialism, freedom, patriotic, realistic, justice* have each of them several different meanings which cannot be reconciled with one another. In the case of a word like *democracy*, not only is there no agreed definition, but the attempt to make one is resisted from all sides. It is almost universally felt that when we call a country democratic we are praising it: consequently the defenders of every kind of regime claim that it is a democracy, and fear that they might have to stop using that word if it were tied down to any one meaning. Words of this kind are often used in a consciously dishonest way. That is, the person who uses them has his own private definition, but allows his hearer to think he means something quite different. Statements like *Marshal Pétain was a true patriot, The Soviet Press is the freest in the world, The Catholic Church is opposed to persecution*, are almost always made with intent to deceive. Other words used in variable meanings, in most cases more or less dishonestly, are: *class, totalitarian, science, progressive, reactionary, bourgeois, equality.*

Now that I have made this catalogue of swindles and perversions, let me give another example of the kind of writing that they lead to. This time it must of its nature be an imaginary one. I am going to translate a passage of good English into modern English of the worst sort. Here is a well-known verse from *Ecclesiastes:*

> I returned and saw under the sun, that the race is not to the swift, nor the battle to the strong, neither yet bread to the wise, nor yet riches to men of understanding, nor yet favour to men of skill; but time and chance happeneth to them all.

Here it is in modern English: 10

> Objective considerations of contemporary phenomena compel the conclusion that success or failure in competitive activities exhibits no tendency to be commensurate with innate capacity, but that a considerable element of the unpredictable must invariably be taken into account.

This is a parody, but not a very gross one. Exhibit (3) above, for instance, contains several patches of the same kind of English. It will be seen that I have not made a full translation. The beginning and ending of the sentence follow the original meaning fairly closely, but in the middle the concrete illustrations—race, battle, bread—dissolve into the vague phrases "success or failure in competitive activities." This had to be so, because no modern writer of the kind I am discussing—no one capable of using phrases like "objective considerations of contemporary phenomena"—would ever tabulate his thoughts in that precise and detailed way. The whole tendency of modern prose is away from concreteness. Now analyze these two sentences a little more closely. The first contains forty-nine words but only sixty syllables, and all its words are those of everyday life. The second contains thirty-eight words of ninety syllables: eighteen of those words are from Latin roots, and one from Greek. The first sentence contains six vivid images, and only one phrase ("time and chance") that could be called vague. The second contains not a single fresh, arresting phrase, and in spite of its ninety syllables it gives only a shortened version of the meaning contained in the first. Yet without a doubt it is the second kind of sentence that is gaining ground in modern English. I do not want to exaggerate. This kind of writing is not yet universal, and outcrops of simplicity will occur here and there in the worst-written page. Still, if you or I were told to write a few lines on the uncertainty of human fortunes, we should probably come much nearer to my imaginary sentence than to the one from *Ecclesiastes*.

As I have tried to show, modern writing at its worst does not consist in picking out words for the sake of their meaning and inventing images in order to make the meaning clearer. It consists in gumming together long strips of words which have already been set in order by someone else, and making the results presentable by sheer humbug. The attraction of this way of writing is that it is easy. It is easier—even quicker, once you have the habit—to say *In my opinion it is not an unjustifiable assumption that* than to say *I think*. If you use ready-made phrases, you not only don't have to hunt about for the words; you also don't have to bother with the rhythms of your sentences since these phrases are generally so arranged as to be more or less euphonious. When you are composing in a hurry—when you are dictating to a stenographer, for instance, or making a public speech—it is natural to fall into a pretentious, Latinized style. Tags like *a consideration which we should do well to bear in mind* or *a conclusion to which all of us would readily assent* will save many a sentence from coming down with a bump. By using stale metaphors, similes, and idioms, you save much mental effort, at the cost of leaving your meaning vague, not only for your reader but for yourself. This is the significance of mixed metaphors. The sole aim of a metaphor is to call up a visual image. When these images clash—as in *The Fascist octopus has sung its swan song, the jackboot is thrown into the melting pot*—it can be taken as certain that the writer is not seeing a mental image of the objects he is naming; in other words he is not really thinking. Look again at the examples I gave at the beginning of this essay. Professor Laski (1) uses five negatives in fifty-three words. One of these is superfluous, making nonsense of the whole passage, and in addition there is the slip—*alien* for *akin*—making further nonsense, and several avoidable pieces of clumsiness which increase the general vagueness. Professor Hogben (2) plays ducks and drakes with a battery which is able to write prescriptions, and, while disapproving of the everyday phrase *put up with*, is unwilling to look *egregious* up in the dictionary and see what it means; (3), if one takes an uncharitable attitude towards it, is simply meaningless: probably one could work out its intended meaning by reading the whole of the article in which it occurs. In (4), the writer knows more or less what he wants to say, but an accumulation of stale phrases chokes him like tea leaves blocking a sink. In (5), words and meaning have almost parted company. People who write in this manner usually have a general emotional meaning—they dislike one thing and want to express solidarity with another—but they are not interested in the detail of what they are saying. A scrupulous writer, in every sentence that he writes, will ask himself at least four questions, thus: What am I trying to say? What words will express it? What image or idiom will make it clearer? Is this image fresh enough to have an effect? And he will probably ask himself two more: Could I put it more shortly? Have I said anything that is avoidably ugly? But you are not obliged to go to all this trouble. You can shirk it by simply throwing your mind open and letting the ready-made phrases come crowding in. They will construct your sentences for you—even think your thoughts for you, to a certain extent—and at need they will perform the important service of partially concealing your meaning even from yourself. It is at this point that the special connection between politics and the debasement of language becomes clear.

In our time it is broadly true that political writing is bad writing. Where it is not true, it will generally be found that the writer is some kind of rebel, expressing his private opinions and not a "party line." Orthodoxy, of whatever color, seems to demand a lifeless, imitative style. The political dialects to be found in pamphlets, leading articles, manifestoes, White papers and the speeches of undersecretaries do, of course, vary from party to party, but they are all alike in that one almost never finds in them a fresh, vivid, homemade turn of speech. When one watches some tired hack on the platform mechanically repeating the familiar phrases—*bestial, atrocities, iron heel, bloodstained tyranny, free peoples of the world, stand shoulder to shoulder*—one often has a curious feeling that one is not watching a live human being but some kind of dummy: a feeling which suddenly becomes stronger at moments when the light catches the speaker's spectacles and turns them into blank discs which seem to have no eyes behind them. And this is not altogether fanciful. A speaker who uses that kind of phraseology has gone some distance toward turning himself into a machine. The appropriate noises are coming out of his larynx, but his brain is not involved as it would be if he were choosing his words for himself. If the speech he is making is one that he is accustomed to make over and over again, he may be almost unconscious of what he is saying, as one is when one utters the responses in church. And this reduced state of consciousness, if not indispensable, is at any rate favorable to political conformity.

In our time, political speech and writing are largely the defense of the indefensible. Things like the continuance of British rule in India, the Russian purges and deportations, the dropping of the atom bombs on Japan, can indeed be defended, but only by arguments which are too brutal for most people to face, and which do not square with the professed aims of the political parties. Thus political language has to consist largely of euphemism, question-begging and sheer cloudy vagueness. Defenseless villages are bombarded from the air, the inhabitants driven out into the countryside, the cattle machine-gunned, the huts set on fire with incendiary bullets: this is called *pacification*. Millions of peasants are robbed of their farms and sent trudging along the roads with no more than they can carry: this is called *transfer of population* or *rectification of frontiers*. People are imprisoned for years without trial, or shot in the back of the neck or sent to die of scurvy in Arctic lumber camps: this is called *elimination of unreliable elements*. Such phraseology is needed if one wants to name things without calling up mental pictures of them. Consider for instance some comfortable English professor defending Russian totalitarianism. He cannot say outright, "I believe in killing off your opponents when you can get good results by doing so." Probably, therefore, he will say something like this:

> "While freely conceding that the Soviet regime exhibits certain features which the humanitarian may be inclined to deplore, we must, I think, agree that a certain curtailment of the right to political opposition is an unavoidable concomitant of transitional periods, and that the rigors which the Russian people have been called upon to undergo have been amply justified in the sphere of concrete achievement."

15 The inflated style itself is a kind of euphemism. A mass of Latin words falls upon the facts like soft snow, blurring the outline and covering up all the details. The great enemy of clear language is insincerity. When there is a gap between one's real and one's declared aims, one turns as it were instinctively to long words and exhausted idioms, like a cuttlefish spurting out ink. In our age there is no such thing as "keeping out of politics." All issues are political issues, and politics itself is a mass of lies, evasions, folly, hatred, and schizophrenia. When the general atmosphere is bad, language must suffer. I should expect to find—this is a guess which I have not sufficient knowledge to verify—that the German, Russian and Italian languages have all deteriorated in the last ten or fifteen years, as a result of dictatorship.

But if thought corrupts language, language can also corrupt thought. A bad usage can spread by tradition and imitation even among people who should and do know better. The debased language that I have been discussing is in some ways very convenient. Phrases like *a not unjustifiable assumption, leaves much to be desired, would serve no good purpose, a consideration which we should do well to bear in mind,* are a continuous temptation, a packet of aspirins always at one's elbow. Look back through this essay, and for certain you will find that I have again and again committed the very faults I am protesting against. By this morning's post I have received a pamphlet dealing with conditions in Germany. The author tells me that he "felt impelled" to write it. I open it at random, and here is almost the first sentence I see: "[The Allies] have an opportunity not only of achieving a radical transformation of Germany's social and political structure in such a way as to avoid a nationalistic reaction in Germany itself, but at the same time of laying the foundations of a co-operative and unified Europe." You see, he "feels impelled" to write—feels, presumably, that he has something new to say—and yet his words, like cavalry horses answering the bugle, group themselves automatically into the familiar dreary pattern. This invasion of one's mind by ready-made phrases (*lay the foundations, achieve a radical transformation*) can only be prevented if one is constantly on guard against them, and every such phrase anaesthetizes a portion of one's brain.

I said earlier that the decadence of our language is probably curable. Those who deny this would argue, if they produced an argument at all, that language merely reflects existing social conditions, and that we cannot influence its development by any direct tinkering with words and constructions. So far as the general tone or spirit of a language goes, this may be true, but it is not true in detail. Silly words and expressions have often disappeared, not through any evolutionary process but owing to the conscious action of a minority. Two recent examples were *explore every avenue* and *leave no stone unturned,* which were killed by the jeers of a few journalists. There is a long list of flyblown metaphors which could similarly be got rid of if enough people would interest themselves in the job; and it should also be possible to laugh the *not un-* formation out of existence,[3] to reduce the amount of Latin and Greek in the average sentence, to drive out foreign phrases and strayed scientific words, and, in general, to make pretentiousness unfashionable. But all these are minor points. The defense of the English language implies more than this, and perhaps it is best to start by saying what it does *not* imply.

To begin with it has nothing to do with archaism, with the salvaging of obsolete words and turns of speech, or with the setting up of a "standard English" which must never be departed from. On the contrary, it is especially concerned with the scrapping of every word

---

[3] One can cure oneself of the *not un-* formation by memorizing this sentence: *A not unblack dog was chasing a not unsmall rabbit across a not ungreen field* [Orwell's note].

or idiom which has outworn its usefulness. It has nothing to do with correct grammar and syntax, which are of no importance so long as one makes one's meaning clear, or with the avoidance of American-isms, or with having what is called a "good prose style." On the other hand, it is not concerned with fake simplicity and the attempt to make written English colloquial. Nor does it even imply in every case preferring the Saxon word to the Latin one, though it does imply using the fewest and shortest words that will cover one's mean-ing. What is above all needed is to let the meaning choose the word, and not the other way around. In prose, the worst thing one can do with words is surrender to them. When you think of a concrete ob-ject, you think wordlessly, and then, if you want to describe the thing you have been visualizing you probably hunt about until you find the exact words that seem to fit it. When you think of something abstract you are more inclined to use words from the start, and un-less you make a conscious effort to prevent it, the existing dialect will come rushing in and do the job for you, at the expense of blurring or even changing your meaning. Probably it is better to put off using words as long as possible and get one's meaning as clear as one can through pic-tures and sensations. Afterward one can choose—not simply *accept*—the phrases that will best cover the meaning, and then switch round and decide what impressions one's words are likely to make on another person. This last effort of the mind cuts out all stale or mixed images, all prefabricat-ed phrases, needless repetitions, and humbug and vagueness generally. But one can often be in doubt about the effect of a word or a phrase, and one needs rules that one can rely on when in-stinct fails. I think the following rules will cover most cases:

CONVERSATIONS: ADVICE FOR WRITERS

In criticizing common writing style and offering advice for good writing, Orwell is joining an age-old conversation among writers, teachers, grammarians, and other language experts about what is proper language usage. You can trace this conversation back to the ancient Greeks. Aristotle, for example, criticized some of his contemporaries for the way they taught their students to use language in public speaking. If you do a quick search of a web site like Amazon.com, you'll find dozens of current books critiquing contemporary writing styles and offering advice for good writing. The specific advice offered in such books varies, but the six rules that Orwell lists in this paragraph routinely show up in various forms in books and articles about writing today, more than sixty years later. It's worth considering why there seems to be a never-ending conversation about how to write well—a conversation that often focuses on how much "bad" writing people produce. What might that say about the nature of writing? And how might Orwell's essay continue to influence our thinking about writing today?

(i)   Never use a metaphor, simile, or other figure of speech which you are used to seeing in print.

(ii) Never use a long word where a short one will do.

(iii) If it is possible to cut a word out, always cut it out.

(iv) Never use the passive where you can use the active.

(v)   Never use a foreign phrase, a scientific word, or a jargon word if you can think of an everyday English equivalent.

(vi) Break any of these rules sooner than say anything outright barbarous.

These rules sound elementary, and so they are, but they demand a deep change of attitude in anyone who has grown used to writing in the style now fashionable. One could keep all of them and still write bad English, but one could not write the kind of stuff that I quoted in those five specimens at the beginning of this article.

I have not here been considering the literary use of language, but merely language as an instrument for expressing and not for concealing or preventing thought. Stuart Chase and others have come near to claiming that all abstract words are meaningless, and have used this as a pretext for advocating a kind of political quietism. Since you don't know what Fascism is, how can you struggle against Fascism? One need not swallow such absurdities as this, but one ought to recognize that the present political chaos is connected with the decay of language, and that one can probably bring about some improvement by starting at the verbal end. If you simplify your English, you are freed from the worst follies of orthodoxy. You cannot speak any of the necessary dialects, and when you make a stupid remark its stupidity will be obvious, even to yourself. Political language—and with variations this is true of all political parties, from Conservatives to Anarchists—is designed to make lies sound truthful and murder respectable, and to give an appearance of solidity to pure wind. One cannot change this all in a moment, but one can at least change one's own habits, and from time to time one can even, if one jeers loudly enough, send some worn-out and useless phrase—some *jackboot, Achilles' heel, hotbed, melting pot, acid test, veritable inferno,* or other lump of verbal refuse—into the dustbin, where it belongs.

CONVERSATIONS: POLITICAL LANGUAGE THEN AND NOW

Orwell writes that "political language . . . is designed to make lies sound truthful and murder respectable, and to give an appearance of solidity to pure wind." Some critics charged that the "war on terror" declared by President George W. Bush in the aftermath of September 11, 2001, involved the same kind of language that Orwell criticized after World War II. Indeed, many such critics invoked Orwell's work, especially his famous novel *1984,* in which a totalitarian government controls its citizens in large part by controlling language. In that novel, "doublespeak" referred to language that seems to say one thing but means another; it is language that seems clear but isn't—language that makes the good seem bad, and vice versa. Note how the button below, which criticizes the U.S. government's Patriot Act, uses Orwell's ideas about language to convey its criticism.

© BORDC, 2005

Understanding the Text

1. Why does Orwell assert that there has been a "decline" in the English language at the beginning of his essay? What is the nature of this decline? What causes the decline, in his view? What does this decline have to do with politics, according to him?

2. What are the "mental vices" that Orwell believes are reflected in the examples of bad writing that he provides in this essay? Why are these mental vices important, in his view? Do you think he's right? Why or why not?

3. What is "the special connection between politics and the debasement of language" that Orwell refers to at the

end of paragraph 12? Why is this connection important?

4. In what ways does language corrupt thought, according to Orwell? Why does this kind of "corruption" concern him? Do you agree? Explain.

5. What does Orwell mean when he writes that "the worst thing one can do with words is surrender to them" (par. 18)? How can a writer avoid this problem, in his view?

Exploring the Issues

1. Examine the examples of "bad" writing that Orwell includes in this essay. What specifically is bad about them, as Orwell sees it? Do you think they are bad in the ways Orwell describes? Explain, referring to specific passages to support your answer. You might also look at your own writing to see whether it has any of the characteristics that Orwell criticizes.

2. Orwell identifies two main problems in writing: "staleness of imagery" and "lack of precision" (par. 4). Examine Orwell's own prose. Does he avoid these two problems? Support your answer with references to specific passages in his essay.

3. Some of the expressions that Orwell criticizes as examples of "bad" writing in this essay are no longer commonly used (for example, *ring the changes on, the hammer and the anvil, jackboot,* and *mailed fist*), but many are. For example, expressions like *Achilles' heel, play into the hands of, status quo, extramarital,* and *utilize,* all of which Orwell criticizes, are common expressions that often appear in popular and academic writing today. Keeping in mind that Orwell wrote this essay more than sixty years ago, how might you explain the fact that so many expressions Orwell criticized are still in wide use today? What might this suggest about the nature of the English language and how it is used?

4. At the end of his essay, Orwell writes that "the pres- ent political chaos is connected with the decay of language." He is referring to the complex and tense political situation in Europe after World War II. Do you think this statement is still true today, given the current political situation in the world? Explain.

5. Explain the connection between language use and the process of power, as Orwell understands it. What role does language play in the use or abuse of power as Orwell sees it? Do you think Orwell's understanding of this connection still applies today? Explain.

Entering the Conversations

1. Write an essay responding to Orwell's assertion that we can improve our political situation by using language properly (par. 19). In your essay, explain Orwell's reasoning and offer your own position on whether our ways of using language can positively affect our political situation. Include in your essay current examples of political language to support your position.

2. Orwell argues that "political writing is bad writing" and explains some of the specific ways that this is true (par. 13). Examine some contemporary examples of political speeches and writing and analyze them using some of Orwell's criticisms of writing. Then write an essay in which you offer your analysis of contemporary political discourse (speech or writing, including political ads on television, radio, or the Internet). In your essay, discuss what you found when you analyzed current political discourse and offer examples to support your points. Draw conclusions about the nature of contemporary political discourse.

3. Take an essay you have written and edit it using the advice for good writing that Orwell offers in this essay.

4. Create a web site, PowerPoint presentation, or some other kind of document in which you identify current examples of the four "tricks" of bad writing that Orwell describes in this essay (dying metaphors, operators or verbal false limbs, pretentious diction, and meaningless words).

5. In paragraph 9, Orwell rewrites a passage from the Bible in "bad" prose. Following his example and using his analysis of the specific features of bad writing, take a passage from a piece of writing that you consider good and rewrite it in bad style. Once you have finished your rewrite, consider what you have learned about writing by intentionally trying to write bad prose.

6. In today's newspaper or a news web site of your choice, locate an article in which the writer has used one of the following words: *democracy, socialism, freedom, patriotic, realistic,* or *justice.* Examine how the word has been used. Then, drawing on Orwell's essay, write an analysis of the author's use of this word. Has the author made clear what the word means? Is the word used in a way that obscures the author's point? How might Orwell have judged the author's use of the word? Address these questions in your essay.

Most Americans accept majority rule as the *way things should be. In the U.S. political system, for example, the party that wins more seats in the House of Representatives or the Senate controls that body. If more Republicans win seats, then all Senate committees are chaired by Republicans and the Senate is effectively run by Republicans. This*

THE Tyranny OF THE Majority

winner-take-all approach to political power is a basic principle of the American style of democracy—so basic that many Americans assume that democracy is equivalent to majority rule. But some democracies distribute power proportionally, assigning a portion of political power to each party based on the percentage of votes that party received in an election. In parliamentary democracies like Canada or Israel, several parties will compete in elections, and the percentage of the vote that each party receives determines how much power that party will have in the government. Such a system requires that the party with the largest percentage of votes form coalitions with other parties in order for the government to function.

Some political scientists and legal scholars believe that such parliamentary democracies avoid some of the problems associated with the winner-take-all process in the

LANI GUINIER

I have always wanted to be a civil rights lawyer. This lifelong ambition is based on a deep-seated commitment to democratic fair play—to playing by the rules as long as the rules are fair. When the rules seem unfair, I have worked to change them, not subvert them. When I was eight years old, I was a Brownie. I was especially proud of my uniform, which represented a commitment to good citizenship and good deeds. But one day, when my Brownie group staged a hatmaking contest, I realized that uniforms are only as honorable as the people who wear them. The contest was rigged. The winner was assisted by her milliner mother, who actually made the winning entry in full view of all the participants. At the time, I was too young to be able to change the rules, but I was old enough to resign, which I promptly did.

To me, fair play means that the rules encourage everyone to play. They should reward those who win, but they must be acceptable to those who lose. The central theme of my academic writing is that not all rules lead to elemental fair play. Some even commonplace rules work against it.

United States. In her carefully reasoned essay, Lani Guinier (b. 1950) explains how American-style majority rule is not always fair and does not necessarily best serve the needs and interests of the minority, especially in a diverse society. Guinier reminds us that some of the founding fathers expressed concerns about the possibility that the American political process could result in a "tyranny of the majority," and she suggests some steps to make the American political process fairer. Her essay is part of an ongoing debate in American society about how to interpret the Constitution and how best to manage the process of power.

Lani Guinier, a distinguished legal scholar, taught at the University of Pennsylvania before becoming the first black woman tenured professor at Harvard Law School in 1998. She has written extensively about political and legal issues and has published several books, including The Tyranny of the Majority *(1994), in which the following essay first appeared.* ▼

The professional milliner competing with amateur Brownies stands as an example of rules that are patently rigged or patently subverted. Yet, sometimes, even when rules are perfectly fair in form, they serve in practice to exclude particular groups from meaningful participation. When they do not encourage everyone to play, or when, over the long haul, they do not make the losers feel as good about the outcomes as the winners, they can seem as unfair as the milliner who makes the winning hat for her daughter.

Sometimes, too, we construct rules that force us to be divided into winners and losers when we might have otherwise joined together. This idea was cogently expressed by my son, Nikolas, when he was four years old, far exceeding the thoughtfulness of his mother when she was an eight-year-old Brownie. While I was writing one of my law journal articles, Nikolas and I had a conversation about voting prompted by a *Sesame Street Magazine* exercise. The magazine pictured six children: four children had raised their hands because they wanted to play tag; two had their hands down because they wanted to play hide-and-seek. The magazine asked its readers to count the number of children whose hands were raised and then decide what game the children would play.

Nikolas quite realistically replied, "They will play both. First they will play tag. Then they will play hide-and-seek." Despite the magazine's "rules," he was right. To children, it is natural to take turns. The winner may get to play first or more often, but even the "loser" gets something. His was a positive-sum solution that many adult rulemakers ignore.

The traditional answer to the magazine's problem would have been a zero-sum solution: "The children—all the children—will play tag, and only tag." As a zero-sum solution, everything is seen in terms of "I win; you lose." The conventional answer relies on winner-take-all majority rule, in which the tag players, as the majority, win the right to decide for all the children what game to play. The hide-and-seek preference becomes irrelevant. The numerically more powerful majority choice simply subsumes minority preferences.

In the conventional case, the majority that rules gains all the power and the minority that loses gets none. For example, two years ago Brother Rice High School in Chicago held two senior proms. It was not planned that way. The prom committee at Brother Rice, a boys' Catholic high school, expected just one prom when it hired a disc jockey, picked a rock band, and selected music for the prom by consulting student preferences. Each senior was asked to list his three favorite songs, and the band would play the songs that appeared most frequently on the lists.

Seems attractively democratic. But Brother Rice is predominantly white, and the prom committee was all white. That's how they got two proms. The black seniors at Brother Rice felt so shut out by the

"democratic process" that they organized their own prom. As one black student put it: "for every vote we had, there were eight votes for what they wanted. . . . [W]ith us being in the minority we're always outvoted. It's as if we don't count."

Some embittered white seniors saw things differently. They complained that the black students should have gone along with the majority: "The majority makes a decision. That's the way it works."

In a way, both groups were right. From the white students' perspective, this was ordinary decisionmaking. To the black students, majority rule sent the message: "we don't count" is the "way it works" for minorities. In a racially divided society, majority rule may be perceived as majority tyranny.

10

That is a large claim, and I do not rest my case for it solely on the actions of the prom committee in one Chicago high school. To expand the range of the argument, I first consider the ideal of majority rule itself, particularly as reflected in the writings of James Madison and other founding members of our Republic. These early democrats explored the relationship between majority rule and democracy. James Madison warned, "If a majority be united by a common interest, the rights of the minority will be insecure." The tyranny of the majority, according to Madison, requires safeguards to protect "one part of the society against the injustice of the other part."

For Madison, majority tyranny represented the great danger to our early constitutional democracy. Although the American revolution was fought against the tyranny of the British monarch, it soon became clear that there was another tyranny to be avoided. The accumulations of all powers in the same hands, Madison warned, "whether of one, a few, or many, and whether hereditary, self-appointed, or elective, may justly be pronounced the very definition of tyranny."

As another colonist suggested in papers published in Philadelphia, "We have been so long habituated to a jealousy of tyranny from monarchy and aristocracy, that we have yet to learn the dangers of it from democracy." Despotism had to be opposed "whether it came from Kings, Lords or the people."

The debate about majority tyranny reflected Madison's concern that the majority may not represent the whole. In a homogeneous society, the interest of the majority would likely be that of the minority also. But in a heterogeneous community, the majority may not represent all competing interests. The majority is likely to be self-interested and ignorant or indifferent to the concerns of the minority. In such case, Madison observed, the assumption that the majority represents the minority is "altogether fictitious."

STRATEGIES: SUMMARY
Notice how Guinier uses her summary of James Madison's political ideas to help explain the problems with majority rule. In these paragraphs and for much of the rest of her essay, she relies on Madison's ideas to lay out her own position on this issue, using quotations from his writings. She also relies on Madison's status as one of the founding fathers, which gives his words more weight with many American readers than the words of a less revered political figure or scholar.

CONVERSATIONS: TYRANNY IN HISTORY
The quotation Guinier includes here from a colonist in the late eighteenth century indicates that the historical context within which James Madison and the other founding fathers were writing the U.S. Constitution was very different from our own time. This colonist's concerns about tyranny were based on the many examples of powerful monarchs who ruled European nations at the time of the American Revolution. As Americans formed their own government, the world had many tyrannical governments but no examples of the kind of democracy Americans were trying to create. As a result, the idea of the "tyranny of the majority," which may seem odd to many contemporary readers, would have been a very real concern at the time Madison and his colleagues were debating how to form a new government. Today, few Americans have such concerns, which makes Guinier's argument in this essay a little harder to make. Consider how she uses historical information to help her modern readers appreciate the significance of her concerns about majority rule.

15   Yet even a self-interested majority can govern fairly if it cooperates with the minority. One reason for such cooperation is that the self-interested majority values the principle of reciprocity. The self-interested majority worries that the minority may attract defectors from the majority and become the next governing majority. The Golden Rule principle of reciprocity functions to check the tendency of a self-interested majority to act tyrannically.

So the argument for the majority principle connects it with the value of reciprocity: You cooperate when you lose in part because members of the current majority will cooperate when they lose. The conventional case for the fairness of majority rule is that it is not really the rule of a fixed group—The Majority—on all issues; instead it is the rule of shifting majorities, as the losers at one time or on one issue join with others and become part of the governing coalition at another time or on another issue. The result will be a fair system of mutually beneficial cooperation. I call a majority that rules but does not dominate a Madisonian Majority.

The problem of majority tyranny arises, however, when the self-interested majority does not need to worry about defections. When the majority is fixed and permanent, there are no checks on its ability to be overbearing. A majority that does not worry about defectors is a majority with total power.

In such a case, Madison's concern about majority tyranny arises. In a heterogeneous community, any faction with total power might subject "the minority to the caprice and arbitrary decisions of the majority, who instead of consulting the interest of the whole community collectively, attend sometimes to partial and local advantages."

"What remedy can be found in a republican Government, where the majority must ultimately decide," argued Madison, but to ensure "that no one common interest or passion will be likely to unite a majority of the whole number in an unjust pursuit." The answer was to disaggregate the majority to ensure checks and balances or fluid, rotating interests. The minority needed protection against an overbearing majority, so that "a common sentiment is less likely to be felt, and the requisite concert less likely to be formed, by a majority of the whole."

20   Political struggles would not be simply a contest between rulers and people; the political struggles would be among the people themselves. The work of government was not to transcend different interests but to reconcile them. In an ideal democracy, the people would rule, but the minorities would also be protected against the power of majorities. Again, where the rules of decisionmaking protect the minority, the Madisonian Majority rules without dominating.

But if a group is unfairly treated, for example, when it forms a racial minority, *and* if the problems of unfairness are not cured by conventional assumptions about majority rule, then what is to be done?

The answer is that we may need an *alternative* to winner-take-all majoritarianism. In this book, a collection of my law review articles, I describe the alternative, which, with Nikolas's help, I now call the "principle of taking turns." In a racially divided society, this principle does better than simple majority rule if it accommodates the values of self-government, fairness, deliberation, compromise, and consensus that lie at the heart of the democratic ideal.

In my legal writing, I follow the caveat of James Madison and other early American democrats. I explore decisionmaking rules that might work in a multi-racial society to ensure that majority rule does not become majority tyranny. I pursue voting systems that might disaggregate The Majority so that it does not exercise power unfairly or tyrannically. I aspire to a more cooperative political style of decisionmaking to enable all of the students at Brother Rice to feel comfortable attending the same prom.

In looking to create Madisonian Majorities, I pursue a positive-sum, taking-turns solution.

Structuring decisionmaking to allow the minority "a turn" may be necessary to restore the reciprocity ideal when a fixed majority refuses to cooperate with the minority. If the fixed majority loses its incentive to follow the Golden Rule principle of shifting majorities, the minority never gets to take a turn. Giving the minority a turn does not mean the minority gets to rule; what it does mean is that the minority gets to influence decisionmaking and the majority rules more legitimately.

Instead of automatically rewarding the preferences of the monolithic majority, a taking-turns approach anticipates that the majority rules, but is not overbearing. Because those with 51 percent of the votes are not assured 100 percent of the power, the majority cooperates with, or at least does not tyrannize, the minority.

25   The sports analogy of "I win; you lose" competition within a political hierarchy makes sense when only one team can win; Nikolas's intuition that it is often possible to take turns suggests an alternative approach. Take family decisionmaking, for example. It utilizes a taking-turns approach. When parents sit around the kitchen table deciding on a vacation destination or activities for a rainy day, often they do not simply rely on a show of hands, especially if that means that the older children always prevail or if affinity groups among the children (those who prefer movies to video games, or those who prefer baseball to playing cards) never get to play their activity of choice. Instead of allowing the majority simply to rule, the parents may pro-

---

CONVERSATIONS: TURN-TAKING AND THE 2004 U.S. PRESIDENTIAL ELECTION

Ten years after Guinier's essay was published, one of the closest and most controversial presidential elections in U.S. history ended with George W. Bush being reelected by historically slim margins. His party controlled both the U.S. House of Representatives and the U.S. Senate, also by slim margins. In many ways, the 2004 election illustrates some of Guinier's concerns about the winner-take-all approach in American politics: A very small majority effectively gained full power to rule everyone. But circumstances in 2004 were different from 1994, when Guinier's essay was first published. In 2004, many groups who felt that their concerns were being ignored by both the Republican and Democratic Parties began to use alternative ways of voicing their concerns and participating in the political process. One way was the use of alternative media like the Internet to mobilize opposition to the two main political parties, as MoveOn.org, one of the most visible of such groups, did. Consider how the emergence of groups like MoveOn.org might complicate—or lend support to—Guinier's argument for an alternative to simple majority rule in the United States. Consider, too, how the rise of new technologies like the Internet might affect her proposals.

pose that everyone take turns, going to the movies one night and playing video games the next. Or as Nikolas proposes, they might do both on a given night.

Taking turns attempts to build consensus while recognizing political or social differences, and it encourages everyone to play. The taking-turns approach gives those with the most support more turns, but it also legitimates the outcome from each individual's perspective, including those whose views are shared only by a minority.

In the end, I do not believe that democracy should encourage rule by the powerful—even a powerful majority. Instead, the idea of democracy promises a fair discussion among self-defined equals about how to achieve our common aspirations. To redeem that promise, we need to put the idea of taking turns and disaggregating the majority at the center of our conception of representation. Particularly as we move into the twenty-first century as a more highly diversified citizenry, it is essential that we consider the ways in which voting and representational systems succeed or fail at encouraging Madisonian Majorities.

To use Nikolas's terminology, "it is no fair" if a fixed, tyrannical majority excludes or alienates the minority. It is no fair if a fixed, tyrannical majority monopolizes all the power all the time. It is no fair if we engage in the periodic ritual of elections, but only the permanent majority gets to choose who is elected. Where we have tyranny by The Majority, we do not have genuine democracy.

Understanding the Text

1. What specific problems does Guinier see with majority rule in American politics? How serious are these problems, in your view?

2. What is a "Madisonian Majority," according to Guinier? Why are James Madison's ideas about democracy and specifically about majority rule so important, in her view?

3. How would Guinier's alternative "turn-taking" approach to government and political power be fairer to political minorities than the current

"winner-take-all majoritarianism" in U.S. politics, in her view? Under what circumstances does Guinier believe that we might need such an alternative? Do you agree with her that these circumstances would require such an alternative? Why or why not?

4. What fundamental values does Guinier hold that shape her view of how government should work? Do you think most Americans share these values? Explain.

Exploring the Issues

1. Guinier uses several examples to illustrate the problems with majority rule and to sup-

port her argument for changes in the American political process. How effective do you think these examples are in helping her make her case? What might her examples suggest about her sense of her audience?

2. In 1993, when President Bill Clinton nominated Guinier to serve on the U.S. Supreme Court, her nomination was strenuously opposed by many critics who disagreed with her views about affirmative action and "proportional representation," which is the belief that power should be distributed proportionally according to the percentage of the vote received by each party. Based on this essay, why do you think some Americans would have such severe objections to a person with Guinier's views serving on the U.S. Supreme Court? To what extent do you think this essay might address—or worsen—the concerns of such critics?

3. Guinier includes several anecdotes from her personal life in this essay. How do you think these anecdotes might affect a reader's sense of Guinier as a person and as an authority on the legal issues she is addressing in this essay? Do you think these anecdotes make her essay more or less effective? What might your answer to that question reveal about you as a reader?

4. How would you sum up Guinier's view of democracy? Do you think most Americans share her view? Why or why not?

Entering the Conversations

1. Write an essay for an audience of your classmates in which you discuss your basic concerns about the current American political process. In your essay, draw on Guinier's ideas and on any other essays in this cluster to explain or support your position.

2. Visit the web sites of several active political groups, such as MoveOn.org. Try to get a sense of their political views and what their organizations seem to believe about the American political process. Then write a report about what you learned about these groups and their uses of the Internet to participate in the political process. Alternatively, create a web site on the basis of your research.

INFOTRAC

3. In this essay, Guinier is calling for reforms to the American political process. In recent years, a number of related political reforms have been proposed and debated, including changes to the rules governing campaign funding and even abandoning the electoral college for U.S. presidential elections. Using InfoTrac College Edition and any other relevant resources, investigate current proposals for political reform in the United States, perhaps focus-

ing on one particular reform, such as campaign finance reform or changes in the electoral college system. Try to get a sense of what kinds of reforms are being proposed, by whom, and why. What advantages or disadvantages might the proposed reforms have compared to the current political process? Then write a report for an audience of your classmates in which you discuss what you learned through your research and offer your conclusions about political reform.

4. On the basis of your research for Question 3, write a letter to the editor of your local newspaper (or another appropriate publication) in which you make an argument for or against a specific political reform. In your letter, identify what you believe is the basic problem with the political process today and propose your reform as a way to address that problem.

5. Create a pamphlet (or a web site) whose purpose is to explain what you believe to be the most important aspects of the process of political power in the United States today.

Wendell Berry (b. 1934) has been called *"perhaps the greatest moral essayist of our day"* and *"the unimpeachable Jeffersonian conscience of American public discourse."* He's also been called much less flattering things. When you read the following essay, which Berry wrote shortly after the terrorist attacks of September 11, 2001, you'll begin to see why his

Thoughts IN THE Presence OF Fear

writing provokes such strong emotions. Berry is often thought of as a voice for rural values and an advocate for an environmentally conscious lifestyle, but he sees politics and lifestyle as inseparable; in his view, how we live on the land reflects ethical and moral choices that affect our social, economic, and political lives. So it is no surprise that Berry would see in the terrible events of September 11, 2001, something more than political or ideological conflict between America and its enemies. In this essay, Berry takes direct aim at what he considers the causes of those terrorist attacks. Characteristically, he insists that we not simply condemn those who perpetrated such horrific acts but ask how our consumer-driven lifestyle and our choices as individuals and as a society might have given rise to these acts. In making this argument, Berry risked the anger of Americans. Indeed,

WENDELL BERRY

The time will soon come when we will not be able to remember the horrors of September 11 without remembering also the unquestioning technological and economic optimism that ended on that day.

II. This optimism rested on the proposition that we were living in a "new world order" and a "new economy" that would "grow" on and on, bringing a prosperity of which every new increment would be "unprecedented."

III. The dominant politicians, corporate officers, and investors who believed this proposition did not acknowledge that the prosperity was limited to a tiny percent of the world's people, and to an ever smaller number of people even in the United States; that it was founded upon the oppressive labor of poor people all over the world; and that its ecological costs increasingly threatened all life, including the lives of the supposedly prosperous.

IV. The "developed" nations had given to the "free market" the status of a god, and were sacrificing to it their farmers, farmlands, and communities, their forests, wetlands, and prairies, their ecosystems and watersheds. They had accepted universal pollution and global warming as normal costs of doing business.

V. There was, as a consequence, a growing worldwide effort on behalf of economic decentralization, economic justice, and ecological responsibility. We must recognize that the events of September 11 make this effort more necessary than ever. We citizens of the industrial countries must continue the labor of self-criticism and self-correction. We must recognize our mistakes.

VI. The paramount doctrine of the economic and technological euphoria of recent decades has been that everything depends on innovation. It was understood as desirable, and even necessary, that we should go on and on from one technological innovation to the next, which would cause the economy to "grow" and make everything better and better. This of course implied at every point a hatred of the past, of all things inherited and free. All things superseded in our progress of innovations, whatever their value might have been, were discounted as of no value at all.

VII. We did not anticipate anything like what has now happened. We did not foresee that all our sequence of innovations might be at once overridden by a greater one: the invention of a new kind of war that would turn our previous innovations against us, discovering and exploiting the debits and the dangers that we had ignored. We never considered the possibility that we might be trapped in the webwork of communication and transport that was supposed to make us free.

VIII. Nor did we foresee that the weaponry and the war science that we marketed and taught to the world would become available, not just to recognized national governments, which possess so uncannily the power to legitimate large-scale violence, but also to "rogue nations," dissident or fanatical groups and individuals—whose violence, though never worse than that of nations, is judged by the nations to be illegitimate.

IX. **WE HAD ACCEPTED UNCRITICALLY THE BELIEF THAT TECHNOLOGY IS ONLY GOOD;** that it cannot serve evil as well as good; that it cannot serve our enemies as well as ourselves; that it cannot be used to destroy what is good, including our homelands and our lives.

X. We had accepted too the corollary belief that an economy (either as a money economy or as a life-support system) that is global in extent, technologically complex, and centralized is invulnerable to terrorism, sabotage, or war, and that it is protectable by "national defense."

XI. We now have a clear, inescapable choice that we must make. We can continue to promote a global economic system of unlimited "free

you may find yourself angry as you read this unflinching essay. But Berry's thoughts about the events of September 11, 2001, are worth considering for what they might reveal about our beliefs about ourselves and our way of living, and they can help us understand the complexities and consequences of power.

Wendell Berry is the award-winning author of more than forty novels, collections of poetry, and books of essays, and he has written widely for many magazines and newspapers, including Orion, *in which this essay originally appeared in 2001.* ◪

CONVERSATIONS: UNQUESTIONING TECHNOLOGICAL AND ECONOMIC OPTIMISM

The optimism Berry discusses in the first few paragraphs of his essay refers to the surging U.S. economy and its influence on the changing global economy in the 1990s and the early years of the twenty-first century. Although the U.S. stock market suffered a serious decline after 2000, the U.S. economy continued to grow, and business leaders and politicians spoke of a "new world order." Obviously, Berry has grave concerns about these developments, concerns shared by others in what he describes in paragraph 5 as "a growing worldwide effort on behalf of economic decentralization, economic justice, and ecological responsibility." Others have called this an antiglobalization movement, and its proponents organized large protests at meetings of international economic organizations like the World Bank. Readers of *Orion,* a magazine focusing on environmental and social issues in which this essay was first published, would recognize Berry's references to this "worldwide movement." You might consider whether you recognized these references. Think about how your understanding of this larger context might influence the way you read Berry's essay.

trade" among corporations, held together by long and highly vulnerable lines of communication and supply, but now recognizing that such a system will have to be protected by a hugely expensive police force that will be worldwide, whether maintained by one nation or several or all, and that such a police force will be effective precisely to the extent that it oversways the freedom and privacy of the citizens of every nation.

XII. Or we can promote a decentralized world economy which would have the aim of assuring to every nation and region a local self-sufficiency in life-supporting goods. This would not eliminate international trade, but it would tend toward a trade in surpluses after local needs had been met.

XIII. One of the gravest dangers to us now, second only to further terrorist attacks against our people, is that we will attempt to go on as before with the corporate program of global "free trade," whatever the cost in freedom and civil rights, without self-questioning or self-criticism or public debate.

XIV. This is why the substitution of rhetoric for thought, always a temptation in a national crisis, must be resisted by officials and citizens alike. It is hard for ordinary citizens to know what is actually happening in Washington in a time of such great trouble; for all we know, serious and difficult thought may be taking place there. But the talk that we are hearing from politicians, bureaucrats, and commentators has so far tended to reduce the complex problems now facing us to issues of unity, security, normality, and retaliation.

XV. National self-righteousness, like personal self-righteousness, is a mistake. It is misleading. It is a sign of weakness. Any war that we may make now against terrorism will come as a new installment in a history of war in which we have fully participated. We are not innocent of making war against civilian populations. The modern doctrine of such warfare was set forth and enacted by General William Tecumseh Sherman, who held that a civilian population could be declared guilty and rightly subjected to military punishment. We have never repudiated that doctrine. 15

XVI. It is a mistake also—as events since September 11 have shown—to suppose that a government can promote and participate in a global economy and at the same time act exclusively in its own interest by abrogating its international treaties and standing apart from international cooperation on moral issues.

XVII. And surely, in our country, under our Constitution, it is a fundamental error to suppose that any crisis or emergency can justify any form of political oppression. Since September 11, far too many public voices have presumed to "speak for us" in saying that Americans will gladly accept a reduction of freedom in exchange for greater "security." Some would, maybe. But some others would accept a reduction in security (and in global trade) far more willingly than they would accept any abridgement of our Constitutional rights.

XVIII. In a time such as this, when we have been seriously and most cruelly hurt by those who hate us, and when we must consider ourselves to be gravely threatened by those same people, it is hard to speak of the ways of peace and to remember that Christ enjoined us to love our enemies, but this is no less necessary for being difficult.

XIX. Even now we dare not forget that since the attack of Pearl Harbor—to which the present attack has been often and not usefully compared—we humans have suffered an almost uninterrupted sequence of wars, none of which has brought peace or made us more peaceable.

XX. The aim and result of war necessarily is not peace but victory, and any victory won by violence necessarily justifies the violence that won it and leads to further violence. If we are serious about innovation, must we not conclude that we need something new to replace our perpetual "war to end war"? 20

XXI. What leads to peace is not violence but peaceableness, which is not passivity, but an alert, informed, practiced, and active state of being. We should recognize that while we have extravagantly subsidized the means of war, we have almost totally neglected the ways of peaceableness. We have, for example, several national military academies, but not one peace academy. We have ignored the teachings and the examples of Christ, Gandhi, Martin Luther King, and other peaceable leaders. And here we have an inescapable duty to notice also that war is profitable, whereas the means of peaceableness, being cheap or free, make no money.

XXII. The key to peaceableness is continuous practice. It is wrong to suppose that we can exploit and impoverish the poorer countries, while arming them and instructing them in the newest means of war, and then reasonably expect them to be peaceable.

XXIII. We must not again allow public emotion or the public media to caricature our enemies. **IF OUR ENEMIES ARE NOW TO BE SOME NATIONS OF ISLAM, THEN WE SHOULD UNDERTAKE TO KNOW THOSE ENEMIES.** Our schools should begin to teach the histories, cultures, arts, and language of the Islamic nations. And our leaders should have the humility and the wisdom to ask the reasons some of those people have for hating us.

XXIV. Starting with the economies of food and farming, we should promote at home, and encourage abroad, the ideal of local self-sufficiency. We should recognize that this is the surest, the safest, and the cheapest way for the world to live. We should not countenance the loss or destruction of any local capacity to produce necessary goods.

CONVERSATIONS: ARABS AND ISLAM
Paragraph 23 may be the most provocative of the essay because Berry challenges his readers to try to understand America's enemies and to resist ridiculing those enemies. After September 11, 2001, anger toward Arabs intensified in the United States, and reports of anti-Arab bias increased. But some advocacy groups pointed out that negative images of Arabs had been common in the American media for many years. Consider how American attitudes toward Arab peoples and toward Islam after September 11, 2001, might affect readers' responses to this passage. Do you think Berry meant to provoke readers with this passage?

25   XXV. We should reconsider and renew and extend our efforts to protect the natural foundations of the human economy: soil, water, and air. We should protect every intact ecosystem and watershed that we have left, and begin restoration of those that have been damaged.

XXVI. The complexity of our present trouble suggests as never before that we need to change our present concept of education. Education is not properly an industry, and its proper use is not to serve industries, either by job-training or by industry-subsidized research. Its proper use is to enable citizens to live lives that are economically, politically, socially, and culturally responsible. This cannot be done by gathering or "accessing" what we now call "information"—which is to say facts without context and therefore without priority. A proper education enables young people to put their lives in order, which means knowing what things are more important than other things; it means putting first things first.

XXVII. The first thing we must begin to teach our children (and learn ourselves) is that we cannot spend and consume endlessly. We have got to learn to save and conserve. We do need a "new economy," but one that is founded on thrift and care, on saving and conserving, not on excess and waste. An economy based on waste is inherently and hopelessly violent, and war is its inevitable by-product. We need a peaceable economy.

Understanding the Text

1. What was the state of the world before September 11, 2001, in Berry's view? What led to the conditions he describes? Do you agree with his description? Why or why not?

2. What is the "inescapable choice" that Americans must now make, according to Berry? Are these the only two available choices facing us? Explain.

3. Berry writes that "the substitution of rhetoric for thought, always a temptation in a national crisis, must be resisted by officials and citizens alike." What does he mean by that statement? What exactly does he think

Americans must resist? Why must they resist it?

4. What is the connection between war and the economic policies that Berry criticizes in this essay? How can peace be achieved, in his view? How feasible do you think Berry's proposals for achieving peace are?

5. What is the role of education in bringing about the changes that Berry advocates? Do you think education can achieve these goals? Explain.

Exploring the Issues

1. Based on this essay, how would you describe Berry's political views? How does he view the power of governments and the power of citi-

zens? Refer to specific passages in your answer.

2. Berry charges that Americans have an uncritical view of science and technology. Do you agree? Explain. Do you think most Americans would share his criticisms of science and technology? Why or why not?

3. In paragraph 5, Berry asserts that "we citizens of the industrial countries must continue the labor of self-criticism and self-correction. We must recognize our mistakes." Why does Berry believe this labor of self-criticism and self-correction is necessary? To what extent do you think Berry's essay is part of this self-criticism and self-correction? In what ways might the

American political process come into play in this labor? Do you think most Americans would agree with Berry about the need for such self-criticism and self-correction? Do you? Why or why not?

4. This essay first appeared in *Orion* magazine, which promotes an environmentalist perspective and reflects a progressive view of social and political issues. It is unlikely that Berry would moderate his voice for a particular audience, but it is also likely that readers of *Orion* would be a sympathetic audience for his essay. How do you think Berry's voice might be received by a more general audience, such as readers of widely circulated publications like *USA Today* or *Newsweek?*

Entering the Conversations

1. Write an essay for a general audience, such as readers of your local newspaper or a regional publication, in which you offer your own views about what happened on September 11, 2001. In your essay, try to address the role of government and the workings of power as you discuss those events and their impact. Alternatively, create a video, web site, PowerPoint presentation, or some other kind of document in which you present your view of the state of the society or the world after September 11, 2001.

2. Berry concludes his essay by describing the steps that he believes we must take to address "the complexity of our present trouble" (par. 24–27). Write an essay in which you offer your own views of what we should do to address the social, political, and environmental problems that Berry describes in this essay.

INFOTRAC

3. In paragraph 23, Berry refers to American attitudes toward Arabs and Islam (see *Conversations: Arabs and* *Islam* on page 477). Using InfoTrac College Edition, your library, and any other relevant resources, investigate American attitudes toward Arabs and toward Islam. You might focus your investigation on the popular media or on some other aspect of American society, such as immigration rules or new security measures adopted after September 11, 2001. Look into how Arab people and Islam are portrayed, understood, and treated. You might consider speaking with someone on your campus who might have insight into this issue, such as staff members in your school's office for international students or faculty members who specialize in these issues. Then write a report for your classmates on the basis of your research.

4. Drawing on Berry's essay and any other relevant readings in this book, write an essay in which you discuss what you see as the connections among science, technology, and political power.

CHALLENGING POWER

A FEW YEARS AGO, ON A TYPICAL SCHOOL DAY IN DECEMBER, STUDENTS AT MY LOCAL HIGH SCHOOL HAD A KIND OF REBELLION. AT A DESIGNATED TIME DURING A REGULAR MORNING CLASS PERIOD, ABOUT THREE DOZEN STUDENTS GOT UP FROM THEIR SEATS, WALKED OUT OF THEIR CLASSROOMS, AND GATHERED AT THE FRONT OF THE SCHOOL BUILDING. THERE THEY MADE A STATEMENT VOICING

their concerns about a proposal to implement a new "block" schedule, in which the traditional school day would be restructured from seven 45-minute class periods to four 75-minute class periods. This proposal had been brought before the school board several months earlier and had been discussed at various meetings between parents and school officials. The students, however, felt that the decision to adopt the new block schedule had already been made and that the public meetings were held to give the illusion that school officials were accepting input from the community. The students wanted their voices to be heard. So they walked out of class and stood together at the school entrance to declare their protest before school officials appeared, along with local police, to inform them that they were suspended from school for violating school safety policies.

This incident is one small example of a challenge to power. The students had genuine concerns that they believed were ignored by school officials, even though school officials were following standard procedure in implementing a policy change. They believed that those in power had already made up their minds and would do what they wanted regardless of the strong opposition to the proposal. In fact, polls showed that a majority of teachers at the school opposed the proposal, and many parents did, too. So the students decided that they had to step outside the rules to challenge those in power.

Those students were acting in a very American way. In many respects, American history is the story of people who were willing to challenge power. Indeed, the country was founded when the American colonists challenged the great-

est military power on earth at the time, Great Britain. Like the students at my local high school, the colonists believed that their British rulers were not acting in the colonists' best interests, and the only way to change that was to challenge those rulers. I'm not sure that the students who walked out of my local high school thought of themselves as revolutionaries, but in an important way, they were. They were doing what so many Americans and so many people around the world have done for centuries: challenging power to right a wrong or to claim something that is rightfully theirs.

The following essays explore what it means to challenge power. They explore the complexities and consequences of the decision to resist, to break laws that seem unjust, and to challenge ways of thinking about or treating people who are different.

It is an appropriate time to think about challenging power. Recent events, such as the terrorist attacks on September 11, 2001, and the war in Iraq, have led to controversial decisions by the U.S. government that many critics believe amount to abuses of power. During this time, we have seen numerous protests and new strategies for challenging power, such as the use of the Internet and new kinds of grass-roots organizing. But all these developments share something basic with the protest by the students at my high school: They all grow out of a need to change something by challenging those in power. To challenge power in this way may be a very American thing to do, but it is neither easy nor simple. I hope the essays in this cluster will help you appreciate that. I also hope they will help you appreciate the usefulness of writing as a way to challenge power.

When I began working on this section, Amy, who helped put together this book, confessed that she was having trouble with the following essay by famed American writer Henry David Thoreau (1817–1862). Although she had read the essay before and found its argument provocative, she complained that this time she found herself slogging through the essay.

Resistance to *Civil* Government

The problem, she said, was that Thoreau's writing is often difficult to follow, which makes his complex argument that much harder to understand.

My guess is that you may have similar complaints about this famous essay, which was first published in 1849. And it's worth wondering why. This is one of the most widely reprinted and influential essays ever written. It has become part of the canon of American literature as well as of international discussions of human rights. Important figures like Martin Luther King, Jr., and Mahatma Gandhi have acknowledged that it deeply affected their own thinking about power, justice, and change. Why, then, is it so difficult for so many readers today?

I'll let you answer that question for yourself, but keep in mind that any text is a reflection of its time. Some of the features of Thoreau's writing style that you may find

HENRY DAVID THOREAU

I HEARTILY ACCEPT the motto,—"That government is best which governs least"; and I should like to see it acted up to more rapidly and systematically. Carried out, it finally amounts to this, which also I believe,—"That government is best which governs not at all"; and when men are prepared for it, that will be the kind of government which they will have. Government is at best but an expedient; but most governments are usually, and all governments are sometimes, inexpedient. The objections which have been brought against **A STANDING ARMY**, and they are many and weighty, and deserve to prevail, may also at last be brought against a standing government. The standing army is only an arm of the standing government. The government itself, which is only the mode which the people have chosen to execute their will, is equally liable to be abused and perverted before the people can act through it. Witness the present Mexican war, the work of comparatively a few individuals using the standing government as their tool; for, in the outset, the people would not have consented to this measure.

This American government—what is it but a tradition, though a recent one, endeavoring to transmit itself unimpaired to posterity, but each instant losing some of its integrity? It has not the vitality and

HENRY DAVID THOREAU, "RESISTANCE TO CIVIL GOVERNMENT" (1849).

difficult were common in his day. Also, part of the challenge in reading a text like this one is placing it in historical context so that its references make sense. It may take a bit more effort for readers today to appreciate Thoreau's complex arguments.

Most important, though, is considering what has made this essay such an important piece of writing. Thoreau's argument challenges us to examine our individual responsibilities when it comes to government power, and this challenge may be especially important today, an era when the power of some governments, including that of the United States, extends beyond anything Thoreau could have imagined in 1849. There is little question that Thoreau's message is still relevant today. In that sense, his essay is still part of the important conversations that we are always having about how to live together and how to understand power. ◪

CONVERSATIONS: A STANDING ARMY AND THE MEXICAN WAR
For American readers today, the idea of a "standing army"—that is, a military that exists permanently, whether or not there is a war—seems commonsensical. In 1792, a law was passed that gave the U.S. government some authority over local and state militias, but it was not until 1903 that the National Guard was officially formed as an army separate from the state militias. When Thoreau wrote this essay in 1849, a standing army was a controversial idea. Many Americans were skeptical about a standing army, which they feared the U.S. government leaders would use for their own purposes. Notice that Thoreau suggests that the United States was doing exactly that by waging war with Mexico at that time, a war that many Americans, including Thoreau, opposed because it was fought to bring Texas into the United States as a slave state. Consider how Thoreau's arguments about government power are shaped by the historical moment when he was writing. Do the political circumstances today make his arguments more or less valid?

force of a single living man; for a single man can bend it to his will. It is a sort of wooden gun to the people themselves. But it is not the less necessary for this; for the people must have some complicated machinery or other, and hear its din, to satisfy that idea of government which they have. Governments show thus how successfully men can be imposed on, even impose on themselves, for their own advantage. It is excellent, we must all allow. Yet this government never of itself furthered any enterprise, but by the alacrity with which it got out of its way. *It* does not keep the country free. *It* does not settle the West. *It* does not educate. The character inherent in the American people has done all that has been accomplished; and it would have done somewhat more, if the government had not sometimes got in its way. For government is an expedient by which men would fain succeed in letting one another alone; and, as has been said, when it is most expedient, the governed are most let alone by it. Trade and commerce, if they were not made of India rubber, would never manage to bounce over the obstacles which legislators are continually putting in their way; and, if one were to judge these men wholly by the effects of their actions, and not partly by their intentions, they would deserve to be classed and punished with those mischievous persons who put obstructions on the railroads.

But, to speak practically and as a citizen, unlike those who call themselves no-government men, I ask for, not at once no government, but *at once* a better government. Let every man make known what kind of government would command his respect, and that will be one step toward obtaining it.

After all, the practical reason why, when the power is once in the hands of the people, a majority are permitted, and for a long period continue, to rule, is not because they are most likely to be in the right, nor because this seems fairest to the minority, but because they are physically the strongest. But a government in which the **MAJORITY RULE** in all cases cannot be based on justice, even as far as men understand it. Can there not be a government in which majorities do not virtually decide right and wrong, but conscience?—in which majorities decide only those questions to which the rule of expediency is applicable? Must the citizen ever for a moment, or in the least degree, resign his conscience to the legislator? Why has every man a conscience, then? I think that we should be men first, and subjects afterward. It is not desirable to cultivate a respect for the law, so much as for the right. The only obligation which I have a right to assume is to do at any time what I think right. It is truly enough said that a corporation has no conscience; but a corporation of conscientious men is a corporation *with* a conscience. Law never made men a whit more just; and, by means of their respect for it, even the well-disposed are daily made the agents of injustice. A common and natural result of an undue respect for law is, that you may see a file of soldiers, colonel, captain, corporal, privates, powder-monkeys, and all, marching in admirable order over hill and dale to the wars, against their wills, ay, against their common sense and consciences, which makes it very steep marching indeed, and produces a palpitation of the heart. They have no doubt that it is a damnable business in which they are concerned; they are all peaceably inclined. Now, what are they? Men at all? or small movable forts and magazines, at the service of some unscrupulous man in power? Visit the Navy Yard, and behold a marine, such a man as an American government can make, or such as it can make a man with its black arts—a mere shadow and reminiscence of humanity, a man laid out alive and standing, and already, as one may say, buried under arms with funeral accompaniments, though it may be

    "**NOT A DRUM WAS HEARD,** not a funeral note,
    As his corse to the rampart we hurried;
    Not a soldier discharged his farewell shot
    O'er the grave where our hero we buried."

5   The mass of men serve the state thus, not as men mainly, but as machines, with their bodies. They are the standing army, and the militia, jailers, constables, *posse comitatus,* etc. In most cases there is no free exercise whatever of the judgment or of the moral sense; but they put themselves on a level with wood and earth and stones; and wooden men can perhaps be manufactured that will serve the purpose as well. Such command no more respect than men of straw or a lump of dirt. They have the same sort of worth only as horses and dogs. Yet such as these even are commonly esteemed good citizens. Others, as most legislators, politicians, lawyers, ministers, and office-holders, serve the state chiefly with their heads; and, as they rarely make any moral distinctions, they are as likely to serve the devil, without *intending* it, as God. A very few, as heroes, patriots, martyrs, reformers in the great sense, and *men,* serve the state with their consciences also, and so necessarily resist it for the most part; and they are commonly treated as enemies by it. A wise man will only be useful as a man, and will not submit to be "clay," and "stop a hole to keep the wind away," but leave that office to his dust at least:—

    "**I AM TOO HIGH-BORN TO BE PROPERTIED,**
    To be a secondary at control,
    Or useful serving-man and instrument
    To any sovereign state throughout the world."

He who gives himself entirely to his fellow-men appears to them useless and selfish; but he who gives himself partially to them is pronounced a benefactor and philanthropist.

CONVERSATIONS: MAJORITY RULE
In this paragraph (par. 4), Thoreau writes that "a government in which the majority rule in all cases cannot be based on justice." Compare Thoreau's ideas about majority rule and justice with those of Lani Guinier, whose essay appears on page 467 in this chapter. Guinier wrote her essay almost 150 years after Thoreau wrote his, yet the basic issue they address is the same. What might that say about how societies work out problems related to power?

GLOSS: "NOT A DRUM WAS HEARD"
Thoreau is quoting here (par. 4) from "The Burial of Sir John Moore at Corunna," a poem by Charles Wolfe (1791–1823) describing the burial of British General John Moore, who was killed after defeating French forces at Corunna, Spain, in 1809. Consider how Thoreau uses this quotation to make his point about men who serve the state as soldiers.

GLOSS: "I AM TOO HIGH-BORN TO BE PROPERTIED"
This quotation is from Shakespeare's *King John.*

How does it become a man to behave toward this American government to-day? I answer, that he cannot without disgrace be associated with it. I cannot for an instant recognize that political organization as *my* government which is the *slave's* government also.

All men recognize the right of revolution; that is, the right to refuse allegiance to, and to resist, the government, when its tyranny or its inefficiency are great and unendurable. But almost all say that such is not the case now. But such was the case, they think, in the Revolution of '75. If one were to tell me that this was a bad government because it taxed certain foreign commodities brought to its ports, it is most probable that I should not make an ado about it, for I can do without them. All machines have their friction; and possibly this does enough good to counterbalance the evil. At any rate, it is a great evil to make a stir about it. But when the friction comes to have its machine, and oppression and robbery are organized, I say, let us not have such a machine any longer. In other words, when a sixth of the population of a nation which has undertaken to be the refuge of liberty are slaves, and **A WHOLE COUNTRY IS UNJUSTLY OVERRUN** and conquered by a foreign army, and subjected to military law, I think that it is not too soon for honest men to rebel and revolutionize. What makes this duty the more urgent is the fact that the country so overrun is not our own, but ours is the invading army.

PALEY, a common authority with many on moral questions, in his chapter on the "Duty of Submission to Civil Government," resolves all civil obligation into expediency; and he proceeds to say that "so long as the interest of the whole society requires it, that is, so long as the established government cannot be resisted or changed without public inconveniency, it is the will of God that the established government be obeyed, and no longer"—"This principle being admitted, the justice of every particular case of resistance is reduced to a computation of the quantity of the danger and grievance on the one side, and of the probability and expense of redressing it on the other." Of this, he says, every man shall judge for himself. But Paley appears never to have contemplated those cases to which the rule of expediency does not apply, in which a people, as well as an individual, must do justice, cost what it may. If I have unjustly wrested a plank from a drowning man, I must restore it to him though I drown myself. This, according to Paley, would be inconvenient. But he that would save his life, in such a case, shall lose it. This people must cease to hold slaves, and to make war on Mexico, though it cost them their existence as a people.

10   In their practice, nations agree with Paley; but does any one think that Massachusetts does exactly what is right at the present crisis?

> **"A DRAB OF STATE,** a cloth-o'-silver slut,
> To have her train borne up, and her soul trail in the dirt."

GLOSSES
A WHOLE COUNTRY IS UNJUSTLY OVERRUN
The country unjustly overrun is a reference to Mexico, overrun by American military forces.

PALEY
William Paley (1743–1805) was an influential British philosopher and theologian in the eighteenth century. Notice how Thoreau uses ideas from Paley's *Principles of Moral and Political Philosophy* (1785) to justify resistance to government.

"A DRAB OF STATE"
This quotation is taken from a play believed to have been written by Cyril Tourneur (1575–1626) called *The Revenger's Tragedy* (1607). Thoreau seems to use the reference to further his criticism of the laws of Massachusetts regarding slavery.

Practically speaking, the opponents to a reform in Massachusetts are not a hundred thousand politicians at the South, but a hundred thousand merchants and farmers here, who are more interested in commerce and agriculture than they are in humanity, and are not prepared to do justice to the slave and to Mexico, *cost what it may*. I quarrel not with far-off foes, but with those who, near at home, co-operate with, and do the bidding of those far away, and without whom the latter would be harmless. We are accustomed to say, that the mass of men are unprepared; but improvement is slow, because the few are not materially wiser or better than the many. It is not so important that many should be as good as you, as that there be some absolute goodness somewhere; for that will leaven the whole lump. There are thousands who are *in opinion* opposed to slavery and to the war, who yet in effect do nothing to put an end to them; who, esteeming themselves children of Washington and Franklin, sit down with their hands in their pockets, and say that they know not what to do, and do nothing; who even postpone the question of freedom to the question of free-trade, and quietly read the prices-current along with the latest advices from Mexico, after dinner, and, it may be, fall asleep over them both. What is the price-current of an honest man and patriot to-day? They hesitate, and they regret, and sometimes they petition; but they do nothing in earnest and with effect. They will wait, well disposed, for others to remedy the evil, that they may no longer have it to regret. At most, they give only a cheap vote, and a feeble countenance and Godspeed, to the right, as it goes by them. There are nine hundred and ninety-nine patrons of virtue to one virtuous man; but it is easier to deal with the real possessor of a thing than with the temporary guardian of it.

All voting is a sort of gaming, like checkers or backgammon, with a slight moral tinge to it, a playing with right and wrong, with moral questions; and betting naturally accompanies it. The character of the voters is not staked. I cast my vote, perchance, as I think right; but I am not vitally concerned that that right should prevail. I am willing to leave it to the majority. Its obligation, therefore, never exceeds that of expediency. Even voting *for the right* is *doing* nothing for it. It is only expressing to men feebly your desire that it should prevail. A wise man will not leave the right to the mercy of chance, nor wish it to prevail through the power of the majority. There is but little virtue in the action of masses of men. When the majority shall at length vote for the abolition of slavery, it will be because they are indifferent to slavery, or because there is but little slavery left to be abolished by their vote. *They* will then be the only slaves. Only *his* vote can hasten the abolition of slavery who asserts his own freedom by his vote.

I hear of a convention to be held at Baltimore, or elsewhere, for the selection of a candidate for the Presidency, made up chiefly of editors, and men who are politicians by profession; but I think, what is it to any independent, intelligent, and respectable man what decision they may come to? Shall we not have the advantage of his wisdom and honesty, nevertheless? Can we not count upon some independent votes? Are there not many individuals in the country who do not attend conventions? But no: I find that the respectable man, so called, has immediately drifted from his position, and despairs of his country, when his country has more reason to despair of him. He forthwith adopts one of the candidates thus selected as the only *available* one, thus proving that he is himself *available* for any purposes of the demagogue. His vote is of no more worth than that of any unprincipled foreigner or hireling native, who may have been bought. Oh for a man who is a *man,* and, as my neighbor says, has a bone in his back which you cannot pass your hand through! Our statistics are at fault: the population has been returned too large. How many *men* are there to a square thousand miles in this country? Hardly one. Does not America offer any inducement for men to settle here? The American has dwindled into an Odd Fellow—one who may be known by the development of his organ of gregariousness, and a manifest lack of intellect and cheerful self-reliance; whose first and chief concern, on coming into the world, is to see that the almshouses are in good repair; and, before yet he has lawfully donned the virile garb, to collect a fund for the support of the widows and orphans that may be; who, in short, ventures to live only by the aid of the Mutual Insurance company, which has promised to bury him decently.

It is not a man's duty, as a matter of course, to devote himself to the eradication of any, even the most enormous wrong; he may still properly have other concerns to engage him; but it is his duty, at least, to wash his hands of it, and, if he gives it no thought longer, not to give it practically his support. If I devote myself to other pursuits and contemplations, I must first see, at least, that I do not pursue them sitting upon another man's shoulders. I must get off him first, that he may pursue his contemplations too. See what gross inconsistency is tolerated. I have heard some of my townsmen say, "I should like to have them order me out to help put down an insurrection of the slaves, or to march to Mexico;—see if I would go"; and yet these very men have each, directly by their allegiance, and so indirectly, at least, by their money, **FURNISHED A SUBSTITUTE.** The soldier is applauded who refuses to serve in an unjust war by those who do not refuse to sustain the unjust government which makes the war; is applauded by those whose own act and authority he disregards and sets at naught; as if the state were penitent to that degree that it hired one to scourge it while it

---

CONVERSATIONS: VOTING

Americans tend to believe that voting is the hallmark of democracy, the right of each individual to voice his or her views and participate in government. But here (par. 11) Thoreau offers his famous criticism that "even voting *for the right* is *doing* nothing for it." Consider what this view might mean in terms of the responsibility it places on individual citizens. In the contentious 2004 U.S. presidential election, some activists argued that citizens could not rely on voting to change what they believed to be misguided or immoral government policies. During that election, these critics developed new techniques for promoting their views, including using the Internet and other mass media to organize citizens. To an extent, such efforts reflect Thoreau's view as he expresses it here, which suggests that Americans are still actively debating these important issues.

GLOSS: SUBSTITUTES FOR MILITARY SERVICE

Thoreau is referring (par. 13) to the practice, which is no longer followed, of allowing a man who was drafted into military service to pay another man to serve in his place as his "substitute." Thoreau argues that paying taxes to the government is equivalent to hiring such a military substitute because tax dollars support the government's war efforts.

sinned, but not to that degree that it left off sinning for a moment. Thus, under the name of Order and Civil Government, we are all made at last to pay homage to and support our own meanness. After the first blush of sin comes its indifference; and from immoral it becomes, as it were, *un*moral, and not quite unnecessary to that life which we have made.

The broadest and most prevalent error requires the most disinterested virtue to sustain it. The slight reproach to which the virtue of patriotism is commonly liable, the noble are most likely to incur. Those who, while they disapprove of the character and measures of a government, yield to it their allegiance and support are undoubtedly its most conscientious supporters, and so frequently the most serious obstacles to reform. Some are petitioning the State to dissolve the Union, to disregard the requisitions of the President. Why do they not dissolve it themselves—the union between themselves and the State—and refuse to pay their quota into its treasury? Do not they stand in the same relation to the State, that the State does to the Union? And have not the same reasons prevented the State from resisting the Union, which have prevented them from resisting the State?

How can a man be satisfied to entertain an opinion merely, and 15 enjoy *it*? Is there any enjoyment in it, if his opinion is that he is aggrieved? If you are cheated out of a single dollar by your neighbor, you do not rest satisfied with knowing that you are cheated, or with saying that you are cheated, or even with petitioning him to pay you your due; but you take effectual steps at once to obtain the full amount, and see that you are never cheated again. Action from principle—the perception and the performance of right—changes things and relations; it is essentially revolutionary, and does not consist wholly with anything which was. It not only divides states and churches, it divides families; ay, it divides the *individual*, separating the diabolical in him from the divine.

Unjust laws exist; shall we be content to obey them, or shall we endeavor to amend them, and obey them until we have succeeded, or shall we transgress them at once? Men generally, under such a government as this, think that they ought to wait until they have persuaded the majority to alter them. They think that, if they should resist, the remedy would be worse than the evil. But it is the fault of the government itself that the remedy *is* worse than the evil. *It* makes it worse. Why is it not more apt to anticipate and provide for reform? Why does it not cherish its wise minority? Why does it cry and resist before it is hurt? Why does it not encourage its citizens to be on the alert to point out its faults, and *do* better than it would have them? Why does it always crucify Christ, and excommunicate Copernicus and Luther, and pronounce Washington and Franklin rebels?

One would think, that a deliberate and practical denial of its authority was the only offence never contemplated by government; else, why has it not assigned its definite, its suitable and proportionate, penalty? If a man who has no property refuses but once to earn nine shillings for the State, he is put in prison for a period unlimited by any law that I know, and determined only by the discretion of those who placed him there; but if he should steal ninety times nine shillings from the State, he is soon permitted to go at large again.

If the injustice is part of the necessary friction of the machine of government, let it go, let it go; perchance it will wear smooth—certainly the machine will wear out. If the injustice has a spring, or a pulley, or a rope, or a crank, exclusively for itself, then perhaps you may consider whether the remedy will not be worse than the evil; but if it is of such a nature that it requires you to be the agent of injustice to another, then, I say, break the law. Let your life be a counter friction to stop the machine. What I have to do is to see, at any rate, that I do not lend myself to the wrong which I condemn.

As for adopting the ways which the State has provided for remedying the evil, I know not of such ways. They take too much time, and a man's life will be gone. I have other affairs to attend to. I came into this world, not chiefly to make this a good place to live in, but to live in it, be it good or bad. A man has not everything to do, but something; and because he cannot do *everything*, it is not necessary that he should do *something* wrong. It is not my business to be petitioning the Governor or the Legislature any more than it is theirs to petition me; and if they should not hear my petition, what should I do then? But in this case the State has provided no way; its very Constitution is the evil. This may seem to be harsh and stubborn and unconciliatory; but it is to treat with the utmost kindness and consideration the only spirit that can appreciate or deserves it. So is a change for the better, like birth and death which convulse the body.

I do not hesitate to say, that those who call themselves Abolitionists should at once effectually withdraw their support, both in person and property, from the government of Massachusetts, and not wait till they constitute a majority of one, before they suffer the right to prevail through them. I think that it is enough if they have God on their side, without waiting for that other one. Moreover, any man more right than his neighbors constitutes a majority of one already. 20

I meet this American government, or its representative, the State government, directly, and face to face, once a year—no more—in the person of its tax-gatherer; this is the only mode in which a man situated as I am necessarily meets it; and it then says distinctly, Recognize me; and the simplest, the most effectual, and, in the present posture of affairs, the indispensablest mode of treating with it on this head, of expressing your little satisfaction with and love for it, is to deny it then. MY CIVIL NEIGHBOR, THE TAX-GATHERER, is the very man I have to deal with—for it is, after all, with men and not with parchment that I quarrel—and he has voluntarily chosen to be an agent of the govern-

CONVERSATIONS: GOVERNMENT WORKERS In this passage, Thoreau refers to two government employees that he himself knew: Sam Staples, the tax collector in Thoreau's region, and Sam Hoar, a Massachusetts legislator who traveled to South Carolina to protest that state's policy of imprisoning freed slaves. Thoreau argues that "it is . . . with men and not with parchment that I quarrel." In other words, Thoreau holds government employees responsible for government actions. A similar argument was made by Timothy McVeigh, the man who bombed a federal building in Oklahoma City in 1995, and by the terrorists who attacked the World Trade Center and the Pentagon on September 11, 2001. Consider what Thoreau's position here suggests about individual responsibility. How do you think these recent terrorist events might affect the way readers react to Thoreau's argument today?

ment. How shall he ever know well what he is and does as an officer of the government, or as a man, until he is obliged to consider whether he shall treat me, his neighbor, for whom he has respect, as a neighbor and well-disposed man, or as a maniac and disturber of the peace, and see if he can get over this obstruction to his neighborliness without a ruder and more impetuous thought or speech corresponding with his action? I know this well, that if one thousand, if one hundred, if ten men whom I could name—if ten *honest* men only—ay, if *one* honest man, in this State of Massachusetts, *ceasing to hold slaves,* were actually to withdraw from this copartnership, and be locked up in the county jail therefor, it would be the abolition of slavery in America. For it matters not how small the beginning may seem to be: what is once well done is done forever. But we love better to talk about it: that we say is our mission. Reform keeps many scores of newspapers in its service, but not one man. If MY ESTEEMED NEIGHBOR, THE STATE'S AMBASSADOR, who will devote his days to the settlement of the question of human rights in the Council Chamber, instead of being threatened with the prisons of Carolina, were to sit down the prisoner of Massachusetts, that State which is so anxious to foist the sin of slavery upon her sister—though at present she can discover only an act of inhospitality to be the ground of a quarrel with her—the Legislature would not wholly waive the subject the following winter.

Under a government which imprisons any unjustly, the true place for a just man is also a prison. The proper place to-day, the only place which Massachusetts has provided for her freer and less desponding spirits, is in her prisons, to be put out and locked out of the State by her own act, as they have already put themselves out by their principles. It is there that the fugitive slave, and the Mexican prisoner on parole, and the Indian come to plead the wrongs of his race, should find them; on that separate, but more free and honorable ground, where the State places those who are not *with* her, but *against* her— the only house in a slave State in which a free man can abide with honor. If any think that their influence would be lost there, and their voices no longer afflict the ear of the State, that they would not be as an enemy within its walls, they do not know by how much truth is stronger than error, nor how much more eloquently and effectively he can combat injustice who has experienced a little in his own person. Cast your whole vote, not a strip of paper merely, but your whole influence. A minority is powerless while it conforms to the majority; it is not even a minority then; but it is irresistible when it clogs by its whole weight. If the alternative is to keep all just men in prison, or give up war and slavery, the State will not hesitate which to choose. If a thousand men were not to pay their tax-bills this year, that would not be a violent and bloody measure, as it would be to pay them, and enable the State to commit violence and shed innocent blood. This is, in fact, the definition of a peaceable revolution, if any such is possible. If the tax-gatherer, or any other public officer, asks me, as one has done, "But what shall I do?" my answer is, "If you really wish to do anything, resign your office." When the subject has refused allegiance, and the officer has resigned his office, then the revolution is accomplished. But even suppose blood should flow. Is there not a sort of blood shed when the conscience is wounded? Through this wound a man's real manhood and immortality flow out, and he bleeds to an everlasting death. I see this blood flowing now.

I have contemplated the imprisonment of the offender, rather than the seizure of his goods—though both will serve the same purpose—because they who assert the purest right, and consequently are most dangerous to a corrupt State, commonly have not spent much time in accumulating property. To such the State renders comparatively small service, and a slight tax is wont to appear exorbitant, particularly if they are obliged to earn it by special labor with their hands. If there were one who lived wholly without the use of money, the State itself would hesitate to demand it of him. But the rich man—not to make any invidious comparison—is always sold to the institution which makes him rich. Absolutely speaking, the more money, the less virtue; for money comes between a man and his objects, and obtains them for him; and it was certainly no great virtue to obtain it. It puts to rest many questions which he would otherwise be taxed to answer; while the only new question which it puts is the hard but superfluous one, how to spend it. Thus his moral ground is taken from under his feet. The opportunities of living are diminished in proportion as what are called the "means" are increased. The best thing a man can do for his culture when he is rich is to endeavor to carry out those schemes which he entertained when he was poor. Christ answered the Herodians according to their condition. "Show me the tribute-money," said he;—and one took a penny out of his pocket;—if you use money which has the image of Cæsar on it, and which he has made current and valuable, that is, *if you are men of the State,* and gladly enjoy the advantages of Cæsar's government, then pay him back some of his own when he demands it; "Render therefore to Cæsar that which is Cæsar's, and to God those things which are God's"—leaving them no wiser than before as to which was which; for they did not wish to know.

When I converse with the freest of my neighbors, I perceive that, whatever they may say about the magnitude and seriousness of the question, and their regard for the public tranquility, the long and the short of the matter is, that they cannot spare the protection of the existing government, and they dread the consequences to their property and families of disobedience to it. For my own part, I should not like to think that I ever rely on the protection of the State. But, if I deny the authority of the State when it presents its tax-bill, it will soon take and waste all my property, and so harass me and my children without end. This is hard. This makes it impossible for a man to live honestly, and at the same time comfortably in outward respects. It will not be worth the while to accumulate property; that would be sure to go again. You must hire or squat somewhere, and raise but a small crop, and eat that soon. You must live within yourself, and depend upon yourself always tucked up and ready for a start, and not have many affairs. A man may grow rich in Turkey even, if he will be in all respects a good subject of the Turkish government. Confucius said, "If a state is governed by the principles of reason, poverty and misery are subjects of shame; if a state is not governed by the principles of reason, riches and honors are the subjects of shame." No: until I want the protection of Massachusetts to be extended to me in some distant Southern port, where my liberty is endangered, or until I am bent solely on building up an estate at home by peaceful enterprise, I can afford to refuse allegiance to Massachusetts, and her right to my property and life. It costs me less in every sense to incur the penalty of disobedience to the State than it would to obey. I should feel as if I were worth less in that case.

25   Some years ago, the State met me in behalf of the Church, and commanded me to pay a certain sum toward the support of a clergy-man whose preaching my father attended, but never I myself. "Pay," it said, "or be locked up in the jail." I declined to pay. But, unfortu-nately, another man saw fit to pay it. I did not see why the schoolmas-ter should be taxed to support the priest, and not the priest the schoolmaster: for I was not the State's schoolmaster, but I supported myself by voluntary subscription. I did not see why the lyceum should not present its tax-bill, and have the State to back its demand, as well as the Church. However, at the request of the selectmen, I conde-scended to make some such statement as this in writing:—"Know all men by these presents, that I, Henry Thoreau, do not wish to be re-garded as a member of any incorporated society which I have not joined." This I gave to the town clerk; and he has it. The State, having thus learned that I did not wish to be regarded as a member of that church, has never made a like demand on me since; though it said that it must adhere to its original presumption that time. If I had known how to name them, I should then have signed off in detail from all the societies which I never signed on to; but I did not know where to find a complete list.

I have paid no **POLL-TAX** for six years. I was put into a jail once on this account, for one night; and, as I stood considering the walls of solid stone, two or three feet thick, the door of wood and iron, a foot thick, and the iron grating which strained the light, I could not help being struck with the foolishness of that institution which treated me as if I were mere flesh and blood and bones, to be locked up. I wondered that it should have concluded at length that this was the best use it could put me to, and had never thought to avail itself of my services in some way. I saw that, if there was a wall of stone between me and my

GLOSS: POLL TAX
In Thoreau's day, the government did not collect a general income tax as it does today; rather, taxes were collected for specific purposes. Poll taxes were essentially voting fees.

townsmen, there was a still more difficult one to climb or break through, before they could get to be as free as I was. I did not for a moment feel confined, and the walls seemed a great waste of stone and mortar. I felt as if I alone of all my townsmen had paid my tax. They plainly did not know how to treat me, but behaved like persons who are underbred. In every threat and in every compliment there was a blunder; for they thought that my chief desire was to stand the other side of that stone wall. I could not but smile to see how industriously they locked the door on my meditations, which followed them out again without let or hindrance, and they were really all that was dangerous. As they could not reach me, they had resolved to punish my body; just as boys, if they cannot come at some person against whom they have a spite, will abuse his dog. I saw that the State was half-witted, that it was timid as a lone woman with her silver spoons, and that it did not know its friends from its foes, and I lost all my remaining respect for it, and pitied it.

Thus the State never intentionally confronts a man's sense, intellectual or moral, but only his body, his senses. It is not armed with superior wit or honesty, but with superior physical strength. I was not born to be forced. I will breathe after my own fashion. Let us see who is the strongest. What force has a multitude? They only can force me who obey a higher law than I. They force me to become like themselves. I do not hear of *men* being *forced* to have this way or that by masses of men. What sort of life were that to live? When I meet a government which says to me, "Your money or your life," why should I be in haste to give it my money? It may be in a great strait, and not know what to do: I cannot help that. It must help itself; do as I do. It is not worth the while to snivel about it. I am not responsible for the successful working of the machinery of society. I am not the son of the engineer. I perceive that, when an acorn and a chestnut fall side by side, the one does not remain inert to make way for the other, but both obey their own laws, and spring and grow and flourish as best they can, till one, perchance, overshadows and destroys the other. If a plant cannot live according to its nature, it dies; and so a man.

The night in prison was novel and interesting enough. The prisoners in their shirt-sleeves were enjoying a chat and the evening air in the doorway, when I entered. But the jailer said, "Come, boys, it is time to lock up"; and so they dispersed, and I heard the sound of their steps returning into the hollow apartments. My room-mate was introduced to me by the jailer as "a first-rate fellow and a clever man." When the door was locked, he showed me where to hang my hat, and how he managed matters there. The rooms were whitewashed once a month; and this one, at least, was the whitest, most simply furnished, and probably the neatest apartment in the town. He naturally wanted to know where I came from, and what brought me there; and, when I had told him, I asked him in my turn how he came there, presuming him to be an honest man, of course; and, as the world goes, I believe he was. "Why," said he, "they accuse me of burning a barn; but I never did it." As near as I could discover, he had probably gone to bed in a barn when drunk, and smoked his pipe there; and so a barn was burnt. He had the reputation of being a clever man, had been there some three months waiting for his trial to come on, and would have to wait as much longer; but he was quite domesticated and contented, since he got his board for nothing, and thought that he was well treated.

He occupied one window, and I the other; and I saw that if one stayed there long, his principal business would be to look out the window. I had soon read all the tracts that were left there, and examined where former prisoners had broken out, and where a grate had been sawed off, and heard the history of the various occupants of that room; for I found that even here there was a history and a gossip which never circulated beyond the walls of the jail. Probably this is the only house in the town where verses are composed, which are afterward printed in a circular form, but not published. I was shown quite a long list of verses which were composed by some young men who had been detected in an attempt to escape, who avenged themselves by singing them.

I pumped my fellow-prisoner as dry as I could, for fear I should never see him again; but at length he showed me which was my bed, and left me to blow out the lamp.

It was like travelling into a far country, such as I had never expected to behold, to lie there for one night. It seemed to me that I never had heard the town-clock strike before, nor the evening sounds of the village; for we slept with the windows open, which were inside the grating. It was to see my native village in the light of the Middle Ages, and our Concord was turned into a Rhine stream, and visions of knights and castles passed before me. They were the voices of old burghers that I heard in the streets. I was an involuntary spectator and auditor of whatever was done and said in the kitchen of the adjacent village-inn—a wholly new and rare experience to me. It was a closer view of my native town. I was fairly inside of it. I never had seen its institutions before. This is one of its peculiar institutions; for it is a shire town. I began to comprehend what its inhabitants were about.

In the morning, our breakfasts were put through the hole in the door, in small oblong-square tin pans, made to fit, and holding a pint of chocolate, with brown bread, and an iron spoon. When they called for the vessels again, I was green enough to return what bread I had left; but my comrade seized it, and said that I should lay that up for lunch or dinner. Soon after he was let out to work at haying in a neighboring field, whither he went every day, and would not be back till noon; so he bade me good-day, saying that he doubted if he should see me again.

When I came out of prison—for some one interfered, and paid that tax—I did not perceive that great changes had taken place on the common, such as he observed who went in a youth and emerged a tottering

30

STRATEGIES: USING NARRATIVE TO MAKE A POINT
Thoreau devotes several paragraphs to his experiences in jail after he refused to pay a poll tax. If you read this passage carefully, you'll see that Thoreau is doing more than just telling the story of his famous night in jail. Writers sometimes use narrative to help convey their ideas in essays, like this one, that are argumentative or analytical. Consider what Thoreau accomplishes with this brief narrative. What ideas does he convey? How does this narrative support main points that he makes elsewhere in his essay? Notice, too, how Thoreau draws lessons from his experience, which he sums up in paragraph 33.

and gray-headed man; and yet a change had to my eyes come over the scene—the town, and State, and country—greater than any that mere time could effect. I saw yet more distinctly the State in which I lived. I saw to what extent the people among whom I lived could be trusted as good neighbors and friends; that their friendship was for summer weather only; that they did not greatly propose to do right; that they were a distinct race from me by their prejudices and superstitions, as the Chinamen and Malays are; that in their sacrifices to humanity, they ran no risks, not even to their property; that after all they were not so noble but they treated the thief as he had treated them, and hoped, by a certain outward observance and a few prayers, and by walking in a particular straight though useless path from time to time, to save their souls. This may be to judge my neighbors harshly; for I believe that many of them are not aware that they have such an institution as the jail in their village.

It was formerly the custom in our village, when a poor debtor came out of jail, for his acquaintances to salute him, looking through their fingers, which were crossed to represent the grating of a jail window, "How do ye do?" My neighbors did not thus salute me, but first looked at me, and then at one another, as if I had returned from a long journey. I was put into jail as I was going to the shoemaker's to get a shoe which was mended. When I was let out the next morning, I proceeded to finish my errand, and, having put on my mended shoe, joined a huckleberry party, who were impatient to put themselves under my conduct; and in half an hour—for the horse was soon tackled—was in the midst of a huckleberry field, on one of our highest hills, two miles off, and then the State was nowhere to be seen.

This is the whole history of **"MY PRISONS."**

I have never declined paying the highway tax, because I am as desirous of being a good neighbor as I am of being a bad subject; and as for supporting schools, I am doing my part to educate my fellow-countrymen now. It is for no particular item in the tax-bill that I refuse to pay it. I simply wish to refuse allegiance to the State, to withdraw and stand aloof from it effectually. I do not care to trace the course of my dollar, if I could, till it buys a man or a musket to shoot one with—the dollar is innocent—but I am concerned to trace the effects of my allegiance. In fact, I quietly declare war with the State, after my fashion, though I will still make what use and get what advantage of her I can, as is usual in such cases.

If others pay the tax which is demanded of me, from a sympathy with the State, they do but what they have already done in their own case, or rather they abet injustice to a greater extent than the State requires. If they pay the tax from a mistaken interest in the individual taxed, to save his property, or prevent his going to jail, it is because they have not considered wisely how far they let their private feelings interfere with the public good.

GLOSS: "MY PRISONS"
Thoreau is referring to *Le Mie Prigioni* by Silvio Pellico (1789–1854), an Italian imprisoned for eight years by his government.

35

This, then, is my position at present. But one cannot be too much on his guard in such a case, lest his action be biased by obstinacy or an undue regard for the opinions of men. Let him see that he does only what belongs to himself and to the hour.

I think sometimes, Why, this people mean well; they are only ignorant; they would do better if they knew how: why give your neighbors this pain to treat you as they are not inclined to? But I think, again, This is no reason why I should do as they do, or permit others to suffer much greater pain of a different kind. Again, I sometimes say to myself, When many millions of men, without heat, without ill-will, without personal feeling of any kind, demand of you a few shillings only, without the possibility, such is their constitution, of retracting or altering their present demand, and without the possibility, on your side, of appeal to any other millions, why expose yourself to this overwhelming brute force? You do not resist cold and hunger, the winds and the waves, thus obstinately; you quietly submit to a thousand similar necessities. You do not put your head into the fire. But just in proportion as I regard this as not wholly a brute force, but partly a human force, and consider that I have relations to those millions as to so many millions of men, and not of mere brute or inanimate things, I see that appeal is possible, first and instantaneously, from them to the Maker of them, and, secondly, from them to themselves. But, if I put my head deliberately into the fire, there is no appeal to fire or to the Maker of fire, and I have only myself to blame. If I could convince myself that I have any right to be satisfied with men as they are, and to treat them accordingly, and not according, in some respects, to my requisitions and expectations of what they and I ought to be, then, like a good Mussulman and fatalist, I should endeavor to be satisfied with things as they are, and say it is the will of God. And, above all, there is this difference between resisting this and a purely brute or natural force, that I can resist this with some effect; but I cannot expect, like Orpheus, to change the nature of the rocks and trees and beasts.

I do not wish to quarrel with any man or nation. I do not wish to split hairs, to make fine distinctions, or set myself up as better than my neighbors. I seek rather, I may say, even an excuse for conforming to the laws of the land. I am but too ready to conform to them. Indeed, I have reason to suspect myself on this head; and each year, as the tax-gatherer comes round, I find myself disposed to review the acts and position of the general and State governments, and the spirit of the people, to discover a pretext for conformity.

40

> "WE MUST AFFECT OUR COUNTRY AS OUR PARENTS,
> And if at any time we alienate
> Our love or industry from doing it honor,
> We must respect effects and teach the soul
> Matter of conscience and religion,
> And not desire of rule or benefit."

GLOSS: "WE MUST AFFECT OUR COUNTRY AS OUR PARENTS"
This quotation is from *Battle of Alcazar* by George Peele, a sixteenth century writer.

I believe that the State will soon be able to take all my work of this sort out of my hands, and then I shall be no better a patriot than my fellow-countrymen. Seen from a lower point of view, the Constitution, with all its faults, is very good; the law and the courts are very respectable; even this State and this American government are, in many respects, very admirable and rare things, to be thankful for, such as a great many have described them; but seen from a point of view a little higher, they are what I have described them; seen from a higher still, and the highest, who shall say what they are, or that they are worth looking at or thinking of at all?

However, the government does not concern me much, and I shall bestow the fewest possible thoughts on it. It is not many moments that I live under a government, even in this world. If a man is thought-free, fancy-free, imagination-free, that which is *not* never for a long time appearing *to be* to him, unwise rulers or reformers cannot fatally interrupt him.

I know that most men think differently from myself; but those whose lives are by profession devoted to the study of these or kindred subjects, content me as little as any. Statesmen and legislators, standing so completely within the institution, never distinctly and nakedly behold it. They speak of moving society, but have no resting-place without it. They may be men of a certain experience and discrimination, and have no doubt invented ingenious and even useful systems, for which we sincerely thank them; but all their wit and usefulness lie within certain not very wide limits. They are wont to forget that the world is not governed by policy and expediency. **WEBSTER** never goes behind government, and so cannot speak with authority about it. His words are wisdom to those legislators who contemplate no essential reform in the existing government; but for thinkers, and those who legislate for all time, he never once glances at the subject. I know of those whose serene and wise speculations on this theme would soon reveal the limits of his mind's range and hospitality. Yet, compared with the cheap professions of most reformers, and the still cheaper wisdom and eloquence of politicians in general, his are almost the only sensible and valuable words, and we thank Heaven for him. Comparatively, he is always strong, original, and, above all, practical. Still, his quality is not wisdom, but prudence. The lawyer's truth is not truth, but consistency or a consistent expediency. Truth is always in harmony with herself, and is not concerned chiefly to reveal the justice that may consist with wrong-doing. He well deserves to be called, as he has been called, the Defender of the Constitution. There are really no blows to be given by him but defensive ones. He is not a leader, but a follower. His leaders are the **MEN OF '87**. "I have never made an effort," he says, "and never propose to make an effort; I have never countenanced an effort, and never mean to countenance an effort, to disturb the arrangement as originally made, by which the

GLOSS: WEBSTER
A reference to Daniel Webster (1782–1852), a U.S. senator at the time. The quotations in this paragraph are taken from a speech about slavery that Webster gave to the Senate.

GLOSS: MEN OF '87
This is a reference to the men who wrote the U.S. Constitution in 1787.

various States came into the Union." Still thinking of the sanction which the Constitution gives to slavery, he says, "Because it was a part of the original compact—let it stand." Notwithstanding his special acuteness and ability, he is unable to take a fact out of its merely political relations, and behold it as it lies absolutely to be disposed of by the intellect—what, for instance, it behooves a man to do here in America to-day with regard to slavery, but ventures, or is driven, to make some such desperate answer as the following, while professing to speak absolutely, and as a private man—from which what new and singular code of social duties might be inferred? "The manner," says he, "in which the governments of those States where slavery exists are to regulate it is for their own consideration, under their responsibility to their constituents, to the general laws of propriety, humanity, and justice, and to God. Associations formed elsewhere, springing from a feeling of humanity, or any other cause, have nothing whatever to do with it. They have never received any encouragement from me, and they never will."

They who know of no purer sources of truth, who have traced up its stream no higher, stand, and wisely stand, by the Bible and the Constitution, and drink at it there with reverence and humility; but they who behold where it comes trickling into this lake or that pool, gird up their loins once more, and continue their pilgrimage toward its fountain-head.

45   No man with a genius for legislation has appeared in America. They are rare in the history of the world. There are orators, politicians, and eloquent men, by the thousand; but the speaker has not yet opened his mouth to speak who is capable of settling the much-vexed questions of the day. We love eloquence for its own sake, and not for any truth which it may utter, or any heroism it may inspire. Our legislators have not yet learned the comparative value of free-trade and of freedom, of union, and of rectitude, to a nation. They have no genius or talent for comparatively humble questions of taxation and finance, commerce and manufacturers and agriculture. If we were left solely to the wordy wit of legislators in Congress for our guidance, uncorrected by the seasonable experience and the effectual complaints of the people, America would not long retain her rank among the nations. For eighteen hundred years, though perchance I have no right to say it, the New Testament has been written; yet where is the legislator who has wisdom and practical talent enough to avail himself of the light which it sheds on the science of legislation?

The authority of government, even such as I am willing to submit to—for I will cheerfully obey those who know and can do better than I, and in many things even those who neither know nor can do so well— is still an impure one: to be strictly just, it must have the sanction and consent of the governed. It can have no pure right over my person and property but what I concede to it. The progress from an absolute to a

CONVERSATIONS: RESISTANCE TO GOVERNMENT
Thoreau advocates individual resistance on the basis of individual conscience, and he himself refused to pay taxes as a protest against U.S. government actions. But there can be many forms of resistance, including individual expressions of protest like this poster, which was created in 2004 to criticize U.S. security policies. Consider the effectiveness of these visual expressions of resistance. To what extent do you think such a visual expression is consistent with Thoreau's argument?

limited monarchy, from a limited monarchy to a democracy, is a progress toward a true respect for the individual. Even the Chinese philosopher was wise enough to regard the individual as the basis of the empire. Is a democracy, such as we know it, the last improvement possible in government? Is it not possible to take a step further towards recognizing and organizing the rights of man? There will never be a really free and enlightened State until the State comes to recognize the individual as a higher and independent power, from which all its own power and authority are derived, and treats him accordingly. I please myself with imagining a State at least which can afford to be just to all men, and to treat the individual with respect as a neighbor; which even would not think it inconsistent with its own repose if a few were to live aloof from it, not meddling with it, nor embraced by it, who fulfilled all the duties of neighbors and fellow-men. A State which bore this kind of fruit, and suffered it to drop off as fast as it ripened, would prepare the way for a still more perfect and glorious State, which also I have imagined, but not yet anywhere seen.

Understanding the Text

1. Early in his essay, Thoreau claims that government itself has not accomplished any of the things we often give it credit for, such as educating people or keeping the nation free. These things, he asserts, are the result of "the character inherent in the American people." If so, what *has* government done, according to Thoreau? What purpose does it serve? Why is it necessary, in his view?

2. Thoreau spends a great deal of time discussing slavery, which was still legal and widespread in the United States when he wrote this essay. Why is the issue of slavery important to his larger point about civil disobedience?

3. What is Thoreau's view of patriotism? How does patriotism figure into his argument about resistance to government?

4. Under what circumstances does Thoreau believe it is acceptable or even necessary for a person to break the law? On what principles does Thoreau base his arguments for breaking the law?

5. How does Thoreau define freedom? How does his definition of freedom inform his arguments about resisting government? Do you think most Americans would agree with his definition of freedom today? Why or why not?

6. What is the ideal state, in Thoreau's view? Do you think most Americans today would agree with Thoreau about the

ideal government? Do you? Why or why not?

Exploring the Issues

1. How would you describe Thoreau's tone in this essay? How effectively do you think his tone helps him convey his arguments? How do you think Thoreau's tone compares with the tone of political debate in the United States today, especially in view of the increase in television and radio political talk shows as well as Internet blogs?

2. In paragraph 20, Thoreau argues that Abolitionists— that is, people who wanted to abolish slavery—were justified in withdrawing their support for the government because "they have God on their side." Today, there are a number of controversies, like those surrounding capital punishment and abortion, in which one side or another claims to have God on its side. In some cases, people concerned about these issues advocate violence, as in the case of some radical antiabortion groups that have bombed abortion clinics. What do you think Thoreau would say about such situations, if he were alive today? In what ways do you think his argument for civil disobedience might intensify these controversies? In what ways might his essay help us address such controversies?

3. Thoreau himself did many of the things that he argues honest people should do. For example, he lived a relatively independent life with few possessions, which he says people of conscience may have to do (par. 24); he refused to pay certain taxes to support a government that he believed was ʻunjust, for which he was jailed (par. 26). Because his writing had made him famous, Thoreau's readers would likely have known these things about him. How might that knowledge have affected the strength of his arguments? Do

you think Thoreau intentionally included references to his own life to make his essay more persuasive to readers of his day? Explain. In what ways does this knowledge about Thoreau affect your response to his arguments?

Entering the Conversations

1. Write an essay in which you discuss what you believe is the relevance (or irrelevance) of Thoreau's argument about civil disobedience today.

2. Write an essay describing an experience in which you resisted authority. In your essay, explain the circumstances you were in and why you decided to resist authority. Try to tell your story in a way that conveys your view of authority and individual responsibility.

 INFOTRAC

3. American history includes famous examples of civil disobedience. But there are many other less famous examples of civil disobedience today. Select one or more instances

of civil disobedience that you know about and investigate those events. What issues were involved? What laws or policies were those who engaged in civil disobedience resisting? What did they hope to accomplish? What led to their actions? How did the authorities respond? What was the outcome of the actions? Try to answer these questions through your research, using InfoTrac College Edition, your library, and other appropriate resources. Then write a report about the events. In your report, describe the situations and issues, and explain the outcomes of the acts of civil disobedience that occurred. Try to draw conclusions on the basis of these events about resisting power. Alternatively, create a web site based on your research.

4. Using Thoreau's main argument in this essay, write a letter to the editor of your local newspaper or some other appropriate publication explaining why you think civil disobedience is (or is not) justified in the case of an important current controversy (such as capital punishment, abortion, or a war involving U.S. troops).

If you consider the fact that only two other Americans have a national holiday celebrating their lives (Presidents' Day honors George Washington and Abraham Lincoln), then it's clear that Martin Luther King, Jr., (1929–1968) occupies a very special place in American history. King was not an elected official or a military leader. In fact, his fame

Letter FROM Birmingham Jail

arose from his resistance to government. His leadership during the Civil Rights Movement helped change discriminatory laws and racist attitudes in the United States, and he is honored for those efforts. But as the following letter reveals, King's views were not limited to racial issues and the desire for racial equality, for which he is most remembered; he was also a political leader of a kind. This letter, which he wrote from a jail cell after being arrested during demonstrations he led against segregation in Alabama in 1963, presents a philosophy of nonviolent resistance to government when that government has unjust policies or laws. King's philosophy of nonviolent resistance, which cuts across racial lines, has been invoked by people facing oppression throughout the world.

It's worth noting that the Martin Luther King, Jr., holiday was controversial from its beginnings. President Ronald Reagan signed it

MARTIN LUTHER KING, JR.

My Dear Fellow Clergymen:

April 16, 1963

While confined here in the Birmingham city jail, I came across your recent statement calling my present activities "unwise and untimely." Seldom do I pause to answer criticism of my work and ideas. If I sought to answer all the criticisms that cross my desk, my secretaries would have little time for anything other than such correspondence in the course of the day, and I would have no time for constructive work. But since I feel that you are men of genuine good will and that your criticisms are sincerely put forth, I want to try to answer your statement in what I hope will be patient and reasonable terms.

I think I should indicate why I am here in Birmingham, since you have been influenced by the view which argues against "outsiders coming in." I have the honor of serving as president of the Southern Christian Leadership Conference, an organization operating in every southern state, with headquarters in Atlanta, Georgia. We have some eighty-five affiliated organizations across the South, and one of them is the Alabama Christian Movement for Human Rights. Frequently we share staff, educational, and financial resources with our affiliates. Several months ago the affiliate here in Birmingham asked us to be on call to engage in a nonviolent direct-action program if such were deemed necessary. We readily consented, and when the hour came we lived up to our promise. So I, along with several members of my staff, am here because I was invited here. I am here because I have organizational ties here.

But more basically, I am in Birmingham because injustice is here. Just as the prophets of the eighth century B.C. left their villages and carried their "thus saith the Lord" far beyond the boundaries of their home towns, and just as the Apostle Paul left his village of Tarsus and carried the gospel of Jesus Christ to the far corners of the Greco-Roman world, so am I compelled to carry the gospel of freedom beyond my own home town. Like Paul, I must constantly respond to the Macedonian call for aid.

Moreover, I am cognizant of the interrelatedness of all communities and states. I cannot sit idly by in Atlanta and not be concerned about what happens in Birmingham. Injustice anywhere is a threat to justice everywhere. We are caught in an inescapable network of mutuality, tied in a single garment of destiny. Whatever affects one directly, affects all indirectly. Never again can we afford to live with the narrow, provincial, "OUTSIDE AGITATOR" idea. Anyone who lives inside the United States can never be considered an outsider anywhere within its bounds.

You deplore the demonstrations taking place in Birmingham. But your statement, I am sorry to say, fails to express a similar concern for the conditions that brought about the demonstrations. I am sure that none of you would want to rest content with the superficial kind of social analysis that deals merely with effects and does not grapple with underlying causes. It is unfortunate that demonstrations are taking place in Birmingham, but it is even more unfortunate that the city's white power structure left the Negro community with no alternative.

In any nonviolent campaign there are four basic steps: collection of the facts to determine whether injustices exist; negotiation; self-purification; and direct action. We have gone through all these steps in Birmingham. There can be no gainsaying the fact that racial injustice engulfs this community. Birmingham is probably the most thoroughly segregated city in the United States. Its ugly record of brutality is widely known. Negroes have experienced grossly unjust treatment in courts. There have been more unsolved bombings of Negro homes and churches in Birmingham than in any other city in the nation. These are the hard, brutal facts of the case. On the basis of these conditions, Negro leaders sought to negotiate with the city fathers. But the latter consistently refused to engage in good-faith negotiation.

into law in 1983 in the midst of intense debate, but some states refused to recognize it. Many people believe that racism explains this opposition to the holiday, but it may also be that many Americans remain uncomfortable with the idea of honoring someone who resisted government. Indeed, in his letter, King argues that all people have a moral responsibility to resist unjust laws, and he charged that complacency amounted to support for injustice. As you read, you might reflect on your own views about your responsibilities as a citizen. How would you respond to King's call for resistance to injustice?

Martin Luther King, Jr.'s, efforts in Birmingham, Alabama, and elsewhere during the Civil Rights Movement helped secure the passage of the Civil Rights Bill in 1963. He was honored for his work with the Nobel Prize for Peace in 1964. An assassin's bullet ended his life in 1968. ▼

5

CONVERSATIONS: "OUTSIDE AGITATOR"
During the Civil Rights Movement in the 1960s and 1970s, this phrase—"outside agitator," which King mentions in paragraph 4—was often used by law enforcement and government officials to describe protesters. Some people considered the phrase an insult intended to suggest that protesters were actually connected to communist organizations and other groups hostile to the United States. Notice in paragraph 4 how King subtly shifts the focus of the phrase from "agitator" to "outsider." He then undermines the phrase by arguing that since we are all interrelated, no one can be considered an "outsider." Although this term is rarely used today, it is a good example of how words or phrases acquire meanings in certain contexts.

STRATEGIES: RESPONDING TO CRITICISM

King's letter was a response to a statement released by eight White Alabama clergymen who objected to the demonstrations King led against segregation in Alabama; they called for both Whites and Blacks to "observe the principles of law and order and common sense." It may be that King originally intended this letter to be read only by those clergy, but given King's stature as a national leader of the Civil Rights Movement, it is likely that he knew his letter would be read by many others. In that sense, his use of the second person *you* may have several meanings. Consider how the apparent rhetorical situation—a letter from one clergyman to others—enables King to accomplish certain goals with this letter that another situation—for example, a letter to the editor of a newspaper or to the governor of Alabama—might not. You might also consider that many of the Christian gospels were written in the form of letters from one of the apostles to specific groups of people (for example, to the Corinthians). Consider, too, how differently we might read this letter today compared with 1963 at the height of the Civil Rights Movement, a time of great social and political conflict in the United States.

Then, last September, came the opportunity to talk with leaders of Birmingham's economic community. In the course of the negotiations, certain promises were made by the merchants—for example, to remove the stores' humiliating racial signs. On the basis of these promises, the Reverend Fred Shuttlesworth and the leaders of the Alabama Christian Movement for Human Rights agreed to a moratorium on all demonstrations. As the weeks and months went by, we realized that we were the victims of a broken promise. A few signs, briefly removed, returned; the others remained.

As in so many past experiences, our hopes had been blasted, and the shadow of deep disappointment settled upon us. We had no alternative except to prepare for direct action, whereby we would present our very bodies as means of laying our case before the conscience of the local and the national community. Mindful of the difficulties involved, we decided to undertake a process of self-purification. We began a series of workshops on nonviolence, and we repeatedly asked ourselves: "Are you able to accept blows without retaliating?" "Are you able to endure the ordeal of jail?" We decided to schedule our direct-action program for the Easter season, realizing that except for Christmas, this is the main shopping period of the year. Knowing that a strong economic-withdrawal program would be the byproduct of direct action, we felt that this would be the best time to bring pressure to bear on the merchants for the needed change.

Then it occurred to us that Birmingham's mayoral election was coming up in March, and we speedily decided to postpone action until after election day. When we discovered that the Commissioner of Public Safety, Eugene "Bull" Connor, had piled up enough votes to be in the run-off, we decided again to postpone action until the day after the run-off so that the demonstrations could not be used to cloud the issues. Like many others, we waited to see Mr. Connor defeated, and to this end we endured postponement after postponement. Having aided in this community need, we felt that our direct-action program could be delayed no longer.

10   You may well ask, "Why direct action? Why sit-ins, marches, and so forth? Isn't negotiation a better path?" You are quite right in calling for negotiation. Indeed, this is the very purpose of direct action. Nonviolent direct action seeks to create such a crisis and foster such a tension that a community which has constantly refused to negotiate is forced to confront the issue. It seeks so to dramatize the issue that it can no longer be ignored. My citing the creation of tension as part of the work of the nonviolent resister may sound rather shocking. But I

must confess that I am not afraid of the word "tension." I have earnestly opposed violent tension, but there is a type of constructive, nonviolent tension which is necessary for growth. Just as Socrates felt that it was necessary to create a tension in the mind so that individuals could rise from the bondage of myths and half-truths to the unfettered realm of creative analysis and objective appraisal, so must we see the need for nonviolent gadflies to create the kind of tension in society that will help men rise from the dark depths of prejudice and racism to the majestic heights of understanding and brotherhood.

The purpose of our direct-action program is to create a situation so crisis-packed that it will inevitably open the door to negotiation. I therefore concur with you in your call for negotiation. Too long has our beloved Southland been bogged down in a tragic effort to live in monologue rather than dialogue.

One of the basic points in your statement is that the action that I and my associates have taken in Birmingham is untimely. Some have asked: "Why didn't you give the new city administration time to act?" The only answer that I can give to this query is that the new Birmingham administration must be prodded about as much as the outgoing one, before it will act. We are sadly mistaken if we feel that the election of Albert Boutwell as mayor will bring the millennium to Birmingham. While Mr. Boutwell is a much more gentle person than Mr. Connor, they are both segregationists, dedicated to maintenance of the status quo. I have hoped that Mr. Boutwell will be reasonable enough to see the futility of massive resistance to desegregation. But he will not see this without pressure from devotees of civil rights. My friends, I must say to you that we have not made a single gain in civil rights without determined legal and nonviolent pressure. Lamentably, it is an historical fact that privileged groups seldom give up their privileges voluntarily. Individuals may see the moral light and voluntarily give up their unjust posture; but, as **REINHOLD NIEBUHR** has reminded us, groups tend to be more immoral than individuals.

GLOSS: REINHOLD NIEBUHR
Protestant theologian Reinhold Niebuhr (1892–1971) examined the relationship between Christianity and modern politics.

We know through painful experience that freedom is never voluntarily given by the oppressor; it must be demanded by the oppressed. Frankly, I have yet to engage in a direct-action campaign that was "well timed" in the view of those who have not suffered unduly from the disease of segregation. For years now I have heard the word "Wait!" It rings in the ear of every Negro with piercing familiarity. This "Wait" has almost always meant "Never." We must come to see, with one of our distinguished jurists, that "justice too long delayed is justice denied."

We have waited for more than 340 years for our constitutional and God-given rights. The nations of Asia and Africa are moving with jet-like speed toward gaining political independence, but we still creep at horse-and-buggy pace toward gaining a cup of coffee at a lunch counter. Perhaps it is easy for those who have never felt the stinging darts of segregation to say, "Wait." But when you have seen vicious

STRATEGIES: A HUMAN FACE
Notice how King moves from abstract
principles to concrete details describing
the impact of racism and the laws he
considers unjust. He includes a series of
vivid images to put a human face on the
abstract arguments that he makes.
Consider how this strategy helps King
make his appeal to his fellow clergy, who
all work with members of their own
congregations and who could appreciate
the human misery that King describes in
this passage.

mobs lynch your mothers and fathers at will and drown your sisters and brothers at whim; when you have seen hate-filled policemen curse, kick, and even kill your black brothers and sisters; when you see the vast majority of your twenty million Negro brothers smothering in an airtight cage of poverty in the midst of an affluent society; when you suddenly find your tongue twisted and your speech stammering as you seek to explain to your six-year-old daughter why she can't go to the public amusement park that has just been advertised on television, and see tears welling up in her eyes when she is told that Funtown is closed to colored children, and see ominous clouds of inferiority beginning to form in her little mental sky, and see her beginning to distort her personality by developing an unconscious bitterness toward white people; when you have to concoct an answer for a five-year-old son who is asking, "Daddy, why do white people treat colored people so mean?"; when you take a cross-country drive and find it necessary to sleep night after night in the uncomfortable corners of your automobile because no motel will accept you; when you are humiliated day in and day out by nagging signs reading "white" and "colored"; when your first name becomes "nigger," your middle name becomes "boy" (however old you are) and your last name becomes "John," and your wife and mother are never given the respected title "Mrs."; when you are harried by day and haunted by night by the fact that you are a Negro, living constantly at tiptoe stance, never quite knowing what to expect next, and are plagued with inner fears and outer resentments; when you are forever fighting a degenerating sense of "nobodiness"—then you will understand why we find it difficult to wait. There comes a time when the cup of endurance runs over, and men are no longer willing to be plunged into the abyss of despair. I hope, sirs, you can understand our legitimate and unavoidable impatience.

15   You express a great deal of anxiety over our willingness to break laws. This is certainly a legitimate concern. Since we so diligently urge people to obey **THE SUPREME COURT'S DECISION OF 1954** outlawing segregation in the public schools, at first glance it may seem rather paradoxical for us consciously to break laws. One may well ask: "How can you advocate breaking some laws and obeying others?" The answer lies in the fact that there are two types of laws; just and unjust. I would be the first to advocate obeying just laws. One has not only a legal but a moral responsibility to obey just laws. Conversely, one has a moral responsibility to disobey unjust laws. I would agree with St. Augustine that "an unjust law is no law at all."

Now, what is the difference between the two? How does one determine whether a law is just or unjust? A just law is a man-made code that squares with the moral law or the law of God. An unjust law is a code that is out of harmony with the moral law. To put it in the terms of St. Thomas Aquinas: An unjust law is a human law that is not rooted in eternal law and natural law. Any law that uplifts human person-

GLOSS: THE SUPREME COURT'S DECISION OF 1954
King refers here to the famous decision
by the U.S. Supreme Court in the case of
Brown v. *Board of Education of Topeka* in
which the Court overturned the policy of
providing "separate but equal" education
for Black children.

ality is just. Any law that degrades human personality is unjust. All segregation statutes are unjust because segregation distorts the soul and damages the personality. It gives the segregator a false sense of superiority and the segregated a false sense of inferiority. Segregation, to use the terminology of the Jewish philosopher Martin Buber, substitutes an "I–it" relationship for an "I–thou" relationship and ends up relegating persons to the status of things. Hence segregation is not only politically, economically, and sociologically unsound, it is morally wrong and sinful. **PAUL TILLICH** has said that sin is segregation. Is not segregation an existential expression of man's tragic separation, his awful estrangement, his terrible sinfulness? Thus it is that I can urge men to obey the 1954 decision of the Supreme Court, for it is morally right; and I can urge them to disobey segregation ordinances, for they are morally wrong.

GLOSS: PAUL TILLICH
Paul Tillich (1885–1965) was a Christian theologian who addressed basic philosophical questions of human existence.

Let us consider a more concrete example of just and unjust laws. An unjust law is a code that a numerical or power majority group compels a minority group to obey but does not make binding on itself. This is *difference* made legal. By the same token, a just law is a code that a majority compels a minority to follow and that it is willing to follow itself. This is *sameness* made legal.

Let me give another explanation. A law is unjust if it is inflicted on a minority that, as a result of being denied the right to vote, had no part in enacting or devising the law. Who can say that the legislature of Alabama which set up that state's segregation laws was democratically elected? Throughout Alabama all sorts of devious methods are used to prevent Negroes from becoming registered voters, and there are some counties in which, even though Negroes constitute a majority of the population, not a single Negro is registered. Can any law enacted under such circumstances be considered democratically structured?

Sometimes a law is just on its face and unjust in its application. For instance, I have been arrested on a charge of parading without a permit. Now, there is nothing wrong in having an ordinance which requires a permit for a parade. But such an ordinance becomes unjust when it is used to maintain segregation and to deny citizens the First-Amendment privilege of peaceful assembly and protest.

20   I hope you are able to see the distinction I am trying to point out. In no sense do I advocate evading or defying the law, as would the rabid segregationist. That would lead to anarchy. One who breaks an unjust law must do so openly, lovingly, and with a willingness to accept the penalty. I submit that an individual who breaks a law that conscience tells him is unjust, and who willingly accepts the penalty of imprisonment in order to arouse the conscience of the community over its injustice, is in reality expressing the highest respect for law.

Of course, there is nothing new about this kind of civil disobedience. It was evidenced sublimely in the refusal of Shadrach, Meshach, and Abednego to obey the laws of **NEBUCHADNEZZAR,** on the ground that a higher moral law was at stake. It was practiced superbly by the early

Nebuchadnezzar was the King of Babylon, described in the Book of Daniel of the Bible, who forced the Jewish people to worship a gold image of himself. He ordered Shadrach, Meshach, and Abednego, who refused his command, thrown into a furnace, but according to the biblical account, they were unharmed.

HUNGARIAN FREEDOM FIGHTERS
In 1956, Hungarian citizens temporarily overthrew the communist dictatorship in their country. Unwilling to confront the Soviet Union, Western democracies stood by as the Red Army suppressed the revolt by force.

Christians, who were willing to face hungry lions and the excruciating pain of chopping blocks rather than submit to certain unjust laws of the Roman Empire. To a degree, academic freedom is a reality today because Socrates practiced civil disobedience. In our own nation, the Boston Tea Party represented a massive act of civil disobedience.

We should never forget that everything Adolf Hitler did in Germany was "legal" and everything the **HUNGARIAN FREEDOM FIGHTERS** did in Hungary was "illegal." It was "illegal" to aid and comfort a Jew in Hitler's Germany. Even so, I am sure that, had I lived in Germany at the time, I would have aided and comforted my Jewish brothers. If today I lived in a Communist country where certain principles dear to the Christian faith are suppressed, I would openly advocate disobeying that country's anti-religious laws.

I must make two honest confessions to you, my Christian and Jewish brothers. First, I must confess that over the past few years I have been gravely disappointed with the white moderate. I have almost reached the regrettable conclusion that the Negro's great stumbling block in his stride toward freedom is not the White Citizen's Counciler or the Ku Klux Klanner, but the white moderate, who is more devoted to "order" than to justice; who prefers a negative peace which is the absence of tension to a positive peace which is the presence of justice; who constantly says, "I agree with you in the goal you seek, but I cannot agree with your methods of direct action"; who paternalistically believes he can set the timetable for another man's freedom; who lives by a mythical concept of time and who constantly advises the Negro to wait for a "more convenient season." Shallow understanding from people of good will is more frustrating than absolute misunderstanding from people of ill will. Lukewarm acceptance is much more bewildering than outright rejection.

I had hoped that the white moderate would understand that law and order exist for the purpose of establishing justice and that when they fail in this purpose they become the dangerously structured dams that block the flow of social progress. I had hoped that the white moderate would understand that the present tension in the South is a necessary phase of the transition from an obnoxious negative peace, in which the Negro passively accepted his unjust plight, to a substantive and positive peace, in which all men will respect the dignity and worth of human personality. Actually, we who engage in nonviolent direct action are not the creators of tension. We merely bring to the surface the hidden tension that is already alive. We bring it out in the open, where it can be seen and dealt with. Like a boil that can never be cured so long as it is covered up but must be opened with all its ugliness to the natural medicines of air and light, injustice must be exposed, with all the tension its exposure creates, to the light of human conscience and the air of national opinion, before it can be cured.

25   In your statement you assert that our actions, even though peaceful, must be condemned because they precipitate violence. But is this

a logical assertion? Isn't this like condemning a robbed man because his possession of money precipitated the evil act of robbery? Isn't this like condemning Socrates because his unswerving commitment to truth and his philosophical inquiries precipitated the act by the misguided populace in which they made him drink hemlock? Isn't this like condemning Jesus because his unique God-consciousness and never-ceasing devotion to God's will precipitated the evil act of crucifixion? We must come to see that, as the federal courts have consistently affirmed, it is wrong to urge an individual to cease his efforts to gain his basic constitutional rights because the quest may precipitate violence. Society must protect the robbed and punish the robber.

I had also hoped that the white moderate would reject the myth concerning time in relation to the struggle for freedom. I have just received a letter from a white brother in Texas. He writes: "All Christians know that the colored people will receive equal rights eventually, but it is possible that you are in too great a religious hurry. It has taken Christianity almost two thousand years to accomplish what it has. The teachings of Christ take time to come to earth." Such an attitude stems from a tragic misconception of time, from the strangely irrational notion that there is something in the very flow of time that will inevitably cure all ills. Actually, time itself is neutral; it can be used either destructively or constructively. More and more I feel that the people of ill will have used time much more effectively than have the people of good will. We will have to repent in this generation not merely for the hateful words and actions of the bad people, but for the appalling silence of the good people. Human progress never rolls in on wheels of inevitability; it comes through the tireless efforts of men willing to be coworkers with God, and without this hard work, time itself becomes an ally of the forces of social stagnation. We must use time creatively, in the knowledge that the time is always ripe to do right. Now is the time to make real the promise of democracy and transform our pending national elegy into a creative psalm of brotherhood. Now is the time to lift our national policy from the quicksand of racial injustice to the solid rock of human dignity.

You speak of our activity in Birmingham as extreme. At first I was rather disappointed that fellow clergymen would see my nonviolent efforts as those of an extremist. I began thinking about the fact that I stand in the middle of two opposing forces in the Negro community. One is a force of complacency, made up in part of Negroes who, as a result of long years of oppression, are so drained of self-respect and a sense of "somebodiness" that they have adjusted to segregation; and in part of a few middle-class Negroes who, because of a degree of academic and economic security and because in some ways they profit by segregation, have become insensitive to the problems of the masses. The other force is one of bitterness and hatred, and it comes perilously close to advocating violence. It is expressed in the various black nationalist groups that are springing up across the nation, the largest and best-known being Elijah Muhammad's Muslim movement. Nourished by the Negro's frustration over the continued existence of racial discrimination, this movement is made up of people who have lost faith in America, who have absolutely repudiated Christianity, and who have concluded that the white man is an incorrigible "devil."

I have tried to stand between these two forces, saying that we need emulate neither the "do-nothingism" of the complacent nor the hatred and despair of the black nationalist. For there is the more excellent way of love and nonviolent protest. I am grateful to God that, through the influence of the Negro church, the way of nonviolence became an integral part of our struggle.

If this philosophy had not emerged, by now many streets of the South would, I am convinced, be flowing with blood. And I am further convinced that if our white brothers dismiss as "rabble-rousers" and "outside agitators" those of us who employ nonviolent direct action, and if they refuse to support our nonviolent efforts, millions of Negroes will, out of frustration and despair, seek solace and security in black-nationalist ideologies—a development that would inevitably lead to a frightening racial nightmare.

30 Oppressed people cannot remain oppressed forever. The yearning for freedom eventually manifests itself, and that is what has happened to the American Negro. Something within has reminded him of his birthright of freedom, and something without has reminded him that it can be gained. Consciously or unconsciously, he has been caught up by the *Zeitgeist,* and with his black brothers of Africa and his brown and yellow brothers of Asia, South America, and the Caribbean, the United States Negro is moving with a sense of great urgency toward the promised land of racial justice. If one recognizes this vital urge that has engulfed the Negro community, one should readily understand why public demonstrations are taking place. The Negro has many pent-up resentments and latent frustrations, and he must release them. So let him march; let him make prayer pilgrimages to the city hall; let him go on freedom rides—and try to understand why he must do so. If his repressed emotions are not released in nonviolent ways, they will seek expression through violence; this is not a threat but a fact of history. So I have not said to my people, "Get rid of your discontent." Rather, I have tried to say that this normal and healthy discontent can be channeled into the creative outlet of nonviolent direct action. And now this approach is being termed extremist.

But though I was initially disappointed at being categorized as an extremist, as I continued to think about the matter I gradually gained a measure of satisfaction from the label. Was not Jesus an extremist for love: "Love your enemies, bless them that curse you, do good to them that hate you, and pray for them which despitefully use you, and persecute you." Was not Amos an extremist for justice: "Let justice roll down like waters and righteousness like an everflowing stream." Was not Paul an extremist for the Christian gospel: "I bear in my body the marks of the Lord Jesus." Was not Martin Luther an extremist: "Here I stand; I cannot do otherwise, so help me God." And John Bunyan: "I will stay in jail to the end of my days before I make a butchery of my conscience." And Abraham Lincoln: "This nation cannot survive half slave and half free." And Thomas Jefferson: "We hold these truths to be selfevident, that all men are created equal. . . ." So the question is not whether we will be extremists, but what kind of extremists we will be. Will we be extremists for hate or for love? Will we be extremists for the preservation of injustice or for the extension of justice? In that dramatic scene on Calvary's hill three men were crucified. We must never forget that all three were crucified for the same crime—the crime of extremism. Two were extremists for immorality, and thus fell below their environment. The other, Jesus Christ, was an extremist for love, truth, and goodness, and thereby rose above his environment. Perhaps the South, the nation, and the world are in dire need of creative extremists.

I had hoped that the white moderate would see this need. Perhaps I was too optimistic; perhaps I expected too much. I suppose I should have realized that few members of the oppressor race can understand the deep groans and passionate yearnings of the oppressed race, and still fewer have the vision to see that injustice must be rooted out by strong, persistent, and determined action. I am thankful, however, that some of our white brothers in the South have grasped the meaning of this social revolution and committed themselves to it. They are still all too few in quantity, but they are big in quality. Some—such as Ralph McGill, Lillian Smith, Harry Golden, James McBride Dabbs, Ann Braden, and Sarah Patton Boyle—have written about our struggle in eloquent and prophetic terms. Others have marched with us down nameless streets of the South. They have languished in filthy, roach-infested jails, suffering the abuse and brutality of policemen who view them as "dirty nigger-lovers." Unlike so many of their moderate brothers and sisters, they have recognized the urgency of the moment and sensed the need for powerful "action" antidotes to combat the disease of segregation.

Let me take note of my other major disappointment. I have been so greatly disappointed with the white church and its leadership. Of course, there are some notable exceptions. I am not unmindful of the fact that each of you has taken some significant stands on this issue. I commend you, Reverend Stallings, for your Christian stand on this past Sunday, in welcoming Negroes to your worship service on a nonsegregated basis. I commend the Catholic leaders of this state for integrating Spring Hill College several years ago.

But despite these notable exceptions, I must honestly reiterate that I have been disappointed with the church. I do not say this as one of those negative critics who can always find something wrong with the church. I say this as a minister of the gospel, who loves the church; who was nurtured in its bosom; who has been sustained by its spiritual blessings and who will remain true to it as long as the cord of life shall lengthen.

35   When I was suddenly catapulted into the leadership of the bus protest in Montgomery, Alabama, a few years ago, I felt we would be supported by the white church. I felt that the white ministers, priests, and rabbis of the South would be among our strongest allies. Instead, some have been outright opponents, refusing to understand the freedom movement and misrepresenting its leaders; all too many others have been more cautious than courageous and have remained silent behind the anesthetizing security of stained-glass windows.

   In spite of my shattered dreams, I came to Birmingham with the hope that the white religious leadership of this community would see the justice of our cause and, with deep moral concern, would serve as the channel through which our just grievances could reach the power structure. I had hoped that each of you would understand. But again I have been disappointed.

   There was a time when the church was very powerful—in the time when the early Christians rejoiced at being deemed worthy to suffer for what they believed. In those days the church was not merely a thermometer that recorded the ideas and principles of popular opinion; it was a thermostat that transformed the mores of society. Whenever the early Christians entered a town, the people in power became disturbed and immediately sought to convict the Christians for being "disturbers of the peace" and "outside agitators." But the Christians pressed on, in the conviction that they were "a colony of heaven," called to obey God rather than man. Small in number, they were big in commitment. They were too God-intoxicated to be "astronomically intimidated." By their effort and example they brought an end to such ancient evils as infanticide and gladiatorial contests.

   Things are different now. So often the contemporary church is a weak, ineffectual voice with an uncertain sound. So often it is an archdefender of the status quo. Far from being disturbed by the presence of the church, the power structure of the average community is consoled by the church's silent—and often even vocal—sanction of things as they are.

   But the judgment of God is upon the church as never before. If today's church does not recapture the sacrificial spirit of the early church, it will lose its authenticity, forfeit the loyalty of millions, and be dismissed as an irrelevant social club with no meaning for the twentieth century. Every day I meet young people whose disappointment with the church has turned into outright disgust.

40   Perhaps I have once again been too optimistic. Is organized religion too inextricably bound to the status quo to save our nation and the world? Perhaps I must turn my faith to the inner spiritual church, the church within the church, as the true **EKKLESIA** and the hope of the world. But again I am thankful to God that some noble souls from

GLOSS: *EKKLESIA*
Ekklesia is a Greek word meaning assembly, congregation, or church.

the ranks of organized religion have broken loose from the paralyz-
ing chains of conformity and joined us as active partners in the struggle for freedom. They have left their secure congregations and walked
the streets of Albany, Georgia, with us. They have gone down the
highways of the South on torturous rides for freedom. Yes, they have
gone to jail with us. Some have been dismissed from their churches,
have lost the support of their bishops and fellow ministers. But they
have acted in the faith that right defeated is stronger than evil triumphant. Their witness has been the spiritual salt that has preserved the
true meaning of the gospel in these troubled times. They have carved
a tunnel of hope through the dark mountain of disappointment.

I hope the church as a whole will meet the challenge of this decisive
hour. But even if the church does not come to the aid of justice, I have
no despair about the future. I have no fear about the outcome of our
struggle in Birmingham, even if our motives are at present misunderstood. We will reach the goal of freedom in Birmingham and all over
the nation, because the goal of America is freedom. Abused and
scorned though we may be, our destiny is tied up with America's destiny. Before the pilgrims landed at Plymouth, we were here. Before the
pen of Jefferson etched the majestic words of the Declaration of Independence across the pages of history, we were here. For more than two
centuries our forebears labored in this country without wages; they
made cotton king; they built the homes of their masters while suffering
gross injustice and shameful humiliation—and yet out of a bottomless
vitality they continued to thrive and develop. If the inexpressible cruel-
ties of slavery could not stop us, the opposition we now face will surely
fail. We will win our freedom because the sacred heritage of our nation
and the eternal will of God are embodied in our echoing demands.

Before closing I feel impelled to mention one other point in your
statement that has troubled me profoundly. You warmly commended
the Birmingham police force for keeping "order" and "preventing
violence." I doubt that you would have so warmly commended the
police force if you had seen its dogs sinking their teeth into unarmed,
nonviolent Negroes. I doubt that you would so quickly commend the
policemen if you were to observe their ugly and inhumane treatment
of Negroes here in the city jail; if you were to watch them push and
curse old Negro women and young Negro girls; if you were to see
them slap and kick old Negro men and young boys; if you were to
observe them, as they did on two occasions, refuse to give us food
because we wanted to sing our grace together. I cannot join you in
your praise of the Birmingham police department.

It is true that the police have exercised a degree of discipline in
handling the demonstrators. In this sense they have conducted themselves rather "nonviolently" in public. But for what purpose? To preserve the evil system of segregation. Over the past few years I have
consistently preached that nonviolence demands that the means we
use must be as pure as the ends we seek. I have tried to make clear

© AP Photo/Bill Hudson

CONVERSATIONS: POLICE BRUTALITY

During the Civil Rights Movement, photographs like the one on the left, taken during King's march on Birmingham, were published in U.S. newspapers, and they helped galvanize national support for the movement. Consider how such images can communicate some of the same messages that King is conveying in his written letter. Consider, too, the effects that images can have in movements such as King's or in more recent events, such as the beating of Rodney King by Los Angeles police in 1991 (shown in the photo on the right).

MAR. 3 1991

GLOSS: JAMES MEREDITH

In the fall of 1962, James Meredith was the first Black student to attend the University of Mississippi. When he enrolled in the university, riots broke out on campus.

that it is wrong to use immoral means to attain moral ends. But now I must affirm that it is just as wrong, or perhaps even more so, to use moral means to preserve immoral ends. Perhaps Mr. Connor and his policemen have been rather nonviolent in public, as was Chief Pritchett in Albany, Georgia, but they have used the moral means of nonviolence to maintain the immoral end of racial injustice. As T. S. Eliot has said, "The last temptation is the greatest treason: To do the right deed for the wrong reason."

I wish you had commended the Negro sit-inners and demonstrators of Birmingham for their sublime courage, their willingness to suffer, and their amazing discipline in the midst of great provocation. One day the South will recognize its real heroes. They will be the **JAMES MEREDITHS,** with the noble sense of purpose that enables them to face jeering and hostile mobs, and with the agonizing loneliness that characterizes the life of the pioneer. They will be old, oppressed, battered Negro women, symbolized in a seventy-two-year-old woman in Montgomery, Alabama, who rose up with a sense of dignity and with her people decided not to ride segregated buses, and who responded with ungrammatical profundity to one who inquired about her weariness: "My feets is tired, but my soul is at rest." They will be the young high school and college students, the young ministers of the gospel and a host of their elders, courageously and nonviolently sitting in at lunch counters and willingly going to jail for conscience's sake. One day the South will know that when these disinherited children of God sat down at lunch counters, they were in reality standing up for what is best in the American dream and for the most sacred values in our Judeo-Christian heritage, thereby bringing our nation back to those great wells of democracy which were dug deep by the founding fathers in their formulation of the Constitution and the Declaration of Independence.

45   Never before have I written so long a letter. I'm afraid it is much too long to take your precious time. I can assure you that it would have been much shorter if I had been writing from a comfortable desk, but what else can one do when he is alone in a narrow jail cell, other than write long letters, think long thoughts, and pray long prayers?

If I have said anything in this letter that overstates the truth and indicates an unreasonable impatience, I beg you to forgive me. If I have said anything that understates the truth and indicates my having a patience that allows me to settle for anything less than brotherhood, I beg God to forgive me.

I hope this letter finds you strong in the faith. I also hope that circumstances will soon make it possible for me to meet each of you, not as an integrationist or a civil-rights leader but as a fellow clergyman and a Christian brother. Let us all hope that the dark clouds of racial prejudice will soon pass away and the deep fog of misunderstanding will be lifted from our fear-drenched communities, and in some not too distant tomorrow the radiant stars of love and brotherhood will shine over our great nation with all their scintillating beauty.

Yours for the cause of Peace and Brotherhood,
Martin Luther King, Jr.

Understanding the Text

1. How does King explain his presence in Birmingham, Alabama? Why is it important for him to do so?

2. In his letter, King explains that there are four steps to a nonviolent campaign (par. 6), the last of which is "direct action." Why is it important for him to explain these steps? What is he able to reveal to his readers about the situation in Birmingham and about his movement by explaining in detail the need for direct action?

3. How does King justify breaking the law? How does he distinguish between a just law and an unjust law? What is the fundamental basis on which to judge laws, in King's view? Do you find his justification for breaking unjust laws persuasive? Why or why not?

4. Why does King criticize "the white moderate"? In what sense are White moderates, who agree with King's demands for civil rights for Blacks, an obstacle to change, in King's view? Why do you think King spends so much time discussing White moderates?

5. What are the advantages of nonviolent resistance for trying to change unjust laws, according to King?

6. Why does King not object to being labeled an "extremist"? How does King's discussion of this term compare with the way the term tends to be used today? Do you think Americans would find his acceptance of the term *extremist* convincing today? Explain.

Exploring the Issues

1. How would you describe King's voice in this letter? To what extent do you think his voice contributes to the persuasiveness (or the lack of persuasiveness) of his arguments? How does his voice in this letter fit in with your own sense of Martin Luther King, Jr., from what you have read or heard?

2. Throughout his essay, King makes references to many writers, thinkers, and well-known texts, including the Bible and works of philosophy. How do these references contribute to King's argument? What do they reveal about King as a writer and a person? What do they suggest about his sense of his audience? Do you think these references are effective? Why or why not?

3. In this letter, King is responding to a written statement by eight White ministers who criticized his efforts to fight segregation in Birmingham, Alabama. As a reader, you do not have that statement in front of you, but King refers to it several times in this letter. What effect do you think these references to the statement have on King's overall argument? Does it make any difference that you do not have the White ministers' statement? Explain.

4. Americans have always been concerned about mixing religion and politics. The U.S. Constitution has several provisions that prohibit the government either from adopting an official religion or from preventing citizens from worshipping as they choose. Yet King bases his arguments for resisting unjust laws largely on his own Christian beliefs. What do you think King's use of religious beliefs might suggest about the role of religion in American society? How do you think Americans today might react to King's views about the relationship between religion and politics?

Entering the Conversations

1. Write an essay describing an experience you've had when you resisted authority as a result of your beliefs or principles.

2. The national holiday honoring Martin Luther King, Jr., was controversial from the time it was first proposed by President Ronald Reagan in 1983. Some Americans still oppose the holiday. Write a letter to the editor of your local newspaper or to one of your state or local elected officials expressing your views about the Martin Luther King, Jr., holiday. In your letter, draw on King's "Letter from a Birmingham Jail" to support your position about the holiday.

INFOTRAC

3. Martin Luther King, Jr., was a controversial figure during his life, and he remains so even many years after his death in 1968. Using InfoTrac College Edition, your library, and other appropriate resources, investigate King's life and his work as a civil rights leader. Try to identify the reasons he was disliked, opposed, and even hated by some people but revered by so many others, and try to understand the opposition to the national holiday that was established in his honor. Then write a report in which you present what you learned about King and the controversy surrounding him. Try to draw conclusions about the consequences of challenging power.

4. Working with a group of classmates, create a web site in which you present your view of Martin Luther King, Jr.'s, efforts as a civil rights activist and especially of his views about nonviolent resistance to government. Design your site for a general audience and emphasize what you think are the most important or problematic of King's ideas about nonviolent resistance.

5. Write an essay in which you analyze King's views about nonviolent resistance in terms of controversies that are occurring today. Select one or more controversies in which citizens object to and oppose their government's policies or laws (such as the war in Iraq, abortion, or environmental policies), and use those situations to discuss what you see as the importance of King's ideas. Discuss as well concerns you might have about his views.

In the following essay, well-known scholar *and cultural critic bell hooks writes that she has long had "the craving to speak, to have a voice, and not just any voice but one that could be identified as belonging to me." That statement might serve as a good summary of the main theme of hooks's impressive body of work: the importance of being heard. And*

Talking Back

being heard is one way to challenge power. hooks grew up poor in the rural American South, where ideas about race and gender were as powerful in shaping her life and the lives of those around her as laws or government policies. To challenge power, then, sometimes means to challenge ways of thinking; it means questioning conventional attitudes and beliefs. And most of all, it means not remaining silent. As she does in this essay, hooks has written relentlessly about speaking out and claiming one's voice. At the heart of her message is the idea that what makes us human, what gives us dignity, is not language itself but the willingness to use it to give voice to our concerns, especially in the face of injustice and inequality.

Although she is an academic, part of hooks's appeal is that her messages about race, gender, and culture reach beyond academic audiences. If she doesn't sound like an academic to you, it may be

BELL HOOKS

In the world of the southern black community I grew up in, "back talk" and "talking back" meant speaking as an equal to an authority figure. It meant daring to disagree and sometimes it just meant having an opinion. In the "old school," children were meant to be seen and not heard. My great-grandparents, grandparents, and parents were all from the old school. To make yourself heard if you were a child was to invite punishment, the back-hand lick, the slap across the face that would catch you unaware, or the feel of switches stinging your arms and legs.

To speak then when one was not spoken to was a courageous act—an act of risk and daring. And yet it was hard not to speak in warm rooms where heated discussions began at the crack of dawn, women's voices filling the air, giving orders, making threats, fussing. Black men may have excelled in the art of poetic preaching in the male-dominated church, but in the church of the home, where the everyday rules of how to live and how to act were established, it was black women who preached. There, black women spoke in a language so rich, so poetic, that it felt to me like being shut off from life, smothered to death if one were not allowed to participate.

because she tries not to so that you can enter the conversations that matter to her. She avoids academic jargon, even when she is writing about complicated or theoretical issues, and she draws on her own experiences in her essays and books in a way that is rare in academic writing. In this way, she uses writing as a powerful way to speak out and to challenge power.

For more information on bell hooks, see the introduction for "On Building a Community of Love" on page 256. ◪

CONVERSATIONS: SILENCE
Here and throughout this essay, hooks refers to silence or to being silent. But those terms mean something more than just being quiet. *Silence* in this context refers to the matter of who is allowed (or not allowed) to speak on the basis of cultural beliefs and social status. Cultural attitudes about race, gender, and related matters influence who can speak, who cannot, and who will listen. For example, White men may have more opportunity or authority to speak out in American culture than, for example, an Arab immigrant woman. So for hooks, to speak out is not just a matter of expressing your individual opinion; it is also a challenge to cultural attitudes, and it is a way to take responsibility for changing those attitudes. Silence, then, is accepting things as they are and acquiescing to unjust cultural attitudes (similar to Martin Luther King, Jr.'s, criticisms of "white moderates" on page 509 in his essay). This more specialized meaning of silence emerges from many academic and cultural discussions about race, gender, and related issues. Writers like hooks have helped give this term its special meanings.

It was in that world of woman talk (the men were often silent, often absent) that was born in me the craving to speak, to have a voice, and not just any voice but one that could be identified as belonging to me. To make my voice, I had to speak, to hear myself talk—and talk I did—darting in and out of grown folks' conversations and dialogues, answering questions that were not directed at me, endlessly asking questions, making speeches. Needless to say, the punishments for these acts of speech seemed endless. They were intended to silence me—the child—and more particularly the girl child. Had I been a boy, they might have encouraged me to speak believing that I might someday be called to preach. There was no "calling" for talking girls, no legitimized rewarded speech. The punishments I received for "talking back" were intended to suppress all possibility that I would create my own speech. That speech was to be suppressed so that the "right speech of womanhood" would emerge.

Within feminist circles, silence is often seen as the sexist "right speech of womanhood"—the sign of woman's submission to patriarchal authority. This emphasis on woman's silence may be an accurate remembering of what has taken place in the households of women from WASP backgrounds in the United States, but in black communities (and diverse ethnic communities), women have not been silent. Their voices can be heard. Certainly for black women, our struggle has not been to emerge from silence into speech but to change the nature and direction of our speech, to make a speech that compels listeners, one that is heard.

5   Our speech, "the right speech of womanhood," was often the soliloquy, the talking into thin air, the talking to ears that do not hear you— the talk that is simply not listened to. Unlike the black male preacher whose speech was to be heard, who was to be listened to, whose words were to be remembered, the voices of black women—giving orders, making threats, fussing—could be tuned out, could become a kind of background music, audible but not acknowledged as significant speech. Dialogue—the sharing of speech and recognition—took place not between mother and child or mother and male authority figure but among black women. I can remember watching fascinated as our mother talked with her mother, sisters, and women friends. The intimacy and intensity of their speech—the satisfaction they received from talking to one another, the pleasure, the joy. It was in this world of woman speech, loud talk, angry words, women with tongues quick and sharp, tender sweet tongues, touching our world with their words, that I made speech my birthright—and the right to voice, to authorship, a privilege I would not be denied. It was in that world and because of it that I came to dream of writing, to write.

Writing was a way to capture speech, to hold onto it, keep it close. And so I wrote down bits and pieces of conversations, confessing in cheap diaries that soon fell apart from too much handling, expressing the intensity of my sorrow, the anguish of speech—for I was always saying the wrong thing, asking the wrong questions. I could not confine my speech to the necessary corners and concerns of life. I hid these writings under my bed, in pillow stuffings, among faded underwear. When my sisters found and read them, they ridiculed and mocked me—poking fun. I felt violated, ashamed, as if the secret parts of my self had been exposed, brought into the open, and hung like newly clean laundry, out in the air for everyone to see. The fear of exposure, the fear that one's deepest emotions and innermost thoughts will be dismissed as mere nonsense, felt by so many young girls keeping diaries, holding and hiding speech, seems to me now one of the barriers that women have always needed and still need to destroy so that we are no longer pushed into secrecy or silence.

Despite my feelings of violation, of exposure, I continued to speak and write, choosing my hiding places well, learning to destroy work when no safe place could be found. I was never taught absolute silence, I was taught that it was important to speak but to talk a talk that was in itself a silence. Taught to speak and yet beware of the betrayal of too much heard speech, I experienced intense confusion and deep anxiety in my efforts to speak and write. Reciting poems at Sunday afternoon church service might be rewarded. Writing a poem (when one's time could be "better" spent sweeping, ironing, learning to cook) was luxurious activity, indulged in at the expense of others. Questioning authority, raising issues that were not deemed appropriate subjects brought pain, punishments—like telling mama I wanted to die before her because I could not live without her—that was crazy talk, crazy speech, the kind that would lead you to end up in a mental institution. "Little girl," I would be told, "if you don't stop all this crazy talk and crazy acting you are going to end up right out there at Western State."

MADNESS, not just physical abuse, was the punishment for too much talk if you were female. Yet even as this fear of madness haunted me, hanging over my writing like a monstrous shadow, I could not stop the words, making thought, writing speech. For this terrible madness which I feared, which I was sure was the destiny of daring women born to intense speech (after all, the authorities emphasized this point daily), was not as threatening as imposed silence, as suppressed speech.

Safety and sanity were to be sacrificed if I was to experience defiant speech. Though I risked them both, deep-seated fears and anxieties characterized my childhood days. I would speak but I would not ride a bike, play hardball, or hold the gray kitten. Writing about the ways we are traumatized in our growing-up years, psychoanalyst Alice Miller makes the point in *For Your Own Good* that it is not clear why childhood wounds become for some folk an opportunity to grow, to move forward rather than backward in the process of self-realization. Certainly, when I reflect on the trials of my growing-up years, the many punishments, I can see now that in resistance I learned to be vigilant in the nourishment of my spirit, to be tough, to courageously protect that spirit from forces that would break it.

CONVERSATIONS: MADNESS
When hooks mentions "madness" here, she is referring to cultural attitudes that expected women to defer to men and to keep their ideas and opinions to themselves. Women who did not do so, like hooks herself, were often believed to suffer from mental disorders. In fact, in the nineteenth and early twentieth centuries, women who were outspoken were often "treated" by doctors for mental illness. In recent decades, of course, such attitudes have been challenged, and many theorists have examined how medicine and other disciplines used science to justify sexist or racist beliefs. Understanding this historical context makes this passage in hooks's essay even more disturbing. It can help us see how frightening and risky it was for her to speak out.

10   While punishing me, my parents often spoke about the necessity of breaking my spirit. Now when I ponder the silences, the voices that are not heard, the voices of those wounded and/or oppressed individuals who do not speak or write, I contemplate the acts of persecution, torture—the terrorism that breaks spirits, that makes creativity impossible. I write these words to bear witness to the primacy of resistance struggle in any situation of domination (even within family life); to the strength and power that emerges from sustained resistance and the profound conviction that these forces can be healing, can protect us from dehumanization and despair.

These early trials, wherein I learned to stand my ground, to keep my spirit intact, came vividly to mind after I published *Ain't I A Woman* and the book was sharply and harshly criticized. While I had expected a climate of critical dialogue, I was not expecting a critical avalanche that had the power in its intensity to crush the spirit, to push one into silence. Since that time, I have heard stories about black women, about women of color, who write and publish (even when the work is quite successful) having nervous breakdowns, being made mad because they cannot bear the harsh responses of family, friends, and unknown critics, or becoming silent, unproductive. Surely, the absence of a humane critical response has tremendous impact on the writer from any oppressed, colonized group who endeavors to speak. For us, true speaking is not solely an expression of creative power; it is an act of resistance, a political gesture that challenges politics of domination that would render us nameless and voiceless. As such, it is a courageous act—as such, it represents a threat. To those who wield oppressive power, that which is threatening must necessarily be wiped out, annihilated, silenced.

Recently, efforts by black women writers to call attention to our work serve to highlight both our presence and absence. Whenever I peruse women's bookstores, I am struck not by the rapidly growing body of feminist writing by black women, but by the paucity of available published material. Those of us who write and are published remain few in number. The context of silence is varied and multi-dimensional. Most obvious are the ways racism, sexism, and class exploitation act to suppress and silence. Less obvious are the inner struggles, the efforts made to gain the necessary confidence to write, to re-write, to fully develop craft and skill—and the extent to which such efforts fail.

Although I have wanted writing to be my life-work since childhood, it has been difficult for me to claim "writer" as part of that which identifies and shapes my everyday reality. Even after publishing books, I would often speak of wanting to be a writer as though these works did not exist. And though I would be told, "you are a writer," I was not yet ready to fully affirm this truth. Part of myself was still held captive by domineering forces of history, of familial life that had charted a map of silence, of right speech. I had not completely let go of the fear of saying the wrong thing, of being punished. Somewhere in the deep recesses of my mind, I believed I could avoid both responsibility and punishment if I did not declare myself a writer.

One of the many reasons I chose to write using the pseudonym bell hooks, a family name (mother to Sarah Oldham, grandmother to Rosa Bell Oldham, great grandmother to me), was to construct a writer-identity that would challenge and subdue all impulses leading me away from speech into silence. I was a young girl buying bubble gum at the corner store when I first really heard the full name bell hooks. I had just "talked back" to a grown person. Even now I can recall the surprised look, the mocking tones that informed me I must be kin to bell hooks—a sharp-tongued woman, a woman who spoke her mind, a woman who was not afraid to talk back. I claimed this legacy of defiance, of will, of courage, affirming my link to female ancestors who were bold and daring in their speech. Unlike my bold and daring mother and grandmother, who were not supportive of talking back, even though they were assertive and powerful in their speech, bell hooks as I discovered, claimed, and invented her was my ally, my support.

That initial act of talking back outside the home was empowering.   15
It was the first of many acts of defiant speech that would make it possible for me to emerge as an independent thinker and writer. In retrospect, "talking back" became for me a rite of initiation, testing my courage, strengthening my commitment, preparing me for the days ahead—the days when writing, rejection notices, periods of silence, publication, ongoing development seem impossible but necessary.

Moving from silence into speech is for the oppressed, the colonized, the exploited, and those who stand and struggle side by side a gesture of defiance that heals, that makes new life and new growth possible. It is that act of speech, of "talking back," that is no mere gesture of empty words, that is the expression of our movement from object to subject—the liberated voice.

Understanding the Text

1. What role did hooks's upbringing as a Black girl have on her beliefs about speaking out? In what ways have her race and gender influenced her thinking about herself and the need to speak out?

2. How did hooks come to writing as a young girl? In what way is her writing related to her upbringing among Black women? What purpose did writing serve for her?

3. What was hooks's reaction to the intense criticisms of her first book, *Ain't I a Woman?* What lessons did she learn from those criticisms? In what ways is this learning on her part important to her larger point about speaking out?

4. Why did hooks feel as though she was not a writer, even after publishing several articles and books? What connection does this feeling have to her upbringing? What might it suggest about writing and the risks associated with it?

5. In paragraph 14, hooks explains why she chose to write under her pseudonym bell hooks. What do you think her

choice might reveal about the risks associated with challenging power through writing?

Exploring the Text

1. hooks refers to Black women who write as "us." What does that way of referring to herself suggest about how hooks imagines her audience for this essay? Do you think she is writing exclusively for other Black women? Why or why not? If so, do you think her essay can still speak to other kinds of readers? Explain, citing specific passages to support your answer.

2. At one point in her essay, hooks states that she writes "to bear witness to the primacy of resistance struggle in any situation of domination (even within family life)." In what way do you think her essay does (or does not) bear witness? Do you agree with her about the importance of doing so? Why or why not? Do you think your own racial background and gender have anything to do with your answer to that question? Explain. How does "bearing witness" challenge power?

3. What do you think hooks's essay suggests about writing as a way to speak out and challenge power?

4. hooks tries hard to write in a way that is accessible to the widest possible audience and not to write in a way that only scholars can understand. Based on her writing in this essay, do you think she succeeds?

Explain, citing specific passages to support your answer.

Entering the Conversations

1. Write an essay for an audience of your classmates in which you tell the story of an experience in which you were silenced in the way that hooks describes being silenced in this essay.

2. In a group of classmates, share the stories you wrote for Question 1. Examine the different situations in which each of you felt silenced or unable to speak out. Can you identify any similarities in those situations? Are there differences based on race, ethnicity, gender, class, or similar factors? What do these stories reveal about the risks and benefits of speaking out in certain situations? Now, drawing on this discussion and the essays written by you and your classmates, write an editorial for your local newspaper (or your school newspaper) about what it means to speak out.

3. Think about social or political issues that matter most to you. Have you ever felt silenced on those issues—unable to voice your opinion about them in certain circumstances (such as in the experience you might have written about for Question 1)? Now consider ways in which you might speak out on those issues. Using whatever medium or means seems appropriate to you, and considering how your voice might affect your

intended audience, make a statement about an issue of concern to you. You might consider writing a letter to the editor of your local newspaper or using some other medium to express your view, such as a flyer or pamphlet that might be posted on your campus, a web site, or even a video (assuming you have access to the appropriate technology).

4. With a group of classmates, review the documents or materials you created for Question 3. Examine them not only for the messages they convey but also for the impact that those messages might have on a specific audience, intended or not. Consider how ethical each effort to speak out is (or isn't). Try to draw conclusions about the consequences of speaking out on complex and important social or political issues.

5. Blogs have become an important way for people to resist the kind of silencing that hooks describes in this essay. Visit several blogs devoted to issues that matter to you and read them for a time to get a sense of how they are used by their authors to speak out on those issues. Then, write a report in which you offer an assessment of blogs as a way to resist silencing. Draw on hooks's essay in your assessment.

Alternatively, maintain your own blog as a way to speak out on issues of importance to you. Write a self-assessment of your blog, using hooks's ideas to evaluate the value of your blog as a means to speak out.

Extending the Conversations

1. Drawing on several of the essays in this chapter, write an essay in which you define power and discuss how power affects our lives.

2. Write your own statement about an individual's responsibility to the government.

3. Write a conventional academic essay in which you compare the views of Henry David Thoreau; Martin Luther King, Jr.; bell hooks; and any other appropriate writers in this chapter regarding resistance to authority. In your essay, identify any major similarities among the writers you chose and discuss the fundamental beliefs that they have about individual rights and government authority. On the basis of your comparison, draw conclusions about resisting government or power.

4. Select three or four authors whose essays appear in this chapter and write a dialogue in which these authors discuss power. In your dialogue, try to draw from the essays written by the authors you've selected and focus your dialogue on what you believe are key issues related to power.

5. Many popular television shows depict government or law enforcement. For example, *The West Wing* focuses on presidential power; *Law and Order* tells stories involving law enforcement and legal professionals. Select several such shows and write an essay in which you discuss how political or legal power—or other kinds of power—is portrayed in these shows. What conclusions can you draw about cultural attitudes regarding power?

6. Artists and others often use images to voice protests or to resist or challenge power. Consider the images on this page as efforts to resist or challenge power. What messages do they convey? How do the images use common images or symbols to make their points? How effective do you think these images are as a way to challenge power? Select several of these images (or other images you can find) and write an essay in which you try to answer these

questions. In your essay, discuss what the images you have chosen say about power and examine the strategies used to convey their messages.

Draw conclusions about the use of images as a tool for resisting power.

7. Photographs often convey powerful messages about power and protest. Select one or more of the photographs on the next page or find other appropriate photographs and examine them for the messages they convey. Analyze the way the images convey their messages. Then write an essay presenting your analysis. Alternatively, take a photograph of your own in which you convey a message about power or protest.

8. It is not uncommon for popular films to portray government power as sinister and oppressive. For example, *The X-Files* (1998) depicted a vast government conspiracy involving experiments to create a race of human-alien hybrids. Films like *Enemy of the State* (1998) depict ordinary citizens caught up in a web of government secrecy and clandestine power, and some films about historical events suggest the existence of similar conspiracies—for example *JFK* (1991). Even classic films, such as *Mr. Smith Goes to Washington* (1939), portray government as somehow less honest than the ordinary citizen. Select several such films and analyze those films for what they suggest about government and its power. Then write an essay presenting your analysis. Draw conclusions about what these films might reveal about American attitudes regarding government power.

9. Student organizations can give voice to students' concerns and serve as a vehicle to challenge the authority of their school administrators. Identify one or more student organizations on your campus (perhaps including one that you belong to) and investigate their activities to get a sense of how they have served as a means to challenge power. If possible, interview members of the organization and explore some of the issues they have been involved in. Then, write an essay in which you offer your perspective on student organizations and their roles in challenging power on your campus.

Alternatively, create a pamphlet or web site (or other appropriate text) that presents your view of the role of a specific student in giving voice to students' concerns on your campus.

Erika Rothenberg, *Freedom of Expression National Monument,* Foley Square, New York, 2004

© Stockbyte/Getty Images

I N THE SUMMER OF 2008, NATIONAL PUBLIC RADIO BROADCAST AN INTERVIEW WITH A MAN NAMED DEREK HUNTER FROM OHIO, WHO WAS DESCRIBING THE IMPACT OF THE INCREASING PRICE OF GASOLINE ON HIS LIFE. AT THE TIME, THE NATIONAL AVERAGE PRICE OF A GALLON OF GAS WAS MORE THAN $4.00,

which was an increase of nearly 30% from the summer of 2007. The rapidly rising cost of gas was beginning to cause hardship for Americans, many of whom depend upon their cars. Derek Hunter lived in Lima, a small city of 40,000 residents in northwest Ohio between Dayton and Toledo. Like so many Americans, he lived in a suburb and drove an SUV, a Ford Excursion, which traveled only 8–10 miles on a gallon of gas. With five children and a job that required him to drive from place to place, he was spending about $200 each week on gas. Such high fuel costs were beginning to affect his life in frustrating ways, he told the interviewer. For instance, he had canceled the family's summer vacation because he simply couldn't afford it that year with gas prices so high. In 2008, that was a familiar story, and like Mr. Hunter, Americans everywhere were beginning to adjust their lifestyles as rising fuel prices were preventing them from living as they were accustomed to doing.

That radio report focused on the rising price of gas, but it revealed a great deal about how Americans live together. For one thing, it underscored how central the automobile has become to the typical American lifestyle. Unless you live in a city with mass transit, you probably rely on a car to get to work, to the supermarket, to school, to the dentist, to church or temple, or anywhere else you might need to go on a typical day. Since the end of World War II, Americans have built their entire lifestyle around the car. Shopping malls are located far from our suburban homes, and their large parking lots indicate that shoppers are expected to drive there. The very idea of a suburb is based on automobile transportation. Few suburbs are served by mass transit such as trains, subways, or buses. And the classic American vacation involves piling the family into a car and driving to the beach or a national park or amusement park.

Derek Hunter of Lima, Ohio, grew up in a nation that took driving (as well as cheap gas) for granted. He told the radio interviewer that when he was a kid, "We went everywhere. We got to see Amish country and the oceans, just because that was what you could do in America. You could get in your car and drive some place." He implied that being able to drive wherever he wanted was almost a basic right that all Americans should enjoy, and he was frustrated that he could no longer do what he and his family did when he was a boy. But in 2008, Americans were being forced to begin thinking about changing how they live together in ways that perhaps they have never done. When the interviewer asked Mr. Hunter whether he had considered moving to another town so that he wouldn't have to drive as much, he replied that he *had* thought about moving somewhere that has mass transit. Then he laughed and said, "I don't know that it would be any cheaper to move me and the kids to New York." New York City was the only place he could think of where he would not have to use his car to do everything he needed to do every day.

If Derek Hunter was frustrated because he didn't see any way out of his costly lifestyle, he was in good company. Most of us probably don't think much about how the most routine activities, like driving to school or work or buying groceries at a supermarket, are part of a complicated and interconnected way of living together on the earth. We do what we need to do every day without having to think much about why things are the way they are. But that began to change in 2007 and 2008 as rising world oil prices and increasingly dire warnings about global climate change forced people all over the world to begin to rethink how they live together: how they use the land, how they create living spaces, how they build communities, how they take care of the places where they live. I suspect you have thought about some of these same things recently, because like Derek Hunter, you too are almost certainly affected by rising energy costs, which influence everything from driving to school to the price of food in our globalized economy.

If you are worried, about how these changes will affect the way you live, that may be a good thing because it will probably mean you will look more carefully at your own life and the way it fits into the lives of others in your community, your country, and indeed the whole world. This chapter may help you do that. The three clusters include readings that examine the many different aspects of how we live together, from our homes and neighborhoods to the places we set aside as special to our entire economic system and the values that shape all of these things. As I was writing this chapter in 2008, I shared Derek Hunter's fears. But I also see possibilities in the problems we are facing. I hope the readings in this chapter can help you see some of those same possibilities. They certainly reveal how writing can help us appreciate the complexities of living together.

CREATING LIVING SPACES

MOVE-IN DAY ON COLLEGE CAMPUSES IS A KIND OF CLINIC ON CREATING SPACES. IF YOU'VE EVER BEEN ON A CAMPUS WHEN STUDENTS ARE MOVING IN FOR THE NEW SCHOOL YEAR, YOU KNOW THAT THE ACTIVITY ISN'T OVER ONCE ALL THE CARS AND VANS ARE UNLOADED. FOR THE NEXT SEVERAL DAYS, STUDENTS WILL ORGANIZE AND DECORATE THEIR DORM ROOMS, AND THEIR CREATIVITY IN DOING SO IS BOUNDLESS. THEY WILL rearrange furniture; hang posters and photos on the walls; set up stereos, computers, televisions, and video games; and stow their clothes and other belongings in every available space. Most dorm rooms that I've seen are small, but their size never seems to limit what students can do in making the rooms comfortable and useful. If you've ever moved into a dorm, an apartment, or another living space, then you know something about what it means to create a personal space that you will use for living and working. But I suspect that most of us never really think about how complex and interesting this process really is.

The readings in this cluster invite you to think about just that. They explore some of the many ways in which human beings create the spaces they inhabit and the spaces they use for all kinds of important purposes. In one sense, each of these readings examines a different kind of space that we create. Melissa Holbrook Pierson, for instance, describes the emotional attachment that most of us develop to our homes, which are perhaps the most important and intimate physical spaces we use in our lives. Brent Staples describes the city neighborhood where he once lived, but his essay is really about how our physical living spaces can be dramatically shaped by who inhabits them—and what we think about them. Will Yandik's essay looks at a much more mundane space: the American lawn. He helps us see that even seemingly ordinary spaces can have more complicated meanings than we might realize. Marcus Renner also looks at a rather mundane space—a freeway—but he explores how that space was transformed into something more by the residents of the nearby neighborhoods. Together, these essays remind us that the living spaces we create are as much in our minds as in the physical world around us.

As you read these essays, you might also consider some of the other spaces in your life: the classroom space you may be in right now, for example, or the room where you're reading this text (maybe a lounge in your campus student center or a coffee shop or diner), or even the "community space" that is created by participating in the writing and reading activities that this book—and your composition course—invite you to do. What kinds of living spaces are these? How do you help create them? And how do they affect your life? These are some of the questions that the essays in this cluster invite you to think about.

If you have ever moved away from home—
or moved from one home to another—
you will probably identify with the
strong emotions that Melissa
Holbrook Pierson describes in this
essay. Pierson tells the story of having
to pack up the home in Ohio where
she was born before it was sold. Even
though she is now middle-aged and
has lived for many years in another

state, she still feels a deep and
powerful connection to her family
home. Her essay is a kind of tribute
to that home, where she still feels she
belongs. It is also an essay about the
importance our homes acquire. We
all have some sense of a home, no
matter what kind of house or
apartment or structure we live in.
And often that sense of home is
attached to the place where we were
born. This essay is a story about that
sense of home.

When I first read Pierson's essay,
I immediately recalled the emotions I
felt when I moved from the home
where my wife and I raised our
children. Maybe because I shared
that experience, I found her essay to
be one of the most powerful pieces of
writing about home that I've yet
encountered. But even if you haven't
moved away from home or had to sell
the home where you were born, you
can still appreciate the intense
connection she feels to her home. Her
ability to convey that connection so

Losing Home

MELISSA HOLBROOK PIERSON

I never kept count of all the times I drove from New York to Ohio. In the twenty-five years since I moved away, it's been a lot, because home was like a magnet whose insistent attraction pulled me across four hundred miles of mid-Atlantic hills as if I were ball bearings on glass. As soon as I got back from a visit to Ohio, I'd start thinking about the next time I would return. The ability to reinsert myself into the house, the town, the countryside that gave birth to me was a thick, comfortable joy. **BUT THIS TIME WAS DIFFERENT.** After this trip there would be no home to which to return. My mother had sold our house.

I took the old route, Route 6, across the top of Pennsylvania. It felt appropriate to drive along a superseded road that itself took you into the past, through one-stoplight towns of brick hotels and lunch cars that don't look like any place they make in this twenty-first century. Because in going west to Ohio, I was going back into my history, to the childhood home—and even, it seemed possible, the childhood itself—that would soon no longer be mine.

What spread before the car's windshield was enchanting in its yesteryearness, but imaginary billboards kept shimmering in the dis-

MELISSA HOLBROOK PIERSON, "LOSING HOME," *ORION MAGAZINE*. SEPTEMBER/
OCTOBER 2007.

vividly is one of the reasons I selected this essay for this textbook.

Melissa Holbrook Pierson (b. 1957) has written three books, including The Place You Love is Gone: Progress Hits Home *(2006). Her articles have appeared in many publications, including* Orion, *where this essay was published in 2007.* ◪

STRATEGIES: ORGANIZING A NARRATIVE
Notice that Pierson tells her story chronologically—that is, from the beginning of her trip back to her childhood home in Ohio up to the point at which she has finished cleaning out the house. But she also fills in background about her past in the house as well as about her more recent life. In writing a narrative, it can be difficult to work such information into a chronological narrative, but Pierson does so in her essay by organizing her story around her trip back home. Notice that the memories and background information she provides are usually tied to the place she arrives at (for example, the street where the house is located or a specific room in that house) or the activity she is doing (such as when she goes through boxes of old things stored in the house). In this way, Pierson can share memories, tell relevant anecdotes, and provide background information without seeming to interrupt the pace of her story about her return home to Ohio.

CONVERSATIONS: A NATION ON THE MOVE
In paragraph 4, Pierson seems to criticize the tendency of Americans to keep moving into new places that they take over and develop. She refers to the fact that the United States began as a nation of European immigrants who settled on land that was already occupied by Native American peoples and is still in a sense a nation of new towns. According to the U.S. Census in 2000, 16% of Americans moved to a new residence during 1999–2000; one fifth of those moved to a different state. (Pierson refers to this "mobile society" in par. 15.) Some observers believe, as Pierson seems to, that this tendency to move is part of the American character, perhaps because of the nation's unique history. Yet, as she acknowledges in paragraph 15, most Americans live near where they were born. Her own experience reveals the deep connection many people have to their birthplace. In this sense, Pierson's essay is part of the larger conversation Americans are always having about who they are.

---

tance. They were the kind that tout the New and Improved that is now concocted to replace the old scenery. Obviously this was a projection of my tremulous inner state—not to mention my persistent fear of the American penchant for destroying anything that dared to get older than a decade or two.

THE DESIRE TO MOVE, TO LEAVE HOME AND NEVER LOOK BACK, IS CARRIED DEEP IN THE NATIONAL DNA. After all, unless we sprang from what little native rootstock was not pulled up and crushed by European interlopers who could not bear to share the promised land with the people who already called it home, we all came from somewhere else. The current carpeting of every last field and forest with subdivisions is testimony in part to the fact that not everyone is hopelessly stuck on her birthplace. As is the attempt to create, all at once, a new town that will purportedly be just like an old town. The attractiveness of "better" may be a remnant of the child's hesitancy before that vast array of candy at the store—which one will taste the sweetest, which? And if it turns out not to be better, but only bigger or newer, we will probably think the solution lies in moving yet again.

If we could be buried in our backyards, right next to the hammock, most of us would forgo the local cemetery, although anywhere in our hometowns would do when it comes to that. But only after we've gone out to see what else there is. Americans, eh? What a perverse bunch. We may forever love the ancient hills of home, but still feel beset by a restlessness to find some sunny California, either of the mind or the map.

Across the road atlas I went toward the dreaded assignment: to pack up the archives of my first twenty years, and those of my parents and miscellaneous forebears, from where they had been stored in the basement, the attic, the many closets and drawers and shelves of the Tudor revival house we had loved so deeply it seemed to love us back. It was witness and shelter, provider and backdrop: sweet sixteens; several youthful groping sessions on the velvet couches downstairs while parents slept upstairs (yeah, right); two weddings; one lovely spring memorial party under a tent, with flowers floating in the punch bowls, for the father who would have loved to have been there with all his friends in the shady green yard he had worked so hard to make peaceful and lush. Dozens of exuberant Christmases, with their package-strewn living room and champagne breakfasts, and countless cocktail parties and dinners and July Fourth post-parade brunches. It was a place to be happy in, despite the occasional house call by the dour German pediatrician carrying his black bag to the bedside of one or another feverish little girl. **IT WAS A HOUSE THAT CONTAINED THE ECHO OF FORTY YEARS' WORTH OF PERIODIC TEARS.**

Nothing prepared me for turning the corner at last and seeing, spearing the soil of a flower bed on this corner lot in a gracious 1929 development, a sign announcing the pending sale of the building thereon. As if it were a commercial transaction, and not something designed to bring surprising pain to the heart of a middle-aged woman who thought she was no longer susceptible to the type of searing emotion she once apparently felt pretty much every waking minute of every day, to judge by the contents of the high school diaries that now must be reread so it can be determined whether they belong in a trash bag on the curb or packed into the car for the journey back, in one week's time, to the present.

Going through those boxes was a voyage of rediscovery, of coming face to face with things I had once known well but had apparently forgotten as I conducted what I now came to see as a surface life, running concurrently over the subterranean life of my past. There were passionate friendships with girls I met on vacation, which spawned several months of long letters, each sealed with wax or stickers, drawn or collaged upon, filled with oblique references to deep matters of the heart that we must have fervently discussed while applying baby oil to each other's backs on the beach. Then the letters sputtered to silence, until they were replaced with another burst of equally eruptive missives to other girls. These contained advice about what to do about boys whose names now perplexed me: *Who was this person who filled my head for months of 1972?*

The most abrupt recollection, however, was also the simplest, for it was overhead, underfoot, all around me. This house itself: it was nothing less than my mother's colossal lifework. Beyond raising her girls, some volunteer work, and the occasional European trip to look forward to, there was mainly the house. She had visions of its potential, and my youth was spent amid a sea of dog-eared *House and Gardens,* stacks of *Architectural Digests* with pictures ripped out. Her girls' bedrooms each had a color theme carried out by vibrant wallpaper—mustard yellow or pink-flowered with kelly-green vines or navy blue with tiny white sprigs—and custom-made bedding to match. The master bathroom became a sparely serene retreat with travertine marble, two sinks with modernist chrome goose-necked faucets, and a shower with a teak seat that dropped from the wall, enclosed by a silver curtain. I had never seen such luxury in someone's house before, and now I know why my father poured himself a drink and read the newspaper before he looked at the day's mail. Its weight of bills would cause his face to get longer and longer with each envelope he opened then set aside.

STRATEGIES: VAGUE OR SPECIFIC DESCRIPTION
In this paragraph, Pierson describes many of the special events that took place in her family home. Although she provides many details in her description, as writing teachers often ask students to do, these details are not always specific and are often somewhat vague (for example, "one lovely spring memorial party"; "dozens of exuberant Christmases"). You might wonder why Pierson chose to be vague rather than more specific in her use of details in this passage. What is the effect of these concrete yet rather vague details? How do they help Pierson convey a sense of the meaning of her family home? Compare Pierson's use of details in this paragraph with the details she includes in paragraph 18.

10 Here was the patio my mother enlarged and repaved in brick—there was an awful lot of brick in this particular corner of Akron—that radiated out around the large shade maple (into which I climbed as a girl to write dreadful short stories about how no one understood the protagonist). She designed a keyhole-shaped pool and fountain so there would always be the gentle sound of splashing. We and our guests spent every rainless hour possible out there, and it became the test I set for every boy I brought home: if he did not find the patio one of the most idyllic spots in the world, I would know he did not suit me. He could not belong here.

I also remembered that I used to take down and look at my parents' wedding album so often and so deeply I became convinced I was there, perhaps at the end of the conga line of smiling friends in satin cocktail dresses. And of course I sort of was, in the intense gaze of joy the newlyweds shared on the day they took a swan dive into their future. Looking at it again finally released the weeping that had only threatened at the sight of that for sale sign. I sat in what we called the Orange Room, the bedroom I for a short while shared with my older sister when we first moved in, and cried until I sounded like a five year old whose balloon was now a thumbtack against the clouds. Everywhere I went I was putting into Mayflower boxes the evidence that my parents had been truly, madly in love. That it was now gone, because he was gone, and soon too the house they had made the manifestation of that love, seemed beyond need to note in its transparent simplicity. Maybe that's why the fact stunned me when I ran into its immovability at speed. *It's all so damn brief.*

Of course it is. Or else it wouldn't be so sweet, would it, or something that I would so desperately want to grab. I mean, just look at the piles of letters from insistent suitors I no longer remember, the anguished verse of a girl who did not know how to get what she wanted, the photos of happy times with friends or on vacations in places that now are ruined, the rejections—why saved?—from schools, jobs, and those who refused to be suitors, the wistful mementos from trips taken by ancestors I cannot even name.

I am attached to my past, and so to the house in which it occurred. How often I longed to return home—from camp, then from boarding school, then from college, from New York.

Nostalgia is a virus that runs in the family. My parents both went east to school, but seemed unable to resist Ohio's call; it sure enough drew them back from New York, from Boston. My aunt tells me that on the day she was due to move from the Utah house in which she raised three children, she sat on the floor in the echoing living room, weeping without end, until her antisentimental husband stood over her and asked, "So, um, how long is this going to take?"

15 If moving is in our veins, we sons of pioneers, daughters of immigrants, why then is homesickness such an unholy ache in the gut? For

some time now, we have been reading of our "increasingly mobile society," as if the modern world had somehow shaken off the morbidly antique notion of Home Sweet Home. But just as teleportation once seemed just around the futuristic corner, so too that increasingly mobile society remains more putative than real: the mass of Americans live no farther from where they grew up than fifty miles. There is duplicity in what we are, expressed in a mighty instinct toward self-preservation that coexists in the same cells as the urge, say, to jump out of planes at ten thousand feet. On second thought, perversity is not just an American quality; it is human.

I have a friend, a woman who grew up in Pittsburgh. Then she (like so many) moved on to another life, or two or three, in another place. Toward the end of the '60s, she went back to visit the street where she was raised. Even though she was armed with the knowledge that the apartment building in which she had spent her childhood had been destroyed in the catastrophes of that city's race riots, it was not until she stopped in front of its blackened remains that she felt it: the sucker punch of loss, as hard to stand up from as the death of someone you knew.

That is because home is physical before it can be metaphorical. It is also personal while being collective. Go figure that. It seeps into your body as you grow, and when it is gone you commune with a ghost. No one else knows what it feels like to you, even if they have their own séances from time to time with the dead places of their own pasts.

For me, every room, every tablecloth in every drawer, every serving bowl and Easter decoration and ancient sled drawn from its burial mound of storage starts a projector whirling. (Never mind the thirty-two actual slide carousels, each of which is a Kodachrome passport to memoryville, us in full '60s mufti and squinting against the sun on trips to Williamsburg, Oglebay Park, Fire Island; at someone's baptism, for which my mother would demand sculpted sherbet roses as the true and just dessert; at every event that made me who I am.) Who could have imagined there would be so much to remember, so much that had remained packed away?

I go outside and walk down the block in this most perfect of neighborhoods and see the house where lived my parents' friends, a family so close to us we called them Aunt and Uncle and went on vacations together. Someone else lives there now, and they are busy gathering their own memories, which will live unrecognized among the bricks and flowers and the gentle air that invades the porch during the twilight hour given over to martinis and the reading of the newspaper. Then one day, they will feel it all rushing over them, while they box the books and the kitchen pots. They too will think about why it has to come to an end. Around the corner, and there's the house of other friends, now elderly and no longer given to the kind of large backyard blowout where the grownups' constant laughter mixed with Dixieland and the little kids—us—took their first sips of frozen whiskey sours when no one looked.

20   I think the behaviorist branch of psychology may have an explanation for the strength of this glue that sticks us evermore to the childhood home. It is the place where we receive so many "primary reinforcers," the stuff we need most in order to live. Food, sleep, safety, comfort, touch. Pleasures, too, like gifts under the tree or a Bach concerto issuing from the hi-fi or the hum of a distant lawnmower on an August evening or the slam of a car door signaling both the promise of an arrival and the possibility of a departure after which one can go home again.

When in a few days I finish packing up, to hit the faster, newer I-80 to home (another home, which will also inevitably refresh this melancholy when I have to leave it or it leaves me), it may all strike me with the finality of a lid closing forever on a trunk, the key handed to a new owner. The child who is still present within me will cry, or maybe throw an untoward fit. But the behavior, like all things children are compelled to do, will not change anything. Ever insistent, I will think: I needed the place to be there always, somehow, and not just in my heart. I want actual bricks, bearing singe marks of originating fire.

Understanding the Text

1. In what sense are Americans a "perverse bunch," according to Pierson (see par. 5)? Do you think she's right? Why or why not?

2. What was special about Pierson's family home? Does her home seem typical of American homes in any way? Explain. Do you think she tries to portray her home as typical? Why or why not?

3. What does Pierson discover about her past as she packs up the items in her family home? What does she learn about herself as she looks through these items? What do you think Pierson reveals about herself in

revisiting her past? What does she reveal about the role of writing in her life?

4. What does Pierson's family home reveal to her about her mother? What do you think her return to her family home suggests about the relationship a person can develop to a house?

5. What is the duplicity that Pierson sees in Americans (par. 15)? Where does she see this duplicity? Do you agree with her? Why or why not?

6. What does Pierson mean when she writes that "home is physical before it can be metaphorical" (par. 17)? In what ways does her essay support this statement?

Exploring the Issues

1. In paragraph 3, Pierson writes about her "persistent fear of the American penchant for destroying anything that dared to get older than a decade or two." What does she mean by this statement? What is the nature of this fear of hers? What do you think this fear suggests about her as a person? How might it influence the way you respond to her as the writer of this essay? Do you think she's right about Americans' "penchant" for destroying things that are old? Explain.

2. How would you describe Pierson's voice in this essay? What features of her writing contribute to her voice? Point to specific passages that you think best illustrate her voice. Do you find her voice appealing in this essay? Why or why not? Is it appropriate for her subject? Explain.

3. This essay is as much about memory as it is about a home. What is the relationship between the past and present as Pierson seems to understand them in this essay? How does the past—or the memory of it—give her family home its meaning? What might her experience in selling her family home suggest about the role of memory in the important places in our lives?

Entering the Conversations

1. Write an essay about your own home. In your essay, try to convey a sense of what your home has meant to you.

Alternatively, write an essay about leaving or returning home.

2. In paragraph 15, Pierson asks, "If moving is in our veins, we sons of pioneers, daughters of immigrants, why then is homesickness such an unholy ache in the gut?" Write an essay in which you answer that question. In your essay, draw on your own experiences or the experiences of people you know to answer Pierson's question.

3. In 2007 and 2008, what came to be known as the "sub-prime mortgage crisis" emerged in the United States as housing values fell and many homeowners were stuck with mortgages they couldn't afford. In many cases, people lost their homes as a result. The crisis affected other components of the U.S. economy, too, such as credit card usage. Using InfoTrac, the Internet, and other appropriate resources (including your local realtor association), look into the mortgage crisis and its impact on American homeowners. Find out what led to the crisis and what effect it had on Americans and the U.S. economy. Then write a report about the crisis on the basis of your research. In your report, explain the crisis and how it affected American homeowners. Draw conclusions about the importance of owning a home in American society.

4. Today, real estate organizations use the Internet to help them sell homes. They maintain extensive listings of homes for sale that often include a great deal of detailed information as well as photos and even videos of the homes. Visit one or more of these web sites and review the kinds of listings there. Get a sense of how realtors present homes to potential buyers: What aspects of a home do they seem to emphasize? What do they assume about potential buyers? If possible, talk to one or more realtors in your area about how they present homes for sale. Then write an essay in which you offer your own analysis of what the real estate market seems to tell us about the role of homes in American culture. What values seem to inform the real estate market? Draw conclusions about the values that seem to shape the real estate market and the place of the home in American society.

5. On the basis of the research you did for Question 4, create a real estate advertisement for your own home that conveys a sense of its importance to you.

A few years ago, a colleague of mine experienced what some people have called "driving while Black." He and a friend, both middle-aged African American men, were driving home late one Saturday evening from another friend's home when they were pulled over by local police. It was never clear why the police pulled them over, but my

Just Walk on By

colleague believes the police were suspicious of two Black men driving through a mostly White neighborhood late at night. My colleague is a college professor with a Ph.D. from an Ivy League school and serves as a trustee for a major state university; he is an accomplished and respected professional. Yet he was apparently suspected of wrongdoing simply for being a Black man

BRENT STAPLES

My first victim was a woman—white, well dressed, probably in her early twenties. I came upon her late one evening on a deserted street in Hyde Park, a relatively affluent neighborhood in an otherwise mean, impoverished section of Chicago. As I swung onto the avenue behind her, there seemed to be a discreet, uninflammatory distance between us. Not so. She cast back a worried glance. To her, the youngish black man—a broad six feet two inches with a beard and billowing hair, both hands shoved into the pockets of a bulky military jacket—seemed menacingly close. After a few more quick glimpses, she picked up her pace and was soon running in earnest. Within seconds she disappeared into a cross street.

That was more than a decade ago, I was twenty-two years old, a graduate student newly arrived at the University of Chicago. It was in the echo of that terrified woman's footfalls that I first began to know the unwieldy inheritance I'd come into—the ability to alter public space in ugly ways. It was clear that she thought herself the quarry of a mugger, a rapist, or worse. Suffering a bout of insomnia, however, **I WAS STALKING SLEEP; NOT DEFENSELESS WAYFARERS.** As a softy who is scarcely able to take a knife to a raw chicken—let alone hold one to a person's throat—I was

STRATEGIES: WORD CHOICE AND METAPHOR

In describing his encounter with the white woman in Chicago, Staples writes that he was "stalking sleep, not defenseless wayfarers." His description of himself in this passage is an excellent example of a writer carefully selecting words not just to describe something but also to convey or reinforce a point. In this case, Staples takes the verb "stalk" and turns it into a metaphor (he was "stalking" sleep), playing on the negative connotations of the word to help convey his point that the woman's fears about him were unjustified.

BRENT STAPLES, "JUST WALK ON BY," MS. MAGAZINE, SEPTEMBER 1986.

surprised, embarrassed, and dismayed all at once. Her flight made me feel like an accomplice in tyranny. It also made it clear that I was indistinguishable from the muggers who occasionally seeped into the area from the surrounding ghetto. That first encounter, and those that followed, signified that a vast, unnerving gulf lay between nighttime pedestrians—particularly women—and me. And I soon gathered that being perceived as dangerous is a hazard in itself. I only needed to turn a corner into a dicey situation, or crowd some frightened, armed person in a foyer somewhere, or make an errant move after being pulled over by a policeman. Where fear and weapons meet—and they often do in urban America—there is always the possibility of death.

In that first year, my first away from my hometown, I was to become thoroughly familiar with the language of fear. At dark, shadowy intersections, I could cross in front of a car stopped at a traffic light and elicit the *thunk, thunk, thunk* of the driver—black, white, male, or female—hammering down the door locks. On less traveled streets after dark, I grew accustomed to but never comfortable with people crossing to the other side of the street rather than pass me. Then there were the standard unpleasantries with policemen, doormen, bouncers, cabdrivers, and others whose business it is to screen out troublesome individuals *before* there is any nastiness.

I moved to New York nearly two years ago and I have remained an avid night walker. In central Manhattan, the near-constant crowd cover minimizes tense one-on-one street encounters. Elsewhere—in SoHo, for example, where sidewalks are narrow and tightly spaced buildings shut out the sky—things can get very taut indeed.

5   After dark, on the warrenlike streets of Brooklyn where I live, I often see women who fear the worst from me. They seem to have set their faces on neutral, and with their purse straps strung across their chests bandolier-style, they forge ahead as though bracing themselves against being tackled. I understand, of course, that the danger they perceive is not a hallucination. Women are particularly vulnerable to street violence, and **YOUNG BLACK MALES ARE DRASTICALLY OVERREPRESENTED AMONG THE PERPETRATORS OF THAT VIOLENCE.** Yet these truths are no solace against the kind of alienation that comes of being ever the suspect, a fearsome entity with whom pedestrians avoid making eye contact.

It is not altogether clear to me how I reached the ripe old age of twenty-two without being conscious of the lethality nighttime pedestrians attributed to me. Perhaps it was because in Chester, Pennsylvania, the small, angry industrial town where I came of age in the 1960s, I was scarcely noticeable against a backdrop of gang warfare, street knifings, and murders. I grew up one of the good boys, had perhaps a half-dozen fistfights. In retrospect, my shyness of combat has clear sources.

As a boy, I saw countless tough guys locked away; I have since buried several, too. They were babies, really—a teenage cousin, a brother

in a White community. Although this kind of "racial profiling" by law enforcement authorities is prohibited in many communities, many African Americans, especially men, claim that the experience is all too common.

In the following essay, writer Brent Staples gives us some insight into what it might be like to experience this kind of prejudice or racism. He shares his own experiences as a Black man in an urban community where he was sometimes suspected of being a criminal simply because of his skin color. His essay helps us understand how attitudes and beliefs as well as deep-seated prejudices can profoundly shape our interactions with one another. It also helps us appreciate the extent to which the living spaces we create are not only physical but psychological and emotional as well. In that sense, his essay is about the complexities of our living spaces, which we create with our minds as much as with our hands.

An editorial writer for the New York Times, *Brent Staples (b. 1951) is the author of the award-winning* Parallel Time: Growing Up in Black and White *(1994). The following essay first appeared in* Ms. *magazine in 1986 and was later republished in* Harper's *magazine as "Black Men and Public Spaces."* ▼

CONVERSATIONS: RACE AND CRIME IN THE UNITED STATES

When Staples writes in paragraph 5 that "young black males are drastically overrepresented among the perpetrators of that violence," he is addressing an issue that has been the subject of intense debate in the United States for decades: the relationship between race and crime. Although young Black men are incarcerated at a much higher rate than young men of other racial or ethnic backgrounds, there is disagreement about whether Blacks actually commit more crimes than people of other groups or are subject to arrest and conviction at a greater rate as a result of inherent racial bias in the U.S. criminal justice system. Statistical evidence also shows that Blacks are more often the victims of crimes, as this chart indicates. And despite popular perceptions to the contrary, this chart reveals that crime rates have actually declined since the early 1990s, according to the U.S. Department of Justice. Essays like Staples' can complicate this debate by reminding us that perceptions about crime can powerfully influence our attitudes and behaviors as we create living spaces together.

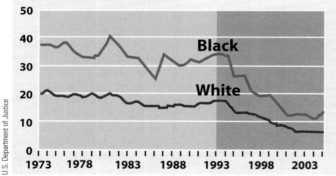

Violent crime rates by race of victim

Adjusted victimization rate
per 1,000 persons age 12 and over

U.S. Department of Justice

of twenty-two, a childhood friend in his mid-twenties—all gone down in episodes of bravado played out in the streets. I came to doubt the virtues of intimidation early on. I chose, perhaps unconsciously, to remain a shadow—timid, but a survivor.

The fearsomeness mistakenly attributed to me in public places often has a perilous flavor. The most frightening of these confusions occurred in the late 1970s and early 1980s, when I worked as a journalist in Chicago. One day, rushing into the office of a magazine I was writing for with a deadline story in hand, I was mistaken for a burglar. The office manager called security and, with an ad hoc posse, pursued me through the labyrinthine halls, nearly to my editor's door. I had no way of proving who I was. I could only move briskly toward the company of someone who knew me.

Another time I was on assignment for a local paper and killing time before an interview. I entered a jewelry store on the city's affluent Near North Side. The proprietor excused herself and returned with an enormous red Doberman pinscher straining at the end of a leash. She stood, the dog extended toward me, silent to my questions, her eyes bulging nearly out of her head. I took a cursory look around, nodded, and bade her good night.

10   Relatively speaking, however, I never fared as badly as another black male journalist. He went to nearby Waukegan, Illinois, a couple of summers ago to work on a story about a murderer who was born there. Mistaking the reporter for the killer, police officers hauled him from his car at gunpoint and but for his press credentials would probably have tried to book him. Such episodes are not uncommon. Black men trade tales like this all the time.

Over the years, I learned to smother the rage I felt at so often being taken for a criminal. Not to do so would surely have led to madness. I now take precautions to make myself less threatening. I move about with care, particularly late in the evening. I give a wide berth to nervous people on subway platforms during the wee hours, particularly when I have exchanged business clothes for jeans. If I happen to be entering a building behind some people who appear skittish, I may walk by, letting them clear the lobby before I return, so as not to seem to be following them. I have been calm and extremely congenial on those rare occasions when I've been pulled over by the police.

And on late-evening constitutionals I employ what has proved to be an excellent tension-reducing measure: I whistle melodies from Beethoven and Vivaldi and the more popular classical composers. Even steely New Yorkers hunching toward nighttime destinations seem to relax, and occasionally they even join in the tune. Virtually everybody seems to sense that a mugger wouldn't be warbling bright, sunny selections from Vivaldi's *Four Seasons*. It is my equivalent of the cowbell that hikers wear when they know they are in bear country.

Understanding the Text

1. What did Staples learn from his encounter with the white woman on a street in Chicago? Why is the lesson he learned from that encounter important? What does it suggest about the living spaces we create and share?

2. What was the "language of fear" with which Staples became familiar as a young graduate student (see par. 3)? What did that "language" reveal to him about how people live together? What did it reveal about how he was perceived by others?

3. What does Staples mean when he writes that he "came to doubt the virtues of intimidation early on" (par. 7)? What led him to feel this way? What irony does he see in his own aversion to violence?

4. How has Staples adjusted his own behavior in response to the experiences he describes in this essay? What do you think his own behavior suggests about him as a person? What might it suggest about how people live together?

Exploring the Issues

1. What do you think this essay suggests about racism and prejudice? Sometimes we hear that only people who experience racism themselves truly understand it—that only Black people, for example, really understand what it means to be discriminated against because of race. Based on this essay, do you think Staples would agree with that viewpoint? Explain, citing specific passages from the essay to support your answer.

2. At the end of paragraph 2, Staples writes, "Where fear and weapons meet—and they often do in urban America—there is always the possibility of death." This essay was first published in 1986. Do you think his statement is valid today? Explain. What might this statement suggest about the role of violence in how we live together in urban communities—or *any* community?

3. Throughout this essay, Staples shares anecdotes from his own past as well as anecdotes about others to illustrate the experiences of Black men who were assumed by Whites to be dangerous. Examine these anecdotes and evaluate their effectiveness in helping Staples convey his point. What do they reveal about how people treat one another and live together? How effective do you think they are in helping Staples convey the experience of being discriminated against in this way?

4. Why do you think Staples ends his essay as he does? What point do you think he intends to convey by comparing himself as a Black man to a hiker in bear country? How does this point relate to his larger themes in this essay?

Entering the Conversations

1. Write an essay about a time when you felt discriminated against.

2. In a group of classmates, share the essays you wrote for Question 1. What do your essays suggest about the nature of racism and prejudice? On the basis of your essays, discuss the implications of your experiences for what it means for people to create living spaces together.

3. On the basis of your discussion for Question 2, create a pamphlet, web site, or other appropriate document offering guidelines for creating living spaces in which racism and prejudice have less impact.

4. In some ways, Staples' essay is a reminder that racism and prejudice arise from a lack of understanding. He describes situations in which people make false or mistaken assumptions about him on the basis of his race, and he seems to suggest that if people could get past their assumptions and take the time to understand one another,

the problems of racism and prejudice would be minimized. Write an essay in which you explore this issue. In your essay, discuss what you see as the causes of racist or prejudiced attitudes, and examine the consequences of these attitudes. Propose solutions to the problems of racism and prejudice as you understand them. Draw conclusions about how people might create living spaces without racism and prejudice.

5. Many popular films and television shows have addressed the issue of racism or prejudice, sometimes causing controversy. *Crash* (2005), which won the Academy Award for Best Picture in 2006, depicts the experiences of several characters of different ra-

cial backgrounds as they encounter racism, often in the midst of intense conflict. *Babel* (2006) also explores problems caused by racial prejudice and language difference. Select these or other appropriate films and write an essay in which you discuss what these films suggest about racism today. Draw conclusions about the role of racism—and other kinds of prejudices—in how we create living spaces together.

6. Design a living space in which racism does not exist. Use any appropriate form for your document: an essay, a web site, a PowerPoint presentation, a video, or some other medium. In your document, describe your living space and explain how it will eliminate racism.

I have come to dislike lawns. When they're taken care of, they look nice. But after years of mowing lawns (first my father's lawn when I was growing up and then my own lawn) and toiling for hours in the summer sun to eliminate weeds, grow grass in shady spots where it doesn't want to grow, and fertilize the grass that does grow, I have

Ridding THE *American* Landscape OF Lawn

come to see lawn care as a burden and a waste of time. Most Americans seem to disagree with me. In most places, when the weather permits, American homeowners spend hours laboring over their lawns. And lawn care is a multibillion-dollar business that keeps growing. Whenever I see someone mowing a lawn or loading bags of fertilizer into the trunk of a car, I can't help but think of all the time Americans spend on this endless task of keeping lawns neat and tidy. So I was pleased when I first read the following essay by Will Yandik. Yandik shares my dislike of lawns. But his reasons are perhaps more complicated than mine. In criticizing the traditional American lawn, Yandik reveals that there's more to the way we think about lawns than it might seem. Although lawns may

WILL YANDIK

One landscape remains unchallenged in our built environment, a vernacular Virgin Mary, worshiped seasonally by millions—the lawn. Anyone who doubts that Americans are willing to place form ahead of function need only observe an August suburb and its throngs sweating their way to a perfect carpet of green. We cultivate more grass than wheat, corn, or tobacco, with almost 50,000 square miles of grass in the U.S. alone—an area roughly the size of New York State. The lawn's adverse effects on the environment are well documented: chemical pollution and runoff, a voracious appetite for water, mowers that belch hydrocarbons. Yet I suggest another reason, an aesthetic one, to rethink the concept of the lawn. It is an outdated pastoral fantasy, a bland backdrop that hinders the imaginative use of landscape. Much of what we dislike about sprawl is simply lawn. It is time for a change, and architects must be part of that change. After

seem natural to most Americans, Yandik shows that they are in fact artificial in a number of ways and that they reflect certain beliefs about how to use the land; they also contribute to serious environmental and social problems. You may disagree with him (especially if you enjoy doing yard work!), but his analysis helps us see that the spaces we create say a lot about us and our relationship to the land we live on.

Will Yandik (b. 1977) is a freelance writer who has written about landscaping and architecture for numerous publications, including Preservation *and* Architectural Record, *in which this essay first appeared in 2001.* ◪

all, the lawn is more architecture than landscape, more design than nature. It is no more natural than the concrete that often forms its border; in fact, we exterminate any real nature (moles, grubs, dandelions) that violates our green. The lawn is the imposition of designed interior space onto an exterior frame (thus the ubiquitous description of a healthy lawn as a "carpet"), and this kind of design may have outgrown its purpose. As new architectural designs break free from strict, boxlike intersections of 90-degree angles, it is less important to provide a horizontal, neutral surface to complement those axes.

The origins of the lawn are in Western Europe, likely in the British Isles, where the Atlantic climate keeps native grasses naturally green and short. What began as practical, enclosed grazing fields evolved into the estate lawn, cultivated by an upper class that was drunk on classical pastoral literature. Wealthy colonial families in North America slavishly imitated the English landscape until the middle class caught on in the 19th century, encouraged by fashion leaders such as A. J. Downing, who urged others to adopt "the unrivaled beauty of [England's] velvet lawns." The lawn flourished in the new suburbs, reaching its icon status after World War II, when Madison Avenue challenged returning soldiers to fight crabgrass instead of an evil empire.

QUEST FOR PERFECTION

The lawn has become a quest for perfection, a singular standard of color, shape, and texture. A flip through a grass seed catalog is initially inspiring and expansive—Bermuda grass, buffalo grass, centipede grass, St. Augustine, zoysia—but the poetry ends with the nomenclature. The seeds are used to produce the same uniform shapes. The aesthetic problem with the lawn is that it allows no room for innovation, growth, or art. The lawn is a front door, a symbolic facade constructed to communicate conformity. It advertises that the owner honors such values as dependability and hygiene. In essence, I shave, therefore I mow. The idea of the lawn has become so universally sacred that in the arid Southwest even gravel and hardscaping have been painted green and arranged in squares.

Must the lawn always be the green canvas, the neutral background for an architectural event—something that unifies brighter, bolder colors and textures? Mark Wigley, author of *The Electric Lawn*, describes architects' renderings: "It is assumed that wherever there is nothing specified in the drawing there is grass. The lawn is treated like the paper on which the projects are drawn, a tabula rasa without any inherent interest, a background that merely clears the way for the main event." A

CONVERSATIONS: SPRAWL

Yandik writes (par. 1) "much of what we dislike about sprawl is simply lawn." In making that statement, he is joining a much larger conversation about what has come to be called *sprawl*. In the 1990s, the rapid development of rural and wilderness areas into suburbs, corporate office parks, strip malls, so-called big box retailers (such as Wal-Mart), and industrial parks created a variety of environmental concerns, including the loss of wilderness and farmland, water and air pollution, and lifestyle problems, such as the increasing reliance on cars to get to and from the places people need to be every day. Some environmental groups began to identify this problem as "suburban sprawl" and called for initiatives to reduce sprawl. Some states and towns implemented "smart growth" ordinances to limit development or require developers to keep "open spaces" available in their developments. Although Yandik's essay does not address the problem of sprawl directly, his complaints about the typical American lawn are similar to the complaints voiced by opponents of sprawl and advocates of "smart growth." You might consider how much you know about the debates about sprawl and how your knowledge (or lack of it) might affect the way you read this essay.

problem arises when we fail to recognize that the periphery in architectural renderings constitutes most of our built environment. As the boundaries of our cities fade into suburbs, we realize that the lawn surrounds more than the single-family bungalow. Our schools, hospitals, libraries, museums, and corporate headquarters have become isolated in lawn.

5   Some successful lawn alternatives already exist. **XERISCAPING** with varied, drought-resistant grasses and cacti has become popular in the West, and some landscapers use native wildflowers and indigenous shrubs creatively in the East. But there must be a stronger relationship between architect and landscaper or, better yet, architects willing to design whole landscapes. Architects rely too heavily on the lawn to sew buildings together. The result is often a predictable composition that triggers our knee-jerk reactions against nonurban environments. The lawn prevents the suburb from achieving a balance of harmonious differences—the juxtaposition of different architectural styles and textures described and admired by critics like **ADA LOUISE HUXTABLE.** By replacing the lawn with an architectural landscape that integrates geometry within existing regional and natural geographic variation, we could advance suburbs beyond the predictable and prosaic.

FUSING STRUCTURE AND LAND

The 1994 Japanese Soft and Hairy House by Ushida-Findlay Partnership illustrates a more ambitious lawn replacement. A simple motif that could be expanded, the design fuses structure and natural topography. An unfussy tangle of native vegetation coils around the roof of the smooth, sculptural frame; the composition cannot be teased apart. Viewed from ground level, the green elements provide a hairy texture against the sky, softening the concrete and stucco and pulling the piece together. A similar example is the 1987

CONVERSATIONS: LAWN LANDSCAPING

In paragraph 1, Yandik states that "the lawn is more architecture than landscape, more design than nature." To what extent might these photographs support his statement—or not? One shows a typical suburban lawn and the other a golf course, which is a different kind of lawn. What do lawns suggest about how we create spaces and our relationship to the land?

© Tony Roberts/CORBIS

© Richard Berenholtz/CORBIS

GLOSSES
XERISCAPING
Xeriscaping (par. 5) is the practice of landscaping with slow-growing, drought-tolerant plants to conserve water and reduce yard waste.

ADA LOUISE HUXTABLE
A Pulitzer Prize–winning architecture critic for the *Wall Street Journal,* Ada Louise Huxtable (par. 5) has written books and many articles about architectural issues.

CONVERSATIONS: AUDIENCE
Yandik wrote this essay for *Architectural Record*, a specialized kind of magazine sometimes called a trade publication. The readers of that magazine are mostly professionals involved with architecture, planning, and design. But most of the readers of *Architectural Record* are also Americans, and many of them are homeowners as well. To what extent do you think Yandik addresses his audience as professionals? To what extent does he address them as part of this larger audience of American homeowners? And how might readers who are not homeowners and who have no lawn (for example, city dwellers who rent an apartment) react to his discussion about the importance of lawns in American culture? This is a good example of an essay in which a writer might address several different audiences at once.

Brunsell Residence by Obie Bowman, AIA, in Sea Ranch, Calif. The house appears to have been raised from the surrounding California grasses. Natural elements are not sacrificed through the introduction of geometry to the landscape, but rather assimilated into the composition. The architectural design expands beyond the four walls and bleeds into its environment. More recently, the Diamond Ranch High School by Morphosis in Diamond Bar, Calif., integrated classrooms into the natural topography of low hill barrens and scrub oak of a Los Angeles suburb. No dirt was removed or added. By cantilevering buildings off a hillside slope and choreographing the irregular rooflines with the natural contour of the landscape, the school campus eliminates the lawn.

If lawn-alternative designs exist, why then have they had such limited impact? One obstacle is zoning ordinances. In many municipalities, homeowners must specifically devote a certain percentage of their property to lawn, and citizens have the right to sue if their neighbor's grass grows a few inches above regulated standards. Another obstacle is simply consumer resistance. Americans have been taught for more than a century that the lawn is a safe, responsible statement of taste. Therefore, this time-tested standard will not vanish overnight. And despite the lawn's negative qualities, the lawn and garden industry successfully markets a familiar, accessible product. It's a reality that is unmistakable, but not immutable. Architects, like all artists, should pride themselves on pushing, rather than following, consumer tastes. Our landscape begs for an alternative to the sea of green.

Understanding the Text

1. Yandik claims that when it comes to their lawns, Americans "place form ahead of function." What does he mean by that statement? What evidence does he offer to support it? Why is this statement important to his larger point about lawns in this essay? Do you agree with him? Why or why not?

2. What are Yandik's primary complaints about American lawns? What do you think these complaints suggest about Yandik's values regarding lifestyle and the way we use the land?

3. How did lawns gain their "icon status" in the United States, according to Yandik? What do you think this status of lawns suggests about the relationship between social class and the spaces people create in American culture?

Exploring the Text

1. How would you describe Yandik's writing style in this essay? What specific features of his writing (for example, his word choice or use of images) contribute to his style? How effective do you think his style is? Does it help make his argument more persuasive? Explain, citing specific passages in your answer.

2. Yandik presents a lot of information in this essay, including facts and figures, historical background, quotations, and examples of special architectural projects. In that sense, you might think of this essay as a kind of research paper in which Yandik uses research to help him make his argument about lawns. Examine the information he includes. How effectively do you think he uses this information to help illustrate and support his arguments?

3. Yandik argues that we need to achieve "a balance of harmonious differences" in the lawns and buildings we create. Explain what he means by this concept of "harmonious differences." What does this concept reveal about his own values regarding the spaces we create and the lifestyles we have? To what extent do you think Americans would agree with Yandik? Do you? Explain.

4. In paragraph 6, Yandik discusses a number of architectural designs that he thinks provide good alternatives to the typical American lawn. What do these descriptions suggest about Yandik's sense of his audience? How do you think knowledge of the projects mentioned in this passage might affect the way readers read this passage? To what extent is Yandik's essay part of a specialized conversation that doesn't include "general" readers?

Entering the Conversations

1. Write an essay in response to Yandik's essay. In your essay, explain why you agree with his complaints about lawns, or offer a rebuttal to his argument. Discuss your own beliefs about how we

should create the spaces we inhabit.

INFOTRAC

2. In the past decade or so, the problem of suburban sprawl has become an important social and environmental issue in the United States (see *Conversations: Sprawl* on page 540). In recent years, many towns and states have attempted to address the problems associated with sprawl through various regulations and land-use measures. Such efforts are sometimes called "smart growth." Using InfoTrac College Edition, the Internet, and any other appropriate resources, find out what you can about the problem of sprawl and the so-called smart growth movement. Write a report on the basis of your research. Describe what sprawl is and the problems it causes, and discuss what efforts have been made to address it. Draw conclusions about what these efforts seem to suggest about how we create and use living spaces in U.S. society.

3. On the basis of your research for Question 4, write a letter to the editor of your local newspaper or some other appropriate publication in which you express your views about efforts to control sprawl.

4. The images in *Conversations: Lawn Landscaping* on page 541 and the image below show a golf course and some typical American suburban homes. In these instances, the lawns are carefully created. Consider what these created spaces suggest about our attitudes toward the land. What do they suggest about how we imagine and use spaces? To what extent are these elaborate spaces necessary or practical? Can these spaces be made differently and still be useful? Write an essay in which you try to answer such questions. Use these photographs or other appropriate photographs you may have of lawns or similar spaces.

© Lester Lefkowitz/CORBIS

Every once in a while I have to walk somewhere designed for cars rather than pedestrians. Whenever I do this, I am struck by how out of place I feel as I try to cross the road with cars zooming by. It becomes clear that this space was intended not for people but for cars. And the fact that people seem so out of place there suggests how much we have

The People's Freeway

designed our living spaces around the automobile. Changing that is no easy task.

Marcus Renner's essay describes an effort to create exactly that kind of change. He tells the story of a community effort to close down one of the busiest stretches of highway in the United States so that the space could be made more livable. In the latter half of the twentieth century, Los Angeles, with its overburdened freeway system, became a symbol of the automobile-centered American lifestyle—and of the problems with that lifestyle. So it is fitting that Renner's story takes place there. If people can make their communities less dependent on cars in Los Angeles, then perhaps they can do so anywhere. Renner's essay may open up your thinking about what kinds of change are possible as people continue to learn about how to create livable communities together.

When this essay was published in Orion *magazine in 2004,*

MARCUS RENNER

"What if we cut the fence?"** Nicole Possert yelled above the roaring traffic. On the other side of a battered chain-link fence clogged with trash, drivers zoomed toward Los Angeles. **NICOLE AND I WERE PONDERING A PROJECT** that would shock most Los Angelenos: shutting down a freeway so that people could walk and ride bikes on a road they normally experience at sixty miles per hour.

The Historic Arroyo Seco Parkway, known to commuters as the Pasadena or 110 Freeway, is the oldest freeway in the western United States. Completed in 1940, it carries 120,000 cars a day through the broad canyon of the Arroyo Seco, which runs southwest from the mountains above Pasadena toward downtown Los Angeles. For much of its length, the parkway's six narrow lanes wind along the concrete channel that holds what's left of the Arroyo's stream. Together, the road and stream pass through a dense urban landscape of pocket parks and arching bridges, leaning sycamores and historic homes.

Shutting down a freeway in Los Angeles—even for a few hours—might seem comparable to driving a lance through a windmill. The effort to close the parkway, however, was part of a broader vision for the Arroyo—a dream that, if realized, could provide a model for creating

MARCUS RENNER, "THE PEOPLE'S FREEWAY," *ORION MAGAZINE*, MAY/JUNE 2004.

© Hector Mata/AFP/Getty Images

Marcus Renner worked for the Urban and Environmental Policy Institute at Occidental College in Los Angeles. He is now director of the Environmental Center at Fort Lewis College in Colorado. The essay reprinted here is an abridged version that was published on Orion's *web site.* ▽

livable communities across southern California. Such places would offer clean and convenient transportation, accessible parks and open space, and would cultivate an appreciation of both local history and wild nature. In short, what had drawn us to the side of the highway on this December morning was a plan for the next Los Angeles.

The closure had a certain magical appeal. In southern California, freeways contribute to sprawl and air pollution and often carve up communities, reinforcing and sometimes creating social and economic divisions. Their effects are made more acute by the fact that Los Angeles has fewer acres of open space per capita than any other large metropolitan area in the country. Perhaps more important, freeways affect how people think about and experience the local landscape, reducing public understanding of place and geography to origins and destinations, with nothing in between. "Freeways," said Bob Gottlieb, head of L.A.'s Urban and Environmental Policy Institute, "are the city's biggest environmental issue."

5   The ad hoc group to which Nicole and I belonged was formed to create a different sort of city. We viewed the act of shutting down L.A.'s first freeway as a symbolic gesture to stimulate **DISCUSSION ABOUT HOW TO CREATE LIVABLE URBAN COMMUNITIES.**

The original vision for the parkway—described to the Los Angeles Chamber of Commerce by landscape architects **FREDERICK LAW OLMSTED, JR.** and **HARLAND BARTHOLOMEW** in 1930—was of a lei-

---

STRATEGIES: IN MEDIAS RES
To organize a story, writers often use a technique called *in medias res,* a Latin phrase meaning "in the middle of things." Using this technique, Renner begins telling his story about ArroyoFest "in the middle" rather than at the very beginning, and then he interrupts the story (at the end of par. 3) to provide necessary background information and to convey a sense of the context for the story (par. 4–13). Then, he resumes the story (around par. 14) and tells it to the end. This technique can be an effective way to draw readers into your story and keep them reading.

CONVERSATIONS: CREATING LIVABLE URBAN COMMUNITIES
In paragraph 5, Renner informs us that his group's effort to close down the freeway was part of a larger effort "to stimulate discussion about how to create livable urban communities." In fact, that discussion was well underway by the time Renner's group was working on ArroyoFest in 2002. At least since the 1970s, politicians, scholars, urban planners, and city residents have been debating the question of how to create safe, healthy urban living environments. In the late 1980s and early 1990s, as the rapid growth of suburbs worsened some of the environmental problems affecting cities, some critics began to advocate "smart growth," a development philosophy by which towns and cities planned their growth more carefully in view of both economic and environmental considerations. Renner's group's efforts can be seen as part of this "smart growth" movement, and his story might be read as part of the ongoing conversation in the United States about how to create more livable urban spaces.

GLOSS: OLMSTEAD AND BARTHOLOMEW
Frederick Law Olmstead, Jr., (1870–1957) designed many famous public spaces, such as the National Mall in Washington, D.C. His ideas about city planning helped shape the creation of many urban parks and developments. Harland Bartholomew (1889–1989) was the first full-time city planner employed by a U.S. city, serving in that role in Newark, New Jersey, and St. Louis, Missouri. He was instrumental in establishing urban planning in the United States.

surely, scenic drive between Pasadena and downtown Los Angeles. A disorganized mix of electric trolleys, buses, and automobiles already clogged city streets; the parkway was the first in a series of modern expressways Olmsted, Bartholomew, and others proposed as part of an integrated transportation system that incorporated trains, buses, and bicycles. Following the architects' lead, engineers who designed the parkway sought to balance efficiency and aesthetics. They eschewed walls to give drivers a better view of the surrounding hills, and built arching bridges over road and stream. Broad curves followed the contours of the canyon and slowed traffic. Tawny gold sycamores leaned over the road. Wooden guardrails and garden plantings helped the parkway blend into the landscape.

By the 1950s, efficiency had become the primary goal of freeway architecture, and in time faster cars overwhelmed the parkway's design. Today, the road carries almost four times its rated capacity and has a much higher accident rate than other local freeways.

But in June 2002, the efforts of state officials and neighborhood activists like Nicole Possert, president of the Highland Park Heritage Trust, a local preservation group, earned the road a **NATIONAL SCENIC BYWAY** designation, making the parkway eligible for grants to improve safety and beautify surrounding communities. Millions of government dollars became available to revive the experience that the parkway's designers had envisioned.

Restoring the parkway to its leisurely splendor is one element of a renewed attempt to create an integrated transportation system, both for the Arroyo and for the region as a whole. In 2003, the new Gold Line commuter train began running between Pasadena and Los Angeles. Proposed bus, bike, and pedestrian routes, if linked to rail stations, would allow people to travel relatively easily without a car and make the Arroyo a transportation model for the rest of Los Angeles.

The stream, too, has drawn attention from those who want to remake the city. The headwaters of the Arroyo Seco fall down a shaded staircase of pools and cascades in the San Gabriel Mountains. Downstream, the Arroyo Seco is confined to a concrete flood-control channel. So disguised, the creek flows for almost eleven miles past soccer fields, golf courses, the Rose Bowl football stadium, and pockets of seminatural, open land. It joins the parkway for the last six miles of its journey before emptying onto the broad concrete flood channel of the moribund Los Angeles River.

At the confluence of these two urban waterways is the Los Angeles River Center and Gardens, home to several environmental groups and government agencies. Every day Anne Dove, a planner with the National Park Service, drives the parkway or rides the Gold Line to work here. "There is something about the Arroyo that just resonates with people," she said. "It's something about the scale of

GLOSS: NATIONAL SCENIC BYWAYS
The National Scenic Byways program of the U.S. Department of Transportation, established in 1991, helps communities preserve and enhance roadways that are identified as especially scenic or distinctive. Currently, there are 126 designated scenic byways in 44 states.

10

the place; that you can see all the boundaries, all the edges within one viewshed."

For three years Anne has helped the Arroyo Seco Foundation and North East Trees with a plan to restore a living stream to the canyon. In 2002, their work piqued the interest of the U.S. Army Corps of Engineers, which may remove portions of the Arroyo's concrete channel— a first for Los Angeles County. This development meshes with plans to enhance and expand existing parks and open space throughout the watershed.

Most of the land along the Arroyo's floodplain, which varies in width from fifty yards to a quarter mile, is publicly owned. By combining this land with the right-of-way that the state owns along the parkway, local environmental groups envision an eleven-mile greenway stretching from the mountains to downtown.

A week after our scouting expedition, Nicole and I described our idea for cutting the fence to twenty people in the parlor of a Craftsman mansion at the canyon's edge. Our job had been to find the best way to get walkers and cyclists off the closed freeway and into Sycamore Grove Park, a fifteen-acre grassy parcel where we planned an all-day festival. The park is between two freeway exits. Cutting the fence was the only answer.

A hundred years ago, boosters extolled the Arroyo as a playground 15 for the white upper class. The communities that share the Arroyo today—and that were represented in that meeting—present a very different face. Forty-two percent of the seven hundred thousand people sharing the Arroyo were born outside the United States. Average household incomes range from less than ten thousand dollars to more than sixty thousand dollars a year, and **THE VARIED TOPOGRAPHY HAS BALKANIZED THE ARROYO** into a place where graffitied parks exist in the shadows of gated mansions.

During ArroyoFest's planning, people's disparate geographies began to merge; their sense of place broadened. But the task of bringing such diverse communities together to care for the shared resources of the twenty-two-mile-long Arroyo is, really, a social experiment. We began to develop an appreciation for how creating "livable communities" means more than just making the Arroyo a pretty place. Social and economic issues such as jobs, gangs, and public safety entered the conversation. For example, conversion of undeveloped open space along the Arroyo into parkland means the likely eviction of numerous people who are homeless. One important question we faced was, "Livable for whom?"

CONVERSATIONS: A BALKANIZED TOPOGRAPHY
Renner describes Arroyo Seco as a "balkanized" place, where low-income households exist near wealthy gated communities. "Balkanization" originally referred to the fragmentation of a region, such as occurred in the twentieth century in the Balkan region of Europe (which includes Croatia, Bosnia, and Serbia) as a result of ethnic and religious conflicts. The term has come to refer to fragmentation in general. Here, Renner relies on its negative connotations to make his point about what has happened in Arroyo Seco. This is a good example of how a term acquires meanings as a result of its use in different contexts (see "Understanding Discourse and Why It is Important" in Chapter 1).

CONVERSATIONS: GENTRIFICATION

When Renner refers to "gentrification" in this passage, he connects his story to an ongoing conversation in the United States about creating urban living spaces that emerged in the 1980s and 1990s as cities began to try to improve previously blighted neighborhoods. In many U.S. cities, such neighborhoods were transformed from slums to upscale housing with shops and restaurants that attracted wealthier residents. Although many people originally viewed this process as a way to create more desirable living spaces in cities, "gentrification" became controversial as low-income residents were forced out by rising housing costs. Some critics charged that gentrification was merely a process of removing the poor from city neighborhoods rather than addressing the problems of poverty. Here, Renner suggests that the groups involved in the effort to transform Arroyo Seco were aware of such criticisms. In this passage, the term *gentrification* carries complicated meanings related to the larger historical context of urban development in the United States in the latter twentieth century.

The arrival of the Gold Line train service has also sent real estate prices skyrocketing, threatening to push out low-income families and businesses. "If you talk to communities that have gone through **GENTRIFICATION,** most will tell you that they didn't see it coming until it was too late," said Beth Steckler, who lives in Highland Park and works for Livable Places. Beth's nonprofit group is trying to get ahead of the gentrification curve in the Arroyo by converting two abandoned factories next to a light-rail stop into affordable housing. The project can't be done soon enough; the median price of a single-family home in Highland Park rose almost 70 percent in three years, topping $250,000. In many ways, success in remaking the Arroyo will depend as much on Beth's project as on restoring the stream.

It will also depend on education. Carmela Gomes has taught public school in the Arroyo for more than twenty years and sits on the Historic Highland Park Neighborhood Council. She's helped develop a weekend workshop called "A River Runs Through It" to integrate the study of the Arroyo into classrooms. "It's something that we have to pass on to our young people, this sense that this place belongs to them, this sense of home and what it means to take care of that," Carmela explained.

ArroyoFest's early meetings connected these efforts and planted seeds for a more comprehensive vision for the Arroyo's future. But the first question that everyone raised was the big one: Would the California Department of Transportation—Caltrans—agree to close the road? Caltrans engineers worried the closure would back up L.A.'s entire freeway system. But a detour plan and helpful letters from elected officials convinced Caltrans to let our group of starry-eyed activists have the freeway from six to ten on a Sunday morning.

20   In April, with two months to go, the printer delivered posters and entry forms, and we called for volunteers to distribute them. Ten people filled the small conference room for instructions. These became fifteen, then twenty, then thirty. People stood in the hallway to listen. Three hours later we shooed the last of them out the door with armloads of materials. Our plan to close the highway was in the fast lane.

The final weeks were a blur of phone calls, media interviews, contracts, and deadlines. Last-minute requests for booth space poured in. A final program draft went off to the printer, and a crew spruced up Sycamore Grove Park. Traffic advisories hit the airwaves, and driving, biking, and bus directions from every corner of the Southland went up on the web. A contractor cut the fence and groomed the entrance where Nicole and I had stood eighteen months before. On June 14, an article about the next day's ArroyoFest appeared in the

Los Angeles Times. The office phone started ringing at six in the morning and didn't stop until midnight.

On the morning of June 15, Claudine Chen got up at five-thirty to bicycle to the intersection that marks the beginning of the freeway in Pasadena. "There was a lot of fog, and it was really quiet and dark," she recalled. "The first person didn't show up until six-fifteen. Then I turned around and suddenly there was this whole mob of people. They just kept coming and coming. It was pretty unreal."

At seven a horn sounded, and ArroyoFest was on. More than two thousand cyclists let out cheers as they rolled past the blue and yellow ArroyoFest banner, down the parkway, and into the mist. Ten-speeds, tandems, and tricycles hit the road as a chorus of birds and clicking bike gears supplanted roaring engines. "I always knew that parks lined the parkway, but seeing and experiencing them as I went by was magical," said one rider.

Down at Sycamore Grove Park, Anne Dove arrived a little before six and began checking in the sixty community groups that had taken booth space. Carmela Gomes was busy setting up school exhibits beneath the coast live oak trees and helping direct volunteers as they covered tables with bottled water and programs. The first cyclist rolled in at seven-thirty, and by eight the park's band shell, which once hosted John Phillip Sousa's brass band concerts, was alive with acoustic folk and Latin soul.

By eight-thirty the veil of mist had lifted for the thousands of enthu-   25
siastic walkers gathered at the parkway's ten ramps along the route. The greens and golden browns of the Arroyo seemed more vivid than usual against the bright blue sky. One volunteer brought her two teenage daughters, both of whom were less than thrilled to be awake so early. By the time the walk started, the spectacle of the event had overcome their cool reserve. One of them ran to the side of the road. "That's a passion flower!" she gasped, pointing to a delicate blossom growing on the shoulder. "I read about them in school, but I never thought I'd actually see one."

Freed from their cars, participants put aside their drivers' defensiveness. One schoolteacher walked four miles from Pasadena with his wife and young children. "For my daughter, it was just a big party," he told me. "It was great. You were able to see things from interesting angles that you normally miss because you're going so fast." Several people said they noticed the shape of the hills and canyon for the first time. The quiet that settled over the road drew people out of their houses. One of my former high school teachers wrote to me, "Once we reached Highland Park and you could see homes and people; it was so cool. They were taking videos and pictures, and waving and smiling."

Instead of being a means to get someplace else, the parkway became the place to be, a tree-lined plaza where residents gathered for a Sunday stroll. Neighbors sat on guardrails and chatted; people walked their dogs. Skateboarders and in-line skaters glided down the road and children raced between the lane lines. "Walking the area was incredible," wrote another participant. "It was an amazing sight to see all the bicyclists on the Arroyo parkway and all that joyous, constructive human energy in action. Without the cars along the parkway you could almost hear the trees breathe a little easier."

The next day, newspapers around the country carried the headline "Thousands Snub Car Culture." From Japan to France, the press was taken with the idea of closing a Los Angeles freeway.

In the months since, Nicole and the rest of the Scenic Byway team submitted a management plan for the parkway to Caltrans. Beth Steckler's Livable Places is close to building its affordable housing. Claudine Chen organized a scouting expedition for a commuter bikeway between Pasadena and Los Angeles, and Carmela Gomes's neighborhood council is trying to create parks out of two vacant lots. The future of these and other projects in the Arroyo depends on funding, political will, and the ability to maintain and strengthen the networks created by the event, but a sense now exists that these initiatives are part of a larger, coordinated movement.

30 "I think it showed the community what they can do," Anne Dove said. "If people from the community can work with Caltrans to close down the freeway, just think about what else they can accomplish."

Understanding the Text

1. What developments led to Renner's group's efforts to close down a section of the Arroyo Seco Freeway? What did they intend to accomplish by their efforts? Do you think they succeeded? Why or why not?

2. How did the freeway system in Los Angeles change over time? Why are these changes important? Why should we be concerned about the history and original purposes of that freeway system, in Renner's view? What might the example of the Los Angeles freeway system suggest about creating living spaces?

3. What challenges did the citizens' groups and government officials face in redesigning the freeways and surrounding land in Arroyo Seco? What do these challenges suggest about creating living spaces, especially in urban settings?

4. Why did Renner believe it was necessary to cut the fence bordering the freeway? What do you think was the significance of cutting the fence?

5. In paragraph 16, Renner writes that he and his group began to appreciate "how creating 'livable communities' means more than just making the Arroyo a pretty place." What does he mean by that

statement? What other considerations did his group take into account as they worked to change Arroyo Seco? What did they ultimately learn about creating livable communities?

6. What was the impact of ArroyoFest according to Renner? Did it have the effect its organizers intended? What do you think this event suggests about the possibilities for changing existing living spaces?

Exploring the Issues

1. In a sense, Renner's essay tells a complicated story of many different groups working to change how people in one big city live together. Based on Renner's descriptions of these efforts, examine the process by which this change was attempted. What different groups were involved in this effort? What were their agendas? How were they able to coordinate? What difficulties did they face? What do you think this example might suggest about how we create living spaces in general? How effectively do you think Renner explained this complex process in his essay?

2. Renner provides a lot of description of the terrain surrounding the Arroyo Seco Freeway. For readers who have never been to that part of the country, his descriptions will have to help them imagine what that landscape is like so that they can appreciate the challenges facing his group as they try to create a new kind of livable urban community. Evaluate these descriptions. What does Renner emphasize in them? How does he tend to describe the landscape around the freeway? How effectively do you think his descriptions convey a sense of that landscape? Explain.

3. In paragraph 16, Renner tells us that as his group worked to make Arroyo Seco more livable, it confronted an important question: "Livable for whom?" How do you think they eventually answered that question? How would you have answered it? What does that question indicate about the process of creating living spaces?

4. Examine how Renner tells the story of ArroyoFest. How does he organize his story?

What does he emphasize? How well do his descriptions convey the main events in the story? How does he present the climactic moment of the story? Do you think he tells the story effectively? Explain.

Entering the Conversations

1. Write an essay in which you tell the story of a community that was changed by the efforts of its members. Select any kind of community that is appropriate for your essay (for example, your own neighborhood or town, your dorm, your apartment building, a summer camp you attended, your school).

2. Based on Renner's essay (and any other relevant texts you choose), write an essay in which you define a "livable community" and what it takes to create such a community.

Alternatively, create a visual or multimedia representation of your vision for a livable community.

INFOTRAC

3. In many ways, Renner's essay is about the challenges of urban planning, which is a professional field that emerged in the early twentieth century as cities began to grow and face new and unfamiliar problems. Using InfoTrac, your library, and other appropriate resources, examine the field of urban planning today and its role in addressing some of the challenges facing American communities (or communities in

other parts of the world). Look into the history of urban planning and identify important movements or events in that history. Examine how urban planners work today and investigate the major challenges they try to address. If possible, talk to an urban planner in your region or a faculty member at your school who is trained in urban planning (such faculty members often work in Geography departments). Then, write a report on the basis of your research. In your report, provide an overview of urban planning today and discuss its role in efforts to solve the most pressing problems facing cities today. Consider how urban planners are trying to address current problems associated with global climate change. Draw conclusions about the role of urban planning in creating living spaces.

4. Write a letter to an official of your town or city in which you express your views about the most important issues facing your region today. In your letter, offer suggestions about how to make your community more livable.

5. Working with a group of classmates, create a web site (or other appropriate document) in which you offer your plan for making your campus more livable.

6. Write an editorial essay for your campus (or town) newspaper in which you propose specific ways to make your campus more livable.

COMMUNITIES

WHAT DO YOU THINK OF WHEN YOU HEAR THE WORD *COMMUNITY?* MY GUESS IS THAT IF YOU POSED THAT QUESTION TO A DOZEN OF YOUR CLASSMATES, YOU'D GET A DOZEN DIFFERENT VERSIONS OF THE SAME BASIC ANSWER. A COMMUNITY IS THE PLACE WHERE YOU LIVE: YOUR NEIGHBORHOOD OR TOWN, YOUR BLOCK or street if you live in a big city, or maybe your apartment complex. A community is that familiar place where you belong, the place where your family is, maybe the place where you grew up, where you know people and they know you. A community is that place where you feel comfortable and safe, the kind of place famed American painter Norman Rockwell depicted in well-known images like the one on this page.

In American culture the idea of community seems to have a special status. We always seem to be talking about community in one way or another. The reporters on the local television news routinely refer to "our community," while reporters for national news shows such as ABC's *World News Tonight* often file their reports about people from this or that "community." Sometimes those same reporters will refer to "the African American community" or "the Muslim community." Politicians often say the same kinds of things. Obviously, community means something a little different in each of these cases.

As these examples indicate, *community* means many things. Yes, it is that place where we live, where we grew up, where we work, go to school, worship, and play. It is our neighborhood, our town, our city, even our state (we describe ourselves as Californians or New Yorkers) or our nation (we are Americans). But it is also the institutions we are part of: our college or university, our church, our workplace, our union. It is the racial or ethnic or cultural group we are part of: the Jewish community, the Asian American community, Italians, Native Americans, and so many more. It is our profession or job: the medical community, the teaching community, the mental health community. It is the group of people who do the same things we do: climbers, runners, dancers, musicians, coin collectors. And it is the virtual communities we belong to on social networking web sites like Facebook or blogs or discussion forums devoted to like-minded people. Community can be all these things—and more.

The essays in this cluster expose the richness and complexity of communities. These writers describe different kinds of communities and they do so in ways that reveal the nuances of those communities. These writers help us think about what those complicated places mean to us. They show us some of the many different ways that we live together in communities, and they pose challenging questions about the communities we have created.

But these writers also reveal that communities are not always the happy, safe, good places depicted in Norman Rockwell's paintings. Communities can be oppressive, intolerant places, too. Communities certainly seem to be at the center of our lives and provide us with many different kinds of support, but they create problems, too. And at the root of those problems may be the very way we think about *community.*

Together, these three essays can deepen our understanding of the communities in our lives. They also serve as examples of how writing itself is not only a way for us to create and maintain communities but to understand them better as well.

Works by Norman Rockwell printed by permission of the Norman Rockwell Family Agency, Copyright 2010, Norman Rockwell Family Entities.

When I first read Judith Warner's essay about her memories of her childhood home, I immediately thought about my grandmother, in whose home I lived for most of my childhood and adolescence. Like the home that Warner describes in this essay, the home I grew up in always seemed to have a relative or neighbor sitting at the kitchen table or on

Memory Refill

the front porch. I can still picture my grandmother in her apron standing over a cutting board and chopping cabbage or making pierogi (a traditional Polish dumpling), while talking to the friend or relative who always seemed to be sitting at the table where she worked. On the stove behind her was a coffee pot that was always on. Friends, neighbors, and relatives were always coming in and out. It was a kind of

JUDITH WARNER

At home, hidden in the bread box, I have a few samples of a "delicious" herb-chicory mix given to me by my acupuncturist to help me break my addiction to coffee.

It has gone untouched for months. Today, I think I will make the bold move of throwing it out.

I love coffee. And though I have, previously, shown myself willing to forgo all kinds of food and drink in the quest to rid myself of migraines, coffee is one habit that I am firmly committed never to break.

It's not about the caffeine. I have largely renounced caffeine. I say largely because I know that the decaf I now drink all day isn't entirely caffeine-free. My attachment to coffee is about the taste, and the smell, and the gesture.

I mean **"GESTURE,"** now, not in the way of French subway ads, where every ice cream pop, car or laundry detergent is either of a "gesture of freshness" or "a gesture towards pleasure." I mean the kind of gesture my mother's brother Mel used to make, waving toward the coffee pot, when you walked into his house in Brooklyn.

There was, first, the gesture toward the pot, always on, always ready, always warm. Then there was a gesture toward a cup, then a gesture

5

STRATEGIES: WORD CHOICE
Notice how Warner calls our attention to the different meanings of the term "gesture" in this passage. She emphasizes that she is using the term to refer to a physical gesture (such as waving an arm) rather than in its metaphorical sense (of making a gesture, say, of friendship or kindness). Writers often choose words carefully to convey an intended meaning, but it is rare for a writer to explain the meaning in this way. What might Warner gain by doing so here?

community all by itself. I have fond memories of that community, and I think many people have similarly fond memories of their own childhood communities.

Or maybe not. Warner writes in her essay, "Early childhood memories are notoriously inaccurate—and incomplete." She's right. So maybe we have fond memories of the communities where we grew up because we somehow need to have fond memories of the neighborhoods that were so much a part of our lives. If so, then it's worth wondering why. Why do we seem to need to think of our communities with fondness—as good places where life was good? Warner may provide some answers to that question. Her essay can help us better understand the importance of communities—or perhaps of our ideas about communities—in our lives.

Judith Warner hosts her own show on satellite radio and writes a column called "Domestic Disturbances" for the New York Times, *where this essay first appeared in 2008. She writes about politics for the* New Republic, *among other publications, and is the author of several books, including* Hillary Clinton: The Inside Story *(1993).* ▼

GLOSS: DAWN AND G.I. JOE
Dawn was a popular doll for girls in the 1970s and 1980s; G.I. Joe was a popular "action figure" for boys during the same period. Note how Warner seems to avoid describing G.I. Joe as a "doll." Why do you think she does so?

toward a chair. Mel had been in World War II. He'd been left with a metal plate in his skull. There was always something formal, something military about his bearing.

At his behest, you'd sit down at the table, in the breakfast room off the kitchen, and you'd gesture into conversation. Or the grown-ups did, at least, while my cousins Michael and Jonathan and I went off and warred with some combination of **DAWN DOLLS** and **G.I. JOES.**

Mel died of a brain aneurism in 1985. He developed a blinding headache driving home from dropping Jonathan off at music camp and slipped into a coma within hours.

"He was always there, with the coffee cup in one hand and the cigarette in the other," my mother said, bitterly, after the funeral.

In the years that followed, Mel's wife, Barbara, and my mother and I   10
spent many hours sitting around in that breakfast room. We'd drink coffee, and we'd jump in unison every hour on the hour, as the clock in the breakfast room opened to the maddening squawk of a cuckoo.

"Mel loved that clock," Barbara would say.

These days, no one is "always there" with a coffee cup in his hand; nor is there anyone around with a cigarette. No decent person keeps the coffee pot brewing all day. No one would dream of drinking that much caffeine. No one would dream of sitting still all day to schmooze.

The only people who would are perhaps just the sort who might sneak out into the garden to smoke an occasional cigarette when their kids aren't looking. Appealing people, I might be tempted to say. People who live in the grip of their passions. But suspect.

My husband, Max, used to smoke. In our early life together, I didn't much mind. But by the time we had children it became a big issue; I did not want my children to have a father who was going to drop dead one day, coffee cup in one hand, cigarette in the other.

Early on, we lived briefly in the bottom two floors of a house in   15
Brooklyn Heights. Max used to open the kitchen door to smoke. Sometimes, on weekend mornings, the smell of cigarette smoke would combine with the smell of coffee and a certain kind of sun-warmed Brooklyn air. And I'd be transported. Farther away than to the Victorian house in Midwood. Further back—to Flatbush, to the late 1960s, to a brick row house overflowing with great-aunts and grandparents, a kitchen filled with the smells of coffee and cookies and smoked fish and, of course, cigarettes. There were so many cigarettes: Pall Malls and Kents and Lucky Strikes, I think. (Or were the Lucky Strikes the chocolate cigarettes that my Aunt Fannie bought for me?)

My Aunt Fannie had a closet filled with secret things; finger paints and shiny paper, and crayons and scissors. In my memory, they are all just for me, but of course they weren't; they were also for Michael and Jonathan.

Many of my memories of the house are false, it seems. The rooms were not arranged the way I remember them. It wasn't a row-house at all, my mother says; it was semi-detached. Early childhood memories are notoriously inaccurate—and incomplete. I hadn't even remembered the smell—that coffee and cigarettes and bagels and cream cheese and, with any luck, a couple of chocolate jelly rings smell—until Max opened the back door and God in his heaven sent in that perfect beam of sunlight.

It was 1994. Mel was dead, but Barbara was then still alive. The World Trade Center was still standing on the other side of the river. My father was still alive, though within a year he would no longer be, after collapsing on the street, on the way to his office from the Gramercy Park Coffee Shop—where he had his first few cups of the day, every day.

I wouldn't be so pretentious as to say that **I HAVE MEASURED OUT MY LIFE IN COFFEE SPOONS.** But it wouldn't be so far from the truth. I began drinking coffee at the age of nine—teaspoons of warm, milky coffee from my father's cup in restaurants after dinner. By age 11, I was drinking it chummily with my Mom over breakfast. I spent my adolescence over never-empty cups in places like Joe Junior's and Lepanto's and the Viand. There was time for this then, in my New York.

20   I miss that world terribly.

When Emilie greets me, after a long day in school, she buries her head in my neck and breathes deeply.

"You smell like coffee," she says with satisfaction.

Every Monday, we have an hour's break between school pickup and Julia's violin lesson. Every Monday, wishing for a coffee shop, I take the girls to our local bakery-café. Julia and Emilie eat ersatz French pastries and I order a decaf. They do their homework, and I read the paper.

On the wall there is a mural of a village scene somewhere that looks something like Provence. There's a cat in the mural who sits on a stone wall. We believe that the cat has magical powers: he can move at will between his wall in Washington and his wall in France.

25   When I get bored with reading the paper, I stare into his eyes. He is an exile of sorts, never entirely at home.

But I still have my coffee.

CONVERSATIONS: MEASURING LIFE I COFFEE SPOONS

In the opening sentence of paragrap Warner quotes a famous line from T. Eliot's poem "The Love Song of J. Alf Prufrock," in which the speaker says have measured out my life with coffe spoons." Eliot's poem is widely interpreted to be about regret and m opportunities in life. Quoting from a famous literary work as Warner does is a way for writers to enrich the mea of their own writing. Consider how Warner's reference to Eliot's poem fit purpose in this essay. Consider, too, h a reader's familiarity—or lack of familiarity—with Eliot's poem might affect the meaning of this passage of Warner's essay.

Understanding the Text

1. How does Warner describe her "attachment" to coffee? What do you think this attachment reveals about her? What might it reveal about how we live together in communities?

2. What has changed about drinking coffee since Warner's childhood? What does this change suggest to her about her life and about contemporary life in general? What doe it seem to reveal about our communities?

3. What does Warner miss about the world she grew u

in? Does it matter that her memories of that world might be false (as she writes in par. 17)? Explain.

Exploring the Issues

1. What do you think coffee symbolizes for Warner? What is its significance to her? What do you think the importance of coffee for her suggests about how we create and maintain communities?

2. In many ways, this essay is about memory. At one point, Warner writes, "Early childhood memories are notoriously inaccurate—and incomplete." Why is this an important idea for Warner? What does it have to do with her main point in this essay? Does it influence your response to her essay in any way to know that she is unsure about the memories she describes in this essay? Explain. Do you think she's right? Why or why not?

3. Warner shares anecdotes about some of the friends and relatives from her past. What do you think she accomplishes by sharing these anecdotes? How do they help her convey her main points in this essay? How effective do you think these anecdotes are in conveying her ideas? Explain, citing specific passages from her essay to support your answer.

4. Why do you think Warner ends her essay as she does? What point do you think she emphasizes by ending her essay as she does? Do you find her ending effective? Why or why not?

Entering the Conversations

1. Write an essay in which you share your memories of the neighborhood or community or home where you grew up.

2. In a *New York Times* column published shortly after this essay first appeared, Warner responded to the many readers who wrote e-mails to her about the essay. She explained that her essay grew out of her "repugnance for a world where, when people stop by your house, on the way from there to there with never a moment for here, they stand in the doorway, cell phone in one hand, water bottle in the other, too peripatetic to even entertain the notion of sitting down for a warm drink." She wrote that she "wanted to capture a sense of lost worlds. I wanted to try to express what it felt like to have the time to be present." Write an essay in which you assess whether Warner succeeded in achieving these goals for her essay. Cite specific passages from her essay to support your evaluation of her piece.

3. In Warner's essay, coffee becomes a symbol of something lost from her past. Write an essay in which you focus on an item (such as coffee) or an activity (such as playing baseball) that becomes a symbol of something lost or a symbol of community.

4. Based on Warner's essay and any other relevant essays in this chapter (or other chapters in this textbook), write an essay in which you define *community.*

5. In a group of classmates, share the essays you wrote for Question 4. Identify similarities and differences in how each of your classmates defines community, and try to reach consensus about what a community is. Then create an appropriate document (for example, a web page, a PowerPoint presentation, a pamphlet, or some other kind of document) in which your group presents its definition of a community.

6. Search appropriate academic sources to find out what experts and scholars have to say about what a community is. (Google Scholar is a good place to begin your search. Your school library web site will likely have links to other appropriate databases.) Focus on relevant academic fields, such as sociology and anthropology, and try to get a sense of the main ways of thinking about communities in those fields. If possible, talk to a faculty member at your school in one of those fields. Then, write a report in which you present what you learned about how community is defined by experts.

7. On the basis of the research you did for Question 6, write an analysis of a community you belong to. In your essay, use the expert definitions of community that you learned through your research to analyze your community. Draw conclusions about the nature and well-being of your community on the basis of your analysis.

Several years ago, I was on a backcountry *trip in the White Mountains in northern New Hampshire. I stayed for a few nights in a log cabin without electricity or plumbing located a few miles from the nearest road and accessible only by a vigorous hike. On the front door of the cabin was a sign: "No cell phones." The caretaker of the cabin*

Disconnected Urbanism

prohibited cell phones because he wanted to preserve the wilderness atmosphere of the cabin. I was glad he did.

Today, cell phones are everywhere, and the traditional telephone, which has been an important means of communication for nearly a century, is being replaced by wireless communications devices. Complaints about cell phone use in public places are almost as common as cell phones themselves, so you probably won't be surprised to read Paul Goldberger's (b. 1950) criticisms of the use of cell phones on city streets. But there's more to Goldberger's essay than complaints about the annoyance of having to listen to someone's private telephone conversation in a public place or hearing a cell phone ring in a place you don't expect it. Goldberger is concerned about something more: how we use public spaces like city streets. He argues that cell phones are changing our relationship to

PAUL GOLDBERGER

There is a connection between the idea of place and the reality of cellular telephones. It is not encouraging. Places are unique—or at least we like to believe they are—and we strive to experience them as a kind of engagement with particulars. Cell phones are precisely the opposite. When a piece of geography is doing what it is supposed to do, it encourages you to feel a connection to it that, as in marriage, forsakes all others. When you are in Paris you expect to wallow in its Parisness, to feel that everyone walking up the Boulevard Montparnasse is as totally and completely there as the lampposts, the kiosks, the facade of the Brasserie Lipp—and that they could be no place else. So we want it to be in every city, in every kind of place. When you are in a forest, you want to experience its woodsiness; when you are on the beach, you want to feel connected to sand and surf.

This is getting harder to do, not because these special places don't exist or because urban places have come to look increasingly alike. They have, but this is not another rant about the monoculture and sameness of cities and the suburban landscape. Even when you are in

PAUL GOLDBERGER, "OBJECT LESSON: DISCONNECTED URBANISM." FROM *METROPOLIS*, NOVEMBER 2003 ISSUE, COPYRIGHT © 2003 BELLEROPHON PUBLICATIONS, INC. PERMISSION GRANTED BY METROPOLIS WWW.METROPOLISMAG.COM.

those spaces, which he believes may be a sign that we ourselves are changing in ways we may not realize. Given the rapid expansion of wireless communications networks in recent years, Goldberger's concerns are worth considering. His essay provides another way to think about how we live together in communities as new technologies continue to shape our lives. And I couldn't help noticing that when I returned to that cabin in New Hampshire's White Mountains in 2005, the sign about cell phones was no longer there.

Pulitzer Prize–winning author Paul Goldberger is the architecture critic at The New Yorker. *He has written many books and articles on urban design, preservation, and architecture. This essay first appeared in* Metropolis *magazine in 2003.* ◪

CONVERSATIONS: CELL PHONE USE
The use of cell phones has increased dramatically worldwide in the past decade. Between 2001 and 2006, cell phone subscriptions in the United States alone nearly doubled, and it is estimated that 90% of the world will have cell phone coverage by 2010. According to a poll by the Pew Internet and American Life Project, 82% of Americans have complained about annoying cell phone use in public places. Figures like these convey a sense of the dramatic growth in cell phone use, but they are also part of the growing conversation about the impact of cell phones on our lives. Goldberger is one of many critics of technologies that seem to be changing the way we live together in our communities. Such criticisms can be seen as part of a larger conversation about the kinds of communities we want to have.

GLOSS: FLANEUR
A *flaneur* is a person who strolls along idly.

---

a place that retains its intensity, its specialness, and its ability to confer a defining context on your life, it doesn't have the all-consuming effect these places used to. You no longer feel that being in one place cuts you off from other places. Technology has been doing this for a long time, of course—remember when people communicated with Europe by letter and it took a couple of weeks to get a reply? Now we're upset if we have to send a fax because it takes so much longer than e-mail.

But the cell phone has changed our sense of place more than faxes and computers and e-mail because of its ability to intrude into every moment in every possible place. When you walk along the street and talk on a cell phone, you are not on the street sharing the communal experience of urban life. You are in some other place—someplace at the other end of your phone conversation. You are there, but you are not there. It reminds me of the title of Lillian Ross's memoir of her life with William Shawn, *Here But Not Here.* Now that is increasingly true of almost every person on almost every street in almost every city. You are either on the phone or carrying one, and the moment it rings you will be transported out of real space into a virtual realm.

This matters because the street is the ultimate public space and walking along it is the defining urban experience. It is all of us—different people who lead different lives—coming together in the urban mixing chamber. But what if half of them are elsewhere, there in body but not in any other way? You are not on Madison Avenue if you are holding a little object to your ear that pulls you toward a person in Omaha.

The great offense of the cell phone in public is not the intrusion of its ring, although that can be infuriating when it interrupts a tranquil moment. It is the fact that even when the phone does not ring at all, and is being used quietly and discreetly, it renders a public place less public. It turns the boulevardier into a sequestered individual, the **FLANEUR** into a figure of privacy. And suddenly the meaning of the street as a public place has been hugely diminished.

I don't know which is worse—the loss of the sense that walking along a great urban street is a glorious shared experience or the blurring of distinctions between different kinds of places. But these cultural losses are related, and the cell phone has played a major role in both. The other day I returned a phone call from a friend who lives in Hartford. He had left a voice-mail message saying he was visiting his son in New Orleans, and when I called him back on his cell phone—area code 860, Hartford—he picked up the call in Tallahassee. Once the area code actually meant something in terms of geography: it outlined a clearly

CONVERSATIONS: THE CONVENIENCE OF CELL PHONES
Goldberger describes cell phones as "infuriating" intrusions in public places, but today, cell phones are commonly portrayed as a convenient and useful technology. Consider what these images, commonly used in advertisements, say about the use of cell phones.

defined piece of the earth; it became a form of identity. Your telephone number was a badge of place. Now the area code is really not much more than three digits; and if it has any connection to a place, it's just the telephone's home base. An area code today is more like a car's license plate. The downward spiral that began with the end of the old telephone exchanges that truly did connect to a place—RHinelander 4 and BUtterfield 8 for the Upper East Side, or CHelsea 3 downtown, or UNiversity 4 in Morningside Heights—surely culminates in the placeless area codes such as 917 and 347 that could be anywhere in New York—or anywhere at all.

It's increasingly common for cell-phone conversations to begin with the question, "Where are you?" and for the answer to be anything from "out by the pool" to "Madagascar." I don't miss the age when phone charges were based on distance, but that did have the beneficial effect of reinforcing a sense that places were distinguishable from one another. Now calling across the street and calling from New York to California or even Europe are precisely the same thing. They cost the same because to the phone they are the same. Every place is exactly the same as every other place. They are all just nodes on a network—and so, increasingly, are we.

Understanding the Text

1. Why is it important to Goldberger that a specific city or place is unique? What might that suggest about his sense of place and our relationship to places like cities?

2. Goldberger writes that "the great offense of the cell phone . . . is the fact that even when the phone does not ring at all, and is being used quietly and discreetly, it renders a public place less public." In what sense does the cell phone render a public place less public? Why is that a problem, in Goldberger's view? Do you agree with him? Why or why not?

3. In what sense does the cell phone help make every place like every other place? Why does this concern Goldberger? Do you think it should concern him? Explain.

Exploring the Issues

1. In a sense, Goldberger is writing about two spaces in this essay: the public space of the city street and the "virtual" space of the cell phone. What basic distinction does Goldberger make between these two spaces? Why is that distinction important? What might it suggest about Goldberger's values regarding lifestyle and the spaces we live in?

2. Goldberger describes walking along a city street as "a glorious shared experience" (par. 6). What is glorious about walking along a city street in Goldberger's view? What does this statement reveal about Goldberger's lifestyle preferences? What does it reveal about his view of cities? Do you think most people would agree with him that walking along a city street is a glorious shared experience? Why or why not?

3. How would you describe Goldberger's voice in this essay? What features of his voice stand out for you? Do you think his voice is effective? Explain, citing specific passages to illustrate your answer.

Entering the Conversations

1. Write an essay in which you express your own views about cell phones and their use today.

INFOTRAC

2. Communications technologies like the cell phone and the Internet have developed rapidly in the past decade or so, and as Goldberger's essay suggests, these technologies can affect our lives in a variety of ways—intended or not. Select one such technology and, using InfoTrac College Edition, the library, and any other appropriate resources, investigate its development and its effects on modern life. Then write a report on the basis of your research. Try to draw conclusions about the impact of the technology you have researched on our communities

3. On the basis of your research for Question 2, write a letter to the editor of your local newspaper or another appropriate publication in which you express your own concerns about an important new communications technology and how it tends to be used today.

4. Write an essay in which you explore the connection between technology and how we live together in communities. Draw on Goldberger's essay and any other essay in this chapter (or on other readings that are not in this book) to help support your points.

5. Create a web site intended to educate people on using their cell phones appropriately in public places. On your site, identify several important common places that people frequent and offer advice for using (or not using) cell phones in those places.

Shortly before I read the following essay, I attended a relative's high school graduation ceremony. The commencement speakers inevitably referred to the school community as well as the larger community of which the school is part, always talking in positive tones about those communities. Indeed, school commencements are among the most

Community Kills

important rituals by which we define ourselves as part of a community. As I listened to these speeches, I wasn't thinking about the terrible shootings that occurred at Columbine High School in Colorado nearly ten years earlier. But writer Cyrus Sanai might have wished that I had been. His essay, published shortly after the Columbine shootings in 1999, which left 14 students and a teacher dead, presents a much different perspective on the idea of a school community than most of the people attending my relative's com-

CYRUS SANAI

The massacre at Columbine High School prompted OP-ED WRITERS ACROSS THE LAND TO diagnose a shocking "lack of community" as the cause of the madness. As if! There is no public institution in America that works harder to forge a sense of belonging than the suburban public high school. Assemblies, homecoming week festivities, car wash fund-raisers, pep rallies, proms, graduation ceremonies—these rituals instill in their participants the "school spirit" that persuades many alumni to return to town every five years for reunions to celebrate high school's glory days.

Representing the "lack of community" position were **ESSAYIST RICHARD RODRIGUEZ AND BIOGRAPHER NEAL GABLER,** writing separately in Sunday's *Los Angeles Times* "Opinion" section.

Rodriguez took the standard communitarian tack, arguing that newly landscaped suburbs such as Littleton produce deracinated teens who can't become individuals because they lack a sense of community: "[Y]ou cannot become an individual without a strong sense of 'we,' " He writes. Gabler

CYRUS SANAI, "COMMUNITY KILLS," *SLATE MAGAZINE,* APRIL 30, 1999.

STRATEGIES: USING CONTEXT TO ENTER A CONVERSATION
In the very first sentence of his essay, Sanai refers to the many "op-ed writers across the land" who published opinion pieces about the events that took place at Columbine High School in 1999. Assuming that his readers would be familiar with the massive press coverage of the shootings, Sanai can quickly focus his readers' attention on his subject and establish his own position without having to provide much background information. In this way, he takes advantage of the historical and cultural context to be concise and efficient as he sets the tone and establishes the subject of his essay.

mencement probably had in mind. Sanai asks us to think about the responsibility that the community itself had for that massacre. Criticizing the intolerance that he sees in school communities, Sanai provokes us to think about the less flattering and even destructive aspects of communities. In that regard, his essay complicates our sense of what a community is—and what it means to be part of one.

Cyrus Sanai's articles have appeared in the Washington Post, *the* Chronicle of Higher Education, *and* Slate, *an online magazine in which this essay was first published in 1999.* ☑

CONVERSATIONS: RICHARD RODRIGUEZ AND NEAL GABLER
Writer Richard Rodriguez (whose essay "The Achievement of Desire" appears in Chapter 6 of this textbook) is a well-known critic who often writes about education. Neal Gabler is the author of many books and articles about popular culture as well as a regular guest on popular television talk shows like *Good Morning America* and *Fox News Watch*. In paragraph 2, Sanai refers to essays that each wrote about the Columbine shootings for the *Los Angeles Times* in 1999. In doing so, Sanai engages directly in the national conversation about those shootings that was occurring at the time. Notice that Sanai summarizes Rodriguez's and Gabler's essays and interprets them as having the same basic position about the Columbine shootings, a position with which he obviously disagrees. This is a common strategy writers use when entering a complex and intense conversation. By summarizing Rodriguez's and Gabler's essays in this way, Sanai makes his criticisms of their viewpoint clear and quickly establishes his own viewpoint.

GLOSS: ERIC HARRIS AND DYLAN KLEBOLD
Eric Harris and Dylan Klebold are the two students who carried out the shootings at Columbine High School. In the aftermath of those shootings, a great deal was written about these two students and why they carried out the attacks on their classmates and teachers. As Sanai suggests here, one explanation is that Harris and Klebold were the victims of favoritism toward athletes that Sanai (and other critics) believe is typical of American high schools.

combined a squishier communitarian criticism ("it may be too simple to say that rootless malleable communities . . . give rise to rootless malleable children with little identity of their own, save the identity borrowed from mass culture, but it may not be too far off, either") with his media monism: Identitiless teens play "Doom" on the PC, then try it out in the enhanced 3-D perspective of real life.

But neither Gabler nor Rodriguez appear to have attended a suburban high school. If they had, they would know that such high schools suffer from an overdose of community, not a deficit. In Columbine, community killed.

Columbine evidently overflowed with this sort of school spirit, most of which revolves around student athletics. The latest consensus from Littleton is that rage directed at student athletes and their perceived protectors, the school administration, drove **ERIC HARRIS** and **DYLAN KLEBOLD** to meticulously prepare and then execute the killings. At Columbine and suburban high schools elsewhere, athletics are the biggest tool in creating the sense of "we" that Rodriguez extols. The community—both on and off campus—worships the basketball and football gods, and favoritism for the top jocks is institutionalized in the name of fostering a sense of community. It's more than curious that at institutions supposedly dedicated to academics, spectator-friendly athletic competitions are the only activities considered to be worthy of regular praise and attention. Gabler notes that Columbine's closed-circuit TV system played sports highlights regularly. Can one imagine the *Rocky Mountain News,* or any other newspaper, replacing high-school sports coverage with debate team transcripts?

The skewed community values created by administrators, teachers, parents, and the media exacerbate the natural volatility of high-school social groups. Just as rape and other felonies committed by star athletes at the NCAA powerhouses are tolerated with wearying predictability, today's high-school administrator will allow the barely controllable gangs from the gridiron free rein to commit verbal and physical **AGGRO** upon the castes below. Most victims of the harassment and ostracism survive. Some drop out of school or transfer. In my day, one hassled student ended his life by hanging himself from a basketball rim. In Harris and Klebold's case, the endgame was a spasm of violence.

While Harris and Klebold have established—one hopes—the extreme end of inappropriate response to high-school hazing, their crimes were anticipated by popular culture. It's particularly strange that the supposedly media-savvy Gabler didn't acknowledge in his

5

piece the popular-kid killing classic *Heathers* and its less acute echo *Jawbreaker.* Even the mild snarkiness of MTV's **DARIA** should have put Gabler, for whom mass entertainment is the only important reality, on notice that high schools are communities that are hardly tolerant, accepting, or even rational. Are the public vows to rebuild Columbine also a vow to resurrect the very community that shaped Harris and Klebold?

You can't feel like an outsider if you don't want to get inside. Viewed from this angle, Harris and Klebold's rampage can be interpreted as an extreme desire to join a community whose values they had bought into. By embracing Nazi sloganeering, Harris and Klebold may have thought that they had cast out Columbine's influence. But they absorbed Columbine's football team community values—aggression, planning, cohesion, and physical sacrifice for the goal—in the methodical planning and execution of their atrocity. Yet right up to their donning black trench coats for the last time, they would probably have preferred being honored at a Columbine pep rally than at the **NUREMBERG** rally.

GLOSS: AGGRO

"Aggro" is a term generally meaning aggression or threatening behavior. The term seems to have evolved from role-playing games like *World of Warcraft.*

GLOSS: DARIA

Daria, a cynical suburban high school student, was the main character on an animated television show that was aired on MTV from 1997 to 2002.

GLOSS: NUREMBERG

In the 1920s and 1930s, the Nazi Party in Germany held an annual rally at Nuremberg that has come to symbolize the mass embrace of racism, intolerance, and violence for which the Nazis eventually became famous. Note how Sanai uses this reference to emphasize his point in this final paragraph.

Understanding the Text

1. What is the "lack of community" viewpoint on the Columbine shootings that Sanai criticizes? Why does he criticize this viewpoint? What does this viewpoint suggest to him about how we tend to understand the idea of a community? Do you think he's right? Why or why not?

2. What does Sanai mean when he writes that suburban high schools suffer from "an overdose of community" (see par. 4)? What is the nature of this "overdose," in his view? What are its effects on students? What do you think his discussion of this "overdose of community" suggests about the communities we create and live in?

3. How does Sanai explain what happened at Columbine? Does he blame the students who carried out the shootings? Explain. Do you find his explanation convincing? Why or why not?

Exploring the Issues

1. Sanai presents a rather negative image of high school in his essay. What do you think his depiction of high school in this essay indicates about his views on communities in general? Do you think he sees communities as inherently problematic? Why or

why not? Do his criticisms of high schools apply to other kinds of communities? Explain.

2. How would you characterize the tone of this essay? What features of Sanai's writing help establish his tone? Do you think his tone is appropriate for his subject matter in this essay? Explain.

3. Sanai makes several references to popular culture in his essay, specifically to films and television shows, as well as to historical events and op-ed essays in major newspapers. What do you think these references suggest about his sense of his audience? Do you think you are part of his intended audience? Explain. (To answer these questions you might review *Slate*, the online publication in which this essay first appeared.)

Entering the Conversations

1. Write an essay in which you draw on your own experience to present your view of high school as a community.

2. In a group of classmates, share the essays you wrote for Question 1. What similarities and differences can you identify in your classmates' viewpoints about high schools as communities? What common experiences do you all share? Are your respective experi-

ences related in any way to the kind of high schools you each attended (urban, suburban, small, large)? What conclusions can you draw about schools as communities? On the basis of your discussion, make appropriate revisions to the essay you wrote for Question 1.

3. In paragraphs 2–4 of this essay, Sanai summarizes essays by Richard Rodriguez and Neal Gabler that were published shortly after the Columbine shootings. Using appropriate databases, find these essays and read them. Evaluate whether Sanai's summaries of them are accurate. Then either write your own response to them (or to Sanai), or write an analysis in which you evaluate Sanai's representation of their arguments.

4. Create a web site (or similar kind of multimedia document) that represents your view of a high school as a community.

5. Write a response to Sanai in which you present your own viewpoint about the nature of high schools as communities.

6. Create a pamphlet, web site, or other appropriate document explaining the nature of the community at the high school you attended. Write your document as a guide for current students at that high school.

VALUING PLACE

FOR A TIME, I LIVED IN THE MIDWESTERN UNITED STATES, AND ALTHOUGH I ENJOYED LIVING THERE, I SOMETIMES FELT OUT OF PLACE. I MISSED THE MOUNTAINS AND FORESTS AND EVEN THE WEATHER OF THE NORTHEASTERN UNITED STATES WHERE I GREW UP. THE LANDSCAPE OF THE MIDWEST SEEMED TO LACK THE FEA-tures or characteristics that I needed to feel at home. Sometimes I would talk about this sense of being out of place with friends who grew up in the Midwest but lived in the East, and they would confide that they had similar feelings. They felt out of place in the eastern states where I grew up. One colleague of mine, who grew up in the Northwest but has now lived in upstate New York for many years, clearly still feels out of place and often talks about Washington State as "home."

> Whatever the specific connection, somehow these places are part of who we are; they shape our sense of identity and purpose.

I was thinking about these feelings as I compiled the readings for this cluster. And the more I thought about them, the more I realized how important a sense of place can be in our lives. Paradoxically, American culture seems to value mobility. As soon as the nation was established, Americans were pushing into the frontier of the West and didn't stop until much of the land between the Atlantic and Pacific oceans had been settled. American history is marked by large migrations of people: waves of immigrants in the nineteenth and early twentieth centuries from European nations and more recent immigrations from Asian and Latin American countries; the movement of millions of Blacks from the American South to northern industrial cities like Chicago and Cleveland after the Civil War; more recently, the shifting of the U.S. population from the Northeast to the Southwest and Southeast, seen in the dramatic growth of cities like Denver, Las Vegas, and Atlanta.

Yet for all this movement, people still seem to need a connection to a place. The essays in this cluster explore that need. They examine the many different ways in which we come to value certain places, as individuals and as members of larger communities or cultures. Sometimes that place is a town or region or even a kind of landscape—like a desert or a lake—that holds emotional importance for us. Sometimes it is a place, like a battlefield or Ground Zero in New York City, where something momentous happened and where we feel a need to remember. Whatever the specific connection, somehow these places are part of who we are; they shape our sense of identity and purpose. We value these places because they help us find value in our lives. These essays are about that kind of value in our lives.

E. B. White (1899–1985) is considered by many to be America's preeminent essayist. He is probably better known for his children's books, Charlotte's Web *(1952) and* Stuart Little *(1945). But if you attended school in the United States, it's possible that you were also assigned to read the following essay. A study published in 2000 revealed that*

Once More TO THE Lake

this essay was the most frequently reprinted essay in composition textbooks during the previous fifty years. It's worth examining why.

White is usually praised for his simple but elegant writing style and carefully crafted descriptions. This essay, which was first published in Harper's *magazine in 1941, may give you some sense of how White earned his reputation as a superb stylist. But certainly this essay has more to offer a reader than an effective writing style. Something about the way White explores his subject continues to resonate with readers more than a half century after he wrote this essay. I first read the essay when I was a new graduate student in my early twenties, and it immediately reminded me of the lake in Pennsylvania where I spent summers during my teenage years. White's descriptions of being on the lake felt familiar to me, almost as if he were describing my own experiences. That sense of familiarity*

E. B. WHITE

One summer, along about 1904, my father rented a camp on a lake in Maine and took us all there for the month of August. We all got ringworm from some kittens and had to rub Pond's Extract on our arms and legs night and morning, and my father rolled over in a canoe with all his clothes on; but outside of that the vacation was a success and from then on none of us ever thought there was any place in the world like that lake in Maine. We returned summer after summer—always on August 1st for one month. I have since become a salt-water man, but sometimes in summer there are days when the restlessness of the tides and the fearful cold of the sea water and the incessant wind which blows across the afternoon and into the evening make me wish for the placidity of a lake in the woods. A few weeks ago this feeling got so strong I bought myself a couple of bass hooks and a spinner and returned to the lake where we used to go, for a week's fishing and to revisit old haunts.

I took along my son, who had never had any fresh water up his nose and who had seen lily pads only from train windows. On the journey over to the lake I began to wonder what it would be like. I wondered how time would have marred this unique, this holy spot—the coves and streams, the hills that the sun set behind, the camps and the paths behind the camps. I was sure that the tarred road would have found it out and I wondered in what other ways it would be desolated. It is strange how much you can remember about places like that once you allow your mind to return into the grooves which lead back. You remember one thing, and that suddenly reminds you of another thing. I guess I remembered clearest of all the early mornings, when the lake was cool and motionless, remembered how the bedroom smelled of the lumber it was made of and the wet woods whose scent entered through the screen. The partitions in the camp were thin and did not extend clear to the top of the rooms, and as I was always the first up I would dress softly so as not to wake the others, and sneak out into the sweet outdoors and start out in the canoe, keeping close along the shore in the long shadows of the pines. I remembered being very careful never to rub my paddle against the gunwale for fear of disturbing the stillness of the cathedral.

The lake had never been what you would call a wild lake. There were cottages sprinkled around the shores, and it was in farming country although the shores of the lake were quite heavily wooded. Some of the cottages were owned by nearby farmers, and you would live at the shore and eat your meals at the farmhouse. That's what our family did. But although it wasn't wild, **IT WAS A FAIRLY LARGE AND UNDISTURBED LAKE AND THERE WERE PLACES IN IT WHICH, TO A CHILD AT LEAST, SEEMED INFINITELY REMOTE AND PRIMEVAL.**

I was right about the tar: it led to within half a mile of the shore. But when I got back there, with my boy, and we settled into a camp near a farmhouse and into the kind of summertime I had known, I could tell that it was going to be pretty much the same as it had been before—I knew it, lying in bed the first morning, smelling the bedroom, and hearing the boy sneak quietly out and go off along the shore in a boat. I began to sustain the illusion that he was I, and therefore, by simple transposition, that I was my father. This sensation persisted, kept cropping up all the time we were there. It was not an entirely new feeling, but in this setting it grew much stronger. I seemed to be living a dual existence. I would be in the middle of some simple act, I would be picking up a bait box or laying down a table fork, or I would be saying something, and suddenly it would be not I but my father who was saying the words or making the gesture. It gave me a creepy sensation.

5   We went fishing the first morning. I felt the same damp moss covering the worms in the bait can, and saw the dragonfly alight on the tip of my rod as it hovered a few inches from the surface of the

may be one reason that readers connect with this essay. But as I've become older and raised my own family, my response to White's essay has changed. Now I read it as a father who shares some of White's joys and fears as a parent. And the ending of the essay, which has generated so much discussion over the years, means something different to me now than it did when I was younger. Maybe what makes an essay great is the way it can prompt us to explore complex ideas or issues that change over a lifetime.

But this essay is also about a place that was special to White. And whatever else we might think about this essay, it may help us appreciate the value of special places in our lives.

Elwyn Brooks White was a columnist for The New Yorker *for many years. His columns were collected in two volumes,* One Man's Meat *(1942) and* The Points of My Compass *(1962). He also published other essay collections in addition to his children's books and* The Elements of Style, *which he coauthored with William Strunk, Jr.* ☑

CONVERSATIONS: WILD LAKES

White describes the lake where he and his family vacationed not as a "wild lake" but one that was "undisturbed" and "seemed infinitely remote and primeval." Such places are increasingly hard to find as regions like the area in Maine where White took his family have become developed for resorts and vacation homes. Real estate values in such places have increased dramatically in the past few decades, so visiting them is not affordable for many people. It's worth considering whether the experience that White describes in this essay requires a remote and undisturbed place like this lake. Or does the nature of the place itself not matter? In other words, can this kind of experience happen in any place? If not, will some readers be unable to appreciate the value of this place to White?

water. It was the arrival of this fly that convinced me beyond any doubt that everything was as it always had been, that the years were a mirage and there had been no years. The small waves were the same, chucking the rowboat under the chin as we fished at anchor, and the boat was the same boat, the same color green and the ribs broken in the same places, and under the floor-boards the same freshwater leavings and débris—the dead helgramite, the wisps of moss, the rusty discarded fishhook, the dried blood from yesterday's catch. We stared silently at the tips of our rods, at the dragonflies that came and went. I lowered the tip of mine into the water, tentatively, pensively dislodging the fly, which darted two feet away, poised, darted two feet back, and came to rest again a little farther up the rod. There had been no years between the ducking of this dragonfly and the other one—the one that was part of memory. I looked at the boy, who was silently watching his fly, and it was my hands that held his rod, my eyes watching. I felt dizzy and didn't know which rod I was at the end of.

We caught two bass, hauling them in briskly as though they were mackerel, pulling them over the side of the boat in a businesslike manner without any landing net, and stunning them with a blow on the back of the head. When we got back for a swim before lunch, the lake was exactly where we had left it, the same number of inches from the dock, and there was only the merest suggestion of a breeze. This seemed an utterly enchanted sea, this lake you could leave to its own devices for a few hours and come back to, and find that it had not stirred, this constant and trustworthy body of water. In the shallows, the dark, water-soaked sticks and twigs, smooth and old, were undulating in clusters on the bottom against the clean ribbed sand, and the track of the mussel was plain. A school of minnows swam by, each minnow with its small individual shadow, doubling the attendance, so clear and sharp in the sunlight. Some of the other campers were in swimming, along the shore, one of them with a cake of soap, and the water felt thin and clear and unsubstantial. Over the years there had been this person with the cake of soap, this cultist, and here he was. There had been no years.

Up to the farmhouse to dinner through the teeming, dusty field, the road under our sneakers was only a two-track road. The middle track was missing, the one with the marks of the hooves and the splotches of dried, flaky manure. There had always been three tracks to choose from in choosing which track to walk in; now the choice was narrowed down to two. For a moment I missed terribly the middle alternative. But the way led past the tennis court, and something about the way it lay there in the sun reassured me; the tape had loosened along the backline, the alleys were green with plantains and other weeds, and the net (installed in June and removed in September) sagged in the dry noon, and the whole place steamed with midday heat and hunger and emptiness. There was a choice of pie for dessert, and one was blueberry

STRATEGIES: METAPHOR

This paragraph (par. 5) is one of the most famous passages in American nonfiction writing. Notice how White describes this seemingly simple scene of him and his son fishing from a rowboat. Consider how White uses the images of the lake surface and the dragonfly as metaphors to convey his ideas in this essay. What ideas do you think he is conveying with these metaphors?

and one was apple, and the waitresses were the same country girls, there having been no passage of time, only the illusion of it as in a dropped curtain—the waitresses were still fifteen; their hair had been washed, that was the only difference—they had been to the movies and seen the pretty girls with the clean hair.

Summertime, oh summertime, pattern of life indelible, the fade-proof lake, the woods unshatterable, the pasture with the sweetfern and the juniper forever and ever, summer without end; this was the background, and the life along the shore was the design, the cottages with their innocent and tranquil design, their tiny docks with the flagpole and the American flag floating against the white clouds in the blue sky, the little paths over the roots of the trees leading from camp to camp and the paths leading back to the outhouses and the can of lime for sprinkling, and at the souvenir counters at the store the miniature birch-bark canoes and the post cards that showed things looking a little better than they looked. This was the **AMERICAN FAMILY AT PLAY**, escaping the city heat, wondering whether the newcomers in the camp at the head of the cove were "common" or "nice," wondering whether it was true that the people who drove up for Sunday dinner at the farmhouse were turned away because there wasn't enough chicken.

It seemed to me, as I kept remembering all this, that those times and those summers had been infinitely precious and worth saving. There had been jollity and peace and goodness. The arriving (at the beginning of August) had been so big a business in itself, at the railway station the farm wagon drawn up, the first smell of the pineladen air, the first glimpse of the smiling farmer, and the great importance of the trunks and your father's enormous authority in such matters, and the feel of the wagon under you for the long ten-mile haul, and at the top of the last long hill catching the first view of the lake after eleven months of not seeing this cherished body of water. The shouts and cries of the other campers when they saw you, and the trunks to be unpacked, to give up their rich burden. (Arriving was less exciting nowadays, when you sneaked up in your car and parked it under a tree near the camp and took out the bags and in five minutes it was all over, no fuss, no loud wonderful fuss about trunks.)

Peace and goodness and jollity. The only thing that was wrong now, really, was the sound of the place, an unfamiliar nervous sound of the outboard motors. This was the note that jarred, the one thing that would sometimes break the illusion and set the years moving. In those other summertimes all motors were inboard; and when they were at a

---

CONVERSATIONS: AMERICAN FAMILY LIFE

In paragraph 8, White offers a description of "the American family at play." It is possible that at the time he wrote this essay, the scene he describes in this passage was common. In other words, perhaps he was describing the typical American family on vacation in the middle of the twentieth century. Many readers might therefore find this scene familiar. But many readers might not. Consider whether White's descriptions focus on a certain kind of American family or a certain segment of American society. And consider how this description might apply today: Is this scene typical of American families today? Such questions may help us see that in describing such scenes, White was participating in a larger conversation about the American family. Some critics would see his descriptions as based on an ideal view of the family, one that is associated with a certain social class and cultural background, and they might charge that such descriptions contribute to false myths about the family in American society. As you read, you might consider whether such criticisms are valid. Consider, too, what White's essay might contribute to this ongoing conversation about the American family.

little distance, the noise they made was a sedative, an ingredient of summer sleep. They were one-cylinder and two-cylinder engines, and some were make-and-break and some were jump-spark, but they all made a sleepy sound across the lake. The one-lungers throbbed and fluttered, and the twin-cylinder ones purred and purred, and that was a quiet sound too. But now the campers all had outboards. In the daytime, in the hot mornings, these motors made a petulant, irritable sound; at night, in the still evening when the afterglow lit the water, they whined about one's ears like mosquitoes. My boy loved our rented outboard, and his great desire was to achieve single-handed mastery over it, and authority, and he soon learned the trick of choking it a little (but not too much), and the adjustment of the needle valve. Watching him I would remember the things you could do with the old one-cylinder engine with the heavy fly-wheel, how you could have it eating out of your hand if you got really close to it spiritually. Motor boats in those days didn't have clutches, and you would make a landing by shutting off the motor at the proper time and coasting in with a dead rudder. But there was a way of reversing them, if you learned the trick, by cutting the switch and putting it on again exactly on the final dying revolution of the flywheel, so that it would kick back against compression and begin reversing. Approaching a dock in a strong following breeze, it was difficult to slow up sufficiently by the ordinary coasting method, and if a boy felt he had complete mastery over his motor, he was tempted to keep it running beyond its time and then reverse it a few feet from the dock. It took a cool nerve, because if you threw the switch a twentieth of a second too soon you could catch the flywheel when it still had speed enough to go up past center, and the boat would leap ahead, charging bull-fashion at the dock.

We had a good week at the camp. The bass were biting well and the sun shone endlessly, day after day. We would be tired at night and lie down in the accumulated heat of the little bedrooms after the long hot day and the breeze would stir almost imperceptibly outside and the smell of the swamp drift in through the rusty screens. Sleep would come easily and in the morning the red squirrel would be on the roof, tapping out his gay routine. I kept remembering everything, lying in bed in the mornings—the small steamboat that had a long rounded stern like the lip of a Ubangi, how quietly she ran on the moonlight sails, when the older boys played their mandolins and the girls sang and we ate doughnuts dipped in sugar, and how sweet the music was on the water in the shining night, and what it had felt like to think about girls then. After breakfast we would go up to the store and the things were in the same place—the minnows in a bottle, the plugs and spinners disarranged and pawed over by the youngsters from the boys' camp, the fig newtons and the Beeman's gum. Outside, the road was tarred and cars stood in front of the store. Inside, all was just as it had always been, except there was more Coca-Cola and not so much Moxie and root beer and birch beer and sarsaparilla. We would walk out with a bottle of pop apiece and sometimes the pop would backfire up our noses and hurt. We explored the streams, quietly, where the turtles slid off the sunny logs and dug their way into the soft bottom; and we lay on the town wharf and fed worms to the tame bass. Everywhere we went I had trouble making out which was I, the one walking at my side, the one walking in my pants.

One afternoon while we were there at that lake a thunderstorm came up. It was like the revival of an old melodrama that I had seen long ago with childish awe. The second-act climax of the drama of the electrical disturbance over a lake in America had not changed in any important respect. This was the big scene, still the big scene. The whole thing was so familiar, the first feeling of oppression and heat and a general air around camp of not wanting to go very far away. In midafternoon (it was all the same) a curious darkening of the sky, and a lull in everything that had made life tick; and then the way the boats suddenly swung the other way at their moorings with the coming of a breeze out of the new quarter, and the premonitory rumble. Then the kettle drum, then the snare, then the bass drum and cymbals, then crackling light against the dark, and the gods grinning and licking their chops in the hills. Afterward the calm, the rain steadily rustling in the calm lake, the return of light and hope and spirits, and the campers running out in joy and relief to go swimming in the rain, their bright cries perpetuating the deathless joke about how they were getting simply drenched, and the children screaming with delight at the new sensation of bathing in the rain, and the joke about getting drenched linking the generations in a strong indestructible chain. And the comedian who waded in carrying an umbrella.

When the others went swimming my son said he was going in too. He pulled his dripping trunks from the line where they had hung all through the shower, and wrung them out. Languidly, and with no thought of going in, I watched him, his hard little body, skinny and bare, saw him wince slightly as he pulled up around his vitals the small, soggy, icy garment. As he buckled the swollen belt suddenly my groin felt the chill of death.

Understanding the Text

1. What exactly made the lake in Maine that White and his family visited so special? Why does White describe it as "this holy spot"? Was there anything special about that particular lake that made it different from other lakes White might have visited? What might the connection White felt to this particular lake suggest about how and why we value specific places?

2. What is the "illusion" that White begins to experience once he has arrived with his family at the lake where he vacationed as a child? What is the "dual existence" he begins to feel? Why is this dual existence important to White?

What does it suggest about the value of special places in our lives?

3. In what ways had the sounds of the lake changed for White? What do you think these changes suggest about that place? What might they suggest about our sense of place in general?

4. Why does White feel "the chill of death" as he watches his son pull on a wet pair of shorts? What do you think White is emphasizing about the experience of returning to the lake by ending his essay with this line?

Exploring the Issues

1. What do you think this essay suggests about relationships, especially the relationship between parent and child? What role does place play in such relationships?

2. In many ways, this essay is about memory. What do you think the essay suggests about our memories and their role in our lives? What does it suggest about the role of memory in the way we understand and value certain places in our lives?

3. A great deal has changed since White wrote this essay more than sixty years ago, including the technologies we now use in our lives and the way Americans spend their leisure time. Many places like the lake White describes have been transformed by rising real estate prices and increasing populations (see *Conversations: Wild Lakes* on page 567). How might these kinds of changes influence the way readers to-

day respond to White's essay? Do you think these changes affect the main ideas White explores? Explain.

4. White has earned much acclaim for his writing style. How would you describe White's writing style? What characteristics of his prose do you think contribute to his style? Do you think his writing deserves its reputation? Explain, citing specific passages to support your answer.

Entering the Conversations

1. Write an essay about a place that was special to you or your family when you were growing up. In your essay, try to convey a sense of why that place was special and what role it seemed to play in your life.

2. This essay has been discussed as an essay about time, memory, place, change, and relationships. Identify the idea or issue in this essay that seems most important or striking to you and write an essay in which you discuss that idea. In your essay, examine how White explores this idea or issue in his descriptions of the lake and the events that took place there.

3. In a group of classmates, share the essays you wrote for Question 2. Identify any similarities and differences in the ideas that each of you took away from White's essay. Draw conclusions about what your group's essays might suggest about how we make sense of essays like White's "Once More to the Lake."

INFOTRAC

4. Like White, many people vacation at a special place that has some meaning for them or their families. But vacationing has changed in many ways since White's essay was published in 1941. Using InfoTrac College Edition, the Internet, your library, and other relevant resources (such as travel organizations like the American Automobile Association), investigate how Americans tend to spend their vacations today. How have vacations changed in the years since White wrote this essay? What kinds of vacations are most popular today? Why do Americans vacation as they do? Try to answer such questions in your research. Then write a report based on your research. In your report, draw conclusions about the role of place in the way people spend vacations.

5. Find several flyers, Internet sites, magazine advertisements, or similar promotional materials that advertise specific vacation spots. Examine how these materials present the places they are promoting. What do they emphasize about these places? What ideas or feelings do they try to convey? What audiences do they seem to target? Then write a report in which you discuss what you found in examining these materials. Try to draw conclusions about the role of place in the way we think about vacations.

6. Create a flyer, web site, or other appropriate kind of document in which you advertise a place that is special to you for some reason.

Recently, I was talking to my brother about his habit of falling asleep each night with the television on. My brother is a busy guy. He's a high school guidance counselor, a football and golf coach, and the father of two active boys. Every night, he has to have the television on to fall asleep. Otherwise, he says, his mind just races and he becomes too restless to sleep.

Stillness

Maybe my brother should read the following essay by Scott Russell Sanders (b. 1945). Sanders describes a problem similar to my brother's: a busy life that leaves him with too much on his mind. He confides to us that what is on his mind is more than just his many professional and family commitments; he is also worried about the many problems in the world beyond his own small place in Indiana, where he makes his home. How, he asks, can we be expected to deal with the frantic pace of our own lives and attend to the pain and suffering in the wider world, too?

One answer is to find stillness, which for Sanders means a small hut that he built on his property. In describing that hut, Sanders is offering us a way to think about how we use space in general and about our relationship to the places we inhabit. My guess is that you have some place where you can take a break from the regular pace of

SCOTT RUSSELL SANDERS

Through the aisle of waving woodland sunflowers and purple ironweed, I approach a cedar hut where I plan to sit quietly for a few hours, gathering the scattered pieces of myself. Resting at the foot of a hill between a meadow and a forest, surrounded by a deck and railing, the tiny cabin seems to float on the earth like a gabled houseboat the color of whole wheat bread. Grasshoppers lurch aside with a clatter as I move along the path, but hummingbirds and butterflies continue blithely feeding. Here in southern Indiana the tall grasses have bent down under the weight of their seeds, the maples and sycamores have begun to release a few crisp leaves, and the creeks have sunk into their stony troughs.

I climb the stairs and leave my sandals on the deck. The boards feel warm against the soles of my feet. The pressure of sunlight draws the fruity smell of cedar from the clapboard siding. I turn a key in the lock, swing the door inward, then hesitate on the threshold, gazing into this room where I hope to recover my balance. The two carpenters, friends of mine, who built this hut for me to use as a studio have removed the last of their tools and swept the place clean. The vacancy both attracts

your life. Maybe it's a room in your home or a spot on your campus; maybe it's a favorite booth in a coffee shop or perhaps a favorite bench in the city park. Whatever that place, Sanders's essay may help you better understand your need for it.

Scott Russell Sanders, who teaches creative writing at Indiana University, has written numerous essays, novels, and short stories for which he has been widely acclaimed. The following essay was published in Orion *magazine in 2001.* ◪

CONVERSATIONS: A CABIN IN THE WOODS

Many cultures have a tradition of going into the wilderness to seek not only solitude but also enlightenment or insight. For example, young men in some Native American tribes would venture into remote mountain areas on "vision quests" to seek insight into their destinies. The Bible tells the story of Jesus going into the wilderness to cleanse his soul and gain strength for his own destiny. In American culture, the idea of living in the wilderness, away from modern society, is perhaps best exemplified by Henry David Thoreau (1817–1862), whose classic book *Walden* (1854) describes his life in a small cabin in the forest outside Concord, Massachusetts, from 1845 to 1847. Thoreau's life in his cabin, a replica of which is shown in this photograph, has come to symbolize this impulse to seek solitude and wisdom in a remote, natural place uncorrupted by human society. Sanders' hut might be seen as part of this tradition and thus also part of a continuing conversation about how to live and the value of specific places in our lives.

© Images & Stories/Alamy

Replica of Thoreau's cabin at Walden Pond.

and daunts me. The pine floor, still unmarked, is fragrant and shiny with varnish, like a bare stage the moment before a play begins. The walls seem watchful, for they, too, are covered with planks of yellow pine, and the knots burn like a constellation of eyes.

Overcoming my wariness, I go inside, carrying with me only a pen, a journal, the clothes on my back, and the buzz in my head. I have come here in hopes of calming that buzz, the better to hear voices aside from my own. I open the windows and sit cross-legged on the floor with my back against a wall and my face to the east, where the meadow brightens with morning. I draw in a deep breath, let it go, and try to shed a feeling of decadence for sitting here alone, idle, on a Sunday morning.

My wife knows I am here, but she is the only one, and she urged me to come. As of one o'clock this afternoon, Ruth and I will have been married thirty-three years, and in that time our lives have been braided together so tightly, so richly, that I cannot imagine myself apart from her. And yet we both recognize my periodic need for solitude and stillness, a need that has grown more acute over the years.

We arranged for the building of this hut on some land we own at the edge of a state forest a few miles from our house in town, so that I would have a place to withdraw. I realize what a privilege it is to have such a refuge, what a luxury to claim a second roof when so many people lack any shelter at all, and I do not know how long I can bear to keep it. "Don't spoil your studio by feeling guilty," says Ruth, who has come to know my guilt all too well since the day of our wedding. She drove me out here this morning to inaugurate this quiet space, dropped me off at the end of the gravel path with a kiss and a blessing, then went on about her errands. We'll rendezvous this evening to celebrate our anniversary by sharing a meal with friends.

Although I must eventually return to house and work and a host of obligations, for a few hours, at least,

5

nobody will disturb me. There is no telephone in this room, no television, no radio, no computer, no electrical device at all except for a light and a fan overhead. I do not switch them on, because the sun gives me all the light I need and a breeze through the windows keeps me cool. Although cars rumble past now and then on a road that skirts the far side of the meadow, they disrupt the stillness only briefly. Otherwise, I hear the churr of cicadas and crickets, the rattle and purl of birdsong, the drumming of a woodpecker, and the trickle of these words as they run from my mind through my fingers onto the page.

Sunlight pouring through a southern window forms a bright rhomboid on the wooden floor. Even without a watch, by tracking this brilliant shape as it changes through the day I could mark noon as the moment when the corners are square. If I stayed longer, if I devoted myself to recording the dance of light over the gleaming boards, I could trace out sunrise and sunset, equinox and solstice, all the cycles of the turning year. But I will not do so, for I wish to shrug off time for a spell, to dwell in the present. I drift so often into past and future, jerked around by memory and expectation, that I lose the savor of the moment. I have come to this empty room to break free of tasks and deadlines, to cast off worry and grief.

Dust motes float lazily before me in a shaft of light, twitching as they collide with one another. I learned in freshman physics class that this perpetual shimmy is called Brownian motion, and the higher the temperature, the faster the particles move. In that same class I was also told that **IF YOU PUT A FROG IN A POT OF COLD WATER ON A STOVE AND THEN GRADUALLY RAISE THE HEAT,** the poor benighted creature will boil before it has the sense to jump out of the pot. I never tested this claim on a frog, but I have come to believe that a version of it holds true for many people, including myself.

As the demands on our time and attention multiply, we move faster and faster to keep up with them, crowding our calendars, shuttling from place to place and deadline to deadline, strapping phones to our belts, carrying chores everywhere in satchels and laptops, working through lunch and supper and weekends and holidays, getting and spending twenty-four hours a day. Many of us take pills to lull us to sleep, pills to wake us up, and pills to soothe our nerves. Many of us hire strangers to raise our children, to buy presents for our loved ones, to clean our houses and cook our food. Instead of slowing down when the pace becomes frantic, we enlarge our highways and pipelines and cables, we buy gadgets and software guaranteed to help us do everything more quickly, we push down on our accelerators. Instead of deciding there's something wrong with this pot as the water roils about us, we flail our arms and thrash our legs to keep from drowning.

I have decided to climb out of the pot, which is why I've come to this empty hut on a Sunday morning. The room is four paces wide by

10

STRATEGIES: EXTENDED METAPHOR
Sanders writes that he once learned in a physics class that a frog will not jump out of a pot of water before the water boils. In the next few paragraphs, he continually refers back to this image of the frog in the pot. Writers sometimes use this strategy, called *extended metaphor,* to convey certain ideas or make a specific point. What ideas or points does Sanders convey through this metaphor of the frog in the pot?

five paces long, about twelve feet by fifteen, and open to the steep rafters overhead. All the surfaces are wood, a reminder that this place is a gift of trees. There are windows in each wall and two skylights in the ceiling. Looking east I see the meadow, a sweep of grasses polished by sun. To the south I see a grove of sycamores, a thicket of blackberries, and a field grown up in goldenrod and ragweed and saplings. The forest begins just beyond the railing of the deck to the west, mainly oak and maple and hickory and beech, rank after rank of big trees rising up a slope into deepening shade and continuing on for several miles before yielding to the next road. Through windows in the north wall I see a welter of blowzy flowers and weeds, and a path leading to the gravel drive where Ruth dropped me off.

On a Sunday morning in town I could have worshiped with any of several dozen congregations, from staid Episcopalians to Holy Rollers, but they are all too noisy for my taste, too intent on scriptures and formulas, too eager to lasso the great mystery with words. I could have sat in silence with Buddhists or Quakers, waiting for insight, and yet even they often quarrel about the truth as soon as they rise from meditation, and over the years their arguments have led to schisms and feuds. The world is manifestly one, and each of us is part and parcel of that unity, so our quarrels about religious doctrine can only estrange us from the reality we seek.

Although I can't let go of language entirely, as witness these lines stretching across the pages of my journal, I do manage to sit for long spells in a wakeful hush. I keep my eyes open because I wish through stillness to enter the world, not escape from it. I wish to bear in mind all the creatures that breathe, which is why I've chosen to make my retreat here within the embrace of meadow and woods. The panorama I see through the windows is hardly wilderness, and yet every blade of grass, every grasshopper, every sparrow and twig courses with a wild energy. The same energy pours through me. Although my body grows calm from sitting still, I rock slightly with the slow pulse of my heart. My ears fill with the pulse of crickets and cicadas proclaiming their desires. My breath and the clouds ride the same wind.

In his **PENSÉES, PASCAL** remarks: "When all are moving precipitously toward excesses, none seems to be so moving. He who stops makes the mad rush of the others perceptible, as would a fixed point." Those others may decide for themselves whether their lives have sped out of control. The mad rush that concerns me is my own. By sitting still, I can measure the crazed motion of my customary days.

GLOSS: PASCAL'S *PENSÉES*
The *Pensées* is a collection of notes written by French philosopher Blaise Pascal (1623–1662) in which he explored his ideas about human nature. These notes, which were published after Pascal's death, were apparently intended to be part of a treatise defending Christianity.

In those customary days, I work almost every waking hour. Even during the rare pauses—while shaving, taking a shower, waiting for the teakettle to boil, pedaling my bicycle to and from the office—I find myself compiling lists and scheduling tasks. I read as I dash from appointment to appointment, jot notes on a clipboard in the car, lug everywhere a backpack stuffed with chores. When I lie down in exhaustion at night, sleep seems like an interruption in the round of toil. So far I haven't swallowed any pills to soothe my frazzled nerves. I've resisted the sales pitches for tools designed to speed up my life. I carry neither beeper nor cell phone nor palm pilot, feeling already too thoroughly connected to other people's demands. And yet, so long as I'm awake I feel driven to accomplish things, to redeem the time.

Why do I keep such a frantic pace? Not to rake in more money, because my wife and I could live quite well on half of what we earn. Nor to win fame, because I recognize how small and brief my life is. Nor to secure happiness, because I realize that happiness comes to me only in the moments when I slow down. Nor to meet the expectations of a boss, because I am my own boss. Then why the endless toil? Maybe I'm still trying to satisfy the insatiable needs of my parents as I sensed those needs in childhood. Maybe I'm still trying to ease the ache that drove my father to drink, even though he is long since dead, and I'm struggling to relieve the dismay and anger my mother felt because of his drinking. Or it could be that I'm trying to placate the Protestant God I learned about as a boy, the stern judge who watches us every moment, recording how we use our days, a God I've tried to banish from my thoughts but who keeps burrowing back in through the mind's basement. Or perhaps, like anyone who can't help seeing damage and pain in every direction, I'm only trying to avoid the bite of conscience.

I've been spared the turmoil of war, the pain of exile, the cramp of hunger. As far as I know, I'm free of disease. No one treats me with spite or scorn. I lead a blessed life, a rarity on this suffering planet, and yet much of the time I feel torn asunder by the needs I see around me, needs that outstrip my power to respond. From the circle of my family and friends, on out through the ever-larger circles of my students, my neighbors, the members of my community, the people in this country and in distant lands, and the earth itself with all its imperiled creatures, there are far more claims on my thought and compassion than I can meet.

I would not speak of this dilemma if it were only mine, but I watch many others race again and again through the cycle of widening concern, frenzied effort, and exhaustion. Whatever the source of conscience—parents, God, solemn books, earnest friends, the dictates of biology—it is adapted to a narrower space than the one we inhabit. Limited to a small tribe or a community of a few hundred people, conscience may prompt us to serve others in a balanced and wholesome way. But when television and newspapers and the Internet bring us word of dangers by the thousands and miseries by the millions and needful creatures by the billions; when pleas for help reach us around the clock; when aching faces greet us on every street—then conscience either goes numb or punishes us with a sense of failure.

I often lie awake at night, rehearsing the names of those I've disappointed by failing to give them all they asked. I don't say this to make myself out as a generous soul. I am hardly that; I feel defenseless rather than virtuous. The truth is that I've come to fear the claims that other beings make on me, because their numbers grow relentlessly. I wish to love my neighbor, but the neighborhood has expanded so far, and the neighbors have become so many, that my love is stretched to the breaking point. I'm tempted to run away, beyond reach of the needy voices. So I make of this hut a hiding place.

Sitting cross-legged, eyes open to this room filled with light, I ride my breath in and out as if it were the swells and troughs of a mild sea, and soon the strings of duty that bind me to the world begin to fall slack. Thoughts of the sea remind me of kayaking in Glacier Bay twelve months ago with my son and his fiancée and an Alaskan friend. Some days the water was choppy and we had hard going, especially into the wind. Other days the water lay as smooth and glossy as the pine floor in this room, and we glided over the surface with ease. My breath now feels like that effortless paddling.

20 I remember the way otters floated on their backs among the kelp beds, the way seals bobbed to the surface beside our kayaks and studied us with their dark eyes, the way humpback whales breached with a snort from their blowholes and a wave of their flukes, and I remember how the water erased all sign of their passage moments after they dove again. Even a storm tousled the sea only so long as the wind blew, leaving no mark after the sky cleared. Gradually I breathed in the equanimity of this imperturbable sea. By the end of our week in Glacier Bay, after camping each night on shore in the neighborhood of bears and eating fresh salmon cooked over driftwood fires and talking under the stars with people I love, I felt as serene as those waters on the calmest days.

We began our trip home from Alaska by taking a sauna and bathing in a creek at my friend's house on an island near Juneau, a house almost as simple and not much bigger than the hut where I record these memories. He had built the cabin and its furniture with timber salvaged from the beaches of Glacier Bay. We ate food from his garden and root cellar, drank water from his cistern, relieved ourselves in his privy with a view into the dripping forest of hemlock and spruce. His place was so close in spirit to the wilderness that it left my newfound tranquility unruffled.

My son and his fiancée and I parted from my friend and flew in a shuddering single-engine plane through rain to Juneau. Already in that small airport I felt dizzy from the onslaught of noise, the blabbing televisions, the clutter of machines, the milling, fretful travelers. From there we flew to Seattle, where the crowds and racket and hard surfaces and bustling carts and droning conveyor belts seemed like the stage props of nightmare. Then we stopped over at the airport in Las Vegas around midnight, and a two-hour delay forced us to leave the plane and make our way into the pandemonium of grunting loudspeakers, maundering drinkers, clanking slot machines, and wailing sirens. I felt I had descended into bedlam. I could not fathom how this midnight delirium and the serenity of Glacier Bay belonged on the same planet. Here was a frenzy beyond anything I had ever seen, and I knew with absolute certainty that it pointed the way to madness.

But was my life back home so different? Was my crowded calendar, my backpack stuffed with chores, my head crammed with duties, any less crazed? What jackpot was I after? Measured against the serenity I had felt in the wilderness, my usual life seemed as hectic and frazzled as this delirium in the casino. The twin images of Las Vegas and Glacier Bay have stayed with me ever since, like the opposite poles in a force field.

The hut creaks as the boards expand in the sun, like an animal stretching as it wakes. Tonight, after the sun goes down, the joints of cedar and pine will creak again as they cool. The hummingbirds will keep darting from blossom to blossom until the cold drives them south for winter. The crickets will keep on singing day and night until the first heavy frost, and then they will carry their song with them into the ground. Even in the depths of winter, beneath soil frozen as hard as iron, hearts will beat in burrows, and the creek will run beneath a skin of ice. There is no absolute stillness in nature. In the nails that hold this building together, electrons whirl. Even the dead yield their substance in a ferment of decay.

As I write these words in my journal, I'm forced to acknowledge a deeper source for the frantic pace of my ordinary days. I suspect I'm trying to stave off death. If I work without ceasing, maybe death will think I'm a good boy, useful and industrious, too valuable for extinction. If I serve others all my waking hours, maybe death will pass by the ones I love. If I write books, teach classes, give speeches, donate money, lobby politicians, and march in the streets, maybe death will spare the millions of species endangered by our prodigal ways.

When I was growing up in the country, a neighbor boy warned me never to lie still for long in an open field, because the turkey vultures would spiral overhead, waiting to feast on me. Especially if you're lying down, he told me, keep fidgeting, so they know you're alive. Except for rare passages of calm, I have kept fidgeting ever since.

On our drive out here this morning, Ruth and I passed a vulture that was tearing bright red strands from a possum flattened on the road. At the sound of our engine, the bird hunched protectively over

25

STRATEGIES: USING DESCRIPTION TO SHIFT FOCUS
At this point in the essay, the focus abruptly shifts from Sanders' hectic life to the quiet of his cabin. Notice that Sanders accomplishes this shift through description. In the preceding two paragraphs, he describes the "pandemonium" of the airports in Seattle and Las Vegas, focusing on the noise in those places, but in paragraph 24 he describes the soothing sounds of his cabin. This shift refocuses our attention on the stillness of his cabin and helps reinforce his larger point in this essay about the need for such stillness in our lives. This passage is an excellent example of a careful use of description to convey more than a physical sense of a place.

its meal and thrust its beak into the bloody mess for another scrap. I found nothing gruesome in the sight, for the vulture was doing necessary work, obeying an appetite as clean and simple as gravity. This gawky black bird with its featherless head the color of blood was not death itself but only one of death's janitors. Without all the dutiful scavengers, from bacteria to wolves, our planet would be layered in corpses. Instead, the living dismantle the dead, and out of the debris new life rises.

Over the past few years, Ruth and I watched Alzheimer's disease whittle her mother to a thin reed, which finally snapped. Month by month, each of our surviving parents has lost certain blessings of body and mind—a range of hearing and sight, fine control of the fingers, strength of legs, precision of memory, the names of familiar things. Ruth and I have ached over this paring down, even as we know our own turn will come if we live long enough. Age strips away our powers as well as our possessions. By giving myself to this empty room, perhaps like the monk who sleeps in his coffin I am only preparing myself for an emptiness over which I will have no choice.

The Hebrew root of sabbath means "to rest." In anticipation of this Sunday morning's retreat, I copied into my notebook the fourth commandment delivered by Moses to the people of Israel:

> Remember the sabbath day, and keep it holy. Six days you shall labor and do all your work. But the seventh day is a sabbath to the Lord your God; you shall not do any work—you, your son or your daughter, your male or female slave, your livestock, or the alien resident in your towns.

30   So keeping the sabbath holy means not only that we should rest from our own labors but also that we should grant rest to all those beings—both human and nonhuman—whose labor serves us.

According to Moses, God went further in demanding restraint from this wandering tribe once they entered the promised land. Every seventh year the land was to be left fallow; the fields were not to be plowed and the grapevines not to be pruned; and whatever grew of itself on the land was to be left alone. Every fiftieth year, slaves were to be set free, leased property was to be restored to its original owners, and the earth was to be granted a solemn rest. Why? Because, God proclaims through Moses, "the land is mine; with me you are but aliens and tenants."

These ancient rules are instructions in humility. For six days we make the Creation serve our needs, but on the seventh day we must leave the Creation alone. We may hold title to the land, but we may not claim it for our own, as if it were ours to do with as we choose. Whatever our religious views, we might do well to recover the idea of the sabbath, not only because we could use a solemn day of rest once a week, but also because the earth could use a respite from our demands. Whether or not we accept the idea of a Creator, we should admit we're not the makers of this bountiful and beautiful earth, we're only guests here, just passing through, and we have no right to devour the promised land.

A spider lowers itself by a thread from a rafter, settling a few inches from my outstretched feet. It's only a smidgen of life, no bigger than a grain of rice, with a bright red dot for a body and legs so fine they're all but invisible. Even in so small a creature—and in ones much smaller, as I know from gazing through microscopes—there is room for hunger and purpose. The spider sets off across the floor, slowing up at the joints between boards like a skier straddling crevasses. Against the caramel grain in the pine, the bright spark of a body glows like a burning coal. It crawls over the carcass of a ladybug, stops to examine a dead wasp, eventually trundles into a dark corner where it begins laying out the warp for a web.

The spider does not rest every seventh day, nor do the warblers singing now from the branches of a sumac just outside the window, nor do the crickets sawing away at their lovelorn tune in the grass. They pursue their passions as long as their breath holds out. They needn't be reminded to restrain themselves, for nature curbs their appetites soon enough with frost or drought or some other calamity. Among all the menagerie, it seems, we alone must be taught to curb our own appetites. We alone need reminding that the condition of our lease on the promised land is that we restrain ourselves.

The industry of the spider makes me notice the stiffness in my legs. 35 How long have I sat here? Two hours? Three? Whenever she finishes her errands, Ruth will be coming to pick me up. I rise and stretch. The gleaming floor, so smooth, tempts my feet. I wonder for a moment if the holy sabbath allows for dancing, then I dance anyway, a slow and clumsy shuffle, the way a bear might dance. My feet brushing the wood make the whispery sound of a broom. Since nobody is around to hear how badly I sing, I go ahead and sing. It's a love ballad that I'll repeat for Ruth tonight when we celebrate our anniversary. At the sound of my voice, the crickets and cicadas and warblers surrounding the hut cease their chorus, but in a little while they resume, overcome by desire, and we sing together our amorous tunes.

Before long the dancing covers me in sweat. I lie on the floor where a breeze from the windows cools me. This room is a haven. Eventually I'll put a table, a chair, a lamp, and a meditation cushion in here, but for now I prefer to leave it bare. The two skylights in the ceiling open onto rectangles of blue. Clouds drift across those openings, coiling and merging like foam at the confluence of rivers. Every few seconds, barn swallows wheel across, there a moment and then gone, like thoughts. Suddenly, through my framed patch of sky, two red-tailed hawks glide past. I leap to my feet and throw open the door and step onto the deck to watch them sail away beyond the rim of trees.

And so, without planning to leave my hermitage, I'm drawn outside by a pair of birds. Standing in the open air, I realize I'm hungry, I'm thirsty, and I'm eager for company. I want to see Ruth, my bride of thirty-three years. I want to walk with her through our neighborhood in the evening as lights come on in the houses. I long to hold my children and catch up on their lives. I want to share food with friends. I want to sit with my students and talk over the ancient questions. I want to walk among crowds at the farmers' market and run my hands over the melons and apples and squash. I want to do good work—not every waking hour, and not for every worthy cause, but enough work to ease some pain and bring some hope and free some beauty in a few lives. I want to carry back into my ordinary days a sense of the stillness that gathers into the shape of a life, scatters into fragments, and then gathers again.

Waiting in the sunshine, I listen to the rumble of cars approaching the hut along the blacktop road, for one of those cars will bring Ruth, who will find a husband more peaceful and joyful and grateful than the one she left here this morning.

Understanding the Text

1. Why did Sanders arrange to have his hut built? What needs does the hut fulfill? What do you think his hut might suggest about the role of special places in our lives?

2. What does Sanders mean when he uses the term *stillness?* Why does he seek this stillness? What does stillness have to do with his hut? Why must he go there in search of stillness? Do you think stillness, as he defines it, can only be found in a specific place? Explain.

3. Why does Sanders wish to "let go of language" (par. 12)? What would it mean to do so? Why is he not able to let go of language?

4. What dilemma does Sanders describe in this essay? What is the source of this dilemma? What does it have to do with Sanders's hut? What do you think this dilemma suggests about Sanders as a person?

5. Sanders writes that the first day he spent in his hut was also his wedding anniversary. What connection does Sanders make between that important event and his need for stillness?

Exploring the Issues

1. What do you think this essay suggests about the relationship between specific places and the emotional life of human beings? What might it suggest about how people use certain kinds of spaces? Cite specific passages to support your answer.

2. Sanders's writing is often praised for its vividness and the effectiveness of his de-scriptions. Select one or more passages from this essay that you think are particularly de-scriptive and analyze them. What words or phrases does Sanders use in his descrip-tions? How does he use sound or imagery to depict the scenes he describes? What ideas about his subject matter does he use his descriptions to convey? How effective do you think his descriptive writ-ing is?

3. Sanders makes a number of references to religion in this essay, and at one point, he muses that he may be "trying to placate the Protestant God I learned about as a boy." He also discusses *conscience* throughout the essay. Based on this essay, what do you think Sanders's view of reli-gion is? What do his views of religion have to do with his desire for stillness? What might religion have to do with Sanders's relationship to his hut?

4. At several points in his essay, Sanders writes about death. For example, in paragraphs 27 and 28, he offers images of death in the natural world and of his own inevitable death. Why does Sanders include these images? What do they have to do with his hut? What do they have to do with his desire for stillness? What do you think Sanders's discussions of death suggest about the role of certain spaces in our lives?

Entering the Conversations

1. Write an essay describing a special place of your own. In your essay, describe that place in a way that conveys its significance for you.

2. Write a conventional academic essay in which you discuss where you think the need for special places, such as

Sanders's hut, comes from. Why do people need such spaces? What is it about these spaces that we need to make us feel comfortable? What does this need suggest about humans—or about our cultures? Discuss such questions in your essay. Refer where appropriate to Sanders's essay and to your own experience with special places in your life.

3. In paragraph 17, Sanders writes, "But when television and newspapers and the Internet bring us word of dangers by the thousands and miseries by the millions and needful creatures by the billions; when pleas for help reach us around the clock; when aching faces greet us on every street—then conscience either goes numb or punishes us with a sense of failure." Write an essay in which you respond to this statement. In your essay, discuss your own view of this problem of conscience that Sanders describes, and try to address the question of what this problem

might suggest about modern life. If appropriate, discuss also whether our use of space has anything to do with this problem.

4. Using whatever appropriate technology you have available (such as computer graphics programs, web authoring software, or video or still photography), create a document that represents an important space in your life. Try to create your document in a way that conveys its importance to you.

5. Find a place where you might have a moment of stillness, such as Sanders describes in his essay. Occupy that place for a time. Then write a brief essay in which you describe what happened when you sought stillness in that place. In your essay, draw conclusions about stillness and how we might use particular spaces to achieve it. Discuss whether you agree with Sanders's view of stillness and place, based on your own experience.

In the months following the terrorist attacks of September 11, 2001, many people I know visited the site of the Word Trade Center in New York City, the place now known as Ground Zero. In every case, those people had few words to say about what it was like to see the place where so many people died in such a horrific way. The words they did use—"amazing,"

Where Nothing Says Everything

"unbelievable," "horrible," "incredible"—seemed inadequate to convey their feelings about that now-sacred place and the magnitude of what happened there. There's just no way to describe it, a few of them said.

Writer Suzanne Berne (b. 1961) would probably agree with that, but the following essay, which she wrote just a few months after September 11, 2001, comes as close as anything I have read to conveying the sense of horror, reverence, and awe that people feel when they visit Ground Zero. In her essay, Berne tells the story of her own visit to that place, and she provides a picture of the impact of the site on those who visit it. Her essay is a powerful statement about the value of such places. As you read, consider not only what Berne seems to be saying about what makes these places special—aside from the events that took place there—but also how Berne conveys a sense of what it's like to be there. Her essay can tell us something about the

SUZANNE BERNE

On a cold, damp March morning, I visited Manhattan's financial district, a place I'd never been, to pay my respects at what used to be the World Trade Center. Many other people had chosen to do the same that day, despite the raw wind and spits of rain, and so the first thing I noticed when I arrived on the corner of Vesey and Church Streets was a crowd.

Standing on the sidewalk, pressed against aluminum police barricades, wearing scarves that flapped into their faces and woolen hats pulled over their ears, were people apparently from everywhere. Germans, Italians, Japanese. An elegant-looking Norwegian family in matching shearling coats. People from Ohio and California and Maine. Children, middle-age couples, older people. Many of them were clutching cameras and video recorders, and they were all craning to see across the street, where there was nothing to see.

At least, nothing is what it first looked like, the space that is now ground zero. But once your eyes adjust to what you are looking at, "nothing" becomes something much more potent, which is absence.

But to the out-of-towner, ground zero looks at first simply like a construction site. All the familiar details are there: the wooden scaffolding; the cranes, the bulldozers and forklifts; the trailers and construction workers in hard hats; even the dust. There is the pound of jackhammers, the steady beep-beep-beep of trucks backing up, the roar of heavy machinery.

5   So much busyness is reassuring, and it is possible to stand looking at the cranes and trucks and feel that mild curiosity and hopefulness so often inspired by construction sites.

Then gradually your eyes do adjust, exactly as if you have stepped from a dark theater into a bright afternoon, because what becomes most striking about this scene is the light itself.

Ground zero is **A GREAT BOWL OF LIGHT,** an emptiness that seems weirdly spacious and grand, like a vast plaza amid the dense tangle of streets in lower Manhattan. Light reflecting off the Hudson River vaults into the site, soaking everything—especially on an overcast morning—with a watery glow. This is the moment when absence begins to assume a material form, when what is not there becomes visible.

Suddenly you notice the periphery, the skyscraper shrouded in black plastic, the boarded windows, the steel skeleton of the shattered Winter Garden. Suddenly there are the broken steps and cracked masonry in front of Brooks Brothers. Suddenly there are the firefighters, the waiting ambulance on the other side of the pit, the police on every corner. Suddenly there is the enormous cross made of two rusted girders.

And suddenly, very suddenly, there is the little cemetery attached to St. Paul's Chapel, with tulips coming up, the chapel and grounds miraculously undamaged except for a few plastic-sheathed gravestones. The iron fence is almost invisible beneath a welter of dried pine wreaths, banners, ribbons, laminated poems and prayers and photographs, swags of paper cranes, withered flowers, baseball hats, rosary beads, teddy bears. And flags, flags everywhere, little American flags fluttering in the breeze, flags on posters drawn by Brownie troops, flags on T-shirts, flags on hats, flags streaming by, tied to the handles of baby strollers.

10   It takes quite a while to see all of this; it takes even longer to come up with something to say about it.

An elderly man standing next to me had been staring fixedly across the street for some time. Finally he touched his son's elbow and said: "I watched those towers being built. I saw this place when they weren't there." Then he stopped, clearly struggling with, what for him, was a double negative, recalling an absence before there was an absence. His son, waiting patiently, took a few photographs. "Let's get out of here," the man said at last.

Again and again I heard people say, "It's unbelievable." And then they would turn to each other, dissatisfied. They wanted to say something more expressive, more meaningful. But it is unbelievable, to stare at so much devastation, and know it for devastation, and yet recognize that it does not look like the devastation one has imagined.

Like me, perhaps, the people around me had in mind images from television and newspaper pictures: the collapsing buildings,

power of writing to evoke the places we value.

Novelist Suzanne Berne's books include A Crime in the Neighborhood *(1997) and* A Perfect Arrangement *(2001). This essay first appeared in the* New York Times *in 2002.* ▼

STRATEGIES: POINT OF VIEW
In paragraph 3, Berne shifts from the third person point of view ("he" or "she" or "they") to the second person ("you"). For the rest of the essay, Berne refers to "you." Consider the effect of this shift on you as a reader. In what ways might the essay be different if Berne had remained with a third-person point of view? What do you think Berne accomplishes by using the second person?

CONVERSATIONS: CREATING A PROPER MEMORIAL
Berne's description in this passage (par. 12) of the dissatisfaction that visitors to Ground Zero felt may help explain some of the controversy that continued to swirl around the proposals for the memorial to be built there. Disagreements about what kind of memorial should be built at Ground Zero were intense from the very moment that government officials decided to build a memorial. At the time Berne's essay was published in 2002, proposals for such a memorial were being submitted and ideas about what should be done with the site were being debated. But even after a design was accepted in 2004, controversy continued. Consider how Berne's perspective on the site might fit into this controversy. Consider, too, how the controversy about what to do with the site might shape how readers respond to this essay.

CONVERSATIONS: A GREAT BOWL OF LIGHT
Berne describes the site of the attacks on the World Trade Center in New York City as "a great bowl of light" (par. 7). Some people have proposed that the memorial to be built on that site use light to memorialize the towers that once stood there. The photograph shown here was taken on September 11, 2003, at a ceremony to commemorate the victims of the attacks. Consider how such uses of light can convey messages that perhaps are difficult to convey in words. To what extent does this photograph coincide with Berne's perspective on Ground Zero?

© AP Photo/John Marshall Mantel

the running office workers, the black plume of smoke against a bright blue sky. Like me, they were probably trying to superimpose those terrible images onto the industrious emptiness right in front of them. The difficulty of this kind of mental revision is measured, I believe, by the brisk trade in World Trade Center photograph booklets at tables set up on street corners.

Determined to understand better what I was looking at, I decided to get a ticket for the viewing platform beside St. Paul's. This proved no easy task, as no one seemed to be able to direct me to South Street Seaport, where the tickets are distributed. Various police officers whom I asked for directions, waved me vaguely toward the East River, differing degrees of boredom and resignation on their faces. Or perhaps it was a kind of incredulousness. Somewhere around the American Stock Exchange, I asked a security guard for help and he frowned at me, saying, "You want tickets to the disaster?"

Finally I found myself in line at a cheerfully painted kiosk, watching a young juggler try to entertain the crowd. He kept dropping the four red balls he was attempting to juggle, and having to chase after them. It was noon; the next available viewing was at 4 P.M. [15]

Back I walked, up Fulton Street, the smell of fish in the air, to wander again around St. Paul's. A deli on Vesey Street advertised a view of the World Trade Center from its second-floor dining area. I went in and ordered a pastrami sandwich, uncomfortably aware that many people before me had come to that same deli for pastrami sandwiches who would never come there again. But I was here to see what I could, so I carried my sandwich upstairs and sat down beside one of the big plate-glass windows.

And there, at last, I got my ticket to the disaster.

I could see not just into the pit now, but also its access ramp, which trucks had been traveling up and down since I had arrived that morning. Gathered along the ramp were firefighters in their black helmets and black coats. Slowly they lined up, and it became clear that this was an honor guard, and that someone's remains were being carried up the ramp toward the open door of an ambulance.

Everyone in the dining room stopped eating. Several people stood up, whether out of respect or to see better, I don't know. For a moment, everything paused.

Then the day flowed back into itself. Soon I was outside once more, joining the tide of people washing around the site. Later, as I huddled with a little crowd on the viewing platform, watching people scrawl their names or write "God [20]

Bless America" on the plywood walls, it occurred to me that a form of repopulation was taking effect, with so many visitors to this place, thousands of visitors, all of us coming to see the wide emptiness where so many were lost. And by the act of our visiting—whether we are motivated by curiosity or horror or reverence or grief, or by something confusing that combines them all—that space fills up again.

Understanding the Text

1. What does Berne mean when she refers to *absence* in this essay? Why is this absence important in reference to Ground Zero in New York City?

2. What activities does Berne describe as taking place around the site of the World Trade Center? What is the significance of these activities? What do they say about places like the site of the attacks on the World Trade Center?

3. In what sense is the space where the World Trade Center once stood filling up again? What do you think this "filling up" suggests about special places like Ground Zero?

Exploring the Issues

1. Examine the way Berne tells the story of her visit to Ground Zero. What information about her visit does she include? What does she seem to leave out? How does she organize her essay? What is the effect of this way of organizing her essay on you as a reader?

2. At several points in her essay, Berne describes the reactions and words of people around her who also came to see the site of the attacks on the World Trade Center. What do these reactions suggest about the impact of that place on those who visit it? What ideas about the value or

meaning of a place does Berne convey through these descriptions?

3. In paragraph 14, Berne writes that a security guard asked her whether she wanted "tickets to the disaster." In paragraph 17, Berne tells us that she finally got her "ticket to the disaster." What do you think she means by this phrase? Does it mean the same thing to her and the security guard? Explain.

4. Throughout this essay, Berne includes much description of what she sees during her visit to the World Trade Center site. What kinds of details does she tend to include in her descriptions? What does she emphasize in these descriptions? What ideas or feelings do you think she conveys through these descriptions? How effective did you find these descriptions in conveying a sense of what it is like to visit that place?

Entering the Conversations

1. Attempting to describe the magnitude of the impact of the death of thousands of people can be overwhelming. If you have never been to the site of the World Trade Center in New York City, you may have visited another place that has great importance, such as a war memorial or a battlefield or cemetery for those who died in bat-

tle or some other kind of tragic event. Or maybe you've seen a place of great natural beauty such as the Grand Canyon. Write an essay about such a place that you have visited. In your essay, try to describe this place in a way that conveys its magnitude and significance.

2. Using photographs, video, web authoring software, PowerPoint, or any other appropriate technology, create a visual representation of a place that you consider sacred or special in some way. In your representation, try to convey a sense of the significance of the place.

3. Write a letter to the editor of the *New York Times* in which you express your views about what should be done with the site of the World Trade Center.

4. Design a memorial for a place that you believe has special meaning—perhaps a place in your community commemorating an important event that took place there. Write an explanation of your design as if you were proposing it to government officials who might decide whether to build it.

5. Visit a memorial in your region, such as a battlefield memorial or statue of a famous person. Write an essay in which you describe that place, conveying a sense of its significance to you or others in your community.

A few years ago, I learned to sail. My wife, *Cheryl, and I were complete novices, but we took sailing lessons, read as much as we could about sailing, and practiced on a small, second-hand sailboat that we kept on Lake George in upstate New York. Before learning to sail, we had visited Lake George many times, so we already knew the lake well. Or so we thought.*

Tea WITH Giants

Sailing gave us a whole new perspective on the lake. From the deck of our sailboat, we began to see things we had never noticed before: coves that were invisible from shore, the varied shapes of the many islands that dot the lake, small beaches and points that we'd walked or driven by countless times without even knowing they were there. And sailing taught us about the lake's wind and weather patterns. We learned how to see subtle wind shifts on the surface of the water and learned what they meant about the changing weather. On our sailboat, the lake became a new place that we

WENDY MITMAN CLARKE

J**ust past sunrise, and I'm waiting for the coffee to perk. There's** a cool, clean westerly riffling the water in this man-made cove off the outer harbor at Port Jefferson, New York. The chart reads **"SPOIL AREA,"** but we heard it was deep. We spent the night here with a couple of **ALBERG 30S**, a lobster-type powerboat, a big **CATANA** catamaran, and a **FREEDOM 36**.

This basin was used for sand mining decades ago. On the east and south sides, ragged brushy slopes climb maybe 100 feet high, topped with a crew cut of hardwood trees. To the north, huge hills of bare sand are as tan and humpbacked as camels. To the west is a narrow channel leading to the outer harbor and a stretch of low-growth forest and marsh flecked with rusted remains of the mining operation. I feel **LIKE I'M FLOATING IN A GIANT'S TEACUP.**

A red-tailed hawk is soaring up the cliffs, playing on the thermals. It's been screaming since first light. I suspect it's a youngster trying its wings, shrieking at the pure joy and peril of flight.

I thought we'd be doing the same at this point in our maiden long-distance cruise. I'm beginning to think, though, that one first has to

GLOSS: SPOIL AREA
In boating, a "spoil area" refers to a section of a body of water where dumping has occurred or debris has collected as a result of activities like dredging. As Clarke tells us in the next paragraph, the cove she describes in this essay was created by a sand-mining operation.

WENDY MITMAN CLARKE, "TEA WITH GIANTS," *CRUISING WORLD MAGAZINE*, JANUARY 2008, PAGE 160. REPRINTED BY PERMISSION OF THE AUTHOR.

define **"CRUISING."** I wonder if its meaning isn't tied up somehow in how we define ourselves, or maybe it's the other way around. Either way, this cruising isn't nearly as clear-cut as I'd thought.

5   I've been sailing most of my life, my husband all of his. We raced together for years, had two kids, bought a Peterson 34 we named *Luna,* and started cruising on Chesapeake Bay. We'd anchor someplace after sailing all day and entertain the perpetual dream that one day we'd just head out and not come back. We *lived* for our time on our boat. But it seemed like what we were doing just wasn't enough. That we weren't challenging ourselves. That we weren't really cruisers until we crossed an ocean or lived aboard for a couple of years or headed south for the winter. And so we bought *Osprey,* our 45-foot steel cutter that's a proven traveler, and set our sights higher and farther.

This dawn isn't unlike one of those Chesapeake mornings, and I realize I enjoy this most about cruising (at least so far): I love waking up surrounded by beauty. I love that I had to work to get here. That maybe five or six other people are seeing what I'm seeing, the early light through the treetops on the cliff, the way that hawk's wingtips flutter on the breeze.

Still, there's this pygmy tyrant in my head: "Hey, Poser. You said you were going all the way to Maine. What are you doing loafing here? Are you cruising, or what?"

STRATEGIES: DESCRIPTION
Describing a place is one of the most basic skills a writer develops (and probably something you've practiced in your writing classes). Here, Clarke describes the small cove off the coast of New York where she and her family anchored their sailboat, and she uses the metaphor of a giant's teacup to help her readers "see" the cove. Consider how effectively her description evokes that cove. Do you think her description would enable you to imagine the cove sufficiently without this photograph, which accompanied her essay when it was originally published?

© Wendy Mittman Clarke

came to know much more intimately than we had before.

Wendy Mitman Clarke understands this intimate connection to a place. In the following essay, she describes a small, unremarkable cove along the coast of New York where she and her family anchored their sailboat. As experienced sailors, they had spent years cruising along many miles of coastline, and no doubt they had visited many coves like the one she describes in this essay. But over time, Clarke began to develop a new appreciation for the places she visited on her sailboat, and she learned to see the beauty of even a nondescript cove that seems to have escaped everyone's notice. In this regard, her essay is about becoming intimate with a place by learning not only to notice what's there but also to appreciate it for what it offers. Her essay is also about how writing can help us gain such insight into the world around us.

Wendy Mitman Clarke is a senior writer for Chesapeake Bay Magazine *and the author of* Window on the Chesapeake: The Bay, Its People and Places *(2002). This essay was published in* Cruising World *magazine in 2008.* ◗

CONVERSATIONS: ALBERG, CATANA, AND FREEDOM
In the opening paragraph and elsewhere in this essay, Clarke refers to brands of sailboats, such as the Alberg, Catana, and Freedom sailboats she mentions here. She mentions other brands elsewhere in her essay (Peterson, in par. 5, and Island Packet, in par. 8). When sailors describe a sailboat, they typically identify its brand followed by its length in feet (for example, an Alberg 34). The boat's name is italicized (as in the case of Clarke's boat *Osprey,* mentioned in par. 5). Since she wrote this essay for a sailing magazine called *Cruising World,* Clarke can assume her readers are familiar with these conventions and with the language of sailing.

CONVERSATIONS: CRUISING
Generally, "cruising" refers to sailing or boating from one point to another over several days, weeks, months, or even years. As Clarke suggests in this paragraph, cruising can mean different things to different sailors. For some, it means leisurely sailing in one area (such as the Chesapeake Bay on the eastern U.S. coast or Puget Sound in Washington state) without specific destinations or schedules. For others, cruising is a way of life that involves exploring new areas and making longer passages between stops. Readers who are familiar with sailing would know that sailors often debate the pros and cons of different approaches to cruising, as Clarke suggests in paragraphs 8 and 9. Notice how Clarke implicitly refers to these debates here and uses them to help make her point about the joy of sailing as a way to become intimately familiar with a specific place.

We met a couple in an Island Packet as we left the Chesapeake, former racers who have been cruising for years and had that enviable attitude born of experience that makes it all look easy. How long, we asked, had they been out? The man assured us that they don't cruise full-time. He learned long ago, he said, that he couldn't stand the boat for more than six months at a stretch. Then he had to reattach to terra firma for a while.

Does that make him any less a sailor? Is the person who winters in the same anchorages in the Bahamas and returns to the Chesapeake every spring any less of a cruiser than the sailor who makes it all the way to Australia? If we spend six weeks this summer meandering along Long Island Sound and through Massachusetts, are we wimping out of some greater achievement? Weren't we supposed to get all the way to Maine?

10   I wonder sometimes whether we've spent so much of our lives racing onward and upward that we can't quite accept that cruising isn't a competition. It seems to me that more than anything, it's a state of mind, a willingness to live not for the future or the past but only for the present moment. The Buddhists among us would say this is a higher state of being. Ironically, it turns out to be harder than it sounds. I'm learning that not only must we pare our physical possessions when we move aboard; we also have to shed the emotional baggage, our clutter of expectations and regret. Only then can we let ourselves explore for the sake of exploring, try out these young wings and shriek at the pure joy and peril of flight.

I've never been here before, in this giant's sandy teacup, and no, it's not a Polynesian atoll that we crossed an ocean to find. But for the moment, it's where I am, and it's exactly where I want to be.

Understanding the Text

1. In what sense is "cruising" not clear-cut, according to Clarke? (See "Conversations: Cruising" on page 590.) How is this uncertainty about cruising related to Clarke's main point in this essay?

2. What is the appeal of cruising for Clarke? How does she ultimately define cruising? How have her own experiences influenced her opinions about cruising?

3. What has Clarke learned through cruising? What has cruising helped her learn about herself? About living in general? What is it about her approach to sailing that enables her to become more intimately familiar with the places she visits?

Exploring the Issues

1. Clarke originally wrote this essay for a magazine called *Cruising World,* which is read by sailors, and she assumes her readers are familiar with sailing, sailboats, and specialized sailing terms like "cruising." But her essay is about more than sailing. Do you think her ideas in this essay are accessible to readers who are not familiar with sailing? Explain. If you are such a reader, consider how accessible Clarke's ideas are to you.

2. How would you describe Clarke's voice in this essay? What characteristics of her writing style contribute to her voice? Do you think her voice is appropriate to her subject matter and her main point in this essay? Explain. Do you find her voice appealing? Why or why not?

3. In this essay, Clarke enters the debate about "cruising" that sailors are always having (see "Conversations: Alberg, Catana, and Freedom" on page 590). Do you think this debate, as Clarke presents it in her essay (and as explained in "Conversations: Alberg, Catana, and Freedom" on page 590), is similar to debates about other important matters in our lives? Identify other debates about how we live together and how we relate to the places we encounter in our lives that might relate to the issues Clarke addresses in this essay. What insights might she offer for those other debates?

Entering the Conversations

1. Write an essay about an activity or experience you had that gave you a different perspective on a place.

2. Describe a place that you are familiar with as accurately as you can. Assume your readers are not familiar with that place. Share your description with a group of classmates who have never visited the place you described and try to determine whether your description enables them to "see" the place. Is anything missing from your description? Is anything unclear? Then revise your description on the basis of your classmates' responses to your description.

3. With a group of classmates, visit a place on your campus (such as a commons, a memorial, the library or student center, or some distinctive area of the campus). Write a description of that place and have your classmates write their own descriptions. Now share those descriptions. Identify similarities and differences in how each of you described that place. What did everyone notice about the place? What surprised you about differences in your classmates' descriptions? What might this activity reveal about how we "see" the world around us?

4. Have each member of your group take a single photograph of the place you described for Question 3, then compare photographs. How did each person in your group choose to "see" that place? Alternatively, create a visual or multimedia representation (for example, a web page or photo essay) of the place.

5. Select a photograph of a place you would like to visit (such as a famous national park like the Grand Canyon or a special building like the Space Needle in Seattle). Then write a brief description of that place on the basis of the photograph.

6. Write a description from memory of a place you are very familiar with. Then visit that place and evaluate your description. Is anything missing or unclear? Do you need to change anything to make your description more accurate or vivid? Then consider whether this exercise helped you see anything differently about that place.

Extending the Conversations

1. Identify an important issue related to the challenges of living together that is explored in several readings in this chapter. Then, drawing on those readings, write an essay in which you discuss that issue and examine its importance in contemporary society.

2. Select one or more of the essays in this chapter, and in a conventional academic essay, discuss the way the writers explore their relationships to a place. Examine how these writers portray that relationship and discuss what these relationships reveal about the value of certain places in our lives.

3. Several of the essays in this chapter describe a return to a place that they left when they were younger. For example, Melissa Holbrook Pierson describes returning to her childhood home. E. B. White describes taking his family to a lake where his father took him as a young child. Drawing on these essays, any other appropriate essays in this book, and your own experience, write an essay about returning to a significant place in your life.

4. Write a letter to the editor of your local paper in which you express your views about preserving a place of importance in the region where you live. In your letter, explain the importance of this place and discuss your ideas for what should be done to preserve that place.

INFOTRAC

5. In the past few decades, the idea of *open space* has gained supporters as many regions of the United States continue to develop rapidly. Commercial and residential development often changes the regional landscape in ways that concern many residents. For example, farms are sometimes sold to developers as suburbs grow out from cities into surrounding rural areas, dramatically changing the character of the area and often resulting in a variety of social, economic, and environmental problems. In response to these developments, many towns have implemented controversial policies that limit or prohibit development in certain areas. Using InfoTrac College Edition, the Internet, your library, and any other relevant resources, investigate the loss of open space and what is being done about it. You might focus your investigation on your own region, if these problems concern people where you live. Then write a report on the basis of your research. Try to draw conclusions about the value of open spaces in our lives.

6. Using appropriate technologies available to you (such as PowerPoint, desktop publishing software, or web authoring software), create a visual representation of a community that is important in your life.

7. Find several magazine or Internet advertisements that depict a specific kind of community. Analyze the way these ads portray certain communities through the use of images. What messages do these images send about those communities? What ideas or values do these image seem to convey? Address such questions in an essay in which you discuss what you learned about how images are used in these documents and what they suggest about our beliefs about certain kinds of communities.

8. Many popular films focus on a specific place or are set in a location that is central to the story told in the film. For example, many of Woody Allen's films focus on New York City as a special place. By contrast, many films take place in wilderness or frontier areas that are depicted as special; for example, films such as *Dances with Wolves* (1990) and *Jeremiah Johnson* (1972) are set in the American West, a location that is important to the stories told in the films. Select one or more films in which a certain place plays an important role and examine how that place is portrayed. What ideas or attitudes about that place does the film convey? What values about place seem to be conveyed by the film? Then write an essay in which you discuss place as it is treated in these films.

9. If you have access to a video camera, create a film about an important community you belong to. Working with a group of classmates, write a script for this film and use appropriate software (such as *iMovie* or *Windows Movie Maker*) to edit your film. Create your film in a way that conveys a sense of the importance of the community you are depicting.

© Jean Luc Morales/Getty Images

Chapter 11 Resources

RECENTLY, MY WIFE AND I BEGAN LOOKING INTO SOLAR ENERGY. WE HAD BECOME CONCERNED ABOUT GLOBAL CLIMATE CHANGE, AND WE WANTED TO MAKE CHANGES IN OUR LIFESTYLE TO REDUCE OUR IMPACT ON THE EARTH. PART OF OUR MOTIVATION CAME FROM LEARNING, that while the United States has only about 5 percent of the world's population, it consumes 20 to 25 percent of the world's resources. That means Americans contribute disproportionately to pollution and to global climate change. Such figures reveal that the American lifestyle is in many ways wasteful and potentially causes serious environmental damage. We wanted to see what we could do in our own lives to try to change that.

As we talked with experts, we learned that it is relatively easy to incorporate solar electricity, which produces no pollution, into a home. We also learned about how much energy we waste ev-

> Such figures reveal that the American lifestyle is in many ways wasteful and potentially causes serious environmental damage.

ery day. Many appliances that we rely on, like our washer and dryer, microwave oven, television, and dishwasher, use electricity inefficiently. The typical light bulbs that illuminate our home also waste electricity. We learned that even when many appliances are turned off, they continue to use power. The more we learned, the more we began to realize that just by living our lives in a typical American way, we are wasting resources needlessly. Alternatives to our wasteful use of resources exist. Solar electricity is one such alternative. Newer, more energy-efficient appliances and compact fluorescent light bulbs use far less electricity than older appliances and conventional light bulbs. Washing dishes by hand rather than in a dishwasher wastes less water and uses less electricity. The new gas-electric hybrid cars use less fuel and cause far less pollution than conventional cars and trucks. More important, small changes in our lifestyle can reduce our use of resources. For example, buying locally grown vegetables and fruits rather than produce that is trucked from hundreds or thousands of miles away, as most groceries sold in the United States are, also reduces pollution.

All this seems straightforward enough. But as we learned about these easy ways to reduce our use of resources and our impact on the earth, we also came to realize that most Americans are unaware of how wasteful their lifestyles are, and many don't care. Many of our family members and friends considered our efforts to change our wasteful lifestyle silly, too expensive, or inconvenient. They agreed that Americans live wastefully, but few were willing to consider small changes in their lifestyles, such as car pooling or using energy-efficient light bulbs. Ultimately, what we learned is that how we Americans use resources is so deeply woven into our way of life that we can't always *see* the impact we have.

The readings in this chapter aren't necessarily about changing your lifestyle, but they may

> Just by living and using the resources we need every day, we affect the land and other people in ways we may never see.

help you begin to appreciate the many ways in which we take basic resources for granted. The food we eat, the water we drink, the land we occupy for our homes, the gas we burn in our cars, the electricity we use for so many purposes—all these uses of resources have consequences, many of which we may be unaware of. For example, Michael Pollan explores what a fast food meal contains and where it really comes from, revealing that the simple decision to eat one kind of food rather than another can have environmental and economic consequences hundreds or even thousands of miles from where you eat that meal. Similarly, David Morris explores the implications of the decision to eat food that is produced locally to show that such a decision can be complicated in ways we very likely do not take into account. And Donella Meadows traces the impact of the items that you might purchase for your ski trip and shows that such recreation can have huge (and mostly unnoticed) costs for our earth.

And that may be the real lesson to be learned from the readings in this chapter: that we are interconnected in a multitude of ways to each other and to everything around us. Just by living and using the resources we need every day, we affect the land and other people in ways we may never see.

NECESSITIES

WHAT DO YOU REALLY NEED TO LIVE? FOOD, WATER, SHELTER, AND AIR? CERTAINLY, THOSE ARE NECESSITIES. WITHOUT THEM, YOU COULD NOT SURVIVE. BUT THE ISSUE IS MORE COMPLICATED THAN THAT. THINK FOR A MOMENT ABOUT FOOD. IF YOU'RE TALKING ABOUT SURVIVAL, THEN YOUR NEEDS ARE PRETTY BASIC. YOU NEED ENOUGH CALORIES TO SUSTAIN YOUR BODY, AND YOU NEED A CERTAIN

combination of proteins, fats, carbohydrates, minerals, and vitamins to stay healthy. Beyond that, you don't actually *need* any specific kind of food to survive. You don't *need* meat, for example. You can get the proteins and vitamins contained in meat from other food sources. And of course, there are big differences in the nutritional value of different kinds of meat. You may have heard, for example, that white meat from chicken is healthier in some ways than beef. Or maybe you've heard that buffalo meat, which has become

> Beyond that, you don't actually need any specific kind of food to survive.

more commonly available in some parts of the United States, is healthier than beef. And some kinds of beef are better than others, depending on how the cattle were raised and processed and which cut of beef you select. The more you look into food, the more there is to see. And the more questions you might have about the foods we consider necessities.

I selected the readings for this cluster to highlight some of these complexities of the necessities we tend to take for granted: food, energy for lights and appliances, shelter. These readings focus our attention on these necessities in ways that perhaps we don't normally do and raise questions about what we consume and why. For example, in describing her efforts to change her family's eating habits, well-known writer Barbara Kingsolver helps us see that there is so much more that goes into producing and consuming the food we eat than we probably realize. Richard Corliss raises a different question about the foods we eat, such as whether or not it makes sense to give up eating meat. Stephen Doheny-Farina tells the story of a storm-caused power outage in the rural region of upstate New York where he lives and reveals how much we take for granted things like electricity that we ultimately depend on for our lives; his story suggests that we overlook so much in our lives because the conveniences of modern life make necessities relatively easy to obtain. And Rick Moranis offers a humorous look at how many things we use and consume in our lives—probably without ever really thinking about them. Together, these essays encourage us to look a little more closely at the necessities around which we have built many beliefs, attitudes, habits, and traditions. They may help you appreciate how much is really involved in getting the things we need for our very survival.

I have a friend who grows apples as a hobby. *He owns several acres of land, on which he has dozens of apple trees. Each fall, he harvests the apples to sell at local markets. Although it isn't his main source of income, growing and selling apples require an enormous effort and a great deal of his time. He does it mostly because he loves it. He enjoys tending the*

A *Good* Farmer

trees, the feeling of being outdoors, and the satisfaction of using the land productively. More than most of us, I suspect, he appreciates what goes into growing the foods we eat, something we tend to take for granted. In some ways, the following essay is about how much we take for granted when it comes to food. In this essay, award-winning writer Barbara Kingsolver (b. 1955) describes her family's attempt to change their lives so that they would live less wastefully and more in line with the agrarian values that she was raised by on her own family's farm. This lifestyle change had a lot to do with food, and Kingsolver describes some of the changes her family made in what they ate, how they ate, and their awareness of food in general. In sharing her experience with us, Kingsolver perhaps raises our awareness about the impact of the choices we make when it comes to the foods we eat. She also helps us see that these choices are not only about

BARBARA KINGSOLVER

Sometime around my fortieth birthday I began an earnest study of agriculture. I worked quietly on this project, speaking of my new interest to almost no one because of what they might think. Specifically, they might think I was out of my mind. Why? Because at this moment in history it's considered smart to get out of agriculture. And because I already embarked on a career as a writer, doing work that many people might consider intellectual and therefore superior to anything involving the risk of dirty fingernails. Also, as a woman in my early 40s, I conformed to no right-minded picture of an apprentice farmer. And finally, with some chagrin I'll admit that I grew up among farmers and spent the first decades of my life plotting my escape from a place that seemed to offer me almost no potential for economic, intellectual or spiritual satisfaction.

It took nigh onto half a lifetime before the valuables I'd casually left behind turned up in the lost and found.

The truth, though, is that I'd kept some of that treasure jingling in my pockets all along: I'd maintained an interest in gardening, always, dragging it with me wherever I went, even into a city backyard where

BARBARA KINGSOLVER, "A GOOD FARMER." FROM *THE NATION*, NOVEMBER 2003.
REPRINTED BY PERMISSION OF THE FRANCES GOLDIN LITERARY AGENCY.

convenience or habit but also about basic values that we may not often think about. For Kingsolver and her family, moving to a family farm was an effort to live by their values. Unlike my friend, Kingsolver states bluntly that farming is not a hobby for her. It is an effort to reject what she believes is the wasteful American lifestyle in favor of a more ethical way of life. As you read, consider whether your own lifestyle reflects your values.

Barbara Kingsolver is the author of eleven books, including the award-winning The Poisonwood Bible *(1998) and* Last Stand: America's Virgin Lands *(2002). The following essay, which first appeared in* The Nation *magazine in 2003, was adapted from an essay that appeared in* The Essential Agrarian Reader: The Future of Culture, Community, and the Land *(2003).* ◪

CONVERSATIONS: THE FAMILY FARM
In paragraph 7, Kingsolver describes some of the scenes she associates with growing up on a family farm, which has been slowly disappearing as agriculture has become an increasingly large-scale, corporate business. According to the Economic Policy Institute, for example, more than 72,000 family farms disappeared between 1993 and 1999, a decline of 8 percent. The U.S. Department of Agriculture reports that in 1978, 87 percent of farms were "sole proprietorships"—that is, owned by one person or family; in 1997, that figure had declined to 52 percent. During the same period, "nonfamily" ownership of farms increased from 0.3 percent to 5.6 percent. These figures reflect the growth of "agribusiness," but they also suggest that agriculture is changing to meet the demands of expanding food markets. Some people believe that the traditional family farm is an outdated lifestyle that can't keep up with a changing agricultural marketplace, a view that Kingsolver alludes to in the following paragraph. But many people share Kingsolver's concern about the disappearance of the family farm, and the images she includes in this paragraph suggest some of the reasons for that concern. Consider what ideas these images convey about the family farm and how Kingsolver depicts the family farmer. Consider, too, what Kingsolver's picture of the family farm might leave out. How might her essay fit into the ongoing conversations about the importance of the family farm in American culture?

a neighbor who worked the night shift insisted that her numerous nocturnal cats had every right to use my raised vegetable beds for their litter box. (I retaliated, in my way, by getting a rooster, who indulged his right to use the hour of 6 AM for his personal compunctions.) In graduate school I studied ecology and evolutionary biology, but the complex mathematical models of predator-prey cycles only made sense to me when I converted them in my mind to farmstead analogies—even though, in those days, the ecology department and the college of agriculture weren't on speaking terms. In my 20s, when I was trying hard to reinvent myself as a person without a Kentucky accent, I often found myself nevertheless the lone argumentative voice in social circles where "farmers" were lumped with political troglodytes and devotees of all-star wrestling.

Once in the early 1980s, when cigarette smoking had newly and drastically fallen from fashion, I stood in someone's kitchen at a party and listened to something like a Greek chorus chanting out the reasons why tobacco should be eliminated from the face of the earth, like smallpox. Some wild tug on my heart made me blurt out, "But what about the tobacco farmers?"

"Why," someone asked, glaring, "should I care about tobacco farmers?" [5]

I was dumbstruck. I couldn't form the words to answer: Yes, it is carcinogenic, and generally grown with too many inputs, but tobacco is the last big commodity in America that's still mostly grown on family farms, in an economy that won't let these farmers shift to another crop. If it goes extinct, so do they.

I couldn't speak because my mind was flooded with memory, pictures, scents, secret thrills. Childhood afternoons spent reading Louisa May Alcott in a barn loft suffused with the sweet scent of aged burley. The bright, warm days in late spring and early fall when school was functionally closed because whole extended families were drafted to the cooperative work of setting, cutting, stripping or hanging tobacco. The incalculable fellowship measured out in funerals, family reunions, even bad storms or late-night calvings. The hard-muscled pride of showing I could finally throw a bale of hay onto the truckbed myself. (The year before, when I was 11, I'd had the less honorable job of driving the truck.) The satisfaction of walking across the stage at high school graduation in a county where my name and my relationship to the land were both common knowledge.

But when pressed, that evening in the kitchen, I didn't try to defend the poor tobacco farmer. As if the deck were not already stacked against his little family enterprise, he was now tarred with the brush of evil along with the companies that bought his product, amplified its toxicity and attempted to sell it to children. In most cases it's just the more ordinary difficulty of the small family enterprise failing to measure up to the requisite standards of profitability and efficiency. And in every case, the rational arguments I might frame in its favor will carry no weight without the attendant silk purse full of memories and sighs and songs of what family farming is worth. Those values are an old currency now, accepted as legal tender almost nowhere.

I found myself that day in the jaws of an impossible argument, and I find I am there still. In my professional life I've learned that as long as I write novels and nonfiction books about strictly human conventions and constructions, I'm taken seriously. But when my writing strays into that muddy territory where humans are forced to own up to our dependency on the land, I'm apt to be declared quaintly irrelevant by the small, acutely urban clique that decides in this country what will be called worthy literature. (That clique does not, fortunately, hold much sway over what people actually read.) I understand their purview, I think. I realize I'm beholden to people working in urban centers for many things I love: They publish books, invent theater, produce films and music. But if I had not been raised such a polite Southern girl, I'd offer these critics a blunt proposition: I'll go a week without attending a movie or concert, you go a week without eating food, and at the end of it we'll sit down together and renegotiate "quaintly irrelevant."

10   This is a conversation that needs to happen. Increasingly I feel sure of it; I just don't know how to go about it when so many have completely forgotten the genuine terms of human survival. Many adults, I'm convinced, believe that food comes from grocery stores. In **WENDELL BERRY'S** novel *Jayber Crow*, a farmer coming to the failing end of his long economic struggle despaired aloud, "I've wished sometimes that the sons of bitches would starve. And now I'm getting afraid they actually will."

Like that farmer, I am frustrated with the imposed acrimony between producers and consumers of food, as if this were a conflict in which one could possibly choose sides. I'm tired of the presumption of a nation divided between rural and urban populations whose interests are permanently at odds, whose votes will always be cast different ways, whose hearts and minds share no common ground. This is as wrong as blight, a useless way of thinking, similar to the propaganda warning us that any environmentalist program will necessarily be antihuman. Recently a national magazine asked me to write a commentary on the great divide between "the red and the blue"—imagery taken from election-night coverage that colored a map according to the party each state elected, suggesting a clear political difference

GLOSS: WENDELL BERRY
Wendell Berry is a well-known writer who advocates a simple, environmentally sound lifestyle and who often writes about rural values. His essay, "Thoughts in the Presence of Fear," appears in Chapter 9.

CONVERSATIONS: RED AND BLUE STATES
During the 2004 U.S. presidential election, "red" and "blue" became a common way to refer to more conservative and more liberal states, respectively. Consider how Kingsolver assumes that her readers understand what red and blue mean in this context; that is, she assumes her readers are familiar with current conversations about the political and cultural divisions in American society. (See Conversations: *The Color Red* on page 373 in Chapter 8 for an image of a map of the red and blue states during the 2004 U.S. presidential election.)

between the rural heartland and urban coasts. Sorry, I replied to the magazine editors, but I'm the wrong person to ask: I live in red, tend to think blue and mostly vote green. If you're looking for oversimplification, skip the likes of me.

Better yet, skip the whole idea. Recall that in many of those red states, just a razor's edge under half the voters likely pulled the blue lever, and vice versa—not to mention the greater numbers everywhere who didn't even show up at the polls, so far did they feel from affectionate toward any of the available options. Recall that farmers and hunters, historically, are more active environmentalists than many progressive, city-dwelling vegetarians. (And conversely, that some of the strongest land-conservation movements on the planet were born in the midst of cities.) Recall that we all have the same requirements for oxygen and drinking water, and that we all like them clean but relentlessly pollute them. Recall that whatever lofty things you might accomplish today, you will do them only because you first ate something that grew out of dirt.

We don't much care to think of ourselves that way—as creatures whose cleanest aspirations depend ultimately on the health of our dirt. But our survival as a species depends on our coming to grips with that, along with some other corollary notions, and when I entered a comfortable midlife I began to see that my kids would get to do the same someday, or not, depending on how well our species could start owning up to its habitat and its food chain. As we faced one environmental crisis after another, did our species seem to be making this connection? As we say back home, Not so's you'd notice.

If a middle-aged woman studying agriculture seems strange, try this on for bizarre: Most of our populace and all our leaders are participating in a mass hallucinatory fantasy in which the megatons of waste we dump in our rivers and bays are not poisoning the water, the hydrocarbons we pump into the air are not changing the climate, overfishing is not depleting the oceans, fossil fuels will never run out, wars that kill masses of civilians are an appropriate way to keep our hands on what's left, we are not desperately overdrawn at the environmental bank and, really, the kids are all right.

15   OK, if nobody else wanted to talk about this, I could think about it myself and try to pay for my part of the damage, or at least start to tally up the bill. This requires a good deal of humility and a ruthless eye toward an average household's confusion between need and want. I reckoned I might get somewhere if I organized my life in a way that brought me face to face with what I am made of. The values I longed to give my children—honesty, cooperativeness, thrift, mental curiosity, physical competence—were intrinsic to my agrarian childhood, where the community organized itself around a sustained effort of meeting people's needs. These values, I knew, would not flow naturally from an aggressive consumer culture devoted to the sustained effort of invent-

ing and engorging people's wants. And I could not, as any parent knows, prohibit one thing without offering others. So we would start with the simple and obvious: eschewing fast food for slow food, with the resulting time spent together in the garden and kitchen regarded as a plus, not a minus. We would skip TV in favor of interesting family work. We would participate as much as possible in the production of things our family consumes and the disposal of the things we no longer need. It's too easy to ignore damage you don't see and to undervalue things you haven't made yourself. Starting with food.

Meal preparations at our house, then, would not begin with products, like chicken tenders and frozen juice concentrate, but with whole things, like a chicken or an apple. A chicken or apple, what's more, with a background we could check up on. Our younger daughter was only a toddler when we first undertook this enterprise, but she seemed to grasp the idea. On a family trip once when we ate in a Chinese restaurant, she asked skeptically, "What was this duck's last name?"

What began as a kind of exercise soon turned into a kind of life, which we liked surprisingly well. It's enough to turn your stomach, anyway, to add up the fuel, money and gunk that can go into food that isn't even about food. Our gustatory industries treat food items like spoiled little celebrities, zipping them around the globe in luxurious air-conditioned cabins, dressing them up in gaudy outfits, spritzing them with makeup and breaking the bank on advertising, for heaven's sake. My farm-girl heritage makes me blush and turn down tickets to that particular circus. I'd rather wed my fortunes to the sturdy gal-next-door kind of food, growing what I need or getting it from local "you pick" orchards and our farmers' market.

In making the effort to get acquainted with my food chain, I found country lanes and kind people and assets I had not known existed in my community. To my amazement, I found a Community Shared Agriculture grower sequestered at the end of a dirt road within walking distance of my house, and he helped me fix an irrigation problem that had stumped me for months. I found others who would help me introduce a gardening program into my children's elementary school. I befriended the lone dairyman in my county who refuses to give hormones to his cows, not because he's paid more for the milk he sells to the cooperative (he isn't) but because he won't countenance treating his animals that way. I learned about heritage breeds, and that one of the rarest and tastiest of all turkeys, the Bourbon Red, was first bred a stone's throw from my hometown in Kentucky. I've come to know this

CONVERSATIONS: "OUR GUSTATORY INDUSTRIES"
In this paragraph (par. 17), Kingsolver complains about the highly processed nature of common foods in the American diet and about the resources used to transport, store, and preserve food. Her complaints are based on increasing evidence that this food system may be both environmentally destructive and unhealthy. In early 2005, for example, a study was released that indicated that the high sodium content of the American diet was contributing to thousands of deaths each year; most of the sodium in the typical American's diet is contained in processed foods. Similarly, the shipping of common foods over long distances uses up resources and contributes to air and water pollution. One study indicated that the average food product in the United States is transported 1,500 miles from where it is produced to where it is consumed. Michael Pollan's "Fast Food Meal," which appears on page 648 of this chapter, addresses some of these issues. Compare his treatment of these issues with Kingsolver's.

bird inside and out, and intend to have my own breeding flock of them. I've become part of a loose-knit collective of poultrywomen who share tools and recipes and, at the end of the day, know how to make a real party out of harvest time. All in the house that good food built.

There is more to the story. It has come to pass that my husband and I, in what we hope is the middle of our lives, are in possession of a farm. It's not a hobby homestead, it is a farm, somewhat derelict but with good potential. It came to us with some twenty acres of good, tillable bottomland, plus timbered slopes and all the pasture we can ever use, if we're willing to claim it back from the brambles. A similar arrangement is available with the seventy-five-year-old apple orchard. The rest of the inventory includes a hundred-year-old clapboard house, a fine old barn that smells of aged burley, a granary, poultry coops, a root cellar and a century's store of family legends. No poisons have been applied to this land for years and, we vow, none ever will be.

20   I've never loved any earthly thing so much. It seems to my husband and me that this farm is something we need to work hard to deserve. As a former tobacco farm, it had a past without a future. But now that its future is in our hands, we recognize that it ought to feed people— more than just our family and those who come to our table. Precisely because of tobacco's changing fortunes, we're now situated in a community of farmers who are moving with courage and good cheer into the production of a regionally distributed line of organic produce. This economic project may be small in the eyes of global capitalism, but it concerns us greatly, for its success or failure will be felt large in our schools, churches and neighborhood businesses, not to mention our soil and streams, as these farmers make choices and, I hope, remain among us on their land. My family hopes to contribute to the endeavor as best we can, as producers as well as consumers, though with regard to the former we acknowledge our novice status. For several years now we've received from each other as gifts, on nearly all occasions, such books as are written by Gene Logsdon, Michael Phillips, Elliot Coleman, Carol Ekarius, Vandana Shiva, Wendell Berry. Some other wife might wish for diamond earrings, but my sweetheart knew I wanted *Basic Butchering*.

Our agrarian education has come in as a slow undercurrent beneath our workaday lives and the rearing of our children. Only our closest friends, probably, have taken real notice of the changes in our household: that nearly all the food we put on our table, in every season, was grown in our garden or very nearby. That the animals we eat took no more from the land than they gave back to it, and led sunlit, contentedly grassy lives. Our children know how to bake bread, stretch mozzarella cheese, ride a horse, keep a flock of hens laying, help a neighbor, pack a healthy lunch and politely decline the world's less wholesome offerings. They know the first fresh garden tomato tastes as good as it does partly because you've waited for it since last

STRATEGIES: REFERENCES
Notice the specific authors that Kingsolver mentions in her list of the kinds of books she and her family give each other as gifts. Selecting references carefully in the way Kingsolver does in paragraph 20 is a strategy by which writers can convey messages to readers. What messages is Kingsolver conveying through this list of authors? An essay by Wendell Berry appears in this book, so you can learn something about him by reading the introductions to his essays. You might want to do a quick Internet search to learn about the other authors. Consider what assumptions about her readers Kingsolver is making here.

Thanksgiving, and that the awful ones you could have bought at the grocery in between would only subtract from this equation. This rule applies to many things beyond tomatoes. I have noticed that the very politicians who support purely market-driven economics, which favors immediate corporate gratification over long-term responsibility, also express loud concern about the morals of our nation's children and their poor capacity for self-restraint. I wonder what kind of tomatoes those men feed their kids.

I have heard people of this same political ilk declare that it is perhaps sad but surely inevitable that our farms are being cut up and sold to make nice-sized lawns for suburban folks to mow, because the most immediately profitable land use must prevail in a free country. And yet I have visited countries where people are perfectly free, such as the Netherlands, where this sort of disregard for farmland is both illegal and unthinkable. Plenty of people in this country, too, seem to share a respect for land that gives us food; why else did so many friends of my youth continue farming even while the economic prospects grew doubtful? And why is it that more of them each year are following sustainable practices that defer some immediate profits in favor of the long-term health of their fields, crops, animals and watercourses? Who are the legions of Americans who now allocate more of their household budgets to food that is organically, sustainably and locally grown, rather than buying the cheapest products they can find? My husband and I, bearing these trends in mind, did not contemplate the profitable option of subdividing our farm and changing its use. Frankly, that seemed wrong.

It's an interesting question, how to navigate this tangled path between money and morality: not a new question by any means, but one that has taken strange turns in modern times. In our nation's prevailing culture, there exists right now a considerable confusion between prosperity and success—so much so that avarice is frequently confused with a work ethic. One's patriotism and good sense may be called into doubt if one elects to earn less money or own fewer possessions than is humanly possible. The notable exception is that a person may do so for religious reasons: Christians are asked by conscience to tithe or assist the poor; Muslims do not collect interest; Catholics may respectably choose a monastic life of communal poverty; and any of us may opt out of a scheme that we feel to be discomforting to our faith. It is in this spirit that we, like you perhaps and so many others before us, have worked to rein in the free market's tyranny over our family's tiny portion of America and install values that override the profit motive. Upon doing so, we receive a greater confidence in our children's future safety and happiness. I believe we are also happier souls in the present, for what that is worth. In the darkest months I look for solace in seed catalogues and articles on pasture rotation. I sleep better at night, feeling safely connected to the things that help make a person whole. It is fair to say this has been, in some sense, a spiritual conversion.

Modern American culture is fairly empty of any suggestion that one's relationship to the land, to consumption and food, is a religious matter. But it's true; the decision to attend to the health of one's habitat and food chain is a spiritual choice. It's also a political choice, a scientific one, a personal and a convivial one. It's not a choice between living in the country or the town; it is about understanding that every one of us, at the level of our cells and respiration, lives in the country and is thus obliged to be mindful of the distance between ourselves and our sustenance. I have worlds to learn about being a good farmer. Last spring when a hard frost fell upon our orchards on May 21, I felt despair at ever getting there at all. But in any weather, I may hope to carry a good agrarian frame of mind into my orchards and fields, my kitchen, my children's schools, my writing life, my friendships, my grocery shopping and the county landfill. That's the point: It goes everywhere. It may or may not be a movement—I'll leave that to others to say. But it does move, and it works for us.

Understanding the Text

1. In paragraphs 2 and 3, Kingsolver mentions "valuables" and "treasure." What is she referring to? What does her use of these terms suggest about her beliefs when it comes to farming and living in general?

2. Why does Kingsolver believe that we must have a conversation about where our food comes from? Do you agree with her? Why or why not?

3. What is the "mass hallucinatory fantasy" that Kingsolver claims most Americans are participating in (par. 14)? What does this claim reveal about Kingsolver's values and her political perspective?

4. In what ways do Americans confuse their needs and their wants, according to Kingsolver? What are the consequences of this confusion? What can be done about it, in her view? Do you agree with her? Why or why not?

5. What are the benefits of living on a family farm, according to Kingsolver? Why are these benefits important not just to her family but to the society in general?

Exploring the Issues

1. Kingsolver discusses an opposition between farmers and city dwellers, between rural and urban populations. In paragraph 11, for example, she refers to "the presumption of a nation divided between rural and urban populations." Examine how Kingsolver uses this opposition between farmer (or rural dweller) and city dweller. What characteristics does she associate with each group? In what ways does she favor one over the other? What values of her own does she reveal in the way she presents these two groups? Do you think her characterization of farmers and city dwellers is accurate or fair? Explain.

2. How would you describe Kingsolver's tone in this essay? What features of her writing contribute to her tone? In what ways do you think her tone reinforces her main point? Do you think her tone strengthens or weakens her essay? Explain, citing specific passages to support your answer.

3. What do you think Kingsolver's title, "A Good Farmer," means? In what sense is a farmer "good," in her view? What does her title suggest about her own values?

4. Kingsolver bases much of her argument about how we think about and consume food on her own experience and her family's experience. How effectively do you think Kingsolver uses these experiences to support her main argument in this essay? Do you think that the kinds of experiences she and her family had would appeal to most people? Would such experiences be possible for most Americans? Explain.

Entering the Conversations

1. Write an essay in which you describe an experience you have had that was somehow related to farming or gardening or the production of food (such as working at a food processing plant, a restaurant, an orchard, or a food market). Describe your experience in a way that conveys an important idea or point about our attitudes toward food.

INFOTRAC

2. In this essay, Kingsolver writes passionately about the experience of living on a family farm in the United States. However, the family farm may be declining (see *Conversations: The Family Farm* on page 598). Using InfoTrac College Edition, your library, and other relevant resources, investigate the state of the American family farm today. Try to find out whether the

family farm is in fact declining. Also, try to get a sense of the role or status of the family farm in American culture. If possible, talk to someone at your school who may have expertise on this subject or talk to local farmers or farming experts. You may wish to focus your research on the situation with family farming in your region or state. Then write a report on the basis of your research. In your report, draw your own conclusions about the status of the family farm and its role in American society.

3. Write a standard academic essay in which you analyze Kingsolver's representation of the family farm. Discuss how Kingsolver presents the experience of living on a family farm, and discuss the basic values and beliefs she holds that shape her view of the family farm. Identify any problems you see in her depiction of the family farm, and offer your own conclusions about attitudes toward farming in American culture.

4. Kingsolver suggests that the choices each person makes affect the larger world to some degree. Write an essay in which you consider the choices you have made as you participate in the consumer culture, focusing specifically on the foods you eat. What are the choices you typically make

about food? Why do you think you make these specific choices? What impact do you think your choices have? What would you like to do differently? Why? Try to address such questions in your essay.

5. Create a web page, PowerPoint presentation, or another kind of appropriate multimedia document that presents your view of a "good farmer." Draw on your own experience, beliefs, and values to define a good farmer, and draw as well on Kingsolver's essay, if appropriate. (Even if you live in a city or somewhere other than what you consider to be "farming country," you can define a "good farmer" in a way that reflects your own values.)

6. Visit several blogs devoted to farming, local food initiatives, and related issues and follow the conversations for several days. Get a sense of the beliefs and values of the people who participate in these blogs as well as their main arguments about food and farming. Then write an essay in which you present what you learned from these blogs. In your essay, draw conclusions about how the bloggers view food, farming, and our food production system. Also comment on how Kingsolver's ideas do or do not coincide with the views of people who participate in the blogs you visited.

A few years ago, a student of mine wrote an essay in which she made a very persuasive argument against eating meat. In her essay, she cited many statistics to support her claim that eating meat was not only less healthy than a vegetarian diet but also contributed to environmental damage because of the way cattle, chickens, and pigs are raised and

Should We *All* Be Vegetarians?

processed. She concluded that becoming a vegetarian was therefore an ethical matter as well as a matter of health. Not long ago, that student, who is now a high school English teacher, contacted me, and we met at a local restaurant to talk about teaching. For her dinner, she ordered a large hamburger.

You might call my former student a hypocrite, but I think the matter is more complicated. I have no doubt that she believed what she wrote in her essay, but I also think she learned how challenging it can be to give up eating meat if you live in the United States. The following article helps explain why. As writer Richard Corliss (b. 1944) points out in this article, meat is not only a major part of the American diet, but it is also part of American culture. Think hamburgers on the Fourth of July and hot dogs at the baseball park. Moreover, despite health risks associated with eating meat, becoming a vegetarian has risks of

RICHARD CORLISS

FIVE REASONS TO EAT MEAT:

1)   It tastes good

2)   It makes you feel good

3)   It's a great American tradition

4)   It supports the nation's farmers

5)   Your parents did it

Oh, sorry . . . those are five reasons to smoke cigarettes. Meat is more complicated. It's a food most Americans eat virtually every day: at the dinner table; in the cafeteria; on the barbecue patio; with mustard at a ballpark; or, a billion times a year, with special sauce, lettuce, cheese, pickles, onions on a sesame-seed bun. Beef is, the TV commercials say, "America's food"—the Stars and Stripes served up medium rare—and as entwined with the nation's notion of its robust frontier heritage as, well, the Marlboro Man.

But these days America's cowboys seem a bit small in the saddle. Those cattle they round up have become politically incorrect: for many, meat is an obscene cuisine. It's not just the additives and ailments connected with the consumption of beef, though a dish of hormones, E. coli bacteria or the scary specter of mad-cow disease might be effective enough as an appetite suppressant. It's that more and more Americans, particularly young Americans, have started engaging in a practice that would once have shocked their parents. They are eating their vegetables. Also their grains and sprouts. Some 10 million Americans today consider themselves to be practicing vegetarians, according to a *Time* poll of 10,000 adults; an additional 20 million have flirted with vegetarianism sometime in their past.

To get a taste of the cowboy's ancient pride, and current defensiveness, just click on South Dakota cattleman Jody Brown's web site, www.ranchers.net, and read the new meat mantras: "Vegetarians don't live longer, they just look older"; and "If animals weren't meant to be eaten, then why are they made out of meat?" (One might ask the same of humans.) For Brown and his generation of unquestioning meat eaters, dinner is something the parents put on the table and the kids put in their bodies. Of his own kids, he says, "We expect them to eat a little of everything." So beef is served nearly every night at the Brown homestead, with nary a squawk from Jeff, 17, Luke, 13, and Hannah, 11. But Jody admits to at least one liberal sympathy. "If a vegetarian got a flat tire in my community," he says, "I'd come out and help him."

For the rancher who makes his living with meat or the vegetarian whose diet could someday drive all those breeder-slaughterers to bankruptcy, nothing is simple any more. Gone is the age of American innocence, or naiveté when such items as haircuts and handshakes, family names and school uniforms, farms and zoos, cowboys and ranchers, had no particular political meaning. Now everything is up for rancorous debate. And no aspect of our daily lives—our lives as food consumers—gets more heat than meat.

5   For millions of vegetarians, beef is a four-letter word; veal summons charnel visions of infanticide. Many children, raised on hit films like *Babe* and *Chicken Run*, recoil from eating their movie heroes and switch to what the meat defeaters like to call a "nonviolent diet." Vegetarianism resolves a conscientious person's inner turf war by providing an edible complex of good-deed-doing: to go veggie is to be more humane. Give up meat, and save lives!

Of course, one of the lives you could save or at least prolong is your own. For vegetarianism should be about more than not eating; it's also about smart eating. You needn't be a born-again foodist to think this. The American Dietetic Association, a pretty centrist group, has proclaimed that "appropriately planned vegetarian diets are healthful, are nutritionally adequate and provide health benefits in the prevention and treatment of certain diseases."

So, how about it? Should we all become vegetarians? Not just teens but also infants, oldsters, athletes—everyone? Will it help us live lon-

its own. Corliss's article explores these complexities and helps us see that a basic necessity like food is not always as basic as it might seem.

Richard Corliss writes about popular culture for Time *magazine, in which the following article appeared in 2002. (Corliss was assisted in writing this article by reporters Melissa August, Matthew Cooper, David Bjerklie, Lisa McLaughlin, Wendy Cole, and Jeffrey Ressner.)* ▾

CONVERSATIONS: POPULAR CULTURE AND OUR FRONTIER HERITAGE

Corliss makes several references (par. 1) that are probably familiar to most Americans. For example, the phrase "special sauce, lettuce, cheese, pickles, onions on a sesame-seed bun" is a reference to a popular advertisement for McDonald's restaurants from several years ago; "America's food" is a reference to an advertising campaign by U.S. producers of beef. These references suggest that writers like Corliss rely on their readers' familiarity with various aspects of popular culture, such as well-known advertisements. They also assume that readers are familiar with certain ideas that are part of the culture. For example, later in this paragraph (par. 1), Corliss associates meat with what he calls "the nation's notion of its robust frontier heritage," which is reflected in the image of the famous Marlboro Man in cigarette advertisements. Here, Corliss assumes his readers understand the idea of the frontier, which is well established in American culture. This brief paragraph provides a good example of how much knowledge readers and writers bring to a text; it also shows how that knowledge helps shape the meaning that readers and writers make in a piece of writing.

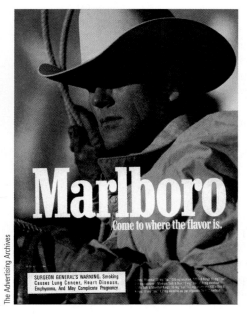

The Advertising Archives

ger, healthier lives? Does it work for people of every age and level of work activity? Can we find the right vegetarian diet and stick to it? And if we can do it, will we?

There are as many reasons to try vegetarianism as there are soft-eyed cows and soft-hearted kids. To impressionable young minds, vegetarianism can sound sensible, ethical and—as nearly 25% of adolescents polled by Teenage Research Unlimited said—"cool." College students think so too. A study conducted by Arizona State University psychology professors Richard Stein and Carol Nemeroff reported that, sight unseen, salad eaters were rated more moral, virtuous and considerate than steak eaters. "A century ago, a high-meat diet was thought to be health-favorable," says Paul Rozin of the University of Pennsylvania. "Kids today are the first generation to live in a culture where vegetarianism is common, where it is publicly promoted on health and ecological grounds." And kids, as any parent can tell you, spur the consumer economy; that explains in part the burgeoning sales of veggie burgers (soy, bulgur wheat, cooked rice, mushrooms, onions and flavorings in Big Mac drag) in supermarkets and fast-food chains.

Children, who are signing on to vegetarianism much faster than adults, may be educating their parents. Vegetarian food sales are savoring double-digit growth. Top restaurants have added more meatless dishes. Trendy "living foods" or "raw" restaurants are sprouting up, like Roxanne's in Larkspur, Calif., where no meat, fish, poultry or dairy items are served, and nothing is cooked to temperatures in excess of 118°F. "Going to my restaurant," says Roxanne Klein, "is like going to a really cool new country you haven't experienced before."

Like any country, vegetarianism has its hidden complexities. 10 For one thing, vegetarians come in more than half a dozen flavors, from sproutarians to pesco-pollo-vegetarians. The most notorious are the vegan (rhymes with intriguin' or fatiguin') vegetarians. The Green Party of the movement, vegans decline to consume, use or wear any animal products. They also avoid honey, since its production demands the oppression of worker bees. TV's favorite vegetarian, the cartoon 8-year-old **LISA SIMPSON**, once had a crush on a fellow who described himself as "a Level Five vegan—I don't eat anything that casts a shadow." Among vegan celebrities: the rock star Moby and Ohio Congressman Dennis Kucinich, who swore off steak for breakfast and insists he feels much better starting his day with miso soup, brown rice or oat groats.

To true believers—who refrain from meat as an A.A. member does from drink and do a spit-take if told that there's gelatin in their soup—a semivegetarian is no vegetarian at all. A phrase like pesco-pollo-vegetarian, to them, is an oxymoron, like "lapsed Catholic" or "semivirgin." *Vegetarian Times,* the bible of this particular congregation, lays down the dogma: "For many people who are working to become vegetarians, chicken and fish may be transitional foods, but they are not vegetarian foods . . . the word 'vegetarian' means someone who eats no meat, fish or chicken."

Clear enough? Not to many Americans. In a survey of 11,000 individuals, 37% of those who responded "Yes, I am a vegetarian" also reported that in the previous 24 hours they had eaten red meat; 60% had eaten meat, poultry or seafood. Perhaps those surveyed thought a vegetarian is someone who, from time to time, eats vegetables as a side dish—say, alongside a prime rib. If more than one-third of people in a large sample don't know the broadest definition of vegetarian, one wonders how they can be trusted with something much more difficult: the full-time care and picky-picky feeding of their bodies, whatever their dietary preferences.

We know that fruits, vegetables, grains, legumes and nuts are healthy. There are any number of studies that show that consuming more of these plant-based foods reduces the risk for a long list of chronic maladies (including coronary artery disease, obesity, diabetes and many cancers) and is a probable factor in increased longevity in the industrialized world. We know that on average we eat too few fruits and vegetables and too much saturated fat, of which meat and dairy are prime contributors. We also know that in the real world, real diets—vegetarian and nonvegetarian—as consumed by real people range from primly virtuous to pig-out voracious. There are meat eaters who eat more and better vegetables than vegetarians, and vegetarians who eat more artery-clogging fats than meat eaters.

The International Congress on Vegetarian Nutrition, a major conference on the subject, was held this spring at Loma Linda (Calif.) University. The research papers presented there included some encouraging if tentative findings: that a predominantly vegetarian diet may have beneficial effects for kidney and nerve function in diabetics, as well as for weight loss; that eating more fruits and vegetables can slow, and perhaps reverse, age-related declines in brain function

CONVERSATIONS: LISA SIMPSON
The author describes Lisa Simpson, a character on the animated television sitcom *The Simpsons,* as "TV's favorite vegetarian." This mention of the character (par. 10) of Lisa Simpson not only suggests how well known this television show was at the time this article was published, but it also indicates how important television can be as a cultural medium. In this case, *The Simpsons,* which is intended to be entertainment, also becomes part of the ongoing conversations in American society about such matters as diet and lifestyle.

CONVERSATIONS: CHARTING VEGETARIANS
This graphic accompanied Corliss's article when it was first published in *Time* magazine. Such charts are commonly used in news magazines and newspapers to illustrate the article or to add information related to the article. Consider what this graphic might contribute to Corliss's article. Does it add anything that cannot be conveyed through writing in the article itself?

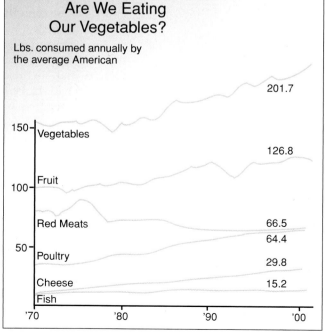

Are We Eating Our Vegetables?

Lbs. consumed annually by the average American

Vegetables — 201.7
Fruit — 126.8
Red Meats — 66.5
Poultry — 64.4
Cheese — 29.8
Fish — 15.2

'70   '80   '90   '00

© 2002 Time Inc.

and in cognitive and motor performance—at least in rats; that vegetarian seniors have a lower death rate and use less medication than meat-eating seniors; that vegetarians have a healthier total intake of fats and cholesterol but a less healthy intake of fatty acids (such as the heart-protecting omega-3 fatty acids found in fish oil).

15   But one paper suggested that low-protein diets (associated with vegetarians) reduce calcium absorption and may have a negative impact on skeletal health. And although several studies on Seventh-Day Adventists (typically vegetarians) indicated that they have a longer-than-average life expectancy, other studies found that prostate-cancer rates were high in Adventists, and one study found that Adventists were more likely to suffer hip fractures.

Can it be that vegetarianism is bad for your health? That's a complex issue. There's a big, beautiful plant kingdom out there; you ought to be able to dine healthily on this botanical bounty. With perfect knowledge, you can indeed eat like a king from the vegetable world. But ordinary people are not nutrition professionals. While some vegetarians have the full skinny on how to watch their riboflavin and vitamins D and B12, many more haven't a clue. This is one reason that vegetarians, in a study of overall nutrition, scored significantly lower than nonvegetarians on the USDA's Healthy Eating Index, which compares actual diet with USDA guidelines.

Another reason is that vegans skew the stats, because their strict avoidance of meat, eggs and dairy products can lead to deficiencies in iron, calcium and vitamin B12. "These nutrients are the problem," says Johanna Dwyer, a professor of nutrition and medicine at Tufts University. "At least among the vegans who are also philosophically opposed to fortified foods and/or vitamin and mineral supplements."

Debates about the efficacy of vegetarianism follow us from cradle to wheelchair. In 1998 child-care expert Dr. Benjamin Spock, who became a vegetarian late in life, stoked a stir by recommending that children over the age of 2 be raised as vegans, rejecting even milk and eggs. The American Dietetic Association says it is possible to raise kids as vegans but cautions that special care must be taken with nursing infants (who don't develop properly without the nutrients in mother's milk or fortified formula). Other researchers warn that infants breast-fed by vegans have lower levels of vitamin B12 and DHA (an omega-3 fatty acid), important to vision and growth.

And there is always the chance of vegetarian theory gone madly wrong in practice. A Queens, N.Y., couple were indicted last May for first-degree assault, charged with nearly starving their toddler to death on a strict diet of juices, ground nuts, herbal tea, beans, flaxseed and cod-liver oils. At 16 months, the girl weighed 10 lbs., less than half the normal weight of a child her age. Their lawyer's defense: "They felt that they have their own lifestyle. They're vegetarians." The couple declined to plea bargain, and are still in jail awaiting trial.

Many children decide on their own to become vegetarians and are   20
declaring their preference at ever more precocious ages; it's often their first act of domestic rebellion. But a youngster is at a disadvantage insisting on a rigorous cuisine before he or she can cook food—or buy it or even read—and when the one whose menu is challenged is the parent: nurturer, disciplinarian and executive chef. Alicia Hurtado of Oak Park, Ill., has been a vegetarian half her life—she's 8 now—and mother Cheryle mostly indulges her daughter's diet. Still, Mom occasionally sneaks a little chicken broth into Alicia's pasta dishes. "When she can read labels," Cheryle says, "I'll be out of luck."

By adolescence, kids can read the labels but often ignore the ingredients. Research shows that calcium intake is often insufficient in American teens. By contrast, lacto-ovo teens usually have abundant calcium intake. For vegans, however, consuming adequate amounts of calcium without the use of fortified foods or supplements is difficult without careful dietary planning. Among vegan youth who do not take supplements, there is reason for concern with respect to iron, calcium, vitamins D and B12, and perhaps also selenium and iodine.

For four years Christina Economos has run the Tufts longitudinal health study on young adults, a comprehensive survey of lifestyle habits among undergraduates. In general, she finds that "kids who were most influenced by family diet and health values are eating healthy vegetarian or low-meat diets. But there is a whole group of students who decide to become vegetarians and do it in a poor way. The ones who do it badly don't know how to navigate in the vegetarian world. They eat more bread, cheese and pastry products and load up on salad dressing. Their saturated-fat intake is no lower than red-meat eaters, and they are more likely to consume inadequate amounts of vitamin B12 and protein. They may think they are healthier because they are some sort of vegetarian and they don't eat red meat, but in fact they may be less healthy."

Jenny Woodson, 20, now a junior at Duke, has been a vegetarian from way back. At 6, on a trip to McDonald's, she ordered a tossed salad. When Jenny lived in a dorm at high school, she quickly realized that teens do not live on French fries and broccoli alone. "We ended up making vegetarian sandwiches with bagels and ingredients from the salad bar, cheese fries and stuffed baked potatoes with cottage cheese." Jenny and her friends were careful to avoid high-fat, calorie-laden fare at the salad bar, but for those who don't exercise restraint, salad-bar fixings can become vegetarian junk food.

Maggie Ellinger-Locke, 19, of the St. Louis, Mo., suburb of University City, has been a vegetarian for eight years and went vegan at 15. Since then she has not worn leather or wool products or slept under

STRATEGIES: EXAMPLES
Notice the examples of two young people who are vegetarians described in paragraphs 23 and 24. Both are women. One attended Duke, a prestigious university; the other lives in a suburb of St. Louis. Consider how the author uses these examples to convey specific ideas about being a vegetarian. Consider, too, whether these two people are in any way typical of Americans.

a down comforter. She has not used cups or utensils that have touched meat. "It felt like we were keeping kosher," says Maggie's mother Linda, who isn't Jewish. At high school Maggie was ridiculed, even shoved to the ground, by teen boys who apparently found her eating habits threatening. She found a happy ending, of sorts, enrolling at Antioch College, where she majors in ecofeminism. "Here," she says, "the people on the defensive are the ones who eat meat."

Maggie hit a few potholes on the road to perfection. Until recently, she smoked up to two packs of cigarettes a day (cigarettes, after all, are plants fortified with nicotine), quitting only because she didn't want to support the tobacco business. And she freely admits to an eating disorder: for the past year she has been bulimic, bingeing and vomiting sometimes as much as once a day to cope with stress. But she insists she is true to her beliefs: even when bingeing, she remains dedicated to vegan consumption.

The American Dietetic Association found that vegetarian diets are slightly more common among adolescents with eating problems but that "recent data suggest that adopting a vegetarian diet does not lead to eating disorders." It can be argued that most American teens already have an eating disorder—fast food, soft drinks and candy are a blueprint for obesity and heart trouble. Why should teens be expected to purge their bad habits just because they have gone veggie? Still, claims Simon Chaitowitz of the pro-vegetarian and animal-rights group Physicians Committee for Responsible Medicine, "Kids are better off being junk-food vegetarians than junk-food meat eaters."

Maybe. According to Dr. Joan Sabate, chairman of the Loma Linda nutrition conference, there are still concerns over vegetarian diets for growing kids or lactating women. When you are in what he calls "a state of high metabolic demand," any diet that excludes foods makes it harder to meet nutrient requirements. But he is quick to add that "for the average sedentary adult living in a Western society, a vegetarian diet meets dietary needs and prevents chronic diseases better than an omnivore diet."

Like kids and nursing moms, athletes need to be especially smart eaters. Their success depends on bursts of energy, sustained strength and muscle mass, factors that require nutrients more easily obtained from meat. For this reason, relatively few top athletes are vegetarians. Besides, says sports nutritionist Suzanne Girard Eberle, the author of *Endurance Sports Nutrition*, "lots of athletes have no idea how their bodies work. That's why fad diets and supplements are so attractive to them."

Eberle notes that vegetarian diets done correctly are high in fiber and low in fat. "But where are the calories?" she asks. "World-class endurance athletes need in excess of 5,000 or 6,000 calories a day. Competition can easily consume 10,000. You need to eat a lot of plant-based food to get those calories. Being a vegetarian athlete is hard, really hard to do right."

25

It's not that easy for the rest of America, either. Middle-aged to el-   30
derly adults can also develop deficiencies in a vegetarian diet (as they
can, of course, with a poor diet that includes meat). Deficiencies in
vitamins D and B12 and in iodine, which can lead to goiter, are common. The elderly tend to compensate by taking supplements, but
that approach carries risks. Researchers have found cases in which
vegetarian oldsters, who are susceptible to iodine deficiency, had dangerously high and potentially toxic levels of iodine in their bodies
because they overdid the supplements.

Meat producers acknowledge that vegetarian diets can be healthy.
They also have responded to the call for leaner food; the National
Pork Board says that, compared with 20 years ago, pork is on average
31% lower in fat and 29% lower in saturated fat, and has 14% fewer
calories and 10% less cholesterol. But the defenders of meat and
dairy can also go on the offensive. They mention the need for B12.
And then they ratchet up the fear factor. Kurt Graetzer, CEO of the
Milk Processor Education Program, scans the drop in milk consumption (not only by vegans but by kids who prefer soda, Snapple and
Fruitopia) and declares, "We are virtually developing a generation of
osteoporotic children."

Dr. Michelle Warren, a professor of medicine at New York Presbyte-
rian Medical Center in New York City—and a member of the Council
for Women's Nutrition Solutions, which is sponsored by the National
Cattlemen's Beef Association—expresses concern about calcium deficiency connected with a vegan diet: "The most serious consequences
are low bone mass and osteoporosis. That is a permanent condition."
Warren says that in her practice, she has seen young vegetarians with
irregular periods and loss of hair. "And there's a peculiar color, a yellow tinge to the skin," that occurs in people who eat a lot of vegetables
rich in beta carotene in combination with a low-calorie diet. "I think
it's very unattractive." She also is troubled by the reasons some young
vegetarians give for their choice of diet. One female patient, Warren
says, wouldn't eat meat because she was told it was the reason her father had a heart attack.

Michael Jacobson, executive director of the Center for Science in
the Public Interest in Washington, sees most of the meat and dairy
lobby's arguments as desperate, disingenuous scare stories. "It un-
masks the industry's self-interest," he says, "when it voices concern
about B12 while hundreds of thousands of people are dying prematurely because of too much saturated fat from meat and dairy products." Indeed, according to David Pimentel, a Cornell ecologist, the
average American consumes 112 grams of protein a day, twice the
amount recommended by the National Academy of Sciences. "This
has implications for cancer risks and stress on the urinary system,"
says Pimentel. "And with this protein comes a lot of fat. Fully 40% of
our calories—and heavy cardiovascular risks—come from fat."

Pimentel argues that vegetarianism is much more environment-friendly than diets revolving around meat. "In terms of caloric content, the grain consumed by American livestock could feed 800 million people—and, if exported, would boost the U.S. trade balance by $80 billion a year." Grain-fed livestock consume 100,000 liters of water for every kilogram of food they produce, compared with 2,000 liters for soybeans. Animal protein also demands tremendous expenditures of fossil-fuel energy—eight times as much as for a comparable amount of plant protein. Put another way, says Pimentel, the average omnivore diet burns the equivalent of a gallon of gas per day—twice what it takes to produce a vegan diet. And the U.S. livestock population—cattle, chickens, turkeys, lambs, pigs and the rest—consumes five times as much grain as the U.S. human population. But then there are 7 billion of them; they outnumber us 25 to 1.

35   In the spirit of fair play to cowboy Jody Brown and his endangered breed, let's entertain two arguments in favor of eating meat. One is that it made us human. "We would never have evolved as large, socially active hominids if we hadn't turned to meat," says Katharine Milton, an anthropologist at the University of California, Berkeley. The vegetarian primates (orangutans and gorillas) are less social than the more omnivorous chimpanzees, possibly because collecting and consuming all that forage takes so darned much time. The early hominids took a bold leap: 2.5 million years ago, they were cracking animal bones to eat the marrow. They ate the protein-rich muscle tissue, says Milton, "but also the rest of the animal—liver, marrow, brains—with their high concentrations of other nutrients. Evolving humans ate it all."

Just as important, they knew why they were eating it. In Milton's elegant phrase, "Solving dietary problems with your head is the trajectory of the primate order." Hominids grew big on meat, and smart on that lovely brain-feeder, glucose, which they got from fruit, roots and tubers. This diet of meat and glucose gave early man energy to burn—or rather, energy to play house, to sing and socialize, to make culture, art, war. And finally, about 10,000 years ago, to master agriculture and trade—which provided the sophisticated system that modern humans can use to go vegetarian.

The other reason for beef eating is, hold on, ethical—a matter of animal rights. The familiar argument for vegetarianism, articulated by Tom Regan, a philosophical founder of the modern animal-rights movement, is that it would save Babe the pig and *Chicken Run*'s Ginger from execution. But what about Bugs Bunny and Mickey Mouse? asks Steven Davis, professor of animal science at Oregon State University, pointing to the number of field animals inadvertently killed during crop production and harvest. One study showed that simply mowing an alfalfa field caused a 50% reduction in the gray-tailed vole population. Mortality rates increase with each pass of the tractor to plow, plant and harvest. Rabbits, mice and pheasants, he says, are the indiscriminate "collateral damage" of row crops and the grain industry.

By contrast, grazing (not grain-fed) ruminants such as cattle produce food and require fewer entries into the fields with tractors and other equipment. Applying (and upending) Regan's least-harm theory, Davis proposes a ruminant-pasture model of food production, which would replace poultry and pork production with beef, lamb and dairy products. According to his calculations, such a model would result in the deaths of 300 million fewer animals annually (counting both field animals and cattle) than would a completely vegan model. When asked about Davis' arguments, Regan, however, still sees a distinction: "The real question is whether to support production systems whose very reason for existence is to kill animals. Meat eaters do. Ethical vegetarians do not."

The moral: there is no free lunch, not even if it's vegetarian. For now, man is perched at the top of the food chain and must live with his choice to feed on the living things further down. But even to raise the question of a harvester Hiroshima is to show how far we have come in considering the humane treatment of that which is not human. And we still have a way to go. "It may take a while," says actress and vegetarian Mary Tyler Moore, "but there will probably come a time when we look back and say, 'Good Lord, do you believe that in the 20th century and early part of the 21st, people were still eating animals?'"

It may take a very long while. For most people, meat still does taste good. And can "America's food" ever be tofu?   40

Understanding the Text

1. Why is the matter of eating meat or being a vegetarian no longer simple, according to Corliss? Do you think it ever was? Explain.

2. What are the main reasons for becoming a vegetarian, according to this article? What do you think these reasons suggest about Americans' eating habits and attitudes toward food?

3. What are some of the challenges of having a true vegetarian diet? Why are these challenges important, according to the author? What do you think these challenges reveal about our habits and attitudes relating to food?

4. What are the reasons for eating meat, according to this article? Do you think these reasons are persuasive? Why or why not? What might your answer to that question suggest about your own values regarding food and lifestyle?

Exploring the Issues

1. How would you characterize the writing style in this article? What specific features of the writing style—such as word choice, figures of speech, sentence structure, or rhythm—are most distinctive in your view? Do you find this writing style effective? Explain.

2. Corliss cites many statistics, refers to scientific studies of nutrition, provides examples, and quotes food researchers. Examine his use of information and evidence in this article. What kinds of information seem to be emphasized? How effectively do you think the specific points raised in the article are supported by information and evidence?

3. This article originally appeared in *Time* magazine, a large-circulation weekly news magazine that reaches a general audience. *Time* is known for informative articles that present an in-depth discussion of timely issues or events. This was intended to be such an article rather than an editorial that presents an opinion about an issue or event. To what extent do you think this article succeeds in presenting its subject fairly and objectively? Do you think the author favors one side or another in the debates about whether or not to eat meat? Explain, citing specific passages to support your answer.

4. Corliss depicts representatives of various groups in this article, including cattle ranchers and beef producers, nutritionists and scientists, and vegetarians. Examine the picture he paints of these groups. What does he seem to emphasize about each? Do you think his picture of these groups is accurate and fair? Why or why not?

Entering the Conversations

1. Write an essay in which you make a case for or against becoming a vegetarian. Base your argument on your own principles for living and for using resources.

2. In a group of classmates, share the essays you wrote for Question 1. Identify the main arguments for and against becoming a vegetarian. Try to draw conclusions about what these arguments might reveal about your attitudes regarding food.

3. Create a web site, PowerPoint presentation, flyer, or some other appropriate kind of document in which you educate a general audience about the pros and cons of eating meat or becoming a vegetarian. Draw on this article and other appropriate resources in creating your document.

4. Write a letter to the editor of your local newspaper indicating why you believe people who live in your region should or should not eat meat.

5. Watch television to find advertisements about food—for example, advertisements for fast-food restaurants, certain snack foods or other food products, or food stores. (Or look for similar advertisements in newspapers, magazines, or on the Internet.) Select several common ads for popular products or restaurants and analyze them for the messages they seem to convey about food in general. Then write a report on the basis of your analysis. Try to draw conclusions about American attitudes regarding food.

In the following essay, writer and teacher *Stephen Doheny-Farina describes his experiences during a powerful winter storm that hit the northeastern United States and southeastern Canada in 1998. I remember that storm well. At the time, I was living near Albany, New York, about a four-hour drive by car from the small town of*

The Grid AND THE Village

STEPHEN DOHENY-FARINA

Potsdam, New York, where Doheny-Farina lives and works. My own neighborhood lost power for a few days, which caused inconvenience but not much more than that for my neighbors and me. However, the news reports we heard at the time described a much more dire situation in the northern part of the state, where communities like Potsdam were without power for much longer—in some cases for several weeks. In addition to lives lost and disrupted, the storm cost millions of dollars in lost business, repairs, and aid. But even after such a destructive and deadly storm, it didn't take long before most people returned to their routines.

For Doheny-Farina, the storm was a lesson in how those routines can hide serious problems in how we live together in our communities. Doheny-Farina began to see that how we use necessities—such as energy for heat and light, gasoline for our cars, and electricity to cook

Early morning, January 1998. In Potsdam, New York, the power was out and the freezing rain was intensifying. Our roof, like all our neighbors' roofs, lay insulated beneath a creamy gray-white icing, rounding off the edges and dripping down every wall. Power and phone lines sagged deeply. Bushes and shrubs bowed gracefully down, embedded in glass. A gently undulating, pebbly white sheet stretched across yards and fields from the western horizon down to the frozen flat expanse of the Raquette River to the east. The only sound I could hear was the constant chattering of ice pellets punctuated by the intermittent gunshots of breaking branches. Tree limbs were snapping all around me.

One of our dogs was sniffing around my feet when I saw an orange flash on the horizon, a fiery flare somewhere in the village. A moment later a brilliant blue explosion lit up the entire dome of the sky: one of the major power circuits supplying energy to our entire town had just blown. Startled, I ducked involuntarily and the dog skittered away from me. A mile away, on the other side of the river, my neighbor's son, Mike Warden, had just opened his eyes when the world outside

"THE GRID AND THE VILLAGE," BY STEPHEN DOHENY-FARINA, AS IT APPEARED IN *ORION MAGAZINE*, AUTUMN 2001 FROM *THE GRID AND THE VILLAGE*. YALE UNIVERSITY PRESS, 2001. REPRINTED BY PERMISSION OF YALE UNIVERSITY PRESS.

our meals—can actually weaken our communities. But when the storm forced him and his neighbors to pool their resources, he began to see his community in a new way. His essay may help you see that there is much more to the necessities we take for granted than most of us ever notice.

Stephen Doheny-Farina is professor of communications and media at Clarkson University and author of a number of articles and books, including The Wired Neighborhood *(1996). This essay, which appeared in* Orion *magazine in 2001, was adapted from his book* The Grid and the Village: Losing Electricity, Finding Community, Surviving Disaster *(2001).* ◙

his bedroom window was suddenly revealed in that silent flash of light. For a moment he could see as clearly as if it were midday, but under a sickly green sun. His wife, Marge, slept on, **THE BABY DUE IN LITTLE MORE THAN A WEEK.**

For the first two days of the ice storm, my family and neighbors were so cut off from the world that we had no concept of the severity of the problem. The storm had arrived with little warning; we didn't know that it had knocked out power grids from the Great Lakes to the North Atlantic, or that thousands of people were already fleeing to makeshift shelters. We didn't know that national emergencies were being declared on both sides of the U.S.-Canada border and utility crews from across both countries were steadily parading into this vast zone of darkness. We simply expected the lights to come back on at any moment.

It was chillingly cold, and so dark at night that the ice seemed to glow. By the third day without power my wife, Kath, and I had begun working with our neighbors, the Centofantis and the Wardens. We needed warmth, in at least one of our houses, and we needed water from at least one of our wells. The only way we could succeed in either of these was to run a generator—and to do that we needed gasoline. As an essential ingredient for all those who had not taken refuge in one of the emergency shelters, finding gas was nearly impossible.

A plan to get some gasoline to us was on the mind of my brother-in-law, Steve, who called us several days into the disaster from one of his service stations downstate. He knew far more about the scale of the storm than we did. He said that he'd be willing to sell a fifty-five gallon drum with gasoline and drive it and a generator to our house. Kath and I were somewhat taken aback by this proposal. It couldn't be that bad, I thought. You can't just wake up one morning and have to live off of a generator for the foreseeable future. That doesn't happen.

But within a day we realized that not only could it happen, it had. We decided to take Steve up on his offer. And when he and Kath's father, Bob, arrived, they told us of a sharp line they had crossed as they descended out of the Adirondack mountains and into the St. Lawrence River val-

5

STRATEGIES: SETTING THE SCENE

In the opening two paragraphs, Doheny-Farina describes the situation he and his family found themselves in during the storm that struck the eastern United States in 1998. Notice that his description in this passage is not limited to the physical surroundings and weather conditions (as in the photograph shown here) but also includes the actions of his neighbors as well as details that convey a sense of the severity of the situation. At the end of paragraph 2, for example, he tells us that his neighbor's son's wife was expecting a baby in a little more than a week. Given the context of the storm, this detail is significant, and Doheny-Farina includes it to help set the scene and establish the tone of this essay. This passage is a good example of how a writer can use description for several purposes in an essay.

© Frank Cezus/Getty Images

ley. After that point, Bob said, the utter destruction of the trees reminded him of photos of European forests that had been shelled in World War II—for as far as he could see there were just tall sticks with craggy, broken branches drooping down. Kath and her father wired the generator into our furnace and water pump, and then set it up so that it could be disengaged and carried over to our neighbor's house intermittently to keep their pipes from freezing, too.

With this it had become clear that the power wasn't just about to come back. We were in the middle of a major storm and we were all starting to realize that we'd better be prepared to take care of ourselves. We emptied the refrigerator and set up a makeshift one on our back deck, which had the effect of putting all our perishables in a freezer. Then we decided to join our neighbors in cooking supper each night at the Wardens' house. The families would pool some key resources.

With a baby due any day, Marge and Mike moved in with their parents. The houses had all become public places; no one needed to knock, and we all moved freely in and out of each other's homes. I heard myself saying things like, "Let's see, with that fifty-five gallons of gas, the twenty-five you have in those cans, the other fifty or sixty gallons we have left in the tanks of all our vehicles, we'll be alright." Twenty-four hours earlier the storm was merely an annoyance that was keeping me from finishing my course syllabi for the coming semester. Suddenly I'm talking about siphoning off gas tanks so we don't freeze; suddenly we're making decisions like having the kids stay in the Wardens' rec room because that's the warmest spot of all our houses.

This was an ironic and deserved fate for me. A couple of years before I had written a book that touted local life while warning people of the potential dangers of global networks. Yet all the while I was continually connected to these networks, participating in global discussions about the **IMPORTANCE OF PROTECTING LOCAL COMMUNITIES**. Now my network extended across one yard to the Wardens' house and across one road to the Centofantis' house. No matter how often I had preached about the importance of geophysical place before, I had never in my adult life been so totally consumed for so long by such a limited here and now. It was a moment-by-moment existence devoted to the people and property around me.

10   Life was focused on keeping generators running, and moving them between our houses. One day when several of us drove a generator over to Mike and Marge's now-abandoned house so that we could pump out its flooded basement, a woman appeared suddenly in the middle of the street and

CONVERSATIONS: PROTECTING LOCAL COMMUNITIES
As globalization has become an accepted reality of contemporary life, many writers, activists, economists, and public policy experts have argued for "the importance of protecting local communities," as Doheny-Farina writes in paragraph 9. These critics have pointed out that while globalization can benefit regions and nations by expanding markets and making consumer goods and services available to more and more communities around the world, it can also destroy local markets and cultures. Doheny-Farina himself has been part of these conversations about the value of local communities. Here, he refers to his book, *The Wired Neighborhood* (1996), in which he warns about the impact of rapidly growing online networks on real local communities. This essay, though, describes his first-hand experiences with the kind of intensely local existence that he advocated in that book. In a sense, by writing this essay he is not only participating in the ongoing global conversation about how we should use the earth's resources, but he is also having a kind of conversation with himself as his own views about these complex issues continue to evolve. By exploring through writing his experience in the ice storm, he can gain new insight into the complicated questions about how we should live together on the earth.

asked me if I knew of anyone who could spare a generator. She was nearly in tears. I hesitated. She said that there was a farm outside of town where the cows were threatened because they couldn't be milked. I didn't know what to say. Our little generator certainly couldn't handle that job. We suggested she contact the police or fire departments. Good Lord, I thought, are we going to find ourselves choosing between keeping our kids warm and fed or helping our neighbors save their livelihoods?

But events quickly pulled us back to our own situation. In the middle of our fourth night without power, Marge went into labor and had to be rushed to the hospital, which itself was operating in emergency mode under generator power. Then, as the temperatures dropped into the single digits, our generators started to falter. Mine had begun to run ragged and stall out under the strain of cold and overuse.

On the morning of the fifth day I awoke to discover that Mike and Marge had a new baby boy and the Wardens' generator was silent and sitting in a pool of oil. Our genuine happiness was tinged with concern. Without some source of heat and water, we, too, might end up at the shelter. So the day was spent working on generators and with the expert help of a friend of the Wardens, we were able to get both of them back online for the moment.

After nearly a week without power, with Mike, Marge, and baby safely ensconced in the hospital, and with two generators barely limping along, we all decided that we should treat ourselves by going to the shelter for supper. We had heard that they offered free food to anyone who could make it there, and although we hesitated to join what we considered a "refugee camp," we realized that we needed help, too.

The building that night had evolved into a kind of place that has largely disappeared, even in small towns and villages; it became a public commons, a place where people met by chance and talked about whatever was on their minds. On this night, of course, conversations were focused. As we pushed our trays along the buffet line, the common question was "how are you doing?"—not the polite and empty how-are-you-doing but one that meant, What kind of heat do you have? How are you holding up? Who are you with? What have you seen? What do you know? The stories spilled out. Some people had generators; some had fireplaces or woodstoves. Those who had were sharing with those who didn't. Multigenerational families far flung across the region were coalescing at one location. Others, like us, found themselves throwing in with small neighborhood groups. Whole households were living in one room, the rest of the house closed off and abandoned to the cold. Some were enjoying the company, others were suffocating. For young kids it was fun while teenagers were getting bored and difficult.

15   There were stories about unexpected predicaments and amazing sights. There was grapevine information about the state of the power grid and who was going to get power first. People stood between tables holding trays of hot food getting cold and just kept talking. Or they

were leaning back in their chairs and talking over their shoulders to someone behind them. Attitudes ranged from a resigned relaxation to a kind of subdued, exhausted agitation. All were shocked by the state of the trees. At one point I realized that each of the adults around our table was turned away talking to a different person whom we may or may not have known before. Talk was easy when everyone was bound by the same necessities. For me it was a simple but powerful night.

On the night of our sixth day without power, a light over the stove in our kitchen suddenly came on. It stayed on. Later I would learn that we were among the first thirty percent to get power back in **ST. LAWRENCE COUNTY.** After that, every day brought more people back online. It would take two more weeks to restore power to everyone in New York. It took until February 8, nearly five weeks after the storm hit, for the complete restoration of power in Quebec's "triangle of darkness" south of Montreal.

A few days after power had been restored to our road, I was home trying to bring myself to begin preparing again for the upcoming semester. At that time there were still large chunks of the north country without electricity, and the word at **CLARKSON** was that the semester's start would be pushed back by a week or more. Even so I had little else to do but to get back at it. The trouble was, I had zero interest in doing so. The job seemed so distant to me. It was almost as if I had changed careers over the course of two weeks from teacher to home handyman—klutzy, semi-clueless, but coachable, very willing to learn new skills like how to run and maintain a two-cycle generator engine.

Suddenly the power went out again. I got up quickly and looked out the window to see if there was evidence of power anywhere in sight. I got on the phone and started calling people. Power seemed to be out across the village. I was alive—it was as if the power left the grid and poured into me. I started to check for essential materials throughout the house: candles, flashlights, et cetera. I turned on the radio. Was it a story yet? I was smiling and excited. But I knew there was something perverse about that. "This is nuts," I told myself. "Calm down. It can't last."

It didn't, of course. About an hour later power was restored and the reality of pre-storm living continued to loom over me. A week or so later I heard a weather forecaster predict that we might be getting hit by another ice storm. That same day I heard the panicky voice of a local caller to North Country Public Radio who was clearly unnerved by the forecast. She said her husband was immobilized by fear of another ice storm. "We have to do something," she said, "to help each other handle all this." A wave of guilt washed over me. No one who lived through it—including myself—wants to live under those conditions. But why was I, like many others I knew, so unsettled by the prospect of returning to the energized grid?

20   Late that afternoon, outside the door to the Wardens' house, I stood holding one of their gas cans that had found its way to my garage. I didn't just open the door and walk in. **I KNOCKED INSTEAD.**

GLOSS: ST. LAWRENCE COUNTY
Located in upstate New York adjacent to the Canadian border, which is formed by the Saint Lawrence River, St. Lawrence County is the state's largest county in terms of geographical area and one of its most rural and sparsely populated. It's also one of the poorest counties in the state. According to the U.S. Census Bureau, more than 15% of the county's residents live below the federal poverty line.

GLOSS: CLARKSON
Clarkson University, where Doheny-Farina teaches, is a private research university with 3,000 students located in Potsdam, New York.

STRATEGIES: USING ANECDOTE TO MAKE A POINT
In paragraph 20, Doheny-Farina shares a brief story about returning a gas can to his neighbors after the ice storm. Notice that he ends this anecdote with the simple statement that he knocked on his neighbor's door rather than just walking in without knocking, as he had done during the storm (see par. 8). Writers often select anecdotes carefully to help make or reinforce a point. You might read this anecdote as Doheny-Farina's answer to the question he poses at the end of the preceding paragraph. If so, what point is he making with this anecdote?

In the end, as in all major disasters, the ice storm numbers were big. In the U.S. alone, the storm damaged about eighteen million acres of rural and urban forests. In New York over one thousand power transmission towers were damaged; power companies replaced over eight thousand poles, 1,800 transformers, and five hundred miles of wires. In Canada over 1,300 steel towers were damaged; power companies replaced over 35,000 poles and five thousand transformers. Dairy farmers in both countries lost millions of dollars in livestock and income. At least thirty-five people were killed by storm-related house fires, falling ice, carbon monoxide poisoning, or hypothermia. The Worldwatch Institute reported that the cost of the damage on both sides of the border totaled 2.5 billion dollars, about half of the cost inflicted by Hurricane Mitch ten months later.

But the impact of this experience goes beyond these quantifiable items. Consider for a moment one more statistic—one small, local, seemingly insignificant item: during the week in which the village of Potsdam was without any type of traffic signals or traffic control, only one minor fender-bender was reported. Only one. Under normal circumstances accidents happen every day around here. Yes, Potsdam is a small town, but as in any active community, urban, suburban, or rural, there is just the right combination of traffic and tricky intersections to bring about a number of serious and sometimes fatal accidents. There were fewer cars on the road, thereby reducing the chance of an accident, but I drove through a few of the most dangerous intersections enough times in the early days of the storm to know that there were plenty of chances for serious accidents to happen.

There was more going on than just fewer drivers on the road. I think drivers were more mindful of the act of driving during that experience. And it was this exercise of storm-induced mindfulness that may have the most lasting impact of the entire event. Like most people before the storm I lived as if electricity came from light switches and power outlets. The storm changed that. It's as if I've started to trace electricity back along the lines from my house to the pole on the road to the local substation to the transmission lines to one of the sources of that bulk power: the massive hydropower dam twenty-five miles away on the St. Lawrence Seaway.

From there I can go a number of places. I can examine the environmental impact of the Seaway to illustrate the price we pay for power. I can explore in depth that growing worldwide movement to oppose the building of large dams, most notably the gargantuan **THREE GORGES PROJECT IN CHINA**, as a way to gauge power's costs. I can follow the changes in the power industry nationwide as state after state is moving to deregulate its utilities. Or I can delve into the newly resurgent world of alternate energy sources, especially the recent advances in home power stations that promise to further atomize the home by removing it from the power grid without sacrificing any electronic convenience. But, ultimately, what I find particularly compelling is

CONVERSATIONS: THREE GORGES DAM
In paragraph 24, Doheny-Farina refers to the controversial Three Gorges Dam project on the Yangtze River in eastern China. Begun in 1994, the dam is expected to be completed in 2011 and will be the largest hydroelectric power station in the world. The dam is intended to provide power for China's rapidly growing economy, but the construction of the dam has sparked intense controversy over the loss of land, archaeological sites, and towns along the river. This controversy is part of a larger global debate about how humans obtain, share, and use necessities for living. Note how Doheny-Farina uses this reference to the dam to position himself in that debate.

the way that community came to the fore in the absence of the grid that under normal conditions enables us to live and work quite independently from one another.

Although all disasters have their unique dangers, in many ways the impact of the ice storm was less a sudden catastrophe than an unforeseen change in the way we had to live. Many other types of disasters leave relatively clear boundaries between destruction and normality. For those who are fortunate enough to emerge safely from the mayhem of, say, an earthquake or tornado, escape is possible. The path of destruction is narrow and capricious. One person's world may be destroyed while a neighbor's goes untouched. Or in the case of all but the largest of hurricanes, a section of a town may be obliterated while others survive largely intact. There is some level of destruction and some level of normal living, and the distinction is clear. In contrast, the ice storm was far less violent, far less lethal, but far more democratic; it afflicted everyone within its vast boundaries. For most of the five million of us who lived through it, there was no escape. The only options were to adapt and endure.

And during that process a fascinating phenomenon evolved: as the power grid failed, in its place arose a vibrant grid of social ties—formal and informal, organized and serendipitous, public and private, official and ad hoc. While national news media reported on the standard three Ds of disaster news—deaths, destruction, and disorder—a spontaneous, ever-shifting group of citizen volunteers, public officials, corporate decision-makers, and neighbors helping neighbors pulled together to weather the storm.

By the time we all returned to the safety of the electrified grid, we had come to realize that there existed in this place at this time a web of support that many people thought had long since withered away from disuse. While the fruits of the power grid may make it seem as though each of us can live an autonomous life, we learned that that is an illusion. It is family and community, not global networks, that truly sustain us.

Understanding the Text

1. Why was Doheny-Farina surprised by the severity of the power outage he and his family experienced during the storm in 1998? What might his surprise suggest about our typical attitudes toward the necessities we depend on? Do you think he intends to convey anything about those attitudes by telling us about his surprise? Explain.

2. What did Doheny-Farina learn when he and his neighbors went to the public shelter for dinner? In what ways are the lessons he learned at the shelter related to his larger point in this essay?

3. In paragraph 19, Doheny-Farina writes that after the power was restored to his community, "the reality of pre-storm living continued to loom over me." What was the "reality of pre-storm living"? How did it differ from the reality he experienced during the storm and power outage? Why did he regret going back to his "pre-storm" reality? What do you think his regret suggests about how we use and share necessities?

4. In what sense was the ice storm "more democratic" than other kinds of natural disasters, such as hurricanes or floods, according to Doheny-Farina? Do you think he is right? Why or why not?

5. Ultimately, what did the storm change for Doheny-Farina? Do you think the lessons he learned from the storm are relevant to the rest of us? Explain.

Exploring the Issues

1. Throughout this essay, Doheny-Farina describes the many ways that he and his neighbors helped each other through the storm and shared their available resources. What do you think Doheny-Farina's experience suggests about our individual and community responsibilities in using resources and providing for the necessities we depend on?

2. In paragraph 15, Doheny-Farina writes, "Talk was easy when everyone was bound by the same necessities." What does he mean by that statement? What do you think he learned about necessities through this experience? What do you think he learned about how necessities shape the communities we live in? Do you think the lessons he learned apply to your community? Explain.

3. In this essay, Doheny-Farina tells the story of his experiences during a powerful winter storm to make a point about how we live together in our communities and how we share necessities. How effectively do you think he tells his story? How effectively does he

use the story to make his point? Do you think his essay would be as effective if he simply presented his views about communities and necessities without telling the story of the storm? Why or why not?

Entering the Conversations

1. Write an essay describing an experience in which you and other people had to provide necessities that you otherwise take for granted.

2. Write a proposal to your mayor or another appropriate official in your town or city to make the use of necessities in your region more fair and efficient. In your proposal, explain the problems you see with how necessities (such as water, food, energy, and shelter) are obtained, distributed, and used in the area where you live, and describe how your proposal would provide solutions to those problems. Justify your proposal on the basis of your beliefs about how people should use resources in their communities. If appropriate, refer to a specific event, such as a storm or power outage, that helps illustrate the problems you see (as Doheny-Farina does in his essay).

Alternatively, write a letter to the editor of a newspaper in your community in which you defend the current ways that necessities are obtained and used there.

3. Choose a necessity, such as food, water, energy, or shelter, that you think is especially important or problematic for some reason in your commu-

nity, and examine the way that necessity is obtained, distributed, and used in your community. For example, there may be a controversy in your community about a local power plant or building new waterlines for a new housing development. Using appropriate resources, including InfoTrac, the Internet, and your library, learn what you can about this necessity and how it is obtained and used in your community today. Try to talk to officials or experts who are involved with the distribution and use of this necessity. You might also talk to residents of your community about their uses of this necessity. Then write a report on the basis of your research. In your report, describe the use of the necessity in your community and draw conclusions about any questions or problems that you encountered in your investigation of this necessity.

4. For several days keep a log in which you describe your own use of the necessity you investigated for Question 4 (or select another necessity). Then write an essay for an audience of your classmates in which you describe your use of that necessity. Draw conclusions about how your use of that necessity affects others in your community or elsewhere.

5. On the basis of your research for Question 4 (or your essay for Question 5), create a web page, pamphlet, or another appropriate document for residents of your community explaining the impact of the uses of necessities in your community.

If you have ever bought a homeowner's or renter's insurance policy, you were probably asked by the insurance agent to make a list of your possessions. The purpose of the list is to estimate how much your possessions are worth. I remember the first time my wife and I made such a list. When we actually listed everything we owned, as our insurance agent asked us to do—

My Days Are Numbered

from big items like a washing machine to things like socks and T-shirts—I was even more surprised. We had a lot of stuff. For me, the whole exercise raised an obvious question: Did we really need all the stuff we had?

The following essay by Rick Moranis poses the same basic question, although in a much more humorous way than my list of possessions did for my insurance agent. Moranis makes a similar list, but the items he includes focus our attention on the many things we own that somehow seem to control our lives rather than make

RICK MORANIS

The average American home now has more television sets than people . . . according to Nielsen Media Research. There are 2.73 TV sets in the typical home and 2.55 people, the researchers said.
— The Associated Press, Sept. 21.

I **have two kids. Both are away at college.**

I have five television sets. (I like to think of them as a set of five televisions.) I have two DVR boxes, three DVD players, two VHS machines and four stereos.

I have nineteen remote controls, mostly in one drawer.

I have three computers, four printers and two non-working faxes.

I have three phone lines, three cell phones and two answering machines.   5

I have no messages.

I have forty-six cookbooks.

I have sixty-eight takeout menus from four restaurants.

I have one hundred and sixteen soy sauce packets.

I have three hundred and eighty-two dishes, bowls, cups, saucers, mugs and glasses.   10

"My Days Are Numbered," by Rick Moranis. *New York Times*, November 22, 2006. Reprinted by permission of the *New York Times*.

STRATEGIES: USING AN EPIGRAPH
Writers use epigraphs (a quotation or inscription placed at the beginning of a book, essay, or chapter) to help establish the theme of an essay or book. Consider how this epigraph from an Associated Press report influences your reading of Moranis's essay. Would it read differently without the epigraph?

our lives easier or better. His list is thus a kind of comment on how we live—and on the many things that define our lives, whether we need them or not. As you read his list, consider how your own days are "numbered" and whether you really need everything on your own list of possessions.

Rick Moranis (b. 1953) is a musician and former actor who appeared in Ghostbusters *(1984),* Spaceballs *(1987), and* Honey, I Shrunk the Kids *(1989), among other films. This essay was published in the* New York Times *in 2006.* ◪

I eat over the sink.

I have five sinks, two with a view.

I try to keep a positive view.

I have two refrigerators.

It's very hard to count ice cubes.   15

I have thirty-nine pairs of golf, tennis, squash, running, walking, hiking, casual and formal shoes, ice skates and rollerblades.

I'm wearing slippers.

I have forty-one 37-cent stamps.

I have no 2-cent stamps.

I read three dailies, four weeklies, five monthlies and no annual   20
reports.

I have five hundred and six CD, cassette, vinyl and eight-track recordings.

I listen to the same radio station all day.

I have twenty-six sets of linen for **FOUR REGULAR, THREE FOLDOUT AND TWO INFLATABLE BEDS.**

I don't like having houseguests.

I have one hundred and eighty-four thousand frequent flier miles   25
on six airlines, three of which no longer exist.

I have "101 Dalmatians" on tape.

I have fourteen digital clocks flashing relatively similar times.

I have twenty-two minutes to listen to the news.

I have nine armchairs from which I can be critical.

I have a laundry list of things that need cleaning.   30

I have lost more than one thousand golf balls.

I am missing thirty-seven umbrellas.

I have over four hundred yards of dental floss.

I have a lot of time on my hands.

I have two kids coming home for Thanksgiving.   35

STRATEGIES: JUXTAPOSITION

Throughout his list, Moranis seems to place related statements next to one another. In paragraph 23, for example, he tells us that there are nine beds in his home (which is apparently occupied by only him and his wife), but in the next paragraph he tells us that he doesn't like having houseguests. Sometimes writers will juxtapose statements, images, or facts to convey a point. What point might Moranis be conveying by juxtaposing the statements in paragraphs 23 and 24?

Understanding the Text

1. What kind of lifestyle does Moranis describe through the items on his list? Is his lifestyle a common or familiar one? Explain.

2. Some of the items on Moranis's list are not really things but activities ("I listen to the same radio station all day.") or statements about his life ("I have a lot of time on my hands."). What do these items tell us about Moranis and his lifestyle? Do you think he includes these items to make a point about his lifestyle? Explain.

3. What do you think the specific items on Moranis's list indicate about how he obtains and uses necessities such as food?

Exploring the Issues

1. What do you think Moranis's list suggests about his social status? Based on his list, would you say he is wealthy, middle-class, of modest income? Does his list suggest he is a city dweller or a resident of a suburb or rural area? To what extent do you think his list is typical of Americans today? Explain. How might your list differ from his? What might those differences suggest about how people of different social and economic backgrounds use necessities in the United States?

2. Why do you think Moranis ends his essay as he does? What point do you think he is trying to make with the last sentence of his essay? How does that last item on his list ("two kids coming home for Thanksgiving") relate to the other items on his list? What do you think it suggests about Moranis and his own values?

3. What might the items on Moranis's list indicate about contemporary American society—specifically, about how Americans obtain and use necessities? What values are implicit in this list?

4. Do you find Moranis's essay funny? Why or why not? What might account for the humor in his essay? What assumptions do you think he makes about his audience in trying to make his essay

funny? How effectively do you think Moranis uses humor to help convey his point in this essay?

Entering the Conversations

1. Make a list of your own "numbered days," similar to Moranis's list but reflecting your own lifestyle.

2. In a group of classmates, share the lists you wrote for Question 1. Try to identify similarities and differences in your lists, and compare them with Moranis's list. What do your lists suggest about contemporary American society? What do they suggest about your own lifestyles?

3. Select one item on the list you wrote for Question 1 and write an essay in which you explore the role of that item in your life. For example, if you included a cell phone or DVD player, describe the role of that item in your daily life and its importance in your life in general. Try to select an item that you think plays a significant role in your life or is somehow typical or reflective of the lifestyle you lead. In your essay, draw conclusions about the nature of your lifestyle and what it

suggests about your own values.

Alternatively, create a web page or some other multimedia document that describes the role of that item in your life.

4. Revise the list you wrote for Question 1 so that it includes only those items that are truly necessities in your life: things you need to stay alive and be safe as well as things you might need to earn your livelihood (or be a student). Then write an essay in which you analyze the things you have in your life and the things that are true necessities. Draw conclusions about your lifestyle and discuss implications of that lifestyle.

5. Based on the work you did for Question 4, write a letter to the editor of your local newspaper (or another appropriate publication) expressing your view about the role of necessities in contemporary American lifestyles.

6. On the basis of the work you did for Question 4, create a web page of your own (or a pamphlet or other appropriate document) in which you present your view of how to live a lifestyle that uses necessities according to your own values.

THE POLITICS OF CONSUMPTION

N THE 1990S, SEVERAL HUMAN RIGHTS ORGANIZATIONS AND OTHER ADVOCACY GROUPS BEGAN A CAMPAIGN AGAINST LABOR EXPLOITATION BY WESTERN CORPORATIONS WITH FACTORIES IN DEVELOPING NATIONS. THESE GROUPS TRIED TO PUBLICIZE THE POOR WORKING CONDITIONS AND LOW WAGES OF WORKERS IN COUNTRIES LIKE INDONESIA, MEXICO, AND THAILAND, WHERE many different kinds of consumer products, including popular brands of clothing and shoes, were made for large Western companies. On the university campus where I work, this campaign energized some student groups, who organized a local campaign to stop the university from selling clothing that is manufactured under such conditions. That campaign was successful, and today, all the clothing with the university's logo is manufactured by companies that have tried to address the problem of exploited workers. In other words, if you buy a T-shirt with my university's logo on it, you should be confident that it was manufactured by a worker who was paid a decent wage and enjoys decent working conditions.

But how would you know for sure? The terrible conditions and the abuse of workers in some factories in developing na-

> But our choices as consumers are not only about price or the quality of the product; those choices are also political.

tions came to light only because some human rights organizations documented the cases through interviews with workers, secret videos and photographs taken at the factories, and other kinds of evidence that was not always easy to obtain. Some of the nations where these factories are located have few laws or regulations to protect workers or the environment, which is one reason that Western corporations build the factories there in the first place. So if a corporation that makes, say, athletic shoes announces that it will make sure workers are treated and paid well, you may simply have to take their word for it.

You may also have to pay more for those athletic shoes. In some cases, companies that manufacture such items close down their factories in the United States and move them to developing nations to lower their costs. If they pay workers less and have lower production costs, they can charge less for their products. Of course, this means that some American workers will be out of jobs. So if you saved some money on a pair of athletic shoes or a popular brand of clothing, you may have done so because someone else is out of a job. And you may have helped maintain a system that exploits workers in other nations and pollutes their land as well.

These circumstances reveal how complicated the matter of consumption can be. Often, you buy something because you need it or want it. You try to get it at the lowest price. That makes sense. But our choices as consumers are not only about price or the quality of the product; those choices are also political. They have consequences that we often cannot see or don't know about. Even if you choose to buy a product—or refuse to buy a product—because of how or where it was made, you may still be doing social, economic, or environmental harm without realizing it. And change often comes only through hard-fought campaigns like the one on my campus.

The readings in this chapter explore some of these complexities of being a consumer. They examine different situations in which the production and consumption of the resources we need—food, water, clothing—have consequences that are sometimes disturbing. They may help you better understand the politics of the choices you make about those resources. I chose these readings because they focus on important matters that affect all of us. But I also chose them because they are part of ongoing and important conversations around the world about how we should live. I hope they'll prompt you to think about your own participation in those conversations.

No doubt you have heard the term *globaliza-*tion. *But what exactly does it mean? The following essay by Helena Norberg-Hodge provides some answers. In fact, you might think of this essay as an extended definition of globalization. Globalization is often defined as the expansion of markets and the increase in social and economic exchanges among people, communities, and nations throughout the world. And certainly, globalization is that. But Norberg-Hodge explores the social, cultural, economic, political, and environmental impacts of globalization. In doing so, she helps us see how complex globalization really is. She is especially concerned about the costs of globalization that may not be obvious as consumerism expands into regions of the world where it previously did not exist. Although she acknowledges that the global consumer culture that is replacing many local cultures may bring more material goods for people, she points out that it may also cause local cultures to disappear. More important, it may not result in greater well-being for individuals. In other words, making more consumer goods available to people in remote places like Ladakh, a mountainous region of northern India that Norberg-Hodge describes in her essay, may not ultimately improve their lives. In*

THE March OF THE Monoculture

HELENA NORBERG-HODGE

Around the world, the pressure to conform to the expectations of the spreading, consumer monoculture is destroying cultural identity, eliminating local economies and erasing regional differences. As a consequence the global economy is leading to uncertainty, ethnic friction, and collapse, where previously there had been relative security and stability.

For many, the rise of the global economy marks the final fulfillment of the great dream of a "Global Village." Almost everywhere you travel today you will find multi-lane highways, concrete cities and a cultural landscape featuring grey business suits, fast-food chains, Hollywood films and cellular phones. In the remotest corners of the planet, Barbie, Madonna and the Marlboro Man are familiar icons. From Cleveland to Cairo to Caracas, *Baywatch* is entertainment and *CNN* news.

The world, we are told, is being united by virtue of the fact that everyone will soon be able to indulge their innate human desire for a Westernised, urbanised consumer lifestyle. West is best, and joining the bandwagon brings closer a harmonious union of peaceable, rational, democratic consumers "like us."

HELENA NORBERG-HODGE, "THE MARCH OF THE MONOCULTURE." THIS ARTICLE FIRST APPEARED IN THE MAY-JUNE 1999 ISSUE OF *THE ECOLOGIST*, VOL. 29, NO. 3, WWW. THEECOLOGIST.ORG. REPRINTED BY PERMISSION.

sharing these concerns, Norberg-Hodge helps us see how interconnected we all are, which makes the political aspects of consumerism even more complicated.

Helena Norberg-Hodge is the founder and director of The International Society for Ecology and Culture, a nonprofit organization promoting biodiversity and local culture. She has written extensively about globalization and its impact on local cultures and the environment. This essay first appeared in The Ecologist *magazine in 1999.* ◪

This world-view assumes that it was the chaotic diversity of cultures, values and beliefs that lay behind the chaos and conflicts of the past: that as these differences are removed, so the differences between us will be resolved. As a result, all around the world, villages, rural communities and their cultural traditions, are being destroyed on an unprecedented scale by the impact of globalising market forces. Communities that have sustained themselves for hundreds of years are simply disintegrating. The spread of the consumer culture seems virtually unstoppable.

CONSUMERS R US: THE DEVELOPMENT OF THE GLOBAL MONOCULTURE

Historically, the erosion of cultural integrity was a conscious goal of colonial developers. As applied anthropologist Goodenough explained: "The problem is one of creating in another a sufficient dissatisfaction with his present condition of self so that he wants to change it. This calls for some kind of experience that leads him to reappraise his self-image and re-evaluate his self-esteem."[1] Towards this end, colonial officers were advised that they should:

1. Involve traditional leaders in their programmes.
2. Work through bilingual, acculturated individuals who have some knowledge of both the dominant and the target culture.
3. Modify circumstances or deliberately tamper with the equilibrium of the traditional culture so that change will become imperative.
4. Attempt to change underlying core values before attacking superficial customs."[2]

It is instructive to consider the actual effect of these strategies on the well-being of individual peoples in the South. For example, the Toradja tribes of the Poso district in central Celebes (now Sulawesi, Indonesia) were initially deemed completely incapable of 'development' without drastic intervention. Writing in 1929, A.C. Kruyt reported that the happiness and stability of Toradja society was such that "development and progress were impossible" and that they were "bound to remain at the same level".[3]

Toradja society was cashless and there was neither a desire for money nor the extra goods that might be purchased with it. In the face of such contentment, mission work proved an abject failure as the Toradjas had no interest in converting to a new religion, sending their children to school or growing cash crops. So, in 1905 the Dutch East Indies government decided to bring the Poso region under firm control, using armed force to crush all resistance. As a result of relocation and continual government harassment, mortality rates soared among the Toradjas. Turning to the missionaries for help, they were "converted" and began sending their children to school. Eventually they began cultivating coconut and coffee plantations and began to acquire new needs for oil lamps, sewing machines, and 'better' clothes. The self-sufficient tribal economy had been superseded, as a result of deliberate government action.

In many countries, schooling was the prime coercive instrument for changing "underlying core values" and proved to be a highly effective means of destroying self-esteem, fostering new 'needs,' creating dissatisfactions, and generally disrupting traditional cultures. An excerpt from a French reader designed in 1919 for use by French West African school-children gives a flavour of the kinds of pressure that were imposed on children:

"It is . . . an advantage for a native to work for a white man, because the Whites are better educated, more advanced in civilisation than the natives . . . You who are intelligent and industrious, my children, always help the Whites in their task. That is a duty."[4]

THE SITUATION TODAY: CULTURAL EROSION

Today, as wealth is transferred away from nation states into the rootless casino of the money markets, the destruction of cultural integrity is far subtler than before. Corporate and government executives no longer consciously plan the destruction they wreak—indeed they are often unaware of the consequences of their decisions on real people on the other side of the world. This lack of awareness is fostered by the cult of specialisation and speed that pervades our society—the job of a public relations executive is confined to producing business-friendly sound-bites—time pressures and a narrow focus prevent a questioning of the overall impact of corporate activity. The tendency to undermine cultural diversity proceeds, as it were, on "automatic pilot" as an inevitable consequence of the spreading global economy.

But although the methods employed by the masters of the "Global Village" are less brutal than in colonial times, the scale and effects are often even more devastating. The computer and telecommunications revolutions have helped to speed up and strengthen the forces behind the march of a global monoculture, which is now able to disrupt traditional cultures with a shocking speed and finality which surpasses anything the world has witnessed before.

PREYING ON THE YOUNG

Today, the Western consumer conformity is descending on the less industrialised parts of the world like an avalanche. "Development" brings tourism, Western films and products and, more recently, satellite television to the remotest corners of the Earth. All provide overwhelming images of luxury and power. Adverts and action films give the impression that everyone in the West is rich, beautiful and brave, and leads a life filled with excitement and glamour.

In the commercial mass culture which fuels this illusion, advertisers make it clear that Westernised fashion accessories equal sophistication and "cool." In diverse "developing" nations around the world, people are induced to meet their needs not through their community or local economy, but by trying to 'buy in' to the global market. People are made to believe that, in the words of one U.S. advertising executive in China, "imported equals good, local equals crap."

Even more alarmingly, people end up rejecting their own ethnic and racial characteristics—to feel shame at being who they are. Around the world, blonde-haired blue-eyed Barbie dolls and thin-as-a-rake "cover girls" set the standard for women. Already now, seven-year-old girls in Singapore are suffering from eating disorders. It is not unusual to find east Asian women with eyes surgically altered to look more European, dark-haired southern European women dying their hair blonde, and Africans with blue- or green-coloured contact lenses aimed at "correcting" dark eyes.

15   The one-dimensional, fantasy view of modern life promoted by the Western media, television and business becomes a slap in the face for young people in the "Third World." Teenagers, in particular, come to feel stupid and ashamed of their traditions and their origins. The people they learn to admire and respect on television are all "sophisticated" city dwellers with fast cars, designer clothes, spotlessly clean hands and shiny white teeth. Yet they find their parents asking them to choose a way of life that involves working in the fields and getting their hands dirty for little or no money, and certainly no glamour. It is hardly surprising, then, that many choose to abandon the old ways of their parents for the siren song of a Western material paradise.

For millions of young people in rural areas of the world, modern Western culture appears vastly superior to their own. They see incoming tourists spending as much as $1,000 a day—the equivalent of a visitor to the U.S. spending about $50,000 a day. Besides promoting the illusion that all Westerners are multi-millionaires, tourism and media images also give the impression that we never work—since for many people in "developing" countries, sitting at a desk or behind the wheel of a car does not constitute work.

People are not aware of the negative social or psychological aspects of Western life so familiar to us: the stress, the loneliness and isolation, the fear of growing old alone, the rise in clinical depression and other "industrial diseases" like cancer, stroke, diabetes and heart problems. Nor do they see the environmental decay, rising crime, poverty, homelessness and unemployment. While they know their own culture inside out, including all of its limitations and imperfections, they only see a glossy, exaggerated side of life in the West.

LADAKH: THE PRESSURE TO CONSUME

My own experience among the people of Ladakh or "Little Tibet," in the trans-Himalayan region of Kashmir, is a clear, if painful, example of this destruction of traditional cultures by the faceless consumer monoculture. When I first arrived in the area 23 years ago, the vast majority of Ladakhis were self-supporting farmers, living in small scattered settlements in the high desert. Though natural resources were scarce and hard to obtain, the Ladakhis had a remarkably high standard of living—with beautiful art, architecture and jewellery. Life moved at a gentle pace and people enjoyed a degree of leisure unknown to most of us in the West. Most Ladakhis only really worked for four months of the year, and poverty, pollution and unemployment were alien concepts. In 1975, I remember being shown around the remote village of Hemis Shukpachan by a young Ladakhi called Tsewang. It seemed to me, a newcomer, that all the houses I saw were especially large and beautiful, and I asked Tsewang to show me the houses where the poor lived. He looked perplexed for a moment, then replied, "We don't have any poor people here."

In recent years external forces have caused massive and rapid disruption in Ladakh. Contact with the modern world has debilitated and demoralised a once-proud and self-sufficient people, who today are suffering from what can best be described as a cultural inferiority complex. When tourism descended on Ladakh some years ago, I began to realise how, looked at from a Ladakhi perspective, our modern, Western culture appears much more successful, fulfilled and sophisticated than we find it to be from the inside.

In traditional Ladakhi culture, virtually all basic needs—food, clothing and shelter, were provided without money. Labour was free of charge, part of an intricate and long-established web of human relationships. Because Ladakhis had no need for money, they had little or none. So when they saw outsiders—tourists and visitors—coming in, spending what was to them vast amounts of cash on inessential luxuries, they suddenly felt poor. Not realising that money was essential in the West—that without it, people often go homeless or even starve—they didn't realise its true value. They began to feel inadequate and backward. Eight years after Tsewang had told me that Ladakhis had no poverty, I overheard him talking to some tourists. "If you could only help us Ladakhis," he was saying, "we're so poor."

Tourism is part of the overall development which the Indian government is promoting in Ladakh. The area is being integrated into the Indian, and hence the global, economy. Subsidised food is imported from the outside, while local farmers who had previously grown a vari-

STRATEGIES: THE EXAMPLE OF LADAKH
Norberg-Hodge describes at length her experiences in the mountainous region of northern India called Ladakh. In doing so, she is employing two common strategies for supporting a position or making an argument: the use of example and the use of personal experience. In this case, she uses Ladakh as an extended example to illustrate what she sees as the damage that Western consumer culture can do to local cultures. But she also discusses Ladakh as someone who has had long experience there. In this way, she speaks as an authority who has greater knowledge of the situation than her readers or others who may be experts on globalization. You might consider how effective you found Norberg-Hodge's use of Ladakh as an example of the impact of globalization and consider as well whether her experience there gives her credibility to write about these issues.

20

CONVERSATIONS: CONSUMER CULTURE

Norberg-Hodge argues that consumer culture changes the ideas about lifestyle and "the good life" that people in various cultures may have. Consider, for example, what this advertisement for clothing might suggest about the good life. To what extent do you think advertisements like this one for common consumer goods might support or complicate Norberg-Hodge's argument?

ety of crops and kept a few animals to provide for themselves have been encouraged to grow cash crops. In this way they are becoming dependent on forces beyond their control—huge transportation networks, oil prices, and the fluctuations of international finance. Over the course of time, financial inflation obliges them to produce more and more, so as to secure the income that they now need in order to buy what they used to grow themselves. In political terms, each Ladakhi is now one individual in a national economy of 800 million, and, as part of a global economy, one of about six billion.

As a result of external investments, the local economy is crumbling. For generation after generation Ladakhis grew up learning how to provide themselves with clothing and shelter; how to make shoes out of yak skin and robes from the wool of sheep; how to build houses out of mud and stone. As these building traditions give way to "modern" methods, the plentiful local materials are left unused, while competition for a narrow range of modern materials—concrete, steel and plastic—skyrockets. The same thing happens when people begin eating identical staple foods, wearing the same clothes and relying on the same finite energy sources. Making everyone dependent on the same resources creates efficiency for global corporations, but it also creates an artificial scarcity for consumers, which heightens competitive pressures.

As they lose the sense of security and identity that springs from deep, long-lasting connections to people and place, the Ladakhis are starting to develop doubts about who they are. The images they get from outside tell them to be different, to own more, to buy more and to thus be "better" than they are. The previously strong, outgoing women of Ladakh have been replaced by a new generation—unsure of themselves and desperately concerned with their appearance. And as their desire to be "modern" grows, Ladakhis are turning their backs on their traditional culture. I have seen Ladakhis wearing wristwatches they cannot read, and heard them apologising for the lack of electric lighting in their homes—electric lighting which, in 1975, when it first appeared, most villagers laughed at as an unnecessary gimmick. Even traditional foods are no longer a source of pride; now, when I'm a guest in a Ladakhi village, people apologise if they serve the traditional roasted barley, ngamphe, instead of instant noodles.

Ironically, then, modernisation—so often associated with the triumph of individualism—has produced a loss of individuality and a growing sense of personal insecurity. As people become self-conscious and insecure, they feel pressured to conform, and to live up to an idealised image. By contrast, in the traditional village, where everyone wore essentially the same clothes and looked the same to the casual observer, there was more freedom to relax. As part of a close-knit community, people felt secure enough to be themselves.

In Ladakh, as elsewhere, the breaking of local cultural, economic   25
and political ties isolates people from their locality and from each other. At the same time, life speeds up and mobility increases—making even familiar relationships more superficial and brief. Competition for scarce jobs and political representation within the new centralised structures increasingly divides people. Ethnic and religious differences began to take on a political dimension, causing bitterness and enmity on a scale hitherto unknown. With a desperate irony, the monoculture—instead of bringing people together, creates divisions that previously did not exist.

As the fabric of local interdependence fragments, so do traditional levels of tolerance and co-operation. In villages near the capital, Leh, disputes and acrimony within previously close-knit communities, and even within families, are increasing. I have even seen heated arguments over the allocation of irrigation water, a procedure that had previously been managed smoothly within a co-operative framework. The rise in this kind of new rivalry is one of the most painful divisions that I have seen in Ladakh. Within a few years, growing competition has actually culminated in violence—and this in a place where, previously, there had been no group conflict in living memory.

DEADLY DIVISIONS

The rise of divisions, violence and civil disorder around the world are the consequence of attempts to incorporate diverse cultures and peoples into the global monoculture. These divisions often deepen enough to result in fundamentalist reaction and ethnic conflict. Ladakh is by no means an isolated example.

In Bhutan, where different ethnic groups had also lived peaceably together for hundreds of years, two decades of economic development have resulted in the widespread destruction of decentralised livelihoods and communities—unemployment, once completely unknown, has reached crisis levels. Just like in Ladakh, these pressures have created intense competition between individuals and

CONVERSATIONS: DEADLY DIVISIONS
In this section, Norberg-Hodge refers to several regions of the world where conflicts have intensified in recent years, including Bhutan, a tiny Himalayan nation to the north of India; the former Yugoslavia, which is now often referred to as the Baltic region and where bloody ethnic and religious conflicts erupted in the 1990s (Kosovo, which Norberg-Hodge mentions in paragraph 32, is in this region); and Rwanda, an African nation where thousands of people were killed in ethnic conflicts in the 1990s. As Norberg-Hodge suggests in this passage, experts have debated the causes of these conflicts, which have occurred in regions where religious and ethnic diversity has existed for hundreds of years. Notice how Norberg-Hodge uses this global political context to help make her argument against globalization. Consider, too, how this context might influence the way readers respond to her argument. You might think about how your own knowledge of these events affects your reaction to her argument.

groups for places in schools, for jobs, for resources. As a result, tensions between Buddhists and Bhutanese Hindus of Nepalese origin have led to an eruption of violence and even a type of "ethnic cleansing."

Elsewhere, Nicholas Hildyard has written of how, when confronted with the horrors of ethnic cleansing in Yugoslavia or Rwanda, it is often taken for granted that the cause must lie in ingrained and ancient antagonisms. The reality, however, as Hildyard notes, is different:

"Scratch below the surface of inter-ethnic civil conflict, and the shallowness and deceptiveness of 'blood' or 'culture' explanations are soon revealed. 'Tribal hatred' (though a real and genuine emotion for some) emerges as the product not of 'nature' or of a primordial 'culture,' but of a complex web of politics, economics, history, psychology and a struggle for identity."[5]

In a similar vein, Michel Chossudovsky, Professor of Economics at the University of Ottawa, argues that the current Kosovo crisis has its roots at least partly in the macro-economic reforms imposed by Belgrade's external creditors such as the International Monetary Fund (IMF). Multi-ethnic Yugoslavia was a regional industrial power with relative economic success. But after a decade of Western economic ministrations and five years of disintegration, war, boycott, and embargo, the economies of the former Yugoslavia are in ruins. Chossudovsky writes:

"In Kosovo, the economic reforms were conducive to the concurrent impoverishment of both the Albanian and Serbian populations contributing to fuelling ethnic tensions. The deliberate manipulation of market forces destroyed economic activity and people's livelihood creating a situation of despair."[6]

It is sometimes assumed that ethnic and religious strife is increasing because modern democracy liberates people, allowing old, previously suppressed, prejudices and hatreds to be expressed. If there was peace earlier, it is thought it was the result of oppression. But after more than twenty years of first-hand experience on the Indian subcontinent, I am convinced that economic 'development' not only exacerbates existing tensions but in many cases actually creates them. It breaks down human-scale structures, it destroys bonds of reciprocity and mutual dependence, while encouraging people to substitute their own culture and values with those of the media. In effect this means rejecting one's own identity—rejecting one's self.

Ultimately, while the myth makers of the "Global Village" celebrate values of togetherness, the disparity in wealth between the world's upper income brackets and the 90 percent of people in the poor countries represents a polarisation far more extreme than existed in the 19th century. Use of the word "village"—intended to suggest relative equality, belonging and harmony—obscures a reality of high-tech islands of privilege and wealth towering above oceans of impoverished humanity struggling to survive. The global monoculture is a dealer in illusions—while it destroys traditions, local economies and sustainable ways of living, it can never provide the majority with the glittering, wealthy lifestyle it promised them. For what it destroys, it provides no replacement but a fractured, isolated, competitive and unhappy society.

References

1. Quoted, John Bodley, *Victims of Progress,* Mayfield Publishing, 1982, pp. 111–112.

2. Ibid., p.112.

3. Ibid., p.129.

4. Ibid., p.11.

5. N. Hildyard, *Briefing 11—Blood and Culture: Ethnic Conflict and the Authoritarian Right,* The Cornerhouse, 1999.

6. M. Chossudovsky, *Dismantling Yugoslavia, Colonising Bosnia,* Ottawa, 1996, p. 1.

Understanding the Text

1. Norberg-Hodge describes some of the effects of colonialism on local cultures throughout the world. What lessons does she see in these examples of the impact of colonialism? What are the differences between the destruction of local cultures as a result of globalization and the destruction caused by colonizing in previous eras? Why is this difference important, according to Norberg-Hodge?

2. Why, according to Norberg-Hodge, do people in developing regions of the world often reject their local cultures and ethnic backgrounds? What might this rejection suggest about the power of consumer culture?

3. What are the most obvious characteristics of Western consumer culture, as Norberg-Hodge sees it? Do you think her description of Western culture is fair and/or accurate? Why or why not?

4. How does monoculture lead to division and conflict, according to Norberg-Hodge? Do you think her analysis of this process is correct? Why or why not?

Exploring the Issues

1. One way to read this essay is as an argument against globalization. To support her argument, Norberg-Hodge cites various kinds of evidence, including examples of situations in which local cultures were affected by Western nations; she also quotes from experts and draws on her own experiences working in Ladakh. Examine the way Norberg-Hodge supports her argument with such evidence. How effectively do you think she supports her claims? What do you think her use of evidence suggests about her assumptions about her readers?

2. Norberg-Hodge describes globalization and consumerism in negative terms, often using figures of speech and colorful phrases to do so. In paragraph 12, she describes the movement of consumerism into less industrialized parts of the world as "an avalanche"; in paragraph 3, she refers to the spread of consumerism as a "bandwagon." Examine Norberg-Hodge's use of figurative language in this essay. What ideas or impressions do you think she conveys through the language she uses to describe globalization? How effective do you think her use of language in this essay is?

3. Early in her essay, Norberg-Hodge writes "we are told" that the world is being united in a global consumer culture. Who is the "we" she refers to here? Is this "we" the same as the "myth makers" that she refers to in her final paragraph? Examine how Norberg-Hodge represents those whom she might consider to be supporters of globalization. Do you think she represents such people fairly? Explain, citing specific passages to support your answer.

4. One of Norberg-Hodge's chief complaints against globalization is that consumer culture reflects certain values that many local cultures do not share. She rejects the idea that a Western-style consumer culture is good for all people, and she describes some of the benefits of non-Western cultures, such as Ladakh. Based on your reading of this essay, what values regarding lifestyle and community do you think Norberg-Hodge holds? Do you think

most Western readers share these values?

Entering the Conversations

1. Write an essay in which you respond to Norberg-Hodge's essay. Focus your response on her view of Western consumer culture and explain why you agree or disagree with her concerns about consumerism.

INFOTRAC

2. Norberg-Hodge refers to *globalization* without explicitly defining what it is. Although you can get a sense of how she defines globalization, it is also true that the term refers to a complicated set of developments and that different people may have different definitions of it. Using InfoTrac College Edition, your library, and other appropriate resources, investigate the idea of globalization. Find out how it tends to be defined, and try to determine how different interest groups (for example, environmental groups, free trade organizations) tend to define and use the term. Visit the web sites of such groups to get a sense of their view of globalization. Write a report

on the basis of your research. Discuss the different ways globalization is defined and describe the different views of it you found. Offer your own definition of the term.

3. Write an essay in which you describe what you see as the benefits and/or drawbacks of a modern consumer-oriented lifestyle. Then, in a group of classmates, share your essays. Identify the main benefits and drawbacks that members of your group believe a modern consumer lifestyle has. Draw conclusions about the values that you and your classmates seem to have regarding lifestyle, and discuss the extent to which these values are influenced by consumer culture. Alternatively, create a web page intended to educate people about the impact of a modern consumer lifestyle.

4. Collect several television, print, or Internet advertisements that you believe convey important ideas about modern consumer culture. Analyze the advertisements you collect to identify the ideas they convey about being a consumer. Create a PowerPoint presentation, a web site, or some other appropriate document in which you present the results of your analysis.

A few years ago, my family and I looked into Community-Supported Agriculture. CSAs, as they are called, are farms that have "members" who buy "shares" in the farm for a season. A share is usually a weekly shipment of produce that is being harvested at that time of year. CSA members pay for their shares in the beginning of the season (usually in the spring), and they assume some of the risk that farmers traditionally shoulder on their own. That means that members pay the same price for a share whether the harvest is good or not. One reason we were interested in joining a CSA is that we came to believe that buying local vegetables was not only less destructive for the environment and healthier for us but also good for local farmers, who are part of our community. Reading the following essay, I suspect that David Morris would support our decision to join a CSA. But he also explains that buying local food may not be as simple as we initially believed.

In his essay, Morris joins a growing debate about the problems with our conventional ways of producing and distributing food, and he adds his voice to the increasing number of people who are calling for alternatives to our conventional food system. Reviewing some of the arguments against

Is Eating Local THE Best Choice?

DAVID MORRIS

Some 30 years ago NASA came up with another BIG idea. Assemble vast solar electric arrays in space and beam the energy to earth. The environmental community did not dismiss NASA's vision out of hand. After all, the sun shines 24 hours a day in space. A solar cell on earth harnesses only about four hours equivalent of full sunshine a day. If renewable electricity could be generated more cheaply in space than on earth, what's the problem?

A number of us argued that the problem was inherent in the scale of the power plant. Whereas rooftop solar turns us into producers, builds our self-confidence and strengthens our sense of community as we trade electricity back and forth with our neighbors, space-based solar arrays aggravate our dependence. By dramatically increasing the distance between us and a product essential to our survival, we become more insecure. The scale of the technology demands a global corporation, increasing the distance between those who make the decisions and those who feel the impact of those decisions. Which, in turn, demands a global oversight body, itself remote and nontransparent to electric consumers.

buying local food, Morris concludes that buying local can create problems, too. Although he still supports the local food movement, he believes that we should be aware of the impact of the choices we make. His essay reminds us that what we decide to eat can have consequences far beyond what we might expect.

David Morris is co-founder and vice president of the Institute for Local Self-Reliance, which supports environmentally sound and equitable community development projects. He wrote this essay for Alternet.org in 2007. ◪

STRATEGIES: USING FIGURATIVE LANGUAGE
Morris ends this paragraph with a statement that is intended to describe the outcome of the U.S. government's proposal in the 1980s to construct a giant solar electricity facility in space. He writes, "The prospect of solar arrays dimmed." In choosing the verb "dimmed" for this sentence, Morris uses figurative language to help reinforce his view of the misguidedness of the government's plan. Consider whether a different verb, such as "diminished," would have the same effect as "dimmed" in this case.

CONVERSATIONS: THE FOOD MILES DEBATE
In the past decade or so, some critics began to analyze the real costs of producing and distributing specific kinds of food for the marketplace. For example, one American researcher concluded that the typical food item in an American meal was transported 1,500 miles to the consumer's plate from the place where it was produced. Such studies have been used as evidence that the modern food system is wasteful and causes environmental damage. So, the argument goes, it is healthier for the planet if we eat foods that are produced close to where we live. In this passage, Morris refers to this debate about "food miles," with which readers of the web site where this essay was originally published would probably be familiar. But notice that he cites other studies that call into question the idea that buying local food is always better for the environment. This passage is a good example of how conversations about important issues like food are carried on; it is also an example of how scientific research can be used in those conversations.

NASA and most of the environmental community were impervious to arguments about scale and community. But environmentalists soon turned against the orbiting solar satellites when they concluded the microwave beams used to transmit the solar electricity to earth would wreak havoc on birds flying through its path. Ronald Reagan cut NASA's budget. **THE PROSPECT OF SOLAR ARRAYS DIMMED.**

My experience with distant solar came to mind when I read James F. McWilliams' recent column in the *New York Times* about food miles. McWilliams, a "passionate" advocate of "eat local," discussed new studies that conclude local is not always environmentally superior. One study he cites found the life cycle impact of a lamb raised in New Zealand and shipped to the United Kingdom was lower than a lamb raised and consumed in the U.K. Another more comprehensive study by University of Wales professors Ruth Fairchild and Andrea Collins found that transporting food from farm to store accounts for only 2 percent of the overall environmental impact of food systems. Food grown locally could have a considerably bigger footprint than food flown halfway around the world.

"I'm a bit worried about **THE FOOD MILES [DEBATE]**, because it is educating the consumer in the wrong way. It is such an insignificant point," says Fairchild.   5

McWilliams' column comes as the U.K. Soil Association (the certification agency for U.K. organics) proposes stripping the organic label from foreign-produced certified organic goods that are flown in. Some food stores in Europe have announced they will label products that have been transported by air.

McWilliams thinks the new studies are beneficial even for **LOCALVORES** because they force us to adopt a more sophisticated and nuanced approach. He begins with the proposition, "[I]t is impossible for most of the world to feed itself a diverse and healthy diet through exclusively local food production—food will always have to travel." . . . And ends with the conclusion, ". . . [W]ouldn't it make more sense to stop obsessing over food miles and work to strengthen comparative geographical advantages? And what if we did this while streamlining transportation services according to fuel-efficient standards?"

For McWilliams, globally efficient food systems trump local food systems. "We must accept the fact, in short, that distance is not the enemy of awareness."

A few days later the *Times* published six letters to the editor in response to McWilliams' article. All disagreed with him, on environmental grounds. But none mentioned the word "community," which, to me, is the most important reason to prefer local food. Distance kills community.

Buying and using local creates a tight-knit interconnection between producers and consumers. It makes us more intimately aware of the impact of our buying and producing decisions on our neighbors. I live in Minneapolis, a few blocks away from a shallow lake. My neighborhood has learned that what we put on our lawns ends up in the lake. We see the impact in increased algae blooms and reduced fish that results from our own individual obsession with perfect lawns. Which has led more and more people to grow nonpolluting gardens rather than manicured lawns. That same awareness leads us to frown upon local farmers who use pesticides and fertilizers that run off into our water table and support those who don't.

Buying locally grown food, as Maiser observes, "is fodder for a wonderful story. Whether it's the farmer who brings local apples to market or the baker who makes local bread, knowing part of the story about your food is such a powerful part of enjoying a meal." Buying local builds relationships, almost organically forcing the consumer to become aware of the plight of the producer and the producer to become familiar with the needs of the consumer.

Buying and producing locally enables accountability. Distance disables accountability. As we have recently discovered, food shipped across the planet, from jurisdictions and by corporations that do not view safety as their highest priority, is virtually untraceable. Or it requires global inspection agencies that themselves become unaccountable.

Still, a growing number of voices, especially from southern countries, criticize advocates of local food on equity grounds. Many developing countries rely on agricultural exports to generate foreign currency to buy products and services essential to their survival and growth, they argue. If the developed world suddenly stopped importing its food, southern farmers would be further impoverished. This could have profound environmental consequences. Poverty is the single biggest factor driving problems like deforestation, biodiversity loss, soil depletion and the endangerment of wildlife. Export earnings—from food flown to Europe and the United States—allow southern farmers to invest in more environmentally friendly agriculture.

I find the equity argument more compelling than the environmental argument against local foods. Yet the equity argument also ignores the dynamics of dependence. The globalization of food has rarely enriched small farmers in the south. For 200 years, the food crops of the New World were cultivated by slaves. When the Spaniards brought bananas to the Caribbean, they needed to get the natives to do the backbreaking work of harvesting them in large plantations. But the natives were food self-sufficient and had little or no need for money.

GLOSS: LOCALVORES
"Localvore" is a term that emerged in the past decade or so to refer to someone who advocates eating local food. Notice that Morris seems to assume that many (if not most) of his readers are localvores. Such an assumption may be a safe one, given that this article was originally published on *Alternet.org*, a progressive web site that usually supports environmental movements. Consider whether Morris should revise this passage in any way if his article were intended for a more general audience, such as readers of *USA Today* or *Newsweek*.

Thus the Spanish outlawed personal gardens. By destroying food self-sufficiency, they created a work force for growing exported food.

15   Today the dynamic of globalization and dependence is more nuanced but no less important. Countries are shifting land use and growing crops for export instead of local consumption. This may enrich some farmers but forces many others into poverty and increases hunger. The developing countries subsidize commodity exports, such as dumping grains on poorer countries, that impoverish small farmers. Indeed, just a few days ago CARE, a nonprofit that works to fight global poverty, refused tens of millions of dollars in federal money for food aid to Africa. CARE argued that the program was counterproductive. By supplying free food, the United States was undercutting domestic farmers, and poverty and hunger was increasing, not decreasing.

Local resources processed by local businesses for local consumption is the ideal. We will never live up to the ideal. But we can always be guided by the need to foster community here and abroad. We will never be completely food self-sufficient on the local or even regional level. Much of our food will come from elsewhere. And when it does, we should use **THE PRINCIPLES OF** fair trade. We should, whenever possible, contract directly with cooperative producer organizations. In return for paying a slightly higher price, we can require them to raise their crops in the most environmentally benign way as possible. But the environmental benefits of fair trade agreements are far less important than the benefits that come from strengthening communities in rural areas of the world: new educational and health networks, local innovation and invention, the preservation of extended families, and the continuation of cultures hundreds and thousands of years old.

Which leads to an odd but comforting conclusion. Just as strengthening community is the most important benefit of buying locally, it is also the most important benefit from buying distant. Public policies should be designed to maximize the use of local resources for local consumption here and abroad while trade rules should be designed to make trade less destructive to, and more supportive of, strong communities here and across the globe.

CONVERSATIONS: FAIR TRADE
When Morris refers to "the principles of fair trade" in this paragraph, he is drawing on a debate that has emerged in recent years about the ethics of producing some food items. For example, large multinational corporations often buy coffee from large coffee growers who employ workers at low wages and sometimes in poor working conditions; buying such coffee keeps the price down. Growers who pay their workers better wages are often unable to make a profit because they must charge higher prices for their coffee. Some critics who have called attention to these practices have urged consumers to buy coffee only from companies that obtain coffee from growers who pay workers decent wages and offer decent working conditions. This coffee has come to be known as "fair trade" coffee. Advocates argue that consumers who pay a slightly higher price for such coffee not only benefit the workers on the coffee plantations but also benefit the environment because many growers who sell such coffee use organic growing methods, which also raises the prices of the coffee. Note that Morris assumes his readers know the term "fair trade." Consider whether this is a fair assumption today.

Understanding the Text

1. Why does Morris believe that the idea of community is the most important reason for deciding to eat local? In what sense does "distance kill community," as he puts it? What do you think this argument suggests about the politics of food consumption?

2. What are the benefits of buying local food, according to Morris? What do these benefits suggest about Morris's own values? Do you agree with him that these benefits of buying local food are important? Explain.

3. Why does Morris find "the equity argument" (par. 14) a compelling argument against buying local food? What problems does he see with that argument? What might Morris's analysis of these arguments indicate about the politics of food consumption?

Exploring the Issues

1. In the first part of this essay (par. 4–10), Morris summarizes a debate about eating local food that took place in the pages of the *New York Times* in 2007. Why do you think he devotes so much attention to that debate? How does his summary help him establish his own viewpoint and make his main point in this essay?

2. In paragraph 16, Morris writes, "Local resources processed by local businesses for local consumption is the ideal. We will never live up to the ideal. But we can always be guided by the need to foster community here and abroad." If we can never achieve his ideal, how can it help guide us? What implications do you see in Morris's view that we should

strive for locally produced food even though we know we can never be "completely food self-sufficient," as he puts it?

3. Evaluate the effectiveness of Morris's argument. What evidence or reasoning does he offer in support of his claim that eating locally produced food is the right thing to do? How persuasive do you find his argument? What might your reaction to his argument suggest about you as a reader and as a consumer?

Entering the Conversations

1. Write a response to Morris in which you offer your own views about eating local food. In your essay, be sure to offer your reasoning for why you agree or disagree that eating local food is the right thing to do.

INFOTRAC

2. As noted in "Conversations: The Food Miles Debate" (page 640), various groups have begun to advocate eating locally produced food. Such advocates have argued that local food has a variety of social, economic, environmental, and personal health benefits; critics have argued that the local food movement is not feasible on a large scale. Using InfoTrac, the Internet, your library, and other appropriate resources, investigate the local food movement. Look into its history and identify some of the major developments that have led to its growth. If possible, interview representatives of one or more organizations that advocate local food. (There may be such an organization on your campus.) Then, write a report about the local food move-

ment. In your report, draw conclusions about what this movement suggests about food production and consumption today.

4. In the final paragraph of this essay, Morris writes, "Public policies should be designed to maximize the use of local resources for local consumption here and abroad while trade rules should be designed to make trade less destructive to, and more supportive of, strong communities here and across the globe." Using the research you did for Question 3 and drawing on your own views about these issues, write a letter to your U.S. senator (or another appropriate political representative) in which you argue in favor of specific steps that you believe the U.S. government should take to promote the use of local food. (If you disagree that such policies should be pursued, your letter should indicate your reasons for your position.)

5. Try to cook a meal exclusively from local foods. Plan your meal as carefully as you can so that as many ingredients as possible are produced as close to where you live as possible. (Some college campuses have tried to serve "100-mile" meals, in which everything in the meal was produced within 100 miles of campus.) Then write an essay about your experience. Describe how you were (or were not) able to obtain local foods for your meal, and draw conclusions about the local food movement on the basis of your experience.

Alternatively, create a photo essay, PowerPoint presentation, or another kind of multimedia document about your local meal.

When it comes to consumer goods, there seems to be something for everyone. But if you look a little closer, you may find that your choices are actually much more limited than they might appear. As Cathy McGuire learned when her friend decided to buy a new refrigerator, consumers may not have as many choices as they believe if they are

Get Me A Vegetable-Friendly Refrigerator!

looking for something just a little out of the ordinary because all the choices may really be variations of "ordinary."

In this light-hearted essay, McGuire reveals that manufacturers design their refrigerators on the basis of certain expectations about the kinds of foods their customers typically eat. For most customers, there are many different styles of refrigerators to choose from, but all those styles are basically slight variations of the same thing and they are all designed for a "typical" consumer—that is, people who eat a typical American diet, which includes meat. If you are not that

STRATEGIES: INTRODUCTORY QUESTIONS
McGuire begins her essay with a question posed directly to her readers. Beginning an essay in this way is a common strategy that enables a writer to draw her readers into the essay and make them feel involved in the subject. It also helps establish a casual voice and informal tone.

CATHY MCGUIRE

When was the last time you bought a refrigerator? I myself don't usually make a habit of shopping for "big ticket" items, but recently I had the opportunity to do so. A friend was in dire need of a new fridge so I offered to help scour the market.

We headed over to the local Sears and wound our way into the gleaming appliance section. At first all the refrigerators looked alike, but gradually we zeroed in on the major difference among them: the freezer. Most freezers are traditionally located at the top of the fridge, some are parallel to the body like a side door, but a select few are positioned at the bottom. You're probably wondering, what does it matter anyway?

Well, as a vegetarian, I say it matters a lot. If you observe closely, you will notice that the majority of refrigerators situate the vegetable bins way at the bottom. At the top of the hierarchy sits the freezer, the compartment which invariably stocks ample meat supplies and pro-cessed, prepackaged fast food. The freezer's premier placement pro-motes easy access to those types of products. Needless to say, fresh vegetables are not freezer material. Instead, vegetables are relegated to a sort of enclosed netherworld where the produce is out of sight, out of mind.

We found a model, however, that deserves more attention. It's called the "bottom mount," (i.e., the freezer is at the bottom). The name itself reveals an industry preoccupation with freezer location. This little baby, though, has the vegetable bins smack dab in the mid-dle, making vegetable accessibility convenient, if not a breeze! No more hunching down, awkwardly opening testy drawers or fumbling for zucchini only to find some rotten carrots hidden down in the bin's back bowels. Of the 25 or so refrigerators on display at Sears, a paltry two or three were bottom mounts. My friend and I wisely lim-ited our selection to these few choices.

5   Yet, even the bottom mount had a few disconcerting features. Draw-ers were constructed to hold "MEAT" and "DAIRY PRODUCTS." At home, with the help of a magic marker, these bins became "EAT" and "AIRY PRODUCTS." The BUTTER box was likewise mislabeled for those of us who use safflower oil margarine. And what's a **VEGAN** sup-posed to store in all those curved slots designed for eggs?

Clearly, the manufacturers of refrigerators market their product to meat eating, freezer foods-oriented consumers. The next time you're shopping for a refrigerator, let the store, the refrigerator industry and consumer groups know that you want a vegetable friendly refrigerator!

typical consumer—if you are a vegetarian, like McGuire's friend—your selection of refrigerators becomes more limited. McGuire's essay thus provides one revealing example of how certain values and lifestyle choices are built into the consumer items we buy. McGuire helps us realize that the politics of con-sumption go beyond high-profile controversies about issues like drilling for oil in the Arctic National Wildlife Refuge or using ethanol as fuel for our cars. Sometimes the politics of consumption are hidden in the design of the things we buy and use every day.

Cathy McGuire is co-founder of Ecofeminist Visions Emerging, or EVE, on whose web site, Eve Online, *this essay appeared. It was originally published in 1994 in* The Far Newsletter, *which is published by FAR, an organization devoted to animal rights.* ◪

CONVERSATIONS: VEGANS

At the end of this paragraph, McGuire poses the question, "And what's a vegan supposed to store in all those curved slots designed for eggs?" In a sense, such a question is part of a much larger debate about what we should eat and how we produce food in the United States. (Michael Pollan's "Fast Food Meal" and David Morris's "Is Eating Local the Best Choice?", which appear in this chapter, can also be seen as part of this debate.) Vegans eat no animal products, including eggs and cheese, whereas vegetarians eat no meat but may consume animal products like cheese or milk. For some people, the choice to become a vegan or a vegetarian is an ethical and even a political one, based on values related to how animals are treated and our impact on the environment; for others, it is a decision based on health concerns. McGuire's complaints about refrigerators underscore the fact that many voices can be part of these conversations, including those, like vegans, who are only a small percentage of the population. At the same time, her complaints reveal that much of what we consume is produced for the mainstream society and therefore reflects the values and habits of those in the mainstream.

Understanding the Text

1. Why does the position of the freezer in a refrigerator matter to McGuire and her friend? What does she believe the position of the freezer indicates about the use of the freezer by the consumer? Why is this issue important to her? Do you think she is right? Why or why not?

2. What are the implications of the way most refrigerators are designed, according to McGuire? Why are these implications important, in her view? Do you agree with her? Explain.

3. What changes in refrigerator design would McGuire recommend? What do you think her recommended changes suggest about the politics of food consumption?

Exploring the Issues

1. McGuire's essay first appeared in the publication of an organization devoted to animal rights, so she could reasonably assume that many, if not most, of her readers were vegetarians. To what extent do you think she writes for an audience of vegetarians? Explain, citing specific passages from the text to support your answer. Do you think her essay would be effective for a more general audience, including people who are not vegetarians? Why or why not? What revisions would you suggest to this essay if it were intended for a more general audience?

2. Much of McGuire's argument is based on her own analysis of the design of common refrigerators (see par. 3–5). How valid or accurate do you think her analysis of refrigerator design is, based on your own experience with refrigerators? How well does she explain the problems she sees in refrigerator design? How effectively do you think she uses this analysis to support her argument in favor of a different kind of refrigerator design?

3. The tone of this essay is rather light and even somewhat humorous, but the issue that McGuire addresses is complicated and serious. How effective do you think McGuire's tone is in this essay? Do you find it appropriate for her subject matter? Why or why not? Do you think her tone strengthens or weakens her essay in terms of her main argument? Explain.

Entering the Conversations

1. Select an item that you regularly use in your daily life, such as an appliance like a refrigerator or toaster or an item such as cell phone. Analyze the design of that item in the way that McGuire analyzes the design of refrigerators. Focus your analysis on what seem to be the assumptions that the manufacturer made about who will use the item, how it will be used, and what is most important to the users of the item. Then, write an essay in which you present your analysis of that item.

2. Using the item you selected for Question 1 (or another appropriate item), propose design changes in that item that reflect your own beliefs about how that item should be used—or how you would like to be able to use it. Try to propose a design that reflects your own values. Describe your proposed design changes in an essay or represent them in a multimedia document such as a web page or PowerPoint presentation.

3. Using the item you selected for Question 1 or Question 2, write a letter to the manufacturer in which you propose changes in the design of the item. Explain your complaints about the current design of the item and present your reasons for proposing changes to that design.

4. Compare the texts you created for Questions 2 and 3. What differences can you identify in these texts? To what extent are these differences related to the form of the text? To what extent are they related to the intended audience?

5. Select an item you regularly use in your life, such as a cell phone, a television, a piece of clothing, or a common appliance. Visit several web sites on which different brands or versions of the item you've selected are discussed and reviewed. For example, if you selected a camera or a printer, you can find many web sites devoted specifically to those products that include product reviews, ratings, and comments by consumers. Review the evaluations of the item on the web sites you visited and get a sense of the priorities and values of the people who post reviews of that item. What do they seem to value most about that particular item? What are they looking for in the different brands or versions of that item? What do their comments suggest about what is important to them about the item and how they use it? Then, write a report about what you learned by visiting these sites. In your report, describe the item you selected and the web sites you visited. Describe as well the nature of the reviews and discussions on those sites. Draw conclusions about what the people who post comments and reviews on those sites seem to value about the items being reviewed. Also, draw conclusions about the nature of product design.

USE AND CONSEQUENCES

I F YOU ARE AT ALL CONSCIOUS OF YOUR HEALTH, YOU PROBABLY PAY ATTENTION TO WHAT YOU EAT. SO WHEN YOU GO TO THE SUPERMARKET, YOU'RE LIKELY TO BUY FRESH FRUITS AND VEGETABLES. YOU MIGHT CHOOSE CHICKEN INSTEAD OF BEEF. AND MAYBE YOU BUY A LOAF

of whole wheat bread instead of white. Today, most supermarkets in the United States offer all these foods and more all year round. There really isn't any season for fresh foods any longer. In the past, you couldn't buy, say, peaches in February because February is not part of the growing season for peaches in the United States. But these days, you can buy peaches any time of year. In the summer, those peaches were probably grown in Georgia or Maryland; if you buy peaches in February, they probably came from Chile or Brazil. The same is true of grapes, plums, and many other kinds of fruits and vegetables. And of course, in addition to these common foods, supermarkets often sell many different specialty foods from all over the world.

At first glance, the availability of these foods seems like a good thing. It means that you have a lot of choices when you shop and that you can buy a variety of fresh, healthy foods all year long. But there are costs to this convenience. For one thing, most of the food Americans buy is grown far from where they live, which means that it must be transported over long distances. Typically, foods grown in the United States are trucked from where they are produced to where they are consumed; those trucks not only consume gas or diesel fuel, but they also contribute to air pollution and greenhouse gases. Foods grown outside the United States may be flown from farm to market, which uses enormous amounts of fuel and also contributes to pollution. Even if foods are transported by ship, the process contributes to the degradation of sea and coastal ecosystems.

Of course, foods must also be stored, and many foods have to be kept cool. Storage, especially cold storage, uses electricity, which adds to the destruction of the environment because most electricity is generated by coal- or oil-fired plants,

which causes air pollution. The packaging used for even the freshest food is often made of plastic, which is manufactured from oil that must be pumped from underground oil wells and transported to manufacturing plants; packaging made of cardboard may be manufactured from recycled materials, but much of it is made from trees. And many foods, especially fresh produce, must be picked by hand, often by poorly paid migrant workers whose working conditions are often bad.

Had enough? All this—and more—goes into your simple choice to buy a peach or a bunch of grapes at your local market. And I haven't even begun to discuss clothing, or the energy you use to keep your home or apartment or dorm room lit and warm, or the impact of the car you drive or the bus you ride.

The point is that everything you consume, every resource you use to stay alive and healthy, has social, economic, and environmental consequences. Living your life in a typical American way causes environmental harm and may do social and economic harm as well—usually to people and places far from where you live. When you buy a shirt or a bunch of grapes, or when you drive your car to school or work, you are part of the problem.

The readings in this cluster explore some of the consequences of our uses of resources. They examine some hidden costs of common foods like corn or of leisure activities like skiing. They help us see that the choices we make every day affect people and the environment throughout the world. And perhaps they will help us be more mindful of the impact we each have on the earth. These readings also illustrate how writing about these issues can contribute to our collective efforts to reduce our impact and live together more responsibly.

When I first read the following essay by Michael Pollan, I thought about what a treat it was when my father would bring home hamburgers and fries from a local fast food restaurant for dinner when I was a kid. To my brother and sisters and me, those fast food meals were better than the elaborate dinners my mother would prepare most days. Over the years I

Fast Food Meal

have come to appreciate that fast food meals aren't really the treat I once thought they were, but it wasn't until I read Pollan's book The Omnivore's Dilemma *(2006), from which the following essay was taken, that I understood just how complicated such a meal really is. In this essay, Pollan traces what he calls the "natural history" of a fast food meal that he and his family ate. He describes the origins of that meal, and he reveals that no matter what they ate—chicken, salad, hamburger—he and his family were mostly eating corn. Pollan explains why that may be a problem and shows that everything we consume has consequences that very likely go far beyond what we realize when we order those fries or that hamburger. His essay is also a wonderful example of how writing can help us explore those consequences and better understand the resources we use every day.*

MICHAEL POLLAN

The meal at the end of the industrial food chain that begins in an Iowa cornfield is prepared by McDonald's and eaten in a moving car. Or at least this was the version of the industrial meal I chose to eat; it could easily have been another. The myriad streams of commodity corn, after being variously processed and turned into meat, converge in all sorts of different meals I might have eaten, at KFC or Pizza Hut or Applebee's, or prepared myself from ingredients bought at the supermarket. Industrial meals are all around us, after all; they make up the food chain from which most of us eat most of the time.

My eleven-year-old son, Isaac, was more than happy to join me at McDonald's; he doesn't get there often, so it's a treat. (For most American children today, it is no longer such a treat: One in three of them eat fast food every single day.) Judith, my wife, was less enthusiastic. She's careful about what she eats, and having a fast-food lunch meant giving up a "real meal," which seemed a shame. Isaac pointed out that she could order one of McDonald's new "premium salads" with the Paul Newman dressing. I read in the business pages that these salads are a big hit, but even if they weren't, they'd probably stay on

"Fast Food Meal," by Michael Pollan. From The Omnivore's Dilemma by Michael Pollan. Penguin Books, 2006. Reprinted by permission of Penguin Books USA.

the menu strictly for their rhetorical usefulness. The marketers have a term for what a salad or veggie burger does for a fast-food chain: "denying the denier." These healthier menu items hand the child who wants to eat fast food a sharp tool with which to chip away at his parents' objections. "But Mom, you can get the salad . . ."

Which is exactly what Judith did: order the Cobb salad with Caesar dressing. At $3.99, it was the most expensive item on the menu. I ordered a classic cheeseburger, large fries, and a large Coke. Large turns out to be a full 32 ounces (a quart of soda!) but, thanks to the magical economics of supersizing, it cost only 30 cents more than the 16-ounce "small." Isaac went with the new white-meat Chicken McNugget, a double-thick vanilla shake, and a large order of fries, followed by a new dessert treat consisting of freeze-dried pellets of ice cream. That each of us ordered something different is a hallmark of the industrial food chain, which breaks the family down into its various demographics and markets separately to each one: Together we would be eating alone together, and therefore probably eating more. The total for the three of us came to fourteen dollars, and was packed up and ready to go in four minutes. Before I left the register I picked up a densely printed handout called "A Full Serving of Nutrition Facts: Choose the Best Meal for You."

We could have slipped into a booth, but it was such a nice day we decided to put the top down on the convertible and eat our lunch in the car, something the food and the car have both been engineered to accommodate. These days 19 percent of American meals are eaten in the car. The car has cup holders, front seat and rear, and, except for the salad, all the food (which we could have ordered, paid for, and picked up without opening the car door) can be readily eaten with one hand. Indeed, this is the genius of the chicken nugget: It liberated chicken from the fork and plate, making it as convenient, waste-free, and automobile-friendly as the precondimented hamburger. No doubt the food scientists at McDonald's corporate headquarters in Oak Brook, Illinois, are right now hard at work on the one-handed salad.

5   But though Judith's Cobb salad did present a challenge to front-seat dining, eating it at fifty-five miles per hour seemed like the thing to do, since corn was the theme of this meal: The car was eating corn too, being fueled in part by **ETHANOL**. Even though the additive promises to diminish air quality in California, new federal mandates pushed by the corn processors require refineries in the state to help eat the corn surplus by diluting their gasoline with 10 percent ethanol.

One of the foremost voices today on food and related issues, Michael Pollan (b. 1955) is the Knight Professor of Science and Environmental Journalism at the University of California at Berkeley. Among his books are The Botany of Desire: A Plant's-eye View of the World *(2001),* In Defense of Food: An Eater's Manifesto *(2008), and* The Omnivore's Dilemma, *in which this essay first appeared.* ▼

CONVERSATIONS: ETHANOL

In paragraph 5, Pollan notes that his car was using fuel that included ethanol, which is made from corn. As he indicates, federal and state regulations have encouraged the use of ethanol as a fuel for cars. The debate about the wisdom of burning ethanol in cars intensified in 2008 (two years after this essay was published) as the world price of oil rose dramatically and gasoline prices in the United States rose accordingly. In view of rising prices, some Americans called for even greater use of ethanol. However, the price of corn also rose dramatically in 2008, in part because of a greater demand for ethanol. Other food prices began to rise as well. These developments reveal the complexity of the food system that Pollan describes in this essay; they also reveal the political nature of that system: policies intended to encourage ethanol use are often adopted for political reasons, not only environmental or economic ones. Pollan's writing is thus part of the ongoing debate about how to use resources, even as it helps us see that the use of resources in the United States affects others around the world—and vice versa.

GLOSS: PRE-WALLERSTEIN ERA
Pollan is referring to David Wallerstein, a member of McDonald's board of directors who is credited with inventing the idea of "super-sizing" items on the McDonald's menu. Pollan discusses Wallerstein, who died in 1993, in a earlier chapter of *The Omnivore's Dilemma,* the book from which this essay is taken.

STRATEGIES: DESCRIPTION
Pollan's description of fast food in paragraph 6 highlights the appeal of a fast food meal. Pollan might have made the same point simply by explaining that these characteristics of fast food are the source of its appeal, but this description may help him make his point more effectively than straightforward explanation. This is an example of a writer's strategic use of description not only to make a point but to do so in a way that is intended for a specific audience (in this case, Americans who grew up with fast food). Note, too, his use of figurative language to make his description of eating fast food in the car more vivid: he describes the milk shake that was spilled in his family's car as flying across the car "in creamy white lariats." Such figurative language can make the descriptions more vivid and engaging.

I ate a lot of McDonald's as a kid. This was in the **PRE-WALLERSTEIN ERA,** when you still had to order a second little burger or sack of fries if you wanted more, and the chicken nugget had not yet been invented. (One memorable childhood McDonald's meal ended when our station wagon got rear-ended at a light, propelling my milk shake across the car in creamy white lariats.) **I LOVED EVERYTHING ABOUT FAST FOOD:** the individual portions all wrapped up like presents (not having to share with my three sisters was a big part of the appeal; fast food was private property at its best); the familiar meaty perfume of the French fries filling the car; and the pleasingly sequenced bite into a burger—the soft, sweet roll, the crunchy pickle, the savory moistness of the meat.

Well-designed fast food has a fragrance and flavor all its own, a fragrance and flavor only nominally connected to hamburgers or French fries or for that matter to any particular food. Certainly the hamburgers and fries you make at home don't have it. And yet Chicken McNuggets do, even though they're ostensibly an entirely different food made from a different species. Whatever it is (surely the food scientists know), for countless millions of people living now, this generic fast-food flavor is one of the unerasable smells and tastes of childhood—which makes it a kind of comfort food. Like other comfort foods, it supplies (besides nostalgia) a jolt of carbohydrates and fat, which, some scientists now believe, relieve stress and bathe the brain in chemicals that make it feel good.

Isaac announced that his white-meat McNuggets were tasty, a definite improvement over the old recipe. McNuggets have come in for a lot of criticism recently, which might explain the reformulation. Ruling in 2003 in a lawsuit brought against McDonald's by a group of obese teenagers, a federal judge in New York had defamed the McNugget even as he dismissed the suit. "Rather than being merely chicken fried in a pan," he wrote in his decision, McNuggets "are a McFrankensteinian creation of various elements not utilized by the home cook." After cataloging the thirty-eight ingredients in a McNugget, Judge Sweet suggested that McDonald's marketing bordered on deceptive, since the dish is not what it purports to be—that is, a piece of chicken simply fried—and, contrary to what a consumer might reasonably expect, actually contains more fat and total calories than a cheeseburger. Since the lawsuit, McDonald's has reformulated the nugget with white meat, and begun handing out "A Full Serving of Nutrition Facts."* According to the flyer, a serving of six nuggets

---

*In 2005 McDonald's announced it would begin printing nutrition information on its packaging.

now has precisely ten fewer calories than a cheeseburger. Chalk up another achievement for food science.

When I asked Isaac if the new nuggets tasted more like chicken than the old ones, he seemed baffled by the question. "No, they taste like what they are, which is nuggets," and then dropped on his dad a withering two-syllable "duh." In this consumer's mind at least, the link between a nugget and the chicken in it was never more than notional, and probably irrelevant. By now the nugget constitutes its own genre of food for American children, many of whom eat nuggets every day. For Isaac, the nugget is a distinct taste of childhood, quite apart from chicken, and no doubt a future vehicle of nostalgia—a **MADELEINE** in the making.

GLOSS: MADELEINE
A madeleine is a small traditional French cake. In using the term here, Pollan seems to be referring to a scene in *Remembrance of Things Past,* a classic novel by Marcel Proust, in which eating a madeleine provokes powerful memories in one of the characters.

10   Isaac passed one up to the front for Judith and me to sample. It looked and smelled pretty good, with a nice crust and bright white interior reminiscent of chicken breast meat. In appearance and texture a nugget certainly alludes to fried chicken, yet all I could really taste was salt, that all-purpose fast-food flavor, and, okay, maybe a note of chicken bouillon informing the salt. Overall the nugget seemed more like an abstraction than a full-fledged food, an idea of chicken waiting to be fleshed out.

STRATEGIES: ORGANIZING AN ESSAY
Notice that Pollan organizes this essay more or less chronologically by telling the story of his family's fast food meal. But here, about halfway through the essay, he interrupts the story of the meal to provide background information about fast food, to describe the larger context of food production and consumption in contemporary American society, and to pursue his main points about how we produce and consume food today. From this point, most of the rest of his essay focuses on the implications of how we produce and consume our food. Notice that Pollan returns to his story periodically (in par. 14, for example) and then again in his final paragraph, a strategy that enables him to end his essay neatly and remind us that his detailed analysis of a fast food meal in paragraphs 11–20 ultimately comes down to individual people and their eating habits.

The ingredients listed in the flyer suggest a lot of thought goes into a nugget, that and a lot of corn. Of the thirty-eight ingredients it takes to make a McNugget, I counted thirteen that can be derived from corn: the corn-fed chicken itself; modified cornstarch (to bind the pulverized chicken meat); mono-, tri-, and diglycerides (emulsifiers, which keep the fats and water from separating); dextrose; lecithin (another emulsifier); chicken broth (to restore some of the flavor that processing leaches out); yellow corn flour and more modified cornstarch (for the batter); cornstarch (a filler); vegetable shortening; partially hydrogenated corn oil; and citric acid as a preservative. A couple of other plants take part in the nugget: There's some wheat in the batter, and on any given day the hydrogenated oil could come from soybeans, canola, or cotton rather than corn, depending on market price and availability.

According to the handout, McNuggets also contain several completely synthetic ingredients, quasi-edible substances that ultimately come not from a corn or soybean field but from a petroleum refinery or chemical plant. These chemicals are what make modern processed foods possible, by keeping the organic materials in them from going bad or looking strange after months in the freezer or on the road. Listed first are the "leavening agents": sodium aluminum phosphate, monocalcium phosphate, sodium acid pyrophosphate, and calcium lactate. These are antioxidants added to keep the various animal and vegetable fats involved in a nugget from turning rancid. Then there are "antifoaming agents" like dimethylpolysiloxene, added to the cooking oil to keep the starches from binding to air molecules, so as to produce foam during the fry. The problem is evidently grave enough to warrant adding a toxic chemical to the food: According to the *Handbook of Food Additives*, dimethylpolysiloxene is a suspected carcinogen and an established mutagen, tumorigen, and reproductive effector; it's also flammable. But perhaps the most alarming ingredient in a Chicken McNugget is tertiary butylhydroquinone, or TBHQ, an antioxidant derived from petroleum that is either sprayed directly on the nugget or the inside of the box it comes in to "help preserve freshness." According to *A Consumer's Dictionary of Food Additives*, TBHQ is a form of butane (i.e., lighter fluid) the FDA allows processors to use sparingly in our food: It can comprise no more than 0.02 percent of the oil in a nugget. Which is probably just as well, considering that ingesting a single gram of TBHQ can cause "nausea, vomiting, ringing in the ears, delirium, a sense of suffocation, and collapse." Ingesting five grams of TBHQ can kill.

With so many exotic molecules organized into a food of such complexity, you would almost expect a chicken nugget to do something more spectacular than taste okay to a child and fill him up inexpensively. What it has done, of course, is to sell an awful lot of chicken for companies like Tyson, which invented the nugget—at McDonald's behest—in 1983. The nugget is the reason chicken has supplanted beef as the most popular meat in America.

Compared to Isaac's nuggets, my cheeseburger is a fairly simple construct. According to "A Full Serving of Nutrition Facts," the cheeseburger contains a mere six ingredients, all but one of them familiar: a 100 percent beef patty, a bun, two American cheese slices, ketchup, mustard, pickles, onions, and "grill seasoning," whatever that is. It tasted pretty good, too, though on reflection what I mainly tasted were the condiments: Sampled by itself, the gray patty had hardly any flavor. And yet the whole package, especially on first bite, did manage to give off a fairly convincing burgerish aura. I suspect, however, that owes more to the olfactory brilliance of the "grill seasoning" than to the 100 percent beef patty.

In truth, my cheeseburger's relationship to beef seemed nearly as metaphorical as the nugget's relationship to a chicken. Eating it, I had to remind myself that there was an actual cow involved in this meal—most likely a burned-out old dairy cow (the source of most fast-food beef) but possibly bits and pieces of **A STEER LIKE 534** as well. Part of the appeal of hamburgers and nuggets is that their boneless abstractions allow us to forget we're eating animals. I'd been on the feedlot in Garden City only a few months earlier, yet this experience of cattle was so far removed from that one as to be taking place in a different dimension. No, I could not taste the feed corn or the petroleum or the antibiotics or the hormones—or the feedlot manure. Yet

15

GLOSS: A STEER LIKE 534
Steer 534 was a steer that Pollan purchased from a ranch in South Dakota so that he could learn more about how beef cattle are raised, slaughtered, and processed for food in the United States today. Garden City, which he mentions later in this paragraph, is the location of the feedlot in Kansas where Steer 534 was taken to be fattened for slaughter. Pollan describes his experiences as a steer owner and follows the life of Steer 534 earlier in *The Omnivore's Dilemma*, the book from which this essay was taken.

while "A Full Serving of Nutrition Facts" did not enumerate these facts, they too have gone into the making of this hamburger, are part of its natural history. That perhaps is what the industrial food chain does best: obscure the histories of the foods it produces by processing them to such an extent that they appear as pure products of culture rather than nature-things made from plants and animals. Despite the blizzard of information contained in the helpful McDonald's flyer—the thousands of words and numbers specifying ingredients and portion sizes, calories and nutrients—all this food remains perfectly opaque. Where does it come from? It comes from McDonald's.

But that's not so. It comes from refrigerated trucks and from warehouses, from slaughterhouses, from factory farms in towns like Garden City, Kansas, from ranches in Sturgis, South Dakota, from food science laboratories in Oak Brook, Illinois, from flavor companies on the New Jersey Turnpike, from petroleum refineries, from processing plants owned by ADM and Cargill, from grain elevators in towns like Farnhamville, and, at the end of that long and tortuous trail, from a field of corn and soybeans farmed in Churdan, Iowa.

It would not be impossible to calculate exactly how much corn Judith, Isaac, and I consumed in our McDonald's meal. I figure my 4-ounce burger, for instance, represents nearly 2 pounds of corn (based on a cow's feed conversion rate of 7 pounds of corn for every 1 pound of gain, half of which is edible meat). The nuggets are a little harder to translate into corn, since there's no telling how much actual chicken goes into a nugget; but if 6 nuggets contain a quarter pound of meat, that would have taken a chicken half a pound of feed corn to grow. A 32-ounce soda contains 86 grams of high-fructose corn syrup (as does a double-thick shake), which can be refined from a third of a pound of corn; so our 3 drinks used another 1 pound. Subtotal: 6 pounds of corn. From here the calculations become trickier because, according to the ingredients list in the flyer, corn is everywhere in our meal, but in unspecified amounts. There's more corn sweetener in my cheeseburger, of all places: The bun and the ketchup both contain high-fructose corn syrup (HFCS). It's in the salad dressing, too, and the sauces for the nuggets, not to mention Isaac's dessert. (Of the sixty menu items listed in the handout, forty five contain HFCS.) Then there are all the other corn ingredients in the nugget: the binders and emulsifiers and fillers. In addition to corn sweeteners, Isaac's shake contains corn syrup solids, mono- and diglycerides, and milk from corn-fed animals. Judith's Cobb salad is also stuffed with corn, even though there's not a kernel in it: Paul Newman makes his dressing with HFCS, corn syrup, corn starch, dextrin, caramel color, and xanthan gum; the salad itself contains cheese and eggs from corn-fed animals. The salad's grilled chicken breast is injected with a "flavor solution" that contains maltodextrin, dextrose, and monosodium glutamate. Sure, there are a lot of leafy greens in Judith's salad too, but the overwhelming majority of the calories in it (and there are 500 of them, when you count the dressing) ultimately come from corn. And the French fries? You would think those are mostly potatoes. Yet since half of the 540 calories in a large order of fries come from the oil they're fried in, the ultimate source of these calories is not a potato farm but a field of corn or soybeans.

The calculation finally defeated me, but I took it far enough to estimate that, if you include the corn in the gas tank (a whole bushel right there, to make two and a half gallons of ethanol), the amount of corn that went into producing our movable fast-food feast would easily have overflowed the car's trunk, spilling a trail of golden kernels on the blacktop behind us.

Some time later I found another way to calculate just how much corn we had eaten that day. I asked Todd Dawson, a biologist at Berkeley, to run a McDonald's meal through his **MASS SPECTROMETER** and calculate how much of the carbon in it came originally from a corn plant. It is hard to believe that the identity of the atoms in a cheeseburger or a Coke is preserved from farm field to fast-food counter, but the atomic signature of those carbon isotopes is indestructible, and still legible to the mass spectrometer. Dawson and his colleague Stefania Mambelli prepared an analysis showing roughly how much of the carbon in the various McDonald's menu items came from corn, and plotted them on a graph. The sodas came out at the top, not surprising since they consist of little else than corn sweetener, but virtually everything else we ate revealed a high proportion of corn, too. In order of diminishing cornness, this is how the laboratory measured our meal: soda (100 percent corn), milk shake (78 percent), salad dressing (65 percent), chicken nuggets (56 percent), cheeseburger (52 percent), and French fries (23 percent). What in the eyes of the omnivore looks like a meal of impressive variety turns out, when viewed through the eyes of the mass spectrometer, to be the meal of a far more specialized kind of eater. But then, this is what the industrial eater has become: **CORN'S KOALA.**

So what? Why should it matter that we have become a race of corn [20] eaters such as the world has never seen? Is this necessarily a bad thing? The answer all depends on where you stand.

If where you stand is in agribusiness, processing cheap corn into forty-five different McDonald's items is an impressive accomplishment. It represents a solution to the agricultural contradictions of capitalism, the challenge of increasing food industry profits faster than America can increase its population. Supersized portions of cheap corn-fixed carbon solves the problem of the fixed stomach; we may not be expanding the number of eaters in America, but we've figured out how to expand each of their appetites, which is almost as good. Judith, Isaac, and I together consumed a total of 4,510 calories at our lunch—more than half as many as we each should probably consume in a day. We had certainly done our parts in chomping through the corn surplus. (We had also consumed a lot of petroleum, and not just because we were in a car. To grow and process those

GLOSS: MASS SPECTROMETER
A mass spectrometer is a sophisticated instrument for identifying the atomic and molecular structure of a substance. It enables a researcher to determine the composition of a substance.

GLOSS: CORN'S KOALA
Koalas, which are small marsupial mammals native to Australia, feed almost exclusively on one thing: eucalyptus leaves. Here, Pollan suggests that humans have become like koalas; we eat primarily one thing: corn.

4,510 food calories took at least ten times as many calories of fossil energy, the equivalent of 1.3 gallons of oil.)

If where you stand is on one of the lower rungs of America's economic ladder, our cornified food chain offers real advantages: not cheap food exactly (for the consumer ultimately pays the added cost of processing), but cheap calories in a variety of attractive forms. In the long run, however, the eater pays a high price for these cheap calories: obesity, Type II diabetes, heart disease.

If where you stand is at the lower end of the world's economic ladder, however, America's corn-fed food chain looks like an unalloyed disaster. I mentioned earlier that all life on earth can be viewed as a competition for the energy captured by plants and stored in carbohydrates, energy we measure in calories. There is a limit to how many of those calories the world's arable land can produce each year, and an industrial meal of meat and processed food consumes—and wastes—an unconscionable amount of that energy. To eat corn directly (as Mexicans and many Africans do) is to consume all the energy in that corn, but when you feed that corn to a steer or a chicken, 90 percent of its energy is lost—to bones or feathers or fur, to living and metabolizing as a steer or chicken. This is why vegetarians advocate eating "low on the food chain": every step up the chain reduces the amount of food energy by a factor of ten, which is why in any ecosystem there are only a fraction as many predators as there are prey. But processing food also burns energy. What this means is that the amount of food energy lost in the making of something like a Chicken McNugget could feed a great many more children than just mine, and that behind the 4,510 calories the three of us had for lunch stand tens of thousands of corn calories that could have fed a great many hungry people.

And how does this corn-fed food chain look if where you stand is in the middle of a field of corn? Well, it depends on whether you are the corn farmer or the plant. For the corn farmer, you might think the cornification of our food system would have redounded to his benefit, but it has not. Corn's triumph is the direct result of its overproduction, and that has been a disaster for the people who grow it. Growing corn and nothing but corn has also exacted a toll on the farmer's soil, the quality of the local water and the overall health of his community, the biodiversity of his landscape, and the health of all the creatures living on or downstream from it. And not only those creatures, for cheap corn has also changed, and much for the worse, the lives of several billion food animals, animals that would not be living on factory farms if not for the ocean of corn on which these animal cities float.

But return to that Iowa farm field for a moment and look at the matter—at us—from the standpoint of the corn plant itself. Corn, corn, corn as far as the eye can see, ten-foot stalks soldiering in perfect thirty inch rows to the far horizon, an 80-million-acre corn lawn rolling across the continent. It's a good thing this plant can't form an impression of us, for how risible that impression would be: the farm- 25 ers going broke cultivating it; the countless other species routed or emiserated by it; the humans eating and drinking it as fast as they can, some of them—like me and my family—in automobiles engineered to drink it, too. Of all the species that have figured out how to thrive in a world dominated by *Homo sapiens,* surely no other has succeeded more spectacularly—has colonized more acres and bodies—than *Zea mays,* the grass that domesticated its domesticator. You have to wonder why we Americans don't worship this plant as fervently as the Aztecs; like they once did, we make extraordinary sacrifices to it.

These, at least, were my somewhat fevered speculations, as we sped down the highway putting away our fast-food lunch. What is it about fast food? Not only is it served in a flash, but more often than not it's eaten that way too: We finished our meal in under ten minutes. Since we were in the convertible and the sun was shining, I can't blame the McDonald's ambiance. Perhaps the reason you eat this food quickly is because it doesn't bear savoring. The more you concentrate on how it tastes, the less like anything it tastes. I said before that McDonald's serves a kind of comfort food, but after a few bites I'm more inclined to think they're selling something more schematic than that—something more like a signifier of comfort food. So you eat more and eat more quickly, hoping somehow to catch up to the original idea of a cheeseburger or French fry as it retreats over the horizon. And so it goes, bite after bite, until you feel not satisfied exactly, but simply, regrettably, full.

Understanding the Text

1. What is the appeal of a fast food meal, according to Pollan? What does the appeal of such a meal reveal about the way Americans eat today, in his view? What problems does Pollan see in the prominent place of fast food in the American diet? Do you think he's right? Why or why not?

2. Why does Pollan describe a McDonald's chicken nugget as "its own genre of food for American children" (par. 9)? What does this kind of food reveal about contemporary food production and consumption in the United States, as Pollan sees it?

3. What does Pollan mean when he describes a McDonald's nugget's relationship to chicken and a McDonald's hamburger's relationship to beef as "metaphorical" (par. 15)? In what sense are these foods "abstractions"? What are the implications of this "metaphorical" relationship between certain fast food items and the sources of those foods, as Pollan sees it?

4. Why does Pollan calculate the amount of corn in the fast food meal he and his family ate? What does the amount of corn in this fast food meal have to do with Pollan's main point in this essay?

5. What are the implications of the modern corn-based diet,

as Pollan describes it? Why do these implications worry Pollan? Do they worry you? Why or why not?

6. Why does Pollan "regret" being full after his fast food meal? What do his feelings about that meal suggest about our contemporary eating habits?

Exploring the Issues

1. At several points in his essay, Pollan mentions nostalgia and recalls memories of his own childhood. What does nostalgia have to do with fast food, in Pollan's view? What do you think his references to nostalgia in this essay suggest about food in general?

2. Pollan includes a great deal of factual information about the ingredients in fast food and how it is manufactured (see especially par. 11–18). Evaluate Pollan's use of this information to help make his point about fast food and the contemporary American diet. How effectively do you think Pollan explains these facts? How well does he use them to support his own views about fast food? What effect do you think he intended these facts to have on his readers? What effect did they have on you? Do you think his use of this information strengthens or weakens his essay? Explain.

3. In paragraph 20, Pollan poses the question of whether a diet based on corn is necessarily a bad thing and writes, "The answer all depends on where you stand." Then he reviews some of the answers that might be given by different people in the world. Why do you think Pollan offers several different answers to his question? What do you think he gains (or loses) in terms of his main point in this essay by reviewing these different perspectives?

Entering the Conversations

1. Write an essay in which you describe your own experience in consuming a fast food meal. Try to convey a sense of the experience and the appeal (or lack of appeal) of fast food from your point of view. (If you do not eat fast food, you might consider interviewing several people who do and describe what you learned from them about their experiences with fast food.)

2. Much of Pollan's attention in this essay is focused on the prominent role of corn in the modern American diet. As best you can, try to determine how much corn you consume in a typical day. Use Pollan's approach to examining the ingredients of the food you eat (see par. 17–19). Then write a report for an audience of your classmates on the basis of your research. Describe what you eat in a typical day and try to identify any corn in your diet. Then draw conclusions about your diet and its environmental, social, or economic impact. If appropriate, draw on Pollan's essay and his own perspective on the role of corn in the American diet.

3. In a group of classmates, share the reports you wrote for Question 2. On the basis of these essays, draw conclusions about the extent to which Pollan's criticisms of our modern corn-based diet are valid. Then, as a group, create a web page, pamphlet, or other appropriate kind of document in which you present your group's insights about the modern American diet. Identify a specific audience for your document, such as other students at your school, and design the document with that audience in mind.

4. If possible, talk to one of the people who is responsible for food service on your campus to get their perspective on the state of the modern American diet. Get their reactions to Pollan's analysis and his criticisms of the modern corn-based diet, and get a sense of the problems they see with modern eating habits, especially on your campus. Then, write a report about what you learned from the person you interviewed.

5. On the basis of the work you did for Question 4, write a letter to an appropriate administrator on your campus in which you convey your viewpoint about the food that is consumed on your campus and the implications of typical eating habits on your campus. Propose changes that you believe will result in a diet that is healthier for students, for the community, and for the environment.

6. Talk to someone you know who was raised in another culture where food traditions and diet are different from those in the United States. (If you do not know such a person, you might be able to meet someone through the office for international students on your campus.) Learn about the typical diet in that person's culture, and find out what they think about the American diet, especially fast food. Then, write an essay in which you explore the differences between the typical American diet and a typical diet in that person's culture. (You may wish to do additional research for this essay to learn more about the person's culture and its food traditions as well as about typical American eating habits.)

In early 2005, I visited Whiteface Mountain *in upstate New York. Whiteface is well known as the site of the alpine ski events in the 1980 Winter Olympic Games, during which American skier Phil Mahre won a silver medal and the U.S. hockey team defeated the formidable Soviet hockey team on its way to a gold medal. But the operators of Whiteface*

THE *Ski* Store AND THE *Real* Cost OF Fun

Mountain also want to be known for something else: being environmentally responsible. While I was there, I learned that Whiteface is a charter member of Sustainable Slopes, an initiative by ski areas to reduce their significant impact on their local and regional environments. This initiative includes reducing the use of water for making snow, employing efficient technologies to reduce electricity use, and educating skiers about how they can reduce their own impact on the environment. I was pleased to learn about Sustainable Slopes because recreation like skiing causes great environmental damage. But as internationally acclaimed environmentalist Donella Meadows (1941– 2001) points out in the following essay, the impact of recreational activities goes well beyond the obvious environmental damage that we can see when we visit a ski area. Her essay offers a lesson in how much we can affect the environment and

DONELLA MEADOWS

A 17-year-old friend convinced me to take her to a ski store on a Saturday afternoon right before the supposed start of the supposed ski season. I guess it's been 20 years since I was last in a ski store.

This one was a happy place, full of torchy colors and young, energetic people. It was packed, but my companion was blonde and tall and slim and beautiful, so three young, energetic salesmen buzzed right up to us.

During the next hour, as she questioned and pondered and tried on and rejected and enthused and racked up many bucks on her papa's credit card, I absorbed the modern world of skiing.

"Are you an aggressive skier?" they asked, and when she said she liked to go really fast, they led her off to the aggressive skis, the aggressive boots, the aggressive bindings. These are made of supermetals and superplastics and superfabrics, bonded in layers with superglues. "Imagine all the toxics," I thought. "And that layered stuff can never be recycled. And it will last in a landfill for a million years."

Donella Meadows, "The Ski Store and the Real Cost of Fun." Copyright © 1998 Sustainability Institute Donella Meadows Archive, http://www .ststainer.org/dhm_archive (accessed 02-11-05).

5 I must have been the only person in the store with such thoughts. My companion had long conversations with the salesmen about shaped skis, cutting edges on sharp turns and what an extra quarter-inch of height in the bindings does for maneuverability. She picked out equipment of steel gray and flaming red.

I pondered, "What if all this care and design, this cleverness, these exotic materials, this money went to ending hunger? Or solar collectors? What if these great young people poured their boundless energy into reforestation or insulating the houses of the poor or at least the kind of skiing where you have to haul yourself to the top of the hill?"

I shared none of these dark thoughts with my bright friend. But all the next week, a week in December during which the temperature in New England hovered between 40 and 60 and the ski areas couldn't even make artificial snow, all through that strangely balmy week I was in a bah! humbug! mood. "They load their pricey skis into their gas-guzzling vans," I harrumphed to myself. "They drive to mountains covered with effluent from diesel-belching, stream-destroying snow guns. They use still more fossil fuel to pull themselves uphill so they can slide down. Then they're surprised when global warming comes along."

Finally I turned to some wise 23-year-olds for enlightenment. "Why is this high-tech, high-expense, high-emission kind of skiing fun?" I asked them. "Or, no, cancel that, I can see why it's fun. But why isn't cross-country skiing just as much fun? Or snowball fights or skating or snowshoeing or any of the less destructive ways to play outside in the winter?"

"Because they're not IN," my friends explained patiently. "Because you can't compare your flashy equipment with your friends' flashy equipment. Because the good parties are on the ski slopes. Because no one sells designer clothes for snowshoeing. Because it's fun to go really fast."

10 I listened, and then I dug out my copy of *Brave New World* (written in 1932 by Aldous Huxley) and found the place where the Director of Hatcheries describes why his society programs children to hate nature.

other people by the simple choices we make, even choices to engage in seemingly wholesome activities like skiing.

Donella Meadows was a professor of biophysics at Dartmouth College and founder of the Sustainability Institute, which promotes environmentally sustainable lifestyles. She authored many books about environmental issues, including The Limits to Growth *(1972) and* Beyond the Limits *(1992), and wrote a column distributed by the Sustainability Institute called* The Global Citizen, *in which this essay was first published in 1998.* ▼

CONVERSATIONS: THE APPEAL OF SKIING
Downhill skiing is a popular pastime in many parts of the world and a multibillion dollar business. Consider what this image might suggest about skiing. How does the message conveyed by this image support or complicate Meadows's argument?

Who	Dani Costandaché
Where	Klosters-Swiss
When	05 February 1977
What	Halfpipe and Big Air Meister
Why	I just live freestyle – Just do whatever you want.

150012 (874) Small Contrast Stripe Snow Jacket

CONVERSATIONS: DYSTOPIAS AND UTOPIAS
In this passage (par. 10), Meadows quotes from the well-known novel *Brave New World* by Aldous Huxley, which describes a frightening future in which everything is controlled through technology, even the characteristics of human beings, who are developed in test tubes. The world described in Huxley's novel is an example of a *dystopia*, a carefully controlled world or community in which the quality of life is undesirable. Dystopias can be thought of as the opposite of *utopias*—that is, ideal worlds in which the most difficult problems of our societies are solved. In referring to Huxley's novel in this way, Meadows is using an ongoing conversation about how to improve our world to help make her point about our current lifestyle. Obviously, she sees in Huxley's terrible imaginary world some similarities to the world we have created. Novels like *Brave New World* are thus an important part of the way ideas about how we should live are examined and discussed. Essays like this one by Meadows are part of that process, too.

"'Primroses and landscapes,' he pointed out, 'have one grave defect: they are gratuitous. A love of nature keeps no factories busy. It was decided to abolish the love of nature . . . but not the tendency to consume transport. For of course it was essential that they should keep on going to the country, even though they hated it. The problem was to find an economically sounder reason for consuming transport than a mere affection for primroses and landscapes. It was duly found.'"

"'We condition the masses to hate the country,' concluded the Director. 'But, simultaneously we condition them to love all country sports. At the same time we see to it that all country sports shall entail the use of elaborate apparatus. So that they consume manufactured articles as well as transport. . . .'"

Old Aldous got our number 66 years ago, didn't he? But he did not foresee the possibility of environmental backlash.

It's easy to label environmentalists as anti-fun grinches. It would be easy to label my young friend as shallow or gullible. Neither she nor I deserve those labels. There is nothing I want more for her than that she should have fun. And she would never deliberately hurt other people or the earth. She is just doing what I did when I was 17, going out with friends, having fun. In my day we had lots of fun without much in the way of fossil fuel, fancy equipment, or credit cards. But the economy had not yet perfected the art of conditioning us to buy elaborate apparatus and consume transport.

15   She's not to blame. If blame is useful here, it should be directed toward an amorphous system that charges her papa a high price, but gives neither him nor her any sense of real, full costs.

And I'm not a killjoy. I've just been educated to see the whole system, to see how those real, full costs fall upon the air and the waters and the land and the climate in ways that will ruin the very fun that is causing the damage in the first place. And I'm old enough to know that there are far less costly, far more sustainable kinds of joy and fun.

Understanding the Text

1. What characterizes "the modern world of skiing," in Meadows's view? What do you think modern skiing reveals about how we spend our leisure time?

2. What is the appeal of a sport like skiing, as Meadows describes it? Do you think this is a fair or accurate depiction of this kind of leisure activity? Explain.

3. Who or what is to blame for the destructive ways that we tend to have fun today, according to Meadows? Do you think she's right? Why or why not?

Exploring the Issues

1. Throughout this essay, Meadows comments on the activities around her in the ski store. What do her comments reveal about her values or her perspective? How do you think her comments affect her credibility? Explain. To what extent do her comments affect the way you respond to her essay?

2. In the final paragraph of this essay, Meadows writes that she has been "educated to see the whole system, to see how those real, full costs fall upon the air and the waters and the land and the climate in ways that will ruin the very fun that is causing the damage in the first place." What exactly does she mean by that statement? How might she have been "educated" in this way, while her seventeen-year-old friend and her friend's father and others have not been? What does this statement suggest about Meadows? What do you think it suggests about how we come to understand the world around us and our impact on it?

3. Meadows bases this essay on one experience with a young friend, with whom she visited a ski store. Examine how Meadows uses this experience in her essay. What ideas or arguments does she convey through telling about this experience? How effective do you think her use of this experience is to convey her point?

4. Some readers might reject Meadows's analysis of skiing as too extreme. If we accept her main premise about the consequences of our leisure activities, it is possible to conclude that *anything* we do for recreation is environmentally destructive and therefore should be avoided. Do you think Meadows's argument is too extreme? Why or why not? If it is, how might we reasonably address her concerns about the impact of our activities?

Entering the Conversations

1. Write a response to Meadows's essay, especially to her point that "there are far less costly, far more sustainable kinds of joy and fun" than skiing (par. 16). If you ski or snowboard, you might draw on your own experience in your response to Meadows. If you don't ski or snowboard, you might draw on your experience with other leisure activities.

2. In paragraph 6, Meadows asks, "What if all this care and design, this cleverness, these exotic materials, this money went to ending hunger? Or solar collectors? What if these great young people poured their boundless energy into reforestation or insulating the houses of the poor or at least the kind of skiing where you have to haul yourself to the top of the hill?" Write an essay in which you respond to her questions.

3. Create a photo essay, web site, PowerPoint presentation, or some other appropriate document that presents your view of the impact of your favorite leisure activity.

4. Write an essay in which you describe a utopian community where the kinds of problems Meadows describes in her essay don't exist.

In the past few years, shrinking glaciers have been getting a lot of attention as worldwide concerns about global climate change increase. Maybe that's why writer Dominique Browning decided to visit Patagonia, Argentina, where some of the world's most spectacular glaciers are located. As she tells us in the following essay, she is well aware that glaciers are

The Melting Point

melting much faster than was predicted even a few years ago, and perhaps that accounts for the many visitors to places like Argentina's Los Glaciares National Park, which she describes in her essay. But Browning didn't find exactly what she expected to see in that beautiful place. She describes its beauty, but her visit also revealed something about how human beings relate to natural places like the glaciers she

DOMINIQUE BROWNING

GLOSS: EL CALAFATE
Located in the Patagonia region of southwest Argentina, El Calafate is a small village that serves as a main access point for visitors to Argentina's Los Glaciares National Park, which contains 47 glaciers, including the Perito Moreno Glacier, which Browning describes visiting in this essay. The Perito Moreno Glacier has become one of the most popular tourist destinations in the world, perhaps in part because of the publicity surrounding the rapidly melting glaciers in Patagonia and elsewhere in the world (which Browning mentions in par. 10).

Los Glaciares National Park, Argentina

The most striking thing about the drive out of **EL CALAFATE** on the way to the Patagonian glaciers is the trash. Sheer, flimsy, white plastic bags, tens of thousands of them, are strewn across acres of land. The harsh wind has blown them in curtains up against the chain-link fences around construction sites; thousands have been tilled into the mud of wide tire tracks; thousands more, tattered by sharp nettles, festoon the low, clumping bushes that cover the landscape.

The plastic bags have become such a problem that the local grocery store will no longer supply them to shoppers. El Calafate exists for glaciers and its proximity to Los Glaciares National Park. The town is a hodgepodge of houses, sheds and stores; the old section is clearly demarcated by **THE ROWS OF TALL, THICK-TRUNKED POPLARS THAT ARE TO YARDS IN PATAGONIA WHAT PRIVET HEDGES ARE TO THOSE IN NEW ENGLAND.** The town is growing rapidly, with cinder-block hotels and vacation condos springing up everywhere, thanks to the tourist dollars pouring into its coffers. The shops are full of souvenirs, their windows plastered with posters of glaciers and ads for boat tours. Finishing touches are being put on a large casino.

Los Glaciares National Park was declared a World Heritage Site by **UNESCO** in 1981. Argentina's park service controls the number of visitors and the modes by which glaciers can be seen. Tour companies run boats of various sizes several times a day across the enormous Lake Argentino. Its peculiar blue-green water, called glacial milk, looks opaque because of the way light refracts off the silt and sediment it contains. We arrive at the boat to which we've been assigned and climb the stairs to the upper level, having paid extra for a V.I.P. area, the better to savor every moment of what we fully expect to become one of those memories of a lifetime.

Before we've even pulled out of El Calafate's harbor, a fight erupts among several passengers over seating; the armchairs aren't arranged in such a way to allow all the couples to be together. An elegant Frenchman, his head and neck swathed in an expensive vicuña scarf, is furiously berating the young boat attendant who, it seems, didn't appreciate just how V.I.P. the man was; he wants the seats being occupied by a hip young British couple, who are not budging but yelling back at him. Their voices grow louder as the engine picks up.

5   To end the tirade, I offer my seat next to my teenage niece; she is plugged into her iPod and isn't going to hear anything outside her own head anyway. The man looks disappointed and barely thanks me; his partner, whose melancholy hauteur is achievable only by elegant Frenchwomen of a certain age, buries her nose in a magazine article called "The Voice of Hamas" and does not look up again.

From the deck outside, I watch chunks of ice bob around us, and it's disconcerting because the water looks as if it should have a Caribbean warmth. The scenery is stunning, a tableau off an inked Chinese screen. Cliffs rise straight up out of the water; evergreens cling to the rocky faces, their forms tortured and extruded by the fierce and unrelenting winds. Eagles soar over the boat. We nose into an inlet and the smell of fuel wafts through the air.

As I am an eco-tourist, I try to calculate how many years of subway rides it will take to atone for the **CARBON MILES** I have burned in the flight from New York City, but I lose track of the decimal points. The sun is so intense that my lips and skin burn even under a thick coat of sunscreen. We are following the exact route of the boats ahead of us, as there are, I suppose, only so many ways to get to a glacier.

Probably a hundred people are on our boat, and as we draw closer to land, the deck grows crowded. All of a sudden loud music blares through the speakers; Argentines seem fond of '80s-era soundtracks and lose no opportunity to pipe them into any space. The disco beat reverberates across the deck, drowning out the engine and the wind. I expect other guests to make a run on the captain's quarters to beg for relief, but instead a few make tentative Village People dance moves. Everyone has to shout to continue conversing.

saw in Argentina. In the end, she may have been more awestruck by her fellow tourists and their behavior than by the spectacular glaciers they came to see.

Dominique Browning is the former editor of House and Garden *magazine and the author of several books, including* Paths of Desire: The Passions of a Suburban Gardener *(2004). This essay appeared in the* New York Times *in 2008.*

STRATEGIES: USING ANALOGIES
Writers sometimes use analogies to compare an unfamiliar thing with something more familiar, as Browning does in paragraph 2 when she compares the "rows of tall, thick-trunked poplars" with privet hedges in New England. Privet hedges are thick shrubs grown close together and trimmed to form a kind of living green wall. This analogy may be ineffective for readers who are unfamiliar with privet hedges. In deciding to use such an analogy, a writer tries to anticipate whether readers are likely to have the appropriate background knowledge or experience to understand the analogy. Given that this essay was first published in the *New York Times,* an internationally distributed newspaper, consider whether Browning could make such an assumption about her readers in this case.

GLOSS: UNESCO
According to its web site, the United Nations Educational, Scientific, and Cultural Organization, or UNESCO, "promotes international co-operation . . . in the fields of education, science, culture and communication." Through its World Heritage Sites program, UNESCO "seeks to encourage the identification, protection and preservation of cultural and natural heritage around the world considered to be of outstanding value to humanity."

CONVERSATIONS: CARBON MILES

In recent years, attention has been focused on how much carbon is released into the atmosphere by common human activities, including transportation. This "carbon footprint" is intended to measure how much our individual activities might contribute to the production of the greenhouse gases that are believed to cause global warming. The chart shown here shows the percentages of the total greenhouse gas output of various activities of a typical person in developed nations like the United States. When Browning mentions the "carbon miles" burned on her flight from New York City, she is referring to the amount of carbon released into the atmosphere by the jet she flew on. Depending upon the method of calculation, her single flight could have released nearly a ton of carbon into the atmosphere. By contrast, driving a mid-size car such as a Honda Accord 10,000 miles during one year will release approximately three tons of carbon into the atmosphere. Such calculations have become more commonplace as people around the world debate the best ways to address the problem of global climate change and reduce the human impact on the atmosphere.

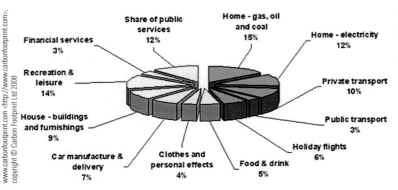

The pieces of ice in the water around us are now larger; their shapes are mesmerizing, as are their colors, varying shades of an intense, crystalline blue that I've never before seen in nature. As if we were children watching clouds float through the sky, we start pointing out ice in the shapes of whales and giraffes, or fallen columns; the larger icebergs, showing only 15 percent of their incredible mass above water, look like ruined temples and amphitheaters.

We come in sight of the first glacier and it is strange and magnificent, a frozen river of jagged peaks. Water pours off the sides. Glaciers worldwide have been receding for more than a century, but the melting has accelerated catastrophically in the last few decades. The tree line has not had time to advance enough to catch up; the ice has left behind wide scars of bare, hardscrabble earth. All the glaciers in Patagonia save one are shrinking more rapidly every year.

To my teenage niece, who has unplugged herself and joined me on deck, I explain all the science of climate change I can muster. Every once in a while a thundering crack is audible over the human din, as a huge piece of ice breaks off the face of the glacier. By the time you've heard it, you've missed it, and can see only the widening ripples radiating from the water where the newly calved iceberg has fallen. We watch melting ice cascade off the glacier's crenellated face. "I guess this gives new meaning to 'a glacial pace,'" my niece remarks.

I try to imagine what it must have been like to see glaciers looming 19 or 20 stories above, as the guide puts it, from a small, fragile craft, rather than from our three-story-high cruiser, and then I realize how strange it is that we resort to the architectural measurements of skyscrapers to wrap our minds around **SUCH GRANDEUR.** Getting to the glaciers in a small boat as a backpacker might have done a mere 20 years ago is now a privilege reserved for the very wealthy. Our cruiser cannot get too close for fear of a chunk of ice breaking off and sinking it—in revenge?

The ancient, mythic language we use to describe the effects of climate is distorting, but hard to resist. We should know better, but we still refer to Mother Earth and her fury at our polluting ways, unleashing hurricanes, hurling tornadoes into strange places, punishing us with heat waves. We can't seem to get past putting ourselves at the center of everything. Gazing at the glacier, I feel as if I am in the presence of a dying beast. But it isn't the glacier that is dying.

By now, the deck is crowded and people are arguing, pushing and shoving each other aside to get pictures of a companion with the ice in the background. We drop anchor at the edge of the park and are told to follow a path to a beachfront on which to picnic and admire the view.

15 Walking the length of the beach is like crossing a city and hearing accents change along the way: there's the German area; the Italian neighborhood; the Japanese block. Next come the Israelis, the British and of course the aloof French in a choice arrondissement. There are surprisingly few Americans on our boat. All along the water's edge men and boys are picking up rocks to try to hit the ice chunks floating past. One child has gone so far as to wade in to drag a piece closer, and he is thwacking it urgently with a stick, desperate to break it. The stick shatters.

At the signal to get back on board we are reminded to leave nothing behind. I linger a bit, trying to steal a quiet moment in front of the glacier. I cannot seem to feel, in a deep way, the awe I know this spectacle deserves, a response more profound than the simple excitement that makes us reach for our cameras—closer perhaps, to a state of grace and wonder, the feeling of being in the presence of something holy. I cannot push aside the clamor of our journey or the mess of my companions. How can we expect anyone to care about melting glaciers in the abstract, in news articles and scientific papers, when even in the face of their stupendous presence we remain careless? Along the path grow exquisite, miniature Alpine flowers in every imaginable color, so tiny you could easily miss them. Among the delicate blossoms are bits of foil, trash, cigarette butts, broken glass and plastic water bottle caps. We can't seem to help ourselves.

On the ship, people settle sleepily into the upholstery. We have four more glaciers to visit, but I suppose the general feeling in the napping class is that if you've seen one, you've seen them all. Meanwhile, life out on deck becomes friendlier, more cooperative. The music is not as loud. People give way at the rails to let others have a turn, and take pictures for one another. The feeling out here seems to be that there are plenty of glaciers to go around, more than enough glaciers for everyone.

By the time we pull up to the last one on the tour, only a few of us are left on deck. Everyone else is below, where I find that Champagne and chocolates are being served. Someone raises a glass.

"To the future!"

CONVERSATIONS: NATURAL GRANDEUR
In this section of her essay, Browning describes the scene she observed as her tour boat neared the glacier. When she writes that she realizes "how strange it is that we resort to the architectural measurements of skyscrapers to wrap our minds around such grandeur," she is not only reminding us how difficult it can be to describe spectacular natural places but she is also making a comment about the relationship between humans and their environment. Sometimes photographs, like the one shown here, can convey the grandeur she refers to, but consider whether her words convey her point effectively without such a photograph.

© Hiroshi Higuchi/Getty Images

Understanding the Text

1. What does Browning find on her visit to Los Glaciares National Park in Argentina? Is she at all surprised by what she sees there? Explain. What lessons do you think she draws from what she finds there?

2. What is Browning's reaction to the actions and behaviors of the other tourists on her visit to the glaciers? What do their behaviors suggest to her about human beings and their relationship to their environment?

3. Why is Browning not able to feel the awe that she knows the spectacle of the glacier she is visiting deserves? What prevents her from feeling a sense of awe? What does she feel instead? What do you think her feelings reveal about her? About human beings in general?

Exploring the Issues

1. This essay describes Browning's visit to a glacier in Argentina's Los Glaciares National Park, but she begins her essay by describing the trash, made up mostly of plastic grocery bags, that she saw on her way to the park. Why do you think she begins the essay in this way? What do the plastic bags have to do with her visit? How might the image of the plastic bags that Browning paints in the opening paragraph relate to her main points in this essay?

2. Browning titled this essay "The Melting Point." What do you think that title means? Obviously, it refers to the melting glaciers that

Browning observed in Argentina, but do you think it carries any other meanings? Explain. How effectively do you think the title introduces her essay?

3. At the end of paragraph 13, Browning confides that while visiting the glacier, she felt as though she were in the presence of a dying beast. Then she writes, "But it isn't the glacier that is dying." If the glacier isn't dying, who or what is? What point do you think she intends to convey with this statement? Do you agree with her? Why or why not?

4. Why do you think Browning ends her essay as she does? What point do you think she is trying to make with her ending? Do you find her ending effective? Why or why not? What might your reaction to her ending reveal about you as a reader and as a person?

Entering the Conversations

1. Write an essay describing a special, unusual, or particularly beautiful place you have visited.

 INFOTRAC

2. In this essay, Browning calls herself an "eco-tourist." Eco-tourism has become a growing industry in many places in the world, such as Los Glaciares National Park, which Browning describes in her essay. Using InfoTrac, the Internet, your library, and other appropriate resources, investigate eco-tourism. Try to find out exactly what people mean by

that term, and describe the different kinds of eco-tourism that have developed in recent years. Try to find out as well whether there are controversies surrounding eco-tourism. Consider talking to someone at a travel agency that specializes in eco-tourism to get their perspective on it. Then write a report on the basis of your research. In your report, define eco-tourism and describe its social, economic, and environmental implications. Draw conclusions about what eco-tourism might suggest about the consequences of the way humans use resources and their environment.

3. On the basis of your research for Question 2, create a pamphlet or web page for people who want to know more about eco-tourism. In your pamphlet or web page, try to convey a sense of what you believe are appropriate concerns about eco-tourism and how potential eco-tourists can address those concerns.

4. On the basis of your research for Question 2, write an argument for or against eco-tourism.

Alternatively, create a pamphlet, web page, or another kind of multimedia document that presents your own perspective on eco-tourism.

5. Browning's essay is essentially the story of her visit to Los Glaciares National Park in Argentina, but she obviously uses that story to make a point. Write a conventional academic essay in which you analyze her story and evaluate its effectiveness in conveying her point.

Meteorologists and climate scientists *remind us that extreme weather events like hurricanes cannot necessarily be connected directly to global climate change, but that doesn't seem to stop people from making that connection. Writer Verlyn Klinkenborg might see that as a good thing. In the following essay, he shares his own musings about global warming after seeing a*

Some Thoughts ON Living THE Combustible Life

wildfire burning in California. Wildfires in the western United States have been getting a lot of attention in the media in recent years, perhaps because they seem to be a symptom of global warming, and like so many other people, Klinkenborg is reminded of global warming when he sees a wildfire. But his musings focus attention on the many other fires that

GLOSS: THE GYPSUM FIRE

In paragraph 2, Klinkenborg is referring to several of the many fires that were burning in southern California in the spring of 2007, when he wrote this essay. As he notes later in the paragraph, 2007 was an exceptionally dry year for that region, which increased the danger of wildfires. The Gypsum fire refers to a wildfire in Orange County, California, that burned 140 acres. Klinkenborg mentions two other fires—in Griffith Park, which is in Los Angeles, and on Catalina Island off the California coast—that were burning at the same time. He also mentions the spectacular fires that burned nearly 800,000 acres in Yellowstone National Park, more than a third of the park's total area, in 1988. Those fires sparked a national controversy about U.S. Forest Service fire policy.

VERLYN KLINKENBORG

Recently, I flew from Denver to Ontario, Calif. The next-to-last leg of that flight is mostly over desert, and at night the desert floor means darkness. Then we came over the mountains, and in the distance I could see a dim line of lights slowly rising to fill the horizon, the leading edge of the luminosity that is Southern California at night. Before long we were descending, wheels down, over a district of low, flat buildings, enormous in scale, their parking lots and loading bays gleaming under mercury and sodium lamps.

But what caught my eye just before we landed was another kind of light. It was the ragged edge of a wildfire off to the south, probably the **GYPSUM FIRE** near Yorba Linda. It was dull orange, highly

we burn every day: the fires that we use for heat and light and transportation. The sight of a wildfire burning out of control prompts Klinkenborg to wonder about how we seem to ignore those many other fires, which may have much greater consequences than the wildfires that get so much attention on the evening news programs. His essay may prompt you to wonder the same thing. It is a good example of how a writer can help focus our attention on important things that might otherwise escape our notice—which, after all, is one of the great uses of writing.

A member of the editorial board of the New York Times, *Verlyn Klinkenborg (b. 1952) writes about rural living and contemporary lifestyles. He is the author of numerous books, including* Making Hay *(1986) and* The Rural Life *(2003), and has written for many publications, including* Harper's, The New Yorker, *and* National Geographic, *as well as the* New York Times, *in which this essay appeared in 2007.* ◪

variable, often obscured by its own smoke and then flaring brightly once again. There was no geometry, no steadiness to it, and that lack of proportion and symmetry was as much a part of the fire's wildness as the fact that it had escaped from human control. Other wildfires have been burning around the region, too, in Griffith Park and on Catalina Island. These have been widely scattered burns, but they raise the fear of a different kind of fire—the kind that begins in separate places with separate names but merges into a single conflagration and is best remembered by the year itself, the way 1988 is remembered in Yellowstone. This year may well bring that kind of fire to Southern California. It is the driest year in the last 120 years. The hills are just waiting to go up. The question is what else will go up with them.

The sight of that wildfire has stuck in my mind. It took the form of a wavering, shallow V on a distant hillside, and, of course, it reminded me of other wildfires I have seen. But whatever that fire was in itself—and it was contained by the next morning—it also helped me visualize global warming in a more literal way than I ever have. I suddenly saw that there are fires everywhere, all around us all the time, but fires so wholly controlled that we no longer think of them as fire at all.

I drove back to my college town that night along the San Bernardino Freeway. The traffic was light and lulling. But there were fires burning in the engines of every vehicle I saw. The lights in our quiet town were themselves a serene combustion, waypoints along a nearly infinite electrical grid that is itself a kind of wire-drawn fire. I got home and saw the porch light burning, its filament kindling in the darkness. The dull-orange haze of night in Los Angeles was the transposed heat of millions of domesticated fires.

A picture came to mind—the familiar sight of a gas flare at the top of the refinery stack in Laurel, Mont., a wavering flame of unwanted gas lighting up the night. I remembered a passage from the journals of John Cheever—a paragraph from 1954 describing "the winter fires of New York burning like the ghats in Benares," the incinerating of mattresses, wooden crates, cardboard cartons, uptown and down.

5

It began to seem to me that we are a species of fire-starters, and that all of our imprisoned fires are just so many versions of **YET ANOTHER COOK-FIRE** on the edge of night in a land where fuel has grown scarce from all the cook-fires of all the people.

I thought about this sudden vision for a couple of days. At first, it seemed almost overwhelming. I tried to picture all the combustions that are essential to the human ways of life in all their global diversity. I wondered what Earth would look like from our neighborhood in space if we could

STRATEGIES: SYMBOLISM

In calling up the image of a cook-fire in a land where fuel is scarce, Klinkenborg seems to be establishing a symbol for global warming: the numerous cook-fires that deplete the area where they are burned symbolize the worldwide combustion of many different fuels by humans that are contributing to global climate change. Interestingly, the image of a cook-fire is usually a positive one; cook-fires heat our food and give us light and warmth in the outdoors or the wilderness. Writers will sometimes establish a symbol to help reinforce or convey a main idea or point. What might Klinkenborg wish to suggest by choosing as a symbol for global warming an image that is not necessarily negative?

see all our incandescences, in all their forms, glowing at once. There would be only a faint corona of anthropogenic combustion, but it would be more than enough to have begun overwhelming the atmosphere, which is, after all, such a thin, faint halo around this planet.

The image of the cook-fire kept coming back to mind—the cook-fires I saw burning last June in a village in Tanzania, where every day the problem of fuel presented itself all over again. Sooner or later a wildfire burns itself out for lack of fuel. The question, I suppose, is whether our species will do the same.

We will see what the summer brings in the way of wildfires in Southern California—and, still worse, what October brings when the winds really begin to stir. The drought that afflicts the region probably has nothing to do with global warming. It may simply be part of the natural pattern of wet and dry cycles in the Southwest. If the hills do go up in smoke, they will add their carbon load to the atmosphere, and it will perhaps crystallize in our minds the effect of all our more domesticated flames. But, eventually, the wildfires will die down, and life will return to normal and that momentary vision will subside.

Understanding the Text

1. How does the sight of a wildfire in California relate to global warming, according to Klinkenborg?

2. What does Klinkenborg mean when he writes that "there are fires everywhere, all around us all the time, but fires so wholly controlled that we no longer think of them as fire at all"? What fires is he referring to here? Why are they important, in his view? Do you think he's right? Why or why not?

3. What is the "momentary vision" that Klinkenborg refers to in the final sentence of his essay? Why is this vision "momentary"? What does this vi-sion suggest about the impact humans have on the earth? Do you think Klinkenborg's use of the term "momentary" here is meant as a comment on humans? Explain.

Exploring the Issues

1. In a sense, this essay is a meditation on the environmental consequences of human living that is sparked by the sight of a wildfire, which Klinkenborg sees from the window of an airplane. In this regard, the essay is one of many examples of writers finding insight or meaning in a common sight or an unusual event. How effectively do you think Klinkenborg uses the sight of the wildfire to convey his insight to us about the situation humans face in the world?

2. The last paragraph of this essay seems ambivalent about the future of the human race. On the one hand he suggests that the drought causing the fires he observes "probably has nothing to do with global warming"; on the other hand, he suggests that the wildfires may contribute to global warming and help us under-stand "the effect of our more domesticated flames." But his last sentence seems fatalistic; in other words, it seems to suggest that once the wild-fires are out, we will pay no more attention to the problem. What point do you think Klinkenborg intends to convey with his ending? Is he fatalistic about the fate of humans in the face of global warming? Or does he see hope for the future? Explain, citing specific passages from the essay to support your answer.

3. Throughout this short essay, Klinkenborg includes careful descriptions of the sights he sees in California and sights he has seen on previous trips to other parts of the world. What do you think is the effect of these descriptions? What ideas do you think Klinkenborg conveys through these descriptions? How effective do you think his descriptions are in this essay? Explain, citing specific descriptions to support your answer.

Entering the Conversations

1. Write an essay in which you describe the "fires" (as Klinkenborg uses that term in his essay) that you burn in your daily life. In your essay, describe those fires and examine their consequences. Draw conclusions about the impact of your own "fires" on your community and the earth.

Alternatively, create a visual representation, such as a photo essay or a web page,

that describes the "fires" you burn in your life.

2. Review Question 2 under "Exploring the Issues." Then write a conventional academic essay in which you offer your interpretation of the ending of Klinkenborg's essay.

3. Share the essays you wrote for Question 2 in a group of classmates. Compare your respective interpretations of Klinkenborg's essay and identify key points of agreement or disagreement. Identify as well each group member's reasons for his or her interpretation. Then, examine the implications of your discussion of Klinkenborg's essay. What might your discussion suggest about how we read and make sense of a piece of writing? What might it suggest about the factors that influence how individual readers make sense of an essay?

 INFOTRAC

4. In recent years, wildfires, especially in the western United States, have been an issue of concern and controversy. Some people believe they are a symptom of global warming; some believe they result from poor forest man-

agement policies. Using InfoTrac and any other appropriate resources, investigate the issue of wildfires in the United States. Find out whether such fires have increased in recent years and try to learn why. Explore the controversies over how to manage forests and how (and whether) to fight such fires. Look into the claims that wildfires somehow relate to global warming. Then write a report on what you learned from your research. Draw your own conclusions about the significance of these fires.

5. Write an essay in which you describe an experience that somehow involved fire.

6. Klinkenborg is a white man who, presumably, lives a mainstream American lifestyle. Rewrite his essay from a different social, cultural, ethnic, or racial background. For example, rewrite his essay from the perspective of someone living in a low-income urban neighborhood or an isolated, poor rural area. Or rewrite it from a racial perspective. Use your own identity or adopt a different identity for the purposes of this assignment.

Extending the Conversations

1. Select a resource, such as food, energy, or water. Drawing on several of the readings in this chapter as well as your own experience, write an essay in which you carefully examine the way that resource is used in contemporary society. Discuss some of the social, economic, political, or environmental issues associated with that resource. Try to examine recent developments that might affect how that resource is used.

2. Identify what you consider an important theme that runs through several of the readings in this chapter and write an essay intended for a specific audience about that theme. Draw on the readings you've selected to support your main point.

3. Select several essays in this chapter and examine them from the perspective of race, class, gender, culture, or some other important factor. Write an essay in which you present your analysis. For example, you might select three or four essays that address issues related to food and examine those essays in terms of gender. In what ways might gender be an issue for these writers? How might gender figure into the argument or analysis in the essay? To what extent do the essays seem to reflect biases or problematic attitudes about gender? If the author does not seem to consider gender, how should the author have addressed gender as part of the issue he or she wrote about? In your essay, try to address such questions.

4. Identify an issue in this chapter about which you feel strongly and about which you disagree with one or more of the authors whose essays are included here. Write an essay in which you present your view of your selected issue, drawing from any appropriate essays in the chapter.

5. Visit the web sites of organizations devoted to issues somehow related to our use of resources. For example, you might visit the sites of environmental groups concerned about the loss of the rain forest or the damage to water resources. Examine how the sites you've selected present the issue. Examine the messages they try to convey and the way they present their own position and the positions of others on that issue. Look at the strategies they seem to use to persuade visitors about the validity of their position. Write an essay in which you present your analysis. Discuss the ideas and messages conveyed by the sites you visited about the resource-related issue you have selected. Draw your own conclusions about what these sites might suggest about current attitudes regarding our uses of resources.

6. Using appropriate computer software or conventional pencil and paper, design a home that reflects your beliefs about how we should use resources. Include some explanation of the specific features of your design and how they reflect your beliefs about how to live responsibly.

7. Drawing on several of the essays in this chapter and any other relevant resources, create a pamphlet, web site, PowerPoint presentation, video, or another appropriate kind of document for a specific audience intended to educate that audience about our uses of specific resources and concerns you may have about those uses of resources.

Alexis Rockman, *The Farm,* 2000

Leo Koenig Inc., New York

8. Alexis Rockman, the artist who created the image on page 671, writes that her artworks are "information-rich depictions of how our culture perceives and interacts with plants and animals, and the role culture plays in influencing the direction of natural history." What messages do you think this work conveys about how American culture perceives plants and animals? Write an essay in which you answer that question. Draw on any appropriate readings in this chapter to develop your ideas about this piece of art. Alternatively, find another work of art that carries messages about our relationship to important resources and write an essay in which you discuss those messages.

9. The following images all have something to do with resources. Some of them send obvious messages about how we use resources; in others, the messages are more subtle. Select several of these images (or others you may have found) and write an essay in which you discuss the messages they convey about using resources. Alternatively, create an image of your own (for example, a photo, a sketch, a painting) that conveys a message about using resources.

10. In the popular film *The Matrix* (1999), the main character Neo (played by actor Keanu Reeves) learns that the world was dramatically altered by a war between human beings and machines. One result of that war was the destruction of Earth's atmosphere. In a sense, this film can be interpreted as conveying certain messages about how humans use resources. Select one or more popular films that you think make some kind of statement about our uses of resources and our responsibility (or lack of) for using resources. Write an essay in which you discuss the messages those films convey.

How can you help protect the prairie and the penguin?

Simple. Visit www.earthshare.org and learn how the world's leading environmental groups are working together under one name. And how easy it is for you to help protect the prairies and the penguins and the planet.

www.earthshare.org

One environment. One simple way to care for it.   Earth Share

© Earth Share

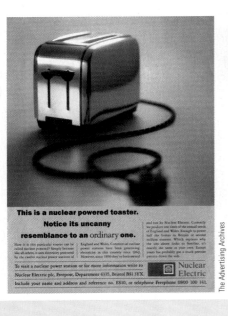

This is a nuclear powered toaster.
Notice its uncanny
resemblance to an ordinary **one.**

Nuclear Electric

The Advertising Archives

Less cars, more world. **Drivers wanted.**®

www.adbusters.org

U. S. 388. New York City, Flatiron Building.

Chapter 12 Change

FEW YEARS AGO, A LARGE INVESTMENT COMPANY RAN A TELEVISION ADVERTISING CAMPAIGN TO PROMOTE ITS RETIREMENT PLANNING SERVICES. THE POINT WAS TO ENCOURAGE POTENTIAL CUSTOMERS TO HIRE THE COMPANY TO HELP PLAN FOR RETIREMENT. THE MESSAGE WAS THAT YOU HAVE TO BE READY FOR ANYTHING BECAUSE YOU never know what might happen. The tag line was, "In life, the only constant is change." As a writer, I enjoyed the paradoxical idea that change is a constant (this kind of paradoxical expression is called an *oxymoron*). But that tag line expresses a profound idea that has been explored for centuries by philosophers, theologians, poets, and even scientists: the idea of change over time.

At first glance, this idea of inevitable change seems simple and commonsensical. Of course things change. Everything changes. Even seemingly permanent things like mountains or oceans

> Everything changes. Even seemingly permanent things like mountains or oceans change over time.

change over time. And our efforts to defeat time, to create permanence or to seek immortality, are futile. That's the message of the famous poem "Ozymandias" (1818) by the great British poet Percy Bysshe Shelley (1792–1822):

> I met a traveller from an antique land,
> Who said—"Two vast and trunkless legs of
>   stone
> Stand in the desert. . . . Near them, on the
>   sand,
> Half sunk a shattered visage lies, whose
>   frown,
> And wrinkled lip, and sneer of cold com-
>   mand,
> Tell that its sculptor well those passions
>   read
> Which yet survive, stamped on this lifeless
>   things,
> The hand that mocked them, and the
>   heart that fed;

And on the pedestal, these words appear:
> My name is Ozymandias, King of Kings,
> Look on my Works, ye Mighty, and despair!
> Nothing beside remains. Round the decay
> Of that colossal Wreck, boundless and bare
> The lone and level sands stretch far away."

Shelley's poem is about the futility and foolishness of our efforts to resist time and the inevitable changes its passage brings; it is also about the deep human desire not only to be recognized and even honored, as reflected in the monument of himself that King Ozymandias had sculpted, but also to feel that our lives have some permanent meaning that transcends time. Shelley's poem gives voice to this need and perhaps reflects how much humans struggle to deal with change.

There was a more recent and humorous television commercial in early 2005 that speaks to this same struggle—an ad for a special promotion by a national pizza restaurant chain by which customers could order three different kinds of pizza for the same price. In the commercial, a pizza deliveryman brings three pizzas to the home of a customer, who announces triumphantly that the special promotion allows him to order any kind of pizzas he wants. When his wife reminds him that despite all the choices he has, he ordered three pepperoni pizzas, the man says dejectedly, "I fear change." Obviously, the commercial is poking fun at a person who, given many different choices, chooses the same old pepperoni pizza. But the fear of change seems to be widely shared. You can see it in the way people follow the same daily routines for years, maybe even for their entire lives. You see it in the way various kinds of reform efforts, such as school reform or Social Security reform, make many people nervous. You see it in the nostalgia that many people feel for the past. And perhaps you see it in rituals that focus on change—rituals like graduation or wedding ceremonies, in which hope and happiness mix with some sadness and anxiety about the uncertainties that lie ahead.

Even science has tried to understand the phenomenon of change. The last three lines of Shelley's poem "Ozymandias" depict an image of the desert as all that remains of Ozymandias's kingdom, suggesting that only Nature itself survives change. Astronomers and physicists have learned how the universe itself is always changing; indeed, Albert Einstein's theory of relativity, one of the most important scientific developments in history, explains that time itself is not constant but can change in relationship to space.

If all this seems abstract, the readings in this chapter may make it more concrete. These readings explore some of the many ways in which we confront change in our lives. From technological developments, such as cell phones and computers, that have dramatically changed the way we communicate and live together, to growing up, to medical discoveries that may change our lives, to global climate change—these readings highlight the kinds of changes that can profoundly shape our lives. They also illuminate the challenges that change

> When his wife reminds him that despite all the choices he has, he ordered three pepperoni pizzas, the man says dejectedly, "I fear change."

presents. How we face those challenges is perhaps one of the most important questions we must answer, individually and together. The varied readings in this chapter may help you appreciate how writers have explored these challenges—and how writing itself is one of the most important ways that humans have tried to meet those challenges.

COMING OF AGE

IF YOU'RE READING THIS BOOK FOR A COLLEGE CLASS, YOU PROBABLY HAVE EXPERIENCED A HIGH SCHOOL GRADUATION CEREMONY—MOST LIKELY YOUR OWN. IF EVER THERE WAS A RITUAL FOR COMING OF AGE, HIGH SCHOOL GRADUATION IS IT. IT MARKS A KIND OF UNOFFICIAL END TO CHILDHOOD AND ADOLESCENCE AND THE BEGINNING OF ADULTHOOD. FOR MOST STUDENTS, HIGH SCHOOL graduation signals the biggest change in their lives up to that point. Whereas high school students are usually given some latitude for "being kids," high school *graduates* are treated as adults and expected to act accordingly. As you have probably discovered, college students are also expected to act like adults, and in my experience, they mostly do. They come to college knowing that it's fundamentally different from high school, and they, too, are now different. They are coming of age.

You've probably heard that phrase before, maybe even in one of the speeches at your high school graduation ceremony. But what does it mean, exactly? For one thing, it means looking at yourself and your responsibilities differently. And very often it means getting advice on how to do that. I'm sure you got some of that advice at your high school graduation: advice on how to work toward your goals, how to go confidently into the future, to meet difficult challenges and learn from them, to appreciate the help you received from your teachers and parents, to become a responsible citizen, to make the world a better place. But I think most of us quickly realize that such advice ends up being pretty useless. I've heard some very good commencement speeches over the years, but I suspect they had almost no effect on the students sitting in the audience. That's partly because it's hard to listen carefully to those somber, serious speeches in all the joy and excitement of graduation day. But I think it's also because advice about coming of age can never really make much sense to the person receiving the advice until that person experiences things for himself or herself. I remember my father giving me advice about being a parent after my first child was born, but it wasn't until years later, when I was in the midst of the difficult challenges of parenting, that I understood what he meant. His advice was well-intentioned, like the advice given in commencement speeches, but I had to learn for myself, just as every high school graduate will have to figure out what it means to come of age.

The essays in this cluster offer three different perspectives on what it means to come of age. They focus on some of the changes that young people face as they make the transition from adolescence to adulthood. Lisa Belkin, for example, tells us about a speech she gave at a school near her home and wonders whether the schoolgirls in her audience have been getting the wrong kind of advice from their mothers about what it means to be a woman today. High school student Zara Kessler describes her ambivalent feelings as she moves on from the dance classes that had been so central to her young life. And Amy Goldwasser shares her faith that young people today will do what young people have always done: find a way through change. All these writers appreciate the complexities of coming of age; they also acknowledge that each of us must confront those complexities for ourselves. I hope these essays will help you make sense of that process as you examine your own coming of age.

Everywhere you look in American culture, you encounter some version of the idea that you can have it all if only you work hard enough. Television commercials about sports drinks tell you that hard work results in winning. The U.S. military invites you to "be all you can be." Teachers tell us that diligence and dedication in school will pay off with a better

Sharing Practical Truths, in Child-Sized Measures

education, a better job, and a better life. This idea of hard work providing rewards seems to be at the very heart of American culture itself. And it seems to make sense, for how can you succeed if you don't work hard? Conversely, the prospect of having it all seems to drive so many Americans to work hard. Studies show that Americans work more (and take fewer vacations) than workers in just about every other developed nation. Maybe that's because so many Americans are trying to have it all.

If so, writer Lisa Belkin has some advice: not so fast. She believes that teaching our children that hard work will always pay off is misleading and maybe even destructive because it's not the whole story. The connection between hard work and having it all is much more complicated, especially for girls who

LISA BELKIN

I RECENTLY HAD A CHANCE TO SPEAK **to a cafeteria full of high** school girls at the Lincoln School in Providence, R.I. Each had been asked to invite a woman she admires, and most brought their moms, making it the first time I spoke to an audience of mothers and daughters.

As I talked about life and work, and how some days the balancing act doesn't go very well, the mothers nodded knowingly while the students were polite, but looked confused.

The evening resonates for me as companies across the country prepare to participate in Take Our Children to Work Day on Thursday. At some offices, there will be just a handful of children, sitting by their parents' side, watching them go through a quasi-typical day. At others, there will be thousands, and they will participate in elaborate programs paid out of the corporate budget.

want to have both careers and families. Belkin highlights the special challenges facing girls as they become women and take their places in the sometimes-conflicting worlds of work and family. And she worries that the well-intentioned advice we give them may cause more problems for them. Belkin believes that we can better prepare young people—especially girls—for adulthood if we stop teaching them that hard work is always the answer. Her essay may complicate your own views about hard work, your future, and having it all.

Lisa Belkin is a columnist for the New York Times, *in which this essay was published in 2007, and the author of* Life's Work: Confessions of an Unbalanced Mom *(2002), a memoir about her own efforts to balance work and family.* ◪

STRATEGIES: ESTABLISHING RHETORICAL CONTEXT
In the first five paragraphs of this essay, Belkin establishes the context for her writing in several ways. First, she uses an anecdote about giving a talk at the Lincoln School (which is an independent college preparatory school for girls in kindergarten through Grade 12). That anecdote not only helps introduce her main point but it also provides a vivid scene that might spark her readers' curiosity. Second, Belkin refers (in par. 3) to "Take Our Child to Work Day," a national event sponsored by the Take Our Daughters and Sons to Work Foundation. Both these events—her speech and the "Take Our Daughters and Sons to Work" day—provide the occasion for Belkin's essay. In other words, she provides her readers with reasons to read her essay. Giving readers a compelling reason for reading a piece of writing can be one of the most difficult challenges facing a writer. Belkin provides a useful example of how to meet that challenge.

STRATEGIES: PARAGRAPHING
Notice that paragraph 10 is made up of a single sentence. Sometimes, writers use paragraphing in this way to emphasize a point or call attention to an idea, as Belkin seems to do here. But the length of paragraphs can also be influenced by the intended audience and the form of the text. In this case, Belkin was writing a column for a newspaper. Conventional newspaper style calls for much shorter paragraphs than is typical of, say, essays for your English class or research papers in your economics class. It's important for writers to know the expectations for format, including paragraphing, for each writing task they do.

I wonder how many of these parents, however, have thought about exactly what they want their sons and daughters to learn about work.

After my talk at the Lincoln School, mothers came up to tell me that this was the first time they had ever thought to talk to their girls about the challenges of combining work and parenting. Do any of us think to have those talks?

When we talk to our children about sex, about alcohol and drugs, or about the dangers of the Internet, we give them limitations and warnings. But when it comes to the subject of work, we tell them that they can be whatever they aspire to be; that they should aim high, work hard and dream big.

What we rarely do is tell them how hard some days are. Or that along the road, they might have to compromise, or detour, or backtrack. To warn them would be to discourage them. Or so our thinking goes.

The morning after my speech I met with smaller groups of students in workshops, where I heard that many of them had learned quite a lot about their mothers during their rides home the night before.

One girl heard for the first time how her mother was still wistful over her choice not to go to medical school after she'd learned she was pregnant. Another mother described a recent itch to get back into the work force after a few years of being away, and the unfamiliar frustration of being seen by employers as too old.

How many of you, I asked, were regularly told by your mothers that you can be whatever you want to be? Every girl in the room raised her hand. Then I asked: "How many of your mothers have worked full time for most of your lives?" In each of two workshops, with about 25 girls each, only one or two hands went up.

THE MESSAGE: DO AS I SAY, NOT AS I HAVE BEEN ABLE TO DO.

We are telling our children only half the truth. We are doing this to both boys and girls—as it happens, the Lincoln School is girls only—and we are leaving them ill-prepared.

Of course we want to tell them that they can achieve all they can envision. But we also need to tell them that those visions may change color and scope along the way. Of course we want to tell them that hard work will pave their way. But we must also warn them that sometimes it won't be enough, and that they will have to choose, because the whole of work and the whole of life rarely fit neatly into every working day.

There is the risk that this will discourage them, but the alternative, I think, is worse. Thinking that we could do it all, then crashing headlong into the wall of "but not at the same time" is part of the reason that so many women have left the work force in frustration in recent years.

15 Thinking that hard work will get them anywhere is what led so many to believe that re-entry would be much easier than it is proving to be.

In her new book, *THE FEMININE MISTAKE,* Leslie Bennetts writes about the destructive assumption that women can leave their jobs without financial risk. Unprepared for the imperfections of the workplace and the "second shift" at home, they assume that their inability to balance is their own failure. So they leave, trusting that their husbands will stay alive and faithful, and that the workplace will remain eager for their return.

Will an understanding that Mom regularly drops the ball give them permission to do so, too? Will frank talk about the bad days provide inoculation against them? Will eyes open to the faults of an inflexible workplace make them more likely to insist on change?

Maybe not. But as parents we must hope that there are more answers for them than there were for us, just as we had more than our mothers. And the only way to find those answers is to teach our children—early and often—how to ask the questions.

CONVERSATIONS: WOMEN AND WORK

Here, Belkin refers to *The Feminine Mistake* (2007) by Leslie Bennetts. Bennetts's book is part of a continuing conversation about the role of women in American society. According to the U.S. Census, only 44% of women age 16 or older were part of the workforce in 1973, as compared with 78% of men; today, approximately 60% of women age 16 or older participate in the workforce, as compared with 73% of men. As more and more women are working outside the home, the debate about the role of women in the workplace and the home has intensified. As Belkin indicates here, Bennetts examines the risks facing women who leave their jobs to raise families. Bennetts's book might be seen as a response to *The Feminine Mystique* (1963), a famous and influential book by Betty Friedan (1921–2006), in which Friedan argued that women can have both family and career. Belkin's essay joins this debate. Your response to it will be shaped by your own knowledge of the debate as well as your beliefs about gender and work.

Understanding the Text

1. Why does Belkin believe it is important to talk to young girls about the challenges of combining work and parenting? What problems does she see with the typical advice girls receive about those challenges?

2. What is the reality facing women who try to balance family and work, according to Belkin? In what sense are adults leaving girls ill-prepared for that reality, in her view? Do you think she's right? Why or why not?

3. What solutions does Belkin offer to the problems she describes in this essay? Do you find these solutions adequate? Do you think they will help young girls come of age today? Explain.

Exploring the Issues

1. Examine Belkin's criticisms of the idea of the value of hard work (see par. 15). On what basis does she believe that common views about the value of hard work are sometimes misleading and even destructive? Do you agree with her? Why or why not?

2. Belkin suggests in this essay that changes in American society have created new challenges for young girls as they come of age. What kinds of changes have contributed to these challenges? How is the world that young women enter today different from the world of their mothers or grandmothers? Do you think it is more difficult for young women to come of age today? Explain. What insights do you think Belkin offers about coming of age in general?

3. How would you describe Belkin's writing style in this essay? What features of her prose contribute to her style? Do you find her writing style effective? Why or why not? Do you think it is appropriate for her intended audience and her subject matter? Explain.

Entering the Conversations

1. Write an essay offering advice to young girls or boys about growing up and entering the adult world today. Your essay should present your own views about the challenges of pursuing your goals or dreams as an adult.

2. Write an essay about an experience that taught you something important about growing up and entering the adult world.

3. In the final paragraph of her essay, Belkin writes that "as parents we must hope that there are more answers for [our children] than there were for us, just as we had more than our mothers. And the only way to find those answers is to teach our children—early and often—how to ask the questions." Write an essay exploring this idea of teaching our children to ask questions. Alternatively, create a web site or other kind of multimedia document intended for girls or boys (or both) to help them ask what you believe are the questions they should learn to ask about coming of age.

4. Interview several women of different ages about their experiences in coming of age, focusing especially on entering the workplace and raising a family. Listen to their stories and try to get a sense of the challenges they faced in going to work, raising a family, and learning to be an adult; ask them for the advice they would give girls who are coming of age today. Then, write a report in which you describe the women you interviewed and present what you learned from them about the challenges facing women as they come of age. Draw conclusions about these challenges and how they may have changed over time. (If appropriate, draw on Belkin's essay and any other relevant essay in this textbook.)

5. On the basis of the work you did for Question 4, write an essay telling the story of one of the women you interviewed. Your essay should tell her story of coming of age and convey the challenges she faced and some of the lessons she learned. Alternatively, create a multimedia document, such as a PowerPoint presentation or web site, in which you tell that woman's story of coming of age.

6. Read *The Feminine Mystique* by Betty Friedan, *The Feminine Mistake* by Leslie Bennetts, or another book about women and work and write a review of that book, evaluating the author's perspective and her advice for women today.

One summer when my children were very young, I signed them up for swimming lessons. Their instructor was a pleasant young man who had just graduated from high school and was earning some extra money for college. In fact, he was good enough as a high school swimmer to have earned an athletic scholarship to the college he would

One Last Day

be attending in a few months. I was impressed. I knew how much hard work, time, and commitment were required to excel at swimming: early-morning workouts, long practices after school, weekend swim meets, summer training. But when I told him that, he surprised me by telling me that he had decided to turn down the scholarship. When I asked why, he told me that because of swimming, he had missed so many things in high school, and he just didn't want to miss out in college.

GLOSS: TEMPS DE FLECHE, ENTRECHAT SIX, AND ROND DE JAMBE

These terms refer to specific moves in ballet dancing. *Temps de fleche* is a jump in which the dancer transfers weight from one foot to the other. In *entrechat,* the dancer jumps into the air and rapidly crosses her legs before landing; *six* refers to the number of times the dancer's legs cross and uncross while in the air. In *rond de jambe,* the dancer makes a circular motion with one leg.

ZARA KESSLER

I heatedly throw my dance bag into the corner, allowing a pair of *pointe* shoes to spill out, and plop down on the hard gray floor to watch the five-hour-long *Sleeping Beauty* rehearsal. One question resounds in my head, pounding like a never-ending hammer: Why am I here? The SAT book perched halfway between my bag and the floor refuses to let me forget the painful practice test that I took this morning, the X after X after X that filled my answer sheet as I checked for the correct responses. I have vocabulary to learn, formulas to memorize, and grammar rules to review. And that is not to mention my schoolwork—essays, math problems, outlines that I want to finish weeks in advance—that awaits me at home.

So, why am I here? The ballet mistress forced me to come. She snatched my part away from me because I tried to be a **NORMAL PERSON,** attempted to spend a week in a world where *TEMPS DE FLECHE,* *ENTRECHAT SIX,* and *ROND DE JAMBE* are meaningless phrases. I went away to Portugal for the holidays with my family and returned to find the glittering costume, the heavy jewelry and the character shoes replaced with one clunky word: understudy. As much as I struggle to restrain the thoughts from entering my head, ruminations that I

"ONE LAST DAY," BY ZARA KESSLER, FROM BEST TEEN WRITING OF 2007, EDITED BY JUSTIN BELTZ. ALLIANCE FOR YOUNG ARTISTS AND WRITERS, INC.

I imagine that his decision must have been difficult because he had worked so hard as a swimmer and had earned a scholarship. Zara Kessler would understand. In the following essay, she tells the story of a similar decision that she made as a young woman: the decision to give up her dream of becoming a world-class ballet dancer. Kessler reveals that, despite her love of dance, the time and hard work she had to devote to dancing diverted her from other commitments in her life, including her desire to succeed in school. Her struggle to decide what to dedicate herself to is not an easy one, but in many ways it is typical: most young people have to make tough decisions about what commitments they should make as they come of age. I suspect that Kessler's struggle will sound familiar to you.

Zara Kessler wrote this essay when she was a sixteen-year-old student at the Trinity School, a private school in New York City. It was published in The Best Teen Writing of 2007 *(2007).* ▣

CONVERSATIONS: A NORMAL TEEN

In paragraph 2, Kessler describes her frustration at trying to be "a normal person" as she struggles to keep up with her schoolwork, prepare for the SATs, and practice dancing. In a sense, Kessler is joining a conversation in modern American society about what a "normal" childhood and adolescence should be. As Kessler demonstrates in her essay, pressures to excel in school and to be involved in activities like dance can force students to make difficult choices and prevent them from enjoying what adults sometimes tell them are the best times of their lives. Some critics have argued that high school students should spend less time trying to enhance their college applications and more time just being kids. Kessler's essay might be seen as one example of the problems created by the pressures teens face today as they come of age.

never could have imagined having two or three years ago, I cannot help feeling that this may not be the right place for me, that perhaps I am not meant to be a dancer. It's something that my actions have been telling me for months but that I have never let enter my head for fear that they might be correct. I arrive at ballet class with no time to warm up because I am finishing a math assignment that isn't due for a week. I edit and re-edit and re-edit even the smallest English paper rather than sew the *pointe* shoes that I desperately need to wear the next day. The other girls, the students who will wear the gowns and the jewels along with the company members, they're not like me. They don't care about school or family; they don't want to go on vacation, to see the world. They are perfectly content with lives that are one-hundred-percent saturated with ballet.

Yet I stay because I can see the ballet mistress gazing at me out of the corner of her eye and because no matter how much my allegiance to school and to my family draw me outside the studio's mirrored walls, there is still one last glimmer of enjoyment that I may be able to get from watching a Manhattan Ballet Company rehearsal.

The director of the company, David Thomson, enters, and a chill goes down my spine as his sharp, blue Russian eyes, resting under a handsome mane of curly blonde-gray hair, scour over the row of sitting ballerinas. He harshly claps his hands together and without a word, the dancers take their places around the studio. Judging from their attire—ripped tights, bright blue bike shorts, leotards with massive holes gracing the sides, hair not controlled in buns but flying everywhere—one would never believe that they are professionals, but as they begin to leap and twirl around the studio, their sharp leg movements, precise footwork, and delicate arms make the fact incontrovertible.

Henry West, playing the king, enters the scene   5
and performs a small pantomime. David immediately smacks his hands together, signaling someone to halt the music. He exclaims in his refined accent, "You are the king. You cannot look like some man running to catch the bus. You are getting the world's attention; you are the king!" He rushes to the center of the studio and hilariously mimics what Henry did and then proceeds to perform what he desires: grand majestic movements and stately facial expressions. Henry repeats the opening scene, imitating each of David's corrections, and the effect is spectacular, regal, enough to make me feel that I am one of his subjects. Within the next thirty minutes, David transforms into a young maiden, a nervous messenger, a fairy, and a page, each of his impressions funnier than the next, each of his changes immensely improving the

scene. As I sit, laughing in enjoyment, I realize that David is not the menacing, villainous, omnipotent director as I have always pictured him. Behind the sharp gaze, he is an affable, approachable boss with a keen sense for detail, an impeccable understanding of what will please an audience, and an innate ability to articulate his expertise.

Jennifer Winger, playing the lead role of Aurora, begins the Rose Adagio, famed throughout the dance world as one of the most strenuous sections of a ballet ever choreographed. Yet, you would never be able to tell that from **JENNY'S MOVEMENTS**. The room becomes silent, everyone left breathless, gazing at Jenny's supple legs and fluid arms. I feel the urge to jump into her shiny pink *pointe* shoes, to have my time to shine amidst a world of observers, to move with the poise that Jenny moves with. She perches in attitude, and one-by-one, four suitors dexterously partner her. I hold my breath as she reaches her final balance, the most challenging component of the arduous section. She removes her hand from the man's shoulder and balances . . . and balances . . . and balances; faces around the room light up as Jenny remains poised in position. When she finally gently rolls down through her *pointe* shoe, the studio bursts into thunderous applause. No longer concerned with recalling the definitions of cantankerous and erudite, I beat my hands together, the tears welling up in my eyes.

Everyone is astounded; words praising Jenny dart like arrows through the large studio. But the action is far from over; four men, playing bugs, pull Melly Baron, a friend of mine, a company member, and today, the nefarious **CARABOSSE,** into the studio on a glittering black cart. Melly's new to the part, and I observe the nerves swarming around her willowy body as the cart flies past David's gaze. Yet, as soon as she dismounts and begins her wicked pantomime, any apprehension vanishes. Melly plunges into the dramatic role, suspending all chatter with her twisting and contorting her hands, a depiction of the spell that she will place on Aurora, and her silent yet deceitful laugh, engrossing her whole body and causing goosebumps to spring up on my arms. Before I know it, Melly is back on her cart and quickly exiting the scene, leaving behind a smiling David, obviously pleased by her striking portrayal of the role.

After a few more minutes of dancing fairies and maidens, the ballet mistress perceives the growing restlessness in the room and loudly announces, "Everybody take ten." I sigh, overjoyed finally to be given the opportunity to move about the studio, even if only walking. I stroll around, gossip with a few of my classmates, and then return to my humble abode, my spot on the floor, and settle down again to observe the groups of beautiful blonde girls with big blue eyes and handsome

STRATEGIES: DESCRIPTION

In this passage, Kessler offers a detailed description of the performance of one of the dancers in the studio. Notice that she describes the dancer's many movements and poses to convey a sense of her movement and the concentration of the audience on those movements. More than just a description of the scene Kessler witnessed, this passage also conveys a vivid sense of what appeals to Kessler about dancing; it presents an image of what she has worked so hard to do, and it helps readers who are unfamiliar with ballet appreciate its appeal. Note, too, that Kessler tells her story in the present tense, which helps give us a sense of immediacy as we read this scene.

GLOSS: CARABOSSE

Carabosse refers to a wicked fairy in traditional fairy tales, especially "Sleeping Beauty." She is one of the characters in the classic ballet *Sleeping Beauty* by the Russian composer Pyotr Tchaikovsky (1840–1893), as is Aurora, who is mentioned in paragraph 6.

brown-haired young men standing around chatting and erupting in laughter. Sophie and Tess, company members crouched a few feet away, discuss the intricacies of their New Year's Eve plans: "I'll come over to your place tonight at seven, and we can get ready and then we can go to his house at like nine thirty or ten. Did I tell you that I got that dress, you know the green one that we saw in the window at Interscoop? It was on a huge sale. I definitely have to wear it tonight. But what shoes? Hmm . . ."

Joey and Masa, two short men with bandanas tied around their long locks, have more practical concerns: "Did you see my jumps and turns? Were they good? . . . Yeah, they looked good. . . . That's a relief. I hope David liked them . . ." The camaraderie, the normalcy of these focused, gifted artists surprises me, and I burn to jump up and tell Sophie that I saw the green dress in the window, and it would look stunning with her complexion, to inform Joey that I noticed David smiling as he pirouetted across the studio. But I am not part of their world, not a member of the company, not a distinguished dancer.

10   The curtain closes on the break, and the next dance to be practiced is a huge waltz containing a flock of small children in addition to virtually all of the members of the *corps de ballet.* As I watch tiny girls, their long blonde curls twisted into French braids, waltz around the studio clutching strings of flowers, nostalgia courses through my body, memories of those former days when I too clung to a garland and danced in the spotlight as a miniscule villager. Yet more than the children, more than the handsome men, the dancers that stand out to me the most are the fresh crop of apprentices nervously twirling about the studio. A few months ago, they were students just like me, and now they are there, dancing amidst the *corps de ballet,* the printer warming to produce their contracts. Erin was in my class last year; we stood next to each other at the barre. I secretly shunned her because she did not go to school; she got to ballet hours before our classes began so that she could stretch, warm up, and prepare for the lesson, while I was left to dash in from school with thirty seconds to spare, barely enough time to tie my *pointe* shoe ribbons. Yet I prided myself with the knowledge that Erin wouldn't know the difference between a linear or exponential function, between an element and a mixture. At 17, lectures, notecards, and college applications were the furthest things from her mind. But the truth is that no one in this studio cares that I know the definition of "garrulous," and she does not; that if someone ran into the room with a complex equation, I could solve it in about half the time that Erin could. And I yearn to be like Erin, to forget the stress of Virgil and the quadratic formula, to twirl and leap across a stage. Because look at her now, she is waltzing along with the professionals, she is part of the magic, and I am shunned in the corner, the student understudy.

For the next half an hour, I sit in a trance, gazing at one long-legged beauty after another gracefully float across the studio or soar up to almost graze the double-height ceilings. It's as though I am in a dream; the hard, grueling work, the sweat, the elegance, and the grace combine before my eyes like the colors in a kaleidoscope shifting into place. "You may leave now. The court couples are finished," the ballet mistress nudges, galvanizing me from my reverie. I stand up and slowly tiptoe out of the studio, looking back over my shoulder, still gazing at the scene, never wanting to return to reality. We're done an hour early. This morning that news would have brought a huge grin to my face; I can go home and edit my papers or pour over the SAT website. But now all I want to do is run back into the studio, stay there until the magic is over, sleep there, wake up tomorrow and watch again. I don't want to learn how to graph a sine curve; I want to study each step of the Rose Adagio.

But I must leave, go out into the December air; the bitter cold trying its hardest to ship me back to reality. Yet my absorption in the galaxy of ballet has not left me completely; the drug still circulates in my veins. I return home and again fling my bag off my shoulder. This time the SAT book falls out completely, but I don't pick it up. I read the Manhattan Ballet Newsletter instead. I browse around the Manhattan Ballet Company web site, reading Jenny and Sophie and Melly's bios. I discover that there is a movie on television tonight about the Company's trip to Russia and sit wide-eyed, watching the dancers pirouette across the Maryinsky stage, gazing at them laughing while sightseeing. When the film finishes, I want more; I am addicted. I find the documentary about the Manhattan Ballet Company's *Nutcracker* that my parents had bought me but that I had left to grow dusty under a stack of vocabulary flashcards and slip it into my computer. I sit enthralled, exhilarated by the endless footage of rehearsals and performances. Ten minutes before midnight, I remember from amidst my fervor that it is New Year's Eve. I watch the ball drop, see the fireworks exploding outside my window, yet quickly return to the movie, yearning to hear the end of an interview with a famous ballerina, seeking to discover all of the secrets of a trade that this morning I was on the road out of.

But it's a new year, and new thoughts are entering my head, new ruminations telling me that I am not ready to give up all of this yet.

Understanding the Text

1. What is the main conflict or struggle that Kessler faces? What does this struggle reveal about her? What might her struggle suggest about the challenges of coming of age?

2. What is it about dancing that appeals to Kessler? Why does she feel that dancing may not be right for her? What do you think her decision to devote time to school and family—rather than to dedicating herself completely to dancing—reveals about her?

3. In what ways is Kessler different from the other girls her age who have become apprentices with the ballet? How does Kessler understand these differences? What does she believe they suggest about her? Do you think she's right? Why or why not?

Exploring the Issues

1. In some ways, the struggle that Kessler describes in this essay is typical of young people, who are often faced with choices about their different responsibilities and commitments. But in other ways, Kessler's challenges may not be so common. How typical do you think her situation is? To what extent does her struggle to balance school, family, and dance reflect her social and economic background? For example, do all teens have the opportunity to become dancers in the way that Kessler experienced? Explain. What might Kessler's situation suggest about the connection between social status and the challenges of coming of age?

2. What do you think Kessler means when she writes at the end of her essay that she is "not ready to give up all of this yet"? Has she changed her mind about staying involved in dancing? Explain. Do you think her final sentence is an effective ending for her essay? Why or why not?

3. Kessler wrote this essay when she was sixteen years old. Unlike almost all the other writers whose essays are included in this textbook, Kessler is not a professional writer. Yet she uses many of the same strategies professional writers use to make their writing effective. Evaluate Kessler's prose. How would you describe her writing style? What strengths or weaknesses do you see in

her writing? Are there features of her writing that suggest that she is inexperienced? Explain, citing specific passages from her essay to support your answer.

Entering the Conversations

1. Write an essay about a time when you made an important decision that was part of your own coming of age.

2. In a sense, Kessler's essay can be seen as her effort to find balance in her life among her many responsibilities and activities. Write an essay in which you present your own philosophy of how to find that balance as a young person today. Draw on Kessler's essay or any other relevant reading selections in this book.

INFOTRAC

3. As indicated in "Conversations: A Normal Teen" on page 682, a debate has emerged in recent years about what a "normal" childhood or adolescence should be. Using InfoTrac College Edition, your library, and the Internet, and drawing from your own experience, investigate this debate. Find out what experts say about the nature of childhood and adolescence and the challenges facing teens today. Try to identify the main arguments among experts in the debate. Also try to find information about how teens spend

their time today and how they feel about the pressures they face. (You might draw on your own experience or interview teens you know.) Then, write a report on the basis of your research. In your report, present your findings and draw conclusions about what it means to come of age today.

4. Several times in her essay, Kessler mentions preparing for the SAT, which most colleges and universities require students to take in order to apply for admission. (Most colleges will also accept the ACT, a similar test that is offered by a different company.) For most high school students who wish to attend college, the SAT or ACT is a rite of passage—another part of coming of age—and as Kessler shows, it creates pressure for many students. Write an essay about your experience with the SAT or ACT. In your essay, draw conclusions from your experience about the impact of that test on your life. (If you have not taken either test, talk to someone who has and focus your essay on his or her experience.)

5. Write an essay about an activity that has required you to make a significant commitment (as Kessler did with dancing). Describe your experience in a way that makes your commitment and investment clear, and discuss what you believe you learned from the experience. Also, try to convey the impact of that commitment on your life.

Complaints about youth by older generations are not only common but age-old. You can find them as far back in Western culture as Plato and Aristotle, and every generation since then has offered its own version of basic worries about the younger generation. It's worth asking why. Is there something about coming of age that inherently makes older people worry?

What's the Matter with Kids Today?

In the following essay, Amy Goldwasser offers her own un-equivocal answer to the question of what's wrong with kids today: nothing, really. Where other older adults see reason for concern about young people of today, Goldwasser sees cause for celebration and optimism. The technologies, such as the Internet, that others blame for what they believe are the failings of today's young people Goldwasser praises as wonderful opportunities of which kids today are taking full

---

STRATEGIES: USING PARENTHETICAL STATEMENTS
Writers sometimes use parenthetical statements to comment on another statement or idea or to make a kind of aside that is related to the main statement but not the focus of attention at that point in the essay. In the first sentence of her essay, Goldwasser includes such a parenthetical statement: "(land line!)." With this statement, she seems to be making an ironic comment on the phone survey she is referring to here. The statement also helps establish the voice and tone of her essay. Although such parenthetical statements are often inappropriate or unusual in formal academic writing, they can be used for several purposes in other kinds of writing, as Goldwasser's statement illustrates.

AMY GOLDWASSER

The other week was only the latest takedown of what has become a fashionable segment of the population to bash: the American teenager. A phone **(LAND LINE!)** survey of 1,200 17-year-olds, conducted by the research organization **COMMON CORE** and released Feb. 26, found our young people to be living in "stunning ignorance" of history and literature.

This furthered the report that the National Endowment for the Arts came out with at the end of 2007, lamenting "the diminished role of voluntary reading in American life," particularly among 13-to-17-year-olds, and **DORIS LESSING'S CONDEMNATION,** in her acceptance speech for the Nobel Prize in literature, of "a fragmenting culture" in which "young men and women . . . have read nothing, knowing only some specialty or other, for instance, computers."

Kids today—we're telling you!—don't read, don't write, don't care about anything farther in front of them than their iPods. The Internet, according to

"WHAT'S THE MATTER WITH KIDS TODAY?" BY AMY GOLDWASSER. *SALON MAGAZINE,* MARCH 14, 2008. REPRINTED BY PERMISSION OF *SALON MAGAZINE.*

advantage. She joins that never-ending discussion about youth and coming of age by pointing out how well kids today are adapting to the changing world they are inheriting. I suspect you will find her argument persuasive. Or maybe not. By this point in your life you have probably heard these debates and participated in them yourself, and you may have made up your own mind about whether people should worry about kids today. If so, Goldwasser would probably be pleased.

Amy Goldwasser is the editor of RED: The Next Generation of American Writers—Teenage Girls—On What Fires Up Their Lives Today *(2007). This essay appeared in* Salon.com, *an online magazine, in 2008.* ◘

CONVERSATIONS: COMMON CORE, DORIS LESSING, AND THE NEA REPORT ON AMERICANS' READING HABITS
In 2007, the National Endowment for the Arts (NEA) released a report titled *To Read or Not to Read: A Question of National Consequence,* which documented a decline in both the reading ability and the habit of regular reading among Americans. The report caused considerable controversy in the United States. Although critics pointed out various flaws in the report's data and conclusions, many educators, scholars, politicians, and experts shared the concern about the decline in reading described in the report. Among them was acclaimed novelist Doris Lessing, who received the Nobel Prize for Literature in 2007. As Goldwasser indicates in paragraph 2, Lessing used her Nobel Prize acceptance speech, which she delivered a few weeks after the NEA report was released, to criticize young people for their lack of reading. Lessing blamed the computer, television, and the Internet for the diminishing interest in reading among young people. Lessing's comments, the controversy sparked by the NEA report, and the report from Common Core, an organization that advocates a common core curriculum for all American high school students (which Goldwasser mentions in par. 1 and 10) are all part of an ongoing conversation about what young people should know and how they should learn.

88-year-old Lessing (whose specialty is sturdy typewriters, or perhaps pens), has "seduced a whole generation into its inanities."

Or is it the older generation that the Internet has seduced—into the inanities of leveling charges based on fear, ignorance and old-media, multiple-choice testing? So much so that we can't see that the Internet is only a means of communication, and one that has created a generation, perhaps the first, of writers, activists, storytellers? When the world worked in hard copy, no parent or teacher ever begrudged teenagers who disappeared into their rooms to write letters to friends—or a movie review, or an editorial for the school paper on the first president they'll vote for. Even 15-year-old boys are sharing some part of their feelings with someone out there.

We're talking about 33 million Americans who are fluent in texting, e-mailing, blogging, IM'ing and constantly amending their profiles on social network sites—which, on average, 30 of their friends will visit every day, hanging out and writing for 20 minutes or so each. They're connected, they're collaborative, they're used to writing about themselves. In fact, they choose to write about themselves, on their own time, rather than its being a forced labor when a paper's due in school. Regularly, often late at night, they're generating a body of intimate written work. They appreciate the value of a good story and the power of a speech that moves: Ninety-seven percent of the teenagers in the Common Core survey connected "I have a dream" with its speaker—they can watch Dr. King deliver it on demand—and eight in 10 knew what "To Kill a Mockingbird" is about.

This is, of course, the kind of knowledge we should be encouraging. The Internet has turned teenagers into honest documentarians of their own lives—reporters embedded in their homes, their schools, their own heads.

But this is also why it's dangerous, why we can't seem to recognize that it's just a medium. We're afraid. Our kids know things we don't. They drove the presidential debates onto YouTube and very well may determine the outcome of this election. They're texting at the dinner table and responsible for pretty much every enduring consumer cultural phenomenon: iPod, iTunes, iPhone; Harry Potter, "High School Musical"; large hot drinks with gingerbread flavoring. They can sell ads on their social network pages, and they essentially made MySpace worth $580 million and "Juno" an Oscar winner.

Besides, we're tired of having to ask them every time we need to find Season 2 of "Heroes," calculate a carbon footprint or upload photos to Facebook (now that we're allowed on). Plus, they're blogging about us.

5

So we've made the Internet one more thing unknowable about the American teenager, when, really, it's one of the few revelations. We conduct these surveys and overgeneralize—labeling like the mean girls, driven by the same jealousy and insecurity.

Common Core drew its multiple-choice questions for teens from a test administered by the federal government in 1986. Twenty-plus years ago, high school students didn't have the Internet to store their trivia. Now they know that the specific dates and what-was-that-prince's-name will always be there; they can free their brains to go a little deeper into the concepts instead of the copyrights, step back and consider what **SCOUT AND ATTICUS** were really fighting for. To criticize teenagers' author-to-book title matching on the spot, over the phone, is similar to cold-calling over-40s and claiming their long-division skills or date of *Jaws* recall is rusty. This is what we all rely on the Internet for.

That's not to say some of the survey findings aren't disturbing. It's crushing to hear that one in four teens could not identify Adolf Hitler's role in world history, for instance. But it's not because teenagers were online that they missed this. Had a parent introduced 20 minutes of researching the Holocaust to one month of their teen's Internet life, or a teacher assigned *The Diary of Anne Frank* (arguably a 13-year-old girl's blog)—if we worked with, rather than against, the way this generation voluntarily takes in information—we might not be able to pick up the phone and expose tragic pockets of ignorance.

The average teen chooses to spend an average of 16.7 hours a week reading and writing online. Yet the NEA report did not consider this to be "voluntary" reading and writing. Its findings also concluded that "literary reading declined significantly in a period of rising Internet use." The corollary is weak—this has as well been a period of rising franchises of frozen yogurt that doesn't taste like frozen yogurt, of global warming, of declining rates of pregnancy and illicit drug use among teenagers, and of girls sweeping the country's most prestigious high school science competition for the first time.

Teenagers today read and write for fun; it's part of their social lives. We need to start celebrating this unprecedented surge, incorporating it as an educational tool instead of meeting it with punishing pop quizzes and suspicion.

We need to start trusting our kids to communicate as they will online—even when that comes with the risk that they'll spill the family secrets or campaign for a candidate who's not ours.

Once we stop regarding the Internet as a villain, stop presenting it as the enemy of history and literature and worldly knowledge, then our teenagers have the potential to become the next great voices of America. One of them, 70 years from now, might even get up there to accept the very award Lessing did—and thank the Internet for making him or her a writer and a thinker.

10

15

GLOSS: SCOUT AND ATTICUS
You probably recognize this reference to the main characters in *To Kill a Mockingbird* (1960), the classic novel by Harper Lee that is one of the most widely assigned books in American middle and high schools. Notice that Goldwasser assumes her readers know these characters—as well as the movie *Jaws* (1975). Consider whether this is a reasonable assumption to make of most American readers.

Understanding the Text

1. What benefits does Goldwasser see in the Internet? How has it affected the writing and reading of teenagers today, in her view? What might her arguments about the Internet's impact suggest about her views regarding reading and writing in general? Do you think she's right about the Internet? Why or why not?

2. What kind of knowledge does Goldwasser believe we should be encouraging young people to acquire today? What role does the Internet play in this kind of knowledge, as she sees it?

3. On what basis does Goldwasser criticize the surveys, such as the ones conducted by Common Core and the NEA, about teenagers' knowledge and reading habits? What flaws does she see in such surveys? What can these surveys really tells us about teens today, in her view?

4. What alternatives does Goldwasser propose to the "teen bashing" that she believes adults often engage in? What solutions does she see to the problems that worry adults about today's teens? Do you think her solutions are practical? Why or why not?

Exploring the Issues

1. Goldwasser rejects the complaints of "the older generation" about teenagers' use of digital technologies and their apparent lack of interest in reading. What evidence does Goldwasser offer in support of her position? To what extent do you think her use of evidence strengthens or weakens her argument?

2. How would you describe the tone of this essay? What features of Goldwasser's prose help create this tone? Is the tone of this essay appropriate for Goldwasser's subject matter and argument, in your view? Explain, citing specific passages from the text to support your answer.

3. What picture does Goldwasser paint of today's teenagers? How accurate do you find her description of teens today? What do you think her description of teens today suggests about her own values? What might it suggest about her views about coming of age today?

Entering the Conversations

1. Write an essay in which you present your view of young people today. Focus your essay on any aspect of the lives of young people that you think is important.

2. To an extent, Goldwasser's essay is an answer to widespread concerns about the reading habits of today's teens and their perceived lack of knowledge about the world. She mentions reports by the National Endowment for the Arts and Common Core that suggest that Americans today read less and know less than Americans did in the past. Using appropriate resources, including InfoTrac College Edition, the Internet, and your library, investigate this controversy. Locate and review the reports by the NEA and Common Core as well as similar reports about the state of knowledge and literacy among teens today, such as those regularly re-

leased by the Pew Internet and American Life Project. If possible, talk to a professor on your campus who is an expert on these issues (most likely a professor in Education, English, or Communications). Try to get a sense of the main perspectives in this controversy. Then, write a report on the basis of your research. Describe what you found through your research and draw conclusions about the state of literacy and knowledge among teens today. Discuss the role of technology in teens' literacy today. Assess whether the concerns expressed in reports like the NEA report are valid.

3. On the basis of your work for Question 2, write a letter to the editor of your local newspaper or another appropriate publication in which you present your views about young people today. Place your views in the context of the ongoing debates about what young people should know.

4. Read the report of the National Endowment for the Arts (*To Read or Not to Read*) and/or the reports released by Common Core and similar organizations. Then write an analysis of these reports. In your analysis, summarize what the reports say about young people today, what information they present, and how they drew their conclusions. Evaluate the reports and their conclusions. Draw your own conclusions about the usefulness of these reports.

5. On the basis of your work for Question 5, write a letter to the organization (or organizations) whose report(s) you analyzed in which you offer your support for or criticisms of their report(s) and share your own views about young people and what they know or should know.

PROGRESS

I N THE PAST DECADE OR SO, MEDICAL RESEARCHERS HAVE BECOME INCREASINGLY ALARMED BY THE EMERGENCE OF SO-CALLED "SUPERBUGS," NEW AND ESPECIALLY VIRULENT STRAINS OF BACTERIA THAT ARE RESISTANT TO ANTIBIOTICS. SCIENTISTS BELIEVE THEY KNOW HOW THESE SUPERBUGS DEVELOP: THROUGH THEIR NATURAL REPRODUCTION CYCLES, THEY MUTATE SO THAT subsequent generations of the bacteria develop immunity to drugs that killed previous generations. It's a classic example of natural selection. Since the development of antibiotics, which were hailed as "miracle drugs" in the early twentieth century, common infections that once killed millions of people could be defeated. And as new bacteria emerged, new drugs were developed to combat them. If you were ever given medication for an ear infection or bronchitis, then you have benefited from these drugs, like millions of other people. For most of the past century, antibiotics have been considered one of medical science's great success stories, an example of the march of modern civilization. Like other

> We tend to believe that we can always find a scientific or technological fix to any problem.

important scientific and technological breakthroughs, such as electricity or anesthetics, antibiotics improved our lives. That's progress.

But the appearance of drug-resistant bacteria is one sign that progress may be a more complicated matter than we usually think. The overuse of antibiotics to defeat dangerous bacteria has ironically helped give rise to even more dangerous bacteria. In the same way, our astonishing technological developments and industrial growth, which have given us the comforts of warm homes, bright lights, and fast cars, have also caused a host of environmental and social problems and seem to be contributing to global warming, which may be a looming catastrophe. Our tech-

nological prowess has enabled us to devise increasingly sophisticated devices for communicating with each other throughout the world, but it has also enabled us to create ever deadlier weapons of awesome power. In short, human progress on so many different fronts is undeniable, but it may also be a mixed bag.

Most of us seem to believe that progress is a good thing, despite the kinds of problems just described. Indeed, our collective belief in progress often seems unshakeable. We tend to believe that we can always find a scientific or technological fix to any problem. After all, we have often done so in the past.

A few years ago at a family gathering, I was talking to a cousin of mine who is a doctor. I told him about a newspaper article I had recently read describing the drug-resistant bacteria, and I expressed my concern that these new strains of bacteria could create a health crisis in the coming decades. I mentioned that some scientists have begun to lobby the medical community to drastically reduce their use of antibiotics so that they do not contribute to the development of other strains of drug-resistant bacteria. My cousin, a smart and caring man who has been a family physician for more than twenty years, dismissed my concerns. The drug companies will eventually come up with new drugs to kill these new bacteria, he said. He had absolute confidence in modern science to meet this challenge.

The readings in this cluster may temper that confidence. They complicate our ideas about progress and they raise questions about our collective belief in progress as a good thing. They also help us see some of the consequences of the amazing scientific and technological developments that we usually consider signs of progress.

As a child, I was terrified of the dentist. Today, I still don't like going to the dentist, but I'm no longer so fearful of it. That's mostly because modern technology and new dental techniques have made most dental procedures almost painless. Clearly, when it comes to dentistry, things are much better than they were twenty or thirty years ago. Similar improvements

THE Myth OF Progress

have occurred in medicine, communications, transportation, and other important areas of our lives. No wonder that for most of us the very idea of progress is a positive one.

Writer Kirkpatrick Sale (b. 1937) would agree that dentistry might be better today, but he has serious doubts about whether progress, *as we usually understand that term, has benefited humanity in general. In the following essay, Sale examines what progress has meant for the world's people, and the picture he paints is not a happy one. Where others may see improvement as a result of scientific or technological progress, Sale sees a more complicated picture. His argument will strike many readers as pessimistic, but his essay may also prompt you to look again at the world that progress has given us.*

Kirkpatrick Sale has written many articles and books on technology and environmental issues. He is also a

KIRKPATRICK SALE

Ican remember vividly sitting at the dinner table arguing with my father about progress, using upon him all the experience and wisdom I had gathered at the age of fifteen. Of course we live in an era of progress, I said, just look at cars—how clumsy and unreliable and slow they were in the old days, how sleek and efficient and speedy they are now.

He raised an eyebrow, just a little. And what has been the result of having all these wonderful new sleek and efficient and speedy cars, he asked. I was taken aback. I searched for a way to answer. He went on.

How many people die each year as a result of these speedy cars, how many are maimed and crippled? What is life like for the people who produce them, on those famous assembly lines, the same routinized job hour after hour, day after day, like **CHAPLIN'S FILM?** How many fields and forests and even towns and villages have been paved over so that these cars can get to all the places they want to get to—and park there? Where does all the gasoline come from, and at what cost, and what happens when we burn it and exhaust it?

Before I could stammer out a response—thankfully—he went on to tell me about an article written on the subject of progress, a concept

KIRKPATRICK SALE, "THE MYTH OF PROGRESS." FROM *EARTH CRASH EARTH SPIRIT*, JULY 22, 2003 HTTP://ECES.ORG/.

I had never really thought of, by one of his Cornell colleagues, the historian **CARL BECKER,** a man I had never heard of, in the *Encyclopedia of Social Sciences*, a resource I had never come across. Read it, he said.

5 I'm afraid it was another fifteen years before I did, though in the meantime I came to learn the wisdom of my father's skepticism as the modern world repeatedly threw up other examples of invention and advancement—television, electric carving knife, microwave oven, nuclear power—that showed the same problematic nature of progress, taken in the round and negatives factored in, as did the automobile. When I finally got to Becker's masterful essay, in the course of a wholesale re-examination of modernity, it took no scholarly armament of his to convince me of the peculiar historical provenance of the concept of progress and its status not as an inevitability, a force as given as gravity as my youthful self imagined, but as a cultural construct invented for all practical purposes in the Renaissance and advancing the propaganda of capitalism. It was nothing more than a serviceable myth, a deeply held unexamined construct—like all useful cultural myths—that promoted the idea of regular and eternal improvement of the human condition, largely through the exploitation of nature and the acquisition of material goods.

Of course by now it is no longer such an arcane perception. Many fifteen-year-olds today, seeing clearly the perils with which modern technology has accompanied its progress, some of which threaten the very continuance of the human species, have already worked out for themselves what's wrong with the myth. It is hard to learn that forests are being cut down at the rate of 56 million acres a year, that desertification threatens 8 billion acres of land worldwide, that all of the world's seventeen major fisheries are in decline and stand a decade away from virtual exhaustion, that 26 million tons of topsoil is lost to erosion and pollution every year, and believe that this world's economic system, whose functioning exacts this price, is headed in the right direction and that direction should be labeled "progress."

E. E. CUMMINGS once called progress a "comfortable disease" of modern "manunkind," and so it has been for some. But at any time since the triumph of capitalism only a minority of the world's population could be said to be really living in comfort, and that comfort, continuously threatened, is achieved at considerable expense.

Today of the approximately 6 billion people in the world, it is estimated that at least a billion live in abject poverty, lives cruel, empty, and mercifully short. Another 2 billion eke out life on a bare subsistence level, usually sustained only by one or another starch, the majority without potable drinking water or sanitary toilets. More than 2 million more live at the bottom edges of the money economy but with incomes less than $5,000 a year and no property or savings, no net worth to pass on to their children.

contributing editor of The Nation *magazine. The following essay was published in* Earth Crash Earth Spirit *in 2003.* ◪

GLOSSES

CHAPLIN'S FILM
Sale is referring to *Modern Times* (1936), a famous silent film directed by Charlie Chaplin, seen as his protest against the industrial age, in which the Tramp, a character played by Chaplin, works at one point on a factory assembly line.

CARL BECKER
American historian Carl Becker (1873–1945) studied intellectual history. The essay Sale refers to was titled "Progress" and appeared in the *Encyclopedia of Social Sciences* in 1934.

E. E. CUMMINGS
Sale is referring in paragraph 7 to "pity this busy monster, manunkind," a poem by e. e. cummings (1894–1962).

That leaves less than a billion people who even come close to struggling for lives of comfort, with jobs and salaries of some regularity, and a quite small minority at the top of that scale who could really be said to have achieved comfortable lives; in the world, some 350 people can be considered (U.S. dollar) billionaires (with slightly more than 3 million millionaires), and their total net worth is estimated to exceed that of 45 per cent of the world's population.

10   This is progress? A disease such a small number can catch? And with such inequity, such imbalance?

In the U.S., the most materially advanced nation in the world and long the most ardent champion of the notion of progress, some 40 million people live below the official poverty line and another 20 million or so below the line adjusted for real costs; 6 million or so are unemployed, more than 30 million said to be too discouraged to look for work, and 45 million are in "disposable" jobs, temporary and part-time, without benefits or security. The top 5 percent of the population owns about two-thirds of the total wealth; 60 percent own no tangible assets or are in debt; in terms of income, the top 20 percent earn half the total income, the bottom 20 percent less than 4 percent of it.

All this hardly suggests the sort of material comfort progress is assumed to have provided. Certainly many in the U.S. and throughout the industrial world live at levels of wealth undreamed of in ages past, able to call forth hundreds of servant-equivalents at the flip of a switch or turn of a key, and probably a third of this "first world" population could be said to have lives of a certain amount of ease and convenience. Yet it is a statistical fact that it is just this segment that most acutely suffers from the true "comfortable disease," what I would call affluenza: heart disease, stress, overwork, family dysfunction, alcoholism, insecurity, anomie, psychosis, loneliness, impotence, alienation, consumerism, and coldness of heart.

GLOSS: LEOPOLD KOHR

Austrian economist Leopold Kohr (1909–1994) (par. 13) argued in his book *The Breakdown of Nations* (1957) that the most pressing problems facing modern society were largely a result of governments or institutions becoming too big. He is often credited with coining the phrase "small is beautiful." In recent years, there has been renewed interest in Kohr. Why? Consider, too, how Sale's reference to him (par. 13) might be part of a larger conversation about the direction of modern society that Kohr was part of during his lifetime.

LEOPOLD KOHR, the Austrian economist whose seminal work, *The Breakdown of Nations,* is an essential tool for understanding the failures of political progress in the last half-millennium, often used to close his lectures with this analogy.

Suppose we are on a progress-train, he said, running full speed ahead in the approved manner, fueled by the rapacious growth and resource depletion and cheered on by highly rewarded economists. What if we then discover that we are headed for a precipitous fall to a certain disaster just a few miles ahead when the tracks end at an uncrossable gulf? Do we take advice of the economists to put more fuel into the engines so that we go at an ever-faster rate, presumably hoping that we build up a head of steam so powerful that it can land us safely on the other side of the gulf; or do we reach for the brakes and come to a screeching if somewhat tumble-around halt as quickly as possible?

15   Progress is the myth that assures us that full-speed-ahead is never wrong. Ecology is the discipline that teaches us that it is disaster.

Consider the following two images, which show automobile assembly lines. The first shows an assembly line from the mid-twentieth century, when each job along the line was performed by a worker. The second shows a current assembly line, on which almost every job is performed by a machine. Such technological change is often presented as progress. What is the nature of such progress? What are its consequences? To what extent do such images support or complicate Sale's point?

Ford automobile assembly line, 1935

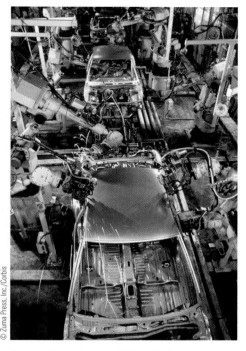

Computerized auto assembly line, 1995

Before the altar of progress, attended by its dutiful acolytes of science and technology, modern industrial society has presented an increasing abundance of sacrifices from the natural world, imitating on a much grander and more devastating scale the religious rites of earlier empires built upon similar conceits about the domination of nature. Now, it seems, we are prepared to offer up even the very biosphere itself.

No one knows how resilient the biosphere, how much damage it is able to absorb before it stops functioning—or at least functioning well enough to keep the human species alive. But in recent years some very respectable and authoritative voices have suggested that, if we continue the relentless rush of progress that is so stressing the earth on which it depends, we will reach that point in the quite near future. The Worldwatch Institute, which issues annual accountings of such things, has warned that there is not one life-support system on which the biosphere depends for its existence—healthy air, water, soil, temperature, and the like—that is not now severely threatened and in fact getting worse, decade by decade.

Not long ago a gathering of elite environmental scientists and activists in Morelia, Mexico, published a declaration warning of "environmental destruction" and expressing unanimous concern "that life on our planet is in grave danger." And recently the U.S. Union of Concerned Scientists, in a statement endorsed by more than a hundred Nobel laureates and 1,600 members of national academies of science all over the world, proclaimed a "World Scientists' Warning to Humanity" stating that the present rates of environmental assault and population increase cannot continue without "vast human misery" and a planet so "irretrievably mutilated" that "it will be unable to sustain life in the manner that we know."

The high-tech global economy will not listen; cannot listen. It continues apace its expansion and exploitation. Thanks to it, human beings annually use up some 40% of all the net photosynthetic energy available to the planet Earth, though we are but a single species of comparatively insignificant numbers. Thanks to it, the world economy has grown by more than five times over in the last 50 years and is continuing at a dizzying pace to use up the world's resources, create unabating pollution and waste, and increase the enormous inequalities within and between all nations of the world.

Suppose an Objective Observer were to measure the success of Progress—that is to say, the capital-P myth that ever since the **ENLIGHT-ENMENT** has nurtured and guided and presided over that happy marriage of science and capitalism that has produced modern industrial civilization.   [20]

Has it been, on the whole, better or worse for the human species? Other species? Has it brought humans more happiness than there was before? More justice? More equality? More efficiency? And if its ends have proven to be more benign than not, what of its means? At what price have its benefits been won? And are they sustainable?

The Objective Observer would have to conclude that the record is mixed, at best. On the plus side, there is no denying that material prosperity has increased for about a sixth of the world's humans, for some beyond the most avaricious dreams of kings and potentates of the past. The world has developed systems of transportation and communication that allow people, goods, and information to be exchanged on a scale and at a swiftness never before possible. And for maybe a third of these humans longevity has been increased, along with a general improvement in health and sanitation that has allowed the expansion of human numbers by about tenfold in the last three centuries.

On the minus side, the costs have been considerable. The impact upon the earth's species and systems to provide prosperity for a billion people has been, as we have seen, devastatingly destructive—only one additional measure of which is the fact that it has meant the permanent extinction of perhaps 500,000 species this century alone. The impact upon the remaining five-sixths of the human species has been likewise destructive, as most of them have seen their societies colonized

GLOSS: THE ENLIGHTENMENT
Sale is referring (par. 20) to the great intellectual and social movement in the eighteenth century usually called the Enlightenment, during which many of the most important scientific and philosophical ideas on which modern society is based were developed.

or displaced, their economies wrenched and shattered, and their environments transformed for the worse in the course of it, driving them into an existence of deprivation and misery that is almost certainly worse than they ever knew, however difficult their times past, before the advent of industrial society.

And even the billion whose living standards use up what is effectively 100 percent of the world's available resources each year to maintain, and who might be therefore assumed to be happy as a result, do not in fact seem to be so. No social indices in any advanced society suggest that people are more content than they were a generation ago, various surveys indicate that the "misery quotient" in most countries has increased, and considerable real-world evidence (such as rising rates of mental illness, drugs, crime, divorce, and depression) argues that the results of material enrichment have not included much individual happiness.

25   Indeed, on a larger scale, almost all that Progress was supposed to achieve has failed to come about, despite the immense amount of money and technology devoted to its cause. Virtually all of the dreams that have adorned it over the years, particularly in its most robust stages in the late 19th century and in the past twenty years of computerdom, have dissipated as utopian fancies—those that have not, like nuclear power, chemical agriculture, manifest destiny, and the welfare state, turned into nightmares. Progress has not, even in this most progressive nation, eliminated poverty (numbers of poor have increased and real income has declined for 25 years), or drudgery (hours of employment have increased, as has work within the home,

CONVERSATIONS: IMAGES OF PROGRESS
Since the onset of the Industrial Revolution in the nineteenth century, progress in Western culture has been associated with industrialization and technology. This image shows a poster from the 1879 Cincinnati Industrial Exposition. Consider what messages about progress the image of the factory on the poster convey. To what extent might these messages be similar to current beliefs about progress?

Poster from Cincinnati Industrial Exposition

STRATEGIES: PLACING NUMBERS IN CONTEXT
In paragraphs 8 and 10, Sale is citing figures to support his claim, which he states in the previous paragraph, that those who live comfortably under capitalism do so "at considerable expense." Notice how the first figure he provides is 6 billion, the approximate total world population. This figure provides a context for the figures he provides later in this paragraph and elsewhere in the essay. Consider how the impact of those latter figures might be changed if Sale had not included the figure of 6 billion here.

for both sexes), or ignorance (literacy rates have declined for fifty years, test scores have declined), or disease (hospitalization, illness, and death rates have all increased since 1980).

It seems quite simple: beyond prosperity and longevity, and those limited to a minority, and each with seriously damaging environmental consequences, progress does not have a great deal going for it. For its adherents, of course, it is probably true that it doesn't have to; because it is sufficient that wealth is meritorious and affluence desirable and longer life positive. The terms of the game for them are simple: material betterment for as many as possible, as fast as possible, and nothing else, certainly not considerations of personal morality or social cohesion or spiritual depth or participatory government, seems much to matter.

But the Objective Observer is not so narrow, and is able to see how deep and deadly are the shortcomings of such a view. The Objective Observer could only conclude that since the fruits of Progress are so meager, the price by which they have been won is far too high, in social, economic, political, and environmental terms, and that neither societies nor ecosystems of the world will be able to bear the cost for more than a few decades longer, if they have not already been damaged beyond redemption.

HERBERT READ, the British philosopher and critic, once wrote that "only a people serving an apprenticeship to nature can be trusted with machines." It is a profound insight, and he underscored it by adding that "only such people will so contrive and control those machines that their products are an enhancement of biological needs, and not a denial of them."

An apprenticeship to nature—now there's a myth a stable and durable society could live by.

CONVERSATIONS: HERBERT READ AND CONTROLLING MACHINES
Many popular films have explored the relationship between humans and the machines they create. In recent years, among the best-known of such films have been *The Matrix, The Matrix Reloaded,* and *The Matrix Revolutions,* a trilogy that tells the story of a future generation of humans fighting to regain control of the world from a race of sophisticated machines. These films can be seen as part of longstanding conversations in modern society about the nature of progress and the role of technology in human life. British philosopher and art critic Herbert Read (1893–1968), whom Sale mentions here (par. 28), was also well known as an anarchist who was deeply skeptical of government and technological progress. Thinkers like Read have been part of these conversations for centuries, and it is worth considering how their writing, as well as essays like this one by Sale, relates to visual art, such as film, in these conversations. In what ways do films like *The Matrix* carry on these conversations?

Understanding the Text

1. In what sense is progress a "cultural construct," in Sale's view? In what sense is it a useful myth? What's wrong with this myth, as Sale sees it? Do you agree with him? Why or why not?

2. In paragraph 5, Sale writes that "the modern world repeatedly threw up other examples of invention and advancement—television, electric carving knife, microwave oven, nuclear power—that showed the same problematic nature of progress." What do these examples of invention and advancement have in common? What does Sale believe they indicate about the problematic nature of progress? Do you think most people would agree with him about these examples? Explain.

3. What is "comfortable disease," according to Sale? What might this idea suggest about Sale's own values regarding lifestyle and progress?

4. In what sense is the record of progress "mixed," according to Sale? Do you think he's right? Why or why not?

5. Who is the "Objective Observer" to which Sale refers in paragraph 20 and later in his essay? How does this Objective Observer fit into Sale's main argument about progress?

Exploring the Issues

1. How would you characterize Sale's tone in this essay? What specific features of his writing help create this tone? Do you think his tone is appropriate for the main point he makes in this essay? Explain, citing specific passages to support your answer.

2. At the end of his essay, Sale refers to a "stable and durable society." What do you think he means by that phrase? Based on this essay, what do you think he believes such a society might look like? Do you think most people would share his view of such a society? Explain.

3. What do you learn about Sale and his own background in this essay? How does this information about Sale influence the way you read his essay? Does it affect your response to his argument in any way? Explain.

4. Throughout this essay, Sale supports his claims with many statistics and related factual information. Examine this information. What kinds of information does he tend to use as evidence to support his claims? How effectively do you think this information supports his claims? To what extent does it make his argument more or less persuasive, in your view?

Entering the Conversations

1. Write an essay in which you define *progress*. Draw on Sale's essay and any other relevant resources to support your definition.

2. In paragraph 21, Sale poses a series of questions about the results of progress in modern industrial society: "Has it been, on the whole, better or worse for the human species? Other species? Has it brought humans more happiness than there was before? More justice? More equality? More efficiency? And if its ends have proven to be more benign than not, what of its means? At what price have its benefits been won? And

are they sustainable?" Write an essay in which you offer your answer to these questions. In your essay, draw on Sale's essay and any other relevant readings to help support your position on these issues.

3. Write a response to Sale's essay in which you explain why you agree with his viewpoint on progress or offer your perspective on why progress, as you understand it, has been beneficial to humanity.

4. Create a visual representation of progress. Use PowerPoint, web authoring software, camera or video technology, or any other appropriate medium for your representation.

 INFOTRAC

5. Throughout his essay, Sale refers to a number of problems that he associates with progress in modern industrial society. For example, he refers to environmental destruction, poverty among a majority of the world's population, and great inequities in the way the world's wealth and resources are distributed. Select one of the problems Sale identifies in his essay and use InfoTrac College Edition, the Internet, your library, and other appropriate resources to investigate that problem. Try to determine the extent of the problem as well as its apparent causes. Examine the current state of the problem. Then write a report on the basis of your research. Draw conclusions about whether Sale's concerns about and representation of the problem are valid.

In August 2003, the largest power outage in U.S. history occurred, leaving a vast region of the northeastern United States without electricity for most of a day and, in some areas, for more than a week. When the power went out, I was in my kitchen preparing dinner for some friends who were at that moment driving from Ohio to my home in upstate New York. Not

A Shock to the System

long after the power went out, they called me from a gas station about an hour away from my home. They were nearly out of gas and afraid they wouldn't make it to my home. But they couldn't fill their tank because the gas pumps at the station weren't working. The pumps needed electricity to pump gas.

When I first read the following essay by Anna Quindlen (b. 1953), which was published a week after that power outage, I thought about my friends' situation: They needed one form of energy (electricity) to get another form of energy (gasoline) to get to my home; without electricity, they were stranded, even though their car did not use electricity to run. Their situation illustrated the energy dependence that has become part of the American lifestyle. As Quindlen notes in her essay, we have become so accustomed to using energy to do just about anything that we think of energy as our "birthright," as Quindlen calls it; rarely do we think about the larger

ANNA QUINDLEN

Whenever you run into a bear out here in the country, some-one will invariably ask if it was big. I never really know how to answer. All bears appear large to me, even the cubs. Something about the slope of the forehead, the glint of the eyes, the teeth and the claws. I don't take the time to assess relative size because I am so agog at the sheer bearness of the thing. Unlike Harrison Ford, a bear is not a creature you peer at in passing, thinking, 'Is that really . . . ?' It has a certain unmistakability.

The bear have become yet another species on the list of inconvenient animals in **THIS PART OF AMERICA,** right up there with the trash-picker possums and, of course, those loathsome shrubbery eaters, the deer. My favorite bear anecdote was the animal accused of getting physical after a man had proffered a bagel to get the bear to stick around for a photograph. The bear wanted more. What I want is an answer to this question: who gives a 250-pound wild animal baked goods?

The way in which modern people interact with their animal counterparts is one of those things that make us look as though our evolution took place on a bell curve and it's currently on the downside. Most of us now act toward native creatures the way our ancestors once acted toward Native Americans: we know that they were here first so we're willing to tolerate them as long as they don't demand to share when we build unattractive structures atop their former homes.

If they don't cooperate, we slaughter them.

5   Ultimately the deer **ABATTOIRS** along the highway, or the pest-control experts pulling bats out of attics, are, as one town official in New Jersey said of the bears not long ago, signs of a 'people problem.' Beneath it all is a cosmic question: how do Americans plan to live over the long haul? This was reinforced last week when, all over the Northeast, the power went out and millions found themselves suddenly humbled by their sheer reliance on electricity. What was remarkable was that the reaction was much the same as it is, on a smaller scale, to the animals. No talk of changing behavior, of finding a balance. Once the biggest power outage in history had begun, the only concern was for getting the juice back as quickly as possible. There was a faint undercurrent of revoked privilege. Where was the air conditioning, the pizza delivery, the ballgame on TV, all the things once seen as gifts and now assumed as birthrights?

What you saw time and time again was hubris brought low, people accustomed to instant communication without phone service, people accustomed to flying anywhere and at any time grounded at the airport. It was also hubris writ large. Office buildings, designed with windows that will not open, turning into saunas in the August sun. Office systems utterly dependent on computers turning into ghost towns in ghost cities.

Americans have been careless and casual with our natural resources for a long time. Can an accounting be long delayed? You could look at middle-class travelers sleeping like the homeless on the steps of public buildings during the blackout and see a vision of future unnatural disasters. The delivery grid is poorly conceived.

The fail-safe systems must be improved. But not a word about a world so profligate with its power that it uses as much to fuel the advertising glitz of Times Square as it once used to sustain an entire town.

Watch great cities fade to black, look at the unchecked and unsightly over development all around them, and it is hard to imagine this will be a livable country a hundred years from now. The battle between human and animal is merely a reflection of that. Public officials are notoriously leery of the long view, but ordinary people are no better. The great contradiction: all those alleged nature lovers who fall for a forested range, then bring in the bulldozers. According to the National Association of Home Builders, the average American

impact of how we use energy. Quindlen believes that we should be thinking about that impact because it is our lifestyle, which we tend to think of as a sign of progress, that has created problems leading to events like the power outage of 2003. Her essay is a call for us to reexamine our ideas about progress—and part of a long-standing debate in Western culture about progress.

Anna Quindlen is a best-selling author and Pulitzer Prize–winning columnist for Newsweek, *in which the following essay appeared in 2003.* ▼

CONVERSATION: THIS PART OF AMERICA
Quindlen is referring to New Jersey (par. 2) when she mentions "this part of America." Specifically, she is referring to a landscape of expanding towns and suburbs that have crept into the remaining forested areas of this populous state—areas that are still home to many kinds of wildlife, including bears. In the summer of 2003, when this essay was first published, several New Jersey towns were trying to address problems with deer and bears, as Quindlen notes in this paragraph. But these problems are not unique to New Jersey. In many parts of the United States where residential and commercial development is encroaching on wilderness areas, similar problems have arisen. So although Quindlen is writing specifically about "this part of America," she is addressing a problem that is occurring in many other places as well. This is an example of how a writer can draw on a local context to make a larger point about an important issue.

STRATEGIES: FORMATTING FOR EMPHASIS
One way writers can emphasize a point or an idea is to use formatting, as Quindlen does here (par. 4). By setting off this sentence as a separate paragraph, Quindlen makes it more noticeable than it would be as part of the preceding paragraph, thereby focusing her readers' attention on her point.

GLOSS: ABATTOIR
Abattoir (par. 5) is another term for slaughterhouse.

CONVERSATIONS: PROGRESS

Quindlen's brief parenthetical (par. 9) reference to a report titled a "Century of Progress" suggests that she is joining a much larger and longstanding conversation about the nature of progress and the relationship between humans and the earth. Earlier, in paragraph 5, she poses what she calls a "cosmic" question that is part of this conversation: "How do Americans plan to live over the long haul?" In one way or another, all the essays in this cluster are part of this conversation about progress, and it is worth thinking about how Quindlen uses the term here in comparison to how other writers use it. In what ways does her essay contribute to our collective effort to answer the question she has posed about how we will live over the long haul?

CONVERSATIONS: THE PRICE OF COMFORT

Quindlen's complaints about the wasteful American lifestyle are part of an ongoing debate in the United States about how we should live and about our responsibilities as consumers. Consider how these cartoons contribute to that debate.

home has doubled in size in the past century. (Its report calls this a Century of Progress. Guess it depends on your definition.) This is not because families are larger. Quite the contrary. The three-car-garage-and-great-room trend—a great room being a living room on steroids—reflects family life that has devolved into individual isolation, everyone with his own TV and computer, centrally cooled to a frosty edge or heedlessly heated.

Irony of ironies, New York City may soon   10
have a greater unbroken stretch of green (Happy 150th Birthday, Central Park!) than the suburbs that once lured its people with the promises of grass and trees. The animals thus become more and more of a nuisance: get out of our way! Occasionally, we are forcibly reminded that human beings have created an environment in which, in some ways, we have less control than ever before; after all, the lack of power is, by definition, powerlessness. Meanwhile New Jersey, the most densely populated state (in case you hadn't noticed), wants very much to allow the hunting of bears. No one seems to have considered the obvious alternative: instead of issuing hunting permits, call a moratorium on building permits. Permanently.

Understanding the Text

1. Why does Quindlen describe the bear as an "inconvenient" animal? What do you think this term suggests about the relationship between humans and wildlife? How does this idea of inconvenient animals fit into Quindlen's main argument?

2. What was the main reaction to the power outage in 2003, as Quindlen sees it? What does that reaction suggest about our attitudes toward natural resources, wildlife, and lifestyle, in her view? Do you think she's right? Why or why not?

3. What is the main lesson Quindlen sees in the power outage that occurred in 2003? Do you think her views about this situation are common views? Explain.

4. What would be gained by adopting a moratorium on building permits, as Quindlen proposes in her final paragraph? What does such a proposal suggest about Quindlen's own values?

Exploring the Issues

1. Summarize Quindlen's main point in this essay, citing specific passages to support your answer. Do you agree with her? Why or why not?

2. How would you characterize Quindlen's writing style in this essay? What features of her prose contribute to her style? How effective do you find her writing style? Explain, citing specific passages to support your answer.

3. In paragraph 9, Quindlen writes that "public officials are notoriously leery of the long view, but ordinary people are no better." In fact, she seems to criticize Americans in general in this essay. What is the basis of her criticisms?

Do you think her criticisms are valid? Why or why not? What might your answer to that question suggest about your own views regarding lifestyle?

Entering the Conversations

1. Write a response to Quindlen's essay in which you offer your own view of the American lifestyle and the progress it represents.

2. Visit the web sites of several advocacy groups or organizations concerned about issues of lifestyle, environmental protection, or the use of resources. For example, you might visit sites for groups advocating "smart growth" to control suburban sprawl or the sites of organizations advocating more responsible uses of resources. In searching for sites, consider using the following terms: *smart growth, sustainability, lifestyle, environmental impact.* Try to visit sites representing different viewpoints on these issues. Examine these sites for the messages they send about lifestyle and its impact on the environment. Examine, too, how they convey their messages. Consider whether they promote change, or progress, or not. Then create your own web site in which you offer a guide to these various sites. On your site, explain the purpose of your site and include links to the sites you have reviewed. Convey your own viewpoint about the impact of the American lifestyle.

Alternatively, write an essay in which you present your review of the web sites you visited.

🖋 INFOTRAC

3. In paragraph 9, Quindlen mentions that the size of the average American home has doubled in the past century. (It

is now about 2,400 square feet.) This fact is sometimes cited by advocates of "smart growth," who are concerned about reducing the environmental impact of the American lifestyle; these advocates argue that typical American homes are wasteful and use space in environmentally unsound ways. Quindlen refers in this paragraph to some other ways that the American is wasteful—for example, the excessive use of air conditioning or heating or an unnecessary number of inefficient electric appliances, such as televisions. Use InfoTrac College Edition, the Internet, and other appropriate resources to investigate Quindlen's claims. Try to find out the environmental impact of common components of the American lifestyle, such as housing, transportation, and entertainment. How do these components affect the environment? How are resources typically used in the American lifestyle? What common activities or practices are wasteful? You might focus your research on one component of the American lifestyle, such as housing, food, entertainment, or transportation. Try to find out what impact people have by engaging in typical American activities, such as driving a car or living in a typical home. Then write a report on the basis of your research. In your report, present what you learned about the impact of the American lifestyle and draw conclusions about whether or not Quindlen's claims are valid.

4. Write a letter to the editor of your local newspaper or another appropriate publication in which you express your viewpoint about the impact of the American lifestyle (or the lifestyle in another country where you may live); propose solutions to the problems you see with that lifestyle.

"Community-based agriculture," or CSA, *refers to small, locally owned farms that produce fruits, vegetables, meats, and other products for sale in local markets. Usually, these products are raised organically, so community-based agriculture does less damage to the local environment than conventional farming methods. In addition, because the products*

Ecological Destruction AND A *Vermont* Farm IN May

are sold locally, they do not require much energy (such as gasoline) to transport them. Many community-based farms operate on the basis of "memberships." If you become a member, you not only can buy the farm's products, but you can also volunteer to work on the farm, which enables the farmers to keep their costs lower by not having to hire many workers or use large machines to grow and harvest their crops. CSAs provide a way to support local farmers and reduce our impact on the environment.

Such small-scale farms are often considered "alternative" or "back-to-the-land" operations. They are not usually thought of as progress. The following essay by internationally known environmentalist Donella Meadows might convince you that

DONELLA MEADOWS

The timing is unbearable. Here on my desk in the middle of the blooming, buzzing month of May is the best report yet on the state of the world's ecosystems. Best not because it contains good news—it doesn't—but because it's short and clear and blunt.

The report evaluates the health of our life support system with a simple grid of colored squares. Five columns across the top list the five kinds of ecosystems from which we live—agricultural land, coastal waters, forests, freshwater, grazing land. Four rows down rank each of these systems according to their ability to produce what we need from them: food and fiber, water (both quality and quantity), and biodiversity (the support of other species). The colors of the squares cover a range from "excellent" to "bad."

One glance reveals that there's no "excellent." There's one "bad" (freshwater biodiversity) and four "poors" (ag land water quality, ag land biodiversity, forest biodiversity, freshwater quality). Eight "fairs," only three "goods" (ag land production, forest production, freshwater production). Three squares are blank, meaning not relevant or not assessed.

That's all I can take in one dose. I sigh and wander outside, where our farm is twittering. Warblers migrate through in waves, barn swallows swoop for black flies, an oriole pours forth joy from a blooming apple tree. Wow! The song of an oriole is liquid gold, and then to see its brilliant orange and black against white blossoms! The colors on that grid may be gloomy, but the colors in this little spot in Vermont are amazing.

5   The story isn't over yet. The planet is still full of magnificent things worth saving.

That oriole fortifies me to study the chart more carefully. The colors of the boxes show the present state of each ecosystem. Within each box is an arrow showing its direction of change. The arrow slopes up if the ecosystem's capacity is increasing, down if it is decreasing, both up and down if the trend is mixed. Of the seventeen squares two are mixed (coastal water quality, freshwater production). One is improving (forest production—the legend says that forest plantations and natural forest cutting are increasing and there's no fiber scarcity in sight.) Fourteen, including forest biodiversity and water quality and quantity, are pointing down.

That's on a global scale. These are the systems that sustain human life. Whew! Time to go outside again.

There's some nice bottomland on this farm, one of the main reasons we came here. For one year we left it in alfalfa and grass, then we plowed under seven acres, sowed a cover crop, plowed that down, picked out the big rocks, spread manure and lime, harrowed. Stephen and Kerry, our vegetable farmers, are planting it now to supply 50 subscribing families with fresh-picked produce from June through October. Next year we'll be able to certify the land as organic. I'd call it "good"; we're aiming to get it up to "excellent."

The story isn't over. At least in small places people are actively building resources instead of tearing them down.

10   The report was put out by a page-long list of scientists and advisors convened by the UN Development Program, the UN Environmental Program, the World Bank, and the World Resources Institute. Just in case their grid doesn't convey the point, these august bodies conclude in italics, "The current rate of decline in the long-term productive capacity of ecosystems could have devastating implications for human development and the welfare of all species."

such operations are indeed progress— just the kind of progress we need in the face of the global destruction of the ecosystems on which we depend. In her essay, Meadows discusses a discouraging report on the state of the world's ecosystems, but she also describes some of the efforts she has made on her own farm to reduce the impact on the environment. It may be that the small, positive steps Meadows describes in her essay represent a new way of thinking about progress.

Donella Meadows (1941–2001) wrote widely about environmental issues. The following essay first appeared in 2000 in her column, Global Citizen, *which was distributed by the Sustainability Institute.* ◪

STRATEGIES: REPETITION
The first line of paragraph 14 is a statement that Meadows repeats, in slightly different versions, three times in this essay (see also par. 5 and 9). Often, writers will use repetition to emphasize a point or call attention to an idea. Consider what Meadows accomplishes by repeating this statement.

CONVERSATIONS: THE BEST REPORT YET

The report Meadows refers to throughout her essay is *World Resources 2000–2001: People and Ecosystems: The Fraying Web of Life*, released jointly by the United Nations Development Programme, United Nations Environment Programme, the World Bank, and the World Resources Institute. Here is the graphic from the report that Meadows describes. Consider not only the information conveyed in this graphic (which, as Meadows notes, is not good news) but *how* the information is conveyed: In what ways might this visual representation present information more effectively than a verbal description? This graphic was not included in Meadows's original essay. Consider how effectively she describes this graphic in paragraph 2—and whether or not her description captures the visual impact of the graphic.

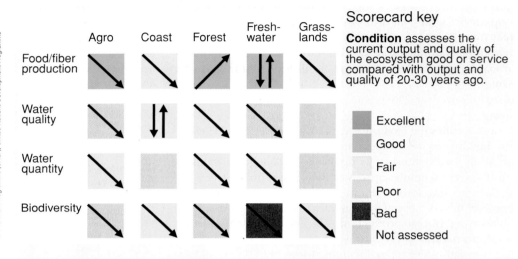

© World Resources Institute (WRI) in collaboration with United Nations Environment Programme (UNEP), United Nations Development Programme (UNDP), and World Bank, 2000.

Changing capacity asses the underlying biological ability of the ecosystem to continue to provide the good or service.

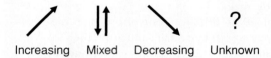

Scores are expert judgements about each ecosystem good or service over time, without regard to changes in other ecosystems. Scores estimate the predominant global condition or capacity by balancing the relative strength and reliability of the various indicators described in the notes on data quality. When regional findings diverge, in the absence of global quality, weight is given to better-quality data, larger geographic coverage, and longer time series. Pronounced differences in global trends are scored as "mixed" if a net value cannot be determined. Serious inadequacy of current data is scored as "unknown."

Dozens of groups have come to a similar conclusion over the past decade, but somehow it hasn't sunk in. Listen to the chatter of the media, the pronouncements of politicians, the forecasts of economists, and you don't hear any recognition of what must be the most important fact of the present world. We are undermining the systems that support all people and all production. Why don't we even TALK about this? Why can't we FOCUS on it?

The pastures sloping up from the bottomland are that intense May green, spangled with yellow dandelions. Our three horses and ten cows are in heaven up there. We're keeping the stock count low; we'll do rotational grazing to help build fertility.

High up on the ridge the forest is light-green lace. We worry about that forest. Acid rain falls on it. Climate change encourages the spread of pests like the woolly adelgid, which kills hemlocks and is moving north toward us. The chestnuts, elms, butternuts are already gone. Though we hope to make our forest more productive, it's not possible to move a small place toward "excellent," if systems all around are crashing down from "fair" to "poor" to "bad."

The story is far from over. Life is bursting forth, pushing, throbbing, aiming toward fertility, productivity, purity and the most astonishing beauty. It's an awesome force working in our direction, if we would let it do so.

Understanding the Text

1. Why is the timing of the report on the state of the world's ecosystems "unbearable," according to Meadows? What do you think her use of that term suggests about her own perspective? What might it suggest about her as a person?

2. What does Meadows's own farm have to do with the report on the world's ecosystems? What does that connection suggest about the relationship between local and global environments?

3. What are Meadows's concerns about the report on the state of the world's ecosystems? Do you think her concerns are valid? Why or why not?

Exploring the Issues

1. In a sense, in this essay Meadows is telling the "story" of her experience of reading the report on the state of the world's ecosystems. Examine how she tells that story. How does she organize the essay? What information, images, or events does she include? How does she present the information, images, or events to her readers? How does she use this "story" to make her main point? How effective do you find this way of presenting her point? Explain.

2. Throughout this essay, Meadows discusses and describes colors. Examine her references to color. What colors does she refer to and why? What ideas or messages does she convey through her repeated references to color. What do you think she accomplishes through these references?

3. In her final paragraph, Meadows repeats the statement, "The story is far from over." She then discusses the "awesome force" of life. What message do you think she emphasizes in this concluding paragraph? Do you find her message valid? Explain, citing specific passages to support your answer.

Entering the Conversations

1. In paragraph 9, Meadows writes, "At least in small places people are actively building resources instead of tearing them down." Her own Vermont farm is one such place. Write an essay about another such "small place" that you know about. The place you write about may be a place you have direct experience with, a place you have read about, or a project that someone you know is involved in. In your essay, describe that place and how it is "building resources." Draw conclusions about what this place might suggest about progress.

2. Write a proposal for a project that would make your school campus the kind of "small place" that Meadows describes in paragraph 9. Address your proposal to the appropriate officer on your campus (such as the dean of campus life or the director of buildings and grounds). Include any appropriate visual components, such as graphs or photos, to support your proposal.

INFOTRAC

3. In paragraph 11, Meadows states that the issue of the destruction of ecosystems is not being talked about. She made

that claim in 2000. Investigate whether it is still valid today, especially in view of the attention now being paid to the problem of global warming and related environmental concerns. Using InfoTrac College Edition, the Internet, your library, and other appropriate resources, try to determine whether and how the issue of the destruction of ecosystems is addressed in various media and by various groups and/or governments. Find out if states or the U.S. government has tried to address these problems with any recent programs or laws. Talk to faculty members at your school who may have expertise in these areas (for example, environmental studies, biology, business, public policy, or political science). You might also talk to representatives of appropriate government agencies (such as your state department of environmental conservation) or advocacy groups (such as the Environmental Defense Fund or the Sierra Club). Then write a report on the basis of your research. In your report, describe your research and present your findings. Draw conclusions about the extent to which the destruction of the world's ecosystems is being addressed.

4. On the basis of your research for Question 3, write a letter to the editor of a widely circulated publication, such as *USA Today,* expressing your views about the state of the world's ecosystems today.

5. Drawing on Meadows's essay and any other appropriate essays in this book, write an essay discussing progress. In your essay, define progress and offer your own viewpoint about it.

Not long ago I developed an infection in *one of my teeth and ended up at the dentist for a root canal procedure. When I arrived there, I was in excruciating pain and eager to have the dentist fix the problem. Once he examined my tooth and determined the necessary treatment, he gave me an injection of Novocain, a widely used anesthetic*

MY Bionic Quest
FOR *Bolero*

that numbs the tooth. Within seconds, the pain in my tooth stopped and I relaxed. I joked to the dentist that Novocain is my favorite invention.

Most of us have benefited from the development of sophisticated technologies like those used by dentists. Such technologies are generally considered progress and few of us would want to live without them. I can't imagine having to endure a dental procedure like a root canal without the use of anesthesia or the highly sophisticated tools dentists use today. I also cannot imagine living without the ability to hear, as writer Michael Chorost has had to do. As Chorost tells us in the following essay, he lost his hearing completely when he was in his thirties. Losing his hearing affected his life in a number of ways, but one of the hardest things for him to accept was not being able to listen to his favorite piece of music: Bolero, *a famous classical composition. Chorost's essay is the story of his*

MICHAEL CHOROST

WITH ONE LISTEN, I WAS HOOKED. I was a fifteen-year-old suburban New Jersey nerd, racked with teenage lust but too timid to ask for a date. When I came across *Bolero* among the LPs in my parents' record collection, I put it on the turntable. It hit me like a neural thunderstorm, titanic and glorious, each cycle building to a climax and waiting but a beat before launching into the next.

I had no idea back then of *Bolero's* reputation as one of the most famous orchestral pieces in the world. When it was first performed at the Paris Opera in 1928, the fifteen-minute composition stunned the audience. Of the French composer, Maurice Ravel, a woman in attendance reportedly cried out, "He's mad . . . he's mad!" One critic wrote that *Bolero* "departs from a thousand years of tradition."

I sat in my living room alone, listening. *Bolero* starts simply enough, a single flute accompanied by a snare drum: *da-da-da-dum, da-da-da-dum, dum-dum, da-da-da-dum.* The same musical clause repeats seventeen more times, each cycle adding instruments, growing louder and more insistent, until the entire orchestra roars in an overpowering finale of rhythm and sound. Musically, it was perfect for my ear. It had a structure that I could easily grasp and enough variation to hold my interest.

"MY BIONIC QUEST FOR BOLERO," BY MICHAEL CHOROST. *WIRED MAGAZINE*, NOVEMBER 2005. VOL. 13 NO. 11. REPRINTED BY PERMISSION OF MICHAEL CHOROST.

70

*...at music again. It
...about the challenges
...g the sophisticated
...hat we sometimes take
..., such as anesthetics,
...ools, eyeglasses, and for
people with hearing loss, hearing
devices like the one Chorost uses.
Chorost is a believer in such
technologies, but his experiences
reveal that technology is not always
exactly what we want or expect it to
be. In that regard, his essay might
help us rethink our attitudes toward
technology—and complicate our
beliefs about progress.*

Michael Chorost has written
Rebuilt: How Becoming Part
Computer Made Me More
Human *(2005) and many articles
for such publications as the*
Washington Post, Technology
Review, *and* Wired, *in which this
essay first appeared in 2005. It was
reprinted in* The Best American
Science and Nature Writing
(2006). ◾

STRATEGIES: DESCRIBING *BOLERO*
In the first three paragraphs of this essay, Chorost describes the
experience of listening to the famous classical orchestral
composition *Bolero* by French composer Joseph-Maurice Ravel
(1875–1937). It's not easy to describe what music sounds like or
what the experience of listening to it feels like. If you have ever
heard *Bolero*, decide whether Chorost's description matches your
experience of that piece. If you haven't heard it, listen to it (if
possible) to see whether Chorost's description feels accurate to
you. Either way, his description is intended not only to convey his
experience but also to set up his main themes in this essay. This
passage is a good example of a writer's use of descriptive writing
to serve several purposes at once. Notice, too, that Chorost returns
to describing *Bolero* later in this essay (par. 40–46). This early
passage helps prepare readers for that later description.

It took a lot to hold my interest; I was nearly deaf at the time. In
1964 my mother contracted rubella while pregnant with me. Hearing aids allowed me to understand speech well enough, but most
music was lost on me. *Bolero* was one of the few pieces I actually enjoyed. A few years later I bought the CD and played it so much it
eventually grew pitted and scratched. It became my touchstone. Every time I tried out a new hearing aid, I'd check to see if *Bolero*
sounded okay. If it didn't, the hearing aid went back.

And then, on July 7, 2001, at 10:30 A.M., I lost my ability to hear 5
Bolero—and everything else. While I was waiting to pick up a rental
car in Reno, I suddenly thought the battery in my hearing aid had
died. I replaced it. No luck. I switched hearing aids. Nothing.

I got into my rental car and drove to the nearest emergency room.
For reasons that are still unknown, my only functioning ear had suffered "sudden-onset deafness." I was reeling, trying to navigate in a
world where the volume had been turned down to zero.

But there was a solution, a surgeon at Stanford Hospital told me a
week later, speaking slowly so I could read his lips. I could have a
computer surgically installed in my skull. A cochlear implant, as it is
known, would trigger my auditory nerves with sixteen electrodes that
snaked inside my inner ear. It seemed drastic, and the $50,000 price
tag was a dozen times more expensive than a high-end hearing aid. I
went home and cried. Then I said yes.

For the next two months, while awaiting surgery, I was totally deaf
except for a thin trickle of sound from my right ear. I had long since
become accustomed to not hearing my own voice
when I spoke. It happened whenever I removed my
hearing aid. But that sensation was as temporary as
waking up without my glasses. Now, suddenly, the
silence wasn't optional. At my job as a technical
writer in Silicon Valley, I struggled at meetings. Using the phone was out of the question.

In early September, the surgeon drilled a tunnel
through an inch and a half of bone behind my left
ear and inserted the sixteen electrodes along the
auditory nerve fibers in my cochlea. He hollowed a
well in my skull about the size of three stacked
quarters and snapped in the implant.

When the device was turned on a month after 10
surgery, the first sentence I heard sounded like
"Zzzzzz szz szvizzz ur brfzzzzzz?" My brain gradually learned how to
interpret the alien signal. Before long, "Zzzzzz szz szvizzz ur brfzzzzzz?"
became ''What did you have for breakfast?" After months of practice,
I could use the telephone again, even converse in loud bars and cafeterias. In many ways, my hearing was better than it had ever been.
Except when I listened to music.

I could hear the drums of *Bolero* just fine. But the other instruments were flat and dull. The flutes and soprano saxophones sounded as though someone had clapped pillows over them. The oboes and violins had become groans. It was like walking colorblind through a **PAUL KLEE** exhibit. I played *Bolero* again and again, hoping that practice would bring it, too, back to life. It didn't.

The implant was embedded in my head; it wasn't some flawed hearing aid I could just send back. But it *was* a computer. Which meant that, at least in theory, its effectiveness was limited only by the ingenuity of software engineers. As researchers learn more about how the ear works, they continually revise cochlear implant software. **USERS AWAIT NEW RELEASES WITH ALL THE ANTICIPATION OF APPLE ZEALOTS LINING UP FOR THE LATEST MAC OS.**

About a year after I received the implant, I asked one implant engineer how much of the device's hardware capacity was being used. "Five percent maybe." He shrugged. "Ten, tops."

I was determined to use that other 90 percent. I set out on a crusade to explore the edges of auditory science. For two years I tugged on the sleeves of scientists and engineers around the country, offering myself as a guinea pig for their experiments. I wanted to hear *Bolero* again.

15 **HELEN KELLER** famously said that if she had to choose between being deaf and being blind, she'd be blind, because while blindness cut her off from things, deafness cut her off from people. For centuries the best available hearing aid was a horn, or ear trumpet, which people held to their ears to funnel in sound. In 1952 the first electronic hearing aid was developed. It worked by blasting amplified sound into a damaged ear. However, it (and the more advanced models that followed) could help only if the user had some residual hearing ability, just as glasses can help only those who still have some vision. Cochlear implants, on the other hand, bypass most of the ear's natural hearing mechanisms. The device's electrodes directly stimulate nerve endings in the ear, which transmit sound information to the brain. Since the surgery can eliminate any remaining hearing, implants are approved for use only in people who can't be helped by hearing aids. The first modern cochlear implants went on the market in Australia in 1982, and by 2004 approximately 82,500 people worldwide had been fitted with one.

When technicians activated my cochlear implant in October 2001, they gave me a pager-sized processor that decoded sound and sent it to a headpiece that clung magnetically to the implant underneath my skin. The headpiece contained a radio transmitter, which sent the processor's data to the implant at roughly 1 megabit per second. Six-

GLOSS: PAUL KLEE
Swiss painter Paul Klee (1879–1940) is known for the unusual and innovative way he used color in his art. Note that Chorost uses the image of visiting an exhibit of Klee's work as a simile to help convey his experience of listening to *Bolero* after he first received a cochlear implant. He uses the same metaphor again in paragraph 19.

STRATEGIES: USING APPROPRIATE METAPHORS FOR YOUR AUDIENCE
This essay was originally published in *Wired* magazine, one of the world's foremost publications devoted to computers and related technologies. Readers of that magazine would be familiar with all the excitement that is generated by the release of new operating system (OS) software for the Mac computer by Apple, which Chorost refers to here. Notice that Chorost compares people who await new versions of hearing devices software with the "zealots" waiting for new Mac software. Writers use metaphors like this to convey a point, and the most successful metaphors are those that are appropriate for their intended audience, as this metaphor seems to be for readers of *Wired*. Consider whether it would be effective for a different audience.

GLOSS: HELEN KELLER
Helen Keller (1880–1968) was an author, an activist for women's and workers' rights, and an advocate for people with disabilities. She became famous when she published her autobiography, *The Story of My Life* (1903), in which she described her experiences as a child who had lost the ability to see and hear as a result of an illness when she was not yet two years old.

teen electrodes curled up inside my cochlea strobed on and off to stimulate my auditory nerves. The processor's software gave me eight channels of auditory resolution, each representing a frequency range. The more channels the software delivers, the better the user can distinguish between sounds of different pitches.

Eight channels isn't much compared with the capacity of a normal ear, which has the equivalent of thirty-five hundred channels. Still, eight works well enough for speech, which doesn't have much pitch variation. Music is another story. The lowest of my eight channels captured everything from 250 hertz (about middle C on the piano) to 494 hertz (close to the B above middle C), making it nearly impossible for me to distinguish among the eleven notes in that range. Every note that fell into a particular channel sounded the same to me.

So in mid-2002, nine months after activation, I upgraded to a program called Hi-Res, which gave me sixteen channels—double the resolution! An audiologist plugged my processor into her lap top and uploaded the new code. I suddenly had a better ear, without surgery. In theory, I would now be able to distinguish among tones five notes apart instead of eleven.

I eagerly plugged my Walkman into my processor and turned it on. *Bolero* did sound better. But after a day or two, I realized that "better" still wasn't good enough. The improvement was small, like being in that art gallery again and seeing only a gleam of pink here, a bit of blue there. I wasn't hearing the *Bolero* I remembered.

20   At a cochlear implant conference in 2003, I heard Jay Rubinstein, a surgeon and researcher at the University of Washington, say that it took at least one hundred channels of auditory information to make music pleasurable. My jaw dropped. No wonder. I wasn't even close.

A year later I met Rubinstein at another conference, and he mentioned that there might be ways to bring music back to me. He told me about something called stochastic resonance; studies suggested that my music perception might be aided by deliberately adding noise to what I hear. He took a moment to give me a lesson in neural physiology. After a neuron fires, it goes dormant for a fraction of a second while it resets. During that phase, it misses any information that comes along. When an electrode zaps thousands of neurons at once, it forces them all to go dormant, making it impossible for them to receive pulses until they reset. That synchrony means I miss bits and pieces of information.

Desynchronizing the neurons, Rubinstein explained, would guarantee that they're never all dormant simultaneously. And the best way to get them out of sync is to beam random electrical noise at them. A few months later Rubinstein arranged a demonstration.

An audiologist at the University of Iowa working with Rubinstein handed me a processor loaded with the stochastic-resonance software. The first thing I heard was a loud whoosh—the random noise.

It sounded like a cranked-up electric fan. But in about thirty seconds, the noise went away. I was puzzled. "You've adapted to it," the technician told me. The nervous system can habituate to any kind of everyday sound, but it adjusts especially quickly to noise with no variation. Stochastic-resonance noise is so content-free that the brain tunes it out in seconds.

In theory, the noise would add just enough energy to incoming sound to make faint details audible. In practice, everything I heard became rough and gritty. My own voice sounded vibrato, mechanical, and husky—even a little querulous, as if I were perpetually whining.

We tried some quick tests to take my newly programmed ear out for   25
a spin. It performed slightly better in some ways, slightly worse in others—but there was no dramatic improvement. The audiologist wasn't surprised. She told me that in most cases a test subject's brain will take weeks or even months to make sense of the additional information. Furthermore, the settings she chose were only an educated guess at what might work for my particular physiology. Everyone is different. Finding the right setting is like fishing for one particular cod in the Atlantic.

The university loaned me the processor to test for a few months. As soon as I was back in the hotel, I tried my preferred version of *Bolero,* a 1982 recording conducted by Charles Dutoit with the Montreal Symphony Orchestra. It sounded different but not better. Sitting at my keyboard, **I SIGHED A LITTLE AND TAPPED OUT AN EMAIL** thanking Rubinstein and encouraging him to keep working on it.

> **STRATEGIES: ORGANIZING AN ESSAY**
> Chorost has organized his essay as a narrative, telling the story of his experience with his cochlear ear implant and his effort to be able to listen to *Bolero* again. But he also tells another story: the story of the development of technologies such as cochlear implants. He weaves the two stories together, using his personal story to tell the other story. At the end of paragraph 26, for example, he interrupts his personal story to continue the more technical story of the development of hearing technologies, which he continues in the next few paragraphs. This way of organizing an essay enables a writer to incorporate a great deal of information while at the same time keeping readers interested, even when the technical material is complex.

Music depends on low frequencies for its richness and mellowness. The lowest-pitched string on a guitar vibrates at 83 hertz, but my Hi-Res software, like the eight-channel model, bottoms out at 250 hertz. I do hear something when I pluck a string, but it's not actually an 83-hertz sound. Even though the string is vibrating at 83 times per second, portions of it are vibrating faster, giving rise to higher-frequency notes called harmonics. The harmonics are what I hear.

The engineers haven't gone below 250 hertz because the world's low-pitched sounds—air conditioners, engine rumbles—interfere with speech perception. Furthermore, increasing the total frequency range means decreasing resolution, because each channel has to accommodate more frequencies. Since speech perception has been the main goal during decades of research, the engineers haven't given much thought to representing low frequencies. Until Philip Loizou came along.

Loizou and his team of postdocs at the University of Texas at Dallas are trying to figure out ways to give cochlear implant users access to more low frequencies. A week after my frustratingly inconclusive encounter with stochastic resonance, I traveled to Dallas and asked Loizou why the government would give him a grant to develop software that increases musical appreciation. "Music lifts up people's spirits, helps them forget things," he told me in his mild Greek accent. "The goal is to have the patient live a normal life, not to be deprived of anything."

30   Loizou is trying to negotiate a trade-off: narrowing low-frequency channels while widening higher-frequency channels. But his theories only hinted at what specific configurations might work best, so Loizou was systematically trying a range of settings to see which ones got the better results.

The team's software ran only on a desktop computer, so on my visit to Dallas I had to be plugged directly into the machine. After a round of testing, a postdoc assured me, they would run *Bolero* through their software and pipe it into my processor via Windows Media Player.

I spent two and a half days hooked up to the computer, listening to endless sequences of tones—none of it music—in a windowless cubicle. Which of two tones sounded lower? Which of two versions of "Twinkle, Twinkle, Little Star" was more recognizable? Did this string of notes sound like a march or a waltz? It was exacting, high-concentration work—like taking an eye exam that lasted for two days. My responses produced reams of data that they would spend hours analyzing.

Forty minutes before my cab back to the airport was due, we finished the last test and the postdoc fired up the programs he needed to play *Bolero*. Some of the lower pitches I'd heard in the previous two days had sounded rich and mellow, and I began thinking wistfully about those bassoons and oboes. I felt a rising sense of anticipation and hope.

I waited while the postdoc tinkered with the computer. And waited. Then I noticed the frustrated look of a man trying to get Windows to behave. "I do this all the time," he said, half to himself. Windows Media Player wouldn't play the file.

35   I suggested rebooting and sampling *Bolero* through a microphone. But the postdoc told me he couldn't do that in time for my plane. A later flight wasn't an option; I had to be back in the Bay Area. I was crushed. I walked out of the building with my shoulders slumped. Scientifically, the visit was a great success. But for me, it was a failure. On the flight home, I plugged myself into my laptop and listened sadly to *Bolero* with Hi-Res. It was like eating cardboard.

It's June 2005, a few weeks after my visit to Dallas, and I'm ready to try again. A team of engineers at Advanced Bionics, one of three companies in the world that makes bionic ears, is working on a new software algorithm for so-called virtual channels. I hop on a flight to their Los Angeles headquarters, my CD player in hand.

My implant has 16 electrodes, but the virtual-channels software will make my hardware act like there are actually 121. Manipulating the flow of electricity to target neurons between each electrode creates the illusion of seven new electrodes between each actual pair, similar to the way an audio engineer can make a sound appear to emanate from between two speakers. Jay Rubinstein had told me two years ago that it would take at least 100 channels to create good music perception. I'm about to find out if he's right.

I'm sitting across a desk from Gulam Emadi, an Advanced Bionics researcher. He and an audiologist are about to fit me with the new software. Leo Litvak, who has spent three years developing the program, comes in to say hello. He's one of those people of whom others often say, "If Leo can't do it, it probably can't be done." And yet it would be hard to find a more modest person. Were it not for his clothes, which mark him as an Orthodox Jew, he would simply disappear in a roomful of people. Litvak tilts his head and smiles hello, shyly glances at Emadi's laptop, and sidles out.

At this point, I'm rationing my emotions like Spock. Hi-Res was a disappointment. Stochastic resonance remains a big if. The low-frequency experiment in Dallas was a bust. Emadi dinks with his computer and hands me my processor with the new software in it. I plug it into myself, plug my CD player into it, and press Play.

Bolero starts off softly and slowly, meandering like a breeze through 40 the trees. *Da-da-da-dum, da-da-da-dum, dum-dum, da-da-da-dum.* I close my eyes to focus, switching between Hi-Res and the new software every 20 or 30 seconds by thumbing a blue dial on my processor.

My God, the oboes d'amore do sound richer and warmer. I let out a long, slow breath, coasting down a river of sound, waiting for the soprano saxophones and the piccolos. They'll come in around six minutes into the piece—and it's only then that I'll know if I've truly got it back.

As it turns out, I couldn't have chosen a better piece of music for testing new implant software. Some biographers have suggested that *Bolero's* obsessive repetition is rooted in the neurological problems Ravel had started to exhibit in 1927, a year before he composed the piece. It's still up for debate whether he had early-onset Alzheimer's, a left-hemisphere brain lesion, or something else.

But *Bolero's* obsessiveness, whatever its cause, is just right for my deafness. Over and over the theme repeats, allowing me to listen for specific details in each cycle.

At 5:59, the soprano saxophones leap out bright and clear, arcing above the snare drum. I hold my breath.

At 6:39, I hear the piccolos. For me, the stretch between 6:39 and 45 7:22 is the most *Bolero* of *Bolero*, the part I wait for each time. I concentrate. It sounds . . . *right.*

Hold on. Don't jump to conclusions. I backtrack to 5:59 and switch to Hi-Res. That heart-stopping leap has become an asthmatic whine. I backtrack again and switch to the new software. And there it is again, that exultant ascent. I can hear *Bolero's* force, its intensity and passion. My chin starts to tremble.

I open my eyes, blinking back tears. "Congratulations," I say to Emadi. "You have done it." And I reach across the desk with absurd formality and shake his hand.

There's more technical work to do, more progress to be made, but I'm completely shattered. I keep zoning out and asking Emadi to repeat things. He passes me a box of tissues. I'm overtaken by a vast sensation of surprise. I did it. For years I pestered researchers and asked questions. Now I'm running 121 channels and I can hear music again.

That evening, in the airport, sitting numbly at the gate, I listen to *Bolero* again. I'd never made it through more than three or four minutes of the piece on Hi-Res before getting bored and turning it off. Now, I listen to the end, following the narrative, hearing again its holy madness.

50   I pull out the Advanced Bionics T-shirt that the team gave me and dab at my eyes.

During the next few days I walk around in a haze of disbelief, listening to *Bolero* over and over to prove to myself that I really am hearing it again. But *Bolero* is just one piece of music. Jonathan Berger, head of Stanford's music department, tells me in an email, "There's not much of interest in terms of structure—it's a continuous crescendo, no surprises, no subtle interplay between development and contrast."

"In fact," he continues, "Ravel was not particularly happy that this study in orchestration became his big hit. It pales in comparison to any of his other music in terms of sophistication, innovation, grace, and depth."

So now it's time to try out music with sophistication, innovation, grace, and depth. But I don't know where to begin. I need an expert with first-rate equipment, a huge music collection, and the ability to pick just the right pieces for my newly reprogrammed ear. I put the question to craigslist—"Looking for a music geek." Within hours, I hear from Tom Rettig, a San Francisco music producer.

In his studio, Rettig plays me Ravel's String Quartet in F Major and Philip Glass' String Quartet no. 5. I listen carefully, switching between the old software and the new. Both compositions sound enormously better on 121 channels. But when Rettig plays music with vocals, I discover that having 121 channels hasn't solved all my problems. While the crescendos in Dulce Pontes' *Cancao do Mar* sound louder and clearer, I hear only white noise when her voice comes in. Rettig figures that relatively simple instrumentals are my best bet—pieces where the instruments don't overlap too much—and that flutes and clarinets work well for me. Cavalcades of brass tend to overwhelm me and confuse my ear.

55   And some music just leaves me cold: I can't even get through Kraftwerk's *Tour de France*. I wave impatiently to Rettig to move on. (Later, a friend tells me it's not the software—Kraftwerk is just dull. It makes

me think that for the first time in my life I might be developing a taste in music.)

Listening to *Bolero* more carefully in Rettig's studio reveals other bugs. The drums sound squeaky—how can drums squeak?—and in the frenetic second half of the piece, I still have trouble separating the instruments.

After I get over the initial awe of hearing music again, I discover that it's harder for me to understand ordinary speech than it was before I went to virtual channels. I report this to Advanced Bionics, and my complaint is met by a rueful shaking of heads. I'm not the first person to say that, they tell me. The idea of virtual channels is a breakthrough, but the technology is still in the early stages of development.

But I no longer doubt that **INCREDIBLE THINGS CAN BE DONE** with that unused 90 percent of my implant's hardware capacity. Tests conducted a month after my visit to Advanced Bionics show that my ability to discriminate among notes has improved considerably. With Hi-Res, I was able to identify notes only when they were at least 70 hertz apart. Now, I can hear notes that are only 30 hertz apart. It's like going from being able to tell the difference between red and blue to being able to distinguish between aquamarine and cobalt.

My hearing is no longer limited by the physical circumstances of my body. While my friends' ears will inevitably decline with age, mine will only get better.

CONVERSATIONS: INCREDIBLE TECHNOLOGY

When Chorost writes in this passage that "incredible things can be done" with the hearing restoration technology he uses, he not only refers to the often remarkable capacity of technology to improve our lives, but he also reveals our deep faith in technology to make life better. His essay may also reveal the high expectations we have for technology. It might be seen as part of the conversations we are always having about the role of technology in our lives.

Understanding the Text

1. Why is the musical composition *Bolero* so important to Chorost? What role does that composition play in his efforts to deal with his hearing loss?

2. What does Chorost mean when he describes his quest for an improved hearing device as "a crusade to explore the edges of auditory science" (par. 14)?

To what extent does he succeed? What does his "crusade" suggest about medical technologies such as hearing aids?

3. What limitations of hearing restoration technology did Chorost encounter in his quest to hear music again? Why did these limitations matter to him, despite improving his hearing? What do you think his experiences with hearing res-

toration technologies suggest about technology in general?

4. What is the process by which advances in hearing technologies have been made, as Chorost describes it in this essay? What do you think this process tells us about the development of technology in general? What might it suggest about the nature of progress?

5. What do you think Chorost ultimately learns about technology from his experiences? Explain, citing specific passages from his essay to support your answer.

Exploring the Issues

1. Evaluate the passages in this essay in which Chorost discusses the science and technology of hearing loss (for example, par. 15–17 and 20–21). How clear are these technical explanations? How effectively does Chorost convey complex technical concepts? To what extent do you think his discussions of science and technology strengthen or weaken his essay?

2. One noticeable feature of Chorost's writing style is his use of similes and metaphors to help explain a technical idea or describe a feeling. For example, at the end of paragraph 35, he writes that listening to *Bolero* on the Hi-Res device was "like eating cardboard." Look for other similes and metaphors in this essay and evaluate their effectiveness. To what extent do you think they strengthen or weaken Chorost's writing? Do they appeal to you as a reader? Why or why not? What might your answer to that question suggest about you as a reader?

3. The climax of Chorost's story is the point at which he is able to listen to *Bolero* again with new software that enables him to hear the richness of the music that he heard before he completely lost his natural hearing (par. 40–50). Evaluate that passage and how Chorost leads up to it. How does he create a sense of anticipation for that moment? How does he describe the moment? Do you think his description of that moment is ef-

fective? Does it do justice to the impact of his experience on him? Explain, citing specific passages from the essay to support your answer.

4. To what extent do you think Chorost's experiences resulted in progress for him? What do you think his experiences might teach us about the nature of progress?

Entering the Conversations

1. Write an essay about an experience in which technology played a prominent role in your life. You might choose an experience with a technology that you believe somehow improved your life, as Chorost does in his essay. Or, you might choose an experience with technology that was less positive. In your essay, describe the experience and convey a sense of what you learned from it.

2. In a group of classmates, share the essays you wrote for Question 1. Look for similarities and differences in the experiences you each wrote about and in your perspectives on technology. What do your experiences suggest about the role of technology in our lives? What might they reveal about our attitudes toward technology? What might they suggest about the nature of progress?

INFOTRAC

3. Select a technology of importance or interest to you and, using appropriate resources such as InfoTrac College Edition, your library, and the Internet, research the history and development of that technology. Then, write a report about that technology. In your report, convey a sense of the

role of that technology in our lives and draw conclusions about what it might suggest about the nature of progress.

4. Find print, Internet, radio, or television advertisements for the technology you wrote about in Question 3 (or another technology of interest to you). Examine those ads for what they seem to suggest about our attitudes regarding technology and progress. Then, write an essay in which you present your analysis of these ads.

Alternatively, create your own advertisement for the technology you researched that conveys your sense of the role of that technology in our lives.

5. Many popular television shows and films depict technologies that somehow change the human body or create humanlike creatures. For example, *The Six Million Dollar Man* was a popular television show in the 1970s in which a man's body is rebuilt and improved through surgery and special technologies after an accident, giving him extraordinary physical capabilities. *The Terminator* (1984) and follow-up films depict cyborgs, robots that appear human but have superhuman powers. View these or other films or television shows in which the human body is somehow improved or enhanced by technology. Then, write an essay in which you analyze the way technology is depicted in such films. Draw conclusions about what these films might reveal about our attitudes toward technology and progress.

6. Identify a technology that is somehow integral to your life. Imagine your life without that technology. Write an essay describing your life if you did not have that technology.

GLOBAL CHANGE

IN 2007, THE INTERGOVERNMENTAL PANEL ON CLIMATE CHANGE (IPCC) RELEASED AN ALARMING REPORT. ON THE BASIS OF HUNDREDS OF SCIENTIFIC STUDIES, THE IPCC CONCLUDED THAT "WARMING OF THE CLIMATE SYSTEM IS NOW UNEQUIVOCAL"; MOREOVER, THE IPCC ASSERTED THAT "MOST OF the observed increase in globally averaged temperatures since the mid-twentieth century is very likely due to the observed increase in anthropogenic greenhouse gas concentrations." In other words, humans are causing global warming. For the past two decades, many environmentalists and scientists have warned about the potentially disastrous effects of global climate change, but the idea that humans were causing the earth's atmosphere to become warmer was controversial. By 2007, however, most people seemed to believe what the IPCC was telling us: that the scientific evidence indicated that human activity was probably responsible for the documented increase in average global temperatures.

Suddenly, it seemed, everyone was worried about global warming. People began talking about reducing their "carbon footprints," decreasing the production of greenhouse gases, and "living green." If you were paying attention to these developments, you probably noticed that "going green," which used to be associated with alternative lifestyles, was becoming part of the mainstream culture. Many companies began to advertise products—such as compact fluorescent light bulbs or more efficient appliances—that minimize our impact on the earth. Some automobile companies began to market gas–electric hybrid vehicles not only as more fuel efficient but also as less dangerous because they released fewer greenhouse gases into the atmosphere. If Americans weren't necessarily changing their lifestyles to try to stop global warming, they were at least taking the problem much more seriously.

At the same time, critics warned that even if Americans reduced their impact on the atmosphere, other nations, such as China and India, were pumping more greenhouse gases into the air than ever before as they expanded their economies in their efforts to attain the lifestyle that Americans have long enjoyed. Some business leaders argued that measures to reduce Americans' impact on the atmosphere could weaken the U.S. economy while other nations increased their own production of greenhouse gases; in the end, the world would be no better off and maybe even worse. The debates about what to do continue.

Such developments underscore how much the world we are living in is changing. The atmosphere is changing, the environment is changing, and human society itself is changing. You are living in a globalized world, where the decision by a Chinese citizen in Shanghai to buy a car can affect changes in the weather in California. A drought in Africa might mean that you will pay higher prices for foods at your local market. A hurricane in the Gulf of Mexico can send world oil prices soaring. Such an interconnected world means greater challenges—and opportunities—for all of us.

The readings in this chapter explore those challenges and illuminate some of those opportunities. They can help us appreciate the complexity of our changing world and may help you think differently about your place in the world and your connection to other human beings—as well as to the earth we all share. They will also, I hope, help you appreciate the complex process by which we try to make sense of the greatest challenges facing us—and how writing itself is an integral part of that process.

Al Gore delivered this lecture in 2007 when *he received the Nobel Peace Prize, one of the world's most prestigious awards recognizing the efforts of individuals and organizations to improve human life. Gore received the Nobel Peace Prize for his work to educate the world about global climate change. Earlier in that same year, he also won an Academy*

Nobel Lecture

Award for his film An Inconvenient Truth, *which depicts the potentially devastating effects of global warming. Clearly, Gore has been working in many different media—film, speech, the Internet, and print—to convey his message about global climate change. And more people seem to be listening. As I was writing this chapter in the summer of 2008, for example, Gore gave a speech in Washington, D.C., outlining a proposal to eliminate all carbon-emitting forms of electricity production in the United States within ten years and to replace them with alternative forms of energy, including solar and wind power. His speech received as much attention as the U.S. presidential campaign, which was in full swing at the time. Whether you agree with him or not, Gore has profoundly shaped perhaps the most important conversation of our time.*

That's one reason I included his Nobel speech in this textbook. It's a good example of how writers join

AL GORE

Your Majesties, Your Royal Highnesses, Honorable members of the Norwegian Nobel Committee, Excellencies, Ladies and gentlemen.

I have a purpose here today. It is a purpose I have tried to serve for many years. I have prayed that God would show me a way to accomplish it.

Sometimes, without warning, the future knocks on our door with a precious and painful vision of what might be. One hundred and nineteen years ago, a wealthy inventor read his own obituary, mistakenly published years before his death. Wrongly believing the inventor had just died, a newspaper printed a harsh judgment of his life's work, unfairly labeling him **"THE MERCHANT OF DEATH"** because of his invention—dynamite. Shaken by this condemnation, the inventor made a fateful choice to serve the cause of peace.

Seven years later, Alfred Nobel created this prize and the others that bear his name.

Seven years ago tomorrow, I read my own political obituary in a judgment that seemed to me harsh and mistaken—if not premature. But that unwelcome verdict also brought a precious if painful gift: an opportunity to search for fresh new ways to serve my purpose.

5

Unexpectedly, that quest has brought me here. Even though I fear my words cannot match this moment, I pray what I am feeling in my heart will be communicated clearly enough that those who hear me will say, "We must act."

The **DISTINGUISHED SCIENTISTS** with whom it is the greatest honor of my life to share this award have laid before us a choice between two different futures—a choice that to my ears echoes the words of an ancient prophet: "Life or death, blessings or curses. Therefore, choose life, that both thou and thy seed may live."

We, the human species, are confronting a planetary emergency—a threat to the survival of our civilization that is gathering ominous and destructive potential even as we gather here. But there is hopeful news as well: we have the ability to solve this crisis and avoid the worst—though not all—of its consequences, if we act boldly, decisively and quickly.

However, despite a growing number of honorable exceptions, too many of the world's leaders are still best described in the words Winston Churchill applied to those who ignored Adolf Hitler's threat: "They go on in strange paradox, decided only to be undecided, resolved to be irresolute, adamant for drift, solid for fluidity, all powerful to be impotent."

10   So today, we dumped another 70 million tons of global-warming pollution into the thin shell of atmosphere surrounding our planet, as if it were an open sewer. And tomorrow, we will dump a slightly larger amount, with the cumulative concentrations now trapping more and more heat from the sun.

As a result, the earth has a fever. And the fever is rising. The experts have told us it is not a passing affliction that will heal by itself. We asked for a second opinion. And a third. And a fourth. And the consistent conclusion, restated with increasing alarm, is that something basic is wrong.

We are what is wrong, and we must make it right.

Last September 21, as the Northern Hemisphere tilted away from the sun, scientists reported with unprecedented distress that the North Polar ice cap is "falling off a cliff." One study estimated that it could be completely gone during summer in less than 22 years. Another new study, to be presented by U.S. Navy researchers later this week, warns it could happen in as little as 7 years.

SEVEN YEARS FROM NOW.

15   In the last few months, it has been harder and harder to misinterpret the signs that our world is spinning out of kilter. Major cities in North and South America, Asia and Australia are nearly out of water due to massive droughts and melting glaciers. Desperate farmers are losing

and influence important conversations; it also a good example of how to make an argument about a complex and controversial topic. But I also included this speech because Gore's voice has become such an important one in a conversation that I suspect has become part of your own life.

Elected to the U.S. Congress in 1977, Al Gore (b. 1948) served as U.S. Representative from Tennessee until 1985 and then as U.S. Senator from 1985 to 1993, when he became Vice President under President Bill Clinton, a post he held until 2001. He is the author of many books on environmental policy, government, and family, including Earth in the Balance *(1992),* The Spirit of Family *(2002), and* The Assault on Reason *(2007).* ☑

GLOSS: THE MERCHANT OF DEATH
Alfred Nobel (1833–1896), a Swedish chemist and businessman, was sometimes called "The Merchant of Death" for inventing and selling dynamite. Nobel used his fortune to establish the Nobel Foundation, which since 1901 has been awarding annual prizes for achievements in medicine, physics, chemistry, and literature and for work toward peace. In this passage, Gore relates the story about an obituary for Nobel that was prematurely published in a French newspaper. Nobel reportedly decided to establish the Nobel prizes after reading the reference to himself as the Merchant of Death in that obituary. Note how Gore uses this story to refer to his own "political obituary" in paragraph 5. There he is referring to the "unwelcome verdict" in the U.S. Supreme Court case *Bush v. Gore,* handed down on December 12, 2000, a day after oral arguments were heard in the case. That decision effectively allowed the results of the U.S. presidential election in the state of Florida to stand, giving Republican presidential candidate George W. Bush the victory over Al Gore, the Democratic candidate. Gore suggests that that decision was considered by some people to be the end of his political career.

GLOSS: DISTINGUISHED SCIENTISTS
The "distinguished scientists" who shared the 2007 Nobel Peace Prize with Al Gore were the scientists of the Intergovernmental Panel on Climate Change, a scientific organization established in 1988 by the World Meteorology Organization and the United Nations Environmental Program to review scientific evidence regarding climate change.

STRATEGIES: EMPHASIZING A POINT
Paragraph 14 is composed of a single phrase—"seven years from now"—that Gore repeats from the previous paragraph. Writers often employ several techniques to emphasize an important point, including repetition, rhythm, sentence structure, and even paragraphing. Gore uses all these techniques here, signaling to his readers that this is a crucial point in his argument. In the next paragraph (15), he uses additional techniques to reinforce this point. There he presents a sequence of images that convey a picture of the changing climate. Notice that he presents these images in seven sentences that all have the same basic structure. The repetition of that sentence structure helps convey the seriousness of these images. It focuses our attention on these sentences in a way that more varied sentence structure might not.

GLOSS: SVANTE ARRHENIUS
Swedish scientist Svante Arrhenius (1859–1927) won the Nobel Prize for chemistry in 1903.

GLOSS: ROGER REVELLE AND DAVE KEELING
Roger Revelle (1909–1991) was one of the first scientists to investigate the effects of carbon dioxide in the atmosphere. He and scientist Charles David Keeling (1928–2005) helped explain the greenhouse effect, by which carbon dioxide and other gases "trap" heat at the earth's surface, much as the glass of a greenhouse traps the sun's heat. Their research helped create awareness of global warming and the impact of human activities on the atmosphere.

their livelihoods. Peoples in the frozen Arctic and on low-lying Pacific islands are planning evacuations of places they have long called home. Unprecedented wildfires have forced a half million people from their homes in one country and caused a national emergency that almost brought down the government in another. Climate refugees have migrated into areas already inhabited by people with different cultures, religions, and traditions, increasing the potential for conflict. Stronger storms in the Pacific and Atlantic have threatened whole cities. Millions have been displaced by massive flooding in South Asia, Mexico, and 18 countries in Africa. As temperature extremes have increased, tens of thousands have lost their lives. We are recklessly burning and clearing our forests and driving more and more species into extinction. The very web of life on which we depend is being ripped and frayed.

We never intended to cause all this destruction, just as Alfred Nobel never intended that dynamite be used for waging war. He had hoped his invention would promote human progress. We shared that same worthy goal when we began burning massive quantities of coal, then oil and methane.

Even in Nobel's time, there were a few warnings of the likely consequences. One of the very first winners of the Prize in chemistry worried that, "We are evaporating our coal mines into the air." After performing 10,000 equations by hand, **SVANTE ARRHENIUS** calculated that the earth's average temperature would increase by many degrees if we doubled the amount of CO_2 in the atmosphere.

Seventy years later, my teacher, **ROGER REVELLE,** and his colleague, **DAVE KEELING,** began to precisely document the increasing CO_2 levels day by day.

But unlike most other forms of pollution, CO_2 is invisible, tasteless, and odorless—which has helped keep the truth about what it is doing to our climate out of sight and out of mind. Moreover, the catastrophe now threatening us is unprecedented—and we often confuse the unprecedented with the improbable.

We also find it hard to imagine making the massive changes that are now necessary to solve the crisis. And WHEN LARGE TRUTHS ARE GENUINELY INCONVENIENT, whole societies can, at least for a time, ignore them. Yet as George Orwell reminds us: "Sooner or later a false belief bumps up against solid reality, usually on a battlefield." 20

In the years since this prize was first awarded, the entire relationship between humankind and the earth has been radically transformed. And still, we have remained largely oblivious to the impact of our cumulative actions.

Indeed, without realizing it, we have begun to wage war on the earth itself. Now, we and the earth's climate are locked in a relationship familiar to war planners: "Mutually assured destruction."

More than two decades ago, scientists calculated that nuclear war could throw so much debris and smoke into the air that it would block life-giving sunlight from our atmosphere, causing a **"NUCLEAR WINTER."** Their eloquent warnings here in Oslo helped galvanize the world's resolve to halt the nuclear arms race.

Now science is warning us that if we do not quickly reduce the global warming pollution that is trapping so much of the heat our planet normally radiates back out of the atmosphere, we are in danger of creating a permanent "carbon summer."

25 As the American poet Robert Frost wrote, "Some say the world will end in fire; some say in ice." Either, he notes, "would suffice."

But neither need be our fate. It is time to make peace with the planet.

We must quickly mobilize our civilization with the urgency and resolve that has previously been seen only when nations mobilized for war. These prior struggles for survival were won when leaders found words at the 11th hour that released a mighty surge of courage, hope and readiness to sacrifice for a protracted and mortal challenge.

These were not comforting and misleading assurances that the threat was not real or imminent; that it would affect others but not ourselves; that ordinary life might be lived even in the presence of extraordinary threat; that Providence could be trusted to do for us what we would not do for ourselves.

No, these were calls to come to the defense of the common future. They were calls upon the courage, generosity and strength of entire peoples, citizens of every class and condition who were ready to stand against the threat once asked to do so. Our enemies in those times calculated that free people would not rise to the challenge; they were, of course, catastrophically wrong.

30 Now comes the threat of climate crisis—a threat that is real, rising, imminent, and

CONVERSATIONS: INCONVENIENT TRUTHS
When Gores writes in paragraph 20 of "large truths [that] are genuinely inconvenient," he is making a subtle reference to his Academy Award–winning film about the impact of global climate change, *An Inconvenient Truth* (2006), which was advertised as "the most terrifying film you will ever see." Gore's film might be seen as another important part of the ongoing conversations about global climate change, in which Gore has been a key figure. Consider how a speech like his Nobel lecture compares to a film like *An Inconvenient Truth* as a way to participate in these important conversations.

CONVERSATIONS: NUCLEAR WINTER
In 1985, an organization called International Physicians for the Prevention of Nuclear War won the Nobel Peace Prize for their work in educating the world about the likely effects of a nuclear war, which according to some scientific studies would result in an environmental catastrophe that came to be described as "nuclear winter." At the time, many people believed that nuclear war was the greatest threat to humankind. According to International Physicians for the Prevention of Nuclear War, an exchange of nuclear bombs by the United States and the Soviet Union, the two nations with the largest nuclear arsenals, would destroy ecosystems, contaminate the atmosphere, and block sunlight such that the world could be launched into a kind of permanent winter. This idea of a "nuclear winter" became shorthand for the dangers associated with nuclear arms, in the same way that "global warming" has become a kind of shorthand to refer to the severe environmental problems being caused by human activities. In their Nobel Prize acceptance speech, the International Physicians for the Prevention of Nuclear War spoke out against building more nuclear weapons and urged governments to destroy their nuclear stockpiles, as Gore suggests in this paragraph. In a sense, like the International Physicians for the Prevention of Nuclear War, Gore is engaged in a conversation about how to live together peacefully and solve the most serious problems facing humankind.

universal. Once again, it is the 11th hour. The penalties for ignoring this challenge are immense and growing, and at some near point would be unsustainable and unrecoverable. For now we still have the power to choose our fate, and the remaining question is only this: Have we the will to act vigorously and in time, or will we remain imprisoned by a dangerous illusion?

Mahatma Gandhi awakened the largest democracy on earth and forged a shared resolve with what he called "Satyagraha"—or "truth force."

In every land, the truth—once known—has the power to set us free.

Truth also has the power to unite us and bridge the distance between "me" and "we," creating the basis for common effort and shared responsibility.

There is an African proverb that says, "If you want to go quickly, go alone. If you want to go far, go together." We need to go far, quickly.

We must abandon the conceit that individual, isolated, private actions are the answer. They can and do help. But they will not take us far enough without collective action. At the same time, we must ensure that in mobilizing globally, we do not invite the establishment of ideological conformity and a new lock-step "ism." 35

That means adopting principles, values, laws, and treaties that release creativity and initiative at every level of society in multifold responses originating concurrently and spontaneously.

This new consciousness requires expanding the possibilities inherent in all humanity. The innovators who will devise a new way to harness the sun's energy for pennies or invent an engine that's carbon negative may live in Lagos or Mumbai or Montevideo. We must ensure that entrepreneurs and inventors everywhere on the globe have the chance to change the world.

When we unite for a moral purpose that is manifestly good and true, the spiritual energy unleashed can transform us. The generation that defeated fascism throughout the world in the 1940s found, in rising to meet their awesome challenge, that they had gained the moral authority and long-term vision to launch the **MARSHALL PLAN,** the United Nations, and a new level of global cooperation and foresight that unified Europe and facilitated the emergence of democracy and prosperity in Germany, Japan, Italy and much of the world. One of their visionary leaders said, "It is time we steered by the stars and not by the lights of every passing ship."

In the last year of that war, you gave the Peace Prize to a man from my hometown of 2000 people, Carthage, Tennessee. **CORDELL HULL** was described by Franklin Roosevelt as the "Father of the United Nations." He was an inspiration and hero to my own father, who followed Hull in the Congress and the U.S. Senate and in his commitment to world peace and global cooperation.

My parents spoke often of Hull, always in tones of reverence and 40 admiration. Eight weeks ago, when you announced this prize, the

GLOSS: THE MARSHALL PLAN
The Marshall Plan was the U.S. assistance program to rebuild Europe after World War II. It was conceived by George Marshall (1880–1959), a five-star general in the U.S. Army who served as U.S. Secretary of State from 1947 to 1949. He was awarded the Nobel Peace Prize in 1953 for his plan to rebuild Europe.

GLOSS: CORDELL HULL
A Tennessean like Al Gore, Cordell Hull (1871–1955) served as U.S. Secretary of State from 1933 to 1944 and received the Nobel Peace Prize in 1945 for helping to establish the United Nations.

deepest emotion I felt was when I saw the headline in my hometown paper that simply noted I had won the same prize that Cordell Hull had won. In that moment, I knew what my father and mother would have felt were they alive.

Just as Hull's generation found moral authority in rising to solve the world crisis caused by fascism, so too can we find our greatest opportunity in rising to solve the climate crisis. In the Kanji characters used in both Chinese and Japanese, "crisis" is written with two symbols, the first meaning "danger," the second "opportunity." By facing and removing the danger of the climate crisis, we have the opportunity to gain the moral authority and vision to vastly increase our own capacity to solve other crises that have been too long ignored.

We must understand the connections between the climate crisis and the afflictions of poverty, hunger, HIV-AIDS and other pandemics. As these problems are linked, so too must be their solutions. We must begin by making the common rescue of the global environment the central organizing principle of the world community.

Fifteen years ago, I made that case at the "Earth Summit" in **RIO DE JANEIRO.** Ten years ago, I presented it in **KYOTO.** This week, I will urge the delegates in **BALI** to adopt a bold mandate for a treaty that establishes a universal global cap on emissions and uses the market in emissions trading to efficiently allocate resources to the most effective opportunities for speedy reductions.

This treaty should be ratified and brought into effect everywhere in the world by the beginning of 2010—two years sooner than presently contemplated. The pace of our response must be accelerated to match the accelerating pace of the crisis itself.

45 Heads of state should meet early next year to review what was accomplished in Bali and take personal responsibility for addressing this crisis. It is not unreasonable to ask, given the gravity of our circumstances, that these heads of state meet every three months until the treaty is completed.

We also need a moratorium on the construction of any new generating facility that burns coal without the capacity to safely trap and store carbon dioxide.

And most important of all, we need to put a *price* on carbon—with a CO_2 tax that is then rebated back to the people, progressively, according to the laws of each nation, in ways that shift the burden of taxation from employment to pollution. This is by far the most effective and simplest way to accelerate solutions to this crisis.

The world needs an alliance—especially of those nations that weigh heaviest in the scales where earth is in the balance. I salute Europe and Japan for the steps they've taken in recent years to meet the challenge, and the new government in Australia, which has made solving the climate crisis its first priority.

But the outcome will be decisively influenced by two nations that are now failing to do enough: the United States and China. While India is

---

CONVERSATIONS: RIO DE JANEIRO, KYOTO, AND BALI
In this paragraph, Gore mentions three important events in the ongoing global discussions about protecting the environment and in particular about global climate change. In 1992, the U.N. sponsored the Conference on Environment and Development, held in Rio de Janiero, to discuss international efforts to address environmental problems, including climate change. The agreement reached at that conference led to the Kyoto Protocol, an international agreement adopted in 1997 in Kyoto, Japan, to set emissions limits intended to reduce the greenhouses gases that are thought to cause global warming. That agreement was controversial in the United States, which was one of the few developed nations in the world that did not sign it. In 2007, representatives from 180 countries attended the U.N.-sponsored Climate Change Conference in Bali to continue discussions about how to address climate change. These events reflect the changing nature of the international conversations about how best to address the problem of global climate change. Al Gore has been involved in these events and has been a leading voice in these conversations. His Nobel lecture can be seen as part of those conversations.

also growing fast in importance, it should be absolutely clear that it is the two largest CO_2 emitters—most of all, my own country—that will need to make the boldest moves, or stand accountable before history for their failure to act.

50   Both countries should stop using the other's behavior as an excuse for stalemate and instead develop an agenda for mutual survival in a shared global environment.

These are the last few years of decision, but they can be the first years of a bright and hopeful future if we do what we must. No one should believe a solution will be found without effort, without cost, without change. Let us acknowledge that if we wish to redeem squandered time and speak again with moral authority, then these are the hard truths:

The way ahead is difficult. The outer boundary of what we currently believe is feasible is still far short of what we actually must do. Moreover, between here and there, across the unknown, falls the shadow.

That is just another way of saying that we have to expand the boundaries of what is possible. In the words of the Spanish poet, Antonio Machado, "Pathwalker, there is no path. You must make the path as you walk."

We are standing at the most fateful fork in that path. So I want to end as I began, with a vision of two futures—each a palpable possibility—and with a prayer that we will see with vivid clarity the necessity of choosing between those two futures, and the urgency of making the right choice now.

55   The great Norwegian playwright, Henrik Ibsen, wrote, "One of these days, the younger generation will come knocking at my door."

The future is knocking at our door right now. Make no mistake, the next generation *will* ask us one of two questions. Either they will ask: "What were you thinking; why didn't you act?"

Or they will ask instead: "How did you find the moral courage to rise and successfully resolve a crisis that so many said was impossible to solve?"

We have everything we need to get started, save perhaps political will, but political will is a renewable resource.

So let us renew it, and say together: "We have a purpose. We are many. For this purpose we will rise, and we will act."

Understanding the Text

1. What is Gore's stated purpose in this speech? What actions is he encouraging human beings to take? Why do you think he emphasizes his purpose in his speech in this way? Do you think his purpose is appropriate for his Nobel acceptance speech? Explain.

2. Does Gore blame human beings for the dire situation that they are facing as a result of global climate change? Explain. What do you think Gore's analysis of the problem of climate change suggests about his views of human beings and his hope (or lack of it) for the future?

3. What does Gore mean when he states that "we often

confuse the unprecedented with the improbable" (par. 19)? Why is that confusion important to his main point in this speech?

4. How were the most difficult problems facing humans solved in the past, according to Gore? What lessons can we learn from the past to help us solve the problem of global warming, in his view? Do you think Gore is right about these lessons? Why or why not?

5. In what sense is the problem of climate change linked to major social problems facing humans today, according to Gore? Why is this connection so important, in his view?

Exploring the Issues

1. In this speech, Gore makes a vigorous argument that we must act to address the problem of global climate change. What evidence does he provide to support his argument? How persuasive do you find this evidence? How effective do you think Gore's argument is? Explain, citing specific passages from his text to support your answer.

2. How would you describe Gore's voice in this speech? What features of his text help create his voice? How does his voice in this text compare with your sense of him as a politician? How effective do you think his voice is in this speech? Explain, citing specific passages from his text in your answer.

3. In paragraph 37, Gores advocates a "new consciousness" that he believes is necessary to solve the problem of global warming. What exactly is this "new consciousness"? What impact can it have, in his view? Do you think his

views about this new consciousness are shared by many people? How encouraged does his discussion of this new consciousness make you feel? Explain.

4. In this speech, Gore makes many references to important scientists, political leaders, writers, and historical events. What do you think these references suggest about Gore's view of history? How should we use history as a guide, in his view? What might his view of history reveal about his views about humankind in general?

Entering the Conversations

1. Write an essay in which you present your own views about the problem of global climate change and what should (or shouldn't) be done about it. In your essay, draw on Gore's Nobel lecture and any other appropriate text to help make and support your main points.

2. Rewrite the essay you wrote for Question 1 as a speech to be given to a specific audience (for example, students at your university or members of your town or city Chamber of Commerce). Then compare your speech and your essay. What changes did you feel you had to make to turn your essay into a speech? What conclusions can you draw about differences or similarities in writing an essay to be read or a speech to be heard by an audience?

INFOTRAC

3. Although few people today dispute that global warming is happening, there is still much debate about the extent to

which it is being caused by human activity and perhaps even more debate about what to do about it. Using InfoTrac College Edition, the Internet, your library, and any other available resources, investigate this issue. Try to identify the main perspectives on what is causing global warming and what should be done about it. If possible, talk to a faculty member at your school who might be an expert in these issues. Then write a report in which you present an overview of the current debates about global warming. Draw your own conclusions about what can (or should) be done (if anything) about this problem.

4. Using Gore's speech as a guide and drawing on your research for Question 3, create a pamphlet, flyer, web site, or other appropriate document in which you present your ideas about what individual students at your school can do about global warming.

5. Write a conventional academic essay in which you analyze and evaluate Gore's speech. In your essay, describe the techniques Gore uses to make his case and evaluate the evidence he uses to support his claims. Draw conclusions about the effectiveness of his argument.

6. Watch *An Inconvenient Truth* and write an essay in which you evaluate the effectiveness of that film, as compared with Gore's Nobel lecture, in conveying his concerns about global warming. Identify what you believe are the strengths and weaknesses of the film and the speech, and draw conclusions about the influence of the medium in conveying a message.

In the debates about global climate change in recent years, attention often has been focused on the scale of the problem: the millions of tons of carbon dioxide and other greenhouse gases pumped into the atmosphere by millions of cars and hundreds of power plants. Arguments focus on the potential costs, usually calculated in millions or billions of dollars, of

Climate Migration

various proposals to stop global warming. We are told how many square miles of glaciers are disappearing each year as the atmosphere gets warmer. We are told how many millions of barrels of oil are consumed every day by the millions of cars and trucks driving on millions of miles of roads. These numbers are always big. And maybe that's why it can be so hard to acquire a real sense of what climate change might mean for us as we try to live our daily lives.

The following essay by aid worker Nicki Bennett may help us acquire the necessary perspective to appreciate the impact of global warming. She introduces us to a rickshaw driver in Bangladesh whose life has been directly affected by global climate change—one human being among the millions who are (or will be) similarly affected. Bennett shares some big numbers, too: 300,000 rickshaws, 150 million people, millions of square miles of coastal

NICKI BENNETT

© Corey Wise/Lonely Planet

THIS WEEK I'M BACK IN DHAKA, **the world's undisputed rickshaw** capital. With more than 300,000 of these brightly colored bicycle contraptions plying the city's streets for trade, I rarely walk for more than a block before a rickshaw driver (known as "rickshaw-wallah") pulls up next to me and urges me to hop on board.

I've learned it's almost impossible to refuse a ride. This is partly because the rickshaw-wallahs are very persistent, partly because I feel I should be supporting people struggling to make a living (one in five of the city's inhabitants depends on the rickshaw business for their

© Rosemary Behan/Alamy Limited

land threatened by rising seas. But she reduces those numbers to one man who represents a new category of human being: people whom Bennett calls "climate migrants" because their migration from their homes has been forced by a changing climate. Her essay brings him to us and thus helps make climate change real—another example of the power of writing.

Nicki Bennett works for Oxfam, a coalition of aid organizations working to fight poverty and injustice throughout the world. This essay appeared in 2008 on a blog maintained by Nicholas Kristoff, a columnist for the New York Times. ▼

income) and partly because Dhaka is now starting to get unbearably hot and humid (and I'm starting to get horrendously lazy).

Coming back from a meeting near my office this afternoon, I start chatting (well, mainly hand-gesturing) with my rickshaw-wallah and ask him where he's from. I've heard lots of stories about families in the cyclone-affected coastal areas sending sons or brothers to urban centers like Dhaka to make a little bit of cash driving rickshaws (many people have not been able to return to their regular jobs as the cyclone destroyed their fishing boats and nets or washed away their crops). I'm wondering if my rickshaw-wallah is one of them.

Instead, he names a district that I've never heard of. We manage to establish that it's somewhere north of Dhaka, near a river. "Floods," he tells me. "In my village. Village underwater." Finally the penny drops—he's not just an economic migrant, he's also a "climate migrant."

5   Few countries in the world are more acutely threatened by climate-related disasters and climate change than Bangladesh. The country (70 percent of which consists of flood plain) is already sinking—within the next two decades Bangladesh may lose as much as 20 percent of its land to rising sea levels and melting Himalayan glaciers. This is not good news in a country of 150 million people—even a relatively moderate 10 or 20 centimeters rise in sea level could displace millions within the next 15 years. Population density is already high, with approximately 1045 Bangladeshis crammed into each square kilometer of land.

Following last year's scientific breakthrough (and the publication of **THE IPCC CLIMATE CHANGE REPORT**), it's no longer possible for anyone to deny that global warming is happening. It's also pretty clear that the biggest polluters are not poor countries like Bangladesh, but wealthy nations like the United States, Saudi Arabia, Australia and

STRATEGIES: BEGINNING AN ESSAY
Notice how Bennett jumps right into her description of her experience in Dhaka, Bangladesh. Sometimes such an abrupt beginning effectively draws a reader into the writing. But there is another consideration in this case: Bennett originally wrote this essay as a guest blogger for "On the Ground," a blog maintained by *New York Times* columnist Nicholas Kristoff. As a guest blogger, Bennett posted regular essays to Kristoff's blog, so her readers would already know that she was writing from Bangladesh. Her seemingly abrupt beginning is a good example of how the medium can influence a writer's strategies (as discussed in "Using Multimedia and Online Technologies" in Chapter 2). The writing on blogs is sometimes more informal and personal than a regular newspaper column—almost like a personal letter or e-mail message.

CONVERSATIONS: THE IPCC AND GLOBAL WARMING
When Bennett writes of "last year's scientific breakthrough" in this paragraph, she seems to be referring to international agreements on climate change reached in 2007 as well as to the conclusions of the Intergovernmental Panel on Climate Change (IPCC), a scientific organization established by the World Meteorology Organization and the United Nations Environmental Program that is considered the world authority on climate change. In 2007, the IPCC released the latest of several reports it has issued since its founding in 1988. Its 2007 report, which was based on a review of hundreds of scientific studies of climate change, left little doubt that the earth's atmosphere is getting warmer, almost certainly as a result of human activity. Perhaps Bennett uses the term "breakthrough" because the IPCC report seemed to silence many global warming skeptics by providing overwhelming scientific evidence of human-induced global warming. That report and the discussions it provoked are part of ongoing international conversations about how to address climate change. As Bennett notes here and in the next paragraph, those discussions include debate about the responsibilities of wealthier nations to take a greater role in trying to solve the problem of global warming. The "adaptation fund" she mentions is the Kyoto Protocol Adaptation Fund, a fund established to help so-called Least Developed Countries (LDCs) such as Bangladesh deal with some of the social and economic effects of climate change. Bennett criticizes the candidates in the 2008 U.S. presidential election for not discussing this fund or the poor people affected by climate change whom she sees in her work for Oxfam. Her criticisms reveal how complex and far-reaching these discussions about climate change have become.

Canada. The rich countries have committed themselves to doing two things—cutting their greenhouse gas emissions and setting up a fund that helps poor countries cope with the damage already being caused by climate change.

Back at the office, feeling curious, I decide to conduct a quick (and totally unscientific) experiment to check how much people in the United States actually care about the issue: I log onto the web sites of the main U.S. presidential candidates to see if they have a position on climate change. Some of them talk about cutting greenhouse gas emissions. None talk about paying money into the climate change "adaptation" fund. And none are talking about the impact of climate change on poor people—or what they might do about the fact that places like Bangladesh and New Orleans are already being bashed by climate-related disasters and slowly losing land to rising sea levels.

I'm sure my rickshaw-wallah is not exactly thinking about climate change or politics as he reaches for a grimy piece of cloth to wipe his sweaty brow at the end of my journey. But as someone who spends his waking hours inhaling a potent mix of lead and carbon monoxide and has a life expectancy of only 45 years, he may be thinking about other ways of making a living. I have a feeling he would not be averse to discussing alternative job opportunities with those who have the power to provide the scale of finance Bangladesh needs to help it adapt to climate change. Unfortunately, I'm not sure if we are ready to listen to him just quite yet.

Understanding the Text

1. Why is Bennett unable to refuse a rickshaw ride when she returns to Dhaka? What does she learn from her rickshaw ride? How does she relate the rickshaw ride to her main point in this essay?

2. What significance does Bennett see in the weather-related problems in Bangladesh? In what sense is Bangladesh unique in terms of these problems? In what sense is it representative of the rest of the world?

3. What does Bennett believe we might learn from the rickshaw driver she meets? Do you think she's right? Why or why not?

Exploring the Issues

1. Bennett supports several of her assertions with references to studies, facts, and other kinds of evidence. For example, in paragraph 2, she tells us that "one in five of the city's inhabitants depends on the rickshaw business for their income." In her original post to the blog where this essay first appeared, Bennett included hyperlinks to other web sites where readers could find the sources of this information (similar to a footnote in a conventional research paper). Evaluate the evidence she provides to support her assertions. What effect do you think this evidence is intended to have on her readers? Does this evidence make her essay more persuasive, in your view? Explain, citing specific passages from her essay to support your answer.

2. Although Bennett tells the story of the "climate migrants" in this essay, she also shares her own views at times and reveals something about herself as a person. What do you learn about Bennett in this essay? What do you learn about her views on the subjects that matter to her? Do you get a favorable impression of her from this essay? Why or why not? How credible do you find her as the writer of this essay? Explain, citing specific passages to support your answer.

3. How would you describe Bennett's writing style in this essay? What features of her writing characterize her style? To what extent do you think her style indicates that she originally wrote this essay for a blog?

Entering the Conversations

1. Write an essay in which you describe an experience from which you might learn a lesson about climate change (or another environmental issue that concerns you).

INFOTRAC

2. As Bennett indicates in this essay, climate change is likely to have different effects on different parts of the world, and people living in poverty may suffer the worst effects of all. Use InfoTrac College Edition, the Internet, your library, and other available resources to look into the potential impact of climate change on different people living in different parts of the world. Visit the web site of the Intergovernmental Panel on Climate Change (IPCC) and review their reports about the

impact of a warming atmosphere on different ecosystems and different regions. Try to learn what experts believe about the impact of climate change and its relationship to social status and geographical location. Then write a report on the basis of your research. Present what you found about the different ways that climate change might affect different people, and draw conclusions about the role of social and economic factors in the effects of climate change.

3. On the basis of your research for Question 2, write a letter to an appropriate government official (such as one of the U.S. senators from your state) in which you express your views about what the United States should be doing to address climate change. In your letter, present your perspective on the role of social and economic factors in climate change and how those should influence U.S. policy.

4. Visit several blogs devoted to the issue of climate change or related issues such as those that Bennett discusses in her essay. Read these blogs to get a sense of the various perspectives on the issues addressed by the bloggers. Then, write an essay in which you discuss what you believe these blogs reveal about attitudes regarding climate change.

5. Write an essay in which you define "climate migrant" and discuss what climate migration suggests about the future.

6. Create a multimedia document, such as a web site or PowerPoint presentation, in which you depict the effects of climate change on a single person.

As I was writing this section of Chapter 12 *in the summer of 2008, few reports in the mainstream media raised questions about whether climate change is really happening or whether it is being caused by the burning of fossil fuels. Instead, the debates seemed to shift toward what steps should be taken to solve the problem and adapt to a warming climate.*

Climate Policy: A Reality Check

These debates have grown increasingly complicated, but they are all based on the same assumption: that global warming is a reality.

In the following essay, William O'Keefe offers a check on that reality. Without denying global climate change, O'Keefe questions the widely held view that we have incontrovertible scientific evidence to support the conclusion that humans have caused the earth's atmosphere to become warmer. He calls for a more careful and skeptical

WILLIAM O'KEEFE

The climate debate has been driven mostly by rhetoric and advocacy and what Nobel economist **FREDERICK HAYEK** termed the "fatal conceit."

If any environmental issue was in need of a reality check, it is climate change. Doing so, however, requires distinguishing reality from image and myth. That is not easy, as evidenced by the fact that most of what passes for conventional wisdom about climate change bears little resemblance to either scientific or economic reality. Journalists face a daunting task in getting it right.

Much of the climate change debate and the international policy to address asserted human influence on it are driven by assumptions and complex computer models reflecting those assumptions.

A certain amount of fact based reality is beginning to replace what has passed as reality since the late 1980s. I hold no illusions, however. The special interests and advocates who gain from an

GLOSS: FREDERICK HAYEK
The influential Austrian economist Friedrich (or Frederick) August von Hayek (1899–1992) was a vigorous defender of free-market capitalism and classical, or *laissez faire,* liberalism, a political philosophy emphasizing individual freedom and limited government. Hayek, who won the Nobel Prize for Economics in 1992, helped revive this philosophy in the late twentieth century and influenced current economic policy in the United States. He believed the idea that government planners could solve economic problems better than the free market is a "fatal conceit"—that is, it is based on a fundamentally flawed and arrogant view that governments know best. Consider what O'Keefe's reference to Hayek here might reveal about O'Keefe's own political philosophy.

apocalypse scenario will fight hard to maintain the illusions that have proven profitable.

5   For almost two decades, the climate debate has been dominated by advocates and environmental ministries, primarily those from the European Union. They used the image of a distant environmental apocalypse caused by human activity to fashion an unsustainable and unachievable treaty and to demonize anyone who questioned their orthodoxy.

That orthodoxy holds that climate science is settled, that humans are the major cause of warming in recent decades, and that there is only one way to avoid a climate-induced apocalypse later this century. That one way is to drastically reduce greenhouse gas emissions to levels 60% below 1990 levels by 2050. That orthodoxy is not built on observation, measurement, validation, and objective analyses, which are the bases of scientific information and sound policy.

There is not enough time, nor is this the place, to discuss how this state of self-delusion came about. But it is not a new phenomenon. It has long been the case that prophesies and uncertainty about the future have put bread on the table.

THE ART AND HISTORY OF MANIPULATING THE PUBLIC OPINION ARE WELL DOCUMENTED IN TWO BOOKS. The first is *Extraordinary Popular Delusions and the Madness of Crowds* by Charles Mackay, which was written in 1841. Even then, Mackay made the point that crowds of people become simultaneously impressed with one delusion and run after it until their attention is caught by some new folly more captivating than the first. And, Mark Twain once observed that he was not troubled by what people didn't know, only what they knew that wasn't so.

Our capacity for being bamboozled must be hard wired.

The second book is *The Image: A Guide to Pseudo Events in America* by the late historian Daniel Boorstin. He documented how the gap between what an informed citizen needs to know and can know is being filled with deceptive illusions.

In addition, MICHAEL CRICHTON and others have made the case that environmentalism has replaced religion. The environmental orthodoxy divides the world into angels and demons with the demons being anyone who expresses skepticism about the asserted climate consensus.

As it becomes ever more clear that the Kyoto Protocol is flawed beyond repair, the policy debate will gradually and grudgingly become more realistic and shaped by objective realities. Some of that is already taking place as evidenced by THE RECENT G-8 MEETING declaration, the one from THE RECENT GREENLAND SUMMIT and Tony Blair's surprise admission that Kyoto is unworkable.

The fact that virtually all developed country KYOTO signatories will miss their 2012 obligations and have no hope of meeting the more stringent ones that would follow will be sobering. As Samuel Johnson observed, there is nothing like a hanging to concentrate the mind.

review of available evidence before we take any dramatic steps to address global warming. Although several important developments have changed the debate about climate change somewhat since he wrote this essay in 2005, he represents a perspective on the issue that is still widely shared.

O'Keefe first delivered this essay as a speech at the annual meeting of the Society of Environmental Journalists on September 30, 2005. As you'll see, he has special concerns about the media's role in the debates about climate change, and it's worth considering whether he conveys those concerns effectively to his audience of journalists. It's also worth considering how effectively his essay conveys his concerns to a wider audience that might include you.

William O'Keefe is the CEO of the George Marshall Institute, a non-profit organization that examines scientific issues affecting public policy. He is also president of Solutions Consulting, Inc., which provides engineering and environmental consulting services. This speech was published in the Marshall Institute Policy Outlook *in 2005.*

STRATEGIES: USING SUMMARY TO SUPPORT A POINT
In paragraphs 8 and 10, O'Keefe presents brief summaries of two books, *Extraordinary Popular Delusions and the Madness of Crowds* by the Scottish poet and journalist Charles Mackay (1814–1889) and *The Image: A Guide to Pseudo Events in America* (1962) by American historian and social critic Daniel Boorstin (1914–2004). Note how O'Keefe uses these summaries to support his view of the problems he sees with the current debate about climate change. Writers often use the work of other writers to strengthen their arguments. Consider whether O'Keefe strengthens his argument with these references.

CONVERSATIONS: MICHAEL CRICHTON

In 2005, best-selling author Michael Crichton, whose novels (such as *Jurassic Park*) often have scientific themes, gave a speech to the National Press Club in Washington, D.C., in which he questioned mainstream views about global warming. Crichton claimed that available scientific data do not support the conclusion that humans are causing the earth's atmosphere to become warmer. His speech intensified the ongoing debates about global warming at the time, especially because he claimed to refute the conclusions of the Intergovernmental Panel on Climate Change (IPCC), which is considered the world authority on the issue (and which O'Keefe mentions in par. 14). (See "Conversations: The IPCC and Global Warming" on page 730.) By referring to Crichton here, O'Keefe signals his own agreement with Crichton's call for more skepticism about climate change. O'Keefe reflects the views of many businesspeople who have questioned some environmentalists' warnings about global warming, and his essay might be seen as an example of how such questions have been raised in this ongoing debate.

CONVERSATIONS: KYOTO, G-8, AND GREENLAND

O'Keefe refers here (and in par. 12) to the Kyoto Protocols, an international agreement to reduce the production of greenhouse gases believed to contribute to global warming. (See "Conversations: Rio de Janeiro, Kyoto, and Bali" on page 725.) One hundred eighty nations signed the agreement; the United States was not one of them. O'Keefe suggests that the nations who signed will fail to meet their obligations to reduce greenhouse gases, which they agreed to do by 2012. That likelihood was one of the main criticisms of the Kyoto Protocols by businesspeople like O'Keefe, who argued that signing the agreement would weaken the U.S. economy yet would not result in the reduction of greenhouse gases. Such issues were a focus of discussion at the meetings of the G-8 (which O'Keefe mentions in par. 12), or Group of 8, an annual international forum at which representatives from the United States, Canada, the United Kingdom, France, Germany, Italy, Japan, and Russia discuss economic issues. It was at such a meeting in 2005 that British Prime Minister Tony Blair stated that although he supported international efforts to address global warming, he believed that few nations would seriously try to meet the targets set by the Kyoto agreement (as O'Keefe notes in par. 12). These disagreements also arose at the Greenland Summit (also mentioned in par. 12), a meeting of nations bordering the Arctic to discuss issues such as oil exploration in the Arctic as the sea ice continues to melt. All these meetings reflect the complex and ongoing nature of the conversations about global climate change. O'Keefe's references in these paragraphs are a good example of how a writer's own ideas are shaped by—and contribute to—these conversations.

The debate over future climate change and human attribution is an important one and it will go on for a long time because significant uncertainties will not be resolved soon. Claims that climate science is settled do not square with the many uncertainties documented by the IPCC or the strong support for the Bush Administration Climate Science Strategic Plan by the National Academy of Sciences. Some like climate sensitivity and natural variability may never be completely resolved.

Science will not soon resolve the extent of human influence on the climate system or illuminate an unambiguous path forward. Policy making in the fog of uncertainty is how the world works and we will get better policy if we acknowledge that. Uncertainty complicates decision making but need not paralyze it.

We know that average global temperature is warmer than it was a century ago. We know that CO_2 emissions are higher and increasing. We know that human activity has contributed to a warmer world but not whether the longer term impact will be trivial or serious. And we know that reducing emissions involves reducing fossil fuel use. Beyond that, almost everything else is speculation, professional judgment and the circular process of climate modeling.

The cold hard realities are that we are where we are, there is no politically viable way of turning the greenhouse gas clock back, the world is not about to turn away from fossil fuels, and we cannot predict the future, as much as we pretend otherwise.

Inevitability can be reality forcing. According to the International Energy Agency, the world will need about 50% more energy by 2025. Like it or not, fossil fuels will remain the dominant source of energy then and or some time beyond. That means that emissions will be higher, not lower. The best we can hope for is to slow their growth and increase the world's resiliency. Increased energy efficiency and the introduction of new energy-generation technology are the only politically viable means of achieving those objectives but they will not lead us to a world of increased prosperity with zero or negative emissions growth.

Since most of the future growth in emissions will be from developing countries, a major focus must be to help them realize their economic aspirations, while also lowering their carbon intensity. That is clearly doable and cost-effective. In addition, it is the right thing to do. There can be no justification for ignoring serious human and environmental problems that we know how to solve—malnutrition, high mortality and disease rates, and polluted water for example—while focusing on one that we do not adequately understand and, at best, is distant.

As a nation, and as a group of developed nations, we can do better going forward than we have done in the past. We can do better by testing image against reality and not the reverse. We can do better by being more humble about our ability to will outcomes. We may not be able to abandon Hayek's "fatal conceit" but we can do better in keeping it in check. We can do better by not demonizing those who raise legitimate issues for debate. After all, challenge and skepticism are the hallmarks of good science and the source of new knowledge.

Today, we pretend that we know enough to predict what the world and its climate will be in 2100. We cannot and the sooner we admit it, the better off we will be. Models are useful tools for research and can help illuminate policy issues. But models that have not been validated and can only simulate are instruments of mischief.

Planning the world's economic and climate future, if they could be planned, is not like planning a long vacation where there is little uncertainty and a lot of predictability. Instead, the right model is how Lewis and Clark carried out their charge from Thomas Jefferson to explore and map the territory west of the Missouri. Jefferson set the objective but Lewis and Clark had little knowledge about how they were going to achieve it. They succeeded by an iterative process of taking small steps, acquiring and analyzing new information and then taking their next steps based on what they had learned. Distant predictions of dread and policies reflecting them are not based on this model.

Policies that are based more on facts and objectivity and the acquisition of new knowledge stand a better chance of success and sustainable public support. But, expecting such policies is probably a triumph of hope over experience.

Healthy skepticism makes good journalism and is recognized as a virtue. In the climate debate, unfortunately, it has been treated as a vice. It should not be.

Understanding the Text

1. What complaints does O'Keefe make about the on-going debate about climate change? Why does the nature of this debate concern him? Do you agree with his assessment of this debate? Why or why not?

2. What is the "orthodoxy" in this debate, in his view? Why does he reject this orthodoxy? What does his criticism of this orthodoxy suggest about his own view about how best to resolve complicated problems such as climate change?

3. Why does O'Keefe believe that science will not resolve the controversies about global warming? What do you think his view suggests about the nature of such controversies? Do you think he's right? Why or why not?

4. What problems does O'Keefe believe governments should try to solve rather than taking steps to address global warming? Why, in his view, does it make more sense to address these problems rather than global warming? Do you agree with him? Why or why not?

Exploring the Issues

1. In this essay, O'Keefe presents a harsh, critical view of those he describes as "special interests," "advocates," and "environmental ministries." Who exactly is O'Keefe criticizing in this essay? Who are the advocates and special interests that he refers to? What do you think he gains by criticizing them as harshly as he does? Do you think his criticisms strengthen or weaken his essay? Explain, keeping in mind that he initially wrote

this speech for an audience of environmental journalists.

2. What role does science play in O'Keefe's argument about global climate change? What view of science does he have, based on this essay? Do you think most Americans share his view of science? Explain. Do you? Why or why not?

3. In paragraph 20, O'Keefe writes, "We can do better by not demonizing those who raise legitimate issues for debate." Do you think he follows his own advice in this essay? Explain, citing specific passages from his essay in your answer. What do you think his essay—and particularly his criticism of those with whom he disagrees—suggests about the nature of debate about controversies like global warming?

Entering the Conversations

1. Write a response to O'Keefe's essay in which you present your own view of the debate about global climate change and explain why you agree or disagree with him.

2. In a group of classmates, share the essays you wrote for Question 1. Identify the main reasons that members of your group agree or disagree with O'Keefe, and look for similarities and differences in the views of your classmates about climate change. Draw conclusions on the basis of your discussion about the nature of debates regarding global climate change.

 INFOTRAC

3. As O'Keefe's essay indicates, the debate about global

climate change is complicated and intense. His essay and the others in this cluster present some of the perspectives on this issue. Using InfoTrac College Edition, your library, the Internet, and other available resources, investigate the current debate about global climate change. Visit the web sites of major organizations involved in the debate to get a sense of how they present their positions and what they say about opposing positions. Identify key points of view and key points of disagreement. Try to get a sense of the main issues that have emerged in these debates. Then write a report in which you present an analysis of the debate. Explain the main issues and summarize the main perspectives. On the basis of your research, assess O'Keefe's representation of the issue. Draw your own conclusions about the nature of this debate.

4. On the basis of your research for Question 3, create a guide to the current debates about global climate change. Design your guide as a web site, pamphlet, PowerPoint presentation, or other kind of multimedia document that would be accessible to a general audience who are not experts on the issue.

5. In paragraph 18, O'Keefe writes, "Like it or not, fossil fuels will remain the dominant source of energy then and or some time beyond. That means that emissions will be higher, not lower. The best we can hope for is to slow their growth and increase the world's resiliency." O'Keefe wrote his essay in 2005, and since then a number of important developments have influenced the ongoing debate about global climate change. Write an essay in which you respond to O'Keefe's statement based on what we know (or believe) today. In your essay, discuss developments that have occurred since 2005 that might affect O'Keefe's position about the importance of fossil fuels. Offer your own view about whether O'Keefe is right, based on your perspective and on the current situation regarding fossil fuels and global climate change.

6. O'Keefe argues for a "healthy skepticism" in the debate about global climate change, and he states that such skepticism also makes good journalism (see par. 24). Write an essay in which you define "healthy skepticism" and offer your own view of whether such a skepticism should be recognized as a virtue, as O'Keefe believes it should. In your essay, identify

other debates about important issues in which such skepticism does—or should—play a role, in your view.

7. Many people believe that global warming is a hoax. This image reflects this widespread view. The cartoon pokes fun at Al Gore (whose essay also appears in this chapter) in a way that questions the validity of his position on global

warming. Using this image and others you find on the Internet and elsewhere, evaluate the ways in which such images are used in the ongoing debates about global warming and especially about the idea that it is a hoax. Write a conventional academic essay presenting your analysis and conclusions about the debate and the use of images in it.

© The Mike Lester Studio

Extending the Conversations

1. Write an essay about an important change you have experienced in your life. Tell the story of that change in a way the reveals its importance in your life and how you dealt with it.

2. Write a proposal for a change that you believe should happen in your school or community. Address the proposal to the appropriate audience (such as your school president, your local town council or school board, or some other government official). In your proposal, describe the situation that you believe needs to be changed and explain why you think change is needed. Justify the change you are proposing and explain how it will address the problems you have described in your proposal.

3. Interview several older people you know who have witnessed momentous events in their lifetime. Ask them about the changes they have seen over the course of their lives and get a sense of how they believe these changes have affected them and their communities. Then write an essay discussing what you learned from your interviews.

4. Create a flyer or brochure presenting your perspective about a change that you believe is affecting your local community. For example, you might live in a place that is experiencing controversy about building a new school, allowing the construction of a new shopping mall, or changing a law that affects where local teens can ride their skateboards. Select such an issue that is affecting your community and focus your flyer or brochure on that issue.

5. Drawing on any appropriate essays in this chapter and on other relevant resources, create a PowerPoint presentation, video, or another appropriate kind of presentation for a specific audience (for example, students at your school or people at your workplace) intended to educate that audience about an important change that is occurring in your community.

6. Many popular films tell stories about how people have dealt with difficult changes in their lives. For example, *About Schmidt* (2002), starring Jack Nicholson, describes the challenges facing a nondescript actuary from Omaha whose wife dies soon after he retires; the film explores his struggle to deal with such momentous life changes as retirement and the death of a loved one. Similarly, *One True Thing* (1998) tells the story of a young professional woman (played by Renee Zellweger) who returns to her small hometown to care for her terminally ill mother; she is dealing with several difficult changes that force her to reevaluate her own life and her relationships to those around her. Select one or more such films that examine change and analyze what these films seem to suggest about change in human life. Then write an essay in which you present your analysis of these films. Draw conclusions about what these films might suggest about prevailing attitudes in American culture regarding change in our lives.

7. The idea of progress implies change that is positive. However, as several of the readings in this chapter (especially in Cluster 2) indicate, the idea of progress is complex. Not everyone agrees that progress means change for the better. That complexity has sometimes been explored in film. For example, science-fiction films such as *The Matrix* (1999) present a more pessimistic view of technological change. Films like *The Mosquito Coast* (1986) explore some of the harmful effects of technological progress—in this case, the effects of technological progress on an indigenous community in Central America. Select several films that you believe explore the ideas of progress or change associated with technology, and examine the messages that these films convey about technology, society, and progress. Write an essay in which you discuss some of the insights you believe these films might offer.

8. Select several of the authors whose essays appear in this chapter and write a dialogue in which they debate climate change (or another important change facing humankind today).

9. Create a pamphlet, web site, or other appropriate document in which you present advice to teens who are coming of age; focus your advice on how they should confront the challenges facing them and deal with the changes occurring in the world today.

CREDITS

Chapter 2. 17: top, From *Psycholinguistics,* 2nd Edition by Dan I. Slobin. Copyright © 1979, 1974 by Scott, Foresman and Company. Reprinted by permission of Addison Wesley Longman, Inc. **30:** "Dialogue Boxes You Should Have Read More Carefully," by Evan Eisenberg. *New York Times,* Sept. 0, 2004.

hapter 5. 71: Sojourner Truth, "Ain't I a Woman?" 1851). **74:** N. Scott Momaday, "The Way to Rainy Mountain" From *THE REPORTER* (1967). Reprinted by permission of University of New Mexico Press. **81:** Bobbie Ann Mason, "Being Country." From *CLEAR SPRINGS* by Bobbie Ann Mason. Copyright © 1999 by Bobbie Ann Mason. Used by permission of Random House, Inc. **87:** Maxine Hong Kingston, "No Name Woman." From *THE WOMAN WARRIOR* by Maxine Hong Kingston, copyright © 1975, 1976 by Maxine Hong Kingston. Used by permission of Alfred A. Knopf, a division of Random House. Inc. **98:** Dagoberto Gilb, "You Know Him by His Labors, But Not His Face." Reprinted by kind permission of the author. **101:** Gregory Jay, "Who Invented White People," from speech given by Gregory Jay, reprinted by permission. **110:** Erin Aubry Kaplan, "Black Like I Thought I Was" *LA Weekly,* October 3, 2003 http://www.laweekly.com/. Reprinted by permission. **115:** Oscar Casares, "Crossing the Border Without Losing Your Past." Copyright © 2003 by The *New York Times* Company. Reprinted with permission. **119:** Bharati Mukherjee, "American Dreamer." Copyright © 1997 by Bharati Mukherjee. Originally published in *Mother Jones.* Reprinted by permission of the author. **126:** Orenstein, Peggy. "Mixed Messenger," *New York Times,* April 6, 2008 Sunday. Reprinted by permission of the *New York Times.*

Chapter 6. 137: Richard Wright, "The Library Card." From *BLACK BOY* by Richard Wright. Copyright © 1937, 1942, 1944, 1945 by Richard Wright; renewed © 1973 by Ellen Wright. Reprinted by permission of HarperCollins Publishers, Inc. **147:** Annie Dillard, "Living Like Weasels" from *TEACHING A STONE TO TALK: EXPEDITIONS AND ENCOUNTERS* by ANNIE DILLARD. Copyright © 1982 by Annie Dillard. Reprinted by permission of HarperCollins Publishers, Inc. **152:** D. Winston Brown, "Both Sides of a Gun Barrel," Creative Nonfiction, 2005. Reprinted with the permission of Creative Nonfiction. **164:** Maya Angelou, "Graduation," copyright © 1969 and renewed 1997 by Maya Angelou, from *I KNOW WHY THE CAGED BIRD SINGS* by Maya Angelou. Used by permission of Random House, Inc. **176:** Paulo Freire, "Banking Concept of Education." From *PEDAGOGY OF THE OPPRESSED,* copyright © 1970, 1993 Continuum International Publishing Group. Reprinted by permission of The Continuum International Publishing Group. **191:** Richard Rodriguez, "The Desire of Achievement." From *HUNGER OF MEMORY* by Richard Rodriguez. Reprinted by permission of David R. Godine, Publisher, Inc. Copyright © 1982 by Richard Rodriguez. **213:** Adrienne Rich, "Taking Women Students Seriously." From *ON LIES, SECRETS, AND SILENCE: SELECTED PROSE 1966–1978* by Adrienne Rich. Copyright © 1979 by W. W. Norton & Company, Inc. Used by permission of the author and W. W. Norton & Company, Inc. **224:** Langston Hughes, "Salvation," from *THE BIG SEA* by Langston Hughes. Copyright © 1940 by Langston Hughes. Copyright renewed 1968 by Arna Bontemps and George Houston Bass. Reprinted by permission of Hill and Wang, a division of Farraf, Straus and Giroux, LLC. **228:** Joel Engardio, "Learning The True Tolerance," From NPR, Weekend Edition, November 25, 2007. **231:** Paul Davies, "Talking Science on Faith," *New York Times,* November 24, 2007, Section A: Column 0, OP-ED.

Chapter 7. 241: John Allen Paulos, "God and Girls in Thailand" Excerpt from *Irreligion: A Mathematician Explains Why the Arguments for God Just Don't Add Up.* Hill and Wang 2007. **245:** Kristin van Ogtrop, "Attila the Honey I'm Home." From *THE BITCH IN THE HOUSE* (2002) by Cathi Hanauer. Reprinted by permission of the author. **256:** bell hooks, "On Building a Community of Love: bell hooks Meets with Thich Nhat Hanh to Ask: How Do We Build a Community of Love." From *Shambhala Sun Online,* January 2000. From the *Shambhala Sun Magazine:* www.shambhalasun.com. Reprinted by permission.

AUTHOR AND TITLE INDEX